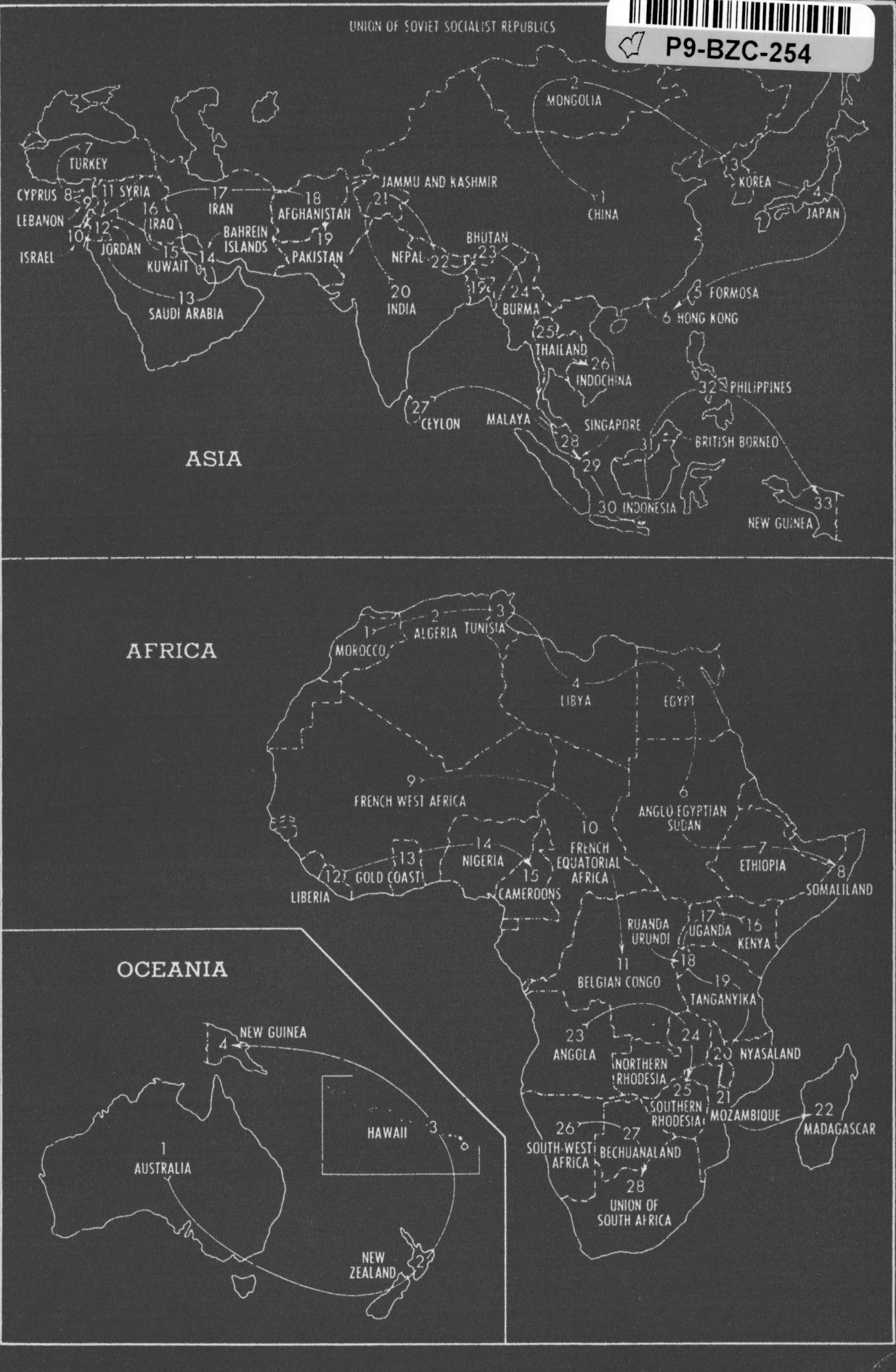

UNION OF SOVIET SOCIALIST REPUBLICS

P9-BZC-254

ASIA

MONGOLIA 2

1 CHINA

3 KOREA

4 JAPAN

7 TURKEY

CYPRUS 8

11 SYRIA

LEBANON

16

10 12 IRAQ

ISRAEL

JORDAN

15 KUWAIT 14

13 SAUDI ARABIA

17 IRAN

18 AFGHANISTAN

BAHREIN ISLANDS

19 PAKISTAN

20 INDIA

JAMMU AND KASHMIR

21

NEPAL 22

BHUTAN

23

19

24 BURMA

25 THAILAND

26 INDOCHINA

5 FORMOSA

6 HONG KONG

32 PHILIPPINES

27 CEYLON

MALAYA

SINGAPORE

28

29

31

BRITISH BORNEO

30 INDONESIA

33 NEW GUINEA

AFRICA

1 MOROCCO

2 ALGERIA

3 TUNISIA

4 LIBYA

5 EGYPT

9 FRENCH WEST AFRICA

6 ANGLO-EGYPTIAN SUDAN

10 FRENCH EQUATORIAL AFRICA

13 NIGERIA 14

12 GOLD COAST

LIBERIA

15 CAMEROONS

7 ETHIOPIA

8 SOMALILAND

17 UGANDA 16 KENYA

RUANDA URUNDI

11 BELGIAN CONGO

18

19 TANGANYIKA

23 ANGOLA

24

20 NYASALAND

NORTHERN RHODESIA

25 SOUTHERN RHODESIA

21 MOZAMBIQUE

22 MADAGASCAR

26 SOUTH-WEST AFRICA

27 BECHUANALAND

28 UNION OF SOUTH AFRICA

OCEANIA

4 NEW GUINEA

HAWAII 3

1 AUSTRALIA

2 NEW ZEALAND

WORLD COMMERCE AND GOVERNMENTS

TRENDS AND OUTLOOK

WORLD

COMMERCE AND

GOVERNMENTS

TRENDS AND OUTLOOK

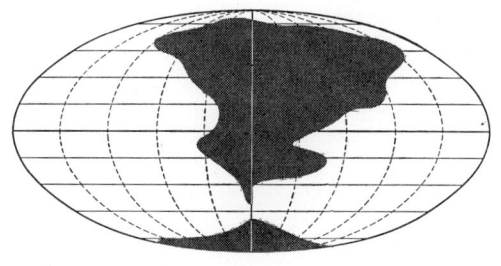

W. S. Woytinsky AND *E. S. Woytinsky*

THE TWENTIETH CENTURY FUND

NEW YORK · 1955

COPYRIGHT, © 1955 BY THE TWENTIETH CENTURY FUND, INC.

Library of Congress Catalog Number: 55–8797

PRINTED IN THE UNITED STATES OF AMERICA BY
THE LORD BALTIMORE PRESS, INC., BALTIMORE, MARYLAND

FOREWORD

THIS VOLUME completes the work begun by the authors eight years ago, the first fruits of which appeared in *World Population and Production,* published by the Twentieth Century Fund in 1953. This comprehensive project constitutes a survey of the population, the needs and resources, the agriculture, industry, transportation and trade, and the governmental systems of all the regions and nations of the world.

The research has been jointly financed by the Rockefeller Foundation, through a grant administered by the Johns Hopkins University, and the Fund. A committee consisting of Robert T. Crane, former executive director of the Social Science Research Council, Fritz Machlup, of the faculty of the Johns Hopkins University, and J. Frederic Dewhurst, of the Fund staff, served in an advisory capacity in the inauguration of the project.

Mr. and Mrs. Woytinsky are the sole authors of this volume, as well as the preceding one. They are wholly responsible for planning and carrying to completion this vast undertaking and for the opinions expressed in the survey. Their professional training and years of study and observation in the United States and many other countries have given them exceptional qualifications for this important and difficult enterprise. The Fund is deeply indebted to them, not only for their knowledge and experience, but for their patience and diligence in pursuing and successfully completing this task — which required much more time than originally contemplated by the authors and covered by the funds available.

The two authors bear joint responsibility for the project as a whole and for this volume. Mrs. Woytinsky is primarily responsible for Chapters 7–11 (Transportation), and Mr. Woytinsky for Chapters 1–6 (Trade) and 12–17 (Governments).

The reception accorded *World Population and Production* by the general and technical press in the United States and abroad and by readers has vindicated the Fund's conviction that there was a real need for such an over-all survey of world trends and prospects as the authors planned. The book has required a second printing and has been translated into Japanese. The Fund hopes this second volume will equally meet the needs of the public.

J. FREDERIC DEWHURST, *Executive Director*
The Twentieth Century Fund

330 WEST 42ND STREET
NEW YORK 36, NEW YORK
SEPTEMBER 1, 1955

ACKNOWLEDGMENTS

THE AUTHORS are deeply indebted to Dr. Joseph Willits of the Rockefeller Foundation for his confidence in the feasibility of their plan for this study; to the Johns Hopkins University, under whose auspices the Rockefeller grant was administered; and to the Twentieth Century Fund for carrying out the publication of the study in its present form.

While the authors had no contributors or collaborators in their work, they had the generous aid of many experts. We fully appreciate how much we are indebted to them for their criticisms and suggestions.

We also acknowledge with deep gratitude the assistance of various governmental and international agencies and, in particular, the Secretariat of the United Nations. During our study in Europe, covering the United Kingdom, France, Scandinavia, the Low Countries, Switzerland, Western Germany and Italy, we received the generous cooperation of many individuals and agencies — too numerous to mention here by name.

To the following persons goes our grateful appreciation for having read various parts of the manuscript and given comments and suggestions on questions pertaining to their special fields of interest and experience:

> D. W. Bluestone, Defense Air Transportation Administration
> Henry Chalmers, U.S. Department of Commerce
> Gerhard Colm, National Planning Association
> Ben Dorfman, U.S. Tariff Commission
> Irwin M. Heine, Maritime Administration
> Colonel R. Henry, Association of American Railroads
> Folke Hilgerdt, United Nations
> Dal Hitchcock, economic consultant
> Harold Gosnell, American University
> David Levin, Bureau of Public Roads
> David Lynch, U.S. Tariff Commission
> Fritz Machlup, Johns Hopkins University
> Fritz Mann, American University
> Wilfred Owen, Brookings Institution
> J. H. Parmelee, Association of American Railroads
> Pitnam B. Porter, American University
> James J. Robbins, American University
> Robert L. Sammons, U.S. Department of Commerce
> Paul Studenski, New York University
> M. Twiss, International Road Federation
> Simon N. Whitney, Twentieth Century Fund

Our warm appreciation also goes to Mary Ross Gannett for her unsparing efforts in editing this study.

We recognize with gratitude the work of the Twentieth Century Fund in handling the difficult task of publishing a volume of this size and scope, and our deep appreciation goes to the Fund staff as a group for the tremendous amount of effort entailed in preparing the manuscript for the printer. Acknowledgment is also given to I. J. Starworth for his competent and careful work in drawing and preparing most of the maps and charts included as illustrative material in the book. A further word of credit is due to Minn Radner, who prepared the index.

In a study of this scope, with its vast amount of detail, covering worldwide problems and some of the most controversial issues of our time, we are aware that errors are unavoidable. We accept full responsibility for possible mistakes and inconsistencies that may have occurred during the long course of preparing the original draft of the manuscript and revising it in the light of new sources of statistical data that became available before the book was published. We have, however, tried to make use of the most reliable sources of information at our disposal and have employed them to the best of our ability.

W. S. WOYTINSKY
E. S. WOYTINSKY

CONTENTS

PART I. TRADE

PART II. TRANSPORTATION

TABLES

PART I. TRADE

Chapter 1. Trade in the World Economy

PART III. GOVERNMENTS

Chapter 12. Nations and Governments

Chapter 13. Elections and Parliaments

CHAPTER 14. COLONIAL EMPIRES

CHAPTER 15. GOVERNMENT EXPENDITURES AND REVENUES

FIGURES

PART I. TRADE

PART II. TRANSPORTATION

CHAPTER 7. TRANSPORTATION IN THE WORLD ECONOMY

CHAPTER 8. LAND TRANSPORTATION: THE PREMECHANICAL ERA AND THE RAILROADS

CHAPTER 9. LAND TRANSPORTATION: MOTOR VEHICLES AND HIGHWAYS

INTRODUCTION

THIS BOOK is closely related to the volume by the same authors published by the Twentieth Century Fund in 1953 under the title *World Population and Production*. It starts from the same historical premises, uses the same methods of analysis and presentation and carries the world survey forward into fields not covered in the first volume.

The purpose of both volumes is the same: to study world trends during the fateful era in which the mechanized economy originated on the two coasts of the North Atlantic is becoming the universal civilization of mankind. A long and winding road has brought the world to this turn, and the turn itself is marked by violent clashes — revolutions, wars, disintegration of old empires and the rise of new world powers.

In the preceding volume we have examined the current transformation of the world in the field of population (in the broad sense of the term); human needs, consumption, national income and forms of economy; agriculture, including forestry and fisheries; mining and energy supply; and manufacturing industries. The present volume deals with the exchange of goods among peoples; transportation within national communities and in the world as a whole; governments and their interrelationships — supranational organizations and international cooperation.

BACKGROUND: THE TECHNICAL REVOLUTION

As long as the mechanized economy was a monopoly of a few nations, it gave them tremendous advantage over the rest of mankind. The world economy of the nineteenth century was like a pyramid, with a broad foundation and narrow top: at the base, hundreds of millions of poverty-stricken men and women, mostly illiterate, haunted by disease, many condemned in advance to premature death; at the top, the industrialized nations with steadily rising standards of living, declining mortality, increasing expectation of life.

The gap between the have and have-not nations was the most characteristic feature of this system. Its transformation began when modern methods of agriculture, mining, manufacturing and transportation began to invade the underdeveloped regions. The spread of industrialism over the world has not brought equality and freedom from want to the awakening nations, but it has given them hope of a better life. They feel — or believe — that improvement is within their reach. Thus, to the technological and economic dynamism of the industrial, prosperous nations is added the political dynamism in the traditionally underdeveloped, slumbering areas.

The new economic techniques challenge the patriarchal, semifeudal patterns of life that prevail in these areas. The foundations and landmarks of the primitive subsistence economy, old customs and social institutions inherited from time immemorial, are disappearing in fires blazing in all parts of the world. The process is long — even now, more people live under the conditions of a subsistence economy than in the areas dominated by mechanized civilization. One civilization is on its way out; the other is advancing.

The economic transformation of the world implies far-reaching social and political changes. Whether violent or orderly, they are revolutionary in the sense of a complete and irrevocable break with the past. Such are the land reforms — or land revolutions — and emancipation of colonies sweeping the underdeveloped areas of the world.

Some changes are bound to bring disillusionment to the people. Their desires are growing more rapidly than the means at their disposal. Moreover, along with obsolete customs and institutions, the new mechanized civilization is destroying traditions that made life worth living. Liberated peoples of former colonial empires are facing most difficult problems of economic development and cultural adjustment.

The progress of mechanized civilization is the central topic of this study. We have tried to describe, measure and explain this development but have not attempted to appraise it.

The expansion of mechanized civilization has destroyed the foundation of international relationships that existed in the nineteenth century — the domination by the industrial countries of colonial and semicolonial areas in Middle and South America, Asia, Africa and Oceania. A new pattern of division of labor and international cooperation must be found to assure stability to the world which emerges from the clashes of our time. To be acceptable to the peoples that are entering — or re-entering — the historical scene, the new system of international relations must promise them equality of opportunity with their former masters. They will settle for nothing less. Equal opportunity, however, does not mean equality of wealth and income. The latter will depend on how the awakening peoples utilize the new economic and political tools being placed in their hands. Their first steps along the new road in the new environment are discussed, described and analyzed in the following pages.

The transformation of the world economy has had a deep impact also on the pattern of international trade.

The Mechanized Economy

Recent economic changes are characterized by steadily increasing momentum. The mechanized economy born some two centuries ago has been growing ever since at a continuously increasing rate. The beginning was slow, from the timid, not too successful experiments with the steam engine in the second half of the eighteenth century to the huge but poorly equipped mills and rudimentary railways in the first half of the nineteenth. Even in the most progressive countries, the economic system of the middle of the past century was a clumsy, slowly moving affair without very bright promise for the future — wooden sailing vessels on the oceans, horse and buggy transportation on land, gas and whale-oil lights on the streets and in homes, cities scattered like islands amid borderless expanses of primitive farming.

Contrary to the prophetic vision of Adam Smith, most scholars of that time believed that the capitalistic system of production had only limited possibilities. So slow were the changes that many keen observers failed to notice them. Thus, the capitalism which Karl Marx described was an economy bound to collapse because of internal contradictions and inability to grow and expand.

The economic world portrayed at about the same time by Friedrich List was more dynamic. It was planning railroads and beginning to build them. List brought his dynamic concept of an industrial system to slumbering provincial Germany from the United States, where he had witnessed the revolutionary impact of the new means of transportation on business. Unlike Marx, who, as an economist, never ceased to represent the capitalist system of production by a model fitting best the primitive manufacture of the eighteenth century, List was fascinated by the new technological trends. But how old-fashioned even his world looks to the modern reader!

Technological Progress

Acceleration of technological and economic progress came simultaneously on both sides of the Atlantic in the second half of the nineteenth century, especially the latter part of this period. The quickening came with electricity, steel and petroleum; with the steamship that linked nations, with railways that crossed the continents and linked towns and villages to the thoroughfares. The last two or three decades of the nineteenth century brought more technological and economic changes to the nations of the West than the preceding hundred and twenty or thirty years. So stupendous was the progress that by the end of the century some students, in America as well as in Europe, believed that the industrial system had reached maturity — that every conceivable machine had been invented and put in action, all necessary railroads had been built, all major projects of urbanization completed. The speed of progress was bound to decrease.

Actually what they had seen was only the prologue to an explosive economic expansion. Unprecedented progress began after the turn of the century with the penetration of applied sciences into all fields of human activity. Inventions and discoveries followed in close succession. Cars and trucks appeared on the roads, calling to life a new system of highways. Airplanes rose in the sky and found their way into areas hitherto inaccessible by highway and railroad. Scientific agriculture came to the aid of the farmer. New, man-made materials invaded the markets. The complete story of the role of chemistry and electronics in the modern economy cannot be told within the compass of this work, but the study outlines the main developments in each field of economic activity.

The "Know-how" Formula

What has happened in the past few decades, since World War I, has been more than acceleration of the former long-range trend. The problems of struggle against hunger and want and of prosperity and economic progress have been reduced to a simple formula: *know-how*. People have discovered that skill and organization rather than accumulated wealth are the clues to economic progress, and this has been the most revolutionary discovery of our time. The tree of knowledge has been shown to the have-not peoples and there are no cherubim with flaming swords to keep them away from it.

The turn in our economic thinking and the growing emphasis on know-how as the basis of prosperity implies recognition of the supremacy of the searching, alert, flexible and free human mind and of the unlimited possibilities beyond the visible horizons of our knowledge of today. Moreover, while accumulated wealth is the possession of a few, economic and technical know-how is widespread in modern society, belonging to all and denied to none.

Indeed, the facility with which it can be transferred characterizes modern mechanized civilization. Air transportation epitomizes this. A plane can land almost anywhere and in a short time it can bring all the accessories of an efficient airfield to a selected site at a crossing of caravan trails, on a tiny island or in an oasis surrounded by bare desert. A country too rugged and too poor to build railroads and highways can have a network of airfields. The radio penetrates the wilderness ahead of the telephone and telegraph, indeed ahead of the elementary school. A hydroelectric station can be built in a region too remote from modern civilization to use a steam engine fed by coal. Modern technology spreads as widely as gaseous matter released from a container.

Natural Resources

The technological progress initiated in the modern industrialized countries and now spreading to the remotest corners of the world is the answer to questions on the carrying capacity of our planet, the depletion of its natural resources and the pressure of overpopulation. In some limited areas, scarcity of land and other natural resources, combined with a rapidly growing density of population, has doubtless produced a Malthusian situation — poverty due largely to overpopulation. Such a situation is particularly disturbing on some islands in each hemisphere — for example, in Puerto Rico, Japan and Indonesia. This is a local phenomenon, however, similar to other sources of poverty, such as obsolete customs, rigid stratification of society, concentration of lands in the hands of large landowners.

But overpopulation is no more responsible for poverty in a large part of the world than technological progress is to blame for mass unemployment during a depression. This question was examined in detail in the first volume. No evidence has been found of a general tendency of mankind to outgrow available resources. There is evidence, however, that the short-sighted destructive exploitation of land, forests and other resources characteristic of the ruthless nineteenth century is being brought under control in recent times. The present phase of economic history is characterized by reclamation of the soil, irrigation of deserts, drainage of swamps, flood control, conquest of malaria and other environmental diseases, protection of cattle and plants against parasites and diseases. Further progress, including purification of sea water for irrigation of arid areas, is in sight.

Long-Range Economic Trends

This description of the present phase of our civilization may impress the reader as too optimistic. The authors are aware of the other side of the picture: of the contradictions within the modern industrial system; of the gap between technological progress and other aspects of civilization; of international tensions and the imminent danger of a new world war. These issues are not within the scope of this study. Its purpose is to outline long-range and recent trends in the world's economic structure — a broad but still limited task that provides a background for the discussion of other problems.

The trends in the world economy are presented by topic rather than by country. The elucidation of particular subjects, however, is not the final aim of the study but mainly a medium for giving an over-all picture of the world. This objective has determined the selection of single topics: the space given to each depends not on its importance alone but on its relation to the whole picture.

A study of economic trends in the world requires a broad historical approach to each topic. Our economic civilization is both older and younger than most people believe. Its roots penetrate deep into the past, but most of our machines and technical methods and many of our raw materials were unknown to the generations just before us.

Modern technology is heavily concentrated in the two North Atlantic regions. The United States leads in many fields; never before has a single nation controlled so large a percentage of the world's industrial capacity. The incomparable industrial plant of the country, however, has been built on the foundation of a rich inheritance from the Old World. The United States itself is an emanation of European culture, and its superlative techniques in agriculture, mining, manufacturing and transportation rest largely on ingenious practical adaptations of theoretical ideas originated in a dozen old countries. Although the immediate concern of this study is the present and the future rather than the past, it stresses the international genealogy of many modern inventions and occasionally refers to times as remote as those of the Bible and ancient Greece. Apart from tracing the historical roots of the modern economy, such references are designed to emphasize the dynamism of the modern economy in contrast to the slowness of economic progress in the preceding millenniums.

A historical approach is particularly necessary in considering the unique position of the United States in world economics and politics. So rapid and so radical have been the changes that the present generation has been unexpectedly catapulted into the center of unfamiliar events and problems. How did the country reach this position? What are the foundations of its economic power? What are its responsibilities? A survey of historical development will aid the reader in his search for answers to these and related questions.

Scope of the Study

The present volume consists of three parts.

Part I. Trade. This section deals with the exchange of goods within national economies and among nations, and with relations resulting from this exchange. The role of trade in the economy of nations and the status of traders in communities in different stages of historical development are examined. Methods of measuring the volume of trade are discussed and variations in the volume and value of foreign trade are surveyed. Under the heading "Direction of World Trade" the reader will find an analysis of the distribution of exports and imports among continents and single nations, bilateral and multilateral trade, and trade balances between different countries and regions. Next, the composition of world trade by groups of commodities and the role of the principal raw materials and finished goods in the flow of world trade are explored and the main routes of these products are traced. The analysis of merchandise trade is supplemented by a survey of balances of payments, international capital movements, foreign investments and debts. The concluding chapter of Part I deals with customs, tariffs and trade agreements and their measurement and comparison. It also contains a brief survey of other trade restrictions.

Part II. Transportation. The first chapter of Part II contains an analysis of the economic, social and political effects of progress in transportation and a survey of employment in transportation services and the share of these services in the national income of various countries. Other chapters deal with specific types of transportation, on land, water and in the air. They trace the historical development of each branch of transportation in the world and in single countries and describe the main routes, the equipment used (rolling stock, motor fleets and ships) and the volume of passenger and freight traffic in each branch of transportation. They also explore the main aspects of the economics of transportation — investments, revenues and expenditures, ownership, public subsidies and the problem of competition among single branches of transportation, as well as the types of government control in the various countries.

Part III. Governments. This section begins with a survey of types of government, suffrage systems, elections and parliaments. Next, the origins and roles of colonies are discussed and the history of the rise and fall of colonial empires is outlined, with particular emphasis on the present phase of liquidation of colonial relationships. Then public finances, as an outstanding feature in the operation of governments, are examined: trends in the size of national budgets in relation to population and national income; sources of public revenues; trends in taxation, especially in income taxes; public debts, their origin and impact on the economy of nations. The last chapter of the book covers the supranational organizations — the League of Nations, the United Nations and other organizations. Special attention is given to the international aid activities of the United Nations and the United States.

Statistical and Tabular Methods

World economic trends do not all incline in the same direction, nor do they move at the same pace. Some are waning as others are becoming increasingly important. The component trends that make up the over-all pattern of development must be weighted, and this is a task for statistics. This consideration has determined the character of the study; synthetic and interpretative in purpose, it is largely statistical in form. It not only makes extensive use of statistics, but is also intended to serve as an introduction to the realm of international statistics.

Statistical tables on the following pages are designed for laymen. They are accompanied by methodological explanations that would be omitted in a more technical publication, but the technician will miss the customary array of footnotes.

This omission is intentional. In a ten-column table that covers some fifty countries, only a few figures are strictly comparable and each line, each column and almost each figure calls for a footnote.[1] Such paraphernalia, however, would appear as unbearable pedantry to the general reader. Moreover, after having read — or skipped — all the

---

1. The United Nations *Demographic Yearbook, 1954* contains a table with more than 148 numbered footnotes, plus explanations of six methods of classification of base data and ten methods of time adjustment.

footnotes the reader would learn not much more than that the figures differ from one another in concept, method of computation and the exact date to which they refer and are to be used with caution. Since this warning applies to almost all international tables, it can be given directly, here and now, without repetitious footnotes.

This study makes a point of presenting statistics in the simplest possible form, with illustrative charts and brief analytical summaries in the text but with a minimum of technical detail. The reader interested in omitted details is referred to the original sources.

World Totals and Averages

The study as a whole contains frequent references to world totals and national and regional averages — for population, exports and imports, foreign debts and investments, transportation facilities, and so on. Most of these data are presented in the conventional form: population with precision to the nearest thousand or million; value to the closest million dollars. These precise figures should not be taken too seriously, however, for most of the data have a considerable margin of error.

In fact, more or less reliable and detailed current population statistics are available for only two dozen countries, with an aggregate population of less than 600 million, about a fourth of mankind. Even these data are not strictly comparable because of significant differences in methods of enumeration and classification. For an area embracing another fourth of the world's population, including India and large parts of South America, statistics are less abundant. For the rest of the world — notably China, the Near and Far East, the USSR and a large part of Africa — statistical information is extremely meager.

When the precise number of inhabitants in an area is unknown, its other statistics become doubtful. Statistics of per capita trade and comparisons of exports and imports, transportation and public finances and public debts with per capita income in different areas are, necessarily, only rough approximations.

The reader is cautioned that international surveys covering a large number of countries are not selective and contain figures of unequal reliability; inclusion of a figure in the survey does not mean its endorsement by the authors.

This observation applies also to economic statistics. Official data on exports and imports, international financial transactions, investments and debts, finances of railroads and highways depend on the methods of measurement and classification, which vary from country to country. They always contain an appreciable margin of error, and these errors are not always distributed at random; there may be a definite tendency toward understatement or overstatement in certain series.

Despite these limitations in international statistics, they are the only available tool for quantitative appraisal of the divergent trends in world affairs — indeed, the cornerstone of any exploration in the field of world economy. Their indisputable service is to give the reader a sense of magnitude and relative values.

Life Behind the Iron Curtain

The United Nations and its specialized agencies have made serious attempts to develop modern statistical reporting throughout the world and to increase the comparability of national statistics. The Kremlin has met these efforts with a resolute veto and a statistical blackout in the areas under its control. Besides boycotting the inquiries of the United Nations, the Kremlin is flooding the world with reports of its own which contravene all principles of modern statistics. These reports are usually indexes of production computed in an unknown way and related to an unknown base.

There is no way to segregate truth from falsehood in these communications, but their purpose is obvious. Some of them have scarcely more than accidental similarity to the statistics used by the Soviet authorities in the economic planning and operation of their industrial plant and are concocted as instruments of propaganda at home and abroad. Moreover, most of the Soviet statistics are presented in such a form as to be effective as propaganda without revealing the facts of life behind the Iron Curtain.

Apart from the lack of more or less trustworthy statistics, it is difficult to discuss the economy of the USSR in an economic survey of the world because of the basic differences between totalitarian and free economies.

The incentive in the free economy is profit, but the producer cannot make a profit unless he sells his product and cannot sell the product unless it incites or satisfies demand and meets the needs of consumers. Thus, the enterprise system is ultimately oriented toward satisfaction of people's needs. In a totalitarian state, in contrast, all economic activities are subordinated to the interests of the party or clique that controls the government. The perpetuation and expansion of its power become the ultimate goals of the national economy and determine production plans. The remaining surpluses are used for private consumption and are distributed among various groups of the population according to political expediency.

This economic system, although perfectly logical when observed according to the scale of values of the totalitarian state, seems full of contradictions from the Western viewpoint. It combines an extremely low level of living and real wages with a formidable heavy industry. In contrast to the free economy, it permits only insignificant improvement — or no improvement at all — in civilian consumption while its munitions industries are among the most dynamic and efficient in the world.

It is noteworthy that the repercussions of World War II on the economic system of the USSR have conformed to its militaristic nature. The vast conquests in the west have brought little improvement to the working population in the USSR but have put at the disposal of the Soviet the arsenals of Skoda, the munitions factories of Eastern Germany and an army of Czech and German technicians who were the brains of the war industry under Hitler. The duality of the Soviet economy is clearly revealed by the ranking of the USSR among other industrial nations: close to the bottom in per capita consumption and close to the top in capacity of iron and steel mills.

Estimates and Projections

Despite the limitations of international statistics, they permit certain generalizations and projections. The writer must judge how far he should go in this direction. The only rigid rule is that he must warn the reader when he shifts from the thin ice of official statistics to the still thinner ice of extrapolation. Throughout the two volumes, the reader will find warning signs wherever they seem appropriate.

This study includes numerous estimates of the distribution of world population by type of government, the distribution of world trade by continent, of transportation facilities and operations, of foreign investments and debts, and so on. All these estimates are, of course, open to criticism and are presented as rough approximations. They cannot be more precise than the statistics on which they are based. The projections ventured here and there require an additional reservation: they express simply the opinion of the authors on the probable course of events.

International Tables

A major problem in arranging international statistical tables is the order in which individual countries are listed. The Statistical Office of the United Nations lists the continents and broad geographic regions *alphabetically* — from Africa to Oceania and the USSR — and arranges the countries alphabetically within each division: first, sovereign countries by the first letter of their English name; then colonies and possessions grouped by the first letter of the name of the colonial power and, within each group, by the first letter of their name.[2]

This system is very convenient for reference, for the reader knows where to find the area in which he is interested. The weak point of the system, however, is that each area is handled as an unrelated unit, like names in a telephone directory.

The purpose of the present study calls for a different arrangement. Alphabetical order is incompatible with the approach to national data as elements of the world picture illustrative of the pattern and trends prevailing in different parts of our planet. Most of our tables are therefore arranged *geographically,* following the outline shown on the key maps used as end papers and in the table on the following page.

This arrangement has certain weaknesses. The geographic principle, from north to south and from west to east, cannot always be followed consistently; the starting point for each continent must be selected arbitrarily; and the whole arrangement is less clear than the alphabetical order. It is recognized also that tables arranged in this way may seem confusing to the reader accustomed to the alphabetical system.

Essentially, the two arrangements are analogous to the two patterns used by the United States Bureau of the Census in its arrangement of state statistics. Some of its tables are arranged alphabetically, running from Alabama to Wyoming; in others the states are arranged by geographic division, from New England to the Pacific. The latter pattern is followed in most of the tables in this study.

In some analytical tables, however, countries are arrayed by a definite statistical feature, for example, by population, per capita income or value of foreign trade.

Units of Measurement

Most statistics in this study are expressed in the units used in the United States: miles, short and long tons, dollars, etc. Metric units have been used, however, in

2. The complete list begins with Africa, from Egypt to the Union of South Africa; next comes an array of African colonies, from the Belgian Congo and France's Algeria to the United Kingdom's Zanzibar; this is followed by a third alphabetical listing of trust territories, from the Cameroons to Togoland; and, finally, a fourth list of military governments, condominiums and so on. Similarly, the list for North America begins with independent nations, from Canada, Costa Rica and Cuba to the United States; next, non-self-governing territories are listed, from Denmark's Greenland to the United States' Virgin Islands. The same procedure is used for other continents.

ARRANGEMENT OF COUNTRIES AND AREAS, BY CONTINENT [a]

NORTH AMERICA	EUROPE	ASIA	AFRICA
1. United States	1. United Kingdom	1. China	1. Morocco
2. Alaska	2. Ireland	2. Mongolia	2. Algeria
3. Canada	3. France	3. Korea	3. Tunisia
4. Newfoundland	4. Luxembourg	4. Japan	4. Libya
5. Greenland	5. Belgium	5. Taiwan (Formosa)	5. Egypt
	6. Netherlands	6. Hong Kong	6. Sudan
MIDDLE AMERICA	7. Denmark	7. Turkey	7. Ethiopia
1. Mexico	8. Sweden	8. Cyprus	8. Somaliland
2. Guatemala	9. Norway	9. Lebanon	
3. El Salvador	10. Finland	10. Israel	9. West Africa
4. Honduras			10. Equatorial Africa
5. Nicaragua	11. Germany	11. Syria	11. Congo
6. Costa Rica	12. Poland	12. Jordan	
7. Panama	13. Czechoslovakia	13. Saudi Arabia	12. Liberia
		14. Bahrein Islands	13. Gold Coast
8. Cuba	14. Switzerland	15. Kuwait	14. Nigeria
9. Jamaica	15. Austria	16. Iraq	15. Cameroons
10. Haiti	16. Hungary	17. Iran	
11. Dominican Republic	17. Portugal	18. Afghanistan	16. Kenya
12. Puerto Rico	18. Spain	19. Pakistan	17. Uganda
	19. Italy		18. Ruanda-Urundi
SOUTH AMERICA	20. Yugoslavia	20. India	19. Tanganyika
1. Venezuela	21. Romania	21. Jammu and Kashmir	20. Nyasaland
2. Colombia	22. Bulgaria	22. Nepal	21. Mozambique
3. Ecuador	23. Albania	23. Bhutan	22. Madagascar
	24. Greece	24. Burma	
4. Brazil			23. Angola
5. Peru	USSR	25. Thailand	24. Northern Rhodesia
6. Bolivia		26. Indochina	25. Southern Rhodesia
7. Paraguay			
		27. Ceylon	26. South-West Africa
8. Chile		28. Federation of Malaya	27. Bechuanaland
9. Uruguay		29. Singapore	28. Union of South
10. Argentina		30. Indonesia	Africa
		31. Borneo	
		32. Philippines	OCEANIA
		33. New Guinea	1. Australia
			2. New Zealand
			3. Hawaii
			4. New Guinea

a. Order numbers are the same as in the end-paper maps.

some of the United Nations series which are continued in their current publications. The conversion factor is given under most of these tables.

Foreign currency units appear in historical surveys for single countries where the conversion of original data into dollars would have introduced a new source of uncertainty and erratic fluctuations.

Symbols

A dash (—) in the table columns means zero or less than half the smallest unit recorded in the respective column.

Dots (...) indicate "no information available" or "unknown."

The footnote "preliminary data" is used in some cases for recent years and shows that final data are expected to appear in the near future. This note is omitted when statistics for remote years are used.

Maps and Their Use

The purpose of this survey has determined the choice of its standard world map. Neither a map showing the hemispheres as two circles nor the Mercator projection could be used, since both give a false picture of the spatial interrelation of the different parts of the world.[3]

The same objection is valid in relation to the popular equal-area projections, such as Goode's homolosine projection and its modifications. Excellent for portraying single continents, they fail to represent the world as a continuity. For similar reasons, the authors could not use Van der Grinten's projection, which shows the Americas in the middle of the world, with Europe, Africa and the western parts of the USSR and Asia (including India) to the right, and eastern Asia (including another part of the USSR, China, Indochina and Indonesia) and Australia to the left.

The projection developed by Dr. Erwin Raisz best meets the requirements of this study. Dr. Raisz describes his map as the "armadillo projection" and stresses its realism, rather than its theoretical perfection. Like all continuous maps of the world, it admits deviations from the principle of equal areas, but its main distortions are confined to the Pacific Ocean and polar regions, while the shape and relative location of all continents except Australia are preserved fairly well.[4] (See map on the following page.) The great advantage of this map is that it shows the world as two huge masses of land on both sides of the Atlantic, brings the North Atlantic regions into sharp focus and presents Europe in the middle of the conflicting forces of the West and the East.

Distorted Maps

Among other graphic devices, this study uses *distorted maps* on which continents, geographic regions and countries are drawn to the scale of population, income, exports or some other characteristic. The method is not new, but a feature that distinguishes these distorted maps from the usual ones requires explanation.

Since a distorted map shows some areas on a larger scale than others, it cannot locate countries and regions at the correct longitudes and latitudes. It would be logical, therefore, to draw distorted maps without the network of meridians and parallels. Such a map would look like a diagram, however, and would not suggest clearly enough the spatial relationships of each region to the rest of the world. It seems preferable, therefore, to project the distorted continents and countries against the background of our planet, with the conventional network of longitudes and latitudes. (See map on page li.) The justification for this unorthodox course is that all maps of this

---

3. A few official maps, however, based on the Mercator projection are reproduced. They serve to stress certain features of world economics that can be successfully represented in this way despite the distortion of the regions close to the poles.

4. In the arrangement of contents, this map has a vague resemblance to the Mollweide equal-area elliptical projection, but ingeniously avoids some of its distortions and makes more economical use of the space, permitting a larger scale in presenting continents on a given-size page.

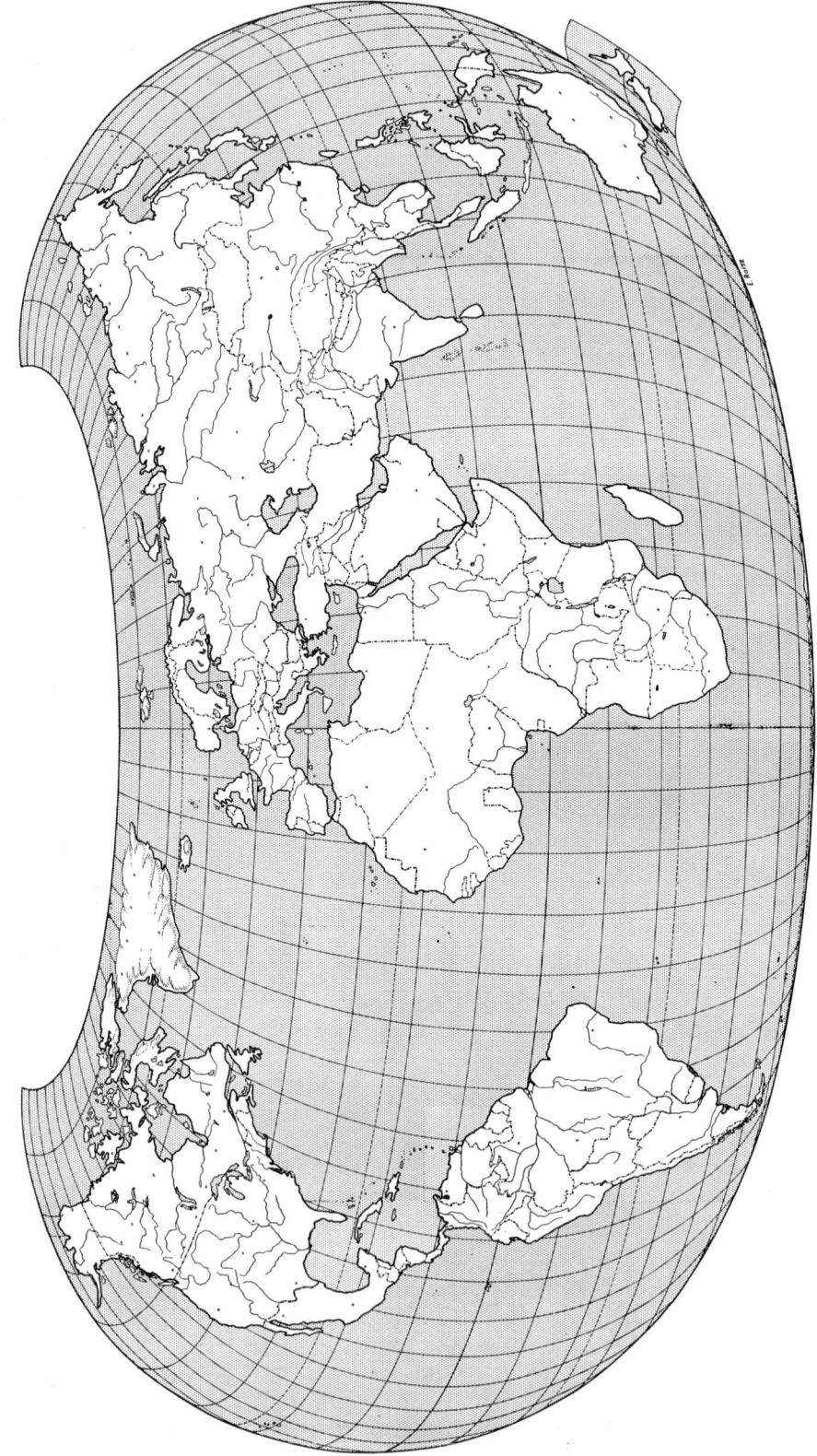

KEY MAP: OUTLINE OF CONTINENTS ACCORDING TO THE PROJECTION OF ERWIN RAISZ

1

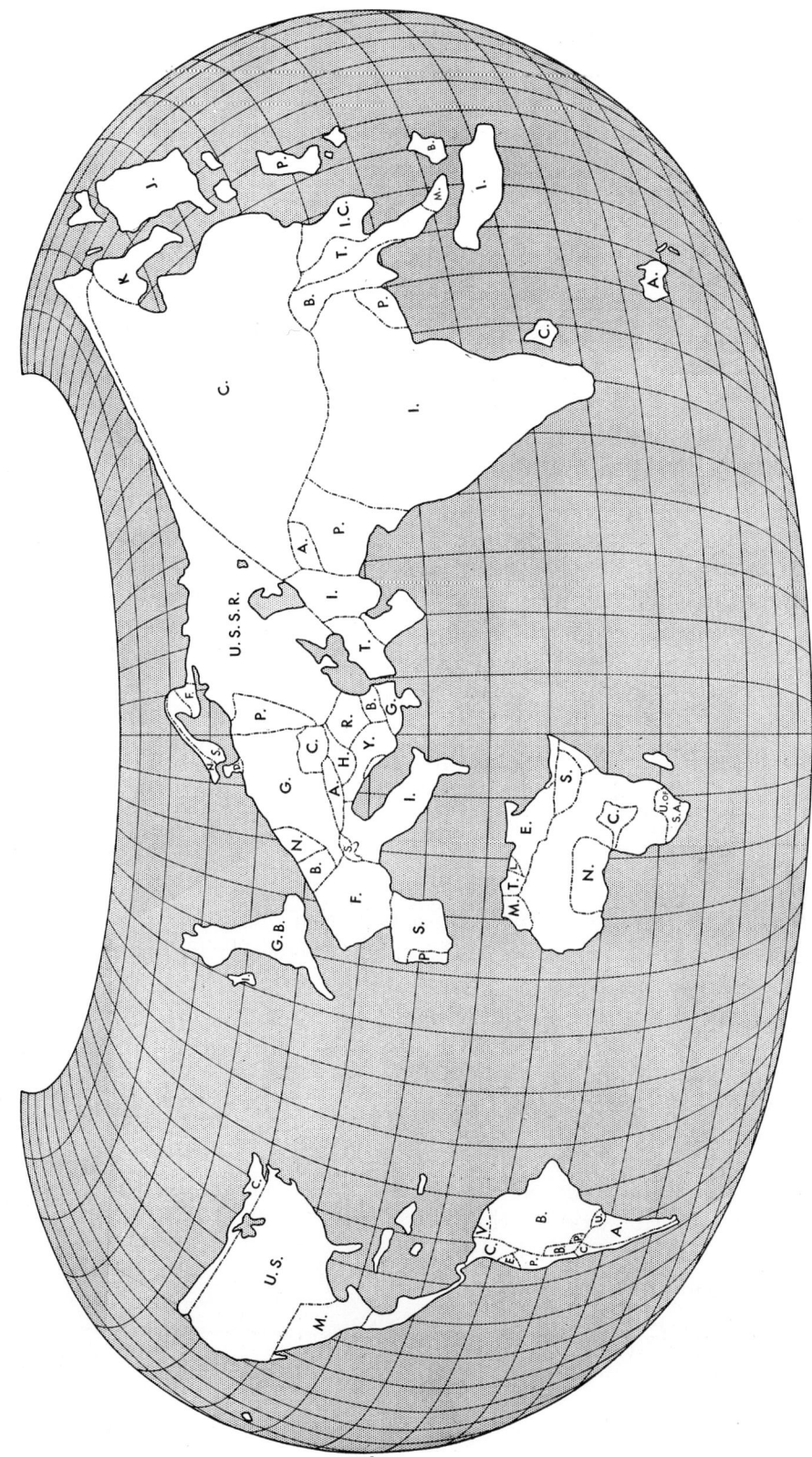

KEY MAP: CONTINENTS AND SELECTED COUNTRIES ON THE SCALE OF THEIR POPULATION, AROUND 1950

type try to picture the relative location of different areas. Once this principle is accepted, why not draw the distorted map of the world in a form reminiscent of maps of the conventional type?

SOURCES AND REFERENCES

Because the broad scope of this volume makes exhaustive discussion of each subject impossible, the reader's attention is directed to the lists of sources at the end of the book. A separate list has been prepared for each chapter; the numbers in these lists correspond to the boldface source number given in the footnotes. Only publications used in the study are listed. Although the lists do not meet all the requirements of a selected bibliography, they should be a helpful guide to the reader.

Many of the international tables are based on publications of the United Nations and its agencies — the Economic Commission for Europe, the International Bank for Reconstruction and Development, the International Monetary Fund, the International Civil Aviation Organization and other specialized agencies. Statistical series of these agencies are not all of the same quality, and some of them are subject to frequent revisions. Occasionally these sources may contradict one another. All in all, however, publications of the United Nations contain the largest and most systematic collection of international statistics ever assembled by any organization.

There is a special reason for using United Nations sources in the present study. Most of the tables in the first volume are carried through 1950 and a few through 1951, while others could not be carried further than 1949. Wherever a table for recent years is derived from the United Nations, its continuation can be found in the current publications of the agency cited as the source.

The manuscript of the present volume was completed in mid-1953, when international statistics were available only up to 1952. Later, many tables were revised and updated and new facts were included in the text. It was impossible, however, to revise the entire book and refresh all the data — a limitation of all statistical volumes, including the yearbooks of the United Nations. The ever-changing data for the latest year, month and day can be supplied only by current periodical publications. This survey is primarily designed to provide background information, give the over-all picture of the world, convey the sense of dynamism of our time and bring the general direction of developments into focus.

Geographic Names

In the transcription of geographic names the study follows the nomenclature established by the United Nations, which is, in most cases, identical with *Webster's Geographical Dictionary* (1949). In tables covering a period in which a country's name has been changed, only the recently established name is listed, as, for example, Thailand, Iran, Jordan, Indonesia. When the new name appears only at the end of a long period covered by the survey, both the old and new names are shown, as in Russia (USSR). Names of Russian authors and titles of books follow the transliteration of the Library of Congress.

PART I. TRADE

CHAPTER 1

TRADE IN THE WORLD ECONOMY

THE EXCHANGE of goods and services is the means through which independent economic units enter into relation with one another and become part of a local or national economic community. As exchange passes beyond a country's boundaries, national economic systems become parts of a broader regional, continental or world economy.

Trade has undergone a long evolution from primitive barter to the modern worldwide network of exports and imports combined with an intricate system of international credits, loans and investments. In this evolution, primitive forms of trade have not disappeared completely but have continued to exist through the centuries with various degrees of adjustment to the changing economic environment.

TRADE IN ECONOMIC HISTORY

Trade has always been one of the main vehicles of human progress. The political structure and the economic organization of our modern world were created in "a vast process of commercial expansion," writes J. B. Condliffe. "From the earliest times, traders have spread knowledge and transplanted plants, animals, products, processes, and ideas." [1]

Regional, national and international trade accounted for the development of urban centers and the formation of centralized national governments. Trade was the mainspring of the great travels of the fifteenth and sixteenth centuries and of the colonial expansion which followed the discovery of the New World. It has played a decisive role likewise in the political and economic history of the world in modern times.

THE ANCIENT WORLD

The Origin of Exchange

In its rudimentary form — the exchange of things — trade is as old as any other economic activity of man. Adam Smith considered the "propensity to truck, barter, and exchange one

thing for another" to be the cause and foundation of the division of labor among individuals and tribes, declaring:

Whether this propensity be one of those original principles in human nature, of which no further account can be given, or whether, as seems more probable, it be the necessary consequence of the facilities of reason and speech, it . . . is common to all men. [2]

Modern anthropology has shown that the propensity to exchange one thing for another is not more inherent in human nature than the propensity to drive a car or fly a plane. Some of our economic propensities were acquired earlier than others, but all are the result of a long evolution. Primitive trade may have developed from the exchange of gifts within a tribe or between tribes as a display of friendliness in the course of making peace after a war or of celebrating religious festivities. [3] Indeed, rudimentary traces of trade are found at a level of historical development at which economic activities are not differentiated from other functions, such as religious rites or war. Trading in a narrow sense of the word — buying to resell at a profit — presumes a comparatively high level of economic development. [4]

Regular trade postulates division of labor and some specialization among individual households or communities — a differentiation which develops within a community later than among different communities. Thus commercial exchange among communities remote from each other, and often speaking different tongues, is older than the exchange of local products. Foreign trade is older than domestic trade. [5]

2. **31**, p. 6.
3. **22**, pp. 116–36.
4. As late as the fourth century B.C., Athens, the center of the civilized world, considered the business of trade an unnatural mode of acquiring wealth. According to Aristotle, it was "justly censured" as a dishonorable occupation in contrast to the honorable ways of getting wealth through the work of slaves in the fields, mines or forests. (**16**, Book I, Chapters 9 and 10.)
5. **24**, Vol. V, p. 244.

1. **17**, p. 14.

While division of labor and economic specialization are prerequisites of trade, differentiation does not always result in commercial exchange of goods. Communities with widely different patterns of production and consumption — for example, pastoral and agricultural tribes — may exist side by side without exchange. On the other hand, members of a primitive tribal community may perform specialized functions without commercial exchange of products.

Within a community, trade passes through three typical phases: barter among producers; direct sale of products by the producer — farmer or craftsman — to consumers;[6] and trade as a specialized business. The last form predominates in modern industrialized nations, but direct sale has been preserved in town and village markets and small handicraft shops. Moreover, the market in which consumers and other prospective buyers meet not only traders but also producers displaying their produce is still the prevailing form of exchange for a large part of mankind — in Middle and South America, Africa and Asia.

Trading as an Occupation

As a rule, a producer can personally reach consumers in only a limited area. If he lives in a city or suburb, he has direct access to the local market; if in a rural area, he has to seek buyers within the distance he can cover in a day. Direct sale by producers is, therefore, short-distance trade. When trade becomes a specialized occupation, the trader can move his merchandise from market to market, covering larger distances in search of profitable outlets. In the markets of Middle and South America and the Orient, such traders mingle with producers who bring their own products for sale. Perhaps the main difference between the two types of sellers is in the distance they can cover.

In early trade the specialized trader combines three functions: purchase of the product; its transportation over a distance which the original producer cannot easily cover; and its sale to consumers whom the producer cannot reach readily. In the past, a trader was associated with travel.[7]

He traveled with his merchandise from market to market, from community to community, selling and buying, a stranger and guest wherever he stopped with his bundle, pack horse, cart or ship. Transporting the merchandise was no less his function than buying and selling.

Foreign Trade

Very early traders discovered that long-distance trade was the most profitable and that they could cover great distances with the primitive means of transportation at their disposal.

In the times of Homer and the Bible, trade as a distinct economic activity was a combination of import and export, transportation, adventurous travel and occasional piracy.[8]

Sea-borne trade. Since overland roads were poor, if not wholly lacking, sea-borne trade prevailed in the Mediterranean Basin, the cradle of Western civilization. The Phoenicians, Carthaginians and Greeks led, and Tyrus (modern Tyre) was probably the main center of international trade in this area between the ninth and sixth centuries B.C.

The scope and diversity of Tyrus' commercial operations are revealed by the famous text of the prophet Ezekiel in which he predicts the destruction of the city. He depicts its past glory, enumerating the foreign products displayed at its fairs: rare timber — fir trees, cedars, oaks and ebony; metals — gold, silver, iron, tin, lead and brass; slaves, horsemen, mercenary mariners; horses, mules, lambs, rams and goats; wheat, wines, spices, honey, oil and balm; ivory, purple dyes, coral, agate and precious stones; embroidered and blue- and purple-dyed fabrics from many countries, fine clothing and linen, white wool and chests of rich apparel.[9] In terms of our modern statistical classifications, Tyrus in its glory traded in a great variety of raw materials and finished goods, staple commodities as well as luxuries. Its international trade was handled partly by private merchants in open fairs such as those described by the prophet, partly by exchange between the rulers of various kingdoms.[10]

---

6. This form of trade includes the operations of itinerant craftsmen who sell their services or products directly to consumers.

7. According to Aristotle, commerce consisted of three operations: the provision of a ship, the conveyance of goods, and exposure for sale. (**16**, Book I, Chapter 11.) Characteristically, transportation comes first in this description.

8. In *The Odyssey,* the aged Nestor asks Telemachus and his companions in the friendliest way: "Strangers, who are you? Whence sail you over the wet ways? On some trading enterprise, or at adventure do you rove as sea robbers?" (**21**, *The Odyssey,* Book III.)

9. Ezek. 27.

10. The Bible records an agreement between King Solomon and Hiram, the king of Tyrus. Hiram was to deliver cedar and fir trees to Israel for building the Tem-

Caravan routes. While sea trade was flourishing in the Mediterranean Basin, commerce in the East followed caravan routes. "Transport by camels across the desert was reckoned a far safer and more trustworthy method of conveyance than that by ship, and it was mostly by means of caravans that the products of India, of Arabia, and even those of Central Africa were dispatched from Arabia to Babylonia, to Syria, to Egypt, or even much farther to north and south." [11]

In the fourth century B.C. the conquests of Alexander brought the classical West and the Far East into contact: Bactria, which was the eastern limit of Alexander's advance, was within the reach of Chinese merchants.[12] At that time, world trade was expanding from two centers, from Greece and Rome eastward and from China southward and westward. Chinese merchants reached Malaya, Java, Ceylon and the eastern coast of India by sea and pushed overland across the expanses of Asia to the valleys of the Indus and to Persia, Syria and the Black Sea. Herbert Allen Giles describes six commercial routes that crossed China before the beginning of the Christian era, some of them a thousand years old at the time of Alexander the Great.[13]

Selfridge lists articles of Chinese domestic trade and export: rice, wheat, maize, millet and barley; tea in different forms, tobacco, opium, rhubarb, groundnuts, walnuts, bean cakes, peas; melons, oranges and other fruit and preserves; silk, cotton and hemp; timber and bamboo; wool and the skins of deer, goats and lambs, hides and leather; sheep, goats, yaks, pigs and camels; eggs, bristles, feathers; coal and pitch; silver, quicksilver, copper, antimony and steel; salt and sugar; paper, fans and other articles of paper; cloth and lace, ivories, indigo and varnishes, camphor, medicines, umbrellas, hats, porcelain and pottery, jade; ships.[14] Some of these articles were too bulky to be handled over long distances and transported over the forbidding

ridges of the Himalayas or Hindu Kush, but many were designed for transcontinental caravan trade.

West and East. Greek, and later Roman, merchants were active on the coasts of the Mediterranean, Black and Red Seas, in northern Africa, southern Europe and the Levant. At the time of the Roman Empire, Greeks, Syrians and Jews were the middlemen between Europe and the East in trade which extended from the British Isles and Spain to the Yellow and East China Seas.

The basis of this trade, writes George Unwin, lay in the more precious commodities, the price of which would repay the long transportation, the many profits and the great risk involved in passing from the heart of one continent to the extremities of another. In such traffic Asia, and even Africa, had the advantage over Europe. Apart from perishable products and those too bulky for long-distance hauling overland, Europe had few products to trade for the gold and ivory of Ethiopia, the frankincense and myrrh of Arabia, the pearls and spices of the Indies and the silk of China.

The distinctive exports of European countries at that time were amber, tin, furs from the northern forests, and slaves. European slaves appeared on African and Asiatic markets long before Europe became a market for slaves from other continents. The eastern trader who made his way northward across Europe must have been a dealer in slaves or have sought his gain in local trade in the necessities of life — salt, iron, wine and cloth. Trade routes across classical Europe, including the lanes across the Mediterranean, were only tributaries of the broad stream of commerce that flowed in many channels between Africa and Asia and converged in the Red Sea.[15] (See Figure 1.)

The Mediterranean was the main thoroughfare of the trade of the Western world and the bulwark of the economic unity of the Roman Empire,[16] but the center of *world trade* at that time lay further to the east, in the Red Sea.

The Social Status of the Trader

The ruins of temples and buildings related to trade, stock exchanges and sea traffic attest the importance of trade in the classical world. Long-distance trade from abroad was limited to valu-

---

ple, in exchange for wheat and oil. He was to supply labor to cut the trees in the mountains of Lebanon and bring them down to the sea and convey them by rafts to the place appointed by Solomon. The king of Israel would provide hire for the workers supplied by Hiram. (I Kings 5.)

11. **29**, p. 13.
12. **34**, p. 231.
13. "It must not be understood," he remarks, "that caravans made regular journeys from end to end along these courses. Trade was done by goods being passed from hand to hand along the way." (Quoted in **30**, pp. 28–29.)
14. **30**, p. 45.

15. **34**, p. 226. Cf. **33**, *passim.* For a description of the old "silk route" in China see **20**.
16. **26**, p. 1.

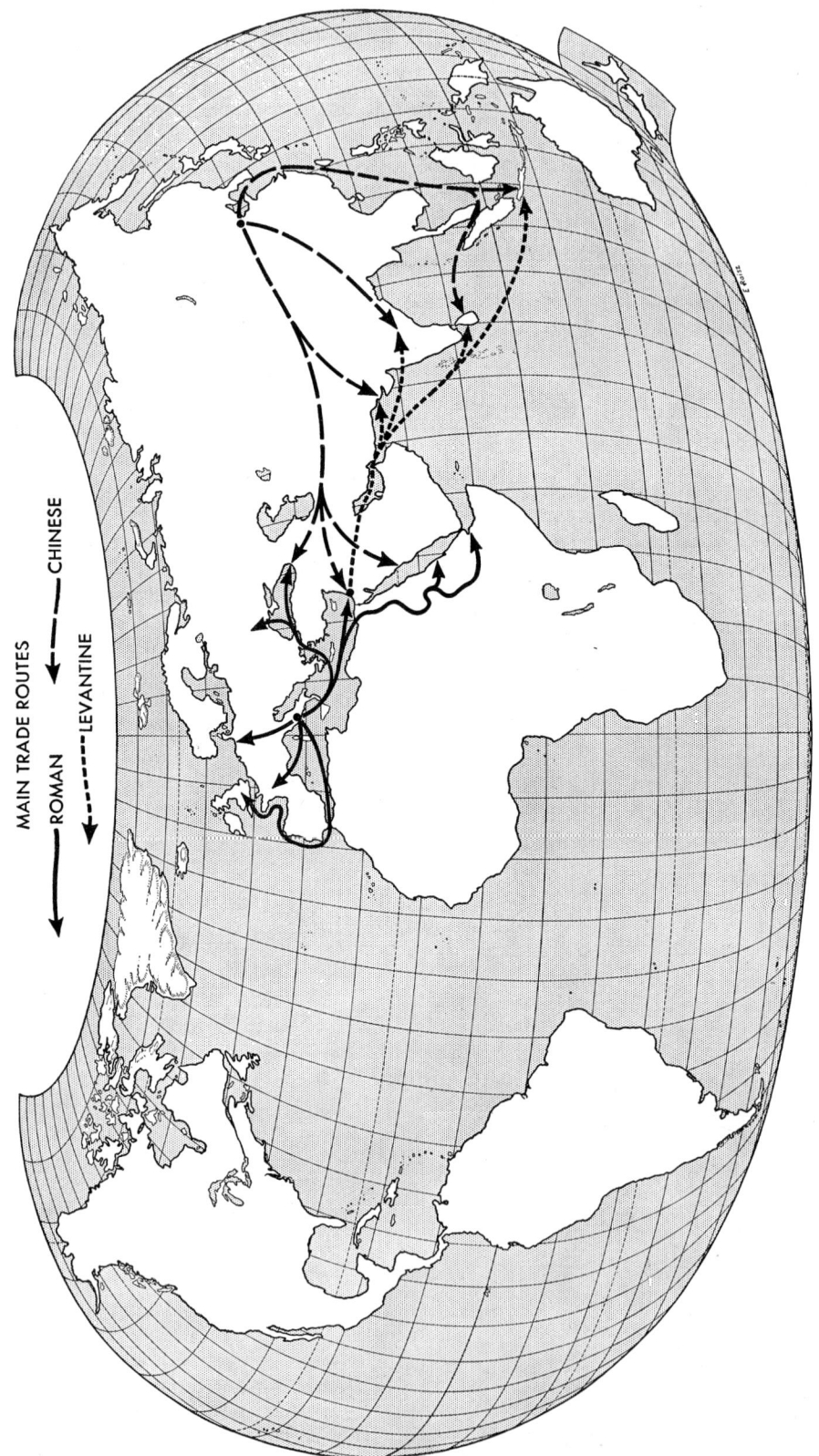

FIGURE 1. WORLD TRADE: MAIN ROUTES IN THE WEST AND EAST IN THE THIRD CENTURY A.D.

This map shows schematically the main routes of Roman and Chinese foreign trade in the third century of the Christian era, the time of full expansion of the Roman Empire. Chinese caravans reached the valleys of the Indus and Ganges and the shores of the Black Sea, Mediterranean Sea and Red Sea. Chinese sailing vessels carried merchandise to Malaya, Java and Ceylon, where they met merchants from the Levant.

Roman merchants went as far as the British Isles in the north, Ethiopia in the south and the coasts of the Black Sea in the northeast. The Levantine merchants traded with both the Romans and the Chinese. (After George Unwin.)

The general direction of the trade thoroughfare in China follows the old "silk route" described by Albert Herrmann. (Cf. **20**.)

MAIN TRADE ROUTES

ROMAN →

CHINESE →

LEVANTINE →

able luxury articles, but coastal commerce in the Mediterranean included a great variety of more bulky products — wine, olives, salt, wheat, fish, timber, tin, iron and so on.

There is ample evidence that traders represented a fairly large and wealthy group in the Roman Empire but did not belong to the ruling classes. Traveling from country to country and from city to city with his ships or caravans, the trader remained a stranger to the community he visited with his merchandise and a stranger to his home when he returned after a long absence. The public authorities encouraged trading, but traders were hardly more than tolerated. In the Roman Empire, as in ancient Greece, the owners of land, cattle and slaves constituted the upper class in the community. They were ready to multiply their wealth by usury and participation in trade ventures and speculation. Mingling with them, a trader could become a member of the upper class through marriage, public service or personal connections, but the wealthy slave owners and landlords did not recognize traders — as an occupational or social group — as their equals.

THE MIDDLE AGES

The role of Rome as the center of trade in the Western (Mediterranean) world depended less on its geographic location and the acumen of its traders than on the political and military power of the Eternal City. After the disintegration of the Roman Empire, the Mediterranean lost its significance as the main commercial thoroughfare of the Western world. Under the impact of wars, internal strains and onslaughts of the Germanic tribes, exchange of goods between the former provinces of the Empire declined. The Mediterranean remained a link between them and the East, but its commerce shrank. At the same time, the famous Roman roads, which had extended from the capital to the borders of the Empire, began to decay since no longer was any authority interested in maintaining them.[17] Although the pavements and bridges proved more durable than the political institutions of the Roman era, a thousand years after the eclipse of the Empire only disjointed portions remained of this engineering wonder of the ancient world.

The period following the invasions by the Germanic tribes — from the fourth to the sixth century A.D. — was characterized by far-reaching political and economic regression in Europe, but the general pattern of economic relations survived. This was not broken down and destroyed until the seventh century, with the onslaught of the Moslems from the east and south.[18] In no more than fifty years, Islam spread from the China Sea to the Atlantic Ocean, engulfing the Persian Empire, Syria, Egypt and northern Africa and reaching into Spain. This offensive cut the Western world off from Asia and Africa and closed to European trade the Mediterranean, which became, for the most part, a Moslem lake.[19]

This was the most important turning point in European history. Greece and Italy never recovered from the blow. The center of European trade shifted northward, from the Mediterranean to the areas along the Atlantic coast. The Crusades and the great voyages of the fifteenth and sixteenth centuries, which culminated in the discovery of America, were Europe's response to the challenge of the Moslem kingdoms that had risen in the seventh and eighth centuries as a wall between the West and the East.

Local Markets

The political decentralization of medieval Europe favored the development of market places for the exchange of goods among surrounding rural areas, monasteries and seignioral castles. Some of these local markets prospered and extended their influence and trade far beyond the customary day's travel of 15 to 20 miles with a pack horse or mule.

The network of cities developed slowly but steadily. Although feudalism was essentially the political organization of a rural economy, cultural life under this system was concentrated in towns, which were primarily local markets. The growing wealth of the cities was a main factor in the revival of foreign trade.

Foreign trade of that time was somewhat like that of the ancient world — long-distance commerce in rare and valuable luxuries.[20] It followed intricate routes by sea and land, usually starting from Mediterranean ports visited by Moslem merchants or from the Levant. Gold from Ethiopia, silk from China and spices from the Indies changed hands many times before

---

17. Cf. Chapter 8.

18. **26**, p. 23.
19. **26**, p. 24.
20. **26**, p. 127.

they reached European markets, where they commanded exorbitant prices.

In the cities of medieval Europe traders remained foreigners, but they were greeted with respect in conformity with their wealth and enjoyed special privileges. The corporations they established for mutual financial support increased their influence. The close relations between traders in different communities gave them relative security in a time of unsettled political conditions. Thus, the rise of cities was accompanied by the rise of traders as a social class. By the fourteenth century, the end of the Middle Ages, merchants had become a powerful social group in urban communities all over Europe and had developed into the ruling aristocracy of many Italian and Germanic cities.

From the point of view of world trade, however, Europe was still a colonial market of the Moslems.

The Search for a Route to the East

By the fifteenth century, European commerce had passed into the hands of traders from Portugal, Spain, the Netherlands, England and the Hanseatic League. In commerce with the East, they all paid tribute to the Arabs, who had a monopoly over trade with India and China. The Moslems held all the many known routes to the East. By that time, however, European merchants and navigators became convinced that the East could be reached by sea without passing through waters and lands under Moslem control. The Portuguese prince, Henry the Navigator, initiated a systematic search for a maritime route to the Orient.[21] Between 1415 and 1460, his captains, advancing slowly along the western coast of Africa, discovered, for the Portuguese crown, the Madeira and Canary Islands, Senegal and Guinea and penetrated into the Gulf of Guinea. Exploration of the African coast by the Portuguese continued after Henry's death in 1460.

A maritime route to the Indies was the main objective of successive expeditions, but more immediate assignments were added to this long-range goal — to establish trade with the natives, to lay a foundation for Portuguese settlements at strategic points along the coast, to acquire, by purchase or kidnaping, slaves for the domestic market. After eighty years of continuous effort, the Portuguese reached their goal: in 1497, Vasco

da Gama rounded the Cape of Good Hope and brought his ships into the Indian Ocean.

At the same time, the daring attempt of Columbus to reach India by sailing westward from Europe ended in the discovery of the West Indies.[22] Thus, by the end of the fifteenth century, Europe had broken the Moslem blockade. The whole world — Africa, Asia and America — lay open to European trade and colonization.

MODERN TIMES

Europe's foreign trade, revived by the great discoveries at the end of the fifteenth century and the beginning of the sixteenth, was directed chiefly, as in earlier times, toward the East. Trade with the Caribbean islands and the American mainland fell far below expectations, although the New World proved to be an excellent source of plunder and its mines and plantations were a promising market for the slave trade. Mexican gold and silver flowed to Spain and Portugal and from there to other European countries, providing specie to buy the luxuries imported in increasing quantities from the East.

At that time, Europe lagged behind Asia in industrial skill.[23] In exchange for silk, cotton, sugar and spices, Europe could export only small arms, which were hardly better than those made in the East, small quantities of tin and silver, furs and linen fabrics. Europe was too poor to gain any considerable advantage from trade over da Gama's route around the Cape of Good Hope. The flow of precious metals from America changed the situation. With American gold, and

---

22. To the end of his life, Columbus was convinced that the land he had discovered was China or some Chinese island. Amerigo Vespucci was the first to identify the discovered land as a new continent, to determine its location and to give an exact geographic description of the eastern coast of South America, covering approximately two thirds of the distance from the Caribbean Sea to Cape Horn. Dissipating the illusion of the western maritime route from Europe to Asia, Vespucci "discovered America" to contemporary geographers, who honored him by giving his name to the New World. (**27**, *passim*.)

23. The superiority of commerce, handicraft and administration in China in comparison with Italian cities was the theme of the fascinating story Marco Polo told his countrymen when, languishing in a Venetian jail, he recalled his travels to the Far East and his triumphs at the court of Kublai Khan. (**28**.) His story relates to the end of the thirteenth century, but there is no indication that Europe was catching up with China in the following century and a half.

---

21. **25**, pp. 45ff.

newly invented firearms, Europe ruled the world ocean.

European ships were not impressive, according to our standards — small, two-masted, half-decked boats dependent on wind and tide, with very imperfect nautical instruments and crews which seldom exceeded thirty men.[24] Their captains were hardly superior to the Arabs in navigating skill, but they had a common goal and, in their drive to remote and unknown lands, they made full use of the compass and nautical map — two marvelous devices developed by the Moors.[25] They were animated by an aggressive spirit similar to that of the Moslems in their conquests in the seventh and eighth centuries.

The history of European commerce in the sixteenth century is the history of the slave trade, the plunder of Mexico and South America and the colonial conquests in Africa and the Indian Ocean. By the end of the century, a pattern of multilateral foreign trade developed, as Spanish-American gold flowed to India and the Spice Islands in the Pacific in payment for Oriental produce.[26]

This pattern began to change in the second half of the seventeenth century, which can be considered the beginning of the Industrial Revolution in England. The development of new forms of foreign trade was accelerated in the following century, after the steam engine and new textile machines had opened undreamed-of perspectives to the British textile industry, first to wool mills and later to cotton. Factory towns sprang up. Manufacturers combed the world for raw materials and markets. New times required a radical revision of foreign trade policy. The emphasis shifted from the search for foreign products — the mainspring of foreign trade until the sixteenth century — to the search for outlets for domestic merchandise.

The Search for Markets

Lack of outlets for fabrics, which were turned out in greater quantities than the domestic markets could absorb, brought a remarkable change in the colonial policy of the seafaring European nations.

When Columbus landed in the West Indies and Vasco da Gama reached India, Europe had stretched its tentacles to the end of the world. The objective of subsequent expeditions and further exploration became more practical. Cortez and Pizarro set the goal of Spanish colonization in America — the plunder of treasure accumulated by the old native civilizations. At the same time, the Indian Ocean became the scene of desperate rivalry among European nations for control over the export of local products — mainly spices — to Europe. Now, in the seventeenth century, the British and Dutch discovered the value of overseas colonies as monopolistically controlled markets. (See Chapter 14.) By this time, factories — without mechanical power — had begun to appear in Western Europe, and their comparatively inexpensive products found outlets in the Orient. With the beginning of the eighteenth century — long before the technical revolution in England was completed — Europe began to export manufactured goods, mainly textiles, in exchange for tropical and semitropical products largely supplied by colonial plantations.

Modern times — beginning in the sixteenth century — have brought conspicuous changes in the social position of merchants. Although the standards of colonial business, including the slave trade, were not puritanical, people successful in such business gained a prominent social status. Stock companies engaged in overseas trade, and especially in trade with colonies, generously shared their profits with influential backers. Overseas trade, piracy and high policy went hand in hand, as exemplified by the career of Queen Elizabeth's brilliant captain, Sir Francis Drake.[27] Adventure and close association with politics continued to characterize foreign and

---

24. **25**, p. 45. Cf. Chapter 10.

25. The place and time of the invention of the compass are unknown. A floating magnetic needle had been used occasionally by seamen in various parts of the world since the thirteenth century, but there are indications that the Arabs were the first to realize the advantages of the compass in navigating according to a nautical map plotted on the network of meridians and parallels. Vasco da Gama learned the use of such maps from the Moors. (**18**.)

26. **23**, Vol. VI, p. 284.

27. Drake's voyage around the world was financed by a joint stock company which invested £5,000 in outfitting, arming and manning his ships. The objective of the expedition was discovery of new lands, sea routes and possibilities for colonization, and trade with the natives. The sideline was to plunder Spanish ships bringing the spoils from colonies to Europe. The business proved profitable; back home, the admiral paid out 4,700 per cent on the capital ventured by his backers and made a present of £300,000 to the Queen. The total returns from his voyage were estimated at £1,500,000 to £1,750,000, or £300 to £350 on each pound invested. (**17**, p. 91.)

colonial trade in the eighteenth century, but the emphasis shifted toward export of inexpensive domestic fabrics and other manufactured articles and import of products of colonial plantations and mines operated by European capital with benefit of cheap native labor.

At the beginning of the eighteenth century Great Britain was the leading colonial power. The American colonies were its most valuable overseas possession and the most promising market for its manufactures. However, control over this market and its monopolistic exploitation were becoming increasingly difficult. The colonies were growing economically and politically. Local capital appeared on the scene and the drive of the population for economic independence foreshadowed serious troubles for Great Britain.

Free Trade vs. Protectionism

Rebellion of British colonies in North America, followed by upheaval in Latin America, marked the end of the old colonialism in the Western Hemisphere and compelled Great Britain to revise its trade policy. There was only one alternative to the policy of monopolistic control over limited overseas markets — free trade, which would ultimately give control of the world market to the most efficient nation. This was the trade policy that had been recommended to Great Britain by Adam Smith and his school before the rebellion of the American colonies. Reorientation of British foreign trade was interrupted, however, by the French Revolution and the Napoleonic wars.

Repercussions of the long struggle between England and France for supremacy in Europe were felt all over the world, from South America and the Caribbean to the Indian Ocean. As in the recent world wars, the clash of arms was combined with a series of revolutions and counterrevolutions, wanton destruction and a long period of reconstruction, revision of the political map and redistribution of colonial possessions. England emerged from the conflict impoverished, exhausted by high taxes, saddled with a heavy national debt, but with largely increased productive capacity, elated by victory, politically strong, supreme on the seven seas.[28]

After the secession of the American colonies, commercial interests in Great Britain turned again toward the East, where the British were building up a new colonial empire around the Indian Ocean. The goal of British trade policy, however, remained the world market.

The new policy required keen competition, cuts in production costs of exported merchandise, and cheap food, but, first of all, elimination of trade barriers. Powerful interests opposed these measures and demanded protection of domestic agriculture, industry and trade by customs duties. The clash between the protectionists and free traders remained the main issue of the domestic policy in Great Britain for a quarter of a century and ended in the 1840's with the victory of the free traders. In other countries, including the United States, the dispute continued with intermittent successes for one party or the other, and has never been settled.[29]

The controversy between free trade and protectionism has often been presented as a clash between selfish nationalism and internationalism. Actually, the two schools of thought reflect the interests of different groups of the population in different phases of national economic growth. The nations that lag behind in technology and efficiency are inclined to encircle themselves with protective or prohibitive tariffs; those with a superior industrial plant and trade organization, although occasionally using high tariffs to support certain groups of domestic producers, tend to condemn this policy when it is practiced by weaker and less developed countries.

Adam Smith, the spokesman of exuberant and aggressive British industry, was the most eloquent proponent of free trade. The idea of protecting young and weak industries by import duties was brilliantly expressed by Alexander Hamilton [30] and later elaborated by Friedrich

---

28. Condliffe compares Great Britain at the end of the Napoleonic wars with the United States after World War II. Free from invasion, Britain "had developed productivity, technical skill, and financial strength. . . .

Instead of a debtor, it had become practically the sole creditor country in the world. . . . Refugee capital had flowed to Britain, and London had taken the place of Amsterdam as the leading money market of the world. Britain had been the arsenal and the paymaster of the enemies of Napoleon. The credit to restore their currencies and the skilled workmen to reorganize their industries could come only from her." (**17**, p. 203.) Like all historical comparisons, the parallel between Britain of 1820 and the United States of 1950 requires some reservation, but the similarity of the situation cannot be denied.

29. See Chapter 6.

30. **19.** In many points, Hamilton fell back on the ideas of the mercantilists, but he gave them a new slant.

List, the German economist, who referred to American experience to convince his countrymen of the advantages of industrialization.[31] The arguments of these two have remained the gospel of protectionism. They have been used to justify import duties in economically weak countries, while the industrialized, high-wage nations have portrayed their own tariffs as a defense against unfair competition of foreign underpaid labor, the same argument that the English wool weavers brandished against the import of Indian cotton fabrics in the eighteenth century.[32]

Customs were not fully abolished in even the industrial countries most inclined to this doctrine, but revenue duties predominated in their tariffs. Moreover, thanks to the system of trade treaties, the world as a whole was never closer to the freedom of sea traffic and trade than on the eve of World War I.

Economic Expansion

Growth of world trade in the nineteenth century was stimulated by technological progress. Railroads knit together Western Europe and the states of the United States. Steamers conquered the Atlantic and the Pacific. Raw materials and finished goods could be shipped cheaply in large quantities and over long distances.[33] Mass production on an unprecedented scale began in the United States and Europe, especially in Germany, which was rapidly becoming the leading industrial power in the Old World. In the Far East, Japan was emerging as a great power. In Africa and Asia, Great Britain and France built up their colonial possessions into world-encircling empires.[34] The gold standard assured the stability of international exchange rates which favored the flow of foreign investments.

Under these conditions, a definite pattern of world trade developed in the latter part of the nineteenth century. It rested on the division of labor between the industrial and the agrarian countries and tended to perpetuate the contrast in their economic structure. In the Old World, this was a division between western and central Europe, on the one hand, and the rest of Europe, Africa and Asia, on the other. The role of the United States in this system was vague. Its share in world trade was rather small in comparison with its growing industrial power and its wealth and population.[35] Unlike the industrial countries of Europe, the United States had an export surplus, and such products as wheat, corn, cotton and tobacco were its leading exports.

The New Pattern of World Trade

Just before the outbreak of World War I, the structure of world trade differed appreciably from the pattern which had prevailed in the nineteenth century. Bulky staple commodities, such as coal, petroleum, iron ore, timber, wheat and cotton, became the most important articles of international exchange. The simple geographical pattern of exchange between countries of the tropical and temperate climatic zones yielded to another and more complex pattern controlled largely by differences in the level of economic development.

London was the center of world trade. The mainspring of international exchange of commodities was Britain's demand for foodstuffs and raw materials and its ability to pay for them with coal, machines and fabrics.

The network of world trade had been changing since the turn of the century, and some of these changes contributed to international tensions and precipitated armed conflict in 1914. The economic growth of the United States was not among these factors. The United States was largely self-sufficient, and its increasing share in world industry did not affect the interests of other nations. The main source of international unrest lay in the rise of Germany and Japan.

Political Frictions

After its victory over France in 1871, unified Germany entered the political scene as the strongest military power of Europe. A generation later, growing population and industrialization also made it the leading economic power. However, long before Germany arrived at this predominance in continental Europe, world markets and overseas colonial areas had been distributed among other industrial nations. The German nationalists therefore felt that the

---

31. **23**, Vol. IV.

32. A publication of English woolen interests in 1719 referred to these fabrics as "a tawdry, pie spotted, flabby low-priced thing, called Callicoe . . . made by a parcel of Heathens and Pagans, that worship the Devil and work for half penny a day." (**17**, p. 58.) The language is somewhat old-fashioned, but the thinking quite modern.

33. See Chapters 8 and 10.

34. See Chapter 14.

35. Cf. Chapter 2.

Fatherland did not have a fair share of the overseas possessions and would have to fight for a "place in the sun." This became the goal of German policy. Using a moment of political confusion and conflict between Great Britain and France, Germany succeeded in getting a foothold in Africa in the 1880's.[36] Its colonies there were not very valuable from the purely economic point of view, but they could become the nucleus of a new colonial empire.

With this objective in sight, Germany began to build up its navy and merchant fleet. By the end of the nineteenth century, it had become a first-rate sea power. It was no less successful in the policy of economic penetration. After having established commercial relations with South America, China and Japan, Germany could challenge Great Britain in the latter's customary overseas markets and even in the British colonies. Germany's commercial organization proved to be more flexible than Great Britain's and its merchandise cheaper. At the same time, Germany exercised pressure on Russia in an effort to prevent its industrialization, and to exploit its agricultural resources. After the turn of the century, largely under the impact of the economic and political offensive of Germany, an armament race developed in Europe. Long before the shot at Sarajevo, the lines of the imminent conflict were set — the Central Powers, Germany and its satellites, against the Triple Alliance. Russia, Britain and France represented the old order which had prevailed in Europe since the end of the Napoleonic wars, while Germany sought a redistribution of colonial possessions and of the world's raw materials and markets. Japan refrained from joining forces with Germany because its aspirations had been satisfied temporarily by the victory over Russia in 1905.

The war touched off by a dispute between Russia and Austria over Serbia developed into a world conflagration and opened a long period of war and revolution of unprecedented violence.

RECENT TRENDS

Aftermath of World War I

World War I left Europe in political and economic chaos. Revolution swept over the central and eastern parts of the continent. Runaway inflation developed in a dozen countries. In the course of disputes over the new political boundaries and the hypothetical German reparations payments, the victorious alliance disintegrated. Its dissolution destroyed the old balance of power in Europe, but no substitute for it was in sight: no nation could assume leadership, no group of nations was sufficiently strong to police peace. The League of Nations, based on the shaky foundation of the Versailles Treaty and weakened by the abstention of the United States and the split among the former Allies, could not cope with the situation.

As at the time of the Napoleonic wars, European nations lost their grip over colonial and semicolonial areas. Deep cracks appeared in the structure of the two largest colonial empires — the British and the French. The principle of trusteeship (mandate) developed by the League of Nations for administration of former German colonies and parts of the Ottoman Empire was a heavy blow to the old system of colonial relations.[37]

Interwar Years

Disorganization of currencies, instability of the new political system in Europe, the protracted controversy about reparations payments and inter-Allied debts [38] and continuous trouble in the colonies made the restoration of world trade difficult. Moreover, the war shattered the great empires of the nineteenth century — Russia, Austria-Hungary and Turkey — and replaced them with a cluster of smaller independent nations.[39] Thousands of miles of new international boundaries, protected by customs barriers, were drawn across the traditional routes of intra-European trade. Each new state aspired to economic self-sufficiency and tried to achieve it by hedging itself with protective tariffs. The drive in Europe toward higher tariffs and the regimentation of international commerce was strengthened by the highly protective tariff established by the United States in 1922.[40]

Despite these difficulties, the economic reconstruction of Europe after the war of 1914–18 was much more successful than the attempts to restore its political life on a foundation of lasting peace. By 1928–29 the international flow of goods had returned to the prewar pattern.

In the fall of 1929, the collapse of the stock

---

36. See Chapter 14.

37. See Chapter 14.
38. See Chapter 16.
39. See **35,** Vol. I, pp. 21–22.
40. See Chapter 6.

market in the United States signaled the beginning of the great depression. The fall of prices, disorganization of international credit and depreciation of national currencies resulted in disintegration of the world market. In all parts of the world, nations besieged by economic and financial difficulties sought solution for their problems in the policy of self-sufficiency and isolationism. Goods continued to flow across political boundaries, but free competition, vital for determining economically sound international prices and exchange rates, was replaced by restrictive regulations and bilateral agreements.

Despite the disorganization of international markets, the ratio of the volume of international trade to world production of raw materials and foodstuffs did not decline appreciably in the 1930's. Its characteristic features remained the exchange of raw materials and foodstuffs for manufactured goods between the industrially developed and the primarily agricultural areas; regional trade within Europe, Asia and the British Commonwealth; long-distance trade in tropical products, coal, petroleum and rare metals. The deterioration of world trade at that time became apparent, however, in the change in its direction among the continents and geographic regions. The multilateral trade of the latter part of the nineteenth century, which had reached full development between the end of that century and the outbreak of World War I, began to lose ground to bilateral transactions reminiscent of barter exchange.

Repercussions of World War II

World War II has again changed the political setting of international trade. The defeat of Germany and Japan opened the way for expansion of the USSR and provided the Kremlin with an opportunity to establish political and military control over smaller countries adjacent to the Soviet Union. A new superempire has been emerging out of the ruins left by the war, and the resurrection of aggressive totalitarian militarism in the USSR has signaled the threat of a new world war.

This danger has had far-reaching implications for the world economy. Leadership in the resistance of the Western world to new aggression passed to the United States, and the goal of its policy became the strengthening of the free nations economically and militarily and the promo-

tion of economic progress in underdeveloped areas.

Postwar Recovery

In contrast to the early 1920's, the campaign for reconstruction after World War II has been carried out largely as a coordinated international action. Its goals have included stabilization of exchange rates, support of national currencies, increase in productivity, elimination of obstacles to international trade, limitation of quantitative restrictions on imports, reduction of tariffs, restoration of exports disorganized by the war, promotion of multilateral trade agreements. The financial foundation of this international action has been provided by the United States, in the form of foreign credits and grants of aid.[41] At the same time, far-reaching programs have been developed to help the underdeveloped areas to improve health conditions, establish efficient financial and economic administrations, modernize local means of transportation, develop natural resources and increase agricultural production.[42]

For international trade, the ultimate objective of this policy has been restoration of a freer, more competitive world market. This goal, however, could not be reached simply by repeal of restrictions accumulated in the past three or four decades. The situation required a combination of negative and positive measures. While some regulations have been repealed, other economic controls, introduced during World War II, have been maintained and strengthened.

The Split World

The meaning of the terms "world market," "world trade" and "world economy" has changed in the last four decades. Before the war of 1914–18, the concept of "world" applied to the globe as a whole. In the interwar years, "world trade" included all countries except the USSR. Today the Iron Curtain has split the world in two. Approximately 30 per cent of mankind, occupying one fourth of the land surface of our planet and controlling about 15 per cent of the world's income, is isolated from the rest. Although this fourth did not have a large share in world trade before World War II, the split has had a serious effect on the world econ-

41. See Chapter 5.
42. See Chapter 17.

omy. In Europe, the Iron Curtain has cut off the heavily industrialized areas from those with agricultural surpluses; in Asia, it has cut China off from the rest of the continent.

The splitting of the world has influenced the goals of economic policy on both sides of the Iron Curtain. The goal of Moscow — to knit together the new superempire as its strictly centralized domain — requires conversion of all newly conquered nations into hinterlands and buffer areas subordinated to Russia proper, the hard core of the Communist state. The goal of the free world — to heal the wounds inflicted upon the world economy by the split — requires full utilization of available resources and wide distribution of the advantages of economic progress among all peoples.

This policy for the free world is dictated not by altruistic motives but by the impending struggle for survival. The economically prosperous free nations represent a minority of mankind, and they realize that superior technology alone will not protect them against the assault of communism unless they succeed in uniting around them peoples who so far have had only a small share in the advantages of modern mechanized civilization. Thus the leading industrial nations are compelled to seek the friendship of the so-called underdeveloped areas, to share with them their know-how, to meet them on terms of equality. This need opens a new era in the history of international cooperation.[43]

EMPLOYMENT IN TRADE

Approximately 100 million persons — 10 per cent of the world's total labor force and more than 20 per cent of its nonagricultural labor force — are employed in trade in the broad sense, including finance and insurance.[44]

TRADE AS AN OCCUPATION AND BUSINESS

In the regions where a subsistence economy prevails, trade is not clearly differentiated from other pursuits, especially farming.[45] Most of the vendors in Oriental or Middle and South American markets sell their own produce; others sell their own products and those of their neighbors, and only a few are professional traders. When a country with this economic structure takes a census of population, it is likely to record as engaged in trade only those whose main or sole occupation is buying and selling.

Similarly, at an early stage of economic development, trade is not clearly differentiated from the transportation business. Transportation developed into a specialized business in the nineteenth century, the age of railroads, but its distinction from trade has become less clear in recent years as a result of progress in trucking. Since distributive trade has resumed its old function of carrying goods from producers to ultimate consumers, it is not always possible to distinguish persons employed in commerce from those working in transportation. In some countries, censuses count the two industrial divisions together.

Long-Range Trends

Increase in industrialization and urbanization has been marked by an increase in the proportion of the labor force employed in trade and transportation. The increase seems very rapid when the number of workers in these pursuits is compared with the total labor force, but appears less impressive when compared with the labor force in other nonagricultural occupations or when comparison is restricted to the urban population.

In Sweden, for example, only 5.2 per cent of the population made their living from trade, transportation and communication in 1870 while in 1945, 20.9 per cent were thus engaged.[46] The proportion of the nonagricultural population attached to these pursuits, however, increased only from 18.9 per cent in 1870 to 29.7 per cent in 1945, and the share of trade, transportation and communication in the urban population, from 25.7 to 32.1 per cent. (See Table 1.) Nonetheless, it is true that employment in trade has increased in Sweden more rapidly than in industrial production (manufacture, handicraft and building construction). Sweden had 35.6 persons attached to trade and transportation per 100 attached to industrial production in 1870, 52.6 per 100 in 1945; for urban communities alone, the corresponding increase was from 49.7 to 70 per 100.

In the United States, the trend is somewhat obscured by the classification of gainful workers in the censuses from 1870 to 1920, which re-

---

43. See Chapter 17.
44. Cf. p. 21, Table 5.
45. Cf. **38**, pp. 413ff; and especially Figures 134 (p. 421) and 137 (p. 434).

---

46. These figures include gainful workers and their dependents.

TABLE 1

EMPLOYMENT IN TRADE: NUMBER AND PROPORTION OF PERSONS LIVING FROM TRADE,[a] IN SWEDEN, 1870–1945

| | Number, in Thousands | | | | Persons Living from Trade [b] as Percentage of: | | |
| | All Occupations | | Trade [b] | | | | |
Year	Total Population	Urban Population	Total Population	Urban Population	Total Population	Urban Population	Nonagricultural Population
1870	4,169	540	217	139	5.2	25.7	18.9
1880	4,566	691	334	196	7.3	28.4	22.8
1890	4,785	900	414	253	8.7	28.1	22.8
1900	5,136	1,104	535	322	10.4	29.2	23.2
1910	5,522	1,367	741	425	13.4	31.1	26.0
1920	5,904	1,743	898	565	15.2	32.4	27.1
1930	6,142	1,996	1,117	697	18.2	34.9	30.0
1940	6,371	2,381	1,245	788	19.5	33.1	29.7
1945	6,674	2,807	1,396	900	20.9	32.1	29.7

Source: Computed from **15**, 1950, pp. 32–33.

a. Workers and dependents. Persons retired from work are distributed by industrial division according to their former occupation; domestic servants are distributed according to the occupation of the head of the household.

b. Includes finance, transportation and communication.

corded as a separate group "clerical occupations" — agents, collectors and credit men, bookkeepers, cashiers and accountants, clerks, stenographers and typists, messengers, errand and office boys and girls. In 1930, approximately 40 per cent of all clerical workers were employed in trade, including finance and insurance.[47] In analyzing the long-range trend in the industrial distribution of the labor force it seems advisable, therefore, to allocate to trade the same proportion of the persons recorded in "clerical occupations" in the censuses of 1870–1920. On that basis, it appears that trade employed 7.0 per cent of all gainful workers in 1870, 11.6 per cent in 1900, and 15.7 per cent in 1930. The percentage increased in the two following decades but the data for 1940 and 1950 are not strictly comparable with those for 1870–1920. (See Table 2.)

All in all, despite the differences in classification, the trends in the United States and Sweden have been similar:

1. The share of trade in employment (labor force attached to trade or number of persons engaged in the respective pursuits, with their dependents) has been increasing rapidly.

2. Its share in the nonagricultural labor force also increased, slowly but steadily, until around 1910–20 in Sweden and until 1930 in the United States, but has not changed appreciably since those years.

47. **37**, pp. 13–16.

The available data for other countries, most of which cover only two or three decades, confirm these general observations. Employment in trade increases with increase in industrialization and

TABLE 2

EMPLOYMENT IN TRADE: NUMBER AND PROPORTION OF GAINFUL WORKERS [a] IN TRADE, IN THE UNITED STATES, 1870–1950

| | Number, in Thousands | | Workers in Trade [b] as Percentage of: | |
Year	All Industries	Trade [b]	All Workers	Nonagricultural Workers
1870	12,925	911	7.0	15.0
1880	17,392	1,435	8.2	16.3
1890	23,318	2,238	9.6	18.1
1900	29,073	3,380	11.6	18.7
1910	37,371	4,350	11.6	16.2
1920	42,434	5,937	14.0	19.2
1930	48,830	7,691	15.7	20.0
1930 [c]	47,400	7,660	16.2	20.6
1940	53,300	8,730	16.4	19.7
1950	59,583	10,925	18.3	19.5

Sources: 1870–1930, computed from **8**, pp. 100–01; 1930 and 1940, from **9**, p. 64; 1950 from preliminary releases of the Bureau of the Census.

a. For 1940 and 1950 persons in labor force according to the Census.

b. For 1870–1930, gainful workers in trade, plus 40 per cent of persons in clerical professions.

c. Data of the 1930 Census adjusted to the classification used in the 1940 Census.

TABLE 3

EMPLOYMENT IN TRADE: INDEXES OF EMPLOYMENT IN TRADE, ALL INDUSTRIES AND MANUFACTURING, IN THE
UNITED STATES, 1929–52 ANNUAL AVERAGE

(1929 = 100)

Year	Indexes of Employment			Employment in Trade as Percentage of Employment in:	
	Wholesale and Retail Trade	All Industries	Manufacturing	All Industries	Manufacturing
1929	100.0	100.0	100.0	16.9	73.3
1930	96.1	95.7	89.2	17.0	78.9
1931	90.0	88.9	75.6	17.1	97.1
1932	82.4	81.4	63.9	17.1	94.4
1933	82.0	82.4	68.9	16.9	87.2
1934	88.9	89.6	80.0	16.8	81.4
1935	91.7	92.4	85.1	16.8	79.0
1936	97.6	99.2	92.2	16.7	77.6
1937	104.2	101.9	101.2	17.3	75.4
1938	103.2	98.1	87.4	17.8	86.4
1939	107.0	101.0	95.5	17.9	82.0
1940	111.8	105.3	104.3	18.0	78.5
1941	117.5	114.9	125.7	17.3	68.5
1942	114.8	125.6	146.1	15.5	57.5
1943	110.0	138.0	166.2	13.5	48.5
1944	110.3	140.9	162.9	13.3	49.6
1945	114.6	137.6	145.4	14.1	57.7
1946	133.4	125.4	139.0	18.0	70.3
1947	140.8	126.7	145.8	18.8	70.7
1948	144.6	128.4	146.4	19.1	72.3
1949	142.9	125.5	135.7	19.3	77.1
1950	145.1	128.0	143.1	19.1	74.3
1951	148.8	136.9	154.3	18.4	70.7
1952	151.5	139.8	157.1	18.4	70.7

Sources: For 1929–1950, **7**, National Income Supplement, 1951, pp. 188–89; for 1951 and 1952, **7**, July 1953, p. 21. All figures refer to the number of persons engaged in production in the respective industries as estimated by the U.S. Department of Commerce.

urbanization, but there is no general economic law of increase in the number of workers in commerce in comparison with that in manufactures.

Short-Range Variations

The long-range trend in the proportion of labor force engaged in trade is overlapped by short-range fluctuations. Apart from the seasonal rhythm, employment in trade changes with the business cycle, and its cyclical changes differ from those in industrial production and other activities.

In the United States, employment in trade is less sensitive to ups and downs in the business cycle than employment in manufacturing. In the early 1930's, the initial phase of the depression, it did not drop as much as factory employment.

On the other hand, in 1942–45, during the war boom, it did not rise as did employment in manufacturing. During the war, indeed, employment in trade fell below the 1941 level, and it did not begin to rise until the reconversion period, when total industrial production was declining but production of consumer goods was going up.

Moreover, during most of this time the share of trade in total employment in nonagricultural establishments has fluctuated within a comparatively narrow range. It was between 16.7 and 18.0 per cent in 1929–41, dropped to 13.3 per cent in 1944, reached a new peak of 19.3 per cent in 1949 and dropped to 18.4 in 1951–52.

In 1929, 73.3 persons were engaged in trade per 100 persons in manufactures; the ratio rose to 94.4 per 100 at the depth of the depression

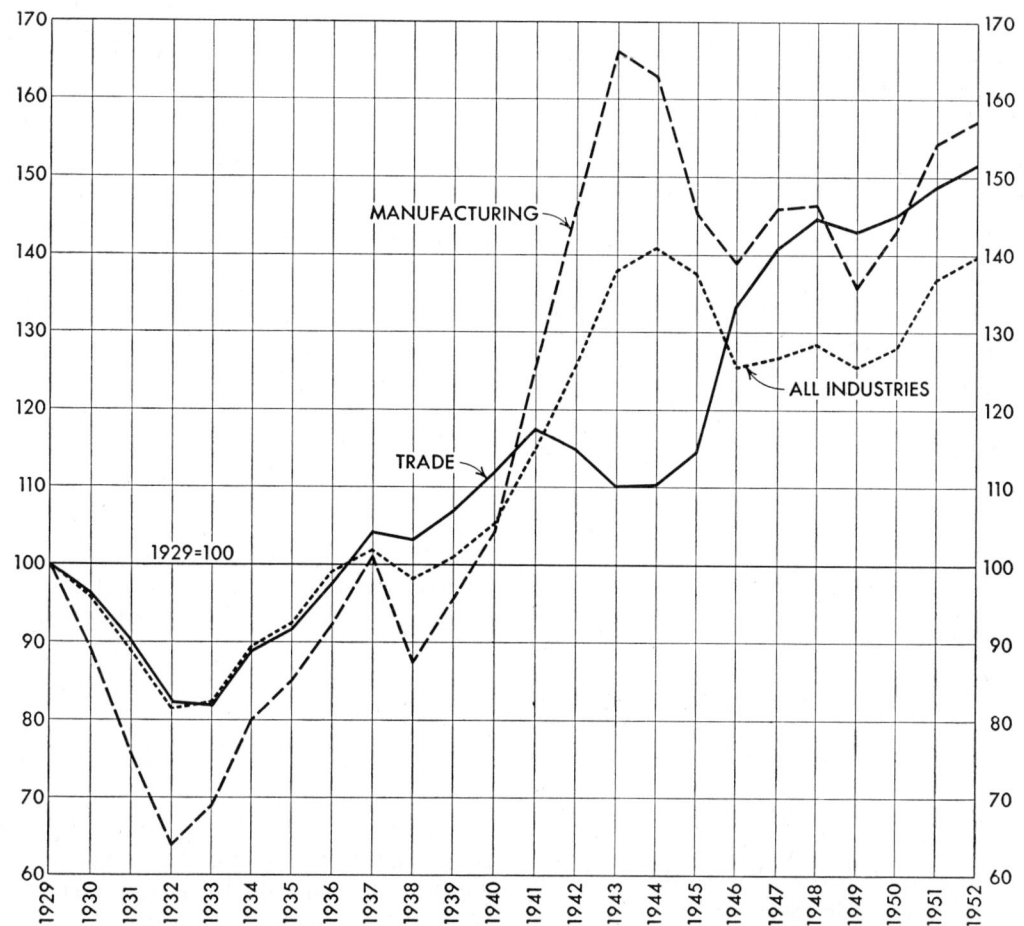

FIGURE 2. EMPLOYMENT IN TRADE: INDEXES OF EMPLOYMENT IN ALL INDUSTRIES, TRADE AND
MANUFACTURING, IN THE UNITED STATES, 1929–52 ANNUAL AVERAGE

The indexes in this chart represent the series computed by the U.S. Department of Commerce in its estimates of national income. The figures include all "persons engaged in production" — employers, self-employed persons and family workers as well as salaried and wage workers. (See Table 3.)

In peacetime, short-range variations in employment in wholesale and retail trade have been close to those in total employment. In the long run, however, employment in trade has kept pace with the growth of employment in manufacturing industries.

(1932), averaged 73.5 in 1940–41, fell to 48.5 per 100 at the peak of war boom (1943), and averaged 72.3 in 1946–52, about the same as in 1929 and 1940-41. (See Table 3; cf. Figure 2.)

Selected Countries

Comparison of employment patterns in countries widely different in economic structure cannot be very precise. Employment in trade cannot be measured satisfactorily in the areas where a subsistence economy prevails. A city in such an area is primarily a commercial center and becomes an ant hill of traders on market day. Trade is relatively more dominant in such a city than in a modern metropolis.

International surveys of the distribution of workers by industry, inaugurated by the International Labor Office [48] and continued by the United Nations,[49] cover more than two score countries. In most of these, "commerce" includes not only wholesale and retail trade but also banking and finance, even when this fact is not explicitly stated. As a general rule, the classification likewise includes eating and drinking places, which often employ more labor than any other branch of retail trade. On the other hand, hotels and lodging houses, craftsmen's shops and repair

48. **5**, 1942, pp. 6–17; 1951–52, pp. 10–34.
49. **1**, 1949–1950, pp. 254–75; **4**, 1949–1950, pp. 64–85; **5**, 1951–52, pp. 10–34.

and service businesses are not counted in this group. Differences in the census definition of the scope of "commerce" and "trade" are perhaps less significant, however, than the difficulty of classifying people who divide their time between trade and other pursuits.

According to recent censuses, trade absorbs more than 13 per cent of the total labor force in countries highly developed economically, such as the United States (18.3 per cent, 1950), Germany (17.5 per cent in 1939), Canada (16.1 per cent, 1951), Australia (15.2 per cent, 1947), New Zealand (14.3 per cent, 1945), the Netherlands (14.1 per cent, 1947), Belgium (13.4 per cent, 1947) and Austria (13.3 per cent, 1951). At the other extreme, less than 5 per cent of the gainful workers are reported in trade in underdeveloped, primarily agricultural countries such as Peru (4.5 per cent, 1940), Thailand (4.4 per cent, 1937), Turkey (3.7 per cent, 1945), Colombia (3.5 per cent, 1938), Romania (3.4 per cent, 1930), Yugoslavia (2.6 per cent, 1931) and Bulgaria (2.3 per cent, 1934). The pattern is less clear in the middle of the distribution. The share of trade in the national labor force varies between 9 and 11 per cent in widely different countries — Mexico, Cuba and Chile, on the one hand, Norway and Switzerland, on the other. (See Table 4; cf. Figure 3.)

The range is narrowed when the number of persons engaged in trade is related to the total nonagricultural labor force. The countries listed in Table 4 rank as follows in the percentage of the total nonagricultural labor engaged in trade:

Thailand (1937)	39.0
Mexico (1940)	27.2
Egypt (1937)	25.8
Germany (1939)	23.5
Hawaii (1950)	22.9
Japan (1950)	22.0
United States (1950)	21.0
Canada (1951)	20.5
Austria (1951)	19.5
Ireland (1946)	18.6
France (1946)	18.5
Australia (1947)	18.0
New Zealand (1945)	17.9
Brazil (1940)	17.5
Netherlands (1947)	17.5
Denmark (1940)	17.1
Cuba (1943)	16.7
Venezuela (1941)	16.6
Italy (1936)	16.2
India (1931)	16.2

Romania (1930)	16.0
Sweden (1945)	15.6
Turkey (1945)	15.4
Belgium (1947)	15.3
Norway (1950)	14.9
United Kingdom (1951)	14.8
Chile (1940)	14.4
Puerto Rico (1940)	13.6
Philippines (1948)	13.4
Spain (1940)	13.1
Colombia (1938)	12.9
Finland (1940)	12.8
Switzerland (1941)	12.5
Yugoslavia (1931)	12.3
Portugal (1940)	12.2
Peru (1940)	12.1
Panama (1950)	12.0
Bulgaria (1934)	11.7
Czechoslovakia (1947)	10.3

All in all, there is no close correlation between the level of economic development and the share of trade in the total nonagricultural labor force or in nonagricultural employment.

The World

For a rough estimate of the number of persons engaged in trade in the world, the data for underdeveloped countries should be adjusted upward to allow for understatement in the reported figures and the increase in urbanization and industrialization since the latest census. The rate of correction must be a guess; there is no convincing reason why it should be set at 2 per cent or 3 or 5 per cent. It seems likely, however, that the census reports for Cuba, Mexico, Chile, Puerto Rico, Venezuela and Egypt are more realistic in this respect than those for Brazil, India, Peru and the Philippines, which show a very low proportion of persons in commercial activities.

When the necessary adjustments are made, it appears likely that primarily agricultural, industrially underdeveloped areas employ not less than 6–7 per cent of the labor force in commercial pursuits, in the broad sense of that term. Rates of 8–10 per cent are probably more common and typical in more developed primarily agricultural areas; rates of 10–14 per cent, in primarily industrial areas; and of 14–16 per cent, in most commercialized countries. The rate for the USSR probably is particularly low.

For the world as a whole 10 per cent seems a plausible average. When the world's total labor force is estimated at one billion (as in midyear

TABLE 4

EMPLOYMENT IN TRADE: NUMBER AND PROPORTION OF GAINFUL WORKERS IN TRADE, IN SELECTED
COUNTRIES, MOST RECENT DATA

| | Number in Thousands | | Gainful Workers in Trade as Percentage of Gainful Workers in: | |
Country and Year	*All Pursuits*	*Trade*	*All Pursuits*	*Nonagricultural Pursuits*
United States, 1950	59,583.0	10,925.0	18.3	21.0
Canada, 1951	5,415.0	873.0	16.1	20.5
Mexico, 1940	5,858.1	552.5	9.4	27.2
Panama, 1950	264.6	19.6	7.4	12.0
Cuba, 1943	1,520.9	149.0	9.8	16.7
Puerto Rico, 1940	602.0	50.5	8.4	13.6
Colombia, 1938	4,566.2	160.6	3.5	12.9
Venezuela, 1941	1,240.7	100.6	8.1	16.6
Brazil, 1940	14,020.1	800.9	5.7	17.5
Peru, 1940	2,475.3	112.1	4.5	12.1
Chile, 1940	1,741.5	162.3	9.3	14.4
United Kingdom, 1951	22,578.5	3,176.8	14.1	14.8
Ireland, 1946	1,298.4	135.4	10.4	18.6
France, 1946	20,520.5	2,415.9	11.8	18.5
Belgium, 1947	3,481.0	467.5	13.4	15.3
Netherlands, 1947	3,866.4	545.3	14.1	17.5
Denmark, 1940	1,971.4	240.9	12.2	17.1
Sweden, 1945	2,987.3	352.1	11.7	15.6
Norway, 1950	1,394.0	153.0	11.0	14.9
Finland, 1940	2,017.2	110.5	5.5	12.8
Germany, 1939[a]	34,268.6	6,008.1	17.5	23.5
Czechoslovakia, 1947	5,852.4	377.0	6.4	10.3
Switzerland, 1941	1,992.5	198.5	10.0	12.5
Austria, 1951	3,352.3	445.4	13.3	19.5
Portugal, 1940	3,049.9	190.5	6.2	12.2
Spain, 1940	9,254.1	589.0	6.4	13.1
Italy, 1936	18,754.7	1,605.4	8.6	16.2
Yugoslavia, 1931	6,477.8	170.0	2.6	12.3
Romania, 1930	10,457.6	357.3	3.4	16.0
Bulgaria, 1934	3,433.1	80.9	2.3	11.7
Japan, 1950	36,280.0	4,190.0	11.4	22.0
Turkey, 1945	7,626.4	279.7	3.7	15.4
India, 1931	148,816.9	7,913.6	5.3	16.2
Thailand, 1937	6,823.6	303.5	4.4	39.0
Philippines, 1948	7,415.8	340.4	4.6	13.4
Egypt, 1937	6,095.0	460.1	7.5	25.8
Union of South Africa,[b] 1946	888.8	140.0	15.8	22.6
Australia, 1947	3,238.2	493.1	15.2	18.0
New Zealand, 1945	679.5	97.5	14.3	17.9
Hawaii, 1950	166.3	30.5	18.3	22.9

Sources: **5,** 1951–52, pp. 10–34; **1,** 1949–1950, pp. 254–75.

a. 1937 borders. **13,** p. 35.   b. Europeans.

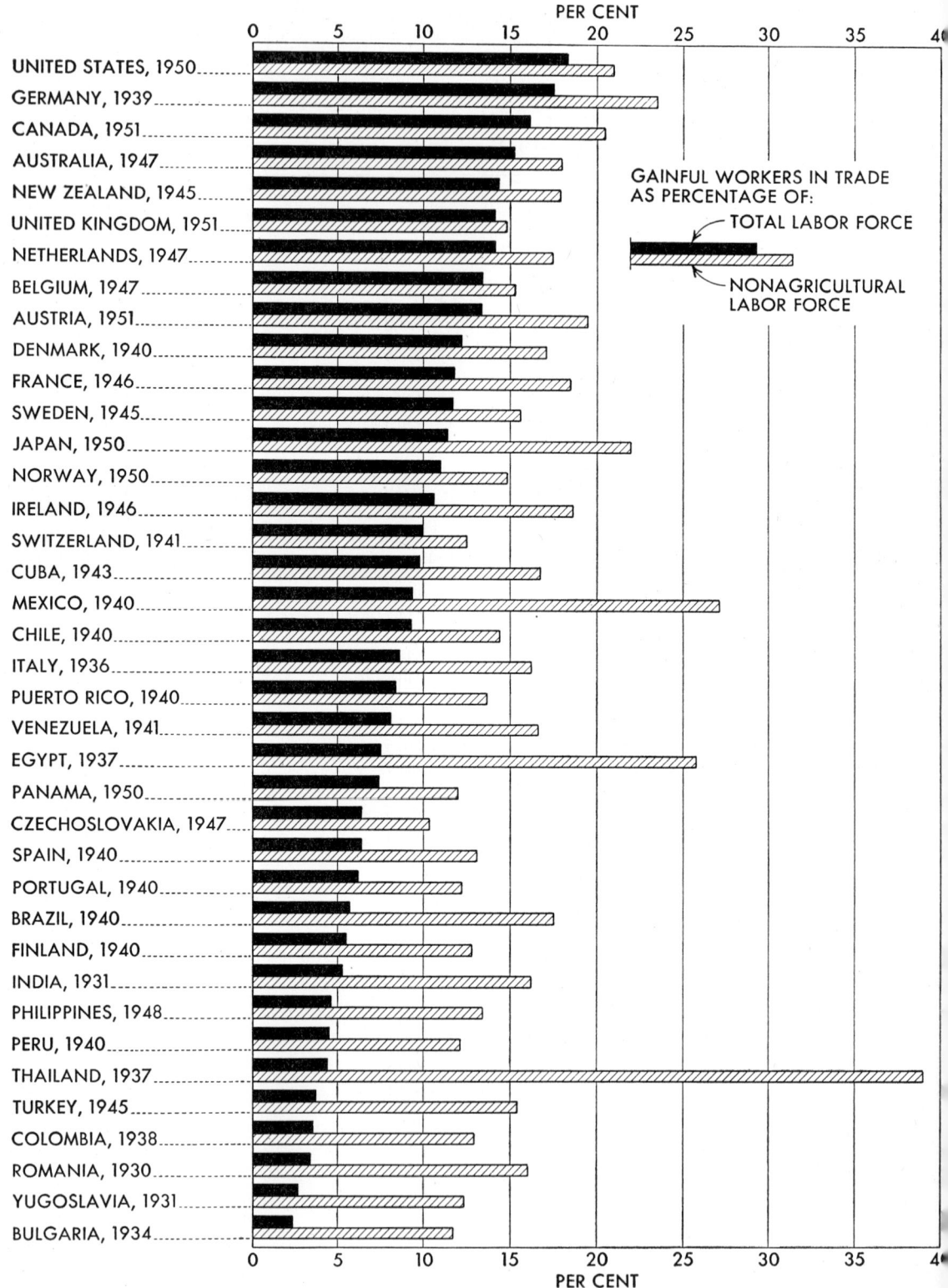

FIGURE 3. EMPLOYMENT IN TRADE: SHARE OF TRADE IN TOTAL AND NONAGRICULTURAL LABOR FORCE, IN
SELECTED COUNTRIES, MOST RECENT DATA

Source: Table

TABLE 5

EMPLOYMENT IN TRADE: POPULATION AND GAINFUL
WORKERS IN ALL INDUSTRIES AND IN TRADE,
THE WORLD AND CONTINENTS, 1950

| | Number, in Millions | | | Workers in Trade as Percentage of All Workers |
| | | Workers | | |
Continent	Population	All Industries	Trade	
Total	2,400	1,000	100.0	10.0
North America	166	70	11.2	16.0
Middle America	51	23	2.3	10.0
South America	111	47	4.2	9.0
Europe	396	200	30.0	15.0
USSR	193	90	6.3	7.0
Asia	1,272	496	39.8	8.0
Africa	198	70	5.6	8.0
Oceania	13	4	0.6	15.0

Sources: For population, **1**, 1951, p. 103; for labor force in all industries, **38**, Chap. 11, p. 365. Labor force in trade estimated by the authors as explained in the text.

1950),[50] the number of gainful workers in trade therefore may be close to 100 million (as suggested in Table 5). A tentative distribution of this total by continent must be largely illustrative. Table 5 shows a pattern in conformity with what is known about the occupational distribution of the labor force in countries with different economic structures but has a considerable margin of error for areas for which we have only fragmentary or doubtful statistics.

Employers and Employees

Even in modern commerce, small family establishments hold their ground in competition with larger concerns. Indeed, in retail trade, especially in the sale of food and drinks, small establishments still prevail in even the most industrialized countries. There are obvious reasons for their vitality in competition with larger concerns. Certain types of trade require wide decentralization, and small establishments can come closer to the local consumers than local branches of large firms. Through personal relations, an independent grocer, for example, can catch business that would not interest a large firm.

50. **38**, Chapter 11.

The structure of trade in different countries is characterized by the distribution of persons engaged in commercial pursuits by class of work: employers and self-employed; unpaid family workers; wage and salary workers.

It is likely that the statistics of unpaid family workers in trade are incomplete. A census enumerator, canvassing people at their homes, often fails to record as a family worker the housewife who helps her husband in operating a small store. Family workers are seldom recorded in eating and drinking places that have no hired help. It is probable, likewise, that most of the persons whom censuses report as engaged in commerce without specifically designating them as employers or employees are small storekeepers or itinerant traders working on their own account.

With correction for such omissions, it appears that not only in primarily agricultural areas in South and Middle America and eastern Europe, but also in such economically developed countries as France and Italy, about half the total labor force engaged in trade and related pursuits represents self-employed or family workers. A larger proportion of salary and wage workers in commercial pursuits — 3 or more employees per employer — is recorded in the countries with highly developed banking and insurance, such as the United States and Canada, and in areas where retail trade is largely controlled by co-operative associations, as in Sweden, Australia and New Zealand. (See Table 6.)

Small establishments predominate in retail trade, especially among food stores, filling stations and eating and drinking places. In the United States, one of the countries with the highest proportion of employees in commercial pursuits, the ratio of employees to employers and persons working on their own account in 1940 was 5.6 in wholesale trade and only 2.7 in retail trade. The ratio averaged 1.7 in food and dairy products stores, 1.6 in filling stations, 2.0 in mixed retail stores and 3.2 in eating and drinking places.

The number of employers and self-employed persons combined is close to the number of trade establishments. Most small shops are family enterprises, however, and it is fairly probable that they use more family workers, on a part-time basis, than the census indicates. With this correction, self-employed persons, employers and unpaid family workers are likely to represent not

TABLE 6

EMPLOYMENT IN TRADE: NUMBER OF WORKERS IN TRADE AND THEIR DISTRIBUTION BY CLASS OF WORK, IN SELECTED COUNTRIES, MOST RECENT DATA

Country and Year	Workers in Trade, in Thousands	Percentage Distribution			
		Employers and Self-employed	Unpaid Family Workers	Employees	Unknown
United States, 1950	10,925	17.5	1.2	81.3	...
Canada, 1951	873	20.5	...	79.5	...
Mexico, 1940	552	...	...	...	...
Cuba, 1943	149	43.5	...	41.5	15.0
Colombia, 1938	161	77.2	...	20.1	2.7
Venezuela, 1941	101	57.3	...	38.4	4.3
Chile, 1940	162	60.4	...	39.6	...
United Kingdom, 1951	3,177	15.9	0.5	82.1	1.5
France, 1946	2,416	52.1	...	47.9	...
Belgium, 1947	467	45.4	9.2	45.4	...
Netherlands, 1947	545	32.4	16.6	51.0	...
Denmark, 1940	241	25.8	6.1	68.1	...
Sweden, 1945	352	19.6	2.8	77.6	...
Norway, 1946 [a]	139	28.7	...	71.3	...
Finland, 1940	111	43.4	5.3	51.3	...
Germany, 1939	6,008	19.5	8.7	71.8	...
Czechoslovakia, 1947	377	28.1	4.0	67.9	...
Switzerland, 1941	199	25.2	4.4	70.4	...
Austria, 1951	445	17.8	5.5	76.7	...
Portugal, 1940	191	36.5	1.8	43.9	17.8
Italy, 1936	1,605	47.1	16.2	36.7	...
Romania, 1930	357	39.5	12.9	46.5	1.1
Bulgaria, 1934	81	51.7	7.4	40.8	...
Japan, 1950	4,190	37.7	22.2	40.1	...
Philippines, 1948	340	56.9	...	43.1	...
Egypt, 1937	460	77.4	...	22.6	...
Australia, 1947	493	20.7	0.4	76.7	2.1
New Zealand, 1945	98	16.3	0.4	82.1	1.1

Sources: **5,** 1951–52, pp. 10–34; **1,** 1949–50, pp. 254–75.

a. The 1950 Census did not record distribution of workers by class of work. (Cf. Table 4.)

less than 40 per cent of all workers in retail trade in the United States. (See Table 7.)

TRADE ESTABLISHMENTS

International statistics of trade establishments are fragmentary but in agreement on one point: despite the development of nationwide chains and huge department stores which dominate the scene in a modern city, small establishments, often one-man shops or family enterprises, prevail in retail trade and are not uncommon in wholesale business, such as brokerage agencies, and even in finance (real estate and insurance agencies).

The United States

From 55 to 60 per cent of the nonagricultural business establishments in the United States are in retail and wholesale trade, finance, insurance and real estate. Most of them either employ no salary and wage workers or have only one employee — a stenographer-secretary or errand boy.

Detailed information on the size of these establishments was supplied by the Censuses of Business in 1929 and 1933 and, in particular, 1935.[51] Current data are provided by the statistics of "business population" and records of the

51. See **36,** pp. 199–203 and 286–88.

TABLE 7

EMPLOYMENT IN TRADE: NUMBER OF EMPLOYED WORKERS IN VARIOUS BRANCHES OF TRADE AND THEIR DISTRIBUTION BY CLASS OF WORK, IN THE UNITED STATES, 1940 [a]

| | | Percentage Distribution | | |
Branch of Trade	*Workers Employed,*[b] *in Thousands*	*Employers and Self-employed*	*Recorded Unpaid Family Workers*	*Wage and Salary Workers*
Wholesale trade	1,198.2	15.3	0.5	84.2
Retail trade	6,341.9	25.9	2.9	71.2
Food and dairy products stores	1,492.2	34.5	5.5	60.0
General merchandise and variety stores	811.9	10.2	1.4	88.4
Apparel and accessory stores	489.9	25.7	1.7	72.6
Furniture and furnishing stores	267.6	21.9	1.7	76.4
Motor vehicle stores	327.0	15.8	0.6	83.6
Filling stations	407.7	38.1	1.7	60.2
Drugstores	225.3	22.5	2.4	75.1
Eating and drinking places	1,115.5	23.0	3.7	73.2
Hardware, farm implements and building materials, retail	367.0	20.2	1.4	78.4
Other retail stores	837.8	32.8	2.0	65.2
Finance, insurance and real estate	1,485.6	12.6	0.3	87.1

Source: **9**, pp. 66–68.

a. Comparable data for 1950 are not available.　　　b. Excludes persons seeking work.

Bureau of Old-Age and Survivors Insurance (OASI). According to the business population statistics, the United States had more than 4 million nonagricultural firms in 1952 and among these, close to 210,000 in wholesale trade, 1,660,-000 in retail trade and 350,000 in finance, insurance and real estate, a total of more than 2.2 million in all commercial pursuits.[52] On the other hand, in 1947 only 1.3 million reported to the Bureau of Old-Age and Survivors Insurance that they employed hired labor, and of these, 757,000 reported 0–3 employees in the first quarter of 1947. (See Table 8.) Firms of this size had 1.3 million persons on their payrolls during the first quarter of 1947, including temporary and casual workers.

This suggests that three quarters of the 2.2 million commercial establishments in 1952 were one-man or family enterprises and used little hired help, while one quarter employed some 10 million salary and wage workers, about 18 workers per establishment. In 1947 more than 5.5 million workers were employed by 532,000

middle-sized firms with 4–49 employees per establishment.[53]

Other Countries

Germany. Establishments with not more than 5 workers, including the owner and members of his family, predominated in retail trade and related services in prewar Germany. Assuming the same pattern of sales per worker as in the United States, 70–75 per cent of Germany's retail trade was handled by establishments with not more than 5 workers, including family workers. Establishments with more than 50 workers accounted for less than 10 per cent of retail business. In wholesale trade, firms with more than 50 workers employed about 15 per cent of the labor force and represented a much larger part of the business. (See Table 9.)

52. Annual averages, excluding professional service. **7**, Supplement, Business Statistics, 1953, p. 23; **10**, 1952, p. 441.

53. The Census of Business in 1933 showed that the amount of sales per full-time employee is about the same in small and middle-sized retail establishments and declines as one moves to the larger concerns. (**36**, pp. 200, 323.) On this basis, it is likely that about 60 per cent of all retail trade is carried on by establishments with less than 20 employees; 20 per cent, by large firms with 20–99 employees; and 20 per cent, by some 4,600 concerns with more than 100 workers.

TABLE 8

COMMERCIAL ESTABLISHMENTS: NUMBER OF ESTABLISHMENTS AND EMPLOYED WORKERS IN MAJOR
BRANCHES OF COMMERCE, BY SIZE OF ESTABLISHMENT, IN THE UNITED STATES, 1947

(*Thousands*)

Item	All Commercial Pursuits	Wholesale Trade	Retail Trade	Finance, Insurance, etc.
Firms, total [a]	2,214.3	196.6	1,673.0	344.7
Firms reporting to OASI, first quarter 1947 [a]	1,314.7	235.5	862.9	216.3
Size of reporting establishment by number of employees				
0–3	757.1	108.2	499.5	149.4
4–7	298.8	54.3	210.4	34.1
8–19	172.4	44.8	107.3	20.3
20–49	60.4	19.5	32.9	8.0
50–99	16.1	5.5	8.1	2.5
100–499	8.7	2.9	4.0	1.8
500 or more	1.0	0.2	0.6	0.2
Workers with wage credits in establishments of each size				
Total employees	10,918.7	2,721.1	6,515.0	1,682.8
0–3	1,333.4	193.4	908.6	231.6
4–7	1,589.4	289.9	1,121.1	178.4
8–19	2,100.5	552.1	1,301.0	247.4
20–49	1,833.0	597.2	991.6	244.2
50–99	1,105.2	379.5	555.6	170.1
100–499	1,608.5	511.4	758.0	339.1
500–999	461.4	113.3	249.1	99.0
1,000 or more	887.2	84.2	630.0	173.0

Sources: For firms, total, **10**, 1951, p. 435; for establishments reporting to OASI, special release of OASI Bureau.

a. Industrial classification in statistics of "business population" (first line in the table) differs from that in the statistics of OASI. The totals for all commercial pursuits are probably more comparable.

Nevertheless wholesale trade was rather decentralized in Germany, in comparison with the United States, where more than 40 per cent of the workers in this field are on the payrolls of firms with more than 50 employees.[54]

France. The last prewar census of population (1936) enumerated in trade, including finance and insurance, 2.7 million gainful workers, among them 722,000 employers, 1.4 million employees (either at work or seeking a job) and

54. The classification in both cases refers to establishments (*Niederlassungen*) rather than firms, which may have several establishments. The total labor force in wholesale trade in the United States is estimated here by adding the number of employees and the number of establishments.

some 600,000 persons working on their own account. It appears, however, that the number of employers was overstated and that of persons working on their own account, understated. The census of business taken simultaneously with the census of population counted only 291,100 commercial establishments with salary or wage workers, showing that some 430,000 persons who reported themselves as employers were actually self-employed. All in all, French commerce probably included more than 2.6 million persons: more than a million persons working on their own account without hired help, and nearly 300,000 employers, with about 1.3 million salary and wage workers. Information on the distribu-

TABLE 9

COMMERCIAL ESTABLISHMENTS: NUMBER OF ESTABLISHMENTS AND WORKING PERSONS BY SIZE OF
ESTABLISHMENT, IN GERMANY, 1933

(Thousands)

Size of Establishment [a]	*All Commercial Pursuits*	*Wholesale Trade*	*Retail Trade*	*Warehouses, Agencies, etc.*	*Finance, Insurance, etc.*
	Establishments				
All classes, number of workers:	1,250.6	150.6	852.7	199.3	48.0
1–5	1,173.1	123.2	821.9	190.4	37.6
6–10	45.8	15.4	21.1	4.6	4.7
11–50	27.8	10.9	8.5	3.8	4.6
51–200	3.4	1.0	1.1	0.5	0.9
More than 200	0.6	0.1	0.2	0.1	0.3
	Persons Working [a]				
All classes, number of workers:	3,449.4	681.2	1,937.4	432.3	398.5
1–5	1,998.7	248.5	1,427.3	256.4	66.5
6–10	337.0	115.3	152.5	33.8	35.4
11–50	541.4	209.4	159.3	79.2	93.5
51–200	302.7	81.8	93.9	46.9	80.1
More than 200	269.7	26.2	104.4	16.0	123.1

Source: **14**, 1938, pp. 146–47.   a. Includes owners, family workers and employees.

tion by size of establishment in 1936 was provided for nearly 1,270,000 employees: [55]

Size of Establishment, by Number of Employees	*Establishments*	*Employees*
Total	291,082	1,268,218
1–5	256,016	451,446
6–10	18,963	142,602
11–20	9,137	132,527
21–50	4,672	144,106
51–100	1,363	93,791
101–200	578	75,724
201–500	255	74,007
501–1,000	64	45,029
1,001 or more	34	108,986

In brief, of all persons engaged in commercial activities, some 11 per cent were employed in establishments with more than 100 employees and 13 per cent in establishments with 11–100 employees, while the rest were in small establishments or worked on their own account.

In France as in other countries, many small shops depend, in varying degree, on large concerns but commerce remains primarily the realm of small business.

THE SHARE OF TRADE IN NATIONAL INCOME

One of the main factors controlling the share of wholesale and retail trade in the national income is the length of the road from producer to ultimate consumer that must be traveled by raw materials, semifinished goods and finished products. As Paul W. Stewart and J. Frederic Dewhurst put it,

The agrarian family worked at production and distribution without distinguishing one process from the other. . . . In this new economy the jobs are all divided . . . Goods have to be distributed not only for personal consumption but for consumption by the organizations engaged in production and distribution. . . . On the old homestead with little machinery and no steam or electric power very little could be produced. But distributing the products of a family to the family was a relatively small job compared with distributing the products of a modern factory to all the people who want those products, scattered as they are throughout the whole United States.[56]

This factor tends to increase the share of trade in national income when a country shifts from a subsistence economy or mixed economy to a

55. **12**, Vol. I, Part 3, p. 96.   56. **32**, pp. 69–70.

TABLE 10

INCOME ORIGINATED IN WHOLESALE AND RETAIL TRADE AS PERCENTAGE OF NATIONAL INCOME ADJUSTED FOR INTERNATIONAL PAYMENTS, IN SELECTED COUNTRIES, 1936–52

Country and Year	Per Cent	Country and Year	Per Cent	Country and Year	Per Cent
United States		Argentina		Hungary	
1938	17	1938	21	1938	9
1946	19	1942	21	1946	10
1948	19	1945	22	Italy	
1950	18	United Kingdom		1938	11
1951	17	1950	13	1948	11
1952	18	1951	13	1951	13
Canada		Ireland [b]		Bulgaria	
1938	13	1946	22	1939	15
1948	15	1951	18	1944	27
1950	15	France		1946	12
Guatemala		1938	14	Greece	
1949	8	1946	12	1938	12
Honduras		1949	12	1946	14
1951	13	Netherlands		1949	11
Mexico		1938	12	Japan [d]	
1939	24	1943	11	1946	17
1944	29	1946	13	1949	14
1950	31	1948	13	1950	19
Dominican Republic [a]		1950	13	1951	18
1946	21	Denmark		Turkey	
Puerto Rico		1938	16	1938	10
1939	11	1948	15	1951	10
1948	20	1952	17	India [b]	
1950	21	Norway		1949	19
Colombia		1938	15	Israel [c]	
1946	7	1948	12	1950	15
1948	8	1952	13	Philippines	
1950	9	Finland		1951	12
Peru		1938 [e]	12	Egypt	
1942	15	1943 [e]	11	1938	7
1946	21	1948	11	1948	11
1948	18	1951	12	1950	10
1951	16	Western Germany		Kenya [d]	
Paraguay		1936	9	1950	16
1951	17	1949	10	Southern Rhodesia	
Chile		1952	9	1950	14
1938	14	Poland		Union of South Africa	
1944	17	1948	18	1938	14
1948	16			1948	17
1950	16			1951	14

Sources: **4,** 1951, pp. 435–38; **3,** pp. 20–27 and **2,** 1953, various issues.

a. Trade includes professions and service industries.
b. Trade includes finance, insurance, transportation.
c. Trade includes hotels and motion pictures.
d. Trade includes finance and business services.
e. National income includes receipts from abroad.

money economy and when the economic and financial structure of the nation becomes increasingly complex.

Contrary to this tendency, however, the share of trade in national income is higher in Chile than in France, higher in Kenya than in the United Kingdom and higher in Puerto Rico than in the United States. (See Table 10.)

The large share of trade in national income in underdeveloped countries is attributable to two factors, one purely statistical, the other economic. The statistical factor is the understatement of income derived from agriculture in areas where subsistence agriculture predominates. The economic factor is the contrast between income in urban and rural pursuits.

Measurement

To permit more or less precise comparison of the share of trade in national income in different countries, statistics on the distribution of national income by industrial origin must be consistent in two respects — in measuring national income and in defining trade.

To improve the comparability of the available data, the Statistical Office of the UN applies the distribution by industrial origin not to national income but to an aggregate it describes as the *net geographic product* of the nation — national income excluding the income from investments abroad but including payments to the rest of the world. This correction is not very significant for the United States, where the net income originated abroad averaged only 0.2 per cent in 1940–50,[57] but is important for nations with large foreign investments and especially for underdeveloped areas dominated by foreign capital. When income from abroad is excluded, the relative share of trade in national income is increased. When the income originated in mines and plantations operated by foreign capital and paid to stockholders abroad is added to the national income of an underdeveloped area, the relative share of trade in national income is diminished.

This adjustment of national income data seems commendable, although the designation of the new aggregate as a net geographic product is not very happy. In Table 10 and on the following pages, this aggregate is described as national income adjusted for international payments.

In defining the scope of trade, the Statistical Office tends to include only wholesale and retail trade and to exclude finance, insurance and real estate. This classification cannot be followed consistently, however, because the national income statistics in many countries do not distinguish distributive trade in the narrow sense from other commercial activities.[58]

Various Countries

As a general rule, the share of trade in national income is somewhat larger than its share in the labor force. In most countries the ratio ranges approximately between 10 and 20 per cent, but the extremes do not connote predominance of subsistence agriculture, on the one hand, or a high level of industrial development, on the other. The rate is comparatively low in Western Germany, the United Kingdom, France and the Netherlands and high in the United States, Puerto Rico, Peru and Argentina. (See Figure 4.)

The United States

Apart from a brief period during World War II, the share of wholesale and retail trade in national income in the United States fluctuated within a comparatively narrow range between 1929 and 1952.[59] It averaged 16.5 per cent before the war (1936–40); fell to 13.2 per cent in 1943; increased to an average of 19.1 per cent after the reconversion (1948–49); was 17.2 per cent in 1951; and rose to 17.4 per cent in 1952.[60] It is not clear whether the difference between the prewar and postwar rates reflects structural changes or is due to temporary factors. (See Table 11.)

Income from trade includes considerable amounts of earnings of unincorporated enterprises, mostly small businesses. In 1950, wholesale and retail trade represented 20.3 per cent of all income originated in nonagricultural pursuits.[61] Trade accounted for 18.9 per cent of wage and salary income, 46.4 per cent of entrepreneurial income from unincorporated business, and only 16.7 per cent of corporate income. Moreover, a sizable part of corporate income reflected the rise in value of inventories. The share of trade in dividends distributed by nonagricultural corporations was only 11.3 per cent. (See Table 12.)

The World

The share of wholesale and retail trade in

India — national income statistics include in trade not only finance but also transportation.

59. For earlier periods cf. **11**, p. 14.

60. In the United States income originated abroad is relatively small and does not appreciably affect the share of trade in national income.

61. Excluding rental income of persons.

57. **7**, National Income Supplement, 1951, p. 159. The ratio was close to 0.3 per cent in 1951. (**7**, July 1952, p. 18.) Cf. Table 10, footnote a.

58. In some countries — for example, Ireland and

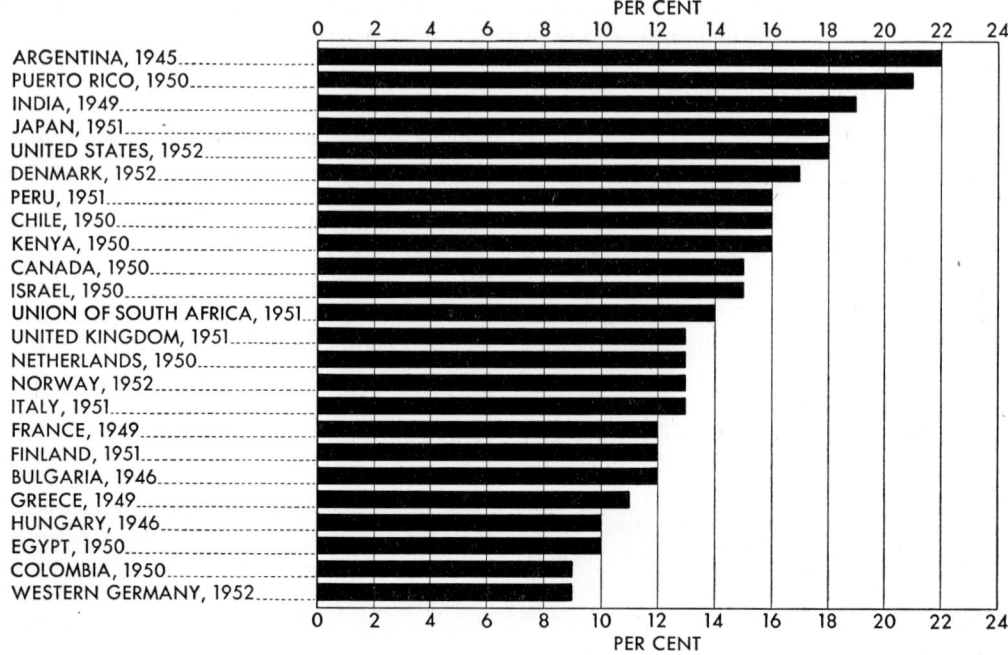

Source: Table 10

FIGURE 4. INCOME ORIGINATED IN WHOLESALE AND RETAIL TRADE AS PERCENTAGE OF NATIONAL INCOME, IN
SELECTED COUNTRIES, MOST RECENT DATA

world income in 1950 was probably 14–15 per cent. This estimate rests on extrapolation of the rates shown in Table 10 and Figure 4 and application of these rates to areas with a similar economic structure. Trade's share in national income slightly exceeded 17 per cent in the United States and a few other countries, in an area controlling approximately half the world's income. It was less than 15 per cent in the United Kingdom (13 per cent in 1951), France (12 per cent in 1949), Western Germany (9 per cent in 1952), Italy (13 per cent in 1951) and some

other countries. If the share of trade in national income is 17 per cent in an area which accounts for half the world's income and 13 per cent in the rest of the world, the average for the world economy as a whole would be 15 per cent. If the share for the latter group of nations is as low as 11 per cent — which is highly improbable — the world average would be 14 per cent.

Measured by the spread between the prices charged by producers and the retail prices paid by ultimate consumers the visible cost of distribution is often several times greater.

TABLE 11

INCOME ORIGINATED IN WHOLESALE AND RETAIL TRADE AS PERCENTAGE OF NATIONAL INCOME, IN THE
UNITED STATES, 1929–52

Year	Per Cent	Year	Per Cent	Year	Per Cent	Year	Per Cent
1929	14.9	1935	15.8	1941	15.3	1947	18.8
1930	16.0	1936	15.4	1942	13.9	1948	18.9
1931	16.4	1937	16.2	1943	13.2	1949	19.2
1932	15.1	1938	17.3	1944	13.6	1950	18.1
1933	13.6	1939	16.7	1945	15.3	1951	17.2
1934	16.2	1940	16.9	1946	18.7	1952	17.4 [a]

Source: Computed from 7, National Income Supplement, 1951, pp. 158–59, and July 1953, p. 16.

a. Because of adjustment of basic data and rounding, Table 10 gives a higher ratio (18 per cent) for 1952.

TABLE 12

INCOME ORIGINATED IN WHOLESALE AND RETAIL TRADE, BY DISTRIBUTIVE SHARE, IN THE
UNITED STATES, 1950

Item	Income, in Millions of Dollars			Income from Trade as Percentage of Income from:	
	Wholesale and Retail Trade	All Nonagricultural Pursuits	All Pursuits	All Nonagricultural Pursuits	All Pursuits
Total income	$43,269	$213,267 [a]	$238,963	20.3	18.1
Wages and salaries [b]	28,447	150,207	153,333	18.9	18.6
Income of unincorporated enterprise	10,968	23,622	37,516	46.4	29.2
Corporate income [c]	6,869	41,213	41,367	16.7	16.6
Tax liability	3,230	18,522	18,593	17.4	17.4
Dividends distributed	1,033	9,114	9,169	11.3	11.3
Undistributed profits	2,606	13,577	13,605	19.2	19.2
Inventory valuation adjustment	−2,992	−6,678	−6,678	44.8	44.8
Rental income of persons	. . .	. . .	8,039	. . .	. . .
Net interest	−23	4,903	5,386	. . .	. . .

Source: Computed from **7**, National Income Supplement, 1951, pp. 150–79.

a. Excludes rental income of persons.
b. Includes supplementary payments.

c. Before federal and state income and excess profit taxes.

THE FLOW OF GOODS IN DOMESTIC TRADE

The total value of goods sold and bought during a year in a country with a prevailing subsistence economy is likely to be less than the national income. In industrially developed modern nations, it greatly exceeds national income. The United States exemplifies the flow of goods in domestic trade in modern countries.

The United States

According to the Department of Commerce, the United States had a national income of $277.6 billion in 1951 but the gross national product or total expenditure amounted to $329.8 billion. The latter included (in billions):

Personal consumption expenditures	$208.1
Investments, including foreign investments (gross)	58.8
Government expenditures	62.9

Each group of expenditures consisted of outlays for goods and for services. Personal consumption accounted for $140.7 billion in goods and $67.4 billion in services, including rental of houses, transportation, educational and health service and so forth. Government (federal, state and local) spent $32.4 billion for goods. After adjustment for foodstuffs consumed by producers, it appears that outlays for goods totaled approximately 80 per cent of the gross national product or roughly $260 billion, in round numbers.

Only a small fraction of the goods was either consumed by producers or delivered by them directly to consumers. Most articles reached the ultimate destination through the channels of trade. They were sold at least twice — by producers to retailers and by the latter to consumers, and a large part of the goods was purchased and sold three times, moving from producers to wholesalers, to retailers and finally to consumers.

Moreover, raw materials, semifinished goods and parts likewise passed through the channels of trade and most of them were sold and purchased more than once. Industrial materials produced by farmers were purchased by the agents of wholesalers and resold to factories. Coal and ore moved from mines to blast furnaces, smelters and refineries, and then, in the form of metals, to rolling mills; the latter sold the semifinished products — sheets, wire, rails and so forth — to factories, which converted them and other materials into machinery, automobiles, airplanes and other finished goods. In addition, factories purchased parts from one another. In this way, some components of manufactured articles may have changed hands four or five times before they reached the wholesaler, or six to seven times before they were sold to the final consumer.

The value of goods increases as the raw materials are converted into semifinished goods and finished articles and the latter are moved from the original producers to wholesalers and retailers. The amount of sales-purchases is therefore larger at the end of the road than at its beginning. Moreover, not all goods pass through all typical phases of trade (from primary production to intermediate trade, to manufacturer, to wholesaler, to retailer, to consumer). It is, therefore, highly improbable that the sales and purchases of goods in a nation would total four or five times the amount paid by ultimate consumers, but in a commercially developed industrial country they must be more than double the value of ultimate consumer expenditures and may be more than triple.

Thus, the total amount of sales and purchases effected in the United States in 1951 is likely to have topped $650 billion, approximately two and a half times the national income.[62]

Domestic and Foreign Trade

Imported and domestic products are intermingled in the flow of goods in modern nations, in everyday consumption, on the shelves of any grocery and in the flow of raw materials and semifinished products. The value of world exports fluctuated in 1948–52 between $55 and $80 billion[63] and averaged 10–12 per cent of world income and hardly more than 5 or 6 per cent of the value of domestic trade in the world in the same years.

These rates may convey the impression that foreign trade is a comparatively unimportant supplement to domestic trade, but such a conclusion would be false. Imported goods are no longer luxuries for the rich, as in the sixteenth and seventeenth centuries. Imported products of tropical countries have become a part of the customary diet in the temperate zone. Modern textile mills use imported fibers; shoe factories depend on imported hides; steelmakers need imported alloys to produce high-quality steel; automobile and airplane factories need materials originated in a dozen countries in all parts of the world; chemical industries depend on a continuous flow of imported rare minerals. To quote a few examples of international interdependence of modern industries, the raw materials for production of atomic energy in the United States, the United Kingdom and France come from the Belgian Congo; British coal mines and American newspapers depend on Canadian and Swedish lumber; the iron and steel industry in France and all manufacturing industries in Italy, Switzerland, and Japan depend on imported coal.

In brief, international trade is vital for the operation of the industrial plant in the modern world. Indeed, international division of labor and exchange of commodities are cornerstones of our economic system and the present geographic distribution of population and our economic civilization are unthinkable without international trade.

The ratio of exports to national income varies widely from country to country.[64] The share of exports in production varies also from industry to industry. Some industries, especially in underdeveloped countries, are operated exclusively for foreign markets; for others, export is only a sideline.[65] The operation of the world economy is characterized by the movement of raw materials and finished goods between certain regions and countries.[66] Each disturbance in the flow of for-

---

62. A more detailed estimate of sales and purchases in the United States was prepared by Paul W. Stewart and J. Frederic Dewhurst for 1929 on the basis of the Censuses of Distribution, Mines and Quarries and other data. In that year, national income amounted to $87.4 billion, and consumer expenditures for goods to $47.1 billion. (7, National Income Supplement, 1951, pp. 150, 198.) But retail sales totaled $49.2 billion, intermediate trade sold goods for $69.3 billion, the sales of manufactures totaled $69.6 billion ($38.2 billion to intermediate and retail trade establishments, $20.8 billion in interfactory trade, the rest in direct sales to consumers, export, and so on). The grand total, including sales by agriculture to intermediate trade, manufacturing industries, private consumers, transportation charges and the like, is estimated at $218.6 billion, two and one half times the national income.

63. **6**, February 1953, p. xviii. These figures do not include the countries behind the Iron Curtain.

64. See Chapter 2.

65. See Chapter 3.

66. See Chapter 4.

eign trade affects not only the exporting and importing nations but also countries which maintain commercial relations with them. The measures taken by a country to regulate its imports or exports affect the interests of the exporters and importers as well as producers and consumers abroad, often in countries with which the country in question has no direct economic relationship.

To sum up, the role of foreign trade in the world economy and international affairs is immeasurably larger than is suggested by the relation between its volume and that of domestic commerce.

CHAPTER 2

THE VALUE AND VOLUME OF FOREIGN TRADE

IN DISCUSSING the exchange of goods among nations, we have been using the terminology established in the seventeenth and eighteenth centuries by the forerunners of the classical school. We speak of trade between the United States and Great Britain or between Great Britain and France as if the countries themselves were carrying on export and import operations. Actually — except for emergencies, occasional governmental purchases of strategic materials and staple foodstuffs, and monopolistic control over export of certain commodities — foreign trade, like domestic trade, is carried on under an enterprise economy by individuals or firms operating in the respective countries.[1] The difference between foreign and domestic trade is only that the former moves merchandise across national boundaries. What is the significance of this distinction?

CHARACTERISTICS OF FOREIGN TRADE

The classical school believed that the fundamental contrast between domestic and international trade was that labor and capital could move freely from one branch of production into another and from one district into another within a nation, while mobility between different countries was largely or totally lacking.[2]

The perfect market of the classical school is, in fact, a market in which "every individual must be considered as exchanging from a pure regard to his own requirements or private interests, and there must be perfectly free competition, so that any one will exchange with any one else for the slightest apparent advantage."[3] The classical writers thought that since international trade does not meet this definition, it differs from domestic trade and requires special theoretical consideration.

The contrast between the mobility of labor and capital within national boundaries and across the border, however, is only one of degree. Labor can move across the border between the United States and Canada more easily than from the Atlantic to the Pacific coast in either country. Capital equipment can be transferred from Trenton, New Jersey, to Rio de Janeiro more readily than from the latter to the upper Amazon basin. Moreover, if the fundamental difference between foreign and domestic trade were in the mobility of labor and capital, the distinction would disappear whenever the international mobility of labor and capital increases to a degree comparable to their mobility within national boundaries.[4] It can also be argued that often the difficulties of transferring labor and capital across national boundaries depend largely on the policy of the respective governments, a factor which can hardly be recognized as fundamental in the sense that this term is used by economists of the classical school.

As Haberler has pointed out, it is characteristic of foreign trade that the areas of dispatch and destination of merchandise fall under the jurisdiction of different governments while home trade means exchange within an area, the prosperity of which interests the national government or is subject to its jurisdiction.[5] Thus, the flow of goods over a nation's frontiers differs from its domestic trade in that the nation can regulate its import and export to some extent without regard to the interests of the other party or a broader community of nations.

Even when a government makes no use, or very moderate use, of its ability to regulate foreign trade, individuals engaged in it are continuously reminded of the possibility of such regulation by the universal practice of customs inspection and registration of merchandise crossing international boundaries.

Since the seventeenth century, the problem of international exchange of goods has been one of the most controversial topics in economic science. No economist has seriously questioned the right of governments to regulate the flow of foreign trade by customs duties and other meas-

---

1. **26**, p. 6.
2. **45**, p. 26; **26**, p. 5; **31**, p. 39; **33**, p. 4; **47**, p. 10.
3. **36**, p. 86.

4. **33**, p. 5.
5. **33**, p. 6.

ures, but there have been conflicting opinions on the economic effect and desirability of such measures.

FACTORS CONTROLLING FOREIGN TRADE

The simplest case of international — or inter-tribal — trade is the exchange of products which are found in only one area and are coveted by those who lack them. This type of trade prevailed in ancient times and perhaps until the eighteenth century in Europe and America, and occurs even now in the exchange between modern industrial countries and underdeveloped areas rich in certain raw materials. Essentially, the exchange of British or German tools and machinery for Ceylonese tea or Brazilian coffee is of the same type as the exchange of European amber and lead for Chinese silk or Indian ivory at the time of Alexander the Great. There is nothing controversial in the economic effect of exchange based on the natural or actual monopoly of certain areas in the production of certain commodities: through such trade, a country uses its surplus produce to obtain articles it cannot produce itself.

In modern international trade, however, most of the goods which flow across international boundaries *can* be produced in the importing country or can be replaced by domestic products. Such goods appear in international trade because the importing country finds it more advantageous to buy them abroad than to produce them. In other words, a large part of modern foreign trade is based on the international division of labor rather than on the geographical incidence of certain rare commodities. The objectives of foreign trade theory since Adam Smith have been to determine the conditions under which the international division of labor takes place and the limits to which it can and must go.

THE PRINCIPLE OF COMPARATIVE COST

Adam Smith pointed out that "natural advantages which one country has over another in producing particular commodities" are essentially a question of the cost of production:

By means of glasses, hotbeds, and hotwalls, very good grapes can be raised in Scotland, and very good wine too can be made of them at about thirty times the expense for which at least equally good can be brought from foreign countries. . . . Whether the advantages which one country has over another, be natural or acquired, is in this respect of no consequence. As long as the one country has those advantages, and 'the other wants them, it will always be more advantageous for the latter, rather to buy of the former than to make. It is an acquired advantage only, which one artificer has over his neighbour, who exercises another trade; and yet they both find it more advantageous to buy of one another, than to make what does not belong to their particular trade.[6]

Smithian reference to grapes and wine, however, fails to explain the mechanism of exchange between two countries when one of them exceeds the other in efficiency in all branches of production. The exchange depends in this instance on the *comparative cost* of production of various commodities. This principle was formulated by David Ricardo as follows:

Two men can both make shoes and hats, and one is superior to the other in both employments; but in making hats, he can only exceed his competitor by one-fifth, or 20 per cent, and in making shoes he can excel him by one-third, or 33 per cent; — will it not be for the interest of both, that the superior man should employ himself exclusively in making shoes, and the inferior man in making hats?[7]

It is very doubtful, of course, that so small a difference in relative cost of production as Ricardo describes could originate international division of labor and result in a regular exchange of hats for shoes between two countries. Probably all the gains that could result from such an exchange would be absorbed by transportation and selling costs and the advantages the domestic producer could obtain by adjusting his production to the changing demand of local consumers. But most students recognize the general principle stressed by Ricardo: the difference in *comparative* cost is the essential condition of international exchange.[8] Indeed a large part of foreign trade is carried on within the limits set by the comparative cost of producing various articles in various countries. In an extreme case, it may be to a country's interest to import a commodity which it could produce at less cost than the exporting country.[9]

In fact, the exchange of commodities among nations depends not on the comparative cheapness — in terms of money converted at existing

6. **45**, pp. 200–01.
7. **42**, p. 77.
8. **27**, p. 372; **26**, p. 15.
9. **26**, pp. 11–12.

exchange rates — of producing the same articles in different areas but on the ratios between the costs of producing different commodities in different countries.

Modern economic theory introduces an important correction into this thesis — the assumption that the comparative production cost of different commodities may depend largely on the volume of production. In some cases, the cost per unit rises when the volume of production increases, in others it declines. The cost rises, for example, when a country increases the acreage under an export crop by using less suitable land or land which, except for the possibility of export, could be used for more lucrative purposes. It rises also when a country increases its output of coal or ore designed for foreign markets by mining comparatively poor deposits. It declines when the availability of new outlets permits application of mass-production methods or diminishes the fixed cost per unit of merchandise. Variation in the cost of production per unit of different articles affects the ratios of costs between the goods which can be exported and imported. Ultimately, this mechanism, combined with the elasticity of demand of the importing country for foreign products, determines the limits of international division of labor.

To increase its exports, the exporting country may be compelled to cut prices to the limit at which export ceases to be profitable. On the other hand, when the exporting country keeps its prices high, the importing countries may be induced to develop a domestic industry which would free them from dependence on foreign produce. In the long run, the tendency is often toward equalization of cost ratios in the countries participating in free exchange of goods.

A country should expand or curtail the production of different commodities until her ratios of cost are the same as those abroad, and export the surplus or import the deficiency so generated. (In some lines production may be abandoned entirely, and some goods may be imported which were not consumed, before trade was opened, owing to the excessive cost or impossibility of producing them at home.) [10]

In this modified form, Ricardo's *law of comparative cost* does not require the assumption of perfect mobility of labor and capital within a nation and lack of mobility across international boundaries. Migration of labor and capital appears simply as a factor which may change both the cost ratios in the affected countries and the limits to which import of foreign merchandise and export of the home product are advantageous to these countries.

INTERNATIONAL VALUES

After allowance for transportation costs, customs duties and other factors affecting the margin of profit in international trade, the ratio in which goods are exchanged between two countries must fall within the margin between the cost ratios and the production costs of the respective goods in these countries. If, for example, it costs one country as much to produce one ton of wheat as two tons of coal and the cost ratio is $1 \div 4$ in another country, the first country will exchange its wheat for coal produced in the second. However, the trade will bring no profit to the country exporting wheat if it obtains only two tons of coal for one ton of wheat. Similarly, the second country will have no interest in an exchange if it has to pay four tons of coal for each ton of wheat. The exchange ratio between weights of wheat and coal must therefore be between $1 \div 2$ and $1 \div 4$.[11]

Actually the margin is narrowed by costs of transportation and marketing, customs duties and so forth. Assuming that all these factors increase the cost of exported goods by approximately 25 per cent, the first country will not export wheat unless it obtains more than 2.5 tons of coal for a ton of wheat, and the second will not export coal if it has to give more than 3.2 tons of coal for one ton of wheat. Within this margin (from 2.5 to 3.2 tons of coal for a ton of wheat), the international price ratio is determined by bargaining — a general and somewhat vague term which includes, among other factors, the intensity of demand for both commodities in the importing countries, the competitive position of both commodities in relation to other goods,[12] the efficiency of the trading organizations of both parties,[13] and conditions in each country tending toward monopoly.[14]

The relation between prices of two commodities, or the ratio in which they are exchanged (in physical units) on the world market, determines in what proportion the economic gains resulting

---

10. **35**, pp. 19–20.

11. **41**, Part III, p. 18; **42**, p. 134.
12. **41**, Part III, p. 18; **38**, p. 275.
13. **36**, pp. 134–35.
14. **26**, p. 42.

from foreign trade are distributed among the trading nations. Moreover, part of the gain which seems to accrue to the weaker country may flow to foreign firms exploiting its natural resources so that the local economy gains little from booming export trade.

These features of foreign trade weaken the claims that both parties gain from a free exchange of their produce. Ultimately, under ideal conditions, both parties must win, but this fact does not imply that free exchange is to their advantage under any conceivable conditions, always and everywhere.

The classical theory of free trade was developed in England at a time when British industry and commerce were supreme in the world and was abandoned by the British a century and a half later, after the United Kingdom had lost its lead in the world economy. Moreover, there are many examples of economic progress in countries that use tariffs to protect domestic industries. Such was the case in England in the seventeenth century and in the United States, Germany and France in the nineteenth.

THE BALANCE OF TRADE

Generally, each country's export is limited by (1) the ability and willingness of other nations to absorb its products at prices that make export profitable; and (2) by the ability or willingness of the exporting country to deliver its produce to other nations at prices acceptable to foreign buyers. When either of these conditions is missing, the flow of exports must stop.

The imports and exports of individual countries do not necessarily balance each other, but in the long run the export of merchandise and services of each country determines the limits of its imports of merchandise and services. Profits from foreign investments, earnings from foreign trade, insurance, tourism and other invisible exports, remittances of immigrants, private and public loans and credits make all the difference between the modern highly intricate international balances of payment and the simple barter exchange of older times. The general principle of exchange remains the same, however: each country has to pay for the goods and services it acquires abroad with goods and services it offers to other countries. A net balance in merchandise trade must be offset either by a balance in invisi-

ble export and import, payment in cash, or transfer of capital.[15]

CUSTOMS AND OTHER RESTRICTIONS

Although the idea of using customs duties as a means of controlling foreign trade can be traced back to the sixteenth and seventeenth centuries, the main objective of foreign trade policy at that time was to accumulate and protect monetary reserves. Protection of domestic industries was a by-product rather than the purpose of customs duties until the beginning of the eighteenth century.

Alexander Hamilton was probably the first to visualize the role of protective tariffs [16] as a means of promoting industrial progress and accelerating the growth of particular branches of production. His ideas were transplanted to Europe by Friedrich List.[17] Both men considered industrialization as the principal goal of economic policy and a protective tariff the best policy for countries that aspire to economic independence. Protection of young and weak industries in "infancy" was not a hollow slogan of the founders of the protectionist philosophy: at that time industries in the United States and Germany were too weak to face British competition. Very soon, however, protectionism acquired another meaning. In the last quarter of the nineteenth century, the argument for "infant industry" became a pretext for giving tariff protection to any economic group that could muster sufficient political pressure.[18]

It is extremely difficult to appraise the long-run effect of protectionism on world trade. Many protective import duties — for example, those imposed on agricultural products, which have a highly inelastic demand — resulted in supporting agricultural prices and redistributing national income in favor of farmers although the effect on imports of the respective commodities was not overwhelming. In other cases, reduction of imports of a certain commodity was offset by increase in imports of competing articles. At the same time, protective and often prohibitive duties established by customs tariffs have been lowered by commercial treaties.[19] In the race of tariffs and treaties, increases and cuts in customs

15. **1**, 1937, pp. 47–48; cf. Chapter **5**.
16. **34**, pp. 79–103; cf. **48**.
17. **37**, *passim*.
18. **33**, p. 284.
19. Cf. Chapter **6**.

duties run neck and neck. After the beginning of the twentieth century the general trend in the level of tariffs was downward rather than upward, and on the eve of World War I, the world market, especially the market for finished articles and industrial raw materials, was as free as at any time in the past. If the growth of world trade then lagged behind world industrial growth, it was not because of customs barriers.

After the depression of the 1930's, the effect of protective tariffs on world trade was overshadowed by disorganization of monetary systems, political insecurity, the widespread practice of restricting and regulating exports and imports and so on. In countries with regulated exchange rates and a system of import and export licenses, tariffs ceased to be the major factor controlling foreign trade.[20]

Measuring Foreign Trade

In considering international statistics of foreign trade, attention should be given to the coverage of the data (that is, the items included in or excluded from the concept of foreign trade), the system of classifying certain operations related to foreign trade, the methods of valuing merchandise and the methods of computing index numbers for the volume (quantum) of foreign trade.

COVERAGE

In addition to merchandise commercially imported and exported, foreign trade statistics generally include merchandise imported or exported on government account, postal trade (parcel and letter post), ships and aircraft bought and sold (whether or not newly built) and silver in all forms. When a country exports finished products fabricated from imported raw materials, they are registered at their full value. Reimports are treated similarly. On the other hand, the repair trade (for example, repair of a foreign ship) is registered at "added value." Fresh fish and other sea products brought directly from the high seas are registered in foreign trade if they are imported on foreign vessels but not when they are carried by domestic vessels. Similarly, ships' stores (including bunker fuel) are registered in foreign trade only if they are exported on foreign ships.

Foreign trade generally does not include direct transit, merchandise imported for temporary use (such as articles for exhibition and tourists' cars), frontier trade (such as farm produce transported to a depth of approximately six miles from the border), consular and diplomatic supplies and passengers' baggage (unless dutiable). It does not include railroad cars in international traffic, gold (bullion and specie), paper currency and war reparations and restitutions.

There is no uniform treatment of such items as relief shipments (for example, deliveries under UNRRA and the European Recovery Program), sales and purchases of surplus war property, and merchandise exported and imported under the lend-lease program.[21]

GENERAL AND SPECIAL TRADE

The main difference in the practice of various countries in classifying trade is in recording general and special trade. *General trade* includes in imports all merchandise unloaded in the country, whether for home consumption or for reexport. It likewise includes reexports in export figures. Usually it does not record direct-transit trade in either imports or exports.[22]

The concept of *special trade* is narrower. It includes in imports merchandise unloaded for home consumption, plus goods customs-cleared from warehouses. It records as exports only national (or domestic) produce exported, plus foreign products reexported after transformation or supplementary treatment other than merely repacking, sorting or blending. Special trade also includes reexports of foreign products which have been cleared by customs and recorded as imported.

The distinction between the two concepts is of importance for countries with extensive intermediate trade — for example, industrial countries which import goods from tropical areas and distribute them among other nations. It is immaterial for most underdeveloped areas, which have no substantial warehousing and reexport trade.

The concept of general trade is used in the United States and the United Kingdom. It is widespread in Middle and South America (Mexico, Guatemala, El Salvador, Honduras, Nic-

---

20. Cf. Chapter 6.

21. **13,** p. 59.

22. In some countries general trade includes direct transit. In such countries foreign trade excluding direct transit is described as "total own trade" (*Gesamteigenhandel* in Germany). (**49,** Vol. V, p. 173.)

aragua, Costa Rica, Panama, Cuba, Jamaica, the Dominican Republic, Venezuela, Colombia, Ecuador and Brazil) and in most British dominions and colonies (Australia, New Zealand and the Union of South Africa; India, Pakistan and Ceylon; Hong Kong and Malaya; the Gold Coast, Northern and Southern Rhodesia and Tanganyika). Other countries that record general trade include Ireland, the Philippines, Burma, Thailand, Korea, Iraq and Ethiopia.

The practice of recording only special trade prevails in continental European countries and their colonies (Algeria, Morocco, Tunisia, Mozambique and Indochina; the Belgian Congo; Canary Islands). This practice is also followed by Canada, Argentina, Chile, Peru and Paraguay, Egypt, Indonesia, Iran, Syria, Lebanon and Israel.[23]

In international surveys of world trade, some countries are often represented by their general trade and others by special trade. Since the concept of general trade is broader than that of special trade, exports and imports of the first group of nations are overstated in comparison with those of the second.

VALUATION

Imports are generally valued *c.i.f.* (that is, "cost, insurance, and freight") ex ship (or other means of international transport), at the port or other place of arrival at the frontier of the importing country, without customs duty and other import charges. There are important exceptions, however. In the United States, the major British dominions and certain other countries, ad valorem import duties are assessed upon the value of the goods on the home market which may differ from the value c.i.f.

Exports are valued *f.o.b.* (that is, "free on board") of a ship (or other means of transport), port or place of dispatch at the frontier of the exporting country (including export duties and other charges passed on to the importer).[24]

According to these definitions, the same merchandise must be valued higher by the importing than by the exporting country. Theoretically, the import value must include the export value, plus cost of freight and insurance. Actually, the

procedures are more complicated. In both exporting and importing countries, customs authorities often evaluate the merchandise according to intricate and sometimes arbitrary definitions and instructions.

In trade between two countries, the two parties often give widely different values for merchandise passing between them. One source of disparity is the difference in the value of the same merchandise at the export station, f.o.b., and the import point, c.i.f. The disparity may be increased by difference in methods of converting foreign currencies, since the conversion rates used by the customs officials are not necessarily those used in financial transactions.[25] There is also a considerable margin of uncertainty in determining the destination and origin of commodities in foreign trade. The destination of goods may be changed after they leave the exporting country, and customs authorities may register as the place of origin either the port where the merchandise was loaded or the last port touched by the ship which brought it.[26]

For the world as a whole, the total value of imports usually exceeds the total for exports. The difference fluctuated around 15 per cent and occasionally reached 20 per cent or more in the second half of the nineteenth century and has narrowed to approximately 10 per cent in more recent years. (See Tables 13 and 14.)

VOLUME

Index numbers of the *volume* (quantum) of foreign trade (Table 14) are designed for measuring changes in the *value* of external trade after allowance is made for the effects of price movements. The objective is the same as in measuring changes in real wages. However, the cost-of-living (or consumers' price) index used to "deflate" wages cannot be applied to the values of exports and imports.[27] Many important items of everyday consumption do not appear in international trade. Likewise changes in prices of staple foodstuffs and raw materials which predominate in world imports and exports often deviate from changes in the wholesale price index. As a gen-

---

23. **13**, pp. 58–70.

24. The United States, Argentina and Finland use a slightly different basis of valuation which is called *f.a.s.* (free alongside ship) and includes all the items of f.o.b. except loading charges.

25. **13**, p. 58.

26. Cf. **40**, pp. 371–72.

27. The cost-of-living index is best used in measuring short-run changes in real wages. The results are less satisfactory when it is used in measuring the long-range trend in real wages (**51**, pp. 182–84) and especially when it is applied to national income. (See **18**, January 1951, pp. 6–11.)

TABLE 13

WORLD TRADE: EXPORTS AND IMPORTS IN U.S. DOLLARS AND WHOLESALE PRICE INDEX, 1867–68 TO 1920

Year [a]	Exports, in Millions	Imports, in Millions	Wholesale Price Index [b]	Year [a]	Exports, in Millions	Imports, in Millions	Wholesale Price Index [b]
1867–68	$4,979	$5,554	137	1894	$7,564	$8,815	88
1872–73	6,355	7,405	151	1895	7,949	9,005	86
1877	6,457	5,826	129	1896	8,171	9,524	84
1880	7,042	8,162	122	1897	8,480	9,799	86
1881	7,197	8,142	117	1901		22,291	97
1882	7,430	8,560	116	1902		23,055	96
1883	7,513	8,653	113	1903		24,392	96
1884	7,248	8,256	103	1904		24,999	97
1885	6,864	7,832	100	1905		26,940	100
1886	6,540	7,525	96	1906		29,704	106
1887	6,777	7,760	94	1907		31,752	111
1888	7,053	8,056	97	1908		29,620	101
1889	7,542	8,750	100	1909		31,561	102
1890	7,771	9,052	100	1910		34,980	110
1891	7,853	9,178	100	1911		36,761	111
1892	7,730	9,074	94	1912		40,287	117
1893	7,763	8,941	94	1913	19,800	20,800	117
				1920	31,600	34,200	261

Sources: **44**, p. 680; **4**, 1911–25, pp. 132-33 and 1913–27, p. 12; **50**, pp. 156–57.

a. No computations were made for 1898–1900 and 1914–19. For 1901–12 only totals for world exports and imports are available.

b. Index of *The Economist* (London). 1890 = 100

eral rule, prices of imported and exported articles are more sensitive to changes in business conditions and exchange rates; occasionally, they do not move in the same direction and they often change in the same direction but at different rates.

Since the existing cost-of-living and wholesale indexes cannot be used to deflate foreign trade figures, special methods have been developed to measure changes in the volume of foreign trade.

The simplest method is to reevaluate the imported or exported goods at prices in the base period and to express the computed aggregate as a percentage of the value for that period. This ratio is described as "quantum index with fixed weights" (Laspeyres formula).[28]

Sometimes, instead of reevaluating foreign trade in the current year, current prices are applied to imports or exports in the base period. In this way, the current value of foreign trade is compared with the value it would have had in the base period if the new (current) prices had prevailed at that time. The index computed in this way is described as the "index with moving current weights" (Paasche formula).[29]

The quantum index with fixed weights is more widely used, especially in Europe. In 1950, it was in use in the United Kingdom, France, Belgium-Luxembourg, the Netherlands, Denmark, Norway, Western Germany, Poland, Czechoslovakia, Switzerland, Austria, Spain and Turkey. It was also used in Chile, Malaya and Ceylon (for exports only). The index with moving weights was used in Ireland (for monthly reports), Sweden (for quarterly statistics), Finland, Indochina, Australia and New Zealand.

Several countries use a more complicated formula — an average of the quantum indexes obtained by the Laspeyres and Paasche methods.[30] This formula is applied in the United States,

28. In this formula, the quantities of imported or exported commodities are considered as variables, while the prices serve as weights.

29. In this formula, as in that of Laspeyres, prices are the weights of the varying quantities of commodities.

30. The average used in this formula is a geometrical mean, that is, the square root of the product of the two indexes.

TABLE 14

WORLD TRADE: EXPORTS AND IMPORTS IN DOLLARS, AND INDEX OF QUANTUM OF EXPORTS, 1913–52

Year [a]	Exports, in Millions	Imports, in Millions	Index of Quantum of Exports (1929 = 100)
In Gold Dollars			
1913	$19,800	$20,800	74.0 [b]
1920	31,600	34,200	53.5
1921	19,700	22,100	55.0
1922	21,700	23,600	59.0
1923	23,800	25,900	65.5
1924	27,850	28,980	75.7
1925	31,550	33,150	83.2
1926	29,920	32,120	85.2
1927	31,520	33,760	91.9
1928	32,730	34,650	95.2
1929	33,024	35,595	100.0
1930	26,480	29,080	93.0
1931	18,910	20,800	85.5
1932	12,885	13,970	74.5
1933	11,710	12,460	75.4
1934	11,300	12,000	78.2
1935	11,600	12,200	81.8
1936	12,600	13,100	85.8
1937	15,000	16,100	96.5
1938	13,400	14,300	89.0
In U.S. Dollars			
1938 [b]	$20,700	$23,200	89.0
1947	48,200	50,100	89.0
1948	52,800	58,400	92.7
1949	53,700	58,500	100.1
1950	55,400	58,200	112.1
1951	75,400	80,200	124.2
1952	72,500	79,100	122.2

Sources: 1913–23, estimated by the authors on the basis of **25**, various years (cf. **49**, Vol. V, p. 176); 1924–38, **5**, 1937, p. 77 and 1938, p. 8; 1938–52 (lower part of the table), **15**, 1952, pp. 16–17.

a. In the upper part of the table (1913–38) values in gold dollars; in the lower part (1938–52) U.S. dollars. Figures for 1938–52 do not include China, USSR and nonreporting countries of eastern Europe.

b. Adjusted for comparability with later data.

Cuba, Ireland and Sweden (for annual data), Italy, Anglo-Egyptian Sudan and Ceylon (for imports).[31]

TRENDS IN WORLD TRADE

Only fragmentary statistics of foreign trade are available for periods before the nineteenth century. The United States is the only country which has continuous records of imports and exports from 1790 to the present. The records of England and France go back to the beginning of the nineteenth century; those of Belgium, to 1831; and of Sweden, to 1836.

BEFORE WORLD WAR I (1820–1913)

With reservation for a broad margin of error, an estimate of world exports may be ventured for the period after the Napoleonic wars. In 1820 Great Britain's exports amounted to $238 million; those of France, to $105 million, and those of the United States, to $52 million. These three countries led in international trade. Other countries with appreciable exports were Belgium, the Netherlands and Austria-Hungary, followed, at a considerable distance, by Russia, Germany, Italy, Switzerland and Sweden. World exports at that time probably totaled between $550 and $600 million, a little more than one per cent of the dollar value in 1950 and somewhat less than 2 per cent of the gold equivalent.

Less than half a century later, in 1867–68, the total value of world exports was close to $5 billion and of world imports, more than $5.5 billion.[32] The growth of world trade slowed down in the 1870's and 1880's but quickened again at the end of the century and, especially, after 1900.[33] The annual increase averaged 1.3 per cent in 1865–1900 and 5.0 per cent from 1895 to 1912–13. (See Table 13; cf. Figure 5.)

The uneven growth of the value of world trade was due partly to fluctuations in prices. Wholesale prices went up about 10 per cent between 1867–68 and 1872–73; declined, with minor fluctuations, until the middle 1890's and subsequently rose rather steadily. Wholesale prices in Great Britain, then the main center of world trade, were some 20 per cent lower in 1913 than in 1867–68.[34]

With rough correction for changes in prices, where the volume of world trade in 1913 equals 100, the index numbers for 1867–68 are 20–25 and for 1880, 35–40.

There is no way to compare the growth of world trade in that period with the rise in world income. We can, however, venture a comparison

31. **13**, pp. 71–81.

32. Based on Jurashek's estimate in **44**, p. 680.

33. **44**, p. 680; **49**, Vol. V, p. 176; for 1913 see **5**, 1937, p. 76.

34. Price index of *The Economist* (London). (See **50**, pp. 26–27, 156–57.)

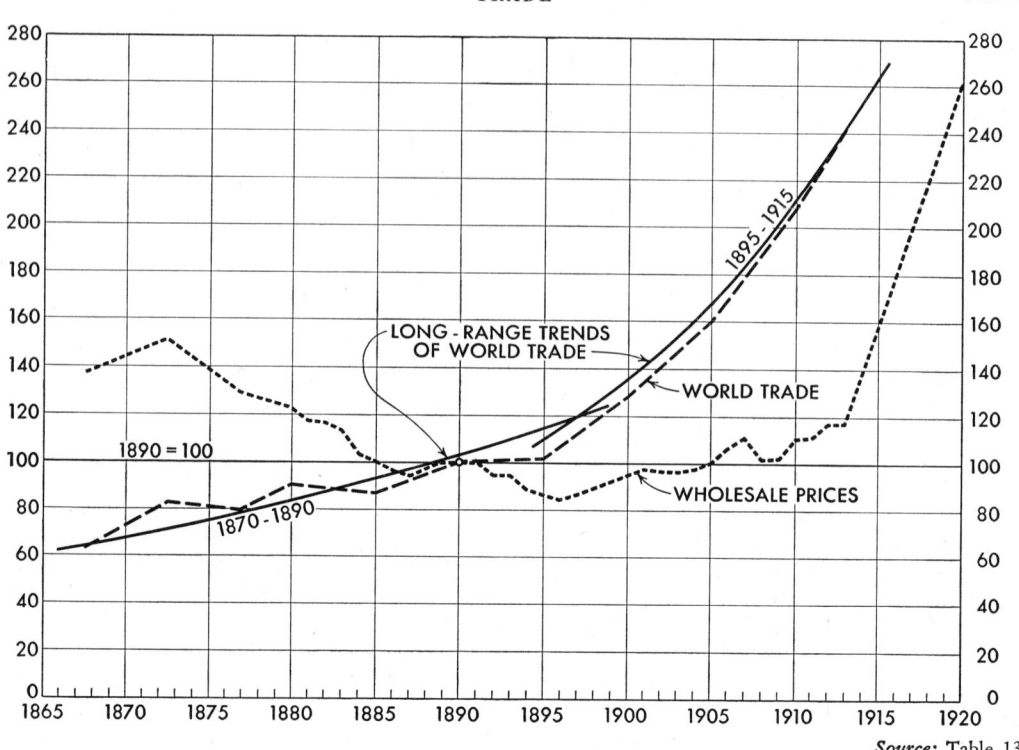

FIGURE 5. WORLD TRADE: INDEXES OF VALUE AND WHOLESALE PRICES, 1867–68 TO 1920

Source: Table 13

between the trend in international trade and in world industrial production. According to the estimates of the German Institute for the Study of Business Conditions, the index number for the world's industrial output (1913 = 100) was 14 in 1860, 19 in 1870, 26 in 1880 and 43 in 1890.[35]

Comparison of the two series suggests that the growth of world trade lagged behind the expansion of world industrial production. For the whole period from 1867–68 to 1913, the value of world trade increased, on the average, 34 per cent per decade, and the volume, probably about 36–37 per cent, while the decennial rate of growth in world industrial production was close to 47 per cent. It can be argued that only a part of international trade is directly related to manufacturing production while the other part consists of foodstuffs. It is an undeniable fact, however, that world trade was expanding at a slower pace than industrial production in the period of spectacular progress in the means of

transportation and the rise of the new colonial empires in Africa and Asia, at a time when world currencies were stable and wars and revolutions were comparatively rare.[36]

DURING AND AFTER WORLD WAR I (1914–52)

The world's economic progress has been interrupted three times in the last four decades, by two world wars and the intervening severe depression. World War I resulted in extensive changes in the political map of Europe and the Near East, a series of revolutions and the almost complete isolation of the USSR from the world economy. World War II left the world split between the West and the East with only

36. Folke Hilgerdt reached similar conclusions when comparing trends in world manufacturing and world trade in primary products and manufactured articles from 1876–80 to 1926–29. He estimates the average rate of growth of world manufacturing output at 3.5 per cent per year, and the rate of growth of the quantum of world trade at 2.6 per cent for primary products and 2.4 per cent for manufactured articles. (**2**, p. 14.) According to his estimate, the ratio of export to world output of manufactured articles declined by more than 40 per cent from 1876–80 to 1926–29. The loss was almost evenly distributed between the periods from 1876–80 to 1913 and from 1913 to 1926–29.

35. **23**, p. 69. The Institute pioneered in computing a world index of industrial production. Its series was carried on, with minor adjustments, by the League of Nations and later by the UN.

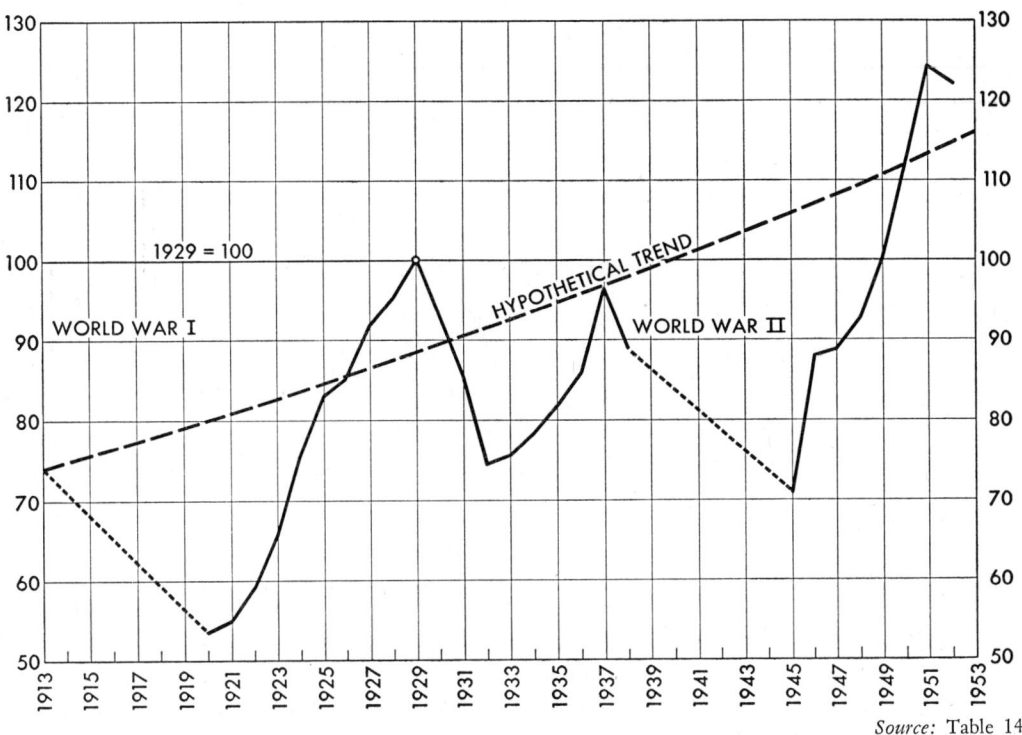

FIGURE 6. WORLD TRADE: INDEX OF QUANTUM OF EXPORTS, 1913–52

feeble vestiges of trade between the two groups of nations.

Changes in the volume of world trade in this period may be pictured as a curve with three waves, one stretching from 1913 to 1929, the second covering the great depression and subsequent recovery, the third extending from the outbreak of World War II to the present.

It is difficult to draw a smooth trend line through this period. When such a line is drawn through the years 1913 and 1937, the high point of 1929 towers above the line and the average rate of growth of the volume of world exports appears very low — less than 12 per cent per decade. (See Figure 6.) For a closer analysis, the three phases of the period 1914–1952 should be examined separately.

World War I and Postwar Prosperity (1914–29)

There are no reliable estimates of the value and volume of world trade in 1914–19. The blockade of the British Isles by German submarines and the encirclement of the Central Powers by the Allied armies did not stop international exchange of goods but changed its direction and form. Foreign trade was dominated by

the movement of military goods and raw materials from the United States to the Allies.

It is fairly certain that the total volume of world trade declined sharply during the war but it is difficult to measure the loss. In the early 1920's, in the period of universal confusion following Armistice Day, the volume was probably 25 per cent less than in 1913.[37] By 1924, world trade had about regained its prewar volume. It continued to increase despite the rising tariffs and in 1929 reached a peak.[38] (See Table 14.)

---

37. When the value of foreign trade in 1920 recorded by individual countries is converted into a hard currency and deflated by a conventional wholesale price index, the real value of world exports and imports in that year appears approximately 28 per cent less than in 1913. Application of the same method to data for 1924 suggests that the real value of world exports and imports in that year was approximately 5 per cent less than before the war. (**49**, Vol V, p. 176.) This conclusion, however, is at variance with the quantum index of world trade of the League of Nations, which shows that world trade in 1924 was only 2 per cent below the prewar volume. (**4**, 1911–1925, p. 133.) Comparison of the two estimates for 1924 suggests that the estimate of world trade volume in 1920 based on a wholesale price index is too low.

38. The quantum of world trade as calculated by the

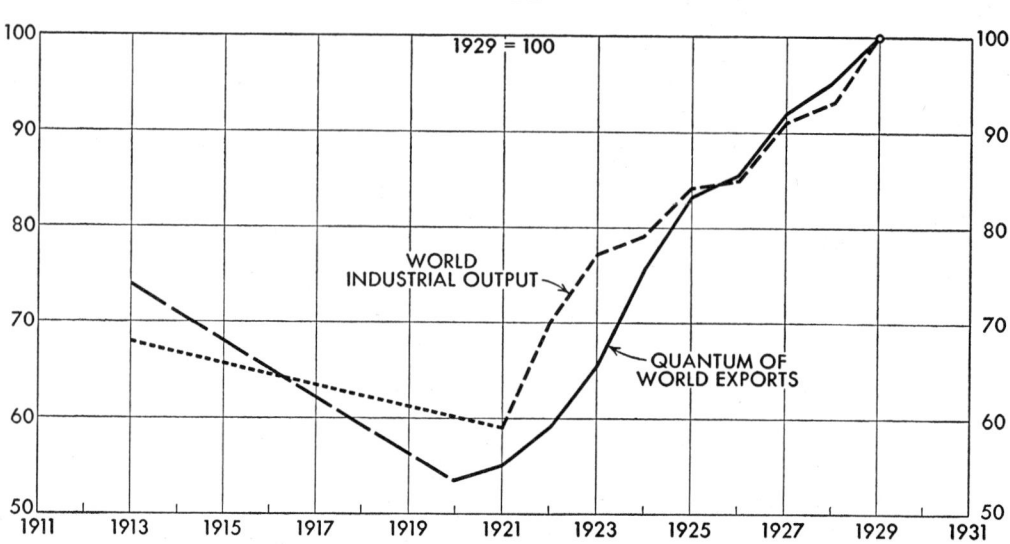

FIGURE 7. WORLD TRADE: INDEXES OF QUANTUM AND OF WORLD INDUSTRIAL OUTPUT, 1913–29

The index of the quantum of world trade shown here was computed by the League of Nations; that of indus- trial production by the German Institute for the Study of Business Conditions. Both indexes exclude the USSR.

The late 1920's were marked by a boom in world trade as well as in industrial output: the volume of each nearly doubled from the low point of 1920–21 to the peak in the autumn of 1929. In that year, world industrial production was 47 per cent above the 1913 level, while the quantum of international trade had risen 35 per cent. (See Figure 7.)

Depression and Recovery (1929–38)

After the autumn of 1929 world trade declined rapidly from month to month. The Austrian Institute for the Study of Business Conditions has presented this course graphically in a chart which has been reproduced by many authors.[39] The chart represents the monthly values of world trade by a spiral revolving clockwise from the peripherical values of 1929 toward the center. It shows that the value in each month was less than in the preceding year and conveys the impression that international trade was shrinking to the zero point. (See Figure 8.) Closer analysis indicates, however, that the loss in the volume of international trade at that time was less than the decline in world industrial output: although the value of foreign trade, in gold dollars, dropped nearly 60 per cent

from 1929 to 1932, the quantum declined only 25 per cent, while world industrial production fell 37 per cent.[40]

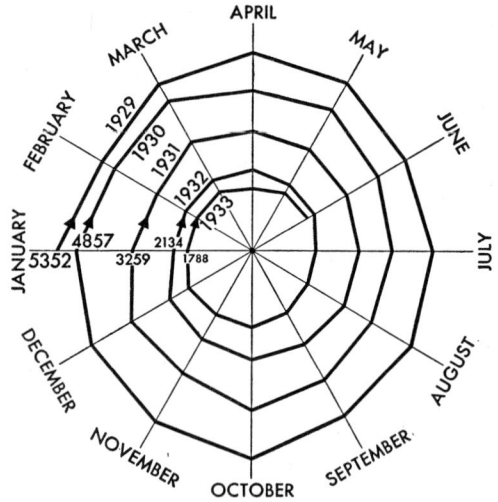

Source: 21

FIGURE 8. WORLD TRADE: THE CONTRACTING SPIRAL, JANUARY 1929–JUNE 1933

(Exports and Imports in Millions of Gold Dollars)

Similarly, after the upturn in 1933, world industrial production recovered more rapidly than the volume of international trade. The two

experts of the League of Nations on the basis of the Paasche formula.

39. **21**, 1933, No. 4, p. 63; cf. **7**, 1932–1933, p. 8; **28**, p. 495.

40. **5**, 1938, p. 60; **8**, 1938–39, p. 66; cf. **51**, pp. 65–68.

TABLE 15

WORLD TRADE: INDEXES OF QUANTUM OF EXPORTS AND OF WORLD INDUSTRIAL OUTPUT, 1913–38

(*1929 = 100*)

Item	1913	1929	1930	1931	1932	1933	1934	1935	1936	1937	1938
Quantum of world exports	74	100	93	86	75	75	78	82	86	97	89
Industrial output [a]											
Total	68	100	86	74	63	72	78	87	97	104	93
Consumption goods	...	100	91	87	80	87	90	94	101	105	99
Capital goods	...	100	82	61	43	55	64	77	93	103	85

Sources: For 1913, Table 14 and **23**, p. 67; for 1929–38, **8**, 1938–39, p. 7.

a. Excludes the USSR.

index curves crossed in 1934, at a point approximately 22 per cent below the 1929 peak. Further recovery brought the world production index high above that of international trade. The recession of 1938 temporarily closed the gap. (See Table 15; cf. Figure 9.)

In the middle of 1938, before the outbreak of World War II, both the quantum of international trade and the index of world manufacturing production (excluding the USSR) were around 10 per cent below the 1929 peak. The index numbers for the average of four quarters in 1938 were 93 for production and 89 for the quantum of trade (1929 = 100). It appears that in the twenty-five years following 1913, the world (without the USSR) increased its manufacturing output approximately 37 per cent and the quantum of international trade, 20 per cent. Increase in the volume of trade lagged behind that in production but not much more than in the period from 1867–68 to 1913.

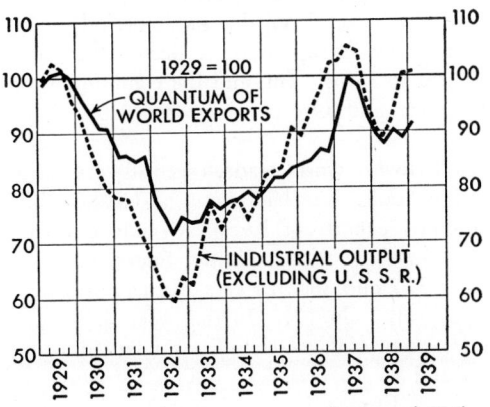

FIGURE 9. WORLD TRADE: QUARTERLY INDEXES OF QUANTUM AND OF WORLD INDUSTRIAL OUTPUT, 1929–39

World War II and Its Aftermath (*1939–52*)

Statistics for 1939–45 are fragmentary and inconclusive. As during World War I, the general pattern of international trade was dominated by war deliveries. Restoration of peacetime trade proved to be a tremendous task. Germany and Japan were knocked out, the British colonial empire was crumbling, the USSR directed all its economic resources and those of conquered areas toward increasing its military power. The economic life of France and Italy was greatly disorganized by the double ordeal of occupation and liberation.

In relation to the prewar peak in 1937, recovery in industrial production preceded that in international trade. (See Table 16.) In 1952, world industrial production, excluding the USSR, was 63 per cent above the 1937 level. Excluding also the United States the gain was 42 per cent. Everything considered, this is a highly satisfactory record even with allowance for the growth of population and long-range industrial progress.

At the same time, the volume of world exports (excluding the USSR and other satellite countries) had risen 35 per cent above the 1937 level. When the United States, too, is excluded, the quantum of exports appears only 22 per cent above that in 1937.

Thus, a gap developed between the growth of world industrial production and international trade. The lag in international exchange of goods seemed to be a major obstacle to the further increase of production and improvement in the standard of living, especially in Western Europe.[41]

---

41. See Chapter 5.

TABLE 16

WORLD TRADE: INDEXES OF QUANTUM OF EXPORTS AND OF WORLD INDUSTRIAL OUTPUT,[a] 1946–52

(1937 = 100)

Area	1946	1947	1948	1949	1950	1951	1952
Quantum of World Exports							
World total	97	98	101	109	123	137	135
United States	191	252	197	201	180	225	215
Europe	49	64	80	95	122	138	133
Other countries	66	75	87	96	115	124	122
Industrial Output							
World total	105	117	127	128	141	159	163
United States	150	165	170	156	177	195	193
Europe	66	76	91	104	117	132	137
Other countries	73	83	97	108	121	137	142

Sources: **11**, August 1953, pp. xxviii, 23; July 1953, p. xiii; **6**, 1949–50, p. 68.

a. Excludes the USSR, Eastern Germany, Hungary, Romania, Bulgaria and China.

THE DISTRIBUTION OF WORLD TRADE AMONG THE CONTINENTS

Western Europe completely dominated world trade in the nineteenth century. In the 1820's, Great Britain alone accounted for more than 40 per cent of all exports. International trade consisted largely of the exchange of Great Britain and continental European countries among themselves and with overseas areas, especially the tropics. Europe's predominance in world trade remained unchallenged until World War I. In 1909–13, Europe (including Russia) took 64–67 per cent of the world's imports and accounted for 58–60 per cent of its exports.[42]

World War I brought a decrease in Europe's foreign trade and an increase in America's. In 1920, the share of the Americas in world trade amounted to 32.1 per cent (as compared with 21–23 per cent in 1909–13), while the European share was 49.2 per cent. (See Table 17.)

Europe regained its predominant position during the depression in the early 1930's, which almost paralyzed economic life in the United States but was less severe in most of the old countries. Thus, the percentage distribution of international trade among the continents in 1932 had returned to practically the 1913 pattern.

A new setback in European trade followed World War II. The share of the Western Hemisphere in world trade increased from 24.1 per cent in 1937 to 38.8 per cent in 1947; Europe's share (excluding the USSR) shrank from 50.2 per cent to 38.8 per cent and the share of Asia, Africa and Oceania combined, from 24.7 per cent to 20.4 per cent. As after World War I, the distribution of world trade in recent years has tended to resume the prewar pattern. (See Figure 10.)

The combined shares of the Americas, Asia, Africa and Oceania amounted to 41.6 per cent in 1913, 47.6 per cent in 1929 and 59.4–59.5 per cent in 1951 and 1952. In 1913 the Western Hemisphere accounted for 54 per cent of this total (non-European trade if the USSR is considered as a part of Europe); in 1951 and 1952, 57–58 per cent. Over the same period, Asia's share in non-European trade declined from 29 per cent to 25 per cent, and the combined share of Africa and Oceania increased from 17 to 18 per cent.

In 1946–47, world trade, especially European foreign trade, was badly out of balance. The combined exports of European countries were less than those of the United States and Canada — 32.2 and 36.1 per cent of the world total, respectively — in 1947. In that year the United States exports of merchandise totaled $15.2 billion and its imports, $5.7 billion. Western and southern Europe imported merchandise worth $23.2 billion and had exports valued at $13.6 billion.[43]

42. According to an estimate published in **25**, 1931, p. 94. The League of Nations gives slightly different figures for 1913. (See Table 17.)

43. **16**, 1951, p. xxii.

TABLE 17

WORLD TRADE: PERCENTAGE DISTRIBUTION OF EXPORTS AND IMPORTS AMONG THE CONTINENTS, 1913–52

Year	World [a]	North America	Middle America	South America	Europe	USSR	Asia	Africa	Oceania
				Exports					
1913	100	15.8	2.4	6.7	50.9	4.3	12.5	4.7	2.7
1920	100	...	...	...	...	...	...	...	...
1923	100	...	...	...	...	...	...	...	...
1926	100	20.7	3.0	6.4	42.9	1.2	18.1	4.4	3.3
1929	100	19.5	9.6		47.4	1.4	14.9	4.5	2.7
1932	100	16.3	9.1		48.8	2.3	13.7	6.7	3.1
1937	100	17.1	10.3		44.8	1.1	16.2	7.1	3.4
1947	100	36.1	3.9	8.8	32.2	1.0	9.7	5.5	2.9
1948	100	27.9	3.9	9.0	36.7	1.5	11.2	6.5	3.3
1949	100	27.7	3.7	8.0	37.0	...	12.2	7.0	4.4
1950	100	23.7	4.1	9.0	36.7	...	15.8	7.1	3.7
1951	100	25.0	3.5	8.0	37.8	...	14.9	6.8	4.0
1952	100	27.1	3.8	7.3	38.6	...	13.7	6.1	3.4
				Imports					
1913	100	12.4	1.9	5.7	57.9	3.6	11.8	4.1	2.6
1920	100	...	...	...	...	...	...	...	...
1923	100	...	...	...	...	...	...	...	...
1926	100	17.6	2.2	5.5	50.6	1.2	15.3	4.4	3.2
1929	100	16.1	7.7		54.2	1.3	13.2	4.8	2.7
1932	100	14.2	7.2		53.7	2.5	13.7	6.2	2.5
1937	100	15.5	8.6		50.2	1.0	14.9	6.7	3.1
1947	100	26.4	4.1	8.3	38.8	2.1	11.3	6.5	2.6
1948	100	22.4	4.0	8.1	40.6	2.3	12.3	7.3	3.0
1949	100	22.6	3.8	7.4	40.8	...	13.4	8.0	4.0
1950	100	23.0	4.2	7.7	39.7	...	14.5	7.3	3.6
1951	100	22.7	3.6	7.5	40.6	...	14.8	7.1	3.6
1952	100	20.2	4.2	6.7	42.7	...	15.5	7.1	3.6
				Total Foreign Trade					
1913	100	14.1	2.1	6.2	54.5	3.9	12.1	4.4	2.7
1920	100	32.1			49.2		13.4	3.4	1.9
1923	100	27.0			51.9		14.2	3.8	3.1
1926	100	19.1	2.6	6.0	46.9	1.2	16.6	4.4	3.2
1929	100	17.7	8.6		51.1	1.3	14.0	4.6	2.7
1932	100	14.2	7.2		53.7	2.5	13.7	6.2	2.5
1937	100	15.5	8.6		50.2	1.0	14.9	6.7	3.1
1947	100	26.4	4.1	8.3	38.8	2.1	11.3	6.5	2.6
1948	100	22.4	4.0	8.1	40.6	2.3	12.3	7.3	3.0
1949	100	22.6	3.8	7.4	40.8	...	13.4	8.0	4.0
1950	100	23.0	4.2	7.7	39.7	...	14.5	7.3	3.6
1951	100	22.7	3.6	7.5	40.6	...	14.8	7.1	3.6
1952	100	23.5	4.0	7.0	40.5	...	14.7	6.8	3.5

Sources: For 1913 and 1926, **4**, 1913–1927, p. 42; for 1920 and 1923, **49**, Vol. V, p. 177; for 1929–37, **5**, 1937, p. 18; for 1947–52, **16**, January 1952 and May 1953.

a. Through 1948, trade of the USSR and its European satellites is included in world totals (as a part of European trade). Beginning with 1949, in view of the statistical blackout, the USSR, Eastern Germany, Bulgaria and Romania are omitted.

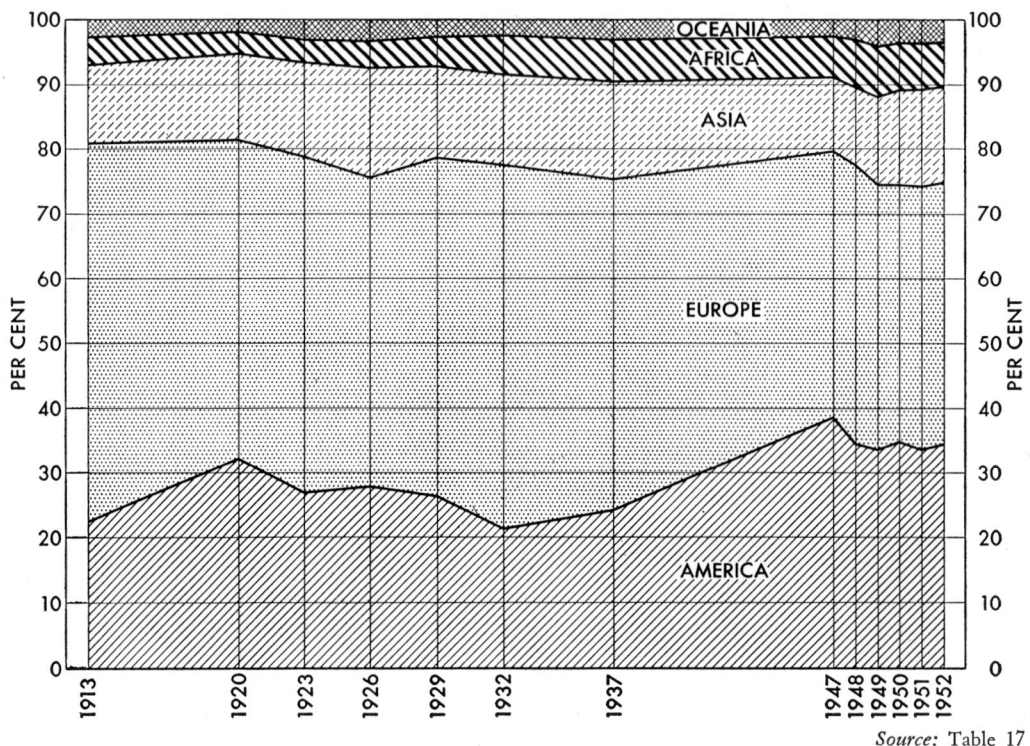

Source: Table 17

FIGURE 10. WORLD TRADE: PERCENTAGE DISTRIBUTION AMONG THE CONTINENTS, 1913–52

World trade as shown on this chart includes exports (f.o.b.) and imports (c.i.f.) of all countries for which statistical data or more or less reliable estimates are available. Through 1948, the totals include the trade of the USSR and its European satellites as a part of the European share in the world total. Beginning with 1949, the USSR, Eastern Germany, Romania, Bulgaria and China have been omitted.

Europe, impoverished and economically disorganized by the war, was unable to pay for the imported foodstuffs and raw materials urgently needed to maintain the customary consumption level of the population and to keep the factories working. Yet a sudden interruption or curtailment of the flow of imports would threaten dangerous economic and political dislocations. Since the crisis of 1947–48 was essentially a crisis of balance of payments, the solution was sought in emergency measures supporting Europe's payment balance, with the United States underwriting the bill.[44]

By 1950, the gap between the imports and exports of European countries and the United States had narrowed and a new equilibrium of world trade was in sight, but in 1951 the gap broadened again. (See Table 18.)

The gap between exports and imports is not peculiar to Europe and the United States: similar disparities between the values of exchange merchandise exist in most countries and geographical regions. (See Table 19.) The smooth flow of international trade requires only that the export or import surplus be balanced by other payments (invisible items of the balance of payments) or by capital movement.[45]

TRENDS IN SELECTED COUNTRIES

Foreign trade has been growing in value and volume in all modern countries since the beginning of the nineteenth century. The expansion has been due to the rise in industrial production and standards of living and improvement in the means of transportation (development of railroads since the middle of the century and of steamships since the 1870's). Despite this general trend, foreign trade lagged behind the growth of national income in many cases so that a steadily declining proportion of a nation's produce was exported and a steadily declining proportion of the needs of the population was

44. See **15**, 1948, *passim.* Cf. Chapter 5.

45. Cf. Chapter 5.

TABLE 18

TRADE BALANCES: EUROPE AND THE UNITED STATES, 1947–52

(*Millions of U.S. Dollars*)

Area and Year	Exports (f.o.b.)	Imports (c.i.f.)	Surplus of Exports (+) or Imports (−)
Western and southern Europe			
1947	$13,585	$23,207	−$9,622
1948	18,057	26,613	− 8,556
1949	20,019	26,134	− 6,115
1950	20,540	25,225	− 4,685
1951	28,448	34,910	− 6,462
1952	28,030	33,451	− 5,421
United States			
1947	$15,191	$ 5,735	+$9,456
1948	12,545	7,163	+ 5,382
1949	11,959	6,667	+ 5,292
1950	10,149	8,853	+ 1,296
1951	14,888	10,921	+ 3,967
1952	15,030	10,812	+ 4,218

Sources: For Europe, **16**, May 1953, pp. 16–17; for the United States, **15**, 1952, pp. 12–13.

covered by imported goods. The United States is a striking example of this pattern of development, while New Zealand exemplifies the opposite pattern of change in the ratio of foreign trade to national income.

THE UNITED STATES

The United States entered the political scene with considerable foreign trade, mainly with Great Britain. In 1800, with a population of about 5 million and a national income of approximately $670 million,[46] the country recorded general imports of $91.3 million and exports of $71.0 million.[47] At that time imports per capita of population amounted to $17.2, or 13.1 per cent of per capita income, and exports per capita, to $13.4, or 10.2 per cent of income. The aggregate value of foreign trade (import and export) was more than 23 per cent of national income, nearly three times the average ratio for 1948–50.

In the period from 1790 to 1870, the United

46. **38**, pp. 6–7.
47. **19**, p. 245. Includes reexport. Taking into account the state of transportation facilities at that time, it appears that the transit traffic cannot have accounted for a large part of reexport.

States had a surplus of imports over exports in merchandise trade in 14 years and a surplus of exports in 67 years. The net surplus of imports accumulated in this period approached $1.6 billion. More than half the deficit ($823 million net) was covered by export of gold, after the middle of the century. (See Table 20.) Since the 1870's, exports have exceeded imports. Between 1871 and 1900 the United States had a surplus of exports in merchandise trade in 23 years and a surplus of imports in only 7 years. Its net surplus of imports in these three decades totaled $3.8 billion. This was partly offset by payments for invisible imports, remittances of immigrants, and so on, but by the turn of the century, the United States had begun to reduce its indebtedness to the old countries. It had substantial export surpluses year after year following 1900, but not until World War I did it become a creditor country. In more recent years, the balance of the merchandise trade of the United States has remained strongly active.

TABLE 19

TRADE BALANCES: SELECTED REGIONS, 1950–52

(*Millions of U.S. Dollars*)

Area and Year	Exports (f.o.b.)	Imports (c.i.f.)	Surplus of Exports (+) or Imports (−)
Middle and South America			
1950	$7,372	$6,356	+$1,016
1951	8,838	8,952	− 114
1952	8,156	8,635	− 479
Middle East			
1950	2,473	2,185	+ 288
1951	2,922	2,622	+ 300
1952	2,575	2,793	− 218
Far East			
1950	6,744	6,197	+ 547
1951	9,657	9,804	− 147
1952	7,516	9,545	− 2,029
Africa			
1950	4,036	4,475	− 439
1951	5,239	6,185	− 946
1952	5,061	6,450	− 1,389
Oceania			
1950	2,276	2,190	+ 86
1951	2,849	3,169	− 320
1952	2,463	2,848	− 385

Source: **16**, May 1953.

TABLE 20

FOREIGN TRADE:[a] EXPORTS AND IMPORTS OF MERCHANDISE AND GOLD, THE UNITED STATES, 1790–1952

(*Millions of Dollars*)

Year [b]	Merchandise [c] Export	Merchandise [c] Import	Gold [d] Export	Gold [d] Import	Year [b]	Merchandise [c] Export	Merchandise [c] Import	Gold [d] Export	Gold [d] Import
1790	$ 20.2	$ 23.0	. . .	. . .	1920	$ 8,341.6	$ 5,366.5	$322.1	$ 417.1
1795	48.0	69.8	. . .	. . .	1921	4,536.6	2,572.4	23.9	691.2
1800	71.0	91.3	. . .	. . .	1922	3,894.6	3,183.6	36.9	275.2
1805	95.6	120.6	. . .	. . .	1923	4,240.0	3,867.0	28.6	322.7
1810	66.8	85.4	. . .	. . .	1924	4,700.9	3,683.9	61.6	319.7
1815	52.6	113.0	. . .	. . .	1925	5,009.0	4,291.2	262.6	128.3
1820	69.7	74.5	. . .	. . .	1926	4,900.9	4,500.5	115.7	213.5
1825	99.2	95.8	$ 0.3	$ 0.5	1927	4,941.0	4,239.8	201.5	207.5
1830	72.4	70.1	1.4	0.8	1928	5,215.7	4,159.6	560.8	168.9
1835	120.3	147.6	1.4	2.3	1929	5,324.4	4,463.3	116.6	291.6
1840	128.4	104.0	3.7	3.1	1930	3,897.3	3,108.7	116.0	396.1
1845	111.6	116.4	3.1	0.8	1931	2,450.7	2,119.3	466.8	612.1
1850	147.3	176.4	4.6	1.8	1932	1,624.9	1,342.4	809.5	363.3
1855	220.0	260.4	55.1	1.1	1933	1,694.0	1,509.8	366.7	193.2
1860	341.6	359.7	58.4	2.5	1934	2,149.4	1,757.8	52.8	1,186.7
1865	175.3	242.1	58.4	6.5	1935	2,301.7	2,402.0	2.0	1,741.0
1870	417.3	450.3	33.6	12.1	1936	2,467.9	2,605.4	27.5	1,144.1
1875	538.6	540.2	67.0	13.7	1937	3,361.2	3,175.5	46.0	1,631.5
1880	849.1	680.2	3.6	80.6	1938	3,101.5	2,191.0	5.9	1,979.5
1885	775.9	594.1	8.5	26.7	1939	3,191.8	2,403.4	0.5	3,574.7
1890	892.7	810.3	17.3	12.9	1940	4,024.8	2,683.8	5.0	4,749.5
1895	854.8	752.2	66.5	36.4	1941	5,152.8	3,392.1	0.0	982.4
1900	1,451.2	885.2	48.3	44.6	1942	8,079.0	2,755.9	0.1	315.8
1905	1,567.4	1,145.0	92.6	53.6	1943	12,964.9	3,381.5	32.9	101.8
1910	1,800.3	1,602.2	118.6	43.3	1944	14,258.7	3,928.9	959.2	113.8
1911	2,114.1	1,573.2	22.5	73.6	1945	9,805.6	4,159.1	200.0	93.7
1912	2,269.2	1,700.3	57.3	48.9	1946	9,738.3	4,942.1	221.5	532.7
1913	2,537.5	1,854.3	77.7	69.2	1947	15,191.3	5,724.5	213.2	2,079.6
1914	2,419.5	1,924.3	112.0	66.5	1948	12,544.5	7,162.9	300.8	1,981.2
1915	2,819.5	1,703.3	146.2	171.6	1949	11,929.4	6,667.2	84.9	771.4
1916	5,553.2	2,423.9	155.8	686.0	1950	10,148.7	8,853.1	534.0	162.7
1917	6,317.6	3,005.8	371.9	552.5	1951	14,888.1	10,920.7	630.4	81.2
1918	6,401.9	3,102.6	41.1	62.0	1952	15,030.1	10,811.8	55.9	734.2
1919	8,159.4	3,993.8	368.2	76.5					

Sources: **19**, pp. 243–45; **15**, 1952, pp. 10–17.

a. General trade; includes reexport.
b. 1790–1840: fiscal years ending September 30; 1845–1915: fiscal years ending June 30; thereafter calendar year.

c. Includes silver and, until 1820, gold.
d. Until 1820 gold is included in merchandise.

From 1876 to 1950, exports of merchandise exceeded imports by more than $100 billion. The total for exports, however, includes more than $40 billion of military goods delivered to the Allies in 1941–45 under the lend-lease program.[48] These deliveries were financed by taxes

48. Outlays based on the lend-lease program totaled $50.2 billion, of which $47 billion is the value of materials charged to foreign governments. (**17**, p. 34.)

and credit operations in the same way as other military expenditures. Of the rest, amounting to approximately $60 billion, some $16 billion was financed by foreign aid grants, including UNRRA and the Marshall Plan, and some $20 billion, by imports of gold. The remainder, approximately $24 billion, went in part for pay-

There is no evidence, however, that all these shipments were recorded at the same value in United States exports.

ment of interest on old loans of the United States; in part for remittances of immigrants to their old countries; and in part for reducing the country's foreign debts and building up assets abroad.[49]

LEADING COMMERCIAL NATIONS

From the early eighteenth century to the 1920's, Great Britain led in world trade. It controlled about 25 per cent of all international trade in the middle of the nineteenth century; 20 per cent at the turn of the century; and 18 per cent before the outbreak of World War I.

France ranked second through most of the nineteenth century, followed, at a short distance, by the United States. In the 1890's Germany advanced to second place, overtaking both France and the United States, and just before World War I Germany was ready to challenge Great Britain's supremacy in the world market. (See Table 21; cf. Figure 11.)

World War I changed the situation. Germany was knocked out for a short time, then came back. Great Britain maintained its lead, but the United States gained on it rapidly. In the late 1920's, the two countries were running neck and neck in total value of foreign trade, the United States leading in exports, Great Britain in imports.[50]

In the early 1930's the depression brought a catastrophic contraction in the dollar value of the foreign trade of all countries, due in part to the collapse of prices. The losses of the United States were particularly heavy and Great Britain regained the lead in foreign trade, followed by the United States, Germany and France, in that order. During World War II, supremacy again passed to the United States. (See Figure 12.)

OTHER COUNTRIES

In most countries, there has not been a continuous and consistent trend toward either increase or decrease in the ratio of the value of

foreign trade to national income. Increases prevailed before the turn of the century, while the value of trade has lagged behind the rise in national income in more recent times, especially since World War I.

At the beginning of the twentieth century, the foreign trade of the Netherlands, which included considerable reexport and straight transit business, nearly equaled that of France. Excluding reexport, the Netherlands stood fifth in aggregate value of exports and imports. Russia ranked sixth; Belgium-Luxembourg, seventh. (See Table 21.) These were followed by Austria-Hungary, Italy and Switzerland; Canada, Argentina and Brazil; British India, China and Japan; the Union of South Africa and Australia. In 1913, the value of the foreign trade of these countries (exports plus imports) was as follows (in millions of U.S. dollars):[51]

Great Britain	$6,837
Germany	4,970
United States	4,392
France	2,953
Netherlands	2,814
Belgium-Luxembourg	1,612
Russia	1,491
British India	1,383
Austria-Hungary	1,319
Italy	1,170
Canada	1,026
Argentina	1,007
Australia	755
China	710
Japan	679
Brazil	643
Switzerland	614
Union of South Africa	520

Most of these countries still play a prominent role in international trade, but their ranking has changed. Trade of the former Austria-Hungary has been distributed among Czechoslovakia, Austria, Hungary, Romania and Yugoslavia; China and Russia have practically disappeared from the world market.

The evolution of the foreign trade of the USSR deserves particular attention. It shrank nearly to zero in the period of civil war and war communism (1919–22), but was rebuilt under the New Economic Policy (NEP). The share of the USSR (Russia) in world trade was close to 2 per cent in 1913, approximately 1.5 per cent in the late 1920's and fluctuated between 1 and 1.5

---

49. See Chapter 5.

50. Figure 11 shows the United States ahead of the United Kingdom in 1926–29. This comparison is based on the League of Nations statistics of foreign trade converted into gold dollars; there are, however, serious doubts about the strict comparability of these data. The International Monetary Fund tried to reduce them to a more comparable basis (f.o.b. for exports and c.i.f. for imports) and found that in 1928 Great Britain was slightly ahead of the United States. (**16**, 1951, pp. xxii–xxiii.)

51. See Tables 20 and 21 and **3**, 1928, p. 128.

TABLE 21

FOREIGN TRADE: EXPORTS AND IMPORTS, IN SELECTED COUNTRIES, 1820–1952

(Millions of Dollars)

Year	United Kingdom (G.T.) [a] Exports	Imports	Germany (S.T.) [a, b] Exports	Imports	France (S.T.) [a] Exports	Imports	Netherlands (S.T.) [a] Exports	Imports
1820	$ 238	$ 158	...	...	$ 105	$ 65	...	...
1830	339	225	...	...	87	94	...	...
1840	567	328	...	...	134	144	...	...
1850	347	...	...	...	206	153	$ 55	$ 75
1860	806	1,024	...	...	439	366	97	122
1870	1,190	1,476	...	...	541	553	154	187
1875	1,366	1,820	$ 593	$ 840	747	683	215	277
1880	1,394	2,001	696	665	669	971	251	333
1885	1,321	1,806	680	697	596	789	358	439
1890	1,597	2,047	792	989	724	856	437	522
1895	1,391	2,028	790	982	651	719	474	580
1900	1,725	2,546	1,098	1,373	793	907	681	791
1905	1,984	2,750	1,365	1,698	939	922	801	1,039
1910	2,599	3,301	1,780	2,128	1,203	1,384	1,058	1,313
1911	2,710	3,310	1,931	2,312	1,173	1,557	1,098	1,340
1912	2,915	3,624	2,133	2,547	1,295	1,588	1,251	1,452
1913	3,096	3,741	2,405	2,565	1,328	1,625	1,239	1,575
1914	2,561	3,390	...	...	940	1,236	1,007	1,161
1915	2,355	4,145	...	...	769	2,130	703	848
1920	7,578	9,406	884	936	1,587	2,944	703	1,354
1921	3,943	5,283	...	1,365	1,475	1,646	592	920
1922	4,006	4,882	1,474	1,498	1,751	1,960	505	817
1923	4,311	5,335	1,454	1,463	1,847	3,198	529	814
1924	4,579	6,217	1,560	2,164	2,216	2,100	724	956
1925	4,514	6,427	2,213	2,945	1,746	1,683	727	987
1926	3,173	5,421	2,328	2,380	1,925	1,938	...	...
1927	3,447	5,330	2,428	3,360	2,165	2,072	...	...
1928	3,521	5,233	2,924	3,335	2,042	2,103	798	1,079
1929	3,549	5,407	3,212	3,203	1,965	2,282	800	1,106
1930	2,777	4,568	2,867	2,476	1,680	2,058	691	972
1931	1,772	3,585	2,286	1,602	1,193	1,654	527	761
1932	1,279	2,276	1,363	1,108	774	1,171	341	524
1933	1,220	2,073	1,155	996	724	1,117	292	487
1934	4,189	2,044	991	1,045	700	905	286	417
1935	2,641	3,925	1,728	1,681	1,034	1,398	434	645
1936	2,586	4,304	1,925	1,709	932	1,530	383	432
1937	2,999	5,185	2,384	2,205	960	1,703	550	735
1938	2,744	4,585	2,266	2,440	881	1,333	553	594
1939	2,198	3,983	2,280	2,100	807	1,119	569	542
1940	1,774	4,646	1,948	2,006	400	1,045	581	666
1941	1,528	4,621	2,737	2,771	339	536	750	593
1942	1,116	4,025	3,038	3,493	627	548	847	741
1943	970	4,979	3,452	3,319	...	...	426	453
1944	1,139	5,288	1,581	1,741	570	218	...	...
1945	1,818	4,456	20	96	229	1,146	...	...
1946	3,915	5,267	143	643	854	2,222	...	...
1947	4,593	6,978	319	734	1,879	3,333	715	1,609
1948	6,379	8,114	592	1,400	2,011	3,443	1,024	1,872
1949	8,620	8,228	1,092	2,089	2,722	3,291	1,312	1,845
1950	6,080	7,066	1,977	2,697	3,081	3,068	1,412	2,055
1951	7,223	10,575	3,465	3,493	4,175	4,551	1,948	2,550
1952	7,228	9,346	4,037	3,854	3,890	4,431	2,108	2,222

a. G.T. = general trade; S.T. = special trade.   b. Since 1945, Western Germany.

(Continued on facing page)

TABLE 21—*continued*

Year	Belguim (S.T.) [a]		Russia (USSR) (S.T.) [a]		Canada (S.T.) [a]		Japan (G.T.) [a]	
	Exports	Imports	Exports	Imports	Exports	Imports	Exports	Imports
1830	$ 19	$ 17	. . .	. . .	. . .	. . .	. . .	. . .
1840	27	40	$ 43	$ 39	. . .	. . .	. . .	. . .
1850	40	43	43	39	. . .	. . .	. . .	. . .
1860	91	100	85	70	. . .	. . .	. . .	. . .
1870	133	178	177	159	$ 59	$ 67	$ 7	$ 17
1875	213	252	197	273	70	117	9	15
1880	235	324	257	321	73	70	14	18
1885	232	260	277	224	79	100	18	15
1890	277	323	362	214	85	112	28	41
1895	267	324	355	277	103	101	68	64
1900	371	428	369	323	169	172	102	143
1905	450	592	855	327	191	252	160	243
1910	658	823	746	558	279	370	228	231
1911	691	870	820	598	274	452	223	256
1912	763	957	782	603	290	521	262	309
1913	717	895	783	708	356	670	315	364
1914	. . .	. . .	492	565	432	614	295	297
1915	. . .	. . .	207	586	409	472	353	265
1920	. . .	. . .	. . .	. . .	1,239	1,065	971	1,165
1921	. . .	. . .	. . .	. . .	1,189	1,240	624	805
1922	702	724	42	139	740	762	816	942
1923	506	688	106	74	1,015	893	721	989
1924	642	812	156	112	1,058	797	901	1,223
1925	690	848	290	381	1,271	1,240	1,149	1,282
1926	707	750	348	390	1,270	1,031	929	1,086
1927	688	806	397	367	1,253	1,109	906	995
1928	859	889	416	490	1,433	1,222	886	990
1929	884	988	482	453	1,225	1,299	970	995
1930	725	861	533	545	905	1,008	706	744
1931	643	660	417	569	623	605	547	589
1932	411	450	290	360	487	398	388	394
1933	391	411	261	182	422	288	366	380
1934	376	381	215	120	461	312	377	397
1935	587	623	320	210	737	552	940	884
1936	664	720	271	269	952	639	1,036	1,051
1937	860	932	329	256	1,012	811	1,200	1,363
1938	730	767	251	268	844	675	1,109	1,070
1939	736	654	. . .	. . .	901	723	1,317	1,073
1940	370	283	. . .	. . .	1,085	975	1,260	1,080
1941	171	234	. . .	. . .	1,491	1,305	1,009	934
1942	149	206	. . .	. . .	2,160	1,481	809	674
1943	273	201	. . .	. . .	2,729	1,563	. . .	. . .
1944	171	116	. . .	. . .	3,166	1,585	. . .	. . .
1945	91	313	. . .	793	2,970	1,430	. . .	. . .
1946	682	1,294	400	604	2,241	1,838	103	305
1947	1,406	1,939	430	. . .	2,812	2,574	174	524
1948	1,690	1,986	. . .	. . .	3,110	2,637	258	684
1949	1,775	1,793	. . .	. . .	2,945	3,699	510	905
1950	1,653	1,942	. . .	. . .	2,910	2,926	820	974
1951	2,650	2,535	. . .	. . .	3,767	3,877	1,355	2,044
1952	2,445	2,444	. . .	. . .	4,453	4,120	1,273	2,028

Sources: Through 1925 (for the Netherlands, through 1927) data computed from **22**, 1938, pp. 426–29 and **25**, various years. For 1926–34 (for the Netherlands, 1928–34), data published by the League of Nations, in old gold dollars (**6**, 1928, 1933–1934 and 1938–1939). From 1935, data published by the United Nations, in U.S. dollars, at current exchange rates, **10**. Data for 1947–52 from **15**, 1952, pp. 10–17. The data for the last six years are not strictly comparable with those for preceding periods, but conform with Tables 14 and 17.

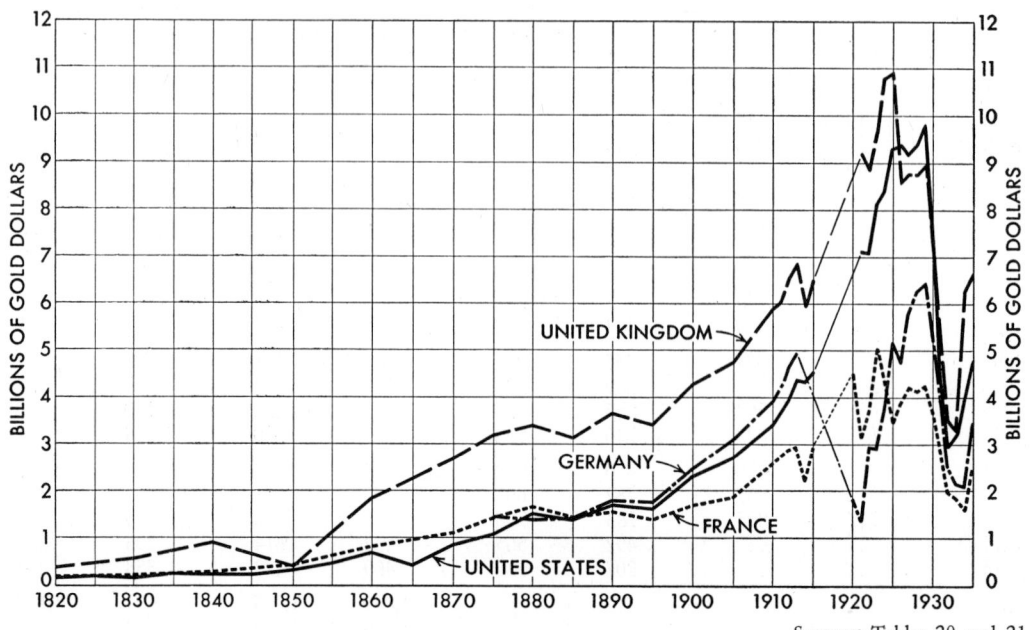

Sources: Tables 20 and 21

FIGURE 11. FOREIGN TRADE: EXPORTS AND IMPORTS OF FOUR LEADING COMMERCIAL NATIONS, 1820–1935

This chart illustrates general trends in the relative position of the four leading commercial nations and therefore shows only data for selected years. The World War I period and the subsequent years marked by inflation and general political and economic confusion have been omitted. The data used here reflect the value of foreign trade rather than the volume (quantum) and are affected by variations in prices, adjusted to exchange ratios. Moreover, because of the differences in methods of valuation, data for individual countries are not strictly comparable.

per cent before World War II. In 1943, thanks to lend-lease shipments from the United States, the imports of the USSR were six times as much as in 1936–40, while exports fell to one fourth the 1940 level.[52] Information for the immediate postwar years is fragmentary and inconclusive. For 1946, Soviet exports have been estimated at $400 million and imports at $604 million.[53] These figures suggest that the USSR controlled approximately 1 per cent of world trade at that time.[54]

FOREIGN TRADE IN RECENT YEARS

For more precise comparative analysis of foreign trade in various countries, the International Monetary Fund has adjusted the data published by countries to include freight and insurance in the value of imports (c.i.f.). At the present time its series covers some ninety countries and areas that represent more than 92 per cent

of world trade. For areas controlling about 2 per cent of world imports and exports, current estimates are made. No data are available for the USSR, Eastern Germany, Poland, Hungary, Bulgaria, Romania and China. In 1928, 1938 and 1948, these countries accounted for 5–6 per cent of world imports and exports.

INTERNATIONAL SURVEY

The survey of the International Monetary Fund reveals considerable annual variations in the value of imports and exports of individual countries. These ups and downs are caused partly by divergent fluctuations in prices and partly by changing business conditions in importing and exporting countries. (See Table 22.[55])

52. **43,** pp. 508–11.

53. **32,** p. 87.

54. An exact comparison is impossible, because of gaps in world trade statistics for 1946 and the absence of data on Russian exports in 1947.

55. Table 22 lists countries geographically, by continent. In the original tabulation they are grouped by geographic regions; sterling countries are separated from other areas, and countries are listed alphabetically within each group. World totals and data for some countries as shown in this table differ slightly from the data published by the UN (for example in **11** and **10**). The source of discrepancies is in adjustments made by the Monetary Fund in order to improve the comparability of reported figures.

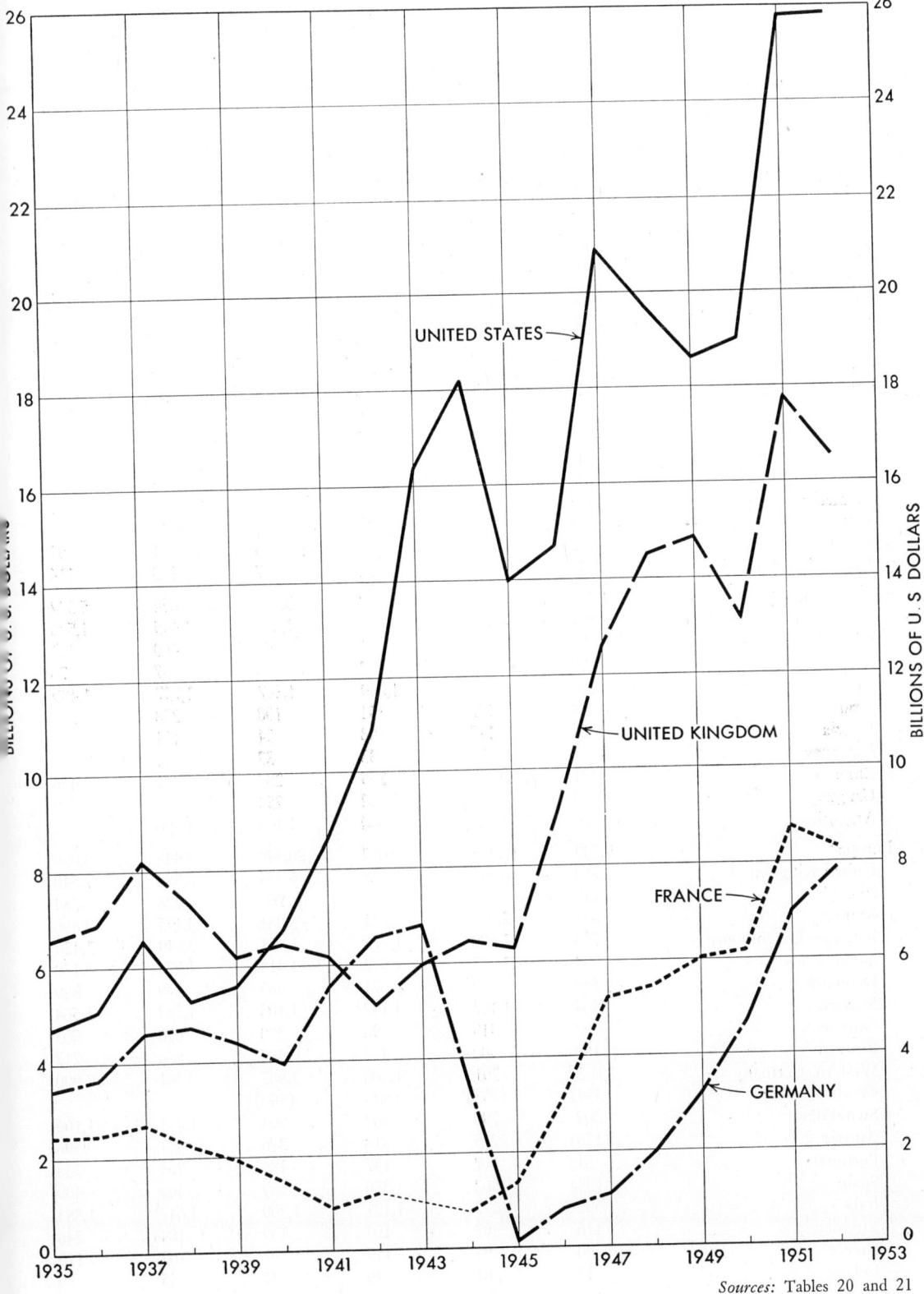

FIGURE 12. FOREIGN TRADE: TOTAL OF MERCHANDISE EXPORTS AND IMPORTS, FOUR LEADING COUNTRIES, 1935–52

TABLE 22. FOREIGN TRADE: EXPORTS AND IMPORTS IN U.S.

(*Millions of*

A. Exports (f.o.b.)

Country [a]	1938	1948	1949	1950	1951	1952
World	$21,027	$54,066	$54,769	$56,453	$76,536	$73,474
North America	4,020	16,018	15,154	13,376	19,083	19,893
United States	3,102	12,666	12,074	10,281	15,041	15,164
Canada [b]	918	3,352	3,080	3,095	4,042	4,729
Middle America	651	2,160	2,048	2,295	2,814	2,814
Mexico	147	466	437	466	572	581
Guatemala	18	50	52	68	76	87
El Salvador	10	45	54	68	85	87
Honduras	11	54	55	58	66	. . .
Nicaragua	4	19	16	27	37	42
Costa Rica	9	32	31	35	39	47
Panama	7	15	14	13	15	16
Cuba	143	724	593	657	786	692
Netherlands Antilles	187	407	431	550	703	. . .
Jamaica	25	46	46	42	48	. . .
Haiti	7	31	35	39	51	52
Dominican Republic	15	83	74	87	109	114
South America	1,282	5,190	4,363	5,077	6,024	5,342
Venezuela	181	1,114	1,078	1,248	1,455	1,546
Colombia	81	289	321	396	460	461
Ecuador	9	46	33	66	57	76
Brazil	289	1,173	1,089	1,347	1,757	1,409
Peru	68	157	151	190	248	236
Bolivia	34	113	103	94	151	. . .
Paraguay	7	28	33	33	. . .	. . .
Chile	131	328	295	282	371	456
Uruguay	62	178	192	254	236	209
Argentina	408	1,700	1,000	1,100	1,190	. . .
Europe [c]	9,739	18,057	20,019	20,540	28,448	28,030
United Kingdom	2,764	6,645	6,858	6,334	7,580	7,540
Ireland	119	199	221	203	228	284
France	881	2,011	2,722	3,081	4,175	3,896
Belgium–Luxembourg	733	1,690	1,776	1,653	2,649	2,426
Netherlands	594	1,025	1,312	1,414	1,978	2,130
Denmark	334	569	671	665	839	849
Sweden	464	1,107	1,142	1,103	1,782	1,564
Norway	192	415	396	390	620	565
Finland	180	500	472	392	866	717
Western Germany	2,162 [d]	791	1,300	1,987	3,461	3,990
Czechoslovakia	(354)	(753)	(806)	(800)	. . .	. . .
Switzerland	302	799	803	903	1,081	1,100
Austria	(178)	215	318	326	451	506
Portugal	51	172	157	186	263	238
Spain	(98)	362	380	389	462	409
Italy	553	1,077	1,121	1,209	1,647	1,383
Yugoslavia	116	302	192	159	184	246
Greece	90	94	115	91	102	119
Iceland	13	61	40	31	45	39

(*Continued on page 56*)

DOLLARS, IN SELECTED COUNTRIES, 1938 AND 1948–52

U.S. Dollars)

B. Imports (c.i.f.)

Country [a]	1938	1948	1949	1950	1951	1952
World	$23,709	$60,183	$59,894	$59,113	$81,357	$79,543
North America	3,259	11,085	10,465	12,844	16,141	16,090
United States	2,465	8,058	7,529	9,642	11,946	11,632
Canada [b]	794	3,027	2,936	3,202	4,195	4,458
Middle America	727	2,477	2,366	2,536	3,291	3,328
Mexico	114	561	493	556	823	739
Guatemala	21	68	68	71	81	76
El Salvador	9	41	41	50	62	68
Honduras	12	36	42	38	51	. . .
Nicaragua	6	27	24	28	34	44
Costa Rica	13	42	43	46	56	68
Panama	20	73	71	71	76	88
Cuba	119	569	487	556	691	675
Netherlands Antilles	253	549	610	706	906	. . .
Jamaica	32	79	72	63	86	. . .
Haiti	8	32	34	38	44	53
Dominican Republic	13	72	51	48	64	63
South America	1,219	4,593	4,065	3,820	5,662	5,307
Venezuela	107	768	749	601	719	809
Colombia	89	337	265	364	416	402
Ecuador	12	57	53	48	64	65
Brazil	295	1,134	1,116	1,098	2,011	2,010
Peru	58	168	167	175	261	288
Bolivia	25	79	90	64	9,101	. . .
Paraguay	9	27	32	21	. . .	. . .
Chile	103	269	305	248	329	371
Uruguay	62	200	181	200	316	237
Argentina	440	1,485	1,040	930	1,360	. . .
Europe [c]	12,992	26,613	26,134	25,225	34,910	33,451
United Kingdom	4,600	8,451	8,522	7,398	10,923	9,733
Ireland	203	549	481	446	573	482
France	1,324	3,443	3,291	3,068	4,591	4,431
Belgium-Luxembourg	765	2,046	1,803	1,942	2,535	2,424
Netherlands	803	1,872	1,846	2,063	2,567	2,251
Denmark	354	714	807	853	1,013	962
Sweden	525	1,377	1,171	1,182	1,776	1,730
Norway	292	750	779	679	877	873
Finland	183	489	410	388	676	722
Western Germany	(2,222 [d])	(1,765)	(2,237)	2,701	3,494	3,818
Czechoslovakia	(292)	(754)	(788)	(713)	. . .	. . .
Switzerland	366	1,163	881	1,048	1,364	1,202
Austria	(289)	484	594	483	657	654
Portugal	102	415	351	275	320	350
Spain	(152)	468	454	392	384	526
Italy	593	1,539	1,545	1,487	2,167	2,313
Yugoslavia	114	362	314	262	391	372
Greece	131	546	484	422	435	346
Iceland	11	71	59	38	57	56

(*Continued on page 57*)

TABLE 22—*continued*

A. Exports (f.o.b.)

Country [a]	1938	1948	1949	1950	1951	1952
USSR	$ (257)	$ (880)	...	...	...	...
Asia [c]	3,425	6,568	$7,076	$8,853	$12,079	$9,871
China [e]	(324)	(170)	...	...	...	...
Japan	767	258	510	820	1,355	1,274
Hong Kong	185	404	564	657	780	510
Turkey	115	196	248	264	314	363
Cyprus	12	23	31	31	43	51
Lebanon–Syria	17	36	51	119	165	178
Iraq	68	81	92	141	186	286
Iran	140	490	588	700	590	152
Pakistan	}621{	565	460	496	763	533
India		1,363	1,309	1,146	1,611	1,296
Burma	181	229	222	158	206	291
Thailand	89	223	271	288	...	...
Indochina	81	92	68	79	135	...
Ceylon	104	306	293	328	400	315
Malaya and Singapore	327	813	718	1,311	1,984	1,280
Indonesia	380	395	517	777	1,258	981
Philippines	117	327	261	337	409	336
Africa	1,099	3,834	3,857	4,036	5,239	5,061
Canary Islands	(17)	151	162	146	125	120
French Morocco	43	174	185	190	252	272
Algeria	161	420	325	333	383	410
Tunisia	39	57	92	114	108	...
Egypt	147	591	515	504	583	417
Anglo-Egyptian Sudan	29	99	108	95	184	123
Ethiopia	(8)	31	29	29	47	43
French West Africa	37	155	203	177	221	...
French Equatorial Africa	7	50	41	43	58	40
Belgian Congo	50	245	235	261	387	394
Gold Coast	52	201	163	189	232	216
Nigeria	70	252	304	253	365	355
French Cameroons	7	36	40	47	65	...
Kenya–Uganda	48	137	141	138	209	...
Tanganyika	17	66	70	68	111	134
Mozambique	8	40	37	37	44	...
Madagascar	23	50	54	71	77	...
Angola	15	44	69	75	111	96
Northern Rhodesia	50	116	123	140	188	231
Southern Rhodesia	30	99	109	117	128	153
Union of South Africa	161	565	587	724	995	954
Oceania	812	2,239	2,252	2,276	2,849	2,463
Australia	522	1,656	1,596	1,676	2,040	1,691
New Zealand	225	493	556	512	693	672

a. Regional totals include countries listed in the table and some other areas in the respective region.
  b. Includes Newfoundland.
  c. Turkey, classified in Europe by the International Monetary Fund, is included in Asia, in this table. The totals for Europe and Asia therefore differ from those shown in the source.
  d. Prewar Germany.
  e. Includes Manchuria.

TABLE 22—*continued*

B. Imports (c.i.f.)

Country [a]	1938	1948	1949	1950	1951	1952
USSR	$ (268)	$(2,055)	...	...	...	...
Asia [e]	3,227	8,135	$9,359	$8,023	$11,999	$12,069
China [e]	(604)	(387)	...	...	...	...
Japan	759	684	905	974	1,995	2,027
Hong Kong	188	523	666	666	856	663
Turkey	119	347	346	313	402	556
Cyprus	11	63	41	38	54	57
Lebanon–Syria	37	214	277	174	275	289
Iraq	46	183	148	105	143	174
Iran	79	167	232	262	248	165
Pakistan	} 575 {	304	478	385	536	609
India		1,616	2,027	1,150	1,816	1,661
Burma	79	180	113	101	137	192
Thailand	57	144	205	209	...	...
Indochina	56	188	231	210	305	...
Ceylon	86	300	289	245	327	358
Malaya and Singapore	315	842	797	952	1,554	1,265
Indonesia	255	465	536	431	805	972
Philippines	153	666	657	384	539	453
Africa	1,452	5,319	5,350	4,475	6,185	6,450
Canary Islands	(10)	135	137	134	137	128
French Morocco	62	389	369	329	456	516
Algeria	143	482	457	434	573	638
Tunisia	45	157	142	146	170	...
Egypt	184	663	664	564	667	608
Anglo-Egyptian Sudan	29	92	89	77	120	...
Ethiopia	24	38	35	30	42	...
French West Africa	47	177	252	241	350	...
French Equatorial Africa	8	53	83	77	104	115
Belgian Congo	35	191	229	193	310	392
Gold Coast	50	121	164	134	177	186
Nigeria	56	169	214	173	233	313
French Cameroons	6	42	65	60	94	...
Kenya–Uganda	46	182	244	138	212	...
Tanganyika	17	91	102	67	78	103
Mozambique	21	75	68	58	71	...
Madagascar	17	78	86	86	128	...
Angola	10	49	51	58	76	91
Northern Rhodesia	28	71	88	84	111	132
Southern Rhodesia	51	192	224	184	269	277
Union of South Africa	503	1,567	1,314	946	1,445	1,294
Oceania	833	1,961	2,155	2,190	3,169	2,848
Australia	571	1,415	1,592	1,623	2,423	1,984
New Zealand	225	451	453	456	596	739

Source: **16,** May 1953. Because of adjustments for international comparability, data in this table differ appreciably from those published by the respective governments and appearing in current publications of the UN. The arrangement of countries by continent in this table differs from that used by the International Monetary Fund. Countries in each continent are here arranged geographically, without distinction between "sterling countries" and other areas. Mexico is included in Middle America; Turkey, in Asia; Egypt, Sudan and Ethiopia, in Africa. Figures in parentheses are estimates.

The years 1948–52 were a period of postwar reconstruction in Europe and of progress toward equilibrium in world trade. This development is reflected in the growth of European exports and United States imports and especially in the increase of the foreign trade of Germany and Japan.

THE GEOGRAPHIC PATTERN

When the value of exports from each country or area is marked on a world map by dots, each one representing a definite value, the dots cluster most closely in northwestern Europe, especially around the United Kingdom. The cluster on the other side of the North Atlantic, in the United States, is less dense. On a conventional map the dots are more widely dispersed in the Western Hemisphere and over the world than similar dots on a world map showing the geographic distribution of income, industrial production or energy.[56] (See Figure 13.)

When exports from different areas are dotted on a distorted map that shows continents and countries on the scale of their income the dots are much more densely clustered in Middle and South America and Africa than in the United States. (See Figure 14.) In relation to its national income the United States has less foreign trade than many less developed areas.

The geographic distribution of world trade can also be pictured by means of a distorted map on which each area is represented on the scale of the value of its exports. Such a map differs characteristically from the distorted world map of income. On a distorted trade map, Canada, South America and, in particular, Middle America appear larger in comparison with the United States than on a map of world income. On the other side of the Atlantic, the USSR and satellite countries are smaller than on the distorted map which pictures the distribution of world income. (See Figure 15.)

RANKING OF COUNTRIES

The countries with the largest foreign trade in 1952 ranked as follows in exports and imports (in millions of U.S. dollars):[57]

56. Cf. Figure 127 in **53**.
57. Countries arrayed by exports. Adjusted figures (cf. Table 22).

	Exports	Imports
United States	$15,164	$11,632
United Kingdom	7,540	9,733
Canada	4,729	4,458
Western Germany	3,990	3,818
France	3,896	4,431
Belgium–Luxembourg	2,426	2,424
Netherlands	2,130	2,251
Australia	1,691	1,984
Sweden	1,564	1,730
Venezuela	1,546	809
Brazil	1,409	2,010
Italy	1,383	2,313
India	1,296	1,661
Malaya and Singapore	1,280	1,265
Japan	1,274	2,027
Argentina	1,190[a]	1,360[a]
Switzerland	1,100	1,202
Indonesia	981	972
Union of South Africa	954	1,294
Denmark	849	962
Finland	717	792
Cuba	692	691[a]
New Zealand	672	739
Mexico	581	739
Norway	565	873
Pakistan	533	609
Hong Kong	510	663
Austria	506	654
Colombia	461	402
Chile	456	371
Egypt	417	608
Algeria	410	638
Spain	409	526

a. 1951.

In 1952, the five nations at the top of this list accounted for 48 per cent of world exports and 43 per cent of the imports. The five following countries controlled 13 per cent of world exports while the countries which ranked from 6 to 10 in imports accounted for 12 per cent of world imports. Fifteen countries maintained two thirds of the world's trade while the remaining third was distributed among some seventy-five countries and areas.

PER CAPITA FOREIGN TRADE AND INCOME

TRENDS IN THE LEADING COMMERCIAL NATIONS

The ratio of the value of foreign trade to national income has varied widely in leading commercial nations.

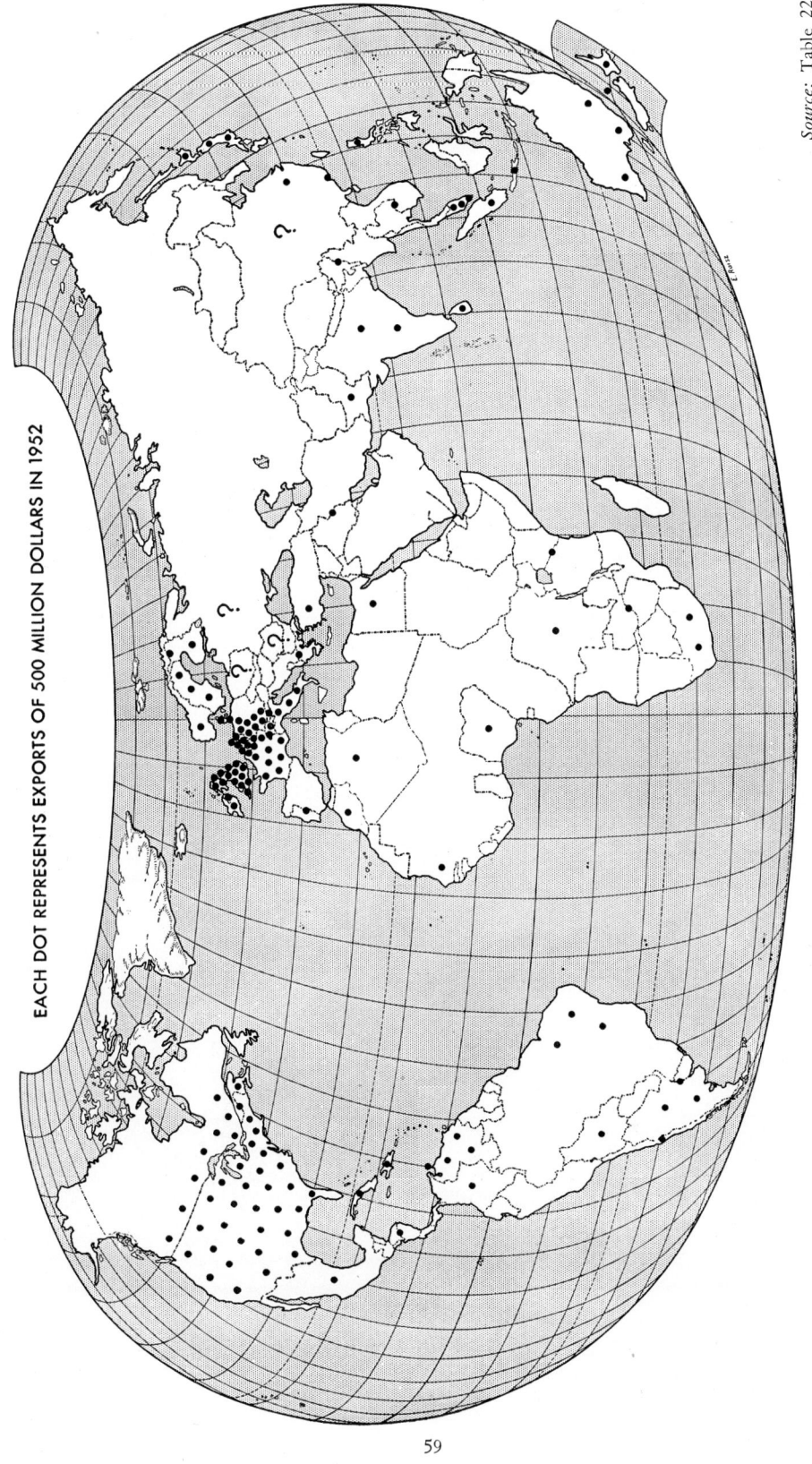

EACH DOT REPRESENTS EXPORTS OF 500 MILLION DOLLARS IN 1952

Source: Table 22

Figure 13. World Trade: Geographic Distribution of Exports, 1952

59

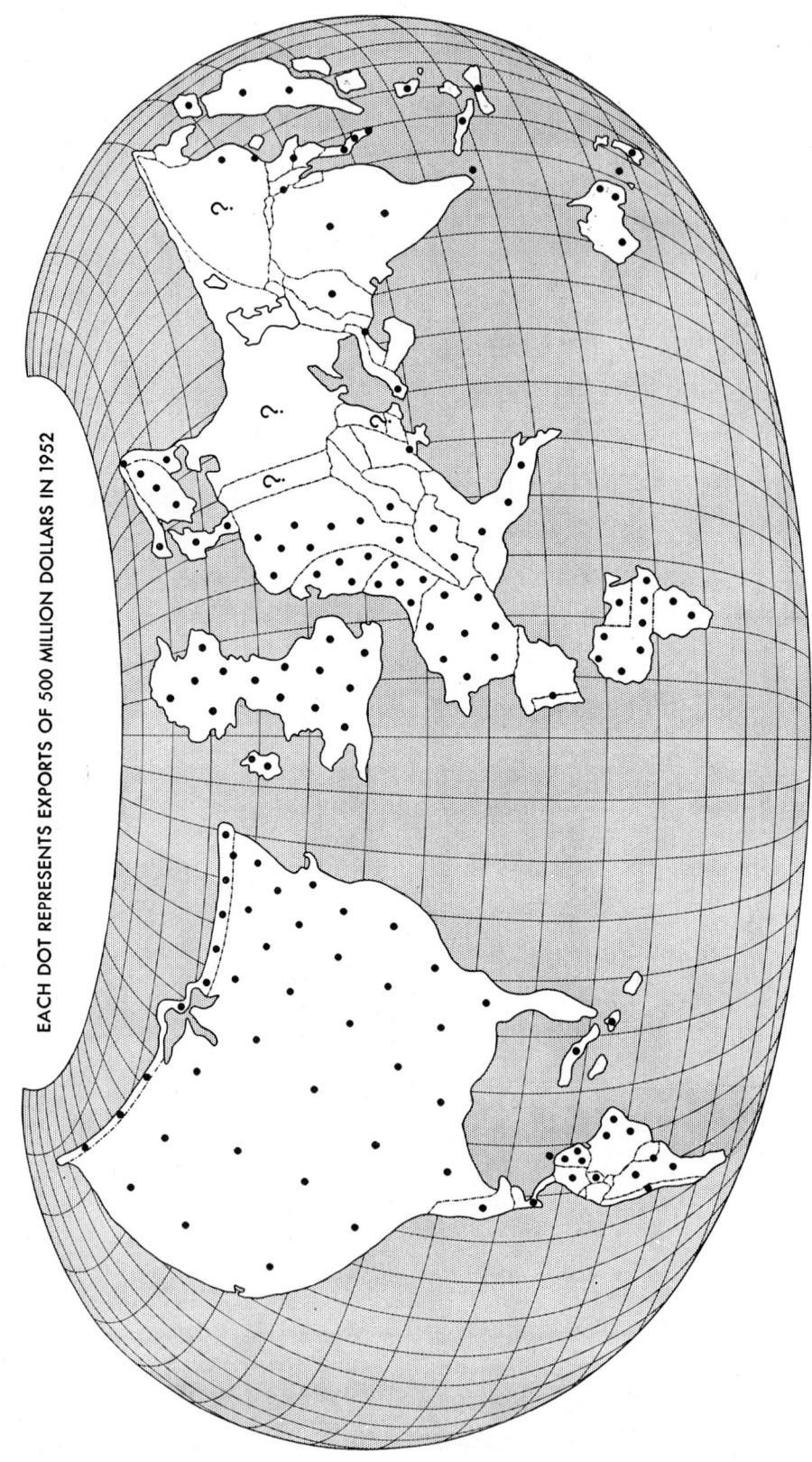

EACH DOT REPRESENTS EXPORTS OF 500 MILLION DOLLARS IN 1952

Source: Table 22

FIGURE 14. WORLD TRADE: GEOGRAPHIC DISTRIBUTION OF WORLD TRADE IN RELATION TO NATIONAL INCOME AS SHOWN ON A DISTORTED MAP REPRESENTING CONTINENTS AND COUNTRIES ON THE SCALE OF THEIR INCOME, AROUND 1950

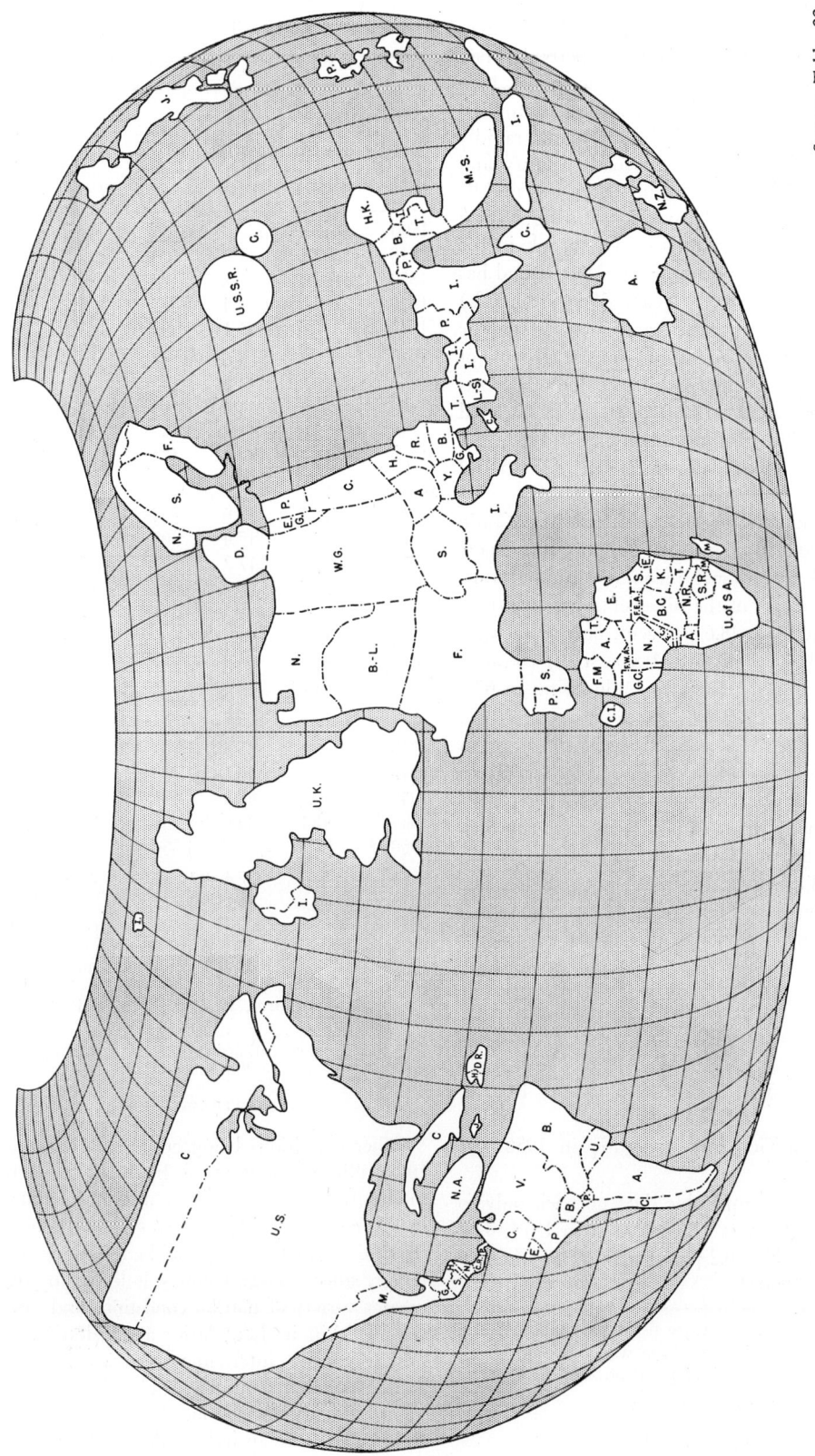

Figure 15. World Trade: Geographic Distribution of World Trade as Shown on a Distorted Map Representing Continents and Countries on the Scale of Their Exports, 1952

Source: Table 22

In the United States the trend has been downward. The sum of imports and exports declined from 20.8 per cent of national income in 1880 to 8.0 per cent in 1950. The value of foreign trade per capita of population decreased rapidly in the first half of the nineteenth century and inched up slowly but steadily after the middle of the century. It skyrocketed during World War I, went down after its end, shrank in the 1930's, rose again during World War II and has declined in more recent years. (See Table 23.)

In the long run, the foreign trade of the United States has lagged behind the growth of national income. The combined value of exports and imports averaged 16.7 per cent of national income in 1800–40, 15.6 per cent 1850–1900, 14.7 per cent in 1900–20, 9.9 per cent in 1925–45 and 9.0 per cent in 1946–52.[58]

In the United Kingdom, the trend in the ratio of the value of foreign trade (import and export combined) to national income was downward in the latter part of the nineteenth century: 66.7 per cent in 1880, 48.6 per cent, on the average, for 1896–1900. This trend was reversed after the turn of the century, the ratio rising to 62.1 per cent in 1911, then declining after World War I. In 1929, the ratio was 52.5 per cent; in 1932, 30.0 per cent; in 1938, 33.4 per cent; in 1950, 43.3 per cent and in 1952, 37.9 per cent.[59]

In Germany, apart from violent short-run fluctuations, the trend was upward before World War I and downward in more recent years. The value of Germany's foreign trade has represented the following percentages of national income: [60]

1891	29.5	1913	41.6
1896	29.3	1925	36.1
1901	31.5	1929	35.4
1906	38.1	1934	16.3
1911	34.7	1938	13.2

For Western Germany, the ratio in 1950 was 27.3 per cent.

For France, comparable data go back only to 1913. The ratio was 42.5 per cent in 1913; 44.2 per cent in 1929; 30.2 per cent in 1938; and 29.0 per cent in 1950.[61]

---

58. Averages for the years listed in Table 23. The figures were much higher in the war years and appreciably lower at the depth of the depression.

59. **46**, pp. 6–45, and **11**, 1953.

60. **24**, pp. 67-68.

61. **29**, p. 549; **30**, p. 959; **14**, p. 2.

TABLE 23

PER CAPITA EXPORTS, IMPORTS AND INCOME, IN THE UNITED STATES, 1800–1952

Year	Per Capita			Percentage of National Income	
	Exports	Imports	National Income [a]	Exports	Imports
1800	$ 13.4	$17.2	$ 131	10.2	13.1
1810	9.2	11.8	130	7.1	9.1
1820	7.2	7.7	93	7.7	8.3
1830	5.6	5.4	78	7.2	6.9
1840	7.5	6.1	98	7.6	6.2
1850	6.3	7.6	107	5.9	7.1
1860	10.9	11.4	140	7.7	8.1
1870	10.5	11.3	180	5.8	6.3
1880	16.9	13.6	147	11.5	9.3
1890	14.1	12.9	173	8.1	7.5
1900	19.1	11.6	212	9.0	5.5
1905	18.7	13.6	254	7.4	5.4
1910	19.6	17.4	305	6.4	5.7
1915	28.5	17.2	327	8.7	5.3
1920	78.4	50.4	642	12.2	7.8
1925	43.2	37.0	610	7.1	6.1
1930	31.7	25.2	588	5.4	4.3
1935	18.1	18.9	441	4.1	4.3
1940	30.5	20.3	616	5.0	3.3
1945	74.3	66.9	1,384	5.4	4.8
1946	69.6	35.3	1,307	5.4	2.7
1947	100.6	40.1	1,385	7.3	2.9
1948	86.6	48.8	1,531	5.7	3.2
1949	81.1	44.6	1,458	5.6	3.1
1950	67.9	58.5	1,580	4.3	3.7
1951	97.4	77.4	1,798	5.4	4.3
1952	96.6	74.1	1,847	5.2	4.0

Sources: Export and import data are computed on the basis of Table 18; national income figures for 1799–1925, **39**, pp. 6–7; for 1930–50, **18**, National Income Supplement, 1951, p. 151; for 1951–52, **18**, July 1953.

a. For 1800–90 national income for preceding year.

INTERNATIONAL SURVEY

Other conditions being equal, a country with 100 million inhabitants is likely to have more foreign trade than one with a million inhabitants. It is very improbable, however, that the foreign trade of the first country will be a hundred times larger, since a large country is likely to have a greater variety of natural conditions and can develop within its boundaries a division of labor similar to the international division of labor among smaller countries. The United States exemplifies this situation. If each of its forty-eight states were an independent nation about as developed economically as it is now, the division of labor among these nations would hardly have gone as far as the actual division of labor among the states but the total foreign trade of the forty-eight nations would be many times larger than the present foreign trade of the United States.

Thus, other conditions being equal, the value of foreign trade is likely to increase and that of per capita trade, to decrease, as one goes from smaller to larger countries.

Similarly, among countries about equal in population, the more prosperous are likely to have more foreign trade than those with a more primitive economic structure. There is no evidence, however, that the ratio of the value of foreign trade to national income necessarily increases as one moves from poorer to richer nations.

The same observation holds for the relationship between foreign trade and industrial production. Progress in manufacturing tends to increase a country's demand for imported raw materials and to provide it with surplus produce for export, but foreign trade does not necessarily increase at the same rate as national income when one moves from less developed countries to more developed countries with about the same population.

Since the foreign trade statistics of different countries are not strictly comparable, minor differences between individual countries are meaningless. No conclusion can be drawn from the statement, for example, that in 1929 export per capita of population in the USSR was 20 cents less than in India ($3.10 and $3.30, respectively) and in 1938, 10 cents more ($1.60 and $1.50). Because of the unavoidable margin of error, figures in Table 24 are rounded to the nearest dollar except for the five countries at the bottom of the list. The range between the per capita values of foreign trade in various countries is so wide, however, that the disparities due to statistical differences are of secondary importance. (See Table 24.)

TABLE 24

PER CAPITA EXPORTS AND IMPORTS, IN SELECTED COUNTRIES, 1913, 1929, 1938, 1952

(*U.S. Dollars*)

Country [a]	Exports				Imports			
	1913	1929	1938	1952	1913	1929	1938	1952
New Zealand	$99	$176	$139	$336	$ 91	$158	$135	$370
Iceland	. . .	155	110	267	. . .	160	100	384
Denmark	57	122	89	197	69	130	89	224
Belgium–Luxembourg	91	106	86	269	116	119	88	269
Canada	58	119	77	328	83	129	66	310
Australia	77	91	75	195	78	108	75	229
Sweden	39	79	73	219	40	78	83	243
Switzerland	69	99	72	228	93	127	86	249
Malaya [b]	54	128	65	168	100	120	63	166
Netherlands	. . .	103	65	205	. . .	142	89	217
Norway	41	71	65	170	59	102	100	269
Germany	40	50	55	82 [c]	43	50	57	79 [c]
United Kingdom	59	77	54	150	75	118	94	193
Finland	24	44	49	175	29	48	50	194
Ireland	. . .	77	39	96	. . .	99	68	164
Southern Rhodesia	10	31	34	62	9	13	17	125
Cuba	69	75	31	123	59	60	26	120
Argentina	65	82	31	. . .	62	74	31	. . .
Uruguay	56	50	29	87	41	50	29	99
Chile	60	67	29	77	35	47	24	63
Austria	. . .	46	26	73	. . .	69	43	94
United States	25	42	24	97	18	35	17	74
Algeria	17	25	22	46	23	36	20	71
France	31	47	21	92	39	54	32	104
Jamaica	13	23	21	. . .	16	34	28	. . .

(*Continued on following page*)

TABLE 24—*continued*

Country [a]	Exports				Imports			
	1913	1929	1938	1952	1913	1929	1938	1952
Hungary	...	$21	$17	...	...	$21	$13	...
Northern Rhodesia	...	20	17	$116	...	32	29	$ 66
Ceylon	$18	25	17	40	$14	24	15	45
Costa Rica	24	36	15	57	22	40	21	80
Union of South Africa	51	29	14	80	32	48	49	100
Iraq	...	6	13	54	...	11	10	33
Italy	13	19	13	29	19	28	14	49
Greece	4	14	13	16	6	27	19	46
Tunisia	17	24	12	...	14	34	14	...
Peru	10	21	11	27	6	12	9	33
Honduras	5	28	11	...	9	18	12	...
Bolivia	15	16	11	...	8	9	8	...
Bulgaria	4	8	11	...	8	11	10	...
Japan	6	19	11	15	7	20	11	24
Romania	8	10	10	...	7	9	10	...
Paraguay	...	15	10	...	...	16	11	...
Dominican Republic	14	21	9	50	13	20	8	24
Colombia	6	16	9	41	5	16	9	35
Iran	4	9	9	8	6	5	6	8
Egypt	13	18	9	20	11	19	11	30
Gold Coast	16	21	8	54	15	17	9	46
Yugoslavia	...	10	8	15	...	11	7	22
Kenya–Uganda	1	6	8	...	3	6	7	...
Brazil	13	12	8	26	13	11	8	36
Philippines	5	13	7	...	6	12	10	...
Panama	...	9	7	19	...	41	27	105
Turkey	5	5	7	18	10	8	7	27
Portugal	6	7	7	28	14	17	13	41
Guatemala	7	11	6	29	5	14	7	26
El Salvador	6	13	6	44	4	12	5	34
Poland	...	10	6	...	...	11	7	...
Mexico	10	15	6	21	6	11	6	27
Madagascar	...	5	6	...	...	9	4	...
Indonesia	6	10	6	13	4	8	3	13
Thailand	5	8	5	...	4	8	4	...
Belgian Congo	1	5	5	34	1	6	3	34
French Morocco	2	9	5	31	7	19	7	60
Nicaragua	...	13	4	38	...	15	6	40
Haiti	4	7	4	26	3	7	4	27
Indochina	3	6	4	...	3	6	2	...
Ecuador	...	7	3	24	...	7	6	22
French West Africa	2.1	3.1	2.5	...	2.5	3.8	3.1	...
Nigeria	2.0	4.0	2.5	15.2	1.8	3.1	1.7	9.7
USSR	5.5	3.1	1.6	...	4.8	2.9	1.6	...
India [d]	2.5	3.3	1.5	3.6	1.9	2.6	1.5	4.7
China [e]	0.7	1.4	0.7	...	0.9	1.9	1.3	...

Sources: Data for 1913 computed from **3**, 1926, pp. 10–15 and 1928, pp. 128–29; for 1929, **25**, 1938, p. 149; for 1938 and 1952, from Table 22, and from **16** and **9**, 1951, pp. 91–127.

a. Countries are arrayed by per capita exports in 1938.
b. Includes Singapore.
c. Western Germany.

d. In 1913, 1929 and 1938, includes Pakistan.
e. Includes Manchuria.

The ranking of individual countries by per capita foreign trade changes from year to year, and countries rank differently in exports and imports. In Table 24, countries are arrayed by per capita exports in 1938. The common feature of the eleven countries at the top of the list is that they are all comparatively small in terms of population; only Canada had a population of as much as 10 million in 1938.

In 1938 Germany ranked twelfth in per capita exports, the United Kingdom thirteenth, the United States twenty-second, and France twenty-fourth. Similar values for per capita exports, ranging from $21 to $55 for these four nations, were recorded in that year in Finland, Ireland, Southern Rhodesia, Cuba, Argentina, Uruguay and Chile.

At the other extreme, at the bottom of the list, are India and China, economically underdeveloped countries with large populations, and the USSR, a nation which has deliberately isolated itself from the rest of the world. In 1938 several areas with primitive economies and small populations had per capita exports similar to those of the colossi, China, India and the USSR, but most of these have increased their foreign trade tremendously in recent years.

In the middle of the list, with per capita exports of $10–$20 in 1938, are such countries as Italy and Japan with about the same per capita trade as small countries on a much lower level of economic development, such as Northern Rhodesia, Tunisia, Honduras.

PATTERNS OF RATIOS BETWEEN FOREIGN TRADE AND NATIONAL INCOME

The ratio of foreign trade to national income (or of per capita foreign trade to per capita income) depends on many factors. In small countries which have only one industry, such as Iceland, or have industries controlled by foreign capital, the value of foreign trade may exceed the national income. On the other hand, in large countries with efficient and diversified industry and strong agriculture, like the United States, the ratio of foreign trade to national income is comparatively low. The ratio is still lower in large countries where a subsistence economy prevails.

Comparable data on national income and foreign trade in 1949 are available for 61 countries (Table 25), which rank as follows in the ratio (percentage) of foreign trade to national income:

Indonesia	244.0
Southern Rhodesia	163.4
Iceland	149.5
Venezuela	123.6
Ceylon	119.4
Philippines	109.0
Israel	90.2
Bolivia	81.8
Dominican Republic	73.3
Honduras	72.4
Thailand	72.2
Belgium	71.3
Costa Rica	70.4
Cuba	69.9
Lebanon	69.6
Netherlands	63.3
Finland	63.2
New Zealand	62.6
Ecuador	62.5
Norway	61.8
Australia	61.1
Panama	60.6
Austria	60.2
Greece	59.3
Egypt	59.0
Union of South Africa	58.7
Paraguay	58.3
Iran	56.5
Iraq	56.5
Ireland	55.9
Chile	55.8
El Salvador	54.3
Syria	54.0
Burma	52.7
Guatemala	51.9
Canada	51.0
Denmark	50.6
Uruguay	47.7
Switzerland	42.7
Sweden	42.5
Haiti	42.5
Brazil	40.2
Colombia	40.1
United Kingdom	39.4
Peru	39.0
Nicaragua	38.2
Argentina	35.5
Czechoslovakia	34.5
Mexico	31.4
France	30.3
Italy	24.6
Portugal	24.0
Turkey	24.0
Western Germany	22.2
Pakistan	22.0
Yugoslavia	20.5

Japan	17.0
India	14.0
Ethiopia	10.5
United States	9.0
China	4.4

It appears that a ratio of foreign trade to national income of 75 per cent or more is characteristic of one-sided, poorly balanced economic systems. Among the modern prosperous nations, Belgium was the only one in which this ratio was more than 70 per cent in 1949. The typical

ratio was about 50–65 per cent for industrially developed countries with a population of not more than 10 million (Denmark, Austria, Australia, Norway, New Zealand, Finland, the Netherlands); 30–40 per cent for the industrialized nations with larger populations (France, Czechoslovakia, the United Kingdom); and much lower — 9.0 per cent — for the United States. In 1949, the ratio was also very low for Western Germany and Japan, but in both countries the value of foreign trade more than doubled from 1949 to 1951 and the ratio to national

TABLE 25

PER CAPITA FOREIGN TRADE AND NATIONAL INCOME, IN SELECTED COUNTRIES, 1949

Country	Per Capita Foreign Trade [a]	Per Capita Income	Trade as Percentage of Income	Country	Per Capita Foreign Trade [a]	Per Capita Income	Trade as Percentage of Income
Iceland	$712	$476	149.5	Honduras	$ 67	$ 83	72.4
New Zealand	536	856[b]	62.6	Indonesia	61	25	244.0
Canada	444	870	51.0	Portugal	60	250	24.0
Australia	415	679[c]	61.1	Egypt	59	100	59.0
Belgium	415[d]	582	71.3	Italy	58	235	24.6
Venezuela	398	322	123.6	Dominican Republic	55	75	73.3
Switzerland	363	849	42.7	Colombia	53	132	40.1
Norway	363	587	61.8	Syria	54	100	54.0
Israel	351	389	90.2	El Salvador	50	92	54.3
Denmark	349	689	50.6	Paraguay	49	84	58.3
Sweden	332	780	42.5	Philippines	48	44	109.0
Netherlands	318	502	63.3	Iran	48	85	56.5
United Kingdom	305	773	39.4	Iraq	48	85	56.5
Ireland	235	420	55.9	Bolivia	45	55	81.8
Finland	220	348	63.2	Brazil	45	112	40.2
Cuba	207	296	69.9	Guatemala	40	77	51.9
Southern Rhodesia	165	101	163.4	Peru	39	100	39.0
Uruguay	158	331	47.7	Mexico	38	121	31.4
Union of South Africa	155	264[c]	58.7	Nicaragua	34	89	38.2
France	146	482	30.3	Yugoslavia	30	146	20.5
United States	131	1,453	9.0	Turkey	30	125	24.0
Austria	130	216	60.2	Thailand	26	36	72.2
Czechoslovakia	128	371	34.5	Ecuador	25	40	62.5
Argentina	123	346	35.5	Burma	19	36	52.7
Panama	111	183	60.6	Haiti	17	40	42.5
Chile	105	188	55.8	Japan	17	100	17.0
Costa Rica	88	125	70.4	Pakistan	11	51	22.0
Lebanon	87	125	69.6	India	8	57[c]	14.0
Ceylon	80	67	119.4	Ethiopia	4	38	10.5
Greece	76	128	59.3	China	1.2	27	4.4
Western Germany	71	320	22.2				

Sources: Data for foreign trade from **16**; population and per capita national income, from **12**, pp. 14–26.

　a. Total of exports and imports.　　　　　　　c. 1948–49.
　b. 1949–50.　　　　　　　　　　　　　　　d. Belgium–Luxembourg.

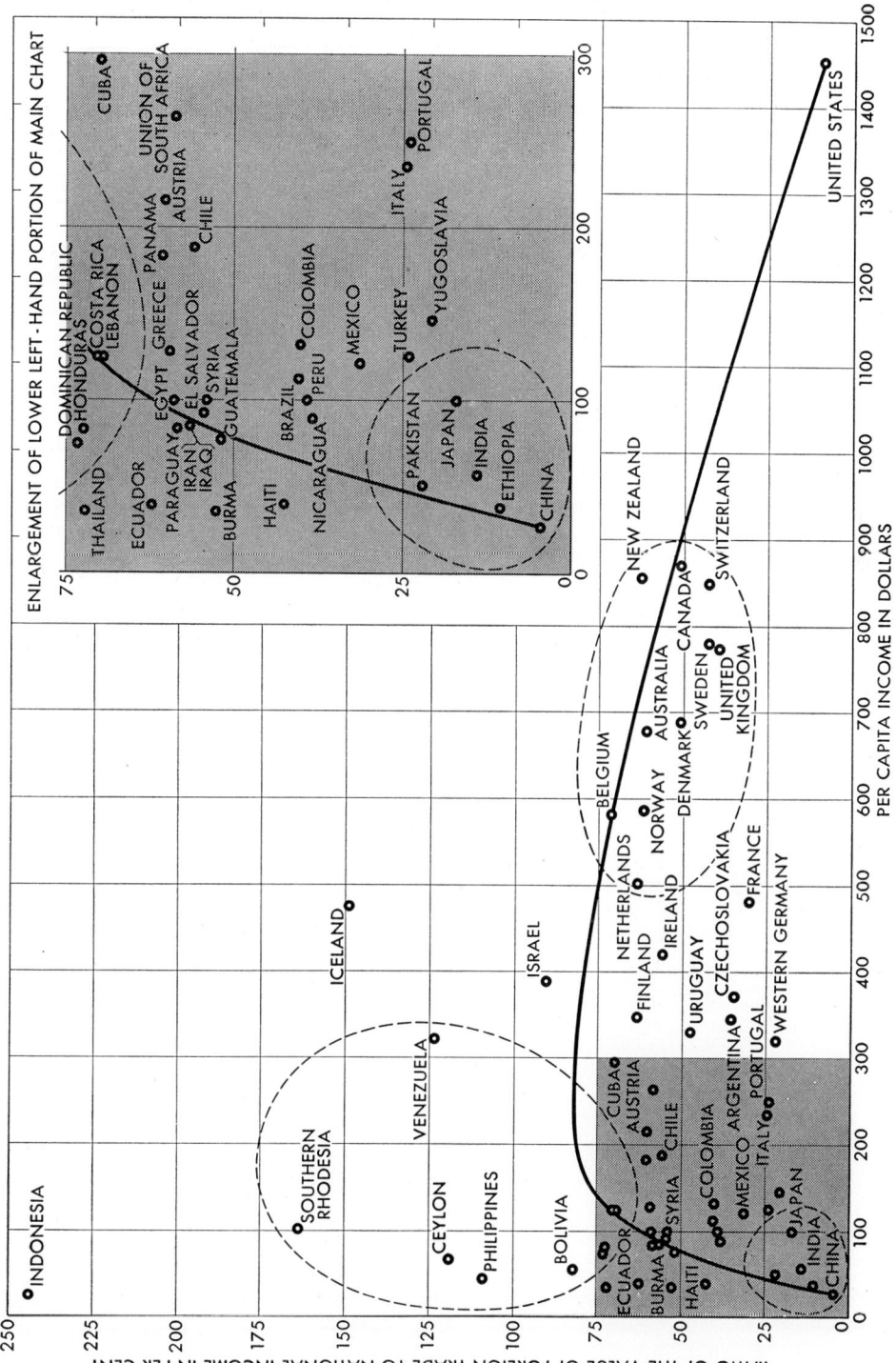

FIGURE 16. FOREIGN TRADE: RELATIONSHIP BETWEEN PER CAPITA INCOME AND RATIO OF THE VALUE OF FOREIGN TRADE TO NATIONAL INCOME, IN SELECTED COUNTRIES, 1949

Source: Table 25

income rose to a level similar to that of France and the United Kingdom.

Except for the United States, Western Germany and Japan, at one extreme, and Belgium, at the other, the ratio in most modern prosperous countries with per capita income of $500 or more ranged from a little less than 40 per cent to 65 per cent, while much higher and much lower ratios were characteristic of underdeveloped areas.

A scatter chart which shows the relationship between per capita income and the ratio of the value of foreign trade to income in 1949, suggests that there is no straight linear correlation between the two values. In fact, the points which represent individual countries in such a chart are scattered all over the plot in such a way that it is impossible to draw a straight line along which most points, or at least the most typical points, are clustered. (See Figure 16.) There is, how-ever, an area of concentration of points which represents typical modern prosperous countries. The foreign-trade-to-income ratio of these countries is appreciably higher than that in the United States, at the one extreme, and China, India, Pakistan, and Ethiopia at the other. There is also a group of countries with a very low per capita income and a comparatively high foreign-trade-to-income ratio.

With due reservation the correlation between this ratio and per capita income may be represented by a bell-shaped curve line as in Figure 16. No particular significance should be attached to this "regression curve," but it is fairly probable that economic growth of countries with very high ratios of foreign trade to income — such as Ceylon, the Philippines, Bolivia, Southern Rhodesia and Indonesia — would result in a shift of their points on the scatter chart in the general direction of the right lower corner of the plot.

CHAPTER 3

DIRECTION OF WORLD TRADE

THE SECOND major characteristic of the pattern of world trade is its direction. This is determined by the distribution of world exports and imports among geographic regions and countries and by the provenance of each area's imports and the destination of its exports.

THE PROBLEM

In a uniform world market with perfectly convertible national currencies, any merchandise imported to any area returns to the exporting country currency or credit which the latter can use to purchase goods or meet obligations in any part of the world. Under such conditions, the interest of the exporting nation in the destination of its exports resembles that of a manufacturer in the distribution of his sales among different sections of the domestic market. A record of the geographic distribution of his business helps him plan sales campaigns, appraise potential new outlets and so forth, but one sale is as good as another. On a free and uniform world market, therefore, the direction of foreign trade has no immediate bearing on the trade and payments balance of individual countries.

As long as all currencies are convertible, each country sells its produce wherever it can obtain the best price and purchases wherever it can find the articles it needs at the lowest price. Under these conditions, multilateral trade is taken for granted.

The pattern of world trade is very different when national currencies cease to be convertible or their conversion becomes subject to special regulations. It changes, for example, when the exporting country demands a particular currency in payment for its merchandise, refusing to take the currency of the country which wishes to purchase its produce. It changes likewise when the importing country requires the importer to take local produce in payment.[1]

Inconvertibility of currencies increases the significance of the direction of imports and exports and, in particular, of trade balances, between each pair of nations. The export industries of a nation may be able to turn out all the goods needed to pay for imported merchandise; there may be sufficient demand for the nation's products abroad and a sufficient supply of the merchandise it wishes to import, but both import and export may be blocked by the inconvertibility of currencies. In brief, while the trade balance between any two countries is almost irrelevant to their ultimate balances of trade and payments as long as foreign trade is carried on in terms of a universal currency, as before World War I and again in the late 1920's,[2] bilateral balances become of vital significance for both countries when their currencies are not mutually convertible or cannot be converted into the "hard" currency which has replaced the universal world currency in a section of the world market.

The classical school of political economy paid little attention to the direction of trade because this issue did not arise in a generalized analysis of a "model" world market in which gold was the universal medium of exchange. The protectionists, too, interested in prices at which the imported products were sold on the national market, gave little thought to the issue of bilateral and multilateral trade; some of them seem to

1. A distinction has sometimes been made between exchange control and other trade regulations, such as tariffs and quotas, on the ground that the former restricts payment for imports while the latter restrict the actual movement of goods. The experience of the 1930's and more recent years has proved that exchange and trade controls tend to go hand in hand, each supplementing the other. Protection of an overvaluated currency calls for control over imports, exports and the flow of capital and may reduce foreign trade to a series of bilateral barter operations supervised by the government. (2, pp. 175ff.)

2. As O. M. W. Sprague, the American monetary expert, points out, the gold standard emerged triumphant from the confusion and disorganization of currencies during World War I and by the late 1920's became "more universally than ever before the foundation of credit structure throughout the world." (8, p. 53; cf. 31.) The system of international currencies before the great depression amounted, for all practical purposes, to a universally accepted world currency. It began to crumble in the 1930's, collapsed under the strain of World War II and has not been restored, despite recent significant improvements.

have favored bilateral trade as a type of transaction that can be more readily controlled by a national government.[3] The issue arose after the great depression when trade regulations introduced by countries with weak currencies became a serious obstacle to the multilateral exchange of goods.

After World War II the problem crystallized in a new form. Attention was focused on the trade between the dollar area, the sterling area and the rest of the world. In this form, the issue of the direction of international trade has become the core of the problem of restoring the world market.

Origin of the Modern System of Multilateral Trade

There is little doubt that the foreign trade of ancient Phoenicia, Egypt, India and China included multilateral transactions. International markets such as Tyrus, in which precious metals served as universal currency, invited operations of this type. The Dark Ages practically obliterated multilateral trade. The new system of international trade, based essentially on the exchange of goods between the industrial and primarily agricultural areas and between the temperate climatic zones and the tropics, was an outgrowth of the Industrial Revolution and the colonial expansion of Europe in the nineteenth century. It matured in the last two or three decades of that century and reached full development before World War I.

Folke Hilgerdt, who has provided the most penetrating analysis of this system,[4] links its origin to the development of the British Empire. Until the middle of the nineteenth century, the United Kingdom had an active trade balance. To the net balance of exports over imports were added invisible exports — services of the British fleet, profits from foreign trade, yield of investments in colonies and other areas. In this way, the United Kingdom accumulated considerable assets in all parts of the world. After the middle of the century, when the yield of these assets began greatly to exceed new British capital exports, the amounts due by the debtor countries began to be transferred to Great Britain in part through Europe and the United States:

Industrial growth in these areas rendered them

dependent upon net import of primary products from overseas, paid for by the excess of exports to the United Kingdom that arose when their dependence upon British manufactures declined.[5]

Hilgerdt distinguishes two phases in the development of the new pattern of world trade. In the 1860's and 1870's triangular trade prevailed, with colonial tropical areas at one end, Great Britain at the other end and the United States or some European countries in the middle. Multilateral features appeared in the 1880's as a result of the growth of Germany's economic power:

From the eighties Germany emerges as a separate link in the transfer chain leading to the United Kingdom. The rapid growth of German industry and the ensuing increase in German net imports from continents other than Europe were accompanied by an increase in German net exports, not to the United Kingdom, but to other European countries which in their turn had a net export to the United Kingdom.[6]

Shortly after Germany emerged on the world market, Canada, Argentina, Australia and New Zealand entered into the system as a separate group between the United States and Germany. All these countries [7] exported agricultural products — meat and wheat — to Europe and used their export surpluses with Europe to purchase iron and steel, machinery and other capital goods in the United States.

In the late 1890's, the United States became a net exporter of manufactured goods, mainly to Canada, Argentina and other countries of Latin America, and a net importer of industrial raw materials, mainly from the tropics. Thus, it had an active trade balance with one group of countries and a passive balance with other countries. The growth of these balances was an outstanding factor in restoring the system of multilateral trade in the 1920's. As Hilgerdt describes it:

The development of the system of multilateral trade, accomplished over a period of a few decades, was similar to the unfolding of a fan. More and more countries became involved, and their insertion took place in a given order, each country being farther away from the United Kingdom on the transfer routes to that country from its debtors.[8]

---

3. See **28**.
4. See **1** and **6**.

5. **27**, p. 397.
6. **27**, p. 399.
7. Hilgerdt describes them as countries "of recent settlement in the temperate belts."
8. **27**, p. 400.

Multilateral trade probably reached its peak development on the eve of World War I and this general pattern of international trade reappeared in the late 1920's. Hilgerdt has pictured the mechanism of trade of that time in two charts which differ from each other only in the treatment of Germany: in one, Germany is handled as a separate party in the system;[9] in the other, its trade is merged with that of the rest of continental Europe.[10] The latter, which has been widely used in discussion of multilateral trade, is reproduced in Figure 17.[11]

Foreign Trade Before and After World War I

Supremacy of Europe, 1913

Europe predominated overwhelmingly in international trade before World War I. Including Russia, it accounted for 55.2 per cent of the world's exports and 61.5 per cent of its imports in 1913.[12] The percentage distribution of the flow of merchandise in world trade was as follows (cf. Figure 18):[13]

Total	100.0
Intra-European trade	40.0
Imports to Europe from non-European countries	21.5
Imports to non-European countries from Europe	15.2
Trade among non-European countries	23.3

Thus trade among non-European countries accounted for less than one fourth of the international exchange of merchandise. Moreover, this figure includes the transactions among European colonies and their trade with non-European nations. As importers, exporters or masters of colonial areas, the old European nations controlled an overwhelming part of world trade. It is true that Europe's share in world trade was increased by the political boundaries that crisscross this promontory of the Eurasian continent and the fact that, despite these partitions, Europe re-

mained largely an economic unity.[14] Indeed, a part of intra-European trade is comparable to interstate commerce in the United States.

Two facts are noteworthy: first, the value of trade among European nations before World War I was almost twice that of trade among non-European countries, including the United States, Japan, the British dominions and European colonies; second, about half of all exports from non-European countries were directed toward Europe.

Imports and Exports of Selected Countries

Before World War I

Before World War I Europe absorbed more than 80 per cent of the exports of Belgium, the Netherlands and Argentina; 75–80 per cent of those of Germany, Russia and Australia; more than 60 per cent of those of France, Italy and the United States; and more than half of Canada's and India's. The foreign trade of the United Kingdom was distributed almost evenly among its dominions and colonies, continental Europe and the rest of the world. Europe's share in the imports of these and other countries was somewhat less than its share in their exports.[15]

Considering both exports and imports, it appears that China and Japan had the strongest commercial ties with other Asiatic countries; Canada belonged to the American economic community; the United Kingdom carried on extensive trade with all parts of the world; and almost all other trading nations gravitated toward European markets. (See Table 26,A; cf. Figure 19.)

In the 1920's

World War I interrupted the customary trade among continents and nations. The situation remained confused for two or three years after the Armistice. Recovery started in 1923, after the inflation in Germany was brought under control.

The postwar trade of individual countries differed somewhat from their prewar trade. The general orientation of their exports and imports, as reflected in their trade balances with different parts of the world, remained unchanged, but Europe's share in the imports and exports of almost all regions and countries declined. (See Table 26; cf. Figure 19.)

---

9. **27**, p. 395.

10. **6**, p. 78.

11. For the method followed by Hilgerdt, his classification of countries, and the statistics underlying his charts, see pp. 80ff.

12. **5**, 1913, and 1923–1927, p. 60.

13. Estimated by the authors on the basis of **5** and **6**.

14. **33**, pp. 33–54.

15. **32**, pp. 198–99.

A. 1928

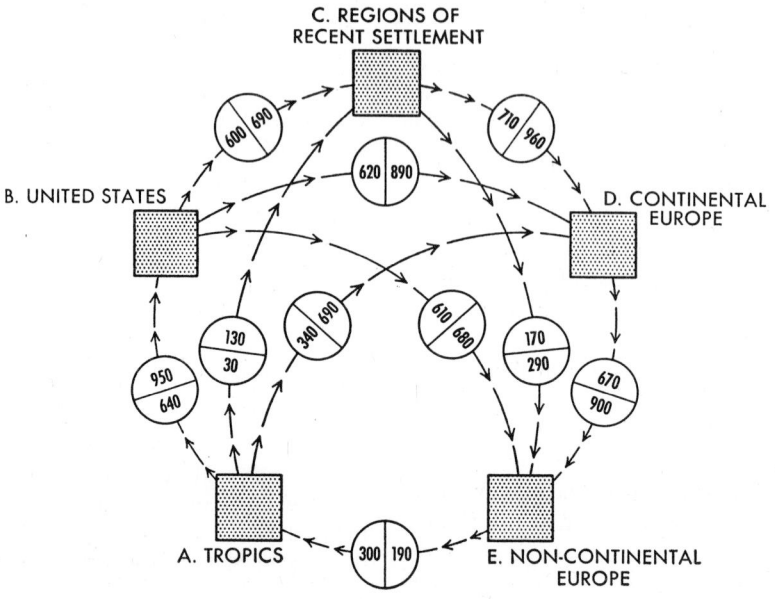

B. 1938

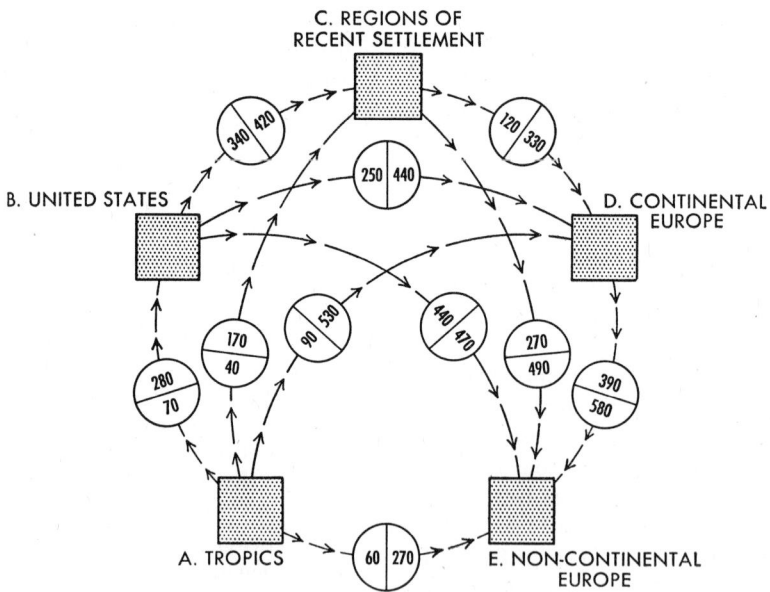

Source: **6,** pp. 78, 90

FIGURE 17. MULTILATERAL TRADE: TRADE BALANCES BETWEEN EACH TWO OF FIVE GROUPS OF COUNTRIES, 1928 AND 1938

The chart uses the balances derived from Table 31, in millions of dollars. Both import and export balances are shown: the first (following the direction of the arrows), and the smaller, of the two figures in each circle represents the export balance of the group from which the arrows emerge; the larger figure represents the import balance of the group to which the arrows point. The difference between the two sets of totals is due largely to the inclusion in imports of transport costs between the frontiers of the exporting and importing countries. In certain cases in 1938, however, it appears due to the over-valuation of imports or undervaluation of exports by countries that apply exchange control and official rates of exchange in converting local currency into dollars.

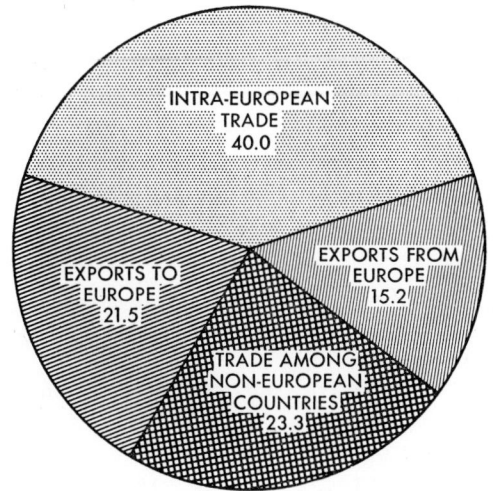

Source: See p. 71

FIGURE 18. WORLD TRADE: EUROPEAN AND NON-
EUROPEAN COUNTRIES, 1913, PERCENTAGE
DISTRIBUTION

DECLINE IN EUROPE'S SHARE IN WORLD TRADE

In 1927 the volume of international trade was approximately 20 per cent greater than in 1913. The total, however, included commerce crossing the new political boundaries — between the United Kingdom and Ireland, among the countries carved out of the old Austro-Hungarian and Ottoman empires, between Poland and the Baltic states, and so on. Without these transactions, the volume of imports and exports across the old political boundaries in 1927 was about 15 per cent above the 1913 level.

Europe's share in world imports fell from 61.5 per cent in 1913 to 54.6 per cent in 1927 and in exports, from 55.2 per cent to 46.1 per cent.[16] Without commerce across the new boundaries, the 1927 ratios would be 52.6 per cent for imports and 43.7 per cent for exports. The share of non-European countries in Europe's imports and exports was larger than in 1913, while Europe's share in imports and exports of the rest of the world had declined. (See Table 26 and Figure 19.)

TRADE BALANCES OF SELECTED COUNTRIES

Few of the nations listed in Table 26 kept their trade with any continent in balance before World War I.

The United States had a relative surplus of exports to Europe and Canada and a relative

16. **5**, 1913 to 1923–1927, p. 60.

surplus of imports from the rest of the world.[17] Canada and Argentina had a strongly active balance with Europe and a passive balance with most of the rest of the world. The pattern of the trade of France, Belgium, the Netherlands and Germany was similar; all had a surplus of exports in trade with the rest of Europe and an import balance with other parts of the world, especially the Americas. On the other hand, the United Kingdom had a passive trade balance with continental Europe and North America and an active balance with Latin America, Africa, Oceania and, in particular, Asia.

China and Japan had an export balance with the United States and a surplus of imports in trade with other areas, including Asia.

India covered its net import balance with Europe by net exports to all other parts of the world, and Australia paid for imports from North America by exports to Europe, Africa and other regions. (See Table 27.)

With a few minor exceptions, the direction of trade balances in 1927 was essentially the same as in 1913 and even the amounts, in relation to the value of imports and exports, had not changed significantly. Europe was still smarting under the repercussion of war, and its supremacy in world trade was shaken, but multilateral trade along the customary lines was resumed as soon as the convertibility of currencies was restored.

If this pattern of world trade represented "normalcy," normalcy was short-lived this time. The great depression was around the corner.

POSITION OF THE UNITED STATES

The United States has been an important partner in the world's multilateral trade since the 1860's.

In the first half of the nineteenth century trade with Europe predominated in the country's foreign transactions, but its imports from the old countries, mainly the United Kingdom, were roughly in balance with its exports. In 1850 the imports of the United States from Europe amounted to $123 million and its exports to Europe, to $109 million. In transactions with other parts of the world, its imports amounted to $50 million and its exports, to $36 million.

17. To eliminate the effect of the difference in the valuation of exported and imported merchandise and other factors of disparity in import and export, the relative percentage shares of different continents in the exports of each nation are compared here with their relative shares in that nation's imports.

TABLE 26. FOREIGN TRADE OF SELECTED COUNTRIES: PERCENTAGE

A. 1913

Country	North America	Middle America	South America	Europe	Asia	Africa	Oceania
Imports from Each Continent							
United States	8.0	13.8	11.1	48.2	16.7	1.3	0.9
Canada	64.2	2.1	1.5	29.2	2.1	0.1	0.8
Argentina	15.4	0.6	3.8	79.6	0.3	0.0	0.3
United Kingdom	24.4	1.3	9.0	44.3	9.7	4.8	6.5
France	11.4	1.6	9.5	52.2	12.8	9.0	3.5
Belgium	9.8	0.3	10.9	64.1	7.9	2.4	4.6
Netherlands	11.7	0.2	5.1	65.4	16.4	0.9	0.3
Germany	16.6	1.0	10.2	54.1	10.5	4.6	3.0
Italy	14.7	0.3	7.1	65.4	9.1	2.4	1.0
China	6.4	0.0	0.0	26.4	67.1	0.0	0.1
Japan	17.3	0.0	0.4	30.7	48.5	1.0	2.1
India	2.6	0.0	0.0	80.3	14.6	2.0	0.5
Australia	14.9	0.3	0.3	70.9	8.8	0.5	4.3
Exports to Each Continent							
United States	16.4	7.7	5.9	60.4	6.2	1.2	2.2
Canada	38.9	1.8	0.9	54.7	1.1	1.0	1.6
Argentina [a]	6.2	0.3	9.8	83.7	0.0	0.0	0.0
United Kingdom	10.3	1.8	9.5	34.7	25.2	9.8	8.7
France	6.6	1.1	5.7	69.0	3.9	13.3	0.4
Belgium	3.5	0.6	5.4	81.7	5.3	2.7	0.8
Netherlands	4.5	0.1	0.5	88.0	5.7	1.1	0.1
Germany	7.7	1.0	6.6	75.2	6.4	2.1	1.0
Italy	11.1	0.6	11.6	63.7	5.4	7.1	0.5
China	9.2	0.0	0.0	25.3	65.4	0.0	0.1
Japan	30.0	0.1	0.3	23.3	43.8	0.3	2.2
India	9.5	0.4	2.0	58.0	25.3	2.8	2.0
Australia	3.6	0.0	1.1	77.7	9.3	3.6	4.7

a. Excludes exports for unknown destination.

Distribution of Imports and Exports, by Continent, 1913 and 1927

B. 1927

Country	North America	Middle America	South America	Europe	Asia	Africa	Oceania
			Imports from Each Continent				
United States	11.6	12.0	12.4	30.5	30.0	2.2	1.3
Canada	65.1	2.6	2.9	24.5	2.9	0.4	1.6
Argentina [a]	27.3	2.1	9.5	60.3	0.6	0.1	0.1
United Kingdom	21.1	2.2	9.3	39.3 [c]	13.0	6.9	8.2
France [a]	14.1	2.4	8.6	44.3	13.1	13.2	4.3
Belgium [a]	13.8	0.6	10.1	66.4	4.0	2.5	2.6
Netherlands	12.2	2.6	11.1	62.0	9.1	2.5	0.5
Germany	17.9	1.6	10.8	52.9	10.0	4.3	2.5
Italy [a]	24.1	0.5	9.0	49.6	10.1	4.1	2.6
China	17.4	0.2	0.0	16.7	65.6	0.0	0.1
Japan	33.6	0.5	0.5	17.9	40.2	1.7	5.6
India	9.8	0.0	0.0	67.1	20.7	1.6	0.8
Australia	27.9	0.1	0.1	53.0	14.7	0.7	3.5
			Exports to Each Continent				
United States	17.4	8.4	9.0	47.5	11.5	2.2	4.0
Canada	40.0	2.2	2.2	46.9	5.4	1.2	2.1
Argentina [a, b]	12.0	0.4	8.2	79.0	0.3	0.1	0.0
United Kingdom	10.7	1.8	8.4	34.0 [c]	22.3	11.3	11.5
France [a]	7.3	1.3	4.7	63.6	7.3	15.1	0.7
Belgium [a]	12.5	0.5	5.3	68.6	7.2	5.3	0.6
Netherlands	6.1	0.9	2.0	76.4	11.1	2.9	0.6
Germany	7.8	1.1	6.3	74.0	7.6	2.4	0.8
Italy [a]	10.7	0.9	10.2	62.4	8.6	6.4	0.8
China	13.4	0.0	0.1	19.2	67.2	0.0	0.1
Japan	43.2	0.3	1.0	7.4	42.4	2.6	3.1
India	12.0	1.6	3.5	48.4	27.9	4.1	2.5
Australia	13.7	0.0	0.3	63.5	13.8	4.4	4.3

Source: **5**, 1913–1927, Vol. I, pp. 58–59.

a. 1926.
b. Excludes exports for unknown destination.

c. Includes trade with Ireland (3.5 per cent for import and 5.1 per cent for export).

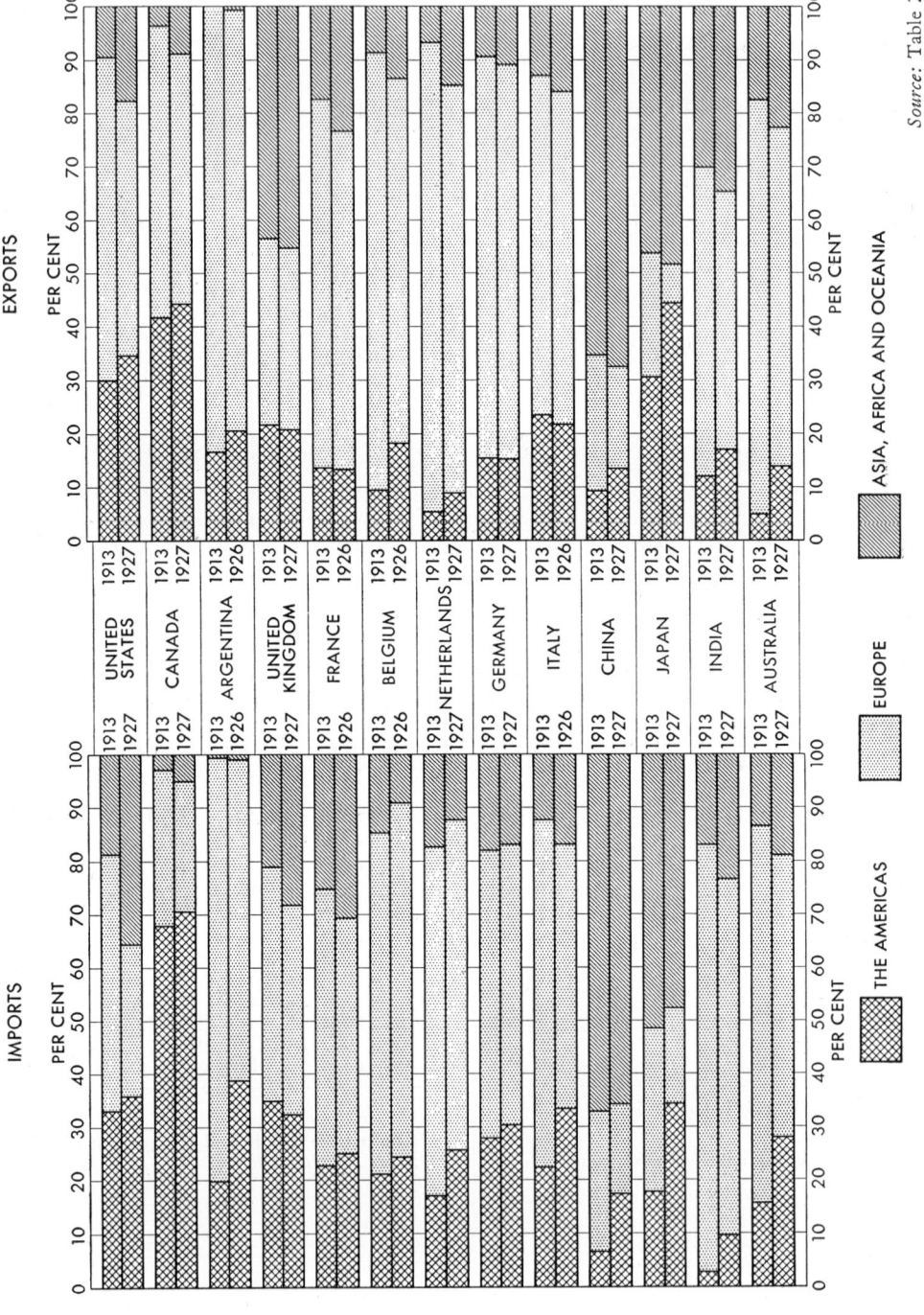

IMPORTS

EXPORTS

Source: Table 26

FIGURE 19. FOREIGN TRADE OF SELECTED COUNTRIES: PERCENTAGE DISTRIBUTION OF IMPORTS AND EXPORTS, BY CONTINENT, 1913 AND 1927

THE AMERICAS   EUROPE   ASIA, AFRICA AND OCEANIA

TABLE 27

TRADE BALANCES OF SELECTED COUNTRIES WITH EACH CONTINENT, 1913 AND 1926–27

(*Exports to Each Continent as Percentage of Total Exports, Minus Imports from the Same Continent as Percentage of Total Imports*)

	North America	Middle America	South America	Europe	Asia	Africa	Oceania
United States							
1913	+8.4	−6.1	−5.2	+12.2	−10.5	−0.1	+1.3
1927	+5.8	−3.6	−3.4	+17.0	−18.5	0.0	+2.7
Canada							
1913	−25.3	−0.3	−0.6	+25.5	−1.0	+0.9	+0.8
1927	−25.1	−0.4	−0.7	+22.4	+2.5	+0.8	+0.5
Argentina							
1913	−9.2	−0.3	+6.0	+4.1	−0.3	0.0	−0.3
1926	−15.3	−1.7	−1.3	+18.7	−0.3	0.0	−0.1
United Kingdom							
1913	−14.1	+0.5	+0.5	−9.6	+15.5	+5.0	+2.2
1927	−10.4	−0.4	−0.9	−5.3	+9.3	+4.4	+3.3
France							
1913	−4.8	−0.5	−3.8	+16.8	−8.9	+4.3	−3.1
1926	−6.8	−1.1	−3.9	+19.3	−5.8	+1.9	−3.6
Belgium							
1913	−6.3	+0.3	−5.5	+17.6	−2.6	+0.3	−3.8
1926	−1.3	−0.1	−4.8	+2.2	+3.2	+2.8	−2.0
Netherlands							
1913	−7.2	−0.1	−4.6	+22.6	−10.7	+0.2	−0.2
1927	−6.1	−1.7	−9.1	+14.4	+2.0	+0.4	+0.1
Germany							
1913	−8.9	0.0	−3.6	+21.1	−4.1	−2.5	−2.0
1927	−10.1	−0.5	−4.5	+21.1	−2.4	−1.9	−1.7
Italy							
1913	−3.6	+0.3	+4.5	−1.7	−3.7	+4.7	−0.5
1926	−13.4	+0.4	+1.2	+12.8	−1.5	+2.3	−1.8
China							
1913	+2.8	0.0	0.0	−1.1	−1.7	0.0	0.0
1927	−4.0	−0.2	+0.1	+2.5	+1.6	0.0	0.0
Japan							
1913	+12.7	+0.1	−0.1	−7.4	−4.7	−0.7	+0.1
1927	+9.6	−0.2	+0.5	−10.5	+2.2	+0.9	−2.5
India							
1913	+6.9	+0.4	+2.0	−22.3	+10.7	+0.8	+1.5
1927	+2.2	+1.6	+3.5	−18.7	+7.2	+2.5	+1.7
Australia							
1913	−11.3	−0.3	+0.8	+6.8	+0.5	+3.1	+0.4
1927	−14.2	−0.1	+0.2	+10.5	−0.9	+3.7	+0.8

Source: Table 26.

The situation changed in the second half of the century, especially after the Civil War. Europe remained the main export market of the United States, but the European share in its imports declined steadily. In 1901–10, United States exports to Europe averaged $1,132 million a year and its imports from Europe, $594 million, while in commerce with other parts of the world, exports averaged $484 million a year and imports, $564 million.

World War I brought a reorientation of the country's foreign trade, with increased exchange with Canada and Latin America. These areas ranked first in the imports of the United States after 1920, and after World War II in its exports as well. (See Table 28.)

Annual Average or Year	Total	North America	Middle America	South America	Europe	Asia	Africa	Oceania
			Millions of Dollars					
1821	$ 55	$ 2	$ 12	$ 2	$ 36	$ 2	—	—
1830	72	3	15	5	47	2	—	—
1840	124	6	17	6	92	2	$ 1	—
1850	144	10	14	8	109	3	° 1	—
1860	334	23	29	16	249	8	3	$ 5
1870	393	22	31	15	313	6	2	4
1871–80	589	33	36	21	482	8	3	5
1881–90	765	41	44	30	614	19	4	14
1891–1900	1,025	65	63	34	798	33	11	20
1901–10	1,616	153	126	64	1,132	87	23	31
1911–15	2,371	337	182	122	1,517	133	27	52
1916–20	6,521	780	503	361	4,124	562	82	109
1921–25	4,397	627	445	297	2,318	499	70	141
1926–30	4,777	830	403	448	2,237	573	110	177
1931–35	2,025	300	162	141	960	350	62	49
1936–40	3,220	522	291	317	1,333	535	132	89
1941–45	10,051	1,297	575	500	5,674	799	842	364
1946	9,738	1,462	1,072	1,149	4,122	1,327	489	117
1947	14,430	2,115	1,715	2,354	5,187	1,918	821	320
1948	12,653	1,945	1,451	1,912	4,279	2,130	785	153
1949	12,051	1,959	1,340	1,562	4,118	2,256	622	195
1950	10,275 [b]	1,996	1,419	1,347	2,893	1,505	349	133
1951	15,032 [b]	2,587	1,703	2,069	4,093	2,188	578	244
1952	15,164 [b]	2,785	1,700	1,832	3,339	2,119	565	224
			Percentage					
1821	100.0	4.4	22.0	4.1	65.3	3.6	0.6	0.1
1830	100.0	3.9	20.5	6.4	66.1	2.7	0.3	—
1840	100.0	4.9	13.9	4.6	74.4	1.3	0.6	0.3
1850	100.0	6.6	9.9	5.4	75.2	2.1	0.7	0.1
1860	100.0	6.9	8.8	4.7	74.8	2.4	1.0	1.5
1870	100.0	5.5	7.9	3.9	79.8	1.5	0.5	1.0
1871–80	100.0	5.6	6.2	3.6	81.8	1.4	0.5	1.0
1881–90	100.0	5.3	5.7	3.9	80.2	2.5	0.5	1.8
1891–1900	100.0	6.3	6.2	3.4	77.9	3.2	1.1	2.0
1901–10	100.0	9.4	7.8	4.0	70.0	5.4	1.4	1.9
1911–15	100.0	14.2	7.7	5.2	64.0	5.6	1.1	2.2
1916–20	100.0	12.0	7.7	5.5	63.2	8.6	1.3	1.7
1921–25	100.0	14.3	10.1	6.8	52.7	11.3	1.6	3.2
1926–30	100.0	17.4	8.4	9.4	46.8	12.0	2.3	3.7
1931–35	100.0	14.8	8.0	7.0	47.4	17.3	3.1	2.4
1936–40	100.0	16.2	9.0	9.9	41.4	16.6	4.2	2.7
1941–45	100.0	12.9	5.7	5.0	56.4	8.0	8.4	3.6
1946	100.0	15.0	11.0	11.8	42.3	13.6	5.0	1.2
1947	100.0	14.7	11.9	16.3	35.9	13.3	5.7	2.2
1948	100.0	15.4	11.5	15.1	33.8	16.8	6.2	1.2
1949	100.0	16.3	11.1	13.0	34.2	18.7	5.2	1.6
1950	100.0 [b]	19.4	13.8	13.1	28.1	14.7	3.4	1.3
1951	100.0 [b]	17.2	11.3	13.8	27.2	14.5	3.8	1.6
1952	100.0 [b]	18.4	11.2	12.1	22.0	13.9	3.7	1.5

a. Exports include reexports.
b. Includes exports not distributed by destination due to security regulations; $632 million in 1950; $1,570 million in 1951; $2,599 million in 1952.

CONTINENTS, BY PROVENANCE AND DESTINATION, 1821–1952

B. Imports [a]

Annual Average or Year	Total	North America	Middle America	South America	Europe	Asia	Africa	Oceania
			Millions of Dollars					
1821	$ 55	...	$ 12	$ 2	$ 35	$ 5	...	...
1830	63	...	11	5	40	6	...	...
1840	98	$ 1	15	9	62	11	...	...
1850	174	5	16	16	123	12	$ 1	...
1860	354	24	44	35	217	29	4	$ 1
1870	436	36	74	43	240	38	3	2
1871–80	535	31	91	66	284	56	3	4
1881–90	692	41	98	79	385	72	4	14
1891–1900	763	37	102	107	394	97	7	20
1901–10	1,158	66	155	139	594	177	14	13
1911–15	1,712	131	249	220	798	271	24	19
1916–20	3,358	425	588	591	682	910	91	70
1921–25	3,450	397	514	421	1,050	943	71	54
1926–30	4,033	480	460	546	1,207	1,196	91	53
1931–35	1,713	236	177	244	516	491	32	16
1936–40	2,482	369	246	338	627	785	81	36
1941–45	3,514	953	589	801	288	478	218	187
1946	4,942	911	733	1,118	804	887	306	183
1947	5,756	1,128	1,016	1,254	820	1,055	327	156
1948	7,124	1,594	946	1,560	1,121	1,346	394	164
1949	6,622	1,552	941	1,501	925	1,239	338	125
1950	8,852	1,962	1,139	1,963	1,387	1,699	494	208
1951	10,967	2,278	1,220	2,327	2,119	1,989	585	450
1952	10,714	2,388	1,351	2,283	2,023	1,819	601	243
			Percentage					
1821	100.0	0.7	21.7	2.9	64.2	9.8	0.7	0.1
1830	100.0	0.6	17.2	7.8	64.0	10.0	0.4	...
1840	100.0	1.2	15.7	8.8	62.8	10.9	0.5	0.2
1850	100.0	3.0	9.3	9.2	71.0	7.2	0.4	...
1860	100.0	6.7	12.5	9.9	61.5	8.3	1.0	0.3
1870	100.0	8.3	17.1	9.9	55.1	8.7	0.6	0.4
1871–80	100.0	5.7	17.1	12.3	53.1	10.4	0.6	0.8
1881–90	100.0	5.9	14.1	11.4	55.6	10.4	0.5	2.0
1891–1900	100.0	4.8	13.4	14.1	51.6	12.7	1.0	2.6
1901–10	100.0	5.7	13.4	12.0	51.3	15.3	1.2	1.1
1911–15	100.0	7.7	14.5	12.8	46.6	15.8	1.4	1.1
1916–20	100.0	12.7	17.5	17.6	20.3	27.1	2.7	2.1
1921–25	100.0	11.5	14.9	12.2	30.4	27.3	2.1	1.6
1926–30	100.0	11.9	11.4	13.5	29.9	29.7	2.3	1.3
1931–35	100.0	13.8	10.3	14.3	30.1	28.7	1.9	0.9
1936–40	100.0	14.8	9.9	13.6	25.3	31.6	3.3	1.5
1941–45	100.0	27.1	16.8	22.8	8.2	13.6	6.2	5.3
1946	100.0	18.4	14.8	22.6	16.3	17.9	6.2	3.7
1947	100.0	19.6	17.6	21.8	14.2	18.3	5.7	2.7
1948	100.0	22.4	13.3	21.9	15.7	18.9	5.5	2.3
1949	100.0	23.4	14.2	22.7	14.0	18.7	5.1	1.9
1950	100.0	22.1	12.9	22.2	15.7	19.2	5.6	2.3
1951	100.0	20.8	11.1	21.2	19.3	18.1	5.3	4.1
1952	100.0	22.3	12.6	21.3	18.9	16.9	5.7	2.3

Sources: 23, 1951, pp. 842–44 and 1952, pp. 856–57; 22, pp. 250–51; 10, Annual Issue, 1953, pp. 6–9; cf. 19 and 21.

a. General trade.

THE NETWORK OF WORLD TRADE BEFORE AND
AFTER THE GREAT DEPRESSION

Multilateral trade in the late 1920's was conditioned by a complex system of international economic relations — the division of labor among nations and differences among them in the level of economic development, natural resources, climate, mutual indebtedness and so on. The system of multilateral trade also depended on relative freedom in the flow of goods and services in the world and, as has been mentioned repeatedly, on the convertibility of currencies. The return of world trade to multilateralism after a decade of war and postwar confusion shows in itself how solidly this system was incorporated in the fabric of the world economy. Under normal peacetime conditions, the direction of the flow of each commodity in the channels of international trade is largely determined by the physical requirements and economic facilities of various regions and each commodity follows the same route year after year.

Owing to this constancy of trade routes, the claims and liabilities arising out of merchandise trade tend to arrange themselves according to a pattern of a certain permanence. Each country is likely, year after year, to have an excess of imports from certain countries, and an excess of exports to others.[18]

This system, however, proved incompatible with the practice of currency control and import and export licensing which most trading nations accepted in the 1930's as a means of protecting domestic employment, their currency and their payment balances.

IMPORTS AND EXPORTS, BY CONTINENT,
1928 AND 1938

The depression in the early 1930's affected the United States more severely than any other country, and America suffered from economic dislocations long after recovery had been achieved in other parts of the world. As a result, from 1928 to 1938, the American share in world production and trade declined and that of Europe increased. According to the experts of the League of Nations, nonagricultural primary production in Europe increased 22 per cent from the average between 1925–29 and 1938, and in North America declined 3 per cent.[19] Similarly,

Europe's share in world imports increased from 53.9 per cent in 1928 to 55.7 per cent in 1938, while that of North America decreased from 16.3 per cent to 12.3 per cent.[20]

Apart from the general contraction of world trade in comparison with production [21] and the decline in North America's share in world imports and exports, the distribution of international trade among continents did not change appreciably between 1928 and 1938. (See Table 29.) In both years intra-European trade, including the trade between continental and noncontinental Europe, accounted for approximately 29 per cent of world imports. European imports from other parts of the world amounted to 25–27 per cent; imports to other parts of the world from Europe, to some 17 per cent; and the trade among non-European countries, to 27–29 per cent. More precisely the percentage distribution of imports was as follows: [22]

	1928	1938
World trade	100.0	100.0
Intra-European trade	29.2	29.1
Imports to Europe	24.7	26.6
Imports from Europe	17.2	17.5
Trade among non-European countries		
Intracontinental imports	11.9	11.2
Intercontinental imports	17.0	15.6

These figures, although not strictly comparable with the data given for 1913 and 1927 on the preceding pages, suggest that the decline in Europe's share in world trade was reversed in the 1930's and that its import surplus in transactions with the rest of the world went up.

IMPORTS AND EXPORTS BY GROUP OF COUNTRIES

Hilgerdt's survey, *The Network of World Trade,* which has become a classic in the literature on world trade,[23] divides the world into seventeen more or less homogeneous but not necessarily contiguous groups of countries as follows: [24]

Africa

1. North Africa (Morocco, Algeria, Tunisia, Libya and Egypt)

---

18. **6**, p. 76.
19. **7**, 1938–1939, p. 16.

20. **6**, pp. 39–40; cf. Table 29.
21. **7**, 1938–1939, p. 65.
22. See Table 29.
23. Cf. **26**. pp. 282–85; **30**, pp. 10–19.
24. **6**, pp. 11–13 and 99–101.

TABLE 29

WORLD IMPORTS: PERCENTAGE DISTRIBUTION AMONG CONTINENTS, BY PROVENANCE AND
DESTINATION, 1928 AND 1938

		Destination							
Provenance	*World*	*North America*	*Latin America* [a]	*Noncontinental Europe* [b]	*Continental Europe*	*USSR*	*Asia*	*Africa*	*Oceania*
		1928							
World	100.0	16.3	7.7	15.6	38.3	1.4	13.6	4.6	2.5
North America	19.6	4.2	2.9	3.4	5.4	0.3	2.2	0.5	0.7
Latin America	9.9	3.4	1.0	1.9	3.4	0.1	0.0	0.1	0.0
Noncontinental Europe	11.5	1.3	1.2	1.1	3.1	0.0	2.4	1.3	1.1
Continental Europe	34.9	2.8	2.3	5.5	19.5	0.5	2.0	2.0	0.3
USSR	1.4	0.0	0.0	0.3	0.8	. . .	0.3	0.0	0.0
Asia	15.9	3.9	0.2	1.4	3.1	0.3	6.3	0.4	0.3
Africa	4.0	0.3	0.0	0.9	2.3	0.1	0.1	0.3	0.0
Oceania	2.7	0.3	0.0	1.1	0.8	0.1	0.3	0.0	0.1
		1938							
World	100.0	12.3	7.8	17.8	37.9	1.1	13.7	6.3	3.1
North America	18.3	3.2	2.7	3.9	4.1	0.4	2.6	0.7	0.7
Latin America	9.4	2.5	1.4	1.9	3.4	0.0	0.1	0.1	0.0
Noncontinental Europe	11.0	1.0	0.9	0.8	3.3	0.2	1.8	1.6	1.4
Continental Europe	35.6	2.3	2.5	5.3	19.7	0.3	2.4	2.8	0.3
USSR	1.1	0.1	0.0	0.3	0.6	. . .	0.1	0.0	0.0
Asia	15.9	2.7	0.3	2.2	3.1	0.2	6.2	0.7	0.5
Africa	5.1	0.3	0.0	1.2	3.0	0.0	0.2	0.4	0.0
Oceania	3.6	0.2	0.0	2.2	0.7	0.0	0.3	0.0	0.2

Source: **6**, pp. 39–40.

a. Includes Middle and South America.

b. Includes the United Kingdom, Ireland, Iceland and some minor islands.

2. South Africa (South West Africa, Northern and Southern Rhodesia, Nyasaland and the Union of South Africa)
3. Other African countries

North America

4. Northern North America (Canada, Newfoundland, Greenland)
5. The United States

Latin America

6. Mineral-producing countries (Mexico, Venezuela, Curaçao, the Guianas, Ecuador, Peru, Bolivia and Chile)
7. Tropical agricultural countries (Central American republics, Colombia, Brazil, the West Indies)

8. Nontropical agricultural countries (Argentina, Paraguay and Uruguay)

Asia

9. India, Burma, Ceylon
10. Southeast Asia (Thailand, Indochina, Malaya, the Philippines, Indonesia)
11. Japan, Korea, Formosa [Taiwan]
12. China, Manchuria and the rest of continental Asia

13. *USSR*

Europe

14. Continental Europe: industrial countries (France, Belgium–Luxembourg, the Netherlands, Sweden, Germany, Czechoslovakia, Switzerland, Austria, Italy)
15. Continental Europe: other countries

TABLE 30

WORLD IMPORTS: DISTRIBUTION AMONG SEVENTEEN GROUPS OF COUNTRIES, BY PROVENANCE AND DESTINATION, 1928 AND 1938 [a]

(Millions of U.S. Dollars)

Prove-nance	World	Imports to Group [b] of Countries																
		1	2	3	4	5	6	7	8	9	10	11	12	13	14	15	16	17
								1928										
World	$35,480	$660	$450	$510	$1,380	$4,410	$670	$1,130	$920	$1,060	$1,250	$1,070	$1,460	$490	$10,560	$3,020	$5,520	$920
1	610	20	—	10	—	40	—	—	—	—	—	10	10	20	300	50	80	10
2	310	—	30	10	—	30	—	—	—	—	10	—	—	10	140	—	80	10
3	500	—	10	30	—	60	—	—	—	10	—	—	10	—	240	20	120	—
4	1,380	—	10	10	20	560	10	40	10	10	10	40	20	10	240	60	290	40
5	5,600	30	70	40	930	—	270	480	220	60	160	300	180	90	1,310	340	910	210
6	960	10	—	—	10	380	110	30	40	—	—	10	—	10	180	30	150	—
7	1,240	10	—	—	30	660	10	10	40	—	—	—	—	10	300	40	130	—
8	1,370	—	—	—	10	120	10	60	30	—	—	—	—	20	640	70	410	—
9	1,590	10	20	30	20	220	10	20	30	70	80	130	100	20	420	60	300	50
10	1,680	10	10	—	10	500	—	—	—	100	390	90	150	20	260	50	60	40
11	1,000	10	10	10	10	420	10	10	10	60	70	—	270	10	50	—	30	20
12	1,370	20	—	20	10	200	—	10	—	50	110	220	330	70	200	20	100	10
13	430	10	—	—	—	20	—	—	—	10	—	10	50	—	170	70	90	—
14	9,910	390	70	170	90	730	150	250	320	190	250	110	160	160	3,900	1,580	1,300	90
15	2,440	50	10	10	10	150	10	40	40	10	—	10	20	30	1,160	280	600	10
16	4,060	80	200	170	210	250	80	180	180	470	150	80	150	10	720	340	400	390
17	1,030	10	10	—	20	70	—	—	—	20	20	60	10	20	330	10	400	50
								1938										
World	24,580	500	580	490	820	2,190	670	730	520	600	860	800	1,100	270	7,140	2,170	4,370	770
1	500	10	—	10	—	10	—	—	—	10	—	10	10	—	320	30	90	—
2	280	—	30	10	—	30	—	—	—	—	—	—	—	—	110	10	90	—
3	480	10	10	20	—	30	—	—	—	20	—	—	10	—	260	20	100	—
4	990	—	20	—	10	290	10	20	10	—	10	30	10	10	110	20	380	60
5	3,490	20	100	30	490	—	240	290	90	50	150	270	110	80	700	190	570	110
6	840	10	—	10	20	170	160	20	40	—	—	10	—	—	230	20	150	—
7	850	10	—	—	30	340	20	10	30	—	—	10	—	—	250	30	120	—
8	640	—	—	—	—	50	20	40	10	—	—	10	—	—	270	30	210	—
9	940	10	10	20	20	90	—	10	20	30	50	60	50	10	190	30	300	30
10	1,210	20	10	10	20	310	—	—	—	40	230	70	60	10	270	20	80	50
11	890	10	20	30	—	140	10	10	20	70	70	—	380	—	40	10	40	40
12	870	20	10	10	10	70	—	—	—	30	50	190	120	40	190	10	110	10
13	270	—	—	—	—	30	—	—	—	—	—	—	20	—	100	40	80	—
14	6,560	290	110	220	50	370	160	210	180	110	180	80	160	60	2,400	1,150	760	70
15	2,180	40	10	20	10	130	10	20	20	10	10	10	30	10	1,080	220	530	10
16	2,700	50	250	100	140	110	40	100	100	220	90	20	100	30	480	320	220	230
17	890	—	—	—	20	20	—	—	—	10	20	30	20	10	140	20	540	60

Source: **6**, pp. 44–48.

a. Totals adjusted to represent "frontier values"; provenance adjusted to show origin of imports; figures rounded to nearest $10 million.

b. The 17 groups of countries listed in this table are Hilgerdt's 17 groups (see p. 80).

16. Noncontinental Europe (the United Kingdom, Ireland, Iceland)

17. *Oceania*

The imports of each of these groups of countries from each other group as well as the imports within each group in 1928 and 1938 are shown in Table 30.[25]

The flow of goods among the seventeen groups of countries reveals that most of them are complementary to Europe in their trade. Hilgerdt declares:

Historically, their trade has developed as a result of the inflow of European capital and their exchange of foodstuffs and raw materials against European manufactured products. Without this exchange, the rapid industrial development in Europe and the increase in Europe's population over the last few generations would not have been possible. With the growth of industrial centers outside Europe, particularly in the United States, and the steady integration of economic activities in different continents, the pattern of world trade became more complicated — it

25. Exports are distributed similarly by provenance and destination with only the difference that the values of exports in transactions between any two areas are usually 5–10 per cent less than the values of the imports flowing between them.

was no longer to the same extent as previously determined by the exchange of goods between Europe and other continents. Still this exchange even during the 'twenties and 'thirties remained a central factor in the mechanism tending to render the world an economic unit.[26]

Exhaustive analysis of the trade among these groups of countries is outside the scope of this study. Many cross tabulations of international trade by provenance and destination have been prepared by the League of Nations, the UN and other agencies. Some of these are voluminous,[27] while others attempt to simplify the picture by grouping countries in geographical areas or on the basis of other characteristics.[28] Hilgerdt's tabulation has an advantage in that it permits further condensation and, in the new form, shows the operation of international trade in a world market with convertible currencies as a continuous flow of goods.

THE MAIN PARTNERS IN MULTILATERAL TRADE

The core of the problem of world trade today is in multilateral operations, that is, trade between countries which cannot balance their accounts without clearing them through other parties. Is there some meaningful relationship between the direction of the trade balances of different countries and areas and their physical and economic characteristics?

Hilgerdt has offered an ingenious answer to this question by combining the seventeen areas listed earlier in six large groups as follows:[29]

A. Tropics: regions 3, 6, 7, 9 and 10 (Central Africa; all Latin America, excluding Argentina, Paraguay and Uruguay; India, Burma, Ceylon; and southeastern Asia)

B. United States: region 5

C. Other regions of recent settlement: regions 2, 4, 8 and 17 (South Africa; Canada, Newfoundland and Greenland; Argentina, Paraguay and Uruguay; and Oceania)

D. Continental Europe: regions 14 and 15

E. Noncontinental Europe: region 16

F. All other areas: regions 1, 11, 12 and 13 (North Africa, USSR and all Asia excluding India, Burma, Ceylon and tropical southeastern areas)

Group F appears tremendous on the conventional world map. (See Figure 20,A.) It represents, indeed, one third of the land surface of the globe and nearly 40 per cent of the population. Its ties with the world market are comparatively slight, however. It controlled approximately 10 per cent of world trade in 1928 and 9 per cent in 1938. (Cf. Figure 20,B.) The other five groups, which represent two thirds of the land surface and 60 per cent of the population, controlled 90 per cent or more of world trade. They can be regarded as the five main partners in world multilateral trade, each playing a definite role with the other.

THE ROUTE OF WORLD MULTILATERAL TRADE

Trade among the five big groups followed a circular route. When the five are arranged in a circle, so that, moving clockwise, one passes from A to B, from B to C and so on, and returning ultimately from E to A, it appears that in 1928 each group had an export balance with each following group and an import balance with each preceding group. In 1938, the system worked less smoothly. (See Table 31.)

The balances of trade between each two groups — for example, groups A and B — can be represented either as the surplus of exports from A to B over imports from B to A (the export balance of A) or as the surplus of imports from A to B over exports from B to A (the import balance of B). The two balances usually are different. In 1928, for example, the "tropics" exported merchandise valued at $1,650 million to the United States and imported goods valued at $1,010 million from the United States, thus having an export balance of +$640 million. At the same time the United States, in trading with the "tropics," had imports of $1,820 million and exports of $870 million, and an import balance of −$950 million. In the circular flow of merchandise, the import balance usually is larger than the export one.

Hilgerdt shows the system of multilateral trade in 1928 and 1938 by diagrams indicating the orientation and amount of the trade balances be-

---

26. **6**, p. 67.

27. See, for example, **3**, 1936, pp. 304–47 for 1929, 1932 and 1934–36 and **8**, pp. 112–71 for 1928, 1935 and 1938.

28. See **15**, 1949–1950, table following p. 210. Cf. **10**, various issues.

29. No particular significance is attached to the names of the six groups. The "tropics" group includes Chile, a country located in the temperate zone. The "regions of recent settlement" might be better described as the "regions of young capitalism."

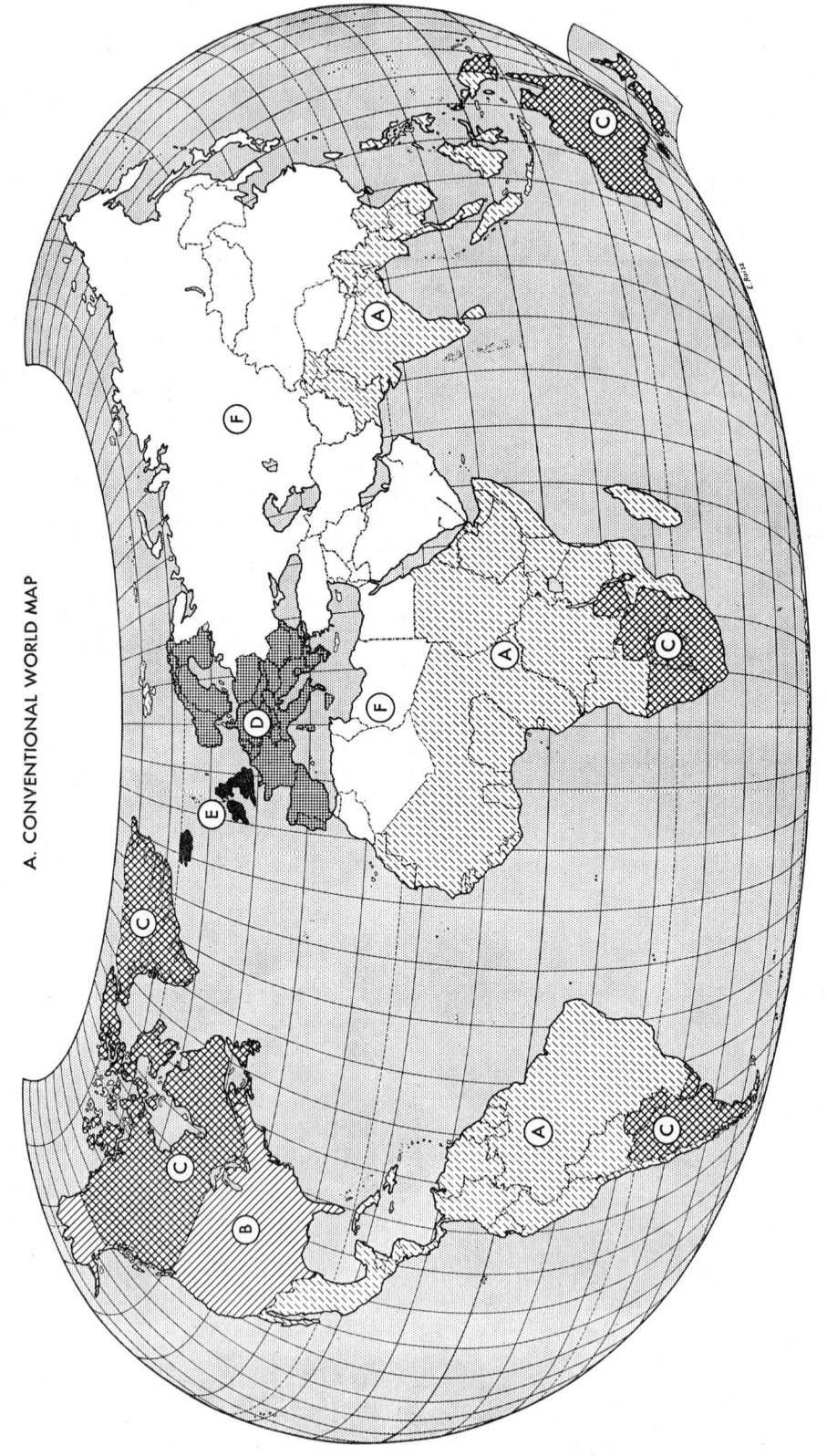

A. CONVENTIONAL WORLD MAP

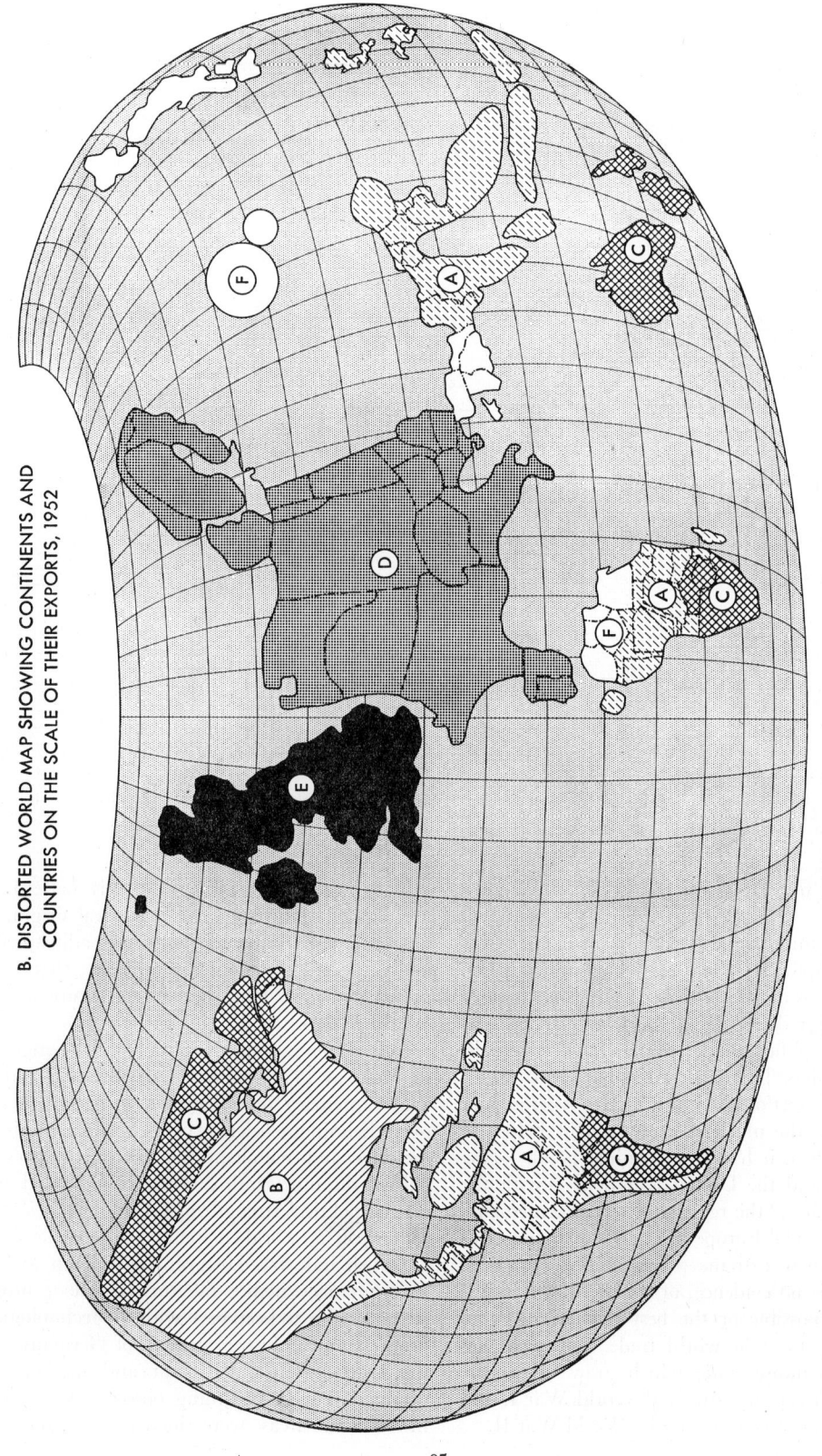

B. DISTORTED WORLD MAP SHOWING CONTINENTS AND
COUNTRIES ON THE SCALE OF THEIR EXPORTS, 1952

FIGURE 20. SIX REGIONS OF WORLD TRADE (AFTER FOLKE HILGERDT)

The six regions shown in this chart are as follows: A. Tropics; B. United States; C. Regions of recent settlement; D. Continental Europe; E. Noncontinental Europe; F. Rest of the world.

TABLE 31

IMPORTS, EXPORTS AND TRADE BALANCES:[a] SIX GROUPS OF COUNTRIES, 1928 AND 1938

(*Millions of U.S. Dollars*)

A. Tropics. B. United States. C. Regions of Recent Settlement. D. Continental Europe.
E. Noncontinental Europe. F. Rest of the World.

Prove-nance	1928 World	A	B	C	D	E	F	1938 World	A	B	C	D	E	F
					Imports									
World	$35,480	$4,620	$4,410	$3,670	$13,580	$5,520	$3,680	$24,580	$3,350	$2,190	$2,690	$9,310	$4,370	$2,670
A	5,970	900	1,820	310	1,600	760	580	4,320	650	940	290	1,320	750	370
B	5,600	1,010	—	1,430	1,650	910	600	3,490	760	—	790	890	570	480
C	4,090	210	780	240	1,490	1,180	190	2,800	140	390	220	710	1,220	120
D	12,350	1,080	880	640	6,920	1,900	930	8,740	950	500	460	4,850	1,290	690
E	4,060	1,050	250	980	1,060	400	320	2,700	550	110	820	800	220	200
F	3,410	370	680	70	860	370	1,060	2,530	300	250	110	740	320	810
					Exports									
World	32,610	5,360	5,160	3,810	11,390	3,750	3,140	21,920	3,610	3,110	2,440	8,060	2,410	2,290
A	4,030	800	870	180	910	950	320	2,990	660	660	120	790	480	280
B	3,950	1,650	—	740	760	230	570	1,970	830	—	370	450	100	220
C	3,310	240	1,380	220	530	890	50	2,290	180	730	200	380	730	70
D	12,710	1,420	1,500	1,350	6,630	1,000	810	8,300	1,040	750	580	4,600	710	620
E	5,210	750	860	1,150	1,730	390	330	3,940	610	550	1,090	1,190	210	290
F	3,400	500	550	170	830	290	1,060	2,430	290	420	80	650	180	810
					Balance									
World	-2,870	+740	+750	+140	-2,190	-1,770	-540	-2,660	+260	+920	-250	-1,250	-1,960	-380
A	-1,940	-100	-950	-130	-690	+190	-260	-1,330	+10	-280	-170	-530	-270	-90
B	-1,650	+640	—	-690	-890	-680	-30	-1,520	+70	—	-420	-440	-470	-260
C	-780	+30	+600	-20	-960	-290	-140	-510	+40	+340	-20	-330	-490	-50
D	+360	+340	+620	+710	-290	-900	-120	-440	+90	+250	+120	-250	-580	-70
E	+1,150	-300	+610	+170	+670	-10	+10	+1,240	+60	+440	+270	+390	-10	+90
F	-10	+130	-130	+100	-30	-80	—	-100	-10	+170	-30	-90	-140	—

Source: **6**, pp. 77 and 90.

a. Adjusted "frontier values," rounded to the nearest $10 million. Figures in frames represent imports, exports and net balances in international trade within each group. The negative balance represents essentially the cost of transportation and differences in valuation, as does also the difference between total world imports and exports.

tween the five groups of countries. (See Figure 17.)

Actual multilateral trade is, of course, far more complicated than this diagram suggests. Transactions of some 200 areas with one another cannot be reduced to 10 principal routes, but only a simplified model can reveal a system in the countless bilateral, triangular and multilateral transactions. As the system operated at the end of the nineteenth century, in 1913 and even in 1928, it had two terminal points — the "tropics" and the United Kingdom — with the United States, "the regions of recent settlement" and continental Europe in intermediate positions between these extreme points.

There is no evidence, of course, that this was the only possible or the best theoretically conceivable pattern of world trade. But such was the merchandise trade which grew up in the nineteenth century, survived World War I, and was put out of commission by World War II.

The force and weakness of this pattern of multilateral trade lay in its historical origin. It had emerged from a long chain of adjustments and reflected economic conditions that had ceased to exist long before the outbreak of World War I.

Indeed, the supremacy of the United Kingdom in trade in 1928 was based on Britain's industrial supremacy in times past. It rested on the overwhelming efficiency of British coal mines, factories and merchant marine in the second half of the nineteenth century. It depended also on the political strength of Great Britain as the center of a world-encircling colonial empire.

British industry, however, had begun to lose its supremacy before the turn of the century. It was unable to keep pace with the technological progress and industrial growth of Germany and the United States. Its plant and methods of production were becoming obsolete. Difficulties in colonial areas were increasing with each decade. Great Britain had come to a standstill and was losing ground in comparison with more dynamic world powers, but its vast assets abroad made it possible to maintain the splendor of former times — a huge import balance in transactions with the rest of the world and a level of living higher than was indicated by its current productive capacity.

The change in the position of Great Britain in the world was bound to destroy the customary flow of world trade sooner or later.

DETERIORATION OF THE MULTILATERAL TRADE SYSTEM

The experts of the League of Nations describe the changes in the pattern of world trade in the 1930's as a deterioration of the system of multilateral trade. In *The Network of World Trade,* Hilgerdt summarizes the events as follows:

The system of trade balances described above deteriorated rapidly during the early 'thirties and did not recover appreciably during the general improvement of business conditions from the middle of the decade.

In 1928, noncontinental Europe had a net export of $190 million to the tropics, but in 1938 a net import of $270 million. This reorientation of balances had two chief causes. First, new capital exports of the United Kingdom to the tropics fell to a fraction of what they had been in 1928 and may even have been exceeded by receipts on account of amortization and other capital imports from the same region. Secondly, a portion of the interest and dividend payments which in 1928 had been financed by exports to other countries, especially those in Europe, were in 1938 performed through net exports to the United Kingdom.

The United States net imports from the tropics fell from $950 million in 1928 to $280 million in 1938. This decline . . . was due largely to price movements and to the fact that after the 1936–37 boom the United States demand for industrial raw materials and other primary goods fell off temporarily while exports to tropical countries were maintained on a high level. For similar reasons the United States export surplus to the regions of recent settlement was higher than might have been expected.

The last-mentioned regions, indebted largely to the United Kingdom, increased their export balance to that country from $170 million in 1928 to $270 million in 1938. This implied a short-circuiting of transfer, affecting particularly trade with continental Europe, export surplus to which fell from $710 to $120 million.

Similarly, the short-circuiting of payments to noncontinental Europe from the tropics was reflected in

a decline from $340 to $90 million in the export surplus of that group to continental Europe. The corresponding import surplus of continental Europe from the tropics, however, declined only from $690 to $530 million.

The reduction in continental Europe's net imports from various oversea regions is naturally connected with the simultaneous decline in its net exports to noncontinental Europe from $670 to $390 million.

We may characterize the change that occurred as a disintegration of world trade: while previously international settlement took place within a world-wide network of multilateral transactions, there was in the 'thirties a tendency to achieve settlement either in bilateral exchange between two countries, or within the limited range of countries attached to each other by political or other ties.[30]

These explanations do not minimize the significance of the more general historical trend. The economic rise of other areas and Europe's political and economic difficulties undermined the foundations of the multilateral system of world trade that was primarily a business of Western European countries headed by Great Britain before World War I.

RECENT DEVELOPMENTS

The lack of economic balance in the world following World War II was reflected in contraction of international trade and disequilibrium in the foreign transactions of many countries.[31] While United States exports increased tremendously, exports from the Eastern Hemisphere lagged behind imports. For the whole world except the United States, the quantum of exports in 1946 was 57 (1938 = 100).[32]

Because of the urgent demand for foodstuffs, industrial raw materials, fuel and capital goods in countries devastated by the war, imports from the United States, Canada, Argentina, Cuba, Brazil, Australia and New Zealand were readily absorbed by the world market, although the importing areas had little to offer in exchange.

Thus the early period of postwar recovery was marked by accumulation of huge trade deficits in many countries, especially in Europe. Increase in production in deficit areas seemed to promise the restoration of equilibrium in their trade in a not too remote future. It seemed that these areas, after having satisfied their most urgent needs and resumed full-scale production, would be able

30. **6,** pp. 89–91.
31. **11,** p. 12.
32. **15,** 1948, p. 47.

to cut their imports, increase exports and continue foreign trade on a pay-as-you-go basis. New difficulties arose, however, from changes in the financial position of various countries and the disorganization of international currencies.

In the past, Europe had covered its import balance in the trade with the New World partly by exports to the tropics and partly by income from investments abroad, shipping and other services.[33] War and disintegration of colonial empires seriously jeopardized these sources of income. Commercial loans could not be obtained because of the collapse of the system of international credit. The outlook for restoration of confidence and private investment in commercial and industrial operations abroad was gloomy. Temporarily, the trade deficits were covered by shipments of gold and by government credits, but this method of financing imports in 1946–47 resulted in a rapid decline in Europe's remaining gold and dollar resources.[34]

Furthermore, the deficit countries found it extremely difficult to increase their exports. The main obstacle was not their limited production capacity or shortage of raw materials but the apparent absence of outlets. To increase their exports, the deficit countries had to find other nations that were able and willing to buy their goods at the price demanded and in the currency the deficit countries needed to pay for their imports. The question of price was probably even more important than that of currency. The deficit countries could not afford to sell their produce below their production cost converted into international currency. Where production cost was high and national currency overrated, they saw themselves priced out of the world market. On the other hand, the deficit in the trade balance, combined with a high, artificially maintained exchange rate, was the main source of inconvertibility of currencies of deficit countries. The ultimate cause of the inconvertibility of weak currencies was the temporary disorganization of the respective economies.

THE PROBLEM OF CURRENCY

Disorganization both of currencies and international trade after World War II was due to deep economic dislocations, and could be over-

come only by readjustments in production and consumption.

In the short run, however, deficit countries felt that they did not have enough dollars and could not get them by selling their products at their price. For them, the serious difficulties they suffered in 1946–47 appeared to result from a bad monetary situation inherited from the 1930's and only aggravated by World War II and its aftermath.[35]

The situation of the United Kingdom at the beginning of 1947 was particularly difficult. At that time the British had an export balance with the Eastern Hemisphere but could not use it to meet their deficit with the Western Hemisphere, partly because many countries of the Eastern Hemisphere had no gold or dollars with which to pay the British and partly because British surpluses in trade with other countries (for example, India) were mortgaged for payment of debts to these countries.[36] The simplest solution would have been to increase exports to the United States and other dollar countries, but Great Britain had little merchandise to offer them at competitive prices. Since a sound economic solution of the problem seemed impossible, the British felt that the only thing they could do was to protect their balance of payment and dwindling gold reserve by restrictive measures, as in the 1930's.

Other European countries were in a similar situation. Most of them had restricted foreign trade and regulated exchange rates in the 1930's in the hope of restoring and maintaining their balance of foreign transactions. World War II started before this aim was achieved. During the war, the existing controls were tightened and new restrictions and regulations were introduced, and few countries were able to repeal or relax these measures after the war.

The task of rebuilding multilateral trade in a world without universal currency was complicated by the significant change in the trade position of the United States, the principal country able to supply the rest of the world with hard currency. Before the war, the United States had an import balance with many tropical areas, and the latter used their dollar balances to pay for merchandise imported from European countries, which, in turn, transferred dollars earned in the tropics to the United States in payment for sur-

---

33. See **4**, *passim.*
34. **11**, p. 16.

35. **11**, p. 18.
36. **25**, p. 19.

plus imports. Since the war, the flow has been reversed. An export balance has developed in the trade of the United States with many countries which supply it and Europe with vital raw materials. Selling their products to Europe, these countries required either dollars or gold in payment.[37]

On July 15, 1947, in an attempt to break the vicious circle and restore the free flow of goods and capital in the world, the United Kingdom suspended most restrictions on exchange of sterling against other currencies, but five weeks later it was compelled to introduce a series of regulations to curtail domestic consumption, imports and other transactions involving currency outlays.[38] Several other countries were forced to take similar steps. The shift in the monetary policy of the United Kingdom and other countries from liberalization to stricter controls marked the end of the premature optimism of the early postwar period.[39] Since that time, the foreign transactions of many countries have been held in precarious balance by means of governmental aid and restrictions on trade and payments. In some countries lack of confidence in the domestic currency has led to the private hoarding of gold and dollars. A twofold shift has developed in the geographical distribution of foreign trade: from hard-currency countries to soft-currency countries as sources of supply; from soft-currency to hard-currency areas for exports.

By 1948 the problem of hard and soft currencies had boiled down to "dollar shortage." This concept has been widely used in discussions of the current problems of world economics, especially since the inauguration of the European Recovery Program (Marshall Plan) and related programs. It may seem self-explanatory but is elusive and even misleading when applied indiscriminately to every situation in which the dollar transactions of a country are out of balance.[40]

The real meaning of the dollar shortage in Europe and other areas was that, because of inconvertibility of currencies, arbitrarily established exchange rates, disorganization of multilateral trade, contraction of triangular transactions, overexpansion of exports from the United States and high import duties preventing large-scale imports to the United States, Europe was unable to cover its imports from that country with exports, with dollars or with gold.

Ultimately, however, this imbalance in international trade was due to imbalance in production and consumption in the areas complaining of dollar shortage. These areas would have suffered no dollar shortage if they had had sufficient produce for export to pay for all their desired imports from countries with convertible currencies. In this sense, the "dollar shortage" in Europe in 1947–50 was a production shortage.[41]

Various countries have tried to ease their dollar shortage by controls over trade and exchange, devaluation of currency, subsidies to production for export, restriction of consumption, bilateral agreements and similar measures. At the same time the United States has made an effort to release the pressure of dollar shortage on the world economy without prejudice to its protectionist policy. From the point of view of world trade, the policy of foreign aid inaugurated by the United States can be described as balancing part of the United States exports by grants and credits to foreign governments. From the point of view of production and national income, it has amounted to a straight transfer to other nations of part of the real income produced in the United States. From a broad political point of view, this action has been justified as the only possible way to import capital equipment and raw materials into European deficit countries to enable them to increase the productivity of labor, improve the efficiency of their economy and thus overcome their dollar shortage.

The total amount of United States foreign aid in the period from the end of the war through the fiscal year 1952–53 is estimated at $41 billion net.[42] This amount, however, includes programs for military aid, civilian supply and surplus property and similar operations, which have not directly affected the balance of payments of the countries to which the aid was extended. Excluding such operations, the United States exports

---

37. **15,** 1948, pp. 50ff.
38. **11,** p. 19.
39. **15,** 1948, p. 64.
40. F. Machlup distinguishes dollar shortages in relation to three types of balance: market balance, which reflects the relation between supply and demand; program balance, which is nothing but a tentative description of what the programing agency or individual student considers desirable; and accounting balance, which is a very complex and vague term. (See **29.**)

---

41. See Henry Chalmers in **18,** February 18, 1948.
42. After deduction of returns, reverse grants and principal collected on credit. See Table 87 in Chapter 5. To this amount approximately $5 billion was added in the fiscal year 1953–54.

covered by grants (i.e., taxpayers' money) and credits may have totaled $33 billion from 1945 to the middle of 1954. This was a major item in the settlement of international accounts after the end of the war, when European countries were unable to pay for their imports with their own produce. Essentially, this unilateral operation replaced the movement of capital which helped to balance international payments in the late 1920's, when multilateral trade functioned on an almost worldwide scale and practically all currencies were convertible.[43]

The acute phase of the postwar disequilibrium in world trade was over by the end of 1950. In 1951, new difficulties developed in Europe, especially in the United Kingdom, the Netherlands, Denmark, Norway and Italy, largely as a result of the general rise of prices for raw materials imported from overseas.[44] There was nothing unusual in this deterioration of trade conditions for one part of the world, but the lack of reserves, the weakness of the international credit structure and the political tensions made the situation more alarming than it would have been in normal circumstances. By the end of 1951, the imbalances had been ironed out, partly as a result of the rearmament program in the United States, and partly at the cost of restrictive measures taken by many countries against imports from dollar areas.

In 1953–54 the United States foreign aid program was continued more as a part of international military and economic cooperation than as a measure for insuring balances of trade and maintaining the currencies of European nations.

UNDERDEVELOPED AREAS

The underdeveloped countries, mainly in the tropical zones of South America, Africa and Asia, were an important link in the circular flow of multilateral trade in the last decade of the nineteenth century and the first three decades of the twentieth. Most of them had an export balance with the United States and the rest of the Western Hemisphere and an import balance with Europe.

During World War II the clash among the great powers gave the underdeveloped areas an opportunity to sell their products at high prices, to liquidate external debts and to accumulate

sizable financial assets.[45] The grip of foreign capital over these areas was weakened, their drive for economic independence gained momentum, and the position of Middle and South America, Asia and Africa in world trade changed radically. Excluding Argentina, Japan and the Union of South Africa (because of the comparatively high level of their economic development), and China (because of the lack of information for recent years), the "underdeveloped" areas in both hemispheres accounted for 22.4 per cent of world exports in 1938 and 27.6 per cent in 1952. They absorbed 19.7 per cent of world imports before the war and 28.8 per cent in 1952. (See Table 32.)

The expansion of the foreign trade of this group of countries is comparable only to the spectacular gains of the United States and Canada, as shown by the following figures on imports and exports (in millions of dollars):[46]

	1938	1950	1951	1952
Exports				
United States	$3,102	$10,283	$15,041	$15,164
Canada and New-foundland	918	3,095	4,042	4,729
Underdeveloped areas [a]	4,636	17,434	22,038	20,290
Imports				
United States	2,465	9,624	11,946	11,632
Canada	794	3,202	4,195	4,458
Underdeveloped areas [a]	4,561	15,685	21,928	22,863

a. As shown in Table 32.

The improvement in the position of underdeveloped areas has enabled some of them to carry on a trade policy in line with their aspirations for a greater degree of economic self-sufficiency. During the war and early postwar years, their orientation was toward the United States. In 1947 the United States predominated in the imports and exports of most Latin American nations and had made inroads into African and Asiatic markets.[47] It accounted for more than 70 per cent of the imports of Mexico, Guatemala, El Salvador, Honduras, Costa Rica, Nicaragua, Panama, Cuba, Haiti and Venezuela; for more

---

43. **15**, 1948, p. 49.
44. **13**, 1951, pp. 68–70.

45. **15**, 1948, p. 50; **14**, 1948, pp. 223–24.
46. **17**, June 1952. These figures have been adjusted by the International Monetary Fund, on the basis of f.o.b. values for exports and c.i.f. values for imports. They differ slightly from the official data of the respective countries and from data compiled by the UN.
47. **18**, 1949, pp. 264ff.

TABLE 32

EXPORTS AND IMPORTS IN UNDERDEVELOPED AREAS, 1938 AND 1950–52

Exporting or Importing Region	Exports (f.o.b.)				Imports (c.i.f.)			
	1938	1950	1951	1952 [a]	1938	1950	1951	1952 [a]
Millions of U.S. Dollars								
World	$20,486	$56,453	$76,540	$73,479	$23,015	$59,113	$81,357	$79,543
Middle America	598	2,291	2,807	2,807	690	2,530	3,284	3,321
South America [b]	903	3,977	4,834	5,142	794	2,890	4,302	4,500
Middle East [c]	481	2,558	2,661	2,575	693	2,185	2,622	2,793
Far East [d]	1,974	5,924	8,302	6,242	1,714	5,223	7,809	7,518
Africa [e]	680	2,684	3,434	3,524	670	2,857	3,911	4,331
Percentage of World Total								
World	100.0	100.0	100.0	100.0	100.0	100.0	100.0	100.0
Middle America	2.9	4.1	3.7	3.8	3.0	4.3	4.0	4.2
South America [b]	4.4	7.0	6.3	7.0	3.4	4.9	5.3	6.2
Middle East [b]	2.3	4.5	3.5	3.5	3.0	3.7	3.2	3.5
Far East [d]	9.6	10.5	10.8	8.5	7.4	8.8	9.6	9.5
Africa [e]	3.2	4.8	4.5	4.8	2.9	4.8	4.8	5.4
Total	22.4	30.9	28.8	27.6	19.7	26.5	26.9	28.8

Source: **17**, May 1953, pp. 16–20.

a. Partly preliminary figures.
b. Excludes Argentina.
c. Cyprus, Lebanon, Israel, Syria, Iraq, Iran, Egypt, Sudan, Ethiopia and some other areas.

d. Excludes China and Japan.
e. Excludes Union of South Africa, Egypt, Sudan and Ethiopia.

than 50 per cent of those of Brazil, 45 per cent of Argentina, and more than 30 per cent of those of Bolivia, Chile and Uruguay.[48] Since 1948–49 Latin American countries have used import licenses as a means of reducing dollar shortages, restoring an active trade balance with the United States and resuming large-scale trade with Europe.[49]

Many Asiatic countries — India, Pakistan, Burma, Ceylon and Malaya, among others — adopted a similar policy in 1949, when they decided to join the United Kingdom in devaluating their currencies. One of the purposes of this measure was, indeed, to curtail imports and encourage exports in trade with the United States and thus assure an active dollar balance. Canada, declining membership in the sterling group, strengthened its ties with the dollar area.

FOREIGN TRADE OF PRINCIPAL CURRENCY AREAS

Recent developments have made the conventional classification of countries by continent less significant for many purposes than a grouping by currency system. Combination of the two classifications — continent and currency — has been widely used by the UN and the International Monetary Fund in recent publications.[50]

In the UN's publications, the direction of world foreign trade is described in terms of the distribution of exports by provenance and destination among fourteen areas consolidated into six large groups: [51]

A. Sterling area
 1. United Kingdom
 2. Ireland and Iceland
 3. Australia, New Zealand and Union of South Africa
 4. Other areas: India, Pakistan and Ceylon; Hong Kong, Malaya and Singapore; Iraq and Burma; Jamaica, Trinidad and Tobago; other British possessions and trust territories in all parts of the world.

48. **14**, 1948, p. 214; **18**, 1949, pp. 268–420.
49. **18**, 1949, *passim.*

50. See **10, 15, 17**.
51. **15**, 1949–1950, table following p. 210.

B. Dollar area
   5. United States
   6. Canada
   7. Other areas: Mexico and the rest of Middle America, excluding dependencies of European powers in the Caribbean; Netherlands Antilles; Colombia, Venezuela, Ecuador and Bolivia; Philippines

C. Latin American nondollar countries
   8. Brazil, Paraguay, Chile, Uruguay, Peru and Argentina

D. Continental countries of the OEEC (Organisation for European Economic Cooperation)
   9. France, the Netherlands, Denmark, Sweden, Norway and Italy
   10. Belgium-Luxembourg, Switzerland, Portugal
   11. Western Germany
   12. Austria, Greece and Turkey

E. Eastern Europe
   13. Finland, Poland, Czechoslovakia, Hungary, Yugoslavia, Romania, Bulgaria, Albania and the USSR

F. Rest of the world
   14. Spain, China, Japan, Indonesia and all other areas of Asia, Africa and Oceania not listed above

A look at the world map reveals the haphazard character of this classification. The sterling area is essentially the British Commonwealth minus Canada and plus Ireland, Iceland, Burma and Iraq. The area of continental OEEC countries is determined by participation in the Marshall Plan organization. "Eastern Europe" includes the USSR and its European satellites and Finland. "Rest of the world" comprises, along with underdeveloped areas of Africa, Asia and Oceania, such countries as Eastern Germany, Japan and Spain. (See Figure 21.) In general, the classification seems to be based on primarily economic characteristics in the Western Hemisphere and on political orientation in the Eastern Hemisphere.

In the opinion of the experts of the UN this classification, bewildering at first sight, fits the present structure of world trade better than the geographical classification or the Hilgerdt model.

The distribution of world exports among the "currency areas" in 1938 and 1949 reveals sig-

nificant changes in the pattern of world trade:

1. There has been a shift toward a more extensive exchange of merchandise within the sterling and dollar areas (an increase from 11.3 per cent of world exports in 1938 to 14.1 per cent in 1949 in the former, and from 8.3 to 14.9 per cent in the latter).

2. Excluding these intraregional transactions, exports from and to these areas have changed as follows in terms of a percentage of total world exports: [52]

	1938	1949
Exports from sterling area	11.5	11.5
Exports to sterling area	18.0	14.9
Balance	−6.5	−3.4
Exports from dollar area	14.4	17.4
Exports to dollar area	7.4	7.5
Balance	+7.0	+9.9

The general direction of the trade of both areas has remained the same as before the war — an import balance in the sterling area and an export balance in the dollar area — but the passive balance of the sterling area, in terms of a percentage of world exports, has been almost halved, while the positive balance of the dollar area, measured in the same way, has increased by more than 40 per cent.

3. The direction of the balance between the two areas has remained unchanged, but the surplus of exports from dollar countries to the sterling area over the exports flowing in the opposite direction has declined from 3.8 per cent of world exports to 2.7 per cent.

4. Most striking have been the changes in the position of continental Western Europe (continental OEEC countries in Table 33). Its percentage share in total world exports has changed as follows: [53]

	1938	1949
Exports within the OEEC area	13.2	9.1
Exports from the OEEC area	16.9	11.8
Exports to the OEEC area	18.0	17.5
Balance	−1.1	−5.7

Continental Western Europe absorbed about the same percentage of world exports in 1949 as in 1938 but its exports declined so that its import balance increased out of proportion to its

52. Table 33.
53. This area includes Turkey but not Spain and Finland.

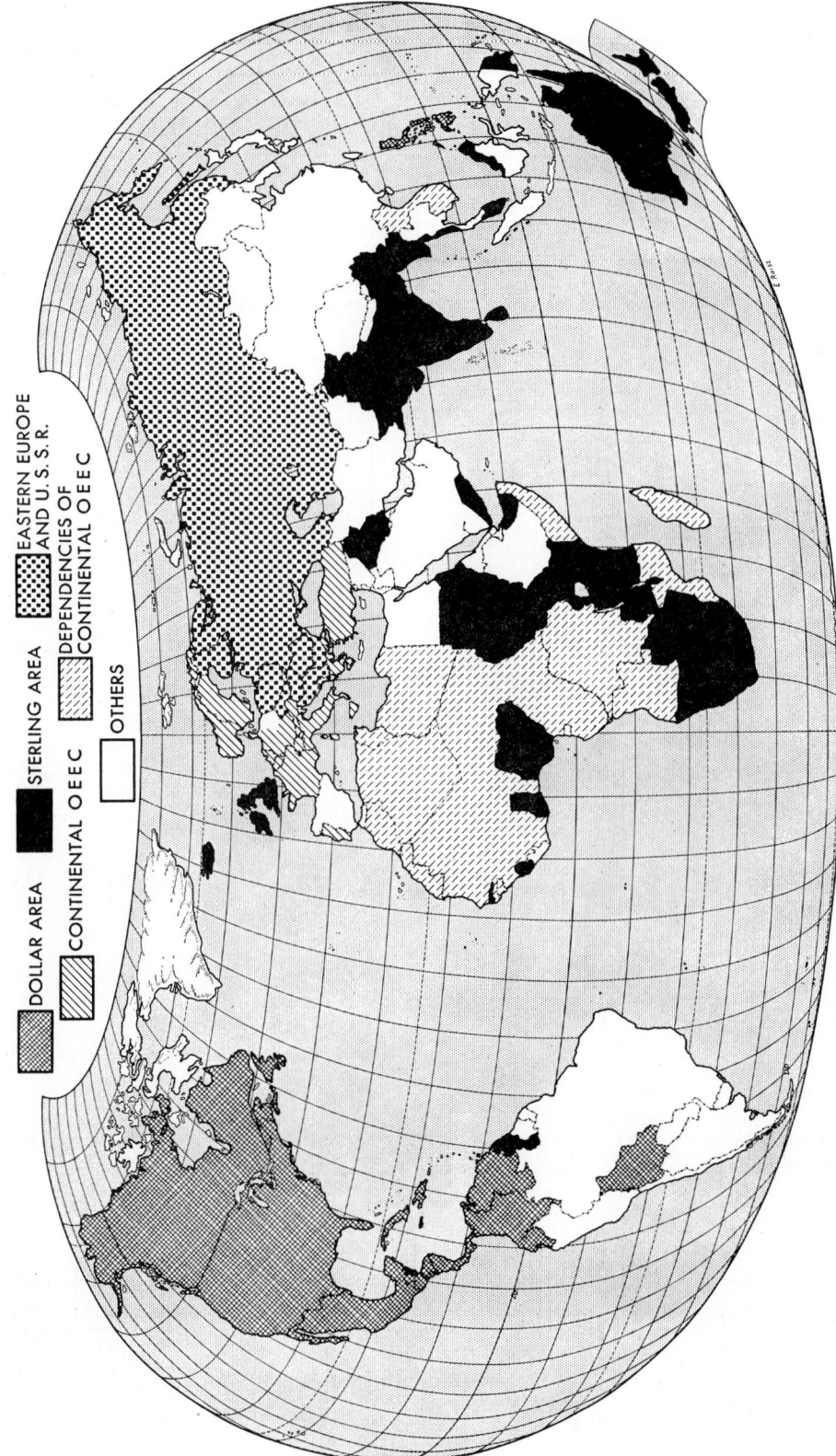

FIGURE 21. GEOGRAPHIC DISTRIBUTION OF PRINCIPAL CURRENCY SYSTEMS IN THE WORLD, 1951

DOLLAR AREA

STERLING AREA

CONTINENTAL OEEC

EASTERN EUROPE AND U. S. S. R.

DEPENDENCIES OF CONTINENTAL OEEC

OTHERS

TABLE 33

WORLD EXPORTS: DISTRIBUTION AMONG CURRENCY AREAS,[a] BY DESTINATION AND PROVENANCE, 1938 AND 1949

Destination	World	Provenance					
		Sterling Area	Dollar Area	Latin American Nondollar Countries	Continental OEEC Countries	Eastern Europe	Rest of World
Millions of Dollars							
World							
1938	$21,934	$ 5,005	$ 4,981	$1,021	$ 6,601	$1,617	$2,709
1949	56,604	14,480	18,284	2,825	11,813	3,509	5,693
Sterling area							
1938	6,430	2,471	1,405	247	1,221	349	737
1949	16,400	7,987	3,228	542	2,244	401	1,998
Dollar area							
1938	3,447	562	1,829	212	509	98	237
1949	12,692	1,678	8,449	985	844	126	610
Latin American non-dollar countries							
1938	890	166	234	94	348	26	22
1949	2,450	460	947	343	622	51	27
Continental OEEC countries							
1938	6,836	1,054	886	404	2,885	827	780
1949	15,096	2,425	3,873	695	5,138	957	2,008
Eastern Europe							
1938	1,340	167	161	29	743	196	44
1949	3,465	394	126	98	903	1,812	132
Rest of world							
1938	2,991	585	466	35	895	121	889
1949	6,501	1,536	1,661	162	2,062	162	918
Per Cent							
World							
1938	100.0	22.8	22.7	4.7	30.1	7.4	12.3
1949	100.0	25.6	32.3	5.0	20.9	6.2	10.0
Sterling area							
1938	29.3	11.3	6.4	1.1	5.6	1.6	3.4
1949	29.0	14.1	5.7	1.0	4.0	0.7	3.5
Dollar area							
1938	15.7	2.6	8.3	1.0	2.3	0.4	1.1
1949	22.4	3.0	14.9	1.7	1.5	0.2	1.1
Latin American non-dollar countries							
1938	4.1	0.8	1.1	0.4	1.6	0.1	0.1
1949	4.3	0.8	1.7	0.6	1.1	0.1	0.0
Continental OEEC countries							
1938	31.2	4.8	3.9	1.8	13.2	3.8	3.6
1949	26.6	4.3	6.8	1.2	9.1	1.7	3.5
Eastern Europe							
1938	6.1	0.8	0.7	0.1	3.4	0.9	0.2
1949	6.1	0.7	0.2	0.2	1.6	3.2	0.2
Rest of world							
1938	13.6	2.7	2.1	0.2	4.1	0.5	4.0
1949	11.5	2.7	2.9	0.3	3.6	0.3	1.6

Source: **15,** 1949–1950, table following p. 210.

a. Figures in frames show foreign trade among countries of the same group.

ability to cover it with invisible exports. The contraction of intra-European trade at that time also reflected the predicament of Western Europe.

5. The intraregional trade of eastern Europe and the USSR increased from 0.9 per cent of world exports in 1938 to 3.2 per cent in 1949. At the same time, the trade of this area with the rest of the world declined from 6.5 per cent to 3.0 per cent of world exports classified by provenance, and from 5.2 per cent to 2.9 per cent classified by destination. These shifts reflect the political domination of the eastern European countries by the USSR. As independent nations, these areas were part of the European community and played an important role in intra-European trade. Moscow has directed their exports eastward.

6. The changes in the trade position of the area described as the "rest of the world" reflect local shifts, often running in opposite directions. The group is too heterogeneous to permit meaningful generalizations on the orientation of its trade. It is noteworthy, however, that in 1949 as in 1938, this area had an export balance in merchandise trade with the sterling area and an import balance with the dollar area. Its percentage of world exports has been as follows:

Area	1938	1949
Exports from sterling area	2.7	2.7
Exports to sterling area	3.4	3.5
Balance	+0.7	+0.8
Exports from dollar area	2.1	2.9
Exports to dollar area	1.1	1.1
Balance	−1.0	−1.8
Exports from continental OEEC countries	4.1	3.6
Exports to continental OEEC countries	3.6	3.5
Balance	−0.5	−0.1
Exports from other areas	0.7	0.6
Exports to other areas	0.3	0.2
Balance	−0.4	−0.4

The direction of the trade balances of this vast area in 1949 was surprisingly close to the prewar pattern.

RETURN TO "NORMALCY"

Multilateral trade with a circular flow of goods as in 1913 or 1928 has not been restored since World War II, and its restoration in the near future is not in sight.

Experts of the UN doubt whether world trade in 1947–52 can be presented in the form of a "system," as a continuous movement or several continuous movements independent of the decisions of this or that government. There is no doubt, however, that substantial progress has been achieved since 1947–48 in the general direction of balancing imports and exports, stabilizing currencies and adjusting the flow of merchandise to the needs and potentialities of the respective geographic areas and individual countries. With the support of international organizations,[54] world trade has been moving in the last five years toward equilibrium on a steadily rising "level of mutually beneficial" transactions.[55]

The devaluation of overvalued currencies in 1949, grants and credits extended by the United States to the deficit countries in the Eastern Hemisphere and international agreements [56] have contributed toward ironing out the main dislocations in trade and payments balances. In many instances the recent adjustments of trade balances between different groups of countries have seemed to be a shift back to prewar patterns with minor changes necessitated by current political and financial conditions. It should be kept in mind, however, that international trade was out of balance before World War II. The objective of a world-trade policy is a system of continuous international transactions which would be better integrated than in 1938, would provide sufficient leeway for temporary disequilibrium in bilateral trade, and would assure an eventual clearing of export and import balances in the multilateral flow of goods, services and capital.[57]

EXPORTS AND IMPORTS OF SELECTED COUNTRIES

There is a great variety in the direction of imports and exports of the countries listed in Table 34, which represent some 87 per cent of

---

54. See Chapter 17.

55. **9**, p. 1.

56. As, for example, the Articles of Agreement of the International Monetary Fund, which protect stability of exchange rates, and the General Agreement on Tariffs and Trade, which provides for reduction in customs duties and looks toward ultimate relaxation of all trade restrictions.

57. See Chapter 5.

TABLE 34. EXPORTS AND IMPORTS OF SELECTED COUNTRIES:

(Millions of

A. Exports

Exporting Country and Year	World	Destination									
		North America	Middle and South America	North-western Europe	Southern Europe	Eastern Europe and USSR	Middle East	Rest of Asia	Rest of Africa	Oceania	Miscellaneous
United States											
1949	12,000	1,958	2,899	3,242	881	109	408	1,750	538	195	19
1950	10,275	1,996	2,765	2,282	583	87	253	1,232	311	133	632
1951	15,032	2,587	3,771	3,154	783	156	383	1,890	493	244	1,570
1952	15,164	2,785	3,532	2,583	645	110	382	1,822	480	224	2,599
Canada											
1949	2,916	1,485	167	890	42	7	36	145	90	50	4
1950	2,874	1,877	166	589	35	5	18	88	51	44	...
1951	3,719	2,200	239	889	60	6	27	156	74	69	...
1952	4,397	2,376	323	1,178	75	27	47	229	71	71	...
Mexico											
1949	463	368	22	34	3	6	10	19	2	...	...
1950	502	438	27	21	5	2	3	5	1	...	...
1951	630	449	37	95	9	1	24	13	2	...	...
1952	726	606	24	48	7	1	20	19	2	...	...
Cuba											
1949	578	370	17	148	16	2	10	8	7	...	...
1950	642	382	16	186	14	2	6	22	13	...	...
1951	766	423	35	200	32	5	5	53	12	...	...
1952	...	...	...	...	...	...	...	...	...	...	...
Colombia											
1949	321	268	26	22	1	4	...	...	...	...	...
1950	396	326	27	31	2	...	...	...	...	...	...
1951	460	379	28	42	1	...	...	2	...	...	9
1952	461	389	32	40	1	...	...	...	...	...	...
Brazil											
1949	1,089	547	134	277	67	18	8	15	13	9	...
1950	1,346	737	125	358	55	23	8	16	16	8	...
1951	1,757	882	154	545	72	26	9	34	17	18	...
1952	1,409	749	128	381	53	31	10	41	13	2	...
Chile											
1949	308	150	37	79	18	2	13	7	1	1	...
1950	294	154	50	48	23	1	17	...	1	1	...
1951	377	194	57	85	24	1	13	1	1	1	...
1952	462	265	71	86	22	2	10	5	...	...	...
Uruguay											
1949	190	52	24	93	10	3	4	4	...	...	...
1950	254	131	8	96	6	2	1	5	2	2	...
1951	236	103	14	91	15	2	...	6	2	2	...
1952	209	51	32	100	16	2	...	4	4	...	...

(Continued on page 98)

DISTRIBUTION BY GEOGRAPHIC AREAS,[a] 1949–52

U.S. Dollars)

B. Imports

Importing Country and Year	World	North America	Middle and South America	North-western Europe	Southern Europe	Eastern Europe and USSR	Middle East	Rest of Asia	Rest of Africa	Oceania	Miscellaneous
United States											
1949	6,622	1,552	2,442	686	181	110	120	1,089	293	125	23
1950	8,852	1,962	3,102	1,052	262	134	206	1,507	420	208	...
1951	10,967	2,278	3,548	1,647	330	142	246	1,816	510	450	...
1952	10,714	2,388	3,634	1,579	339	110	257	1,659	504	243	...
Canada											
1949	2,699	1,911	252	364	14	7	15	71	15	43	6
1950	2,926	1,966	275	447	15	6	28	105	32	51	...
1951	3,876	2,674	341	538	24	7	41	143	29	78	...
1952	4,120	3,049	357	497	21	7	27	94	24	42	...
Mexico											
1949	457	411	3	31	5	1	...	3	...	3	...
1950	509	441	5	44	8	1	...	5	...	5	...
1951	783	651	7	84	15	2	...	16	1	7	...
1952	808	697	6	82	10	3	...	5	...	5	...
Cuba											
1949	451	382	26	21	10	...	...	12	...	...	...
1950	515	414	37	30	10	1	...	21	1	...	...
1951	640	510	30	58	18	3	...	20	1	...	...
1952	...	...	...	...	...	...	...	...	...	...	...
Colombia											
1949	264	200	18	40	3	1	...	1	...	...	...
1950	364	265	23	66	4	2	...	2	...	...	...
1951	416	279	26	92	5	...	...	1	...	...	12
1952	402	278	23	84	4	...	...	8	4	...	...
Venezuela											
1949	669	512	27	108	15	3	...	4	...	...	...
1950	537	389	19	89	13	2	...	...	...	...	25
1951	642	459	20	119	14	1	...	...	...	...	29
1952	723	528	12	134	14	1	...	...	...	...	33
Brazil											
1949	1,116	488	253	310	31	21	1	7	4	...	...
1950	1,098	391	258	382	30	17	...	8	10	1	...
1951	2,010	875	339	645	67	28	...	39	14	2	...
1952	2,010	839	354	695	56	21	...	34	8	3	...
Chile											
1949	304	167	75	47	9	...	...	4	1	...	...
1950	248	121	54	56	10	1	4	2	...	1	...
1951	329	186	59	65	10	1	2	5	...	...	...
1952	371	203	78	79	7	1	...	3	...	...	...
Uruguay											
1949	185	42	45	80	7	2	...	8	1	...	...
1950	202	41	41	95	10	4	...	7	3	...	...
1951	373	146	70	125	15	2	1	10	2	...	...
1952	257	66	65	101	10	2	1	10	2	...	...

(*Continued on page 99*)

TABLE 34—*continued*

A. Exports

Exporting Country and Year	World	Destination									
		North America	Middle and South America	North-western Europe	Southern Europe	Eastern Europe and USSR	Middle East	Rest of Asia	Rest of Africa	Oceania	Miscellaneous
United Kingdom											
1949	6,830	526	627	1,632	318	218	493	995	1,019	956	46
1950	6,317	717	551	1,668	270	165	409	773	796	969	. . .
1951	7,578	822	599	1,878	327	237	423	1,029	1,030	1,233	. . .
1952	7,541	866	590	1,785	435	279	456	1,070	1,110	949	. . .
France											
1949	2,715	66	212	900	133	106	99	179	941	38	39
1950	3,065	139	238	1,168	155	60	104	209	946	37	8
1951	4,225	273	328	1,412	206	90	160	369	1,311	61	21
1952	4,047	177	243	1,237	240	129	169	422	1,370	36	24
Belgium–Luxembourg											
1949	1,770	94	159	1,000	109	115	44	88	130	18	12
1950	1,651	145	131	934	115	77	48	77	97	19	8
1951	2,651	221	208	1,491	143	97	60	146	202	60	15
1952	2,451	218	149	1,373	173	97	60	97	224	34	26
Netherlands											
1949	1,311	43	54	762	65	108	27	192	36	9	13
1950	1,414	68	70	915	52	58	32	130	46	11	31
1951	1,973	120	125	1,197	72	78	47	195	69	29	40
1952	2,129	147	131	1,245	98	66	69	220	93	20	41
Denmark											
1949	672	14	10	545	22	55	8	11	5	1	2
1950	666	17	20	536	23	40	9	12	8	1	. . .
1951	838	26	35	629	44	60	10	20	12	3	. .
1952	849	32	47	634	43	49	11	20	11	2	. . .
Sweden											
1949	1,139	70	91	655	74	122	27	45	22	28	5
1950	1,103	73	103	654	55	101	25	32	32	29	. . .
1951	1,779	104	196	1,038	96	150	33	49	49	63	. . .
1952	1,562	96	119	952	88	148	29	47	49	33	. . .
Norway											
1949	396	28	16	228	21	55	8	23	4	11	2
1950	390	39	24	230	29	28	10	12	9	10	. . .
1951	619	45	60	353	45	33	12	26	20	24	. . .
1952	565	47	47	335	34	34	11	18	27	13	. . .
Finland											
1949	473	30	20	233	12	153	8	6	5	6	. . .
1950	392	34	19	213	14	80	11	6	7	5	2
1951	866	56	67	497	29	147	21	15	13	17	5
1952	717	38	50	391	20	174	12	15	6	7	3
Western Germany											
1949	1,129	49	36	787	96	61	13	35	29	12	11
1950	1,981	112	157	1,137	235	129	41	87	48	28	6
1951	3,474	257	379	1,845	339	173	77	210	120	65	8
1952	4,037	272	415	2,113	491	222	110	221	140	44	9
Poland											
1948	528	1	3	283	18	217	4	. . .	. . .	. . .	1

(*Continued on page 100*)

TABLE 34—*continued*

B. Imports

Importing Country and Year	World	North America	Middle and South America	North-western Europe	Southern Europe	Eastern Europe and USSR	Middle East	Rest of Asia	Rest of Africa	Oceania	Miscellaneous
United Kingdom											
1949	8,431	1,646	941	1,734	302	318	484	753	829	1,261	162
1950	7,303	1,097	938	1,587	291	303	488	742	802	1,009	44
1951	10,931	1,797	1,214	2,384	447	567	849	1,331	1,100	1,192	49
1952	9,748	1,789	749	2,225	292	458	875	982	1,209	1,128	40
France											
1949	3,278	620	243	717	139	95	299	120	795	221	28
1950	3,065	400	296	705	159	58	318	152	811	166	...
1951	4,592	571	394	1,055	212	110	516	372	1,082	280	...
1952	4,547	535	371	1,081	219	123	618	238	1,127	235	...
Belgium–Luxembourg											
1949	1,803	379	158	831	58	58	32	38	176	65	9
1950	1,950	365	156	907	61	57	46	65	200	92	2
1951	2,544	490	180	1,166	74	67	55	132	273	103	2
1952	2,460	450	164	1,237	67	54	73	77	272	66	1
Netherlands											
1949	1,851	317	157	878	49	147	58	171	54	14	5
1950	2,069	250	142	1,093	43	78	111	208	96	31	16
1951	2,575	308	183	1,314	59	89	170	289	120	26	17
1952	2,270	325	143	1,150	46	78	175	199	110	30	14
Denmark											
1949	805	136	23	495	37	87	4	12	5	5	1
1950	854	82	24	599	38	69	9	19	9	5	...
1951	1,013	113	36	704	35	90	5	20	5	5	...
1952	962	84	41	736	30	52	2	9	8	1	...
Sweden											
1949	1,168	120	117	596	66	115	40	48	30	22	14
1950	1,179	108	132	645	55	87	48	44	41	20	...
1951	1,775	178	188	972	77	134	53	85	53	35	...
1952	1,729	180	202	991	69	118	38	59	53	18	...
Norway											
1949	778	126	41	473	29	62	14	16	4	6	7
1950	679	95	47	408	23	38	18	21	19	10	...
1951	876	144	45	539	30	38	17	25	24	12	...
1952	869	135	30	567	26	34	4	26	23	4	...
Finland											
1949	410	31	37	237	12	71	3	4	9	6	...
1950	388	23	39	213	19	65	5	9	4	8	4
1951	676	43	69	379	32	103	6	24	10	11	4
1952	792	64	47	466	24	145	5	12	13	7	8
Western Germany											
1949	2,248	846	157	627	149	107	30	138	94	53	47
1950	2,704	441	193	1,167	204	114	85	200	213	83	4
1951	3,503	699	338	1,200	281	152	155	231	235	111	...
1952	3,854	721	338	1,452	349	194	167	264	302	66	...
Poland											
1948	528	1	3	283	18	217	4	...	...	...	1

(*Continued on page 101*)

TABLE 34—*continued*

A. Exports

Exporting Country and Year	World	North America	Middle and South America	North-western Europe	Southern Europe	Eastern Europe and USSR	Middle East	Rest of Asia	Rest of Africa	Oceania	Miscellaneous
Czechoslovakia											
1948	753	28	29	260	49	292	44	23	9	12	8
Switzerland											
1949	804	111	99	330	92	70	21	51	19	10	2
1950	903	135	99	345	150	66	29	46	24	9	...
1951	1,081	155	127	438	116	68	34	87	36	20	...
1952	1,100	182	110	441	150	51	34	81	39	12	...
Austria											
1949	301	9	9	96	88	76	13	9	1	1	...
1950	305	18	17	116	74	58	10	7	3	2	...
1951	451	28	25	207	84	71	16	7	5	6	...
1952	506	28	26	239	94	87	15	6	5	4	...
Spain											
1949	384	23	33	183	14	2	12	9	104	4	...
1950	405	64	42	158	11	2	13	4	108	2	...
1951	653	127	27	333	61	95	3	3	2	1	...
1952	...	...	...	...	...	...	...	...	...	...	...
Italy											
1949	1,121	50	190	484	40	88	101	114	18	15	20
1950	1,199	93	195	574	51	89	94	80	55	30	6
1951	1,647	123	146	772	90	111	115	135	88	59	7
1952	1,383	149	105	591	121	90	112	125	61	17	12
Japan											
1949	511	90	6	69	2	8	30	239	37	17	13
1950	820	201	44	87	7	2	18	365	70	26	...
1951	1,355	205	93	135	6	2	39	663	108	102	1
1952	1,273	249	75	165	12	...	...	...	...	...	...
Hong Kong											
1949	529	56	4	49	2	1	3	386	4	12	12
1950	650	56	6	55	4	...	2	506	6	8	7
1951	776	31	5	63	3	...	2	637	8	14	11
1952	507	23	4	35	4	...	...	420	72	3	5
Turkey											
1949	248	45	...	116	25	31	24	1	...	...	5
1950	263	46	1	143	26	22	22	2	...	...	...
1951	314	70	1	161	22	29	25	3	1	1	2
1952	363	59	...	196	32	39	20	15	...	...	...
Pakistan											
1949	304	40	3	119	14	23	3	95	1	3	3
1950	402	45	7	160	42	29	2	106	1	7	2
1951	764	33	...	248	61	33	1	343	5	9	31
1952	...	...	...	...	...	...	...	...	...	...	...
India											
1949	1,266	223	64	438	27	22	87	260	49	82	13
1950	1,172	247	55	359	22	6	87	282	46	68	...
1951	1,646	337	104	546	45	20	88	324	67	115	...
1952	1,312	287	63	361	37	8	90	343	65	58	...

(*Continued on page 102*)

TABLE 34—*continued*

B. Imports

Importing Country and Year	World	North America	Middle and South America	North-west-ern Europe	South-ern Europe	Eastern Europe and USSR	Middle East	Rest of Asia	Rest of Africa	Oceania	Miscel-laneous
Czechoslovakia											
1948	753	28	28	260	49	292	44	23	9	12	8
Switzerland											
1949	881	215	79	365	82	53	27	30	20	7	4
1950	1,048	176	116	467	94	50	39	46	50	8	...
1951	1,365	254	118	677	116	52	38	62	39	11	...
1952	1,205	246	85	629	110	46	24	40	18	6	...
Austria											
1949	594	175	23	182	69	105	8	17	5	5	4
1950	431	103	22	174	47	62	7	8	4	2	...
1951	657	147	21	334	57	81	6	5	3	1	...
1952	653	127	27	333	61	95	3	3	2	1	...
Spain											
1949	457	41	132	140	11	2	17	12	99	3	2
1950	390	55	62	125	8	2	16	10	105	7	...
1951	387	63	41	152	7	2	27	20	75	...	...
1952	...	...	...	...	...	...	...	...	...	...	...
Italy											
1949	1,545	546	162	385	26	98	130	56	49	88	5
1950	1,442	344	165	475	27	79	159	70	55	67	1
1951	2,169	504	211	644	34	103	260	181	97	131	1
1952	2,313	535	141	792	52	123	307	136	114	110	3
Japan											
1949	900	581	14	50	14	3	27	157	13	30	9
1950	970	442	67	35	2	4	28	297	13	81	...
1951	1,995	771	259	131	29	2	131	501	8	147	16
1952	2,028	879	170	99	39	3	128	535	25	151	...
Hong Kong											
1949	629	145	1	136	6	4	2	294	6	18	16
1950	663	123	3	122	7	4	1	374	3	14	11
1951	852	81	11	254	26	6	3	433	7	16	16
1952	661	52	2	179	22	1	3	376	9	10	6
Turkey											
1949	290	74	5	119	17	38	19	7	1	10	1
1950	286	74	6	130	14	25	22	8	1	4	1
1951	402	50	9	240	29	25	25	11	2	9	2
1952	556	48	9	370	44	29	29	13	5	8	...
Pakistan											
1949	410	41	3	144	29	10	15	138	...	3	27
1950	351	35	2	121	19	8	20	137	4	1	4
1951	535	32	...	160	30	9	23	210	2	1	68
1952	...	...	...	...	...	...	...	...	...	...	...
India											
1949	1,925	322	56	627	50	42	254	438	61	70	6
1950	1,137	234	7	341	20	12	176	194	59	95	...
1951	1,814	470	12	472	48	16	241	453	61	42	...
1952	1,667	634	8	473	26	11	135	283	63	35	...

(*Continued on page 103*)

TABLE 34—*continued*

A. Exports

Exporting Country and Year	World	Destination									
		North America	Middle and South America	North-western Europe	Southern Europe	Eastern Europe and USSR	Middle East	Rest of Asia	Rest of Africa	Oceania	Miscellaneous
Ceylon											
1949	293	44	3	124	7	...	35	17	14	34	14
1950	328	90	5	118	10	...	26	18	15	32	13
1951	400	57	5	184	17	2	35	39	17	36	18
1952	296	48	1	109	13	...	13	18	13	26	56
Malaya and Singapore											
1949	718	197	9	183	22	40	7	181	12	65	1
1950	1,312	373	27	358	55	56	5	338	22	57	19
1951	1,985	440	72	648	94	69	7	475	39	113	28
1952	1,280	236	28	432	91	33	...	...	...	...	...
Indonesia											
1949	505	81	...	209	2	1	5	154	3	9	40
1950	722	118	2	239	4	1	6	294	5	16	37
1951	1,231	207	7	428	12	2	9	486	7	35	38
1952	911	235	10	277	12	10	4	301	6	28	28
Philippines											
1949	254	183	5	29	8	1	1	22	2	3	...
1950	337	247	12	38	7	...	2	30	1	...	...
1951	410	263	8	79	10	...	3	36	4	6	...
1952	352	239	6	44	10	...	4	46	3	1	...
Egypt											
1949	516	13	1	196	49	70	19	148	6	2	13
1950	504	45	9	223	58	54	16	89	1	2	7
1951	583	57	2	229	65	56	16	142	3	6	7
1952	417	50	1	134	68	66	10	79	1	2	5
Union of South Africa											
1949	547	40	10	257	27	5	31	22	101	9	46
1950	686	63	10	358	32	3	23	13	109	10	9
1951	950	99	17	522	38	5	32	19	192	14	2
1952	912	67	15	539	49	4	9	24	193	10	2
Australia											
1949	1,591	124	...	907	63	31	37	215	9	55	151
1950	1,676	169	...	948	65	24	37	215	8	53	157
1951	2,049	380	...	966	119	45	47	272	9	81	129
1952	1,720	177	7	970	98	13	17	269	16	115	39
New Zealand											
1949	555	20	8	467	6	12	1	8	1	18	14
1950	513	52	10	402	5	3	...	7	1	16	18
1951	695	105	5	504	12	28	1	16	1	20	2
1952	...	...	...	...	...	...	...	...	...	...	...

a. North America includes areas north of the Rio Grande; Middle and South America include the Caribbean; Northwestern Europe includes the United Kingdom, Ireland and Iceland, France, Belgium–Luxembourg, the Netherlands, Denmark, Sweden, Norway, Western Germany, Switzerland, Austria and some other areas; Southern Europe includes Portugal, Spain, Italy, Greece, and Turkey; Eastern Europe and the USSR include all countries in the Soviet bloc; the Middle East includes the area from Cyprus, Egypt, Anglo-Egyptian Sudan and Ethiopia to Saudi Arabia, Iraq and Iran. The three other regions are self-explanatory.

TABLE 34—*continued*

B. Imports

Importing Country and Year	World	Provenance									
		North America	Middle and South America	North-western Europe	South-ern Europe	Eastern Europe and USSR	Middle East	Rest of Asia	Rest of Africa	Oceania	Miscellaneous
Ceylon											
1949	290	23	5	66	6	2	28	111	2	37	8
1950	245	12	3	60	3	2	23	117	10	17	...
1951	328	21	...	97	5	4	25	127	23	26	...
1952	358	40	...	99	4	...	1	125	1	26	63
Malaya and Singapore											
1949	810	58	3	200	17	3	27	379	5	108	9
1950	952	35	2	212	15	4	14	617	9	37	8
1951	1,554	83	1	376	25	6	13	970	20	48	12
1952	1,265	73	7	351	11	4	9	729	20	55	8
Indonesia											
1949	535	138	7	217	9	6	1	119	1	28	8
1950	402	86	3	138	6	3	1	157	6	3	1
1951	806	165	2	251	16	6	3	335	17	10	...
1952	914	162	29	294	25	6	7	364	12	13	...
Philippines											
1949	569	472	5	18	2	...	5	57	...	8	...
1950	342	264	1	16	4	...	13	42	...	2	...
1951	480	355	4	24	4	...	13	79	...	1	...
1952	418	320	1	19	5	...	13	58	1	2	...
Egypt											
1949	674	79	35	272	72	34	57	55	30	39	1
1950	611	41	23	275	58	46	40	63	27	37	...
1951	803	193	18	292	60	62	50	47	26	54	...
1952	628	156	26	249	50	60	33	41	9	5	...
Union of South Africa											
1949	1,195	381	11	583	9	5	61	55	56	12	21
1950	861	174	17	427	19	7	52	56	78	8	13
1951	1,316	304	25	628	52	15	53	111	108	10	8
1952	1,176	296	24	570	24	10	41	83	106	9	12
Australia											
1949	1,385	190	...	795	16	...	39	184	9	13	138
1950	1,417	150	...	840	30	...	54	195	11	11	125
1951	2,111	216	13	1,190	57	15	61	376	11	26	145
1952	1,742	301	18	969	36	23	57	237	42	35	25
New Zealand											
1949	436	59	1	254	1	...	12	30	2	63	15
1950	442	42	1	280	1	...	15	26	5	59	13
1951	578	71	1	343	3	...	13	60	7	63	17
1952	...	...	...	...	...	...	...	...	...	...	...

Source: **10,** Quarterly issues, January-December 1951, and Annual Issue 1953. Although distributed by the Statistical Office of the UN, this is a joint publication of that office, the International Monetary Fund and the International Bank for Reconstruction and Development. Statistics are prepared by the International Monetary Fund but may deviate in some cases from other series released by the same agency which are adjusted for better comparability.

world trade. These countries, however, can be grouped in accordance with the predominant orientation of their exports and imports toward one of the three main geographical regions: the Western Hemisphere, Europe and Asia, including the Middle East.

These three regions account for approximately 85 per cent of world trade. In the flow of world trade they are not clearly separated from one another. Some countries are equally attached to two of them or change orientation from year to year, following the variations in prices, currency rates and other trade conditions. Despite these limitations, the classification of different countries of the world by their prevailing attachment to one of the three principal regional markets is helpful in showing general characteristics of the structure of world trade.

The remaining 15 per cent of international trade is distributed among Africa, Oceania and countries within the Soviet orbit. Very little is known about the last, which can be regarded as a separate region.

Regional Markets

Despite its world-wide commercial operations, the realm of the foreign trade of the United States is the Western Hemisphere. On the average, for 1949–52, this region accounted for more than 40 per cent of the country's exports and 55 per cent of its imports. Roughly half of these operations were in trade with Canada and Mexico.

Exchange of merchandise within the Western Hemisphere — practically exchange with the United States — predominates in the foreign trade of Canada, Mexico, Cuba, Colombia, Brazil and Chile. The Western Hemisphere accounted for the following percentages of the exports and imports of these countries in 1952:

	Exports	Imports
Canada	62	83
Mexico	87	87
Cuba (1951)	60	84
Colombia	21	75
Brazil	62	59
Chile	73	76

Similarly, the foreign trade of Guatemala, El Salvador, Honduras, Nicaragua, Costa Rica, Haiti, the Dominican Republic, Venezuela and Bolivia is oriented toward the United States.

European markets, especially the United Kingdom, have more significance for Peru, Paraguay, Uruguay and especially for Argentina. The last country divides its exports almost equally between the Western Hemisphere and Europe.[58]

Northwestern Europe is the principal market for Belgium-Luxembourg, the Netherlands, Denmark, Sweden, Norway and Finland, on the one hand, and for Australia, New Zealand and the Union of South Africa, on the other. In their foreign trade, all these countries appear as members of the community of Western Europe, and their strongest commercial ties are with the United Kingdom. Northwestern Europe accounted for the following percentages of their exports and imports in 1952:

	Exports	Imports
Belgium–Luxembourg	56	50
Netherlands	59	51
Denmark	75	77
Sweden	61	57
Norway	59	65
Finland	55	59
Union of South Africa	59	48
Australia	56	56
New Zealand (1951)	73	59

Northwestern Europe is also the most important market for Western Germany, Switzerland, Austria, Spain and Italy. In this respect the position of France differs from that of other nations of Western Europe in that it has important colonial possessions in Africa and maintains extensive trade both with them and other parts of that continent. The percentage shares of Northwestern Europe and Africa (including the Middle East) in the French foreign trade in 1952 were as follows:

	Northwestern Europe	Africa and the Middle East
Exports	31	38
Imports	24	38

The foreign trade of African and Asiatic colonial areas is oriented toward the respective colonial powers. French colonies are tied commercially to France, British to Great Britain, Spanish to Spain. Belgium predominates in the foreign trade of the Belgian Congo, with the

---

58. It is noteworthy that the sea route from the Atlantic ports of Brazil and other South American countries to Gibraltar is shorter than to New York.

United States and the United Kingdom disput-ing second and third places. In brief, the foreign trade of most of the colonies of European powers belongs to the European regional market.

Malaya and Singapore, Hong Kong, Ceylon, Indonesia, Japan and China are the great centers of intra-Asiatic trade. After World War II, their trade was diverted toward the United States as the only country able to purchase their products and to supply them with the goods they wanted. This was a temporary deviation from the cus-tomary pattern, however, and the trend in 1949–52 was clearly toward resumption of intra-Asiatic trade.[59]

The United Kingdom

The United Kingdom holds a unique posi-tion in the world market. Its commercial inter-ests and operations are dispersed over the whole globe. None of the large regional markets repre-sents as much as one fourth of its foreign trade. In 1952 the principal markets and other geo-graphical areas accounted for the following per-centages of its exports and imports:[60]

	Exports	Imports
Western Hemisphere	19	26
Northwestern Europe	24	23
Southern Europe	6	3
Eastern Europe and USSR	4	5
Middle East	6	9
Other Asia	14	10
Other Africa	15	12
Oceania	12	12

So wide is the geographic dispersion of Brit-ish imports and exports that it is difficult to classify the United Kingdom by the predomi-nant orientation of its trade. In 1952, the Middle East, Asia, Africa and Oceania together absorbed 47 per cent of its exports, as compared with 30 per cent for northwestern and southern Europe and 19 per cent for the Americas. At the same time, 43 per cent of Britain's imports came from Asia, Africa and Oceania, 26 per cent from Europe (excluding Soviet satellites) and 26 per cent from the Western Hemisphere.

Apart from the United Kingdom, most coun-tries of the world can be roughly classified by the general orientation of their exports as shown in Figure 22.

The Two Giants of World Trade

The United Kingdom and the United States are the two giants of the world market. Together they control approximately 30 per cent of world trade. Both carry on trade in all parts of the world, but they differ greatly in the geographic distribution of their imports and exports and the role of foreign trade in their economy. Of the two countries, the United States leads in the Western Hemisphere, including Canada but ex-cluding the European colonies in the Caribbean, and also in Japan, Indonesia and the Philippines. The United Kingdom leads in the markets of northern Europe (Ireland, Sweden, Norway, Finland and Denmark), southern Asia, Aus-tralia and New Zealand.

The two countries compete with each other in Argentina, France, Belgium, the Netherlands, Germany, southern Europe, the Middle East and parts of Africa. (See Table 35; cf. Figures 23 and 24.)[61] Most of these areas belonged in the sphere of British commercial predominance be-fore the war. The United States has made deep inroads into these markets in the last decade, but it is too early to decide whether or not the current boom in American trade is merely temporary.

In the United States, imports and exports fluc-tuate in amount and direction from year to year in a much wider range than in the United King-dom. The foreign trade of the United States was overexpanded after the war; exports were maintained on a high level by grants and credits to foreign countries and, in 1951 and 1952, by the vast defense and rearmament program. Sta-bilization of military expenses may be followed by a reduction of United States exports, but such a reduction would not necessarily endanger full employment and a high level of economic ac-tivity in the country. Indeed, if it were possi-ble to divorce commercial policy completely from broad considerations of world peace and welfare, a strong argument could be made in favor of balancing the United States foreign trade at a comparatively low level — perhaps no higher, or even lower, than $10 billion, without endangering the continuous growth of its indus-trial production and rise of its standard of liv-ing. The United States depends, of course, on imports of certain metals and minerals[62] and

---

59. **5,** 1911–26, p. 166.
60. Table 34.

61. Cf. **24,** pp. 40–41.
62. For deficiencies of the United States in minerals, see **34,** p. 333.

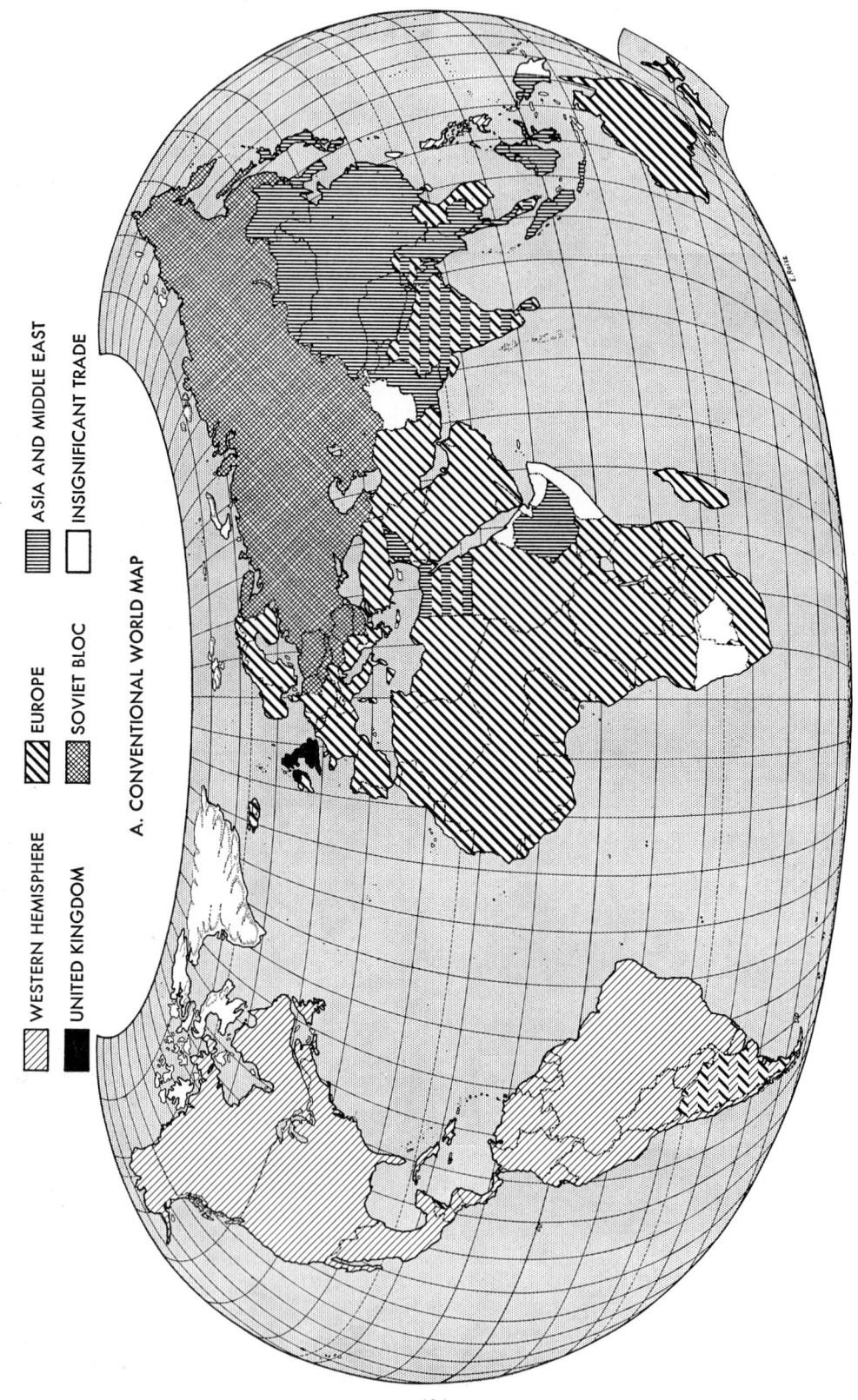

WESTERN HEMISPHERE

UNITED KINGDOM

EUROPE

SOVIET BLOC

ASIA AND MIDDLE EAST

INSIGNIFICANT TRADE

A. CONVENTIONAL WORLD MAP

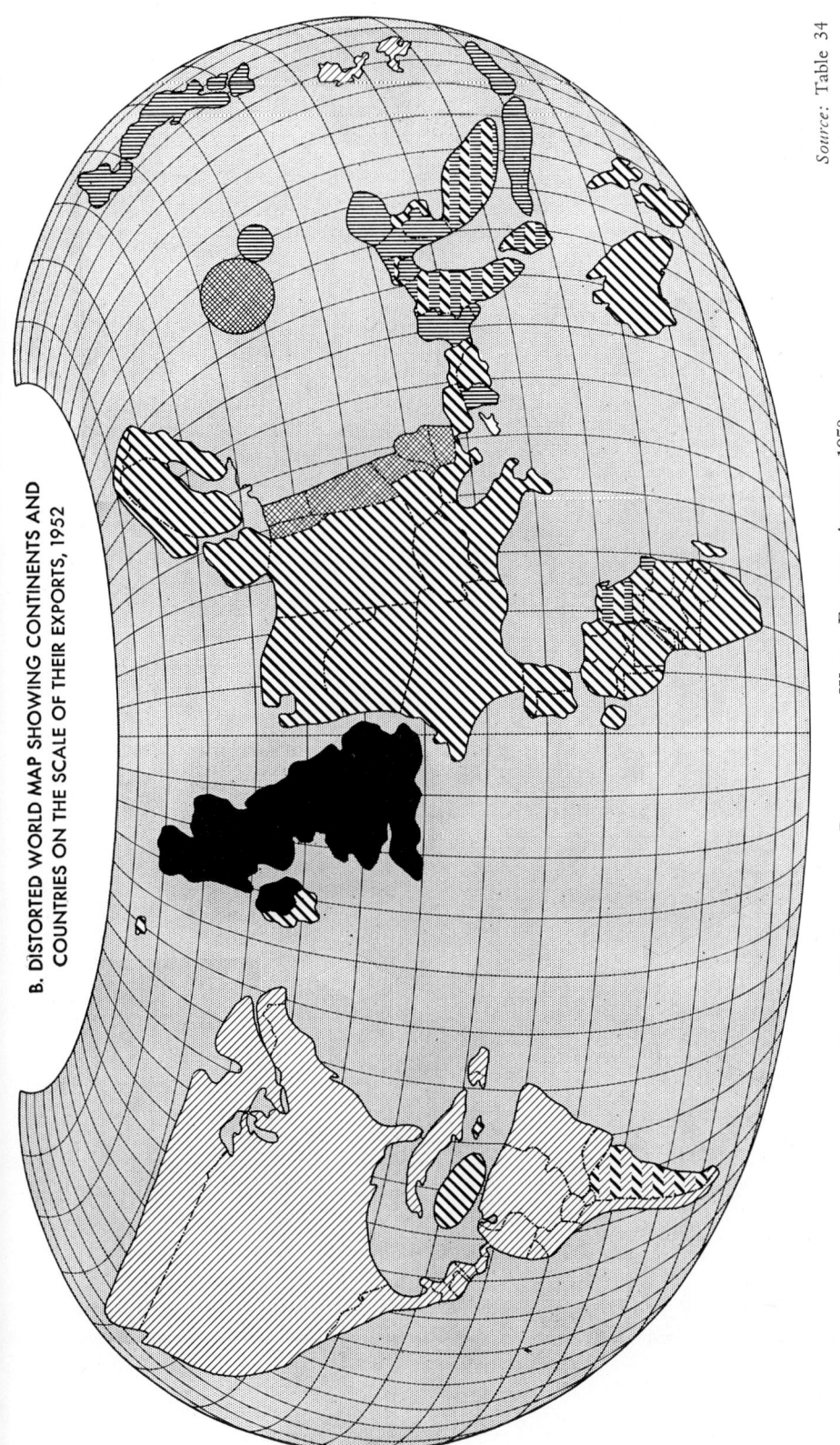

B. DISTORTED WORLD MAP SHOWING CONTINENTS AND COUNTRIES ON THE SCALE OF THEIR EXPORTS, 1952

FIGURE 22. PREVAILING DIRECTIONS OF WORLD EXPORTS, AROUND 1950

Source: Table 34

The bulk of the exports of all American countries — except Argentina and the European colonies in the Caribbean — remains in the Western Hemisphere. America likewise absorbs most of the exports from the Philippines.

Europe, especially the United Kingdom and other industrial countries of north-western Europe, takes the largest part of the exports of continental European countries, Africa, the Middle East, Australia, New Zealand, Indochina and the European colonies in the Caribbean.

Egypt, India, Ceylon and Malaya share their exports between Asia and Europe.

The foreign trade of China, Japan, Korea, Pakistan, Burma, Thailand and Indonesia is normally oriented toward Asiatic and Middle Eastern markets.

This classification does not apply to the United Kingdom (black on the map) whose exports are dispersed to all parts of the world without clear predominance of any single regional market.

A conventional world map (A) fails to show the relative significance of these groups of countries, and especially of the United Kingdom, in world exports.

The distorted world map (B) stresses this aspect of the direction of world exports.

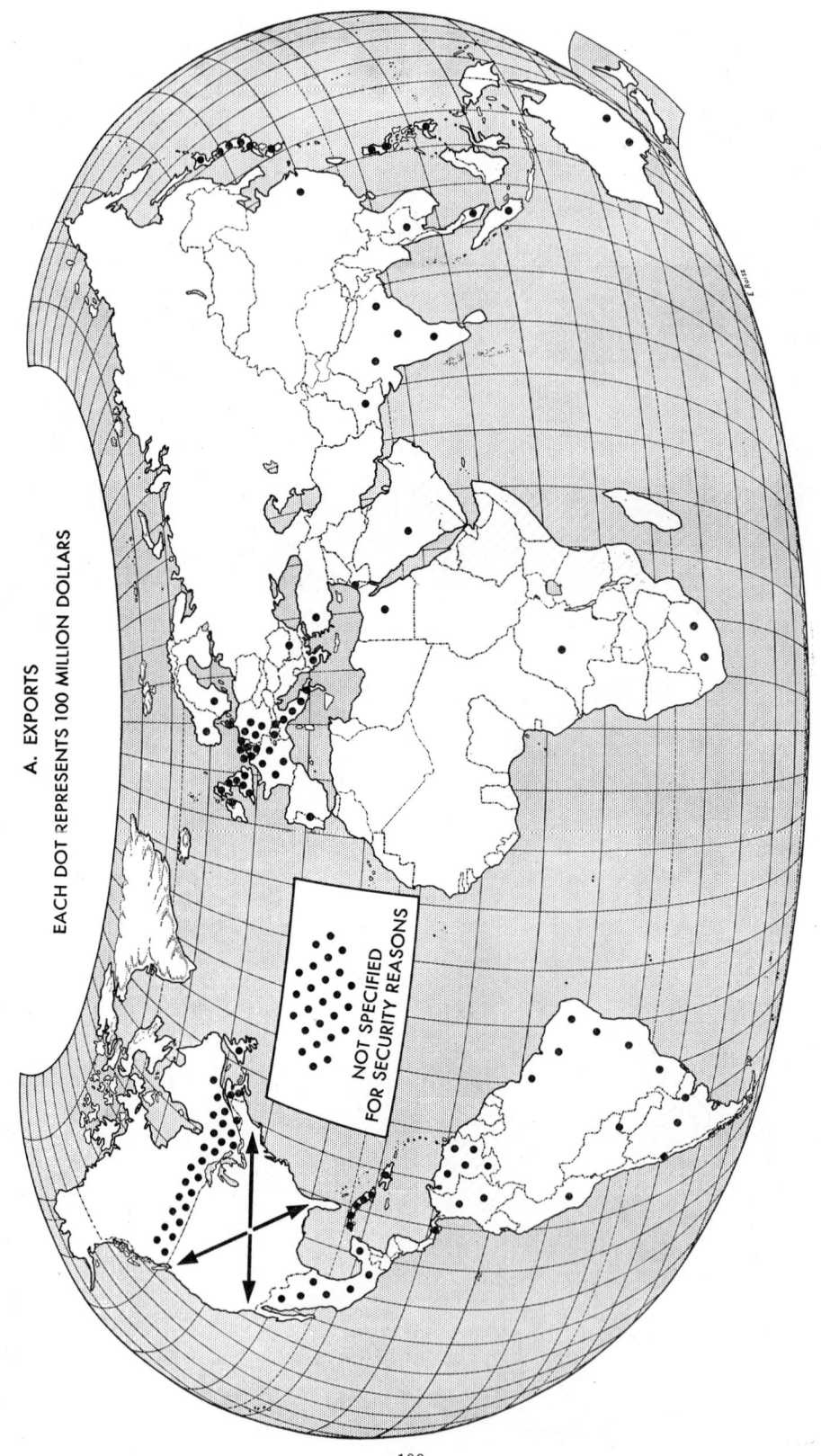

A. EXPORTS

EACH DOT REPRESENTS 100 MILLION DOLLARS

NOT SPECIFIED
FOR SECURITY REASONS

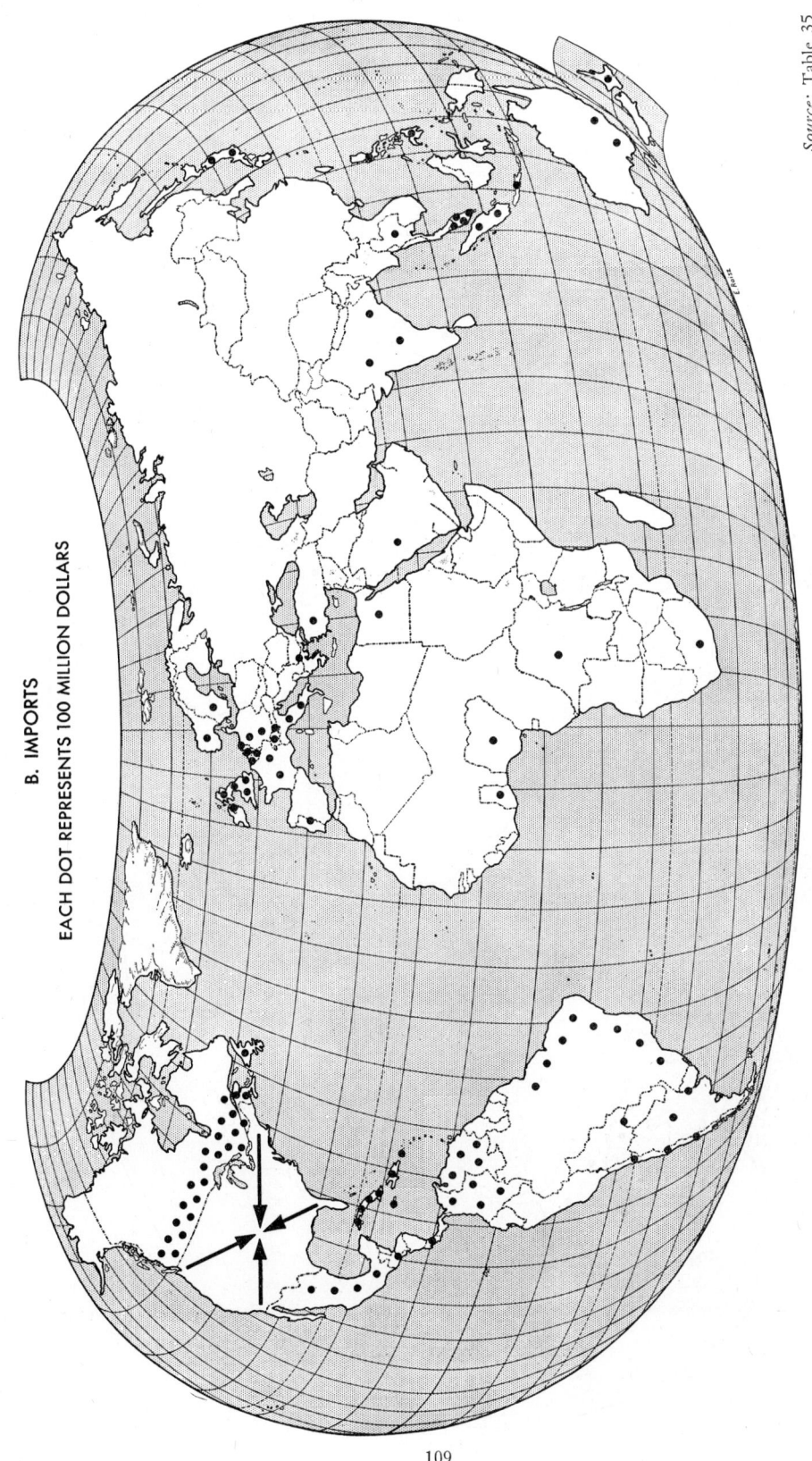

B. IMPORTS

EACH DOT REPRESENTS 100 MILLION DOLLARS

Source: Table 35

FIGURE 23. GEOGRAPHIC DISTRIBUTION OF FOREIGN TRADE OF THE UNITED STATES, 1952

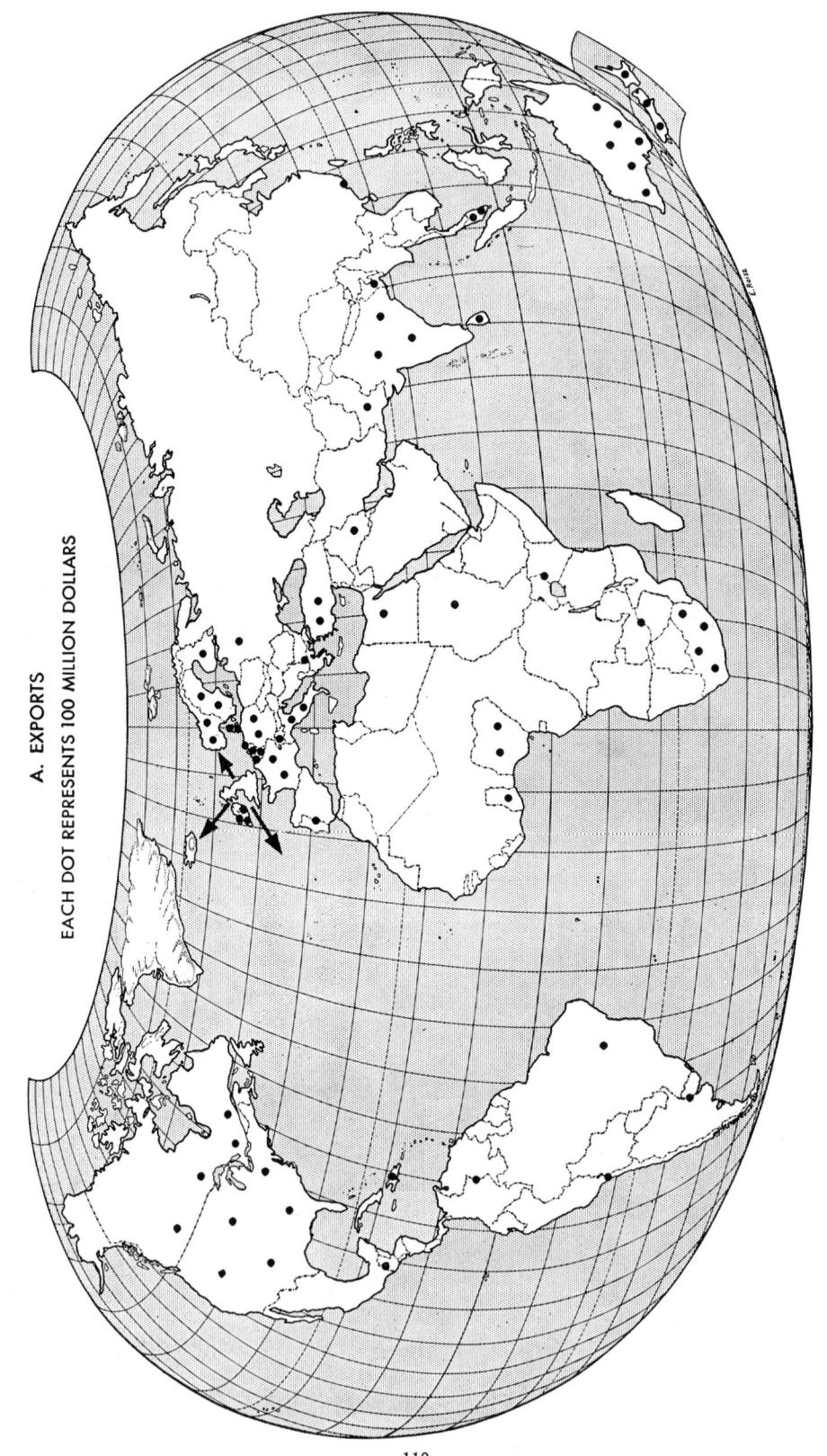

A. EXPORTS

EACH DOT REPRESENTS 100 MILLION DOLLARS

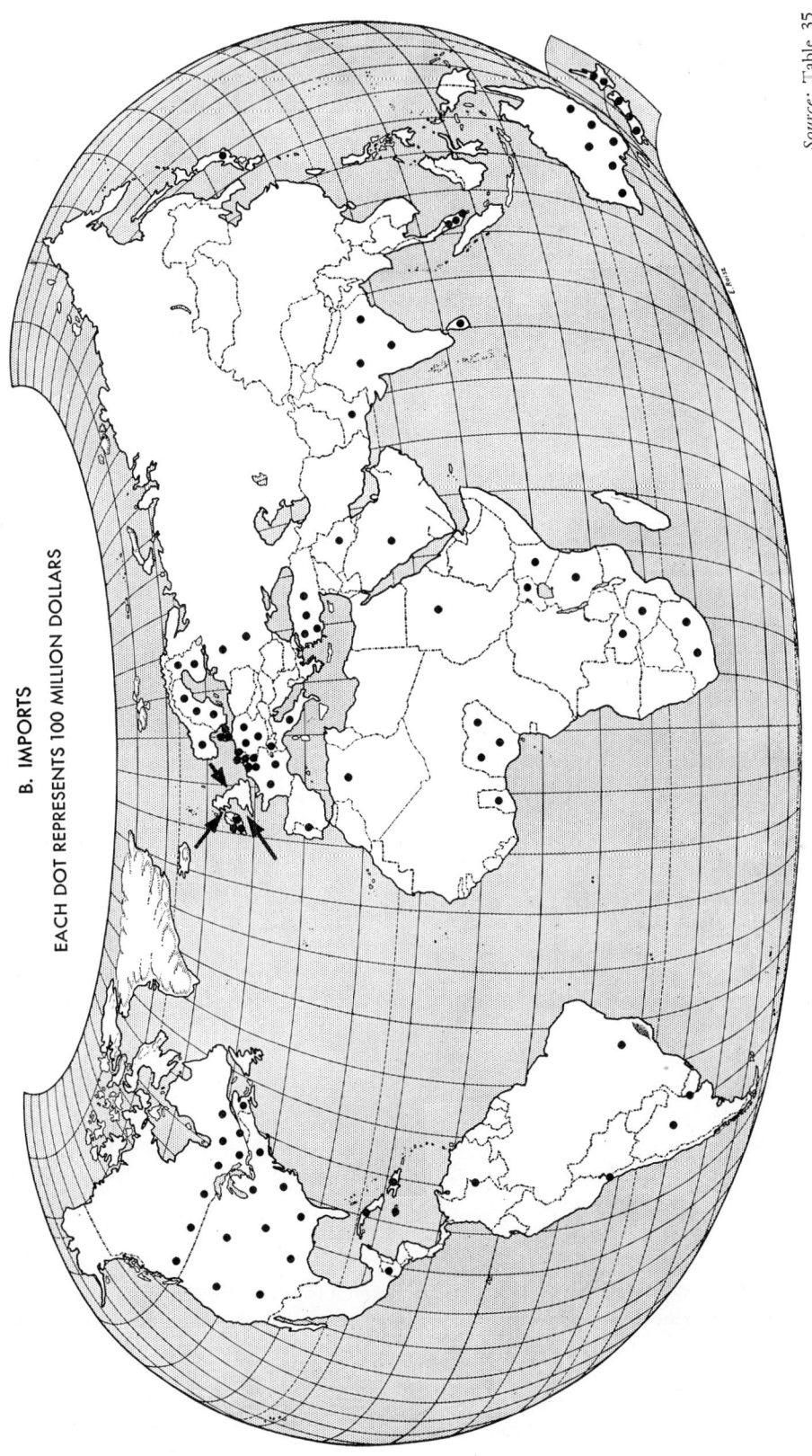

B. IMPORTS

EACH DOT REPRESENTS 100 MILLION DOLLARS

Figure 24. Geographic Distribution of Foreign Trade of the United Kingdom, 1952

Source: Table 35

111

Table 35

DIRECTION OF FOREIGN TRADE OF THE UNITED STATES AND THE UNITED KINGDOM, 1950–52

(Millions of Dollars)

| | United States | | | | | | United Kingdom | | | | | |
| | Exports | | | Imports | | | Exports | | | Imports | | |
Trade with	1950	1951	1952	1950	1951	1952	1950	1951	1952	1950	1951	1952
World	$10,275	$15,032	$15,164	$8,852	$10,967	$10,714	$6,317	$7,578	$7,541	$7,303	$10,931	$9,748
United States	—	—	—	—	—	—	357	430	501	592	1,066	894
Canada	1,996	2,587	2,785	1,960	2,275	2,385	359	392	364	505	731	894
Mexico	512	712	666	315	326	411	14	18	20	16	49	12
Cuba	456	540	516	406	418	438	10	21	16	105	134	74
Jamaica	8	17	20	2	3	5	25	32	38	31	32	41
Netherlands Antilles	69	68	88	158	160	178	10	11	17	119	162	102
Colombia	229	224	230	313	362	384	17	10	20	1	2	4
Venezuela	392	456	500	324	324	396	40	46	54	45	54	27
Bolivia	20	40	30	35	51	56	3	5	5	32	45	45
Brazil	343	700	564	715	911	808	121	155	148	114	185	44
Chile	70	166	130	160	203	286	18	22	21	16	23	23
Argentina	142	233	147	206	220	159	109	81	60	268	241	149
United Kingdom	511	901	676	335	466	485	—	—	—	—	—	—
Ireland	44	53	38	2	8	10	253	286	264	175	196	251
France	334	423	365	132	263	167	155	202	198	307	378	243
Belgium-Luxembourg	266	377	291	140	216	191	163	177	170	182	256	284
Netherlands	234	286	276	85	112	157	214	219	216	240	364	290
Denmark	55	66	50	12	20	25	184	168	181	283	319	331
Sweden	97	134	123	71	105	90	230	273	236	185	385	312
Norway	71	89	78	41	50	52	150	187	170	78	133	125
Finland	21	34	37	35	56	38	59	93	107	95	280	184
Germany (Federal Republic)	439	519	444	104	233	212	156	170	179	116	217	251
Switzerland	128	193	151	110	134	142	87	103	89	36	57	60
Portugal	36	42	41	24	32	37	48	51	54	33	55	36
Spain	44	111	57	50	60	63	28	35	57	70	109	86
Italy	340	456	412	109	140	157	89	100	150	143	233	128
Greece	91	97	65	17	21	20	44	42	37	10	15	19
Turkey	59	61	63	61	76	63	30	63	101	33	30	21
China	68	41 [a]	59 [a]	150	6 [a]	6 [a]	10	8	4	30	24	14
Japan	416	598	622	182	205	229	8	27	26	22	49	81
Hong Kong	103	29	27	5	9	12	79	101	80	34	39	17
Israel	92	107	90	8	12	12	28	34	24	14	17	16
Saudi Arabia	32	53	93	24	30	50	8	10	21	23	104	100
Iran	33	35	17	24	35	23	85	55	16	134	92	8
Pakistan	30	38	55	31	44	23	115	129	158	73	113	81
India	212	463	381	259	297	272	272	324	316	275	427	321
Ceylon	6	19	26	66	49	41	48	67	73	78	122	98
Malaya and Singapore	20	58	36	310	426	382	152	246	240	162	406	278
Indonesia	78	162	132	156	266	276	24	37	48	36	90	35
Philippines	235	350	283	235	284	236	5	7	6	4	12	9
Egypt	32	78	76	55	47	76	120	115	91	112	133	36
Sudan	1	2	2	3	6	3	26	37	58	61	174	95
Belgian Congo	40	61	70	46	63	81	16	23	30	22	28	29
Gold Coast	6	8	10	61	88	67	67	84	99	52	74	66
Nigeria	6	9	10	35	49	42	97	115	155	207	264	310
Kenya and Uganda	…	…	…	…	…	…	68	91	81	43	66	63
Northern Rhodesia	2	3	4	31	20	15	19	20	30	63	113	160
Southern Rhodesia	4	8	7	7	6	9	68	87	90	47	44	60
Union of South Africa	120	247	215	142	138	105	341	467	401	145	178	191
Australia	100	178	174	141	350	154	719	912	618	615	706	630
New Zealand	27	58	43	65	97	84	243	312	320	375	461	464

Source: **10**, Annual Issue 1953, pp. 6–9 and 100–03.   a. Taiwan.

tropical products but could pay for them with 2–3 per cent of its production.

The United Kingdom, on the contrary, cannot maintain a high level of production and employment or restore and improve its prewar level of consumption without an appreciable expansion of foreign trade. It must build up financial assets abroad in order to restore the flow of invisible imports and assure its people of their daily bread, without ration cards. Geographic conditions, favorable in some respects but highly unfavorable in others, have determined the role of the United Kingdom as the mainspring of world trade.

The United States, with vast stretches of land, variety in climate, abundance of natural resources and two oceans washing its shores, can expand its exports on short notice. When the political state of the world makes it necessary, the United States can supply the world market with almost all the commodities usually exported by the United Kingdom, Germany, France and half a dozen other industrially developed countries. The United States is unable, however, after the emergency ends, to take its payment for these deliveries in the form of increased imports. Increase of exports is therefore only a temporary and limited goal of its commercial policy. Its ultimate goal is a flexible equilibrium of exports and imports which assures the necessary imports and provides outlets for key industries best fitted for exporting their production surpluses.

OUTLOOK

Orderly world trade — a circular multilateral exchange of merchandise — which existed, with only a brief interruption, from the last two or three decades of the nineteenth century to the late 1920's, has not been operative since the 1930's. It cannot be resumed unless the convertibility of currencies is restored, restrictions on the flow of merchandise and capital are eliminated, and Europe, especially Great Britain, expands industrial capacity.

Considerable progress has been achieved in these directions in recent years, and there is a chance that multilateral transactions will be resumed in a large part of the world market in the not-too-remote future. More time will elapse before these operations can expand to the dimensions which would assure a high standard of living for Europe and all the advantages of

modern economic progress for the primary producers in underdeveloped areas.

The United States assumed leadership in world trade in the critical postwar years. Indeed, the country financed the world trade recovery from the stalemate in 1946–47 to the comparative equilibrium in 1951–52. After restoration of multilateral world trade, however, the leading role in international trade may return to the United Kingdom.

The new network of world trade will differ from that in 1913 or 1928. A politically important sector of the world may remain — at least temporarily — outside this system and form a regional market of its own, behind the Iron Curtain. The underdeveloped areas may exercise more influence on the flow of goods than in the past. Dissolution of colonial empires will probably result in a temporary contraction in output of industrial raw materials once produced by plantations and of mines operated by foreign capital. Changes in supply-demand conditions may cause a shift in the structure of world prices that could seriously affect industrially developed countries. It will become increasingly difficult for such countries to find sufficient outlets for their produce and to acquire raw materials and foodstuffs from less developed areas. But the law of relative cost of production will remain the mainspring of foreign trade. It will be to the advantage of the areas rich in raw materials to continue production for their own use and for export. They will increasingly use modern techniques, trading their produce for necessary equipment and articles that can be produced more advantageously in the old industrial areas.

The spread of mechanized economy over the world will change the pattern of the international division of labor, but it will not reduce the world economy to an agglomeration of self-sufficient national cells.

CHAPTER 4

THE COMPOSITION OF FOREIGN TRADE

THE EXTREME variety of goods in foreign trade, the differences in national nomenclature and usage, and the frequent changes in patterns of merchandise make precise analysis of the composition of world trade very difficult. After half a century of discussion, the problem of a universal international classification of commodities is still unsolved. Many nations still record their exports and imports according to their own classification.[1] There is, therefore, a considerable margin of error in any attempt to estimate the share of particular commodities or groups of articles in world trade or the trade of a continent.[2]

CLASSIFICATION OF COMMODITIES

The first attempt to establish uniformity in international trade statistics was made by the International Bureau of Trade Statistics (Brussels) in 1910–13. The Bureau's classification had 186 commodity headings grouped in five broad classes. The broad classification was widely used in the interwar years, but the complete Brussels list of commodities has exercised little influence on international trade statistics.

It was left to the League of Nations and the United Nations to try to persuade governments to accept a uniform classification of commodities, at least in addition to the lists currently used by customs officials. The Minimum List developed by the League was accepted before the outbreak of World War II by twenty-five countries.[3] It did not prove very satisfactory, however, and was radically revised after the war. In July 1950, the Economic and Social Council of the UN established a new Standard International Trade Classification (SITC). This has been officially accepted by two dozen countries[4] and many other governments have expressed the intention of using it. However, only a few countries have rearranged their foreign trade records for previous years according to the new pattern. For analytical purposes, therefore, especially for historical comparison, one must rely on the older classifications, which are briefly discussed in the following pages.

BROAD CLASSES

The Brussels classification (1913) distinguished five broad classes of commodities: (1) live animals; (2) foodstuffs and beverages; (3) materials, raw or partly manufactured; (4) manufactured articles; (5) gold and silver, specie.

The first class represents a very small part of world trade and, since live animals are exported largely for slaughter, can be merged with foodstuffs.[5] Gold is usually excluded from reports on merchandise trade. Practically, therefore, the Brussels classification has been reduced to three large groups. Although very rough, this classification has proved useful in an analysis of major currents in world trade and has been widely used in historical surveys of foreign trade.[6]

The League of Nations Minimum List, drawn up in the 1920's as part of a general campaign to improve international statistics, was based on cross-classification of goods by economic characteristics and stage of production.[7]

The classification of commodities by economic characteristics distinguished five broad groups: [8] (1) materials for production; (2) oils and fats; (3) fuels, electric energy and lubricants; (4) capital equipment for agriculture, industry and commerce; (5) articles ready for retail sale or consumers' use. Within this grouping, all commodities were classified by stage of production

---

1. See **9, 26**.
2. For such estimates see **3**, p. 32 (32 commodities, 1938); and **35**, 1938, pp. 156*–62* (more than 200 commodities, 1929–37).
3. **3**, pp. 21ff.
4. The United States, Canada, Mexico, Dominican Republic, Trinidad and Tobago, Panama, Colombia; the United Kingdom, Ireland, Iceland, France, Belgium-Luxembourg, the Netherlands, Denmark, Sweden, Norway,

Germany, Austria, Portugal, Italy, Greece; Turkey, Japan, Hong Kong, Australia. (**9**, 1952.)
5. **3**, pp. 21–24.
6. **34**, various years; **40**, p. 213. A slightly modified classification has been used in the United States. (**28**, p. 246.)
7. See **2**.
8. **1**, 1936, p. 352.

as "crude materials"; "simply transformed articles"; or "more elaborately transformed articles."

It is a matter of opinion whether the selection of the five broad classes was happy or whether it would be better to combine classes 1, 2 and 3 under a single heading as industrial raw materials and subdivide class 5. One can also argue whether the "stages of production" as described here are preferable to the customary distinction between raw materials, semifinished goods and finished or fabricated articles. In any event, the Minimum List has not gained the popularity of the abbreviated Brussels classification.

The German Central Statistical Office (Statistisches Reichsamt) developed another, and perhaps better, broad classification, grouping world exports, 1929–37, by the industrial division in which a commodity is produced. This classification distinguished four branches of agriculture and related pursuits (field and plantation economy; forestry; husbandry and hunting; fishery) and thirteen branches of industrial production, including mining.[9]

Another broad classification used by the German Central Statistical Office distinguished four types of foodstuffs and four stages of industrial production—raw materials, transformed materials, semifinished articles and finished articles.[10]

INTERNATIONAL COMMODITY LISTS

Minimum List of the League of Nations

The complete minimum list of the League of Nations was divided into 17 sections, 50 chapters and 456 items. The sections correspond roughly to branches of industry, and the chapters, to types of products. The immediate purpose of this classification was to provide a list which would be acceptable to a large number of countries despite the differences in the composition of their trade. When classification is carried only to the level of "chapters," it cannot be used for cross-tabulation by economic characteristics and the stage of production. Such an analytical tabulation (even for the simple Brussels classification) requires that "chapters" of the Minimum List be divided into single items and regrouped.

Standard Industrial Trade Classification (SITC)

The new standard classification sponsored by the UN is purely empirical. It starts with 570 items which cover all commodities of international trade in summary form, in such a way that each item clearly excludes commodities included in other items.[11] The items are arranged into 150 groups designed to distinguish the commodity data normally sought in international trade returns. Only these groups are used in UN statistics of international trade.[12]

The groups, in turn, are assembled into 52 divisions according to their broader characteristics, such as the type of commodity, its use, the industry in which it is produced, and so on. The divisions are finally consolidated into 10 sections which serve to subdivide imports and exports according to broad economic groups. The main differences between the Minimum List and SITC are that the latter has an abbreviated list of 150 groups inserted between the 52 "divisions" and 570 single items, and that its divisions are better integrated and more clearly distinguishable than the chapters of the Minimum List. These are the broad sections of SITC:

0. Food
1. Beverages and tobacco
2. Crude materials, inedible, except fuels
3. Mineral fuels, lubricants and related materials
4. Animal and vegetable oils and fats
5. Chemicals
6. Manufactured goods, classified chiefly by material [13]
7. Machinery and transport equipment
8. Miscellaneous manufactured articles [14]
9. Miscellaneous transactions and commodities.

Meaningful generalizations can be deduced from combining the "divisions" of SITC, without splitting them into "groups."

---

9. **35**, 1938, p. 154*. Articles which pass through several industries are classified according to the last industry.

10. **35**, 1938, p. 154*. The headings are freely translated. A literal translation of the German terms (*Rohstoffe, Halbwaren, Fertigwaren-Vorerzeugnisse,* and *Fertigwaren-und-Erzeugnisse*) would make little sense in English.

11. **7**, pp. viii-ix. Although the basic list is supposed to be exhaustive, provision is made for expanding it, on the basis of special international agreements, within the system of the adopted five-digit numerical code.

12. **5**.

13. Leather; rubber; wood; paper; textiles; nonmetallic minerals; metals, subdivided in three groups (silver, platina, gems and jewelry; base metals; manufactures of metals).

14. Classified chiefly by use: prefabricated buildings, sanitary plumbing, etc.; furniture and fixtures; travel goods, etc.; clothing, footwear; professional, scientific and controlling instruments, photographic and optical goods, watches and clocks; miscellaneous.

Table 36

Exports and Imports of the World and the Continents by Main Commodity Group,
Value and Percentage, 1929 and 1937

Continent [a]	Exports				Imports			
	Total	Food-stuffs [b]	Materials	Fabricated Articles	Total	Food-stuffs [b]	Materials	Fabricated Articles
Millions of Gold Dollars [c]								
1929								
World	$32,443	$7,861	$11,338	$13,244	$35,230	$8,909	$13,029	$13,292
America	9,290	2,835	3,692	2,763	8,099	1,691	2,882	3,525
Europe	16,078	2,906	3,883	9,290	19,842	5,764	8,337	5,741
Asia	5,074	1,334	2,596	1,143	4,883	1,120	1,429	2,334
Africa	1,143	381	738	24	1,477	262	214	1,000
Oceania	858	405	429	24	929	72	167	691
1937								
World	14,959	3,359	5,693	5,907	16,102	3,764	6,574	5,764
America	3,954	1,024	1,739	1,191	3,287	738	1,191	1,358
Europe	7,075	1,167	1,953	3,954	9,123	2,477	4,311	2,334
Asia	2,739	691	1,310	738	2,453	405	881	1,167
Africa	691	238	429	24	810	119	95	596
Oceania	500	238	262	. . .	429	24	95	310
Percentage								
1929								
World	100.0	24.2	35.0	40.8	100.0	25.7	37.0	37.3
America	100.0	30.5	39.8	29.7	100.0	20.8	35.6	43.6
Europe	100.0	18.1	24.2	57.7	100.0	29.1	42.0	28.9
Asia	100.0	26.5	51.0	22.5	100.0	22.4	29.6	48.0
Africa	100.0	32.4	63.7	3.9	100.0	17.5	14.2	68.3
Oceania	100.0	46.6	51.4	2.0	100.0	8.5	18.6	72.9
1937								
World	100.0	22.4	38.1	39.5	100.0	23.3	40.9	35.8
America	100.0	25.7	44.4	29.9	100.0	22.7	36.3	41.0
Europe	100.0	16.6	27.8	55.6	100.0	27.2	47.3	25.5
Asia	100.0	24.8	48.0	27.2	100.0	15.9	36.2	47.9
Africa	100.0	35.2	61.0	3.8	100.0	13.7	13.5	72.8
Oceania	100.0	47.4	49.3	3.3	100.0	7.4	18.4	74.2

Source: Computed on the basis of **35**, 1938, pp. 149*–50*.

a. Europe includes the USSR.
b. Includes live animals.

c. For 1929, U.S. dollars at current prices are identical with gold dollars. For 1937, conversion of foreign currencies into current U.S. dollars would show a total value of world exports close to $25 billion, and of world imports close to $26.5 billion.

Main Groups of Commodities in Foreign Trade

The composition of imports and exports of individual countries varies from year to year under the impact of changing business conditions, divergent movements of prices and other factors. In the quantum of foreign trade, industrial raw materials and manufactured articles are most sensitive to the business cycle, while foodstuffs depend on weather and harvest conditions.

The World and the Continents

In 1929 foodstuffs (including live animals) represented 24 per cent of the value of world exports; raw materials (including semifinished goods) comprised 35 per cent, and manufactured articles, 41 per cent. The share of foodstuffs and raw materials in world imports was 26 and 37 per cent, respectively, and that of manufactured articles, 37 per cent. The discrepancy was due to the cost of transportation, which is the main item in the difference between the export and import values of each commodity. Since foodstuffs and raw materials are much more bulky than manufactured articles, the cost of transporting them is usually greater in relation to their export value.

In 1937 foodstuffs represented 22 per cent of the value of world exports and 23 per cent of that of imports. The comparable figures for raw materials were 38 and 41 per cent; for manufactured articles, close to 40 and 36 per cent.[15] (See Table 36.)

In both 1929 and 1937, Europe had a large import surplus in foodstuffs and raw materials, partly covered by its export surplus in manufactured articles. All other continents had an active trade balance in foodstuffs and materials and a passive balance in fabricated articles. The net trade balances of each continent were as follows (in millions of dollars): [16]

	1929	1937
America		
Foodstuffs	+$1,144	+$286
Materials	+810	+548
Fabricated articles	−762	−167
Europe		
Foodstuffs	−2,858	−1,310
Materials	−4,454	−2,358
Fabricated articles	+3,549	+1,620
Asia		
Foodstuffs	+214	+286
Materials	+1,167	+429
Fabricated articles	−1,191	−429
Africa		
Foodstuffs	+119	+119
Materials	+524	+334
Fabricated articles	−976	−572
Oceania		
Foodstuffs	+333	+214
Materials	+262	+167
Fabricated articles	−667	−310

15. These data, based on the estimates of world trade prepared by the German Central Statistical Office, are very close to the estimates of the League of Nations. (Cf. Table 37.)

16. Computed from Table 36.

World trade in the interwar years, as before World War I, was largely a flow of foodstuffs and materials from all parts of the world to Europe and a flow of fabricated articles from Europe to other continents. The consolidated trade balances of Europe and the rest of the world were as follows (in millions of dollars):

	1929	1937
Europe		
Foodstuffs and materials	−$7,312	−$3,668
Fabricated articles	+3,549	+1,620
All other continents		
Foodstuffs and materials	+4,573	+2,382
Fabricated articles	−3,597	−1,477

In these totals, however, Europe's passive balance in foodstuffs and materials is overstated because of the addition of transportation costs to the value of imported goods. Since the largest part of world trade was carried by European merchant ships, the cost of transporting imported goods is not a liability of Europe to other continents. The picture is more realistic, therefore, if the value of imported foodstuffs and materials is cut by, say, 12 per cent.[17] With this correction, the trade balances of Europe and other continents were as follows (in millions of dollars):

	1929	1937
Europe		
Foodstuffs and materials	−$5,620	−$2,853
Fabricated articles	+3,549	+1,620
Total	−2,071	−1,233
All other continents		
Foodstuffs and materials	+5,513	+2,808
Fabricated articles	−3,597	−1,477
Total	+1,916	+1,331

The role of the principal groups of commodities in world trade appears clearer when we examine smaller and economically more homogeneous areas.

SEVENTEEN GEOGRAPHICAL AREAS

When all the countries of the world are distributed among seventeen geographical areas ac-

17. This rate corresponds roughly to the difference in the values of world imports and exports of foodstuffs and materials in both 1929 and 1937. No correction is required for fabricated articles since, in world totals, their import value appears, roughly, in balance with export value. (See Table 36.)

TABLE 37
FOREIGN TRADE OF SEVENTEEN GEOGRAPHICAL AREAS: PERCENTAGE DISTRIBUTION BY MAIN
COMMODITY GROUP, 1928 AND 1937

	Exports			Imports		
Geographical Area	Food-stuffs [a]	Materials	Manufac-tured Goods	Food-stuffs [a]	Materials	Manufac-tured Goods
1928						
World	25	35	40	26	36	38
North America						
Canada	51	22	27	17	28	55
United States	15	43	42	25	50	25
Latin America						
Mineral-producing countries	13	85	2	15	19	66
Tropical agricultural countries	80	18	2	24	12	64
Other agricultural countries	63	34	3	13	20	67
Europe						
Continental industrial countries	13	23	64	27	48	25
Other continental countries	54	33	13	20	31	49
Noncontinental countries	10	18	72	45	33	22
USSR	21	63	16	10	48	42
Asia						
India, Burma, Ceylon	25	51	24	19	12	69
Southeast Asia	41	54	5	24	22	54
Japan, Korea, Formosa	9	43	48	12	64	24
Other continental countries	21	52	27	23	22	55
Africa						
Northern	36	59	5	21	17	62
Southern	17	76	7	12	10	78
Other countries	39	61	0	20	10	70
Oceania	44	54	2	9	17	74
1937						
World	22	39	39	23	41	36
North America						
Canada	32	40	28	15	32	53
United States	8	42	50	29	51	20
Latin America						
Mineral-producing countries	9	90	1	11	27	62
Tropical agricultural countries	69	30	1	20	13	67
Other agricultural countries	62	35	3	11	19	70
Europe						
Continental industrial countries	11	26	63	23	54	23
Other continental countries	43	39	18	13	39	48
Noncontinental countries	10	18	72	41	41	18
USSR	24	58	18	12	50	38
Asia						
India, Burma, Ceylon	30	49	21	15	20	65
Southeast Asia	25	71	4	17	27	56
Japan, Korea, Formosa	11	19	70	5	74	21
Other continental countries	27	55	18	14	18	68
Africa						
Northern	42	54	4	21	21	58
Southern	28	65	7	7	10	83
Other countries	36	62	2	19	8	73
Oceania	45	51	4	8	18	74

Source: **3**, pp. 23–24.   a. Includes live animals.

TABLE 38

EXPORTS AND IMPORTS OF COLONIAL POWERS AND THEIR DOMINIONS AND COLONIES: PERCENTAGE
DISTRIBUTION BY MAIN COMMODITY GROUP, 1937

	Exports			Imports		
Countries	*Food-stuffs* [a]	*Materials*	*Fabricated Articles*	*Food-stuffs* [a]	*Materials*	*Fabricated Articles*
United Kingdom and Ireland	10	18	72	41	41	18
Total Commonwealth	28	33	39	24	40	36
France	15	29	56	26	59	15
France and its colonies	32	31	37	25	48	27
Belgium, Italy, Portugal, Spain and colonies	21	35	44	21	50	29
Netherlands	37	31	32	18	42	40
Netherlands and its colonies	27	57	16	16	37	47

Source: **3,** pp. 27–29.   a. Includes live animals.

cording to the classification used by Hilgerdt in analyzing the network of world trade, the following typical patterns of foreign trade can be distinguished:

1. Exchange of raw materials for fabricated articles: mineral-producing countries of Latin America, India, Burma, Ceylon, southeastern and continental Asia, southern and central Africa.

2. Exchange of foodstuffs for fabricated articles: agricultural countries of Latin America.

3. Exchange of industrial materials and foodstuffs (without decisive predominance of either group) for fabricated articles: Canada, eastern and southern Europe, northern Africa, Oceania.

4. Exchange of fabricated goods for materials: United States, industrial countries of continental Europe, Japan.

5. Exchange of fabricated goods for materials and foodstuffs: United Kingdom.

In the foreign trade of the USSR materials predominate in both exports and imports. (See Table 37.)

The main feature in the classification of countries by composition of foreign trade is the share of fabricated articles in their exports and imports.

Export of foodstuffs and raw materials and import of fabricated articles by an area are not necessarily associated with poverty and backwardness. Oceania has a higher percentage of fabricated articles in its imports and a higher percentage of foodstuffs and raw materials in its exports than the USSR or continental Asia. The share of fabricated goods in Canadian imports does not differ much from that in North Africa and southeastern Asia.

The controlling factor in the composition of exports and imports of each nation or geographical area is the relative cost of production.[18] This factor favors export of foodstuffs and agricultural raw materials from young and rather sparsely populated areas and forces industrially developed and densely populated areas to import foodstuffs and raw materials. (See Figure 25.)

The contrasts in the composition of exports and imports of different geographical areas show the mutually complementary character of their economies. The industrial and agricultural areas are also economically integrated, to some extent, regionally and in the scope of colonial empires.

The situation of the British Commonwealth is striking. The United Kingdom has a huge deficit in foodstuffs and raw materials and an active balance for fabricated articles. But when the Commonwealth is considered as an economic unit, its consolidated imports of each broad group of commodities are roughly in equilibrium with exports. (See Table 38.[19]) The United Kingdom, of course, cannot absorb all the foodstuffs and raw materials exported by British colonies and dominions, and British industry cannot obtain all needed materials within the Commonwealth, but in transactions with the rest of world, the Commonwealth as a whole pays for imported foodstuffs and raw materials with the foodstuffs and materials it produces and for imported fab-

18. See Chapter 2, p. 33.

19. The current balances of trade between various areas differ from the prewar conditions described in Table 38. The general pattern of trade between the colonial powers and their colonies and associated areas, however, has not changed substantially.

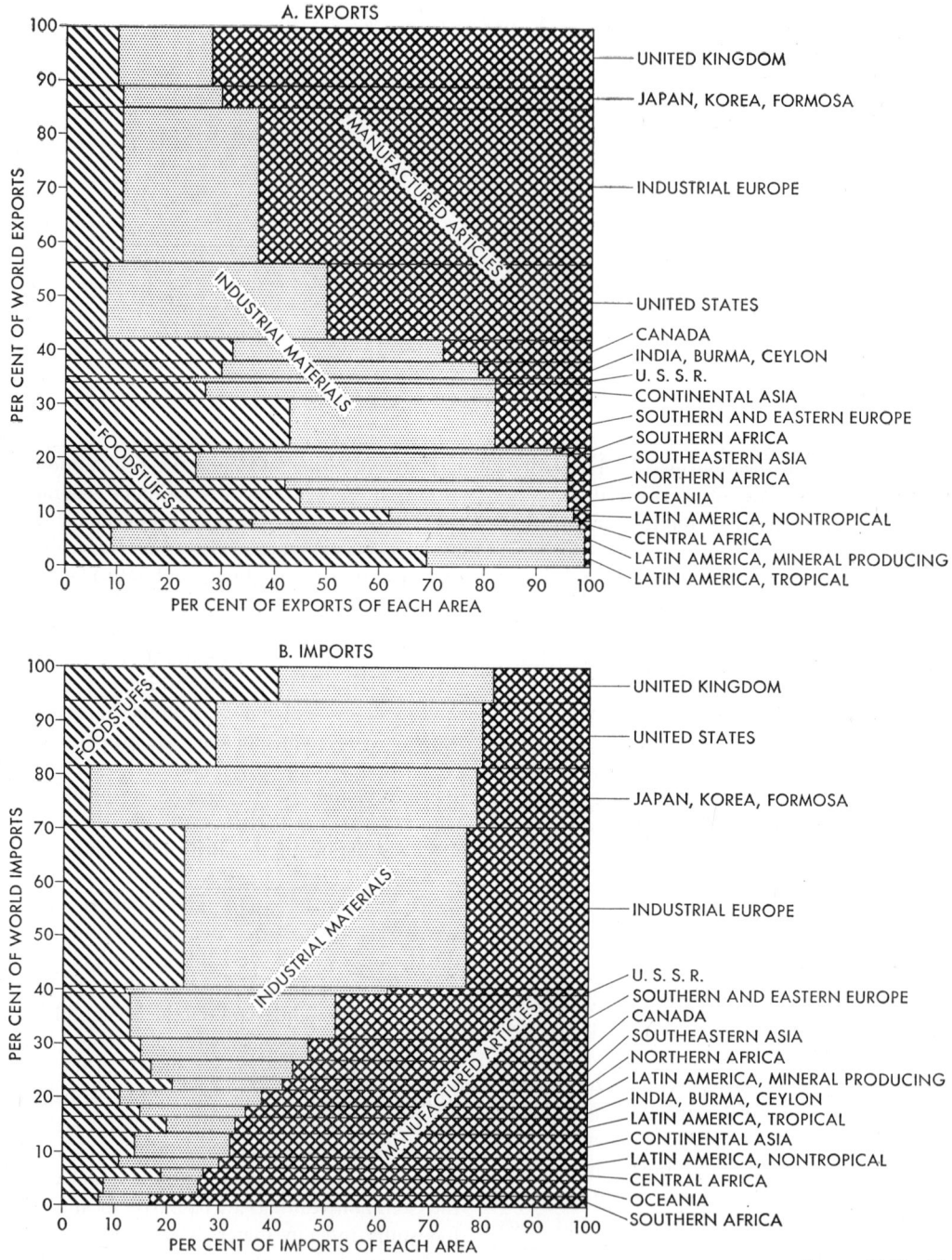

FIGURE 25. EXPORTS AND IMPORTS OF SEVENTEEN GEOGRAPHICAL AREAS: PERCENTAGE DISTRIBUTION BY
MAIN COMMODITY GROUP, 1937

ricated articles with its own fabricated products.

This is likewise the situation for France and its overseas possessions, mainly in northern and central Africa, and to some extent for Belgium, Italy (before World War II), Portugal and Spain and their colonies. On the contrary, the Dutch colonies were not economically complementary to the Netherlands, and when the Dutch were masters of the present Indonesia, exports of foods, raw materials and fabricated articles were not in equilibrium with imports in the consolidated foreign trade of the Dutch colonial empire. (See Table 38.)

SELECTED COUNTRIES

The composition of the exports and imports of individual countries reveals the same variety of patterns as in the seventeen geographical areas.

Foodstuffs predominate in the exports of Cuba (sugar), Colombia (coffee), Brazil (coffee) and Argentina (corn, wheat, meat); Ireland (cattle) and Spain (fruit, olive oil, wine); Algeria (fruit, wine) and the Gold Coast (cocoa); the Philippines (sugar) and New Zealand (meat, butter, cheese). All these countries exchange their surplus in foodstuffs for fabricated articles.

To this list should be added countries which trade foodstuffs for raw materials: Denmark (specializing in export of meat, butter, eggs), Hungary (cattle, hogs, wheat, corn, rye) and Portugal (fish, wine). In Ceylon, which trades tea for rice and fish, foodstuffs predominate in both exports and imports. (See Table 39.)

Among countries that trade industrial materials for fabricated articles, two groups can be distinguished: producers of vegetable raw materials (including timber, naval stores, rubber) and producers of minerals. Some areas export materials of both types. Among the exporters of vegetable raw materials are Turkey (tobacco), India (cotton, jute), Malaya (rubber), Egypt (cotton), and Nigeria (groundnuts, palm kernels). Minerals prevail in the exports of Venezuela (petroleum), Peru (petroleum, copper), Bolivia [20] (tin), Chile (copper, sodium), Iran (petroleum) and the Union of South Africa (gold). Norway's exports include wood pulp, ferroalloys and aluminum; the main materials exported by Indonesia (Netherlands Indies in Table 39) are rubber, tobacco, petroleum and tin.

---

20. Not listed in Table 39.

These patterns of foreign trade — exchange of foodstuffs or industrial materials or both for fabricated articles — prevail in an area which includes at least three fourths of the world's population. In the *fourth* sector of the world commodities flow in the opposite direction. Fabricated articles are traded for imported foodstuffs and materials by the United States, United Kingdom, France, Belgium, Germany, Switzerland, Austria, Czechoslovakia, Italy and Japan — a surprisingly brief list which does not include such economically developed nations as the Netherlands, Denmark, Sweden, Norway, Australia and New Zealand.

The countries with an export surplus in fabricated articles represent about one sixth of the world population but about half of world trade. On the world map, areas with export balances of fabricated goods look like three islands surrounded on all sides by countries with import balances of these commodities. (See Figure 26,A.) All these areas except the United States are densely populated. On the distorted map of world population, therefore, they appear larger in relation to other areas than on a conventional geographical map. (See Figure 26,B.) When countries are classified according to the balance of exports and imports of fabricated articles on a distorted map which shows each country on the scale of its foreign trade, it appears that countries with net export of fabricated articles keep fairly well in balance with the countries which have a net import of these articles. (See Figure 26,C.)

Net export of fabricated articles does not necessarily imply an absolute predominance of commodities of this type in a country's exports. The United States and Belgium-Luxembourg have a considerable net export of finished products, but before the war such commodities accounted for less than half the value of their exports. (See Table 39.)

The foreign trade of the world as a whole cannot be classified by stage of production and use of exported and imported goods. Applied to single countries, this classification splits foodstuffs among all three stages of production, recording live animals and grains as "crude materials," flour as "simply transformed materials" and bacon or cheese as "more elaborate articles." In the classification by use, foodstuffs are split between materials and articles ready for retail sale to consumers, while the "fabricated articles"

TABLE 39

EXPORTS AND IMPORTS OF SELECTED COUNTRIES: PERCENTAGE DISTRIBUTION BY MAIN COMMODITY GROUP, AROUND 1937 [a]

	Exports			Imports		
Pattern of Trade, and Country	Food-stuffs	Materials	Fabricated Articles	Food-stuffs	Materials	Fabricated Articles
Foodstuffs for fabricated articles						
Cuba	78.9	17.7	3.4	29.0	11.7	59.3
Colombia	69.8	29.7	0.5	9.0	7.0	84.0
Brazil	63.8	35.8	0.4	21.3	19.2	59.5
Argentina	66.2	30.9	2.9	10.3	18.3	71.4
Ireland	86.6	9.3	4.1	27.2	24.6	48.2
Spain	69.8	14.5	15.7	20.2	37.1	42.7
Algeria	80.9	14.3	4.8	25.9	13.5	60.6
Gold Coast	83.6	16.4	...	16.2	8.8	75.0
Philippines	57.7	35.7	6.6	18.6	11.7	69.7
New Zealand	64.8	34.9	0.3	10.9	11.0	78.1
Foodstuffs for other foodstuffs or materials						
Denmark	76.8	8.7	14.5	14.5	45.3	40.2
Hungary	57.0	13.0	30.0	5.7	57.6	36.7
Portugal	55.3	30.3	14.4	17.0	46.1	36.9
Ceylon	65.5	33.2	1.3	43.9	15.8	40.3
Materials for fabricated articles						
Venezuela	7.4	92.3	0.3	10.4	2.0	87.6
Peru	9.6	89.8	0.6	17.4	9.5	73.1
Chile	9.1	89.4	1.5	13.0	20.4	66.6
Norway	20.3	56.8	22.9	15.2	29.0	55.8
Greece	29.3	63.3	7.4	32.7	26.8	40.5
Turkey	3.5	62.5	34.0	4.0	13.9	82.1
Manchukuo	17.5	78.4	4.1	11.1	15.1	73.8
Iran	13.0	80.0	7.0	17.9	10.1	72.0
British India	20.8	51.1	28.1	11.4	22.3	66.3
Netherlands Indies	21.8	75.9	2.3	13.7	5.7	80.6
Egypt	10.1	86.1	3.8	12.3	29.7	58.0
Belgian Congo	15.3	82.8	1.9	13.3	8.2	78.5
Nigeria	33.2	65.2	1.6	12.2	5.7	82.1
Union of South Africa	30.9	60.0	9.1	6.1	10.5	83.4
Foodstuffs and materials for fabricated articles						
Canada	32.6	38.8	28.6	14.4	30.3	55.3
Romania	40.4	58.1	1.5	4.4	17.6	78.0
Bulgaria	49.4	46.8	3.8	3.4	25.9	70.7
Yugoslavia	46.3	49.6	4.1	5.2	26.0	68.8
China	32.8	49.0	18.2	11.0	28.8	60.2
Korea	43.1	33.7	23.2	13.3	22.8	63.9
Morocco	46.3	49.9	3.8	33.9	15.3	50.8
Tunisia	53.3	44.3	2.4	26.0	20.2	53.8
Australia	38.7	57.0	4.3	6.7	21.1	72.2

a. For Cuba, Brazil, New Zealand, Portugal, Venezuela, Iran and Belgian Congo: 1936; for Spain: 1932.

(*Continued on facing page*)

TABLE 39—*continued*

Pattern of Trade, and Country	Exports			Imports		
	Food-stuffs	Materials	Fabricated Articles	Food-stuffs	Materials	Fabricated Articles
Fabricated articles for materials						
United States	8.0	42.1	49.9	29.5	50.2	20.3
France	15.2	29.4	55.4	25.7	58.8	15.5
Belgium–Luxembourg	5.6	45.0	49.4	19.7	57.5	22.8
Germany	1.4	16.5	82.1	29.1	60.2	10.7
Czechoslovakia	8.2	19.8	72.0	12.8	57.4	29.8
Italy	30.1	13.2	56.7	22.1	55.7	22.2
Japan	9.4	19.8	70.8	17.0	63.3	19.7
Fabricated articles for foodstuffs and materials						
United Kingdom	6.9	18.3	74.8	41.5	42.0	16.5
Other patterns						
Netherlands	36.6	31.1	32.3	17.8	41.5	40.7
Austria	4.2	29.9	65.9	27.9	42.7	29.4
Poland	31.6	45.1	23.3	9.1	57.0	33.9
Malaya	7.4	88.6	4.0	21.3	48.6	30.0
Sweden	5.9	52.5	41.6	11.8	38.9	49.3
Switzerland	6.4	8.6	85.0	26.6	31.6	41.8

Source: Computed from **35**, 1938, pp. 151*–53*.

of the Brussels classification appear partly as consumers' articles, partly as capital equipment. (See Table 40.)

Not more than a dozen countries export large quantities of capital goods. The rest of the world imports such articles. Before World War II capital goods represented the following percentages of the exports and imports of countries for which information is available:

	Exports	Imports
United States	21.3	1.4
United Kingdom	17.4	2.9
Sweden	15.4	9.1
Czechoslovakia	11.0	8.8
France	10.1	4.9
Denmark	8.8	7.7
Belgium	6.0	6.0
Norway	4.2	18.9
Canada	2.5	12.2
Poland	1.6	12.0
Australia	0.6	17.3

FLUCTUATIONS AND TRENDS

In the World

The relationship between the three groups of commodities — foodstuffs, materials and manu-factured articles — was almost exactly the same in 1938 as in 1929. During that decade, however, the composition of world trade was fluctuating in a wide range under the impact of the depression and recovery.

In 1932 the quantum of trade in manufactured articles was less than 60 as compared with 100 in 1929. The index number for industrial raw materials went down to 81.5 and that for foodstuffs, to 89. Producers of manufactured articles had been able to protect themselves to some extent by adjusting production to the declining demand, while farmers and planters were defenseless against the collapse of prices. Thus in 1933 the dollar prices of exported manufactured articles were some 30 per cent under the 1929 level, while prices of foodstuffs went down 45 per cent and prices of industrial raw materials fell 50 per cent.

As a result of these divergent movements in the quantum of foreign trade and in prices, manufactured products maintained a fairly stable share in the value of foreign trade during the great depression. Their share in world trade, at current prices, was 37.5–38.0 per cent in 1932–33 as compared with 39.5 per cent in 1929, while their share in the quantum of world trade, at

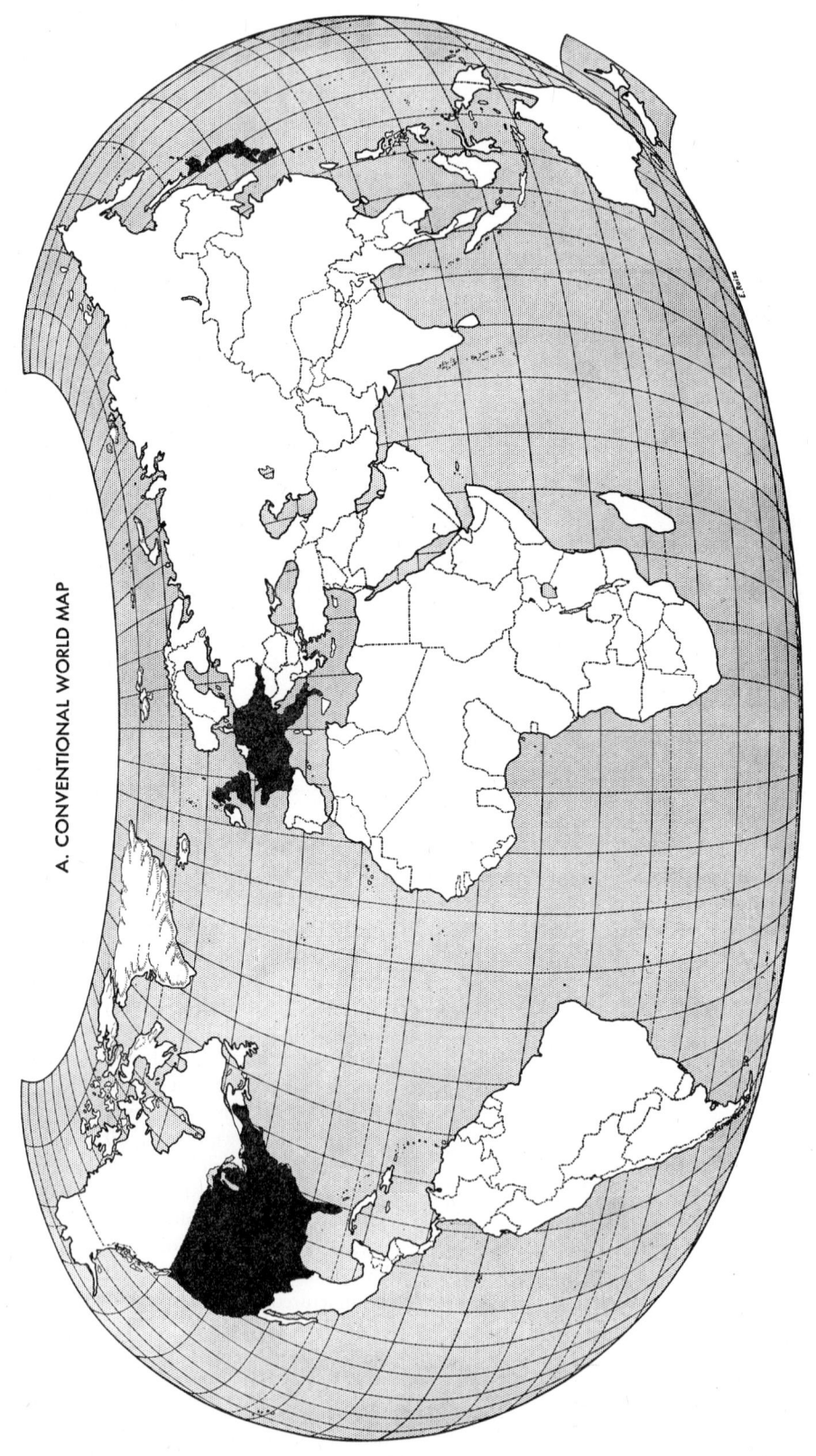

A. CONVENTIONAL WORLD MAP

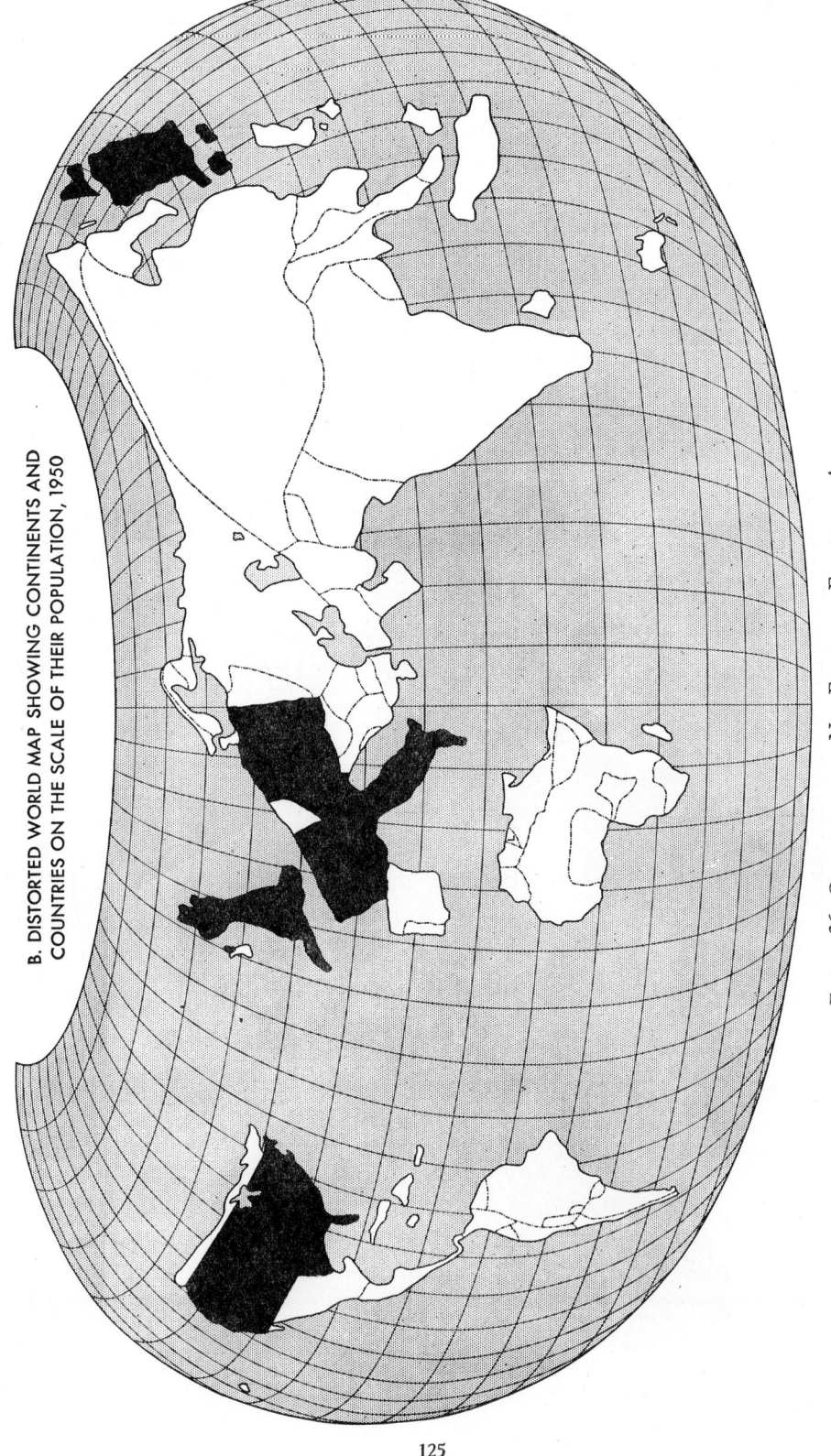

B. DISTORTED WORLD MAP SHOWING CONTINENTS AND
COUNTRIES ON THE SCALE OF THEIR POPULATION, 1950

Figure 26. Countries with Net Export of Fabricated Articles

For map C, see following page

125

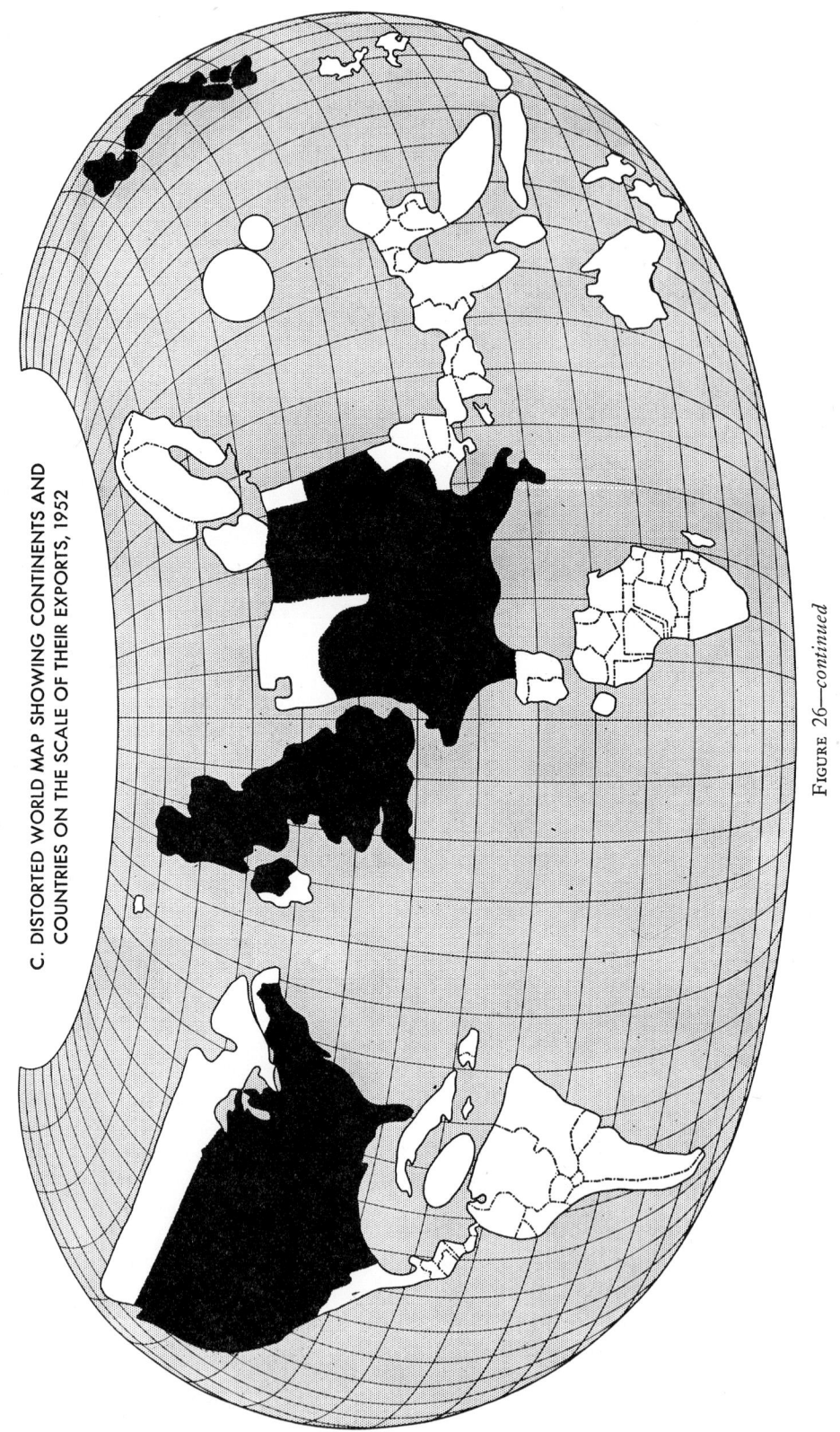

C. DISTORTED WORLD MAP SHOWING CONTINENTS AND
COUNTRIES ON THE SCALE OF THEIR EXPORTS, 1952

FIGURE 26—*continued*

TABLE 40

EXPORTS AND IMPORTS OF SELECTED COUNTRIES: PERCENTAGE DISTRIBUTION BY STAGE OF
PRODUCTION AND USE, 1936

	Stage of Production			Use				
Country	Crude Materials	Crudely Trans- formed	More Elaborate	Materials	Oils and Fats	Fuels, Lubri- cants	Capital Equip- ment	Retail, Con- sumers
United States								
Exports	32.5	23.9	43.6	45.3	0.9	13.6	21.3	18.9
Imports	43.4	30.9	25.7	72.8	5.7	2.4	1.4	17.7
Canada								
Exports	37.1	37.8	25.1	79.4	0.5	0.8	2.5	16.8
Imports	36.3	17.8	45.9	42.8	2.3	14.5	12.2	28.2
United Kingdom								
Exports	12.4	21.7	65.9	41.8	1.2	9.6	17.4	29.9
Imports	44.2	36.8	19.0	49.5	3.6	4.8	2.9	39.2
France								
Exports	19.8	25.1	55.1	54.8	2.1	2.3	10.1	30.7
Imports	56.5	21.6	21.9	49.6	7.1	15.7	4.9	22.7
Belgium								
Exports	21.8	41.7	36.5	72.5	0.7	7.5	6.0	13.3
Imports	51.5	25.6	22.9	67.2	2.8	7.1	6.0	16.9
Denmark								
Exports	23.2	62.6	14.2	16.1	5.2	0.1	8.8	69.8
Imports	31.1	37.6	31.3	58.4	8.4	14.3	7.7	11.2
Sweden								
Exports	16.0	48.7	35.3	72.8	0.6	0.4	15.4	10.8
Imports	31.4	28.1	40.5	48.3	4.2	14.4	9.1	24.0
Norway								
Exports	26.3	50.0	23.7	68.9	7.6	0.1	4.2	19.2
Imports	24.4	28.7	46.9	47.1	5.2	11.0	18.9	17.8
Poland								
Exports	45.1	41.5	13.4	58.0	1.3	16.3	1.6	22.8
Imports	49.7	20.5	29.8	68.8	3.2	0.7	12.0	15.3
Czechoslovakia								
Exports	16.8	22.4	60.8	54.7	0.2	5.5	11.0	28.6
Imports	49.8	23.9	26.3	65.3	7.2	5.7	8.8	13.0
Australia								
Exports	64.7	28.5	6.8	70.9	1.0	0.3	0.6	27.2
Imports	14.0	17.3	68.7	44.4	1.6	8.1	17.3	28.6

Source: **1,** 1936, pp. 360–63.

1929 prices, had declined from 39.5 per cent to 31.0–31.5.[21] (See Table 41.)

In the United States

The distribution of exports and imports of individual countries changes with their economic progress and fluctuates widely from year to year. A striking example of such changes is the com-

position of foreign trade in the United States from the beginning of statistical records — 1821 — to our day.

Until the 1870's, crude materials, mainly cotton, predominated in American exports, while finished manufactures led in imports. Later in the nineteenth century, foodstuffs, crude and manufactured, advanced to the top position in the list of exports; and crude materials increased to head the list of imports. The decisive change

---

21. Cf. **41,** pp. 58–68.

TABLE 41

WORLD TRADE: PERCENTAGE DISTRIBUTION BY MAIN
COMMODITY GROUP AT CURRENT AND
CONSTANT PRICES,[a] 1929–38

	At Current Prices			At 1929 Prices		
Year	Food-stuffs	Materi-als	Manu-fac-tured Arti-cles	Food-stuffs	Materi-als	Manu-fac-tured Arti-cles
1929	24.5	36	39.5	24.5	36	39.5
1930	25.5	34.5	40	26	36.5	37.5
1931	27.5	32.5	40	28	37	35
1932	29	33	38	29.5	39.5	31
1933	26.5	36	37.5	27	41.5	31.5
1934	25	37	38	26	40.5	33.5
1935	24.5	37.5	38	25.5	41	33.5
1936	24.5	38	37.5	25.5	40	34.5
1937	23	39.5	37.5	24	40.5	35.5
1938	24	36	40	25	38.5	36.5

Source: **4,** 1938, p. 61.

a. Sum of exports and imports.

came in the 1890's, when exports of finished and
semifinished manufactures (including foodstuffs) for the first time exceeded imports of
such products. (See Table 42.)

In recent years, the United States has shifted
from crude materials and semifinished goods toward fabricated articles in exports and from
fabricated articles toward crude materials in imports in trade in both agricultural and nonagricultural products. (See Table 43.)

After the turn of the century, the United
States had a continuous export balance in finished manufactures in both dollar value and the
percentage share of such commodities in total
imports and exports. It usually had a negative
balance in crude materials in relation to total
imports and exports — that is, in the relation
between the percentages of crude materials in
the total value of imports and exports. In terms
of dollar value, however, the balance between
imports and exports was positive in some years
and negative in others.

The difference between the two measurements
is illustrated by the following data showing the
surplus of exports (+) or imports (−) of
crude materials and finished manufactures in
U.S. foreign trade: [22]

22. Table 42; cf. **28,** p. 246; **29,** 1953, p. 904.

Year	Crude Materials	Finished Manufactures
	Percentage of Total Imports and Exports	
1900	−8.3	+0.3
1905	−3.3	+4.3
1910	−3.5	+5.6
1915	−13.5	+9.6
1920	−10.5	+13.1
1925	−11.9	+19.5
1930	−10.8	+25.5
1935	+1.8	+24.4
1940	−20.0	+43.1
1945	−19.6	+44.9
1950	−9.6	+39.7
1951	−14.5	+39.6
1952	−14.1	+42.6
	Millions of Dollars	
1900	+$58	+$129
1905	+83	+150
1910	−4	+131
1915	0	+20
1920	+99	+2,328
1925	−306	+1,048
1930	−173	+1,141
1935	+101	+588
1940	−555	+1,921
1945	−300	+5,425
1950	+579	+4,270
1951	+894	+6,605
1952	+954	+7,223

The pattern became clearer in the late 1930's
and especially after World War II. Now the
United States, like the industrialized countries
of Europe, imports not only crude materials but
also crude foodstuffs and semimanufactured
goods, offering manufactures in exchange.

It is noteworthy that the increase in the proportion of finished nonagricultural products in
U.S. exports in 1942–44 was due largely to shipments of military goods, which began on a small
scale in 1941 when the United States, although
not a belligerent, assumed the role of "arsenal of
democracy." (See Figure 27.)

NATIONAL DIFFERENCES

Contrasts in the composition of the foreign
trade of individual countries are evident when
their exports and imports are classified in accordance with the UN Standard International
Trade Classification (SITC). This classification
is available for 1951 and 1952 for most of the
leading commercial nations of the world, including the United States and Canada; the United

TABLE 42

EXPORTS AND IMPORTS OF THE UNITED STATES: PERCENTAGE DISTRIBUTION BY STAGE OF PRODUCTION, 1821–1952

	Exports					Imports				
Year	*Crude Materials*	*Crude Food-stuffs*	*Manufactured Food-stuffs*	*Semi-manufactures*	*Finished Manufactures*	*Crude Materials*	*Crude Food-stuffs*	*Manufactured Food-stuffs*	*Semi-manufactures*	*Finished Manufactures*
1821	60.6	4.8	19.5	8.4	5.7	4.7	11.2	19.8	7.5	56.8
1830	62.6	4.7	16.3	7.0	9.3	7.6	11.8	15.4	8.2	57.0
1840	67.8	4.1	14.3	4.3	9.5	12.4	15.5	15.5	11.6	45.1
1850	62.4	5.6	14.8	4.5	12.7	7.2	10.4	12.4	15.1	54.0
1860	68.6	3.8	12.3	4.0	11.4	11.3	13.0	17.0	9.9	48.8
1870	56.8	11.1	13.5	3.7	14.9	13.0	12.4	22.0	12.7	39.8
1880	29.5	32.3	23.5	3.5	11.3	21.3	15.0	17.7	16.5	29.4
1890	36.6	15.6	26.6	5.5	15.7	22.8	16.3	16.9	14.8	29.1
1895	33.9	12.5	27.6	7.8	18.1	25.6	19.3	14.6	13.2	27.3
1900	24.8	16.5	23.3	11.2	24.2	33.1	11.5	15.6	15.8	23.9
1905	32.1	7.9	19.0	14.1	26.9	35.4	13.1	13.0	15.9	22.6
1910	33.6	6.4	15.1	15.7	29.2	37.1	9.3	11.7	18.3	23.6
1915	21.8	18.7	16.7	13.1	29.7	35.3	13.4	17.1	14.2	20.1
1920	23.3	11.4	13.8	11.9	39.7	33.8	10.9	23.5	15.2	16.6
1925	29.5	6.6	11.9	13.7	38.3	41.4	11.7	10.2	17.9	18.8
1926	26.8	7.1	10.7	13.9	41.5	40.5	12.2	9.4	18.1	19.8
1927	25.1	8.8	9.7	14.7	41.6	38.2	12.1	10.8	17.9	21.0
1928	25.7	5.9	9.3	14.2	44.9	35.8	13.4	9.9	18.6	22.1
1929	22.2	5.2	9.4	14.1	49.1	35.4	12.2	9.6	20.1	22.6
1930	21.9	4.7	9.6	13.6	50.2	32.7	13.1	9.6	19.9	24.7
1931	23.8	5.3	10.4	13.4	47.1	30.7	14.6	10.6	17.8	26.3
1932	32.6	5.7	9.6	12.5	39.6	27.1	17.6	13.1	16.4	25.7
1933	35.8	2.9	9.4	14.4	37.4	28.8	14.9	13.9	20.1	22.2
1934	31.1	2.8	8.0	16.3	41.8	28.2	15.5	16.1	18.8	21.4
1935	30.4	2.6	7.0	15.6	44.3	28.6	15.8	15.6	20.1	19.9
1936	27.7	2.4	5.9	16.2	47.7	30.2	14.4	15.9	20.2	19.2
1937	22.2	3.2	5.4	20.3	49.0	32.3	13.7	14.6	21.1	18.3
1938	19.8	8.1	6.0	16.2	49.8	29.6	13.3	15.9	19.7	21.4
1939	17.4	3.5	6.5	19.2	53.4	32.7	12.7	13.8	21.4	19.3
1940	11.6	1.9	4.2	23.1	59.2	39.8	11.2	10.9	22.0	16.1
1941	7.1	1.7	8.3	15.5	67.4	42.7	11.7	10.0	22.5	13.1
1942	5.2	0.8	11.6	11.5	70.9	37.9	12.6	9.9	23.1	16.5
1943	5.2	0.8	12.1	8.5	73.4	30.6	17.2	12.4	20.0	19.8
1944	3.9	0.9	11.5	7.7	75.9	27.5	21.7	13.4	18.2	19.1
1945	9.1	4.5	13.0	8.1	65.3	28.9	16.9	11.3	22.7	20.3
1946	14.9	6.8	16.0	9.4	52.8	35.8	16.9	10.4	19.3	17.6
1947	11.1	6.0	10.4	12.2	60.4	31.2	17.9	11.6	22.0	17.3
1948	11.9	10.1	10.5	10.9	56.6	30.3	17.9	10.3	23.0	18.5
1949	14.9	11.2	7.4	11.4	55.1	28.1	20.2	11.2	21.5	18.9
1950	18.6	7.5	5.9	11.1	56.9	28.2	20.0	10.3	24.3	17.2
1951	16.6	9.4	5.7	11.2	57.1	31.1	19.2	9.4	22.7	17.5
1952	13.2	9.1	4.8	10.8	62.1	27.3	19.3	10.1	23.9	19.5

Sources: For 1821–1944, **28,** pp. 246–47; for 1945–52, **29,** 1953, p. 903. Cf. **27,** pp. 4–5.

TABLE 43

EXPORTS OF THE UNITED STATES: PERCENTAGE DISTRIBUTION AMONG AGRICULTURAL AND NONAGRICULTURAL
PRODUCTS AND BY STAGE OF PRODUCTION, 1936–38 TO 1949

		Agricultural Products				Nonagricultural Products			
Year	All Commodities	Total	Crude	Semimanu- factured	Manu- factured	Total	Crude	Semimanu- factured	Manu- factured
1936–38	100.0	26.6	21.0	0.1	5.5	73.4	6.7	17.6	49.2
1939	100.0	21.0	14.6	0.2	6.2	79.0	6.4	19.0	53.6
1940	100.0	13.1	9.0	0.1	4.0	86.9	4.7	22.8	59.4
1941	100.0	13.3	5.1	0.1	8.2	86.7	3.9	15.2	67.6
1942	100.0	14.8	3.1	0.2	11.5	85.2	2.9	11.3	71.0
1943	100.0	16.3	3.9	0.4	12.0	83.7	2.0	8.1	73.5
1944	100.0	15.1	3.0	0.4	11.7	84.9	1.8	7.3	75.8
1945	100.0	23.9	10.7	0.1	13.1	76.1	2.9	8.1	65.1
1946	100.0	33.4	17.2	0.2	17.0	66.6	4.5	9.3	52.8
1947	100.0	26.1	14.2	0.3	11.7	73.9	5.2	11.5	57.2
1948	100.0	27.7	16.7	0.3	10.7	72.3	5.3	10.7	56.3
1949	100.0	30.1	22.4	0.4	7.3	69.9	3.9	11.0	55.0

Source: **27,** pp. 4–5.

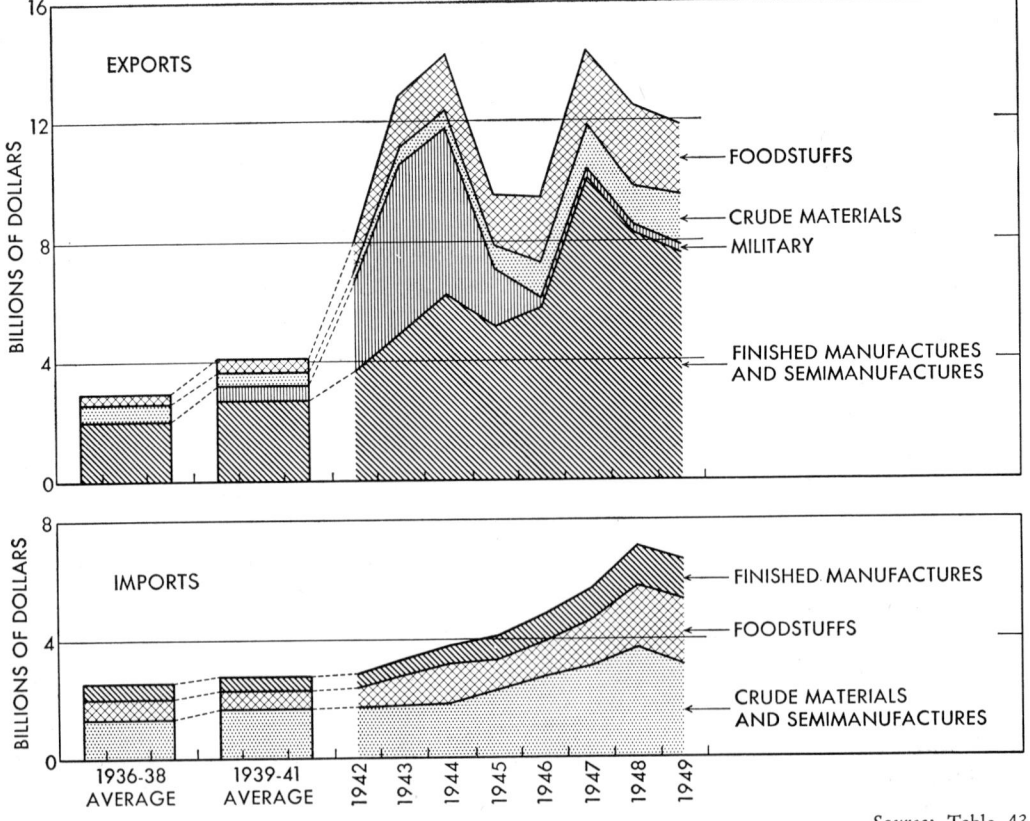

Source: Table 43

FIGURE 27. EXPORTS AND IMPORTS OF THE UNITED STATES: DISTRIBUTION BY ECONOMIC CLASS, 1936–49

TABLE 44

EXPORTS AND IMPORTS OF SELECTED COUNTRIES: PERCENTAGE DISTRIBUTION BY COMMODITY GROUP ACCORDING TO SITC, 1951

Country	Total	0	1	2	3	4	5	6	7	8	9
				Exports							
United States	100.0	14.5	2.6	11.7	9.3	1.6	6.6	14.5	31.0	6.7	1.3
Canada	100.0	26.3	1.8	29.1	0.4	0.3	4.0	29.3	7.6	0.8	0.5
Mexico [a]	100.0	24.9	0.1	32.3	6.8	0.8	1.1	32.3	0.6	1.0	0.1
United Kingdom	100.0	3.7	2.4	4.0	2.7	0.2	7.7	35.8	34.5	7.0	2.0
Ireland	100.0	66.1	6.7	7.3	...	...	0.3	6.6	0.8	2.0	10.1
France	100.0	9.7	3.5	8.4	6.3	0.5	8.7	38.9	15.4	5.5	3.1
Belgium–Luxembourg	100.0	4.6	...	10.3	2.8	1.7	7.8	60.6	8.6	3.1	0.5
Netherlands	100.0	32.6	1.4	7.9	7.9	2.4	8.2	22.7	12.4	3.9	0.6
Denmark	100.0	68.7	1.1	4.2	...	1.3	3.2	6.0	12.8	1.7	1.0
Sweden	100.0	4.0	0.1	47.9	0.1	0.6	1.9	25.6	17.3	2.5	...
Norway	100.0	17.9	0.1	21.0	0.3	10.5	7.0	31.3	11.0	0.9	...
Western Germany	100.0	2.6	0.3	4.5	11.6	0.3	12.2	34.5	27.4	6.5	0.1
Austria	100.0	0.9	0.2	30.3	1.4	...	4.7	45.1	12.3	5.1	...
Portugal	100.0	15.4	9.2	31.4	0.2	2.9	3.2	33.0	1.9	2.0	0.8
Italy	100.0	17.5	1.6	7.5	2.7	0.5	5.5	43.1	16.8	4.8	...
Turkey	100.0	26.2	21.3	45.8	0.1	1.0	1.2	4.2	...	...	...
Japan [b]	100.0	5.0	0.1	5.9	...	1.0	2.7	69.7	7.9	7.6	...
				Imports							
United States	100.0	27.4	2.0	34.0	5.6	1.2	3.1	20.9	2.3	2.5	1.1
Canada	100.0	9.8	0.5	13.1	13.1	1.1	5.0	21.1	27.1	6.0	3.1
Mexico [a]	100.0	8.8	1.1	8.5	4.0	0.2	12.8	19.1	40.0	5.6	...
United Kingdom	100.0	30.3	2.8	36.1	8.1	2.8	2.9	13.4	2.1	1.0	0.4
Ireland	100.0	20.9	2.8	10.4	11.9	1.2	4.7	25.3	14.1	5.8	2.7
France	100.0	16.8	4.4	35.3	17.2	2.9	3.4	10.1	8.2	1.5	0.4
Belgium–Luxembourg	100.0	16.8	1.6	30.4	8.3	1.9	4.8	19.8	12.4	3.6	0.2
Netherlands	100.0	15.3	1.5	22.6	11.6	2.6	4.6	24.6	12.2	3.2	0.1
Denmark	100.0	11.6	2.0	16.5	18.3	1.3	6.4	30.4	11.3	2.2	...
Sweden	100.0	11.8	1.5	13.3	18.6	1.3	5.7	26.8	15.9	5.1	...
Norway	100.0	11.1	0.9	13.8	10.4	1.2	4.4	27.5	27.6	3.0	...
Western Germany	100.0	30.8	2.1	36.6	8.1	4.7	2.2	11.7	2.6	1.4	...
Austria	100.0	25.1	1.5	19.0	16.7	3.3	6.7	15.2	11.1	1.5	...
Portugal	100.0	16.5	1.2	18.8	11.2	1.4	8.7	18.3	19.9	2.7	1.2
Italy	100.0	17.9	0.3	35.9	19.3	2.8	4.2	10.3	7.5	1.6	0.2
Turkey	100.0	6.1	...	8.5	7.6	...	6.4	33.4	33.5	4.4	...
Japan [b]	...	...	...	...	...	...	...	...	...	...	...

Source: Computed from **9**, *passim.* SITC sections: 0. Food; 1. Beverages and tobacco; 2. Crude materials, inedible, except fuels; 3. Mineral fuels, lubricants, related materials; 4. Animal and vegetable oils and fats; 5. Chemicals; 6. Manufactured goods classified by material; 7. Machinery and transport equipment; 8. Miscellaneous manufactured articles; 9. Miscellaneous transactions and commodities.

a. 1950.　　　　　　　　　　　　b. Only exports were classified on the basis of SITC.

Kingdom, France, Western Germany, Belgium, the Netherlands and Japan. Primarily agricultural countries are represented by Mexico, Ireland, Portugal and Turkey. (See Table 44.)

Manufactured articles (sections 6, 7 and 8 of SITC) represented the following percentages of the value of all 1951 exports and imports of the countries listed in Table 44: [23]

	Exports	Imports
Japan	85.2	
United Kingdom	77.3	16.5
Belgium–Luxembourg	72.3	35.8
Western Germany	68.4	15.7
Italy	64.7	19.4
Austria	62.5	27.8
France	59.8	19.8
United States	52.2	25.7
Sweden	45.4	47.8
Norway	43.2	58.1
Netherlands	39.0	40.0
Canada	37.7	54.2
Portugal	36.9	40.9
Mexico	33.9	64.7
Denmark	20.5	43.9
Ireland	9.4	45.2
Turkey	4.2	71.3

Countries with an inadequate supply of raw materials and foodstuffs, rather than those with the greatest industrial capacity, top the list. Manufactured articles constitute a smaller share in the value of exports of such prosperous countries as the United States, Canada, the Netherlands, Denmark and Sweden than of Japan and Italy.

Leading Commodities

The ranking of single commodities in world trade depends largely on classification. Before World War II, for example, exports of wheat were estimated at $580 million and those of wheat flour at $130 million, while exports of coal amounted to $575 million and those of coke and coal briquettes to $140 million.[24] Wheat grain and flour, combined, rank above coal in world trade; grain counted separately is below the total for coal, coke and briquettes. Similar discrepancies in ranking arise through classification of iron and steel articles, machinery, transportation equipment and so forth. Ranking of various fabricated articles is particularly difficult because of lack of uniform classification.

In round numbers, world exports in 1937 totaled $25 billion, distributed as follows by broad class or industrial origin (in millions of dollars):[25]

A. Broad class
Live animals and foodstuffs	$5,600
Materials, crude and semifinished	9,600
Fabricated articles	9,800

B. Industrial origin
Agriculture:	
Production of crops	5,000
Animal husbandry	2,475
Forestry (except saw mills) and fisheries	400
Mining	2,850
Manufactures:	
Food and beverage	1,925
Textile and apparel	2,250
Leather	275
Lumber	650
Paper	850
Rubber	125
Chemical, including petroleum products	2,000
Glass and porcelain	250
Metals	1,750
Machinery	1,125
Transportation equipment	1,000
Electrical, optical, precision instruments	675
Other	1,400

In this classification, the distinction between finished products and raw materials cannot be followed consistently. For example, foodstuffs include both the materials and the products of the food and beverage industries. (See Table 45.)

Of all foodstuffs in international trade, some 30 per cent are tropical products (southern fruits, cane sugar, coffee, tea, cocoa and spices, and some vegetable oils); others are native to the temperate zones.

Industrial materials of agricultural origin also form an important section in international trade. The most important of these products are cotton and wool. Rubber and timber are likewise classified in this section. (See Table 45.)

Another important section of foreign trade includes fuels and other minerals. Few of these are exported as extracted from the soil. More often, minerals appear on the world market in the form of semimanufactured or manufactured articles — coke and coal briquettes, ore concentrates, metals,

---

23. Countries are arrayed by declining share of manufactured articles in total value of 1951 exports.

24. Data for 1937. See **35**, 1938, pp. 156, 159.

25. Based on **35**, 1938, p. 154*. Value in current U.S. dollars. The equivalent in gold dollars was about $15 billion.

TABLE 45

LEADING ARTICLES IN WORLD TRADE: VALUE OF EXPORTS, 1937

(*Millions of Dollars*)

Article	Exports	Article	Exports	Article	Exports
Foodstuffs		**Fuels and Other Minerals**		**Fabricated Articles**	
Wheat [a]	$710	Coal	$575	Yarn, cotton	$200
Corn	290	Coke and briquettes	140	Yarn, wool	100
Rice [a]	280			Yarn, silk	100
Other grains [a]	200	Crude petroleum	300		
		Petroleum products	600	Fabrics, cotton	740
Vegetables	160			Fabrics, wool	250
Vegetable oils	200	Iron ore	150	Fabrics, silk	230
Southern fruits	400	Other ores [d]	160		
Sugar	400			Apparel	350
		Iron scrap	120	Leather and footwear	180
Coffee	300	Pig iron	160	Fur	60
Tea	200				
Cocoa	100	Copper	400	Articles made of wood	
Spices	220	Tin	200	and the like	160
		Lead	100		
Live animals	200	Nickel	65	Paper and paper prod-	
Meat [b]	500	Zinc	60	ucts	460
Fish [b]	200	Aluminum	40	Printed matter	100
Fats	60			Film	80
		Fertilizers, raw	280	Rubber, fabricated	130
Milk	60				
Butter	280	Cement	40	Chemicals [e]	440
Cheese	100	Sulfur	25	Paints and varnishes	210
Eggs	100	Asbestos	25	Soap, and the like	100
Brandy, wine, beer	360	Precious, semiprecious		Paraffine, explosives	70
		stones	110	China and glass	220
Industrial Materials of					
Agricultural Origin				Iron and steel products	1,350
				Machinery [f]	1,100
Cotton, raw	880			Electrical machinery [g]	400
Flax and hemp	80			Automobiles and parts	640
Jute	60			Other transportation	
				equipment	300
Wool and hair	700			Arms, munitions	80
Silk	160			Precision instruments	100
Oil seeds and nuts	400			Musical instruments	30
Oil cakes	100			Toys and sport articles	50
Hides and skins	310			Clocks and watches	80
Furs [e]	120			Cigars and cigarettes	60
Tobacco [e]	300				
Timber	450				
Wood pulp	280				
Rubber [e]	520				

Source: Computed from **35**, 1938, pp. 166*–72*.

a. Includes flour.
b. Includes preserved food.
c. Nonfabricated.

d. Copper, zinc, tin, bauxite and manganese.
e. Includes pharmaceutical products.
f. Other than electrical.
g. Includes equipment.

petroleum products and the like. Moreover, the same article may be regarded by the producer as a manufactured article while it serves the buyer as a material for further manufacture.

A completely satisfactory classification of fabricated articles according to clear, economically meaningful features is impossible.[26] For purposes of the present analysis, 30 clearly distinguishable types of fabricated articles are listed in Table 45.

The 83 types of four general classes of commodities enumerated in this table represented more than 90 per cent of world exports in 1937. In terms of value, iron and steel products and machinery (other than electrical) outrank all other commodities, followed by raw cotton, cotton fabrics, wheat, wool and hair, automobiles and parts, petroleum products, coal and rubber (nonfabricated). These are the "big ten" of the world market. Next in order of value are meat, paper and paper products, timber, chemical and pharmaceutical products, southern fruits, sugar, oilseeds and nuts, electrical machinery and equipment, copper, alcoholic beverages, apparel, hides and skins.

The leading articles in world trade thus include products of all climatic zones and all continents: crops, products of husbandry, forestry products, minerals and products of several branches of manufacturing. (See Table 45 and Figure 28.)

AGRICULTURAL PRODUCTS IN WORLD TRADE

Agricultural products — foodstuffs and industrial materials, including rubber but excluding the products of forestry and fisheries — represent approximately one third of the total value of world trade. Continuous importation of these products is vital for densely populated industrial countries, and many underdeveloped countries have no other products to export.

EXPORT RATES

The proportion of total production used for export varies widely among agricultural products.

Since two thirds of mankind live on farms, farmers and their families consume a large part of staple agricultural foodstuffs. The rest is marketed, but except for a few products, the lion's share of what is sold is consumed within the producing country and only a small part is exported. On the other hand, certain agricultural commodities are produced mainly for export. In 1934–38, the following percentages of the output of various agricultural products were exported: [27]

Food Crops and Tobacco			*Animal Foodstuffs*	
Oats	1.4		Pork	3.1
Rye	2.2		Mutton	4.1
Barley	5.3		Beef	7.3
Rice	5.8			
Corn	9.1		Milk	0.1
Wheat	10.7		Butter	11.8
			Cheese	15.0
Sugar	43.8			
Tea	50.6		*Industrial Raw Materials*	
Coffee	70.8			
Cocoa	93.2		Hemp	13.3
			Flax	22.5
Cottonseed	6.6		Cotton	47.7
Soybeans	8.3		Jute	53.3
Peanuts	13.3		Wool	64.7
Olive oil	22.2		Silk	66.0
Palm oil	83.3			
			Hides	21.5
Tobacco	18.3		Skins	23.6
			Rubber	100.0

The direction of international trade in agricultural products is determined by the interplay of numerous factors: the geographical distribution of agricultural resources and the climatic conditions required by certain crops (such as coffee, tea, cocoa, cotton and rubber); the distribution of population; the insufficient carrying capacity of certain areas (such as western Europe, Japan and southeastern Asia) and the surplus carrying capacity of other areas (the United States, Canada, Argentina and Australia); differences in agricultural technology, costs of production, prices, consumption habits, purchasing power and so forth; transportation costs and facilities; trade policies of exporting and importing nations.

DISTRIBUTION AMONG THE CONTINENTS

There is a striking difference between the patterns of geographical distribution of imports and exports of agricultural products, on the one hand, and of manufactured goods, especially machinery and other engineering products, on the other. Half a dozen industrial nations export most of

---

26. No attempt at such classification has been made in the new Standard Industrial Trade Classification of the United Nations. (See **5** and **7**.)

27. **23**, *passim;* **22**, *passim;* **25**, August 1946, pp. 2–4; **32**, pp. 18–19; **17**, pp. 64–67.

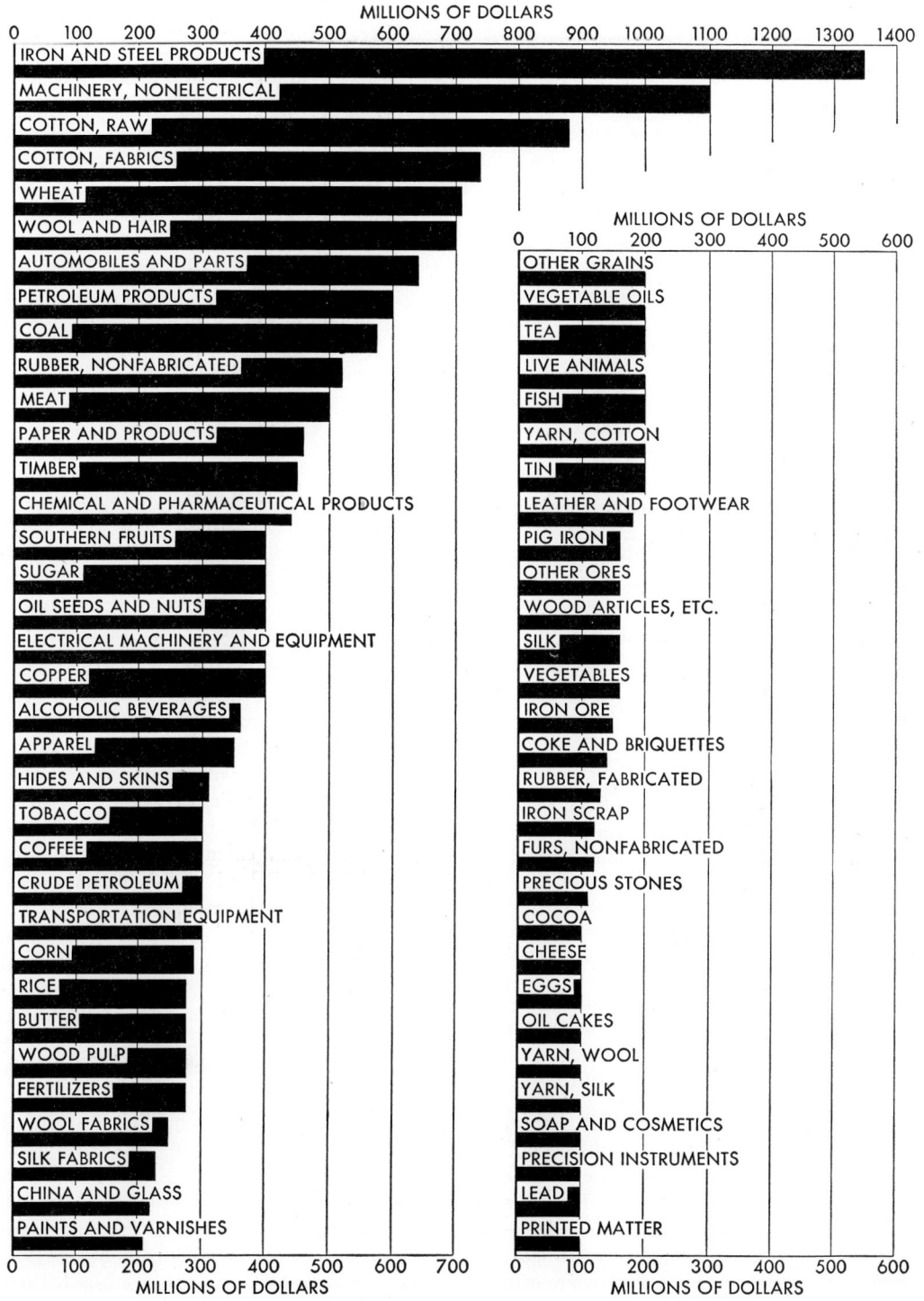

MILLIONS OF DOLLARS

IRON AND STEEL PRODUCTS	
MACHINERY, NONELECTRICAL	
COTTON, RAW	
COTTON, FABRICS	
WHEAT	
WOOL AND HAIR	
AUTOMOBILES AND PARTS	
PETROLEUM PRODUCTS	
COAL	
RUBBER, NONFABRICATED	
MEAT	
PAPER AND PRODUCTS	
TIMBER	
CHEMICAL AND PHARMACEUTICAL PRODUCTS	
SOUTHERN FRUITS	
SUGAR	
OIL SEEDS AND NUTS	
ELECTRICAL MACHINERY AND EQUIPMENT	
COPPER	
ALCOHOLIC BEVERAGES	
APPAREL	
HIDES AND SKINS	
TOBACCO	
COFFEE	
CRUDE PETROLEUM	
TRANSPORTATION EQUIPMENT	
CORN	
RICE	
BUTTER	
WOOD PULP	
FERTILIZERS	
WOOL FABRICS	
SILK FABRICS	
CHINA AND GLASS	
PAINTS AND VARNISHES	

MILLIONS OF DOLLARS

MILLIONS OF DOLLARS

OTHER GRAINS	
VEGETABLE OILS	
TEA	
LIVE ANIMALS	
FISH	
YARN, COTTON	
TIN	
LEATHER AND FOOTWEAR	
PIG IRON	
OTHER ORES	
WOOD ARTICLES, ETC.	
SILK	
VEGETABLES	
IRON ORE	
COKE AND BRIQUETTES	
RUBBER, FABRICATED	
IRON SCRAP	
FURS, NONFABRICATED	
PRECIOUS STONES	
COCOA	
CHEESE	
EGGS	
OIL CAKES	
YARN, WOOL	
YARN, SILK	
SOAP AND COSMETICS	
PRECISION INSTRUMENTS	
LEAD	
PRINTED MATTER	

MILLIONS OF DOLLARS

Source: Table 45

Figure 28. Leading Articles in World Trade: Value of Exports, 1937

the manufactured articles in world trade and ship them to all parts of the world. Agricultural products, however, stream from all parts of the world and flow largely to the two industrial regions on both shores of the North Atlantic. Thus, agricultural exports are highly dispersed and agricultural imports are centralized, just the opposite of exports and imports of finished manufactures. This generalization refers, of course, to total agricultural imports and exports rather than to single products.

In 1937 the four largest exporters of agricultural products (the United States, Argentina, Australia and India) accounted for 27.3 per cent of world agricultural exports, while the four largest importers (the United Kingdom, the United States, Germany and France) absorbed 59.5 per cent of world imports.

The mainspring of world trade in agricultural products is Europe, especially its densely populated northwestern part, an area of about a million square miles with a population of about 250 million. In 1950, Europe absorbed the following percentages of world imports of essential foodstuffs: [28]

Mutton, lamb	99	Cheese	80
Palm kernels	96	Raisins	79
Butter	94	Barley	77
Bacon	91	Apples	72
Palm oil	90	Grapes	71
Beef	89	Tobacco	69
Corn	88	Oats	68
Linseed oil	88	Groundnut oil	66
Wine	88	Onions	65
Groundnuts	86	Potatoes	59
Oilseed cakes	86	Canned meat	57
Soybean oil	84	Wheat and flour	53
Eggs	84	Tea	49
Linseed	83	Copra	46
Oranges, tan-		Dry beans, edi-	
gerines, grape-		ble	44
fruit	83	Sugar	40

Moreover, Europe ranks first in imports of cocoa beans, coconut oil, olives and olive oil. The foodstuffs transferred to Europe are produced in part on plantations established by Europeans in tropical areas and are raised in part by native farmers who have been taught by Europeans to adjust production to the needs of white men.

This is only one aspect of world trade in foodstuffs, however. The trade in rice is essentially an intracontinental trade among surplus and deficit areas of Asia. The trade in sugar and bananas is largely between tropical areas of Middle America and the United States. The main flow of coffee is from South to North America. Intracontinental exchange predominates in the trade in cattle and pigs. Europe and Asia are net importers of dairy products and North America, a net exporter.

In trade in agricultural products used as industrial materials, Europe is the largest importer of cotton (66 per cent in 1950), silk (37 per cent) and wool (65 per cent). North America ranks first in import of rubber. Jute is largely an object of trade between Asia and Europe and among Asiatic nations. (See Table 46.)

SELECTED COMMODITIES

Within the general framework of world trade, each commodity customarily follows its own route. Although the patterns vary from year to year, the routes of agricultural commodities in 1949–52 were mostly the same as in 1934–38.[29]

Grains

Wheat. The main exporters of wheat and wheat flour are the United States, Canada, Argentina, and Australia. Their exports totaled 26.6 million metric tons in 1951, leaving 2.6 million tons to all other exporters, among which only the USSR and France exported a sizable net amount. (See Figure 29.) Before the war, eastern European countries — Romania, Hungary, Bulgaria, Poland and Yugoslavia — also exported considerable amounts of wheat.

Imports of wheat are widely dispersed. The largest importers are the United Kingdom, industrial countries of northwestern Europe and Italy; the Caribbean countries; Brazil, Peru and Venezuela; Japan and the Asiatic Middle East; Egypt and the Union of South Africa. (See Table 47.)

Trade in wheat is essentially an intercontinental, transoceanic exchange. Its main routes cross the Atlantic Ocean, from Canada, the United States and Argentina to the two gateways to the Old World — the English Channel and the Mediterranean. Other important routes are from the United States across the North Pacific to Japan, the Philippines, Indonesia and India; from the United States southward to the Caribbean and South America; and from Australia to

---

28. **20**, 1951, *passim*.

29. See **18**, *passim;* **26**, *passim;* **20**, 1952, *passim*.

TABLE 46

AGRICULTURAL PRODUCTS: EXPORTS AND IMPORTS OF EACH CONTINENT, 1950

(Thousands of Metric Tons)

Commodity	World	North and Middle America	South America	Europe	USSR	Asia	Africa	Oceania
Wheat (incl. flour)								
Exports	21,360	12,440	2,790	1,430	400	600	270	3,430
Imports	20,530	1,420	1,940	10,940	...	4,700	1,340	190
Corn								
Exports	4,600	810	2,480	500	350	100	320	40
Imports	4,890	30	270	4,300	...	70	220	...
Rice								
Exports	4,320	520	210	260	...	3,090	200	40
Imports	4,010	390	60	570	...	2,780	180	30
Oranges, tangerines, grapefruit								
Exports	1,685	260	90	650	...	210	460	15
Imports	1,730	190	60	1,430	...	30	10	10
Bananas								
Exports	2,185	1,330	470	155	...	10	210	10
Imports	2,060	1,230	150	640	...	10	20	10
Sugar								
Exports	11,550	6,650	520	2,010	40	1,170	660	500
Imports	11,180	3,940	360	4,480	200	1,320	750	130
Coffee								
Exports	1,770	240	1,200	11	...	34	280	4
Imports	1,780	1,150	40	490	...	40	58	2
Tea								
Exports	418	1	1	7	...	393	16	...
Imports	411	81	3	200	...	40	54	33
Cocoa beans								
Exports	771	77	182	5	...	3	501	3
Imports	753	317	14	405	...	3	4	10
Wine (thousands of hectoliters)								
Exports	17,392	7	70	4,300	...	150	12,800	65
Imports	17,445	300	100	15,400	...	200	1,400	45
Tobacco								
Exports	565	257	43	60	...	130	75	...
Imports	536	46	10	370	...	60	36	14
Groundnuts								
Exports	893	40	...	3	...	200	630	...
Imports	920	30	...	790	...	80	20	...
Copra								
Exports	1,477	2	...	...	...	1,220	65	190
Imports	1,398	450	40	650	...	220	5	33
Cattle (thousands of head)								
Exports	2,040	520	170	870	...	80	400	1
Imports	1,950	520	150	900	...	80	300	1
Pigs (thousands of head)								
Exports	970	60	5	510	...	370	25	1
Imports	947	60	7	500	...	370	10	...

(Continued on following page)

Table 46—*continued*

Commodity	World	North and Middle America	South America	Europe	USSR	Asia	Africa	Oceania
Meat products [a]								
Exports	1,722	161	468	431	. . .	15	21	626
Imports	1,701	165	30	1,436	. . .	40	24	6
Dairy products [b]								
Exports	1,347	292	15	690	. . .	16	7	327
Imports	1,338	88	26	907	. . .	282	32	3
Eggs								
Exports	327	19	. . .	250	. . .	35	12	11
Imports	316	7	10	270	. . .	28	1	. . .
Cotton (lint)								
Exports	2,965	1,510	230	5	160	410	650	. . .
Imports	2,726	160	55	1,790	30	670	8	13
Jute								
Exports	973	1	. . .	2	. . .	970		. . .
Imports	843	82	20	380	25	330	3	3
Silk (metric tons)								
Exports	8,400	200	. . .	800	. . .	7,400	. . .	
Imports	8,070	3,500	300	3,000	. . .	1,000	200	70
Wool (greasy)								
Exports	1,407	7	270	170	. . .	90	110	760
Imports	1,406	390	6	920	20	60	7	3
Rubber								
Exports	2,356	10	2	36	. . .	2,250	56	2
Imports	2,289	875	23	610	85	630	24	42

Source: **20,** 1951, *passim.* World totals here do not agree exactly with the respective totals in Tables 47–58. Disparities are due to revision of figures for various countries and divergent estimates for areas for which no direct information is available.

a. Beef, mutton and lamb, pork, bacon and ham, other prepared meats, canned meat.

b. Milk, butter, cheese.

South Africa, India, the Near East and, via Suez, Great Britain and continental Europe.

Rice. Asia's staple food plays a predominant role in the trade among countries of that continent. Asia accounts for two thirds of all exports and three fourths of all imports of rice. Before World War II, Burma, Thailand, Indochina and Korea were the main exporters. Taiwan and Pakistan also exported sizable quantities. Now Burma–Thailand is the only area with large net exports of rice, and its surplus cannot meet the demand of the rice-importing Asian countries — Japan, India, Indonesia, Malaya, Ceylon and so on. (See Table 48.)

The geographical pattern of international trade in rice is comparatively simple. Most of the exports from Burma and Thailand are absorbed by the surrounding area; a small part reaches Europe. The United States exports small quantities of rice, mainly to Cuba.

Unlike the trade in wheat, international trade in rice has not recovered since World War II and in 1951 was only about half the customary prewar volume.

Corn. The United States accounted for more than half of all exports of corn in 1949–51, while imports were distributed among two dozen countries. Most of the exports (usually 80–85 per cent) go to Europe. The main importers, in order of their imports in 1951, are the United Kingdom (well in the lead), France, Belgium-Luxembourg, the Netherlands, Germany, Austria, Ireland, Canada, Italy and Mexico. (See Table 49.)

Like the trade in wheat and unlike that in rice, trade in corn is essentially intercontinental and transoceanic. The two main routes run from the Atlantic coasts of the United States and Argentina across the Atlantic Ocean to the English Channel. A third route crosses the Pacific, from

TABLE 47

FOODSTUFFS: WHEAT AND WHEAT FLOUR, EXPORTS AND IMPORTS OF SELECTED COUNTRIES, 1934–38
AVERAGE, AND 1949–51

(Thousands of Metric Tons)

Country	1934–38 Average	1949	1950	1951	Country	1934–38 Average	1949	1950	1951
Exports									
World	17,300	26,000	21,200	29,200	France	499	363	884	819
					Hungary	496	...	...	100
United States	1,259	11,208	6,812	12,902	Romania	550	...	...	150
Canada	4,771	6,873	5,633	7,883	USSR	725	1,400	400	700
Argentina	3,341	1,854	2,783	2,491	Australia	2,787	3,193	3,428	3,345
Uruguay	81	202	8	108	Other	4,417	1,472	2,144	1,879
Imports									
World	16,800	25,700	20,500	27,300	Austria	244	510	378	462
Mexico	19	262	425	364	Portugal	35	308	253	201
Cuba	121	182	190	204	Spain	...	280	254	196
British West Indies	124	161	160	192	Italy	709	2,040	1,094	1,636
					Greece	447	418	393	574
Venezuela	30	118	151	171	China	748	...	...	...
Brazil	990	981	1,237	1,120	Japan	314	2,008	1,576	1,676
Peru	128	230	245	198	Hong Kong	97	95	105	64
Bolivia	36	54	57	...	Syria, Lebanon	21	93	113	185
Chile	13	6	69	70	Iraq, Iran	...	252	114	2
United Kingdom	5,681	5,659	3,896	4,832	India	}50{	28	...	...
Ireland	427	140	206	300	Pakistan		287	1,463	3,078
France	646	641	223	279	Ceylon	25	213	225	290
Belgium–Luxembourg	1,166	645	637	960	Malaya	85	134	173	178
Netherlands	615	531	725	868	Indonesia	105	92	68	168
					Philippines	107	257	234	288
Sweden	49	2	76	210	Egypt	16	465	561	1,137
Norway	219	250	283	375	Union of South Africa	20	205	283	156
Germany [a]	697	2,762	1,734	2,961	New Zealand	39	156	159	149
Switzerland	461	443	361	384	Other	2,316	4,784	2,379	2,972

Source: **20**, 1952 (Trade sec.), pp. 30–32; cf. **19**.

a. For 1949–51, Western Germany.

the American coast to Japan and other parts of the Far East.

The geographical distribution of exports and imports of corn in recent years is unlike that before the war. In 1934–38, the United States had a net import balance in corn; now it accounts for more than half of world exports. The United Kingdom and Germany have cut their imports of corn to less than one third. Changes in international trade in corn have been caused mainly by changes in the orientation of agriculture. Some countries can expand their animal husbandry by diverting more acreage to production of fodder while others must rely increasingly on imported corn.

Sugar

Approximately one third of the sugar consumed in the world is produced from sugar beets, grown in the temperate climatic zone, and two thirds, from sugar cane in tropical regions. The two products are, for all practical purposes, almost identical, but they play different roles in trade and local economic life. The production of sugar beets and beet sugar is usually integrated with the local crop-agriculture and animal husbandry. Most beet sugar is consumed within the producing country; hardly more than 10–15 per cent is exported, mainly in intracontinental trade. On the other hand, sugar cane is raised, and cane sugar produced, mainly for export. In the

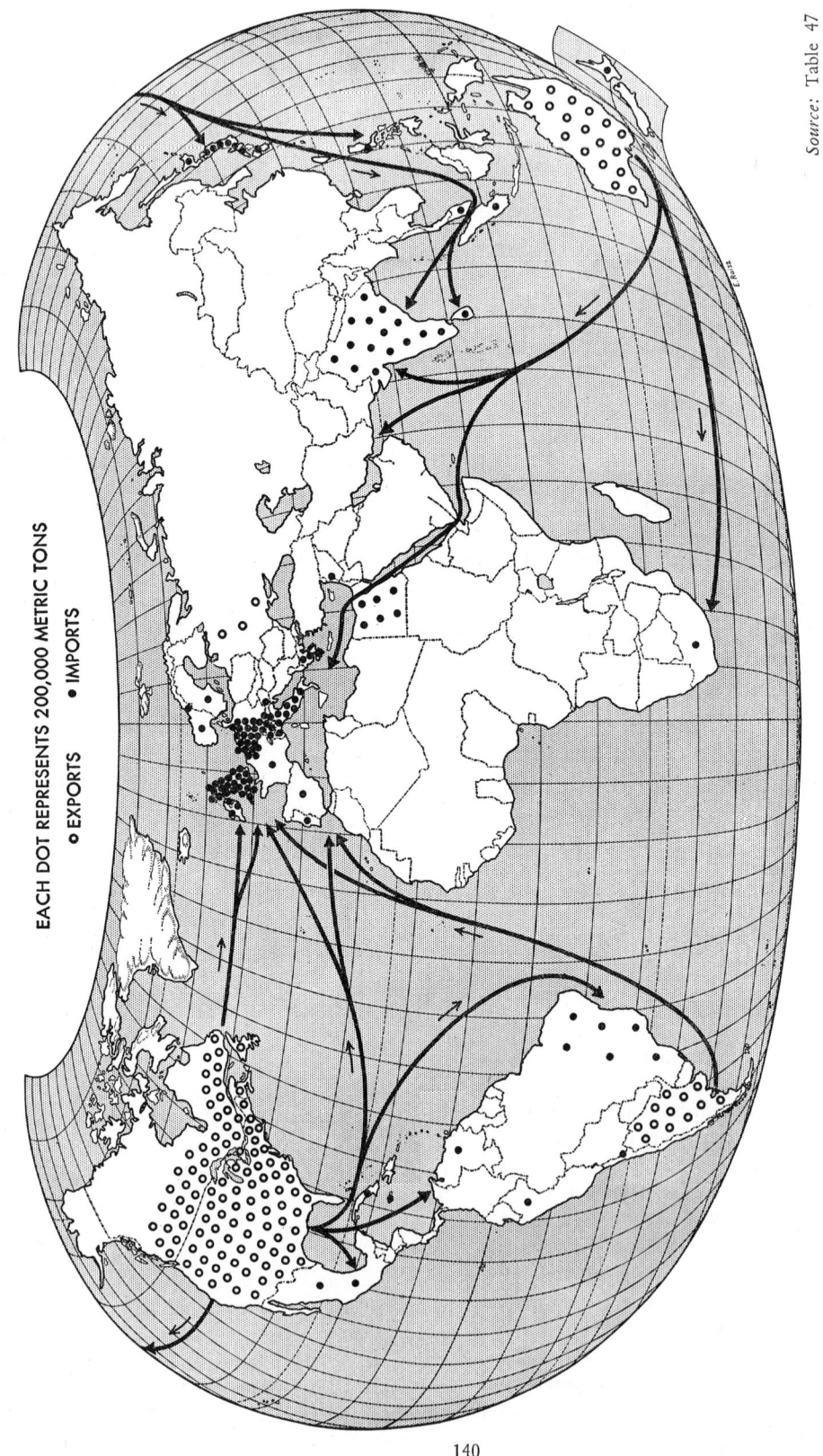

EACH DOT REPRESENTS 200,000 METRIC TONS

○ EXPORTS ● IMPORTS

FIGURE 29. FOODSTUFFS: WHEAT AND WHEAT FLOUR IN WORLD TRADE, 1951

The main routes of wheat in world trade cross the Atlantic Ocean eastward (from Canada, the United States and Argentina to the United Kingdom, the English Channel and Gibraltar) and the Pacific and Indian Oceans westward (from the United States to Japan, the Philippines and India; and from Australia to India, South Africa, the Near East and the Mediterranean).

In 1950–51 France likewise had a net export of wheat.

Source: Table 47

140

TABLE 48

FOODSTUFFS: RICE, EXPORTS AND IMPORTS OF SELECTED COUNTRIES, 1934–38 AVERAGE, AND 1949–51

(*Thousands of Metric Tons*)

Country	1934–38 Average	1949	1950	1951	Country	1934–38 Average	1949	1950	1951
				Exports					
World	9,650	4,100	4,250	5,250	Pakistan	393	—	—	206
					Burma	3,070	1,194	1,198	1,325
United States	72	516	492	491	Thailand	1,388	1,215	1,508	1,612
Brazil	54	1	95	165	Indochina	1,320	105	115	333
Italy	149	160	230	232	Egypt	100	344	178	313
Korea	1,158	12	90	—	Other	1,271	293	317	488
Taiwan	675	260	27	85					
				Imports					
World	9,250	3,800	4,100	5,050	Ceylon	530	404	498	402
					Malaya	719	527	465	581
Cuba	201	271	293	291	Indonesia	281	276	332	409
China	704	410	90	20	Philippines	38	146	3	130
Japan	1,757	130	671	792	Africa	400	130	190	220
Hong Kong	522	76	197	185	Other	1,938	646	982	1,129
India	2,160	784	379	950					

Source: **20**, 1952 (Trade sec.), pp. 54–56; cf. **16**.

TABLE 49

FOODSTUFFS: CORN, EXPORTS AND IMPORTS OF SELECTED COUNTRIES, 1934–38 AVERAGE, AND 1949–51

(*Thousands of Metric Tons*)

Country	1934–38 Average	1949	1950	1951	Country	1934–38 Average	1949	1950	1951
				Exports					
World	10,200	5,800	4,600	4,500	China	126	...	...	200
					Indochina	492	29	40	65
United States	798	3,402	2,446	2,543	Indonesia	123	—	38	—
Brazil	46	—	12	295	Angola	98	92	189	137
Argentina	6,527	1,063	794	304	Union of South				
Yugoslavia	469	317	225	129	Africa	334	99	20	167
USSR	—	200	350	250	Other	1,187	598	482	410
				Imports					
World	10,100	5,900	4,900	4,400	Norway	137	135	131	53
					Germany [a]	979	1,439	273	286
United States	835	20	17	19	Czechoslovakia	112	...	...	...
Canada	305	214	238	193	Switzerland	95	96	99	87
Mexico	5	—	—	118	Austria	369	144	224	276
United Kingdom	3,285	712	992	1,040	Portugal	40	71	150	32
Ireland	299	295	354	203	Spain [b]	57	—	—	—
France	688	469	745	570	Italy	153	93	95	175
Belgium–					Japan	196	257	19	56
Luxembourg	799	410	381	355	India	—	—	136	—
Netherlands	934	424	430	344	Egypt	3	145	166	20
Denmark	332	209	69	49	Other	360	651	267	435
Sweden	117	116	114	89					

Source: **20**, 1952 (Trade sec.), pp. 46–48.

a. For 1949–51, Western Germany.   b. Includes Canary Islands.

TABLE 50

FOODSTUFFS: SUGAR, EXPORTS AND IMPORTS OF SELECTED COUNTRIES, 1934–38 AVERAGE, AND 1949–51

(*Thousands of Metric Tons*)

	Exports					Imports			
Country	1934–38 Average	1949	1950	1951	Country	1934–38 Average	1949	1950	1951
World	11,500	12,150	13,600	13,400	World	11,350	12,200	13,450	13,050
United States [a]	81	25	216	97	United States [a]	4,365	5,123	5,201	5,031
Cuba	2,560	4,951	5,148	4,777	Canada	433	565	580	484
Dominican					Chile	123	106	204	173
Republic	420	442	438	482	Uruguay	51	100	75	90
British West					United Kingdom	2,203	2,221	2,125	2,290
Indies	355	534	683	555	France	362	254	332	303
Puerto Rico	776	1,042	832	870	Belgium–				
British Guiana	172	177	176	183	Luxembourg	132	75	65	99
Peru	306	285	291	264	Netherlands	136	244	289	336
United Kingdom	350	576	764	736	Sweden	8	54	107	66
France	234	189	250	363	Finland	93	90	111	107
Belgium–					Germany [b]	14	450	596	463
Luxembourg	104	74	179	150	Switzerland	152	157	297	153
Netherlands	63	104	189	106	Portugal	67	106	108	96
Poland	81	183	231	...	USSR	34	200	200	400
Czechoslovakia	213	206	...	...	China	352	...	...	12
USSR	108	25	50	100	Hong Kong	171	55	126	87
China	...	...	...	3	Japan	970	242	380	554
Taiwan	873	327	608	281	Iraq	38	52	87	76
Hong Kong	123	34	74	66	Iran	69	154	154	114
Indonesia	1,045	43	2	6	India	}152{	...	6	11
Philippines	862	415	439	633	Pakistan		150	110	150
French African					Malaya,				
colonies	414	613	595	530	Singapore	127	154	177	172
Union of South					Egypt	37	40	140	2
Africa	182	77	65	59	French African				
Australia	430	486	389	294	colonies	300	350	400	395
Fiji	131	113	116	74	New Zealand	80	73	120	94
Hawaii	841	698	1,039	854	Other	881	1,185	1,460	1,292
Other	776	530	826	1,917					

Source: **20,** 1952 (Trade sec.), pp. 59–62; cf. **6,** 1950, pp. 34–35.

a. Including trade of the United States with non-contiguous territories.

b. For 1949–51, Western Germany.

Caribbean, India, Indonesia and the Philippines, large-scale production was established in colonial times. Before World War II, 60 per cent of the cane sugar produced in these areas was exported. The rate fell to 50 per cent in 1949–51.

Australia and Czechoslovakia are the main exporters of beet sugar. Small quantities are exported by Belgium, France and the Netherlands, but these countries, in turn, import cane sugar from Cuba, which is the world's largest exporter of this product. Puerto Rico, Hawaii, the Philippines and the Dominican Republic also export cane sugar. (See Table 50; cf. Figure 30.)

Coffee, Tea, Cocoa

The value of these three products in world trade totaled more than $3 billion, at U.S. prices, in 1951.

The main exporting areas are South and Middle America for coffee (about 80 per cent of total world exports), equatorial Africa for cocoa (two thirds of world exports), and India, Ceylon and Indonesia for tea (about 80 per cent of world exports). North America and Europe take more than 90 per cent of the imports of coffee and cocoa. Imports of tea are distributed more widely: Africa takes 12 per cent; Asia

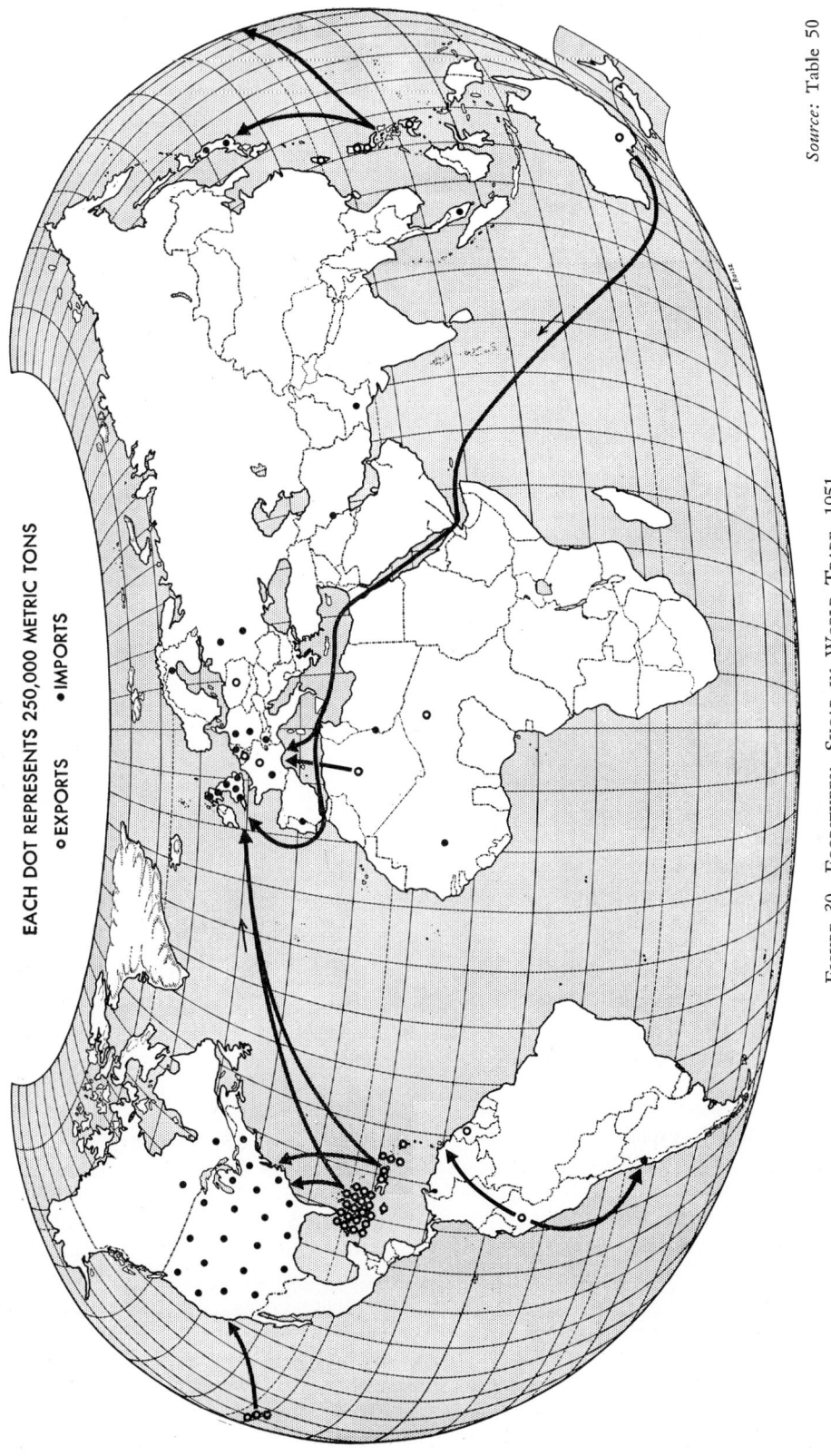

EACH DOT REPRESENTS 250,000 METRIC TONS

○ EXPORTS   ● IMPORTS

FIGURE 30. FOODSTUFFS: SUGAR IN WORLD TRADE, 1951

The main routes of cane sugar in world trade run from the Caribbean area to the United States and the United Kingdom. Another important route brings cane sugar from the Philippines and Hawaii to the United States. Beet sugar is exported from Australia to the United Kingdom and continental Europe.

Source: Table 50

143

some 8 per cent; Australia and New Zealand together, about an equal amount; the rest goes to Europe and America.

The United States is the largest consumer of coffee and cocoa, taking approximately 60 per cent of the coffee exported and 40 per cent of the cocoa. The largest importer of tea is the United Kingdom, which takes more than 40 per cent of exports. (See Table 51.)

Trade in coffee, tea and cocoa is essentially intercontinental. The main routes run from the tropical zone to the industrial countries of the northern temperate zone. (See Figure 31.)

Oilseeds, Nuts and Vegetable Oils

Oilseeds, nuts and vegetable oils are exported from North and South America, Asia and Africa, mainly to Europe, especially the United Kingdom and the industrial countries of northwestern and central Europe, though appreciable quantities follow other routes.

Groundnuts were exported before World War II from Asia and Africa, with India ranking first, and French West Africa second, among exporters. Export from India, interrupted during the war, has not been resumed on a large scale. The main exporters are now French West Africa (26 per cent in 1951) and Nigeria (23 per cent). Europe takes 85–90 per cent of the exports. The largest importers are France and the United Kingdom. (See Table 52.)

Copra comes to the world market from southeastern Asia — the Philippines, Indonesia and Malaya. More than half the exports go to Europe, about 25–30 per cent to North America. The United States is the largest single importer (30 per cent of the world total in 1949 and 1950, 25 per cent in 1951); the Netherlands ranks second (16 per cent in 1951), the United Kingdom, third (11 per cent).

Soybeans were an outstanding item in Chinese (chiefly Manchurian) export before World War II. On the average for 1934–38, China exported 2,036,000 tons a year out of total exports of 2,280,000 tons. Now the United States is the largest exporter: it accounted for 75 per cent of world exports in 1949; 57 per cent in 1950; and 51 per cent in 1951. In 1951, Europe absorbed about 58 per cent of the imports, and Asia 31 per cent. Japan is the largest single importer.

Cottonseed is exported from Africa (Anglo-Egyptian Sudan, Uganda, Mozambique and other areas) and Asia (Pakistan and Turkey).

Before the war (1934–38), the United Kingdom took 628,000 metric tons out of the world total of about 790,000, leaving 162,000 metric tons for all other importers. In 1950 the United Kingdom imported 152,000 metric tons of the total of about 380,000; in 1951, 128,000 metric tons of the total of about 340,000. India and Egypt are also large importers.

Linseed. Before World War II, more than three fourths of the linseed came from Argentina. In recent years, exports from that country have declined sharply. The main exporters are now the United States, Canada and India. Belgium, France and Japan had the largest imports in 1951, followed by the Netherlands, the United Kingdom, Norway, Western Germany and Canada.

Vegetable oils usually follow the same routes as oilseeds, but some countries process imported oilseeds and nuts and export oils.

Groundnut oil. Before the war, nearly half of the world exports came from France and the Netherlands, which crushed groundnuts imported from Asia and Africa. Now the oil is produced in the countries that raise the nuts. The main exporters are India, French West Africa and the United States. Two thirds of the total exports are taken by Europe (France, Belgium, Italy and other countries).

Coconut oil is shipped from Ceylon, Malaya, the Philippines, the Netherlands Indies and Fiji to the United Kingdom, the United States, Germany, Italy, Czechoslovakia, India and Pakistan, Egypt and the Union of South Africa.

Palm oil, a typical tropical product, comes from Africa (Nigeria and the Belgian Congo) and southeastern Asia (Indonesia and Malaya) to Europe (the United Kingdom, the Netherlands, Belgium, Germany, Italy and others) and the United States and Canada.

Soybean oil. The trade in this oil has changed direction since the war. In 1934–38, China was the main exporter (57 per cent of the world total), followed by Denmark, the United Kingdom and the Netherlands, all three of which imported soybeans from China and Korea for processing. The United States accounted for less than 2 per cent of world exports. After the war, the United States became the greatest exporter of soybean oil (90 per cent of the world total, on the average, in 1949–51). Europe remains the principal market. Germany, Spain, Italy, the Netherlands, Greece, Austria and Belgium are the largest importers.

TABLE 51

FOODSTUFFS: COFFEE, TEA AND COCOA, EXPORTS AND IMPORTS OF SELECTED COUNTRIES, 1934–38
AVERAGE, AND 1949–51

(*Thousands of Metric Tons*)

	Exports					Imports			
Country, Area	1934–38 Average	1949	1950	1951	Country, Area	1934–38 Average	1949	1950	1951
Coffee									
World	1,650	2,070	1,780	1,940	World	1,640	2,000	1,790	1,910
Middle America	228	258	253	250	United States	790	1,323	1,106	1,219
Brazil	875	1,162	890	982	France	185	88	150	151
Colombia	230	325	269	288	Belgium–				
Asia	103	24	37	39	Luxembourg	50	90	60	55
Africa	130	254	272	320	Germany [a]	166	26	27	40
Other	84	47	59	61	Rest of Europe	307	262	253	254
					Other	142	211	194	191
Tea									
World	444	451	419	476	World	431	436	407	457
China	40	9	10	10	United States	38	43	52	39
Taiwan	10	12	8	11	Canada	18	20	25	19
Ceylon	100	135	137	138	United Kingdom	225	215	167	211
Pakistan	} 157 {	13	8	21	Ireland	11	8	11	17
India		223	184	204	Netherlands	13	8	9	8
Indonesia	68	21	31	45	Rest of Europe	11	11	13	10
Japan	19	7	7	9	Egypt	7	16	16	16
Kenya, Uganda	3	4	5	5	Australia	21	22	28	27
Nyasaland	3	6	7	7	New Zealand	5	6	5	11
Other	44	21	22	26	Other	82	87	81	99
Cocoa									
World	690	750	770	710	World	680	710	770	700
Middle America	58	41	48	44	United States	250	285	299	275
Venezuela	17	14	16	14	Canada	12	19	18	12
Brazil	114	132	140	96	United Kingdom	104	149	132	109
Ecuador	20	19	27	24	France	43	66	70	56
Gold Coast	266	268	272	233	Belgium–				
Nigeria	91	118	93	123	Luxembourg	10	11	8	8
French African					Netherlands	65	39	66	55
colonies	81	108	112	112	Germany [a]	81	18	55	57
Rest of Africa	26	25	24	20	Switzerland	8	8	8	22
Other	17	25	38	44	Italy	9	9	14	13
					Rest of Europe	40	55	52	45
					Other	58	51	48	48

Source: **20**, 1952 (Trade sec.), pp. 141–56.   a. For 1949–51, Western Germany.

Olive oil is exported mainly from North Africa (Tunisia), Spain and Italy. Imports are widely dispersed throughout the world. (See Table 52.)

Linseed oil. Argentina and Uruguay lead in exports; the United Kingdom and Germany are the largest importers of the oil.

Meat and Dairy Products

Live cattle. Ireland, Denmark and Canada are the main exporters (480,000, 329,000 and 228,000 head, respectively, of world exports of 1,900,000 head in 1951). Other large exporters are Argentina, the British and French African colonies, Turkey and France. The principal import mar-

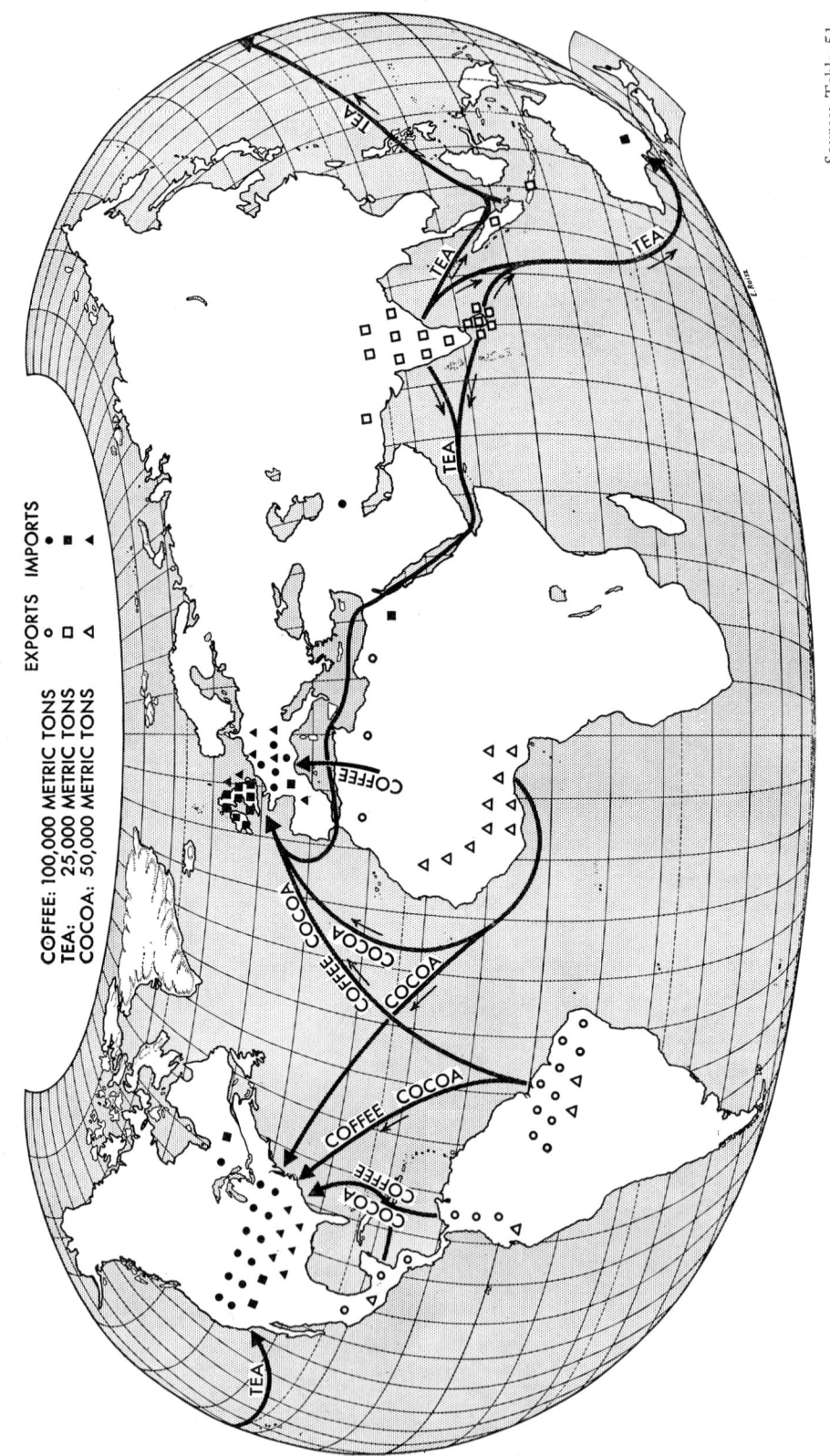

FIGURE 31. FOODSTUFFS: COFFEE, TEA AND COCOA IN WORLD TRADE, 1951

The main routes of coffee in world trade run from South and Middle America to the United States, Canada, Australia and other countries. Cocoa follows routes from the United States and from South America and Africa to continental Europe. Tea is Africa and South and Middle America to the United States and Europe. shipped from the Far East (India, Ceylon and Indonesia) to the United Kingdom,

Source: Table 51

TABLE 52

FOODSTUFFS: OILSEEDS, NUTS AND VEGETABLE OILS, EXPORTS AND IMPORTS OF EACH CONTINENT, 1934–38 AVERAGE, AND 1949–51

(*Thousands of Metric Tons*)

Commodity and Year		World [a]	North and Middle America	South America	Europe	Asia	Africa	Oceania
Groundnuts								
1934–38	Export	1,826	—	2	4	1,050	770	—
Average	Import	1,757	20	5	1,620	80	30	2
1949	Export	981	170	—	1	100	710	—
	Import	985	25	—	880	50	30	2
1950	Export	913	40	—	3	240	630	—
	Import	932	30	1	800	80	20	1
1951	Export	625	40	2	3	150	430	—
	Import	637	25	—	540	55	15	2
Copra								
1934–38	Export	1,369	7	1	1	1,080	70	210
Average	Import	1,355	240	9	880	190	15	21
1949	Export	1,293	3	—	—	1,050	70	170
	Import	1,377	420	15	720	170	15	37
1950	Export	1,492	2	—	—	1,230	70	190
	Import	1,420	450	40	650	240	3	33
1951	Export	1,781	6	—	30	1,470	65	210
	Import	1,700	440	30	1,020	170	5	35
Soybeans								
1934–38	Export	2,280	53	—	6	2,220	—	—
Average	Import	2,177	1	—	1,336	840	—	—
1949	Export	840	636	20	—	180	4	—
	Import	852	59	—	475	300	18	—
1950	Export	915	520	21	—	370	4	—
	Import	705	109	—	280	310	6	—
1951	Export	1,303	670	40	. . .	590	3	—
	Import	1,347	127	. . .	790	420	10	—
Cottonseed								
1934–38	Export	784	2	120	2	110	550	—
Average	Import	788	2	40	650	90	5	1
1949	Export	329	9	. . .	—	110	210	—
	Import	340	5	—	170	120	45	—
1950	Export	385	17	. . .	3	160	205	—
	Import	330	5	—	190	130	5	—
1951	Export	338	8	—	—	140	190	—
	Import	326	6	—	190	110	20	—
Linseed								
1934–38	Export	1,950	1	1,615	12	290	16	—
Average	Import	1,970	483	17	1,400	28	6	33
1949	Export	433	223	27	12	90	81	—
	Import	472	4	3	420	21	7	17
1950	Export	523	201	139	10	100	73	—
	Import	487	11	—	400	31	10	35
1951	Export	457	176	185	16	50	30	—
	Import	511	24	1	390	70	7	19

(*Continued on following page*)

TABLE 52—*continued*

Commodity and Year		World [a]	North and Middle America	South America	Europe	Asia	Africa	Oceania
Groundnut oil								
1934–38	Export	183	—	—	123	57	3	—
Average	Import	174	55	2	37	36	43	1
1949	Export	167	30	—	6	50	81	—
	Import	147	5	1	100	26	14	1
1950	Export	198	18	1	22	75	82	—
	Import	202	6	1	135	42	17	1
1951	Export	232	29	2	25	106	70	—
	Import	238	17	—	165	24	31	1
Coconut oil								
1934–38	Export	347	7	—	61	277	1	1
Average	Import	339	172	4	93	51	18	1
1949	Export	291	10	—	31	225	14	11
	Import	273	59	5	132	65	12	—
1950	Export	283	14	—	32	215	11	11
	Import	286	76	8	125	65	12	—
1951	Export	365	19	—	62	265	7	12
	Import	376	65	9	220	60	22	—
Palm oil								
1934–38	Export	460	—	—	12	205	243	—
Average	Import	456	164	1	275	3	13	—
1949	Export	502	4	2	4	158	334	—
	Import	470	43	1	410	6	10	—
1950	Export	501	1	—	7	149	344	—
	Import	510	33	1	460	5	11	—
1951	Export	477	1	—	7	144	325	—
	Import	494	52	1	425	5	11	—
Soybean oil								
1934–38	Export	120	2	—	45	73	—	—
Average	Import	97	11	2	70	6	8	—
1949	Export	181	163	—	12	6	—	—
	Import	168	10	1	150	6	1	—
1950	Export	147	136	—	6	5	—	—
	Import	124	11	1	105	6	1	—
1951	Export	259	227	—	13	19	—	—
	Import	229	16	10	185	8	10	—
Olive oil								
1934–38	Export	180	—	—	110	12	58	—
Average	Import	188	54	29	87	2	14	2
1949	Export	53	—	—	27	3	23	—
	Import	55	14	3	25	2	11	—
1950	Export	172	1	—	77	2	92	—
	Import	187	46	15	90	3	32	1
1951	Export	87	—	—	50	4	33	—
	Import	96	29	11	45	1	10	—
Linseed oil								
1934–38	Export	112	—	—	110	2	—	—
Average	Import	103	5	2	75	8	9	4
1949	Export	153	22	101	22	7	1	—
	Import	160	2	2	130	7	7	12
1950	Export	302	20	229	45	6	2	—
	Import	256	3	3	225	9	7	9
1951	Export	362	13	279	48	19	3	—
	Import	353	10	2	300	16	9	16

Source: **20**, 1952 (Trade sec.), pp. 98–156.　　　　　　　　a. Includes the USSR.

kets are the United Kingdom (451,000 head in 1951), continental Europe (470,000), the United States (220,000), the Union of South Africa (108,000), Chile (117,000).

Pigs appear mainly in intracontinental trade, such as trade between Honduras and El Salvador or China and Hong Kong.

Meat and meat products. The pattern of international trade in these is as intricate as that in vegetable oils. (See Table 53.)

Argentina, Uruguay and Canada in the Western Hemisphere and Australia and New Zealand in the Eastern account for 80 per cent of the exported *beef* (1951). New Zealand is the main provider of *mutton* and *lamb* (75 per cent of the world exports in 1951); it is followed by Australia and Argentina. *Pork* is largely concentrated in intra-European trade, Denmark being the largest exporter and the United Kingdom and Germany, the largest importers. The United Kingdom also imports considerable amounts of pork from Australia and New Zealand.

The leading exporters of *prepared and canned meat* are Denmark, Australia, Mexico, the United States, Canada, Poland, the Netherlands and Uruguay.

The largest import market is the United Kingdom, which accounts for about 60 per cent of world imports of all kinds of meat (1949–51). (See Table 53.)

Poultry comes from Australia (43 per cent of world exports in 1950, 29 per cent in 1951), New Zealand, Argentina, the United States, Ireland, Denmark and other areas. (See Table 53.)

Milk. Approximately one third of the international trade in milk is an intra-European affair, the Netherlands leading in exports and the United Kingdom in imports; the remaining two thirds is intercontinental. The world's largest exporter of condensed and powdered milk is the United States, which shipped abroad 280,000 metric tons in 1949; 212,000 in 1950; and 180,000 in 1951 out of world exports averaging 650,000 metric tons. More than half of the milk exported by the United States goes to the Far East (the Philippines, Malaya and Indonesia); the rest to Europe, mainly to the United Kingdom.

Butter. Nearly half of the world's exports of butter comes from New Zealand and Australia, and the largest part of the other half, from Denmark, the Netherlands and Sweden. More than 90 per cent of world export was taken by Europe in 1951. The United Kingdom alone took two thirds of world exports.

Cheese follows a similar route. Of the total of over 370,000 metric tons exported in 1951, 128,000 were provided by Australia and New Zealand; about 190,000 by Europe; 50,000 by North America. Europe absorbed 305,000 tons, or over 80 per cent; the United Kingdom alone accounted for 197,000 tons or more than half the world total.

The main flow of dairy products in world trade is from continental Europe and Oceania to the United Kingdom. (See Table 53.) Excluding trade among the countries of continental Europe, world exports of milk, butter and cheese averaged 1.1 million metric tons in 1949-51. Of this total, 570,000 metric tons went to the United Kingdom.

Tobacco

Tobacco can be raised in both tropical and temperate zones. All continents except Europe and Australia have an export balance in this product, which is shipped from North America and Brazil, the Middle and Far East, South Africa (Southern Rhodesia and Nyasaland) and southern Europe (Greece, Italy, Yugoslavia and Bulgaria) to northwestern and central Europe. Other important movements are from the Caribbean (Cuba and the Dominican Republic) to the United States; from Brazil to Argentina and other areas of South America; from India to other Asian countries and from Indonesia to Australia.[30] (See Table 54; cf. Fig. 32.)

Fibers

Cotton and wool are the most important fibers in world trade. Silk, flax, hemp and jute rank next and are of considerable importance for certain limited areas.

Cotton has been among the leading articles in the world trade since the eighteenth century, especially in the trade of Europe with North America and India. The largest exporter, the United States, accounted for 42 per cent of world exports in 1934–38 and for 44 per cent, on the average, in 1949-51. Egypt is the second largest exporter (12 per cent both before World War II, and on the average in 1949–51). India provided 20 per cent of the world's exports in 1934–38, mainly from the province of Bengal (particularly East Bengal, now part of Pakistan). Combined exports from India and Pakistan declined after

30. **20,** 1952 (Trade sec.), pp. 162–64; cf. **6,** 1950, p. 411.

Table 53

Foodstuffs: Meat and Dairy Products, Exports and Imports of Each Continent,
1934–38 Average, and 1949–51

(*Thousands of Metric Tons*)

Commodity and Year		World [a]	North and Middle America	South America	Europe		Asia	Africa	Oceania
					Continent	United Kingdom			
Beef									
1934–38	Export	736	7	517	92	4	8	23	155
Average	Import	806	7	3	103	572	16	5	—
1949	Export	641	56	407	31	2	1	8	136
	Import	578	44	23	120	370	10	10	1
1950	Export	471	51	244	40	2	1	4	129
	Import	485	40	10	80	340	9	11	1
1951	Export	396	47	176	59	1	...	6	107
	Import	359	52	7	111	159	15	14	1
Mutton, lamb									
1934–38	Export	352	—	67	10	1	—	2	272
Average	Import	352	1	—	12	338	1	—	—
1949	Export	416	2	75	3	1	—	—	335
	Import	381	3	—	9	366	3	—	—
1950	Export	388	2	56	8	1	—	—	321
	Import	409	3	—	5	400	1	—	—
1951	Export	276	1	31	6	1	—	5	232
	Import	267	5	—	8	252	2	—	—
Pork									
1934–38	Export	100	9	12	41	1	—	—	37
Average	Import	102	4	—	39	59	—	—	—
1949	Export	88	7	15	41	—	—	6	19
	Import	73	2	—	39	31	1	—	—
1950	Export	103	3	11	70	—	—	3	16
	Import	106	3	—	72	31	—	—	—
1951	Export	106	12	16	64	—	—	1	13
	Import	86	12	—	57	16	1	—	—
Poultry									
1934–38	Export	119	18	34	23	—	—	—	44
Average	Import	131	3	1	20	106	1	—	—
1949	Export	206	26	26	43	—	—	—	111
	Import	223	8	3	57	143	12	—	—
1950	Export	203	22	21	55	—	—	—	102
	Import	155	8	2	37	96	12	—	—
1951	Export	186	25	31	59	1	—	—	70
	Import	181	7	2	37	121	14	—	—
Bacon, ham, etc.									
1934–38	Export	403	100	5	290	5	1	1	1
Average	Import	417	19	2	5	385	4	2	—
1949	Export	187	52	4	124	1	—	2	4
	Import	167	10	3	9	141	3	1	—
1950	Export	302	60	5	229	1	—	4	3
	Import	317	24	3	37	248	3	2	—
1951	Export	280	37	1	234	1	—	4	3
	Import	285	33	3	20	225	2	2	—

(*Continued on facing page*)

TABLE 53—*continued*

Commodity and Year		World [a]	North and Middle America	South America	Europe		Asia	Africa	Oceania
					Conti-nent	United Kingdom			
Other prepared meats									
1934–38	Export	35	7	13	10	2	1	1	1
Average	Import	28	12	2	7	1	2	4	—
1949	Export	56	9	28	10	—	1	1	7
	Import	56	10	3	22	13	2	5	1
1950	Export	55	8	24	14	—	1	1	7
	Import	43	12	5	14	6	2	4	—
1951	Export	58	26	15	13	—	1	1	2
	Import	77	36	2	11	19	4	5	—
Canned meat									
1934–38	Export	181	10	123	33	2	1	4	8
Average	Import	141	41	2	9	71	7	10	1
1949	Export	254	53	75	69	1	—	10	46
	Import	255	50	9	39	116	22	14	5
1950	Export	290	20	111	104	1	—	7	47
	Import	283	75	9	22	153	9	10	5
1951	Export	396	16	124	182	3	2	10	59
	Import	380	90	12	12	233	13	15	5
Milk									
1934–38	Export	304	30	1	223	17	14	—	19
Average	Import	291	25	8	15	105	120	17	1
1949	Export	637	315	. . .	218	7	14	1	82
	Import	647	50	40	152	118	260	25	2
1950	Export	627	240	. . .	270	10	15	1	91
	Import	587	45	45	124	66	270	35	2
1951	Export	651	200	—	307	13	24	1	106
	Import	638	60	50	95	95	295	41	2
Butter									
1934–38	Export	554	3	8	284	6	4	9	240
Average	Import	627	9	1	102	488	17	10	. . .
1949	Export	434	2	1	201	4	1	6	219
	Import	429	5	2	77	323	10	11	1
1950	Export	494	2	9	249	1	2	6	225
	Import	475	5	6	99	341	10	13	1
1951	Export	446	4	8	239	1	2	8	184
	Import	474	13	5	117	313	10	15	1
Cheese									
1934–38	Export	278	34	2	142	3	1	1	95
Average	Import	277	28	2	85	145	4	13	—
1949	Export	348	69	9	149	1	1	1	118
	Import	347	19	4	84	216	10	14	—
1950	Export	362	50	6	179	1	1	1	124
	Import	342	34	5	118	157	8	20	—
1951	Export	374	50	3	189	1	2	1	128
	Import	372	35	4	108	197	6	22	—

Source: **20**, 1952 (Trade sec.), pp. 191–225.   a. Includes the USSR.

TABLE 54

TOBACCO: EXPORTS AND IMPORTS OF SELECTED COUNTRIES, 1934–38 AVERAGE, AND 1949–51

(Thousands of Metric Tons)

Country	Exports 1934–38 Average	1949	1950	1951	Country	Imports 1934–38 Average	1949	1950	1951
World [a]	540	570	570	620	World [a]	550	560	560	600
United States	198	226	216	237	United States	30	40	41	48
Canada	5	7	12	13	United Kingdom	125	137	139	161
Cuba	12	12	12	13	Ireland	6	11	9	8
Dominican Republic	6	21	15	16	France	29	34	21	32
Colombia	3	4	4	4	Belgium-Luxembourg	19	19	22	25
Brazil	31	27	36	30	Netherlands	30	31	29	29
Paraguay	4	7	3	3	Denmark	8	12	14	10
Italy	6	7	9	8	Sweden	6	7	9	12
Yugoslavia	4	13	8	6	Norway	3	4	4	4
Bulgaria	24	14	9	. . .	Finland	3	2	4	5
Greece	44	28	26	32	Germany [b]	97	46	46	47
China	15	. . .	. . .	1	Poland	8	4	11	. . .
Turkey	29	80	51	58	Czechoslovakia	9	. . .	. . .	. . .
India, Pakistan	21	34	50	50	Switzerland	7	10	11	11
Indonesia	48	8	12	13	Austria	8	15	8	10
Philippines	14	5	4	6	Portugal	3	4	5	5
Algeria	12	13	11	14	Spain	22	19	25	21
Nyasaland	6	12	11	12	Italy	3	4	4	3
Southern Rhodesia	9	31	41	31	China	36	. . .	. . .	3
Other	49	21	40	73	Japan	5	—	7	1
					Philippines	1	—	13	5
					Egypt	6	14	13	13
					Australia	9	10	12	12
					Other	77	137	113	135

Source: **20,** 1952 (Trade sec.), pp. 162–64.

a. Partly estimated and rounded.

b. For 1949–51, Western Germany.

the partition to 11 per cent of world exports in 1949–51. Smaller quantities are exported by Mexico, the USSR, Brazil, Peru, Turkey, the Anglo-Egyptian Sudan, Kenya-Uganda and other areas.

The largest importers, in order of their imports in 1949–51, are the United Kingdom, Japan, France, Germany, Italy and India, followed by Belgium, Canada, Poland, the Netherlands and Czechoslovakia.

Exports of cotton from the United States to the United Kingdom, the rest of northwestern Europe and central Europe represent about 40 per cent of world trade in this fiber. An additional 30 per cent is comprised of exports to Europe from Mexico, Brazil, Peru, Egypt, the Anglo-Egyptian Sudan and British West Afri-

can colonies and other areas. Shipments from the United States to Japan, Canada, China and other non-European countries represent 10 per cent. The rest is shipped in intracontinental trade in South America, Asia and Africa and in exports from the USSR to satellite countries, from Brazil to Australia, from Egypt, Pakistan and Peru to the United States, and in some other operations of local importance.[31] (See Table 55; cf. Figure 33.)

Jute comes almost exclusively from Pakistan, which supplied more than 95 per cent of all shipments in 1950–51. India took one third of this export. Distribution of export by destination,

31. **6,** 1950, p. 22.

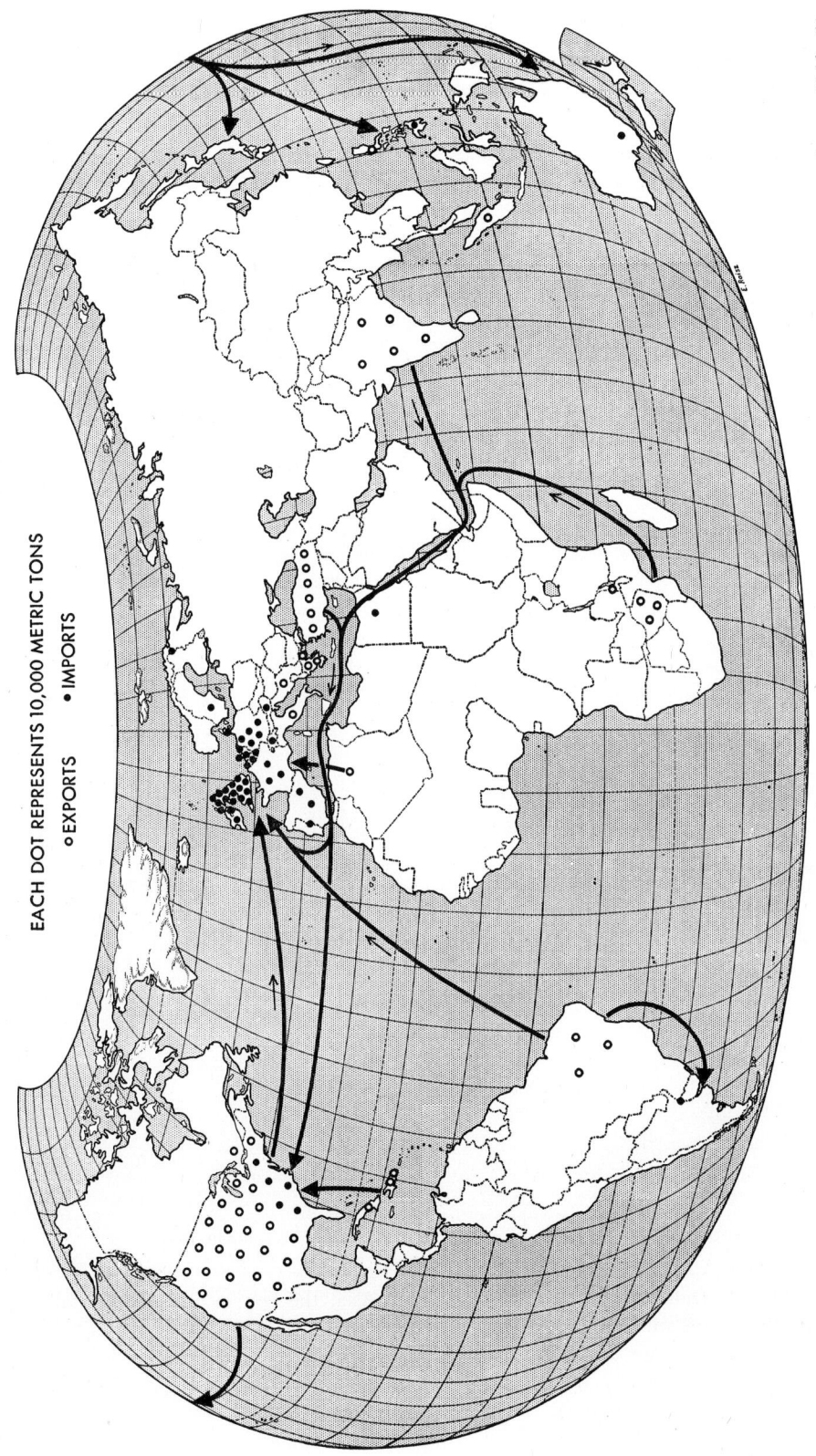

EACH DOT REPRESENTS 10,000 METRIC TONS

○ EXPORTS ● IMPORTS

FIGURE 32. TOBACCO IN WORLD TRADE, 1951

The main routes of tobacco in world trade are from the United States across the Atlantic to the United Kingdom and continental Europe and across the Pacific to the Far East; from Brazil, southeastern Africa and India to Europe; from Turkey to the United States and Europe; from Brazil to Argentina; from the Caribbean to the United States; from Algeria to France.

Source: Table 54

TABLE 55

FIBERS: COTTON, EXPORTS AND IMPORTS OF SELECTED COUNTRIES, 1934–38 AVERAGE, AND 1949–51

(*Thousands of Metric Tons*)

Country	1934–38 Average	1949	1950	1951	Country	1934–38 Average	1949	1950	1951
Exports									
World	3,070	2,520	2,960	2,670	Pakistan	}613{	161	216	206
United States	1,294	1,168	1,341	1,163	India		52	33	28
Mexico	23	123	163	178	Burma	18	4	6	13
Haiti	6	2	1	1	Egypt	375	359	387	255
Brazil	194	140	129	143	Anglo-Egyptian Sudan	50	65	67	97
Peru	75	42	66	62					
Paraguay	9	8	2	7	French Equatorial Africa	7	24	24	27
Argentina	30	—	35	36	Belgian Congo	30	47	49	40
USSR	11	130	160	180	Uganda, Kenya	60	72	64	64
China	53	…	…	11					
Japan	38	—	—	—	Tanganyika	10	11	7	8
Turkey	18	32	76	56					
Iran	18	6	20	9	Mozambique	5	28	24	24
					Angola	2	4	7	4
					Other	131	42	83	58
Imports									
World	3,090	2,490	2,770	2,540	Switzerland	28	30	42	31
United States	38	32	46	36	Austria	36	22	18	21
Canada	64	93	104	93	Hungary	24	29	30	28
					Portugal	25	38	33	36
Colombia	3	17	22	7	Spain	103	73	55	50
Chile	2	18	21	13	Italy	153	196	207	189
Uruguay	—	5	6	5	Yugoslavia	18	29	32	8
United Kingdom	630	467	459	459	Romania	12	16	17	14
France	268	259	280	247	Bulgaria	9	7	7	7
Belgium–Luxembourg	110	86	115	104	USSR	37	50	30	2
Netherlands	50	60	67	58	China	77	119	87	50
Denmark	9	7	11	11	Korea	24	12	11	8
Sweden	33	29	27	26	Japan	779	192	356	381
Norway	3	4	4	5	India	93	205	206	168
Finland	14	12	9	13	Indochina	8	3	4	3
Germany [a]	272	160	216	204	Union of South Africa	—	4	5	4
Poland	70	87	93	98					
Czechoslovakia	83	60	60	65	Australia	3	10	13	20
					Other	12	63	87	76

Source: **20**, 1952 (Trade sec.), pp. 168–71.

a. For 1949–51, Western Germany.

however, varies widely from year to year. The largest importers in Europe are the United Kingdom, France, Belgium, Germany and Italy. The United States and France vie for third place (after India and the United Kingdom). About 50 per cent of foreign trade in jute is effected within Asia, the rest in intercontinental shipments. (See Table 56.)

Silk comes to the world market largely from Japan. Italy provides about 10 per cent. The largest consumers are the United States (25–30 per cent of world imports), France, the United King-

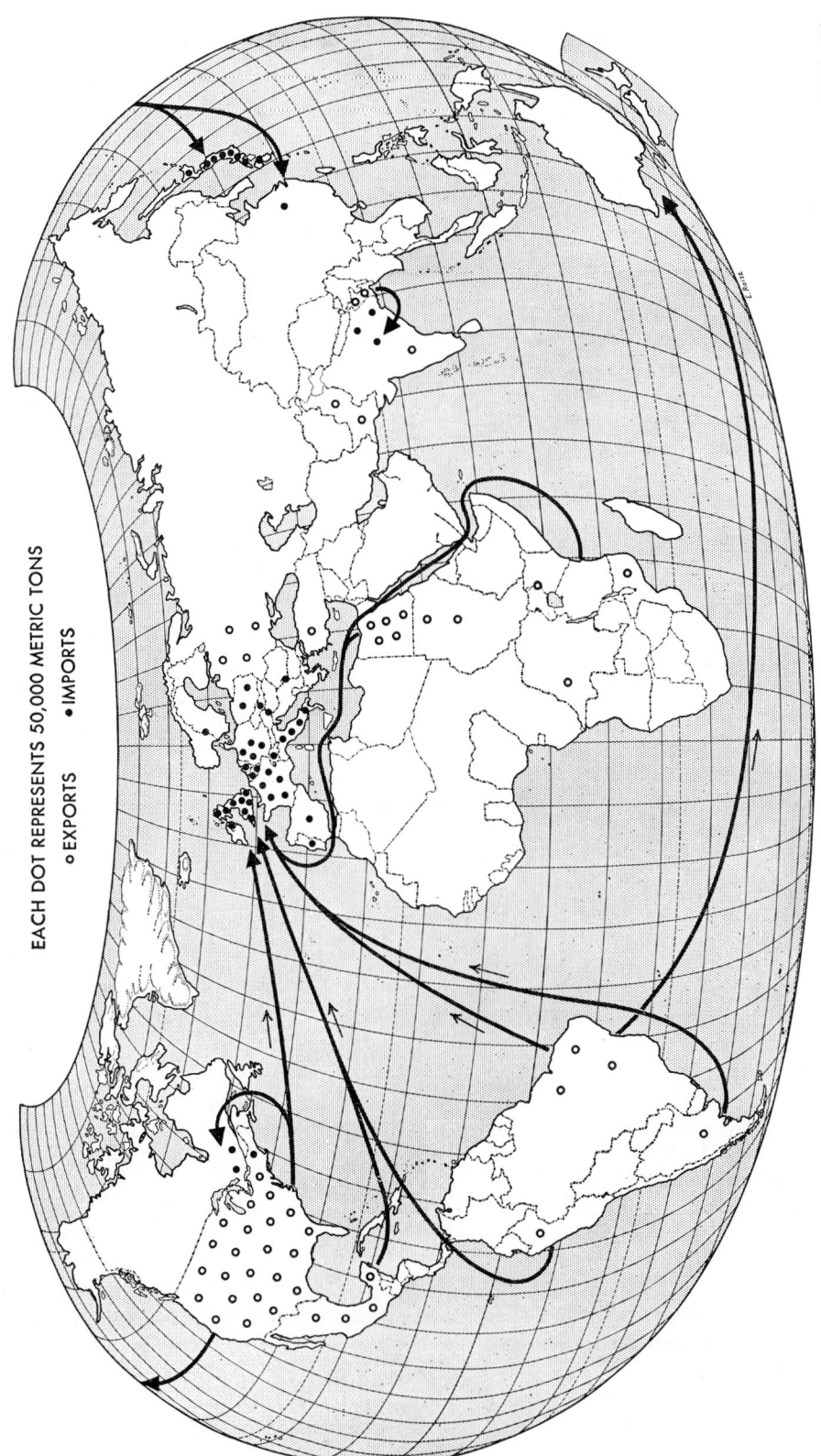

EACH DOT REPRESENTS 50,000 METRIC TONS

○ EXPORTS   ● IMPORTS

FIGURE 33. FIBERS: COTTON IN WORLD TRADE, 1951

The main routes in the cotton trade cross the Atlantic, running eastward and northward from the United States, the Caribbean and South America to the United Kingdom and Western Europe. Other important directions of trade are from the United States to Japan and the Far East; from Egypt and southeastern Africa to Europe; from eastern Pakistan to India; from Brazil to Australia.

Source: Table 55

155

TABLE 56

FIBERS: JUTE AND SILK, EXPORTS AND IMPORTS OF SELECTED COUNTRIES, 1934–38 AVERAGE, AND 1949–51

(Thousands of Metric Tons)

Country	1934–38 Average	1949	1950	1951	Country	1934–38 Average	1949	1950	1951
JUTE									
Exports					*Imports—continued*				
World	820	650	1,150	1,100	Belgium	54	55	56	80
Pakistan	}769{	445	1,112	1,053	Netherlands	10	8	10	14
India		186	7	—	Sweden	8	4	5	6
Other	51	19	31	47	Germany [a]	109	51	53	73
					Poland	14	...	...	...
Imports					Czechoslovakia	35	...	...	...
World	840	730	870	1,220	Hungary	10	...	...	...
United States	73	63	79	107	Portugal	4	2	9	11
Canada	1	4	3	5	Spain	44	4	2	11
Brazil	23	10	5	11	Italy	49	24	35	65
United Kingdom	191	97	114	116	India	...	253	319	450
France	94	55	74	119	Other	120	100	106	152
SILK									
Exports					Canada	1.18	0.06	0.06	0.03
World	40.90	5.20	8.40	6.50	United Kingdom	2.02	0.64	0.81	0.73
Italy	2.29	0.42	0.65	0.63	France	3.06	0.79	0.97	1.03
China	4.66	...	...	...	Germany [a]	1.19	0.08	0.40	0.28
Korea	2.49	—	—	0.30	Switzerland	0.28	0.30	0.53	0.39
Japan	30.19	3.21	5.76	4.29	Italy	0.29	0.15	0.30	0.27
Other	1.27	1.57	1.99	1.28	Korea	1.04	—	—	—
					Japan	2.61	—	—	—
Imports					India	0.91	0.05	0.31	0.54
World	41.70	4.80	8.50	6.40	Egypt	...	0.24	0.19	0.08
United States	27.00	1.26	3.48	2.18	Australia	0.44	0.06	0.07	...
					Other	1.68	1.17	1.38	0.87

Source: **20**, 1952 (Trade sec.), pp. 176–77, 181–82.   a. For 1949–51, Western Germany.

dom, India and Switzerland. Italy, although an exporter of silk, imports Japanese silk. The competition of rayon, nylon and other artificial fibers has reduced the demand for natural silk to a fraction of the prewar volume. (See Table 56.)

Wool is a major item in world trade. The leading exporters are the sparsely populated sheep-raising countries — Australia and New Zealand (about half of world exports in 1949–51); Argentina and Uruguay (more than 10 per cent); and the Union of South Africa (usually about 5 per cent).

Northwestern Europe takes 65–70 per cent of the exports. Domestic consumption and the trade balance of this area depend largely on the supply of overseas wool. The largest importers are the United States and the United Kingdom, which account together for half of world imports. Other large importers are France, Germany, Belgium and Italy. (See Table 57.)

Rubber

Like jute and silk, rubber comes to the world market from Asia, almost exclusively from Malaya, Indonesia, Thailand, Ceylon, British Borneo and Indochina. Brazil, once the main producer of rubber, now provides only 0.2 per cent of world exports. The United States is the largest single importer (40 per cent of total recorded imports or 45 per cent of net imports, excluding

TABLE 57

FIBERS: WOOL, EXPORTS AND IMPORTS OF SELECTED COUNTRIES, 1934–38 AVERAGE, AND 1949–51

(Clean Basis, Thousands of Metric Tons)

	Exports					Imports			
Country	1934–38 Average	1949	1950	1951	Country	1934–38 Average	1949	1950	1951
World	660	770	820	590	World	670	770	830	600
Chile	6	4	5	5	United States	61	124	212	164
Uruguay	28	31	58	22	Canada	7	11	12	10
Argentina	77	65	91	48					
					United Kingdom	245	240	211	153
United Kingdom	80	50	46	30	France	83	111	94	78
Ireland	4	4	5	2	Belgium-				
					Luxembourg	44	41	49	28
France	12	10	14	10	Netherlands	5	14	14	7
Belgium-					Sweden	5	10	9	6
Luxembourg	25	13	18	12	Germany [a]	71	39	53	32
Turkey	4	1	4	2	Poland	12	17	10	9
Syria, Lebanon	2	2	5	6	Czechoslovakia	10	6	9	6
Iran	3	1	2	5	Austria	6	5	5	3
Pakistan	} 18 {	7	11	7	Italy	25	43	37	29
India		9	9	7	USSR	19	30	19	11
Union of South					Japan	49	12	22	35
Africa	45	48	47	44	India	7	5	4	3
Australia	206	330	316	258					
New Zealand	87	141	129	104	Other	21	62	70	26
Other	63	54	60	28					

Source: **20,** 1952 (Trade sec.), pp. 183–86.   a. For 1949–51, Western Germany.

reexports). Other large importers include the United Kingdom, France, Western Germany, the USSR, Canada, Italy and Czechoslovakia. (See Tables 58 and 59.[32])

Rubber is raised exclusively for export. Practically the entire crop passes through the channels of intercontinental trade before it reaches the mill. The main trade routes run from the Far East westward (across the Indian Ocean, via the Red Sea, the Suez Canal and the Mediterranean) to northwestern Europe, and eastward, across the Pacific, to the United States.

Despite the competition of synthetic rubber, the demand for natural rubber for automobiles, tractors and airplanes is growing steadily. The volume of international trade in natural rubber in 1949–51 was nearly 75 per cent above the average for 1934–38.

32. Minor differences between the data in Tables 58 and 59 are accounted for by revision of original figures by the respective statistical services.

FOREST PRODUCTS IN WORLD TRADE

Lumber appears in international trade in different stages of production: raw materials, in the form of poles and posts, fuelwood, pit props and sawlogs; prefabricated materials, as sawn and planed lumber, veneers and plywood, pulpwood and wood pulp; fabricated articles, as newsprint and other paper and paperboard. Because of the bulkiness of raw timber, wood is usually exported in prefabricated or fabricated form, although round wood is also an important item of foreign trade.

International trade in forest products is largely an intra-European and intra-American business: Sweden, Norway and Finland export lumber to the United Kingdom and other European countries; Canada is the main supplier of the United States. Processed wood — such as Canadian, Finnish, Swedish and Norwegian newsprint and paper — is shipped all around the globe.

The relative volume of intracontinental and intercontinental trade in lumber products is

TABLE 58

RUBBER: EXPORTS AND IMPORTS OF SELECTED COUNTRIES, 1934–38 AVERAGE, AND 1949–51

(Thousands of Metric Tons)

Country	1934–38 Average	1949	1950	1951	Country	1934–38 Average	1949	1950	1951
					Exports				
World	1,230	1,760	2,360	2,410	Indochina	39	42	53	48
					Ceylon	64	92	120	104
United States	—	6	9	3	Malaya, Singapore	609	914	1,124	1,072
Brazil	13	1	—	—	Indonesia	347	429	703	807
United Kingdom	51	32	32	61	British Borneo	33	61	84	68
Hong Kong	1	23	42	38	Liberia	2	29	32	35
India	9	—	1	—	Nigeria	2	7	14	21
Burma	6	6	10	12	Belgian Congo	1	7	8	12
Thailand	32	96	114	111	Other	21	15	14	18
					Imports				
World	1,230	1,760	2,290	2,510	Czechoslovakia	11	28	23	11
					Switzerland	2	4	5	8
United States	494	671	817	746	Austria	5	8	8	9
Canada	30	41	47	55	Hungary	3	9	7	—
Mexico	3	10	11	17	Spain	6	8	6	7
Argentina	7	7	18	26	Italy	23	30	37	51
United Kingdom	153	177	257	366	USSR	36	105	85	60
France	57	92	97	126					
Belgium-Luxembourg	14	14	15	19	China	7	28	71	74
					Japan	61	40	58	47
Netherlands	5	11	14	14	Hong Kong	2	24	42	42
Denmark	3	5	6	7	Malaya, Singapore	188	224	456	556
Sweden	7	22	14	19	Union of South Africa	4	18	23	27
Norway	2	4	4	5					
Finland	3	4	5	6	Australia	13	23	37	57
Germany [a]	79	91	92	91	Other	106	50	29	52
Poland	6	12	6	12					

Source: **20**, 1952 (Trade sec.), pp. 153–54.　　　　　　a. For 1949–51, Western Germany.

illustrated by the following distribution of the value of exports and imports in 1949 and 1951 (in millions of dollars): [33]

	1949		1951	
	Exports	Imports	Exports	Imports
World	$2,479	$2,274	$4,644	$4,363
North and Middle America	1,069	882	1,709	1,365
South America	42	40	76	100
Europe	1,316	1,171	2,721	2,543
Asia	34	105	82	146
Africa	13	76	51	89
Oceania	5	1	6	119

Both in 1949 and 1951 North America and Europe together accounted for 96 per cent of the

exports and 90 per cent of the imports. These totals include comparatively few shipments from America to Europe and still fewer from Europe to America.

Lumber products in international trade are classified differently in different countries. The classification used by the Food and Agriculture Organization results in the following distribution of the value of exported and imported lumber products in 1949 (in millions of dollars): [34]

	Exports	Imports
Total	$4,644	$4,363
Wood, lumber and cork	1,421	1,535
Pulp and wastepaper	1,337	1,258
Wood and cork manufactures	269	297
Paper, paperboard and manufactures thereof	1,617	1,273

33. **21**, 1952, pp. 112–15. For prewar years see **24**; cf. **15**.

34. **21**, 1950, pp. 116–25.

TABLE 59

RUBBER: DESTINATION OF EXPORTS FROM PRINCIPAL EXPORTING COUNTRIES, 1951

(*Thousands of Metric Tons*)

| Destination | Total | Exporting Country | | | | | | | Reported Net Import |
		Malaya	Indo-nesia	Thai-land	Ceylon	Cambo-dia	Sara-wak	Other[a]	
Total	2,635.7	1,173.8	806.5	112.5	105.3	52.8	44.1	340.7	1,872.4
United States	723.4	365.6	166.1	103.4	21.0	12.5	0.1	54.7[b]	743.6
Canada	42.9	36.0	0.1	—	4.1	—	—	2.7	48.8
Mexico	11.8	9.6	0.9	—	1.0	—	—	0.3	13.2
Argentina	25.5	21.9	2.6	—	0.2	—	—	0.8	25.6
United Kingdom	396.1	285.3	32.9	—	32.3	3.9	2.5	39.2	304.3
France	130.7	70.2	10.3	—	4.0	34.8	0.3	11.1	125.8
Belgium	43.6	8.5	9.8	—	2.4	0.3	—	22.6	18.8
Netherlands	65.8	7.3	50.4	—	7.0	—	0.1	1.0	14.7
Sweden	18.6	12.9	0.9	—	1.2	—	0.5	3.1	19.5
Western Germany	103.9	44.8	16.4	—	10.0	—	0.4	32.3	90.4
Czechoslovakia	15.9	9.7	—	—	—	—	—	6.4	11.2
Italy	60.4	48.0	2.6	—	8.3	—	0.2	1.3	51.0
USSR	68.7	17.8	—	—	—	—	—	50.9[c]	63.5
China	66.5	23.1	—	—	5.6	—	—	37.8[d]	74.4
Japan	57.3	31.0	25.7	0.5	0.1	—	—	—	59.6
Hong Kong	36.9	35.1	—	—	0.1	—	0.2	1.5	2.1
Malaya	555.9	—	478.2	8.6	—	1.3	39.5	28.3	—
Union of South Africa	26.1	23.3	1.0	—	1.0	—	—	0.8	27.3
Australia	54.6	49.9	3.1	—	1.2	—	0.2	—	57.2
Other	131.1	73.8	5.3	—	5.8	—	0.1	46.1	121.4

Source: **6**, 1952, p. 34.

a. Reexports from the United Kingdom, the Netherlands and Hong Kong and transit trade.

b. Includes 35,000 metric tons from Liberia.
c. From the United Kingdom and the Netherlands.
d. From Hong Kong.

The largest net exporters are Canada, Sweden, Finland, Norway and Austria. The United States exports considerable quantities of sawn and planed lumber and paper, but imports much larger quantities of raw, sawn and planed lumber, pulpwood, wood pulp, newsprint and other wood products. Similarly, in France, export of raw and sawn and planed lumber is more than offset by import of pulpwood and wood pulp.

The United Kingdom ranks first in net imports of forest products, the United States, second. Other large importers are the Netherlands, Belgium, Italy and Western Germany. (See Table 60.)

The main routes of international trade are from Canada to the United States and Europe and from Sweden, Norway and Finland to the United Kingdom and continental Europe. Other important routes are from Canada to South America, Africa and the Far East; from the United States to Canada; and from Sweden and Finland to the Far East and Australia.

In 1950, European countries exported 49 million cubic meters of industrial wood (round-wood equivalent) and imported 40 million cubic meters in round numbers, the export surplus of 9 million cubic meters being absorbed mainly by the Western Hemisphere. Intra-European trade in wood followed an intricate pattern. (See Figure 34.) In 1950 European countries ranked, by

TABLE 60

FOREST PRODUCTS: EXPORTS AND IMPORTS, SELECTED COUNTRIES, 1951

Continent and Country	Total Value, in Millions of Dollars	Raw Lumber [a]	Prefabricated Lumber			Further Processed Lumber			
			Sawn, Planed or Dressed [b]	Sleepers, Veneers, Plywood	Pulp-wood	Wood-pulp	News-print	Other Paper	Fiber-board
			Thousands of Cubic Meters			Thousands of Metric Tons			
Exports									
World	$4,644	9,190	26,950	1,300	11,480	6,180	5,640	2,500	360
North and Middle America	1,709	1,060	11,210	260	7,360	2,200	4,700	530	20
United States	378	399	2,188	157	33	183	65	393	. . .
Canada	1,326	579	8,831	103	7,322	2,017	4,635	137	20
Other countries	5	82	191	—	5	—	—	—	—
South America	76	360	1,330	40	—	—	—	—	—
Brazil	58	93	1,144	13	—	—	—	—	—
Other countries	18	267	186	27	—	—	—	—	—
Europe	2,721	4,950	13,400	900	4,120	3,980	910	1,890	340
France	190	1,322	1,355	310	17	2	21	131	3
Sweden	940	389	4,145	52	169	2,008	199	473	183
Norway	197	134	124	1	9	564	138	76	24
Finland	714	2,038	3,983	385	3,496	1,191	382	141	68
Western Germany	90	212	165	26	13	73	—	53	26
Austria	155	105	2,449	12	—	105	50	27	8
Yugoslavia	58	186	904	66	396	2	—	1	1
Other countries	377	564	275	48	20	35	120	988	28
Asia	82	1,550	710	60	—	—	30	50	—
Africa	51	1,240	210	30	—	—	—	20	—
Oceania	6	30	90	10	—	—	—	10	—
Imports									
World	$4,363	10,220	26,390	1,560	11,780	5,860	5,460	2,040	290
North and Middle America	1,365	1,980	6,420	190	6,520	2,180	4,500	200	30
United States	1,275	1,502	5,966	156	6,401	2,144	4,500	19	22
Canada	82	444	325	25	119	33	—	16	8
Other countries	8	34	129	9	—	3	—	165	—
South America	100	390	920	. . .	150	240	220	140	. . .
Europe	2,543	6,270	15,330	1,090	5,100	3,260	360	1,210	210
United Kingdom	1,332	2,579	8,760	734	313	1,706	174	271	131
Ireland	49	16	352	41	—	22	22	8	4
France	258	159	255	8	523	452	28	58	9
Belgium–Luxembourg	138	608	612	88	184	205	24	95	13
Netherlands	213	566	1,868	81	438	169	3	72	31
Denmark	90	46	770	28	. . .	66	47	38	16
Sweden	34	514	126	11	745	1	—	9	. . .
Western Germany	215	406	836	67	1,253	299	42	39	2
Switzerland	60	463	166	10	407	60	. . .	17	1
Austria	12	2	9	1	157	19	—	. . .	—
Italy	90	545	1,000	. . .	434	155	3	13	. . .
Other countries	52	366	576	21	646	106	17	590	3
Asia	146	1,240	760	160	10	130	130	140	10
Africa	89	200	1,910	90	—	10	90	200	10
Oceania	119	140	1,050	30	—	40	160	150	30

Source: **21**, 1952, pp. 104–15.

a. Pit props; poles, piling and posts; saw logs and veneer logs; fuel wood.   b. Includes boxboard.

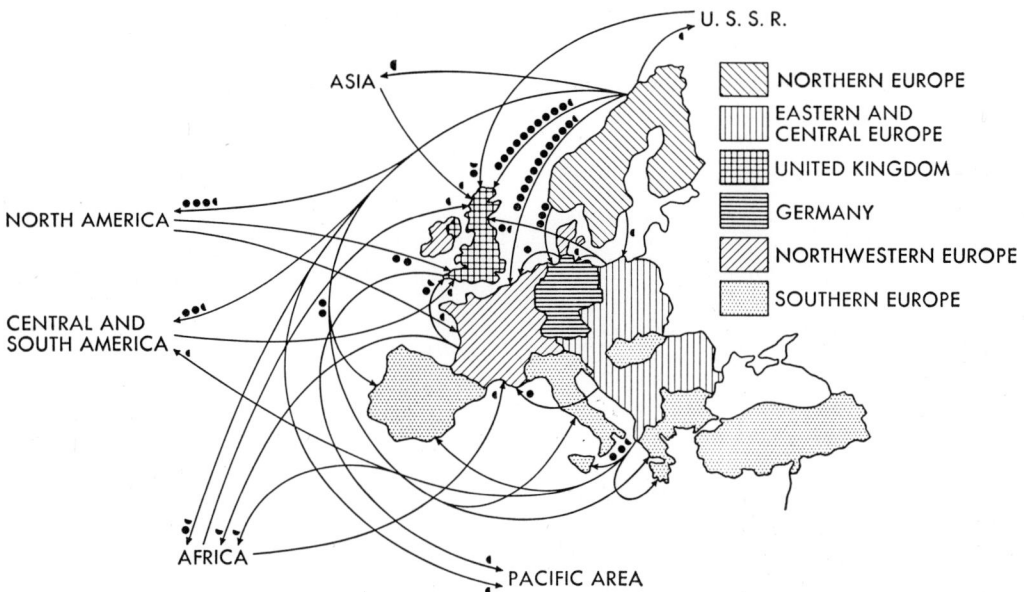

EACH DOT REPRESENTS 1,000,000 CUBIC METERS
(ROUNDWOOD EQUIVALENT)

Food and Agriculture Organization

FIGURE 34. FOREST PRODUCTS: INDUSTRIAL WOOD IN EUROPEAN INTERREGIONAL TRADE, 1950

net export (+) or net import (−) of wood, as follows (in millions of cubic meters): [35]

Sweden	+19.1	Turkey	−0.3
Finland	+16.8	Switzerland	−0.5
Austria	+4.5	Greece	−0.9
Norway	+2.9	Ireland	−1.0
Yugoslavia	+2.2	Hungary	−1.2
Czechoslovakia	+1.2	Western Germany	−1.3
Romania	+1.0	Denmark	−2.8
Poland	+0.8	Belgium−	
France	+0.3	Luxembourg	−3.1
Portugal	0.0	Italy	−3.7
Bulgaria	−0.2	Netherlands	−5.4
Spain	−0.3	United Kingdom	−19.2

MINERAL PRODUCTS IN WORLD TRADE

A detailed survey of all mineral products in foreign trade is outside the scope of the present study, and the following discussion is limited to coal, petroleum products and selected ores and metals.

FUELS

International trade in mineral fuels is of paramount importance for the world economy. The industry and transportation systems of many areas rely wholly on imported fuels. In both tonnage and value, fuels rank high in international freight traffic.

Coal

Before the war, international trade in coal, briquettes and coke was primarily intracontinental. Three fourths of the shipments were among European countries, including their North African colonies. Shipments from the United States to Canada accounted for 10 per cent of the world total. China, Manchuria, Indochina, India and Indonesia supplied coal to Japan, Malaya and other areas in Asia, Australia, New Zealand and New Caledonia. Intercontinental trade was mainly from Europe to South America.[36]

The situation changed after the war. Canadian imports doubled; European exports declined; the shortage of coal in Europe stimulated imports from the United States. (See Table 61.)

Information on the distribution of imports of coal by provenance and of exports by destination is incomplete because of gaps for the countries within the Soviet bloc. In the free world, Canada and Latin America rely on coal from the United States, while in imports of continental Europe,

---

35. **15**, p. 210.   36. **31**, p. 51.

TABLE 61

MINERAL FUELS: COAL AND COKE, EXPORTS AND IMPORTS OF SELECTED COUNTRIES, 1938 AND 1949-51

(*Thousands of Metric Tons*)

Country	1938	1949	1950	1951	Country	1938	1949	1950	1951
					Exports				
World	146,400	...	...	...	Germany [a]	46,200	22,700	25,700	25,200
United States	14,200	29,700	26,600	56,900	Poland	10,200	32,500	30,700	...
Canada	400	...	600	400	Other European				
United Kingdom	43,700	17,000	17,300	...	countries	5,300	5,200 [b]	4,200 [b]	...
France	900	5,300	6,300	5,900	USSR	1,300	...	...	...
Belgium–									
Luxembourg	5,800	1,800	3,200	2,500	Asia	10,100	...	...	...
Netherlands	6,400	1,000	1,200	1,300	Africa	1,400	...	...	...
					Oceania	400	...	...	...
					Imports				
World	140,400	...	...	...	Germany [a]	5,700	3,100	5,100	10,400
United States	800	500	700	400	Czechoslovakia	1,400	...	3,700	...
Canada [c]	14,000	20,100	24,500	27,000	Austria	3,200	6,100	5,600	5,800
Ireland	2,500	1,700	...	2,000	Portugal	1,400	800	900	600
					Spain	1,100	1,000	700	400
France	29,100	18,700	10,500	14,100	Italy	12,800	10,000	8,300	10,800
Belgium–					Other European				
Luxembourg	9,100	1,800	3,200	5,800	countries	16,500	23,000 [b]	...	...
Denmark	5,400	4,900	6,700	6,100	Japan	4,200	1,900	800	1,900
Sweden	8,600	5,200	7,200	7,600	India	1,300	1,200	...	...
Norway	3,000	1,700	1,800	1,500	Africa	5,600	...	...	...
Finland	2,200	1,200	1,900	2,400	Oceania	300	...	...	...

Sources: For 1938, **31**, p. 48. Data include coal, lignite, briquettes and coke, evaluated at coal equivalent. Although internally consistent, these data are not strictly comparable to those for more recent years. For the latter, see **9**, 1951 and 1952, *passim,* and **10**, Fourth Quarter 1951, p. 70.

a. For 1949–51, Western Germany.   c. Includes Newfoundland and Labrador.
b. Includes the USSR.

U.S. coal represents not more than 20–25 per cent and the rest is provided by Germany, Great Britain, Poland and other European producers. According to a report of the British Ministry of Fuel and Power the main shipments are from the United States to Canada (24.6 million metric tons in 1951), to France (4.5 million) and Italy (3.7 million); from Germany to France (10.9 million), to Italy (3.6 million) and Belgium-Luxembourg (3.3 million); from Poland to Scandinavia (4.5 million) and to Czechoslovakia (3.7 million). Exports from Great Britain are widely dispersed among continental European countries and British colonies and dominions. (See Table 62.)

Figure 35 shows the principal routes of world trade in coal in 1951 in accordance with the British report. It fails to show some short-distance shipments.[37] The pattern changes from time to time.

Efforts are being made to restore European self-sufficiency in coal, and it is anticipated that European exports to former markets, at least in the Mediterranean Basin, will be resumed.

Petroleum

Shipments of crude petroleum from an area usually indicate that all or part of the oil produced in the area is taken by purchasers who intend to process it in their own refineries. Such an arrangement may be due to the insufficient capacity of local refineries or to the policy of the

37. Imports and exports of individual countries (as shown by dots on the map) conform to Table 62 but deviate in some cases from Table 61.

TABLE 62

MINERAL FUELS: COAL AND COKE, IMPORTS OF SELECTED COUNTRIES AND THEIR PROVENANCE, 1951

(*Thousands of Metric Tons*)

Importing Country	Total [a]	Supplying Country				
		United States	Great Britain	Germany	Poland	Other
Canada	24,853	24,588	265	—	—	—
Brazil (1950)	1,079	912	113	1	—	53
Uruguay	142	92	25	1	—	24
Argentina	2,205	1,355	424	37	120	269
Ireland	2,039	654	1,170	28	161	26
France	18,365	4,490	593	10,905	967	1,410
Belgium–Luxembourg	5,572	1,411	378	3,348	7	428
Netherlands	5,818	2,071	360	2,589	21	777
Denmark	5,986	829	1,947	1,113	1,935	162
Sweden	7,649	920	1,098	2,297	2,879	475
Norway	2,158	1,073	411	115	130	429
Finland	2,489	314	232	163	1,547	233
Austria	4,583	814	—	2,363	1,094	312
Czechoslovakia (1950)	3,720	—	—	—	3,720	—
Switzerland	3,063	873	106	1,097	179	808
Portugal	633	126	263	84	26	134
Spain	428	72	189	11	—	156
Italy	10,799	3,726	624	3,585	1,061	1,803
Greece	395	—	—	394	—	1
Egypt (1949)	325	1	209	—	7	109

Source: A report of the British Ministry of Fuel and Power, March 1953. These figures deviate appreciably from those in Table 61.

a. Based on import records. The data include hard coal, coke, breeze and briquettes.

importing countries and companies controlling the local petroleum fields. Venezuela, Colombia, Kuwait, Saudi Arabia and Brunei (British Borneo) export mainly crude oil, while Iran and Iraq have large refineries.

Nearly one third of the petroleum in world trade is exported in crude form; the rest, as gasoline, fuel oil, lubricants and other petroleum products.[38] This statement refers, however, to the form in which petroleum crosses political boundaries rather than to the exports from the broader area in which the oil fields are located. For example, most of Venezuela's petroleum output is exported in crude form to the islands of the Netherlands West Indies (Aruba and Curaçao), located just off the coast of Venezuela. From the point of view of the world economy, such shipments can hardly be considered as an export-import transaction between Venezuela and the Netherlands West Indies, but represent,

rather, only the first stage of the road which petroleum travels from the oil wells to the world market. It appears on the market when it leaves the Caribbean area. The same considerations apply to the shipments of crude oil from Saudi Arabia to Bahrein or from Brunei to Sarawak. (See Table 63.)

All in all, approximately one third of the petroleum exported in crude form goes to refineries not very far from the border of the exporting country. The rest, some 90 million metric tons in 1950, is exported to countries which refine imported crude oil for domestic consumption and export part of the distillation products.

The United States is the largest producer of crude oil and the largest exporter of petroleum products. When the values of crude petroleum and refined oils are combined, it appears that the United States imports and exports of these products were in rough equilibrium in 1946. In more recent years, the United States has had an

38. **39,** pp. 406–48.

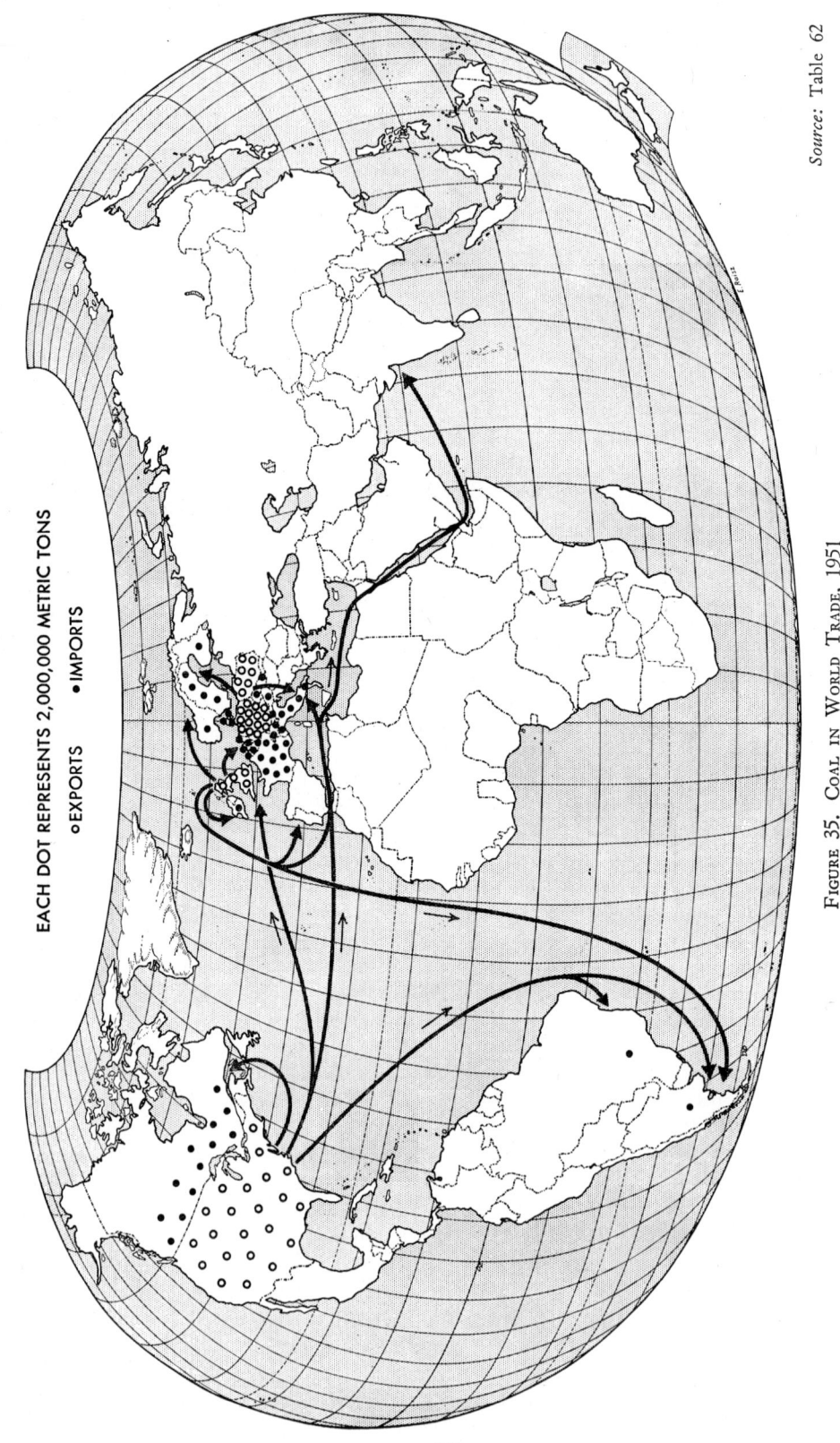

EACH DOT REPRESENTS 2,000,000 METRIC TONS

∘EXPORTS   •IMPORTS

FIGURE 35. COAL IN WORLD TRADE, 1951

Only the main routes are shown on this map. Other important routes of international trade in coal are: from the United States to Japan, Latin America and the Belgian Congo; from the United Kingdom to North Africa and the Far East; from France and Belgium to all European countries.

Source: Table 62

TABLE 63

MINERAL FUELS: CRUDE PETROLEUM, OUTPUT AND EXPORTS OF SELECTED COUNTRIES, 1950

Country	*Output*	*Exports*	*Percentage Exported*	*Destination of Exports*
	Thousands of Metric Tons			
World [a]	489,100	136,100	28.1	——
United States	270,100	4,700	1.7	Japan, Canada
Canada	3,750	—	—	——
Mexico	10,300	—	—	——
Trinidad	3,000	—	—	——
Colombia	4,800	3,600	75.0	United States, Canada
Venezuela	78,250	66,100	84.5	Netherlands West Indies, United States, Canada
Peru	2,000	—	—	——
Argentina	3,400	—	—	——
Austria	1,500	—	—	——
Romania	3,800 [b]	—	—	——
Iran	32,250	6,600	20.5	Europe
Kuwait	17,300	16,100	93.1	Europe, United States
Bahrein	1,500	—	—	——
Iraq	6,500	6,100	93.8	Europe
Saudi Arabia	26,900	20,600	76.6	Europe, United States, Bahrein
Brunei	4,100	4,100	100.0	Sarawak
Egypt	2,350	—	—	——
Other	17,300	8,200	...	——

Sources: For production, see **8**, 1951, pp. 140–41; for export see **6**, 1951, p. 28.

    a. Excludes the USSR.   b. 1947.

active dollar balance in foreign trade in petroleum — crude and refined oils combined.[39]

The largest net exporters of crude petroleum are Venezuela, Saudi Arabia, the United States, Kuwait and Iraq; the largest net importers, the United Kingdom, France, Italy, Canada, and the Netherlands. In foreign trade in petroleum products, the United States and the Netherlands Antilles lead as net exporters; France, the Netherlands and Venezuela are next in line. Sweden, Canada, the United Kingdom and Denmark have the largest net imports. (See Table 64.)

Europe's imports of petroleum and related products have increased since 1946 in absolute volume as well as in relation to total world imports. The net import of twenty-four European countries [40] was close to 56 million metric tons

in 1950; 70 million in 1951; and 74 million in 1952.[41]

The direction of world trade in petroleum is characterized by the distribution of markets among two principal supply areas. (1) The Caribbean and South American areas (Venezuela, Colombia, the Netherlands Antilles, Trinidad, Mexico) supply crude petroleum mainly to the United States and Canada. (2) The Near East (Saudi Arabia, Lebanon, Syria, Kuwait, Iran, Iraq) exports petroleum mainly to the United Kingdom, France, the Netherlands, Germany, Italy and other European countries. Shipments from the Near East to the United States and from the United States, the Caribbean and Venezuela to Europe are of minor significance in comparison with the traffic within each hemisphere.

39. **36**, 1950, pp. 335–37.
40. The United Kingdom, Ireland, Iceland, France, Belgium-Luxembourg, the Netherlands, Denmark, Sweden, Norway, Finland, Germany, Poland, Czechoslovakia, Switzerland, Austria, Hungary, Portugal, Spain, Italy, Yugoslavia, Romania, Greece, Turkey. For 1951, no data

available for Poland, Czechoslovakia, Yugoslavia and Romania.
41. **11**, 1951, p. 206; **10**, Fourth Quarter 1951, p. 70, and First Quarter 1953, p. 106.

TABLE 64

MINERAL FUELS: CRUDE PETROLEUM AND PRODUCTS,
EXPORTS AND IMPORTS OF SELECTED COUNTRIES,
1952

(*Value in Millions of U.S. Dollars*)

Country	Crude Petroleum		Petroleum Products	
	Exports	Imports	Exports	Imports
Total [a]	$3,000	$3,000	$2,500	$2,500
United States	869	445	697	250
Canada	4	215	7	130
Mexico [b]	24	—	—	—
Trinidad	4	42	10	3
Netherlands Antilles	20	3	393	27
Colombia [b]	44	—	—	4
Venezuela [b]	500	—	111	3
United Kingdom	—	669	167	276
Ireland	—	—	—	34
Iceland	—	—	—	9
France	—	557	253	46
Belgium-Luxembourg	—	64	61	87
Netherlands	—	188	173	46
Denmark	—	1	—	73
Sweden	—	31	1	144
Norway	—	1	—	62
Western Germany	—	98	25	30
Austria	—	—	1	4
Portugal	—	13	2	19
Italy	—	225	27	30
Greece	—	—	—	45
Turkey	—	—	—	40
Hong Kong	—	102	1	17
Japan	—	—	1	49
Iraq [b]	371	—	—	—
Saudi Arabia [b]	430	—	—	—
Other Arabian [b]	920	—	—	—
Syria, Lebanon [b]	60	—	—	—
Australia	—	2	—	—

Source: Computed from **5,** January-December 1952, pp. 75–76 and 239.

a. Rough estimate.   b. Incomplete data.

Two thirds of the United States exports remain in the Western Hemisphere and about one fourth goes to Europe. France exports petroleum products to its African colonies; the Netherlands supplies European markets.

Current statistics on exports and imports of petroleum products are incomplete. Many countries report only the value of imported or exported products but fail to report the volume or the equivalent of crude petroleum. Not all imports and exports are classified by destination and provenance.

ORES AND METALS

Ores and metals represent 6–8 per cent of the value of world trade. Some shipments are in intracontinental trade, like the export of iron ore from Sweden and Spain to the United Kingdom, Belgium and Germany; from France to Belgium; from Canada to the United States. Others are in transoceanic trade, often of the same type as exports of tropical products to industrial nations in the temperate zone.[42]

Iron

Shipments of iron ore in international trade can be described, in a general way, as a movement of ore toward coalfields. Approximately 80 per cent of the ore is processed in the country in which it is mined; the rest is exported. In 1950, world output of iron ore was estimated at 93 million metric tons, metal content, which represents about 180 million metric tons of ore or concentrates. Exports of ore and concentrates in that year totaled 36 million tons, including shipments from Canada to the United States and vice versa but excluding the trade between the USSR and its satellites.

On the world map, the routes followed by iron ore in international trade form two systems, one converging in the United States, the other in northwestern Europe — the United Kingdom, Belgium, the Netherlands and Western Germany. (See Table 65 and Figure 36.)

Pig iron and steel are produced in three dozen countries, but the United States, the USSR, the United Kingdom, France, Germany and Belgium-Luxembourg account for 85 per cent of world output and practically all exports.[43] In 1950, the United States produced 88 million metric tons of crude steel; Europe, 61 million, and other countries (excluding the USSR and China), 13 million.[44]

The United States exports 6–7 per cent of its output of crude and finished steel; European countries, 20–25 per cent, although Belgium-

42. **38,** pp. 44–50 and 60–86 and *passim;* **42,** pp. 783ff.
43. **30,** 1949, p. 648. Cf. **42,** p. 785.
44. **8,** 1951, pp. 253–54.

TABLE 65

ORES AND METALS: IRON ORE AND CONCENTRATES, EXPORTS OF SELECTED COUNTRIES AND THEIR
DESTINATION, 1950 AND 1951

(Iron Content, Thousands of Metric Tons)

Exporting Country	Total	United States	United Kingdom	Belgium-Luxembourg	Nether-lands	Western Germany	Others
				1950			
Canada	2,020	2,020	—	—	—	—	—
Brazil	1,200	703	—	—	43	—	454
Chile	2,600	2,600	—	—	—	—	—
France	7,810	—	370	6,870	170	400	—
Sweden	13,000	2,070	3,500	1,520	210	3,750	1,950
Spain	920	—	730	14	116	60	—
Algeria	2,500	500	1,500	—	180	—	320
				1951			
Canada	2,927	1,981	704	—	—	137	105
Brazil	1,320	1,054	—	10	13	10	233
Chile	2,686	1,812	—	—	—	—	874
France	10,599	—	382	9,089	212	905	11
Sweden	14,991	2,561	3,549	1,880	286	4,665	2,050
Spain	3,090	62	785	40	101	602	1,500
Algeria	2,841	453	1,439	172	206	32	539

Source: **6,** 1951, p. 24; 1952, p. 26.

Luxembourg exports up to 80 per cent. Belgium is the largest exporter in Europe and second only to the United States in the world. France and Germany are also large exporters. The United Kingdom and the Netherlands are the largest importers.[45] (See Table 66.)

One third of the United States exports go to Canada, and the rest is distributed among two-score countries. About half of European exports remain within intra-European trade, and the rest is sold throughout the world.[46]

45. Foreign trade in finished steel is discussed here only from the point of view of the mineral interdependence of nations. This approach justifies lumping shipments of iron ore (metal content), pig iron and steel. Actually, steel appears in world trade in many forms: hoops and strips, structural shapes, tin plate and terneplate, rails, railway ties, wheels and axles, tubes, pipes and fittings, wire and wire manufactures and so on. In world trade, different kinds of steel follow different directions. (Cf. in **37** cross tabulations of exports and imports of iron and steel products by group of articles and destination and provenance.)

46. Cf. **12**, p. 7, and **14**, December 1951, *passim.*

TABLE 66

ORES AND METALS: STEEL, EXPORTS AND IMPORTS OF
NINETEEN EUROPEAN COUNTRIES,[a]
1938 AND 1950–52

(Thousands of Metric Tons)

Country	1938	1950	1951	1952
		Exports		
Nineteen countries, total	7,210	11,770	14,010	12,100
United Kingdom	1,300	2,520	2,070	2,020
France	1,160	2,130	3,900	2,780
Belgium-Luxembourg	2,200	3,370	4,880	4,760
Germany	2,140	1,790	2,060	1,800
		Imports		
Nineteen countries, total	4,290	5,320	6,100	7,380
United Kingdom	830	470	550	1,560
Netherlands	800	1,150	1,240	1,060

Sources: **10,** Fourth Quarter 1951, p. 70; and First Quarter 1953, p. 107; **11,** 1951, p. 200.

a. Includes crude and finished steel. Totals include the United Kingdom, Iceland, Ireland, France, Belgium-Luxembourg, the Netherlands, Denmark, Sweden, Norway, Finland, Germany, Switzerland, Austria, Portugal, Spain, Italy, Greece, Turkey.

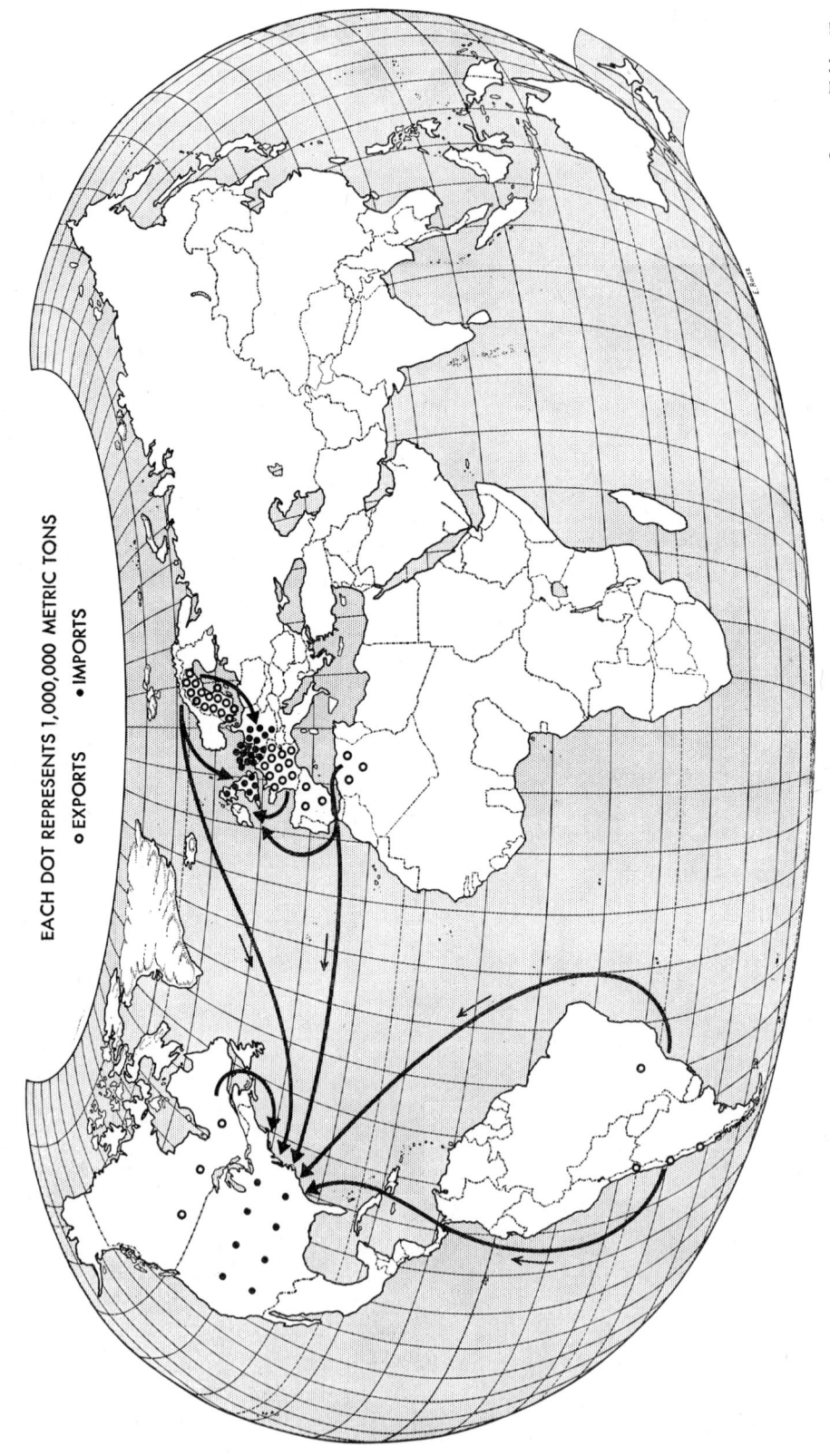

EACH DOT REPRESENTS 1,000,000 METRIC TONS

○ EXPORTS   ● IMPORTS

FIGURE 36. ORES AND METALS: IRON ORE AND CONCENTRATES IN WORLD TRADE, 1951

Iron ore is shipped to the United States from Canada, Chile, Sweden and Algeria; to the United Kingdom from Sweden, Algeria, Spain and France; to Belgium, the Netherlands and Western Germany mainly from France and Sweden.

The flow of ore from France to Belgium is not shown on the map. The very promising route from Venezuela to the United States had not yet come into operation in 1951. (Cf. **42**, pp. 1109–10.)

Source: Table 65

Copper

Since most copper ore is smelted and refined in the country in which it is mined, international trade in ore and concentrates is relatively small. The largest importer, the United States, receives annually 100,000–120,000 metric tons of ore and concentrates (metal content), mainly from Canada, Chile, Cuba and Mexcio.[47]

In 1950, world exports of unwrought copper metal (crude and refined) amounted to about 1.4 million metric tons,[48] while world output (excluding the USSR) was close to 2.5 million metric tons.[49]

These figures seem to indicate that more than 60 per cent of the world output of copper was brought to the world market and less than 40 per cent was used directly in producing countries. Such a conclusion is unwarranted, however, in view of the considerable duplications in statistics of copper exports. Crude copper is shipped, for example, from the Belgian Congo to Belgium for refining, then exported to the United Kingdom and other countries. The United States imports copper from Chile, Northern Rhodesia and Canada and exports copper to Europe. When such transactions are excluded, net exports of copper in 1950 hardly exceeded a million metric tons or 44–45 per cent of world output.

The main exporters of crude copper are Chile, Canada and Mexico in the Western Hemisphere; Northern Rhodesia and the Belgian Congo in the Eastern. The United States is the largest importer but reexports refined copper. Belgium reexports nearly all the copper obtained from the Belgian Congo. The United Kingdom is the largest European importer. (See Figure 37.)

In 1950 the exports and imports of countries with considerable foreign trade in copper were as follows (in thousands of metric tons): [50]

Exports

World	1,400
United States	190
Canada	130
Mexico	60
Chile	320
Belgium	150
Belgian Congo	175
Northern Rhodesia	300
Other	75

Imports

World	1,400
United States	690
United Kingdom	275
Belgium	175
Other	260

In value, copper represented in 1950 about 85 per cent of all exports of Northern Rhodesia, 50 per cent of Chile's and 25 per cent of those of the Belgian Congo.[51]

Data for 1951 on the distribution of exports from principal exporting countries by destination are shown in Table 67.

Nickel

Nickel is largely a natural monopoly of Canada, which in 1950 produced 112 million metric tons (metal content) out of the world total (excluding the USSR) of 119 million tons.[52]

Almost all the Canadian output is exported. Most of it goes to the United States, the rest to the United Kingdom, France, Germany and other countries.

Lead

Lead is usually smelted and refined in the country in which the ore is mined. Not more than 6–7 per cent of the mine output, in terms of metal content, is exported in the form of ore or concentrates. Of the smelter output, however, 15 to 20 per cent is exported. Mexico, Canada and Australia are the principal exporters. Smaller quantities are shipped from Bolivia and Peru, South-West Africa, the Union of South Africa and French Morocco. The largest importer is the United States, which in 1952 absorbed — in addition to its own production — approximately 60 per cent of world exports or one tenth of world output. The United Kingdom ranks second as an import market, followed by the Netherlands and France. (See Table 68.)

Tin

Tin is essentially a product of the tropics, no less so than coffee, tea and cocoa. Of the total world output of 170,000 metric tons (metal content) in 1950, hardly more than 4 per cent was used in the countries where the ore was mined. The rest was exported — 134,000 metric tons in

---

47. **30**, 1949 pp. 478ff; 1951, preprint, pp. 21ff.
48. **6**, 1951, p. 18.
49. **42**, p. 797.
50. **30**, 1949, pp. 478–92; 1950, preprint, p. 21; cf. **6**, 1951, p. 16.

51. **9**, 1951, pp. 33, 62 and 193.
52. **8**, 1951, p. 157. The output of the USSR was estimated at 25 million tons in 1950. **30**, 1951, preprint, p. 6.

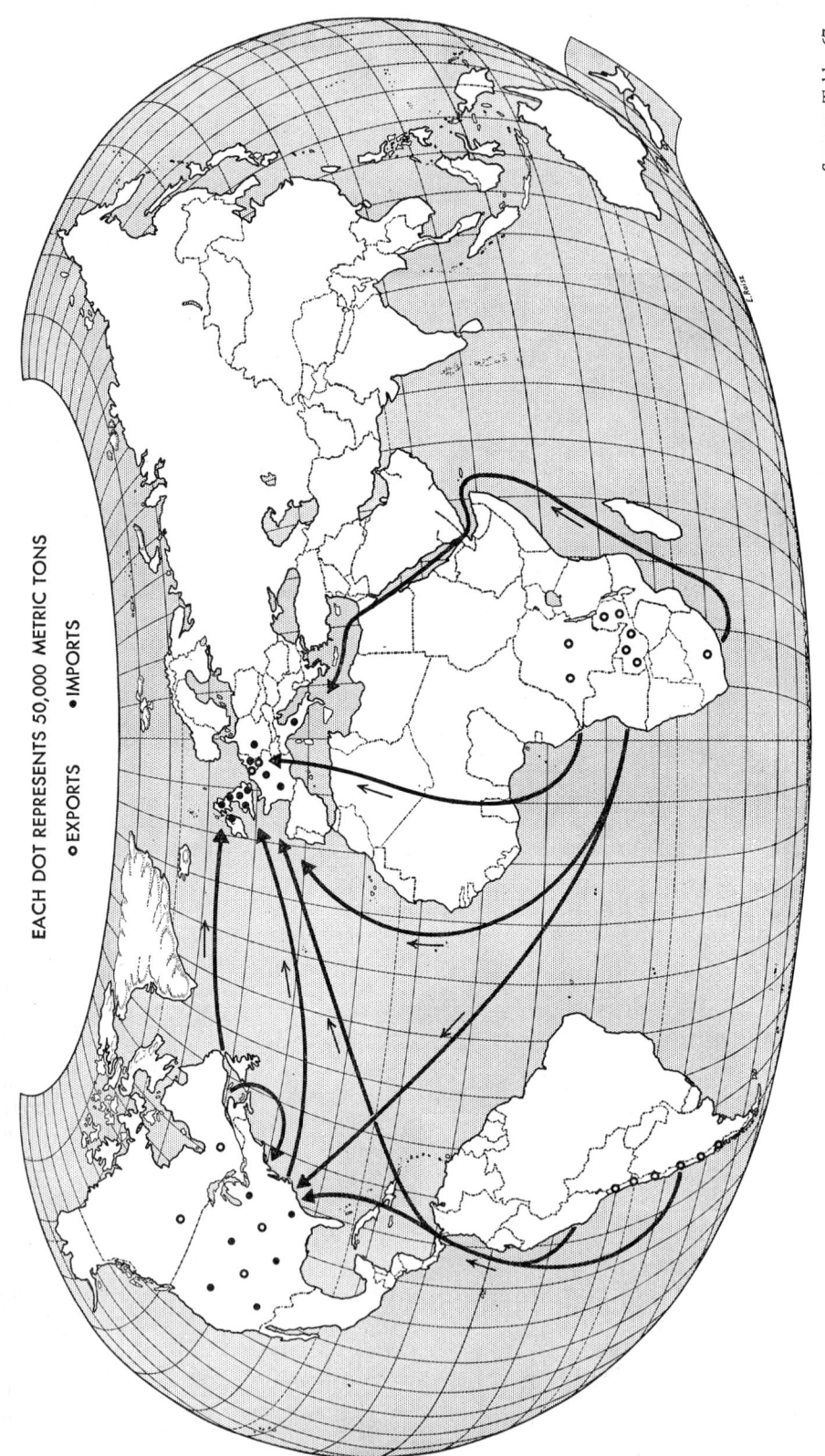

EACH DOT REPRESENTS 50,000 METRIC TONS

○ EXPORTS   ● IMPORTS

FIGURE 37. ORES AND METALS: COPPER IN WORLD TRADE, 1951

Copper ore and metal flow from Canada, Chile, Mexico and Northern Rhodesia to the United States and from the United States, Chile, the Union of South Africa, Northern Rhodesia and the Belgian Congo to the United Kingdom, Belgium and other European countries. Reexports of refined copper from the United Kingdom and Belgium are not shown on the map.

Source: Table 67

TABLE 67

ORES AND METALS: COPPER EXPORTS OF SELECTED COUNTRIES AND THEIR DESTINATION, 1951

(*Thousands of Metric Tons*)

	Exporting Country						
Destination	*United States*	*Canada*	*Chile*	*Belgium*	*Belgian Congo*	*Northern Rhodesia*	*Union of South Africa*
Total	120.9	93.3	308.8	105.7	91.2	225.5	30.8
United States	—	26.2	239.6	—	. . .	35.3	3.7
Brazil	3.3	2.4	6.8	4.5	. . .	—	—
United Kingdom	63.6	47.1	10.0	14.5	. . .	160.9	—
France	16.9	5.2	15.1	39.9	7.8	—	4.5
Belgium	0.5	—	0.7	—	11.2	10.7	4.0
Netherlands	7.4	1.1	0.1	10.9	. . .	—	. . .
Denmark	1.2	0.5	—	—	. . .	—	0.7
Sweden	0.5	3.6	—	7.6	. . .	—	—
Western Germany	9.3	1.1	8.0	7.4	. . .	14.8	2.9
Austria	0.6	0.4	—	—	. . .	—	—
Switzerland	4.9	0.2	1.6	8.2	. . .	—	0.8
Italy	7.2	2.2	13.8	1.7	. . .	—	11.0
India	0.2	3.3	—	—	. . .	0.4	—
Union of South Africa	—	—	—	—	. . .	—	—
Australia	—	—	—	—	. . .	—	—
Other	5.3	5.9	13.1	11.0	72.2	3.4	3.2

Source: **6,** 1952, p. 18.

TABLE 68

ORES AND METALS: LEAD [a] EXPORTS OF SELECTED COUNTRIES AND THEIR DESTINATION, 1952

(*Metal Content, Thousands of Metric Tons*)

		Destination						
Exporting Country	*Total*	*United States*	*Brazil*	*United Kingdom*	*France*	*Denmark*	*Netherlands*	*Other Countries*
Total	267.2	153.6	2.2	67.7	6.7	3.6	9.4	24.0
Canada	55.0	41.1	0.9	12.6	—	—	—	0.4
Mexico	103.5	90.6	—	—	3.1	—	—	9.8
Belgium	28.8	—	0.9	5.6	2.8	3.3	8.6	7.6
Western Germany	18.7	7.7	—	5.4	0.8	0.3	0.8	3.7
Italy	0.9	—	0.4	—	—	—	—	0.5
Australia	60.3	14.2	—	44.1	—	—	—	2.0

Source: **6,** 1952, p. 28.

a. Unwrought lead and concentrates. Metal content of concentrates is estimated at 50 per cent of weight.

TABLE 69

ORES AND METALS: TIN [a] EXPORTS OF SELECTED COUNTRIES AND THEIR DESTINATION, 1950 AND 1952

(Metal Content, Thousands of Metric Tons)

						Destination						
Exporting Country	*Total*	*United States*	*Canada*	*United Kingdom*	*France*	*Belgium*	*Netherlands*	*Germany*	*Italy*	*India*	*Malaya*	*Others*
1950												
Total	181.6	86.6	3.7	18.6	6.7	7.8	15.7	6.8	8.7	3.3	4.8	18.8
Bolivia	15.7	8.7	...	7.0	—	—	—	—	—	—	—	—
United Kingdom	15.9	8.3	0.5	—	0.6	0.5	0.2	0.7	0.1	—	—	5.0
Belgium	10.2	7.8	1.0	—	0.5	—	—	0.7	0.1	—	—	0.1
Netherlands	18.1	5.4	—	—	2.3	—	—	3.9	0.8	—	—	5.7
China	1.8	1.5	—	—	—	—	—	—	—	—	—	0.3
Hong Kong	1.2	0.6	—	—	—	—	—	—	—	—	—	0.6
Burma	0.9	0.1	—	0.1	—	—	—	—	—	—	0.7	—
Thailand	5.4	1.2	—	—	—	—	—	—	—	—	4.1	—
Malaya	83.1	45.3	2.2	7.4	3.3	0.9	4.4	1.5	7.7	3.3	—	7.1
Indonesia	15.9	4.8	—	—	—	—	11.1	—	—	—	—	—
Nigeria	4.1	—	—	4.1	—	—	—	—	—	—	—	—
Belgian Congo	9.3	2.9	—	—	—	6.4	—	—	—	—	—	—
1952												
Total	115.5	54.2	2.5	18.5	6.4	...	...	4.9	4.3	...	...	24.6
United Kingdom	12.5	9.1	0.2	—	0.2	...	...	—	0.2	...	...	2.8
Belgium	12.2	10.1	0.8	—	0.3	...	...	0.7	—	...	...	0.3
Netherlands	25.6	15.4	—	1.9	3.3	...	...	2.7	0.2	...	...	2.1
Malaya	65.2	19.7	1.6	16.6	2.7	...	...	1.4	4.0	...	...	19.3

Source: **6,** 1951, p. 40, and 1952, p. 40.

a. Metal and concentrates. Metal content of concentrates is estimated at 50 per cent of weight.

the form of crude or refined metal, the remainder in the form of concentrates. Many industrial countries import concentrates and export metal.

If the metal content of concentrates is counted at half the weight, it appears that 182,000 metric tons of tin were exported in 1950, including duplications for such countries as the United Kingdom, Belgium, the Netherlands and a few others. Malaya provided 83,000 metric tons; Indonesia and Thailand, 21,000; the Belgian Congo and Nigeria, over 13,000; Bolivia, 16,000. The United States took 87,000 metric tons, nearly 50 per cent of the world's net exports; the United Kingdom, 19,000; the Netherlands, 16,000; Italy, 9,000; France and Germany, nearly 7,000 each. (See Table 69.[53])

On the world map, the routes that tin follows in international trade form a very intricate pattern. If exports from countries which import crude tin or ore concentrates are omitted, the picture becomes clearer. There is only one major export center — the Far Eastern area including Malaya, Thailand and Indonesia. Export routes run from this area eastward across the Pacific and westward across the Indian Ocean. The eastbound routes start from China, Indonesia, Malaya and Thailand and converge in the United States. The main westbound route crosses the Indian Ocean, heading toward the Red Sea, the Mediterranean, the United Kingdom and Western Europe but also branching out to Australia, India and South America. Tin also is shipped from the Belgian Congo to Belgium, from Nigeria to the United Kingdom, and from Bolivia to the United States and the United Kingdom.

53. Data on foreign trade in tin for 1952 as shown in Table 69 are less comprehensive than those for 1950.

TABLE 70

ORES AND METALS: ZINC [a] EXPORTS AND IMPORTS OF SELECTED COUNTRIES, 1950

(Metal Content, Thousands of Metric Tons)

Exporting Country	*Total*	Destination				
		United States	*United Kingdom*	*France*	*Belgium*	*Netherlands*
Total	763.7	219.1	234.7	95.9	181.9	32.1
Canada	211.8	133.9	46.7	11.0	19.3	0.9
Mexico	53.4	52.7	—	0.7	—	—
Peru	51.0	8.0	—	9.1	26.5	6.8
Belgium	78.3	3.3	46.7	20.3	—	8.0
Sweden	20.2	—	. . .	. . .	18.0	2.2
Norway	20.9	7.2	9.1	3.0	—	1.6
Spain	17.7	3.5	. . .	11.0	1.5	1.7
Italy	23.4	2.6	5.0	6.3	9.1	0.4
Australia	122.1	—	104.6	. . .	17.5	—
Other	164.9	7.9	22.6	33.9 [b]	90.0 [c]	10.5

Source: **6,** 1951, p. 45.

a. Metal and ore and concentrates. Metal content of the latter is estimated at 45 per cent of weight.

b. Includes imports from the French colonies.

c. Includes imports from the Belgian Congo.

Zinc

Zinc ores are widely dispersed in the world. A large part of the mine output, unlike that of tin, is smelted, refined and further processed in the countries in which the ore is mined. From 35 to 40 per cent is exported, either as ore and concentrates or as unwrought metal.

The largest exporters of ore are Australia, Canada, Mexico, Peru, the Belgian Congo and the French colonies in Africa. Metal is exported from Belgium (which imports ore), Canada, Australia and other countries.

The largest importer of ore and concentrates is Belgium; of metal, the United States and the United Kingdom.

The United States meets two thirds of its demand for zinc from domestic ore (565,000 metric tons, metal content, in 1950) and imports annually some 240,000–300,000 metric tons of ore (metal content: 100,000–125,000 metric tons) and 120,000–140,000 metric tons of metal. The United Kingdom receives 70,000–80,000 metric tons of metal in imported ores (mainly from Australia) and imports double that amount of metal. Belgium has no domestic ore but operates large smelters and refineries for African ores. In 1950 French smelters produced 12,400 metric tons of zinc from domestic ore and 60,000 from ore imported from African colonies.

Imported ore plays an auxiliary role in the combined output of zinc in the United States and Canada, but is vital for production of zinc in Europe.[54] (See Table 70.)

THE NETWORK OF WORLD TRADE IN FOODSTUFFS AND RAW MATERIALS

When the patterns of international trade in foodstuffs, tobacco, fibers, rubber, forest products, mineral fuels, ores and metals are examined as parts of world trade, not one by one as in the preceding pages, they form an extremely intricate network of exports and imports. Superimposed on one another, the comparatively simple routes followed by the individual commodities, as illustrated by Figures 29 to 37, crisscross all oceans and run from continent to continent in a seemingly haphazard way.

Many routes carry several commodities and the composition of the cargo determines the branches at both ends among the ports where the merchandise is loaded and unloaded.

In the most general way, five main transoceanic routes carry the trade in staple commodities examined on the preceding pages:

1. Across the North Atlantic. This route car-

54. See **8,** 1951, pp. 150–51 and 257; **30,** 1949, pp. 1289–93. Cf. **42,** pp. 797ff.

ries wheat, corn, cotton, tobacco, mineral fuels and many other articles from the United States and sugar from the Caribbean to the Old World.

2. Across the Atlantic, from South America to western Europe. This route brings corn, meat and coffee from Argentina and Brazil to the Old World.

3. Across the Atlantic, from Africa to North America. This route carries, among other products, cocoa, uranium and copper to the United States.

4. Across the Indian Ocean and the Mediterranean, from Australia and the Far East to the United Kingdom and continental Europe. This route provides Europe with meat, butter, cheese and wool from Australia, rubber and tin from Malaya, tea from Ceylon. The western part of this route also carries petroleum from the Near East.

5. Across the Pacific, from Australia, the Far East and Japan to the United States. This route carries wool, silk, tin and rubber to the United States.

A large part of the intercontinental trade in foodstuffs and raw materials is carried across the North Atlantic, which includes the northern part of the transatlantic routes (2) and (3). (See Figure 38.)

An over-all picture of the prevailing directions of foodstuffs and industrial materials in world trade can be given only in terms of the value of exports and imports of the respective groups of commodities. In 1937 foodstuffs and raw materials represented the following percentages of the value of imports and exports of countries belonging to the two North Atlantic regions: [55]

	Per Cent
United States	
Imports	80
Exports	50
Balance	— 30
United Kingdom	
Imports	82
Exports	28
Balance	— 54
Industrial countries of	
continental Europe	
Imports	77
Exports	37
Balance	— 40

These import balances give an over-all measurement of the predominance of foodstuffs and raw materials in world trade on the transoceanic routes from South America and the Caribbean, the Middle East and Far East, the East Indies and Australia to the two North Atlantic regions. This, however, is only one half of the picture of world trade. The other is the movement of manufactured articles.

MANUFACTURED ARTICLES IN WORLD TRADE

World trade in manufactured goods comprises a great variety of articles, each of which has its own customary routes. Most of them radiate from the two North Atlantic regions to all other parts of the world. Essentially, export of manufactured goods is the price a dozen industrialized nations pay to the rest of the world for its primary produce — staple foodstuffs, tropical products, fibers, timber, rubber, mineral fuels, ores and metals. However, the shipment of manufactured goods from industrialized to primarily agricultural areas represents only a part of world trade in manufactured goods. Such trade also includes exchange among industrialized nations, such as the shipment of automobiles from the United States to Switzerland and of clocks and watches and precision instruments from Switzerland to the United States.

For purposes of the present analysis, two groups of manufactured articles in world trade require particular attention: (1) engineering products (machinery, including electrical goods, vehicles and other transportation equipment); and (2) textiles and related products.

In 1937, world exports of metals and manufactures amounted, in round numbers, to $1,000 million; of engineering products, $1,525 million; textiles and apparel, $1,300 million; and all other fabricated articles, $1,425 million. Fabricated articles, including metals ready for further fabrication, constituted a little more than one third of the total value of exports. When metals are excluded, fully fabricated articles represented nearly one fourth of all exports.[56]

MACHINERY AND TRANSPORTATION EQUIPMENT

World exports of machinery, including electrical goods, passenger vehicles and other transportation equipment, as classified by the SITC, were probably close to $7.7 billion in 1950; $11.1

---

55. Table 37.

56. **35**, 1938, pp. 160*–62*.

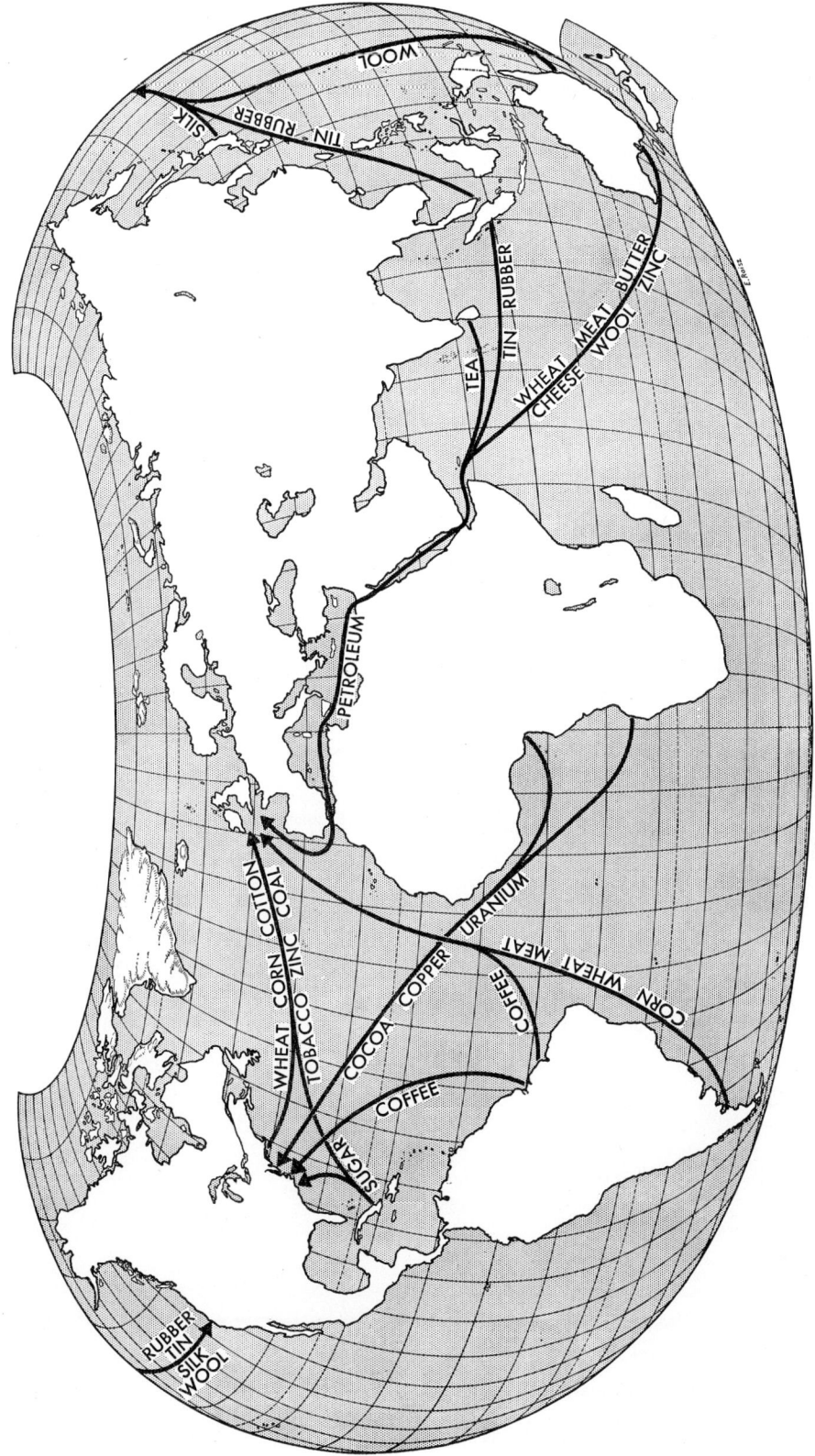

FIGURE 38. PRINCIPAL TRANSOCEANIC ROUTES IN FOREIGN TRADE: FOODSTUFFS AND RAW MATERIALS

Sources: Figures 29–33, 35, 37

billion in 1951; and $12.7 billion in 1952. These totals include some duplications — as in the case of Hong Kong, which reexports machinery received from Europe — and make allowance for exports from countries which are not listed in Table 71.

The United States accounts for more than 40 per cent of world exports of machinery and vehicles; Europe, for nearly 55 per cent. In Europe, the United Kingdom ranked first in 1950–52, but Germany was increasing its exports by leaps and bounds.

A sizable part of machinery and transportation equipment exported by European countries remains in intra-European trade. The UN Economic Commission for Europe has published data showing the destination of "engineering products" exported from eight leading European countries in 1950. In most countries, the figures used by the Commission include some products which are not in the group of "machinery and transportation equipment" according to the SITC, but this does not affect the general pattern of distribution of these products by destination. The eight countries and the United States exported engineering products worth $8,058 million in 1950, and of this total Europe absorbed $2,911 million, and the sterling area (principally the British dominions), $1,345 million. (See Table 72.)

Apart from the very extensive intra-European trade in machinery (see Table 73) the main routes of engineering products in world trade

TABLE 71

MANUFACTURED ARTICLES: MACHINERY AND TRANSPORTATION EQUIPMENT, EXPORTS OF SELECTED COUNTRIES, 1950–52

(Millions of Dollars)

Country	1950	1951	1952
World	$7,700	$11,100	$12,700
United States	3,208	4,613	5,056
Canada	160	. . .	. . .
Mexico	3	2	2
United Kingdom	2,175	2,488	2,699
Ireland	1	1	1
France	441	627	711
Belgium-Luxembourg	164 [a]	315	373
Netherlands	207 [a]	240	263
Denmark	100	114	143
Sweden	250	308	357
Norway	20	68	46
Western Germany	93	947	1,453
Czechoslovakia	234	300	399
Switzerland	183	217	231
Austria	33	45	53
Portugal	5	. . .	. . .
Italy	207 [a]	274	291
Greece	8	3	. . .
Japan	90	106	116
Hong Kong	25	40	. . .
Union of South Africa	18	25	28
Australia	11	13	19

Sources: Estimated by the authors on the basis of **9**, 1952 and **13**, pp. 183–84; cf. **5**, January-December 1952, pp. 136–50 and 344–78.

a. Engineering products.

TABLE 72

MANUFACTURED ARTICLES: ENGINEERING PRODUCTS, EXPORTS OF SELECTED COUNTRIES, BY DESTINATION, 1950

(Millions of Dollars)

Exporting Country	Total	Destination				
		Europe [a]	Dollar Area [b]	Latin America	Sterling Area [c]	Other Areas
Total	$8,058	$2,911	$1,447	$769	$1,345	$1,586
United States	3,226	712	1,140	358	201	815
United Kingdom	2,880	909	256	201	1,093	421
France	453	155	4	25	8	261
Belgium–Luxembourg	163	114	3	11	3	32
Netherlands	207	142	10	19	5	31
Sweden	255	208	4	36	7	—
Western Germany	455	381	13	31	18	12
Switzerland	211	170	9	24	6	2
Italy	207	119	8	64	4	12

Sources: For Europe, **13**, pp. 32, 183–84. Total for the United States, **29**, 1951, p. 836.

a. Includes USSR.
b. United States, Canada, Mexico, Colombia, Venezuela.
c. Iraq, Pakistan, India, Burma, Ceylon, Union of South Africa, Australia, New Zealand.

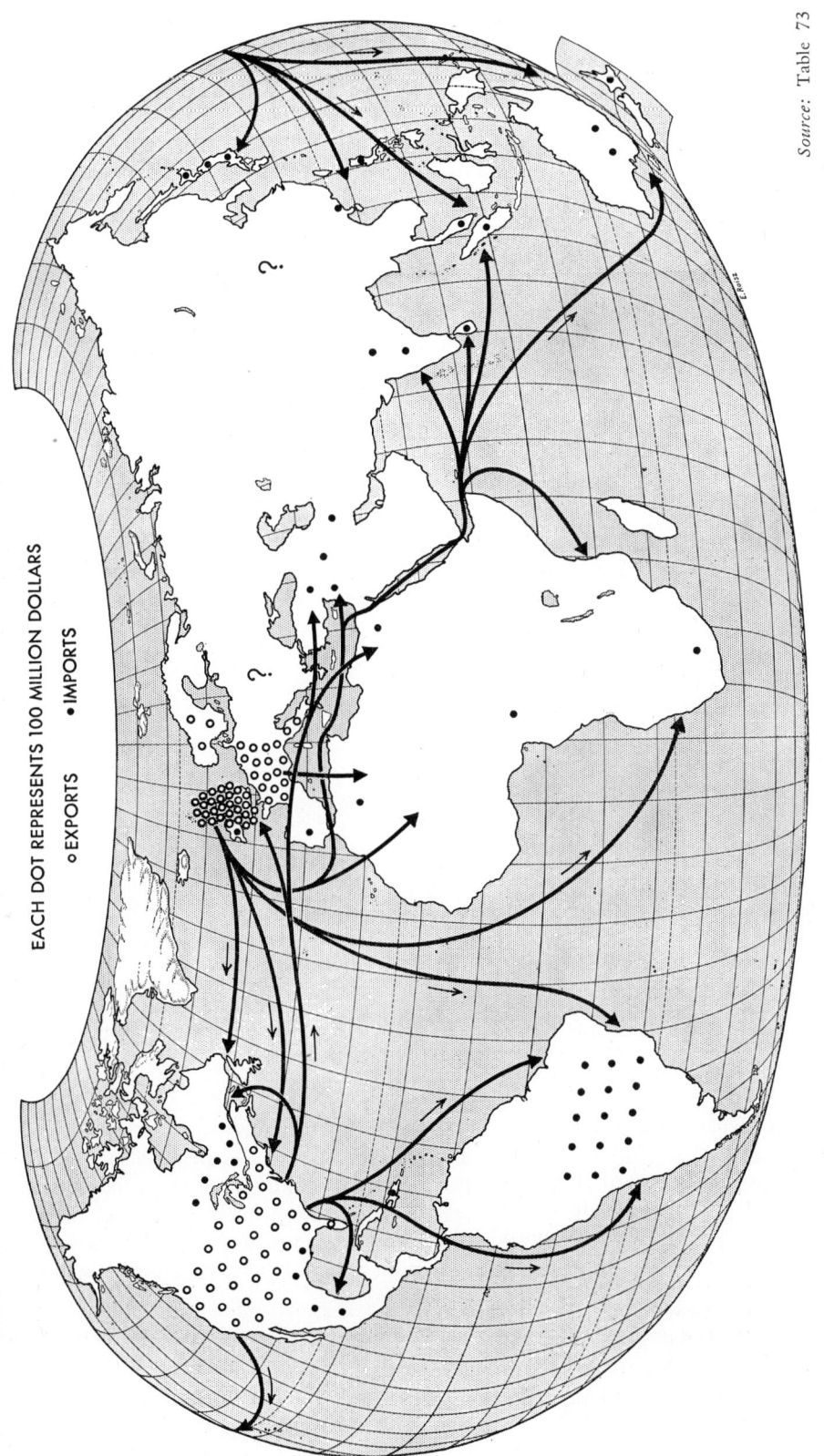

EACH DOT REPRESENTS 100 MILLION DOLLARS

o EXPORTS   • IMPORTS

Source: Table 73

FIGURE 39. MANUFACTURED ARTICLES: ENGINEERING PRODUCTS IN WORLD TRADE, 1950

In world trade in machinery, vehicles and other transportation equipment, all important routes radiate either from the United States or from the United Kingdom and northwestern Europe. Both areas ship engineering products to the rest of the world. The United States predominates in the markets of Middle America and the Far East (Japan, the Philippines and other areas). European, especially British, machinery predominates in Africa, the area of the Indian Ocean and in European markets. Markets in South America, the Near East, Indonesia and Australia are in dispute. Imports into European countries (except for Ireland and Spain–Portugal) and to the USSR and its satellites are not shown.

TABLE 73

MANUFACTURED ARTICLES: ENGINEERING PRODUCTS, EXPORTS [a] OF SELECTED COUNTRIES TO EUROPE AND THE USSR, 1950

(*Millions of Dollars*)

Destination	Total	Exporting Country									
		United States	United Kingdom	France	Belgium-Luxembourg	Netherlands	Denmark	Sweden	Western Germany	Switzerland	Italy
Europe, total	$2,898.3	$711.2	$866.1	$154.9	$102.3	$141.6	$65.2	$207.5	$380.9	$167.6	$101.0
United Kingdom	133.6	82.6	—	4.1	2.7	11.5	2.6	9.3	7.2	10.6	3.0
Ireland	93.5	4.9	84.4	0.1	0.4	0.7	. . .	. . .	1.3	1.5	0.2
Iceland	7.6	1.3	2.6	. . .	. . .	. . .	3.1	. . .	0.3	0.2	0.1
France	357.9	128.6	71.5	—	24.1	20.8	9.3	10.9	50.5	31.6	10.6
Belgium–Luxembourg	310.9	96.4	78.1	36.0	—	25.5	1.4	5.8	43.7	20.0	4.0
Netherlands	323.0	44.3	118.4	18.9	36.2	—	3.5	12.8	72.2	12.9	3.8
Denmark	123.8	13.1	60.1	4.2	1.1	5.0	—	16.9	19.4	3.0	1.0
Sweden	212.1	37.0	118.8	13.1	2.0	9.2	8.6	—	16.4	4.1	2.9
Norway	271.7	18.3	96.9	6.0	3.9	17.8	13.1	98.4	9.3	3.7	4.3
Finland	69.9	14.6	21.2	1.8	0.6	4.3	8.6	11.2	4.1	1.8	1.7
W. Germany	89.9	15.5	16.0	5.0	5.3	12.4	1.8	8.3	—	17.0	8.6
Poland	80.8	1.2	15.3	13.0	2.4	3.3	5.9	21.2	3.1	6.6	8.8
Czechoslovakia	36.5	1.6	6.3	2.0	1.2	3.2	0.7	. . .	8.0	9.6	3.9
Switzerland	134.8	29.5	32.6	14.8	5.2	4.7	1.2	3.9	32.2	—	10.7
Austria	55.3	19.9	7.1	1.8	1.1	2.7	0.1	. . .	13.9	3.9	4.8
Hungary	28.8	0.1	4.6	2.4	—	0.6	0.2	. . .	13.5	4.4	3.0
Portugal	79.4	7.2	40.9	6.6	8.8	3.1	1.5	. . .	3.7	5.5	2.1
Spain	58.5	8.2	16.1	11.6	1.5	3.1	1.9	4.5	4.5	5.8	1.3
Italy	181.2	101.3	23.3	6.1	2.1	2.9	1.7	4.3	23.2	16.3	—
Yugoslavia	54.7	17.8	3.7	1.5	0.3	6.1	. . .	. . .	15.9	1.9	7.5
Romania	11.9	—	1.6	—	0.9	—	—	—	3.6	3.2	2.6
Bulgaria	5.2	—	0.1	0.2	0.1	. . .	. . .	. . .	1.5	1.4	1.9
Greece	71.5	22.8	22.5	2.9	2.0	2.3	. . .	. . .	12.8	0.6	5.6
Turkey	105.8	45.0	24.0	2.8	0.4	2.4	. . .	. . .	20.6	2.0	8.6
USSR	72.4	0.4	39.2	—	12.3	0.1	0.3	—	—	2.6	17.5

Source: **13**, pp. 179–82.

a. The scope of exports included in this table differs from that of Table 72. The list of exporting countries includes Denmark, which is not listed in the preceding table. Totals for Europe include exports to Turkey but do not include the USSR.

can be visualized as two systems of lines criss-crossing the globe:

1. From the United States toward all points of the compass: north to Canada; south to the Caribbean and Latin America; east to the United Kingdom, continental Europe, the Middle East and Africa; west to Japan, the Philippines, the Far East, Indonesia and Australia.

2. From the United Kingdom and continental Europe to Canada, the United States and South America, Africa, the Near and Far East, Indonesia and Australia.

Engineering products are shipped both east-ward and westward over the North Atlantic. The westward stream predominates. On the Pacific, the westward shipments of the United States predominate, while routes across the Indian Ocean carry machinery and transportation equipment eastward from the United Kingdom. (See Figure 39.)

TEXTILES AND RELATED PRODUCTS

Exports of textiles and related fabricated articles were valued at $2,250 million in 1937, 9 per cent of total world exports ($25 billion) or

TABLE 74

MANUFACTURED ARTICLES: TEXTILES AND RELATED PRODUCTS, EXPORTS AND IMPORTS OF
SELECTED COUNTRIES, 1952

(*Value in Millions of Dollars*)

Country	Exports					Imports				
	Total	Yarn	Fabrics	Other Textiles	Clothes	Total	Yarn	Fabrics	Other Textiles	Clothes
World [a]	$5,500	...	...	...	...	$5,750	...	...	...	...
United States	613.8	$ 54.9	$355.1	$106.2	$97.6	408.3	$13.4	$222.5	$ 96.9	$75.5
Canada	25.3	2.1	6.4	12.7	4.1	244.0	22.5	123.7	66.3	31.5
United Kingdom	1,037.2	163.8	598.6	180.6	94.2	246.8	15.0	163.8	50.3	17.7
Ireland	6.6	0.3	2.2	1.8	2.3	33.8	8.5	14.8	6.8	3.7
France	495.7	98.0	276.0	80.1	41.6	70.5	14.8	33.0	16.8	5.9
Belgium– Luxembourg	271.4	93.2	103.2	54.9	20.1	102.9	19.5	38.8	19.1	25.5
Netherlands	211.2	38.4	114.2	30.4	28.2	123.7	44.8	39.5	19.2	20.2
Denmark	14.6	3.2	2.1	4.3	5.0	98.8	23.3	51.0	14.4	10.1
Sweden	17.9	2.5	8.1	4.6	2.7	123.4	29.3	49.4	24.5	20.2
Norway	2.7	0.6	1.2	0.7	0.2	93.9	21.8	46.6	14.6	10.9
Western Germany	235.7	31.0	153.1	34.4	17.2	162.0	57.1	50.8	22.9	31.2
Austria	35.5	9.9	8.0	9.5	8.1	22.9	13.5	6.6	2.3	0.5
Portugal	35.2	0.9	22.3	10.6	1.4	9.1	2.6	3.2	2.5	0.8
Italy	293.9	85.0	140.5	36.8	31.6	31.4	7.3	15.6	6.1	2.4
Greece	3.9	0.2	3.5	0.1	0.1	11.1	3.4	4.9	2.0	0.8
Japan	423.2	50.4	257.8	76.0	37.7	12.1	1.0	5.1	2.1	3.9
Hong Kong	133.4	32.1	51.0	12.6	39.0	97.5	24.3	51.6	17.0	4.6
Turkey	5.3	—	—	—	5.3	69.0	16.6	43.7	7.4	1.3

Source: **5,** January–December, 1952, pp. 107–14, 153–55, 290–304 and 385–87.

a. Rough estimate.

24 per cent of all exports of fabricated articles.[57] In 1952 world exports of textiles amounted to about $5.5 billion, representing approximately 8 per cent of the value of all exports and approximately one fifth that of exports of fabricated goods. The change may be due in part to differences in classification.[58]

Textiles as defined here include yarns, fabrics and made-up articles other than footwear. They exclude textile fibers not manufactured into yarn, fibers used in making furniture, tires, cars and so on.[59]

The United Kingdom, the United States and India are the largest exporters of textiles, followed by Western Germany, France, Japan, Italy, Belgium-Luxembourg, and the Netherlands. (Cf. Table 74.) The ranking of individual countries changes from year to year.

Textiles and related products represent more than 40 per cent of the total value of exports of India (jute) and Japan (mainly cotton); one third of those of Italy; 15–20 per cent in the foreign trade of the United Kingdom, Portugal and Belgium-Luxembourg; and approximately 10 per cent in the Netherlands, France and Austria.

Hong Kong, which is among the large export-

57. Values in current U.S. dollars. Expressed in gold dollars, world exports were close to $15 billion in 1937. Cf. p. 4–38.

58. For 1937 the classification of the German Central Statistical Office is used (**35,** 1938, p. 154*), while the estimate for 1951 is based on the data given in the UN *Yearbook of International Trade Statistics.* In the latter, the foreign trade of twenty countries is classified in accordance with the SITC, while for other areas only principal export and import commodities are recorded.

59. The SITC lists textiles in two divisions: numbers

65 and 84. The first comprises textile yarn and thread; cotton fabrics of standard type; other fabrics of standard type; small wares; special textile products and related products such as felts, hat bodies, cordage, cables and ropes; made-up articles other than clothing and footwear; floor coverings and tapestries. Division 85 includes hosiery, underwear, outerwear, hats and gloves, including leather and fur clothing. (**7,** pp. 19–20 and 26–27.)

ers of textiles, conducts intermediary trade, importing yarn and fabrics from Japan, India and Europe and reexporting them to China. The Netherlands imports yarn and exports fabrics and apparel. Most other exporters of textiles import raw fibers.

Imports of textiles are widely dispersed through the world and available statistics are less complete than those for exports. The ranking of states by import of textiles and related products varies from year to year. In 1952, the United States, Australia, the United Kingdom, Canada, Pakistan and the Union of South Africa were at the top of the list. Along with the two largest exporters of textiles — the United Kingdom [60] and the United States — this group includes four members of the British Commonwealth which have traditionally relied on British textiles. Other large importers of textiles are Peru and Mexico in the Western Hemisphere; Western Germany, the Netherlands, Sweden, Belgium-Luxembourg, Denmark, Yugoslavia and Norway in Europe; Indonesia, Indochina, Malaya and Hong Kong in Asia; and New Zealand.

Textiles represent a large part — 40 per cent or more — of the imports of such countries as Peru, Burma and Pakistan; 20 to 30 per cent in Madagascar, Nigeria, Indochina, Iran, Yugoslavia, Tanganyika, Panama, Kenya-Uganda and the Gold Coast. (See Table 75.) This does not imply, however, that the prominent position of textiles in imports is characteristic of underdeveloped areas: some highly economically developed countries — for example, Australia and New Zealand — have found it to their advantage to import textiles in exchange for their agricultural products. In most cases, however, textiles represent 2–6 per cent of imports of industrially developed countries. The rate is particularly low for Japan, Italy and France. It is, however, very low likewise for Greece, Portugal and India. In any country, the demand for imported textiles depends on the availability of fibers, industrial development, climatic conditions and many other factors which affect the relative costs of producing various articles.

LEADING ARTICLES IN UNITED STATES
FOREIGN TRADE

As in world trade, the ranking of various articles in United States imports and exports depends largely on the way in which these articles are defined and grouped in official statistics. Despite this limitation, a listing of the articles that lead in the country's imports and exports seems enlightening. (See Table 76.)

The list of the principal imported articles (arrayed in accordance with value in 1951) is topped by tropical products (cocoa, coffee, tea and rubber), which represent nearly 25 per cent of United States imports. These are followed by raw materials (wool, crude petroleum, nonferrous metals and paper) of about equal total value.

Some of the products in this list are not produced in the United States or cannot be produced in sufficient quantities; others supplement an insufficient domestic supply of competitive articles. It is in the nature of trade that the import of such products not only meets the demand of consumers but prevents a rise of prices of identical or similar domestic products. Ultimately competition between imported and domestic products stimulates technical progress in the respective branches of industry. In the short run, however, competition of imported goods may affect the interests of producers adversely. Their resentment of competition — in the United States, as in other countries — finds expression in the demand for protection.

The "big four" of United States exports are industrial machinery and automobiles, on the one hand, and grains and cotton, on the other. These four groups of articles account for approximately 40 per cent of the total value of exports.

They are followed by petroleum products, coal, electrical machinery, semimanufactured iron and steel, agricultural machinery, tobacco, and cotton fabrics, which represent an additional 25 per cent of exports.

The stake of farmers throughout the nation in exports is shown by the percentage of the agricultural output sold abroad in 1951: wheat, 48 per cent; dried milk, 45 per cent; rice, 37 per cent; dried peas, 35 per cent; cotton, 34 per cent; soybeans, 28 per cent; lard, 24 per cent; tobacco and hops, 23 per cent; plums and prunes, 21 per cent.

Moreover, under a competitive economic system, different elements in foreign trade are interdependent. Some currents in import trade may affect the interests of a group of producers adversely, but the exchange of commodities benefits the economy as a whole. The continuous

---

60. The United Kingdom imports fabrics, in part, for further processing.

TABLE 75

MANUFACTURED ARTICLES: TEXTILES AND RELATED PRODUCTS,[a] IMPORTS OF SELECTED COUNTRIES, 1952

Country [b]	Value, in Millions of Dollars	Percentage of Total Imports	Country	Value, in Millions of Dollars	Percentage of Total Imports
United States	$408	4	French Morocco	$51	10
Australia	369	21	Cuba	50	8
United Kingdom	247	3	Kenya–Uganda [c]	50	22
Canada	244	6	Belgian Congo	45	11
Pakistan	244	40	Switzerland	42	3
Union of South Africa	204	18	Gold Coast	42	20
Indonesia	185	19	French West Africa	42	17
Western Germany	162	5	Ceylon	42	13
Peru	158	55	Southern Rhodesia	41	17
Mexico	140	19	Madagascar	40	30
Netherlands	124	6	Egypt	37	6
Sweden	123	7	Ireland	34	7
Indochina	119	27	Italy	31	2
New Zealand	115	20	Iraq	28	18
Malaya	115	10	Austria	23	5
Belgium–Luxembourg	103	4	Iran [c]	20	27
Denmark	99	10	Uruguay [c]	19	10
Yugoslavia	99	26	Tanganyika [c]	19	24
Hong Kong	98	19	Israel [c]	17	5
Norway	94	11	Lebanon	16	11
India [c]	80	5	Northern Rhodesia	14	14
Philippines	80	19	Panama [d]	14	23
Finland	80	11	Japan [c]	12	1
Algeria [c]	78	12	Chile [c]	12	5
Argentina	74	10	Greece	11	2
France	71	2	Portugal	9	3
Turkey	69	13	Iceland	7	12
Nigeria	65	27	Dominican Republic	7	13
Burma	60	44	Jamaica	7	8
Colombia	56	14			

Sources: **5**, January–December 1952, *passim;* **9**, 1952, *passim.*

a. This table follows the classification of the UN. For countries listed in Table 74 the classification may be assumed to be reasonably comprehensive. For other countries, the enumeration of textiles and related articles may be incomplete. In many cases, for example in Latin American republics, the gaps in classification are obvious.

b. Arrayed by value of import of textiles and related articles.

c. 1951.

d. 1950.

flow of exports and imports in the United States is represented graphically in Figure 40. The picture is not peculiar to that country. With a change in outline and legends, a similar diagram can be made for any trading nation.

OUTLOOK

The composition and direction of foreign trade is bound to change with changes in the relations between the needs and resources of nations and the relative costs of production. In particular, they must alter as a result of changes in the complementary character of different economic systems. The composition of world exports and imports and the routes that some commodities follow in world trade will change, for example, if the contrast between the old industrial countries and the sparsely populated and underdeveloped areas is reduced as a result of the wider extension of mechanical civilization over the globe.

It seems reasonable to expect that the growing demand of industrialized nations for minerals and other industrial raw materials will

TABLE 76

FOREIGN TRADE OF THE UNITED STATES: PRINCIPAL IMPORTED AND EXPORTED ARTICLES, 1949–52

(*Value in Millions of Dollars*)

A. Imports   B. Exports

Article [a]	1949	1950	1951	1952	Article [a]	1949	1950	1951	1952
Cocoa, coffee, tea	$970	$1,322	$1,613	$1,909	Industrial machinery	$1,367	$1,295	$2,014	$2,547
Rubber	250	475	822	635	Grains & preparations	1,457	834	1,484	1,478
Wool and other animal					Automobiles & other				
hair	248	469	779	453	vehicles	1,055	930	1,265	1,122
Petroleum	478	589	602	695	Cotton	890	1,040	1,190	902
Nonferrous metals,					Petroleum products	441	385	683	699
except precious	531	654	587	989	Coal, coke, briquettes	308	278	606	510
Paper, paperboard	457	471	542	597	Electrical machinery &				
Sugar	396	408	444	477	appliances	453	410	571	679
Pulp, waste paper	182	240	352	271	Iron, steel	611	405	534	647
Iron, steel	48	124	346	217	Agricultural machinery				
Industrial chemicals	113	198	339	320	& tractors	419	352	451	430
Wood, round and					Tobacco & manufactures	309	229	382	304
shaped	153	311	301	291	Cotton fabrics	244	168	301	236
Nonferrous ores and					Medicinal & pharmaceu-				
concentrates	262	235	296	484	tical preparations	198	211	281	222
Machinery & trans-					Manufactures of metals	297	217	272	261
portation equipment	136	160	246	359	Animal & vegetable				
Petroleum products	130	210	217	250	oils & fats	147	145	238	132
Meat products	72	113	191	162	Dairy products	263	138	190	122
Fruits, nuts	147	169	172	167	Power generating ma-				
Fish	112	157	158	181	chinery	146	121	185	184
Crude minerals	86	125	154	162	Chemical materials	187	119	183	163
Hides, skins	73	118	133	60	Paper, paperboard	90	92	183	157
Grains & preparations	75	77	131	165	Organic chemicals	97	101	173	167
Vegetable & animal oils					Fabrics, except cotton	147	101	136	119
& fats	89	121	129	112	Margarine & shortenings	94	65	134	89
Fabrics, except jute	78	104	125	102	Nonferrous metals, except				
Beverages	90	117	125	102	precious	132	100	129	180
Vegetable fibers, except					Rubber, fabricated	100	76	123	132
jute	64	99	122	124	Fruits, nuts	106	116	121	144
Precious stones & imita-					Wood, round & shaped	66	53	106	88
tions	76	111	118	111	Clothing	89	88	105	96
Oilseeds & oil nuts	95	105	104	37	Oilseeds & oil nuts	131	70	105	83
Crude vegetable materials	86	95	102	90	Pigments, paints, varnishes	76	79	103	79
					Petroleum, crude & partly				
					refined	116	107	90	87
					Vegetables	69	58	89	105

Source: **9,** 1952, pp. 365–72; cf. **29,** 1952, pp. 848–51.

a. Based on SITC. Articles arrayed by value of exports and imports in 1951.

compel them to rely increasingly on imports.[61] The example of the United States is in point. In the 1930's, the United States became a net importer of zinc and copper. Since the middle 1940's, it has imported crude petroleum and lumber; it is ready to start large-scale imports of iron ore and concentrates.[62] The challenge of the increasing demand of industrial countries for

61. **33,** Volume I, pp. 11–12.

62. **33,** Volume I, p. 12.

IMPORTS

BANANAS SPICES
COPPER MERCURY COFFEE
MAHOGANY CHROME ZINC
OLIVE OIL TUNGSTEN RUBBER
HIDES & SKINS SILK TIN TEA
TUNG OIL MANGANESE
BAUXITE NEWSPRINT
CANE SUGAR PEPPER
JUTE COCONUT OIL
WOOL & MOHAIR WINES & SPIRITS
WOOD PULP DIAMONDS
NICKEL SISAL
LEAD

EXPORTS

APPLES
LUMBER
WHEAT
WHEAT
CANNED FRUITS & VEGETABLES
WHEAT
MEAT
AIRCRAFT
PETROLEUM REFINING PRODUCTS
COTTONSEED CAKE & MEAL
SOYBEANS
CORN
MEAT
PHOTOGRAPHIC GOODS
COTTON
SULFUR
PAPER & PAPERBOARD
AGRICULTURAL MACHINERY
AUTOMOBILES & PARTS
COAL
INDUSTRIAL MACHINERY
TOBACCO
CIGARETTES
COTTON GOODS
NAVAL STORES
BOOKS
PAINTS
STEEL

U.S. Department of State

FIGURE 40. FOREIGN TRADE OF THE UNITED STATES: COMPOSITION OF IMPORTS AND EXPORTS, 1951

raw materials will be met by the development of raw-material production and the improvement of local means of transportation in other areas. The economic cooperation of the two groups of countries would increase the volume of intercontinental trade to the advantage of both. Technological progress and new uses of metals such as uranium, molybdenum and zirconium would also stimulate long-distance trade.

At the same time, the rise in the standard of living, both in the industrial countries of the temperate zone and in tropical regions where a subsistence economy prevails, is likely to stimulate exchange among them. As the demand of the temperate zone for tropical fruits, nuts, choice lumber and so on increases, the people in tropical regions can and will take an increasing quantity of the staple industrial products of

the temperate zone. These are factors that make for expansion of international trade. Other forces, however, press in the opposite direction.

Progress in chemistry enables industrial countries to replace imported materials with products derived from domestic raw materials. Since the turn of the century, chemical dyes have replaced indigo, and more recently synthetic fibers have crowded out natural silk. Butylene, recovered from gases of petroleum cracking, is a serious threat to natural rubber; hydrogenated coal and shales may replace natural liquid fuels. Substitution of products derived from domestic resources for imported raw materials often is only a matter of cost. Thus, many products that play an important role in international trade may disappear from the world market as a result of the progress in chemistry.

It is also fairly probable that in the near future

some underdeveloped countries will learn how to process local fibers and minerals to meet their needs for staple textiles and iron and steel products. Export of raw cotton and wool and import of fabrics, the typical pattern of world trade in the nineteenth century, have been losing ground since the turn of the century.

Thus, the flow of various goods in world trade will be exposed to divergent influences: The volume of trade will increase with the growth of the worldwide economic system, but exports and imports of some raw materials and staple manufactures may decline; some products will disappear from world trade, and some ocean lanes described in this chapter will be abandoned as have the caravan routes of older times.

CHAPTER 5

BALANCES OF PAYMENTS AND INTERNATIONAL
INVESTMENTS

THE TERM "balance of payments" is used in modern economic literature to mean *a systematic record of all economic transactions during a given period between residents of the reporting country and residents of other countries.*[1] More exactly, the balance of payments records the economic transactions of residents, business concerns and the government of the reporting country with residents, business concerns and governments of other countries.[2]

In such a formal balance, debit and credit are always in equilibrium. For some types of analysis, however, it appears preferable to deal with only a part of the balance, for example, with only current transactions in goods and services, excluding such other items as changes in debts. In such a partial balance, debit and credit are seldom in equilibrium and the gap between them suggests an equal difference — but with the opposite sign — in the part omitted. For example, a surplus of credits in current transactions in goods and services indicates a surplus of debits in the account of the movement of the external debts of the nation.

The balance of current transactions in goods and services is frequently termed the "balance of trade."

BALANCES OF TRADE AND PAYMENTS: THEORY AND PRACTICE

England originated the doctrine that a country which has no gold and silver mines must export more than it imports in order to increase its stocks of precious metals or at least must avoid an excess of imports so as to preserve its gold and silver reserves. This precept was firmly established in England in the fourteenth century, more than a century before Columbus' first voy-

age. Parliament was worried at that time about the drain of gold from England, and an inquiry was ordered as to the cause of this phenomenon and the remedy for it. A mint spokesman explained to Parliament that

> . . . the land spends too much in merchandise, as in grocery, mercery and poltry, or wines, red, white and sweet, and also in exchanges made to the Court of Rome in divers ways. Wherefore the remedy seems . . . to be that each merchant bringing merchandise into England take out of the commodities of the land as much as his merchandise aforesaid shall amount to; and that none carry gold or silver beyond the sea.[3]

The term "balance of trade" was coined much later, in 1615, and came into common use almost immediately. According to Viner, Sir Francis Bacon was the first or one of the first to use it. Sir Francis wrote:

> This realm is much enriched of late years, by the trade of merchandise which the English drive in foreign parts; and, if it be wisely managed, it must of necessity very much increase the wealth thereof; care being taken, that the exportation exceed in value the importation; for then the balance of trade must of necessity be returned in coin or bullion.[4]

This general doctrine gave rise to the concepts of "favorable" and "unfavorable" trade balances, the first meaning an excess of exports and inflow of bullion; the latter, an excess of imports and drain on monetary reserves. This terminology played a prominent role in the economic thinking in the seventeenth and eighteenth centuries. Indeed, the pre-Smithian economists — described as "mercantilists" by Adam Smith and his school — were mainly concerned with the means of maintaining a favorable balance of trade.

It is noteworthy that their concept of "balance of trade" was very close to the modern idea of "balance of payments" when this term is applied to all current transactions. In speaking of "trade,"

---

1. **18,** 1949–50, p. 1. Cf. **17.**
2. The Economic Intelligence Service of the League of Nations, inaugurating the series of international studies of balance of payments, stressed that its records showed economic transactions *booked* rather than payments *effected.* (**1,** 1936, p. 46.)

3. **44,** p. 6.
4. **44,** p. 8.

they thought not only of export and import of merchandise but also of other transactions which would be settled ultimately in gold or coin: remittances to foreign governments or the Church, expenditures of British merchants and travelers abroad, profits from fishery and freight charges, payments on foreign loans, military expenditures abroad, marine insurance premiums, absentee incomes, losses from bad debts, earnings of migratory labor and so on.[5] Statistics on most of these items were lacking, however, and the economists of the time could only list such items as factors affecting the balance of international transactions. Some writers spoke of the *balance of trade,* others of the *balance of accounts.* In 1767, a decade before Adam Smith's great treatise was published, a distinction had already been made between the "balance of trade" as a balance between imports and exports of merchandise and the "balance of payments" as a record of all current economic transactions of a nation with other countries.

FAVORABLE VS. UNFAVORABLE BALANCES

Like the mercantilists of the eighteenth century, we still speak of the "favorable" or "unfavorable" trade balance of a nation in its transactions with another nation or all other countries. Even when these terms are replaced by "active balance" vs. "passive balance" or "export balance" vs. "import balance" (in the sense of export or import surplus) the original connotation remains: an excess of exports over imports seems to be "favorable" in some vague sense, while an excess of imports is taken to be "unfavorable" and to imply a threat to the welfare of the nation.

The British mercantilists advanced a great variety of arguments in support of their contention that England should have a surplus of exports over imports. Some authors stressed that exports ensure high employment, while imported goods compete with products of domestic industry and displace labor.[6] This argument sounds somewhat like the full-employment argument of modern days. It does not rhyme, however, with the mercantilists' obsession with thrift and saving. The prevailing form of saving at that time was to hoard precious metals and coins, and this was what the mercantilists recommended to

the government and to private citizens — a practice more detrimental to employment in a nation than a flood of imported goods.

It seems, therefore, that Jacob Viner is right in playing down the employment argument and stressing the gold-and-money argument in the mercantilist doctrine. According to his interpretation, the real foundation of the doctrine was to accumulate economic reserves through thrift and hoarding. The main difference between the mercantilists' and our concept of the balance of payments is that the idea of wealth in the form of invested capital was foreign to their thinking.

In a curious way, this difference was concealed by the dual role of the surplus of exports over imports in international transactions. Such a surplus may be offset by the inflow of gold or money into the country, which would be "favorable" from the mercantilist point of view. On the other hand, it may indicate that the exporting country transfers capital abroad to build up its foreign investments which, later, will enable it to increase its imports of merchandise far above exports without endangering its monetary reserves. The "favorable" (or active) trade balance may thus become advantageous since it puts the nation into a position where it can afford to have a passive ("unfavorable") balance without prejudice to its currency.

CONTROLLED VS. SELF-REGULATING BALANCES

The mercantilist doctrine assigned a dual task to foreign trade policy — to promote exports and to discourage imports. This was a self-destroying policy: since each article exported from a country must be imported by another, it entailed a continuous clash of interests among the trading nations and led, practically, to a race of import duties and export subsidies.

Doubts as to the soundness of this doctrine developed within the mercantilist school and were summarized by David Hume (1711–76), immediate predecessor of Adam Smith.[7] The core of Hume's theory was the idea of the self-regulating operation of the balance of payments:

A country with a metallic currency will automatically get the amount of bullion it needs to maintain its prices at such a level relative to the prices prevailing abroad as to maintain an even balance between its exports and imports. Should more money than this happen to come into that country,

5. **44**, pp. 13–14.
6. **44**, p. 51.

7. **36**, p. 117.

its prices would rise relatively to those of other countries; its exports, consequently would fall, and its imports increase; the resultant adverse balance of payments would have to be met in specie; and the excess of money would thus be drained off. If, on the other hand, a country's money supply should happen to fall below the amount necessary to maintain equilibrium, its prices would fall relative to those abroad, exports would rise and imports fall, and the resultant favorable balance of payments would bring in an amount of specie from abroad sufficient to restore equilibrium.[8]

This theory was a departure from the fundamental philosophy of mercantilism. Instead of trying to unbalance merchandise trade by import duties and export bounties, each government was invited to let the self-regulating process of balance of payments take its course.

Hume's theory, fully accepted by Adam Smith and his school, was never applied in its pure form. In England, where this theory has been recognized as the Bible of trade policy since the middle of the nineteenth century, responsibility for regulating the supply of money in the nation and maintaining equilibrium in its balance of payments passed to the Bank of England. Opinions are divided on the wisdom of its decisions [9] but all actions taken by the Bank have rested essentially on the theory of the self-regulating mechanism of international balances of payments. Indeed, two centuries after its formulation, this theory remains predominant. As Viner declares, "No strikingly different mechanism . . . has yet been convincingly suggested, although there has been gain in precision of analysis and some correction of undoubted error." [10]

THE BALANCING PROCESS IN THE NINETEENTH
CENTURY

The idea of a self-regulating balance does not postulate automatic adjustment of economic processes independent of the will and decisions of men. It implies, rather, that people and institutions being what they are, the thinking of businessmen, their reactions to economic pressures and their decisions on crucial points of the economic system are predictable. The self-regulating economic process is therefore nothing but a definite pattern of response of individuals in the business community to the challenge of adverse economic conditions.

It is easy to identify the individuals who were making the decisions which constituted the self-regulating mechanism of balance of payments in the nineteenth century and the first decade and a half of the twentieth. As Condliffe puts it:

At that time the London money market was not only the agent of the greatest importing country but also the center where international payments were ultimately cleared. Sterling was not only an important national currency but also the medium for settling international payments. Therefore the movement of interest rates in London was of particular importance: Those interest rates were fixed by bargaining processes in highly competitive specialized markets, but they clustered about one central rate — the rate at which the Bank of England would discount approved bills. The Bank rate, as it was called, was fixed every Thursday and if it was changed, the structure of interest rates in the market went up or down with it. Thus the ultimate control of the money market lay in the hands of the Bank directors, and these men were primarily interested in international trade and finance. The whole marketing process for capital as well as for commodities was dispersed and impersonal. . . . The banker who foreclosed an overdraft, the trader who quoted a price, the financier who floated a loan, did not regard himself as more than the interpreter and agent of impersonal and irresistible market forces. . . . At the top of the pyramid the Bank of England directors held the same view. They were the custodians of the reserves not simply of the London money market, but of the world-wide trade and investment which were cleared through that market. . . . Even when they took positive action—by lowering or raising the Bank rate to correct what they regarded as a departure from equilibrium— they regarded themselves not as the managers of the market but as brokers or middlemen responding to market pressures.[11]

INTERNATIONAL INVESTMENTS BEFORE
WORLD WAR I

International transfer of capital, chiefly bank balances, became a part of international trade and an important item of the balance of payments in the nineteenth century. Short-term credits serve to balance temporary disequilibriums or to bridge over the time between requested payments and offsetting receipts. Some of these credits are self-liquidating, especially in trade in agricultural products and other seasonal operations. Others tend to accumulate, creating a situation of dangerous uncertainty for both the

8. **44**, pp. 74–75.
9. **44**, pp. 118–289.
10. **44**, p. 291.

11. **36**, pp. 358–59.

debtor and creditor country. In order to eliminate this uncertainty, both parties may prefer to transform short-term credits into loans with proper guarantees of repayment. This is one of the sources of international middle-term and long-term indebtedness. The other and more important source is international investment, which does not result from export or import surpluses but creates conditions favorable for the development of such surpluses and often serves to unbalance the current merchandise and service transactions.

TYPES OF INTERNATIONAL INVESTMENTS

Long-term loans constitute the most important type of international investment. They usually appear in the form of stocks or bonds offered to the public in the lending nation by local banks acting on behalf of the government or private concern, but investors may also purchase domestic securities of a foreign nation. Thus, for example, British investments in United States railroads in the nineteenth century consisted of bonds floated in New York through local banks and payable in U.S. dollars. Similarly, United States investments in Canada consisted largely of Canadian bonds payable in Canadian dollars.

From the viewpoint of investors it is not very important whether the borrower is the central government, a municipality, a province, a bank or an industrial firm; or whether the loan is designed to finance a particular operation (for example, railway construction, re-equipping commercial harbors, acquiring a merchant fleet or modernizing mines) or is distributed among several vaguely defined projects. The essential point is that there are sufficient guarantees of payment of interest and repayment of the principal.

Insofar as a loan transfers purchasing power of the lending country to the borrowing country, its immediate financial effect is the same as if the borrowing country had sold merchandise or services to the lending country. Accordingly, a foreign loan appears in the balance of payments of the borrowing nation on the credit side of the ledger, on the same side as exports. In the balance of payments of the lending nation, it is listed as a debit, on the same side as imports.

The further financial impact of the receipt of a foreign loan is likewise similar to that of an export operation. The borrowing country may use the loan to purchase produce of the lending country — for example, a railway loan may be used to purchase rails, rolling stock and other equipment in the lending country. Ordinarily the borrowing country may also use the funds for purchases in other markets. In this event, the country which sells its produce to the borrowing country is paid with the money of the lending country and ultimately will use this money for purchases in that country. The operation thus is completed in the course of triangular or multilateral trade.

Investments of this type are usually called *portfolio* investments. This term stresses that the lending country holds in its "portfolio" obligations of residents, business concerns or government of the borrowing country.

As long as currencies are convertible, no special provisions for transfer of interest and capital repayment are required. It is enough that the banks of the borrowing nation honor the matured coupons of the bonds. The situation changes, of course, if the currency of the borrowing country softens or if the government imposes restrictions on its use in international transactions.

Another form of international investment occurs when a bank or business concern acquires a controlling share of all stock of a foreign concern, or establishes a branch abroad, purchases land, develops plantations or mines, builds railroads and so on.[12] Such *direct* investment ordinarily implies no specific obligation on the part of government or private concerns of the country in which the operation is effected toward the country whose capital has been invested. The rights of investors are determined by local laws or private contracts under these laws.

The distinction between direct and portfolio investments is not always clear. Purchase of the stock of a foreign concern (which appears usually as a portfolio investment) may be a means of establishing control over industrial plants abroad, exactly as if these plants were bought or built by the investing concern. Moreover, the distinction between the two types of investments does not always have the same meaning in different countries. Some authors stress that portfolio investments are initiated by the borrower, who offers his securities on foreign capital markets, while direct investments are initiated by the lender.[13] This definition, however, leaves many intermediate cases unclassified.

---

12. **41**, p. 8.
13. **35**, pp. 156ff.

International loans and investments of the portfolio type were inaugurated by the British banks after the Napoleonic wars. A few decades later, France and Germany and, on a smaller scale, other countries entered the international investment business. The amount of foreign long-term loans grew steadily, and by the end of the nineteenth century, interest on loans became a regular item in international balances of payments.

The growth of private international investment was interrupted by World War I and resumed in the 1920's.[14] Their dollar value in 1938 and 1952 exceeded that in 1914. In relation to prices, however, or the volume of world trade and income, the value of international investments has never regained the level it had before World War I. The chronological limits of the period of growth of international loans and investments are therefore clear enough: the period lasted a century, from 1816 to 1914.

Great Britain

The first large-scale international investment operation handled by London bankers was to finance the pecuniary indemnity exacted by the allies from France after the defeat of Napoleon. The operation, conducted by the famous firm of Baring Brothers, consisted of a series of loans offered (1816–18) to the public, totaling approximately $150 million.[15] It was highly successful, and lending money to foreign governments became popular with the British public.

Loans to Russia, Austria, Prussia and later to Spain, Portugal, Greece and the young South American republics followed in rapid succession. Savings accumulated in England during the Napoleonic wars flowed to Chile, Peru, Mexico, Guatemala, Argentina, Brazil.[16] The foreign loan mania ended in financial collapse in 1825. Jenks has thus described the results of this first venture in international investments:

Not only the South American mines proved a graveyard for British fortunes. Within two years of

the panic of 1825, Spain, Portugal, Greece and every country of South America to which money had been lent — except Brazil — were in default upon their interest payments. For thirty years their financial affairs were in hopeless confusion. An even longer period elapsed before some of these states approached solvency.[17]

All in all, between 1816 and 1830 the British public and bankers invested at least $250 million in the securities of most of the stable European governments, more than $100 million in Latin America and some $25–$30 million in the United States.

After a spell of active participation in speculation in the United States in the 1830's, British capital found a new field for investment in railroad building in France and Belgium. Some $120 million was invested this way in the 1840's. The crises and revolutions of 1848 interrupted this new investment venture.

In the 1850's, British capital sought investment in railroads and other business all over the world — in the United States, Canada and Brazil; France, Belgium, Denmark and Sweden; Austria and Switzerland; Spain and Portugal; Piedmont (later part of Italy); Russia and Turkey; Algeria, British India and Australia. Great Britain was building up a financial empire and its export surplus was financed by loans to foreign countries. Thus British investments in foreign railroad loans stimulated export of railway iron and machinery. The export, however, did not always go directly to the borrowing country; many transactions were settled in triangular and multilateral trade.[18]

According to Jenks, in 1854 England had accumulated foreign investments totaling approximately $1 billion, distributed as follows (in millions of dollars):

United States	$250–$300
French, Belgian, Dutch and Russian government securities	225– 275
Spain and Portugal	175– 225
Latin America	175– 200
French railways	125– 150
Belgian railways	25

By 1875 the amount of British capital lent or invested abroad was close to $6 billion, the bulk of it in bonds of foreign governments and railway shares and debentures. About $2.5 billion

---

14. International capital transactions continued in 1914–19 but the depreciation of old investments — as a result of repudiation of debts, inflation, destruction of industrial installations and so forth — outran the formation of new international investments.

15. **39**, pp. 31ff.

16. **39**, pp. 44ff.

17. **39**, p. 58.

18. **39**, pp. 174–75.

was invested in Europe and Egypt, the remainder distributed among the United States, India, South America and the dominions in that order.[19] Unlike the early phase of the "investment mania," British foreign investments of 1850–75 proved to be reasonably secure. In the 1870's, all countries punctually returned interest at a rate of at least 6 per cent.

At that time, London was the largest financial center in the world but no longer the sole money lender. French and German banks were gaining ground in operations with European governments.

In the latter part of the nineteenth century the British began to redirect their investments from European to non-European countries and financed a part of new investments in Asia and Africa by liquidating their old investments in continental Europe. By 1914 investments in Europe represented only about 6 per cent of all British foreign holdings.[20]

France

In the 1850's and 1860's the French underwrote numerous loans to the governments of Italy, Spain, Austria-Hungary and Portugal. French capital completed the building of the Suez Canal in 1869, and French syndicates were operating gas works, mines, tramways and banks in a dozen countries.[21] The defeat of France by the Prussian armies in 1871 interrupted the accumulation of French assets abroad. Export of capital was not resumed until the 1880's (the Panama Canal and gold mines in South Africa).

Germany

Germany entered the scene of international investments in the 1880's. Operations were shrewdly directed by the leading banks. Herbert Feis writes:

When there were new lines to be established for the Hamburg American line or Norddeutscher Lloyd, concessions to be developed in Shantung or Asia Minor, a colonial chartered company to be sustained, submarine cables to be laid, petroleum companies in Romania to be combined and strengthened, it was these banks that stepped forward, or were called forward to respond to the opportunity. Always in their vaults there was a great volume of securities, not yet distributed to the general investing public, or held to secure representation or control of direction.[22]

Great Britain, Germany and France were the largest sources of capital before the outbreak of World War I. On a smaller scale, foreign investments were made by Belgium, the Netherlands, Switzerland and the United States.

The United States

The United States was a debtor nation before World War I in the sense that its indebtedness to foreign countries exceeded its assets abroad. In the nineteenth century the United States had an import balance in merchandise and service trade, which largely accounted for the growth of its indebtedness to Europe, mainly to Great Britain. American railway loans were particularly popular with European investors at that time.

In the middle of that century, however, after the discovery of gold in California, the United States became an exporter of the yellow metal. Its net exports totaled $170 million in 1851–55, $256 million in 1856–60, $212 million in 1861–65, $192 million in 1866–70, $205 million in 1871–75 — more than $1 billion in 25 years. This operation amounted to export of gold as a product of domestic mining and like any other export brought foreign currency to the United States, offsetting the import balance in foreign merchandise trade.

It has been estimated that the foreign long-term debts of the United States totaled $1,400 million after the Civil War. By 1897, the amount had increased to $3,150 million, but by that time United States capital had found its way to Canada and Mexico and by the turn of the century, to South America. The net indebtedness of the United States in 1897 amounted to $2.7 billion — $2.5 billion in long-term obligations, the rest in short-term credits. Great Britain and France were the main creditors.

The period from 1897 to 1914 was marked by rapid economic expansion in the United States. British, French and German capital was flowing into the United States, while its own capital was seeking profits in Mexico, Central and South America — an operation in conformity with the general pattern of the flow of capital from the more developed to less developed areas.

---

19. **39**, p. 335.
20. **9**, p. 3.
21. **37**, p. 44.

22. **37**, p. 63.

From 1897 to 1908 foreign investments in the United States grew from $3.4 to $6.4 billion and its investments abroad, from $700 million to $2.5 billion, increasing the country's net long-term indebtedness from $2.7 to $3.9 billion. The United States, however, was then entering the phase of development characterized by net outflow of capital and consequent surplus of exports in merchandise trade.

On June 30, 1914, just before the outbreak of war in Europe, the United States' foreign debts totaled $7.2 billion, and its foreign assets (mainly south of the Rio Grande and in Canada), $3.5 billion. Thus the net long-term indebtedness of the country had declined by $200 million in six years.[23]

Although the United States was then a debtor in relation to Europe, it was a creditor and important capital market in relation to the countries of the Western Hemisphere. Indeed, it was the fourth largest investor in the world.

STATUS OF INTERNATIONAL INVESTMENTS, 1914

The total amount of international long-term investments before World War I has been estimated by experts of the United Nations at $44 billion, distributed as follows (in millions of U.S. dollars): [24]

Creditor Country

Total	$44,000
United Kingdom	18,300
France	8,700
Germany	5,600
United States	3,500
Belgium, Netherlands, Switzerland	5,500
Sweden, Portugal, Russia, Japan and other	2,400

Investment Area

Total	$44,000
Europe	12,000
North America	10,500
Middle and South America	8,500
Asia	6,000
Africa	4,700
Oceania	2,300

(Cf. Figure 41.)

These figures do not include short-term credits and obligations. Before World War I such items

normally consisted of revolving mercantile and similar credits.

The heavy and frequently erratic movements of vagrant short-term capital which developed after World War I as a result of political and economic uncertainty in Europe became a major obstacle in appraising the creditor-debtor position of individual nations. Contrary to long-term investments, which are usually widely publicized by the underwriting financial groups, vagrant capital prefers privacy and often takes care to conceal its provenance and destination. A precise estimate of the status of short-term claims and obligations of a country is therefore extremely difficult, and discrepancies in such appraisals are a main source of conflicting statements on the *net* debtor-creditor position of a country. This source of uncertainty, however, was less important in 1914 than it is now.

The UN estimate of total foreign investments in 1914 ($44 billion) is probably on the conservative side. It does not cover all participation of foreign capital in commercial and industrial enterprises. On the other hand, it may contain some duplication. The distribution of foreign investments by continents offered above is admittedly approximate.[25] There was, however, a clear geographic pattern in the distribution of the investments of each of the great creditor nations at that time.

The French preferred loans to governments and were usually unwilling to venture their money in countries more remote than America, Russia and the Middle East, including Egypt and the Suez. Their favorite and most trusted customer was the Russian czar. The British preferred to invest in their dominions and colonies — Canada, Australia, New Zealand, South Africa, India and Ceylon. They also held large investments in the United States and Latin America (especially Argentina).

The growth and wide geographic distribution of German foreign investments reveal the strength of the German economy. A latecomer in international finance, Germany had acquired assets in Latin America as well as in the Middle

23. **28**, pp. 242–45; cf. **41**.
24. **9**, p. 2. The computation is based largely on the data presented in **2**, *passim*.

25. A creditor country may hold securities widely scattered all over the world and sometimes the destination of capital invested in each security cannot be ascertained with precision. Many loans have been handled by international groups of bankers and issued simultaneously in several capital markets so that foreign capital held in a country could be invested in securities of another country.

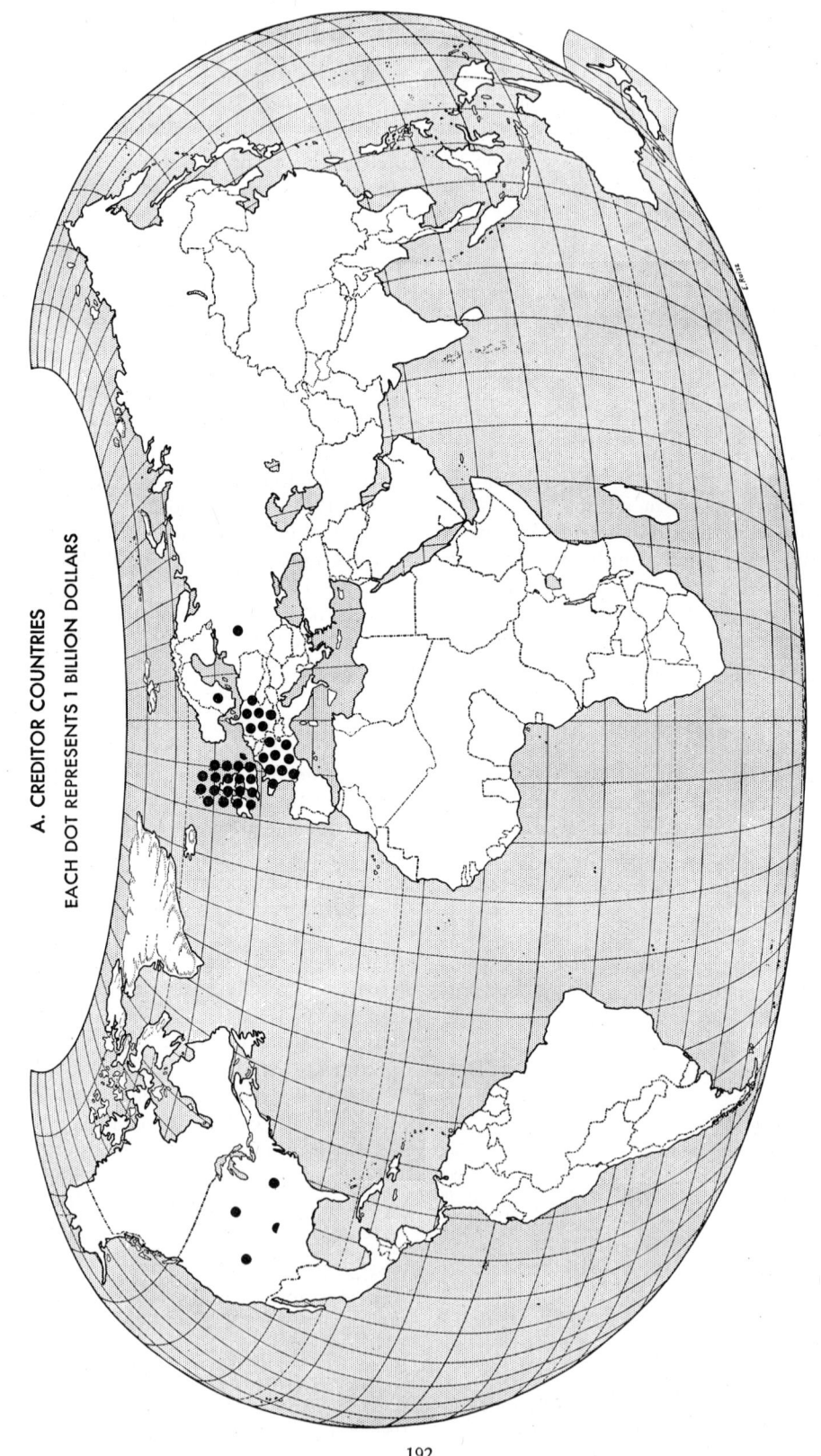

A. CREDITOR COUNTRIES

EACH DOT REPRESENTS 1 BILLION DOLLARS

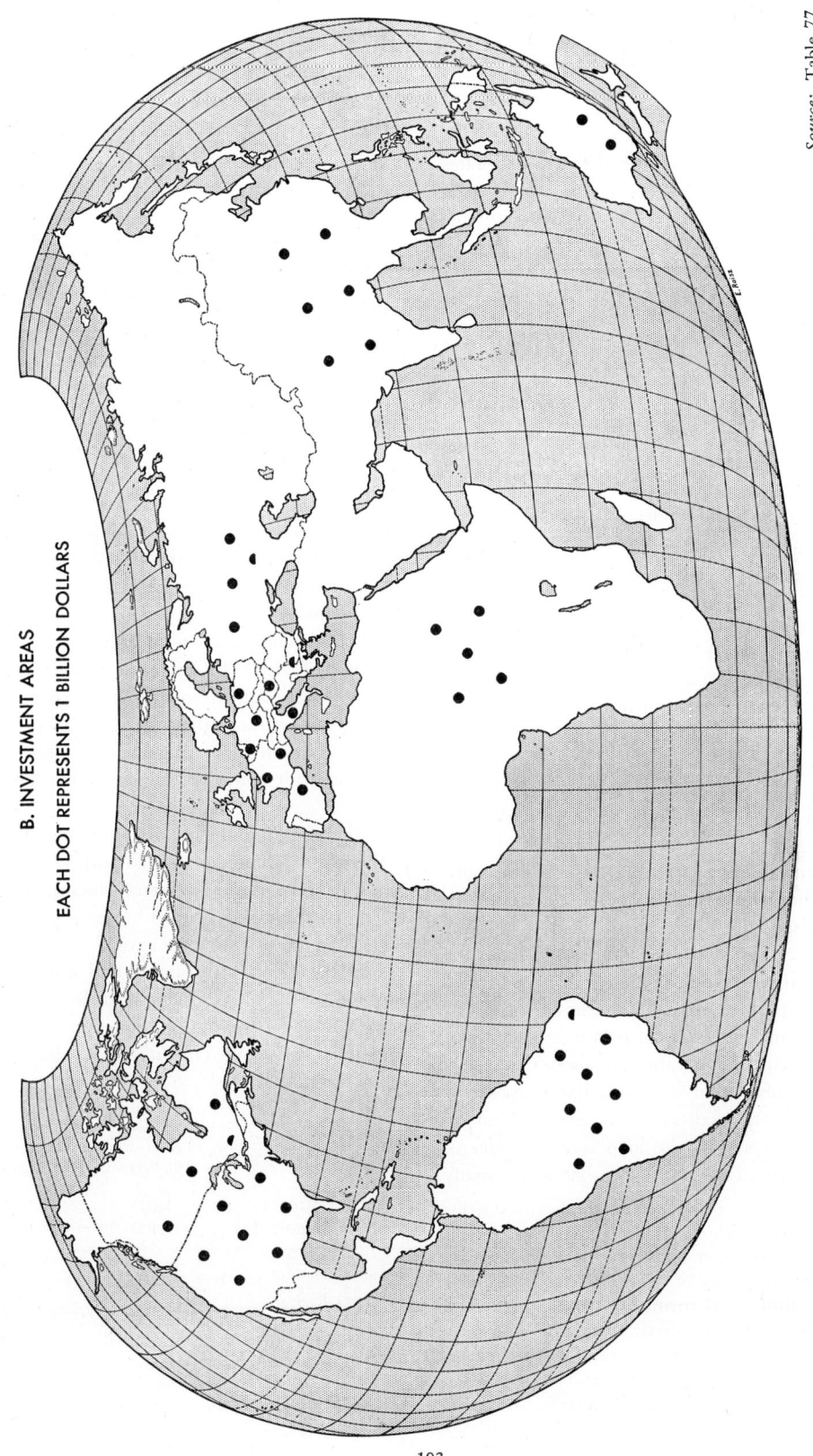

B. INVESTMENT AREAS

EACH DOT REPRESENTS 1 BILLION DOLLARS

Source: Table 77

FIGURE 41. FOREIGN INVESTMENTS: GEOGRAPHIC DISTRIBUTION IN THE WORLD, 1914

and Far East. It had even succeeded in becoming a creditor of the United States, France and Great Britain, though France and Great Britain, in turn, had invested money in German business. (See Table 77; cf. Figure 42.)

The direct investments of the United States went mainly to Canada, Mexico, the Caribbean and South America. Portfolio investments (mainly in the form of loans to foreign governments) were scattered more widely, but South American securities prevailed.

PURPOSES AND RESULTS OF FOREIGN INVESTMENTS

Apart from the formal distinction between "direct" and "portfolio" investments, long-term international loans and debts can be classified as private and public, productive (that is, designed for a definite economic purpose) and nonproductive, and in many other ways.

In the flow of merchandise in international trade, each foreign loan can be described as a long-term postponement of payments for exported goods or services. Through such an arrangement, the exporters are paid with the money advanced by the investors with the understanding that the latter will be compensated with interest in due time.

The simplest pattern of foreign investment is exemplified by railway bonds through which the borrowing country obtains railway steel, machinery and rolling stock from the creditor country or other areas, and producers are paid with funds raised among residents of the creditor country who expect to be compensated from the profits of the new railroad.

This simple pattern is not common, however. When a loan is guaranteed by foreign banks or governments, this guarantee replaces the expectation of profits from the particular purpose for which the loan is launched. Whether or not to stress the purpose of the loan is a question of policy. Herbert Feis points out that in Germany

. . . there was a bent toward those investments which would produce an economic development beneficial for German industry and commerce. By loans to governments of countries with promising economic futures, German finance might win a place which would indirectly yield opportunity to German industry and commerce. By the creation of banks, the establishment of branch factories, the building of railways, the same purpose would be served. The whole operation of the German eco-

nomic system, between 1870 and 1914, became increasingly dependent upon the development of foreign markets for German goods.[26]

The character of French investments was very different. Apart from political considerations, doubtful risks attracted French investors by the lure of high returns:

Paris kept its gates open more widely than any other money market to the governments whose treasuries were perpetually empty, whose expenditure was determined autocratically, whose national vitality seemed corrupted and declined. . . . It kept its gates open, also, for the governments of Europe. . . . living in their ambitions beyond the resources of their tax systems — Italy (in earlier days), Russia, and the Balkan states.[27]

In contrast to French investors, who gambled on bad debts of bad governments, and the Germans, who let their hard-boiled bankers direct the flow of investments, the British preferred to invest money in definite projects — mines, railways, industrial plants, power stations, tramways, canals and docks, telegraph and telephone systems and so on. In 1914, not more than one fourth of the British investments abroad consisted of government securities. Moreover, most of the latter were of the type of productive loans earmarked for definite economically desirable purposes.[28]

Of the total amount of foreign funds invested in the United States before World War I, less than 20 per cent was in direct investments, the rest in portfolio securities. On the contrary, of United States investments abroad, 75 per cent represented direct investments and only 25 per cent, the portfolio type. Long-term foreign assets and liabilities of the United States in 1914 were distributed as follows (in millions of dollars): [29]

	Foreign Investments in the U.S.	*U.S. Investments Abroad*
Total	$6,700	$3,500
Direct investments	1,300	2,600
Portfolio investments	5,400	900

26. **37**, p. 78.
27. **37**, p. 57.
28. This statement refers especially to British colonial investments. Whether these were in the form of direct or portfolio investments, they were usually designed for a definite economically profitable purpose. (Cf. the description of British investments in Africa in **38**, *passim*.)
29. **28**, p. 242.

TABLE 77

FOREIGN INVESTMENTS OF THE UNITED KINGDOM, FRANCE AND GERMANY: GEOGRAPHIC DISTRIBUTION, 1914

(*Millions of Dollars*)

Investing Country and Direction of Investment	Amount	Investing Country and Direction of Investment	Amount
United Kingdom, total [a]	$18,351	France, total [a]	$8,686
		French colonies	772
Within the Empire	8,670		
Canada & Newfoundland	2,508	United States, Canada & Australia	386
India and Ceylon	1,845	Latin America	1,158
Straits Settlements	133		
South Africa	1,803	Belgium, Netherlands & Switzerland	290
West Africa	182	Austria–Hungary	425
Australia & New Zealand	2,028	Portugal & Spain	753
Other countries	171	Italy	251
		Balkan states	483
Outside the Empire	9,681	Other European states	290
United States	3,675		
Mexico	482	Russia	2,180
Cuba	162		
Brazil	721	Turkey	637
Peru	167	Asia	425
Chile	297		
Uruguay	176	Egypt, Suez & South Africa	637
Argentina	1,556		
Other Latin America	124	Germany, total [a]	5,593
France	39	United States & Canada	881
Denmark	54	Latin America	905
Germany	31		
Austria–Hungary	39	Great Britain & France	310
Portugal	39	Austria–Hungary	715
Spain	93	Portugal & Spain	405
Italy	61	Balkan states	405
Balkan states	83	Other European states	286
Other European states	91		
		Russia	426
Russia	536		
		Turkey	426
China	214	Asia [b]	238
Japan	306		
Turkey	117	Africa [b]	476
Egypt	219		
		Other countries	119
Other countries	399		

Source: Computed on the basis of **37**, pp. 23, 51 and 74.

a. The totals for the United Kingdom, France and Germany in this table differ slightly from the estimates of the UN experts quoted on p. 191. The difference is due partly to the rounding of numbers to the next billion or next $100 million in the latter.

b. Including German colonies.

It is noteworthy that in many cases the ultimate result of foreign investments of different types was the same.

In the escort of the capital that travelled from western Europe went the business practices, the technical ways of western Europe. Where it went, old economic habits and relationships vanished, new ones formed. The civilization of large commercial centers, distant exchanges, specialization, round about production took as its own the areas where its capital was employed. Of all the consequences of the capital movement this was the most permanent and the most fertile of future consequence.[30]

---

30. **37**, p. 464.

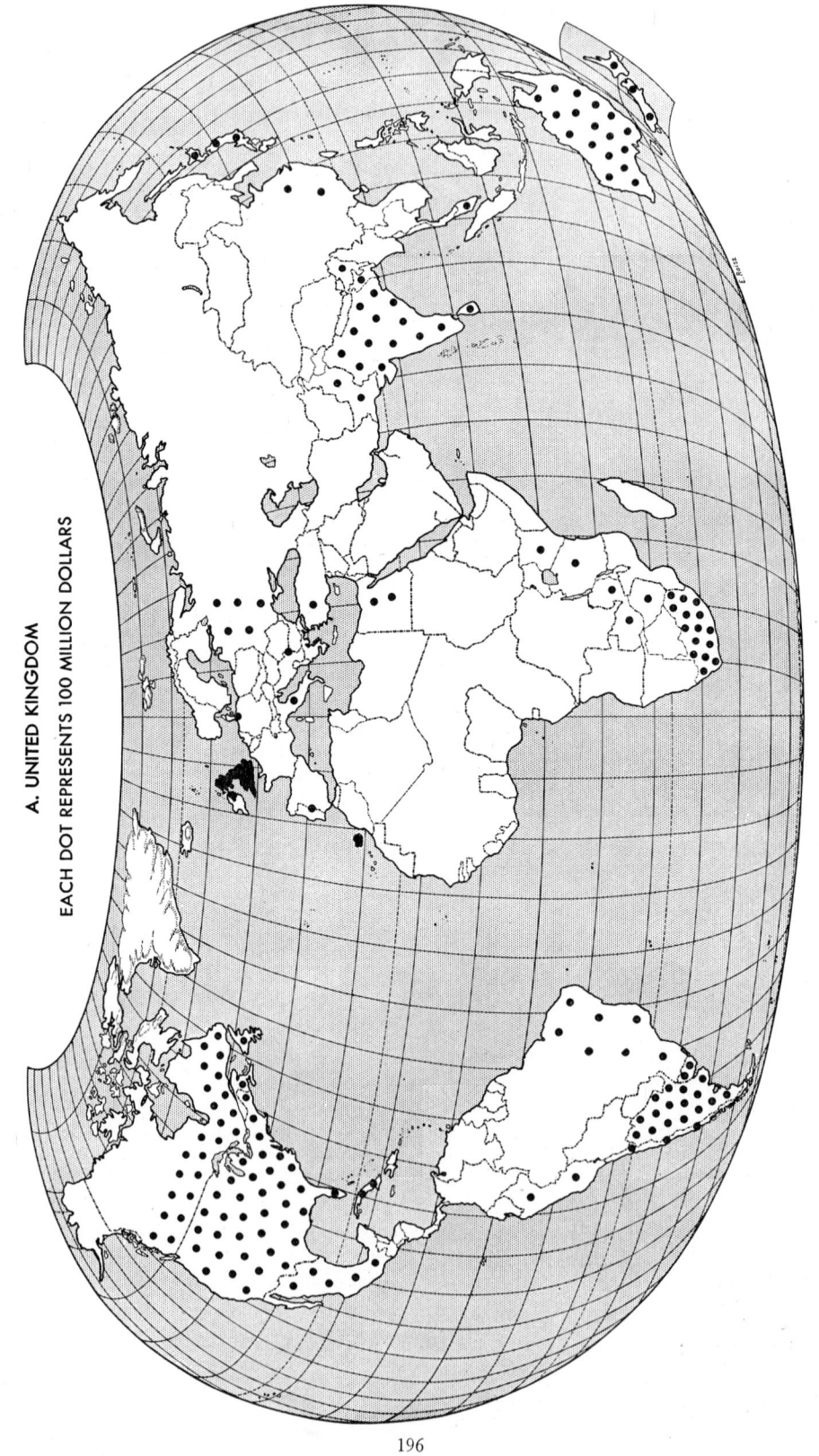

A. UNITED KINGDOM

EACH DOT REPRESENTS 100 MILLION DOLLARS

196

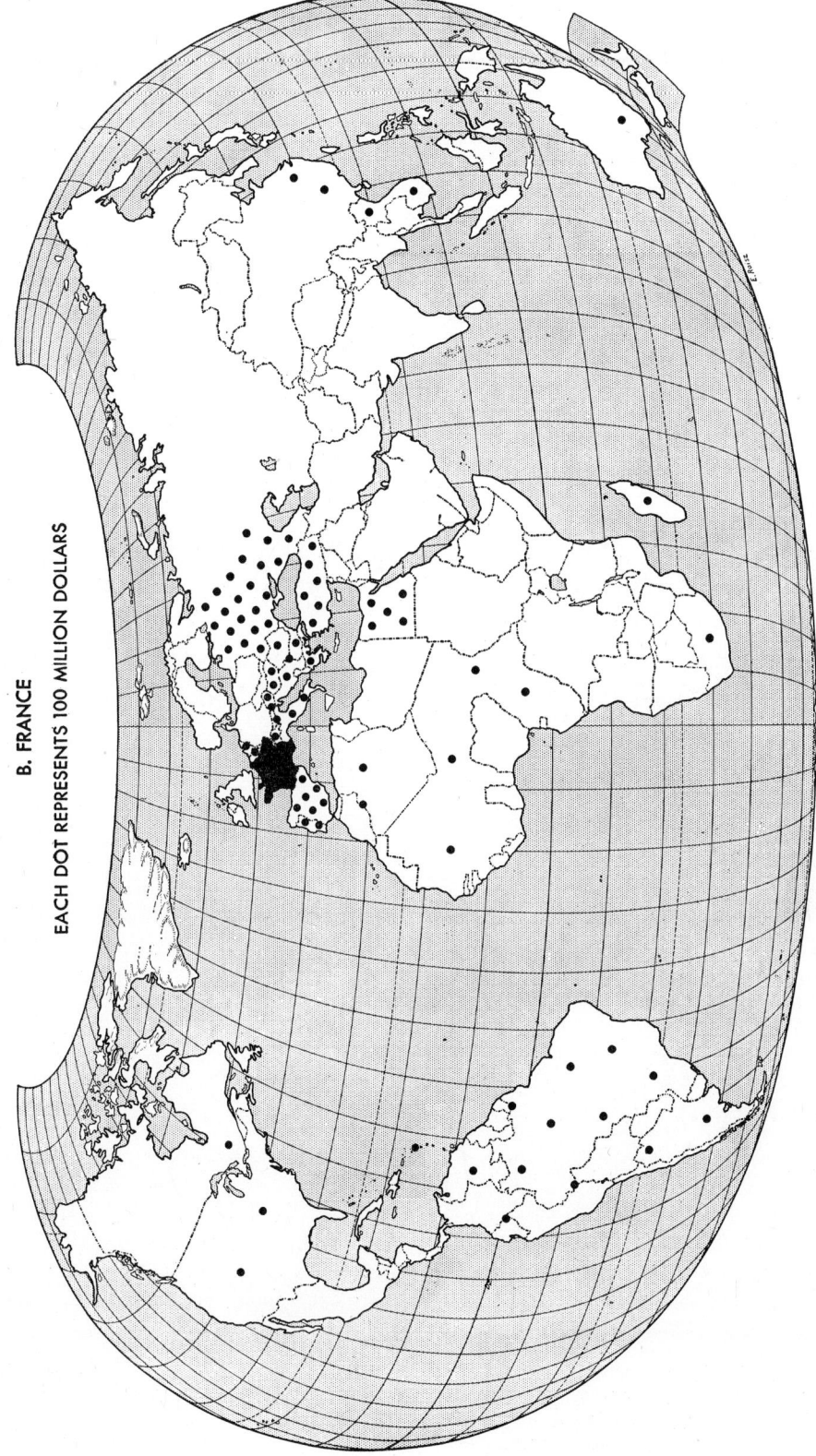

B. FRANCE

EACH DOT REPRESENTS 100 MILLION DOLLARS

FIGURE 42. FOREIGN INVESTMENTS OF THE UNITED KINGDOM, FRANCE AND GERMANY: GEOGRAPHIC DISTRIBUTION, 1914

For Germany (C), see following page

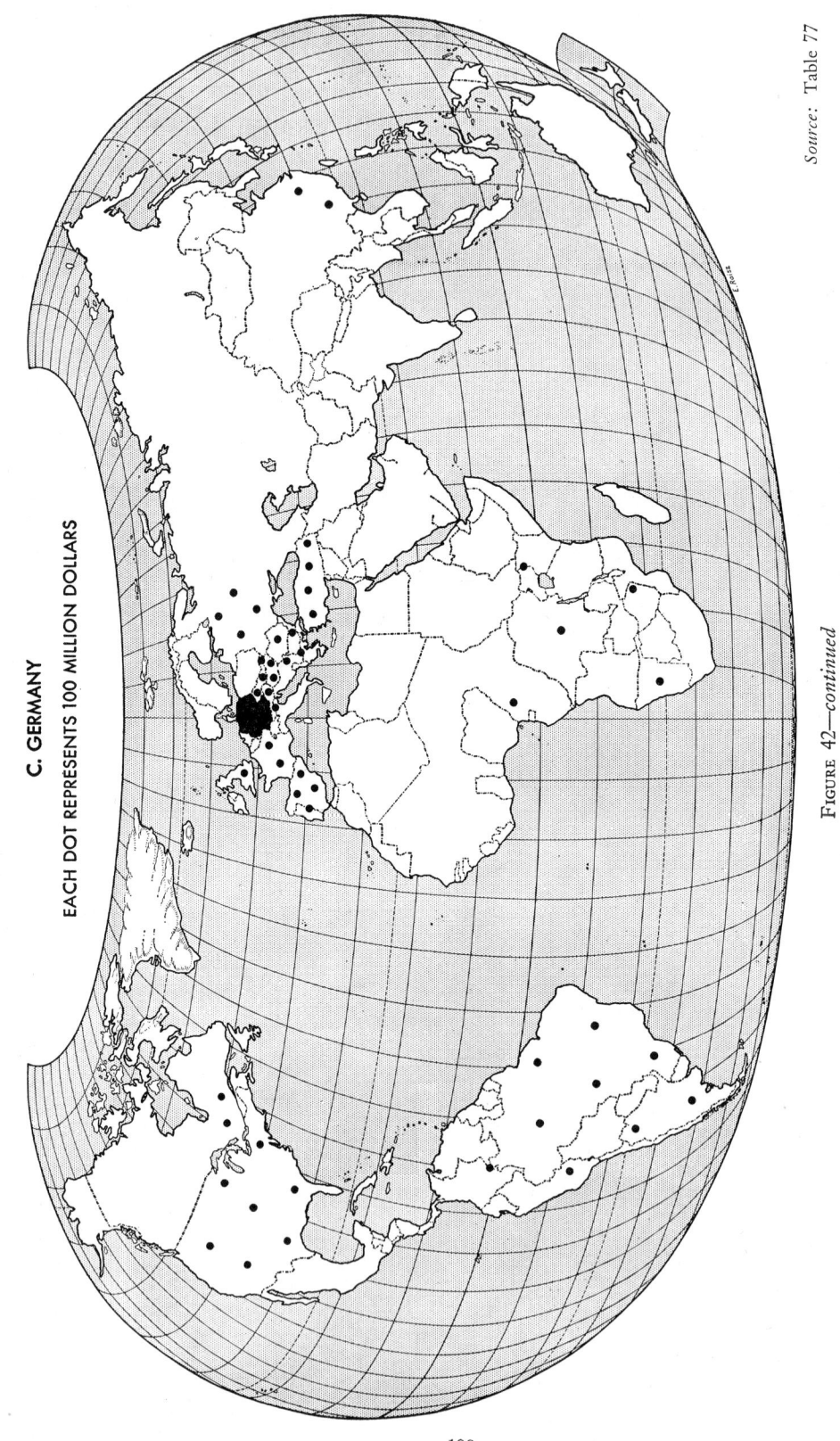

C. GERMANY

EACH DOT REPRESENTS 100 MILLION DOLLARS

Source: Table 77

FIGURE 42—*continued*

The three maps show the geographic distribution of foreign long-term investments of the three leading investor nations at the time of the greatest expansion of foreign investments, on the eve of World War I. All three maps are on the same scale, and comparison of them gives a rough picture of the relative economic strength of the three investing powers in different regions of the world.

THE ROLE OF FOREIGN INVESTMENTS IN THE
BALANCE OF PAYMENTS

Before World War I foreign investments
played a very important role in the balance of
payments of Great Britain, France and Germany
and represented a sizable item in the settlement
of payments of Belgium, the Netherlands and
Switzerland.

Such a role is illustrated by the example of
the balance of payments of Great Britain in 1913.
In this year the United Kingdom exported merchandise valued at £635 million and had imports
totaling £769 million.[31] In addition, it imported
gold worth £24 million and thus had an import surplus of £158 million in the movement
of merchandise and gold. To offset this deficit,
the British had items totaling £129 million on
the other side of the ledger as follows (in millions of pounds):

Earnings of the merchant marine	£94
Earnings of traders (commissions)	25
Other earnings	10

The British thus would have had a deficit of
£29 million except for interest and dividends
from their investments abroad, which amounted
to £210 million. Addition of this item to other
"invisible" exports reversed the balance of payments in favor of the United Kingdom, giving
a net surplus of £181 million. Theoretically, the
British could take this balance in increased imports of merchandise and still have the balance
of payments in equilibrium. Actually they left
the whole net balance abroad as a new investment. In fact, in 1913 London advanced to colonial and foreign concerns long-term loans for
£198 million — almost exactly the amount of
current profits from former investments abroad.[32]

In general, current profits from foreign investments can be used by investors in several ways:
as a means of payment for surplus of purchases
(imports) over sales (exports); as a means of
payment on obligations of a creditor country; as
funds for reinvestment abroad so that foreign
assets of the lending country increase without
prejudice to capital formation at home from current domestic production.

The last operation, plowing profits from foreign investments into new financial ventures
abroad, was a usual practice before 1914. Ger-

many, for example, had an import balance in
1912 of some $170 million in merchandise trade
and an additional $100 million, in round num-
bers, was remitted abroad by foreign workers
employed in Germany. These items were largely
offset by $240 million earned by the German
merchant marine and banks.[33] So far, the balance of payments was about in equilibrium. But
Germany also had profits from investments
abroad — estimated at $250–$300 million —
which remained almost entirely at the disposal
of German banks for new investments abroad.[34]

THE INTERWAR YEARS

World War I drastically changed the creditor-
debtor relations of nations and reshaped their
balances of payments. Changes in France, Germany and the United States were spectacular.

IMPACT OF WORLD WAR I ON INTERNATIONAL
TRANSACTIONS

Information about international transactions
and capital movements during World War I, in
1914–19, is fragmentary. Early in the war, the
belligerent countries were selling their securities
to neutral nations to pay for foodstuffs and military materials. Most such transactions were completed in secrecy, however, and the provenance
of the transferred claims was not always recorded. To these transactions were added, in the
later phase of war, changes in the value of old
investments.

The repudiation of debts by the Soviet government wiped out foreign investments of approximately $3.5 billion in Russia. The total includes
$2,180 million lent by the French investors to
the czarist government and private concerns in
Russia, $536 million invested by the British and
$426 million invested by the Germans. (See
Table 77.) Losses of the United States, Belgium,
the Netherlands and minor creditors are estimated conservatively at $350 million.

In all, the United Kingdom, France and Germany each lost foreign assets in the amount of
$4–$5 billion. The decrease in the value of the
British and French holdings was compensated
to only a small degree by seizure of German assets abroad. Joint net losses of the three Euro-

---

31. **33,** 1908–22, pp. 86–87.
32. **32,** January 29, 1925, p. 145.

33. Net earnings, i.e., surplus of earnings over payments for services of foreign shipping and banks to
Germany.
34. **42,** pp. 30–31; cf. **45,** p. 236.

pean creditor countries may have totaled $12 billion, more than 35 per cent of the foreign investments they had piled up since the middle of the nineteenth century.

At the same time, foreign holdings of the United States increased, mainly as a result of accepting foreign securities in payment of exports. The international transactions of the United States from July 31, 1914 to December 31, 1919, can be summarized as follows (in millions of dollars):

Exports, total	$33,958
Merchandise	31,865
Services	2,093
Imports, total	19,269
Merchandise	15,161
Services	4,108

The surplus of exports over imports thus was $14,689 million. To this surplus were added net receipts, resulting from foreign investments as follows (in millions of dollars):

United States receipts from investments abroad	+$1,619
Payments for foreign investments in the United States	−670
Net receipts	+949

With allowance for unilateral transfers in kind and cash (−$1,442 million) it appears that current transactions in the period from June 30, 1914 to December 31, 1919, left the United States with net claims for about $14.2 billion.[35] This balance of current transactions was offset by the movement of capital as follows (in billions of dollars):

Total	$14.1
Decrease in foreign investments in the United States	2.4
Increase in United States investments abroad	11.7

The minor discrepancy between the balances of current transactions and capital movement is due partly to shipments of gold and partly to statistical errors and omissions, the two factors largely offsetting each other.

---

35. **28**, pp. 242–43. It is mere coincidence that this net balance in favor of the United States is close to total losses in foreign investments of Great Britain, France and Germany.

As a result of the tremendous surplus of exports in 1914–19, the position of the United States was reversed: from a debtor nation, the country was transformed — temporarily — into a creditor nation.

The records of the movement of capital in this period show, however, that during the war the investment balance of the United States increased much less than $14 billion. According to the official estimates, from June 30, 1914 to the end of 1919, the United States reduced its debts to foreign countries by $3.9 billion (from $7.2 to $3.3 billion) and increased its assets abroad by $3.5 billion (from $3.5 to $7.0 billion) so that the net improvement in its foreign position amounted to only $7.4 billion.

The main source of this discrepancy is in the different handling of war debts. In current international transactions, the export surplus of the United States in 1914–19 is offset by the increasing debts of foreign countries to the United States. Most of the war debts, however, proved "bad," and inclusion of them in the picture of the debtor-creditor position of the country proved unrealistic. Their exclusion from the account reduced the increment in net holdings of the United States abroad by nearly half.

All in all, the dollar value of international debts and investments in the world at the end of 1919 was probably close to $39–$40 billion, some $4–$5 billion less than in mid–1914. On the other hand, the real value of each dollar — as well as other currency units converted into dollars at prevailing exchange rates — had declined as a result of the general rise of prices, so that each billion dollars in 1919 had only 50–60 per cent of the real value of a billion dollars in the middle of 1914. Thus World War I resulted not only in a redistribution of international debts and investments but also in a drastic reduction of their total amount.

RECOVERY AFTER WORLD WAR I

Postwar recovery brought a revival of the international movement of capital on a scale that for a time suggested a return to the prewar type of international financial relations. After the economic crisis in the 1930's, however, it became obvious that this would not take place. A landslide of exchange controls and trade restrictions undermined the confidence of investors in foreign ventures unless special guarantees of the security of loans were at hand. Where such guarantees were not given, there was a tendency to liquidate existing foreign investments rather than assume new financial commitments.[36]

For a closer analysis of the movement of international investments, the whole interwar period can be conveniently divided in two sections — before and after the economic crisis of the 1930's.

The principal capital markets — the United Kingdom and the United States — were operating smoothly enough between 1924 and 1930, together providing approximately $800 million in new capital annually. On a smaller scale, foreign investments were made by Canada, Belgium, the Netherlands, Czechoslovakia, Italy and Sweden. The capital market of France was disorganized by protracted inflation. In all, the value of international investments averaged $1,000 million net a year.

The favorite site for international investments at that time was Germany, which absorbed some $4.2 billion worth of foreign loans and credits in 1924–30. Eastern Europe and South America also attracted foreign capital. The United Kingdom continued the traditional policy of long-term investments in colonial areas.

The general flow of international investments is shown in a condensed and simplified form in Table 78, which gives the net balances of inward and outward movement of capital in two dozen countries. Inward movement of capital (borrowing or withdrawal of old investments) is shown with a plus sign, like exports in a trade balance. Outward movement (lending or repayment of old debts) carries a minus sign, like imports.

The data for individual countries are not equally reliable. In some cases, the movement of capital can be ascertained only indirectly, as the balancing item in the account of all other current international transactions of the country, without allowance for errors and omissions in the records of these transactions. This method, among others, has been used in estimating the flow of British foreign investments. Figures computed in this way are shown in parentheses in Table 78 as a warning of the wide margin of error.

The movement of United States foreign investments and debts in the interwar years requires closer examination. The net inflow and outflow of capital was the combined result of several factors. Long-term capital movements include changes in United States investments in foreign securities (portfolio) and direct investments in foreign commercial and industrial enterprises. Portfolio assets change as a result of new issues of securities on the United States market for the account of foreign governments or concerns, amortization payments on outstanding securities, and purchases and sales of foreign securities. Movement of long-term capital investments also include changes in foreign portfolio investments in the United States. It should likewise include changes in direct investments of foreign capital in the United States, which were not recorded before World War II. Short-term capital movement reflects changes in the United States current claims abroad and foreign claims on the United States (fluctuations in banking and brokerage balances, holdings of United States currency abroad and movement of other short-term funds).

Each of these items depends upon the interplay of numerous forces related to business conditions in the United States and abroad. As an illustration of the complexity of the mechanism which controls movement of capital, it suffices to mention that there is a clear negative correlation between the fluctuation of foreign bonds in the United States and the volume of domestic industrial production: an increase in production is followed in the next calendar quarter by a setback in the volume of new foreign issues and vice versa. (See Figure 43.)

The United States was a capital-exporting country from 1919 to 1930, fell back to its prewar position of capital importer during the depression, and remained in this position until the outbreak of World War II. (See Table 79.[37])

In its survey of the place of the United States in the world economy in the interwar years, the U.S. Department of Commerce stressed the role of capital transactions in balancing the world supply of, and demand for, U.S. dollars. (See Figure 44.) The Department pointed out:

The relatively close correspondence between the supply and use of dollars and their common upward movements from 1922 to 1929 suggests the existence and successful operation of a balancing mechanism relating the various items through forces inherent in the economic system of the period. Our imports, loans, and other payments undoubtedly helped to sustain and promote economic growth and

---

36. **9,** p. 6.

37. The totals in this table differ appreciably from the data shown in Table 78.

TABLE 78

CAPITAL MOVEMENT: NET ANNUAL CHANGE, SELECTED COUNTRIES,[a] 1923–38

(*Inward Movement* (+); *Outward Movement* (-). *Millions of Dollars*)

Year	United States	Canada	Argentina	United Kingdom	Ireland	France
1923	+21	-45.9	+32.4	-700	(-17.0)	-54.5
1924	-329	-109.3	+85.3	-380	(-17.1)	+22.3
1925	-520	-176.7	+31.4	-261	(-14.8)	...
1926	-219	-85.3	+134.2	+34	...	...
1927	-511	-11.0	+72.0	-385	...	(-504)
1928	-899	-86.7	+110.0	-569	...	(-236)
1929	-185	+162.4	-6.7	-574	...	(+20)
1930	-678	+308.5	+233.3	-112	...	(+257)
1931	-485	+33.1	-88.7	-313	-7.0	(+791)
1932	-242	-10.0	-20.6	(+231)	-7.5	(+917)
1933	-344	-23.7	+59.4	(+650)	+12.2	(+30)
1934	+215	-69.7	+22.8	(+421)	+13.0	(+102)
1935	+908	-102.5	+7.0	(+111)	-1.7	(-555)
1936	+699	-150.0	+60.8	(+724)	-7.3	(-698)
1937	+518	-117.4	-85.6	(+394)	+6.0	(-98)
1938	+194	-94.0	+26.5	(-23)	-1.5	(+122)

Year	Netherlands	Denmark	Sweden	Norway	Finland	Germany
1923	...	+14.6	+33.1	+34.7	(+6.2)	...
1924	...	+2.4	+12.7	+22.7	(-6.7)	+468
1925	...	-2.7	-32.2	+27.2	(-2.3)	+927
1926	...	+11.7	+7.5	+6.6	(-0.5)	+208
1927	...	+11.3	-24.4	+22.7	(-1.9)	+1,037
1928	...	0.0	-38.9	+33.5	(+40.4)	+967
1929	(+26.9)	-9.4	-26.0	+13.0	(+12.0)	+482
1930	(+43.0)	+2.1	-83.9	+37.2	(-4.8)	+129
1931	(+286.6)	+29.1	+113.1	+34.6	(-23.5)	-540
1932	(+122.6)	-17.7	-19.0	-17.5	(-18.2)	-103
1933	(+58.7)	-10.9	-33.5	-14.4	(-19.7)	-131
1934	-27.3	+5.8	-45.5	-11.8	(-20.9)	-82
1935	-59.5	-0.6	-3.4	+4.8	(-14.4)	+50
1936	-10.3	-1.5	-5.5	-3.0	-15.8	...
1937	-69.9	-16.3	-28.6	-22.3	-15.1	...
1938	+41.3	+17.8	-8.2	-9.4	-5.7	...

(*Continued on facing page*)

the rise in incomes abroad and thus supported foreign demand for our goods and services during the period as a whole. There is also some evidence of year-to-year adjustments of a compensating nature between the various transactions.[38]

The weakness of United States investment operations in the 1920's was their haphazard character. The Department of Commerce describes them as follows:

One of the most critical features in this country's international transactions was the behavior of capi-

tal. To regard the United States' position as a lending country as artificial or improper would be totally unwarranted. There was no inherent reason why there should have been an immediate adjustment in foreign trade to the newly acquired creditor status at the end of the war period (although the higher tariffs of 1921 and 1922 could only increase the difficulty of the eventual adaptation). Foreign countries needed and demanded American goods and American capital, and it was natural that the United States should have supplied both. The mistakes were rather in the particular behavior of our lending operations — not so much in our investment policy as in the lack of one.

---

38. **26**, p. 3.

TABLE 78—*continued*

Year	Poland	Czechoslovakia	Hungary	Italy	Greece	Japan
1923	+23.0	. . .	. . .	. . .	. . .	. . .
1924	+36.1	−10.2	+14.7	−23.9	. . .	+225.7
1925	+119.2	−55.3	+26.7	−17.0	. . .	+67.9
1926	−1.7	−43.1	+25.7	−25.7	. . .	. . .
1927	+56.7	−68.6	+83.9	. . .	. . .	+22.1
1928	+124.6	−56.4	+87.9	(+133.1)	. . .	+54.0
1929	+66.6	−25.0	+36.4	+96.9	+44.6	−26.2
1930	−46.7	−9.4	+36.6	+46.5	+34.3	−145.9
1931	−0.4	+25.2	+50.2	−50.0	+36.8	−153.3
1932	−3.6	+8.7	+1.1	−23.0	+11.6	−92.6
1933	−9.0	+9.7	+0.1	. . .	−3.0	−49.5
1934	−13.2	−4.6	−2.8	. . .	+6.1	−22.8
1935	−12.1	−5.8	−8.1	. . .	+6.8	−63.3
1936	−7.0	−8.4	−10.1	. . .	+17.2	−46.2
1937	−0.7	−12.3	. . .	. . .	+16.3	. . .
1938	+18.5	. . .	. . .	. . .	+12.8	. . .

Year	Iraq [b]	India	Netherlands Indies [b]	Union of South Africa	Australia [b]	New Zealand
1923	. . .	. . .	. . .	+4.4	+17.8	+25.0
1924	. . .	−18.6	. . .	+37.7	+212.7	+24.6
1925	. . .	+81.9	. . .	. . .	+0.6	+33.1
1926	. . .	−70.1	. . .	. . .	+182.4	+67.2
1927	+3.3	+177.9	−24.9	+30.4	(+257)	−2.9
1928	+0.2	+29.7	−7.6	+13.8	(+193)	−4.6
1929	+3.7	+4.5	+31.8	−8.6	(+166)	+53.3
1930	+2.9	+63.6	+31.8	+48.2	+192	+49.1
1931	+3.6	+138.3	+32.2	+1.9	+15	+1.8
1932	−3.7	+9.6	+41.8	+22.2	−52	−11.7
1933	+2.8	−38.3	+19.3	−7.0	−64	+47.1
1934	+4.1	−75.7	−10.4	+36.4	−64	−108.8
1935	−1.6	−42.7	−11.7	−9.9	−4	+85.2
1936	+3.1	−26.7	−33.8	−29.6	−69	−10.0
1937	+1.9	−73.8	−21.6	+12.8	+15	+17.8
1938	+7.0	+11.7	−10.1	. . .	. . .	. . .

Sources: **4**, 1913–1927, pp. 251–53 and *passim;* **1**, 1936, p. 101, 1937, p. 104, 1938, pp. 14–19; cf. **3**, 1911–1925 and **5**, 1931–1932.

a. Many countries, among them the United States, have revised the original estimates of international capital transactions reproduced in this table. Some figures therefore deviate from those given in more recent sources.

b. Fiscal year ended in the respective calendar year.

Under the high-pressure salesmanship methods by which foreign issues were solicited and sold, our loans proved to be their own undoing. The flotation of one loan frequently came to be regarded as adequate justification for further issues to the same borrower or the same country without adequate regard to the growing burden of indebtedness. In some instances, notably in loans to Germany, new lending was vigorously prosecuted long after warnings from high places were sounded. The very operations that expanded the incomes and consumption of foreign countries and made them increasingly dependent on an unfailing source of exchange thus helped to ensure the inevitability of a change and the probability that it would be disastrously abrupt and complete.

Another weakness in American investment activity was that our issuing houses never really regarded foreign issues as more than a side line, which they exploited for a time but felt free to drop when more attractive opportunities presented themselves at home. In these circumstances it is not surprising that, under the intense competition of the stock-market boom, new flotations for foreign countries were suddenly curtailed in the middle of 1928 and,

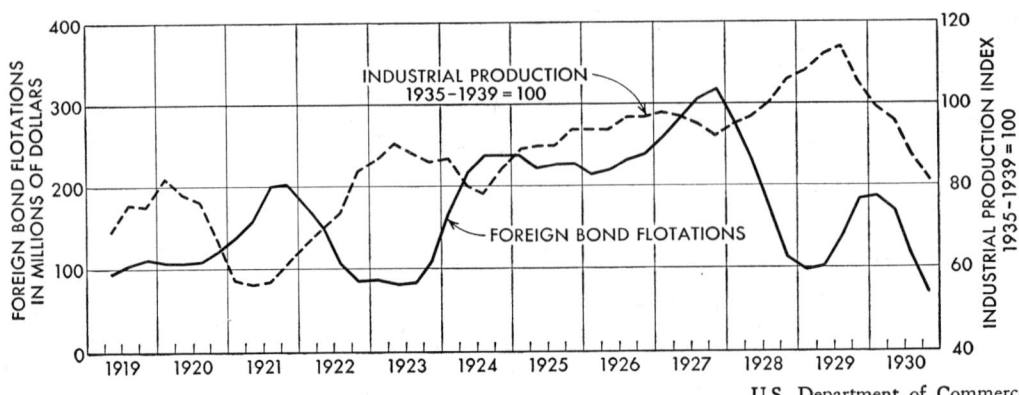

U.S. Department of Commerce

FIGURE 43. FOREIGN INVESTMENTS: VALUE OF QUARTERLY FOREIGN BOND FLOTATIONS AND INDEX OF INDUSTRIAL PRODUCTION, UNITED STATES, 1919–30

The bond series, a quarterly moving average, has been shifted one quarter to the left in charting. The index of industrial production is a quarterly average of seasonally adjusted monthly data.

TABLE 79

CAPITAL MOVEMENTS BETWEEN THE UNITED STATES AND FOREIGN COUNTRIES, 1919–39

(Millions of Dollars)

	Long-term Capital Movement										
	United States Investments Abroad						Forign Portfolio Investments in the United States [a]			Net Long-term Capital Movement	Net Short-term Capital Movement	Grand Total, Net
	Portfolio				Direct Investments	Total						
Year	New Issues	Amortization	Transactions	Net Flow			Amortization	Transactions	Net Flow			
1919	−$371	+$335	−$39	−$75	−$94	−$169	−$20	−$195	−$215	−$384	...	−$384
1920	−500	+581	−481	−400	−154	−554	−20	−258	−278	−832	...	−832
1921	−567	+285	−195	−477	−111	−588	−20	+16	−4	−592	...	−592
1922	−666	+134	−137	−669	−153	−822	−20	+27	+7	−815	...	−815
1923	−317	+82	b	−235	−148	−383	−20	+358 c	+338	−45	−$33	−78
1924	−823	+120	b	−703	−182	−885	−20	+205 c	+185	−700	+119	−581
1925	−824	+221	b	−603	−268	−871	−20	+322 c	+302	−570	−106	−676
1926	−921	+296	+155	−470	−351	−821	−20	+115	+95	−726	+419	−307
1927	−1,114	+285	+193	−636	−351	−987	−20	−30	−50	−1,037	+585	−452
1928	−1,019	+361	−94	−752	−558	−1,310	−20	+483	+463	−847	−348	−1,195
1929	−415	+276	+105	−34	−602	−636	−20	+378	+358	−278	−4	−282
1930	−775	+300	+405	−70	−294	−364	−20	+86	+66	−298	−479	−777
1931	−190	+257	+283	+350	−222	+128	−20	+86	+66	+194	−637	−443
1932	−51	+172	+146	+267	−16	+251	−20	−6	−26	+225	−446	−221
1933	−83	+123	−120	−80	+32	−48	−15	+140	+125	+77	−419	−342
1934	−17	+114	+105	+202	−17	+185	−15	+30	+15	+200	+222	+422
1935	−53	+185	−50	+82	+34	+116	−15	+335	+320	+436	+1,072	+1,508
1936	−47	+181	+55	+189	−12	+177	−15	+615	+600	+777	+431	+1,208
1937	−13	+190	+64	+241	+35	+276	−15	+260	+245	+521	+356	+877
1938	−53	+87	−10	+24	+16	+40	−15	+72	+57	+97	+344	+441
1939	−53	+93	+64	+104	+9	+113	−15	−71	−86	+27	+1,470	+1,497

Source: **26**, Table 3.

a. No data available on direct investment of foreign capital in the United States.

b. Included in transactions in foreign investments in the United States.

c. Includes transactions in U.S. portfolio investments abroad.

aside from a brief upturn in the first half of 1930, failed to recover thereafter.[39]

Before the great depression, the United States had accumulated foreign investments with a book value of $17.2 billion. Foreign assets of the

39. **26**, p. 4.

United Kingdom amounted at that time to $18.1 billion. The total — $35.3 billion — represents the bulk of international investments at the peak of prosperity after World War I. The foreign assets of other countries were estimated at $14.6 billion, distributed as follows (in billions): France, $3.5; the Netherlands, $2.3; Germany,

BILLIONS OF DOLLARS

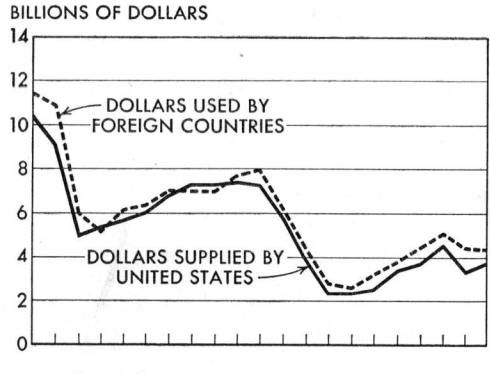

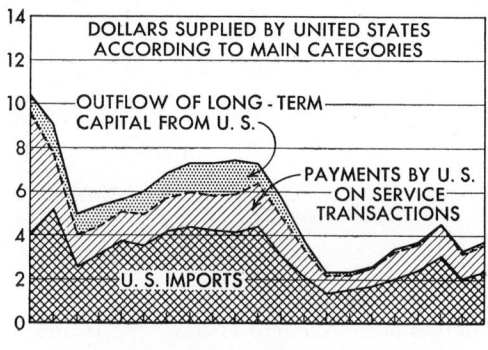

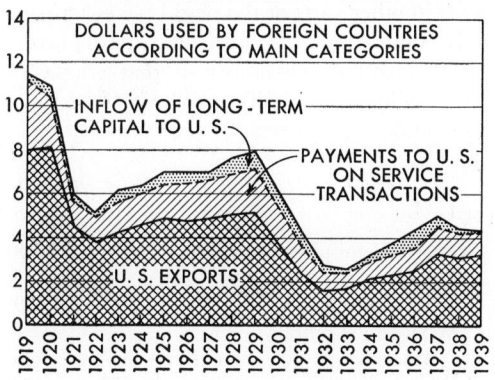

U.S. Department of Commerce

FIGURE 44. INTERNATIONAL TRANSACTIONS OF THE
UNITED STATES: DOLLARS SUPPLIED TO
FOREIGN COUNTRIES, 1919–39

$1.1; Switzerland, $2.0; other countries (including Canada, Belgium, Sweden, Japan, India, Australia and New Zealand), $5.7.[40]

These figures give a total value of foreign investments in 1929 close to $50 billion. It is possible, however, that this total includes some dubious items, for example, French vagrant capital which was transferred abroad in flight from inflation and taxes but was hardly invested abroad.

On the other hand, the total agrees fairly well with our estimate of the flow of foreign investments after World War I.

To judge from the recorded movement of capital, total investments may have increased in the decade 1919–29 by approximately $10 billion, from $39–$40 billion to $49–$50 billion.

To sum up, it seems that the dollar value of international investments in 1929 was some 12–14 per cent higher than in 1914. On the other hand, the real value of the 1929 dollar was 75 to 80 prewar cents. It is fairly certain, therefore, that the real value of foreign investments in 1929 was less than in 1914.

THE GREAT DEPRESSION

The great depression, heralded by the collapse of the stock market in the United States in the autumn of 1929, was an important turning point in the flow of international transactions. New York was knocked out as a capital market. After a brief spell of exceptionally active investment business in the first half of 1930, flotation of foreign loans in the United States ceased almost completely for more than a decade.

If perhaps the exhaustion of favorable investment opportunities near the close of the twenties was more apparent than real, it quickly became a reality because of the rapid spread of the depression and of a depression psychology, by defaults on outstanding loans, and by unfavorable political and exchange developments abroad. Thus little basis or possibility for a renewed outflow of American capital was afforded. On the contrary, from 1931 on there was a substantial reverse flow through a reduction in previous investments abroad.[41]

Reduction of United States imports and cessation of investment activity left the world at large short of dollars and necessitated far-reaching readjustments in payment balances. The problem was aggravated by the existence of fixed obligations, including war-debt payments of some $900 million a year due to the United States.

Although the term "dollar shortage" had not yet been coined, the developments in Europe in 1930–32 can be properly described as an increasing shortage of dollars. To the extent that debtor countries tried to meet their dollar obligations, at the same time defending their exchange parity and monetary reserves, their domestic economy was increasingly exposed to deflationary pressure.[42]

40. **43**, Appendix A.

41. **26**, p. 5.
42. **26**, p. 6.

TABLE 80

FOREIGN ASSETS AND LIABILITIES OF THE UNITED STATES, 1931–39 [a]

(*Millions of Dollars*)

	United States Private Investments Abroad (+)				Foreign Private Investments in the United States (−)				
	Long-term		Short-term		Long-term		Short-term		Net Creditor Position
Year	Port-folio	Direct	term	Total	Port-folio	Direct	term	Total	
1931	$6,235	$7,815	$ 780	$14,830	—	—	$ 965	...	...
1932	5,525	7,840	595	13,960	...	...	...	...	...
1933	5,730	7,485	620	13,835	...	...	...	...	...
1934	5,300	7,820	1,235	14,355	$3,145	$1,800	680	$5,625	$8,730
1935	4,490	7,555	410	12,455	2,035	680	795	3,510	8,945
1936	4,435	6,475	315	11,225	2,975	740	1,120	4,835	6,390
1937	4,205	6,870	720	11,795	4,230	1,880	1,920	8,030	3,765
1938	4,050	7,020	690	11,760	4,575	1,895	2,230	8,700	3,060
1939	3,785	7,110	595	11,490	4,310	1,980	3,295	9,585	1,905

Sources: **1**, 1936, p. 226 and 1938, p. 144; **24**, p. 110. Original figures have been adjusted to 1939 data largely on the basis of the 1941 census of foreign-owned assets in the United States. (See **28**; cf. **6**, 1939–1945, pp. 102–07). Figures given here are comparable to those in **9**, p. 110.

a. For more recent years, see Table 86.

The severe depression in Germany further strengthened the deflationary forces in the world economy. Prices, falling lower and lower, acted as carriers of depression.[43]

The striking feature of the depression of the 1930's was its lasting effect on the balance of payments and international position of the United States. After 1932 the United States ceased to be an active capital market; after 1934, it became an importer of capital. It is true that a large part of the funds transferred to the country was not invested in productive enterprises but was held in American banks and used occasionally in stock-exchange speculations.[44]

In brief, the creditor-debtor position of the United States changed under the impact of the depression as follows: in 1931, its private investments abroad totaled $14.8 billion as compared with relatively small liabilities. In 1939, its foreign investments had shrunk to $11.5 billion, while its indebtedness had increased to $9.6 billion. The net creditor position of the United States was estimated at $13–$14 billion in 1931 and at $1.9 billion in 1938. The depression had wiped out most of its assets abroad. (See Table 80.)

In 1939 the United States was a debtor in relation to Europe and a creditor in relation to the countries of the Western Hemisphere. Its investments in other parts of the world were comparatively unimportant. Private long-term investments abroad in December of that year were distributed geographically as follows (in millions of dollars): [45]

Area	Total	Direct	Portfolio
Total	$10,895	$7,110	$3,785
Western Hemisphere	7,734	4,986	2,748
Canada and Newfoundland	3,722	2,023	1,699
Mexico and Central America	663	637	26
West Indies	836	752	84
South America	2,513	1,574	939
Europe	2,081	1,332	749
Asia	590	420	170
Africa	117	98	19
Oceania	222	123	99
International Bank capital	26	26	—
Unknown	125	125	—

On the other hand, almost all foreign investments in the United States were held by European nations. In capital accounts, the United States was in debt to Europe for nearly $4 billion

43. **46**, p. 300.
44. **26**, p. 9.

45. **6**, 1939–45, p. 95. The totals agree with the data for 1939 in Table 80. For definition of direct and portfolio investments see p. 188.

TABLE 81

FOREIGN INVESTMENTS OF THE UNITED KINGDOM, 1929–37

(Millions of U.S. Dollars [a]*)*

		Investments				
Year	Total	Loans to Central and Local Governments	Investments in British Companies	Investments in Foreign and Colonial Companies	Investments Not Covered by the Inquiry [b]	Income from Investments
1929	$18,233	$6,890	$5,793	$4,090	$1,460	$1,127
1930	18,093	6,981	5,851	3,801	1,460	1,015
1931	12,482	4,861	4,082	2,561	978	569
1932	11,937	4,695	3,951	2,357	934	513
1933	18,753	7,570	6,195	3,556	1,432	767
1934	18,370	7,414	6,074	3,398	1,484	786
1935	18,665	7,408	6,092	3,440	1,725	846
1936	18,472	7,072	5,988	3,449	1,963	903
1937	18,752	7,120	6,045	3,589	1,998	988

Source: **1**, 1938, p. 135.

a. Converted at exchange rates at the end of the respective year. £1 equals $4.882 in 1929; $4.857 in 1930; $3.374 in 1931; $3.279 in 1932; $5.116 in 1933; $4.946 in 1934; $4.929 in 1935; $4.908 in 1936; $4.996 in 1937.

b. I.e., the source of this table: **1**.

and had net assets close to $6 billion in other parts of the world.

The United Kingdom emerged from the depression with increased assets abroad. According to the widely accepted estimates published annually by the *Economic Journal,* British holdings of foreign securities and direct investments abroad totaled £3,753.4 million in 1937 as compared with £3,734.7 million in 1929. Converted into dollars at the actual exchange rate, the increase was from $18.2 billion at the peak of prosperity to $18.7 billion after the depression. (See Table 81.) Moreover, both wholesale prices and living costs were lower in 1937 than in 1929, so that the real value of British investments abroad in 1937 appears appreciably higher than before the depression.

Growth of investments abroad in the decade 1929–38 was recorded likewise in Canada (a gain of $130 million), Sweden ($90 million), Norway ($60 million), New Zealand ($70 million), India ($200 million) and in Japan.

BALANCES OF PAYMENTS, 1927–38

Balances of payments in the late 1930's were deeply affected by the measures taken by various governments in fighting depression.

The U.S. Department of Commerce describes the situation as follows:

Foreign countries could halt the drop in their economic activity and institute measures for domestic expansion only by freeing themselves from external deflationary pressure. While in many countries the immediate force was exerted by the wild flight of capital, the basic strain emanated largely from this country's crippled economy and the drastic cut in the supply of dollars.

The principal measures of adjustment resorted to by other countries, most of which involved a radical departure from the gold standard and the previous world commercial system in general, were as follows: (1) Abandonment of gold parities and depreciation of foreign currencies with respect to the dollar; (2) general tariff increases aimed at curtailing total imports and promoting domestic production; (3) preferential tariff and commercial arrangements designed to foster trade among the participants and to divert trade from other sources of supply; (4) direct trade and exchange control through quotas and licensing requirements for the purpose of forcing trade along selected channels and restricting the use of foreign exchange to the available supply.

These methods were used in various combinations according to place and time. They were accompanied, moreover, by various types of measures for internal expansion and were frequently carried far beyond the requirements of external adjustment. In some countries, notably Germany, they eventually became instruments for violent political as well as economic nationalism.[46]

International transactions on the eve of World War II were largely controlled by governments through licenses and regulations. The general

46. **26**, pp. 6–7.

tendency was toward greater equilibrium in single bilateral accounts, such as merchandise trade and exchange of services. The flow of interest and dividends slowed down. The movement of capital proceeded on a reduced scale. The general picture of international transactions was as confusing as the network of trade balances. (See Chapter 3.) The balance of payments in this period in selected countries is presented briefly in Table 82, which records the balances of the

TABLE 82

BALANCES OF PAYMENTS OF SELECTED COUNTRIES, 1927–38

(*Net Export or Inward Movement of Capital* (+); *Net Import or Outward Movement of Capital* (−). *Millions of U.S. Gold Dollars*)

Country and Year	Merchandise, Services, Interest and Dividends				Gold	Movement of Capital	Errors and Omissions
	Total	Mer-chandise Trade	Services	Interest, Dividends			
United States							
1928	+$734	+$738	−$684	+$680	+$272	−$899	+$107
1930	+575	+386	−580	+769	−278	−678	−381
1933	+174	+67	−218	+325	−139	−344	−31
1936	−192	−152	−235	+195	−608	+699	−101
1938	+474	+451	−174	+197	−968	+194	−300
Canada							
1927	+37	+83	+172	−218	+26	−11	+52
1930	−282	−188	+194	−288	+3	+308	+39
1933	−48	+75	+41	−164	+64	−24	−8
1936	+106	+158	+86	−138	+77	−150	+32
1938	+17	+56	+103	−142	+92	−94	+15
Argentina							
1927	+22	+278	−70	−186	−83	+72	+11
1930	−313	−98	−43	−172	+26	+233	−54
1933	−62	+58	−13	−107	—	+59	−3
1936	+22	+131	−16	−92	—	+61	+83
1938	−99	+9	−27	−81	—	+26	−73
United Kingdom							
1927	+399	−1,883	+1,066	+1,217	−15	...	...
1930	+136	−1,878	+944	+1,071	−24	...	...
1933	0	−871	+341	+530	−650	...	...
1936	−53	−1,015	+359	+603	−671	...	...
1938	−159	−1,089	+352	+578	+182	...	...
France							
1927	+483	+4	+451	+28	+21	...	...
1930	+202	−506	+634	+74	−460	...	...
1933	−112	−353	+169	+72	+81	...	...
1936	−111	−325	+64	+150	+809	...	...
1938	−5	−239	+97	+137	+117	...	...
Netherlands							
1930	−49	−281	... +232 ...		+6	...	...
1933	−86	−201	... +115 ...		+27	...	...
1936	+15	−111	+66	+60	−23	+10	+2
1938	+7	−123	+78	+52	+80	−41	+46
Denmark							
1927	−11	−52	+54	−13	+7	+11	+7
1930	−5	−31	+40	−14	—	+2	−3
1933	+7	−8	+26	−11	—	−11	−4
1936	0	−14	+26	−12	—	−2	−2
1938	+14	−11	+35	−10	—	−18	−4

(*Continued on facing page*)

TABLE 82—*continued*

Country and Year	Merchandise, Services, Interest and Dividends				Gold	Movement of Capital	Errors and Omissions
	Total	Mer-chandise Trade	Dividends	Interest, Services			
Sweden							
1927	+$65	+$8	+$52	+$5	—	–$24	+$41
1930	+26	–31	+52	+5	—	–84	–58
1933	+36	–3	+26	+13	–$7	–33	–4
1936	+19	–18	+25	+12	–32	–5	–18
1938	+4	–36	+40		–25	+8	–13
Norway							
1927	–17	–62	+61	–16	—	+23	+6
1930	–28	–72	+63	–19	—	+37	+9
1933	+14	–11	+39	–14	+1	–14	+1
1936	+8	–27	+46	–11	–4	–3	+1
1938	+13	–53	+75	–9	–6	–8	–1
Finland							
1927	+2	–2	+12	–8	—	...	...
1930	+6	+5	+11	–10	–1	...	...
1933	+19	+20	+7	–8	—	...	...
1936	+16	+13	+7	–4	–2	–16	–2
1938	+7	–1	+10	–2	—	–6	+1
Germany							
1927	–1,012	–688	–242	–82	–24	+1,036	—
1930	–125	+392	–279	–238	–3	+129	—
1933	+27	+157	+37	–167	+103	–131	—
1935	–24	+27	+80	–131	–25	...	...
Spain							
1932	–23	–52	+34	–5	—	–16	–39
Hungary							
1927	–89	–66	–2	–21	—	+84	–5
1930	–21	+13	–1	–33	–1	+37	+15
1933	+6	+12	–1	–5	–1	—	+5
1936	+12	+12	+4	–4	—	–10	+2
Italy							
1928	–131	–385	+305	–51	–3	...	...
1930	–41	–275	+285	–51	–5	...	...
1932	+27	–75	+125	–23	–4	...	...
Greece							
1930	–28	–64	+29	+7	—	+34	—
1933	+3	–17	+24	–4	—	–3	—
1936	–17	–24	+9	–2	—	+17	—
1938	–12	–29	+17	—	—	+13	—
Yugoslavia							
1927	–23	–32	+29	–20	—	+20	–3
1935	–1	+4	+9	–14	–1	—	–2
Turkey							
1927	–22	–21	+3	–4	—	+21	–1
1930	+6	+7	+2	–3	—	+1	+7
1933	+12	+6	+6	—	—	–2	+10
China							
1928	–89	–187	+213	–115	–4	+47	–46
1930	–125	–181	+151	–95	+15	+62	–48
1933	–103	–163	+82	–22	+39	+6	–58
1936	+56	–7	+82	–19	+8	+11	+75

(*Continued on following page*)

TABLE 82—*continued*

Country and Year	Merchandise, Services, Interest and Dividends				Gold	Movement of Capital	Errors and Omissions
	Total	Mer-chandise Trade	Services	Interest, Dividends			
Japan							
1927	−$67	−$134	−$69	−$2	+$17	+$22	−$28
1930	−14	−76	+75	−13	+142	−146	−18
1933	+6	−11	+28	−11	+7	−50	−37
1936	+22	−16	+34	+4	—	−46	−24
India							
1927–1928	−55	+187	−127	−115	−66	...	...
1930–1931	−45	+136	−58	−123	−47	...	...
1933–1934	−46	+66	−30	−82	+139	...	...
1936–1937	+12	+125	−41	−72	+62	...	...
1938–1939	−87	+12	−41	−58	+28	...	...
Netherlands Indies							
1927	+63	+300	−87	−150	−6	−25	+32
1930	−61	+107	−64	−104	+1	+32	−28
1933	−30	+58	−46	−42	+15	+19	+4
1936	+44	+123	−34	−45	+8	−34	+18
1938	−35	+65	−35	−65	+6	−10	−39
Union of South Africa							
1927	−238	−136	−22	−80	+212	+30	+4
1930	−257	−161	−22	−74	+225	+48	+16
1933	−160	−89	−13	−58	+229	−7	+62
1936	−255	−174	−17	−64	+241	−30	−44
Australia							
1928–1929	−221	−45	+5	−181	+13	+169	−39
1931–1932	+15	+122	+9	−116	+35	−52	−2
1934–1935	−56	+27	+2	−85	+19	+59	+22
1937–1938	−72		−72		+26	+15	−31
New Zealand							
1928–1929	+4	+48	−2	−42	+5	+32	+41
1931–1932	−8	+32	−4	−36	+5	+7	+4
1934–1935	−1	+25	−3	−23	+10	+52	+61
1937–1938	−11	+12	−2	−21	+3	+15	+7

Source: **1**, 1938, pp. 14–19.

main types of transactions rather than the transactions themselves; that is, the balance of merchandise trade rather than exports and imports of merchandise; the balance of services (freight, commission earnings of banks, travel and tourist expenditures, and so forth); the balance of interest and dividend receipts and payments; the balance of gold shipments. In all these accounts, plus (+) indicates an export balance and minus (−), a surplus of imports over exports. Earnings of merchant fleets, expenditures of foreign travelers in the reporting country, remittances of workers employed abroad and shipments of gold — either as domestic produce, as in the Union of South Africa, or as a means of settlement of current accounts — are handled in the same way.

The total of these balances (the first column in Table 82) indicates whether all current transactions — except gold shipments — during the calendar (or fiscal) year brought to the reporting country more credit (claims against other parties) or debit (commitments). Theoretically the balance must be offset by the movement of gold and capital in the opposite direction — inward movement (−) if the balance on current transactions is positive and outward movement (+) if it is negative. The transfer of capital takes place either in the form of a change in long-term assets and obligations of the country or as a change in short-term debts and credits. The actual movement of capital, however, does not necessarily equal the balance of current transactions. Wherever direct records of movement of capital are available, it appears that there is some discrepancy between the two movements, due to statistical errors and omissions. The magnitude and direction of error is indicated in the last column of the table.

Table 82 shows a striking reduction in the customary surplus of imports in the merchandise trade of the United Kingdom, France, the Netherlands, Denmark, Norway, Italy, Greece, China and Japan. For most of these countries, the deficit in merchandise trade was offset by the surplus in the account of services: shipping and related services in the United Kingdom, France, the Netherlands, Denmark, Norway and Japan; expenditures of tourists and remittances of emigrants in Italy and Greece; a combination of various service incomes in China. Most of the export balances in service accounts declined in the 1930's.

The balances of interest and dividends in Table 82 reflect the debtor-creditor position of the reporting countries: the United States and especially the United Kingdom have large receipts (+); France, the Netherlands and Sweden have smaller but regular receipts; most other countries listed in Table 82, including Canada, Australia, New Zealand, Germany, Denmark and Norway — all of them debtor countries — record payments (−) under this heading.

Total balances of current transactions in merchandise trade, services, interest and dividend payments were highly unstable at that time. Few countries had throughout 1927–38 an export balance (+) which would suggest a continuous growth of their assets abroad or reduction of their indebtedness (in both cases, outward capital movement) and a negative balance in movement of capital. Likewise there were few countries in which the balance of current transactions was continuously negative (−) and the flow of capital was directed inward (plus in the column showing capital movement). In most countries the movement of capital was directed outward in some years and inward in others, as in the United States, Canada, the Netherlands, Denmark, Norway and Australia. (See Table 82.)

STATUS OF INTERNATIONAL INVESTMENTS, 1938

Data on international investments in 1938, strictly comparable with those cited on the preceding pages, are available for the United States and the United Kingdom. The book value of the combined investments of these two countries went down from about $35 billion in 1929–30 to $30 billion, in round numbers, in 1937–38. There are indications that the foreign assets of other countries were moving in opposite directions at this time. Gains — especially in the Netherlands and Japan — outweighed withdrawals of investments recorded by other countries, especially Switzerland and Germany. The balances of foreign assets and liabilities recorded by banks do not always give a clear picture of the balance of foreign investment: very often such transactions cannot be segregated from migration of idle capital seeking a safe place in an increasingly unsafe world.

If foreign assets of all nations except the United States and the United Kingdom totaled $14–$15 billion in 1929–30, the total was likely to have increased to $17 or even $18 billion by 1938. This would bring the grand total of all international investments to $47 or $48 billion on the eve of World War II. The total is somewhat larger than in 1914 but the difference is within the margin of error of both estimates. When the general upward shift in prices is taken into account, it appears that the real value of international investments did not increase from 1914 to 1938 and the value in relation to the value of world trade and income rather declined.

The preceding estimate — $47–$48 billion in 1938 — is open to criticism, however. The Brookings Institution, on the basis of a careful study of foreign debts and assets of more than fourscore countries, arrived at $53 billion for foreign investments, loans and credits (claims) and $55 billion for foreign obligations.[47] These totals, however, seem too high.[48] Indeed, they are likely to include considerable amounts of debts in default, though not repudiated officially, and repatriated bonds. They show some depreciated bonds and stocks at parity value rather than market price. In the opinion of the present writers, a more realistic estimate of total international loans and investments in 1938 is likely to lie not far from $50 billion.

This judgment, however, does not belittle the value of the Brookings survey, especially in the analysis of composition of foreign assets and liabilities. This study shows that before World War II the British controlled 59 per cent of

---

47. **40**, pp. 52–53.
48. This refers particularly to British holdings.

foreign investments in Asia and Oceania, 54 per cent in Africa, 42 per cent in North America, 45 per cent in Middle and South America. The British share in foreign investments in Europe was surprisingly low — 18.5 per cent as compared with 25.4 per cent for the United States.[49] (See Table 83.)

The net foreign investments (claims minus obligations) of the United Kingdom amounted, according to this estimate, to $21.6 billion in 1938 as compared with $4.5 billion for the United States.[50]

The general geographic distribution of foreign investments of the two nations remained the same as in 1914. The bulk (69 per cent) of United States foreign investments was in the Western Hemisphere. (See Figure 45.)

Impact of World War II

World War II brought deep and far-reaching changes in the status of foreign investments in the world. The United Kingdom sold some 20 per cent of its foreign assets and incurred new debts so that its net credits abroad have been reduced to one fourth of the prewar value. The United States, after entering the war, waived all claims based on deliveries of military materials to the Allies and emerged from the war with a net indebtedness. Foreign assets of Germany, France, Belgium, the Netherlands, Italy and Japan have either been wiped out or largely reduced. On the other hand, Canada, Australia and New Zealand have paid part of their debts to the United Kingdom. India became a creditor of the British government. Latin American republics accumulated comfortable dollar and sterling balances and used part of them for purchasing foreign securities.

The international transactions of the United Kingdom and United States during World War II deserve particular attention.

INTERNATIONAL TRANSACTIONS OF THE UNITED KINGDOM

Early in World War II, the British tried to finance the war with their long-term securities abroad. Nearly all the marketable dollar securities of British nationals were compulsorily acquired for sale or pledge to finance purchase of

munitions and the construction of war plants in the United States.[51] Similar measures were taken with regard to other marketable securities owned by British nationals and concerns.

However, to offer bonds and stocks representing many billions of dollars at any price would have brought meager returns to the Exchequer. The British therefore restricted sales of securities to amounts that could be absorbed by the respective markets.[52] The largest operation of this type was carried out in India, where the United Kingdom transferred securities worth £332 million to the Indian government to pay for building airfields and other military installations and for equipping, supplying and paying Indian troops serving outside India. Similar arrangements were made with Canada, the Union of South Africa and, on a much smaller scale, Australia. Between 1938 and 1944 the United Kingdom disposed of long-term investments with a market value of £1,090 million. It also obtained long-term loans of £253 million, including an interest-free Canadian loan of £153 million.

These arrangements, however, fell short of the urgent needs of wartime. Under the lend-lease program, the British obtained free of charge all military supplies, foodstuffs and raw materials which the United States could provide for them, though they had to pay for purchases not only in Latin America but also in countries that were members of the Commonwealth. Payment was effected by commitments of the British government for the future, that is, by accumulation of sterling deposits by the creditor countries. Between 1938 and 1944 the United Kingdom incurred such debts totaling £1,930 million.

The results of these transactions may be summarized as follows (in millions of pounds): [53]

Foreign Assets, 1938

Long-term investments	£4,582
Minus: Long-term liabilities	400
Minus: Short-term liabilities	270
Net assets, 1938	3,912

Losses, 1938–44

Repatriation of long-term investments	£1,090
New long-term liabilities	253
New short-term liabilities	1,930
Minus: New short-term investments	275
Total losses	2,998
Net assets, 1944	914

---

49. Allowance for possible overstatement of British holdings would not change this picture greatly.

50. This figure differs appreciably from the revised figure in Table 80.

51. **34,** p. 4.
52. **40,** p. 19.
53. **34,** p. 22.

TABLE 83

FOREIGN INVESTMENTS: WORLD CREDITS AND OBLIGATIONS, 1938

(Millions of Dollars)

A. Credits Classified by Creditor Country and Investment Area

| Creditor Country | Total | Investment Area | | | | | | |
		North America [a]	Middle America	South America	Europe	Asia and Oceania	Africa	Not Identified [b]
World	$52,823	$15,136	$1,502	$7,507	$9,342	$14,581	$4,029	$726
United States	11,491	4,454	977	2,519	2,376	997	158	10
Canada	1,855	1,222	11	22	58	—	—	542
United Kingdom	22,905	6,308	416	3,630	1,725	8,601	2,165	60
Within empire	11,590	2,685	202	18	—	6,825	1,800	60
Other	11,315	3,623	214	3,612	1,725	1,776	365	—
France	3,859	539	10	282	1,035	906	1,044	43
Within empire	1,171	—	5	1	—	394	728	43
Other	2,688	539	5	281	1,035	512	316	—
Belgium–Luxembourg	1,253	156	—	344	314	84	355	—
Within empire	355	—	—	—	—	—	355	—
Other	898	156	—	344	314	84	—	—
Netherlands	4,818	1,016	63	82	1,643	1,998	16	—
Within empire	1,956	—	55	1	—	1,900	—	—
Other	2,862	1,016	8	81	1,643	98	16	—
Sweden	381	51	—	2	326	2	—	—
Germany	676	130	23	109	274	140	—	—
Czechoslovakia	160	5	—	—	155	—	—	—
Switzerland	1,610	767	1	57	780	5	—	—
Portugal	394	2	—	300	—	2	90	—
Spain	82	21	1	58	2	—	—	—
Italy	424	48	—	50	117	8	201	—
Within empire	201	—	—	—	—	—	201	—
Other	223	48	—	50	117	8	—	—
China	770	58	—	10	58	644	—	—
Japan	1,230	48	—	1	48	1,128	—	5
Egypt	106	9	—	—	97	—	—	—
Australia	254	18	—	—	224	12	—	—
Other countries	555	284	—	41	110	54	—	66

B. Obligations Classified by Debtor Country and Creditor Area

| Debtor Country | Total | Creditor Area | | | | | | |
		North America	Middle America [a]	South America	Europe	Asia and Oceania	Africa	Not Identified [b]
World	$54,957	$12,939	$68	$73	$36,733	$2,313	$112	$2,719
United States	7,007	1,214	68	40	5,384	182	15	104
Canada	6,628	3,795	—	—	2,725	—	—	108
Mexico	1,778	686	—	—	1,027	—	—	65
Guatemala	152	73	—	—	49	—	—	30
Cuba	807	638	—	—	144	—	—	25
British West Indies	210	10	—	—	200	—	—	—

(Continued on following page)

TABLE 83—*continued*

Debtor Country	Total	North America	Middle America [a]	South America	Europe	Asia and Oceania	Africa	Not Identified [b]
						Creditor Area		
Netherlands West Indies	$ 105	$ 55	—	—	$ 50	—	—	—
Venezuela	356	262	—	—	90	—	—	$ 4
Colombia	322	250	—	—	72	—	—	—
Brazil	1,964	539	—	—	1,220	—	—	205
Peru	326	136	—	—	160	$ 10	—	20
Bolivia	145	90	—	$ 3	51	1	—	—
Chile	1,288	614	—	—	493	1	—	180
Uruguay	248	47	—	—	185	—	—	16
Argentina	3,193	582	—	—	2,588	—	—	23
United Kingdom	1,299	672	—	—	309	224	$94	—
France	559	132	—	—	427	—	—	—
Belgium– Luxembourg	435	48	—	—	371	—	3	113
Denmark	376	111	—	—	185	—	—	80
Norway	413	110	—	—	160	—	—	143
Germany	2,743	697	—	—	1,982	—	—	64
Poland	730	171	—	—	478	—	—	81
Czechoslovakia	284	16	—	—	113	—	—	155
Switzerland	168	24	—	—	144	—	—	—
Austria	377	43	—	—	273	—	—	61
Hungary	369	57	—	—	204	—	—	108
Portugal	157	7	—	—	150	—	—	—
Spain	285	73	—	—	212	—	—	—
Italy	176	157	—	—	12	—	—	7
Yugoslavia	311	38	—	—	230	—	—	43
Romania	650	52	—	—	553	—	—	45
Bulgaria	110	8	—	—	102	—	—	—
Greece	486	27	—	—	459	—	—	—
China	2,557	230	—	—	1,220	1,060	—	47
Japan	534	155	—	—	269	—	—	110
Turkey	590	23	—	—	496	—	—	71
Syria, Palestine, Iraq	137	31	—	—	106	—	—	—
Iran	197	57	—	—	140	—	—	—
India, Burma, Ceylon	3,113	49	—	—	3,050	14	—	—
Siam	200	—	—	—	100	100	—	—
Malaya	696	24	—	—	444	228	—	—
Netherlands Indies	2,378	71	—	—	2,145	162	—	—
Indochina	477	3	—	—	394	80	—	—
Philippines	306	133	—	—	45	128	—	—
French Africa	754	10	—	—	744	—	—	—
Egypt [c]	513	23	—	—	490	—	—	—
Belgian Congo	428	9	—	—	419	—	—	—
British Africa	1,914	78	—	—	1,836	—	—	—
Italian Africa	201	—	—	—	201	—	—	—
Portuguese Africa	184	2	—	—	182	—	—	—
Australia	3,730	195	—	—	2,650	—	—	885
New Zealand	720	23	—	—	685	12	—	—
Other countries	871	389	—	30	315	111	—	26

Source: Computed from **40**, pp. 48–53.

  a. Includes Mexico.   b. Includes $54 million credited to the USSR.   c. Includes Suez.

Thus the net value of foreign holdings of the United Kingdom, at current exchange rates, was reduced from approximately $18 billion in 1938 to less than $4 billion in 1944.

INTERNATIONAL TRANSACTIONS OF THE UNITED STATES

The international transactions of the United States during the war and immediately afterward included lend-lease deliveries, listed as "unilateral transactions" balancing exports. It is easier, perhaps, to grasp the meaning of these transactions when lend-lease shipments are excluded from exports, as in Figure 46. Thus adjusted "commercial" exports declined during the war, were at the low point in 1943 and returned to the prewar level in 1945. They slightly exceeded general imports in 1942 and fell below imports in the later phase of the war. The gap, however, was not very wide in comparison with the total volume of transactions (including lend-lease shipments) and the import balance during a part of this period was largely offset by the export balance during the remainder. (See Table 84; cf. Figure 46.)

It should be kept in mind, however, that this presentation of international transactions of the United States during World War II excludes lend-lease operations, which amounted — including the more recent settlements of accounts — to a transfer to foreign governments of goods and services representing nearly $49 billion. On the receiving end, the British obtained shipments worth $31.6 billion; the Russians, $11.1 billion; the French, $3.3 billion; the Chinese, $1.6 billion. (See Table 84.) At the same time, Great Britain was credited with $6,752 million in "reverse lend-lease" deliveries, $868 million was credited to France and $100 million to other countries.

When the accounts for merchandise trade are combined with receipts and payments for unilateral transfers, services and income from investments, it appears that United States receipts on these accounts (exports) lagged behind payments (imports) by $1,087 million. The difference had to be offset by shipment of gold and transfer of capital. However, United States holdings in gold stocks increased in this period by $2,284 million, bringing to $3,371 million the cumulative import balance, and this is the amount that had to be covered by capital transfer, i.e., the increase in the United States foreign debts in relation to its holdings abroad. Actually,

the short-term obligations of the United States increased $4,129 million and its long-term foreign investments, $2,372 million. The difference of $1,757 million represents the net inflow of long-term and short-term capital. The gap of $1,614 million between this amount and the cumulative import balance for current transactions and gold shipments is due to statistical errors and omissions in the computation.

Thus, the United States emerged from the war with the following changes in its capital position (in millions of dollars): [a]

Gold stock in the United States (increase)	–$2,284
Long-term investments (total, net)	–2,372
U.S. investments abroad (increase)	–1,858
Foreign investments in the U.S. (decrease)	–513
Short-term capital (total, net)	+4,129
U.S. short-term capital abroad (increase)	–390
Foreign short-term capital in the U.S. (increase)	+4,519

a. Import (–): Increase of holdings abroad or decrease of foreign holdings in the United States. Export (+): Decrease of holdings abroad or increase of foreign holdings in the United States.

In round numbers, from 1940 through 1945 the United States increased gold stocks by $2.3 billion, long-term investments abroad by $1.9 billion and short-term credits to foreign countries by $0.4 billion, at the same time reducing long-term debts (foreign investments in the United States) by $0.5 billion and incurring new short-term debts (mainly foreign deposits in U.S. banks) by $4.5 billion. (See Table 85.[54])

When the government's obligations (mainly for military purchases in 1943–45) are added to private investments, loans and deposits of foreigners in U.S. banks, it appears that World War II left the United States a net debtor.[55]

Significantly, United States holdings abroad were in the form of interest-bearing or income-

---

54. The data for 1945 shown in this table are those published by the U.S. Department of Commerce in 1948. They are consistent with the data for the five preceding years in the table. Later they were revised and rearranged according to a new system of recording of international transactions (cf. Table 89). In a discussion of the U.S. balance of payments through the whole period 1940–45, partial adjustment of the data for 1945 would be misleading. Table 85 therefore reproduces the original data for 1945 without any attempt to reconcile them with the revised data shown in Table 89.

55. **9,** p. 110.

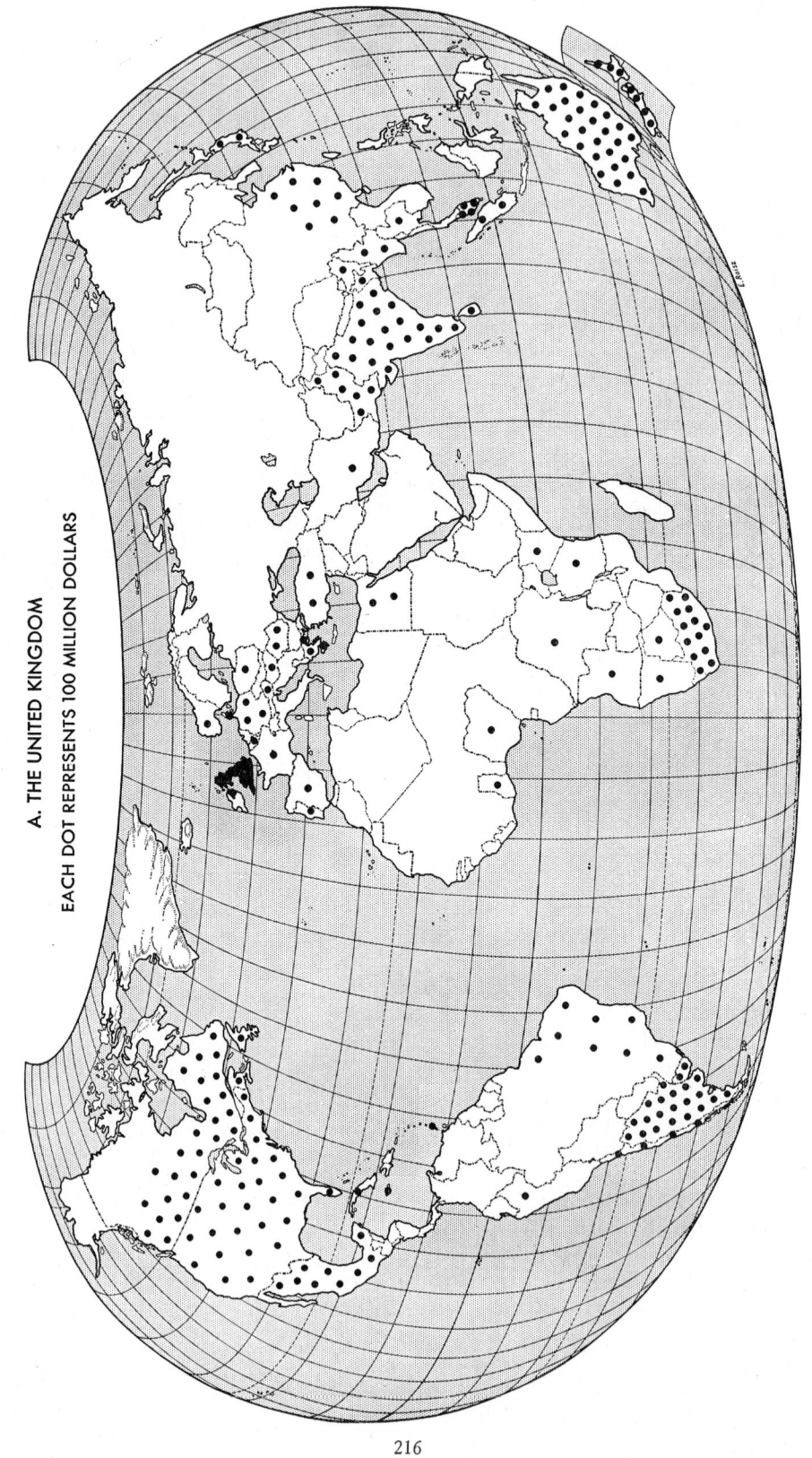

A. THE UNITED KINGDOM

EACH DOT REPRESENTS 100 MILLION DOLLARS

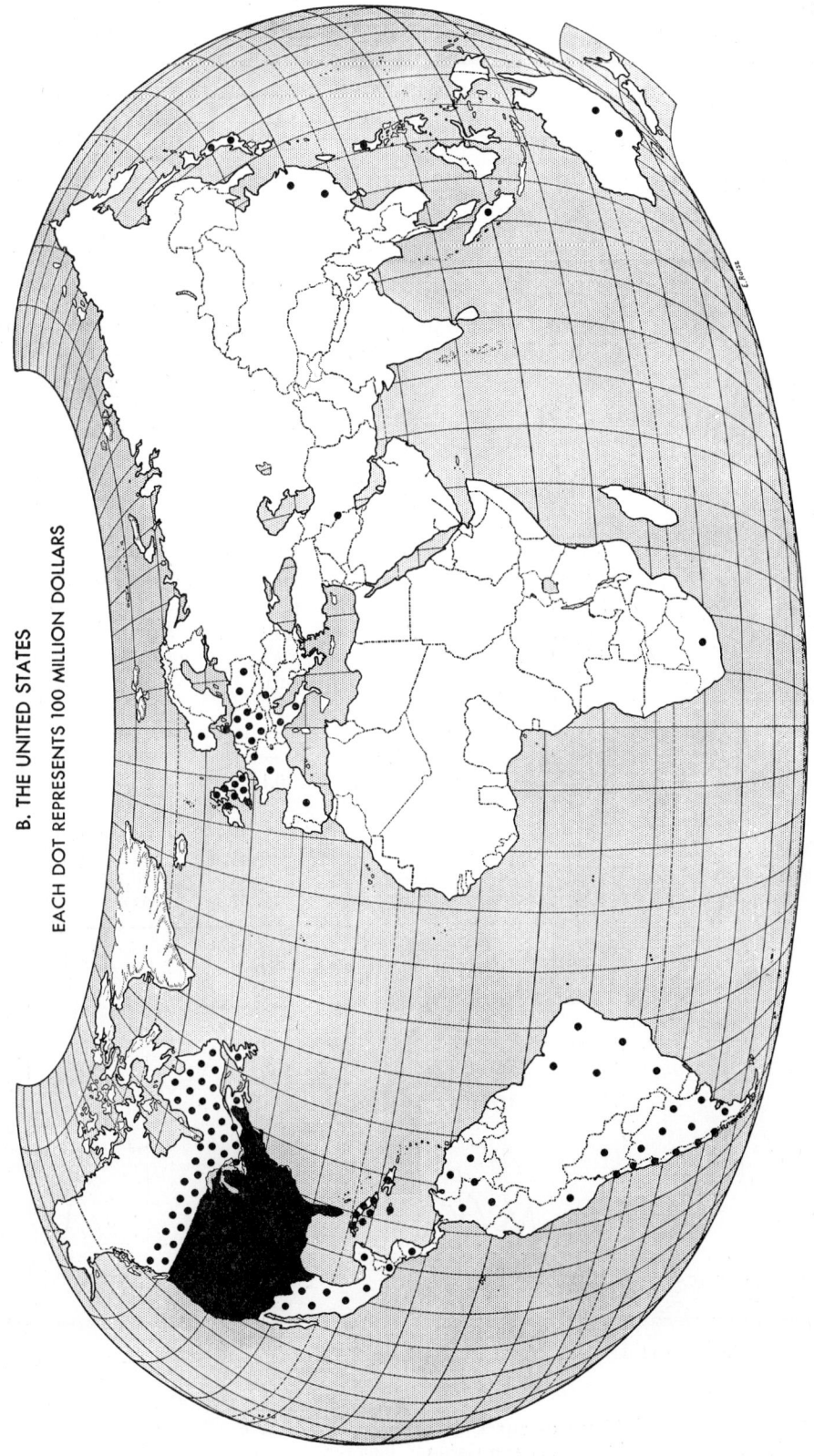

B. THE UNITED STATES

EACH DOT REPRESENTS 100 MILLION DOLLARS

Source: Table 83, based on **40** (All Investments)

Figure 45. Foreign Investments of the United Kingdom and the United States: Geographic Distribution, 1938

TABLE 84

INTERNATIONAL TRANSACTIONS OF THE UNITED STATES GOVERNMENT: LEND-LEASE OPERATIONS THROUGH 1951

(*Millions of Dollars*)

Country	Total	Defense Articles	Testing and Repair of Defense Articles	Agricultural, Industrial and Other Commodities	Services
Total charged to foreign governments	$48,923.8	$31,763.6	$639.4	$15,273.3	$1,247.5
American republics	493.0	437.2	8.8	32.4	14.6
Brazil	361.4	316.6	3.6	29.1	12.1
Mexico	39.3	33.5	2.7	1.5	1.6
Peru	18.9	18.2	0.1	0.5	0.1
Colombia	8.3	6.4	1.0	0.4	0.5
Ecuador	7.8	7.5	0.3	—	—
Uruguay	7.1	7.1	—	—	—
Cuba	6.6	5.7	0.9	—	—
Bolivia	5.5	5.4	—	0.1	—
Venezuela	4.5	4.5	—	—	—
Other	33.6	32.3	0.2	0.8	0.3
Eastern Hemisphere	48,430.8	31,326.4	630.6	15,240.9	1,233.0
British Empire	31,610.8	21,319.2	425.4	9,440.5	425.7
USSR	11,054.4	6,695.1	115.1	4,165.6	78.6
France	3,269.9	2,005.3	61.1	1,106.5	97.0
China	1,627.6	934.4	0.2	84.4	608.6
Netherlands	240.4	131.3	5.2	101.4	2.5
Italy	186.4	36.9	—	132.5	17.0
Belgium	156.3	51.1	—	104.8	0.4
Greece	81.4	42.4	0.1	38.6	0.3
Norway	47.0	18.7	23.1	5.1	0.1
Turkey	42.9	38.9	—	3.7	0.3
Yugoslavia	32.2	17.3	—	14.5	0.4
Saudi Arabia	22.7	2.4	—	20.3	—
Other	58.8	33.4	0.4	23.0	2.1

Source: **20**, Appendix Table 1.

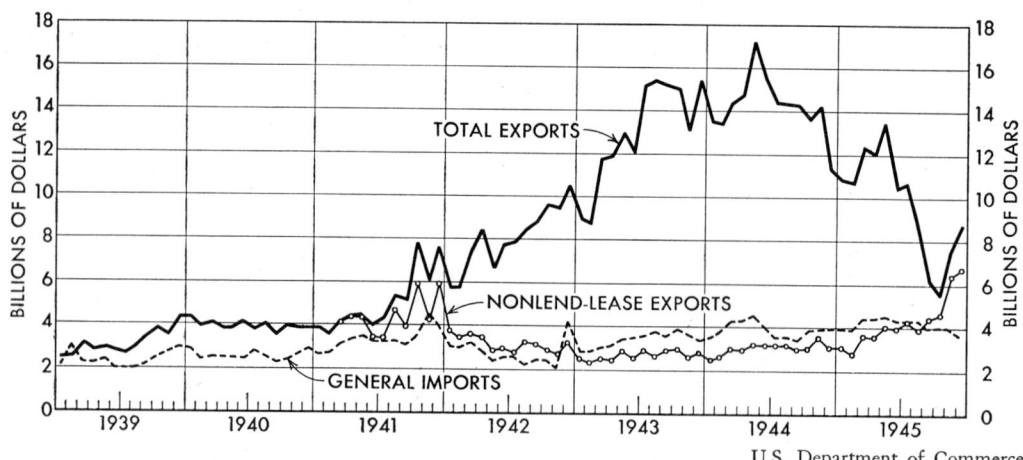

U.S. Department of Commerce

FIGURE 46. INTERNATIONAL TRADE OF THE UNITED STATES DURING WORLD WAR II: TOTAL AND NON-LEND-LEASE EXPORTS AND GENERAL IMPORTS, BY MONTH, 1939–45

TABLE 85

BALANCE OF PAYMENTS OF THE UNITED STATES, 1940–45 [a]

(*Millions of Dollars*)

Item	1940	1941	1942	1943	1944	1945
I. Receipts, total (+)	$5,780	$7,210	$13,077	$21,716	$24,485	$19,249
A. Goods and services, total	5,355	6,896	11,769	19,134	21,438	16,073
1. Goods	4,124	5,343	9,187	15,115	16,969	12,222
2. Income on investments	564	544	514	508	572	555
3. Other services	667	1,009	2,068	3,511	3,897	3,296
B. Unilateral transfers	59	43	1,002	2,137	2,407	2,591
C. Long-term capital movements	366	271	306	445	640	585
II. Payments, total (−)	4,344	6,578	13,159	23,732	26,154	21,009
A. Goods and services	3,636	4,486	5,356	8,096	8,986	9,424
1. Goods	2,713	3,486	3,965	5,427	5,589	5,829
2. Income on investments	210	187	159	155	161	168
3. Other services	713	813	1,232	2,514	3,236	3,427
B. Unilateral transfers	269	1,179	7,338	15,044	16,549	9,628
C. Long-term capital movements	439	913	465	592	619	1,957
III. Excess of receipts (+) or payments (−), total	+1,436	+632	−82	−2,016	−1,669	−1,760
A. Goods and services	+1,719	+2,410	+6,413	+11,038	+12,452	+6,649
B. Unilateral transfers	−210	−1,136	−6,336	−12,907	−14,142	−7,037
C. Long-term capital movements	−73	−642	−159	−147	+21	−1,372
1. U.S. investments abroad	+17	−315	−75	−84	−154	−1,248
2. Foreign investments in the United States	−90	−327	−84	−63	+175	−124
IV. Gold and short-term debts, net inflow (+) and outflow (−)	−2,713	−1,108	+90	+1,982	+1,706	+1,888
A. Net increase (−) or decrease (+) of gold stocks	−4,243	−719	+23	+757	+1,350	+548
B. U.S. short-term capital abroad	+177	+11	−115	+3	−153	−313
C. Foreign short-term capital in U.S.	+1,353	−400	+182	+1,222	+509	+1,653
V. Errors and omissions	+1,277	+476	−8	+34	−37	−128

Source: **24,** p. viii.

a. For more recent trends see Table 89. The two tables are not strictly comparable because of differences in methods of estimating and classification.

TABLE 86

FOREIGN ASSETS AND LIABILITIES OF THE UNITED STATES, 1939–51 [a]

(*Millions of Dollars*)

	United States Investments Abroad					Foreign Investments in the United States					Net Creditor (+) or Debtor (−) Position
	Private					Private					
	Long-term					Long-term					
Year	Direct	Portfolio	Short-term	U.S. Government Claims	Total	Direct	Portfolio	Short-term	U.S. Government Obligations	Total	
1939	$ 7,110	$3,785	$ 595	$ 35	$11,525	$1,980	$4,310	$3,295	$ 325	$ 9,910	+$1,615
1940	7,340	3,970	885	80	12,275	2,875	5,225	5,125	310	13,535	−1,260
1941	7,525	4,110	870	485	12,990	2,700	4,500	4,570	530	12,300	+690
1942	7,740	4,435	755	710	13,640	2,615	4,660	4,370	960	12,605	+1,035
1943	7,845	4,730	765	830	14,170	2,605	4,965	4,990	1,585	14,145	+25
1944	7,960	4,970	835	1,045	14,810	2,630	5,235	5,215	2,005	15,085	−275
1945 [b]	8,369	5,289	1,029	2,179	16,866	2,514	5,517	5,132	4,252	17,415	−549
1946	8,854	5,344	1,337	5,083	20,618	2,548	5,067	5,281	3,556	16,452	+4,166
1947	9,965	5,378	1,533	12,051	28,927	2,650	4,750	5,302	3,944	16,646	+12,281
1948	11,206	5,380	1,649	12,937	31,172	2,843	4,454	5,787	4,003	17,087	+14,085
1949	12,418	5,124	1,427	13,514	32,483	3,066	4,726	5,941	3,835	17,568	+14,915
1950	13,550	5,827	1,631	13,707	34,715	3,293	5,164	6,516	5,195	20,168	+14,547
1951	14,889	6,286	1,765	13,884	36,824	3,499	5,593	6,631	5,443	21,166	+15,658

Sources: **24**, p. 110; **6**, p. 94; **21**, p. 62; **22**, p. 162.

a. For 1931–39 see Table 80. The difference between Table 80 and Table 86 is that the latter includes U.S. government claims and obligations. This item reduces the net credits of the United States in 1939 from $1,905 million to $1,615 million. The significance of this item increased during World War II and in postwar years. In 1945 this item amounted to net obligations of over $2 billion; in 1951 it represented net claims for $8.4 billion.

b. Revised.

producing direct or portfolio investments, while the increase in foreign investments in the United States consisted largely of short-term bank balances. (See Table 86.) Some of these balances represented vagrant capital seeking refuge in the United States. Such balances implied no commitments on the part of residents, banks, business concerns or the government of the country. They were foreign investments in a technical, but not an economic, sense.

FOREIGN INVESTMENTS AND DEBTS OF OTHER COUNTRIES

European long-term investments, before World War II, were largely concentrated within Europe and in the colonial possessions of the European powers. According to the Brookings Institution survey, of the total of $36.8 billion held by Europe, $6.5 billion was invested in European countries and $15.4 billion in colonial empires of the investing countries.[56]

56. **40**, pp. 48–50.

This geographic distribution made European investments highly vulnerable in the event of European war and colonial troubles. On the other hand, war gave non-European debtor countries an opportunity to repay at least a part of their debts, affirm their economic independence and eventually become creditors of their former bankers. Countries exporting strategic materials coveted by belligerent nations had a particularly favorable position in this respect.

France, Belgium and the Netherlands preserved their holdings in the Western Hemisphere but lost a large part of their long-term investments in Europe and Asia. Losses caused by invasion and looting were augmented by losses through inflation and depreciation of direct investments in such areas as Indonesia and Indochina.

There is no reliable information on the value of the foreign investments of these three countries at the end of the war, but in 1947–48 they recorded net income from their foreign investments, which suggests that, despite all losses, they remained creditor countries. In 1945, the value of their long-term assets abroad hardly exceeded half the prewar value.

Of other creditor countries, Sweden and Switzerland suffered only moderate losses in investments in Europe, while Germany, Italy and Japan, as a result of military defeat, lost practically all their foreign assets.

Most of the debtor countries in Middle and South America, Africa, the Middle and Far East have improved their financial and economic positions. Some profited by lend-lease credits and received, free of charge, new highways, airports, harbors, hospitals and power plants. Some accumulated sterling and dollar credits for services rendered to the armed forces of the Allies. Although not designed to stimulate economic progress, military expenditures laid a foundation for future economic growth in some underdeveloped areas.

The redistribution of foreign investments during World War II contributed to undermining colonial and semicolonial relations in underdeveloped areas and helped such areas toward economic independence of creditor nations.

STATUS OF INTERNATIONAL INVESTMENTS, 1944

At the end of World War II the United States and the United Kingdom held the largest direct and portfolio investments abroad. The United Kingdom, thanks to the lend-lease shipments from the United States and its own cautious financial policy, has preserved its most valuable assets — mainly in the Empire and the Western Hemisphere — in the amount of $13–$14 billion. The United States had long-term investments totaling $14 billion at the end of 1944, including a billion in government credits. Both countries had heavy long-term and short-term liabilities. Long-term liabilities of the United Kingdom were estimated at $9–$10 billion, leaving the British approximately $4 billion in net investment. In the United States, long-term liabilities totaled $9.9 billion, with a net creditor position (in long-term accounts) of $4.1 billion. (See Table 86.)

The question of the relative ranking of the two nations as world creditors at that time is pointless. Their gross and net long-term assets were of about the same magnitude, and together they controlled foreign investments — largely direct investments — of approximately $29.5 billion, as compared with $34.3 billion in 1938.

Investments of other nations (some $18.5 billion before World War II) have been drastically depleted. Losses of France, Belgium, the Netherlands, Sweden, Germany, Italy, China and Japan may have totaled $7–$8 billion and were only partly offset by new foreign investments of India and other members of the British Commonwealth. If the total losses of all countries except the United States and the United Kingdom are tentatively estimated at $6 billion, the long-term assets of these countries in 1944–45 must have totaled close to $12.5 billion.

This estimate, admittedly very rough, suggests that all outstanding long-term foreign investments, private and public, direct and portfolio, excluding valueless debts in default, totaled approximately $42 billion in 1944–45. Their dollar value was close to that of international investments on the eve of World War I — $44 billion. The purchasing power of the U.S. dollar, however, declined between 1914 and 1945 at roughly the same rate as its gold content. With reservation for a wide margin of error, $42 billion in 1944–45 was roughly equivalent to $25 billion in 1914.

Meanwhile world population had increased from 1.7 billion to 2.3 billion, in round numbers, and world per capita income likewise had increased — despite the temporary setback in European belligerent countries and Japan. In relation to world income, the value of foreign investments in 1944–45 was less than a third, and probably not much more than a fourth, of that in mid–1914, when the first shot of World War I, fired in Sarajevo, announced the beginning of an era of the bloodiest wars and revolutions in human history.

RECENT CHANGES

The equilibrium of international transactions, undermined by the great depression in the 1930's, was completely destroyed by the economic dislocations caused by World War II. The pattern of world trade and capital movement which developed in the nineteenth century — and was preserved with brief interruptions until the late 1920's — depended on, among other factors, multilateral exchange of goods and services, free flow of capital, convertibility of currencies with a limited flexibility of exchange rates and the availability of monetary reserves as shock absorbers. Payments on investments piled up in the nineteenth century were an important item in balancing current accounts and providing funds for new investments. The war reduced all this structure to a heap of rubble.

THE PROBLEM OF BALANCES OF PAYMENTS

Europe, devastated by the war, was severely affected by the disorganization of international transactions. It urgently needed imports of food-stuffs, feed crops, fertilizers, fuel and industrial raw materials in order to restore the health and strength of the population, rebuild factories, railways and merchant fleets, and resume production. But European industrial nations no longer could pay for imported goods with services and earnings on foreign investments. Moreover, their stocks of gold were depleted, and they had no market in which to raise private loans and credits.[57]

In the absence of a functioning network of world-wide multilateral settlements, a number of payments and trade agreements were signed providing for bilateral exchange of goods and services and in some instances allowing for triangular settlement among European governments and between European and Latin American countries.[58]

These arrangements, however, proved ineffective because Latin American countries could not deliver the goods which Europe needed most urgently during postwar reconstruction — wheat, corn, fertilizers, cotton, coal, petroleum, steel, rails, tractors and cars, industrial machinery, equipment for mining and building. Moreover, the most important primary industries in Latin America, especially in Argentina and Brazil, suffered severe setbacks as the result of ambitious and not fully successful attempts of the governments to accelerate industrialization and achieve economic self-sufficiency. Thus, in none of the postwar years 1946–51 was the volume of Argentine exports to Europe as high as in 1936–38.[59]

Immediately after the end of the war the United States was the only country which could supply Europe with necessary raw materials, capital equipment and staple consumer goods, but Europe had little to offer in exchange. The situation called for emergency measures beyond transactions on a normal commercial basis. The foreign aid advanced by the United States after the end of lend-lease operations was such a meas-

ure. Inspired by humanitarian and political, rather than economic, considerations, the assistance was a purely temporary and self-liquidating measure. Its purpose was to aid Europe to recover sufficient strength to resume production and foreign trade on a sound economic basis. In restrospect, the program appears to have been an unqualified success. Considerable progress was achieved in growth of production and trade in European countries as well as in adjustment of prices and exchange rates, although the economic equilibrium which would permit a smooth and continuous flow of international trade and capital transactions in the world had not been restored at the outbreak of the war in Korea.

The *Annual Report* of the International Monetary Fund for the fiscal year ended April 30, 1952, summarizes the developments as follows:

The attainment of a stable international equilibrium still eludes large parts of the world, and there has been little secure or sustained progress toward the Fund objectives of unimpeded multilateral trade and the general convertibility of currencies.

During the last seven years, balance of payments difficulties have been continuous or recurrent, and most countries have either been unable to make substantial progress toward freer international trade, or have had to reverse from time to time some of the steps taken in that direction.

The first critical situation arising out of the postwar payments disequilibrium occurred in the summer of 1947, and was associated with the short-lived resumption of sterling convertibility. It was temporarily resolved by the U.S. interim aid program and the Marshall Plan, which permitted the European countries to proceed with the restoration of their economies much more rapidly than would otherwise have been possible. Their recovery was in most cases substantial, but, as the most urgent reconstruction and pent-up consumer and producer demands were satisfied, a second exchange crisis began to develop. Its first symptoms were seen in a tendency for some European exporters to find themselves priced out of dollar markets.[60]

The devaluation of the British and other currencies in September 1949 improved the situation. Many countries were able to relax restrictions and some progress was made toward convertibility of currencies.

The *Annual Report* of the International Monetary Fund continues:

Before there had been time for the full effects of the devaluations of September 1949 to be worked

---

57. **8**, p. 16.
58. **9**, p. 20.
59. **11**, p. 26; cf. **7**, *passim*.

60. **16**, 1952, pp. 1, 2.

out, fighting broke out in Korea in June 1950 and initiated a series of new developments to which balances of payments had to be adjusted. . . . The increased demands arising from stockpiling and rearmament raised prices, national income, and world trade to higher levels. It might have been expected that the increased demand for raw materials would, after some adjustments, lead to a new equilibrium, . . . The reserve positions of many countries were, indeed, strengthened, but this trend ceased with the subsequent decline in commodity prices, which reversed part of the initial improvement in terms of trade of raw material producers. The old troubles then reappeared. There were widespread balance of payments difficulties, reserves declined, and the earlier movement toward freer trade was to some extent reversed. While conditions in individual countries in the first half of 1952 vary widely, the reappearance of these difficulties provides a strong indication that the earlier efforts to restore a new world equilibrium had failed to get to the root of the matter.[61]

The Fund sees the main sources of difficulties in the inflationary pressures in various countries and the lack of international cooperation.

UNITED STATES AID TO FOREIGN COUNTRIES

The foreign aid (grants and credits) that the United States extended to other countries during the war and through June 30, 1953 is estimated at $94.3 billion.[62] An additional $5.2 billion was appropriated for the fiscal year 1953–54. Of the $94.3 billion, grants and credits extended after the end of the war and through the fiscal year 1952–53 amounted to $45 billion. This figure, however, shows the gross rather than net outlays of the United States for foreign aid. With allowance for duplication and reverse payments, net aid to foreign countries from July 1, 1945 through June 30, 1953 totaled $41.3 billion — $31.3 billion in grants and $10 billion in loans and credits. (See Tables 87 and 88; cf. Figure 47.) To this aggregate value of goods, services and funds transferred by the United States government to foreign countries were added private donations and transfer of private capital in the amount of $9–$10 billion, bringing the total of grants, donations, loans and credits to more than $50 billion, close to the current aggregate value of all foreign investments in the world.

Not all components of this flow of goods, services, funds and credits are fully recorded in the balances of payments. Many grants were made from military supplies that were abroad or in transit at the end of the war. Neither the export statistics of the United States nor the import statistics of receiving countries recorded all such gifts, and it is fairly probable that the value of many transferred materials was listed among the grants at far less than the market price. The supplies were there; they could not be brought back to the United States because of the lack of shipping. Moreover, if transported home, they would bring a meager return. The sensible thing to do was to give them to people in need. Although not recorded in international trade and payments balances, these supplies, in various countries, were very real items in the nutritional budget of the people and played an important role in the crucial period of postwar reconstruction. To some extent, this situation existed also in the operations of UNRRA and the so-called "interim aid." [63] Essentially, these operations were carried on in kind; only a part went through the channels of regular trade.

In 1946–52 the net trade deficit of the world apart from the United States can be measured roughly by the United States surplus in export of goods and services. (See Table 89.) That surplus changed from year to year as follows (in millions of dollars):

	As Shown in Table 89	Revised
1946	+$ 7,778	+$ 7,778
1947	+11,507	+11,582
1948	+6,736	+6,763
1949	+6,241	+6,373
1950	+2,209	+2,343
1951	+5,164	+5,215
1952	+4,973	+4,972
1953	. . .	+4,709

63. The UNRRA (United Nations Relief and Rehabilitation Administration) program was officially an international program, but three fourths of the cost, to the amount of $2,660 million, was defrayed by the United States. After the completion of the program in the middle of 1947, the U.S. government embarked on two new relief programs. Some $300 million was spent under the post-UNRRA program, mainly in Austria, Greece, Italy, Trieste and China (Public Law 84, approved May 31, 1947) and $546 million, spent mainly in France, under the Interim Aid program (Public Law 389, enacted by Congress in December 1947). (**21**, pp. 119–20.)

61. **16**, p. 3.

62. During the war, $49.2 billion; from the end of the war and until the beginning of the war in Korea, $28.2 billion; after the Korean invasion and to June 30, 1953, $16.9 billion. (**29**, 1952, p. 831; **25**, March 1953, p. 15 and October 1953, p. 15.)

TABLE 87

INTERNATIONAL TRANSACTIONS OF THE UNITED STATES GOVERNMENT: FOREIGN AID, BY PROGRAM, JULY 1, 1945 THROUGH JUNE 1953

(Millions of Dollars)

Item	Total Postwar Period	Before Korean Invasion	July-Dec. 1950	1951	1952	January-June 1953
Gross foreign aid	$45,086	$28,159	$2,223	$5,074	$5,578	$4,042
Grants utilized	33,920	18,824	2,021	4,646	4,756	3,673
Less: credits offsets to grants	1,256	1,256	—	—	—	—
Credits utilized	12,414	10,591	201	428	823	371
Net foreign aid [a]	41,308	25,981	2,006	4,622	5,004	3,695
Net grants	31,316	16,693	1,956	4,506	4,605	3,556
Net credits	9,992	9,287	50	116	399	140
Grants utilized, by program:	34,289	18,824	2,021	4,646	4,756	4,042
Lend-lease	1,932	1,932	—	—	—	—
Civilian supplies	5,341	4,564	257	366	154	—
UNRRA, post-UNRRA and interim aid	3,443	3,443	—	—	—	—
Philippine rehabilitation	635	519	100	12	4	—
Greek-Turkish aid	660	636	15	9	—	—
Chinese stabilization and military aid	243	238	2	3	—	—
Mutual Security Agency [b] economic and technical assistance	13,999	7,004	1,189	2,668	1,850	1,288
Military aid	7,442	63	402	1,484	2,739	2,754
Other	597	426	56	105	10	—
Reverse grants and returns on grants	1,577	874	65	140	151	347
Credits utilized, by program:	12,414	10,591	201	428	823	371
British loan	3,750	3,750	—	—	—	—
Export-Import Bank [c]	3,414	2,651	81	204	478	—
Surplus property [d]	1,486	1,484	—	2	—	—
Credit-agreement offsets to grants	1,256	1,256	—	—	—	—
Mutual Security Agency [e]	1,608	990	78	209	331	—
Lend-lease	71	69	—	—	2	—
Other	457	390	42	13	12	—
Principal collected on credits:	2,422	1,304	152	312	423	231
British loan	89	—	—	44	45	—
Export-Import Bank [c]	1,125	632	88	134	271	—
Surplus property [d]	275	123	25	56	71	—
Credit-agreement offsets to grants	62	22	1	21	18	—
Lend-lease	40	21	6	7	6	—
Other	601	507	33	49	12	—

Source: **25,** March 1953, p. 15; October 1953, p. 16. Discrepancies in addition are due to differences in classification in the most recent period.

a. Gross foreign aid minus reverse grants and returns on grants, minus principal collected on credits, as shown below in this table.

b. Absorbed the European Recovery Program (Marshall Plan) in 1951.

c. Direct loans through agent banks.

d. Includes merchant ships.

e. Includes loans to Spain and India.

TABLE 88

INTERNATIONAL TRANSACTIONS OF THE UNITED STATES GOVERNMENT: NET FOREIGN AID, BY COUNTRY, JULY 1, 1945 THROUGH DECEMBER 1952

(Millions of Dollars)

Country	Total Postwar Period	Before Korean Invasion	July-Dec. 1950	1951	1952
Total	$37,612	$25,981	$2,006	$4,622	$5,004
Western Europe	27,915	19,306	1,497	3,346	3,765
United Kingdom	6,559	5,793	226	129	411
Ireland	146	99	23	24	—
Iceland	26	10	2	9	5
France	4,631	3,712	196	410	314
Belgium–Luxembourg	738	600	84	42	12
Netherlands	1,058	857	55	102	44
Denmark	275	185	25	58	8
Sweden	109	68	18	27	−4
Norway	281	192	26	40	23
Finland	91	101	−4	−3	−3
Germany	3,718	3,057	201	357	103
Austria	956	697	30	147	82
Portugal	45	5	13	20	7
Spain	41	—	—	17	24
Italy	2,478	1,949	97	258	175
Trieste	44	34	3	7	—
Yugoslavia	518	311	24	106	78
Greece	1,502	1,142	56	194	110
Turkey	360	222	23	56	59
Other areas [a]	4,339	275	401	1,348	2,316
Other Europe	1,088	1,107	—	−15	−4
Near East and Africa	296	−6	35	91	176
Asia and Pacific	6,654	4,486	394	920	855
China	1,794	1,642	8	67	76
Korea	704	374	64	118	148
Japan	2,121	1,650	130	283	58
India	217	14	1	108	94
Indochina	35	—	1	13	21
Indonesia	198	164	—	1	33
Philippines	778	620	135	13	9
Other areas [a]	808	21	56	317	414
Canada	7	1	—	1	5
Latin America [a]	637	343	8	159	127
Unspecified [a]	1,015	744	72	120	80

Source: **25,** March 1953, pp. 16–17. Records of military aid awarded to foreign countries in 1953 (see Table 87) are not broken down by country.

a. Includes unspecified areas, and military aid under the Mutual Security Act, which is not designated by country for security reasons.

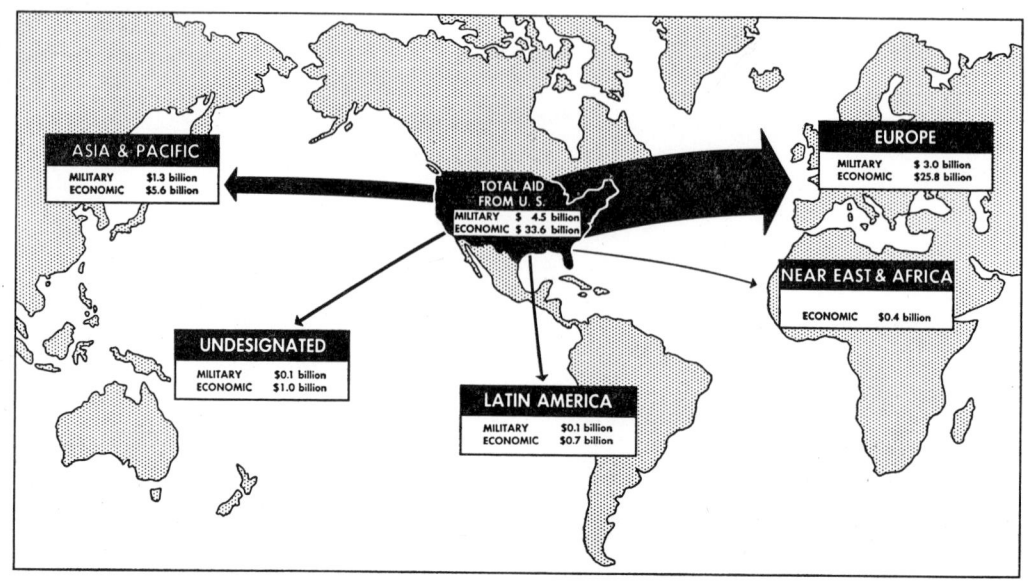

U.S. Department of Commerce

FIGURE 47. INTERNATIONAL TRANSACTIONS OF THE UNITED STATES: POSTWAR FOREIGN AID,
JULY 1945 THROUGH JUNE 1952

The cumulative total surplus for these seven years — $44.6 billion, in round numbers — was only partly balanced by the inflow of gold (some $3.2 billion) and movement of capital (some $13 billion). There remained a gap of more than $28 billion — the amount foreign countries would have had to pay or to commit themselves to pay in the future for American foodstuffs, industrial raw materials, medical supplies, fuel, machinery and other merchandise if this gap had not been filled by the grants enumerated in Table 87.

The outflow of capital (grants or credits) in the balance of payments of the United States was an inflow of purchasing power for the receiving countries. The greatest amounts were transferred to the United Kingdom, France, Germany, Italy and Japan. (See Table 88.) The most important grant operation was the European Recovery Program (Marshall Plan), absorbed in 1951 by operations under the Mutual Security Act.[64] The most important credit operations of the U.S. government were the special loan to the United Kingdom (1947) and appropriations to the Export-Import Bank.

64. The ERP was outlined in June 1947, by George C. Marshall, at that time Secretary of State, and the law was finally approved by the President on April 3, 1948. The Mutual Security Act (June 5, 1951) consolidated most government programs for foreign military and economic aid into one program.

OTHER UNITED STATES TRANSACTIONS

From the standpoint of international accounts, grants by the United States to other countries were a permanent net loss for its economy; but credits extended to foreign governments and international institutions — insofar as repayment could be anticipated — represented a transfer of capital and an increase in United States foreign assets. Moreover, the tremendous expansion of its industrial production enabled the United States to resume private direct investments abroad on a large scale. (See Table 89.)

The postwar net debtor-creditor position of the United States changed as follows (in millions of dollars): [65]

1945	−$ 776
1946	+4,166
1947	+10,931
1948	+12,899
1949	+13,786
1950	+13,385
1951	+14,406
1952	+14,726
1953	+15,838

In 1945–51, the difficult period of postwar readjustment in the world, the United States delivered to other countries goods and services

65. **29**, 1954, p. 895.

TABLE 89

BALANCE OF PAYMENTS OF THE UNITED STATES, 1945–52 [a]

(Millions of Dollars)

Item	1945	1946	1947	1948	1949	1950	1951	1952
I. Exports of goods and services, total (+)	$16,273	$14,741	$19,796	$17,092	$15,956	$14,351	$20,218	$20,701
Merchandise (adjusted)	12,473	11,672	15,977	13,427	12,337	10,679	15,485	15,859
Transportation	1,309	1,420	1,788	1,384	1,289	1,008	1,487	1,373
Travel	162	252	342	308	363	374	420	512
Income on investments								
Private	17	789	1,080	1,273	1,225	1,461	1,800	1,711
Government	572	21	66	102	98	109	192	200
Other services	1,740	587	543	598	644	720	834	1,046
II. Imports of goods and services, total (−)	10,232	6,963	8,289	10,356	9,715	12,142	15,054	15,728
Merchandise (adjusted)	5,666	5,168	6,100	7,833	7,144	9,287	11,668	11,519
Transportation	420	599	761	727	768	846	933	1,051
Travel	309	457	548	600	688	727	722	823
Payments on investments								
Private	17	201	233	267	304	389	351	357
Government	214	15	16	17	25	33	47	64
Other services	3,606	523	631	912	786	860	1,333	1,914
III. Balance on goods and services (I and II)	+6,041	+7,778	+11,507	+6,736	+6,241	+2,209	+5,164	+4,973
Unilateral transfers, net								
Private	−473	−679	−665	−652	· −515	−439	−412	−415
Government	−6,640	−2,288	−1,947	−4,161	−5,304	−4,133	−4,501	−4,628
Balance on current transactions	−1,072	+4,811	+8,895	+1,923	+422	−2,363	+251	−70
IV. Movement of capital, total, net	+516	−4,367	−7,713	−1,405	−1,234	+620	+495	+2?
U.S. foreign investments								
Private, long-term	−454	−59	−810	−761	−800	−950	−963	−?
Private, short-term	−96	−310	−189	−116	+164	−140	−103	
Government, long-term	−842	−3,262	−6,849	−999	−470	−125	−140	
Government, short-term	−178	+250	−108	+92	−173	−34	−23	
Foreign capital in U.S.								
Long-term	−103	−347	−96	−170	+126	+1,001	−543	
Short-term	+2,189	−639	+339	+549	−81	+868	+1,038	
V. Increase (−) or decrease (+) in gold stock	+548	−623	−2,162	−1,530	−164	+1,743	−53	37
VI. Errors and omissions	+8	+179	+980	+1,012	+976	—	+536	+23

Sources: **29**, 1951, p. 817; **25**, March 1953, p. 8.

a. For 1940–45 see Table 85. Figures for 1945 shown in Table 85 have been revised and rearrang[ed] [ac]cordi[ng] to a new system of recording international transactions.

representing some $118 billion and took in exchange goods and services representing $69 billion. The difference of $49 billion was split in two unequal parts: some 60 per cent was delivered free of charge as a gift; the rest, about $16 billion, under conditions of long-term credit (governmental loans and direct investments).

This is when and how the [Un]ited Stat[es] changed from a debtor to a credit[or] nation, i[n-] deed the largest creditor in the w[orl]d. The p[ro-] ducers of goods and services tha[t] were sent [to] foreign countries as grants were [of] course paid [in] full by the government and [t]he price w[as] added to the national debt. Th[e] essential po[int] of the whole transaction was that the amount was invested in the security and peace of the world.[66] As pointed out in Gordon Gray's report to the President, "the United States has provided the critical margin of resources enabling Western Europe and Japan to recover from destruction and disorganization of wartime and to progress far toward a self-sustaining economic position. Largely as a result of this, political conditions have been stabilized and Communist penetration halted." [67]

FOREIGN ASSETS AND LIABILITIES OF THE UNITED STATES

At the end of 1951 the claims of the United States against foreign countries (investments in a broad sense) totaled $36,824 million while its commitments and obligations toward foreign countries (foreign investments in the United States) amounted to $21,166 million. Both amounts include private and U.S. government assets and liabilities of various types. (See Table 90.)

Net long-term investments of the United States totaled $24,881 million — $12,083 million held by private individuals and concerns and $12,798 million held by the U.S. government. In short-term accounts, the United States was in a debtor position in the amount of $9.2 billion.

Approximately 70 per cent of the direct investments of the United States are concentrated in the Western Hemisphere — 30 per cent in Canada and 40 per cent in Latin America, in round numbers. The remainder is almost evenly divided between Western Europe and other areas. A little less than a third of all direct investment is in the petroleum business (mainly in Latin America); a little more than a third, in manufacturing industries (mainly in Canada and Western Europe); the rest is in mining (Canada, Chile, Mexico and other areas), public utilities (Latin America), trade and other industries. (See Tables 91 and 92; cf. Fig. 48.[68])

66.
67. Chapter 17.
68. p. 3.

ments ab... 91 shows the growth of U.S. direct investments for the co... after the end of World War II. The data ternally co... utive years as shown in this table are internally co... tent and comparable despite the broad margin of ... r in each single item. Table 92 summarizes the ... lt of a new estimate of the U.S. direct investments ab... d as at the end of 1950. All its items differ from the ... ta for the same industries and the same areas in Table 9... Data in Table 91, therefore, are not comparable with ... ose for 1946–50 in Table 92.

TABLE 90

FOREIGN INVESTMENTS OF THE UNITED STATES: U.S. DEBTOR-CREDITOR POSITION, END OF 1951

(Millions of Dollars)

Item	U.S. Investments Abroad (+)	Foreign Investments in the United States (−)	Net Debtor (−) or Creditor (+) Position
Total	$36,824	$21,166	$+15,658
I. Private	22,940	15,723	+7,217
Long-term	21,175	9,092	+12,083
Direct	14,889	3,499	+11,390
Securities	4,562	4,112	+450
Other	1,724	1,481	+243
Short-term	1,765	6,631	−4,866
Deposits	447	5,783	−5,336
Other	1,318	848	+470
II. U.S. Government	13,884	5,443	+8,441
Long-term	13,536	738	+12,798
Short-term	348	4,705	−4,358

Source: **22**, p. 162.

Portfolio investments of the United States consist of two types of securities: foreign dollar bonds and securities payable in other currencies. Most of the first type represent loans negotiated by foreign firms or governments with U.S. banks and brokers; foreign-currency securities were floated abroad and either bought by residents of the United States or brought to the United States by immigrants.

Foreign securities of both types owned by residents and firms in the United States at the end of 1951 were distributed as follows (in millions of dollars): [69]

Area	Total	Dollar Bonds	Securities Payable in Other Currencies
Total	$4,562	$2,082	$2,480
Canada	3,275	1,291	1,984
Latin America	192	166	26
OEEC countries	454	80	374
Other	278	182	96
International institutions	363	363	—

United States government loans to foreign countries totaled $10.1 billion as of June 30, 1951 (not including debts of foreign countries to the

69. **22**, pp. 162–63.

TABLE 91

FOREIGN INVESTMENTS OF THE UNITED STATES: DIRECT INVESTMENTS, BY INDUSTRY AND AREA, 1946–50

(*Millions of Dollars*)

Area and Year End	Total	Agriculture	Mining	Petroleum	Manufac-tures	Public Utilities [a]	Trade	Miscel-laneous
All areas								
1946	$ 8,854	$545	$1,062	$1,769	$2,854	$1,277	$ 740	$607
1947	9,965	585	1,109	2,346	3,171	1,268	818	668
1948	11,206	641	1,140	2,981	3,551	1,288	921	684
1949	12,418	651	1,218	3,664	3,831	1,308	977	769
1950	13,550	654	1,324	4,072	4,242	1,338	1,065	855
Canada								
1946	2,663	14	463	178	1,202	378	153	275
1947	2,806	14	481	208	1,328	344	160	271
1948	3,096	13	488	274	1,532	345	186	258
1949	3,359	14	519	349	1,642	343	196	296
1950	3,850	15	580	518	1,853	343	216	325
Latin American republics								
1946	3,146	445	398	768	488	821	165	61
1947	3,705	480	425	1,048	595	846	209	102
1948	4,233	531	441	1,337	685	864	258	117
1949	4,798	535	487	1,721	756	883	284	132
1950	5,065	536	516	1,772	844	907	329	161
ERP countries								
1946	1,768	4	64	310	885	20	281	204
1947	1,887	4	64	346	946	20	293	214
1948	2,019	4	64	390	1,010	20	309	222
1949	2,133	4	64	403	1,079	20	321	242
1950	2,272	4	64	453	1,155	20	321	255
ERP dependencies								
1946	291	55	39	153	13	5	19	7
1947	392	56	38	253	15	5	18	7
1948	499	56	40	351	18	5	20	9
1949	564	57	39	410	22	5	22	9
1950	561	56	42	398	23	5	27	10
Other Europe								
1946	333	2	85	64	108	10	39	25
1947	337	2	83	66	111	10	40	25
1948	324	2	81	63	106	8	39	25
1949	341	2	81	76	109	8	40	25
1950	349	2	81	78	114	8	41	25
All other countries								
1946	653	25	13	296	158	43	83	35
1947	838	29	18	425	176	43	98	49
1948	1,035	35	26	566	200	46	109	53
1949	1,223	39	28	705	223	49	114	65
1950	1,453	41	41	853	253	55	131	79

Sources: **25,** December 1951, p. 13; **31;** and more recent data on the movement of U.S. capital.

a. Includes transportation, communication and electric power.

TABLE 92

FOREIGN INVESTMENTS OF THE UNITED STATES: DIRECT INVESTMENTS, BY INDUSTRY AND COUNTRY, END OF 1950

(Millions of Dollars)

Area	Total	Agri-culture	Mining	Petroleum	Manufac-tures	Public Utilities [a]	Trade	Other
Total	$11,804	$545	$1,114	$3,437	$3,845	$1,428	$759	$678
America	8,239	496	952	1,808	2,655	1,329	480	519
Canada	3,564	21	334	418	1,881	284	240	385
Mexico	399	3	119	13	118	107	30	9
Guatemala	106	b	b	4	b	72	3	b
Honduras	62	b	b	b	b	9	b	b
Costa Rica	62	b	b	4	b	11	3	b
Panama	349	b	b	175	2	139	19	b
Cuba	638	239	b	20	72	271	19	b
Dominican Republic	106	b	b	b	29	11	1	b
Venezuela	981	—	—	846	24	10	24	b
Colombia	194	—	—	112	25	29	9	7
Brazil	627		8	112	270	138	70	29
Peru	140	b	55	b	16	5	13	b
Chile	530	b	341	b	29	137	15	b
Uruguay	55	—	—	3	33	2	4	13
Argentina	355		18	49	146	77	35	30
Other Latin America	71	b	b	b	b	35	b	b
Western Europe	1,774	1	18	441	971	28	186	130
United Kingdom	840	—	3	123	535	11	102	66
France	285	—	3	93	161	5	6	17
Belgium	65	—	—	17	35	—	11	2
Netherlands	84	—	—	43	23	—	13	5
Denmark	32	—	—	20	8	—	4	—
Sweden	58	—	—	25	26	—	5	2
Western Germany	202	—	—	38	121	4	19	21
Spain	31	b	b	6	15	2	b	5
Italy	63	—	—	37	19	—	1	5
Other Europe	114	b	b	39	28	6	b	7
Western European dependencies	430	9	88	292	8	18	13	1
British	302	9	81	172	7	16	9	1
Dutch	94	—	6	87	—	1	2	—
Other	34	—	1	33	—	—	1	—
Other areas	1,361	39	56	896	211	54	79	27
Saudi Arabia, Iraq, Iran	575	b	b	570	b	3	b	b
India	38	—	—	13	16	2	6	1
Indonesia	58	13	—	31	10	—	2	2
Philippines	149	15	b	27	23	47	30	b
Egypt and Sudan	40	—	—	26	8	1	3	2
Liberia	82	b	b	b	b	b	b	b
Union of South Africa	140	—	33	45	44	14	2	2
Other	279	b	b	b	b	b	b	b

Source: **25,** December 1952, p. 8. Data are based on the census of U.S. direct investments abroad made by the U.S. Department of Commerce in 1952 (**27**).

a. Includes communication.   b. Included in totals.

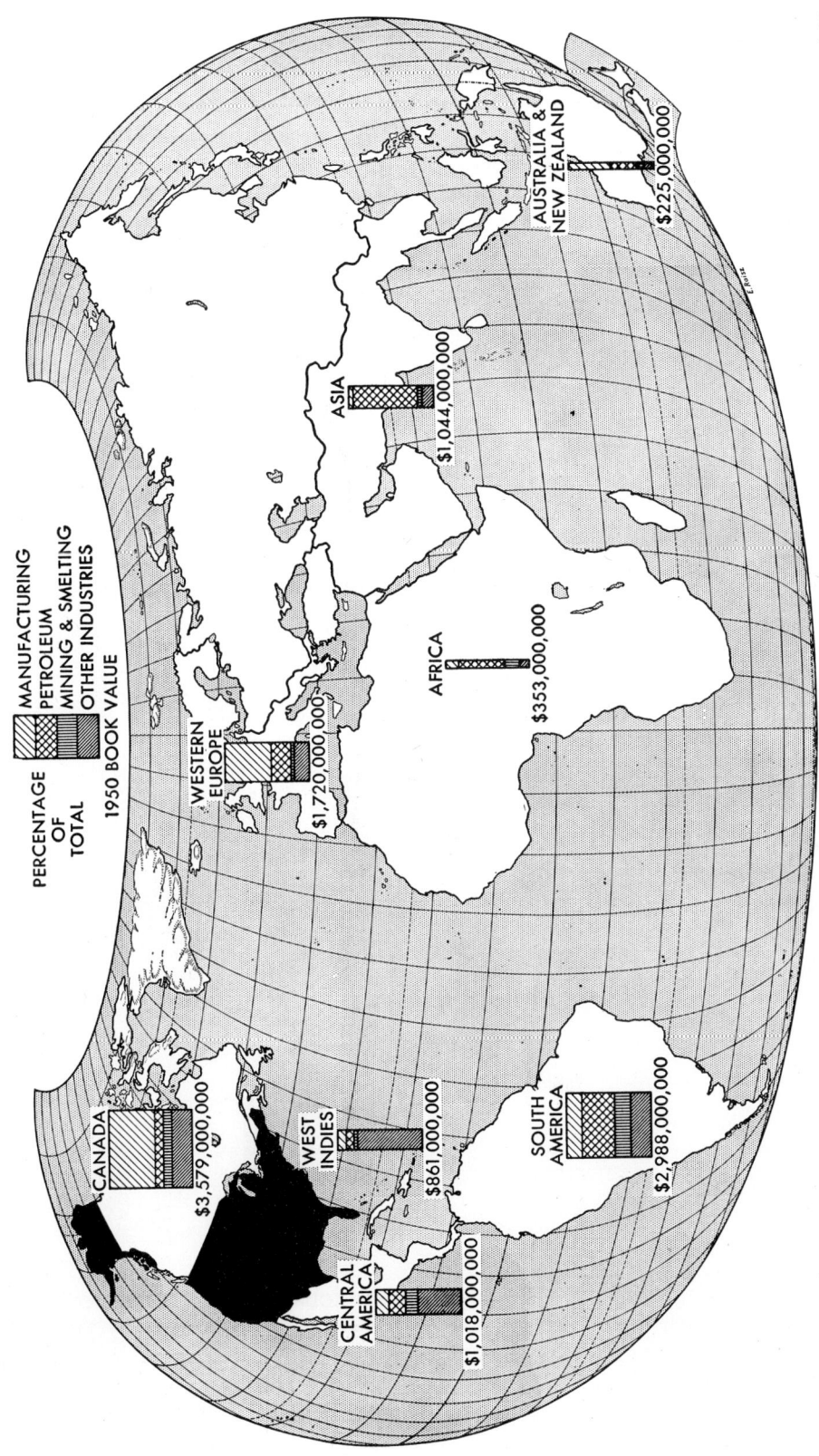

FIGURE 48. FOREIGN INVESTMENTS OF THE UNITED STATES: DIRECT INVESTMENTS, BY INDUSTRY AND AREA, END OF 1950

U.S. Department of Commerce (27)

TABLE 93

FOREIGN INVESTMENTS OF THE UNITED STATES:
GOVERNMENT LOANS TO FOREIGN COUNTRIES,
AS OF JUNE 30, 1951

(*Millions of Dollars*)

Country	Amount
Total	$10,117
American republics	499
Mexico	75
Brazil	108
Chile	85
Argentina	86
Other	109
Undistributed	36
European countries	8,526
United Kingdom	4,784
Ireland	128
France	2,039
Belgium–Luxembourg	171
Netherlands	413
Denmark	52
Norway	96
Finland	117
Germany	69
Poland	79
Italy	343
Greece	98
Yugoslavia	48
Other	89
USSR	223
Far Eastern countries	536
China	161
India	174
Indonesia	63
Philippines	97
Other	41
Other countries	282
Turkey	96
Israel	68
All other	118
United Nations	52

Source: **25,** January 1952, p. 20.

United States originated during World War I).
The loans are heavily concentrated in Western
Europe. (See Table 93; cf. Figure 49.)

Payments of principal and interest on governmental loans were so scheduled that the United
States would receive over $500 million in 1952,
annual payments would decline gradually, and
all loans (except those of the United Kingdom)

OUTSTANDING LOANS AND CREDITS...

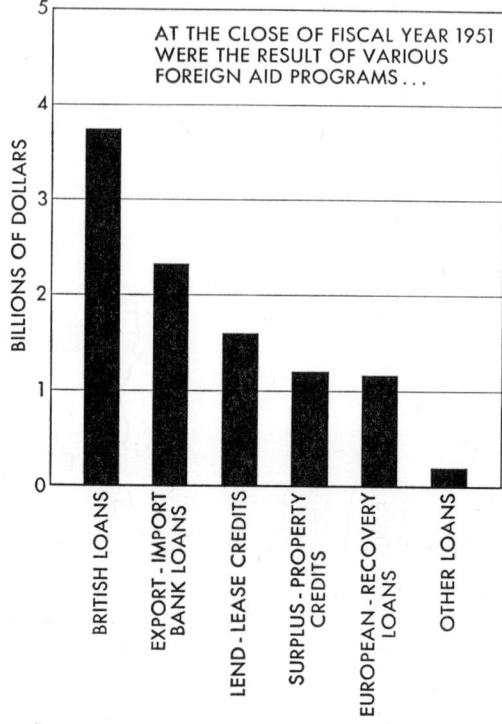

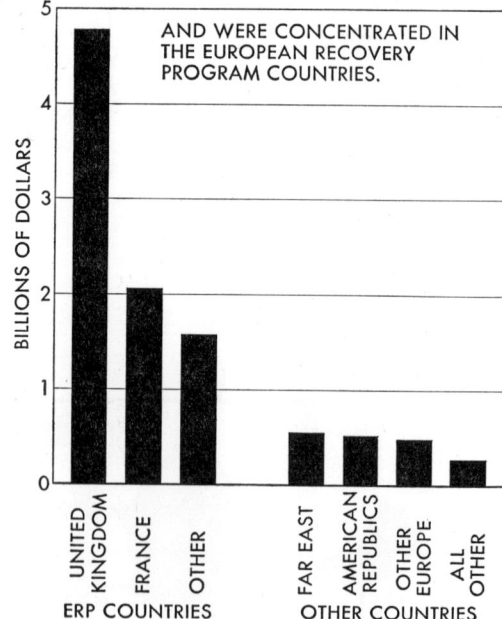

U.S. Department of Commerce (**25,** March 1952)

FIGURE 49.. FOREIGN INVESTMENTS: LOANS OF THE
UNITED STATES GOVERNMENT TO FOREIGN
COUNTRIES, AS OF JUNE 30, 1951

SCHEDULED PRINCIPAL AND INTEREST
PAYMENTS ON FOREIGN CREDITS...

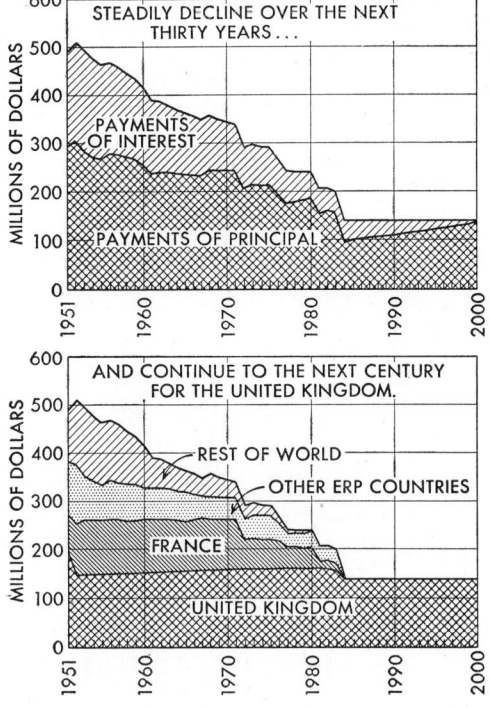

U.S. Department of Commerce (**25,** March 1952)

FIGURE 50. FOREIGN INVESTMENTS: SCHEDULE OF
PAYMENTS ON THE LOANS OF THE UNITED
STATES GOVERNMENT TO FOREIGN
COUNTRIES, 1951–2000

would be repaid in full by the end of the century. (See Figure 50.)

The pattern of the distribution of U.S. government loans among different countries contrasts sharply with the geographic distribution of the country's private investments. (See Figure 51.)

BALANCES OF PAYMENTS AFTER WORLD WAR II

In recent years, international transactions have been kept in balance by a combination of private transactions — such as exchange of goods and services, investment income, remittances and donations and the movement of capital — and official donations (grants) and official capital and gold transfers. The United States, for example, had a huge credit balance in exchange of goods and services year after year, and this surplus was offset by private donations and capital movement (net investment abroad) on the one hand and official donations and official capital transfer (governmental credits) on the other hand.

Most of the Latin American countries have had an unfavorable balance in current private transactions (goods, services and investment interest) and compensated the deficit by private capital movement.

In many European countries (the United Kingdom, France, Belgium, the Netherlands, Norway, Western Germany, Austria, Italy and Greece) the deficit in private transactions was compensated by official donations (U.S. foreign aid). In many cases short-term credits and transfer of gold played an important role in balancing other transactions. (See Table 94.)

In many countries the pattern of balance of payments changed from year to year as a result of changing business conditions. Some visible changes may have resulted from inconsistencies in estimates and differences in treatment of the ultimate balancing items (errors and omissions).

EUROPE'S BALANCE OF PAYMENTS

The huge deficit in Europe's overseas balance of payments was the most critical feature of its economic situation after World War II.[70] (See Table 95.) Three groups of factors were immediately responsible for this deficit:

1. Changes in the volume of imports and exports and an increase in the real import balance in merchandise trade.

2. A rise in prices, which bolstered the dollar deficit in merchandise trade.

3. Changes in the balance of receipts and payments for services, especially on investments and debts.

The UN Economic Commission for Europe attempted to appraise the relative importance of each of these groups of factors and found that the changes in the volume of trade and in prices were even more disastrous for Europe than losses in income from services and foreign investments.

According to the Commission, net losses in Europe's balance of payments in 1946 and 1947, as compared with 1938, were distributed as follows (in millions of dollars):[71]

	1946	1947
Total change in balance on current account	–$5,800	–$7,500
Attributable to:		
Changes in volume of trade	–950	–1,200
Changes in prices	–2,050	–3,600
Losses in income from investments and services	–2,800	–2,700

70. **12,** p. xiii.
71. **12,** p. 58.

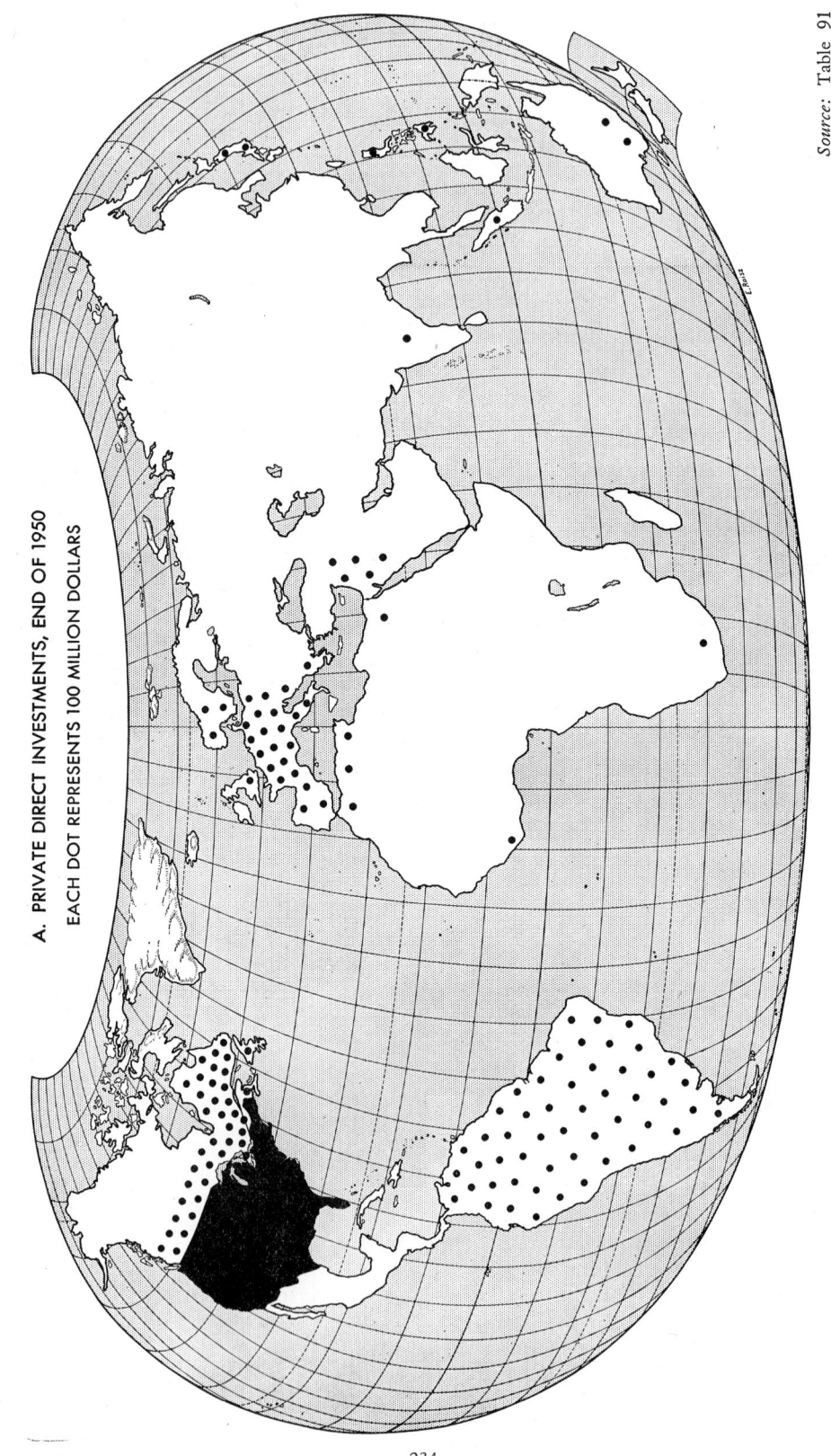

A. PRIVATE DIRECT INVESTMENTS, END OF 1950

EACH DOT REPRESENTS 100 MILLION DOLLARS

Source: Table 91

234

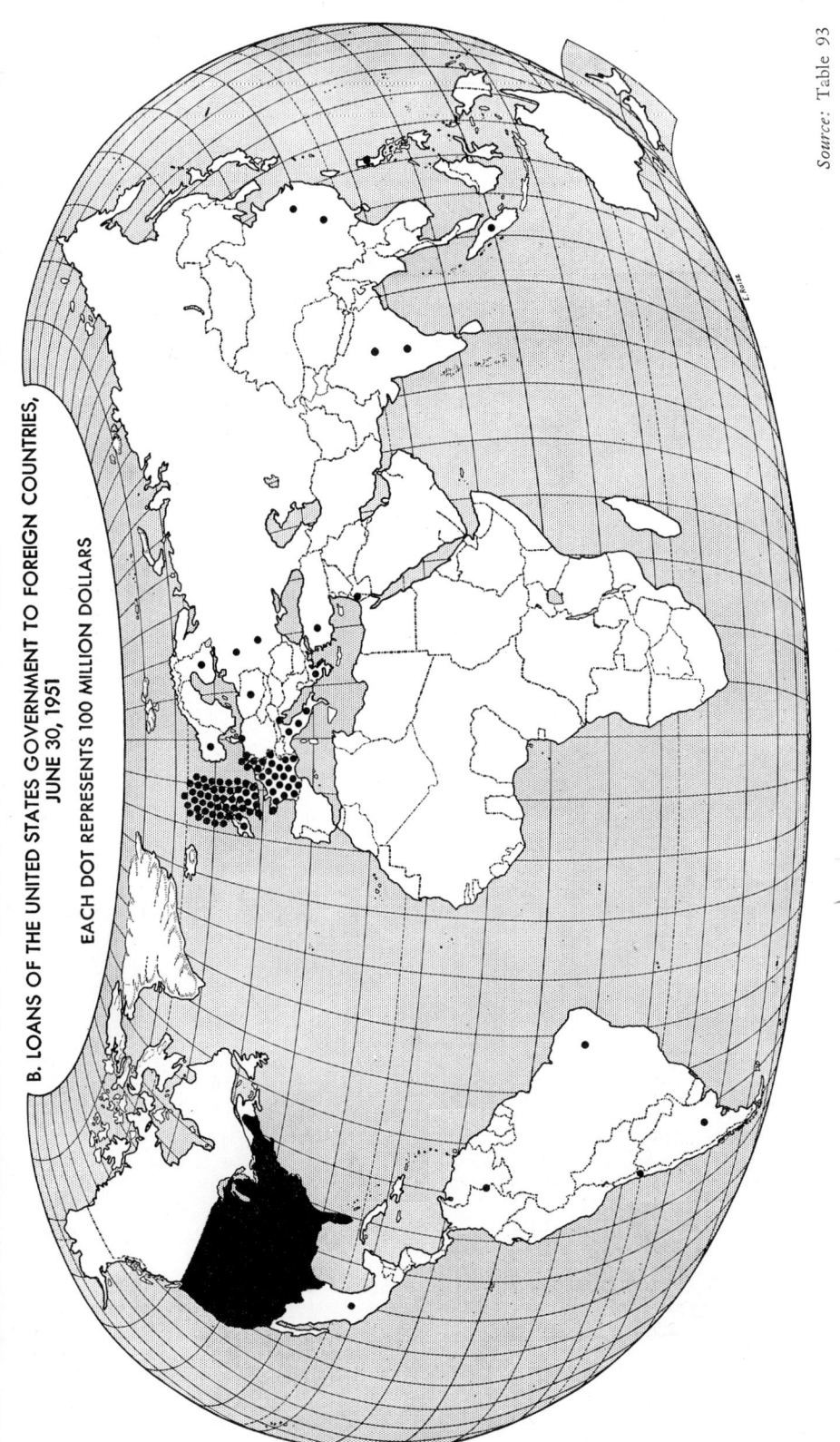

B. LOANS OF THE UNITED STATES GOVERNMENT TO FOREIGN COUNTRIES, JUNE 30, 1951

EACH DOT REPRESENTS 100 MILLION DOLLARS

FIGURE 51. UNITED STATES ASSETS ABROAD: GEOGRAPHIC DISTRIBUTION, 1950–51

A. Private direct investments were heavily concentrated in Canada ($3,850 million in 1950) and Latin America ($5,065 million). Venezuela and Panama have been the favorite areas in recent years.

B. At the end of the fiscal year 1951, 85 per cent of the long-term credits of the U.S. government were extended to European countries; the rest were scattered all over the world — in Latin America (5 per cent), the Far East (5 per cent), and elsewhere.

Source: Table 93

TABLE 94

BALANCES OF PAYMENTS OF SELECTED COUNTRIES, 1938 AND 1948–52

(Millions of Currency Units)

Country and Currency Unit	Year	Goods and Transportation	Investment Income	Other Services	Private Donations	Private Capital	Official Donations	Official Capital and Gold		Errors and Omissions
								Long-term	Short-term and Gold	
United States [a] (U.S. $)	1938	1,030	431	−142	−153	52	−18	—	−1,449	249
	1948	5,768	1,515	−625	−675	−1,380	−3,675	−939	−1,006	1,017
	1949	5,765	1,345	−706	−519	−988	−5,016	−459	−159	737
	1950	1,235	1,577	−806	−480	−1,198	−3,446	605	2,470	43
	1951	3,436	2,157	−1,421	−409	−1,339	−2,912	−861	850	499
	1952	3,636	1,454	−1,839	−430	−791	−1,930	−147	577	470
Canada [b] (Can. $)	1938	346	−241	10	−15	−89	—	−12	−5	6
	1948	616	−255	104	9	17	−23	46	−514	...
	1949	487	−307	14	−11	46	−6	−103	−120	...
	1950	159	−384	−76	−28	901	−5	−72	−495	...
	1951	−5	−335	−154	−14	783	−9	−26	−240	...
	1952	614	−267	−145	−35	−9	−16	39	−181	...
Mexico (U.S. $)	1938	80.1	−40.7	9.7	2.0	5.8	—	−1.6	−7.7	−47.6
	1948	−127.0	−76.9	127.4	...	12.1	9.6	−4.9	64.4	−4.7
	1949	−86.6	−57.0	153.7	...	−6.3	24.7	5.1	−48.9	15.3
	1950	−70.8	−65.9	176.8	...	69.9	12.3	3.5	−176.0	50.2
	1951	−272.9	−38.5	207.0	1.5	56.1	2.9	−4.7	−27.3	75.9
	1952	−193.8	−51.7	216.3	1.5	43.5	1.5	21.5	5.6	−44.5
Venezuela (U.S. $)	1938	70.8	−59.2	−1.1	...	28.0	—	...	−6.6	−31.9
	1948	324.7	−436.7	−0.8	−16.1	318.8	0.4	−0.2	−128.6	−61.5
	1949	199.6	−287.6	−69.8	−17.8	270.3	—	...	−60.0	−34.7
	1950	521.1	−387.7	−75.3	−15.5	−34.0	—	0.1	80.4	−89.1
	1951	566.8	−412.7	−81.9	−17.9	−7.4	—	1.2	−5.1	−43.0
	1952	558.5	−425.3	−89.1	−19.1	118.0	—	3.6	−69.7	−76.9
Colombia (U.S. $)	1938	9.9	...	−17.6	...	3.8	...	...	−5.9	9.8
	1948	−44.5	−6.5	−12.1	...	18.5	...	−0.7	28.7	16.6
	1949	66.9	−13.8	−39.0	...	−1.5	...	−1.0	−33.8	22.2
	1950	51.5	−39.3	−31.3	−0.8	6.4	...	−1.1	25.3	−10.7
	1951	54.1	−36.3	−47.5	13.7	11.6	0.3	8.4	−27.5	23.2
	1952	65.4	−19.4	−42.5	−1.5	0.3	...	47.2	−37.6	−11.9
Brazil (Cruzeiros)	1948	2,265	−1,906	−1,205	−142	2,197	15	−2,313	365	724
	1949	938	−1,806	−1,236	−64	1,008	11	−130	−239	1,518
	1950	5,634	−1,773	−1,615	−60	−1,725	15	−1,323	1,124	−277
	1951	−3,077	−1,575	−2,255	−76	266	16	−406	5,919	1,188
	1952	−9,455	−668	−1,500	−72	10,667	−4	48	1,844	−860
Peru (U.S. $)	1938	15.9	−26.5	0.9	1.0	2.6	—	...	6.3	−0.2
	1948	2.9	−13.5	−0.8	3.1	2.4	0.5	3.9	2.3	−0.8
	1949	8.3	−11.3	1.2	3.5	7.4	0.9	−3.2	−5.8	−1.0
	1950	23.6	−9.6	−21.8	2.2	12.0	1.7	−0.8	−5.1	−2.2
	1951	—	−21.6	−16.8	2.3	40.9	1.7	−4.4	−4.0	1.9
	1952	−38.0	−20.5	−7.5	5.7	56.7	3.0	−5.6	4.3	1.9

(Continued on facing page)

TABLE 94—*continued*

Country and Currency Unit	Year	Goods and Transpor-tation	Invest-ment Income	Other Services	Private Dona-tions	Private Capital	Official Donations	Official Capital and Gold Long-term	Official Capital and Gold Short-term and Gold	Errors and Omissions
Chile (U.S. $)	1948	67.7	−73.1	−1.9	0.1	8.1	—	9.6	−10.4	−0.1
	1949	−31.7	−51.7	−1.6	1.4	49.9	—	23.2	−3.0	13.5
	1950	51.7	−58.1	−4.5	−1.0	−5.6	—	14.3	−4.7	7.9
	1951	26.3	−65.6	2.7	−0.7	34.6	0.1	6.5	−1.2	−2.7
	1952	79.0	−65.6	−3.9	−0.4	33.3	—	−2.2	−23.0	−17.2
Argentina (U.S. $)	1938	−38.0	−122.0	−8.0	...	−23.0	—	40.0	154.0	−3.0
	1946	568.7	−134.3	−9.3	...	−98.0	...	−230.2	−71.2	−25.7
	1947	103.9	−82.2	−50.9	...	−39.9	...	−112.3	294.5	−113.1
	1948	−33.8	−7.6	−39.8	...	5.8	...	−428.6	317.4	186.6
	1949	−106.0	−9.8	−22.2	...	39.4	...	−2.6	36.6	64.6
	1950	140.6	−3.0	−24.0	...	46.6	...	...	−86.4	−73.8
	1951	−232.4	−28.4	−20.2	...	146.6	...	88.4	19.8	26.2
	1952	...	...	...	...	...	...	...	...	...
United Kingdom [e] (£)	1938	−282	175	37	...	−39	...	...	130	−21
	1948	−115	89	86	−34	−145	113	141	−135	...
	1949	−46	94	31	−21	−212	187	−9	−24	...
	1950	11	144	167	4	−82	116	−2	−358	...
	1951	−612	117	96	−5	−261	48	−54	671	...
	1952	7	68	94	−7	−103	107	8	−174	...
France and over-seas areas (U.S. $)	1948	−1,495.4	57.0	−212.3	...	67.3	715.2	275.5	599.6	−6.9
	1949	−627.1	22.1	−96.6	...	20.7	1,025.8	38.3	−382.2	−1.0
	1950	−174.4	−25.3	−17.0	5.1	106.4	527.9	−85.0	−339.5	1.8
	1951	−973.4	−29.7	−41.8	5.1	38.2	467.1	−95.8	595.5	34.8
	1952	−783.1	−19.0	195.9	4.9	49.1	299.8	−61.7	320.7	−6.6
Belgium–Luxembourg (Francs)	1937	−1,405	1,600	875	...	407	...	−26	1,812	−3,263
	1948	−7,223	1,740	−974	763	2,932	223	1,048	1,859	−368
	1949	2,090	275	−529	469	−282	122	869	−2,729	−285
	1950	−12,231	196	−803	895	−2,620	166	−2,474	17,038	−167
	1951	11,656	930	−1,675	624	−2,240	1,107	−436	−10,054	88
	1952	8,179	835	−579	199	−3,643	400	1,309	−7,473	773
Netherlands (Guilders)	1938	−151	245	3	5	−117	—	2	−252	265
	1948	−1,424	132	156	−7	348	551	161	83	—
	1949	−762	215	325	−4	24	−1,371	1,562	43	−32
	1950	−1,474	133	275	7	106	1,141	30	−203	−15
	1951	−810	188	532	−13	208	488	−308	−135	−150
	1952	851	257	676	27	60	224	−183	−1,987	75
Denmark (Kroner)	1938	186	−75	10	−5	−47	—	−45	−35	11
	1948	−268	−67	47	...	99	76	237	−153	29
	1949	−177	−75	−20	...	−111	484	76	−157	−20
	1950	−727	−87	−15	...	110	456	450	−204	17
	1951	−257	−70	40	...	63	421	−145	−125	73
	1952	218	−72	60	...	23	44	−147	−329	203

(Continued on following page)

TABLE 94—*continued*

Country and Currency Unit	Year	Goods and Transportation	Investment Income	Other Services	Private Donations	Private Capital	Official Donations	Official Capital and Gold Long-term	Official Capital and Gold Short-term and Gold	Errors and Omissions
Sweden (Kronor)	1938	−7	104	−13	13	−12	—	−42	−45	2
	1948	326	19	−91	−4	310	−86	−101	207	72
	1949	475	16	−27	−4	61	−32	−32	−446	−11
	1950	181	14	−20	−13	−415	−70	113	201	9
	1951	998	52	−87	−33	327	30	−196	−1,059	−32
	1952	201	70	−115	−35	155	41	−129	−188	...
Norway (Kroner)	1938	69	−60	81	7	−23	—	−53	−35	14
	1948	−712	−63	−29	28	34	203	349	155	35
	1949	−1,099	−59	−86	20	183	630	99	258	54
	1950	−713	−67	−78	11	−42	1,061	132	−254	−60
	1951	423	−78	−187	7	−251	378	64	−312	−44
	1952	195	−61	−131	18	−129	167	−94	−183	218
Finland (Markkaa)	1938	645	−150	−45	80	−425	—	−390	−279	564
	1948	5,040	−1,260	−190	1,390	−1,199	−11,550	3,056	4,860	−147
	1949	13,180	−1,470	180	790	−2,141	−12,230	568	1,501	−378
	1950	6,450	−2,380	−2,420	410	7,198	−7,850	−32	−1,902	526
	1951	54,120	−2,370	−5,990	370	6,279	−12,400	−6,443	−33,717	151
	1952	−7,680	−2,820	−2,800	330	−4,069	−8,220	−2,443	21,988	5,714
Germany, Western (U.S. $)	1948	−1,029.8	...	0.6	125.5	—	929.7	46.2	−89.3	17.1
	1949	−885.2	−0.1	5.6	3.4	—	683.8	−7.9	174.5	25.9
	1950	−654.1	0.1	30.3	7.0	—	490.8	8.6	151.6	−34.3
	1951	126.3	−4.0	28.3	10.6	—	427.7	−37.2	−478.9	−72.8
	1952	413.5	4.6	139.3	11.3	—	116.4	−143.6	−569.2	27.7
Switzerland (Francs)	1948	−1,620	...	400	79	−4	...	...	−389	1,534
	1949	−400	...	300	...	−370	...	...	−326	796
	1950	−674	...	250	...	−321	...	...	514	231
	1951	−1,289	300	300	...	−194	...	...	57	826
	1952	−517	300	340	...	−867	...	...	−308	1,052
Austria (U.S. $)	1948	−278.3	−0.2	11.5	26.8	0.5	260.2	11.5	−19.3	−12.7
	1949	−311.5	−0.6	16.7	9.3	−0.5	290.8	6.0	−11.4	1.2
	1950	−158.5	−0.5	26.9	4.1	−0.5	183.5	−2.2	−10.5	−42.3
	1951	−216.8	0.3	40.3	2.4	−0.8	222.4	−3.4	−27.6	−16.8
	1952	−165.6	1.1	60.0	2.4	—	103.4	−3.9	−58.3	60.9
Portugal, overseas areas (Escudos)	1948	−6,348	120	730	662	1,983	—	−251	2,966	138
	1949	−4,502	114	847	716	805	119	−414	1,917	398
	1950	−1,139	115	711	703	159	387	280	−1,139	−77
	1951	−196	213	726	761	275	515	135	−2,694	265
	1952	−1,637	52	813	299	400	238	39	−659	455
Italy (U.S. $)	1938	−162.0	−8.4	57.1	37.6	...	...	...	16.7	59.0
	1948	−432.2	−12.3	103.4	131.9	157.4	285.1	131.4	−358.5	−6.2
	1949	−353.1	−15.7	114.5	118.4	158.2	288.9	44.1	−386.6	31.3
	1950	−178.2	−9.5	108.6	110.5	−38.0	195.8	−50.6	49.6	−188.2
	1951	−379.1	−7.3	117.7	108.7	173.7	213.9	−33.2	−210.7	16.3
	1952	−784.4	−12.9	166.2	132.4	224.7	166.2	−15.8	101.9	21.7

(*Continued on facing page*)

TABLE 94—*continued*

Country and Currency Unit	Year	Goods and Transportation	Investment Income	Other Services	Private Donations	Private Capital	Official Donations	Official Capital and Gold		Errors and Omissions
								Long-term	Short-term and Gold	
Yugoslavia (Dinars)	1938	1,665	−646	36	299	89	—	−126	−360	43
	1948	−2,624	. . .	−252	885	102	2,749	−1,801	1,148	−207
	1949	−6,344	−124	−281	699	283	1,082	−2,325	6,719	291
	1950	−5,573	−128	−267	1,341	—	1,212	2,347	1,309	−241
	1951	−11,471	−267	−184	1,477	46	9,353	1,225	−98	−81
	1952	−36,783	−1,658	−1,350	6,137	49	30,729	5,407	−2,777	246
Greece (U.S. $)	1938	−38.6	−0.1	9.7	23.7	9.0	—	1.3	−5.1	0.1
	1948	−446.3	−3.8	10.3	11.1	11.1	353.7	38.6	31.2	−5.9
	1949	−390.0	−2.1	3.3	8.6	17.7	373.4	−2.0	−10.6	1.7
	1950	−329.8	−5.0	2.5	14.3	16.0	300.3	−1.6	−0.2	3.5
	1951	−313.9	−3.0	7.2	17.0	14.5	280.0	−2.2	2.5	−2.1
	1952	−143.7	−1.1	1.3	18.0	14.6	126.6	−5.3	−14.0	3.6
China (U.S. $)	1936	2	−25	71	95	18	—	−34	. . .	. . .
	1948	−156	−5	−39	100	55	212	20	−105	−82
China: Taiwan (U.S. $)	1937	28.5	−4.6	—	. . .	8.5	—	. . .	1.4	−33.8
	1950	−94.6	−1.0	−0.3	4.0	. . .	30.5	−4.1	68.1	−2.6
	1951	−42.6	−0.6	−5.8	2.2	0.3	59.2	−4.5	−8.9	0.7
	1952	−84.8	−0.3	−11.5	1.7	0.6	94.6	−1.2	−1.9	2.8
Japan (U.S. $)	1936	54.0	50.8	−34.3	36.9	−86.8	—	−7.0	−6.9	−6.7
	1948	−401.9	−2.2	17.3	0.6	—	461.0	3.6	−105.3	26.9
	1949	−355.9	−1.3	50.8	4.0	—	513.5	−17.5	−178.7	−14.9
	1950	−116.7	−5.6	192.5	43.1	5.4	360.3	−0.2	−456.7	−22.1
	1951	−501.9	−5.3	665.6	15.7	34.2	156.5	−2.4	−369.6	7.2
	1952	−556.0	−4.9	754.2	27.0	37.5	6.4	−77.0	−185.8	−1.4
Turkey (£ T.)	1946	194.5	−0.4	−14.2	6.8	0.7	1.1	−32.8	−20.9	−134.8
	1949	−259.1	−36.6	−22.4	9.5	23.3	194.8	39.1	16.4	35.0
	1950	−124.4	−37.3	−26.0	4.1	25.7	243.1	48.0	131.3	−264.5
	1951	. . .	. . .	. . .	. . .	. . .	. . .	. . .	. . .	. . .
	1952	. . .	. . .	. . .	. . .	. . .	. . .	. . .	. . .	. . .
Israel (£ I.)	1949	−76.2	−0.3	−1.2	42.5	. . .	—	6.6	8.5	20.1
	1950	−89.6	−0.4	−6.3	40.7	. . .	—	16.6	22.2	16.8
	1951	−106.7	−0.3	−8.8	42.3	. . .	5.0	34.3	6.5	27.7
	1952	. . .	. . .	. . .	. . .	. . .	. . .	. . .	. . .	. . .
Iraq (1,000 Iraqi dinars)	1939	3,756	−6.074	1,575	−120	1,007	24	−76	1	−93
	1948	−23,679	−1,573	175	14	11,526	−499	7,654	5,179	1,203
	1949	−11,045	−5,570	1,535	108	9,607	—	637	509	4,219
	1950	13,065	−16,542	1,775	77	11,216	—	3,328	−8,991	−3,928
	1951	15,538	−10,625	−1,421	4	6,627	−53	−944	498	−9,624
	1952	72,530	−78,469	−1,556	9	14,714	—	−605	−11,071	4,448
Iran [d] (Rials)	1946	5,298	−4,716	−205	. . .	. . .	—	−807	96	334
	1949	7,323	−8,921	−384	91	. . .	—	838	877	176
	1950	17,190	−17,642	−132	190	. . .	—	—	−3	397
	1951	3,733	−5,762	−96	114	. . .	75	−41	1,829	148
	1952	−1,039	−62	−21	24	. . .	504	−19	990	−377

(*Continued on following page*)

TABLE 94—*continued*

Country and Currency Unit	Year	Goods and Transportation	Investment Income	Other Services	Private Donations	Private Capital	Official Donations	Official Capital and Gold Long-term	Short-term and Gold	Errors and Omissions
Pakistan [e] (Rupees)	1948	320.3	−4.0	−219.3	−18.2	1.7	—	−108.9	22.1	6.3
	1949	−31.6	−7.9	−381.6	−27.8	8.4	—	—	503.6	−63.1
	1950	266.9	−17.7	−321.7	−26.6	−0.4	—	−139.2	249.9	−11.2
	1951	1,120.5	−18.2	−549.5	−25.3	24.9	−1.7	−812.6	258.7	3.2
	1952	−212.9	−12.1	−553.5	−25.0	−37.8	—	276.4	578.7	−13.8
India [f] (Rupees)	1939	313	−271	−199	. . .	. . .	—	−107	143	121
	1948	−542	−178	−533	99	−154	—	−2,163	3,889	−419
	1949	−1,833	−179	−72	103	−210	—	84	1,666	−416
	1950	478	−236	75	116	−88	21	87	−285	−168
	1951	−861	−241	—	134	−24	14	356	747	−125
	1952	−792	−112	237	168	−19	119	495	215	−311
Burma (Kyats)	1950	185.9	−4.9	−65.1	−101.1	−11.9	. . .	. . .	−15.0	12.1
	1951	324.3	−5.1	−27.1	−49.1	−13.7	21.9	−29.8	−163.7	−57.7
	1952	330.4	−4.5	−44.8	−41.8	−9.6	35.3	—	−240.0	−25.0
Ceylon (Rupees)	1938	56	−47	−13	−24	. . .	—	. . .	9	19
	1948	86	−49	48	−68	2	−4	10	−51	26
	1949	33	−29	24	−58	−22	—	38	18	−4
	1950	258	−55	3	−69	−22	—	11	−148	22
	1951	267	−64	−37	−77	−42	—	−76	−34	63
	1952	−242	−46	−55	−104	25	—	−7	378	51
Indonesia [g] (Rupiah)	1948	−230	−67	−6	. . .	−74	355	−22	158	−114
	1949	−292	−137	−252	. . .	−31	631	160	−13	−66
	1950	872	−92	−177	. . .	−42	148	65	−826	52
	1951	1,062	−169	−251	. . .	−34	2	97	−529	−178
	1952	−2,250	−304	−830	. . .	−218	83	897	2,576	46
Philippines (Pesos)	1946	−720	3	589	3	30	132	61	71	−169
	1949	−762	−60	248	31	12	406	−9	323	−189
	1950	−32	−53	109	22	28	309	68	−267	−184
	1951	−200	−61	122	16	10	25	−7	104	−9
	1952	−215	−37	180	30	44	50	−16	−4	−32
Egypt (£ E.)	1948	−15.4	−3.1	4.7	. . .	−11.2	—	−5.1	26.2	3.9
	1949	3.1	−8.9	9.1	. . .	−2.6	—	0.6	−1.7	0.4
	1950	−5.7	−11.2	6.5	. . .	−2.2	—	−3.2	14.2	1.6
	1951	−11.3	−12.5	7.4	. . .	−3.1	1.2	−29.5	47.8	—
	1952	−37.6	−12.1	−3.7	. . .	−1.2	—	−14.7	69.9	−0.6
Ethiopia ($ Eth.)	1948	−2.7	−1.4	−0.9	−4.0	. . .	—	1.8	−6.5	13.7
	1949	−0.4	−1.7	−0.8	−4.0	. . .	—	10.2	−6.0	2.7
	1950	13.6	−0.4	−3.6	−1.7	0.6	−0.1	8.1	−16.6	0.1
	1951	29.7	−1.2	−13.7	−1.5	. . .	—	−6.0	−7.6	0.3
	1952	10.5	−1.6	−6.1	−2.6	6.9	0.1	−12.6	4.7	0.7

(*Continued on facing page*)

TABLE 94—*continued*

Country and Currency Unit	Year	Goods and Transportation	Investment Income	Other Services	Private Donations	Private Capital	Official Donations	Official Capital and Gold		Errors and Omissions
								Long-term	Short-term and Gold	
Union of South Africa (£ S.A.)	1937	13.1	−21.5	−6.0	−1.1	...	—	1.9	6.9	6.7
	1948	−150.3	−24.0	−1.3	0.5	...	—	−80.0	163.8	91.3
	1949	−82.2	−30.9	−0.4	—	...	—	83.5	−19.6	49.6
	1950	35.9	−34.8	−2.8	1.9	...	—	16.7	−70.1	53.2
	1951	−62.9	−42.5	0.6	3.0	...	—	9.0	34.9	57.9
	1952	−19.8	−46.7	2.2	0.7	...	—	14.6	5.6	43.4
Australia [h] (£ A.)	1939	22.0	−39.6	−5.4	0.7	−3.2	—	2.6	22.9	...
	1948	39.5	−42.2	−2.6	1.6	36.2	8.6	−16.0	−75.4	50.3
	1949	82.3	−39.6	−22.7	7.0	37.8	0.3	−28.9	−143.9	107.7
	1949	41	−40	−24	12	...	−9	−30	−110	160
	1950	32	−57	−31	9	...	19	−61	−77	166
	1951	−118	−58	−45	5	27	10	8	91	80
	1952	−95	−58	−42	4	23	−4	104	12	56
New Zealand (£ N.Z.)	1946	42.3	−4.8	−7.3	−0.7	3.6	4.0	−41.5	−8.2	12.6
	1948	25.7	−6.4	−21.9	−1.4	7.0	—	−9.1	2.6	3.5
	1949	22.8	−6.7	−18.1	−2.8	1.0	—	2.1	2.7	−1.0
	1950	33.1	−5.1	−10.2	−0.9	−2.1	—	5.1	−19.2	−0.7
	1951	33.5	−6.0	−9.1	1.9	0.8	—	−34.5	20.6	−7.2
	1952	−13.8	−2.3	−12.2	2.7	3.3	—	9.4	−0.3	13.2

Source: **10**, 1953, pp. 390–98. The nonmonetary gold movement which is included in "Goods and Transportation" is the difference between net gold transactions with foreigners and the movement in the gold holdings of the official and banking institutions of the reporting country (included in "Official Short-term Capital and Gold"). This difference is the result of gold production and the movement of gold into or out of consumption within the country.

"Other Services" include government expenditure not classified elsewhere, foreign travel, etc.

"Donations" cover one-way transactions, both in cash and kind. "Private Donations" include personal and institutional remittances and migrants' transfers. "Official Donations" include grants such as those under the European Recovery Program and UNRRA, reparations, lend-lease settlements, etc.

"Official Capital and Gold" covers transactions of official and banking institutions of the reporting country.

"Errors and Omissions": in theory, the total credit transactions should equal the total debit transactions. The final balance that occurs in practice represents errors and omissions.

Credits and debits: no sign indicates a credit and a minus sign (−) a debit.

a. For 1948–52, excludes goods and services donated under military aid programs.

b. For 1950–52, excludes military aid donations.

c. "Private Capital," for 1938, shows only transactions with the United States; for 1948–52, includes errors and omissions.

d. Data for 12 months, beginning March 21 of year stated. Private capital movement included in investment income.

e. Excludes military grants.

f. For 1939, data for nonpartitioned India.

g. Excludes transactions of foreign-owned oil companies.

h. For 1939 and 1948–49, data for fiscal year ending June 30.

TABLE 95

EUROPEAN BALANCE OF PAYMENTS WITH THE UNITED STATES AND OTHER NON-EUROPEAN COUNTRIES,
1938 AND 1946–50

(*Billions of Dollars*)

Item	1938	1946	1947	1948	1949	1950
	Total Balance					
Europe's imports	–$5.8	–$9.4	–$13.0	–$14.4	–$13.5	–$12.5
Europe's exports	+3.7	+4.3	+6.1	+8.8	+9.4	+9.6
Balance of trade	–2.1	–5.1	–6.9	–5.6	–4.1	–2.9
Receipts from transportation and other services (net)	+0.7	–1.2	–1.0	+0.3	–0.1	–0.1
Income from investments (net)	+1.4	+0.5	+0.4	+0.4	+0.4	+0.5
Balance on current account	0.0	–5.8	–7.5	–4.9	–3.8	–2.5
	Balance with the United States					
Europe's imports	–1.3	–4.4	–5.9	–4.6	–4.4	–3.6
Europe's exports	+0.6	+0.9	+0.9	+1.3	+1.1	+1.6
Balance of trade	–0.7	–3.5	–5.0	–3.3	–3.3	–2.0
Receipts from transportation and other services (net)	+0.1	+0.1	–0.5	–0.1	+0.1	+0.3
Income from investments (net)	+0.2	–0.8	+0.1	0.0	0.0	+0.1
Balance on current account	–0.4	–4.2	–5.4	–3.4	–3.2	–1.6
	Balance with Other Non-European Countries					
Europe's imports	–4.5	–5.0	–7.1	–9.8	–9.1	–8.9
Europe's exports	+3.1	+3.4	+5.2	+7.5	+8.3	+8.0
Balance of trade	–1.4	–1.6	–1.9	–2.3	–0.8	–0.9
Receipts from transportation and other services (net)	+0.5	–0.4	–0.5	+0.4	–0.2	–0.4
Income from investments (net)	+1.3	+0.4	+0.3	+0.4	+0.4	+0.4
Balance on current account	+0.4	–1.6	–2.1	–1.5	–0.6	–0.9

Sources: **12**, p. 54; **14**, 1949, p. 109; **6**, 1939–1945, p. 33.

Moreover, Europe's deficit in merchandise trade in 1946–47 was no larger than in the first two years after World War I. The difference was in the balance of other current transactions. Europe's consolidated balances for the two-year periods were as follows (in millions of dollars): [72]

	1919 and 1920	*1946 and 1947*
Balance of trade	–$12,000	–$12,000
Europe's imports	–19,700	–22,400
Europe's exports	+7,700	+10,400
Balance of other current accounts	+4,000	–1,300
Receipts from transportation and other services (net)	+2,200	–2,200
Income from investments (net)	+1,800	+900

A closer examination of Europe's balances of payments in 1946–50 reveals that the deficit was due largely to the unbalance in its transactions with the United States. These transactions resulted in a cumulative deficit of $17.8 billion, as compared with a deficit of $6.7 billion in Europe's exchange with all other non-European countries.

This pattern of balances of payments reflected the fact that the United States was the only country in the world able to supply European countries with the commodities they needed most in order to resume industrial production on the prewar scale. On the other hand, the United States was also the only country able to finance Europe's deficit and provide the fresh investment capital required to restore and modernize its industrial plant.

The deficit of $5,800 million in 1946 was balanced as follows (in millions of dollars): [73]

UNRRA and other public and private donations	$2,300
Loans and credits	2,500
Use of European gold stock and dollar balances and liquidation of other external assets	1,000

In more recent years, transactions related to financing the deficit have become increasingly complex, and the International Monetary Fund has devised a new form to record them: [74]

In the new presentation of balances of payment attention is focused on the lack of balance in international transactions and "compensatory financing"

supplied by monetary authorities. Before World War II the reasonably good measure of their action was the movement of monetary reserves. In the post-war period, shipments of gold and similar measures were of minor importance in comparison with official grants and loans. Grants and loans which serve to balance international transactions are therefore separated from investment operations and handled along with movement of monetary gold, under the heading of "Compensatory Official Financing."

In this approach, the balance of payment of a nation is handled as a record of measures taken for balancing the deficit or surplus resulting from the nation's foreign trade, movement of private capital and other international transactions. In the case of a deficit such measures include the sales of monetary gold, reduction of bank balances abroad, special loans and credits from foreign governments and banks, and straight grants received from foreign governments. In the case of a surplus, the balancing items are the grants and loans given to foreign countries, increase of bank balances abroad, purchase of gold and so on.

The general idea of this classification is revealed by the fact that data published by the International Monetary Fund as "Europe's Balance of Payment" [75] appear in the publication of the UN under the title "The Financing of Europe's Overseas Deficit." [76]

According to the new form of presenting international transactions, Europe's deficit on current accounts (including merchandise trade, services and income from private investments), private capital movements, private donations from abroad, public debt settlements and official financing of specific investment projects totaled $19.5 billion in 1947–50.

This deficit was financed as follows (in millions of dollars): [77]

Grants from the U.S. government	+$11,000
Long-term loans (net)	
From the United States	+5,800
From other countries	+900
Loans from international institutions	+1,500
Movement of sterling balances	–400
Movement of U.S. dollar balances	+200
Gold movements	
To and from the United States	+1,700
To and from other countries	–1,200

72. **12**, p. 59.
73. **12**, p. 64.
74. See **18**, 1949–50, pp. 1–27; cf. **17**, *passim*.
75. **18**, 1949–50, p. 33.
76. **14**, 1950, p. 118. The advantage of this system of recording over the conventional registration of international transactions is questionable. Governments that are members of the IMF use the new form in their reports to the Fund but have not accepted it as a basis for current statistics of balance of payments. The *Statistical Yearbook* of the UN uses the IMF data in a condensed and simplified form (**10**, 1952, pp. 379–85).
77. See Table 96.

By 1951, after the devaluation of sterling, the stability and limited convertibility of European currencies were restored, partly thanks to the European Payments Union and the services of the International Monetary Fund. The growth of production, expansion of intra-European trade and shift of European exports to the soft-currency countries of South America and Asia have reduced the dependence of European countries upon the United States for imports, capital and financial assistance.

The outbreak of war in Korea had a dual impact on Europe's balance of payments: it curtailed the flow of economic aid from the United States but at the same time launched a business boom in European countries and their colonial possessions.[78]

Although the upswing was followed by a setback in the latter part of 1951, the trade position of Europe continued to improve. This general tendency is evidenced by the declining amount of the deficit demanding compensatory official financing in France, Belgium-Luxembourg, the Netherlands, Denmark, Sweden, Norway and Western Germany. There were, however, exceptions to this general trend — for example, in the United Kingdom — and difficulties were increasing by the end of 1951 and at the beginning of 1952.[79]

LATIN AMERICAN BALANCES OF PAYMENTS

The economic progress of Latin American republics is reflected in the rapid growth of their share in world trade. Their exports increased from 8.5 per cent of the world total in 1938 to 10.7 per cent in 1951, while their imports rose from 7.7 per cent to 9.3 per cent.[80] The joint balance of trade in merchandise [81] (including transportation cost) of this area shows a slight export surplus, which is more than offset by the import surplus on the account of services, including interest and dividend payments on loans and foreign investments.[82] The remaining net deficit on all current transactions fluctuates from year to year, usually in the range from $100 to $300 million.

This deficit has been almost completely offset by the inflow of private capital. With correction

78. **14**, 1951, p. 3.
79. **13**, 1950–51, pp. 3ff.
80. See **19**.
81. The second column in Table 94.
82. The second and third columns in Table 94.

TABLE 96

EUROPE'S BALANCE OF PAYMENTS: FINANCING THE DEFICIT, 1947–50

(Billions of Dollars)

Item	1947	1948	1949	1950
Balance on goods and services [a]	–$7.4	–$4.9	–$3.8	–$2.5
Private donations	+0.4	+0.3	+0.3	+0.2
Private capital movements	–0.8	+0.1	–0.5	–0.2
Special official financing	–0.7	–0.5	–0.2	+0.2
Total balance	–8.5	–5.0	–4.2	–2.3
Adjusted [b]	–8.8	–5.1	–3.7	–1.9
Compensatory official financing:				
Grants from U.S. government	+1.0	+3.2	+4.1	+2.7
Long-term loans				
United States	+3.8	+1.1	+0.7	+0.2
Other countries	+0.9	+0.5	–0.5	—
Financing by international institutions	+1.2	+0.3	—	—
Movements of sterling balances	–0.6	–0.2	–0.5	+0.9
Movement of U.S. dollar balances	+0.8	–0.3	–0.1	–0.2
Gold movements				
United States	+1.9	+0.9	+0.2	–1.3
Other countries	–0.2	–0.4	–0.2	–0.4
Total compensatory official financing	+8.8	+5.1	+3.7	+1.9

Source: **14**, 1949, p. 116; 1950, p. 118.

a. Cf. balance on current account in Table 95.
b. Corrected for errors and omissions.

for errors and omissions, the balance of payments of Latin America has been in almost perfect equilibrium. Latin America has absorbed foreign investments, mainly from the United States, at a rate of approximately $400 to $500 million a year, chiefly productive investments which have contributed to the development of the natural resources of the respective countries, as in Venezuela, Brazil and Chile. Special loans and grants have not been excessive in relation to the natural resources of Latin American countries and the prospects for their development in the near future.[83] Moreover, some Latin American countries have been able to extend loans and credits to Europe, and they have had at their

83. **15**, *passim*.

disposal adequate stocks of gold to offset temporary deficits in international accounts.

OUTLOOK

The balance of payments is, ultimately, an aggregate of net balances of a number of accounts which depend, in turn, on the interplay of innumerable and often unpredictable factors — economic, political, technological and psychological. An attempt can be made, however, to visualize the probable trends in the general patterns of balances of payments and the international movement of capital in the coming years.

The immediate future is not very bright. The International Monetary Fund declares in its *Annual Report* for 1952:

It is a melancholy fact that seven years after the end of the war the Fund has to report that international payments are still far from having attained a state of balance and that exchange difficulties and exchange restrictions are again, over large parts of the trading world, the order of the day.

Payments pressures have never been entirely absent in many countries, and though the pressures have on occasion been relieved by singularly favorable circumstances — such as very high export prices — exchange difficulties have never been far from the surface, and any adverse change in circumstances has threatened to cause them to emerge in the form of a fresh exchange crisis.[84]

Since one of the immediate causes of disequilibrium is in inflationary pressures and the tendency of many countries to increase their imports beyond their ability to pay for them with domestic produce, a stable equilibrium in world trade cannot be achieved unless a balanced economy is restored in the areas with particularly strong inflationary pressures and weak currencies.

In this situation, the report of the Fund continues:

. . . the use of exchange restrictions and quantitative import controls, frequently of a discriminatory nature, has seemed inevitable to many countries; and during the past year there has been a tendency to extend and intensify these restrictions and controls. Even where the long-term consequences of the measures adopted were clearly understood, the need for immediate action to deal with a critical situation has made it difficult to give adequate attention to them. In consequence, the treatment of exchange problems has frequently been symptomatic rather than radical: it has been aimed at the outward manifestations of balance of payments pressure rather than at its causes.[85]

It is difficult to predict when and how this situation will change. The task of restoring a balanced system of international settlements that will function without periodic breakdowns is indeed formidable. Such a system was in operation before World War I, was restored in the 1920's, collapsed during the great depression and has never functioned since then.

The road back to the "normalcy" which only existed for four or five years out of the past four decades — since the outbreak of World War I — is a long one. The International Monetary Fund expresses its earnest conviction that the problem would be solved if all countries in a strong balance of payments position took all practical means of reducing barriers to international trade as their most effective contribution to the restoration of a balanced world economy.[86]

Will the countries in favorable positions take such measures? Will these measures be effective enough? These are open questions.

It is true that, as the International Monetary Fund puts it,

. . . obstacles placed by the surplus countries on imports, whether in the form of increased tariffs, import quotas and prohibitions, customs administration, or in any other way, may frustrate even the most strenuous efforts of the deficit countries to achieve international balance without resorting to restrictions.[87]

But it is not less true that the most generous policy of the surplus countries may be frustrated by the combination of inflationary measures and restrictions in deficit countries. It seems probable, therefore, that in the years to come the balances of payments of many nations will remain precarious, with an unstable equilibrium, under continuous threat of deficit checked by compensatory financing of various types.

The chances for prompt restoration of the self-balancing process in settlement of international payments are doubtful.

On the other hand, the system of new international institutions — the International Monetary Fund, the International Bank for Reconstruction and Development, the European Payments Union, and the specialized agencies of

---

84. **16**, 1952, pp. 31–32.

85. **16**, pp. 32–33.
86. **16**, p. 37.
87. **16**, p. 37. For trade barriers and restrictions, see Chapter 6. Cf. periodic surveys in **23**.

the UN — has proved efficient enough in handling the situation of unstable equilibrium in the world economy. The self-regulating mechanism of balances of payments has always depended on decisions of individuals in strategic positions. In the future there will probably be more direct intervention of governments and international institutions in economic processes than in the nineteenth century. The classical methods of maintaining the equilibrium of international accounts by regulating exchange and interest rates will be supplemented by other measures under political, national and international control.

Apart from this change in the mechanism of settlement of international accounts, the nineteenth century pattern of balances of payments of old industrial powers will hardly be restored. A large part of the capital invested in colonial systems will be written down. Loss of old investments will be particularly painful for countries which have depended on their colonial possessions and foreign investments for their everyday bread. The liquidation will probably be stretched over a long time, however, and financial losses overseas in this period may be offset by the development of domestic resources, improvement of industrial plant and commercial organization, rise in the productivity of labor, gains in international cooperation. Thus the loss or depreciation of foreign investments will hardly stop economic progress in the affected countries.

This conclusion does not necessarily imply that the system of balances of payments will return to the pattern which prevailed before World War I — the flow of export balances from the areas of colonial and semicolonial economy to the bloc of colonial powers headed by the United Kingdom, and the flow of capital in the opposite direction.

It is highly doubtful that the United States will assume the role which the United Kingdom played in the nineteenth century — when the London market led — in the determination of

prices on staple commodities and the flow of world trade; the Bank of England set the discount and exchange rates; and British investors practically decided how foreign loans would be distributed in the world.

For the British, crowded on their overpopulated and overindustrialized island, control over world trade was of vital importance as a means of assuring an adequate supply of foodstuffs and raw materials for their mills. The economic structure of the United States, on the other hand, does not call for the huge import balance in merchandise trade which it should absorb in order to play the role of the mainspring in world trade and the flywheel in the world capital market.

If the United Kingdom succeeds in consolidating its leadership in the Commonwealth as an association of free and equal nations bound by a community of political and economic interests, it has a good chance of restoring its position in the disputed markets in all parts of the world. The premises of London's absolute supremacy in world trade and finances, however, have been destroyed by the two world wars, the changing character of the British Empire, the rise of the United States and other events in the past forty years.

In brief, neither London nor Washington and New York can qualify in the future for the role of the controlling center of international transactions, the role that London played from 1816 to 1914. It is more probable that this function will be exercised jointly by the United States, the United Kingdom and international institutions and conferences. It seems probable that international agreements — not necessarily of a universal character — could promote and facilitate foreign productive investments by reconciling the urgent need for foreign capital in underdeveloped countries with their reluctance to become "economic colonies" of money-lending nations.

CHAPTER 6

TARIFFS, TRADE AGREEMENTS AND TRADE RESTRICTIONS

SINCE TIME IMMEMORIAL, the rulers of places visited by traders have exacted a share of the profits as toll or protection money. With the passage of time, this primitive tribute developed into import, export and transit duties.

When Marco Polo visited China in the thirteenth century, he found import and export duties to be part of an extensive tax system in the empire of the Great Khan. These were typical revenue duties: 3.33 per cent ad valorem on all goods imported into a city or exported from a city by land or by sea, and 10 per cent of the value of products imported from distant countries and regions.[1]

Eventually came the realization that import duties could also serve as an implement of economic policy, protecting domestic producers against competition of foreign products, encouraging development of local crafts and so forth.

MERCANTILISM AND PROTECTIONISM

Import duties played a prominent role in the policy recommended by British writers of the sixteenth and seventeenth centuries and the first half of the eighteenth, who were to become known as "mercantilists." These writers did not call themselves mercantilists nor pretend to represent a definite school of thought, and on many economic and political issues they professed widely divergent opinions. Their views in the eighteenth century, at the time of industrial revolution in England, had little in common with the ideas which were current among their predecessors two centuries before in the transition period between the Middle Ages and modern times.

The term "mercantilism" was invented in the eighteenth century by the spokesmen of the new industrial era. Originally it had a somewhat contemptuous connotation. Adam Smith, who used it in this sense,[2] was not always fair to the economists of the earlier generation. The main target of his criticism was their preoccupation with the

balance of trade and the policy they recommended to ensure a surplus of exports over imports: duties on imports and direct import restrictions on certain luxuries; subsidies and other forms of assistance to exports; protection of national navigation; prohibition of the export of coin and bullion; an aggressive foreign policy; exploitation of colonies as monopolistically controlled markets.[3]

This policy was widely accepted in England in the sixteenth and seventeenth centuries. Some writers of that time defended it by arguments which suggest that they considered the accumulation of money and gold reserves the main objective of foreign trade; for others, a favorable balance of trade was not the aim but a means of ensuring cheap money, stable or rising prices and full use of the labor force and other national resources; but all agreed that the government should protect a favorable trade balance by import duties and similar measures.

The industrial revolution, the growth of factories, and the search for new outlets for manufactured goods gave rise to criticism of this idea. In the eighteenth century, the physiocrats in France and Adam Smith in England became the spokesmen of free trade. Their ideas gained wide recognition by the end of the century. However, political conditions of the time — the rebellion of the American colonies, the French Revolution and the Napoleonic wars — prevented an immediate practical test of the new economic philosophy. Before it could become a basis of commercial policy, opposition developed.

The new movement, known as protectionism and associated with the names of Alexander Hamilton in the United States [4] and Friedrich List in Germany,[5] appeared to be a return to mercantilism. Actually, it used the old weapon of customs with a new emphasis. The protectionists were only moderately interested in the balance of trade and related problems and considered tariffs primarily as a means of promot-

---

1. **80**, p. 245.
2. **51**, p. 67.
3. Cf. **73**, Vol. 6, p. 651.
4. **66**.
5. **75**.

ing industrial development. Characteristically, Hamilton developed his ideas on trade policy and tariffs in a paper entitled "Report on the Subject of Manufactures."

In the first half of the nineteenth century, the early protectionists supported a tariff with moderate revenue duties on some commodities and much higher protective duties on others. They had little use for export bounties [6] and accepted straight restriction of imports only in exceptional cases and as a temporary measure. Despite this difference in objectives, in actuality the protectionists were defending the heritage of the mercantilists, opposing the repeal of duties and regulations that had been established in the eighteenth century or earlier. From that time to our day, the clash between the protectionists and the low-tariff men has reflected divergences in the interests of different economic groups and often also of different parts of a country.

Once established, each import duty had a tendency to perpetuate itself. The often haphazard schedule of duties in a nation's tariff frequently was made still more chaotic by commercial treaties which reduced certain rates without changing others. It is therefore difficult to understand the tariffs now in force in various countries without examining their origin.

Tariffs and Trade Agreements

Some students believe that the term "tariff" is derived from the name of the little Spanish coast town Tarifa, near the Rock of Gibraltar, from which boats of the feudal lords once sallied forth to demand toll of passing ships.[7] Whether or not this story is true, merchants who were ordered to pay in the name of the king or overlord could hardly perceive the subtle difference between the feudal toll and the import duties exacted by customs officers. In our time, the term is applied to the taxes which must be paid upon various classes of goods when moving across national frontiers. In a broader sense it is also applied to the laws regulating such duties.[8]

6. **57**, p. 36.
7. **57**, p. 110; **87**, p. 199. The *Dictionary of Tariff Information* rejects this story and derives the word "tariff" from old French and, ultimately, Arabic words which mean rates, price lists or notification. (See **28**, pp. 709–10.)
8. **48**; cf. **60**, p. 67.

Some tariffs are very brief, others are embodied in huge volumes with innumerable supplements and appendices. Virtually all are supplemented by commercial treaties or trade agreements. In fact, the treaties serve largely to modify the tariffs, and the latter are often designed as a foundation for negotiating trade agreements.

Commercial treaties may deal with any subject related to trade. Their purpose is usually to provide for mutual concessions intended to promote exchange between the two parties. The concessions that two countries thus make to each other are usually extended to other nations with which the negotiating countries have "most-favored-nation" commitments.

The "most-favored-nation" principle (often referred to as m.f.n.) is essentially an agreement against discrimination in favor of a third party. As the Economic Committee of the League of Nations defines this clause, it

. . . implies the right to demand and the obligation to concede all reductions of duties and taxes and all privileges of every kind accorded to the most favored nation, no matter whether such reductions and privileges are granted autonomously [by a legislative or administrative act of the respective country] or in virtue of a convention with third parties.[9]

This general principle, however, does not usually preclude preferential treatment of certain areas with which the contracting parties have exceptionally close relations, such as those among members of the British Commonwealth. Such exceptions occur even when the most-favored-nation clause is "unconditional and unrestricted."

TYPES OF TARIFFS

Tariffs differ widely in purpose, form, methods of establishing duties and so on. A distinction is usually made between import and export tariffs, revenue and protective tariffs, single-column and double-column tariffs; general-and-conventional and maximum-and-minimum tariff systems. Many tariffs are of intermediate types.

Import and export duties are often combined in a single law.[10] Since the middle of the nineteenth century, however, import restrictions and duties have been the most important and most controversial part of any tariff. Practically, "tariff" means the list of import duties.

9. **2**, p. 69.
10. **62**, p. 67; **64**, p. 308.

Protective and Revenue Tariffs

Any distinction between protective and revenue tariffs is somewhat artificial, since a tariff may contain duties of both types; occasionally the duty on a particular article (for example, sugar) may serve both purposes. For example, the import duties on wine are revenue duties in the United Kingdom, Sweden and Norway but are designed to protect domestic producers in France, Italy, Portugal and Spain. A tariff may also include duties which are neither fiscal nor protective but serve mainly as a basis for bargaining in negotiations with foreign countries and may be reduced or dropped altogether in exchange for concessions granted by the other party.

Single and Multiple Rates

Some tariffs list a single rate for each article described in a general way while others describe dutiable articles with such precision that similar but not identical articles imported from different countries fall into different categories in the schedule.[11]

Tariffs with double or multiple rates are of two basic types — the general-and-conventional tariff, and the maximum-and-minimum system.[12] Under the first, the legislature establishes a general tariff (with a single scale of duties), but the government is authorized to negotiate with foreign countries and to reduce established rates in return for equivalent concessions.[13] Subsequently, under the most-favored-nation clause, the lowest rates are extended to other nations entitled to this privilege. Thus, in addition to the general tariff, a conventional tariff with reduced rates is developed. The rates based on treaties are usually published along with the general rates established by the law. The largest part of the foreign trade of a nation with a general-and-conventional tariff is usually subject to conventional rates, while general rates are applied only to countries which for some reason remain outside the system of treaties with the m.f.n. clause.[14]

A maximum-and-minimum tariff likewise provides for two sets of rates, both of which are established by law. Whereas in the general-and-conventional system the reduced rates are usually applied only to items on which a special agreement has been reached with foreign countries, the maximum-and-minimum system provides for two rates for all commodities and thus sets the range within which actual rates must be established. A tariff of this type is often used as a means for obtaining concessions from other countries, that is, as a weapon in tariff negotiations. The political advantage of a maximum-minimum tariff over the general-and-conventional system is that it leaves the ultimate control of customs rates in the hands of the legislature, setting strict limits to administrative decisions and ensuring interested industries of at least the minimum protection.[15]

Single-column tariffs are sometimes described as "autonomous" in the sense that the rates are established by the nation and are not subject to negotiations and bargaining with foreign countries. However, the government of a country with a tariff of this type can offer to negotiate a commercial treaty with another country and to reduce duties in exchange for similar concessions.

In the first century or more of its history the United States endeavored to obtain favorable treatment for its products in foreign markets by offering other countries equal opportunities of access to its market or by denying access to those who persisted in discriminatory practices against American trade. This policy was not very successful and led to individual bargaining with particular countries, in which equality of treatment of their exports to the United States was in most cases made conditional upon similar treatment of U.S. exports to such countries.[16]

In 1923 Secretary of State Hughes replaced this practice with the principle of offering and expanding m.f.n. treatment unconditionally. The trade agreements program inaugurated in 1934 by Secretary of State Hull added to that principle concessions on general or statutory duties on particular products of other countries in return for reciprocal concessions in favor of selected American products. These concessions the United States then generalized to cover the same

---

11. **62**, p. 68.
12. **64**, p. 318; cf. **68**, p. 3; **31**, pp. 18ff.
13. **57**, p. 122.
14. This system of tariffs was inaugurated by France under Napoleon III, accepted by other European countries in the 1860's, and became predominant in Europe later in the nineteenth century. See pp. 268–69.

15. In the nineteenth century maximum-and-minimum tariffs were less popular in Europe than the general-and-conventional system, but they were used in Spain after 1877 and in France after 1892.
16. **34**, pp. 17ff.

products from all countries that did not materially discriminate against it. There was thus brought into operation a general-and-conventional tariff system. In practice, however, the conventional (reduced) duties have been denied to very few countries. In recent years they have been withheld only from the countries of the Soviet bloc. With this exception the United States tariff operates as a single-column tariff.

Classification of Commodities

Tariffs differ in the classification of commodities in the schedule. The United Kingdom and the Scandinavian countries, for example, use uniform rates for comparatively large groups of commodities. Thus an identical rate is applied to different grains, different kinds of cotton or wool, all makes of automobiles and so on. Other countries, including the United States and France, use a more detailed classification. The French tariff contains individual rates for more than 600 types of cotton yarn.[17] In some cases, the rates depend on the size of the container or package. For example, one rate may be imposed on wine or industrial alcohol in containers no larger than two liters and another rate on the same products in larger containers. Similarly, some tariffs impose a uniform duty per unit of weight on all steam engines or electromotors, and others have different rates per unit of weight for engines and motors of different power.

Tariffs with uniform rates for groups of commodities usually include only a few hundred dutiable items, like those of Great Britain and Sweden. Others list several thousand different items and rates. The French tariff is an example of such elaboration. The United States tariff, with its 3,552 items, is of the intermediate type.[18]

17. **38**, Art. 368A–368R and 369A–369N.
18. The concept of "item" is somewhat vague and is not the same in all countries. In 1927 the Economic and Financial Section of the League of Nations published a comparative survey of customs tariffs of different countries. The survey showed, among other particulars, the number of items in each tariff. Haiti topped the list with 13,300 items. Next in line were France (4,371 items), Argentina (3,811) and Italy (3,574). They were followed by Honduras, Brazil and Belgium (3,000–3,500 items), Hungary, Guatemala, Bolivia, Peru, Germany, Romania, Poland and Austria (2,000–3,000 items). The United States ranked 21st (only 1,635 items at that time) and was followed by Spain, Nicaragua, Paraguay and the Dominican Republic. Canada (1,161 items) was in 31st place; Great Britain (217 items) was close to the bottom, flanked by Persia and Costa Rica (**4**).

Specific, Ad Valorem and Compound Duties

Duty rates may be either *specific,* stated in dollars and cents, shillings or francs per physical unit (for example 20 cents per pound, yard or gallon), or *ad valorem,* expressed as a percentage of the value of the merchandise. The latter basis makes it necessary to appraise the article according to some clearly established formula. The value on which the ad valorem duty is applied is usually calculated close to that in the exporting country plus costs of transportation and insurance (CIF). It can be calculated also as the price of the article in the importing country minus the import duty, unloading cost and similar items (delivered price) or as home market value in the country of origin (foreign value).

Compound duties are often used, combining specific and ad valorem rates — for example, 5 cents per pound plus 15 per cent ad valorem. Sometimes the specific rate is supplemented by a minimum rate ad valorem — for example, 10 cents per pound but not less than 25 per cent ad valorem.

TRADE AGREEMENTS

The German scholar Von Justi was a spokesman for statesmen of the eighteenth century when he declared that "the main purpose of any commercial treaty must be to obtain an advantage in the bargain and this is likewise the aim of the country which is negotiating with us. Thus the whole question is who can outfox whom." [19]

The leading idea of modern treaty negotiation is to make the agreement advantageous for both parties. This official philosophy, however, does not preclude padding rates in the original tariff as a preparation for negotiating conventional reciprocal concessions.

The main clauses of modern commercial treaties are those relating to tariff duties, quotas, and customs laws and regulations. Whether explicitly written into the treaty or not, often the main part of a commercial agreement is the mutual exchange of m.f.n. treatment.

Every state, in entering into a commercial treaty or agreement with another, seeks to gain or to retain certain advantages, to avoid certain disadvantages, or to accomplish both of these objectives. The negotiation of a commercial treaty between states, therefore,

19. **78**, p. 350.

usually involves "bargaining." In making its commercial treaties, a state may or may not seek a privileged position for itself. Most states, however, generally try to obtain treatment from other states which will be at least as favorable as that which those states grant to any other. Accordingly, every state generally asks for all the concessions and guaranties which the other negotiating state has already extended to third states or which it may extend to them in the future.

The most commonly used instrument for automatically assuring to newly contracting states the benefit of existing or future concessions accorded to third states is the so-called most-favored-nation clause. The purpose of this clause has been not to create but to guard against the creation of a "most favored" nation. This clause seeks to make accessible to the contracting parties all the advantages which either of them has granted, or at any future time shall grant, to any third state, i.e., to the "most favored" third state. The most-favored-nation clause has thus been used primarily to prevent the establishment of discriminations in the extending of concessions and guaranties.[20]

Multilateral Agreements

The most-favored-nation principle introduces an element of multilateralism into bilateral agreements; hence in bilateral negotiations each party negotiating for certain concessions or privileges is aware that the same concessions and privileges will be granted to other nations. Because of the m.f.n. principle, the major part of international trade is conducted on the basis of the lowest tariff rates of the respective importing countries.[21] A network of bilateral agreements can therefore achieve the same purpose as a single multilateral treaty. A general multilateral agreement, however, presents obvious advantages. It promises greater security in international trade and investment, eliminates suspicions and frictions, facilitates a peaceful and equitable solution of disputes and favors international cooperation.

Several attempts at multilateral commercial treaties were made in the nineteenth century. The European union engineered by Napoleon I in the struggle against England, as a part of the Continental System, had elements of a regional multilateral agreement. The unification of Germany (1833) began with a multilateral agreement among participating princedoms on a common customs system. A system of multilateral agreements developed later in Europe on the basis of the Anglo-French Trade Agreement of 1860, which promoted reduction of customs and repeal of restrictions of free navigation and commerce.[22] In 1885, fourteen nations entered into a collective agreement on policy in the Congo Basin and Africa in general. This was a multilateral treaty with far-reaching economic and commercial implications.[23] In the 1890's a commercial agreement of Germany with Austria-Hungary and Italy laid the foundation for the future Triple Alliance of Central Europe. Although none of these had lasting success, the idea of broad continental or global multilateral agreements remained alive.

It was natural, therefore, that the League of Nations should give much attention to plans for world-wide collective security based on multilateral economic conventions. Its attempt failed because of the lack of strength and internal cohesion in the Geneva organization. The depression of the 1930's made multilateral agreements particularly difficult. Each country sought security in the policy of self-sufficiency and took measures which ultimately led to the contraction of world trade and disorganization of the world economy. The purpose of these measures in many countries was not so much the protection of domestic industries envisaged by Hamilton and List as preservation of the balance of trade, as in the time of the mercantilists.[24]

After World War II, restoration of world trade began under the aegis of reciprocal supply agreements. Trade negotiations in 1945–46 were often centered on the exchange of goods desired by each party rather than mutual concessions on tariff rates.[25]

HISTORY OF TARIFFS AND TRADE AGREEMENTS

Nations have followed a long road from their first attempts to control foreign trade by methods recommended by the mercantilists to the relative freedom of commerce in the first decade of the twentieth century, and from that time to the present system of trade policy characterized by a combination of tariffs, commercial

---

20. **32**, Part II, pp. 4–5.
21. **31**, p. 6

22. **72**, p. 360.
23. Cf. Chapter 14.
24. Condliffe correctly traces the policy of trade controls during the great depression to the old mercantilism. (**51**, p. 210.)
25. **48**, pp. 353ff.

treaties, quantitative restrictions and exchange regulations.

The discussion of the history of tariffs and trade agreements in the following pages begins with a brief survey of general trends in trade policy from the beginning of the nineteenth century to the present time. Developments in the United Kingdom, the United States, France and Germany are then discussed in greater detail.

GENERAL TRENDS

The trend in the commercial policy of European countries from the beginning of the nineteenth century to the Franco-Prussian war was away from high protectionism and isolationism toward relative freedom of trade. In Great Britain, agricultural duties were repealed in 1846, and most other protective duties were removed in 1860. In France, the government of Napoleon III reduced duties on a number of important articles and, after having signed (1860) a trade treaty with Great Britain, engaged in negotiations for similar treaties with other countries. The German Customs Union was likewise moving toward a liberal trade policy. Before the Franco-Prussian war, a liberal trade policy and a network of trade agreements, all with the m.f.n. clause, predominated throughout Europe except in Russia.

Between the Franco-Prussian War and the outbreak of World War I, Great Britain, Belgium, the Netherlands, Denmark, Sweden and Norway followed a liberal policy more or less consistently, while Russia, Spain and Portugal surrounded themselves with high customs walls and Germany, Austria-Hungary, France and Italy oscillated between a moderate and a restrictive policy. In the United States, protectionism was firmly established as an enduring policy after the Civil War. United States import duties inched up from one tariff act to the next until the 1890's, but the tide receded slightly after the turn of the century.

Before World War I

Apart from considerable differences in the organization and the rates of duties on different articles, the tariffs of Germany, France and Italy approached a common pattern at the beginning of the twentieth century. About half or a little more than half of the imports of these countries were duty-free, while the duties on other articles averaged 10–20 per cent ad valorem. All three countries imposed appreciably higher duties on agricultural products than on manufactured articles.[26]

Contrary to the ideas of Hamilton and List, the main objective of European protectionism before World War I was not to foster new industries but to defend peasant agriculture against the competition of extensive and largely mechanized agriculture overseas. Agricultural protectionism largely served political purposes; it was invoked to preserve the small agricultural holdings and feudal estates which represented the strongholds of conservative forces.[27] Such considerations determined agrarian tariffs not only in Germany, France and Italy, but also in Austria-Hungary, Spain and other European countries.

1914–43

During World War I the leading trading nations split into two camps and the important routes of world trade were cut on both land and sea. Many trade treaties were repealed, others fell into disuse. The collapse of currencies after the end of the war called exchange controls to life, but most of them were repealed after the stabilization of currencies (1923). At the same time a trend toward economic self-sufficiency and high tariffs developed in both Europe and the Western Hemisphere, especially in the young and industrially weak countries. On the other hand, the general rise in prices in the early 1920's reduced the burden of specific duties in relation to the value of the respective goods.

World trade recovered from World War I sooner than most experts had expected, but the

26. **55**, pp. 190, 223, 260.
27. Condliffe explains the role of agricultural protectionism in France as follows:
"Much more was involved in the preservation of national agriculture, for a country like France, than the loss of agricultural capital that would have been involved in a free-trade policy. The land was owned in small parcels, inheritance of which was the cement of the social structure. The peasant lived his own life, relatively independent and hardly troubled by international fluctuations — a life hard but rewarding, limited but safe. To have allowed cheap imported grains and other foodstuffs to have disorganized the national market would have been to destroy this security and the way of life upon which it was based. It would have struck at the most stable and conservative, as well as the most powerful, segment of society, throwing the hard-earned and frugal patrimony of generations into a bottomless pit of economic and social disorder." (**52**, pp. 211–12.)

great depression in the early 1930's wiped out the progress made in the 1920's. Since falling prices on the world market seemed to be a contributing factor in deflation and depression, many countries tried to protect themselves against these disasters behind protective tariff walls.[28] Tariffs skyrocketed in both Europe and America. In the United States the Hawley-Smoot Tariff Act of 1930 was one of the most striking manifestations of the new trend in trade policy. It failed in its aim of halting the fall of prices and contraction of production in the United States but provoked a violent chain reaction throughout the world.

It is very doubtful whether the increase in the import duties of the United States was directly responsible for the deterioration of business conditions in Great Britain, France, Germany, Italy and other European countries. Probably the depression in the United States would have cut down their exports even without the Hawley-Smoot act. It is likewise probable that the increased pressure of protectionist forces in Europe was due primarily to the deteriorating business conditions in European countries rather than the new tariff in the United States. That tariff, however, had both psychological and political effects on Europe. It was decried by the European press as the beginning of an economic war between the New World and the Old.

Spain was among the first to retaliate against the United States by raising duties on automobiles and tires and denying m.f.n. treatment to goods imported from the United States. Italy followed, by increasing duties on automobiles and radio sets and shifting imports from the United States to Germany and the United Kingdom.

France found the Hawley-Smoot tariff a justification for its quota system. The United Kingdom used the same argument in support of its new policy of high duties on products imported from countries other than British colonies and dominions. The British policy met with enthusiastic approval at the Imperial Conference in Ottawa.[29] In restrospect, the contention that the Hawley-Smoot act was "a turning point in world history"[30] appears one-sided, but that is how it was interpreted by contemporaries in Europe.

While it is impossible to determine the extent to which the contraction of United States foreign trade in the early 1930's was due to the new tariff, by 1933 its adverse effect on the nation's economy was widely recognized. One of the early measures of the Roosevelt administration was to shift the emphasis in commercial policy from protection of the domestic market to promotion of exports by reduction of trade barriers. The new policy was embodied in the Reciprocal Trade Agreements Act of 1934. During the following three years the United States concluded trade agreements with 17 countries: Canada, Guatemala, El Salvador, Honduras, Nicaragua, Costa Rica, Cuba (preferential agreement), Haiti, Colombia and Brazil; France, Belgium and Luxembourg, the Netherlands, Sweden, Finland and Switzerland. In the next three years, the agreement with Canada was expanded, and agreements were concluded with Ecuador, Venezuela, the United Kingdom, Czechoslovakia and Turkey. Between 1940 and 1943 Mexico, Peru, Uruguay, Argentina, Iceland and Iran were added to the list.[31]

Through these agreements the United States has granted and obtained substantial concessions in customs duties, but the effect on its foreign trade was retarded by the shift of many countries to the practice of import restrictions through licensing, exchange regulations, quotas and so forth. The importance of tariffs declined. By 1939 a considerable part of all world trade was controlled by such regulations.[32]

Recent Developments

Regulation of foreign trade by government has been a common practice in all modern wars, but the total war of 1939–45 brought stricter regulations than ever before. In some belligerent countries, government became the only importer and exporter. Tariffs on imports became materially less important. In view of the universal shortage of labor, raw materials and foodstuffs, the need for customs duties to protect domestic producers became less urgent or disappeared completely. Many countries reduced duties to ease the cost of living and the cost of raw materials. The United States and Canada agreed to suspend, for the duration of the war, all "legislative and administrative barriers, including tariffs, import duties, customs and other regulations and restrictions of any character which prohibit, prevent, delay or otherwise impede the free flow of necessary munitions and war supplies between

---

28. **89**, p. 300.
29. See **72**, *passim*.
30. **83**, p. 173.

31. **32**, pp. 10–13 and 38.
32. **59**, p. 208.

the two countries." The principal objective of trade regulations during this period was to obtain the most urgently needed goods. In the Atlantic Charter the governments of the United States and the United Kingdom proclaimed the objectives of their trade policy after the war: "to further the enjoyment by all states, great or small, victors or vanquished, of access, on equal terms, to the trade and to the raw materials of the world which are needed for their economic prosperity." [33] Although qualified by "due respect for their existing obligations," these words suggested the tendency toward liberalization of foreign trade. The same idea was restated in a clearer form in the mutual aid arrangements in connection with lend-lease operations. Article VIII of the Master Agreement between the United States and the United Kingdom, concluded on February 23, 1942, pointed to "the elimination of all forms of discriminatory treatment in international commerce, and to the reduction of tariffs and other trade barriers." [34]

After the war, however, it was found that trade barriers established by wartime regulations could be used in the transitional period to implement anti-inflationary policy and help maintain established exchange rates.

The dislocations in the world economy after World War II proved to be much deeper than in the 1920's. The trade position of the United Kingdom, the former center of world trade, was weakened by the disintegration of its colonial empire. The world was split between the West and the East, and the aggressive actions of the USSR after the war were taken by the West as a threat of new conflict.

Tariffs are lower now than in 1937–38. As a result of the rise of prices, the burden of many specific rates of duty, established before the war and reduced by reciprocal agreements, has declined further in relation to the value of the respective goods. Customs walls remain high around some countries but in most cases not so high as to render the restoration of world trade impossible. Something new, however, was added to them during the war — the barbed wire of restrictions, quotas, exchange regulations. These trade restrictions are the main obstacle to the resumption of the multilateral transactions needed to strengthen the ties between Europe and the rest of the world.

In the postwar years, world trade policy has faced two issues — tariffs and quantitative restrictions. Customs walls have been universally regarded as permanent obstacles to the expansion of commercial relations among nations, while other restrictions have seemed to be a temporary aftermath of war. For the United States, the tariff remained the main issue. The United States has made use of direct trade restrictions only for certain farm products for which domestic price supports had been set, but its import duties have remained fairly high on many products even after all the duty reductions granted under the trade agreements program.

Perhaps more than in some other countries, import duties of the United States were supplemented by an "invisible" tariff, and some experts considered the latter the more serious obstacle to expansion of foreign trade.[35] This invisible tariff was considerably reduced by the Customs Simplification Act of 1953 and by various administrative liberalizations. However, the cornerstone of U. S. commercial policy has been the extension of reciprocal trade agreements.

The stated purpose of the Trade Agreements Act of 1934 was to increase the export trade of the United States. At that time it was of no concern to the United States whether its reciprocal agreements with other countries developed into a network of multilateral treaties. After World War II, the situation changed. The United States emerged from the struggle as the greatest economic power; peoples in all parts of the world were eager to obtain its products. The main objective of its foreign policy became the consolidation of international peace and promotion of economic progress in friendly nations. Thus the United States found itself in the position of championing expansion of world trade without

---

33. **49**, p. 280.
34. **49**, p. 286.

35. Shortly before the outbreak of World War II, Percy W. Bidwell wrote about this invisible tariff as follows:

"Today, administrative measures are more comprehensive than the visible tariff, since they affect goods which are on the free list as well as those which are dutiable; they are more effective since they make use of quotas and embargoes as well as tariff duties; they can be put into operation more promptly, since they do not need to wait upon discussion in legislative assembly.

[These] restrictions and prohibitions on American import trade . . . are found in the administrative provisions of the Tariff Act of 1930, as amended in 1938, in customs regulations, in the decisions of customs courts, in regulations of various bureaus and divisions of the Department of Agriculture, the Bureau of Narcotics and other administrative agencies." (**45**, pp. 2–3; cf. **44**.)

increasing its own imports to an appreciable extent. The promotion of exports of European countries was one of the objectives of the Marshall Plan and the United States has done much to strengthen the competitive position of its European allies in foreign markets, even against its own exports.

General Agreement on Tariffs and Trade

In 1945 the U.S. Department of State proposed supplementing the United Nations by an international trade organization and laid down procedures for reducing tariffs and abolishing other obstacles to the flow of international trade.[36] In October 1946 an international Preparatory Committee convened in London, where the United States presented a tentative charter for the new organization. In the spring of 1947, the Preparatory Committee held a second session in Geneva, and tariff negotiations were opened among nineteen nations, including the United States. Four other nations joined the conference later. Negotiations, conducted bilaterally, on a product-by-product basis, resulted in 123 bilateral agreements on reduction of trade barriers. The bilateral agreements were consolidated in the General Agreement on Tariffs and Trade (GATT) and the Final Act was signed on October 30, 1947.[37] A second series of negotiations under the GATT was held in Annecy, France, in the spring and summer of 1949. There the original contracting parties negotiated with other countries that wished to accede to the Agreement. By July 1, 1950, thirty-two countries (including the United States) had become partners of the GATT. In 1952 there were thirty-three participants.[38] In addition, many other countries had signed bilateral agreements, either with the United States or the United Kingdom or other members of the GATT and had become indirectly associated with the organization.

The campaign to establish the International Trade Organization (ITO) with much broader functions has been less successful. In the United States' *Proposals for Expansion of World Trade and Employment* (1945) the need for such an organization was stated as follows:

1. Measures designed to effect an expansion of trade are essential because of their direct contribu-

tion to maximum levels of employment, production and consumption. Since such expansion can only be attained by collective measures, in continuous operation and adaptable to economic changes, it is necessary to establish permanent machinery for international collaboration in matters affecting international commerce, with a view to continuous consultation, the provision of expert advice, the formulation of agreed policies, procedures and plans, and to the development of agreed rules of conduct in regard to matters affecting international trade.

2. It is accordingly proposed that there be created an International Trade Organization of the United Nations, the members of which would undertake to conduct their international commercial policies and relations in accordance with agreed principles to be set forth in the articles of the Organization. These principles, in order to make possible an effective expansion of world production, employment, exchange, and consumption, should:

a. Provide an equitable basis for dealing with the problems of governmental measures affecting international trade;

b. Provide for the curbing of restrictive trade practices resulting from private international business arrangements; and

c. Govern the institution and operation of intergovernmental commodity arrangements.[39]

The draft of the charter of the ITO prepared in Geneva, 1947, was revised and elaborated by the UN Conference on Trade and Employment in Havana, Cuba (November 1947–March 1948), attended by representatives of fifty-seven nations. The document which emerged from this conference became known as the Havana Charter of the ITO.[40] Since some provisions of the Charter differed from the original Geneva draft and the respective sections of the GATT, the latter was amended in accordance with the Havana decision.[41] It was further amended in the international tariff negotiations meeting at Annecy in 1949.[42] However, the enactment of the GATT weakened interest in the ITO. Only two countries announced their adherence to the Havana Charter, and opposition to the project grew in Congress while the GATT gained support in the United States and abroad. In December 1950, during the sessions of the international tariff conference in Torquay, England, the U.S. Department of State announced that the government would no longer seek congressional approval of

---

36. See **25.**
37. See **7.**
38. **16; 17.**

39. **24**; cf. **47,** p. 398.
40. **77,** p. 446; cf. **88.**
41. **33,** April 1948–March 1949, pp. 21–26.
42. **33,** April 1949–June 1950, pp. 32–38.

the Havana Charter but instead would seek appropriate legislative authority to make more effective the country's participation in the GATT.[43] Since the success of the project depended on the participation of the United States,[44] this announcement spelled the end of the ITO.

The Torquay conference followed the procedure established in Geneva. Initial negotiations were conducted bilaterally. In all, 147 such negotiations were completed — 58 between countries which were already contracting parties; 86 between such countries and newly acceding countries; and 3 between the newly acceding parties themselves.[45] After the bilateral agreements had been reached, they were embodied in a series of multilateral declarations which became amendments to the GATT.

Among other questions discussed at the Torquay conference was the application of Article 28 of the GATT. This article permitted members to modify or withdraw any tariff concession they had made at the Geneva or Annecy meetings. Sixteen countries (Cuba, Haiti, Brazil, Chile and Uruguay; the United Kingdom, France, Benelux, Denmark, Sweden, Finland and Italy; the Union of South Africa and New Zealand) had used this privilege, and as a consequence, 295 concessions were withdrawn or modified. To offset the loss of benefits to other participating countries, each government which had availed itself of the escape clause offered compensatory reductions on other duties in its tariff. An agreement was reached at Torquay to consider the new concessions equivalent to those withdrawn.[46]

THE UNITED KINGDOM

Early Customs Duties

In England, temporary and local provisions for import and export duties date from the thirteenth century.[47] King John's attempt to establish a general ad valorem tax on all imported and exported goods (the king's share or "fif-

teenth") at the beginning of the thirteenth century was short-lived.[48] The first national system of customs, established in 1266 in an agreement between Prince Edward and English merchants, entitled the crown to collect on all goods, whether imported or exported, "some reasonable portion, whereby the merchants should not be immoderately burdened." [49] These duties, however, were strongly opposed in England and France, and were finally abolished. A more stable system of import duties developed between 1275 and 1347, with the consolidation of the royal power in England.[50] It included duties on wool, woolfells and hides (1275); a levy on alien traders (1303); a duty on cloth (1347); and so-called "subsidies" on tonnage and poundage. This system remained in force with only minor changes to the middle of the sixteenth century, when England began to raise its import duties.

The Mercantilist Policy

From that time until the end of the eighteenth century, the commercial policy of England was determined by fiscal considerations and the economic philosophy of the mercantilists. Since excessive duties and revenue are natural foes,[51] this policy required that duties should not be such as to bar imports from continental Europe yet should, at the same time, protect the balance of payments effectively.

Severely criticized and ridiculed in retrospect, this policy proved successful in a critical period of British history. It yielded sufficient revenue to the crown and stimulated the growth of the merchant fleet and industry in the seventeenth and eighteenth centuries. Under this system, indeed, England rose from a second-rate state on the fringe of Europe to a leading power.[52] As a

---

43. **33,** July 1950–June 1951, p. 7.
44. **46,** pp. 235–37.
45. **33,** July 1950–June 1951, p. 12.
46. **76,** 1952.
47. There were some earlier levies on imports and exports: "lastage," exacted at fairs and markets; "scavage," collected in seaports on imported and exported goods; customs on imported wine, "wine prise," which required the importers of wine to sell a part of their cargo to the king at a reduced price (**60,** pp. 27–38).

48. **61,** p. 300.
49. **61,** p. 53.
50. **61,** p. 295.
51. **71,** p. 10.
52. In the sixteenth century, in the face of a threat of invasion by the Spaniards, England had to import sulfur for manufacture of gunpowder and bring artisans from the continent to cast guns. Development of ordnance industries was the first preoccupation of the British government. Always feeling the threat from Catholic countries of continental Europe, England strengthened the protectionist features of its commercial policy. By the end of the eighteenth century, the country had reached a level of economic development, in comparison with continental Europe, that no longer required a protective tariff. (**51,** pp. 29–30.)

result of England's economic growth, however, protective duties became more harmful than useful to the British. The obstacles of high tariffs that British merchants met in their search for new markets taught them the advantages of free trade. As long as the Whigs remained in power, however, they continued the restrictive commercial policy in trade with France and the British colonies in America. William Pitt's attempts to change this policy failed. Under Walpole, England treated its colonies in North America in accordance with the mercantilist doctrine until they rebelled.

The Beginning of Free Trade Policy

The idea of free trade gained wide recognition in England at the end of the eighteenth century, in part under the influence of Adam Smith and his school.[53] Political tensions, however, prevented liberalization of British commercial policy. England's opposition, first to the French Revolution, and then to the French Empire under Napoleon, dragged the country into a prolonged war which resulted in an actual blockade of the British Isles. England had to rely increasingly on its own resources; British foreign trade dwindled; the level of living of the majority of the population declined; but the capacity of British factories increased.

After the defeat of Napoleon, when the economic supremacy of England in Europe — and consequently in the world — was firmly established, protectionism became an obstacle to Britain's economic progress. Reorientation of British commercial policy began in the 1820's, with the reduction of duties on certain raw materials, and was completed a quarter of a century later with the repeal of the Corn Laws in 1846.[54]

The English Corn Laws, rooted in medieval local regulations dealing with agriculture and grain marketing,[55] had been revised in 1815. In the new form, they provided that "corn" (wheat, rye, peas and beans, barley and oats) could be imported from abroad or taken out of warehouse duty-free only when prices reached a definite

level.[56] These provisions amounted to conditional protection of corn prices. The amendments of 1822, 1827 and 1828 substituted for prohibition of imports of corn a sliding scale of duties: high rates when home prices were cheap, low or no duties when prices were high.[57] In 1838, Cobden's Anti-Corn-Law League appeared on the English political scene. The campaign found support in the increasing discontent among workers (the Chartist movement). Parliament repealed the Corn Laws in 1846 as part of more inclusive legislation which abolished customs duties on foodstuffs, reduced duties on manufactured articles and foreign timber, and lowered the preference given to colonial and Indian sugar over foreign sugar. Most of the remaining duties were abolished by the trade agreement with France in 1860. Of the 417 commodities liable to duty before the treaty, 371 were removed from the list.[58] All the remaining duties (on 46 articles) served fiscal purposes; none was designed primarily to protect domestic industry against foreign competition.

Revival of Protectionism

In view of the financial strain caused by World War I, the United Kingdom established in 1915 a uniform duty of 33.3 per cent ad valorem on imported luxuries such as watches, jewelry, passenger cars (then a luxury) and motion picture films. These duties (the McKenna duties) remained in force after the war. In 1919 imperial preference on tea, coffee, cocoa and sugar was granted to British colonies and dominions. This gave a new character to the duties and made them protective, in the broad sense of the term. In 1920 Great Britain announced a complete prohibition of imports of dyestuffs and coal-tar dyes as a measure of national security. A year later, the Safeguarding of Industries Act introduced import duties of 33.3 per cent ad valorem on fine mechanical products (optical instruments, barometers, radios and the like). At the same time the Anti-Dumping Act established similar duties on a few manufactured articles imported from countries with temporarily depreciated currencies. Some of these duties were rescinded in 1924 but were reenacted in 1925.

British industrialists, unable to meet the competition of Germany, Japan and the United

---

53. Pitt took the first steps toward liberalizing commercial policy in 1786, concluding a treaty with France which stipulated substantial reciprocal reductions of customs duties. The next year he obtained from Parliament the Consolidation Act, which simplified the whole duty system by codification of existing rates.

54. **53**, p. 52.

55. See **43**.

56. **43**, p. 139.

57. **43**, p. 200.

58. **43**, p. 276.

States on terms of equality in their traditional markets abroad, asked for protection at home and in the colonies. The elections of 1931 brought to power a government committed to adopting whatever measures appeared necessary — including tariff changes — to improve the trade balance and relieve the country's economic depression and financial difficulties.[59] The new government declared as its aim the protection of established industries. The Import Duty Act of 1932 confirmed the duties of 33.3 per cent ad valorem on a long list of commodities and introduced a 10 per cent duty ad valorem on all other imports, with certain exceptions. At the Ottawa Conference (1932), the United Kingdom granted additional preferential treatment to colonies and dominions in exchange for similar concessions for British products. Public opinion accepted the new policy largely as the answer to the Hawley-Smoot tariff in the United States.

Great Britain followed the protectionist policy until World War II. In recent years it has lowered some duties, mainly within the framework of the GATT, but has maintained the system of import restrictions and controls established during the war. The present tariff is that established by the Import Duty Act in 1932, with numerous adjustments and amendments.

This tariff leaves duty-free most foodstuffs and raw materials, including raw cotton, wool, coal and petroleum. Duties on essential articles are graduated as follows:

10 per cent or less ad valorem on tapioca, nuts, some species of fish, kapok, boards, corn starch, fresh vegetables, some metals (including lead and zinc) and metal oxides.

15 per cent on fresh and dried fruits, glass, articles of copper and zinc, tools, agricultural and industrial machinery, refrigerators, handbags, fur, soap, gramophones.

20 per cent on grapes, poultry, iron and steel tubes and pipes, screws, furniture, lighting appliances, cutlery, electrical goods, wireless apparatus, ball bearings, articles of apparel, footwear, various chemicals, paper, cycles, linoleum.

25 per cent on preserved fruits, pig iron, blooms, arms and munitions, cosmetics, spectacles, jewelry.

30 per cent on glassware, gloves.

33.3 per cent on structural iron and steel, forgings, castings, rails, wire and articles manufactured of wire, railroad wagons, automobiles, tires and tubes, clocks, vinegar.[60]

The act of 1932 levied no import duty higher than 33.3 per cent but, independent of this act, much higher revenue charges have been imposed on beer, wine, liquors, coffee, cocoa, playing cards, watches, tobacco, cigars, cigarettes. The duty on spirits is more than £10 per gallon; on cigarettes, £3 3*s.* 8*d.* per pound; cigars, £3 7*s.* 9*d.* per pound; sparkling wines, £3 2*s.* 6*d.* per gallon.

Under the system of imperial preference, duties lower than those in the general column are provided for numerous products imported from countries that are members of the Commonwealth. Among these products are clocks and watches, musical instruments, meat, beer, cocoa, coffee, dried fruits and apparel. A small preference reduction is allowed on spirits and liquors.

During World War II the system of imperial preferences was supplemented by special purchase and delivery agreements between the United Kingdom and other members of the British Empire. The United Kingdom announced its desire to purchase all of Australia's surplus supplies of wool, meat, dairy products, sugar, canned and dried fruits, zinc, and a large part of its surplus of wheat, lead and copper. Similarly, New Zealand declared that all its exports of wool, meat, butter and cheese would be allocated to the United Kingdom. Similar arrangements were made between the United Kingdom on the one side and the Union of South Africa and Canada on the other.[61]

THE UNITED STATES

Early Customs Duties

Customs were an important source of revenue for the British colonies on American soil. Each colony had provisions of its own and collected duties on goods imported from overseas or from other colonies in addition to those imposed by England under the Navigation Acts.[62] Protectionist considerations may have had a part in framing these local tariffs, but the main purpose was fiscal.[63] Moderate duties were levied, mainly on articles considered luxuries such as slaves, sugar, tea and coffee, rum, spirits and wine.

These local customs were maintained after the formation of the Union in 1776. In the next decade the northern states increased their import

59. **49,** p. 101.
60. See **19.**

61. **49,** pp. 196–97.
62. **56,** p. 14.
63. **85,** Vol. I, p. 25.

rates as a means of protecting local business against competition.[64] The Constitution of 1787, however, put an end to local tariffs and declared the regulation of commerce with foreign nations a responsibility of the federal government.

Congress passed the first tariff act in 1789. Its initial purpose was to provide revenue to the Treasury, but in establishing the rates on particular commodities, the demands of northern manufacturers for protection were taken into consideration. Except for seventeen groups of raw materials, all imported goods were taxed, most of them 5–15 per cent ad valorem. The highest rate (15 per cent) was levied on carriages; a 10 per cent duty was imposed on luxuries such as glass, china and lace; from 5 to $7\frac{1}{2}$ per cent was levied on other imports. Specific duties were imposed on 36 articles — some obviously fiscal, as on tea, sugar, salt and spirits; others, protective, as on hemp, cordage and nails.[65]

The tariff of 1789 was supposed to continue in force for seven years but the very next year its rates were revised upward to increase federal revenue.

Alexander Hamilton

In 1791 Hamilton presented to Congress his famous "Report on Manufactures," in which he outlined principles of customs policy as part of a long-range economic program. His leading idea was to foster the development of natural resources and to transform the United States gradually from an agrarian country into an industrial nation like England. Hamilton's recommendations were designed to facilitate the importation of raw materials and protect infant manufactures against foreign competition.

The range of import duties Hamilton envisaged was about the same as in the tariff of 1789 — in most cases, 5–15 per cent — but he demanded the highest rate in this range on many articles which could be manufactured in the United States. All in all, he recommended a higher and more selective tariff than that of 1789.[66]

---

64. **69**, p. 43.
65. Taussig describes the tariff of 1789 as "protective in intention and spirit" but stresses that the "general range of duties was by no means such as would have been thought protective in later days." (**86**, p. 15.)
66. Hamilton recommended, for example, an increase in the duty on books from 5 to 10 per cent, allowing at the same time duty-free importation of books for use in seminaries and public libraries. (**66**, pp. 101–02.)

The Nineteenth Century

Hamilton's report did not exercise an immediate influence on the tariff policy of the United States.[67] Between 1792 and 1816, some twenty-five tariff acts were passed. Individual rates of duty were shifted up and down. Increases were made partly to raise revenue and partly to protect particular groups of producers; cuts were effected to meet the claims of consumers. For a time, as a result of the Napoleonic wars and the War of 1812, the United States found itself practically isolated from Europe. Domestic manufacturers obtained almost complete protection against foreign competition and used it to expand production, especially in the northern states. The resumption of foreign trade threatened to wipe out the new industries and the northern producers asked Congress for protective measures while the agrarian South opposed a substantial rise in import duties. Ultimately the northern states prevailed.

The Tariff Act of 1816 was the first systematic attempt of the country to establish customs duties on a protective, rather than fiscal, basis. It was followed in 1824 and 1828 by new strongly protectionist tariffs; the latter was decried as the "Act of Abominations" by its opponents in the South, who even threatened to withdraw the southern states from the Union. The dispute was settled in 1833 by enactment of a new tariff which provided for immediate repeal of some duties and gradual reduction of others so that all rates would be close to 20 per cent ad valorem by 1842.

The protectionist spirit was revived in the Tariff Act of 1842, but four years later, in 1846, the country returned to a tariff designed primarily to provide revenue, with ad valorem duties ranging from 5 to 40 per cent. The new tariff contained no specific duties and embodied a long list of duty-free articles. It was further liberalized in 1857. In 1861 duties were slightly increased and ad valorem rates were replaced by specific duties.

The Civil War marked a turning point in the commercial policy of the United States. The Customs Act of 1862, which increased duties for fiscal purposes, was followed by the highly protectionist tariff of 1864 and special legislation to protect the wool and copper interests. In 1867, high specific and ad valorem duties were intro-

---

67. **42**, p. 147; **85**, Vol. I, p. 111.

duced on wool and fabrics; in 1870, duties on flax, nickel and marble and steel rails were revised upward.[68] The rise in tariffs was interrupted in 1872 when, in view of a surplus of customs revenues, all rates were reduced by 10 per cent, but this measure was repealed in 1875.[69]

In 1883 a new tariff was established. Taussig characterizes it as follows:

Its general character cannot be easily described; in truth, it can hardly be said to have any general character. On the whole, it may be fairly described as a half-hearted attempt on the part of those wishing to maintain a system of high protection, to make some concession to a public demand for a more moderate tariff system. Some duties were increased, some lowered; nor was any consistent policy followed. Some raw materials, like wool and pig-iron, were admitted at slightly lower rates; others, like iron ore, were charged with higher rates. The same incongruities appear in the duties on more finished goods.[70]

The tariff was one of the central issues in the elections of 1888, and the view of the majority in the new Congress found expression in the high duty rates in the McKinley Tariff Act of 1890. In one respect, however, this tariff differed favorably from all previous tariffs: it was the first tariff in the United States with explicit provisions for negotiations with foreign countries on reciprocal concessions.[71] These provisions were repealed in 1894 but restored and extended in 1897 by a tariff act which raised duties to an unprecedented level and remained in force until 1909.

Tariffs after 1900

The tariff established in 1909 was less aggressively protectionist than those of 1890 and 1897. Taussig comments:

The increases of duties were more furtive, the reductions were more loudly proclaimed. The extreme advocates of protection were on the defensive: . . . High-water mark [of protection] apparently had been reached, and there was reason to expect that the tide, no longer moving upward, might thereafter begin to recede.[72]

In the 1913 tariff enacted in Wilson's administration, many items were put on the duty-free list, many rates were lowered, and specific duties were replaced by ad valorem rates.[73] In all, this was a moderately liberal tariff of approximately the same type as those in force in Germany, Austria-Hungary and France at that time.

The country's liberal commercial policy was reversed after World War I under the pressure of the rising political isolationism and economic nationalism. The depression of 1920–21 gave support to claims for protection against foreign competition and declining agricultural prices. The overwhelming victory of the Republicans in 1920 was followed, in 1922, by the enactment of a tariff with the highest duties the United States had ever had. Moreover, the new tariff looked higher than it actually was because it included duties on articles which are normally exported from the United States and were not likely to be imported in appreciable quantity. For some goods, the tariff prescribed specific duties, for others, ad valorem, often as high as 50, 75 or 100 per cent and occasionally still higher. In many cases a combination of both types of duties was used; recomputed ad valorem for the same unit, some duties ran to 200, 300, 400 per cent or even more.[74]

The Hawley-Smoot Tariff, 1930

The tariff of 1922 was succeeded by a still more protectionist act in 1930, the famous Hawley-Smoot tariff. That act increased practically all duties but made the most drastic changes in the schedule of agricultural products. (See Table 97.)

As a measure of industrial and agricultural protectionism, this tariff was a futile gesture. It brought temporary aid to some industries but it helped neither U.S. agriculture nor the economy as a whole. It did not stop the spiral of falling prices and depression, and at the same time provoked an unfavorable reaction in the trade policies of other countries.[75]

The Trade Agreements Acts, 1934–53

The avowed purpose of Cordell Hull's program in 1934 for reciprocal trade agreements was to stimulate United States exports by mutual agreements to reduce duties. Substantially it was an attempt to revise the Hawley-Smoot tariff

68. **86,** pp. 194–229.
69. **86,** p. 231.
70. **86,** pp. 249–50.
71. **32,** Part II, p. 1.
72. **86,** p. 408.

73. **86,** p. 419.
74. **86,** pp. 470–71.
75. See p. 253.

TABLE 97

TARIFF RATES: THE UNITED STATES, 1922 AND 1930

(Average Percentage Rate Ad Valorem for Each Schedule)

Tariff Schedule	Tariff Act, 1922	Tariff Act, 1930
Chemicals, oils and paints	29.22	31.40
Earths, earthenware and glassware	45.62	53.62
Metals and manufactures of	33.71	35.01
Wood and manufactures of	7.97	10.49
Sugar, molasses and manufactures of	67.85	77.21
Tobacco and manufactures of	63.09	64.78
Agricultural products and provisions	12.86	33.62
Spirits, wines and other beverages	36.48	47.44
Manufactures of cotton	40.27	46.42
Flax, hemp, jute and manufactures of	18.16	19.14
Wool and manufactures of	49.54	59.83
Manufactures of silk	56.56	59.13
Manufactures of rayon	52.68	53.62
Paper and books	24.72	26.06
Sundries	21.97	27.39

Source: **86**, pp. 518–19.

without going through long and tedious tariff hearings in Congress. The act empowered the President to negotiate trade agreements with other nations on the basis of mutual reduction of duties. It gave the Department of State primary responsibility for negotiations with other countries but instructed the Tariff Commission and other agencies to participate in developing lists of concessions that could be made to foreign countries and concessions which should be demanded in return. An interdepartmental committee was designated to conduct public hearings on forthcoming negotiations "in order that any interested person may have an opportunity to present his views to the President."

The President's authority to reduce duties was limited to 50 per cent of the existing rates, and it was provided that every agreement concluded under the act was subject to termination at the end of three years.

The Trade Agreements Act was extended in its original form in 1937 and 1940 and renewed with some amendments in 1943, 1945, 1948, 1951, 1954 (for one year) and 1955.

The amendment introduced in 1945 greatly

extended the authority of the President by empowering him to reduce duties on single commodities up to 50 per cent of the rates in effect on January 1, 1945, even if they were already lower than in 1934. In 1948 the President's authority to reduce tariff rates was limited by introducing the peril-point clause.

The peril-point amendment requires that the Tariff Commission report to the President its views on the depth to which new concessions might be made without causing or threatening serious injury to the domestic industry producing like or directly competitive articles. If the President grants a concession which goes beyond this peril point, he must explain his action to the Congress.[76]

In 1951 Congress took another important step in the same direction through an escape-clause provision. Actually, a provision of this type had been in all U.S. trade agreements since 1943, but before 1951 it expressed the consent of treaty parties; it was limited to "unforeseen developments"; and it had never been used as a reason for withdrawing or modifying concessions agreed upon by the United States. This clause (Section 6,a) was incorporated in the Trade Agreements Extension Act of 1951, as follows:

"No reduction in any rate of duty, or binding of any existing customs or excise treatment, or other concession hereafter proclaimed under section 350 of the Tariff Act of 1930, as amended, shall be permitted to continue in effect when the product on which the concession has been granted is, as a result, in whole or in part, of the duty or other customs treatment reflecting such concession, being imported into the United States in such increased quantities, either actual or relative, as to cause or threaten serious injury to the domestic industry producing like or directly competitive products."

Under the present law, petitions for an escape-clause investigation are submitted to the Tariff Commission which makes an investigation and reports within one year its recommendations for action, if any, to the President. If the President does not carry out the recommendations of the Tariff Commission he must report his reasons for not having done so to the Congress.[77]

The Trade Agreements Extension Act of 1953 introduced minor procedural changes in applying the escape clause. The most important is that

76. **50**, p. 10.
77. **50**, pp. 11–12.

the Tariff Commission must complete its investigation and report within nine months.[78]

Impact of Trade Agreements on U.S. Imports

The immediate effect of the reciprocal-agreements policy was disappointing. The foreign trade of the United States had reached a low level, accounting for only 8 per cent of world imports in 1934.[79] As recovery from the great depression progressed, U.S. exports and imports began to increase, but they rose very slowly, as the following figures show (in millions of dollars): [80]

	Exports	Imports
1929	$5,241	$4,399
1930	3,843	3,061
1931	2,424	2,091
1932	1,611	1,324
1933	1,675	1,450
1934	2,133	1,655
1935	2,283	2,047
1936	2,456	2,423
1937	3,349	3,084
1938	3,094	1,960
1939	3,177	2,318
1940	4,021	2,625

It is not clear to what extent the revival of the country's foreign trade in 1935–40 was due to the reciprocal trade agreements and to what extent, to other economic and political factors. Certainly the change in the commercial policy of the United States was not among the major factors which accounted for the general upturn in world trade in the late 1930's. Moreover, the Trade Agreements Act of 1934 was originally announced as a temporary emergency measure:

In formulating the purposes of the Trade Agreements Act, the Congress explicitly declared the program to be an emergency measure intended primarily to assist in alleviating the pressure of surplus products on the domestic market. The primary objective, it was stated, was to promote United States exports by reducing barriers to, and facilitating the increase of, United States imports contingent upon reciprocal reductions in barriers by other countries. The authority to enter into trade agreements under the act was initially limited to 3 years, and the act provided that every agreement concluded under it should be subject to termination at the end of not more than 3 years after coming into effect.[81]

In the long run, however, the 1934 act was an important event in the history of world trade. Although it did not mark a radical reversal of the commercial policy of the United States it did shift from an aggressively protectionist policy to a more liberal program which can be described as relatively moderate selective protectionism.

The program gave official recognition to foreign trade as an important element in domestic prosperity and in securing a well-balanced relationship among the various components of the domestic economy. Expansion of exports was predicated upon the expansion of imports, and finally, the principle of non-discrimination as between countries, through guaranty of most-favored-nation treatment, was again given full and unreserved expression. Application of the principle, moreover, acquired new practical significance: for the first time it was linked with an active tariff-bargaining policy.[82]

International implications of the reciprocal trade agreements program of the United States are discussed elsewhere, as part of the GATT.[83] The effects of this program on U.S. tariff rates are examined in the following pages.

Reduction of Tariff Rates

After 1934 the United States, without revising its tariff, steadily reduced its customs rates by trade agreements. As a result of these reductions and of the general rise in prices, the ratio of customs collections to the total value of imported merchandise was at a lower level in 1949–52 than at any time in the past except during World War I. (See Table 98.) In the last two decades of the nineteenth century the ratio fluctuated around 25–30 per cent; was around 15–20 per cent before World War I; dropped to an average of 6.9 per cent in 1916–20; [84] rose to nearly 20 per cent under the Hawley-Smoot tariff in the early 1930's; declined to an average of 6.9 per cent in 1946–50; and was at an all-time low — 5.3 per cent in 1952.

Under the trade agreements program, import duties were reduced item by item through negotiations with the foreign countries most interested in exporting the respective articles to the United States. Thus, out of 3,337 rates on duti-

---

78. **27**, 1953, pp. 1–2.
79. **8**, 1936–1937, p. 214.
80. **21**, pp. 243–44.
81. **32**, Part II, p. 9.

82. **32**, Part II, p. 9.
83. See pp. 255–56.
84. The decline in the ratio during World War I was in part due to the changes in the composition of U.S. imports and in part to the suspension of duties on certain strategic goods. All imports from Canada, for example, were exempt from duties.

TABLE 98

DUTY COLLECTIONS: THE UNITED STATES, 1821–1953

Year	Imports (Millions)		Duties		
	Total	Dutiable	Amount (Millions)	As Percentage of:	
				Total Imports	Dutiable Imports
1821	$ 43.7	$ 42.0	$ 18.9	43.2	45.0
1826	57.7	53.0	26.1	45.3	49.3
1831	82.8	77.3	36.6	44.2	47.4
1836	158.8	88.7	31.0	19.5	34.9
1841	114.8	57.7	19.9	17.4	34.6
1846	110.0	91.4	30.5	27.7	33.4
1851	200.5	182.6	48.6	24.3	26.6
1856	295.7	246.0	64.1	21.7	26.1
1861	274.7	207.2	39.0	14.2	18.8
1866	423.5	366.3	177.1	41.8	48.3
1871	499.7	459.7	202.4	40.5	44.0
1876	464.5	324.3	145.2	31.3	44.8
1881	650.6	448.3	193.8	29.8	43.2
1886	624.0	413.8	189.4	30.4	45.8
1891	845.5	466.5	216.9	25.7	46.5
1896	759.7	390.8	157.0	20.7	40.2
1901	807.8	468.7	233.6	28.9	49.8
1906	1,213.4	664.7	293.9	24.2	44.2
1911	1,527.9	751.0	310.0	20.3	41.3
1912	1,640.7	759.2	304.9	18.6	40.2
1913	1,766.7	779.7	312.5	17.7	40.1
1914	1,906.4	754.0	283.7	14.9	37.6
1915	1,648.4	615.5	205.9	12.5	33.5
1916	2,358.6	743.8	214.2	9.1	28.8
1917	2,919.3	778.3	204.6	7.0	26.3
1918	2,951.5	722.9	170.9	5.8	23.7
1919	3,827.7	1,116.2	237.5	6.2	21.3
1920	5,101.8	1,985.9	325.6	6.4	16.4
1921	2,556.9	992.6	292.4	11.4	29.5
1922	3,073.8	1,185.5	451.4	14.7	38.1
1923	3,713.8	1,566.6	566.7	15.2	36.2
1924	3,575.1	1,456.9	532.3	14.9	36.5
1925	4,176.2	1,467.4	551.9	13.2	37.6
1926	4,408.1	1,500.0	590.0	13.4	39.3
1927	4,163.1	1,483.0	574.8	13.8	38.8
1928	4,077.9	1,399.3	542.3	13.3	38.8
1929	4,338.6	1,458.4	584.8	13.5	40.1
1930	3,114.1	1,033.0	461.8	14.8	44.7
1931	2,088.5	696.8	370.8	17.8	53.2
1932	1,325.1	439.6	259.6	19.6	59.1
1933	1,433.0	529.5	283.7	19.8	53.6
1934	1,636.0	644.8	301.2	18.4	46.7
1935	2,038.9	832.9	357.2	17.5	42.9

(*Continued on following page*)

TABLE 98—*continued*

Year	Imports (Millions)		Duties		
			Amount (Millions)	As Percentage of:	
	Total	Dutiable		Total Imports	Dutiable Imports
1936	$ 2,424.0	$1,039.0	$408.1	16.8	39.3
1937	3,009.9	1,244.6	470.5	15.6	37.8
1938	1,949.6	766.9	301.4	15.5	39.3
1939	2,276.1	878.8	328.0	14.4	37.3
1940	2,540.6	891.7	317.7	12.5	35.6
1941	3,222.0	1,191.0	437.8	13.6	36.8
1942	2,780.3	1,001.7	320.1	11.5	32.0
1943	3,390.1	1,197.2	392.5	11.6	32.8
1944	3,887.5	1,169.5	367.3	9.5	31.4
1945	4,098.1	1,348.8	380.8	9.3	28.2
1946	4,824.9	1,889.9	477.9	9.9	25.3
1947	5,666.3	2,211.7	427.7	7.6	19.3
1948	7,032.0	2,917.5	404.8	5.7	13.9
1949	6,591.6	2,708.5	364.6	5.5	13.5
1950	8,743.1	3,976.3	522.3	6.0	13.1
1951	10,817.3	4,823.9	591.3	5.5	12.3
1952	10,747.5	4,490.5	570.1	5.3	12.7
1953 [a]	10,777.4	4,858.7	584.4	5.4	12.0

Sources: **21**, pp. 247–48; **22**, 1954, p. 932.   a. Preliminary.

able items listed in the tariff, 2,532 were reduced between 1934 and January 1, 1953; 148 were bound against increase by treaties, and only 657 remained unaffected by agreements.[85] When the rates of January 1, 1953 are applied to dutiable imports in 1952, it appears that 89.4 per cent of such imports were admitted at reduced rates, 4.0 per cent at rates bound against rise and 6.6 per cent at rates on which no concession had been made.[86]

By January 1, 1953 rates on dutiable items had been reduced by 50 per cent (applying preagreement and 1953 rates to imports in 1952). The reductions averaged more than 50 per cent for chemicals, oils and paints (51 per cent), wood (57), sugar (64), tobacco (56), spirits and other beverages (72), hard fibers (58), paper and books (54). (See Table 99.)

A 1945 amendment to the Trade Agreements Act permits a reduction of 50 per cent on any duties, even those which had been reduced 50 per cent between 1934 and January 1, 1945. Such maximum cumulative reductions have been granted on manganese ore, sawed wood, barley, oats and alfalfa, seed, jute fabrics, cedar siding

and lumber. The law permits further reduction of duties in existence on January 1, 1953 by approximately 30 per cent, on a weighted average.[87]

Duty rates on a large part of the dutiable imports are less than 10 per cent. Merchandise on which 20 per cent or more is levied represented approximately 17 per cent of dutiable imports, or about 7 per cent of total imports in 1952. (See Table 100.) Among articles on which 20 per cent or more ad valorem is levied are certain types of watches, leaf tobacco, meat, whisky, wool and silk manufactures. (See Table 101.) Moreover, Table 101 shows only a few of the individual articles which are imported to the United States in small quantities, in part because of high duties levied on them.[88]

In general a comparison of the preagreement and current duties on the principal dutiable commodities tends to overstate the extent of liberalization of the tariff: it emphasizes reductions in duties on noncompetitive articles and omits consideration of the absence of reductions on highly protected items. Inasmuch as negotiations have adhered to the rule that "no industry shall be

85. **30**, pp. 5 and 18.
86. **30**, pp. 3 and 10.

87. **30**, p. 7.
88. Cf. Table 111.

TABLE 99

CONCESSIONS IN TARIFF RATES: THE UNITED STATES, RATES OF DUTIES BEFORE AGREEMENT AND AS OF
JANUARY 1, 1953

	Number of Rates [a]				Average Rates Ad Valorem, Percentage [b]	
Tariff Schedule	Total	Reduced	Bound against Increase	Unchanged	Preagreement	Jan. 1, 1953
Total	3,337	2,532	148	657	24.4	12.2
Chemicals, oils and paints	427	312	11	104	25.1	12.4
Earths, earthenware, glassware	283	224	12	47	46.0	24.7
Metals & manufactures of	662	566	19	77	23.7	12.1
Wood & manufactures of	52	38	2	12	10.9	4.7
Sugar, molasses & manufactures of	21	16	2	3	25.8	9.4
Tobacco & manufactures of	19	15	—	4	45.6	20.3
Agricultural products & provisions	560	394	43	123	16.2	9.4
Spirits, wines & other beverages	40	30	2	8	81.4	23.1
Cotton manufactures	170	124	3	43	36.8	21.8
Flax, hemp, jute & manufactures of	85	65	3	17	12.2	5.2
Wool & manufactures of	117	104	4	9	36.7	22.4
Manufactures of silk	46	32	1	13	58.8	31.0
Manufactures of rayon & other synthetic textiles	65	61	—	4	32.8	17.7
Paper and books	151	128	1	22	20.4	9.4
Sundries	604	396	41	167	31.8	19.1
Free list taxable [c]	35	27	4	4	10.2	4.1

Source: **30**, pp. 11 and 18.

a. Based on the classification of 1952 and the state of agreement as of January 1, 1953.

b. Specific duties are recomputed as percentage of value of each article at 1952 prices. Averages apply to 1952 imports.

c. Articles on the free list of the tariff act, but subject to import taxes under revenue acts, which have precisely the same effect as duties (**35**, p. 90).

TABLE 100

TARIFF RATES: THE UNITED STATES, IMPORTS
DISTRIBUTED BY RATE OF DUTY, IN 1952

Rate of Duty	Value, in Millions of Dollars	Percentage
Total	$10,747	100.0
Duty-free	6,257	58.2
Percentage:		
10.0 or less	2,349	21.9
10.1–20.0	1,356	12.6
20.1–30.0	515	4.8
30.1–40.0	185	1.7
40.1–50.0	44	0.4
50.1–60.0	26	0.3
60.1–70.0	7	} 0.1
70.1–80.0	5	
80.1 or more	3	

Source: Computed from **30**, pp. 9 and 15.

injured," there has been a strong tendency to grant reductions where such reductions would contribute least to an increase in imports.

Despite all the cuts in import duties the United States market remains a hard nut for importers to crack. It can absorb a large quantity of merchandise if the importer offers the right product at the right time and place and in the right way to reach consumers, but launching merchandise is much more expensive in the United States than in any other country, and the importer faces the danger that consumers may soon lose interest in the new goods. Moreover, successful importers confront additional dangers. In some cases, industry in the United States can beat foreign competition in the domestic market by turning out similar or competitive articles in mass volume at lower prices and, if the products prove inferior to the imported articles or too expensive,

TABLE 101

TARIFF RATES: THE UNITED STATES, PRINCIPAL DUTIABLE COMMODITIES, BEFORE AGREEMENT AND AS OF
JANUARY 1, 1953

Commodity [a]	Value of Imports, 1952, in Millions of Dollars	Duty Rate Ad Valorem, Percentage		Commodity [a]	Value of Imports, 1952, in Millions of Dollars	Duty Rate Ad Valorem, Percentage	
		Before Agreement	Jan. 1, 1953			Before Agreement	Jan. 1, 1953
Ethyl alcohol	$ 12.7	30.0	15.0	Wheat (unfit for human consumption)	$ 49.9	10.0	5.0
Castor oil	17.5	14.5	7.2	Castor beans	12.9	5.4	2.7
Quebracho extract	12.4	15.0	7.5	Raw cotton	24.7	10.6	5.3
Bauxite, crude	20.4	15.0	7.5	Canned beef	41.7	20.0	20.0
Manganese ore	47.9	31.9	8.0	Beef & veal, pickled or cured	18.8	20.0	20.0
Plate, iron or steel	16.6	20.0	10.0	Ham	45.5	4.0	4.0
Beams, girders, etc.	33.9	3.6	1.8	Cottonseed	15.0	9.5	9.5
Tubes, iron & steel	58.9	25.0	12.5	Olives	16.6	17.8	17.8
Automobile parts	10.6	25.0	12.5	Whisky			
Machinery & parts	19.2	27.5	13.8	Scotch & Irish	48.7	92.9	27.9
Aluminum metal	40.4	24.0	9.0	Other	44.2	84.0	21.0
Nickel & alloys	83.2	5.3	2.2	Burlap	113.7	4.2	2.1
Pig iron	17.9	1.9	1.0	Woven fabrics	12.7	40.0	10.0
Sewing machines	19.6	15.0	10.0	Wool & manufactures			
Zinc blocks	16.7	12.9	5.2	Total	462.0	36.7	22.4
Watches (15–17 jewel)	47.1	54.2	33.0	Duty reduced	458.6	36.9	22.4
Lead pigs & bars	48.4	14.6	7.3	Silk manufactures			
Sawn boards, etc.	168.5	3.6	0.9	Total	29.3	58.8	31.0
Molasses from Cuba	29.5	1.0	0.5	Duty reduced	26.2	59.1	27.9
Other	16.4	1.3	0.6	Synthetic textiles, filaments	27.5	25.0	15.0
Sugar from Cuba	316.5	29.0	10.4	Paper and books			
Tobacco leaf	48.5	51.9	22.2	Total	39.1	20.4	9.4
Cigar filler tobacco, stemmed, from Cuba	14.4	27.4	13.7	Duty reduced	38.5	20.2	9.2
Fishery products	118.6	13.3	8.4	Imitation precious stones	13.3	20.0	10.0
Beef, fresh	12.7	34.0	17.0	Synthetic rubber	11.3	20.0	10.0
Barley	26.5	12.5	4.7	Bristles (exc. from Cuba)	11.8	0.8	0.8
Oats	55.3	19.6	4.9				
Bran	21.9	10.0	2.5	Diamonds (exc. from Cuba)	51.7	10.0	10.0
Cashew nuts	19.3	4.4	3.3				

Source: **30,** pp. 20–40.

a. Commodities valued at more than $10 million in 1952. For wool and manufactures, silk manufactures and paper and books, totals and averages for whole groups of commodities are shown.

producers can invoke the escape clause and ask for higher import duties.

The extent of the latter danger to the importers depends on the interpretation of the escape-clause provision by the Administration. In 1951–54 the general tendency was to interpret it in a restricted way. By December 1, 1952, the Tariff Commission had completed investigations on fifteen applications; through July 1954 an additional thirteen reports had been issued. In sixteen cases the Tariff Commission found insufficient reason for application of the escape clause; in twelve cases it recommended modification of concessions awarded through tariff agreements or other action. In five cases the President, after due consultation, rejected the Commission's recommendations,[89] and two were returned to the Commission for further study. Decisions were pending on two cases. In only three cases was action ordered by the President. All three were of minor importance (hatters' fur, dried figs and alsike clover seed). However, these trivial cases were interpreted by some prospective exporters as a warning against expensive promotion campaigns in U.S. markets. Some foreign manufacturers consider large-scale export to the United States a risky business and often prefer to disperse their products in small consignments among a score of markets more familiar to them.

Concessions Granted and Obtained

Through reciprocal agreements the United States has obtained many concessions in duties on its exports, partly in reduction of duties, partly in the binding of existing duties against increase and of the duty-free status of certain commodities. There is no way to compare precisely the scope of the concessions the United States has granted and obtained. Since the starting point of negotiations was the high Hawley-Smoot tariff, it appears that the United States was bound to make larger concessions than other parties to reciprocal trade treaties. In some cases, the United States had to reduce its duties in exchange for the agreement of other partners to bind their duties against increase or to preserve a duty-free status.

The U.S. Tariff Commission describes the scope of concessions obtained by the United States in terms of their application to prewar exports, as follows:

Exports from the United States to thirty-nine trade-agreement countries [90] totaled $2,427 million in 1939. Articles subject to scheduled concessions made at Geneva in 1947 represented a value of $1,498 million, 62 per cent of the total. This value was distributed as follows by the

type and extent of concession (in millions of dollars): [91]

Value of U.S. exports, total	$1,498
Bound to free status	326
Bound against increase	462
With reduced duties	564
Other commitments	146

Value of U.S. exports receiving reduction of:	
100 per cent	80
76–100 per cent	7
51–76 per cent	53
36–51 per cent	117
25–36 per cent	173
Less than 25 per cent	134

The rate concessions affect, in varying degree, almost all groups of U.S. exports — foodstuffs, tobacco, cotton, petroleum products, iron and steel, industrial machinery, automobiles and tractors. (See Table 102; cf. Figure 52.) In recent years, however, United States exports have been affected less by customs walls around foreign markets than by the limited dollar supply of such countries and the restrictions they impose on imports as a means of protecting their balance of payments position and exchange rates.

FRANCE

From 1790 to 1870

Under the kings of France, customs were part of a chaotic agglomeration of local tolls and excises. The first national tariff was enacted by the revolutionary Constituent Assembly in 1790.[92] This tariff was moderately protectionist, with duties on manufactured goods ranging from 5 to 20 per cent but none on foodstuffs and staple raw materials. During the war with England, French commercial policy was determined by military and political considerations. It became strongly protectionist under Napoleon I and remained so for a half century. The original aim under the Bourbons was to maintain industries born during the British blockade of French ports, but in the 1820's protection was extended to agriculture. The change came in 1853–56 under Napoleon III, when the government reduced duties on such commodities as coal, pig iron, steel, wool, dye wood, cotton, cattle, meat, wine

---

89. **50**, p. 12; **33**, 1953, pp. 44–56.

90. Includes all countries with which the United States had negotiated before April 1, 1945, but excludes countries involved in concessions obtained at the Annecy and Torquay conferences.

91. **32**, Part IV, pp. 18–23.

92. **41**, p. 2.

TABLE 102

Trade Agreements: the United States, Value of Selected Exported Commodities Subject to Concessions Obtained under Trade Agreements through 1948

(Exports in 1939 in Millions of Dollars)

Commodity	Total U.S. Exports	Total	Binding To Free Status	Binding Against Increase	Reduction of Duties Total	More than 75	51–75	36–50	25–35	Less than 25	Other Commitments
Total	$2,426.6	$1,498.1	$326.2	$462.1	$564.1	$87.3	$53.0	$116.6	$173.5	$133.7	$145.7
Pork	20.2	16.5	0.9	3.0	4.0	0.3	2.7	0.9	0.1	0.1	8.5
Lard	20.2	19.4	0.7	—	18.6	15.0	—	1.7	1.0	0.9	—
Corn	19.8	2.0	—	—	1.8	—	1.8	—	—	—	0.2
Rice	9.2	8.1	0.9	0.7	6.6	—	—	—	0.8	5.8	—
Wheat and flour	61.4	56.4	18.8	13.6	22.6	14.5	0.6	7.4	0.1	—	1.4
Vegetables [a]	12.2	7.6	—	0.3	7.0	0.8	4.1	1.0	0.9	0.2	0.2
Fruits [a]	76.0	76.2	3.5	10.5	61.1	17.9	2.5	5.7	14.5	20.5	1.1
Leaf tobacco	76.8	67.2	0.2	17.4	2.7	—	—	2.0	0.1	0.7	47.0
Raw cotton	243.0	138.4	126.4	10.9	1.1	—	0.9	0.2	—	—	—
Fish	11.1	7.4	—	0.5	6.8	0.3	0.3	5.0	0.3	0.9	—
Tires and tubes	17.7	7.0	0.1	3.8	3.1	—	0.1	0.2	0.6	2.2	—
Cotton cloth	36.5	12.5	—	1.4	5.4	—	—	2.6	1.9	0.9	5.8
Lumber	39.3	37.7	6.8	15.7	14.8	—	7.7	2.5	0.2	4.4	0.4
Paper	31.7	13.4	0.5	3.3	9.2	—	0.4	0.8	4.9	3.1	0.4
Coal and coke	66.6	34.2	1.0	1.8	31.4	13.5	—	0.1	17.8	—	—
Crude petroleum	92.8	30.9	27.1	2.0	1.5	—	—	—	1.5	—	0.3
Petroleum products	190.3	64.6	1.9	19.4	13.0	0.4	0.4	1.6	4.1	6.5	30.3
Iron and steel products	235.7	54.4	0.8	29.5	19.8	0.4	0.6	1.5	11.5	5.8	4.2
Copper and manufactures	97.2	20.3	17.0	2.1	0.5	—	0.1	0.3	—	0.1	0.6
Industrial machinery	289.9	135.4	8.9	68.4	51.9	1.3	9.3	11.4	25.4	4.6	6.2
Agricultural machinery	20.5	17.7	3.3	9.2	5.2	4.6	—	0.5	—	—	—
Tractors	48.0	32.8	15.7	7.3	6.9	1.5	2.1	1.1	0.5	1.8	2.9
Automobiles	253.7	166.2	0.2	77.7	67.8	0.9	7.3	22.1	11.3	26.3	20.5
Aircraft	117.8	55.3	9.9	41.2	3.4	—	—	2.9	0.4	0.1	0.9
Medical preparations	22.3	7.1	0.4	2.9	3.8	—	—	1.2	0.4	2.2	—
Paints, varnishes	22.8	11.9	0.6	7.3	3.9	0.5	—	0.5	0.7	2.2	—
Fertilizers	17.0	4.8	4.6	—	0.2	—	—	0.1	—	0.1	0.1
Photographic goods	19.1	12.6	0.4	8.4	3.5	0.2	0.5	1.5	0.9	0.4	0.4

Source: **32**, Part IV, pp. 18, 30–33.   a. Fresh and canned.

and other foodstuffs.[93] When the proposal for a new liberal tariff was rejected by the legislature, the government started a campaign to liberalize foreign trade by means of commercial agreements.

In 1860 France signed an important commercial treaty with Great Britain. Each nation guaranteed m.f.n. treatment to the other and agreed to reduce duties on a number of commodities. The treaty was to remain in force for a period of ten years with a provision that it would be extended for an additional decade unless either party should give a year's notice of termination.

After concluding this treaty, France offered other countries the privileges granted to the British in exchange for comparable concessions. In the 1860's France signed such agreements with Belgium, the Netherlands, Austria, the German Customs Union, Portugal, Spain, Italy, Switzerland, Sweden and Norway, and others.[94] This phase of French commercial policy was terminated by the defeat of France in the war with Prussia and the establishment of the Third Republic.

After the Franco-Prussian War

The government of the Third Republic, in search for new sources of revenues, attempted a drastic increase in import duties, but this measure met opposition in the National Assembly.[95] After vehement disputes and a series of parliamentary crises, a compromise was reached in 1881 in a moderately protectionist tariff, supplemented later by a conventional tariff based on trade treaties. The tariff included some revenue duties (on sugar, coffee and cocoa) and left raw

93. **42**, p. 298; **41**, pp. 2ff.

94. **42**, pp. 306–07.
95. **41**, p. 6.

	UNITED KINGDOM	BENELUX	CUBA	FRANCE	NORWAY	CANADA	INDIA	NEW ZEALAND	BRAZIL	CHINA	NEWFOUNDLAND	SOUTH AFRICA	CZECHOSLOVAKIA	CEYLON	AUSTRALIA	LEBANON	BURMA	CHILE	SOUTHERN RHODESIA
GRAINS AND CEREAL PRODUCTS	●	●	●	●	●					●	●	●		●					
FRUITS	●	●	●	●	●	●	●	●	●	●	●	●	●	●		●	●		
VEGETABLES AND PREPARATIONS	●	●	●	●	●	●	●	●	●	●		●			●			●	●
DAIRY PRODUCTS	●		●		●	●			●	●	●			●	●				
MEATS AND MEAT PRODUCTS	●		●	●	●			●			●	●	●	●					
FISH	●	●			●			●	●					●	●				
TOBACCO AND PRODUCTS	●	●	●	●	●	●	●		●				●		●	●			
TEXTILES	●		●		●			●	●		●	●							
AUTOMOBILES AND PARTS	●	●	●	●	●	●	●	●	●	●		●	●		●	●		●	●
AIRCRAFT AND PARTS		●		●	●	●	●		●	●		●	●		●	●		●	
INDUSTRIAL MACHINERY	●	●	●	●	●	●	●	●	●	●	●	●	●	●	●	●	●	●	●

Source: U.S. Department of State

FIGURE 52. FOREIGN TARIFF CONCESSIONS OBTAINED FOR UNITED STATES EXPORTS AT GENEVA, 1947

materials, foodstuffs and certain other commodities practically duty-free.[96] For all dutiable articles, specific rates were established, in most cases some 24 per cent higher than the ad valorem rates in the conventional tariff which had been in force in the late 1860's.

After the enactment of the new tariff, France concluded agreements with most European countries and with Russia and Turkey, all embodying the m.f.n clause. This clause was extended likewise to Great Britain, although the negotiations between that country and France had failed. Thus 1,200 specific rates out of 1,500 listed in the general tariff were reduced.[97] At the same time, however, the government, yielding to the increasing pressure of agrarian interests, introduced protective duties on cereals (1885 and 1887).[98]

In 1892 a new and very elaborate tariff (Méline Act) was established. It provided for two sets of duties on most articles: minimum rates for most favored nations and maximum rates for other countries. The new tariff strengthened protection of agriculture, imposing average rates of 25 per cent ad valorem on agricultural imports, with the provision that these rates could not be reduced by treaty. Rates for fabricated articles in Méline's tariff were likewise higher than in the conventional tariffs of the 1880's.

The new tariff was not changed until 1910, when all rates were increased and the government was empowered to reduce them to half by reciprocal agreements.[99] It has been estimated that before the outbreak of World War I most of the actual rates under the new tariff averaged 10–20 per cent ad valorem.[100]

Méline's tariff became inoperative during World War I and completely obsolete after the war as a result of the rise in prices. After an attempt to combine the old tariff rates with additional ad valorem charges, the government introduced a system of multipliers for adjusting the specific duties of 1910 to current prices (Decree of July 8, 1919).[101]

96. **41**, p. 14.
97. **82**, pp. 186ff.
98. **41**, p. 16.

99. **58**, p. 13.
100. **70**, p. 43.
101. **70**, p. 44.

In 1921 a new temporary tariff was established in which all specific duties were five times those of 1910. In April 1926 all import duties were increased by 30 per cent, and in August of the same year, again increased at the same rate.[102] The next year a new tariff minimum was enacted, based on the duty rates of 1926 but with modifications agreed upon in French-German negotiations. Concessions made to Switzerland, Belgium and Italy were likewise incorporated in the tariff in 1928.[103]

As in other countries, French commercial policy changed in the 1930's under the impact of the depression. From moderate protectionism, France shifted to the policy of subsidies, restrictions of imports, quotas and the like.[104] The new policy, inaugurated in the summer of 1931, applied originally to only a few products, such as fish and meat, but was gradually broadened. In September 1933 negotiated quotas and a series of barter operations actually replaced the free flow of foreign trade. Simultaneously the tariff was supplemented by an ad valorem tax on all imported goods: 2 per cent on raw materials, 4 per cent on semifabricated goods and 6 per cent on fabricated articles.[105] In 1933 some duties were raised and the policy of quotas and allocations was tightened. In 1936, after devaluation of the franc, a tendency toward liberalization of commercial policy developed, but very soon France returned to the strictly protectionist policy and in 1938 proclaimed the restoration of duties to the general level existing before 1936.[106]

The tariff was inoperative during World War II, under the German occupation. It was radically revised after the liberation of France. The new tariff passed the National Assembly in 1947 and came into force on January 1, 1948. It is based on the new Brussels classification. Almost all duties are established in terms of ad valorem rates. The highest rates amount to 35 per cent (on certain agricultural products and automotive

articles) but most range from 15 to 30 per cent. Some of these general rates have been reduced in the course of negotiation under the GATT. In most cases the concessions have amounted to 5–10 points, and it has been estimated that the conventional duties now in force in the French tariff average 15 per cent.

The Customs Union

The consolidation of Germanic princedoms in Central Europe into a national state began with the formation of a Customs Union (Zollverein) in 1833–34. Prussia had blazed the trail in its tariff act of 1818, the most liberal tariff in Europe at that time.[107] This abolished internal customs between the Prussian provinces and established moderate specific import duties up to 20 per cent of value for colonial products and an average of 10 per cent for manufactured goods, leaving raw materials duty-free.[108] By ensuring Prussia's economic unity, this measure accelerated its industrial growth and gave it economic supremacy among the German kingdoms, dukedoms and republics. The customs union of these states came sixteen years later as a result of a series of treaties among them and Prussia.[109]

In 1841 the Union was renewed for twelve years and several minor German states joined it. Austria was eager to become a member but was barred by Prussia. Under the pressure of various economic groups the rates of the Union tariff began to rise. Moreover, the increase of duties in relation to the value of the respective goods was accentuated by the general decline in prices. The trend was reversed in the 1860's by the reciprocal trade agreements campaign launched by France. The treaty between the Customs Union and France provoked vehement opposition in South Germany, and some of the duties it fixed were later adjusted upward. In 1865 the Union signed a series of treaties with foreign countries. All treaties contained the m.f.n. clause and most of them provided for reciprocal concessions.

The German Empire

The German Empire which emerged in 1871 from Prussia's victory over France continued the policy of the Customs Union, keeping a double

---

102. **70**, p. 67.
103. **58**, p. 37.
104. The French government found it difficult to cite international and domestic laws that would entitle it to limit and allocate imports of different commodities in peacetime. Finally, justification of this policy was found in the provision of the tariff of 1910 which empowered the government to take all appropriate emergency measures to counteract actions of foreign countries which endanger French trade. Thus the new policy was explained as retaliation and self-defense (**54**, p. 27).
105. **65**, p. 49.
106. **38**.

107. **67**, p. 1.
108. **42**, p. 4; cf. **84**, p. 1059.
109. **90**, pp. 138ff.

(general-and-conventional) tariff. In 1877 the general tariff of the Empire was revised and simplified. Most of the protective duties were abolished, and only revenue duties and duties on a few finished commodities were retained. Two years later, duties on 43 groups of commodities were established. Although the duties were not very high and served mainly as a source of revenue, they did protect agriculture against the competition of American and Russian grain.[110]

The further development of German commercial policy was determined by the rising power of the agrarian party, which became the chief bulwark of the conservative government against the tide of the social-democratic movement. From 1880 to the end of the century, duties on agricultural products were repeatedly revised upward while the rates on industrial products were bound against increase by trade agreements. The goal of Germany's commercial policy during this period was to promote industrialization, but German industry felt strong enough in the domestic market and needed no protection through import duties. Rather it looked for new outlets abroad.[111]

In order to meet its needs Germany concluded trade agreements with China, Korea, Japan, Siam and all important European countries. Negotiations with Russia proved particularly difficult.[112]

At the end of the century, German commercial policy was strongly protectionist with regard to agricultural products but used a more liberal, general-and-conventional tariff to promote export of industrial products. This dual purpose determined the tariff enacted in 1902, which raised rates on manufactured goods to three and four times those in force in the 1890's but made it clear that these rates were to serve only as the basis for negotiations.[113] This policy largely supported Germany's drive toward economic predominance in Central Europe and the conquest of overseas markets.

World War I and the Interwar Years

World War I revealed the vulnerability of the German economy. Cut off from the sources of supply of strategic raw materials, with practically no reserves and no plans for replacing imports by domestic products, the heavy industry of the Empire proved to be a colossus with feet of clay. Germany met the challenge by administrative regulations imposing thrift, eliminating waste, replacing scarce raw materials by substitutes and rationing foodstuffs. Such measures, largely improvised as the need arose, later became known as the "war economy."[114] Strict regimentation of foreign trade was an important part of this system.

The Versailles Treaty provided m.f.n. treatment for the Allied and associated nations trading with Germany without promising similar treatment of Germans trading with those nations. Then Germany extended an unlimited and unconditional m.f.n. clause to all foreign countries. The provisions of the Versailles Treaty relating to commercial treaties terminated on January 10, 1925 and in the same year Germany enacted a new tariff, of the same type as in 1902. The increased rates gave the government a broad margin for negotiation with foreign countries. Germany signed an agreement with the United States in 1924, a year before the expiration of the five-year period provided by the treaty.[115] By 1930 it had a moderately protectionist tariff and a network of trade agreements with almost all countries. During the depression both the tariff and the trade treaties were submerged under an avalanche of restrictions and regulations. After Hitler's rise to power, Germany drifted from half-free-half-regimented trade to a totally regimented war economy. Formally, however, the tariff and trade agreements of the Weimar Republic remained in force.

---

110. **67**, pp. 2–3.

111. **67**, pp. 14–15.

112. Russia had had an almost prohibitive tariff since the middle of the nineteenth century. Between 1881 and 1891 it increased duties eight times, making some concessions to seaborne trade in comparison with landborne imports. Germany considered such provisions a discrimination against itself in comparison with Great Britain, especially in trade in coal and iron. Moreover, the Russian government was reluctant to bind itself by long-term treaties: Russian diplomats regarded such treaties as incompatible with the principles of an absolute monarchy. In the 1890's, however, Russia decided to join other European nations in the system of treaties. The first step was a treaty with Germany. Negotiations began in 1891, collapsed in 1893 and were followed by a tariff war which ended with a compromise treaty signed in 1894. The main features of the treaty were m.f.n. treatment for Russia and a sizable reduction of duties for 120 groups of articles for Germany (**40**, pp. 52–62 and *passim*).

113. **67**, p. 59.

114. **81**, *passim*.

115. **49**, p. 29.

World War II and Recent Years

During World War II tariffs exercised little influence on the flow of goods within the area controlled by the Nazi government; foreign trade was strictly regulated and goods were shipped in accordance with government orders. The political and economic collapse of Germany left a vacuum in the foreign trade of continental Europe. The Federal Republic of Germany (Western Germany) began recovering freedom of action in 1949–50. Its industrial production was gaining momentum; in 1950 German products reappeared on the world market, and Germany was on the way back to its leading position in Europe.

A tariff was enacted by the Federal Republic in 1951 (August 16) — with approval of the Allies — and came into force the same year. This is a dual, minimum-maximum tariff, moderately protectionist in character, with numerous revenue duties. It specifies the minimum rates, while the maximum rate is double the minimum on dutiable goods and 10 per cent ad valorem on all goods duty-free under the minimum.[116] It gives considerable power to customs authorities to adjust the existing rates in either direction. Like the new French tariff, the German tariff follows the Brussels classification. The duty-free list includes, among other items: cereals (wheat, rye, barley, oats, corn), fish (certain species), oil seed, vegetable materials used in pharmaceuticals and for dyeing, tanning and similar purposes; earth and stone, coal, ores and many other minerals; crude petroleum and some petroleum products; some metals and metal oxides; natural rubber, hides and skins; lumber (round, squared and sawn) and newsprint; raw cotton and other natural fibers; jewelry and works of art. For most other goods ad valorem duties — and, in a few cases, specific duties — are established.

Apart from revenue duties, the highest minimum rates in the original tariff were fixed at 35 per cent, but some were later reduced through negotiations at Torquay. Since the general tariff was approved by the Allies, reductions were kept in a comparatively narrow range rarely exceeding 5–10 points.

Tariff Levels

On the preceding pages, various tariffs have been described as high, moderate, or low —

116. **39**, Art. 3; cf. **18**.

terms which are in universal use and seem self-explanatory. It should be stressed, however, that these designations do not necessarily measure the degree of protection a tariff gives to domestic producers or the obstacles it presents to the import of foreign goods. The tariff is only one implement of a protectionist policy. Others include quantitative restrictions, prohibitions, quotas, licensing, subsidies, the "invisible tariffs" of customs formalities and so forth. Moreover, protection of domestic producers is not the only objective of import duties. Probably the principal purpose of tariffs in most countries is to provide revenue. Some duties serve as indirect taxes on consumption or are designed to equalize excise taxes on domestic products; some protect the balance of trade and the currency exchange rates of the nation.

It is obvious, therefore, that the average level of all duties does not show to what extent a tariff is protectionist. Moreover, when only the protectionist duties in various countries are compared with each other, differences in levels may be due to several reasons. Consider, for example, two countries which base their duties on the same principle of equalizing the price of imported articles with the domestic cost of producing similar or competitive items. It may be that equalization rates estimated in an identical way will be 10 per cent in one country and 30 per cent in another. If the first country establishes a duty of 15 per cent and the second of 25 per cent, it would be fair to say that the first duty is more protectionist and presents a greater obstacle to import than the second.

METHODS OF MEASUREMENT

Import duties are often described as a wall surrounding a national market. The level of the tariff is supposed to represent the height of this wall. Measurement is simple when the wall can be visualized as a fence of uniform heights running along the borders of the nation. When, however, the wall resembles a system of fortifications, with some strong points towering high above the others and bastions and earthworks extending to a considerable depth, computing the average height becomes very difficult.

The Ratio of Duties to Imports

Foreign trade statistics of many nations include data on the value of duty-free and dutiable imports and the amount of import duties collected. The latter is often expressed as a percentage of the value of dutiable imports or of total imports. The United States, among others, uses both forms of reporting. (See Table 98.) Such records are enlightening in some respects but fail to give a correct picture of the level of tariffs and the extent of protection they give to domestic producers.

Suppose, for example, that a country annually imports goods valued at $100 million, half duty-free and half in articles on which 20 per cent ad valorem is imposed. The yield will be $10 million or 10 per cent of total value of imports. Suppose, further, that the rates on half the dutiable goods are raised to 100 per cent ad valorem and these goods practically cease to be imported. If the remaining dutiable and duty-free goods are imported in the same quantities as before, the annual reports will show total imports of $75 million and the amount of duties collected as $5 million or 6.7 per cent ad valorem. Similarly, reduction in duties may increase imports of the items affected and consequently raise the total yield of import duties and the ratio of customs collections to the value of imports. Thus, the increase in protection would result in a decrease in the ratio of customs collections to the value of imports and vice versa.

Average Rates of Duties

The ratio of the total customs collections to the total value of imports amounts, in statistical terms, to the average of individual rates weighted by the value of each commodity imported. Since such weighted averages can be fallacious, it is preferable in some cases to use unweighted averages of duty rates. Such averages, however, become meaningless when they comprise a very wide range of rates including duties which practically bar import of an article. A rate of 200 per cent ad valorem serves this purpose as well as one of 2,000 per cent, but inclusion of one or the other in an average drastically changes the results of computation.

An unweighted average of duty rates is meaningful only when it refers to a list of properly selected commodities, but such selection is difficult. Because of variety in the classification of commodities and assessment of duty rates on them, the ranking of tariffs according to the average rate of duties depends largely on the selection of representative items and the weights given to them.

Hypothetical Average Rates of Duties

Along with the unweighted averages of duty rates, more elaborate methods have been used to measure tariff levels. The current ad valorem rates may be applied to a hypothetical constant distribution of imports — for example, the distribution in a given year.[117] This method is essentially the same as that used in computing price indexes with fixed weights. Its main difficulty is in handling the duties on articles which have disappeared from the imports of a country precisely because of the high duties imposed on them.[118]

This has been the situation, for example, with clocks and watches in the tariff schedule of the United States. Watches, with duties ranging between 18.5 and 39.8 per cent ad valorem (at 1946 prices), appear among the principal dutiable commodities in the surveys of the U.S. Tariff Commission,[119] while the import of clocks is too small to be mentioned. The duties on clocks, however, range from 60 per cent to 155.8 per cent ad valorem,[120] and these rates are one reason why the United States imports few clocks.[121]

---

117. This method is used by the U.S. Tariff Commission for appraising the effect of reducing individual tariff rates on the average level of duties (cf. p. 267).

118. The duties on "pen, pocket and other knives with folding blades and parts" in the U.S. tariff illustrate this point. The tariff distinguishes fifteen types of articles under this title, but only nine of these were imported in 1939 and only six in 1946. The average of 1948 rates for the nine types imported in 1939 was 115 per cent ad valorem and for the six types imported in 1946, 72 per cent. The average rates for the types which were not imported in either year cannot be calculated, but some of them were close to 220 per cent, and the unweighted average for all fifteen types was probably not less than 150–160 per cent. (**36**, Volume 3, Part 3, p. 125.) Which, then, is the average rate of duties on this group of goods for 1948: 72 per cent, 115 per cent, or 150–160 per cent? The probability is that in computing the average rate for the whole group, the duties collected on all types of imported knives with folding blades will be compared with the total value of those actually imported, and the result will be close to the lowest rates in the list, some 40 or 50 per cent ad valorem.

119. **29**, p. 17.

120. **36**, Volume 3, Part 3, p. 237.

121. The structure of duties on watches and clocks in the tariff is extremely complex. Duties are levied on movements and cases separately. Duties on movements are graduated by dimension and number of jewels, with additional duties on each "adjustment" in the mechanism. Compound duties are established on cases. (**37**, pp. 12–13.)

Indexes of Tariff Level

The International Economic Conference of the League of Nations (Geneva, 1927) suggested a standard method for computing indexes of tariff level. Comparison is limited to a list of commodities which play an important role in the foreign trade of the countries in question, and does not include noncompetitive articles on which revenue duties are collected. The ad valorem equivalent of the import duty on each commodity is computed in each country; finally the index of tariff level is calculated as the un-weighted arithmetic mean of these rates.[122] The Conference deserves credit for having carefully selected the list of articles but its allegedly *un-weighted* averages actually were weighted by the numbers of items selected from each economic class of goods and the indexes were biased because of the decisive predominance of finished and semifinished articles over raw materials and foodstuffs.

The comparability of indexes of tariff level is increased when special indexes are computed for each major class and each group of commodities.[123] This method, however, leaves open the question of how to combine the group indexes in an over-all measurement of the tariff level.

When the method of special group indexes is carried to its logical end, it approaches a comparison of particular duty rates for identical goods. As cumbersome as such a comparison may appear, it provides the best basis for quantitative description of tariffs in different countries. The picture becomes confusing when too many items — for example, several thousand — are included, and too fragmentary when only a few are used, but appears enlightening enough when the list of commodities is neither too short nor too long.

Since none of the described methods is completely satisfactory and none is universally recognized, all are used on the following pages.

TARIFF LEVELS BEFORE WORLD WAR I

In 1913–14 some tariffs were higher, others lower, than at the beginning of the century, but the prevailing trend probably had been downward. The United Kingdom had been in the vanguard of the free trade movement since 1846, although it had comparatively high revenue

122. **5**, p. 4.
123. See **74**.

duties (on alcoholic beverages, tea, spices and sugar). The Netherlands, Belgium, Denmark, Switzerland and India were likewise following liberal trade policies and had protective duties on only a few articles; their rates on most staple commodities were low according to our present standards. The German tariff was somewhat higher, and still higher were the tariffs of Austria-Hungary, Sweden, France, Italy, Canada and Australia. Russia, Spain and Portugal had the highest tariffs in Europe. The tariffs of the United States and Argentina, although higher than those in Western Europe, were hardly higher and probably appreciably lower than the Spanish, Portuguese and the Russian.

Duties on Selected Commodities

Josef Grunzel, the German economist, has computed the duties on eight identical commodities in 1912–13 in twenty-one countries (including the United Kingdom, which had all these commodities on the free list), presenting them in the form they had in the respective tariffs — mainly as specific duties but in a few cases as ad valorem rates. Grunzel's survey, reproduced in Table 103 in terms of U.S. dollars per 100 pounds, shows that the tariffs of various nations differed at that time not only in the general level of all duties but also in the relative levels of duties on single articles, as, for example, the following rates per 100 pounds of cotton yarn, cotton fabrics and laces in the United States, France, Germany and Italy:

	Yarn	Un-bleached Fabric	Printed Fabric	Laces
United States	$7.90	$ 6.10	$12.80	$ 5.29
France	1.76	10.20	17.91	47.63
Germany	2.12	8.23	14.11	41.16
Italy	3.14	7.43	15.25	47.63

Of the four countries, the United States had the highest duty on cotton yarn and the lowest on the other three products. France had the lowest duty on yarn and the highest on fabrics.

When comparison is limited to the eight items selected by Grunzel, the 1912–13 tariff of the United States seems fairly low in comparison with those of European countries at that time. This impression, however, is due largely to the selection of commodities. The United States had comparatively low duties on cotton fabrics, laces and sheet iron, but higher duties on machinery

TABLE 103

TARIFF RATES: SELECTED COUNTRIES, EIGHT SELECTED COMMODITIES, 1912–13

(U.S. Dollars per 100 Pounds)

| Country | Wheat | Cotton Yarn [a] | Cotton Fabric [b] | | Laces [c] | Bar Iron | Sheet Iron [d] | Sewing Needles |
			Unbleached	Printed				
United States	0.46	7.90	6.10	12.80	5.29	0.26	0.65	25%
United Kingdom	Free	Free	Free	Free	Free	Free	Free	Free
France	0.67	1.76	10.20	17.91	47.63	0.71	1.29	23.81
Belgium	Free	1.43	7.62	9.53	15%	0.10	0.10	13%
Netherlands	Free	Free	5%	5%	5%	5%	5%	5%
Denmark	Free	0.83	6.68	17.84	26.75	0.14	0.14	8.82
Sweden	0.49	2.65	6.61	14.56	5.29	Free	5.29	5.29
Norway	5.71	1.59	3.30	14.56	79.32	Free	Free	9.93
Germany	6.47	2.12	8.23	14.11	41.16	0.12	5.29	11.76
Switzerland	0.03	1.91	0.95	5.72	9.53	0.04	0.06	4.76
Austria–Hungary	0.63	3.30	—	14.30	65.97	0.50	1.00	17.00
Portugal	—	8.00	10.94	42.68	96.02	0.08	0.80	26.67
Spain	0.76	16.46	41.43	35.24	128.60	0.61	0.76	28.58
Italy	0.72	3.14	7.43	15.25	47.63	0.57	1.14	7.62
Serbia	0.48	4.76	12.38	12.38	57.15	0.24	0.95	11.43
Romania	0.00	0.48	6.67	8.04	38.57	0.29	0.48	19.05
Bulgaria	0.05	3.81	3.81	7.15	33.34	0.24	0.38	10.48
Greece	—	5.72	7.62	11.43	44.65	Free	Free	14.88
Russia	Free	12.74	136.50	165.11	298.59	1.16	1.63	75.41
Japan	0.32	2.62	7.37	10.24	8.18	0.25	0.31	20.69
Turkey	—	11%	7.62	11%	11%	11%	11%	11%

Source: **63**, pp. 155–58.

a. No. 36 English, single, unbleached.
b. Of a weight of 10 kilograms per 100 square meters.

c. Machine-made, unbleached of a weight of 25 kilograms per 100 square meters.
d. Of a thickness of one millimeter.

and some other finished manufactures not represented in Table 103.

Indexes of Tariff Level, 1913

The objective of the League of Nations' Economic Commission was to compare the tariff levels in different countries in 1913 and after World War I. It used as the "index of tariff level" the arithmetic mean of the ad valorem rates of duties on 78 items (or small groups of commodities) distributed among the broad economic classes as follows: [124]

	Number of Items
Foodstuffs	8
Raw materials	9
Semimanufactured goods	18
Manufactured goods	43

Thus, foodstuffs and raw materials, which accounted for more than half the total value of U.S. imports at that time and were largely on the duty-free list, were included with the weight of 22 per cent (17 items out of 78) while semifinished and finished goods, which in most cases were dutiable in the United States tariff, had the weight of 78 per cent.

Two methods were used for calculating the rate of duty on each article in each country. (See Table 104.) In method A, the duty on each article was expressed as a percentage of the import value of the article before duty. In method B, the prices prevailing in the exporting countries were taken as the basis of comparison. The arithmetic means of the two indexes computed

124. **5**, p. 18.

TABLE 104

TARIFF LEVEL INDEXES: SELECTED COUNTRIES,
1913 AND 1925

(International Economic Commission, Geneva, 1927)

| | All Commodities | | | | Manufactured Articles | |
| | Method A | | Method B | | Method B | |
Country	1913	1925	1913	1925	1913	1925
United States	32	26	33	29	44	37
Canada	12	12	18	16	26	23
Argentina	—	—	26	26	28	29
France	14	9	18	12	20	21
Belgium	6	7	6	8	9	15
Netherlands	2	4	3	4	4	6
Denmark	8	6	9	6	14	10
Sweden	13	10	16	13	20	16
Germany	12	15	12	12	13	20
Poland	—	24	—	23	—	32
Czechoslovakia	18	17	18	19	18	27
Switzerland	5	9	7	11	9	14
Austria	11	14	17	25	16	27
Spain	23	28	33	44	41	41
Italy	—	16	17	17	18	22
Hungary	18	19	18	23	18	27
Yugoslavia	—	20	—	23	—	23
India	3	13	4	14	4	16
Australia	11	14	17	25	16	27

Source: 5; for description of method see p. 74.

in this way for the year 1913 show the following percentages, ad valorem: [125]

Country	Tariff Level	Country	Tariff Level
United States	32.5	Australia	14.0
Spain	28.0	Germany	12.0
Argentina	26.0	Denmark	8.5
Italy	17.0	Belgium	6.0
France	16.0	Switzerland	6.0
Canada	15.0	India	3.5
Sweden	14.5	Netherlands	2.5
Austria-Hungary	14.0	United Kingdom	0

In striking contrast to the ranking in Grunzel's survey (Table 103), here the index for the United States appears to be the highest among the countries surveyed — higher than that for Spain, three to four times as high as Denmark's, thirteen times that for the Netherlands. This ranking for the United States is obviously fal-

125. See Table 104.

lacious: the yield of the customs duties in the United States in 1913 amounted to 17.7 per cent of the value of imports.

TARIFF LEVELS IN THE INTERWAR YEARS

Changes, 1913–25

The increase in customs duties after World War I was partly offset by the rise in prices, which tended to cut the ad valorem weight of specific duties. In ad valorem terms, 1925 tariffs were above their prewar level in Belgium, the Netherlands, Germany, Switzerland, Austria, Hungary, Spain, Italy, India and Australia; approximately at the prewar level in Argentina and Czechoslovakia; and below the prewar level in the United States, Canada, France, Denmark and Sweden. Increases predominated in Europe, while the trend in North America was downward. (See Table 104.)

According to the League of Nations survey, the tariff of the United States in 1925 remained one of the highest of those listed, second only to that of Spain. It would have been nearer the middle, in the same class with the tariffs of France, Germany and Italy, if more weight had been given to duties on agricultural products. The United Kingdom was not included in the survey but had fairly high duties at that time on goods imported from outside the British Commonwealth.

In most countries, duties on manufactured goods rose between 1913 and 1925 in comparison with those on agricultural products.

Changes, 1927–31

Tariffs in most countries skyrocketed under the impact of the depression in the early 1930's. By 1931, average ad valorem rates in Germany, France, Italy, Spain and Yugoslavia were approximately double those before World War I.

The increases were very unevenly distributed among different groups of goods. Most striking was the rise for foodstuffs, due in part to increases in specific duties and in part to declines in prices. The average duties on foodstuffs rose in France from 29.2 per cent in 1913 to 53.0 per cent in 1931; in Germany, from 21.8 to 82.5 per cent; in Czechoslovakia, from 29.1 to 84.0; in Switzerland, from 14.7 to 42.2; in Spain from 41.5 to 80.5; in Italy, from 22.0 to 66.0; in Yugoslavia, from 31.6 to 75.0; in Bulgaria, from 24.7 to 133.0.

TABLE 105

TARIFF LEVEL INDEXES: SELECTED EUROPEAN COUNTRIES, 1913, 1927 AND 1931

Country	All Commodities			Foodstuffs			Semimanufactured Goods			Industrial Manufactured Goods		
	1913	1927	1931	1913	1927	1931	1913	1927	1931	1913	1927	1931
France	23.6	23.0	38.0	29.2	19.1	53.0	25.3	24.3	31.8	16.3	25.8	29.0
Belgium	14.2	11.0	17.4	25.5	11.8	23.7	7.6	10.5	15.5	9.5	11.6	13.0
Sweden	27.6	20.0	26.8	24.2	21.5	39.0	25.3	18.0	18.0	24.5	20.8	23.5
Finland	35.0	31.8	48.2	49.0	57.5	102.0	18.8	20.2	20.0	37.6	17.8	22.7
Germany	16.7	20.4	40.7	21.8	27.4	82.5	15.3	14.5	23.4	10.0	19.0	18.3
Poland	72.5 [a]	53.5	67.5	69.4 [a]	72.0	110.0	63.5 [a]	33.2	40.0	85.0 [a]	55.6	52.0
Austria	22.8 [b]	17.5	36.0	29.1 [b]	16.5	59.5	20.0 [b]	15.2	20.7	19.3 [b]	21.0	27.7
Czechoslovakia	22.8 [b]	31.3	50.0	29.1 [b]	36.3	84.0	20.0 [b]	21.7	29.5	19.3 [b]	35.8	36.5
Switzerland	10.5	16.8	26.4	14.7	21.5	42.2	7.3	11.5	15.2	9.3	17.6	22.0
Hungary	22.8 [b]	30.0	45.0	29.1 [b]	31.5	60.0	20.0 [b]	26.5	32.5	19.3 [b]	31.8	42.6
Spain	37.0	49.0	68.5	41.5	45.2	80.5	26.0	39.2	49.5	42.5	62.7	75.5
Italy	24.8	27.8	48.3	22.0	24.5	66.0	25.0	28.6	49.5	14.6	28.3	41.8
Yugoslavia	22.2	32.0	46.0	31.6	43.7	75.0	17.2	24.7	30.5	18.0	28.0	32.8
Romania	30.3	42.3	63.0	34.7	45.6	87.5	30.0	32.6	46.3	25.5	48.5	55.0
Bulgaria	22.8	67.5	96.5	24.7	79.0	133.0	24.2	49.5	65.0	19.5	75.0	90.0

Source: **74**, pp. 413–15.

a. Russia.   b. Austria-Hungary.

Some governments increased both specific and ad valorem duties in a desperate attempt to protect the domestic economy against falling prices, which brought with them mass unemployment.[126] (See Table 105.[127])

Contrasts in the duty rates of France, Germany and Italy in 1931 are characteristic. France had the highest duties on fruits and vegetables, textiles, paper and machines; Germany, the highest on cereals and flour, livestock, alcoholic beverages and tobacco; Italy, the highest on timber, metals, chemicals, mineral oils, glass and china and many other articles. (See Table 106.)

TARIFF LEVELS IN EUROPE, 1950

As a result of reciprocal trade agreements, most duties have been reduced since World War II. At the same time the burdens of specific

duties have been lessened by the rise in prices. On the other hand, many rates have been adjusted upward. The general level of most tariffs is now appreciably lower than in the late 1930's but this statement does not necessarily imply less protection of domestic industries.

The Study Group for the European Customs Union prepared a survey of tariff rates in Europe in 1950. It covers thirteen countries (three included in Benelux), and shows for each the ad valorem rates on some 2,000 articles or groups of articles arranged according to the new Brussels classification. Data for some 200 selected items are presented in Table 107.[128]

Types of Schedules

Three types of tariff schedules can be distinguished in Table 107: (1) schedules with a long list of duty-free articles and comparatively low duties on other goods; (2) schedules with high

126. **89**, p. 300.

127. Indexes in Table 105 are arithmetic means of ad valorem duty rates computed for 144 products widely distributed among all classes of goods. Foodstuffs are represented by 38 items; semifinished industrial goods by 44 articles, manufactured industrial goods by 62 articles. Industrial raw materials are excluded (except for leaf tobacco listed among foodstuffs). Because of the difference in method these indexes for 1913 differ widely from those shown for the same year and 1912–13 in Tables 103 and 104.

128. Five volumes of statistics cannot be condensed in a few pages without sacrificing important details. Table 107 gives only the typical or principal items for most groups of staple foodstuffs and raw materials. For groups of manufactured articles, which often include a great variety of items, the lowest and highest rates are cited. The selection of groups and single articles is open to criticism.

TABLE 106

TARIFF LEVEL INDEXES: FRANCE, GERMANY AND ITALY, GROUPS OF COMMODITIES, 1913, 1927 AND 1931 [a]

Group of Commodities	France			Germany			Italy		
	1913	1927	1931	1913	1927	1931	1913	1927	1931
Foodstuffs									
Cereals and flour	28.6	20.7	100.0	27.5	28.4	186.0	33.8	23.7	110.0
Livestock	14.1	9.1	20.2	13.0	27.3	52.0	11.3	12.8	17.2
Animal foodstuffs	25.0	14.7	31.3	19.0	20.5	28.5	14.5	22.7	22.9
Fruits, vegetables	26.5	12.8	27.1	19.5	15.5	18.0	15.2	16.6	13.9
Other foodstuffs	57.3	29.6	94.5	30.0	45.5	128.5	120.5	36.9	124.0
Alcoholic beverages and tobacco	25.0	28.2	45.0	61.0	58.5	89.5	31.0	35.0	39.8
Semimanufactured goods									
Textiles	37.6	34.9	45.5	11.0	10.5	14.4	12.4	12.7	19.5
Timber, paper, cork	15.2	14.2	28.7	21.0	19.8	17.0	41.8	27.7	61.2
Metals	34.4	38.0	42.7	15.8	17.5	21.0	31.1	50.7	65.0
Chemicals	15.4	10.2	10.5	13.7	10.2	41.3	9.7	23.6	52.1
Mineral oils	166.0	50.2	156.0	23.8	54.0	357.5	103.0	122.0	397.5
Manufactured industrial goods									
Textiles	27.7	24.4	26.6	12.3	37.0	35.5	17.5	24.5	25.6
Paper	21.6	33.0	42.6	17.5	12.1	15.8	22.1	23.9	30.0
Glass, china	10.7	19.6	18.6	14.0	20.0	16.5	28.1	49.0	51.8
Metal goods	15.0	20.1	21.3	9.9	12.3	15.5	13.6	24.1	35.6
Machines	13.8	24.7	23.9	9.3	9.4	9.4	7.0	16.4	20.4
Vehicles	12.5	34.9	43.5	5.8	32.0	15.4	6.8	48.0	102.0
Instruments	12.1	18.7	17.3	6.0	19.3	20.0	6.8	9.9	23.2
Toys and tires	17.4	33.2	38.3	6.1	15.8	18.5	17.4	32.4	45.7

Source: **74,** pp. 385–86.

a. Rates given here are the averages between the highest and the lowest rate reported for single commodities in each group of goods.

duty rates on manufactured articles and comparatively low duties or no duties on agricultural products; and (3) schedules which provide protective duties on both agricultural and industrial products.

The first group includes the tariffs of Denmark and Sweden; the second, of the United Kingdom, and to some extent Benelux and Norway; the third, of all other European countries listed.

A distinction may also be made between two types of agrarian tariffs: Germany's import duties are mainly on meat and dairy products, while other countries chiefly protect cereals, vegetables and fruits.

Application of this classification to the United States tariff is extremely difficult. Its tariff contains high — sometimes prohibitive — duties on certain manufactured articles (such as watches or knives) and a few agricultural products (for example, lemons, walnuts) and admits duty-free

other agricultural and manufactured products which do not compete with domestic produce.

Ranking of Countries by Tariff Level

For all groups of agricultural goods, Denmark, Sweden, Norway, Benelux and the United Kingdom have the lowest tariffs among the European countries included in Table 107. Germany has the highest tariff on dairy products but comparatively low duties on cereals, tallow and margarine; Austria, France, Italy and Greece have the highest tariffs on cereals; Portugal and Greece the highest on vegetables and fruits. Greece ranks first also in duties on fats, tallow and margarine.

It is fairly evident that Denmark, Sweden, Norway, Benelux and the United Kingdom have much lower agricultural duties than other European countries, but it is harder to compare the average levels of agricultural tariffs in France and Germany or Portugal and Greece. There

TABLE 107

TARIFF RATES: THIRTEEN EUROPEAN COUNTRIES, SELECTED COMMODITIES, 1950

(*Per Cent*)

Commodity	United Kingdom	France	Benelux	Denmark	Sweden	Norway	Germany	Austria	Portugal	Italy	Greece
Live animals											
Dairy cows	—	35	9	—	—	4.1	48.9	21	2.2	35	7
Oxen	—	35	9	—	0.9	4.1	35	26	33.3	35	10
Meat											
Beef	—	40	12	—	4.1	26.9	24.9	76	5.4	36	13
Pork	—	40	12	—	4.9	13.9	18.9	121	24.1	40	46
Dairy products											
Milk, fresh	10	15	10	—	—	—	51.1	47	63.2	15	15
Cream	10	10	10	—	—	—	111.5	—	31.4	25	15
Butter	4.5	25	15	—	5.1	—	56.6	65	17.1	30	49
Cheese	15	15	—	3.8	1.6	29.3	56.0	—	51.1	20	3
Vegetables											
Potatoes	16	32	7.5	—	5	7.5	14	36	17.6	20	42
Olives	15	10	12	—	21	16.5	34.5	—	108	10	40
Fruits											
Grapefruit	12	25	13.5	—	—	2.4	43	31.3	108	15	60
Lemons	10	10	15	7.6	10	2.4	—	12.5	108	5	60
Apples	5	9	12	4.1	8.5	35.4	26	22	108	9	50
Colonial products											
Coffee	11	20	27.9	38.9	38.1	20.7	188	303	39.2	50	215
Tea	7.5	45	14.1	12.1	19.5	32.7	188	196	76.9	50	172
Pepper	1.5	30	15	17.6	13.8	11	12.2	577	37.5	60	384
Cereals											
Wheat	—	30	—	—	7.6	—	8	116	—	40	35
Rye	10	50	—	—	6.6	—	7.7	83.1	48.4	30	22
Barley	10	50	—	—	15.4	—	8	98	17.5	35	46
Oats	9.5	50	—	—	—	—	9.6	35.6	57.1	30	35
Corn	13.5	50	—	—	—	—	5.6	—	37.9	30	26
Rice	13.5	30	—	—	2.1	—	5.6	5.3	23.9	30	36
Wheat flour	10	30	3	—	11.8	—	7.3	19.4	—	60	53
Fats											
Tallow	10	15	—	—	—	3.5	7.7	—	3.3	—	112
Margarine	13	25	10	—	3	4.7	7.6	—	4.2	15	80
Fish, preserved											
Sardines	10	35	20	5.2	6.5	31	40	79.3	35.1	42.5	38
Herring	10	25	20	7.9	15.0	31	40	79.3	35.1	30	39
Other foodstuffs											
Sugar	17	130	50.3	—	1.8	22.7	269	226	72.7	105	162
Molasses	6	35	—	—	34	—	34	—	30.7	40	167
Cocoa	6	25	10	0.9	7.6	6.5	54.5	75.7	8.5	20	150
Cacao paste	10	25	10	11	20	17.8	16.0	30.2	108	35	550
Chocolate	17	30	18	9.5	22	17.8	53.4	59.4	92	50	96
Ship biscuits	10	22	—	—	15	18.8	170	132	81.5	50	70
Preserved fruits	—	25	25	27.5	26	29.1	100	112	114	40	310
Orange juice	—	16	18	4.7	30	9.1	130	18.2	50.4	10	104
Beverages											
Beer	10	35	32.1	—	45	52.4	98	94.8	140.6	35	150
Wine	20	30	44.4	31.8	35.6	6.4	104	75.6	81.4	90	14
Vermouth	100	60	73.4	84.3	73	18.3	60	—	86.6	45	129
Rum	14	60	11.9	27.5	27	59.1	190	68.1	418	52.5	65
Whisky	14	30	13	22.5	71	59.1	471	—	418	47.5	80

(*Continued on following page*)

TABLE 107—*continued*

Commodity	United Kingdom	France	Benelux	Den-mark	Sweden	Norway	Ger-many	Austria	Portugal	Italy	Greece
Tobacco											
Nonmanufactured	60	—	10.4	39.8	—	59.9	123	62.5	212	—	70
Manufactured	52	—	35	22.2	—	56.4	1,700	9.3	174	—	190
Cigarettes	32.5	—	45	37.7	—	49.1	525	4.3	180	—	135
Minerals											
Salt	—	60	10	3.1	—	—	95.2	4.6	55.6	—	—
Cement	10	10	3	—	7.3	1.6	33.2	228	15.8	25	49
Mineral oils											
Crude petroleum	7.5	—	—	—	—	—	10	14.7	0.5	10	15
Benzols	41	15	8.9	—	—	—	10.6	—	34.7	18	15
Petroleum oils, crude	142	18	—	—	—	—	290	—	0.4	9	—
Ethers	95	18	11.2	—	1	—	225	—	60.1	18	285
Kerosene	102	18	11.7	—	—	—	343	52.3	28	18	430
Gas oils	103	10	—	—	—	—	176	31.5	4.4	14	14
Fuel oils	129	7	—	1.5	—	—	84	—	6.5	14	14
Lubricating oils	41	15	—	4	—	6.2	140	50.6	5.7	18	63
Chemical elements											
Chlorine	10	15	10	—	20	—	49	—	10.9	15	15
Iodine, crude	33.3	30	—	—	—	—	—	—	24.9	170	8
Sulfur, refined	33.3	14	5	—	—	—	—	—	2.5	35	19
Acids											
Sulfur dioxide	10	35	20	2.6	20	30	50	—	10.9	20	12
Nitric acids	10	15	10	—	8	—	66.6	15.4	28.5	25	8
Phosphoric acids	33.3	20	—	—	5	—	40	10	22.4	30	15
Caustic soda	11	20	8	—	6.4	7	20.4	54.1	4.4	25	—
Zinc oxides	20	20	8	0.7	—	—	10	21.1	9.5	17	20
Iron oxides	20	15	—	—	—	—	23.5	—	26.1	25	35
Tin oxides	20	25	—	—	—	—	1.2	10	21.6	25	20
Copper oxides	33.3	20	—	—	—	—	11.1	10	15.1	8	20
Pharmaceutical products											
Medicaments [a]											
Minimum	}10	10	33{	—	—	—	5	—	5.2	15	}12
Maximum				—	—	15.4	25	—	16.8	75	
Wadding	10	10	33	0.5	—	—	5	—	11	20	20
Fertilizers											
Sodium nitrate	—	—	—	—	—	—	—	—	2.1	25	—
Ammonium nitrate	20	—	—	—	30	—	216	—	0.8	30	5
Phosphates, natural	—	—	—	—	—	—	—	—	0.3	—	25
Superphosphates	20	8	—	—	—	—	83.3	—	—	—	20
Tanning extracts											
Vegetable	10	15	—	—	—	—	—	—	3.7	20	50
Synthetic	10	10	—	—	—	30	—	10	3.5	17.5	52
Coloring matter											
Vegetable & animal											
Minimum	—	0	—	}0.1{	—	—	0	—	1.9	30	45
Maximum	—	30	—		—	—	14	—	3.7	30	120
Chemical											
Minimum	20	10	0	0	—	0	1	0	1.9	15	15
Maximum	33.3	30	8	5.5	—	65	70	31	10.8	30	40
Other chemicals											
Perfumery	15	10	25	26.3	24	19.8	27.2	37.2	118	20	80
Soap	10	25	15	1.8	3	14.9	24.4	14.9	109	30	100
Vegetable glue											
Minimum	}10{	10	}10	2.5{	5	}23.2{	35	0	}17.7{	15	}60
Maximum		25			25		91	46.7		40	
Candles	20	20	12	—	5	11.4	18.1	9	19	25	150

(*Continued on facing page*)

TABLE 107—*continued*

Commodity	United Kingdom	France	Benelux	Den-mark	Sweden	Norway	Ger-many	Austria	Portugal	Italy	Greece
Explosives											
Gun powder	10	—	6	8.4	8.3	3	10	41.9	26.4	25	52
Fuses	20	15	6	1.3	2	11.2	13.4	26.3	14.2	30	50
Matches	350	5	15	9.6	1	6.7	33	—	—	30	—
Photographic goods											
Plates	25	15	18	3	7	10.6	31	24.9	13.1	30	30
Roll films	24	20	12	6.4	4	8.4	29.9	5.8	15.3	24	30
Rubber											
Crude latex	—	—	—	—	—	—	76	—	5.5	—	59
Unvulcanized	10	8	6	—	—	15	65	8.5	4.6	15	30
Tubing	10	14	12	—	10	15	66	22	11.6	25	39
Tires											
Minimum	}33.3{	18	}24{	6.8	20	6.9	}46	60.4	59.9	25	95
Maximum		22		12.9	26	8.2					
Hides and skins											
Hides of cattle	10	12	6	—	15	4	41.6	18.1	38.5	23	20
Calfskins	10	10	6	—	6	7.4	10.1	7.7	19.7	20	18
Sheepskins	10	10	4.5	—	10	7.4	2.3	—	19.7	15	20
Goatskins	10	6	4.5	—	10	7.4	2.4	—	19.7	16.5	20
Dressed leather	15	25	15	0.5	4	6.6	15	5.1	19.7	20	20
Articles of leather											
Coats	20	30	20	5.6	5	9.4	14.9	6	4.3	30	35
Gloves	30	25	18	25.5	8	16.6	30	0	4.4	20	45
Wood											
Round (poles)	—	10	—	1.1	—	—	15	23.3	9.6	20	8
Squared	1.5	10	—	0.9	—	—	30.7	—	5.5	15.6	8
Sawn	1	7	10	0.8	—	—	28	41.5	3.4	10	17
Plywood	10	23	10	7	16	4	50	—	27.6	30	50
Paper											
Wood pulp	—	22	—	—	—	—	17	—	1.2	6	15
Newsprint	—	30	10	—	—	8.8	21.8	—	5.8	14	—
Wrapping paper	20	18	15	2.1	5	4.7	46	—	26.8	20	40
Corrugated paper-board	20	25	18	5.5	8	5.3	40	21.3	23.1	25	110
Silk											
Yarn	29	10	4	1.7	10	4.5	3	—	18.6	6	100
Thread	29	15	12	2.9	4	4.5	14	5.4	18.6	15	80
Tissues, noil silk	26	15	15	11.6	10	6.7	50	35.5	78.3	15	80
Other tissues	28	13	15	11.6	5	6.0	80	37.6	101	22.5	100
Wool											
Greasy	—	—	—	—	—	8.8	—	—	2.5	—	2
Washed	—	1	—	—	—	5.2	—	—	2.9	—	50
Carded [b]	10	2	—	—	—	5.2	3	—	9.8	8	50
Yarn [b]	7.5	8	4	2	25	4.1	8	9.4	18.8	14	20
Tissues	17.5	15	18	6.4	7	8.6	54	35.6	49.8	23	155
Synthetic textiles											
Yarn [b]	35	30	10	12.9	18	23.6	23	65.3	18.6	30	50
Tissues	27	30	18	13	27	15.5	90	30.5	78.3	27.5	70
Cotton											
Crude	—	—	—	—	—	—	—	—	4.7	6	14
Carded	10	8	—	—	3	—	—	15.1	—	10	14
Yarn	7.5	15	4	1.1	25	2.5	25	9.7	9.3	15	70
Gauze	17.5	20	15	—	8	7.7	36	32.6	15.2	25	70
Tissues	17.5	20	16	9	5	7.8	60	27.6	30.5	25	60

(*Continued on following page*)

Tᴀʙʟᴇ 107—*continued*

Commodity	United Kingdom	France	Benelux	Den-mark	Sweden	Norway	Ger-many	Austria	Portugal	Italy	Greece
Carpets											
Silk	43.3	80	30	25	15	6.7	56	10	91.4	45	190
Wool	8	80	24	25	10	24.5	57.9	45	64.9	40	80
Apparel											
Outer garments											
For men											
Minimum	20	}22	24{	0	10	12	28	—	32	}30{	40
Maximum	33.3			11	25	29	35	—	91		120
For women											
Minimum	17.5	}22	24{	0	20	8	22	—	30	}30{	50
Maximum	33.3			16	33.3	16	28	—	91		150
Underwear											
For men											
Minimum	20	}22	24	11.8{	10	8	14	—	30	}30{	50
Maximum	33.3				25	29	25	—	94		150
For women											
Minimum	20	27	}24{	0	10	8	14	—	30	}30{	50
Maximum	33.3	35		15	28	25	23	—	94		120
Footwear											
Shoes	15	20	24	13.8	17	21.3	24	29.1	52.2	35.3	200
Rubbers	20	25	24	—	18	18	50	48.2	16.0	35	50
Ceramic products											
Building brick	10	16	11	—	1	—	12	13.7	10.3	15	50
Tiles	15	12	10	—	2	2.6	16	43.6	10.3	15	50
Tableware	15	15	15	2.3	12	15.9	15	20.3	1	40	40
Glass											
Unworked	20	30	10	3.5	5	17.5	2	24.6	1.5	55	30
Sheet glass	15	20	6	7.3	18	24	80	58.6	37.4	31.5	100
Safety glass	20	20	15	2.6	15	23.8	20	73.2	37.4	35	120
Bottles	25	25	18	8.6	5	10.3	70	27.6	49.6	30	60
Iron and steel											
Pig iron	25	5	1	—	—	—	9	—	1	10	—
Ferromanganese	—	12	—	—	—	—	7	—	1	135	2
Ingots	20	9	1	—	8	—	12.5	10.1	1.4	—	5
Plates, sheets	25	11	3	—	4	—	15	21.3	1.4	20	40
Shapes, sections	25	15	5.5	1.1	6	—	22	24.6	1.4	—	40
Rails	33.3	18	4	—	—	—	23	23.5	4.1	20	15
Cast-iron tubes	20	20	8	8.5	1	2	16	109	33.3	25	40
Hydroelectric conduits	20	25	7	—	5	10.1	8.2	114	5	35	56
Copper											
Wrought bars	10	15	2	2.7	6	2.2	2.8	15.1	2.4	16.5	20
Cables	20	21	10	3.2	4	7.5	12.5	19.1	12.4	21	15
Nickel											
Bars	10	12	4	2.1	3	—	3.4	4.3	5.3	10	25
Tubes, pipes	20	20	4	1.7	7	6.2	3	8.4	5.3	20	55
Aluminum											
Bars	15	20	4	2.5	6	—	24	9.5	4.2	37.5	15
Tubes, pipes	15	20	6	3.8	3	0.2	18.6	7.6	22.2	15	15
Lead											
Bars	10	20	4	0.6	—	—	9	—	23.7	20	20
Plates, sheets	10	19	4	2.2	—	—	10.5	47.5	23.7	20	35
Zinc											
Bars	10	16	4	—	5	—	6	—	1.9	15	25
Plates, sheets	20	18	6	—	—	0.9	18	81.5	35.2	20.5	25

(*Continued on facing page*)

TABLE 107—*continued*

Commodity	United Kingdom	France	Benelux	Den-mark	Sweden	Norway	Ger-many	Austria	Portugal	Italy	Greece
Tools											
Spades, shovels	15	18	10	2.2	4	20	11.5	30.2	4.4	35	20
Handtools	17.5	15	10	0.7	3	20	10	13.3	4.4	35·	20
Lathe tools	15	15	6	—	10	20	5.5	12	5.6	27.6	40
Engines											
Boilers	20	21	6	1.5	15	20	18	26.1	10.8	35	30
Locomotives	20	20	6	6.2	10	20	22	—	5	35	20
Motors	33.3	30	8	5	10	20	48	90.2	5	71.2	20
Aircraft engines	20	35	6	6.2	10	12	20	90.2	5	25	20
Hydraulic engines	20	24	6	6.2	10	20	3	38.5	5	35	20
Pumps for liquids											
Minimum	15	15	}6	6.2	10{	0	3.9	11.5	6.1	32.5	}40
Maximum	20	21				20	12	20.1	7.4	40	
Air pumps											
Minimum	15	12	}6{	3.5	5	11.2	2.4	15.9	6.1	25	}40
Maximum	25	25		6.2	10	20	15	31.2	9.1	37.5	
Machinery											
Agricultural											
Minimum	15	12	}6{	0	5	10	4.8	0	2.9	15	5.5
Maximum	20	22		6.2	12	20	27.5	42.2	20.9	37.5	40
Printing											
Minimum	15	10	}6	6.2{	0	0	4	}13	5{	21.6	}15
Maximum	20	25			15	20	12			35	
Textile											
Minimum	15	15	}6{	0	0.2	0	2.1	0	5	15	}15
Maximum	33.3	25		7.5	10	20	24	21	18.5	30	
Metal working											
Minimum	}20{	6	}6	6.2{	1	}20{	1.5	9.8	3.2	7	}15
Maximum		18			15		4.7	18.1	13.2	25	
Wood working											
Minimum	}20{	12	}6	6.2{	5	15	}4.8{	21.5	}5{	19.5	}15
Maximum		25			15	20		30.7		25	
Typewriters	14	15	8	6.2	10	10	74.7	14	12.7	22	30
Counting machines											
Minimum	15	9	}8	6.2	10	10{	27	5.7	11	15	20
Maximum	20	22					71.5	26.4	13.2	26	40
Electrical machinery											
Motors [e]											
Minimum	15	19	8	0	}10{	12.9	5	26	4.7	34.3	}15
Maximum	20	20	12	5.2		21.9	16	60.3	19.6	47.5	
Accumulators											
Minimum	15	}25{	9	0	3	}5.6{	9	0	5.1	25	9
Maximum	20		20	3.6	17		70	81	35.9	60	44
Microphones	20	18	12	0.5	10	11.4	15	48.5	31.6	50	30
Transportation equipment											
Locomotives											
Minimum	}20{	15	}12	5	10	20{	9	}24.3	0.9	20	10
Maximum		20					32				
Automobiles											
Minimum	}20{	15	}12	5	15{	20	}9{	—	0.9	20	}17.5
Maximum		20				24			3.3	22.5	
Motorcycles	22.5	25	24	7.9	13	30	35.3	62.8	11.2	45	20
Aircraft	20	25	10	7.5	15	30	15	—	3.6	20	9

(*Continued on following page*)

TABLE 107—*continued*

Commodity	United Kingdom	France	Benelux	Den-mark	Sweden	Norway	Ger-many	Austria	Portugal	Italy	Greece
Miscellaneous											
Photographic cameras	50	27	15	10	9	3.7	11	9.9	5.3	40	35
Cinematographic cameras	33.3	18	15	10	2	3.7	12	11.2	5.3	18	35
Watches	33.3	10	10	6.4	5	4	10	14.1	12.4	15	30
Pianos	33.3	36	18	25	17	14	25	27.4	15	37.5	40
Violins	25	45	18	1.2	15	5.3	20.1	3.5	48	30	35
Side arms	20	5	—	12.6	5	5.3	10	19	12	25	50
Revolvers	25	18	12	15	1	21.4	12.5	4.4	2.4	27.5	42
Guns	25	18	12	15	3	10.4	13	22.2	21.1	50	30

Sources: **13** and **14**.

a. Conditioned for retail trade.
b. Bleached or dyed.

c. Includes generators, transformers and related machinery.

is, moreover, a fundamental difference between the primarily protective tariffs of France and Germany and the import duties in Portugal and Greece, some of which are typical revenue duties. The average levels of the typical duty rates on the main groups of agricultural products in each country are shown in Table 108, which suggests also a rough ranking of these countries by the average level of their agricultural duties computed as a mean of the average duties on animal and vegetable products.

The selection of the typical items and the weighting are, of course, open to question, but the range between the lowest and highest rates is so broad that the results do not differ significantly when other items and weights are used.

Equally great are contrasts in the duties on different groups of industrial products. The United Kingdom has practically prohibitive duties on petroleum products. France and Benelux give high protection to musical instruments; Norway has high import duties on motorcycles and aircraft. Germany had very high duties in 1950 on mineral oils, rubber, synthetic fibers, and certain types of machinery. Greece collected duties of more than 50 per cent ad valorem on mineral oils, articles of rubber, silk, wool, synthetic textiles, apparel and glass — most of them, exclusively or primarily, revenue duties.

The eight sets of group indexes of tariff levels in the surveyed countries shown in Table 109 seem typical of the main industrial products. As measured by the unweighted average of the eight group indexes, Denmark, Sweden, Norway and Benelux had the lowest tariffs on industrial goods; France, Austria and Portugal came next, followed by the United Kingdom,[129] Italy

and Germany. Greece had the highest tariff level.

The ranking does not change appreciably when other groups of industrial products are included, such as glass and ceramics, wood and paper, tanning extracts and coloring matter, and leather and footwear. However, as in the case of duties on agricultural products, this ranking by tariff level provides no adequate measurement of the extent of protectionism in the surveyed countries.

The over-all ranking of the European countries in tariff level may be based either on the arithmetic mean of the indexes of agricultural and industrial duties as shown in Tables 108 and 109 or on their weighted average — for example, assigning the weight of 2 to industrial duties and 1 to duties on agricultural products. The results provided by the two methods do not differ markedly:

	Index of Tariff Level	
Country	*Unweighted*	*Weighted*
Denmark	2.0	2.5
Sweden	6.5	7.2
Benelux	9.1	9.8
Norway	9.3	9.8
United Kingdom	16.3	18.6
France	22.2	20.8
Italy	23.4	24.1
Germany	26.5	26.5
Austria	27.1	24.1
Portugal	29.7	25.8
Greece	41.9	40.9

Cf. Figure 53.

This ranking permits some generalizations. At the top of the list are modern states which

129. The high level of duties in the United Kingdom

is due to the many purposes of the tariff: to provide revenue, protect domestic industry, serve as a basis for imperial preferences, safeguard the balance of payments.

TABLE 108

TARIFF LEVEL INDEXES: THIRTEEN EUROPEAN COUNTRIES, 19 AGRICULTURAL PRODUCTS, 1950

(Per Cent)

Country [a]	Animal and Vegetable Products, 19 Items	Animal Products			Vegetable Products		
		Total,[b] 8 Items	Meat and Dairy Products, 6 Items	Tallow and Mar-garine, 2 Items	Total, 11 Items	Vegetables and Fruits, 5 Items	Cereals, 6 Items
Denmark	0.7	0.3	0.4	—	1.2	2.3	—
Sweden	4.6	2.2	2.6	1.5	7.1	8.9	5.3
Benelux	7.1	8.2	9.8	5.0	6.0	12.0	—
Norway	7.8	9.2	11.7	4.1	6.4	12.8	—
United Kingdom	9.3	8.2	6.6	11.5	10.5	11.6	9.4
Italy	21.6	21.0	27.7	7.5	22.2	11.8	32.5
France	26.5	22.8	24.2	20.0	30.2	17.2	43.3
Germany	26.7	38.0	53.2	7.7	15.4	23.5	7.4
Austria	36.3	34.3	51.5	—	38.3	20.4	56.3
Portugal	41.5	22.6	32.1	3.7	60.4	89.9	30.8
Greece	44.8	47.7	23.5	96.0	41.9	50.4	33.3

Source: Table 107.

a. Arrayed by increasing average duty on animal and vegetable products.

b. Weighted average: two thirds for meats and dairy products; one third for tallow and margarine.

TABLE 109

TARIFF LEVEL INDEXES: THIRTEEN EUROPEAN COUNTRIES, 79 INDUSTRIAL PRODUCTS, 1950

(Per Cent)

Country [a]	All Groups,[b] 79 Items	Mineral Oils and Chemicals, 19 Items	Textiles, 16 Items	Apparel, 4 Items	Iron and Steel, 8 Items	Non-ferrous Metals, 10 Items	Tools,[c] 3 Items	Machin-ery, 13 Items	Transpor-tation Equip-ment, 6 Items
Denmark	3.4	0.4	4.5	6.7	1.8	1.9	1.0	5.4	5.9
Sweden	8.5	3.2	9.2	22.7	3.0	3.4	5.7	7.9	13.0
Norway	10.8	2.3	6.9	16.2	1.5	1.7	20.0	13.5	24.0
Benelux	11.2	19.9	8.2	24.0	3.7	4.8	8.7	6.3	13.7
France	17.9	17.4	12.8	22.0	18.4	18.1	16.0	18.4	20.0
Austria	18.0	14.1	19.0	—	37.8	19.3	18.5	16.6	18.6
Portugal	18.0	16.7	28.6	61.0	6.1	13.6	4.8	9.3	3.9
United Kingdom	23.3	33.1	16.3	26.0	42.0	14.0	15.8	19.2	20.4
Italy	25.3	27.0	15.6	30.0	30.6	19.5	32.9	22.6	24.6
Germany	26.4	81.6	27.9	28.2	14.9	10.8	9.0	20.3	18.2
Greece	39.0	53.1	55.9	92.5	24.7	25.0	26.7	19.7	14.0

Source: Table 107.

a. Arrayed by increasing average duty on all industrial groups.

b. Unweighted average of the eight group indexes.

c. Excludes knives.

rely on direct taxation as the basis of public finances.[130] Countries where indirect taxation predominates are at the bottom of the list. The United Kingdom is in the middle, partly because of the revenue duties in its tariff and partly because it uses the tariff as the basis of the policy of preferential treatment of colonies and dominions.

Duties on Raw Materials and Finished Goods

Most European tariffs provide higher duties on finished goods than on raw materials. This difference appears in both protective and revenue duties, as, for example, in the following duties on mineral oils in four European countries (per cent, ad valorem): [131]

	United Kingdom	Germany	Austria	Greece
Crude petroleum	7.5	10	14.7	15
Benzols	41	10.6	—	15
Petroleum oils, crude	142	290	—	—
Ethers	95	225	—	285
Kerosene	102	343	52.3	430
Gas oils	103	176	31.5	14
Fuel oils	129	84	—	14
Lubricating oils	41	140	50.6	63

A similar tendency is evident in a comparison of duties on latex and rubber; fibers, yarn and tissues; ores, crude metals and milling products. There are, however, some conspicuous deviations from this general pattern. (See Table 107.)

Revenue Duties

The items usually subjected to revenue duties are coffee, tea, cocoa and spices; tobacco and alcoholic beverages; and, in some countries, petroleum products, sugar, molasses and salt.

The United Kingdom, like the United States, makes little use of these duties in its tariff. It has only nominal duties on tea, cocoa, pepper and beer; no duty on salt and moderate duties (not above 20 per cent) on rum, whisky and ordinary wine, though it collects 100 per cent on vermouth, 60 per cent on nonmanufactured tobacco, 52 per cent on manufactured tobacco and 32.5 per cent on cigarettes.[132]

Denmark, Benelux, Sweden, Norway and France collect 20–60 per cent ad valorem on most of these articles; Italy, a little more. Germany, Austria, Portugal and Greece impose much higher rates, typified by the following (per cent, ad valorem):

Article	*Germany*	*Austria*	*Portugal*	*Greece*
Coffee	188	303	39	215
Tea	188	196	77	172
Pepper	12	577	38	384
Sugar	269	226	73	162
Cocoa [a]	35	53	58	350
Beer	98	95	141	150
Wine	104	76	81	14
Vermouth	60	—	87	129
Rum	190	68	418	65
Whisky	471	—	418	80
Tobacco Nonmanufactured	123	63	212	70
Manufactured	1,700	9	174	190
Cigarettes	525	4	180	135

a. Average for beans and paste.

Some of these duties are obviously designed as indirect taxes on luxuries. Others should be considered in part as the prohibitive measures designed to bar import of undesirable luxuries, though the distinction between prohibitive and revenue taxes is not always clear.[133]

Since revenue duties and antiluxury duties make the tariffs of some countries look higher, the Study Group for the European Customs Union excludes such items in computing the *average* rates prevailing in each country.[134]

THE UNITED STATES TARIFF

The tariff in force in the United States is the old Hawley-Smoot tariff of 1930 [135] with innumerable amendments and changes, effected mainly through reciprocal trade agreements and duly approved and proclaimed by the President.[136]

---

130. See Chapter 15.
131. Table 107.
132. See Table 107.

133. A revenue tax often becomes prohibitive while a prohibition can become a source of income. In Russia, at the beginning of the eighteenth century, Peter the Great prohibited long beards, which he considered contrary to the spirit of his reforms. Officials armed with scissors hunted violators and cut short their beards. But the owner of a long beard could preserve it by paying a special beard duty. He then obtained as a receipt a copper coin with an image of a beard and scissors which entitled the bearer to let his beard grow as long as he pleased.
134. **12**, pp. 27–38 and *passim*.
135. See **20**.
136. See **23**.

The present tariff is primarily protectionist. It contains practically no revenue duties and no antiluxury duties. Most of its rates were based originally on the idea of equalizing prices of imported goods with the domestic cost of production, including the higher wage rates, social charges, business taxes and so on in the United States. The predominantly protectionist character of the U.S. tariff is revealed by the long list of duty-free goods, which consists mainly of four groups of commodities: (1) consumer goods which are not directly competitive with domestic products (coffee, tea, cocoa, bananas); (2) industrial raw materials which cannot be provided by domestic producers in sufficient quantities (wood pulp, newsprint, natural rubber, silk, tin, nickel, coarse wool and coarse fibers, nonbovine hides and skins, undressed furs); (3) agricultural raw materials and equipment (fertilizers, barbed wire, binder twine, agricultural tools and machinery); (4) products which the United States has in abundance and is unlikely to import (sulfur, certain types of machinery, short-staple cotton).

While there have been few changes in the duty-free or dutiable status of imports since 1930, most of the present rates on dutiable goods are substantially lower than under the original act. It has been estimated that reciprocal trade agreements had reduced rates on items accounting for about 83 per cent of the value of all dutiable imports in 1949–52.

The level of ad valorem duties on different groups and types of products is shown in Table 110, which includes about 220 items classified along the same lines as the typical duties in European countries listed in Table 107 (the Brussels classification).

While the rates listed in Table 110 are roughly comparable with those in Table 107, they may convey a biased impression of the U.S. tariff, which contains high — practically prohibitive — rates for many single items. Indeed, it imposes comparatively low duties on goods which need no protection but maintains very high rates for articles which otherwise could be imported in large quantities and compete with domestic produce.

The partial list of the U.S. tariff rates over 60 per cent ad valorem prepared by the U.S. Chamber of Commerce contains more than 130 items, some of which could have found a large market in the United States if the duty on them did not exceed 30–35 per cent ad valorem. On more than threescore articles mentioned in this list, the import duty exceeds 75 per cent of value. (See Table 111.)

TARIFF LEVELS IN THE UNITED STATES AND EUROPE

In comparing the United States tariff with tariffs of European countries, the unique features of the economic structure of the former country should be kept in mind. Economically, the nation is comparable to the whole western and central Europe or the whole British Commonwealth, rather than to the United Kingdom, France or any other single European country. On the other hand, each European country is more or less comparable in size and economic structure to a single section of the United States.

The tariff of the United States plays the same role in the economic life of the nation as would be played by a tariff of an all-European customs union protecting all European countries as a unit against foreign competition. Since free competition within the union would have eliminated the least efficient producers, normal production costs within the union would be those prevailing in comparatively efficient regions. Therefore, apart from revenue duties, the tariff which such a union would need in order to provide a given degree of protection for both agriculture and industry would be lower than the tariffs required for the same purpose by some of its members.

Agricultural Products

Although the United States has comparatively low duties, on the average, on meat and dairy products, its duties on some articles in this group — such as oleomargarine — are high. Duties on cereals and most vegetables and fruits are low, but there is a very high duty on lemons. The average ad valorem duty rates computed in the same way as for European countries in Table 107 are as follows:

Meat and dairy products (6 items)	13.5
Tallow and margarine (2 items)	22.7
All animal products (8 items)[a]	16.6
Cereals (5 items)[b]	5.7
Fruits and vegetables (6 items)	22.7
All vegetable products (11 items)	14.2

a. Weighted average: two thirds for meat and dairy products; one third for tallow and margarine.
b. Excludes flour.

TABLE 110
TARIFF RATES: THE UNITED STATES, SELECTED COMMODITIES, 1950
(*Per Cent*)

Commodity	Duty	Commodity	Duty	Commodity	Duty
Live animals		Vermouth	20.6	Tanning materials	
Cows (dairy)	10.3	Rum	50.1	Vegetable	7.5–15.0
Oxen	17.1	Whisky	36.1	Synthetic	98.4
Meat		Tobacco		Coloring matter	
Beef	18.0	Unstemmed	33.0–35.0	Chemical and earth	
Pork	4.8	Manufactured	2.8– 8.2	pigments	25.0
Dairy products		Cigarettes	20.0	Paints, enamels and	
Milk, fresh	13.3			stains	12.5
Cream, fresh	13.3	Minerals		Chemicals	
Butter	9.1	Salt	Free	Fish glue	11.5
Cheese	20.0–25.0	Cement	9.2	Vegetable glue	14.3–21.2
Vegetables		Mineral oils		Glycerin	2.2– 4.8
Potatoes	22.3	Crude petroleum	Free	Soap	10.0–15.0
Olives	15.0	Unfinished petroleum		Bath salts	15.0–20.0
Fruits		oils	1.9	Perfumes	
Grapefruit	15.4	Gasoline	6.0–13.9	Not containing	
Lemons	69.9	Naphtha	0.1	alcohol	20.0
Apples	13.6	Kerosene	6.2	Containing alcohol	21.1–52.8
Bananas	Free	Gas oils	7.9	Candles	14.0–27.5
Colonial products		Fuel oils	11.4	Explosives	
Coffee	Free	Lubricating oils	13.7	Dynamite (industrial)	6.4
Tea	Free			Fuses	10.6
Pepper	15.0	Chemicals		Matches	24.9
Cereals		Methyl alcohol	31.7		
Wheat	5.5	Ethyl alcohol	21.3	Photographic goods	
Rye	2.4	Elastic products of		Plates	15.0
Barley	5.1	cellulose acetate	20.0	Roll films	1.3–10.0
Oats	4.2	Boric acid	16.0	Rubber	
Corn	11.1	Phosphoric acid	28.6	Natural, nonmanu-	
Wheat flour	12.1	Ammonium phos-		factured	Free
Rice, milled	2.7	phates	Free	Synthetic	10.0
Fats		Mixed fertilizers	Free	Tubing	12.5–15.0
Tallow	19.5	Sulfur	Free	Tires	10.0–15.0
Margarine	[26] [a]	Caustic soda	4.6	Products of soft	
Fish, preserved		Zinc oxides	5.9	rubber	12.5–25.0
Sardines	15–44	Iron oxides	20.0	Hides and skins and	
Herring	5.3–12.5			leather	
Tuna, frozen	Free	Medicinal preparations		Cattle hides	4.0– 5.0
Other foodstuffs		Not containing alcohol		Nonbovine hides	Free
Sugar (from Cuba)	12.5	Vegetable	12.5–25.6	Sole leather	8.0–10.0
Molasses	7.3	Animal	12.5	Upper leather	8.0–12.5
Cocoa	Free	Other	25.0	Patent leather	10.0
Cocoa paste	6.2	Containing alcohol		Articles of leather	
Chocolate	6.5	Less than 50		Coats	17.5
Biscuits	10.0	per cent	27.0	Gloves	12.5–15.0
Preserved fruits	17.5	More than 50		Wood	
Orange juice	28.4	per cent	81.1	Round (poles)	1.0
Beverages		Vitamins	10.0–12.5	Sawn	0 – 5.0
Beer	Free	Fertilizers		Pulpwood	Free
Wine	8.0	Sodium nitrate	Free	Plywood	20.0
		Ammonium nitrate	Free	Veneers	10.0
		Phosphates, natural	Free		
		Superphosphates	Free		

(*Continued on facing page*)

TABLE 110—*continued*

Commodity	Duty	Commodity	Duty	Commodity	Duty
Paper		Ceramic products		Machinery	
Woodpulp	Free	Building brick	3.3	Steam engines	10.0
Newsprint	Free	Tiles	15.0–30.0	Hydraulic turbines	15.0
Book and printing		Tableware	28.0–65.6	Electric motors	15.0
paper	10.0	Glass		Electric generators	15.0
Wrapping paper	25.0	Unworked	5.7	Internal combustion	
		Sheet glass	11.4	engines	10.0–27.5
Silk		Safety glass	30.0	Plows, harrows, har-	
Raw	Free	Bottles	5.6	vesters, mowers,	
Yarn	20.0			planters, tractors	
Thread	40.0	Iron and steel		and other agricul-	
Tissues (noil)	25.0–65.0	Pig iron	1.9	tural implements	Free
Hosiery	30.0	Ferromanganese	12.2	Linotype machines	Free
Knittings	30.0	Ingots	23.2	Printing	15.0–25.0
		Plates, sheets	10.0–25.0	Textile	10.0–40.0
Wool		Shapes, sections	2.9	Metal working	15.0–20.0
Coarse, for carpets	Free	Rails	3.9	Wood working	15.0
Raw	15.0–20.0	Cast–iron tubes	11.2	Typewriters	Free
Fine and carbonized	48.7	Hydroelectric conduits	30.0	Counting machines	15.0
Yarn	35.7–71.4	Barbed wire	Free	Steam and hydraulic	
Felts	32.3–66.2			turbines	7.5
Fill	35.2–42.0	Bronze		Diesel and similar	
Woolens and wor-		Leaf	12.3	engines	10.0–27.5
steds	36.2–55.5			Sewing machines	10.0–30.0
Outerwear	22.9–67.2	Quicksilver	28.3	Washing machines	17.5
Wearing apparel	29.8–32.4	Copper		Vacuum cleaners	35.0
Carpets and rugs	25.0	Refined	34.1	Electric ranges	10.0
Floor coverings	15.0–40.0	Balls, sheets, rods	7.5		
				Electrical apparatus	
Rayon		Nickel		Radio apparatus	15.0
Staple fiber	20.0	Ores and matter	Free	Telegraph and tele-	
Broad woven fabrics	27.7–56.3	Ingots	4.6	phone apparatus	17.5
Pile fabrics	27.0	Sheets, wire	12.5	X-ray apparatus	10.0
Hosiery	45.8			Other therapeutic	
Knitted outerwear	41.5	Aluminum		apparatus	17.5
Wearing apparel	36.8	Bars	14.0		
		Mill products	14.0	Transportation equipment	
Cotton		Lead		Locomotives	7.5
Short staple	Free	Pigs and bars	10.6	Pleasure boats	15.0
Long staple	9.1–13.7	Mill products	10.9	Automobiles	10.0
Yarn	20.0–25.0			Trucks	12.5
Cloth	30.0	Tin		Bicycles	15.0–30.0
Blankets	30.5	Ores and metal	Free	Motorcycles	10.0
Towels	25.0–40.0	Zinc		Aircraft	15.0
Gloves and mittens	30.0	Blocks, pigs	11.1		
Knitted underwear	35.0	Sheets	14.7	Miscellaneous	
Handkerchiefs	37.7–44.0			Photographic	
Coats and other		Tools		cameras	20.0–25.0
wearing apparel	10.0–20.0	Agricultural	Free	Watch movements	18.5–59.5
		Spades, shovels	7.5	Clocks	60.0–155.8
		Hand tools	7.5–20.0	Pianos	40.0
		Lathe tools	15.0–20.0	Violins	44.9
Footwear		Knives, folding		Phonographs	15.0
Shoes	10.0–20.0	blades	33.5–140.0	Records	15.0
Rubbers	12.5	Knives, fixed		Rifles	36.1–40.1
		blades	15.1–48.9		

Source: **36.**   a. Ad valorem at 1948 prices, estimated by the authors.

TABLE 111

TARIFF RATES: THE UNITED STATES, PARTIAL LIST OF DUTIES OVER 75 PER CENT AD VALOREM, 1950

Abbreviated Description	Imports 1950, in Thousands of Dollars	Duty Rate, Ad Valorem Equivalent in Per Cent
Lemon juice, concentrated	$ 247	104.1
Medical preparations containing over 50 per cent alcohol	6	102.4
Firecrackers over 5⁄16″ diameter, over 1¾″ long	95	117.3
Cotton lace handmade over 2″ in width, valued not more than $50 per lb.	734	90.0
Wool lace over 2″ wide valued not more than $50 per lb.	0	90.0
Synthetic lace handmade over 2″ wide valued not more than $50 per lb.	7	90.0
Synthetic lace handmade not over 2″ wide	2	90.0
Cotton embroidery including edgings, inserts, galloons, n.e.s.	278	90.0
Lace flouncing and all-over, n.e.s., ornamented of cotton	0	90.0
Cotton lace neck rufflings, etc.	0	90.0
Embroideries, n.e.s., of vegetable fiber	83	90.0
Flouncings, etc., of vegetable fiber	4	90.0
Cotton hat braids, etc., n.e.s.	0	90.0
Synthetic textile braid valued at $1 or less per lb.	2	90.0
Braids of other materials, n.e.s., valued at $1 or less per lb.	1	90.0
Wool auto robes valued $1 or less lb., n.e.s.	0	106.9
Cotton articles in part of handmade lace valued not more than $50 lb.	8	90.0
Cotton articles of handmade lace not over 2″ wide	14	90.0
Articles or fabrics embroidered, etc., other than of insertings, etc., of cotton	3,094	90.0
Cotton articles or fabrics ornamented other than of insertings, etc.	57	90.0
Articles of vegetable fiber with handmade lace over 2″ wide and articles valued not more than $50 lb.	53	90.0
Articles of vegetable fiber with handmade lace valued not more than $50 lb.	1	90.0
Ornamented fabrics and articles other than flouncings and neck rufflings, etc., of vegetable fiber	3,093	90.0
Wool articles if all lace is over 2″ wide and articles are valued not more than $50 lb.	0	90.0
Silk articles in part of lace valued not more than $50 lb.	0	90.0
Articles of synthetic textiles in part of lace over 2″ wide and articles valued not more than $50 lb.	1	90.0
China plates, etc., decorated not over minimum value	4,059	78.7
Restaurant china decorated	10	86.0
Gold leaf unmounted	5	144.5
Imitation solid pearls, n.e.s., valued ¼ cent to 1 cent per inch	0	137.3

(Continued on facing page)

The United States index (15.5 per cent) for all agricultural products is higher than in Denmark, Sweden, the United Kingdom, Benelux and Norway, but lower than in other European countries.[137] (Cf. Table 108.) It should be kept in mind, however, that the main device for protecting the U.S. domestic market against competition from foreign agricultural products is not the tariff but the quota system, which is used whenever prices of the respective products drop as the result of pressure of lower world prices.

Industrial Products

As the world's largest producer of mineral oils, the United States has comparatively low duties on this group of products: an average of 6.4 per cent ad valorem (8 items). Its duties on chemicals are apparently higher: 13.5 per cent (11 items). The average rate for 19 items listed in Table 110 under both titles, roughly comparable to the respective group index in Table 109, is 10.0 per cent. Duties on textiles and apparel vary widely, reaching 55.5 per cent ad valorem

137. It should be stressed again that these indexes do not measure adequately the restrictiveness of the respective tariffs or the extent of protection they provide to domestic producers: a moderately low duty on highly competitive articles (for example, dairy products or oils) might be more restrictive and more protective than relatively high duties on less competitive products.

TABLE 111—*continued*

Abbreviated Description	Imports 1950, in Thousands of Dollars	Duty Rate, Ad Valorem Equivalent in Per Cent
Imitation pearl beads valued ¼ cent to 1 cent per inch	0	121.2
Imitation pearl beads valued 1 cent to 5 cents per inch	0	122.9
Tungstic acid and other compounds of tungsten, n.e.s.	2	104.6
Pistols and revolvers valued not over $4 each	5	149.9
Pistols and revolvers valued $4 to $8 each	58	90.6
Razors and parts valued $1.50 to $3 doz.	0	105.6
Razors and parts valued $3 to $4 doz.	0	105.0
Scissors and blades n.e.s., valued over 50 cents not over $1.75 doz.	11	84.6
Pen, etc., knives with folding blades valued 40 to 50 cents doz.	0	86.2
Pen, etc., knives with folding blades valued over 50 cents not over $1.25 per doz.	4	92.0
Pen knife blades or other parts valued not over $1.25 per doz.	0	81.9
Print rollers with brass patterns	0	88.7
Laces handmade over 2″ wide valued not more than $50 per lb. (metallic)	0	90.0
Mechanisms for measuring flowage of electricity	0	79.7
Palm leaf hats blocked, etc.	3	152.9
Other hats not sewed but blocked	5	94.5
Chip hats sewed	1	222.6
Hats of synthetic textile not knit or crocheted, made of braids	17	90.0
Gloves of synthetic textiles knit or crocheted valued less than $1.50 per doz. pairs	4	89.6
Watch parts, assemblies, having more than 1 but not more than 17 jewels, more than ⁹⁄₁₀″ not more than ⁸⁄₁₀″ wide	0	790.2
Knit or crocheted gloves of wool embroidered	1,486	90.0
Clockwork mechanisms, n.e.s., valued not more than $1.10 each	3	176.7
Clockwork mechanisms, n.e.s., valued $1.10 to $2.25 each	5	122.3
Clockwork mechanisms, n.e.s., valued $2.25 to $5.00 each	1	102.8
Clockwork mechanisms, n.e.s., valued $5.00 to $10.00 each	2	105.5
Clockwork mechanisms, n.e.s., valued more than $10.00 each	60	84.0
Clock assemblies consisting of 2 or more parts or pieces fastened, n.e.s.	10	82.8
Decalcomanias, n.e.s., backed with metal leaf	30	75.4
Buttons pearl or shell fresh water	84	82.9
Buttons ocean pearl or shell	311	77.2
Cellulose dolls not having movable parts	10	84.1
Cellulose toys having movable parts	115	84.9
Cellulose toys not having movable parts	53	81.6
Thermostatic bottles over 1 pint not over 2 pints	1	95.4

Source: **50**, pp. 60–65.

on certain types of woolens and worsted, 66.2 on felts, and more than 40 per cent on certain types of knitted goods, outerwear and underwear. All in all, duties on textiles are higher in the United States than in France and the United Kingdom but probably lower than in Germany, while duties on articles of apparel are higher than in most European countries. The average rate for 33 items under the categories silk, wool, rayon and cotton in Table 110 is 30.6 per cent.[138]

A precise comparison of United States duties on other manufactured articles with similar duties in Europe is very difficult because of differences between the classification in the U.S. tariff and the Brussels nomenclature used in Table 107. At a rough approximation, taking from Table 110 the items in the United States tariff closest to those used in computing the group rates in Table 109, the respective average rates in the U.S. tariff are the following percentages:

Iron and steel (9 items)	11.4
Nonferrous metals (14 items)	12.5
Tools (4 items)[a]	9.7
Machinery (19 items)	14.5
Transportation equipment (7 items)	13.1

a.   Excludes knives.

138. Taking the mean of the highest and lowest rate for the groups of commodities for which a range of rates is shown in Table 110.

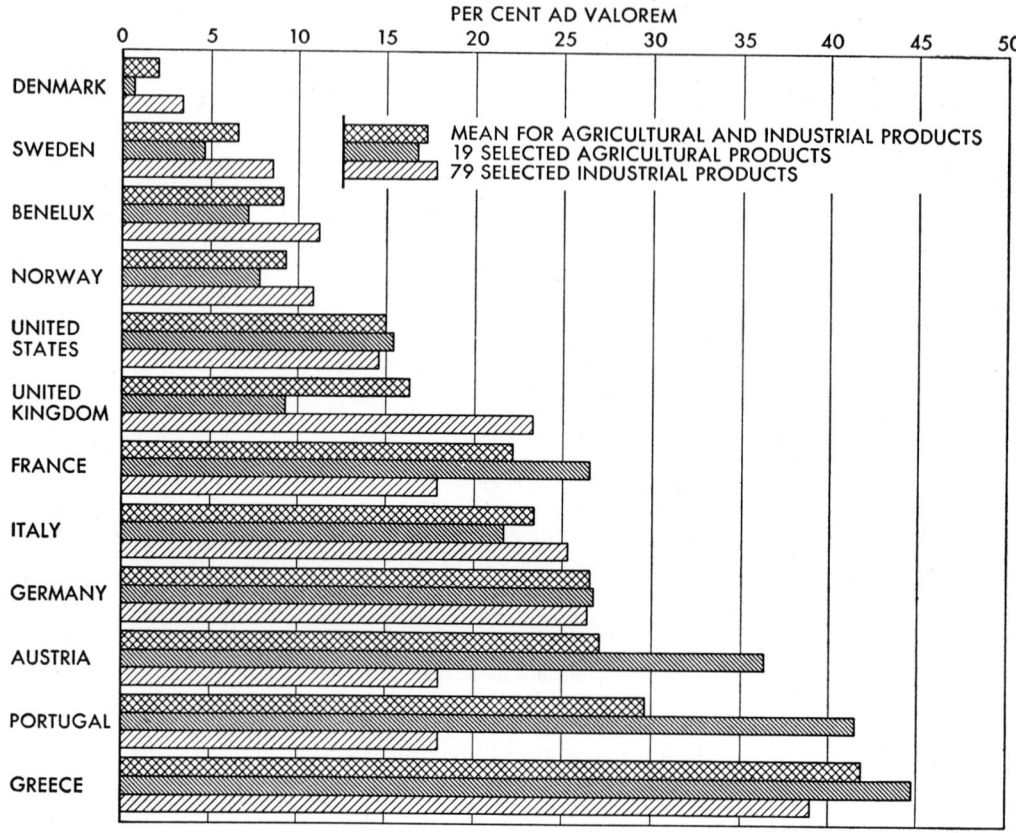

FIGURE 53. TARIFF LEVELS: SELECTED EUROPEAN COUNTRIES AND THE UNITED STATES, 1950

The unweighted average for these five groups, together with the above-mentioned mineral oils, chemicals and textiles, is 14.6 per cent, as compared with 15.5 per cent for agricultural (animal and vegetable) products. Thus, the average level of the U.S. tariff in 1950 (on agricultural and industrial products, combined), measured in the same manner as for European countries in the same year, was approximately 15.0 per cent ad valorem, that is, higher than the tariffs in effect in Denmark, Sweden, Benelux and Norway; fairly close to that in the United Kingdom; and lower than those in France, Germany, Italy and other European countries. (See Figure 53.)

A similar ranking is suggested by the estimate of tariff levels in 1952 prepared by the members of the GATT and based on the mean for 570 items of the Standard International Trade Classification: [139]

Denmark	5
Sweden	6
Benelux	9
Canada	11
United States	16
Germany	16
United Kingdom	17
Austria	17
France	19
Italy	24

These comparisons of tariff levels do not indicate the ranking of the United States among other countries in the degree of protection accorded to its domestic industries. As has been mentioned, protection of domestic production is the absolutely predominant idea of the U.S. tariff, while European import duties largely serve other purposes; hence, an equal degree of protection is likely to entail lower import duties in the United States than in smaller countries with less diversified industries and less regional specialization. Moreover, apart from any artificial trade

139. **17**, p. 62.

barrier, the United States is surrounded by a protective wall as a result of its geographic location, with two oceans separating it from most of the exporting countries.

Nontariff Trade Restrictions

Between the Napoleonic wars and World War I, trade restrictions in the form of prohibition or quantitative limitation of imports and exports, allocation of quotas, exchange controls and licensing were outlawed to a considerable extent by trade treaties. They were used primarily in the time of acute international conflict. In 1914–18 such measures were introduced not only in belligerent countries but in practically all parts of the world. There was a general understanding that restoration of international trade after the war would begin with repeal of trade and exchange controls.[140]

However, inflation and the disorganization of currencies which followed the end of World War I retarded the return to a free flow of international trade. The repeal of wartime restrictions started as late as 1923–24 in many countries, proceeded slowly, and was only more or less completed by 1928–29. Then the depression set in and most nations restored the license and quota systems as means of protecting their markets against the falling prices. These systems were in full force when World War II began.

THE INTERWAR YEARS

In the early 1920's conferences and commissions of the League of Nations repeatedly admonished governments to abolish wartime trade restrictions. The Genoa conference of May 1922 recommended the progressive repeal of import and export prohibitions, holding them one of the gravest obstacles to international trade. Facing the choice between two evils, it recommended customs duties as a better means when limitation of imports was desired.[141]

However, international agreement on this issue could not be reached until the end of the acute inflation in Europe. After the stabilization of currencies in Central Europe in 1924 thirty nations signed a declaration whereby each promised to reduce its export and import prohibitions and restrictions to a minimum "as soon as cir-

cumstances permit" and meanwhile to publish customs regulations in simple and accessible form, publish changes in tariffs and formalities, and not to use formalities for purposes of discrimination and so on.[142] Although this was a declaration of good intentions rather than an international convention, substantial progress was achieved in elimination of trade restrictions in 1926–28 in the period of postwar economic expansion.[143] This trend was reversed in the early 1930's.

The financial crisis in Germany and Austria led to abandonment of the gold standard and introduction of foreign exchange controls in Austria, Bulgaria, Czechoslovakia, Denmark, Estonia, Germany, Greece, Hungary, Latvia, Portugal, Spain, Yugoslavia; Argentina, Bolivia, Brazil, Chile, Colombia, Uruguay; Turkey, Iran. Import quotas were established in Czechoslovakia, France, Italy, Latvia, the Netherlands and Turkey.[144]

In May 1933 an international conference convened in London in an attempt to reduce trade barriers on the basis of restoring a sound international monetary system. A few weeks before the conference, however, the United States abandoned the gold standard. The "gold bloc," which included France, Luxembourg, Belgium, the Netherlands, Poland, Switzerland, Czechoslovakia and Italy, made any consideration of a common trade policy dependent on stabilization of currencies.[145] Such a demand was rejected by the United States, and the conference ended in failure. In 1933–37 the commercial policy of most countries was largely determined by the state of their currencies. At least four currency systems were in operation in the world:

1. The "gold bloc" (France; Switzerland; the Netherlands; Italy until 1934; and Belgium-Luxembourg until 1935);

2. Countries maintaining an "artificial" parity (Germany; Italy after 1934; part of southeastern Europe and various Latin American countries);

3. Countries with depreciated and controlled currencies (mainly in southeastern Europe and Latin America);

4. Countries with depreciated currencies and relatively free exchanges (some twenty countries by 1933, including the United States, the United

140. **1**, p. 17.
141. **1**, p. 22.

142. **1**, p. 26.
143. **49**, pp. 33, 41.
144. **1**, p. 52.
145. **1**, p. 65.

Kingdom, the British dominions, Sweden and Norway).[146]

The League of Nations described the commercial policies of the four groups as follows:

The first and second groups — countries with overvalued currencies and consequently high price-levels — resorted to increasingly stringent measures aimed at restricting imports and encouraging exports. In the "gold bloc" recourse was mainly had to an extensive system of import quotas and export bounties; in exchange control countries such measures were first supplemented by the rationing of foreign exchange and later overshadowed by a rapidly developing technique designed to minimize the need for and maximize the acquisition of free foreign exchange. One of the principal instruments of this technique was the [bilateral] clearing agreement; the growth of a network of these agreements over the European continent and between certain European and Latin-American and Asiatic countries was perhaps the outstanding feature of trade relationships in the period. By 1937 about 12 per cent of world trade, and more than 50 per cent of the trade of Bulgaria, Germany, Greece, Hungary, Yugoslavia, Roumania and Turkey passed through clearings.

Countries of the fourth — and some of the Latin-American countries of the third — group were in a position to pursue policies of domestic reflation without recourse to extreme measures of trade restriction.[147]

During the great depression, the trend throughout the world was toward "planning" of foreign trade as a normal function of the state. Nazi Germany, fascist Italy and the communist USSR spearheaded the movement, and the system of quotas in France, the agricultural quotas and preferential trade policy in Great Britain and the currency controls in Latin America were all proceeding in the same direction.

After the devaluation of the French franc in 1936, the tide seemed to turn. The United States, the United Kingdom and France jointly admonished the world to take measures to revive and expand foreign trade and first of all "to relax progressively the present system of quotas and exchange controls with a view of their abolition." The Assembly of the League of Nations joined in these recommendations (October 1936).

The devaluation of the few remaining gold-standard currencies and readjustment of over-rated currencies brought some order into the international monetary system. World trade began to recover, partly under the impact of Germany's military preparations. A number of primary producing countries relaxed or abolished currency controls. But time ran short; the new war was around the corner.

DURING WORLD WAR II

The last vestiges of free international exchange of goods disappeared during World War II. The League of Nations described the situation as follows:

. . . trade had ceased or was ceasing to be the business of the merchant operating under simple and stable laws and concerned with providing the consumer he served with goods at the lowest available prices. Governments were assuming daily control of all trading operations by means of import prohibitions, varying quotas, exchange control, export subsidies, and by means of trade agreements from which none but the two signatory powers might benefit.

By these treaties, concluded for a few months at a time, the State replaced the merchant in international bargaining.[148]

In its plans for transition from war to a peacetime economy, the League of Nations started with the assumption that governments would be reluctant to abolish their exchange controls for some considerable time after the war:

Countries which have been left seriously impoverished by the war will desire to maintain day-to-day control over imports in order to prevent the expenditure of national resources on goods of a luxury character or goods which, while not luxuries, can be ill afforded during hard times. Countries which have been cut off from their export markets during the war will wish to ascertain how far and how fast they can re-establish their former business connections. Above all, countries in which inflation is taking place or has recently taken place will want to have time in which to restore order in their public finances and domestic monetary situation.[149]

Experts of the United States and of all countries represented in the League agreed that the war would be followed by a long period of economic controls and trade restrictions, and they did not insist on their early abolition. But they recommended putting such measures under the supervision of special international agencies. This point of view played an important role in the blueprints of the International Monetary Fund,

---

146. **1**, p. 69.
147. **1**, pp. 69–70.

148. **3**, pp. 25–26.
149. **3**, pp. 87–88.

the International Bank for Reconstruction and Development, the GATT, the Charter of the proposed International Trade Organization and — later — the European Payments Union.

AFTER WORLD WAR II

Apart from the anticipation of a long period of transition, the program of the postwar commercial policy of the Western bloc of nations envisaged the reduction of tariffs and other trade barriers and the elimination of all forms of discriminatory treatment in international commerce.[150]

Some progress has been made in this direction: exchange rates have been brought closer to the relative purchasing power of the respective currencies and the stability of exchange rates has been increased. The disequilibrium in trade and payments balances has been narrowed and a limited convertibility of national currencies restored. Customs duties have been reduced, customs procedures simplified, quantitative trade restrictions eliminated or liberalized. In one respect, however, the world trade policy announced by the Western bloc has failed: there has been little progress in reviving the international movement of private capital, which is an important basis for the smooth flow of foreign trade.

The cause of the slow progress in eliminating trade barriers was not short-sighted nationalism or lack of good will on the part of individual governments but rather the character of the problems that confronted the world and, most of all, the old countries of Europe after the end of World War II.[151] In the first *World Economic Report* (June 1949) the United Nations fully recognized the situation: "The problem of combining the maintenance of high levels of employment and national prosperity with international integration and equilibrium is one which can hardly be solved in a short time or by schematic methods." [152]

The core of the problem was in the lack of equilibrium in the balances of current transactions of European countries, especially in their transactions with the United States. They urgently needed foodstuffs, raw materials and capital equipment to restore the prewar standard of living and to rebuild industry. The United States was the only place in the world from which they could obtain the coveted goods, but the European countries had too little to offer in exchange. In the critical period of transition, the problem was solved, temporarily, by the aid extended by the United States to its Allies.[153] Such unilateral transactions, however, had to end sooner or later, and the flow of international trade was bound to return to the commercial basis exemplified in the slogan: trade, not aid.

Since 1947–48, both the United States and European countries have been struggling with the problem of closing the gap between imports and exports in their trade. It could be narrowed or closed by an increase in European exports to the United States, by reduction of the United States exports to Europe, or by a combination of both measures. A substantial increase of European exports to the United States proved very difficult, partly because Europe had not enough goods to offer at prices attractive to consumers, and partly because the United States was not ready to relax its tariff so as to accept more European products. Thus, reduction of American exports to Europe became vital for restoration of equilibrium in world trade.

As long as there was a gap between the demand for American goods in Europe and the demand for European goods in the United States, the problem could be approached from two sides — either the United States had to limit its exports to Europe or European countries had to take measures that restricted imports from the United States and forced their foreign trade into new channels. In 1948–49 European countries, especially the United Kingdom, restricted their imports of U.S. products and tried to transfer their orders from the United States to the sterling and soft-currency areas.[154] Before World War I, such a policy would have been considered economic warfare; now it was established by the consent of both parties as a means of restoring equilibrium in foreign trade.

In 1949 the European countries tightened their controls over imports as a means of balancing their foreign transactions. In 1952 France tightened quantitative restrictions, the Netherlands tried to reduce imports by deflationary credit and fiscal policies, and the United Kingdom strengthened direct controls and credit restrictions.[155] Such actions by individual Euro-

---

150. **2**, p. 34.
151. See **6**, pp. 73–74.
152. **9**, 1948, p. 65.

153. See Chapter 5.
154. **10**, 1948, pp. 129–30.
155. **11**, Second Quarter 1952, p. 13.

pean countries inevitably struck at one another's exports, and the effects were aggravated by similar steps taken in a number of important overseas markets.

THE PRESENT STATUS

It is practically impossible to give a systematic picture of current trade restrictions and controls in different countries. It is characteristic of the situation that the principle of governmental control over foreign transactions is universally accepted and there is a tacit agreement that the scope of controls is a question of expediency and should be determined by each government in accordance with its domestic monetary and price policies, the needs of its agriculture and industry, its employment status and outlook and so on. The universal practice of licensing has revived the medieval philosophy of foreign trade: imports are prohibited unless a specific authorization has been granted to the importer. The practice of restrictions and licenses in each country changes from month to month. No legislative act, and in many countries no formal decree of the government, is required for such changes. At times existing restrictions may be interpreted liberally by the customs or monetary authorities, so that licensing becomes a pure formality; on other occasions they may even be used as a form of embargo.

The U.S. Department of Commerce follows the development in import controls in foreign countries. [156] The Department found, however, that only a few formal features of these regulations can be presented in tabular form in an international survey. (See Table 112.) Of eighty-eight countries listed in the survey for April 1953, only ten were admitting imports from the United States without licenses and required no permits for exchanging their currency into dollars. In some of these countries, imports from the United States did not enjoy the privileges extended to other areas.

In the policy of controls and restrictions, the United States is a borderline case: it requires no permit for exchange of currency, but restricts imports of certain agricultural products. Importers also complain of its "invisible" tariff.

OUTLOOK

Slowly, and not without friction, the free na-

tions are moving toward a freer exchange of goods. At three tariff conferences — Geneva, 1947; Annecy, 1949; and Torquay, 1950–51 — some 58,000 concessions (tariff reductions and tariff bindings) were negotiated among the countries which together conduct four fifths of the world's trade. Most conspicuous is the trend toward reduction of customs duties and trade controls in Western Europe. There is some hope that the unification of European markets for iron and steel, under the Schuman Plan, will be followed by similar arrangements in other industries.

There are indications, however, that the process of liberalization of conditions of foreign trade by trade agreements is approaching its end. It has been common practice to make concessions that do not expose domestic industry to dangerous competition from abroad. The development has been toward a selective protectionism — concessions in comparatively unimportant duties and maintenance of rigid protection of industries which might suffer from foreign competition. Water has been squeezed from the tariffs but in many cases the hard core of protection has remained untouched.

Since the Torquay conference efforts have therefore been made to find new methods of reducing tariffs by collective action rather than through bilateral product-by-product negotiations. In 1951 the Benelux governments offered a plan for the reduction of disparities in the tariff levels within Europe.[157] This plan, however, proved unacceptable to high-tariff countries.

The French government suggested another approach to the problem: an international agreement for reducing tariff levels by 30 per cent in three years. This plan, with some modifications, has gained the support of Denmark, Belgium, the Netherlands and Western Germany and has been submitted to participating governments in the GATT. The plan proposes a 30 per cent reduction of the tariff level for each of ten groups of commodities: [158]

I. Primary food products, excluding fish
II. Manufactured food products, excluding fish
III. Fish and fish products
IV. Raw materials, including petroleum products
V. Products of chemical and allied industries

---

156. The "International Trade Controls" section in **20.**

157. **15,** p. 4.
158. **15,** p. 15.

VI. Leather and products of leather, fur skins, rubber, wood, cork, paper and printed matter

VII. Textile products and clothing

VIII. Base metals and manufactures thereof

IX. Machinery, electrical and transportation equipment

X. Miscellaneous manufactures

For each of these groups a level of tariff rates is established, described as the "demarcation line." A country which levies duties averaging less than the demarcation-line rate for a given group of commodities will be committed to reducing these duties by less than 30 per cent.

The demarcation line is tentatively established for each group of commodities at the following percentages, ad valorem:

I.	7	V.	8	VIII.	7
II.	11	VI.	6	IX.	11
III.	8	VII.	14	X.	12
IV.	2				

The plan does not apply to revenue duties and leaves each country free to determine which duties serve fiscal purposes. The plan cannot be brought into operation unless it is accepted by all the main trading countries in Europe and North America.[159]

159. **15**, p. 5.

TABLE 112

TRADE RESTRICTIONS: FOREIGN CONTROL REGULATIONS APPLYING TO IMPORTS FROM THE UNITED STATES IN 88 AREAS, AS OF APRIL 1, 1953

Country	Is Import License Necessary?	Is Exchange Permit Required?
Afghanistan	Yes, for most items	Yes, unless dollars were acquired by sales of commodities other than karakul skins or cotton, or represent only 15 per cent of karakul skin sales, or 90 per cent of cotton sales which are not held by the National Bank of Afghanistan.
Anglo-Egyptian Sudan	Yes	Yes.
Arabian Peninsula areas:		
Saudi Arabia	Yes, on almost all commodities	Yes.
Aden, Bahrein, Qatar, Trucial, Oman	Yes	Yes.
Kuwait, Muscat, and Oman, Yemen	No	No.
Argentina	No, certain products are subject to import quota.	Yes, permit granted only for "listed" products. Application should be filed prior to confirmation of purchase order.
Australia	Yes	Import license carries right to foreign exchange.
Austria	Yes, for most commodities	Yes.
Belgium-Luxembourg	Yes, either a regular import license or a declaration license.	Yes, except for a few items import license carries right to foreign exchange.
Belgian Congo	Yes, a combination import license and exchange authorization is required for all imports except noncommercial parcel post shipments valued at $100 or less.	Yes.
Bolivia	Yes	No, import license authorizes purchase of exchange but is not a guarantee that exchange will be granted.
Brazil	Yes	Yes, exchange granted to holders of import licenses according to availability of exchange in accordance with established priority schedules.
British colonies, not specified elsewhere [a]	Yes	Yes, import license generally assures release of foreign exchange.
Bulgaria	Yes	Import license automatically assures foreign exchange.
Burma	Yes	Yes.
Canada	No, except for a few commodities [b]	No.
Ceylon	Yes, either a general license for commodities under open general license, or an individual license for other commodities.	Yes.
Chile	Yes, must be obtained prior to shipment of goods and copy must be sent to exporter.	Yes, in form of notation on import license.
China (mainland) [c]	Yes	Yes, except for certain Government purchases.
Colombia	Import license takes the form of registry certificate issued without quota or other form of restrictions if merchandise is not included in list of prohibited imports.	No, registry certificate carries the right to foreign exchange.
Costa Rica	No	Yes, for imports with official exchange. No permit required for imports with free-market exchange.

(*Continued on following page*)

TABLE 112—*continued*

Country	Is Exchange Permit Required?	Is Import License Necessary?
Cuba	No, except for wheat, rice, tires, and tubes	No.
Czechoslovakia	Yes	Import license automatically provides for allocation of necessary foreign exchange.
Denmark	Yes, with few exceptions	Yes, for goods subject to license copy of license with customs certification of importation takes place of exchange license.
Dominican Republic	Yes, issued on arrival of imports. Special permits from the Dominican Department of Agriculture required on imports of fertilizers.	No, but all applications for foreign exchange require Government approval, which is granted almost automatically for bonafide commercial transactions.
Ecuador	Yes, must be presented in order to obtain the consular invoice. Some luxury imports prohibited.	Import license carries the right to foreign exchange (Central Bank of Ecuador).
Egypt	Yes, unlicensed imports are subject to confiscation.	Yes.
El Salvador	No	No.
Ethiopia	No, except on products subject to export license in country of origin.	Yes.
Finland	Yes	Yes.
France	Yes, obtainable for "essentials" only	Yes, import license carries right to foreign exchange.
French oversea territories not elsewhere specified	Yes	Import license carries right to foreign exchange.
Germany, Federal Republic (including Western Berlin).	Yes, also purchase authorization	Yes; import and payments license combined in one document.
Germany, Soviet-Occupied Zones	Yes, the government monopolies for foreign trade are the only importers.	No.
Greece	Yes, license granted for limited number of essential products.	Yes, import permit carries right to open letter of credit.
Guatemala	No, but importation of a few items is prohibited.	No.
Haiti	No, except for the required permit on wheat quota imports.	No.
Hashemite Jordan Kingdom	Yes	Yes.
Honduras	No	No.
Hong Kong	Yes, only certain items may be imported directly from hard-currency sources. Licenses to import nonsterling area goods via Hong Kong are issued provided certain exchange regulations are observed.	Yes, for direct imports. For imports from hard-currency areas via Hong Kong no permit is necessary, but payment must be made in a sterling-area currency and shipment effected on a bill of lading issued in Hong Kong.
Hungary	Yes	Yes.
Iceland	Yes, except for items on "special conditional free list" and a limited number of staples.	Yes, except for "special conditional free list" imports.
India	Yes, either a general license for commodities under open general license, or an individual license for other commodities.	Yes, however, foreign exchange is automatically released upon presentation of validated import license to exchange bank.
Indochina	Yes	Import license carries right to foreign exchange.
Indonesia	Yes	Yes, all foreign exchange transactions are controlled by the Foreign Exchange Institute.
Iran	Yes, but only to release goods from Customs; prospective imports must come within annual or supplemental quotas.	Yes.
Iraq	Yes, goods exported before license is obtained are confiscated.	Yes, permits are obtained through licensed dealers.
Ireland	For a few products only	Yes.
Israel	Yes	Yes, import license usually carries right to foreign exchange.
Italy	Yes, from Italian Exchange Office except for list A (mostly industrial raw materials, which require only bank "benestare").	Yes, combined with import permit in same document.
Japan	Yes	Some commodities, as announced by Japanese Government from time to time, require allocation certificate; in other cases import license carries right to foreign exchange.
Korea, Republic of	Yes	Application for import license must be accompanied by certificate from Bank of Korea stating that applicant has sufficient foreign exchange cover on deposit.
Lebanon	Yes	No.
Liberia	For arms, ammunition, and rice only	Yes.
Malaya, Federation of	Yes, only certain items may be imported directly from hard-currency sources. Licenses to import non-sterling-area goods via Hong Kong are issued provided certain exchange regulations are observed.	Yes, for direct imports. For imports from hard-currency areas via Hong Kong no permit is necessary, but payment must be made in a sterling-area currency and shipment effected on a bill of lading issued in Hong Kong.

(*Continued on facing page*)

TABLE 112—*continued*

Country	Is Import License Necessary?	Is Exchange Permit Required?
Mexico	Yes, for an extensive list of articles	No.
Morocco:		
French Zone	Yes [d]	Yes.[d] Import license carries right to foreign exchange.
Spanish Zone	Yes	
Tangier (International Zone)	No	No.
Netherlands	Yes	Yes ("payment attest").
Netherlands West Indies	No, except for certain luxury items	Yes.
New Zealand	Yes	Import license carries right to foreign exchange.
Nicaragua	Yes	No, import permit authorizes purchases of exchange.
Norway	Yes	An authorization to transfer foreign exchange must be obtained from Bank of Norway and will usually be noted on import license.
Pakistan	Yes	Yes, however, foreign exchange is automatically released upon presentation of validated import license to exchange bank.
Panama	No; except for tomato paste; a few items are, however, subject to quota restrictions.	No.
Paraguay	No	Yes, for all shipments except those valued at less than US$133.
Peru	No	No.
Philippine Republic	Yes, except for MSA-financed imports	Possession of a valid import license, if required, entitles holder to exchange cover.
Poland	Yes	Yes.
Portugal (including the Azores and Madeira)	Yes	Yes.
Portuguese colonies	Yes	Yes.
Romania	Yes	Yes.
Singapore	Yes, only certain items may be imported directly from hard-currency sources. Licenses to import nonsterling area goods via Hong Kong are issued provided certain exchange regulations are observed.	Yes, for direct imports. For imports from hard-currency areas via Hong Kong no permit is necessary, but payment must be made in a sterling-area currency and shipment effected on a bill on lading issued in Hong Kong.
Spain, including the Canary Islands	Yes, largely limited to essential raw materials.	Yes, special exchange rates are fixed for many import products.
Spanish colonies	Yes	Import license carries right to foreign exchange.
Surinam	Yes	No, import license carries right to foreign exchange.
Sweden	Yes, except for a few minor products	Yes, however, foreign, exchange, including dollar exchange, is automatically made available if the import license specifies payment in such currency, and if the license is registered with a foreign exchange bank within 2 months after its issuance.
Switzerland	Import licenses are necessary for about 40 percent of Swiss imports. However, licenses for most of these are granted freely.	No difficulty in regard to exchange.
Syria	Yes	Yes.
Taiwan (Formosa)	Yes	Yes, except for Government purchases.
Thailand	No, except for sold passenger cars, motorcycles, and certain paint oils.	No.
Turkey	Yes	Yes, special exchange license from the Control Office, one application suffices for both import permit and exchange control purposes.
Union of South Africa (including Southwest Africa, Basutoland, Bechuanaland, and Swaziland).	Yes, with exception of few specified imports from soft-currency countries, all imports are subject to license issued by the Director of Imports and Exports in the Union. Imports from all countries of a long list of "unessential" items are prohibited.	The import license carries right to foreign exchange up to amount expressed in local currency in relative import license.
United Kingdom	Yes, except for a few products.	Yes.
Uruguay	Yes	No, import license carries right to foreign exchange.
USSR	Yes, importing Government agencies are responsible for securing own permit.	Yes, all exchange allocated by USSR State Bank upon receipt of import license.
Venezuela	No; except for approximately 25 tariff items	No.
Yugoslavia	No, individual import licenses abolished July 1, 1952; since that time only licensed import firms are allowed to carry on import operations.	No, but Government maintains strict control over foreign exchange allocations.

Source: **20**, April 27, 1953, pp. 13-15.

a. Includes Bermuda, British West Indies, British East and West Africa, British Guiana, British Honduras, Northern Rhodesia, Southern Rhodesia, and minor colonies, protectorates, and trusteeship territories.

b. Butter requires individual permits. Swine and uncooked pork from the United States are prohibited under the Animal Contagious Disease Act.

c. All Chinese mainland ports are under Communist control and the U.S. government prohibits exports to Communist China.

d. No license is required when shipment is financed by importer with his own funds held abroad.

The Significance of U.S. Policy

The question of tariff policy is likewise under consideration in the United States.

Referring to the escape clause in the Trade Agreements Extension Act of 1951, various industries are demanding withdrawal of tariff concessions the United States has made since 1934 and restoration of the duties under the Hawley-Smoot tariff of 1930. Opposition to further reduction of import duties has been stiffening.

On the other hand, resolute liberalization of trade policy is advocated by many students of international affairs; by some farseeing business and industrial leaders; and by statesmen concerned with national security.

Practically, the controversy resolves itself into weighing the interests of particular industries and localities against broader economic and political considerations. It is recognized that reduction of import duties on certain commodities can affect the interests of producers, result in laying off workers and adversely affect economic conditions in the area in which the respective industry is located. The controversial question is when does the impact of tariff liberalization constitute a "serious injury" to the industry in the sense of the Extension Acts of 1948 and 1951? Often the dispute boils down to whether the affected industry can readjust and shift to production of other articles.

Spokesmen of strict protectionism consider the readjustment argument contrary to the intent of the escape clause. This view was clearly expressed by two members of the Tariff Commission dissenting from the majority decision regarding a trivial but typical case:

More important . . . in our judgment, is the fallacy involved in the theory that producers of a particular product cannot be found to be seriously injured because of the possibility that they might cease the production of the item in question, and undertake increased production of other items or convert their operations to importing, thus retaining their markets, but abandoning their functions as producers of the product in question. We believe that any such interpretation will defeat the purpose of the escape-clause legislation. An interpretation of the escape clause which results in the elimination of many small industries on the uncertain ground that producers in those industries could shift to other lines of production, leaving the market in the United States for the particular products under consideration to foreign producers, surely does violence to the intent of Congress. [160]

Some people believe that the government must help industries and communities which are seriously affected by competition of foreign products admitted to the domestic market as the result of a reduction in import duties.[161] Others contend that shifts from less to more productive and remunerative activities take place continuously in a growing and dynamic economy; that competition of foreign products is a minor factor in such shifts; that continuous readjustments under the pressure of competition is vital for economic and technical progress. The Chamber of Commerce of the United States summarizes the argument in the general statement that under a free enterprise system, increased competitive pressure impels the flow of capital and labor toward more productive and hence more profitable activities.[162]

From this viewpoint, the competition released by reciprocal concessions in the tariff ultimately has a salutary effect on both parties by compelling them to adjust their production to the conditions of their natural resources, labor supply, means of transportation and other factors.

The problem of orienting trade policy appears less controversial when approached from the angle of broad economic and political interests. The protectionist argument, as developed by Alexander Hamilton and Friedrich List, is valid when it is used by underdeveloped countries attempting to establish new industries especially designed to process local raw materials for the domestic market and for export. In certain cases, a protectionist policy is likewise defensible for political and military reasons. But absolute self-sufficiency cannot be considered a goal of economic policy in a modern nation. As time goes on, the United States and Europe become increasingly dependent on imports of certain raw materials and foodstuffs. The answer to this challenge is a policy of freer interplay of world markets and free access for all to the supplies of respective goods rather than partition of the world economy into isolated quasi-independent units.

---

160. Quoted in **50**, p. 35.
161. This is the substance of the proposal made by David J. McDonald, a member of the Commission on Foreign Economic Policy (Randall Commission).
162. **50**, p. 34.

The most serious implications of U.S. trade policy are political. The common interest of the United States and other free nations confronting the threat of a new war requires strengthening their economic and social fabric and establishing close and continuous cooperation among themselves. With financial and economic aid from the United States, the free nations of the world were able to overcome the dangers they faced in the critical postwar years. The price the United States taxpayers were asked to pay was not too high when compared to the sacrifices which would have been demanded of them in the event of economic collapse and political disintegration in strategic areas of Western Europe. But the problem of lasting economic equilibrium is far from solved. Its new phase is characterized by the dilemma: trade or aid. The choice will be between sporadic aid to areas in extreme need and the liberalization of foreign trade and restoration of the "self-regulating" mechanism of international transactions. A drastic reduction of trade barriers by the United States alone cannot solve this problem but joint efforts of the United States and other free nations can contribute to its solution.

The program of United States trade and tariff policy advanced by the Public Advisory Board for Mutual Security appointed by President Truman in 1952 (Bell Report) was largely inspired by these considerations. The Board made the following recommendations:

1. That decisions on trade policy be based on national interest, rather than the interest of particular industries or groups; that in cases where choice must be made between injury to the national interest and hardship to an industry, the industry be helped to make adjustments by means other than excluding import — such as through extension of unemployment insurance, assistance in retraining workers, diversification of production, and conversion to other lines.

2. That a new, simplified tariff act be adopted, providing for general reductions of duties and eliminating present uncertainties in the classification of goods by consolidating . . . into seven basic schedules: a Free List, . . . bearing duties of 10, 20, 30, and 40 percent ad valorem, a Specific List for basic agricultural and mineral raw materials, and an Extraordinary List where commodities might be placed whose importation, for security or other reasons, should be limited by quotas or other restrictions, or by exceptionally high rates. . . .

3. That the President be authorized to enter into reciprocal trade agreements without limit of time and with power to reduce tariffs, within specified limits, in return for reductions in tariffs or restrictions by other countries.

4. That, as an interim measure, customs procedures be simplified by prompt passage of a bill similar to that recommended by the Treasury and passed by the House of Representatives in 1951; that a commission be created to study and propose further measures of customs simplification.

5. That tariffs be reduced, and quotas on agricultural products be liberalized to allow the freer import of goods that are not produced in this country in sufficient quantity at world prices; that section 104 of the Defense Production Act, restricting the import of certain agricultural products, be repealed.

6. That tariffs be reduced and in some cases ultimately eliminated on metals and minerals of which imports are a major part of the United States supplies; that, where necessary for defense reasons, domestic production be encouraged through special purchases or contracts rather than tariffs.

7. That import excise taxes now applying to petroleum products be dropped; that, if imports reach a level where they impede domestic exploration and development, other measures be taken to assure a domestic industry adequate to defense needs.

8. That cargo preference, by which 50 per cent of the cargo on aid and loan shipments is reserved to domestic carriers, not be applied to countries that let American shippers compete on a fair basis.

9. That the procurement policies of the Government which raise the cost of goods bought by the Government be reconsidered in the light of principles and objectives of a foreign trade policy in the national interest.

10. That the Congress take the necessary steps to enable the United States to join in establishing an international organization to promote the objectives of the General Agreement on Tariffs and Trade (GATT); that active participation be continued in other international organizations to promote fair exchange and fair labor practices and the flow of investment capital.[163]

These recommendations deserve attention more as an expression of the goals of a liberal trade policy than as an outline of forthcoming action by the President and the Congress. The change of Administration called for a general revision of U.S. tariff policy within the framework of its foreign economic policy. In accordance with the Act of Congress of August 7, 1953, a commission was appointed to reexamine the international relationships of the United States in

---

163. **26**, pp. 1–2.

the economic field. This commission, headed by Clarence B. Randall, submitted its report to the President and the Congress on January 23, 1954. The foreign economic policy which it recommended rests on three fundamental principles:

1. The freest possible opportunity for the development of individual talents and initiative in the utilization of private resources and through the free association of workers.

2. The maintenance of vigorous, but fair, competition.

3. The maintenance of a broad free market for goods and services.[164]

The report stressed that "the nations of the free world would be stronger and more cohesive if many of the existing barriers to the exchange of their goods were reduced, if unnecessary uncertainties and delays created by such barriers were eliminated, and if adequate international arrangements for discussing and finding solutions to their common trade problems were developed and maintained." [165]

It recommended liberalization of the Buy American Act, simplification of the tariff and customs regulations, maintenance of the m.f.n. principle and strengthening of the President's power to negotiate trade agreements for reduction of duties. Retaining the escape-clause and the peril-point provisions in the existing Trade Agreements Act, the report advised that the law "should be amended expressly to spell out the fact that the President is authorized to disregard findings under these provisions whenever he finds that the national interest of the United States requires it." [166]

The Randall report thus recommended a liberalization of the foreign trade policy of the United States. Fundamentally, it accepted the principle of protectionism but rejected extreme protectionism and isolationism. It seems fairly certain that the foreign trade policy of the country will be determined by a compromise between the ideas expressed in the report and those of its critics who demand more protection for domestic producers. This suggests a continuation of the trade agreements policy, with only minor deviations from the present course.

The growth of inter-European trade and the restoration of trade between Europe and Asia seem more probable in the near future than does a substantial increase in European exports to the United States. As shown by Howard S. Piquet, suspension of all U.S. tariffs and quotas would have increased imports to the United States by $1.2 to $2.6 billion. Suspension of tariffs alone would have increased imports by $800 million to $1.8 billion. Among the principal beneficiaries would be Cuba and Canada, two countries that have not experienced serious balance-of-payments difficulties.[167] Drastic reductions in U.S. import duties, short of their complete repeal, would provide only a temporary increase in dollar earnings (a few hundred million dollars) for those European countries suffering from balance-of-payments difficulties, but would not solve the problems of world trade. It would leave unsolved such problems as international flow of capital, foreign investment and currency stability. The tariff policy of the United States is a question of considerable significance for the well-being of the free nations, but it is not the key to world peace and prosperity.

---

164. **25**, p. 2.
165. **25**, p. 45.
166. **25**, p. 51.

---

167. **79**, p. 348. The figures refer to 1951.

PART II. TRANSPORTATION

CHAPTER 7

TRANSPORTATION IN THE WORLD ECONOMY

TRANSPORTATION is geared inextricably to the working of the entire economy. It links space-bound agriculture and industry with other parts of a country and the world, and serves them in a thousand and one ways. Trade has always been closely associated with transportation. In early days, production, trade and transportation were often integrated, the producer himself taking his goods to market as he still does in areas with a primitive economy.[1] As distances between producers and consumers lengthened and the volume of trade grew, differentiation — from producer to merchant and from merchant to consumer — became increasingly pronounced.[2] But even after trade became a specialized branch of the economy, differentiated from agriculture and handicrafts, it maintained a close association with transportation. Only at a comparatively high level of economic development did transportation become a specialized economic activity, separated from both production and trade. Today, trade and transportation, though closely integrated, represent highly specialized and complex segments of the national and world economy.

The need for transportation in the technical sense of this term — that is, for overcoming space and conveying goods and persons from one place to another — must have existed even in prehistoric times. Overland means of transportation, however, were limited to human portage, until man learned to domesticate animals and utilize their draft power. Having discovered at an early date how to move on water, men settled preferably along the streams and lake shores.

In land transportation, the most important event was the invention of the wheel; in water transportation, the use of a sail. These discoveries stimulated the movement of goods and people in peacetime, and particularly during war. Though the transit was slow, grain and other foodstuffs were shipped to vast cities in Asia, and from various parts of the Mediterranean to

the large population of Rome. Building materials were transported to erect pyramids and palaces — more often than not at an enormous cost of human effort and life.[3]

In early times, the interests of the state dominated most transport. The road systems of China (about 2000–1500 B.C.), of Persia (500 B.C.) and of Rome were built primarily to serve the state. The governments in Greece and Rome owned vessels for grain transport. A few merchantship owners in Rome operated on their own account, but the state requisitioned the vessels in time of war.[4]

In general, costs of transport were high, the quantities of goods transported comparatively small, and the hazards great, particularly for private business. Caravans and vessels laden with merchandise were frequently ransacked by marauders or fell victim to the power of the elements. Only commodities of high value and relatively light weight could be transported over long distances — tea, spices, silk, precious stones, jewelry — to satisfy the demand of those who could indulge in such luxuries.

With the growth of population and expansion of production and trade, the volume of transportation increased but its basic features remained unchanged. In the 1700's a vehicle moving cargo over the twenty-mile stretch from Halle to Leipzig, Germany, needed from three to four days for the trip because "merchandise articles had to be transported bodily over stones and rocks, or the horse and the vehicle had to be lifted out of a 3–4 foot deep mire." Even in 1850, before railroads were introduced throughout Europe, it took a team of twenty-four horses to move a steam boiler from Aachen, Germany to Warsaw.[5] Adam Smith wrote in his *Wealth of Nations* (1776) that in his time "a broadwheeled wagon, attended by two men, and

---

3. Astonishingly, the Mayas, who did not know the wheel, succeeded in moving huge blocks of stone and marble to build stately monuments to their gods and rulers.

4. **35**, pp. 277–78.

5. **29**, p. 175. Cf. also Chapter 8.

1. Cf. Chapter 1.
2. Cf. **31**, p. 10.

drawn by eight horses in about six weeks' time carries and brings back, between London and Edinburgh, near four tons' weight of goods." [6] Indeed, the means of transport were the same in Napoleon's time as in King David's: shanks' mare and draft animals on land, oar and sail on water.

Revolution in transport came in the nineteenth century, when steam became the motive power, and iron and steel began to be used for equipment. Railroads were built to link land areas, and steamships to girdle the globe. The twentieth century brought two new mediums of transportation — the motor vehicle and the airplane.[7]

Progress in transportation in the past hundred years or so has radically changed the world that men knew previously. There are few inaccessible spots on our planet, and even the atmosphere around us — during all preceding existence of mankind "merely so much air for man to breathe" [8] — has been crisscrossed with thoroughfares in all directions. In terms of time, New York is now closer to Tokyo than it was to Philadelphia in the days of the thirteen colonies.[9]

The revolution in transportation has come through the interplay of many factors — economic, technological and political — such as the growth of industry and commerce; the development of technology and its spread throughout the world; the shift of power from the ruling classes to large groups of the population engaged in productive activities; and the rising standards of living. If the inventions related to transportation had come in the Middle Ages, when production and trade were relatively small and barriers to the movement of people and goods were erected at each estate and town, they probably would have remained on the drawing boards, like so many sketches of Leonardo da Vinci.[10] As it was, innovations in the transport system came when the demand for them was urgent and conditions for their utilization were ripe. Railroads could spread out and shipping could increase because the growing coal industry supplied them abundantly with coal for steam power. Rolling stock and merchant tonnage

could multiply in volume because steel of steadily improving quality was available. Increase in the volume of production stimulated the demand for transportation, and expansion of the transportation system, in turn, aided the growth of production.

PROGRESS IN TRANSPORTATION

Progress in transportation from the middle of the nineteenth century to our day epitomizes the development of the modern economy: the growth of population, particularly in Europe and the Western Hemisphere, mass migration, growth of agricultural and industrial production, advance in the interregional, international and intercontinental division of labor.

The volume of transportation has reflected that of production, not only in its long-range growth but also in short-run fluctuations caused by changes in business conditions. In Germany, for example, the curve for railroad traffic — expressed in passenger- and ton-kilometers per one kilometer of railway — and the curve for pig iron consumption per capita — as a yardstick reflecting business fluctuations — ran parallel between 1872 and 1913.[11] Edwin Frickey has likewise demonstrated the amazingly close relationship between the volume of transportation as a whole and manufacturing production in the United States between 1860 and 1914. (See Figure 54.)

As the rhythm of growth pulsated throughout economic life, the volume of transport swelled from a meandering streamlet to a massive unbroken flow. Speed increased substantially; yet, despite the much greater speed of today's traffic, modern transportation provides greater safety than the slow traffic of earlier times. The regularity and dependability of transportation facilities have become commonplace, while the costs of transporting cargo and of travel have been notably reduced.

Volume

We have no statistical data for comparing the volume of transportation in the world in our time with that at the beginning of the nineteenth century. Only fragmentary records have been preserved in a few countries. The railroads of the United States reported 39.3 billion ton-miles in 1882, 141.6 billion in 1900, 450.2 billion in 1929 and 649.8 billion in 1951. The net tonnage

---

6. **37,** Chapter 3, p. 9.
7. For a more detailed description of development of various types of transportation see Chapter 8 on railroads; Chapter 9 on motor vehicles; Chapter 10 on water transportation; and Chapter 11 on air transportation.
8. **36,** p. 334.
9. **26,** p. 11.
10. Cf. **28,** p. 50.

11. Cf. **35,** p. 173.

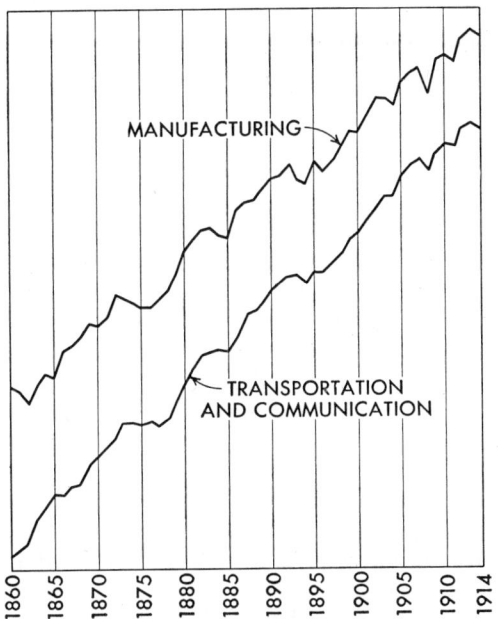

FIGURE 54. TRANSPORTATION AND MANUFACTURING:
INDEXES OF VOLUME OF MANUFACTURING PRO-
DUCTION AND TRANSPORTATION AND COM-
MUNICATION SERVICES, UNITED STATES,
1860–1914

The indexes in this figure are plotted on a logarithmic
vertical scale. A curve plotted in this way has the same
slope when the index changes in the same proportion,
regardless of the level on which the change occurs. Thus,
a change from 100 to 110 is represented by the same
slope as changes from 50 to 55 or from 500 to 550.
The position of the curves in relation to each other is
irrelevant (e.g., the fact that the curve of manufacturing
is plotted above that of transportation and communication). Only the direction of each curve in each period of
time counts.

of ships in foreign trade entering U.S. ports was
3.7 million in 1850, 18.0 million in 1880, 28.2
million in 1900, 82.6 million in 1929, 86.6 million in 1950 and 113.1 million in 1952.[12] Swedish railroads accounted for 648.5 million ton-
kilometers in 1895, 2 billion in 1910, 4.0 billion
in 1935 and 10.0 billion in 1951.[13] In France, the
railroads reported 38 million ton-kilometers in
1841, 16.6 billion in 1900 and 47.7 billion in
1929. Ton-mileage dropped during the depression years, and again during the war and German occupation. In 1947 the volume of operations on the nationalized railroad system began
to grow and in 1951 it considerably exceeded the

prewar level (45.4 and 32.5 billion ton-kilometers, respectively).[14]

The development of passenger traffic has been
no less impressive. Once facilities for faster,
cheaper, and more comfortable travel were established, the number of passengers began to multiply. In France, 6.4 million travelers availed themselves of railroad accommodations as early as
1841, and in 1930 — less than a century later —
812 million.[15] With some variations, this picture
is repeated for every modern type of transportation and in every country that has been improving its transportation system. The total number
of passengers using modern types of transportation today may be many hundred times greater
than when the new era in transportation was
ushered in.

Equipment

In all branches of transportation, growth in
operations went hand in hand with technical
improvement in equipment. Expanding operations required more and larger ships and railroad cars, while improved facilities stimulated
larger shipments.

As long as sea-going ships were built of wood
and propelled by sail, their size was limited to
about 300 feet for stability and because sails
could not move larger vessels. Thus they had
about the same carrying capacity in 1840 as in
antiquity. With the shift to steel and steam, ships
began to increase in size and could handle larger
cargoes. The increase in size has been of particular importance in ocean vessels which carry great
quantities of goods over great distances for distribution among a few ports.

Railroad cars are about four times as large as
the earliest ones, but vary considerably in size
from country to country, depending on the structure of the country's economy and its transportation system. Thus freight cars are comparatively
small in the British Isles, where population is
dense and a limited territory is blanketed with
railroads. Since frequent stops are made to discharge comparatively small shipments, freight
cars with a 12-ton capacity appear to be adequate. In contrast, freight cars in the United
States are several times as large, in line with
the longer hauls, fewer stops and larger shipments. (See Table 113.)

14, 1952, p. 171.
    13. **19**, 1950, p. 163 and 1953, p. 151.

    14. **15**, 1951, pp. 152*–53*. Cf. **25**, p. 292.
    15. **15**, 1951, pp. 152*–53*.

TABLE 113

TRANSPORTATION EQUIPMENT: TYPICAL SIZE OF
VESSELS AND FREIGHT CARS, FROM
ANTIQUITY TO 1930

(*Metric Tons*)

| Period and Year | Vessels | | Freight Cars | | |
	Sea	Inland Waters (Rhine)	Great Britain	United States	Ger-many
Antiquity	400	50	—	—	—
Middle Ages					
(1200–1500)	250	50	—	—	—
1500–1800	300	150	—	—	—
1840	500	250	4	10	4
1860	900	500	4	12	6
1880	2,000	700	6	20	10
1900	4,000	1,000	8	36	15
1913	6,000	1,800	10	40	15
1930	9,000	1,350	12	42	16.5

Source: **35**, p. 149.

Speed

Between 1840 and 1940, the speed of transportation increased considerably, especially in the newer types of transportation. The horse-drawn coach still proceeds much as it always has; the speed of canal tugs and passenger boats on rivers has about doubled. It took a hundred years for the railroad and the steamship to increase their speed threefold or a little more. The automobile, starting from a maximum of about 30 miles an hour in 1900, was capable of 75 or more miles an hour in 1940: two and a half times the speed forty years earlier. The airplane, with an initial 50 miles an hour, now makes 300 and more

miles per hour and promises to increase its speed considerably in a not too remote future. (See Table 114.)

Safety

Every new type of transportation has met with general skepticism and distrust of its safety. Dire predictions were made when the coaches and, later, the railroads, appeared; no less gloomy prognostications greeted the motor vehicle and the airplane. Thus, it was of utmost importance for those responsible for the development of new means of transportation, whether the state or a private company, to minimize the accident rate and establish a favorable safety record. While there can be no absolute safety, the greater the relative safety of a means of transportation the more solidly it establishes itself in the users' esteem.[16] Great progress has been achieved in this respect.

Safety in personal travel is usually measured by the number of fatalities per million passenger-miles. This yardstick provides a reasonable measurement of the safety of a specific means of transportation and of improvement in safety over a period of time. It is less conclusive in comparing safety of transportation in different phases of development — for example, travel on passenger trains and airlines in 1936, the first having had some hundred years of experience and the second, relatively few.

---

16. The private automobile is an exception. Despite the great number of fatal accidents every day, its use is spreading. Its conveniences are so great that few people hesitate to use it on account of accidents to which others fall prey.

TABLE 114

SPEED OF TRANSPORTATION: INCREASE BY BRANCH, 1840–1940

(*Miles Per Hour* [a])

Means of Transportation	1840	1860	1880	1900	1910	1920	1930	1940
Horse coach	5	5	5	5	5	5	5	5
Canal tug	2	2	3	4	4	4	4	4
Passenger ship (Rhine)	5	6	8	10	10	11	11	11
Ocean ship	10	15	20	25	30	30	30	35
Railroad	31	40	50	60	60	65	70	100
Automobile	—	—	—	30	45	55	60	75
Airplane	—	—	—	—	50	110	185	300

Source: **35**, p. 161.

a. Data indicate general maximum speed in the world as a whole, not record-breaking performances.

TABLE 115

SAFETY OF TRANSPORTATION: PASSENGER FATALITY RATES, BY BRANCH, IN THE UNITED STATES, 1936–53

(*Number Per 100 Million Passenger-Miles*)

Year	Railroad Passenger Trains	City and Intercity Buses	Domestic Scheduled Airlines	Private Automobiles and Taxis	Privately Operated Planes
1936	0.10	a	10.1[b]	4.5	146
1937	0.09	a	8.4	4.7	137
1938	0.36	a	4.5	3.9	106
1939	0.14	a	1.2	3.7	88
1940	0.34	a	3.1	3.5	63
1941	0.14	0.23	2.3	4.0	47
1942	0.18	0.23	3.7	2.7	...
1943	0.31	0.22	1.4	2.7	...
1944	0.27	0.22	2.1	2.9	...
1945	0.16	0.17	2.1	2.9	...
1946	0.18	0.19	1.2	3.1	...
1947	0.16	0.21	3.2	3.0	...
1948	0.13	0.18	1.3	2.8	...
1949	0.08	0.21	1.3	2.7	...
1950	0.58	0.14	1.1	2.9	...
1951	0.43	0.15	1.3	3.0	...
1952	0.04	0.12	0.35	2.9	...
1953	0.16	0.11	0.58	2.9	...

Sources: **13**, 1950, p. 109: **34**, 1953, p. 77. Data corrected in accordance with information supplied by the National Safety Council in 1955.

a. Included with private cars and taxis.
b. Series began in 1930 with rate of **28.2**. Rates in 1931–35 were, respectively, 23.5, 15.0, 4.6, 9.0 and 4.8. (**8**, p. 223.)

On the whole, all types of transportation show a declining rate of accidents, apart from somewhat erratic annual fluctuations. The railroads and intercity buses in the United States generally have the lowest rate. Private cars and taxis top the list of accident rates, while scheduled domestic airlines lowered their fatality rate from 23.4 per 100 million passenger-miles in 1931 to 2.3 in 1941, 1.3 in 1951 and 0.58 in 1953. (See Table 115.) Privately operated planes had an exceptionally high fatality rate up to 1941; later data are not available. In the United Kingdom, the number of fatalities per 100 million passenger-miles on all scheduled passenger air services averaged 16.9 in 1936–40, 9.8 in 1941–45, 6.5 in 1946–48 and 3.0 in 1948–52.[17]

Travel by all means of transportation, and particularly by automobile, involves some element of danger due to possible defects in equipment, adverse weather and human failures. Nevertheless, safety seems almost absolute in comparison with conditions a century or so ago,

when many persons made a will before entrusting themselves to a public vehicle.[18]

In freight traffic, the problem is somewhat different. Both the shipper and the consignee are most interested in having merchandise arrive in good condition, with a minimum of handling. Today there are almost no products, no matter how fragile or perishable, which cannot be transported over long distances without breakage or spoilage. This is in sharp contrast to times not so remote when, for example, a glass factory near Paris expected that, on the average, only one out of each six glasses shipped the short distance to the city would arrive unbroken.[19]

Reduction in Cost

The most significant feature of progress in transportation has been the lowering of cost, particularly for freight. Before World War I, it cost about as much to transport one ton of merchandise over a distance of 2,500–3,000 miles as it had cost in 1850 to transport it some 50–

17. **17**, 1953, p. 235. For 1941–45: excludes accidents connected with enemy action and other war operations.

18. **21**, p. 204.

19. **25**, p. 273.

60 miles.[20] On the average, freight rates fell 95 per cent or more in this period; passenger rates, about 50 per cent; and service improved greatly.[21]

The sharp reduction in rates took place in the early period of railroad and steamship growth and was consummated by the end of the nineteenth century. Afterwards, rates continued to decline because of technical and managerial improvements, but much more gradually. For example, the cost of transporting a bushel of wheat from Chicago to New York by rail was 46.1 cents in 1866. It fell to 14.3 cents by 1890, was 12.3 cents in 1897 and 11.3 in 1907.[22]

In the twentieth century, when both the railroads and the steamships became part and parcel of the world's economic system, their rates fluctuated in line with prevailing business conditions and also frequently depended, in the case of railroads, on public regulations.

THE EFFECTS OF PROGRESS IN TRANSPORTATION

Improved transportation has greatly contributed to the economic growth of nations and the world. Its impact has been felt in the specialization and volume of production and trade, the location of industries, equalization of prices and supplies, diversification of consumption. It also has greatly influenced social and political life in individual countries and the world as a whole. It has encouraged migration, stimulated mobility of labor and personal travel, promoted closer contacts among nations and individuals and contributed to the political unification of various countries.

ECONOMIC IMPACT

Specialization

Everything except air — soil, climate and mineral resources — is unevenly distributed over the globe. Differences in soil and climate and in the physical requirements of plants account for the great variety of agricultural products. Minerals, essential to our civilization, are found where the geological development of the earth left them — some in only a few areas of the world, some in areas where there is no demand for them.[23]

Effective and economical transportation enables each area to specialize in the production for which it is best fitted and to exchange its products for those of other regions. In the United States, the nation takes cotton from the South, grain from the Middle West, citrus fruit from California, Florida and Texas, anthracite from Pennsylvania, oil from Texas, Louisiana and some other states; tobacco from Connecticut, Virginia, Kentucky and Maryland. Thanks to the highly developed system of transportation, no state is too far from production centers, and no production center is limited to the adjacent area for its market.

Regional specialization in agriculture was greatly stimulated by the development of railroad systems. As early as 1880, De Foville wrote that, thanks to the great mobility which the French railroads had given to agricultural produce, "the farmer in his selection of crops to plant has today to consult less the particular demand of local consumption than the productive capacity of his soil. Assured of outlets for his produce at good prices and equally certain of ruinous competition for goods produced at too high cost, he now has only one choice: to consult his soil, decide what it can best produce, and plant accordingly. This is, so to speak, to apply to agriculture the fruitful principle of division of labor. We see each region of France becoming more and more specialized. Wheat is grown in the valleys, oats on plateaus . . . sugar beets invade whole districts in the north, colza supplants hemp and flax in Normandy; the south was about to transform itself into one huge vineyard before phylloxera declared war on it." [24]

The people of the United Kingdom depend on foodstuffs brought from all points of the compass; they supply many countries with textiles made of wool from Uruguay, of cotton from the United States, India and Egypt, and of jute from Pakistan. German tanneries depend on hides and skins from Argentina, Uruguay and India. Spanish and Italian peasants specialize in fruits and vegetables and modern transportation makes it possible to move such perishable produce to all corners of Europe. The natives of Java produce rubber and the Malayans extract tin — for which they have little use — and ship their products to the ends of the world. Guatemala raises more coffee and bananas than it can possibly consume

---

20. **29**, p. 1230.
21. **21**, p. 205.
22. **7**, p. 20. The rate for domestic consumption in 1907; that for exported wheat was lower.
23. **41**, Chapters 10, 15 and 22.

24. **25**, pp. 264–65. Authors' translation.

because these products can be shipped to markets which demand them.

Without improved transportation, communities would still live as in primitive times, obliged to produce the sheer essentials of life, whether or not physical conditions favored such production. Local deposits of low-grade ores would have to be mined; small streams would have to be used for power; and crops raised for which soil or climate was ill-adapted.[25] Local materials would have to be used in building, with possibly the same paradoxes as prevailed in medieval France: where marble was available, even barns and stalls were built of it, while in other areas dwellings were built of chalk and covered with mud. As soon as stone could be moved at reasonable prices, Paris, which has no hard stone in the vicinity, began to bring it in from the Côte-d'Or, the Vosges, Brittany and even Belgium.[26] Similarly, valuable deposits of minerals would have remained useless, like some coal and iron ore mines in the United States that were only ten or fifteen miles apart.[27] In contrast, modern transportation enables the United States to utilize iron ore from Venezuela, and various European countries to use coal from the United States.

Some generally available materials can be produced in certain regions only in quantities that are now wholly inadequate to satisfy the demand in urban areas. Kent T. Healy cites the example of New England towns that once were able to obtain fuelwood, building materials and food from neighboring areas. As the small towns grew to large cities, this was no longer possible. Today they get coal from Pennsylvania and West Virginia; oil from Texas; building materials from the forests of the Pacific Coast and the South, and from the limestone quarries of New York and Pennsylvania; grain and meat from the Middle West.[28] In the same way, countries and continents supplement one another. In the world as a whole, this specialization has resulted in a gradual division of countries into primarily agricultural and primarily industrial, with some countries maintaining a mixed economy.[29]

The more countries of different economic structure depend on international division of labor, the greater is their need for efficient and cheap transportation. In general, the areas of greatest specialization and the highest economic development are those with the greatest need and facilities for transportation.[30]

Large-Scale Production

Dependable and cheap transportation has been among the decisive factors encouraging large-scale production. Bulky raw materials that once were space-bound, such as coal, ore, fertilizers and textile fibers, became the main products in international commerce. Reliance on coal supplies for steam power and on cheap assembly of raw materials stimulated industrial production on a large scale. The concomitant factor was the certainty that transport facilities would match the upswing in production and move finished goods to markets anywhere in the world. Factories mushroomed along the railroads, which became a kind of "industry road," and railroad centers became industrial centers.

Steamships bridged the Atlantic between the Western Hemisphere and Europe. Over this bridge moved a continuous stream of tools, machinery, other equipment and various finished goods from Europe. In the opposite direction moved grain, cotton, tobacco and other produce for the rapidly increasing population and expanding industries in the "old countries." Millions of people rushed in over this bridge, to populate the New World, cultivate its soil, process its raw materials and build its factories. With a growing domestic market and world markets, both made accessible by fast and dependable transportation, large-scale production in the United States became feasible and gained increasing momentum.

The Location of Industry

The cost and quality of transportation are among the important factors affecting the location of industry. The site of a factory is usually selected so as to minimize the cumulative cost of assembling raw materials and transporting finished products. Low freight rates on raw materials and relatively high rates on manufactured products tend to draw the plant toward the consuming market, and away from the source of raw materials. For industries which process

25. Cf. **21**, p. 210.
26. **25**, p. 272.
27. **26**, p. 13; **33**, p. 37.
28. **28**, p. 42.
29. Cf. **41**, Chapter 13.

30. Cf. **35**, p. 20.

weight-reducible raw materials — such as ore — high rates on raw materials tend to attract manufacturing to the source of supply, to avoid the costs of transporting waste.

The higher the share of transportation in total production costs, the greater the influence of freight cost. High freight rates on raw materials and other supplies generally encourage decentralization of industries, while low rates permit an industry to establish its plants on a national basis.[31]

Equalization of Prices

As early as 1880 De Foville described the effect of improved transportation on prices. He compared the prices of the same product in different communities to a liquid in connected vessels, which moves until the level is equalized, then remains stable. Prices follow a similar course. When better transportation becomes available, prices in different communities begin to approach one another, falling where they once were relatively high and rising where they were low.[32]

Without cheap transport, bumper crops in one area may be disposed of at any price or be left to rot, while the same crop may command exorbitant prices in a deficiency area. Such a situation was dramatically illustrated in the early 1930's when a severe famine struck the interior section of China. Wheat, a glut on the market in the United States, could have been transported to Shanghai for about a dollar a bushel but it was not sent because it would have cost another $11 per bushel to move the grain from Shanghai to the famine districts.[33]

Effective and cheap transportation tends to equalize prices and makes it possible to establish central markets that rely on many sources for their supplies and a large number of consumers and therefore are less subject to extreme price fluctuations. For some commodities, such as grain, cotton, wool and copper, prices are established on world markets. In such cases, prices in producing areas vary from world prices roughly by the amount of the costs related to transportation.[34]

Diversification of Consumption

As long as the system of self-sufficiency prevailed in the world economy and transportation charges were heavy, patterns of consumption depended on local products and handicrafts. With improvement in transportation, merchandise could be moved at reasonable expense from areas of relatively low production costs to consuming centers. Thus, the coffee of Brazil, cacao of the Gold Coast, copper of the Belgian Congo, tin of Bolivia, hides and skins of Uruguay and India, French textiles, Italy's leather goods and thousands of other products began to move through the channels of international trade by ship, railroad, motor truck and plane. Traders began to search from pole to pole for products to satisfy or incite demand. Goods that cannot be sent in a natural state are processed at the place of production and then shipped to markets wherever demand calls for them.

Today any department store in the United States may reflect the production of the entire world: Panama hats, Mexican shoes and silver, Japanese silk, French perfumes, English china, Swedish glass, Italian scarves, Canadian woolens, Australian angora sweaters and so on. Dime stores offer flower bulbs from Holland and baskets from Cuba; any food store may carry Danish or Polish ham, Dutch cheese, Swiss chocolate, India tea and various other specialties from abroad, to say nothing of a variety of domestic goods from every part of the country. Kings and queens of earlier times could not obtain many of the products that fill shops today and bid for mass consumption. Workers' families eat what once only the rich could afford. Strawberries, for example, which used to come from hothouses in winter to glorify a few illustrious dinner tables, now are marketed in chain stores in off seasons. Bananas from trees thousands of miles away have become as common in the temperate zone as home-grown apples.

Progress in transportation does not deserve the whole credit for these changes in consumption, but it has helped to bring the world's products even to the smallest towns and the farms.

The Value of Land

The value of land suitable for agricultural production or rich in minerals or forests depends, to a great extent, on its distance from adequate transportation facilities. Land that lies close to a railroad or a navigable waterway com-

---

31. **40,** pp. 78–79. For a detailed analysis of the influence of transportation on the location of industry, see **23,** pp. 452–79.

32. **25,** p. 224.

33. **31,** p. 9.

34. **32,** p. 2.

mands a higher price than similar land in a re-mote corner of the country because the cost of transportation may make it impossible to market agricultural products or develop local natural resources.[35] In the prerailroad era, produce on remote farms was of little value. For example, shipment of a ton of grain over 100 miles of highway in the United States cost $15 in the middle of the nineteenth century. With the average price of corn around $25 per ton, its value on a farm 100 miles from the market was about $10; 150 miles away, around $2. Wheat had a higher market value — around $50 a ton — and was still worth some $27 a ton to the farmer if transported over 150 miles, but it brought him only $4–$5 per ton when he raised it 300 miles from the market. In contrast, the railroads charged $4–$5 to transport a ton of grain 300 miles, which enabled the farmer living at that distance from the market to net more than $20 per ton of corn and $45 per ton of wheat.[36] As a result, produce could be brought to markets and the value of land along the railroad or close to it increased. The westward extension of railroads in the United States greatly raised the value of fertile adjacent land. In comparison, less productive agricultural land in the East lost some of its former value as areas distant from eastern markets gained access to western produce. Part of the eastern land, however, later acquired values of a different sort when it began to be used for factories and homes in cities and their suburbs.[37]

SOCIAL AND POLITICAL IMPACT

Improved transportation has produced effective and lasting changes in the composition of population and its social and political structure in vast parts of the world.

Migration

The availability of long-distance transportation has encouraged millions of people to leave overpopulated native lands. More than 36 million left Europe between 1870 and 1915, almost all for the Western Hemisphere. The advertising campaigns of steamship companies helped to sell the New World to workers and peasants of Europe, suffering from limited work opportuni-ties and lack of land.[38] Other millions settled in Australia and other parts of Oceania, while some returned to their native land. On the whole, the world's population underwent widespread redistribution.

Within large countries, transportation has facilitated internal migration to uninhabited areas. Settlement of the West in the United States and Canada gained momentum rapidly after the transcontinental railroads were built.

Labor became more mobile when transportation facilities enabled workers to shift more easily from low-wage areas to more promising places. The automobile, in particular, has made it possible for workers in the United States to go where demand is greater and wages are higher.

Urbanization

Improved transportation has been a significant factor in stimulating urbanization. There were large concentrations of population in antiquity, but providing food and other essentials for them was an onerous task of centralized governments, and their existence often depended on the fortunes of war. Moreover, such centers were always established where water transportation was available. Improved transportation stimulated growth of inland cities, where large populations were assured of supplies from near and far in any needed quantity.[39]

Urban centers, in turn, have created much transportation by the practice of commuting from outlying areas, and the need for intercity and intracity travel and freight transport.

Political Unification

The role of improved transportation in cementing national unity can hardly be exaggerated. Before the railroad to the Pacific was built, the western part of the United States could be reached only by a long hazardous journey across prairies and mountains or by a long ocean passage via Cape Horn. Once the railroad linked West and East, California was drawn much closer to the Union. Likewise, the transcontinental railroads in Canada, Australia and Russia have established closer contacts between parts of their far-flung territories. In Canada, for example, the government undertook to link the Maritime Provinces with Lower and Upper

35. **32**, p. 3; **3**, April–June 1953, p. 24.
36. **30**, November 6, 1852, p. 705.
37. **39**, p. 7.

38. **41**, p. 76.
39. **32**, pp. 9–10.

Canada, its economic heart — areas kept apart through physical barriers and ethnic differences until the railroad joined them.[40]

The political unification of Germany and of Italy was accelerated by the introduction of railways.[41] When Germany was still divided among numerous petty princedoms, Goethe was confident that "good roads and coming railways will do the job of unification." [42]

Culture

Improved transportation has made travel more comfortable, yet cheaper and faster. What was once a luxury, accessible only to a royal purse, is now within reach of modest pocketbooks. When Louis XIV wanted to travel, Colbert had to send the following orders to the country authorities: "Let fill the bad holes with stones if these are at hand; otherwise, with dirt and wood; or you can use the third method, namely of opening the fields and breaking the fences to fill the road for the King's passage. These are means always used to ease the King's voyage in all provinces his Majesty passes." [43]

Now one does not need to be a king to drive a vehicle without worrying about holes in the road. Automobiles and improved highways "have done more in twenty years to develop the habit of travel . . . than any other means of transportation did during a century." [44] The railroad's travel facilities are available to those who will go to a railroad station, but the motor vehicle makes travel from door to door possible.

With the newer means of transportation, travel for pleasure and relaxation has increased both within national borders and among countries. Tourism has become a world-wide industry and has strengthened cultural contacts among peoples and inspired interest in ways of life in other parts of the world. Provincialism and sectionalism still exist but to a far lesser degree than even a few decades ago.

Country people have gained access to specialized medical services and city hospitals, often better equipped than those in small towns. Regular delivery of mail and newspapers has been as-

sured. Buses have made it possible to consolidate schools in sparsely populated areas thereby improving educational opportunities for country children. Life on farms is no longer isolated.

CHARACTERISTICS OF THE FOUR BRANCHES OF TRANSPORTATION

In primitive countries, animals and human beings provide the motive power for a large part of all transportation; in modern systems, railroads, motor vehicles, ships and aircraft are the main transportation facilities.[45]

Each of these four main forms of transportation uses many types of equipment to move freight and people. The equipment of the railroad may include light steam locomotives or giant diesel units; simple platforms for freight or elaborate specialized cars; simple coaches or sleeping cars. Highway transport uses all kinds of vehicles: from ox carts to trucks, passenger cars, trailers, semitrailers and so on. An even greater variety of equipment characterizes transport on water, from junks, rafts and sail boats to luxurious liners. Aircraft may range from a one-seat plane to huge planes capable of carrying nearly a hundred persons.

Within each type of transportation, there are common carriers, serving all patrons; contract carriers, operating according to special arrangements for private companies or individuals; and private carriers owned and controlled by private firms, such as steel companies or distribution enterprises or even private individuals. Some carriers operate on an international scale, such as steamship and air lines; others, on a national, regional or local scale.

The organizational structure within each type of transportation is highly diverse. It may be concentrated in a few great firms, in nationalized systems or dispersed among thousands of small enterprises.[46]

The four branches of transportation vary greatly in their characteristics and capabilities.

Capacity

The railroads' capacity is greater than that of any other type of transportation. They can move a far greater tonnage of freight than ships or

---

40. **26**, p. 9.

41. Friedrich List, who spent many years in promoting the construction of railways in Germany, saw them primarily as the instrument of his country's unification.

42. **29**, p. 1240; cf. **3**, April–June 1953, pp. 25–26.

43. **24**, p. 19.

44. **22**, pp. 25–26.

45. Pipelines, a subsurface type of transportation, are discussed in the first volume of this study. (See **41**, pp. 909–13 and 921.)

46. **22**, p. 65.

trucks can carry. Only exceptional circumstances may force a railroad company to close the gates to passengers, while shortage of passenger space on a ship, bus or plane is common. Thus, the railroads are, in the fullest sense of the term, a *mass transportation* medium.

No type of transportation, however, fully utilizes its capacity. Fluctuations in business conditions create a heavy demand for transport at some times, and at other times, little demand. In addition, the equipment is specialized and therefore not interchangeable.

For example, the railroads cannot use their coal cars to transport foodstuffs and must return them empty if no other suitable cargo, such as ore, is available. A shift in passenger cars from higher-priced to lower-priced accommodations, or vice versa, is rare. A bus cannot take on freight, nor can an oil tanker be used for other purposes than carrying oil. It is estimated that the average utilization of both freight and passenger transportation by all means in the world, taken as a whole, is less than 50 per cent. The lowest utilization in passenger transport is by the railroads — less than 30 per cent; the highest by airplanes (47 per cent) and buses (48 per cent). In moving freight, the equipment on inland waterways is estimated to utilize about 38–39 per cent of its capacity on the average; the railroads use 45 per cent; ocean shipping, airplanes and trucks, about 46 per cent; and canal equipment, more than 51 per cent.[47] Within this range there are many deviations. In moving less-than-carload freight over short distances, the railroads utilize only 18 per cent of car capacity, while trucks in similar traffic may be used to 60–70 per cent of capacity.

Length of Haul

Ocean ships have a longer average haul than any other transportation facility; inland-waterway vessels have the shortest. Therefore, although carrying a relatively small total tonnage of goods as compared to the railroads and canal or river vessels, ocean ships account for the greatest ton-mileage. In contrast, vessels on inland waterways move several times as great a tonnage but report relatively small ton-mileage. The railroads are the greatest carriers of freight in the world, but rank second to ocean ships in

TABLE 116

VOLUME OF WORLD TRANSPORTATION, BY BRANCH, 1930

Type of Transport	Short-Ton-Miles, in Millions	Short Tons, in Millions	Average Length of Haul, in Miles
Railroads	777	4,206	183
Ocean ships	1,294	336	3,852
Inland-water ships	89	1,102	81
Airplanes	0.075	0.018	410

Source: **35**, p. 95.

ton-mileage. Table 116 illustrates these relationships for 1930, the only year for which such an estimate is available.

Weight of Equipment

Weight of equipment in the different forms of transportation varies greatly in relation to passenger or freight capacity.

In passenger transportation, the weight of the equipment per passenger seat is lowest for a bicycle, 15 kilograms, and motorcycle, 60 kilograms. For an intercity bus, it is estimated to average 190 kilograms; an airplane, 330; an automobile, 500; and an express train, with sleeping and dining accommodations, 1,110. The liner, which has to provide facilities for comfort and entertainment during a long voyage, carries 14,300 kilograms of its own weight per passenger berth.

In freight transportation, equipment is much simpler and the weight is much less in relation to cargo. For a river barge, the equipment weighs 290 kilograms per ton of freight capacity and for a canal tug, 400. For a truck, it is 625 kilograms per ton; a freight car, 830; a freighter ship, 470. An airplane represents the greatest weight per ton of freight, 4,160 kilograms.[48]

Life Cycle

The life cycle of equipment, its need for overhauling and the time lost in repairs also differ from one type of transportation to another. The lifetime of a barge may be 35–40 years, of a locomotive 20–25 years, of a bus 8–10 years and of an airplane 3–5 years. The average life of

---

47. **35**, pp. 187–89. This rough estimate for the world as a whole refers to 1930.

48. **35**, p. 150. In this estimate the weight of a passenger is assumed to be 80 kilograms (about 176 pounds) and all figures represent rough approximations.

railroad cars (computed for nine European countries) is 36 years, varying from 25 to 50.[49]

Regular overhauling of a locomotive is considered necessary after every 60,000 miles; of a truck, after every 20,000 miles; and of aircraft, after every 30,000 miles.[50] On the average, tugs and trucks lose ten days annually for repair; cargo tramp ships, twelve days; passenger liners and railroad freightcars, some fifteen days; an airplane may be withdrawn for forty-five days in a year for repairs and a locomotive, for sixty-five days.[51] In general, more complex transport equipment is more expensive and has a shorter life cycle and also requires a greater amount of maintenance.

Investment and Ownership

Several hundred billion dollars are invested in the world's transportation system: $75–$80 billion in the railroads, more than $100 billion in motor vehicles and vast amounts in vessels and planes.[52] Building and maintaining of highways, railways, airways, and navigable waterways with all their necessary installations have absorbed billions of dollars and continue to require huge sums of money each year. Frequent renewal of equipment — determined by its expected life cycle and type of service performed — involves, on a world-wide scale, enormous sums.

Much of this wealth is privately owned, the rest publicly. More than half of the world's railroads are publicly owned.[53] Ocean shipping is almost exclusively in private hands. In 1930 only 6 per cent of the world's gross registered tonnage was publicly owned; today, somewhat more. The same relationship between private and public ownership existed in domestic air transport in 1930, but the public share in international airlines then was 18 per cent. Today, more airlines are publicly owned, particularly international airlines. Transport on highways and inland waterways is essentially a private domain, the main exceptions being in the USSR, its satellites

and, to some extent, the United Kingdom since 1947. In Argentina, as in the United Kingdom, nationalization of the railroads has resulted in the automatic acquisition of a number of road transport undertakings that previously belonged to the railroads.[54] In every country, moreover, government agencies own a greater or smaller fleet of various types of motor vehicles for civil and military purposes.

While highways (except for a few turnpikes), waterways and airways are public property and open to every owner of any kind of vehicle, railroad tracks are monopolized by their owners, private or public.

Geographic Pattern

Railroads and highways have spanned all parts of North America and Europe except the wilderness of Canada, Alaska and remote regions of Scandinavia. Their development in other continents is uneven. They form a rather dense network on limited stretches along the Atlantic and Pacific coasts of South America and on the African and Asian shores of the Mediterranean; in the western part of the USSR and on a long stretch across Asia; in Japan and the coastal region of China, the eastern and southern parts of Australia and New Zealand, and some sections of Indonesia, Malaya, India and South Africa. Areas with approximately 1.2 to 1.5 billion people are provided with railroads and highways to a greater or lesser extent, while the rest of the world relies mostly on inland waters, caravan roads and trails, scattered highways and railways, and a limited number of airlines. (See Figure 55.)

On the other hand, ocean lanes crisscross the seven seas except for the Arctic and Antarctic.

This geographic pattern of prevailing means of transportation makes it possible to classify regions of the world by the speed of surface transportation. Apart from air transit, inhabitants of areas with a well-developed network of railroads and highways may cover from 400 to 800 miles a day; of areas without such facilities, hardly more than 20–60 miles, while the pre-

---

49. **4,** 1952, p. 51.

50. In the United States, time for overhauling is subject to other measurements. (See Chapter 11.)

51. **35,** pp. 150–51. This estimate refers to prewar years.

52. The investment in the public transportation system of the United States is estimated at $110 billion; of this more than half is government investment in basic facilities; the rest, in private installations and equipment. **38,** pp. i–ii.

53. See Chapter 8.

54. **3,** July–September 1952, p. 16. In 1947, the British government took over shareholdings of railway companies in three large truck concerns owning hundreds of vehicles and later it purchased the remaining shares in one of these. In 1951 the British government owned in all nearly 22,000 buses and coaches, about 38 per cent of the total. (**3,** July–September 1951, p. 37.)

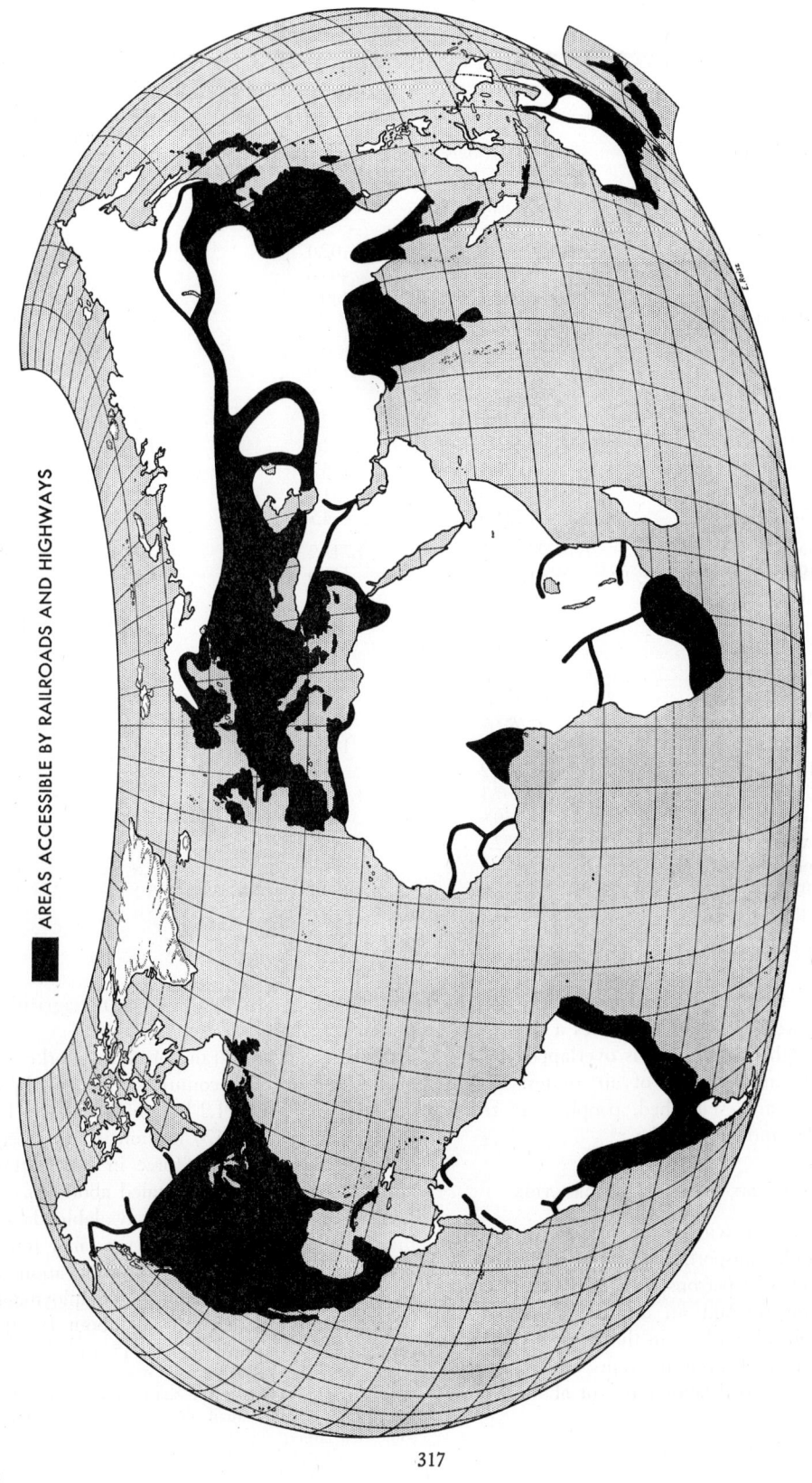

■ AREAS ACCESSIBLE BY RAILROADS AND HIGHWAYS

FIGURE 55. AREAS READILY ACCESSIBLE BY RAILROADS AND HIGHWAYS

Source: Adapted from Carl Pirath (35)

317

TABLE 117

EMPLOYMENT IN TRANSPORTATION: GAINFUL WORKERS IN SELECTED COUNTRIES [a]

| | Number, in Thousands | | Percentage of Transportation Workers to | |
Country and Year	All Pursuits	Transportation	All Pursuits	Nonagricultural Pursuits
United States, 1950	59,583.0	4,107.0	6.9	7.9
Canada, 1951	5,415.0	403.0	7.4	9.4
Mexico, 1940	5,858.1	149.5	2.6	7.4
Nicaragua, 1940	352.7	2.4	0.7	2.5
Panama, 1950	264.6	6.7	2.5	5.0
Cuba, 1943	1,520.9	33.9	2.2	3.7
Puerto Rico, 1940	602.0	18.5	3.1	5.0
Venezuela, 1941	1,240.7	42.8	3.5	7.1
Colombia, 1938	4,566.2	62.8	1.4	5.0
Brazil, 1940	14,020.1	473.7	3.4	10.4
Peru, 1940	2,475.3	51.1	2.1	5.5
Chile, 1940	1,741.5	74.5	4.3	6.6
Great Britain, 1951	22,578.5	1,747.9	7.7	8.2
Ireland, 1946	1,298.4	52.0	4.0	7.3
France, 1946 [b]	20,520.5	1,169.4	5.7	9.0
Saar, 1946	300.5	26.7	8.9	10.1
Belgium, 1947	3,481.0	243.2	7.0	8.0
Netherlands, 1947	3,866.4	240.3	6.2	7.7
Denmark, 1951	2,173.0	128.0	5.9	7.9
Sweden, 1945	2,987.9	219.8	7.4	9.7
Norway, 1950	1,394.0	144.0	10.3	14.0
Finland, 1940	2,017.2	71.6	3.5	8.3
Western Germany, 1950	20,897.1	1,187.8	5.7	7.9
Eastern Germany, 1946	8,139.6	418.1	5.1	7.3
Czechoslovakia, 1947	5,852.4	285.9	4.9	7.8
Switzerland, 1941	1,992.5	76.7	3.8	4.9
Austria, 1939	3,648.9	190.7	5.2	8.6
Portugal, 1940	3,049.9	88.7	2.9	5.7

(*Continued on facing page*)

vailing speed of transportation on the open sea ranges between 250 and 400 miles a day.

This rough classification is overlapped by the fast developing network of air routes. Where such routes are established, people may travel 5,000 miles and more a day.[55]

EMPLOYMENT IN TRANSPORTATION

In comparison with its importance in the life of mankind, transportation employs a relatively small number of persons. Census data and other information warrant an estimate of about 30 million gainful workers in the world's transportation system. This number represents 3 per cent of the world's total labor force, or about 6.5 per

55. Cf. Chapter 11.

cent of all gainful workers in nonagricultural pursuits.

Census data on transportation workers are available for forty-six countries with a total population of more than 1.2 billion and a total labor force of more than 470 million. In these countries the reported labor force in transportation and related pursuits has totaled about 18.5 million. (See Table 117.) The available data for most of these countries cover the labor force in both transportation and communication and sometimes also in warehousing; employment in *transportation* as such must be about 15–20 per cent less,[56] or approximately 15 million work-

56. In some countries the share of communication is considerably smaller than these percentages, in others somewhat larger.

TABLE 117—*continued*

| Country and Year | Number, in Thousands | | Percentage of Transportation Workers to | |
	All Pursuits	Transportation	All Pursuits	Nonagricultural Pursuits
Spain, 1940	9,254.1	310.2	3.4	6.9
Italy, 1936	18,754.7	702.2	3.7	7.1
Yugoslavia, 1931 ᶜ	6,477.8	102.4	1.6	7.4
Romania, 1930	10,457.6	174.4	1.7	7.8
Bulgaria, 1934	3,433.1	43.4	1.3	6.3
Japan, 1950	36,280.0	1,780.0	4.9	9.3
Turkey, 1945	7,626.4	139.8	1.8	7.7
India, 1931 ᵇ, ᵈ		2,341.4	1.6	4.8
Thailand, 1937	6,823.6	57.9	0.8	7.5
Malaya, 1947	1,904.7	67.8	3.6	10.0
Singapore, 1947	534.9	51.9	9.7	10.3
Philippines, 1948	7,415.8	134.9	1.8	5.3
Egypt, 1947	6,728.7	203.3	3.0	8.7
Southern Rhodesia, 1946 ᵉ	33.2	3.0	9.0	10.6
Union of South Africa, 1946				
Europeans	888.8	122.6	13.8	17.0
Non-Europeans	4,269.4	84.8	2.0	4.2
Australia, 1947	3,238.2	297.8	9.2	10.9
New Zealand, 1945	679.5	69.3	10.2	12.7
Hawaii, 1950	166.3	14.2	8.5	10.5

Sources: **6**, 1951–1952, pp. 10–34; **1**, 1949–1950, pp. 64–85; for Western Germany, **16**, 1952, pp. 110–11, 156 and 162.

a. Includes communications; for the United States, Canada, Puerto Rico, Panama, Venezuela, Ireland, Denmark, the Netherlands, Saar and Australia, also includes storage; for Japan and Hawaii also storage and public utilities. Data for the United States, Japan, Austria, Norway and the United Kingdom are based on small sample tabulations of the respective censuses; those for Denmark and Canada, on labor force sample surveys; and for Italy, on estimated figures reported by the International Labor Office.

b. Transport.
c. Communications.
d. Includes Pakistan and Burma.
e. Europeans only.

ers. This figure, however, does not include transportation workers in the USSR (3 million on the railroads alone in 1949),[57] China, Indonesia, Korea, the Middle East, most of Africa and many other areas. It can be reasonably assumed that at least 10 million and probably many more workers are occupied in these parts of the world, where, except for the USSR, transportation is primitive and therefore consumes a relatively large amount of manpower.

In addition, some of the figures shown in Table 117 are too low because of underreporting and the development of transportation since the reports were made. For example, the combined employment reported for India, Pakistan and Burma was 2.3 million in 1931, while according to the International Labor Organization, several million workers are now employed in that area on inland navigation alone.[58] It is therefore believed that many people engaged in activities relating to transportation have not been counted in these industries by the censuses.

The changes brought by the automobile in the process of transporting goods and people have blurred the picture. A substantial proportion of transportation has shifted from specialized enterprises to private persons whose motor vehicles — cars and trucks — have taken over what actually are functions of commercial transportation. The farmer who uses his truck or his car to deliver grain, potatoes or other produce to city customers; the salesman who depends on his car to carry on his business; the small producer who himself moves his products to a larger

57. See Chapter 8.

58. **5**, 1951, p. 98.

firm or store — none of these is gainfully occupied in transportation, but the activities of millions such as these account for a considerable share of transport in advanced countries. This is true of many billions of passenger-miles driven by private cars in the United States, for example.

In countries with a primitive economy and little differentiation among production, trade and transportation, the picture is even more confusing. One may say, with some validity, that a large part of the population of a country like Guatemala is engaged in trade or, with equal justification, in transportation. On market day every family is on the move to the village or town to trade its produce, carrying it, as in very early days, on back or head.

The following discussion deals not with the amount of human energy absorbed in moving goods and people, but with the number of persons gainfully employed in transportation sold to patrons.

Even with this reservation, statistical data are not completely precise. Census data include railroad workers in repair shops in transportation statistics, but garage mechanics are classified in service industries. Railways in "captive" mines are considered part of the mining industry, and so on.[59]

Workers in Selected Countries

The United States has the largest known number of transportation workers — 4.1 million — though it is possible that the unknown figure for the USSR may be higher. Great Britain reports 1.7 million employees — about as many as Japan, with several islands and a much greater population. France and Western Germany each employ about 1.2 million persons. (See Table 117.)

The share of transportation employment in all gainful pursuits ranges from 0.7 to 1.8 per cent in Nicaragua, Thailand, Bulgaria, Colombia, India, Yugoslavia, Romania, Turkey and the Philippines. At the other extreme, it exceeds 10 per cent in Norway and New Zealand. The share of transportation in the employment of Europeans in the Union of South Africa is even higher: 13.8 per cent of all white workers. Within the range where transportation absorbs 6.5 to 8.5 per cent of the total labor force are the United States (6.9 per cent), Belgium (7.0),

Canada and Sweden (7.4), Great Britain (7.7) and Hawaii (8.5).

The share of transportation employment in the nonagricultural labor force is only slightly higher than in the total labor force in industrialized countries, where agriculture accounts for a comparatively small part of total employment. Thus, in Great Britain transportation workers represent 7.7 per cent of the total labor force and 8.2 per cent of the nonagricultural workers. The corresponding figures for the United States are 6.9 and 7.9 per cent; for Belgium, 7.0 and 8.0 per cent. The share of transportation in nonagricultural employment is substantially greater in predominantly agricultural countries. In Turkey, transportation workers account for only 1.8 per cent of the total labor force, but 7.7 per cent of the nonagricultural; in Brazil, for 3.4 and 10.4 per cent, respectively, and in Thailand, for 0.8 and 7.5 per cent.

Male and Female Workers

Transportation, like mining and fishing, is decidedly a male occupation. Even in developed countries where employment figures for transportation include a considerable number of postal, telephone and telegraph workers among whom are many women, the share of women in the total is rather low. In Belgium, female workers account for 6.0 per cent; in Italy, for 5.0 per cent; in the Netherlands, for 7.7; and in Switzerland, for 8.2 per cent. Denmark has the highest proportion — 17.2 per cent; Sweden reports 14.9 per cent; the United States 15.4 per cent; and Finland and Eastern Germany 16.1 and 16.2 per cent, respectively. These figures would undoubtedly be still lower if it were possible to segregate data for transportation as such and for communications. (See Table 118.)

In underdeveloped countries, the share of women in employment in this field is very small: less than one per cent in Egypt, Venezuela and among native transport workers in the Union of South Africa; less than 2 per cent in Mexico, the Philippines and Malaya and less than 3 per cent in Brazil, Spain and Turkey.

Classes of Workers

In contrast to trade, in which about half of all gainfully occupied persons in many countries work on their own account,[60] transportation uses

59. **20**, pp. 10–11.

60. Cf. Chapter 1.

TABLE 118

EMPLOYMENT IN TRANSPORTATION: NUMBER OF GAINFUL WORKERS, BY SEX, IN SELECTED COUNTRIES [a]

Country and Year	Number of Workers, in Thousands		Female Workers, as Percentage of Total	Country and Year	Number of Workers, in Thousands		Female Workers, as Percentage of Total
	Male	Female			Male	Female	
United States, 1950	3,475.0	632.0	15.4	Czechoslovakia, 1947	261.0	24.9	8.7
Canada, 1951	351.0	52.0	12.9	Switzerland, 1941	70.4	6.3	8.2
Mexico, 1940	146.6	2.9	1.9	Austria, 1939	171.7	19.1	10.0
Nicaragua, 1940	2.3	0.1	4.9	Portugal, 1940	80.6	8.2	9.2
Panama, 1950	6.1	0.6	9.6	Spain, 1940 [b]	304.0	6.2	2.0
Cuba, 1943	32.6	1.4	4.3	Italy, 1936	667.0	35.2	5.0
Venezuela, 1941	42.4	0.4	0.9	Yugoslavia, 1931 [c]	94.5	7.9	7.7
Colombia, 1938	59.4	3.4	5.4	Romania, 1930	157.8	16.6	9.5
Brazil, 1940	459.8	13.9	2.9	Bulgaria, 1934	42.0	1.4	3.2
Peru, 1940	48.7	2.4	4.7	Japan, 1950	1,580.0	200.0	11.3
Chile, 1940	70.5	4.0	5.4	Turkey, 1945	136.5	3.3	2.4
Great Britain, 1951	1,529.0	218.9	12.5	India, 1931 [b, d]	2,099.2	242.2	10.3
Ireland, 1946	46.9	5.1	9.9	Thailand, 1937	55.7	2.3	4.0
France, 1946 [b]	997.5	172.0	14.7	Malaya, 1947	67.0	0.8	1.2
Saar, 1946	24.3	2.4	8.9	Singapore, 1947	50.4	1.5	2.9
Belgium, 1947	228.6	14.6	6.0	Philippines, 1948	132.9	1.9	1.4
Netherlands, 1947	221.7	18.6	7.7	Egypt, 1947	201.5	1.9	0.9
Denmark, 1951	106.0	22.0	17.2	Union of South Africa, 1946:			
Sweden, 1945	187.0	32.8	14.9	Europeans	112.5	10.1	8.2
Norway, 1946	116.6	14.2	10.8	Non-Europeans	84.3	0.4	0.5
Finland, 1940	60.1	11.5	16.1	Australia, 1947	267.1	30.8	10.3
Western Germany, 1950	1,057.0	130.8	11.0	New Zealand, 1945	60.3	9.0	13.0
Eastern Germany, 1946	350.9	67.3	16.2	Hawaii, 1950	12.7	1.6	11.3

Sources: **6**, 1951–1952, pp. 10–34; **1**, 1949–1950, pp. 64–85; for Western Germany, **16**, 1952, p. 162.

a. Includes communications; for Canada, the United States, Puerto Rico, Venezuela, the Netherlands and Australia, also includes storage; for Japan, also storage and public utilities. Most recent data available.

b. Transport.
c. Communications.
d. Includes Pakistan and Burma.

predominantly salaried employees and wage earners. In most countries, employees account for more than 85 per cent of all workers and in many for 90–94 per cent or even more, as the following percentages show: [61]

Mexico	66.8
Saar	68.9
Peru	71.2
Bulgaria	72.1
Cuba	72.9
Finland	73.6
Portugal	74.7
Italy	75.3
Colombia	78.7
Singapore	81.5
Netherlands	82.4
Romania	83.9
Denmark	85.9
Yugoslavia	86.0
Ireland	86.5
Australia	86.6
Chile	86.8
Norway	88.6
Belgium	89.6
Sweden	90.2
Canada	90.6
France	90.6
Germany (Soviet Zone)	92.7
New Zealand	92.8
Philippines	93.1
Switzerland	93.9
Czechoslovakia	94.2

61. Table 119. Countries arrayed by increasing rate.

(*Continued on following page*)

TABLE 119

EMPLOYMENT IN TRANSPORTATION: GAINFUL WORKERS, BY CLASS OF WORK, IN SELECTED COUNTRIES [a]

(*Thousands*)

Country and Year	Employers and Workers on Own Account	Salaried Employees and Wage- Earners	Unpaid Family Workers	Status Undefined
United States, 1950	180.0	3,923.0	4.0	—
Canada, 1951	. . .	365.0	. . .	. . .
Mexico, 1940	0.2	99.9	1.0	48.4
Cuba, 1943	4.8	24.7	. . .	4.4
Venezuela, 1941	1.8	40.9	. . .	0.1
Colombia, 1938	10.9	49.4	—	2.5
Peru, 1940	13.6	36.4	0.8	0.3
Chile, 1940	9.8	64.7	. . .	. . .
Great Britain, 1951	47.4	1,667.9	0.9	31.7
Ireland, 1946	2.4	45.0	0.2	4.5
France, 1946	110.1	1,059.3	—	—
Saar, 1946	1.7	18.4	0.2	6.4
Belgium, 1947	19.2	217.8	6.3	—
Netherlands, 1947	34.0	197.9	8.4	—
Denmark, 1951	16.0	110.0	2.0	—
Sweden, 1945	19.6	198.2	1.9	—
Norway, 1946	14.8	115.9	—	—
Finland, 1940	17.3	52.7	1.6	—
Germany, Soviet Zone, 1946	23.8	387.5	6.8	—
Czechoslovakia, 1947	14.4	269.3	2.2	—
Switzerland, 1941	4.1	72.0	0.6	—
Portugal, 1940	7.2	66.3	0.3	14.9
Italy, 1936	155.0	528.8	18.4	—
Yugoslavia, 1931	13.9	88.1	0.4	—
Romania, 1930	23.5	146.4	0.2	4.3
Bulgaria, 1934	11.5	31.3	0.5	—
Japan, 1950	70.0	1,680.0	20.0	—
Singapore, 1947	9.4	42.3	0.1	0.1
Philippines, 1948	9.3	125.6	—	—
Australia, 1947	33.2	257.8	0.4	6.4
New Zealand, 1945	4.2	64.3	. . .	0.7

Sources: **6,** 1951–1952, pp. 12–34; **1,** 1949–1950, pp. 64–85.

a. See footnotes to Table 118.

Japan	94.4
Great Britain	95.4
United States	95.5
Venezuela	95.6

Unpaid family workers, so important in agriculture and trade, have practically no place in transportation. In most countries they account for a fraction of one per cent of all employees, and only in a few, including Italy and Belgium, for more than 2 per cent. (See Table 119.)

Trends in Employment

Precise evaluation of the trend in the labor force in transportation over a long period of time is impossible. In the nineteenth century, the censuses of many countries combined the number of persons working in transportation with those in trade or in public utilities, storage and communications.

Beginning with 1929, data for the United States, published by the Department of Commerce, classify workers by type of transportation. They cover all persons directly engaged in commercial transportation in terms of man-years of full-time employment but exclude the few unpaid family workers.

These data show that the number of persons employed in transportation in the United States was the same in 1951 as in 1929: about 3.0 million.[62] In view of the increase in the volume of traffic of all types, this lack of increase in employment seems to indicate a rise in productivity per transportation worker.[63] This conclusion, however, requires a reservation.

The share of transportation in total employment in the United States declined (in terms of man-years of full employment) from 6.6 per cent in 1929 to 4.8 per cent in 1954. At the same time the ratio between employment in transportation and manufacturing industries went down from 28.7:100 in 1929 to 16.2:100 in 1954. (See Table 120.) This development does not necessarily indicate that transportation has become less important, or productivity of labor in transportation has increased more rapidly than in other industries. It should be kept in mind that transportation establishments lost an appreciable part of their business when farmers, manufacturers, wholesale and retail dealers began to use their own cars and trucks.

In fact, the growth of motor transport has reversed the trend in the share of transportation industries in total employment. Its share began to decline sometime between 1910 and 1930, probably after World War I. This conclusion is suggested by two estimates for the United States — one dating from 1870 for the number of gainful workers in transportation and public utilities, the other dating from 1900 for the labor force in transportation. Though these estimates are differently calculated,[64] both indicate generally that the share of transportation in the total labor force tended to increase somewhat: until 1930 for the first estimate and until 1920 for the second. According to the estimate of the National Bureau of Economic Research, transportation and public utilities together represented 4.5 per cent of the total labor force in 1870, 6.2 per cent in 1890, 8.7 per cent in 1910, 9.9 per cent in

TABLE 120

EMPLOYMENT IN TRANSPORTATION: PERSONS ENGAGED IN THE UNITED STATES, 1929–54 [a]

| Year | *Number, in Thousands* [b] | *Percentage of Workers* | |
		In All Industries	*In Manufactures*
1929	3,035	6.6	28.7
1930	2,795	6.4	29.7
1931	2,444	6.0	30.6
1932	2,100	5.6	31.1
1933	2,008	5.3	27.0
1934	2,077	5.1	24.6
1935	2,102	5.0	23.4
1936	2,218	4.9	22.8
1937	2,333	5.0	21.8
1938	2,073	4.6	22.4
1939	2,169	4.7	21.5
1940	2,252	4.7	20.5
1941	2,435	4.6	18.3
1942	2,585	4.5	16.8
1943	2,774	4.4	15.8
1944	2,959	4.6	17.2
1945	3,056	4.9	20.0
1946	3,080	5.4	21.0
1947	3,099	5.4	20.1
1948	3,044	5.2	19.7
1949	2,846	5.0	19.8
1950	2,889	4.9	19.1
1951	3,051	4.9	18.7
1952	3,041	4.8	18.3
1953	2,763	5.0	16.0
1954	2,592	4.8	16.2

Sources: **12**, 1951, pp. 188–89; **11**, July 1953, pp. 22–23 and February 1955, p. 15.

a. Man-years of full-time employment by wage and salary earners and active proprietors of unincorporated enterprises. Excludes unpaid family workers. Data based essentially on social security records and not comparable with census data used elsewhere.

b. Includes warehousing.

1930 and 7.8 per cent in 1940. The National Industrial Conference Board estimates the share of transportation in the employed labor force at 4.7 per cent in 1900, 5.3 per cent in 1910, 6.2 per cent in 1920 and 4.7 per cent in 1930.[65]

Employment by Branch of Transportation

In all countries with a developed railroad system, the railroads absorb a large part of the labor force directly engaged in transportation. Even in the United States, with its huge highway traf-

---

62. These data from Table 120 deviate from sample data of the census in Table 117, chiefly because they were obtained by calculating man-years of full-time employment.

63. Harold Barger has come to the same conclusion by analyzing railroad data for 1889–1946. Taking the level in 1889 as 100, he obtained indexes of 1,040 for output of the railroad industry in 1946, 260 for the number of workers and 400 for output per worker. (**20**, p. 54.)

64. The first, prepared by the National Bureau of Economic Research, considers all gainful workers in each economic branch and service; the second, published by the National Industrial Conference Board, gives the industrial distribution of the employed (i.e., without the unemployed) and combines all services in one group.

65. **8**, pp. 64–65.

TABLE 121

EMPLOYMENT IN TRANSPORTATION:[a] PERSONS ENGAGED BY BRANCH, IN THE UNITED STATES, 1929–53

(*Thousands*)

Year	Total	Inter-state Railroads	Local Railways and Buses	Highways Passengers	Freight [b]	Water	Air	Pipe Lines	Allied Services
1929	3,035	1,845	280	158	381	168	3	25	175
1930	2,795	1,659	263	151	381	160	4	24	153
1931	2,444	1,405	239	143	369	145	5	21	117
1932	2,100	1,155	214	134	355	131	6	17	88
1933	2,008	1,084	199	127	354	136	6	20	82
1934	2,077	1,122	201	115	373	146	6	22	92
1935	2,102	1,113	202	113	397	150	8	23	96
1936	2,218	1,194	204	115	414	144	10	25	112
1937	2,333	1,251	207	115	437	153	12	26	132
1938	2,073	1,061	187	113	421	136	13	23	119
1939	2,169	1,114	184	112	444	142	15	22	136
1940	2,252	1,160	170	120	476	144	19	23	140
1941	2,435	1,285	161	130	529	146	24	24	136
1942	2,585	1,429	169	144	545	109	34	25	130
1943	2,774	1,534	184	164	519	141	46	25	161
1944	2,959	1,616	188	174	518	207	47	26	183
1945	3,056	1,628	189	184	545	249	53	25	183
1946	3,080	1,564	204	222	614	203	81	27	165
1947	3,099	1,543	199	233	654	181	82	28	179
1948	3,044	1,503	172	240	685	166	78	30	170
1949	2,846	1,349	167	235	683	142	77	29	164
1950	2,889	1,373	158	224	737	129	76	27	165
1951	3,051	1,433	151	227	796	142	85	29	188
1952	3,041	1,382	145	229	828	142	97	30	188
1953	2,958	1,358	141	232	766	138	110	28	185

Sources: For 1929–48, **12**, 1951, pp. 188–89; for 1949–52, **11**, July 1953, pp. 20–21; for 1953, **12**, 1954, p. 203.

a. Man-years of full-time employment by wage and salary earners and active proprietors of unincorporated enterprises. Excludes unpaid family workers. Data based essentially on social security records and not comparable with census data used elsewhere.

b. Includes warehousing.

fic, the railroads rank first, with 1.4 million workers in 1953, as against a million in highway transport. In Western Germany, railroads accounted for much the largest share in 1951.

The share of the railroads in the total labor force engaged in transportation is declining, however, because of technical improvements, on the one hand, and increasing competition from other types of transportation, on the other. In the United States, it amounted to 60.8 per cent in 1929, 51.4 per cent in 1939, 47.4 per cent in 1949 and 45.9 in 1953. The other older type of transportation — the waterways — also employs a decreasing proportion — 5.5 per cent in 1929 and 4.6 per cent in 1953. A reverse trend is evident for the newer means of transport — high-

way and air. Commercial highway transportation in the United States accounted for 17.8 per cent of total employment in transportation in 1929, 25.6 per cent in 1939 and 33.4 per cent in 1953. The corresponding figures for air transportation are 0.1, 0.7 and 3.7 per cent. (See Table 121.)

THE SHARE OF TRANSPORTATION IN NATIONAL INCOME

The share of national income originated in transportation, as in trade, is larger than its share in the labor force because outlays for equipment per worker and wages are high. In the United States, for example, wages of transportation workers are higher than of those in any other major industrial division.

Measurement of Income

The international classification of national income by industrial origin, prepared by the United Nations, combines income from transportation with that from communications and public utilities.

This combination is justifiable to some extent because a major part of communication — the mail — is carried by trains, ships, planes and trucks. Telephone, telegraph and radio use cables and electric wires to "transport" communications. Transmission of electricity and gas is also a kind of transport. Nevertheless, the classification prevents a clear-cut appraisal of the share of transportation as such in national income. Moreover, the definition and measurement vary from country to country, so that data for a country are more meaningful in year-to-year comparisons than in international comparisons.

The UN adjusts national income statistics for payments from and to abroad and thus obtains the "net geographic product," which it distributes among different economic branches in each country.[66]

The Share in Selected Countries

The share of transportation in national income is smaller in underdeveloped countries than in the industrialized.[67] It ranges between 1.6 per cent and about 6 per cent in Paraguay, the Dominican Republic, Honduras, Chile, Peru, Puerto Rico, Bulgaria, the Philippines, Southern Rhodesia, Turkey and Israel. In the United Kingdom, Canada, Western Germany, France, Poland and Italy, the ratio ranges approximately between 7 and 11 per cent. The ratio for the United States is gradually declining, paralleling to some extent the trend in transportation employment. Transportation contributes an exceptionally high share to national income in Norway — between 13 and 17 per cent — and somewhat less in the Netherlands — 11–14 per cent. (See Table 122.)

This tendency can be observed even more clearly from data for *transportation* as such, ex-

cluding communications and public utilities, which are available in national income statistics for the United States. Transportation alone accounted for 7.5 per cent of national income in the United States in 1929, 6.4 per cent in 1935, 6.0 per cent in 1940, 5.7 per cent in 1945. By 1954 it was down to 5.0 per cent (Table 123). In other countries, except perhaps the Union of South Africa, this tendency is less pronounced, fluctuations being due, rather, to the consequences of war, statistical changes and specific local conditions.

The Share of Various Branches

Some countries classify income from transportation by the type of transport. In all cases, except Norway, income from railroad operations is the largest. Norway's income from shipping consistently exceeds that from all other types of transportation combined as the following figures show (in millions of kroner): [68]

	Shipping	All Other Transportation
1938	K.418	K.214
1946	708	394
1948	795	503
1949	715	530
1950	861	551
1951	1,638	564

In no other country does shipping constitute so essential a part of national income as in Norway, where in 1951 it accounted for 10.5 per cent. In 1937, for example, it accounted for 1.3 per cent in the United Kingdom, 2.4 per cent in the Netherlands, 0.7 per cent in Japan, 0.09 per cent in the United States and 0.3 per cent in Germany, as compared with Norway's 11.2 per cent.[69]

As in most countries, the railroads of Western Germany account for a greater income than all other transport services combined: in 1936, for 915 million German marks, as compared to 299 million. The respective figures for 1949 are 3.0 and 1.3 billion German marks; for 1950, 2.8 and 1.4 billion; for the first half of 1951, 1.4 and 0.8 billion.[70] However, the railroads' share in total income originated in transportation in Germany is declining, from 75.4 per cent in 1936 to 66.1 per cent in 1950 and 63.8 per cent in the first half of 1951.

---

66. See Chapter 1.

67. Data for Guatemala, Colombia, Argentina and Peru (1942) seem too high and may point to flaws in statistics or definition rather than to the real importance of transportation as a specialized industry in those countries.

68. **18**, 1952, p. 310.

69. **10**, April 29, 1944, p. 5.

70. **16**, 1952, p. 452.

TABLE 122

INCOME FROM TRANSPORTATION: SHARE IN NATIONAL INCOME IN SELECTED COUNTRIES,[a] 1936–52

Country and Year	Percentage of National Income	Country and Year	Percentage of National Income	Country and Year	Percentage of National Income
United States		Argentina		Bulgaria	
1938	10.0	1938	11.0	1939	4.0
1946	8.3	1942	9.0	1946	4.0
1948	8.4	1945	9.0	Greece [e]	
1950	8.6	United Kingdom		1938	6.0
1952	8.4	1948	10.1	1947	6.3
Canada		1950	9.7	1949	6.1
1938	10.9	1952	10.9	Japan	
1946	11.0	France [c]		1946	4.5
1948	10.0	1938	7.3	1949	8.3
1952	10.2	1946	9.3	1950	7.8
Guatemala		1949	9.4	1951	7.1
1949	14.3	Netherlands [d]		Turkey	
Honduras		1938	13.7	1938	5.6
1950	5.6	1946	11.8	1948	4.8
1951	5.4	1948	11.2	1951	4.6
Nicaragua		1950	10.9	Israel [e]	
1950	4.7	Denmark		1950	6.2
Dominican Republic		1938	8.8	Philippines	
1940	3.0	1948	9.0	1946	3.4
1946	3.0	1951	10.1	1949	3.5
Puerto Rico		Norway		1951	3.7
1939	7.0	1938	16.7	Egypt	
1948	5.5	1948	13.2	1938	3.1
1950	5.1	1951	15.8	1945	3.1
Colombia		Finland		Belgian Congo [f]	
1946	7.8	1938	6.1	1950	7.1
1950	9.5	1946	5.6	Kenya	
Peru [b]		1948	5.9	1949	8.0
1942	12.4	1950	6.5	1950	7.4
1948	5.7	Western Germany		Southern Rhodesia	
1951	5.0	1936	8.6	1948	5.7
Paraguay		1949	9.2	1950	5.8
1950	2.7	1950	8.2	Union of South Africa [g]	
1952	1.6	1952	8.0	1938	6.1
Chile		Poland		1946	10.1
1940	5.5	1948	10.0	1948	9.4
1948	7.6	Italy		1950	8.6
1950	6.2	1938	7.6	New Zealand	
Mexico		1948	7.5	1947	8.2
1939	6.5	1950	8.2	1951	8.0
1950	4.7	1952	8.3		

Sources: **2,** February 1952, pp. 24–30; February 1953, pp. 24–36; February 1954, pp. 27–43; for Hungary, Poland, Bulgaria and Argentina: **1,** 1951, pp. 435–38.

a. Income originated in transportation as percentage of national income, adjusted for payments abroad (net geographical product). Includes communications and public utilities.
   b. Includes construction and miscellaneous services.

c. Public utilities not included.
d. Includes hotels and restaurants.
e. Excludes income from ocean shipping.
f. Includes part of unallocated imports.
g. 1938: railroads and harbors only.

TABLE 123

INCOME FROM TRANSPORTATION:[a] SHARE IN NATIONAL INCOME IN THE UNITED STATES, 1929–54

Year	Percentage of National Income	Year	Percentage of National Income	Year	Percentage of National Income
1929	7.5	1938	5.9	1947	5.8
1930	7.4	1939	6.3	1948	5.7
1931	7.3	1940	6.0	1949	5.5
1932	7.5	1941	6.0	1950	5.5
1933	7.5	1942	6.2	1951	5.3
1934	6.8	1943	6.3	1952	5.4
1935	6.4	1944	6.1	1953	5.2
1936	6.2	1945	5.7	1954	5.0
1937	6.2	1946	5.6		

Sources: **12**, 1951, pp. 158–59; **11**, July 1953, p. 16 and February 1955, p. 13.

a. Does not include communications and public utilities as in Table 122.

TABLE 124

INCOME FROM TRANSPORTATION: DISTRIBUTION, BY BRANCH, IN THE UNITED STATES, 1929–52

Branch of Transportation	1929	1932	1935	1938	1941	1944	1947	1950	1951	1952
				Millions of Dollars						
Total	$6,562	$3,133	$3,612	$3,961	$6,188	$11,197	$11,481	$13,291	$14,888	$15,525
Railroads	4,600	1,965	2,236	2,368	3,779	6,954	6,311	7,150	7,762	7,826
Local railways and bus lines	592	388	337	332	321	571	599	560	581	583
Highways:										
Passenger[a]	231	122	140	166	257	676	773	756	809	838
Freight[b]	482	357	451	569	907	1,305	1,946	2,812	3,163	3,485
Water	267	127	200	206	436	858	876	743	971	1,035
Air (common carriers)	–3	10	15	30	77	177	240	424	542	629
Pipeline	130	56	107	121	145	147	152	260	327	358
Allied services	263	108	126	169	266	509	584	586	733	771
				Per Cent						
Railroads	70.1	62.7	61.9	59.8	61.1	62.1	55.0	53.8	52.2	50.4
Local railways and bus lines	9.0	12.4	9.3	8.4	5.2	5.1	5.2	4.2	3.9	3.8
Highways:										
Passenger[a]	3.5	3.9	3.9	4.2	4.2	6.0	6.7	5.7	5.4	5.4
Freight[b]	7.3	11.4	12.5	14.4	14.7	11.7	16.9	21.2	21.2	22.4
Water	4.1	4.1	5.5	5.2	7.0	7.7	7.6	5.6	6.5	6.7
Air (common carriers)	. . .	0.3	0.4	0.8	1.2	1.6	2.1	3.2	3.6	4.1
Pipeline	2.0	1.8	3.0	3.1	2.3	1.3	1.3	2.0	2.2	2.3
Allied services	4.0	3.4	3.5	4.3	4.3	4.5	5.1	4.4	5.0	5.0

Sources: **12**, 1951, pp. 158–59; **11**, July 1953, p. 16.

a. Passenger transportation not elsewhere classified.   b. Includes warehousing.

The same trend exists in the United States. While the railroads accounted for the greatest share of income from transportation from 1929 through 1952, decline in that share was interrupted only in the war years, when the railroads took on a heavy volume of traffic in carrying armed forces and material. The downward trend was resumed at the end of the war, and the railroads' share in 1952 was 50.4 per cent as compared with 70.1 per cent in 1929.

The opposite trend is particularly evident in two new branches of transportation: highway freight and air traffic. The share in income from highway freight was somewhat affected during two war years (1942–43) due to gasoline and rubber shortages, but air transport's share was practically untouched. The highway's share in income from both passenger and freight transport rose from 10.8 per cent in 1929 to 27.8 per cent in 1952; that of air transport, from a deficit in 1929 to 4.1 per cent in 1952. (See Table 124.)

In all branches of transportation, salaries and wages constitute the largest part of income originated. Thus, in the United States in 1951 salaries and wages represented 82.2 per cent of the income originated by railroad operations, 77.6 per cent of that originated by highway transport, 79.0 per cent by air transport and 74.5 per cent by water transport.[71]

---

71. **11,** July 1953, p. 16. In this respect, coal is the only mining industry that exceeds transportation; salaries and wages account for 87.5 per cent of the income originated in the bituminous coal industry and 89.8 per cent of that in the anthracite industry.

CHAPTER 8

LAND TRANSPORTATION: THE PREMECHANICAL ERA AND THE RAILROADS

MODERN OVERLAND transportation is chiefly by means of railroad and motor vehicle.[1] The first became a cornerstone of our civilization about a century ago; the second has developed in recent decades and has become increasingly important in both industrialized and underdeveloped areas. Each provides some special services, and the availability of both has many advantages for both freight and passenger traffic.

Thousands of years passed before animals were domesticated and the wheel was invented, so that animal draft power could replace human portage; further millenniums, before the invention of the steam engine. After a flanged wheel was placed on rails and steam locomotives were introduced, progress in overland transportation was rapid, and the impact on the world's economic and political life, revolutionary.[2]

THE PREMECHANICAL ERA

Man's movement over the globe and his ability to transport any article from one place to another once depended wholly on the strength and endurance of bone and muscle.

HUMAN AND ANIMAL CARRIERS

In early times, people moved only by shanks' mare to find food and escape danger. They used trails, sometimes trodden by other human beings, sometimes by the migration of animals through dense forests. Even when humanity settled down to live on crops, human bipeds at first carried all the goods. In time, man learned to tie sticks and skins together, put his possessions on the contraption and pull it. Sledges mounted on runners were used on snow.

Domestication of animals somewhat eased the task of human beasts of burden. It is believed that the dog was the first animal in transporting

goods in Egypt and Chaldea; the llama, in the Andes. Either could carry only small loads. When oxen and horses were tamed, they generally displaced human beings in pulling the plow and carrying goods, though the strap around a human forehead continued to be used. Finally, some 4,000 years ago, the wheel was invented. No subsequent event of similar significance for land transportation occurred until the nineteenth century.[3]

The wheel, combined with the use of animal power, ushered in a new era in surface transport. At first, the wheel was simply a disc of solid wood; spokes were introduced later, four at first, then eight. Chariots were built, with two wheels, then with four. Trails were widened and roads constructed as trade developed and wars took conquering armies far beyond their own borders. Relay stations and hostelries were erected at mountain passes or river crossings for troops and trade caravans — in China, Iran, Abyssinia, India, Peru and many other areas. Watchtowers and gates or bars to facilitate the collection of tolls were built, and signs were made of stone to show the direction or distance to another point. Trade with distant countries was conducted over such roads to obtain rare products.[4] The most important need for roads was for defense in time of war, although roads also could invite invasion. For centuries, however, the great mass of the population continued to live in communities that were largely self-sufficient and exchanged comparatively few goods among themselves. Many such communities were completely isolated from the outside world. Travel for pleasure or relaxation was unknown.

Even in modern times, transportation by human carriers has not disappeared. This is still the only power available to millions of people in various parts of the world when they wish to journey or move goods. Abundance of cheap labor in areas where a subsistence economy pre-

---

1. Pipelines, another medium, are discussed in **101**, Chapter 24.

2. Early forms of surface transportation and railroads are discussed in this chapter; motor traffic, in Chapter 9.

3. **85**, p. 313.

4. **64**, pp. 3–32; cf. Chapters 1 and 2.

vails and where time saving is unimportant encourages the use of human carriers.

In Mexico, Guatemala and various other Latin American countries, people walk from village to village with heavy loads — bags of produce, timber, furniture and other goods. A woman with a child on her back, a load on her head and a basket in each hand is a common sight. In Africa, human caravans carry palm oil, ivory, coffee and cocoa bags; a porter with a head load of 60 pounds makes some 15 miles a day. In China the number of human carriers is estimated at many millions.[5] Tea carriers with loads of 50 to 200 pounds on shoulder poles trudge from plantations to distribution centers; hundreds of men drag heavy boats along the coast. To handle particularly heavy articles, such as pieces of machinery, Chinese porters rig up a system of slings and bamboos to distribute the burden on the shoulders of thirty or forty men.[6] Coolies also transport human beings. In Japan, rickshas are commonly used for human transportation.

Animal carriers, too, are still common in the world at large. Camels carry much of Africa's trade; reindeer and dogs are used in subarctic areas. Elephants transport heavy materials in India and other countries in southeastern Asia. Oxen are often employed in South America and some Mediterranean countries. Llamas compete with donkeys in the high altitudes of Peru, while mules and donkeys are commonly used in various countries of Latin America.

ROADS

Most of the ancient roads were primitive and disappeared under the impact of time and weather, but some remain. Of the latter, the Incan and Mayan roads in the Western Hemisphere and the Roman roads in Europe are the best examples of ancient road engineering.

Incan and Mayan Roads

The Incas in Peru and the Mayas in Mexico built paved roads, though they had neither draft animals nor wheels. The Incan roads crossed the entire country, some passing over the mountains buried in snow and others, along the lowlands and the coast. The most remarkable was the road from Quito to Cuzco, 1,500 to 2,000 miles

long. The builders scaled precipices by stairways hewn out of the rock, filled deep ravines with solid masonry, and crossed the turbulent streams by aerial bridges made of ropes fastened at both ends to immense buttresses of stone. Prescott tells us that "all the difficulties that beset a wild and mountainous region, and which might appall the most courageous engineer of modern times, were encountered and successfully overcome," and that the Spanish conqueror, Pizarro, found that "nothing in Christendom equals the magnificence of this road across the sierra."[7] Some of the roads, though intended for fleet-footed messengers and troops as well as for llamas, were so broad that two carriages could have passed abreast.[8] The two main highways of the Inca realm — one some 2,700 miles long and the other only a little shorter — were supplemented by a complex network of feeder roads. One such road led directly from the sea by a series of gigantic steps to the capital (Cuzco), to supply the kings with fresh fish daily.

In Yucatan, too, the Mayas were skillful road builders. They used stone and mortar, and some of their roads, thirty feet wide, are still serviceable when the cover of dense tropical vegetation is removed.[9] Since the Mayas, whose pyramids and temples are noted for the strength and beauty of their construction, did not know the wheel, the huge stones for these monuments and for roads had to be dragged by human carriers. Though the art of road engineering was advanced in the Mayan civilization, shanks' mare was practically the only means of transportation they used.

Roman Roads

The Romans were the greatest road builders of their time and many subsequent centuries. Their maxim was that "the first step in civilization is to make roads."[10] They laid roads in every occupied territory to connect strategic points with one another and the central military post and to connect Rome with the chief trading and producing centers.

Roman roads, straight and wide, usually consisted of four layers. First, large flat stones were laid in two or three courses; on top of these came smaller stones bound with mortar; then

5. **100**, Vol. V, p. 21.
6. **103**, pp. 240–41; **65**, p. 5; **55**, p. 33.

7. **79**, pp. 763 and 954.
8. **79**, p. 920.
9. **34**, p. 2.
10. **82**, p. 23.

A. Italy

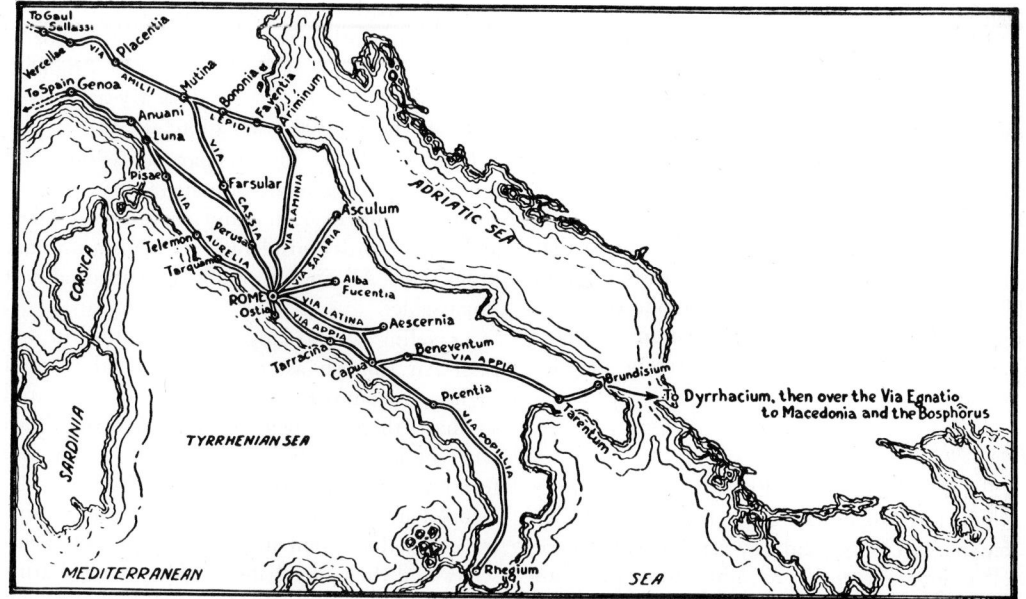

Courtesy of Thomas Y. Crowell Company (**36**)

B. Gaul (France)

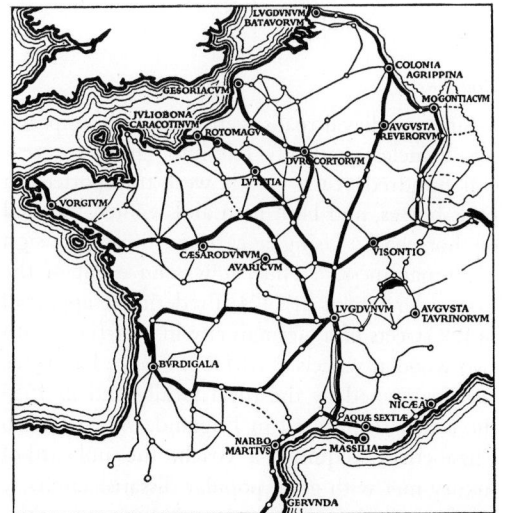

Courtesy of International Road Federation

C. England

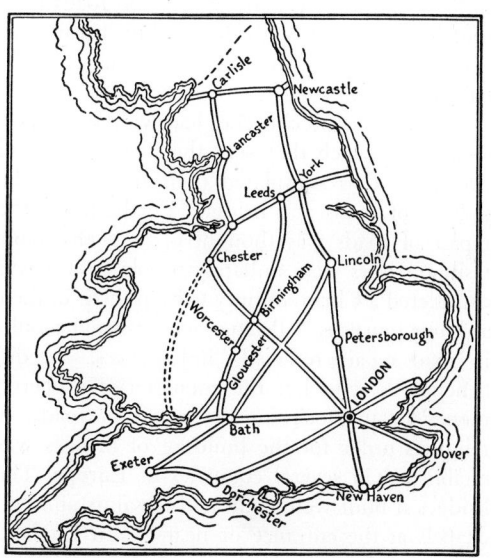

Courtesy of Thomas Y. Crowell Company (**36**)

FIGURE 56. ROMAN ROADS: MAIN ROADS AT THE TIME OF THE ROMAN EMPIRE

pebbles or flints combined with mortar, and finally a layer of polygonal blocks of hard stone. The Roman Empire built 75,000 miles of such roads; 29 of the 372 thoroughfares converged on the Eternal City.[11] (See Figure 56,A.) The most

famous was the Appian Way, about 350 miles long. In Britain, seven highways radiated from London. Though worn ceaselessly by chariot wheels and marching soldiers, these roads served Rome faithfully for four hundred years and lasted throughout the Dark Ages and up to our times. Ronald Syme refers to them as the "finest

11. **29**, p. 1; **36**, pp. 22–27.

roads England has ever known." [12] (See Figure 56,C.)

In Gaul (France) Caesar found small primitive roads built by the Gauls to link their commercial centers with the seaports. Not satisfied with them, the Romans built great stone causeways, five or six yards wide and edged with ditches. Where the ground was boggy, they raised the roads above it. [13] (See Figure 56,B.) Roman engineering was of so high an order that some of the roads built across British marshes 2,000 years ago are still in use despite centuries of neglect and abuse. [14] The foundations of others that have been modernized in recent decades remain as solid as ever.

Routes in the Middle Ages

The fall of the Roman Empire broke the unity in which Europe had been held by the Pax Romana. No longer did any central power need well-maintained roads to administer this vast area. Trade was disrupted and for centuries the upkeep of roads was nobody's concern. Floods and rains washed away the surface, stones were dislodged, bridges collapsed. Holes in roads were occasionally filled with stones but became so deep at some places that even pack horses could barely be seen. [15]

Monasteries and churches had widespread possessions to which they sent their emissaries and overseers. This stimulated their interest in the upkeep of roads and bridges. Furthermore, the repair of roads was thought of as a charitable task: travelers were unhappy people, and it was considered a Christian duty to help them in their arduous journeys. [16] Persons who assisted monks in road repair received "indulgences," as did benefactors who left the monasteries property, money or livestock for the repair of roads. A religious order for the building of bridges was established in several countries of Europe. The bridges it built were dedicated to saints and had chapels at the entrance or near by. In England brotherhoods were formed for the same purpose in the fourteenth century, and trading guilds later took over the task. [17]

But as the roads deteriorated more and more, compulsory labor by the laity gradually replaced pious work. Peasants were ordered to repair and maintain roads around the castle, and parishioners had to work several days a year on roads, under penalty for nonappearance. In England, such "statute labor," for six days a year, was in force for nearly 300 years (1562–1835). [18]

Road repair by forced labor, unwilling and ignorant, proved totally unsatisfactory in most countries. Moreover, in many instances, the rulers and feudal lords considered bad roads a military protection. All in all, roads remained almost impassable.

Traveling was a dangerous adventure in any case. An English act of 1285 directed that all highways from one market to another be cleared so that "there be neither dyke, tree nor bush whereby a man may lurk to do hurt within 200 feet on either side of the way." As trade developed among growing communities, merchants traveling afoot went in groups to protect themselves and their merchandise. They carried arms and often hired guards to repel highwaymen. Others traveled in caravans, with a string of pack horses, making 20–25 miles a day. Conditions were similar throughout Europe, where trade was carried mainly on waterways — rivers, canals and coastal waters. [19]

Coaches

Since medieval roads were practically impassable, vehicles gradually fell into disuse for several hundred years. Goods were transported on pack horses, and both men and women traveled on horseback. Using a carriage became a sign of unmanliness. [20] Thus, it was an event of the first order when, in 1474, Frederic III appeared in the streets of a German city in a carriage with two wooden wheels. [21] In 1550, France had three coaches owned by the royal family and in 1555 the coach reappeared in England. When Queen Elizabeth I acquired a coach, the unheard-of luxury met with great popular dissatisfaction.

A hundred years later, coaches were in common use. In 1658 stagecoaches between London and Edinburgh were introduced and carried a few passengers on each fortnightly journey. The trip should take nine days, according to an adver-

---

12. **89**, p. 3.
13. **58**, Winter 1951, pp. 21–22; **35**, pp. 15–18.
14. **62**, p. 8; **87**, p. 579.
15. **62**, p. 10.
16. **87**, p. 580.
17. **78**, pp. 11–13.

18. **78**, pp. 31–32.
19. See Chapter 10.
20. It was also considered not fit for an honest person in England to use a carriage, but a criminal was taken to prison or to the gallows in a cart. **89**, p. 18.
21. **85**, p. 38.

tisement, but evidently this claim could not be met, since in 1712 a coach company covering the same stretch announced that it would "perform the whole journey in thirteen days without any stoppages (if God permits), having eighty able horses to perform the whole journey." [22] Ordinarily, six horses drew the coach, and more when ruts were deep and descents precipitous. According to Thoresby's diary, the coach trip between London and Leeds at the end of the seventeenth century presented perils that could be matched only by travel to "the Frozen Ocean or to the Desert of Sahara." [23] The roads were so unreliable that when a proposal was made late in the seventeenth century to use horses for postal service, Sir William Petty objected on the ground that men "can go where horses cannot." [24]

In France, public transportation was inaugurated in 1662, and soon thereafter vehicular traffic became common.

Opposition to coaches, denounced in England as "amongst the greatest evils that beset the kingdom," came largely from vested interests. It was claimed that travel by coach, instead of on horseback, would ruin trade in swords, belts, pistols and similar equipment for which there would be little or no occasion. On similar grounds, it was contended that cloth makers would be impoverished, since coach travelers who escaped "the wet and dirt" during the journey would not need an extra suit. Travel in coaches would also reduce the king's revenue by leading to less consumption of beer and ale in the inns. [25]

Opposition to a new medium of transportation was to arise again and again, always on the ground of defending certain established trades. Railways, iron ships, pipelines, motor vehicles and, most recently, the airlines have hurt interests entrenched in existing ways of transport. Among the latest has been the opposition of dog drivers and sled owners in northern Canada to the introduction of air traffic. The outcome has always been the same: the new transportation facilities have come out victorious.

Despite opposition, the use of coaches continued to spread in the eighteenth century. Slowly as the coaches moved — about four miles an hour on the best roads near Paris, London and other capitals — this traffic played havoc with road surfaces. [26] Protection of roads became a matter of administrative and legislative concern. In England Parliament passed new regulations every few years concerning the number of horses to be attached to a coach, the width and position of the wheels, the permissible load and the toll for extra weight. Any person was authorized to seize and keep possession of any horse in excess of three on a cart for hire, or in excess of six on a stagecoach. [27] Parliamentary acts regulated even the shape and size of wheel nails. Harnessing more than three horses to a carriage in winter and more than four in summer was forbidden in France. [28]

As traffic grew, speed increased and more comfortable and speedier coaches displaced mere boxes tied to wheels by leather straps. When the *Flying Coach* appeared on English roads in 1754, its first trip from Manchester to London was advertised as follows: "However incredible it may appear, this coach will actually arrive (barring accidents) in London four days and a half after leaving Manchester." [29]

EIGHTEENTH-CENTURY ROADS

As time passed, the need for good roads became increasingly urgent. Neither religious bodies nor parishioners and statute labor could maintain roads satisfactorily. The problem was who should provide for the upkeep of existing roads and the construction of new. Two different systems were tried in Europe: turnpikes and tolls in England; government responsibility, by taxation and *corvée* (compulsory labor), on the continent.

Turnpikes in England

Introduction of the turnpike system shifted the cost of improving main roads from parishes to road users, though the responsibility of parishes for local roads still remained enforceable by law. The first turnpike act was passed by Parliament in 1663. Turnpike trusts — groups of landlords, merchants, clergy and other citizens — were organized throughout England. They were entitled to raise loans for improving and building roads with hired and statute labor and to establish gates or bars on their roads to exact tolls from the travelers and thus recoup

22. **78**, p. 52.
23. **70**, Vol. I, pp. 345–51.
24. **53**, p. 319.
25. **58**, Spring 1951, p. 27; cf. **70**, Vol. I, Chapter 3.

26. **62**, p. 15.
27. **78**, p. 44.
28. **35**, p. 268.
29. **73**, p. 23.

their expenditures. By about 1770 turnpikes were common, and by 1830 as many as 1,100 turnpike trusts were operating some 20,000 miles or about a sixth of England's road mileage.[30]

Resistance to the toll bars ran high at first, and many were burnt or broken. The opponents considered the bars a bureaucratic attempt to deprive the people of their liberty. This attitude was strengthened by the inefficient and incompetent way in which many turnpike trusts operated. In some instances, 100 to 200 commissioners were in charge of some 10 or 15 miles of road, and each trust employed an attorney, surveyor, treasurer and clerk.[31] Tolls were high, while little was spent on road improvement and upkeep. Cases were reported in which all income was spent on loan interest and management salaries.[32]

Roads in Continental Europe

France pioneered in road construction under government responsibility. In the seventeenth century, first Sully, then Colbert built highways from Paris to the country's borders, in contrast to the practice in England, where roads were laid to connect trading centers with producing areas. Colbert, in particular, initiated a large program which obligated each peasant living near the main road to work one month a year, and each landlord, to maintain the roads leading through his estate. About 15,000 miles of roads were built. The art of road engineering had been lost during the Dark Ages, however, and labor resorted to passive resistance. The new roads were not much better than the old ones in other parts of the country. In 1776 Turgot abolished statute labor and built some 10,000 miles with hired workers. Early in the nineteenth century, France had some 30,000 miles of excellent national highways and many more miles of local roads.

Prussia introduced the principle of state responsibility for roads of military and national importance before the end of the eighteenth century. Local roads remained in charge of local communities. In 1787 the first mile of state road was laid, and by 1816 the network comprised about 2,000 miles.

Sweden had good all-weather roads before new methods of road engineering were introduced

in England. Broken granite was pressed into the roadbeds to provide a durable surface.

Roads in Russia

As in France and Prussia, the first roads laid in Russia tended to connect the administrative center of the country with strategic outposts. From the fourteenth century, the center was Moscow, and the radiating roads extended gradually as Russia's borders moved southward and eastward. The roads were as unsatisfactory as in other countries, and highwaymen and wild beasts were ever-present dangers. The first legal regulations concerning the maintenance of roads and bridges date from the second half of the seventeenth century. Villages and towns bordering the roads were obligated to keep them in good shape and were entitled to exact tolls established by the government agencies. Persons in government service and official mail carriers were exempted from tolls. Toll receivers were legally responsible for any damage caused to travelers by bad road conditions.

Under Peter the Great, a highway was built between Moscow and the newly created capital of Russia — St. Petersburg. Other roads were also laid from the capital to various outposts of the country. Statute labor was used, as in England, with about the same results. It was abolished on government roads in 1817, somewhat earlier than in England. In 1825 the first stretch of the national highway from St. Petersburg to Novgorod, about 100 miles long, was opened and a network of highways was under construction in the western provinces, such as annexed parts of Poland, and in the Crimea.[33]

Roads in the United States

American settlers found road conditions in the New World even worse than in the old countries. There were only Indian trails, mostly in dense uninviting forests where peril confronted the traveler at each step. People traveled on foot or on horseback, and pack horses, tied to one another in a long line like a train of cars, carried the freight. For almost two hundred years, until 1790, there were practically no roads, only trails widened by moving cattle and pack horses.[34]

In 1797 the journey from Baltimore to Philadelphia took five days. The road was frequently

30. **53**, p. 516; **38**, p. 94.
31. **78**, pp. 82–83.
32. **78**, pp. 314–17.

33. **84**, pp. 72–76.
34. **45**, p. 26; **31**, p. 51.

interrupted by "chasms" six to ten feet deep; coaches overturned, and injury to passengers was often reported.[35] Long after the Revolution, there were no bridges over the largest rivers; to attend his presidential inauguration, Thomas Jefferson had to ford five of the eight rivers on his way from Monticello to Washington. Capital and labor were scarce, and pack train operators resisted the construction of better roads. They argued that the American horse was not strong enough to pull a coach, but could move faster than a coach in delivering the mail, and that the stagecoach would deprive many people of their employment.[36]

The nineteenth century was well advanced before coaches came into common use. When roads were laid for their passage, stumps and rocks were usually left. Muddy in winter and spring, laden with dust in summer, impassable in bad weather, the roads made travel uncomfortable and slow — at best a few miles per hour. Charges for transportation of goods were heavy, so that only products of high value and low weight could be shipped over long distances. Salt, sold at one cent a pound at the shore, cost six cents a pound some 300 miles away from the sea, the difference representing the cost of transportation.

The westward movement of the population stimulated road improvement. The first turnpike (Philadelphia-Lancaster, 66 miles) was completed in 1794. Financed by stockholders of the turnpike company, it was so successful that enthusiasm for turnpikes ran high. By 1810, more than 180 turnpike companies had been chartered in New England, and in 1811 New York State had 137 companies. Turnpikes were all-weather roads and permitted faster traffic, but tolls were very high. The freight charge from Philadelphia to Pittsburgh, for example, was $125 per ton; to Erie, $249.[37] Clamor for lower transportation costs led to the construction by the federal government of the National Pike — a through road from the East to the Middle West. At first free, it became a toll highway later, when it was taken over by the states. This pike, or Cumberland Road, played an important role in the country's history by stimulating settlement and commerce along its 834 miles.

While the East had a system of highways (and canals) in the first quarter of the nine-

teenth century, the rest of the territory was crossed only by a few trails. (See Figure 57, A and B.)

Progress in Road Engineering

At the end of the eighteenth century, Thomas Telford and John L. McAdam introduced scientific road building in England.[38] Their main emphasis was on effective drainage of road beds. Telford used three layers — large, medium and small stones. McAdam, whose name is associated with macadamized roads, insisted on breaking the stone into angular shapes and pressing it under a heavy roller. He thus obtained a uniform road surface of sufficient strength and hardness to sustain the traffic. Speed on such roads rose to eight and even ten miles an hour but led to frequent accidents. When a coach between Liverpool and Manchester made fourteen miles an hour, indignation at what was regarded as attempted manslaughter ran so high that the matter was taken to court.[39] Nevertheless, better methods of road making gained ground in England and spread to other countries. They were adopted by many turnpike trusts in the United States.

In the United States a new innovation — to build all-season plank roads with the abundantly available timber — was successful for a time. A few thousand miles of such roads were laid, but maintaining them was expensive and they soon went out of use.

The End of the Turnpike Era

With all its shortcomings and abuses, the turnpike system provided the population with the best roads in many centuries. Initiated in the period of the industrial revolution, it facilitated the development of production and commerce by delivering raw materials to factories and finished goods to distribution centers more rapidly and more nearly on schedule. It gave a fillip to personal travel and postal service and strengthened social interrelationships among persons and among parts of the country.

In the palmiest days of the system, when improved road engineering was opening bright horizons and every ambitious city or town was

35. **82**, p. 25.
36. **82**, p. 45.
37. **46**, pp. 271–72; **82**, p. 21.

38. Metcalf pioneered before them and, although blind from the age of six, built some 200 miles of good roads. He did not suggest an entirely new system of road making, however. **78**, pp. 101–02.
39. **53**, p. 517.

A. MAIN HIGHWAYS IN THE EAST

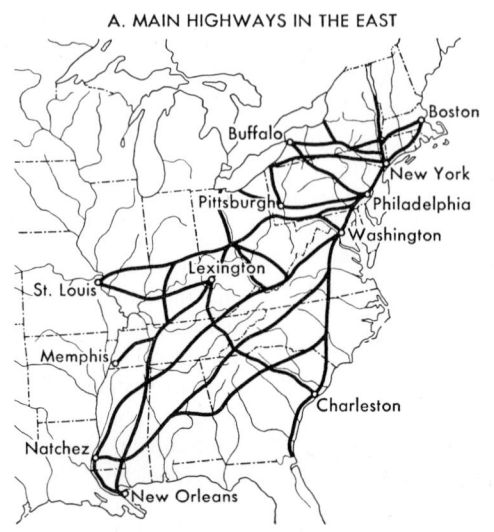

B. TRANSCONTINENTAL TRAILS

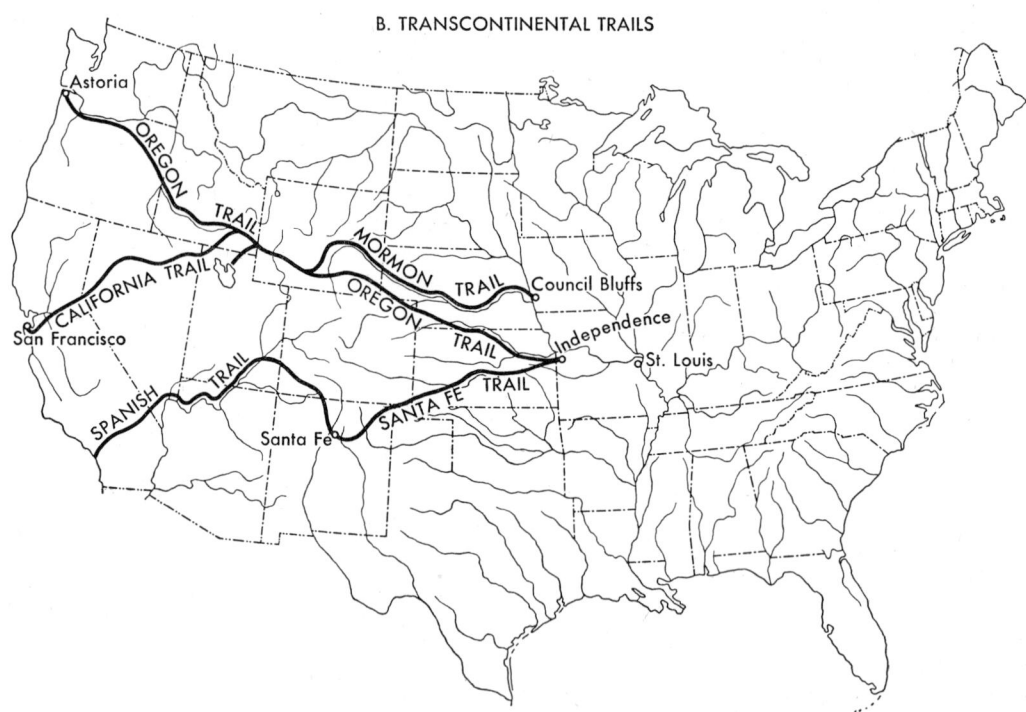

Courtesy of Thomas Y. Crowell Company (36)

FIGURE 57. ROADS IN THE UNITED STATES: HIGHWAYS AND TRAILS AROUND 1820–30

These maps are not intended to give a precise picture of all roads and trails in the United States early in the nineteenth century but to convey a general impression of the road network at that time.

striving to have a chartered turnpike company, a new medium of transportation — the railroad — made its dramatic appearance.[40] Great as were the advantages of turnpikes over dirt roads, they could not match those offered by the railways. Turnpike trusts soon began to feel the pinch and turned to government for support. Some obtained it under varying terms; others soon became bankrupt.[41]

EARLY RAIL CARRIERS

Railways combined two elements — rails and steam power. Both had been used before, but the combination revolutionized transport on land. Ownership of both roadbeds and rolling stock was an innovation of enormous significance and has remained the unique feature of the railroads among all existing mediums of transportation, whether on land, water or in the air.

Railed Roadbeds

Roadbeds with continuous stone rails for the wheels of vehicles and a dirt space between them for horses were laid in Babylonia thousands of years ago. The track gauge was about five feet. This was about the same width as on some modern European and Asiatic railroads and was determined by the same factor — animal traction — that governed construction of the first railways in England and elsewhere. The ancient Greeks learned the importance of permanent roads from the Phoenicians and built parallel stone rails in which they cut ruts to accommodate vehicles. Remains of such rails, with a standard gauge at about five feet four inches, are scattered through Greece — for example, between Athens and Piraeus — and can also be seen in Italy, at Pompeii.[42]

In the sixteenth century, wooden rails were used in Saxony in moving ore from the mines in carts with flanged wheels. Horses, and occasionally, dogs, drew the carts. In the first half of the seventeenth century, coal was drawn from English mines to boats on "tramways";[43] collieries located above the river level used gravity to propel the carts. Wooden planks were laid over the ruts formed by coal carts; later, crossties were pegged to wooden rails, and the space between was filled with ashes and small stones to protect the horses' feet. Such rails wore out rapidly, and were later capped with thin iron strips to keep them in position. Scarcity of lumber and deterioration of the wood under the iron forced a shift to cast-iron rails around 1765–70; these were supported at the joints, first by timber and later by stone. By 1785 iron rails had displaced most of the wooden ones in use for more than a century.[44]

Throughout the eighteenth century, such railways were used in private collieries, quarries and iron works. In 1801 Parliament granted a charter for the first *public* railway in the world, to operate between Wandsworth and Croydon, near London, a stretch of about 9.5 miles. This line was to carry coal, corn and other products "to and from the Metropolis." Traction power was provided by horses, mules and donkeys, and a footpath was laid on each side of the track for the men in charge of animals. Anyone could use this railway with his own carriage and animals, under certain regulations and on payment of tolls. Passenger traffic was not contemplated.[45]

In the United States, wooden rails faced with iron were in use in the nineteenth century in moving coal, brick and stone — for example, on a three-mile stretch in Massachusetts between Quincy and Neponset.[46]

Steam Traction

In 1804, Richard Trevithick built the first steam engine which, mounted on wheels, could move a vehicle.[47] The first locomotive could draw a 10-ton load about 4.5 miles in an hour. It was not a commercial success, however, and horses continued to be used. In 1814 George Stephenson built the first practical locomotive, which could drag a load of 30 tons up a gradient

---

40. The part which canals played in the decline of turnpikes is discussed in Chapter 10.
41. For the revival of turnpikes in recent years, see Chapter 9.
42. **68**, p. 5.
43. Soviet publications claim that Russia originated the railway. The first wooden railways were used in the Urals in 1788, however, and iron rails, in 1810. **76**, pp. 29–31.

44. **78**, pp. 198–208; **39**, p. 47. Wooden rails were retained in some collieries as late as 1860.
45. **78**, pp. 222–23.
46. **46**, p. 285.
47. As is the case with most inventions, the idea of using steam power to move a carriage was conceived long before its practical realization. Watt took out a patent but never tried to make use of it. Various engineers — French, American and English — experimented, but no public trial was made of any of these contraptions until Trevithick's. **41**, pp. 805–06; **62**, pp. 27–30.

at a speed of about 4 miles an hour. To establish the economic advantages of this engine over horse traction, strict accounts were kept for a year; they showed that the locomotive and horses worked at the same cost.

Meanwhile, Stephenson, watching his engine at work, found a way to increase the draft by leading the exhaust steam into the furnace. The improved locomotive of 1815, fitted with an exhaust draft, had all the essentials of the twentieth-century engine. Though this engine was used successfully at the colliery at Killingworth, it was not tried publicly until 1825 at the opening of the Darlington-Stockton line.[48] Weighing nine tons and provided with a single tubular boiler, it moved a 90–ton train at a speed of 4 to 8 miles an hour. During the entire demonstration, its chimney was red hot.[49]

Nevertheless, Stephenson vindicated his claim that his engine *could* move a train and do the work of 40 teams of horses. A public contest for the best locomotive was announced by the Liverpool–Manchester line then under construction and in 1829 Stephenson's *Rocket* won the prize. It had a multitubular boiler and a steam exhaust draft, and drew the train at an average speed of 15 miles an hour, attaining 29 miles over some stretches. That historic day ushered in the railway era.

The United States imported a few English locomotives but they proved too heavy for the light track and could not take sharp curves and heavy grades. Built to burn coal, not wood, they had no spark arresters.[50] The first American-built steam locomotive, *Tom Thumb,* weighing one ton and having one horsepower, made a trial run in a race with a horse-drawn car on the Baltimore & Ohio Railroad, the first railroad in the country for transportation of freight and passengers.[51] Steam traction was so little trusted, however, that the company experimented with cars propelled by sails and with a treadmill locomotive operated by horsepower.[52] Another locomotive built in the United States was the *Best Friend of Charleston,* which reached a speed of as much as 21 miles while hauling four loaded cars. It was put in operation between Charleston and Hamburg, South Carolina, on the first railroad in the Western Hemisphere built specifically for the use of steam traction, without a path for horses. The Philadelphia and Columbia Railroad, which opened in 1834, still assured the public that "the train will depart daily when the weather is fair. . . . On rainy days horses will be attached." [53]

Gauges

The original English gauge, laid on a wooden track in the Northumberland colliery (4 feet 8.5 inches), was determined by the use of horses to haul the coal wagons,[54] but this gauge was not universal; one large English railway company (the Great Western) used the broad gauge of 7 feet. The need for coordinating rail traffic brought the "fight of gauges" to an end in 1892, when the broad gauge disappeared. In time, the English gauge became standard not only on railways in England but also on those in Germany, Belgium and most other parts of Europe, largely because the first locomotives were imported from England.

In the United States, various railways were built with track gauges ranging from 3 to 6 feet. Although some railway companies soon adopted the English gauge and Congress wrote it into the act for construction of the first transcontinental railroad, nineteen different track gauges were in use in 1871. By 1887, however, every important railway had its rails 4 feet 8.5 inches apart.[55] To bring their rails into line with the other railroads, a group of southern companies, by agreement, converted about 15,000 miles of tracks to the standard gauge in two days — May 31 and June 1, 1886.

In 1909 about three fourths of the world's rail mileage had the same gauge — 4 feet 8.5 inches.[56]

Rails

Although iron rails were imported from England around 1831, they were not used widely in the United States until after the 1850's. In the meantime, wooden beams were faced with iron strips which often became loose or even curled up suddenly like "snake heads" and pierced the bottoms of cars, occasionally injuring passengers

48. **62**, pp. 30–31.
49. **78**, p. 226.
50. **82**, p. 94.
51. **31**, p. 67.
52. **39**, p. 65. The treadmill was placed in a car carrying passengers. **82**, p. 103.

53. **82**, p. 65.
54. **98**, p. 23.
55. **54**, p. 16.
56. **97**, p. 100.

or throwing a train off the track. Steel rails appeared considerably later.[57]

Except in England, roadbeds were hurriedly, and not solidly, constructed, with little consideration for inescapable wear and tear. As a result, they often collapsed under heavy loads and train accidents were frequent.

Rolling Stock

The early locomotives were light and low-powered by today's standards. From 1839 to 1854 the weight of locomotives increased from about seven tons to fifteen tons, and the engines had single drivers with two wheels. During the 1850's, engines with four wheels on each side were introduced.[58]

Brakes were mere blocks of hard wood which the engineer pushed down by foot to press on the wheels, as on stagecoaches. Headlights were unknown, and trains ran only in daylight hours. In the United States, the first device for illuminating the track ahead of the train (on the South Carolina Railroad) was a small flatcar in front of the locomotive. A bonfire of pine knots was built on the floor of the car, on a thick layer of sand. Other lines used large candles in glass cases. The Camden and Amboy Railroad in New Jersey adopted an ingenious device to cope with the cows that frequently trespassed on the tracks. A small truck was attached to the front of the locomotive, with a cross, from which evolved a V-shaped "cowcatcher." For many years the cowcatcher remained a fixture on steam locomotives.

Passenger travel presented many discomforts as well as dangers. Coupling carriages caused jolts that threw passengers and luggage from their places. In the United States, until coal displaced the use of wood, flying sparks often started forest fires and ignited the coaches and even the clothing of passengers.[59] Only first-class cars were enclosed. Some coaches had a roof (or awning), and no sides; others with sides had neither windows nor lights. At first the passenger cars had no heat in winter months; later, stoves were installed. Candles, then, successively, whale oil, kerosene and gas lamps were used for lighting. The timetable was a matter of circumstance, the speed slow, and accidents were frequent. All in

all, "a railroad passenger literally took his life into his hands."[60]

Freight cars were of limited capacity, three or four tons. The early type of "wagons" — 4-wheel freight cars — are still used in England, though with great structural changes. In the United States, 8-wheel freight cars were introduced as early as 1831. Until 1870 cars were made of wood. Later, steel underframes were used, and since 1897 metal superstructures have become common.[61]

Opposition to Railroads

As had happened when coaches reappeared after centuries, the railroads were violently opposed by vested interests — turnpike trusts, innkeepers along the roads, coach owners and drivers, horse breeders and livery owners, on the one hand, and the economic groups connected with the building and operation of canals, on the other. In England, the opposition had an ally in the gentry, fearful that railways would destroy game preserves and beautiful lawns.[62] Others felt that to displace the noble animal by a machine which might burst and cause death and destruction was to fly in the face of Providence.[63] The combined forces of the opposition called on Parliament to refuse charters and loans to railroad companies. The latter had to maintain a large staff of attorneys to follow legislative proceedings and secure approval of charters.

Newspapers in many countries ridiculed the railways and printed alarming articles forecasting dire consequences of the new monstrosity for groups of the population and the nation as a whole.[64] Cartoons which reminded the public of the perils inherent in the railway system appeared in the United States, England and continental Europe. Some orators appealed to re-

60. **46**, p. 289; **61**, p. 62.
61. **61**, p. 58.
62. **88**, p. 5.
63. **62**, p. 40.
64. For example, an English editorial declared in 1835: "We denounce the mania as destructive of the country in a thousand particulars — the whole face of the Kingdom is to be tattooed with these odious deformities; huge mounds are to intersect our beautiful valleys; the noise and stench of locomotive steam-engines are to disturb the quietude of the peasant, the farmer and the gentleman; and the roaring of bullocks, the bleating of sheep and grunting of pigs to keep up one continual uproar through the night along the lines of these most dangerous and disfiguring abominations." (Quoted in **78**, pp. 246–47.)

57. **51**, p. 763; **82**, p. 85. See **101**, Chapter 29, p. 1103.
58. **82**, p. 97.
59. **44**, pp. 939–40.

ligious feelings and asserted that investment in railroads was a direct violation of the Scriptures since the Bible did not mention them.[65] In their turn, some railway companies (for example, the Western Railroad in Massachusetts) appealed to churches for help in enlisting public support and asked for sermons approving the moral effect of railroads. Some ministers obliged and others preached that no evil need necessarily be expected, but there were also dissenting sermons.[66] Worried townspeople remonstrated against building railroads in their neighborhood, since being peaceable and orderly people, they did not wish their quiet nights to be interrupted by the noise of steam locomotives.[67]

Skepticism as to the effectiveness of railways was general in France. When the railroad between Paris and Saint-Germain was up for consideration, Thiers said, "We shall have to give it to Paris as a plaything, but it will never carry a single passenger or a single trunk." [68] Blanqui did not mention the railways in his course on economics until 1838, and then only to say that they would be too expensive for freight transport and would never prevent the peasants from traveling afoot, with loads on their back.[69] Arago, the famous scientist, believed that rail travel would make soldiers too effeminate for fighting and that many would incur lung trouble, pleurisy and colds in the railway tunnels.[70]

In the beginning, the opposition met with some success, particularly in England, in influencing the public and government and creating difficulties for railway companies that were trying to issue stock. In the United States, vested interests influenced the stipulations in charters granted to railroads by various states. New York State, for example, had vast investments in the Erie Canal and imposed restrictions and taxes on railroads to be built within its territory. The state either forbade the railroads to carry freight — except the luggage of passengers — or permitted the transport of goods only when navigation on the canal was suspended, requiring payment of tolls equivalent to those obtained from transport on canals. These and similar restrictions were

canceled in New York in 1851 and in Pennsylvania in 1861.[71]

As the railroads improved and their advantages became increasingly evident, the opposition began to retire from a losing cause. Then a railway craze more vehement than that of the turnpikes seized the population in many countries. In England, for example, a wave of speculation, a kind of railway "mania," swept away all opposition around 1845 and stimulated the creation of numerous railway companies. Parliament passed 37 railway acts in 1843, 248 in 1844, and more than 700 in 1845. The scramble for shares reached a point at which "there was scarcely a family in England which was not directly or indirectly interested in the fortunes of the rail." [72] The inevitable reaction, followed by a crisis in railway finance, could not change the fact that in the meantime many lines had been built and others were under construction.

In the United States public interest in railways arose later, with the westward expansion. While much capital came from abroad, the government contributed heavily by grants of land and money. Private subscription for stock also played an important part, as "enterprising citizens" along the railroads bought shares in the expectation of profits from growing business.[73]

THE DEVELOPMENT OF THE RAILROADS

From the day of the *Rocket* demonstration in 1829 to the end of the nineteenth century, nearly half a million miles of rails were laid in the world and the railways became an efficient means of surface transportation.

This progress has required mastery of many technical problems. Roadbeds are better ballasted and graded; sharp curves have been eliminated and efficient traffic control systems established. Automatic coupling has become universal in North America and is used on many railroads elsewhere. The automatic block-signal system has been introduced on most railroads, whereby the train itself operates the signals, and automatic interlocking at train crossings established. Speed has been increased considerably, and the tendency is toward further increase.[74] Heavy steel

---

65. **71**, pp. 20–21.
66. **44**, pp. 939–40.
67. **39**, p. 76.
68. Quoted in **40**, p. 144.
69. **33**, p. 431.
70. **40**, p. 144.

71. **69**, p. 94; **39**, pp. 73–74.
72. **78**, p. 272.
73. See pp. 347–48.
74. In France, for example, the run from Bordeaux to Lyons (615 miles) was reduced between 1939 and 1949 from 34 hours 30 minutes to 25 hours 39 minutes; from

TABLE 125

RAILROAD LINES: LENGTH, BY CONTINENT, 1840–1950

(*Thousands of Miles*)

Continent	1840	1850	1860	1870	1880	1890	1900	1910	1920	1930	1950 [a]
World	5.4	24.4	67.2	130.5	231.4	380.7	491.7	640.4	...	776.6	768.0
North America [b]	3.3	9.1	32.7	55.4	100.2	177.6	211.8	265.8	292.8	294.0	264.7
Middle America	}0.1	}0.3{	0.5	0.7	1.7	7.9	11.0	20.4	20.4	25.6	}85.2 [c]
South America			0.3	1.7	6.2	17.0	26.5	40.3	48.8	58.8	
Europe	1.9	14.6	31.3	58.4	90.4	120.2	146.7	170.9	188.0	192.0	176.0 [e]
Russia (USSR)	0.02	0.4	1.0	7.0	15.0	20.2	31.7	41.2	36.6	52.0	76.6 [d]
Asia	—	—	0.9	5.1	10.1	20.1	36.5	59.5	59.5	82.5	92.1 [e]
Africa	—	—	0.3	1.1	2.9	5.9	12.5	23.0	...	42.4	42.1 [e]
Oceania	—	—	0.2	1.1	4.9	11.8	15.0	19.3	27.3	29.3	31.2

Sources: **100**, Vol. V, p. 35; **95**, pp. 901–02; **24**, 1881, pp. 496–97, 1933, pp. 4–9 and 1938, pp. 267–79; **43**, 1953–1954, pp. 386–87.

a. Data for 1940 are not available.
b. United States, Canada and Newfoundland.
c. 1949.

d. Target. Includes mileage in annexed territory: eastern Poland, the Baltic states and others. (**86**, p. 335.)

rails, averaging more than 100 pounds per yard, have displaced rails of less than half that weight. Heavier and more powerful steam locomotives [75] are in use, with an increasing proportion of diesel locomotives, which are more flexible and consume less fuel. Steel freight cars have replaced wooden boxcars, and their average capacity increased in the United States from the initial 3.5 tons to 29.4 short tons in 1903 and 52.9 in 1951. Specialized cars have been designed for various types of freight: refrigerator cars, tank cars, hopper cars and so on. Passenger cars have undergone great changes to provide travelers with sleeping and eating facilities, air conditioning and other comforts.

EXTENSION OF RAILWAY LINES

Development of the world's network of railways was effected in less than a century. Construction proceeded at a quickening rate — about 5,400 miles of rail lines from the beginning to 1840; 42,800 between 1850 and 1860; nearly 100,900 between 1870 and 1880 and 149,300 in

Versailles to Perpignan (558 miles), from 38 hours 17 minutes to 21 hours. **66**, 1950, p. 147.

75. Around 1900, no locomotive in the United States weighed 100 tons while today some weigh 600 tons or more. The average tractive power rose from less than 22,000 pounds in 1903 to more than 58,000 pounds in 1951. (**14**, 1952, p. 168 and **15**, 1950, p. 155.)

the following decade. The length of the world rail lines increased from 5,400 miles in 1840 to 130,500 miles in 1870, 491,700 miles in 1900 and 776,600 miles in 1930.

Although railroad construction continued after 1930, the total addition (36,000–37,000 miles) was more than offset by abandonment in various countries, particularly the United States, of some lines servicing small traffic. In 1950, the world had 768,000 miles of railroads.

North America and Europe led in railway building. Together they still have a greater mileage than the rest of the world but their relative share has declined with the development of the railway systems of other countries — from 95 per cent in 1860 to 82 per cent in 1880; 73 per cent in 1900; 63 per cent in 1930; and about 57 per cent in 1950. (See Table 125 and Figure 58.)

The decade of most intensive railroad building in England was 1840–50; in France, 1860–70; in Germany, 1870–80; in the United States, 1880–90; in Russia, 1890–1900; in India, 1900–10 and in Australia, 1910–20. After World War I, construction of railroads almost ceased in the United States, the United Kingdom, France, Germany and many other countries. The USSR, Brazil, Argentina and some other countries continued to expand their railway systems, which remain, nevertheless, below their requirements. (See Table 126.)

TABLE 126

RAILROAD LINES: LENGTH IN SELECTED COUNTRIES, 1850–1952

(*Thousands of Miles*)

Country	1850	1860	1870	1880	1890	1900	1910	1920	1930	1940 [a]	1952 [b]
United States	9.0	30.6	52.9	93.3	163.4	193.3	240.3	252.8	249.1	233.7	223.4
Canada	0.1	2.1	2.5	6.9	14.0	17.9	24.8	39.0	42.6	42.6	41.3
Mexico [c]	0.01	0.02	0.02	0.7	6.1	9.1	12.3	13.0	14.8	...	15.0
Cuba	0.2	0.4	0.4	0.9	1.1	1.4	2.3	...	3.0	...	3.7 [d]
Colombia	—	0.1	0.1	0.1	0.2	0.4	0.5	0.8	1.6	...	2.2
Chile	—	0.1	0.5	0.1	1.9	2.9	3.6	5.1	5.5	5.4	6.6
Peru	—	0.1	0.3	1.2	1.1	1.1	1.6	2.0	2.8	2.8	2.8
Brazil	—	0.1	0.4	2.0	5.9	9.2	13.3	17.8	19.7	21.3	23.1
Argentina	—	0.02	0.4	1.4	6.1	10.2	16.5	22.5	23.7	26.6	27.0
Great Britain	6.6	10.4	15.5	18.0	20.0	21.9	23.4	20.3	21.4	19.9	19.4
France	1.9	5.9	10.8	14.7	20.0	22.9	24.2	25.8	26.2	25.2	25.7
Belgium	0.6	1.1	1.9	2.0	2.2	2.7	2.9	3.0	3.2	3.0	3.1
Netherlands [e]	0.1	0.2	0.9	1.4	1.9	2.0	2.0	2.1	2.3	2.1	2.0
Denmark [f]	0.02	0.1	0.5	1.0	1.2	1.8	1.9	2.1	2.1	...	1.6
Sweden	—	0.3	1.1	3.7	5.0	7.0	8.7	4.4	10.4	10.3	9.4
Norway	—	0.04	0.2	0.7	1.0	1.3	1.9	2.1	2.4	2.5	2.7
Finland	—	—	—	—	—	—	—	2.7	3.3	3.6	3.0
Germany	3.7	7.2	12.2	21.0	26.7	31.9	38.0	35.9	36.4	36.7	18.9 [g]
Poland	—	—	—	—	—	—	—	8.6	12.9	11.1	15.8
Czechoslovakia	—	—	—	—	—	—	—	8.5	8.6	8.4	8.1
Switzerland	0.02	0.7	0.9	1.6	2.0	2.4	2.9	3.3	3.7	3.2	3.2
Austria-Hungary	1.0	2.8	6.0	11.5	16.8	22.9	27.6	—	—	—	—
Austria	—	—	—	—	—	—	—	2.7	5.1	3.6	3.7
Hungary	—	—	—	—	—	—	—	5.2	5.9	4.8	4.9
Portugal	—	0.1	0.4	0.7	1.3	1.5	1.8	2.1	2.1	...	2.2
Spain	0.02	1.2	3.4	4.7	6.2	8.3	9.3	9.5	10.1	...	11.1
Italy [f]	0.2	1.1	3.8	5.4	8.0	9.8	10.6	12.7	13.0	10.5	10.4
Yugoslavia	0.1	0.3	0.7	1.2	2.5	3.6	4.7	5.4	6.2	6.9	7.1
Romania	—	—	0.2	0.9	1.6	1.9	2.2	7.3	7.4	7.0	6.4
Bulgaria	—	—	0.1	0.3	0.5	1.0	1.2	1.6	1.8	...	2.0
Greece	—	—	—	—	0.2	0.6	0.9	1.4	1.5	...	1.5
Russia (USSR)	0.4	1.0	7.0	15.0	20.2	31.7	41.2	36.6	52.0	62.5	76.6 [h]
China [i]	—	—	—	—	0.1	0.3	5.0	5.0	8.0	...	11.4
Japan [j]	—	—	—	0.1	1.4	3.7	6.1	8.5	12.8	10.6	12.2
Turkey	—	—	—	...	...	0.4	...	...	...	...	4.8
Pakistan	}—	0.9	4.8	9.3	16.8	23.7	32.1	37.0	41.5	41.0{	5.5
India											34.0
Thailand	—	—	—	—	—	0.2	0.6	1.4	1.9	1.9	2.0
Indonesia	—	—	0.1	0.3	0.9	1.3	1.6	2.2	3.5	4.2	4.5
Egypt	—	0.3	0.7	0.9	0.9	2.1	2.3	2.7	...	...	4.4
Union of South Africa	—	—	0.1	1.0	2.4	5.5	7.5	10.1	12.6	...	13.3
Australia	—	0.2	1.1	3.6	9.8	12.6	16.5	24.1	25.6	26.0	27.7
New Zealand	—	—	—	1.3	1.9	2.3	2.7	3.2	3.7	3.3	3.5

Sources: **100**, Vol. V, pp. 34–37; **95**, pp. 901–02; **24**, various years; **1**, 1926, pp. 121–22; **11**, 1950, *passim;* **8**, 1951, pp. 62–63; **60**, 1951, pp. 18–21; **43**, 1953–1954, pp. 386–87; **2**, 1950, p. 256. For France, see also **77**, p. 185; for the USSR, **49**, p. 79.

(*Notes opposite*)

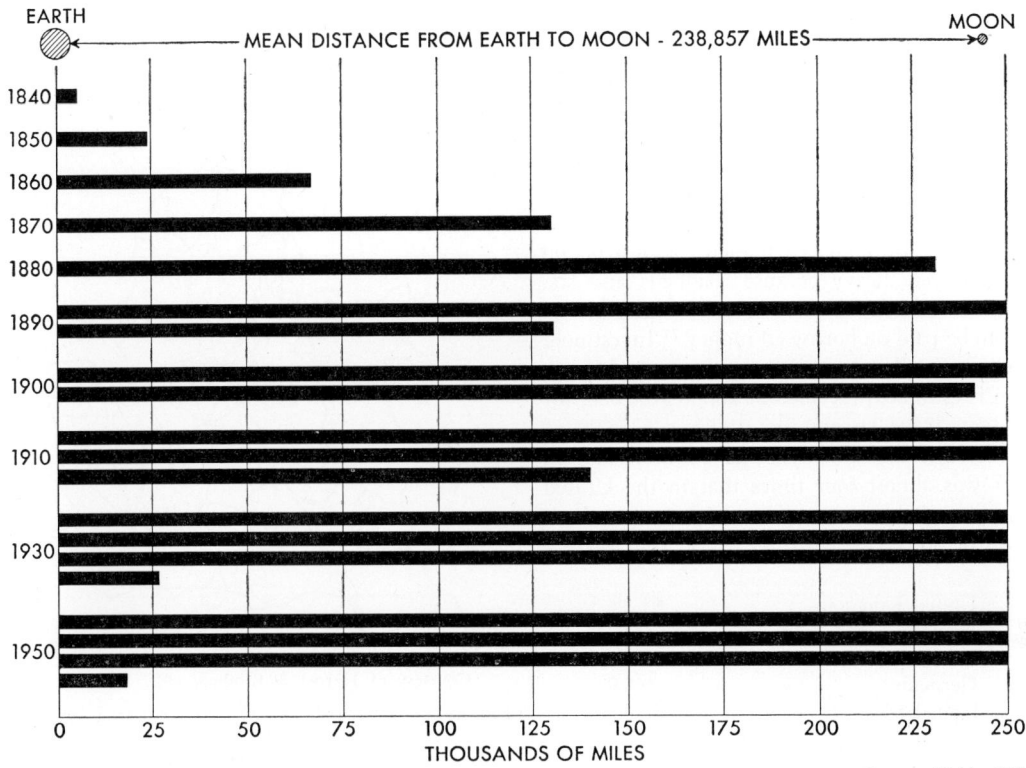

FIGURE 58. RAILROAD LINES: THE WORLD'S MILEAGE, 1840–1950

Source: Table 125

In countries well provided with railroads, the main work in recent decades has consisted in laying parallel tracks and additional sidings, improving the roadbeds and rolling stock, and introducing various devices and facilities for smoother, faster and safer operation.

The total rail trackage operated by railroads in countries with an effective network may be double or almost triple the length of the main lines. Including multiple tracks, sidings and yards, the trackage in the United States approached 400,000 miles in 1951; in the United

Kingdom, 51,703 miles in 1952. For every 100 miles of main line, the United States has 177 miles of track in operation; France, 204 miles; Belgium, 263 miles, in comparison with 114 in Turkey and Greece and 119 in Norway.[76]

DEVELOPMENT IN SELECTED AREAS

England

In England the construction of railways was a private enterprise from the beginning. Neither

76. **14**, 1952, p. 168; **8**, 1952, pp. 82–83.

Notes to Table 126

a. When data for 1940 are not available, those for the nearest year are used.

b. January 1, 1952, or the nearest period. For Romania: 1946; for Poland and Hungary: 1947; for Czechoslovakia: 1948. Canada: includes Newfoundland.

c. Mileage includes operating and nonoperating trunk, branch and auxiliary tracks. Data not comparable with other countries. According to **99** (1950–51, B29–33), the length of main lines is 12,430 miles.

d. Excludes private sugar-mill railways, not open to

general public, with total track mileage: 7,574. (**11**, 1950, p. 587.)

e. Includes some 300 miles for Luxembourg until 1900.

f. State railways only.

g. Western Germany.

h. Target 1950. Includes mileage in annexed territories: eastern Poland, the Baltic states and others. (**86**, p. 335.)

i. Includes Manchuria.

j. Includes Korea until 1940. According to **48** (1946–48, p. 415), the total length of main lines in 1947 was 15,929 miles.

the central government nor local administrations gave the railway companies any financial aid. Nor was there a law of "eminent domain," as in the United States; the acquisition of right-of-way was costly, particularly when speculation in railroad stock ran wild. Obtaining a charter for railway building was another considerable item, since a staff of lawyers was needed to follow the application through Parliament. Construction charges were heavy because roadbeds and stations were built for permanency; high interest had to be paid on borrowed money.[77] Investment per mile in all railway lines in the United Kingdom is estimated for 1863 at about $160,000, for 1883 at $240,000, and for 1907 at $273,000.[78] It exceeded that in any other country, and in 1907 was almost four times that in the United States, as the following figures show (in thousands of dollars): [79]

United Kingdom	$272.6
France	137.2
Italy	126.8
Germany	108.9
United States	70.7
Average:	
Europe	121.5
The world	66.5

Many small railroads, together totaling less than 7,000 miles, had been built in various parts of England by 1850, but they were largely disconnected, and only a few carried through traffic. (See Figure 59.) Later, they were merged into larger units, and then into a nationwide network. It took four more decades before the country was provided with some 20,000 miles of line extending in all directions. The United Kingdom has about the same main-line mileage today but all important lines now have three or four parallel tracks.

The United States

The United States has been the greatest railway builder in the world. In the first decade of railway construction, it laid a larger trackage than the rest of the world together. Even in 1890 the United States had nearly 43 per cent of the world's rail mileage, but afterward its share began to decline, to 39 per cent in 1900. Its mileage

Courtesy of Harper & Brothers (**42,** 1934 edition)

FIGURE 59. RAILROAD LINES: NETWORK IN ENGLAND, 1850

was greatest in 1916 (254,251 miles). Today, the United States has some 223,400 miles of main track, more than a fourth of the world's total.[80]

The short, disconnected tracks built in the 1820's and 1830's were consolidated in the 1840's into a semblance of a network along the Atlantic coast. In 1850, railroad lines were approaching the Mississippi River and the Great Lakes, but no railroad had yet been built west of the Mississippi. (See Figure 60.) Before 1860 a railroad network had pushed beyond the Mississippi at several points; in 1869, the first transcontinental line was put into operation, the East finally joining the West.

Other through lines from the East and the Midwest to the Pacific coast followed in rapid succession. Essentially, the framework of the American railroads was completed in the last decade of the nineteenth century. Though considerable main-track mileage was added until the beginning of World War I, most of the new construction filled out the existing framework.[81] Gradually, a nationwide railway system was developed through mergers and acquisitions, and

77. **87,** p. 589.
78. **81,** p. 18.
79. **13,** p. 7; cf. **81,** p. 189.

80. The mileage has declined somewhat because of abandonment of many small unprofitable lines.
81. **42,** p. 75.

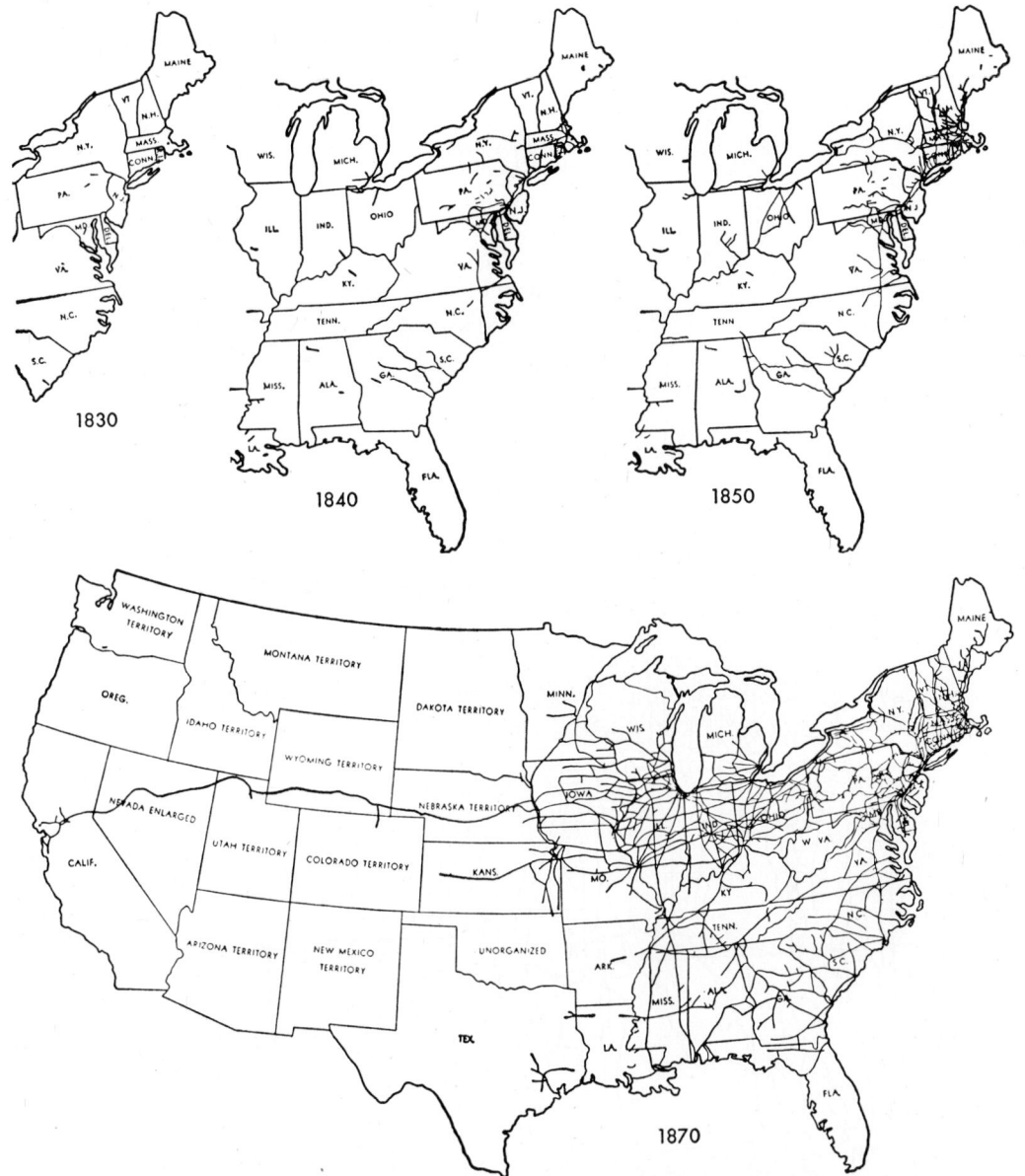

1830   1840   1850

1870

Courtesy of Association of American Railroads

FIGURE 60. RAILROAD LINES IN THE UNITED STATES, 1830–70

1830–50. The early stages of railway development in the United States are shown by this set of maps. During the decade 1830–40, the total length of completed railroad lines increased from 23 to 2,808 miles, and during the next ten years more than 6,200 miles of railroad were opened, bringing the total network up to 9,021 miles in 1850. The most intensive growth during this period was in the Atlantic and seaboard states. In 1850 a trip from Boston or New York to Chicago was made by rail and lake steamers or by stagecoaches, and required several days. One could travel all the way from Boston to Wilmington, North Carolina, by rail, with several changes of cars and a few ferry trips en route.

The population of the United States nearly doubled during these first twenty years of railway development.

1870. Although the Civil War temporarily halted railway development, many projects were resumed or initiated soon after the close of the conflict. The nation's network increased from 30,626 miles in 1860 to 52,922 miles in 1870. An outstanding development of the decade was the construction of the first railroad to the Pacific Ocean, making it possible for the first time to travel all the way across the country by rail. Railway development in the Mississippi and Missouri valleys was especially notable during this period.

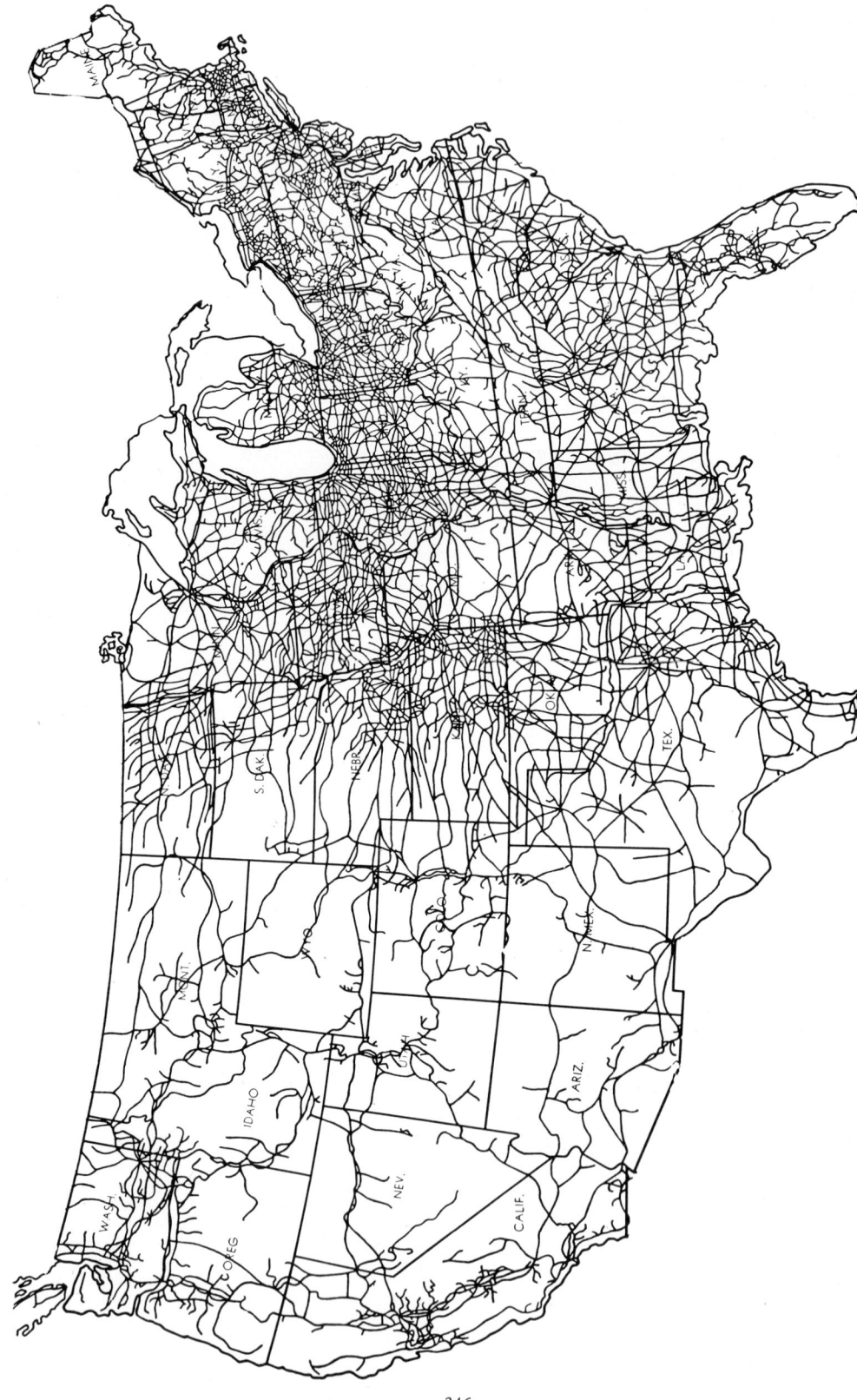

FIGURE 61. RAILROAD LINES: NETWORK IN THE UNITED STATES, 1950

Courtesy of Association of American Railroads

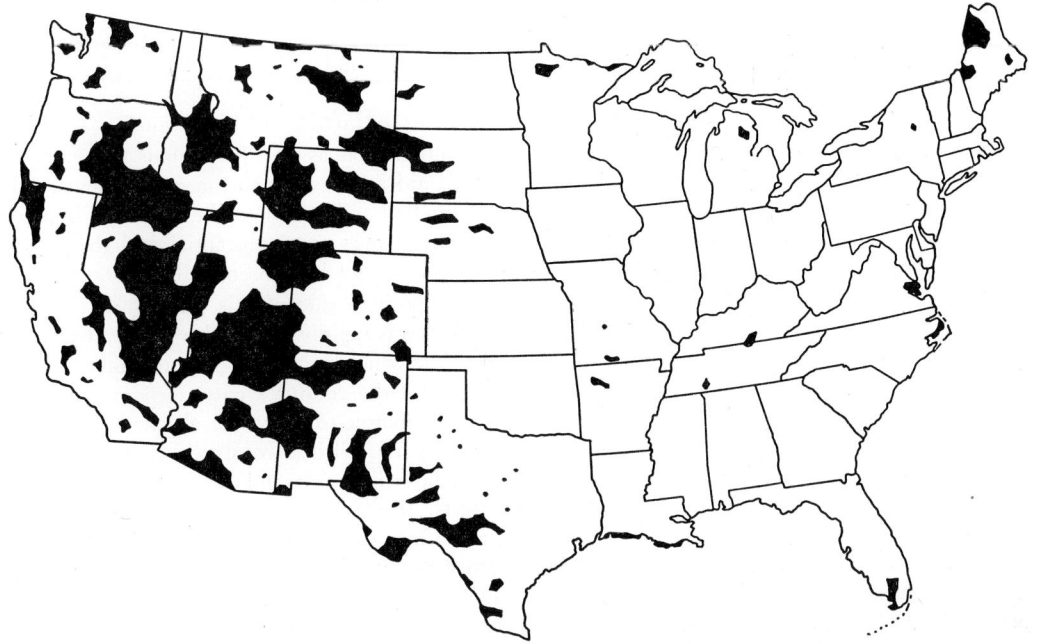

Courtesy of Association of American Railroads

FIGURE 62. RAILROAD LINES: AREAS IN THE UNITED STATES MORE THAN 25 MILES DISTANT FROM A RAILROAD, 1950

The areas shown on this map in black are more than 25 miles (approximately a half hour's drive) from a railroad. They are areas of sparse population.

the construction of link lines, so that now a shipper may load a car for direct movement anywhere in the United States and also in large areas of Canada and Mexico.[82] (Cf. Figure 61.)

Though many railroads have since been built in the western states, the density of the mileage remains uneven in the country as a whole, reflecting the uneven distribution of the population. The eastern part of the country is blanketed with railroads; the West, mostly in its arid and mountainous parts, has many areas more than 25 miles distant from a railroad. (See Figure 62.)

In addition to growth of population and the rapid development of the country, three factors supported the building of railroads in the United States: the law of eminent domain, making it possible to expropriate private property in the public interest against the owner's will but at just compensation; European capital, which controlled half or even more of the stock of some railroads;[83] and generous grants of land and financial aid in various forms (loans, subscription to securities, tax exemptions and so on) by federal and local governments. Although the law of eminent domain freed the railway companies from paying exorbitant prices for property — as the English companies were forced to do — domestic capital was scarce, and the building of many important railways depended on foreign financing. Of the more than $2 billion of foreign capital, English investors alone accounted for nearly $620 million.[84] Railroad stocks and bonds were bought abroad in large quantities. Not until the end of the nineteenth century, when construction of railways was almost completed (193,346 miles in 1900), did American investors begin to repurchase the securities. Some railway corporations placed their stocks on European markets even later, among them the Union Pacific, the Pennsylvania and the Chesapeake and Ohio.[85]

Public aid was lavish and took many forms.

82. **25**, p. 16.

83. For example, Illinois Central, 86 per cent; New York, Ontario and Western, 58 per cent; Reading and Pennsylvania Railroads, 52 per cent; New York Central and Hudson River, 37 per cent, and so on. (**69**, p. 100.)

So much Dutch capital was invested in the Chicago and Northwestern that two foreign directors were on its board for a time. (**93**, p. 45.)

84. **47**, p. 27; **45**, p. 47.

85. **69**, p. 100; **93**, pp. 46–47.

The most important element in federal aid was the land grants, totaling 130 million acres up to June 30, 1940, exclusive of rights-of-way but with allowance for land forfeited because of failure to build the railroad, conflicting titles or other reasons.[86] The Northern Pacific was the largest single beneficiary, with almost 41 million acres.[87] It is estimated that by the close of 1927 the Northern Pacific had obtained $101 million from land sales — more than the initial cost of the road.[88]

Other federal aid consisted in exempting imported iron from the high tariffs then in effect, in granting rights-of-way through the public domain and in according loans, which, however, were almost fully repaid.

State aid took the form of many privileges, such as partial or complete tax exemption, donations, credits, guarantee of bonds and subscription to stock. Land grants were infrequent because few states had much land at their disposal, but Texas, for one, gave away some 35 million acres. State grants of land totaled 49 million acres.[89]

In addition, cities, townships and counties gave railroad companies financial aid amounting to some $140 million, either through subscription to stock of railroad companies or by issuing public obligations. Public aid also included contributions of cash, materials, equipment, labor, banking and lottery privileges, and so on.

There are various estimates of the total amount of public aid to the railroads. One estimate evaluates it at $928.5 million up to 1870, a sum that would have covered some two fifths of all construction costs.[90] The Office of the Federal Coordinator of Transportation estimates public aid up to 1933 at $1.3 billion. The differences in various estimates depend on whether land grants, for example, are to be valued at the very low price per acre at the time of donation ($147.7 million) or at the higher price eventually obtained ($489.3

million) and so on. On the other hand, federal savings from lower rates at which the railroads carried mail and military personnel and equipment (until the repeal of these concessions in 1945) are estimated at $1.2 billion.[91]

Controversial as are the various estimates of public aid and savings to the governments, it is certain that public aid to the railroads in their early years was very substantial and that many lines would not have been built without it.

The positive side of this policy was that the country was rapidly provided with a vast railway network which stimulated the settlement of the West and the country's entire economy. It was no easy matter to overcome all the obstacles in the way of railroad construction, to penetrate into the wilderness and brave mountains and deserts. It was difficult to enlist workers who had to face many dangers and hardships in territory not yet fully conquered. Yet as early as 1880, the United States had a considerably greater railway mileage than the USSR has now. This rapid development benefited every section of the country, every group in the population.

On the negative side were the construction of some unprofitable and superfluous lines, the speculation and fraud sometimes used in obtaining public aid, debts which overburdened the finances of some states and municipalities.[92] Many lines "just grew" like Topsy, in advance of settlements, rather than to meet the requirements of existing traffic. Most of the construction was completed hurriedly, at the minimum outlay, and compared unfavorably with the solidly constructed English railways. While the cost per mile was much lower than in England, the inevitable work of improving the old railways has somewhat lessened the difference.[93]

Public enthusiasm about the railroads gradually subsided and in the 1870's even turned to indignation because of the excessive rates on various lines, discrimination in rates and so on. Under the pressure of public opinion, certain government regulations (the Granger laws) were introduced and in time were modified and strengthened in many respects. Eventually the railroads established themselves as a permanent part of the country's economy and, under government regulation, became more orderly. Even the light construction became something of an

---

86. **31**, p. 619. Including the rights-of-way, the Office of the Federal Coordinator of Transportation counted the land grants to the western railroads alone at 183.2 million acres up to 1933, all of which was granted before 1871. (**17**, Vol. 2, p. 51.)

87. As a rule, 6 square miles of land were allotted for each mile of built railroad; the first Pacific line obtained 10 square miles per mile of line. (**81**, p. 201.)

88. **31**, p. 620.

89. Of the 179 million acres in federal and state grants, the railroads had sold almost 163 million by December 31, 1941. (**31**, p. 620.)

90. **83**, pp. 38–39.

91. **10**, p. 72; cf. **42**, pp. 71–72.

92. **83**, p. 42.

93. **81**, p. 188.

asset, since there was less resistance to modernization. Old light tracks were torn up and replaced; inadequate rolling stock was replaced with improved new equipment.[94]

France

While Great Britain was feverishly building railroads, France was slow in accepting the new medium of transportation. Its roads were in good shape and its canals were developing rapidly, while capital was scarce and hesitant to enter a novel and untried field. A few small steam-powered railroad lines were built, with a total of only 300 miles by 1840. In the meantime, however, administrative and financial foundations for the development of a comprehensive railway network were worked out through cooperation between the government and private companies. The law of 1842 provided for the construction of seven main lines radiating from Paris to the coasts and national borders, and of cross-country lines connecting Bordeaux with Marseilles and Dijon with Mulhouse.

In 1849, France had a few short lines extending from Paris to Le Havre, Calais and other points on the English Channel, and a few other small disconnected lines near the large cities — Lyons, Marseilles, Bordeaux and Strasbourg. (See Figure 63.) Ten years later, France had nearly 6,000 miles in operation, and in another decade — at the time of the Franco-Prussian war — more than twice that mileage. Defeat in that war and financial difficulties slowed progress, but when the government guaranteed interest to stockholders and some moderate dividends to companies, the branching railroads began to extend in various directions from Paris, the focal point. Between 1870 and World War I, France more than doubled its railroad mileage. The lines envisaged in the law of 1842 today form the great trunk lines of the French railway system.[95]

Belgium

While the French system was, from its inception, a kind of a hybrid between government and private companies, Belgium decided as early as 1834 to build a railway network controlled by the state. Two trunk lines were completed in 1844, crossing the country to the borders of

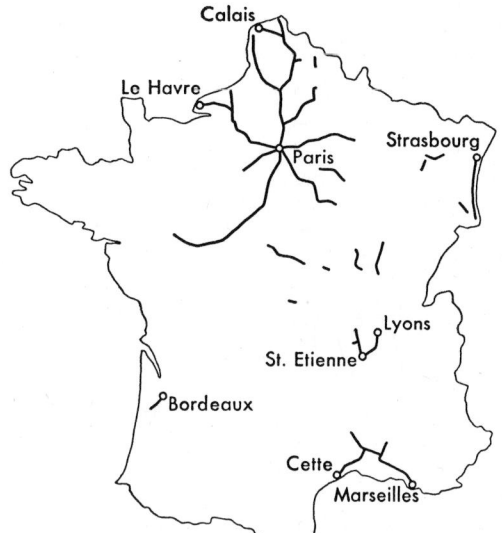

Courtesy of Harper & Brothers (**42**, 1934 edition)

FIGURE 63. RAILROAD LINES: NETWORK IN FRANCE, 1849

France and Germany. The borrowed money was spent carefully; the railroads were built efficiently and speedily. Fares and freight rates were low, and in 1872 Belgium was first to inaugurate cheap weekly tickets to enable workers to live in the environs of industrial centers, taking advantage of low rent and some land to augment their income. Ten years later, a system of narrow-gauge lines was started to facilitate the exchange of goods between rural areas and cities.[96] By 1900, all the essential lines had been built, and the railroad system was only slightly extended thereafter.

Germany

The first railroad in the territory which later formed the German Empire was a 3.5-mile line between Nürnberg and Fürth. The formation of the customs union (Zollverein) among the many petty princedoms in 1834 stimulated railroad building, and in 1849–50 Germany had about 3,700 miles although some lines were less than 20 miles long. (See Figure 64.) Friedrich List, the famous German economist, who had lived in the United States and observed the effect of railways on the American economy and their role in national cohesion, tried, on his return to Germany, to convince his countrymen of the necessity and advantages of a great railroad net-

94. **61**, p. 24.
95. **81**, pp. 63–64.

96. **53**, p. 528.

Courtesy of Harper & Brothers (**42**, 1934 edition)

Figure 64. Railroad Lines: Network in Germany, 1849

work. Military considerations also pointed to the importance of railways, and Prussia soon started a line from Berlin to the Russian border. Other states followed suit with small railroads from the capitals to their frontiers.

Bismarck strove to unify the piecemeal lines in one national system under government ownership, but the hostility of some states made this goal impossible. Then he bought up private companies in Prussia until the entire system became the property of the state. Some railroads crossed Prussia's border, and he purchased these too, so that Prussia finally dominated the German railroad network.[97]

Victory over France and formation of the German Empire gave momentum to railway construction, and Germany more than doubled its mileage between 1870 and 1890, subsequently increasing it further by almost a third before World War I.

German railways were built cheaply, without leveling the roadbeds. They provided the simplest accommodations for passengers of the third, and particularly the fourth, class and also used mixed trains for passengers and freight. Speed was low, but the traffic, nevertheless, very heavy.

The central German government controlled nearly the entire railway system, with 97.5 per cent of the mileage of the main lines and 85 per cent of the branch lines before World War I.[98]

Italy

At the time of the early railroad agitation, Italy represented a group of small independ-

ent city-states. A few short disconnected lines were built in the late 1830's, but the first railway of any practical importance — from Milan to Venice — was not opened until the late 1850's. In 1870, unified Italy had 3,800 miles of railways.[99] Some had a charter from the emperor of Austria, others from the pope. Lines were isolated, running from some city — Naples, Rome, Venice and so on — only to the borders of the former city-state.

The new national government tried to extend the mileage and bring some order into the chaotic conditions among the existing lines and gave the railroads assistance of every kind: guarantees of interest, subsidies for construction and operation, loans. It built some lines and purchased others, either paying or defaulting on payment, according to its financial status. It tried various forms of management — government control, lease to private companies, participation in the profits. Neither the state nor business, however, could make substantial investments.[100] Moreover, the need for railways was less urgent than in some other countries. Goods could be shipped at lower rates from the many adjacent ports; coal, an important item of freight in the United Kingdom and Germany, was almost lacking in Italy. As a result of these and other factors, Italy, with a population about equal to that of Great Britain, had, before World War I, less than half the British railway mileage.

Switzerland

The topography of Switzerland kept it from accepting railroads immediately, and the first short stretch was not built until 1847. After the unification of the country in 1848, construction of railroads encountered less opposition and one line after another was built. The greatest achievement was the Saint Gotthard railroad (1881), an epoch-making enterprise to which Germany and Italy contributed financially. Its nine-mile tunnel was then unique in the world and is still one of the longest.[101]

---

97. **62**, p. 75.
98. **81**, p. 139.

99. Although the Italian state was created in 1860, it was another decade before Venice was ceded to it by Austria and some other provinces by France.
100. **52**, pp. 220–21.
101. The Simplon Tunnel, between Switzerland and Italy, is some twelve miles long. Next come Lötschberg Tunnel, in Switzerland, nine miles long; the Mont Cenis (eight miles) between France and Italy and the Cascade Tunnel (seven miles) in the United States. (**43**, 1953–1954, p. 399.)

In 1910, Switzerland had almost 3,000 miles of railway. Further development has consisted essentially in improvements — building multiple tracks, converting to electric power and so on.

Other European Countries

Austria-Hungary also provided itself with railroads rapidly, although it lagged considerably behind Germany. Spain and Portugal started late but, like other countries, completed the main work before World War I. In the Balkan countries, little was built until the end of the nineteenth century.

Russia (USSR)

With its far-flung territory, Russia needed railways as badly as the United States. Its topography presents few obstacles, while the waterways used for transport since early times have the great disadvantage of being frozen for four or five months a year. Nevertheless, railroad building proceeded very slowly. The first steam railway was built from St. Petersburg, the capital, to Tsarskoe Selo, the Czar's residence, in 1837. But in 1860, when the United States had more than 30,000 miles of main track and Great Britain, more than 10,000, Russia's rail lines extended only about 1,000 miles. The periods of greatest expansion were from 1868 to 1874, after the abolition of serfdom, and again in the last decade of the nineteenth century.

Among the lines which greatly influenced the country's industrial development was the railway from the Donets Basin (coal) to Krivoi Rog (iron ore), completed in 1884. A few years later, Russia initiated its most ambitious project — the Trans-Siberian Railway, still the longest in the world. This trunk line was built simultaneously from the west and the east and extended beyond the Chinese border. When it was completed in 1905, Russia had a direct-line haul from one end of the empire, at Germany's borders, to the other, on the Pacific. This line greatly enhanced the importance of Siberia, stimulated the development of its natural resources and opened new markets for the young Russian industry. It made Russia a Pacific Ocean power, both politically and economically.

The Trans-Siberian line was subsequently continued for more than 1,600 miles through Chinese territory, using the Russian broad gauge, and was operated, by the agreement of 1896, jointly by the Russians and the Chinese. Possibly it was among the immediate causes of the war between Russia and Japan, which was alarmed by the growing might of the czar's empire and its penetration into China.[102]

On the eve of World War I, Russia had almost 50,000 miles of railroad. A considerable mileage was built in 1914–17.[103] After that war, with the loss of the Baltic area, Finland, Poland, and Bessarabia (to Romania), the Russian network shrank to 35,000–36,000 miles.[104]

Between 1918 and 1952, the Soviets built new lines, particularly in the east (the Turksib, 900 miles long, connecting Turkestan with Siberia; the Petropavlovsk-Karaganda-Balkhash line, about 750 miles long, and others), and many feeders to the existing lines. During World War II, more than 6,000 miles were built, and construction is continuing.[105] Many lines, including the largest part of the Trans-Siberian Railway, have been double tracked. More powerful locomotives and better rolling stock have been introduced,[106] and the inventory has been increased considerably. A substantial part of the trackage has been re-equipped with heavier rails, although lighter than those used in most European countries and the United States.[107] The Russian gauge was, from the beginning, wider than that on most European railways, and when traffic across borders developed, a special device was invented for shifting the wider Russian cars to the narrower gauge of other systems. The majority of the main trunk lines in European Russia have moderate grades.

The railroad map of the USSR clearly shows the uneven distribution of the lines and the in-

---

102. The treaty of 1945 provided for the fusion of this Eastern Chinese Railway with that in South Manchuria, to be run jointly for thirty years by the USSR and China and to become Chinese property afterward. The treaty of 1950 stipulated that the USSR would turn over to China its rights of co-administration as soon as a peace treaty with Japan was concluded, and in any case, not later than 1952. On December 31, 1952, the USSR handed over this railroad to China.

103. **63**, pp. 694–96; **27**, pp. 440ff; **76**, pp. 30–31. According to an official Soviet source, Russia had 49,455 miles of railroad, including the Chinese Eastern line, on January 1, 1914. (**75**, p. 3.)

104. **76**, p. 33.

105. **32**, p. 49; **57**, pp. 4–6.

106. The USSR has built locomotives with a tender condenser, capable of running some 625 miles without taking on water. This makes them very useful in arid central Asia and generally in areas with water shortage. **75**, p. 12.

107. **86**, pp. 337–38.

adequacy of the network. The rail system is densest in the west, around Moscow and in the Ukraine. Siberia has one trunk line from east to west; vast northern Siberia has no railroad; central Asia has too few in relation to its territory.[108] (See Figure 65.) The 1950 map of the Russian railways is somewhat similar to the 1870 map for the United States — fairly well-developed network in the areas of the greatest concentration of population and a single line stretching across the continent. The Fifth Five-Year Plan, for 1951–55, schedules the completion of the South Siberian railroad between Akmolinsk and Taishet; a second trans-Siberian line following a more northerly direction than the old one and terminating at Sovetskaya Gavan on the Pacific. Another small line, and further construction work on a few connecting lines (for example, Krasnoyarsk-Yeniseisk in Asia; Gurev-Astrakhan along the Caspian Sea) are also envisaged, as well as the building of double tracks on various lines and improvements in equipment. Of the South Siberian line, 620 miles have been laid, and the latest section, Akmolinsk-Barnaul, was opened at the end of 1951.[109]

Canada

Canada's first railroad, 16 miles long, between Laprairie and Saint-Jean, Quebec, was opened in 1836 and used a locomotive built by Stephenson in England. Another line, 6 miles long, used horsepower for the first few years until a locomotive was brought over in a sailing vessel from England.[110] In 1850 Canada had only 66 miles of railroad; in 1870, 2,500 miles and in 1890, 14,000. Of greatest significance was the completion in 1885 of the first transcontinental line, for which the government contributed money and 25 million acres of land. As in the United States, many lines were built to promote settlement and commerce in remote areas. The federal and provincial governments granted more than 47 million acres, gave cash subsidies of $219 million, and guaranteed railway bonds. The Canadian Pacific Railway alone obtained land grants of 37 million acres.[111]

Between the beginning of this century and World War I Canada almost doubled its railroad mileage. British capital financed a large part of the outlay.[112] Canada built two other transcontinental railways (Grand Trunk Pacific and Canadian Northern). The government undertook to build the eastern section of the former and lease it for fifty years to the Grand Trunk Pacific Company, which obligated itself to build the western section, under government guarantee of interest on bonds up to 75 per cent of construction costs. It was confidently expected that immigration of capital and labor from Europe would rapidly settle areas thus provided with a railroad, as was the case with the region served by the Canadian Pacific. But World War I changed the situation, and the Grand Trunk Pacific could not take over the operation of the railroad completed in 1915. The Canadian Northern also got into financial difficulties. The government undertook the operation of the Grand Trunk and acquired, on the basis of an act of 1917, the capital stock of the Canadian Northern. In 1920, it also took over the insolvent Grand Trunk and formed the Canadian National Railways by merging both systems (Order in Council of 1923).[113]

In addition, the provincial governments of Ontario and British Columbia own some mileage, and some branches of the United States railways also run in Canada. In turn, both major Canadian systems own rail mileage in the United States: the Canadian National has a network in New England, Michigan and Illinois; the Canadian Pacific owns the Duluth, South Shore and Atlantic Railroad and the Minneapolis, St. Paul and Sault Sainte Marie line.[114]

The Canadian railway system, ranking third in the world in length, is closely connected with that of the United States. Rolling stock of all kinds moves freely across the borders. A special feature of the Canadian system is that it operates not only railways but all other transportation facilities — ocean and coastal ships, lake and river vessels, airlines, telegraph, radio and express service, and hotels.

Latin America

Latin America lacks adequate railroads. Construction started late; in 1870, forty years after the appearance of railroads, this vast area had only 2,400 miles. The topography presents great difficulties, particularly in some South American

108. **28**, p. 78.
109. **99**, 1952–53, p. 427.
110. **90**, p. 83; **18**, 1939, p. 630.
111. **18**, 1945, p. 587.

112. **47**, p. 27; **50**, pp. 174–78.
113. **18**, 1939, pp. 630–31 and 640–42.
114. **7**, July–September 1952, p. 27.

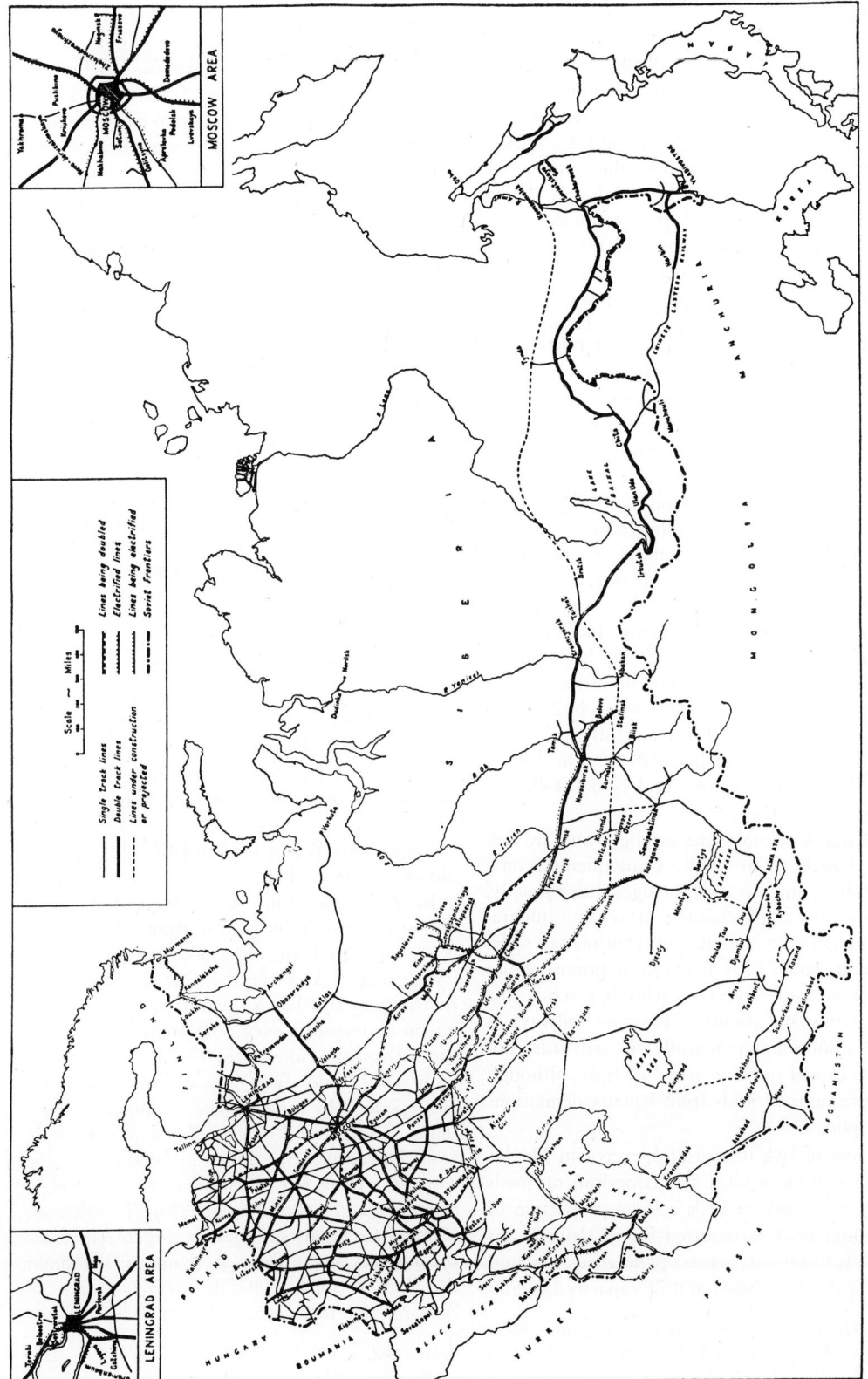

FIGURE 65. RAILROAD LINES: NETWORK IN THE USSR (Target for 1950)

Courtesy of Sampson Low, Marston & Company (99)

353

countries where mountains rise steeply from the sea coast. Trains in Bolivia, Chile and Peru have to climb to the highest roadbeds in the world, over 15,800 feet,[115] and to surmount sharp grades. Climatic conditions, with torrential rains during many months of the year and deep snows in the mountains, impede both the construction and operation of railways. Landslides and washouts occur frequently and disrupt traffic.

Domestic capital is scarce, and railways have been built largely by foreign investors, mainly British but also French. United States capital has been active chiefly in neighboring countries of Latin America, such as Cuba and Guatemala. The participation of foreign capital has exercised considerable influence on the structure of the railway system in Latin American countries. The first lines were built mainly to transport raw materials and agricultural products to the ports for export: minerals from Peru and Bolivia, livestock products and grain from Argentina, coffee from Brazil and Colombia, bananas from Guatemala and Honduras, and so on.

Railway construction proceeded most actively between 1880 and 1913. Panama built its railroad after World War I, when the backbone of the railway system in almost all countries had been completed. Subsequent railway building in Latin America has consisted mostly of feeder roads to main lines built earlier.[116] The largest networks are in Argentina and Brazil, followed by Mexico and Chile.

The tracks of most lines are light and are ballasted largely with earth. Consequently, only light rolling stock is used. Gauges differ greatly, even within a single country, preventing integration on either a national or continental scale. Moreover, some lines between important cities parallel navigable rivers or each other, while vast areas within the countries have no railways at all. Honduras has practically no railroads; not even its capital can be reached by train, although a private railroad leads from banana plantations to the port.

Because of lack of coal and, except in Mexico and Venezuela, of oil, Latin American railroads largely use wood for fuel; a large proportion of the rolling stock is required for its delivery. In Brazil, for example, some of the roads are said to use a third of their ton-mile capacity in hauling their wood fuel supply.[117] Brazilian railroads "use as fuel wood, coal and oil, in the order named. Many roads use wood almost exclusively. . . . Some of the railways . . . have carried on extensive work in reforestation along their lines, preparing for the day when national forests will have been exhausted." [118]

Only a few lines have introduced automatic signaling, and the track is often cleared for the incoming train by telephone from station to station.

Asia

The entire continent of Asia had less than 1,000 miles of railroads in 1860 — all of them in British India.

Japan waited for the famine of 1869, which was aggravated by lack of facilities for transport of rice from surplus areas, to decide to float a railway loan in London and start construction when funds became available. It obtained its first line in 1872, at first using foreign technicians to build the roads, but was soon able to raise domestic capital and employ its own personnel. Main trunk lines have been built along the coast and also in the interior. Ferry steamers, and in some cases train ferries, are used to connect the main islands; an underwater tunnel 2.2 miles long connects Honshu and Kyushu. Before World War I Japan had more than 6,000 miles of railroads and since that time it has doubled the mileage.

China built its first road in 1876, also with the aid of foreign capital.

In *India* the lines have been constructed almost exclusively by British capital. With some 9,300 miles in 1880, India accounted for nearly 93 per cent of Asia's railroads. It has maintained its lead and still has a third of Asia's rail mileage in its territory, even after transfer of part of the network to Pakistan in 1947.

In *Turkey* the first railway lines were built and operated by foreign-owned companies: German, British and French. The first railway — from Haydarpasa, a suburb of Istanbul, on the east side of the Sea of Marmara to Baghdad — was initiated by Germany in 1889. The Ottoman Railway Company of Anatolia, organized under the auspices of the Deutsche Bank, was to build the line in some 200-mile sections — first to Ankara, then to Konya, and so on. The first two

---

115. The highest point reached by a regular steam road in the United States is 11,319 feet.

116. **3**, 1948, pp. 163–65.

117. **102**, p. 194.

118. **56**, p. 315.

sections were completed by 1896. In 1902 Germany obtained the concession for the rest of the project, intended to provide direct communication between Berlin and Baghdad. But political and diplomatic difficulties with Great Britain and France, aware of German expansionist aims, caused delays and interruptions. The agreement reached among these powers in June 1914 was nullified by the outbreak of war, during which construction continued under German military supervision. By 1918 the line ran from Haydarpasa, via Eskisehir, Adana and Aleppo to Nusaybin, and after a gap of some 300 miles, resumed for about 84 miles to end at Baghdad. After the end of World War I, when Iraq and Syria were carved out of former Turkish territory, the railroad was divided between Turkey, Iraq and Syria. If and when Turkey establishes a train-ferry across the Bosporus, from Istanbul to Haydarpasa, London and Baghdad can be connected by railway.

A few other short lines extend westward toward the Aegean plain and eastward toward the Soviet border. The latter provide a connection with Tiflis in Soviet Georgia and, with another route within the USSR's territory, to Iran. Turkey is now extending its network to obtain a connection with Iraq, thereby eliminating the use of the bypass into Syria, and opening a rich agricultural area in the east. The Turkish railway network of less than 5,000 miles consists almost exclusively of single-track lines.[119]

Iran. Except for a 6-mile line from Teheran to a neighboring shrine village, built in 1892, Iran had no railroads before World War I. In 1916 a Russian company completed a 90-mile-long line from Dzhulfa to Tabriz and a shorter branch line. This railway connects Iran with Russia and uses the Russian gauge. Iran's biggest enterprise was the construction of the Trans-Iranian railway, intended to foster the country's own interests rather than to link foreign railways across Iran's territory. This railway, 808 miles long, was completed in 1938, wholly with native capital. It is possible that the difficulties encountered during its construction can hardly be matched anywhere in the world.[120] Hundreds of bridges and nearly 200 tunnels were built; one tunnel, nearly 7,000 feet above sea level, is more than two miles long, and one section of

the line stretches for miles on ledges blasted out of steep walls of deep gorges. Other railways were built in Iran during World War II.

Africa

Construction of railways started in Africa late in the nineteenth century, with the penetration of European colonization deep into the Dark Continent. The first main period of railroad construction lasted until World War I; the second took place in the 1920's. Africa as a whole had the same mileage in 1950 as in 1930.

Not until most of the continent had been divided among the European colonial powers was there interest in building railroads in Africa. Construction was stimulated by the provision of the Berlin Conference of 1884–85 that title to territories in Africa could be maintained by a colonial power only by effective occupancy. Since most African rivers are obstructed by rapids and falls and are unsuitable for uninterrupted navigation, occupancy could be secured largely or only by railways.[121] The developing demand for Africa's raw materials and the prospect of new markets for European goods encouraged railroad construction.

Technical difficulties unknown in other areas faced Africa's railroad builders, however. In some places, the high precipitous topography and unavoidably steep ascents raised engineering problems as to grades and curves.[122] In other areas, an inadequate water supply has been a real barrier to construction. Coal is lacking throughout nearly all the continent, and wood is often used. Heavy seasonal rains wash away whole sections of tracks, and many areas lack good ballast material. Bridges of many spans have had to be built across wide rivers; one, across the Zambezi, is more than four miles long, the longest railway bridge in the world. In densely forested areas such as in the Gold Coast, the Ivory Coast and parts of central Belgian Congo and eastern Nigeria, clearing of forests and undergrowth involves considerable work and expense. About 80,000 trees may have to be cut for 100 miles of railway, and some of them may be 30 feet in circumference at the base and have large buttresses. Even the cutting of undergrowth is

119. **91**, pp. 79–80; **7**, January–March 1953, pp. 16–17.
120. **96**, p. 145.

121. **7**, July–September 1949, pp. 6–7.
122. The Kenya-Uganda railway, for example, reaches about 9,000 feet of altitude, after a descent in the Great Rift Valley to 6,000 feet seventy-five miles away. (**7**, July–September 1949, p. 8.)

difficult. Climatic conditions impose a great strain on non-African personnel, yet labor often has had to be brought from other countries and even other continents, since native labor generally has proved both insufficient and inefficient.

Each European power built lines within its African colonies and deliberately chose a different gauge to discourage trade with other territories. Six main gauges are now in existence, although the standard European gauge is used on some main lines.[123] Lately, some attempts at international cooperation have been made, such as on uniformity of gauge in some areas and on links between separate lines in others.

The largest single railway system is in the Union of South Africa. The system also operates much of the country's highway transport, its domestic and international air services and the main harbors. The government of Southern Rhodesia owns and operates the Rhodesian railways, some 2,500 miles long, running from Bulawayo across Northern Rhodesia via Victoria Falls and Broken Hill to the border of the Belgian Congo. This system has an eastward connection with the Beira railroad, owned by the Portuguese government but operated by the Southern Rhodesian railways. Further links through the continent are provided by the trans-Zambezi line which extends to the Central Africa Railway, and another to Nyasaland. There is a through connection between Capetown, Bulawayo, and Lake Nyasa. There are a few other lines, but connection between Capetown and Cairo has not yet been established. Egypt is served by a small railroad mileage; one of its lines, between Alexandria and Cairo, was the first built in Africa. Almost every territory has some narrow-gauge mileage, but on the whole the continent is meagerly provided with rail transportation and many lines are isolated.

Oceania

Australian railway history began in 1854, with the opening of the first line. Development was sporadic, and the network, depending on the country's physical relief and the policy of individual states, took on a radial and circumferential shape. Along the most populated regions in the southeast, the highlands run parallel to the seacoast and railroads were built inland, behind them. Since the seacoast is well provided with harbors, railways radiate from capitals of the various states or from centers of agricultural production to ports with considerable shipping.

The longest stretch of straight track in the world, more than 300 miles without a curve, is on the Trans-Australian line, crossing the Nullarbor Plain in western and southern Australia. Until the 800-mile-long railroad was built across the barren area to the west, the only communication with the east was by water, along the coast. To build this road, all supplies, including water and even firewood, had to be hauled from the east around the continent.[124]

The Australian network has not yet achieved a truly continental character because of differences in gauges, although some integration was effected when two important breaks in the transcontinental line were closed. The lines reaching into the interior, with the lightest traffic, have been built by the central government to encourage the development of the continent.

New Zealand, too, had many disconnected lines at first but now the network is almost integrated into a national system.

Modern Railroads

DENSITY OF RAIL FACILITIES

The extent to which a nation or an area is provided with railroads is shown by the density of railroads in its territory, usually measured in terms of railroad mileage per 100 square miles (or kilometers) and per 1,000 or 10,000 inhabitants. Because areas differ greatly in density of population, neither of these coefficients alone is sufficient. For example, the United States and Yugoslavia had about the same railroad mileage per 100 square miles in 1950, but per 10,000 inhabitants the United States had five time as many miles of railroads as Yugoslavia. On the other hand, the USSR and Great Britain had about the same mileage per 10,000 inhabitants at that time while the British mileage per 100 square miles was about 27 times the Russian.

In most countries, density per 100 square miles increased between the world wars.[125] In contrast, density per 10,000 inhabitants declined almost everywhere because the slight increase in railway mileage could not match the rapid growth of the population. Thus, in 1950 Canada had 32

---

123. **7**, July–September 1949, pp. 8–9.

124. **93**, p. 13.

125. Data for countries affected by territorial changes are more indicative of shifts in boundaries than of increase in railway building or abandonment of existing lines.

miles per 10,000 inhabitants, in comparison with 43 miles in 1926; for Argentina, the corresponding figures are 17 and 24 miles; for Sweden, 13 and 17 miles; for Australia, 34 and 45 miles. (See Table 127.)

A conventional map reveals the contrasts in the density of railroads in relation to territory. It shows a close and continuous network of railroads in western Europe, eastern North America, the western USSR, Japan and coastal regions of South America and Australia. In contrast, vast areas in other parts of the world are crossed by only a few isolated lines. This difference becomes even clearer when the length of railroads in different regions is marked by dots, one dot representing, say, 1,000 or 5,000 miles of line, independent of the location and direction. (See Figure 66.) Contrasts in the density of railroads in relation to population can be shown similarly by plotting dots on a distorted map of population. (See Figure 67.)

ROLLING STOCK

In 1950, the world as a whole had more than 200,000 locomotives, about 400,000 passenger cars and 6.5–7.0 million freight cars, very unevenly distributed among continents and countries.

INVENTORIES

Comparison of the inventory of rolling stock in various countries is not very meaningful because of great variations in the type, quality, age and serviceability of the actual equipment.[126] A smaller number of modern powerful locomotives, for example, may perform more work than more numerous, but light and obsolete, units.[127] A "passenger car" may have only benches along the wall, like the fourth-class passenger cars on prewar German railroads, or may be a modern, air-conditioned and luxuriously appointed parlor car. Freight cars may be simple platforms for carrying lumber, boxcars, refrigerator cars, or specially equipped tank cars lined with rubber or glass. Freight cars also differ in size and carrying capacity. In Great Britain, Norway, Denmark, Switzerland, Portugal, Spain and Japan, capacity averages 13–16 metric tons. In other European countries, the railway-owned freight cars carry, in general, up to 20 tons or slightly more; some privately owned cars have a capacity of nearly 30 tons. The average capacity of Canadian freight cars is from 38.6 to 43.7 metric tons; in the United States the average is 47.7 metric tons for railway-owned freight cars and 39.5 tons for those privately owned. (See Table 128.) International statistics on rolling stock, however, do offer some insight into the status of railroads in various countries.

The United States has the largest stock of locomotives and freight cars in the world but considerably fewer passenger cars than the United Kingdom. The explanation lies in the much greater use of private automobiles in the United States for general travel and particularly for commuting. Moreover, the American railroad cars are larger and seat more passengers. On the other hand, the volume of production in the United States and the intensive regional specialization and great distances require a substantially larger number of freight cars and locomotives. In its turn, the United Kingdom, although it has only half as many freight cars as the United States, leads all other countries in the number of freight cars. It needs them to transport foodstuffs and raw materials arriving from all parts of the world as well as to haul domestic products throughout its territory. Showing an impressive recovery since World War II, Western Germany ranks third in rolling stock, except for freight cars, of which France and the USSR have more.

During that war, the rolling stock of belligerent countries in Europe was subjected to frequent bombing and excessive wear and tear. Maintenance was inadequate, and replacement of parts almost impossible. When the war ended, much rolling stock had been destroyed and much that remained was obsolete. Most countries have now made a substantial recovery through the repair of old stock and acquisition of new.

Outside the United States and Europe, the USSR, India and Japan lead in rolling stock. Japan has more than before the war, while India still lags behind its peacetime inventory. (See Table 129.) The 1950 target of the postwar plan of the USSR was to build 7,585 locomotives

---

126. The International Union of Railways has now adopted formulae which express the number of locomotives in terms of tractive power and should permit future international comparisons. These formulae are considered to be generally applicable in Europe. **8**, 1952, pp. 48–49.

127. Experience in the United States may illustrate this point: in 1929, the railroads had 61,257 locomotives and produced 31.2 billion passenger-miles and 450.2 billion ton-miles; in 1950, with 18,306 fewer locomotives, they turned out 31.8 billion passenger-miles and 591.5 billion ton-miles. **15**, 1950, pp. 155 and 158.

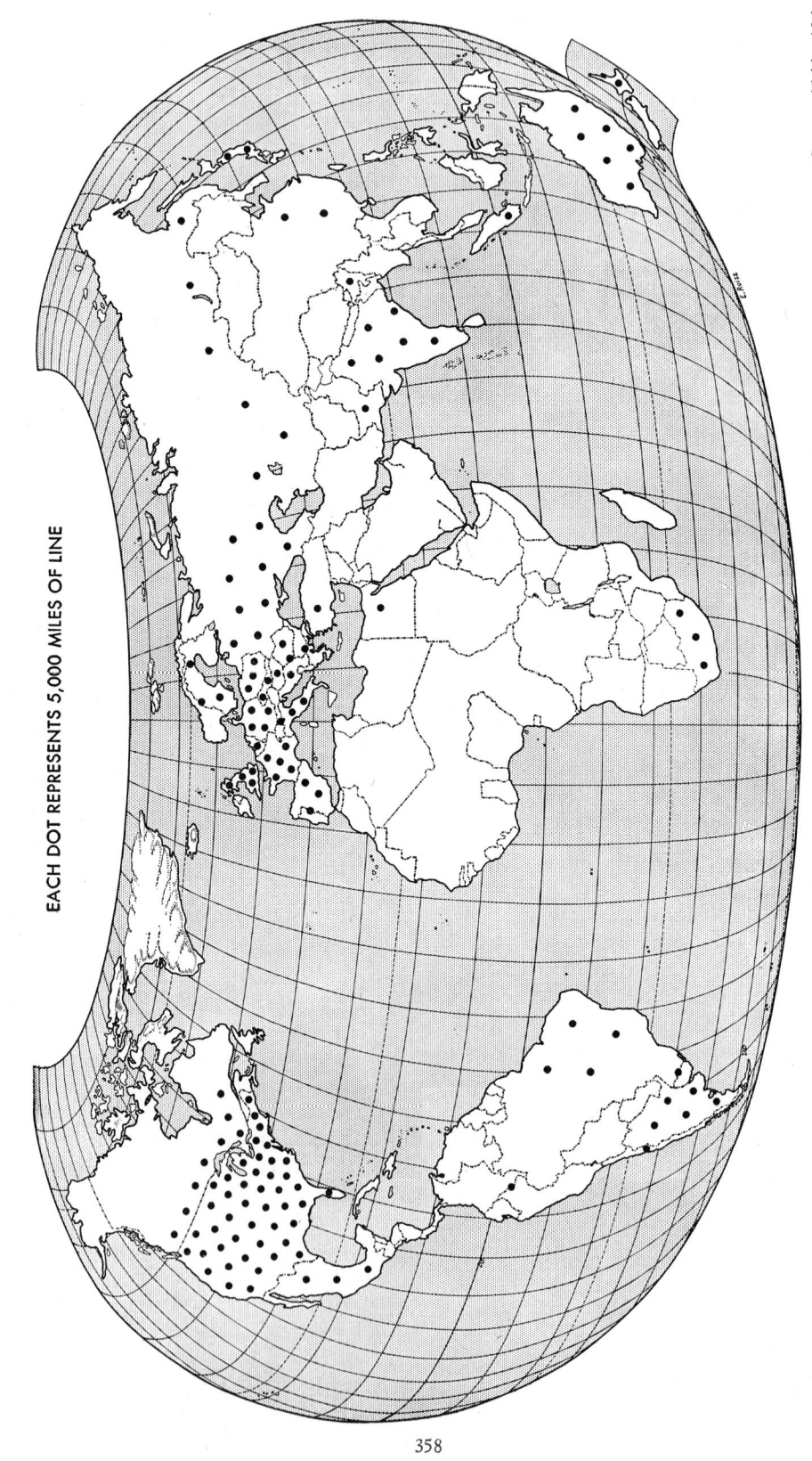

EACH DOT REPRESENTS 5,000 MILES OF LINE

Figure 66. Railroad Lines: Density in the World, 1952

Source: Table 126

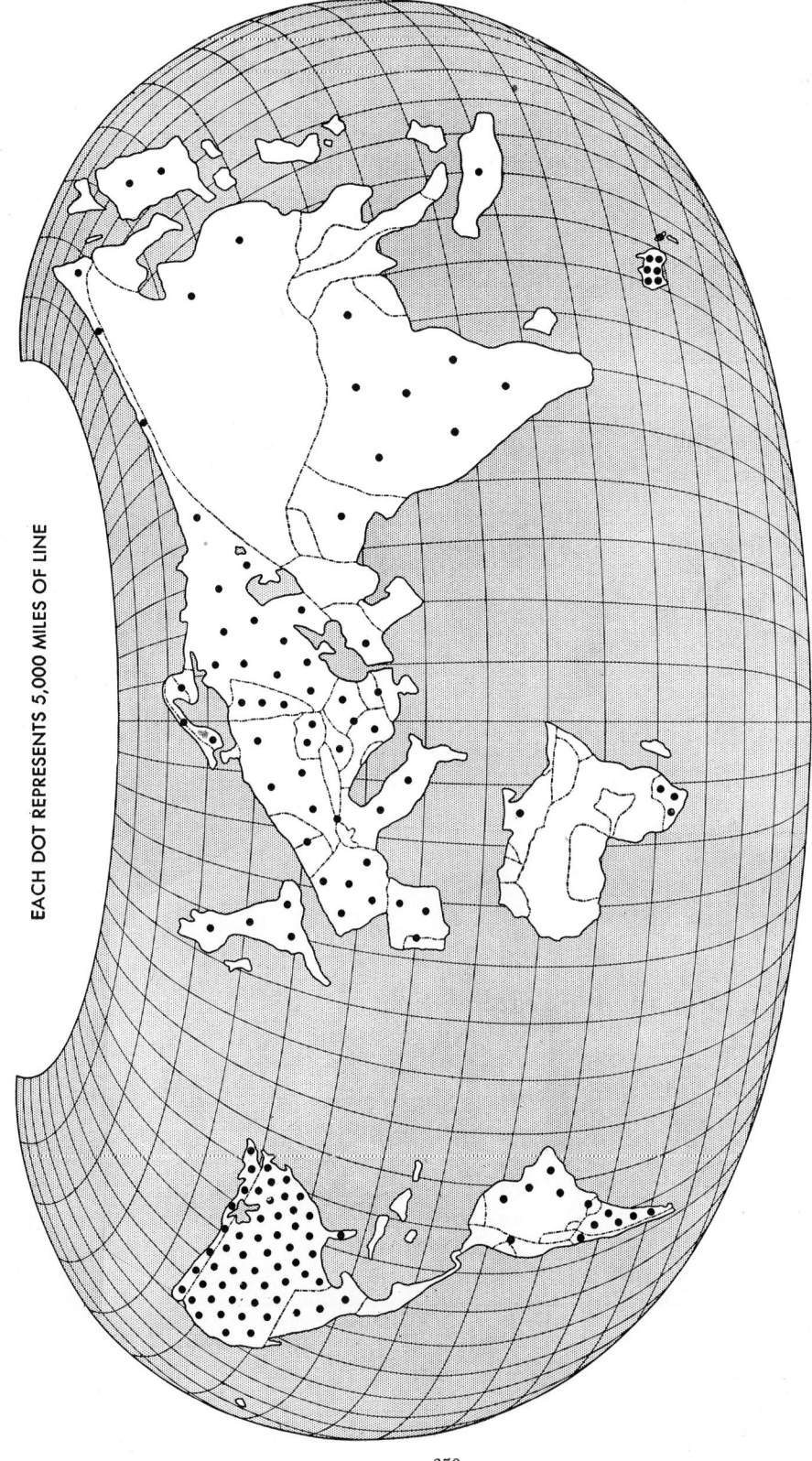

EACH DOT REPRESENTS 5,000 MILES OF LINE

Source: Table 126

Figure 67. Railroad Lines: Density in the World in Relation to Population, 1952

Continents and countries are shown on a scale proportionate to population.

TABLE 127

RAILROAD LINES: DENSITY PER 100 SQUARE MILES AND 10,000 INHABITANTS, IN SELECTED COUNTRIES,
*1901, 1926, 1950

(*Miles*)

Country	Per 100 Square Miles			Per 10,000 Inhabitants		
	1901	1926	1950	1901	1926	1950
United States	6.6	6.9	7.4	25	24	15
Canada	0.5	1.1	1.1	34	43	32
Mexico	1.3	2.1	2.0	7	12	6
Colombia	0.1	0.2	0.5	—	2	2
Chile	1.0	1.9	2.3	9	14	12
Peru	0.2	0.3	0.6	2	4	3
Brazil	0.3	0.6	0.7	6	6	5
Argentina	1.0	2.1	2.5	21	24	17
Great Britain	18.2	20.1	21.6	6	5	4
France	13.0	15.6	12.6	7	7	6
Belgium	22.9	26.3	26.3	6	9	4
Netherlands	14.6	16.2	16.1	4	3	4
Denmark	10.8	12.7	9.6	7	9	4
Sweden	4.2	5.6	5.4	4	17	13
Norway	1.0	1.8	2.0	6	8	8
Finland	—	1.9	2.2	—	10	7
Germany	15.6	20.0	19.8[a]	6	6	4[a]
Poland	—	8.0	11.9	—	6	6
Czechoslovakia	—	16.1	16.2	—	6	7
Switzerland	15.1	22.5	20.0	7	9	7
Austria	}8.9{	13.5	11.5	}5{	7	5
Hungary		16.6	15.0		7	6
Portugal	4.2	6.0	6.1	2	4	3
Spain	4.3	5.0	5.7	5	4	4
Italy	8.9	10.9	8.3	3	3	2
Yugoslavia	—	5.8	7.2	—	5	3
Romania	3.9	6.6	...	3	4	...
Greece	2.4	4.0	3.0	2	4	2
USSR[b]	1.4	1.6	0.8	4	3	3
China	—	0.2	0.3	—	...	...
Japan	2.6	5.1	8.6	—	2	1
Turkey	...	2.4	2.6	...	...	2
India[c]	1.3	2.1	2.7	—	...	1
Thailand	0.1	0.8	1.0	—	2	1
Indonesia	—	0.5	0.5	—	...	...
Egypt	...	0.3	1.3	3	2	2
Union of South Africa	1.0	2.4	2.9	22	...	11
Australia	0.5	0.8	0.9	32	45	34
New Zealand	2.3	3.1	3.4	28	22	18

Sources: **24**, 1903, pp. 502–07; 1929, pp. 2–11. For 1950, Table 126 and **5**, 1951, pp. 21–33.

a. Western Germany.
b. 1901 and 1926: European Russia.
c. 1950: excludes Pakistan. Corresponding figures for

Pakistan: 2.3 miles per 100 square miles; 1 mile per 10,000 inhabitants.

TABLE 128

RAILROAD EQUIPMENT: AVERAGE CAPACITY PER
FREIGHT CAR,[a] 1938 AND 1951

(*Metric Tons*)

Country	1938 Railway Owned	1951	
		Railway Owned	Privately Owned
United States [b]	44.6	47.7	39.5
Canada	...	43.7[c]	—
Great Britain	12.2	13.4	...
France	18.0	19.4	24.4
Belgium	17.8	20.2	20.3
Netherlands	16.3	19.0	23.7
Luxembourg	...	21.0	29.8
Denmark	14.3	16.0	15.6
Norway	14.2	15.1	15.7
Sweden	21.0	19.6	22.1
Finland	...	15.9	13.4
Western Germany	17.0[d]	20.1	19.6
Austria	15.2	18.8	18.0
Switzerland	14.4	15.4	16.0
Portugal	...	14.6	18.3
Spain	...	13.2	17.8
Italy	18.9	18.7	28.7
Japan	...	15.9	...
Turkey	...	18.0	23.2
Iran	...	25.2	...
Syria	...	16.9	...
French Morocco	...	22.3	...
Algeria	...	17.8	28.8

Sources: **8**, 1951, p. 35; **15**, 1950, p. 155; **60**, 1951, pp. 40–45.

   a. Railways of standard and wide gauge.
   b. Class I railways.
   c. National railways. Canadian Pacific: 38.6 tons.
   d. Prewar Germany.

(6,165 for steampower, 555 electric units and 865 diesels), 6,000 passenger cars and 472,500 freight cars.[128] It is estimated that the USSR had 852,000 freight cars in 1948, although the target of its first postwar plan had been 800,000 by 1950.[129]

Types of Locomotives

Steam-powered locomotives have been used for more than a century on at least 95 per cent of the world's railroad mileage and for about 75 per cent of the total traffic.[130] They predominate on almost all railroads except in Switzerland.

In the United States, diesels are being used increasingly and in 1949 accounted for more than 90 per cent of all new locomotives; in 1952, for more than 99 per cent.[131] In 1950, they hauled more than a third of the freight traffic and about half of the passenger traffic; in 1952, more than two thirds of all traffic. The largest locomotive manufacturers in the United States no longer make steam locomotives. Diesels are also gaining ground in the Netherlands, where about one locomotive out of four or five was of this type in 1951, as compared with one in twenty in 1949.

The growing popularity of the diesels comes from their many advantages. They can work longer hours per day and more days per year, yet require much less servicing than steam locomotives. While they are more expensive to build, they can be operated at about half the cost of the steam locomotive and are also cheaper to maintain.[132] According to the Interstate Commerce Commission, "the Diesel locomotive . . . has given railroad operations a marked lift and has made a contribution which will be difficult to match in the immediate future with any other single advance in railroad technology."

The use of electric locomotives is also increasing, though less rapidly. In Switzerland, electric locomotives are rapidly displacing steam locomotives; the latter made up about 30 per cent of the total in 1952 and all were over age and kept largely as an emergency reserve, awaiting replacement by electric units.[133] Italy's railroads also make considerable use of electric power; nearly three locomotives out of ten are electric. Swedish railroads are using diesels and electric locomotives increasingly. (See Table 130.) On the other hand, the United Kingdom and Western Germany still had steam locomotives on order at the end of 1951.[134] In 1950, about a fifth of rail traffic in the USSR was served by electric locomotives and diesel engines.[135]

ELECTRIFICATION

Use of electric traction in the United States began modestly in 1895 on the Baltimore & Ohio Railway when, to reduce the effects of smoke, an electric locomotive was used to draw trains

128. **49**, pp. 27–28.
129. **86**, p. 339.
130. **72**, p. 44.

131. **7**, April–June 1949, p. 26. Data for 1952 supplied by the Association of American Railroads.
   132. **31**, p. 84; **14**, 1952, p. 5.
   133. **8**, 1952, pp. 48 and 93.
   134. **8**, 1951, p. 32.
   135. **32**, p. 117.

TABLE 129

RAILROAD EQUIPMENT: ROLLING STOCK IN SELECTED COUNTRIES, 1929, 1937, 1950

Country	Locomotives			Passenger Cars			Freight Cars, in Thousands		
	1929	1937	1950	1929	1937	1950	1929	1937	1950
United States[a]	61,257	47,555	42,951	61,614	50,440	43,681	2,630.8	2,090.5	2,010.1
Canada	5,531	4,667	4,655	5,597	6,395	6,338	218.0	172.8	175.6
Mexico	1,493[b]	1,300	1,482	1,237[b]	1,642	1,471	18.3[b]	21.4	21.4
Panama[c]	27[b]	21	45	68[b]	65	147	1.0	0.7	1.5
Colombia	. . .	326	332	. . .	773	689	. . .	3.9	4.2
Brazil	3,178[b]	3,556	3,724[d]	3,733[b]	3,652	4,925[d]	43.1[b]	46.0	58.8[d]
Peru	194[b]	225	217	230[b]	267	205	2.2[b]	2.9	3.2
Chile	1,323[b]	1,188	1,149[d]	1,164[b]	1,295	1,269[d]	21.9[b]	19.7	20.0[d]
Argentina	4,067[b]	3,928	3,992	6,834[b]	7,116	6,694	77.8[b]	80.5	81.2
Great Britain	23,454	19,806	19,741	51,243	61,547	58,429	700.0	1,281.0	1,098.0
Ireland[e]	789[b]	745	681	2,470[b]	2,307	1,815	19.0[b]	18.3	18.0
France[f]	20,104	18,730	13,390	35,339	52,750	33,850	531.0	517.8	428.2
Belgium[g]	4,192	3,681	2,728	9,031	8,757	5,257	116.0	112.1	85.7
Netherlands	1,352	1,086	962	5,209	3,322	2,444	34.0	28.7	23.8
Denmark[h]	1,041	836	795	2,725	3,610	3,223	17.0	16.6	18.1
Sweden	2,257	2,151	2,239[i]	4,108	5,216	5,920	57.0	48.4	51.7
Norway	597	547	580	1,226	1,404	1,331	13.3	12.0	12.9
Finland	758	781	857	1,274	1,641	1,874	22.0	24.8	28.1
Germany[j]	24,089	20,482	14,843	66,003	87,710	37,337	682.0	611.6	296.3
Poland	5,269	5,477	6,874[i]	11,913	10,688	7,796[i]	151.0	167.6	144.5[i]
Czechoslovakia	4,235	4,122	3,080[k]	8,947	12,925	9,747[k]	109.0	98.2	72.0[k]
Switzerland	1,284[b]	1,316	1,419	6,130[b]	6,254	6,058	22.5[b]	20.8	23.9
Austria	2,546	2,122	2,148	5,918	7,825	5,069	33.0	36.3	31.3
Hungary	2,100[b]	1,970	1,736	5,048[b]	5,620	3,005[i]	37.1[b]	42.6	18.8[k]
Portugal	541	518	516	1,391	1,674	1,456	9.6	9.4	10.4
Spain	. . .	3,047[i]	3,395	. . .	7,717[i]	6,115	. . .	77.0[i]	73.6
Italy[m]	6,799[b]	5,696	5,484	3,716[b]	12,150	10,841	160.7[b]	133.5	135.1
Yugoslavia[f]	2,839	2,364	2,397	4,188	5,148	5,430	56.0	54.3	63.1
Romania	2,170	3,482	3,048[n]	2,780	4,764	4,177[n]	58.0	64.0	79.4[n]
Bulgaria[f]	440	540	680[n]	535	627	815[n]	10.0	11.0	14.6[n]
Greece	397[b]	448	249	764[b]	678	240	6.2[b]	6.7	5.1
USSR	17,719	25,000[o]	. . .	23,556	34,200	. . .	487.0	650.0[o]	852.0[k]

(Continued on facing page)

through a tunnel section. Some sections of the New York, New Haven and Hartford line were electrified at about the same time.[136]

Before large-scale use of electric power became possible in railroad transportation, many technical problems had to be solved. Today the considerations are economic and financial, rather than technical. Initial investment in power lines and other installations is high, but operating costs are relatively low. Electrification therefore pays in countries with comparatively cheap elec-

tric power and on railways or sections of railways where traffic is heavy, and does not pay on long lines with insufficient traffic. Advanced countries with limited or no coal deposits and with abundant water power naturally are more likely to electrify their railways than countries with plentiful coal supplies. Rising coal prices may also induce the railroads to convert from steam to electric traction.[137]

Nearly all of Switzerland's rail lines and one of every three miles of railroad in Italy are electrically powered. In Sweden, electrified lines ac-

---

136. In London, electric power was used somewhat earlier in the intracity tube (subway). **43**, 1952–1954, p. 398.

137. **92**, p. 53; cf. **7**, October–December 1949, pp. 3–7.

TABLE 129—*continued*

Country	Locomotives			Passenger Cars			Freight Cars, in Thousands		
	1929	1937	1950	1929	1937	1950	1929	1937	1950
China	411	1,000	2,477[k]	459	2,000	3,694[k]	7.0	15.0	31.4[k]
Japan	5,141	4,235	5,692	13,847	9,640	14,009	76.0	73.8	108.7
Turkey[f]	...	878	999	...	1,194	1,606[d]	...	13.1	15.7
Iran	...	...	132[d]	...	...	148[d]	...	...	4.4[d]
India	9,442[p]	8,560	8,437	20,229[p]	26,463	21,198	234.0[p]	221.8	213.0
Burma	395	379	313	1,375	1,183	415	10.7[b]	9.7	4.4
Thailand[f]	182[b]	192	438	310[b]	322	596	3.1[b]	3.5	6.2
Indonesia	...	1,278	809	...	3,614	2,621	...	27.1	20.9
Philippines	161	178[r]	101	359	397[r]	381	2.0	2.4[r]	2.2
French Morocco	...	96	172	...	394	356	...	4.0	4.9
Algeria	771[b]	795	500	1,400[b]	1,290	837	13.5[b]	12.5	11.1
Tunisia[s]	...	236	319	...	370	347	...	3.2	5.3
Egypt	854	849	968[d]	1,691	1,520	1,543[d]	19.0	17.3	18.7[d]
French West Africa	314[b]	341	348	379[b]	401	309	2.9[b]	3.4	3.6
Belgian Congo	355[b]	...	354	138[b]	...	161	3.8[b]	...	5.9
Southern Rhodesia[t]	198[b]	236	236	238[b]	358	373	3.4	4.2	6.4
Union of South Africa	2,139	2,191	2,758	3,758	4,183	5,240	38.0	46.5	76.3
Australia[f]	3,903	3,629	3,536	8,262	8,004	8,170	88.0	86.0	92.4
New Zealand[f]	657	570	656	1,593	1,492	1,555	27.3	27.7	35.2

Sources: **19**, 1931, pp. 75*–77* and 1938, pp. 104*–07*; **8**, 1950, pp. 58–59; **5**, 1952, pp. 279–82; **60**, 1950, pp. 30–45. For the United States: **12**, p. 202; **15**, 1950, p. 155.

a. Passenger stock includes Pullman cars (9,491, 7,776 and 6,322, respectively, for years indicated). Freight stock includes privately owned cars, such as tanks, refrigerator cars, stock cars and other (in thousands: 307.1, 314.1 and 264.3, respectively).
b. 1928.
c. Excludes small lines.
d. 1949.
e. Includes the Great Northern Railway, part of which is in Northern Ireland. Passenger stock includes postal vans.
f. State railways.
g. Standard-gauge railways.
h. Diesel locomotives included in passenger stock.

i. 1947.
j. 1950: Western Germany. Standard-gauge railways, government-owned.
k. 1948.
l. 1935.
m. State railways. **8**, 1951 (p. 70), gives 5,205 locomotives for 1950 and 5,086 for 1951.
n. 1946.
o. 1938.
p. Includes service vehicles.
r. 1939.
s. 1937: Tunisian Railway only.
t. Includes Northern Rhodesia Railway and a small railway in Mozambique.

count for 39.4 per cent of the total mileage and for all the main lines, which carry the bulk of the traffic.[138] In Japan, about 15 per cent of the main track is electrified.

Moreover, the proportion of electrically operated mileage is increasing steadily. In Italy, it was 29.5 per cent in 1938 and 34–35 per cent in 1952. For Norway, the corresponding figures are 10.7 and 23.6; for the Netherlands: 15.2 and 42.2.[139] (See Table 131.)

Shortly after World War II, France decided to electrify its Paris-Lyons railway, which carries one of the heaviest concentrations of passenger traffic in the world. Later, electrification is to be extended to Marseilles. The Paris-Lyon line has been completed, as has that from Lyon to Italy, via Modane. Electric traction between Paris and Rome is to be completed in 1955.[140]

Belgium is planning to electrify a considerable part of its system. The electrification plan envisaged before World War II was to cover some 100 miles of line but has now been extended to about 1,000 miles. Some 30 per cent of the Belgian locomotives are to operate electrically and haul about 70 per cent of total traffic. Electrified

138. **23**, p. 93.
139. **8**, 1949, p. 18 and 1952, p. 42.

140. **66**, 1950, p. 105; **8**, 1953, p. 42.

TABLE 130

RAILROAD EQUIPMENT: LOCOMOTIVES, BY TYPE, IN
SELECTED COUNTRIES, 1951 [a]

Country	Total	Steam	Diesel [b]	Electric
United States	42,473 [c]	22,590	19,014	817
Canada	4,620	4,075	512	33
United Kingdom	19,532 [d]	18,859	211	58
Ireland	631	624	7	—
France	11,224	10,100	160	964
Saar	333	322	11	—
Belgium	2,207	2,176	5	26
Luxembourg	131	131	—	—
Netherlands	899	588	220	91
Denmark	783	726	57	—
Sweden [e]	2,239	1,329	685	225
Norway	571	479	1	91
Finland	814	812	2	—
Western Germany	11,521	10,913	146	462
Austria	1,970	1,677	18	275
Switzerland	917	263	3	651
Portugal	496	461	35	—
Spain	3,446	3,326	3	117
Italy	5,329	3,707	60	1,562
Greece	263	251	6	6
Japan	5,444	5,072	—	372
Turkey	882	882	—	—
Iran	259	230	29	—
India	8,615	8,526	17	72
Morocco	147	79	21	47
Algeria	529	344	154	31
Tunisia	254	221	33	—
Union of South Africa	2,675	2,457	—	218

Sources: **60**, 1951, pp. 26–29; **8**, 1952, pp. 92–93. For
the United States: **14**, 1952, p. 168; for Sweden: **21**,
1950, p. 164.

a. For European countries (except Sweden, the Saar,
Greece, Portugal and Spain) and Turkey: 1952.
b. Includes diesel-electric locomotives and special-system locomotives.
c. Includes 52 other type locomotives.
d. Includes 364 locomotives in store and 40 loaned.
e. 1947.

lines are to reach France, the Netherlands and
Germany.[141] The Netherlands has electrified
almost all main lines, and Norway recently completed electrification of the last section, within its
borders, of the international line between Oslo
and Stockholm.[142] In Western Germany and the
United Kingdom — countries well provided
with coal and poor in water power — electrifica-

141. **80**, January 26, 1953, p. 47.
142. **8**, 1953, p. 43.

tion has gained little ground, and in Poland and
Czechoslovakia, even less. In the United States,
too, electric traction is unimportant; when a
change from steam to another power is made,
diesels are preferred. The first postwar Five-Year
Plan (1946–50) of the USSR provided for the
electrification of 3,309 miles. The chief project
was to electrify the line from the Kuznetsk Basin
to Chita and Ufa.[143] The longest electrified line
in the USSR (1,450 miles) is the Novo Kuz-
netsk-Omsk-Chelyabinsk system. In all, some
5,500 miles of line were converted to electric
traction by the end of 1953.[144]

In many instances, as in the United Kingdom,
France, Belgium, Denmark and the Netherlands, the proportion of train-miles electrically
operated is higher for passenger traffic than for
freight because the suburban lines with very
heavy passenger service have been partly or
wholly electrified. In countries with a considerable proportion of freight-train-miles, the ton-
mileage constitutes a somewhat higher part of
the total, because the average load of an electric
train is greater than that of trains hauled by
other types of power. In 1949 passenger- and
freight-train-miles on electrified lines represented
the following percentages of total train mileage: [145]

	Passenger-Train-Miles	Freight-Train-Miles
Switzerland	96.0	68.6
Sweden	68.0	71.7
Italy	46.3	58.5
Netherlands	42.2	2.5
Norway	33.9	30.4
Austria	27.0	26.6
United Kingdom	24.4	—
France	18.5	15.8
Denmark	10.5	—
Western Germany	9.9	5.8
Belgium	6.8	—

RAILROAD OPERATIONS

The railroads furnish several types of services
in both passenger and freight transport. In passenger traffic, they run long-distance trains with
the highest type of accommodations, local trains
which stop at all points outside the metropolitan

143. **49**, p. 64; cf. **28**, p. 80.
144. **32**, p. 116; **8**, 1953, p. 44.
145. **8**, 1950, pp. 29–30. Countries are arrayed by the
declining percentage of passenger-train mileage. For the
Netherlands the respective figures for 1952 were 58 and
31 per cent (**8**, 1952, p. 43).

TABLE 131

RAILROAD LINES: ELECTRICALLY OPERATED RAILROADS IN SELECTED COUNTRIES, 1952

Country	Length, in Miles	Percentage of Total Rail- road Length	Country	Length, in Miles	Percentage of Total Rail- road Length
United States	2,581	1.2	Poland[b]	209	0.5
Canada	60	0.1	Czechoslovakia[c]	50	0.3
Mexico[a]	79	0.05	Austria	765	20.7
Cuba[a]	144	2.3	Hungary[b]	90	3.9
Brazil	2,474	10.7	Switzerland[a]	3,008	94.0
Chile[a]	217	3.3	Spain	436	3.9
Argentina[a]	70	0.3	Italy	3,580	34.4
Great Britain	924	4.8	USSR	4,575[d]	7.6[d]
France	2,550	9.9	Japan[e]	1,789	14.7
Belgium	112	3.6	India	236	0.7
Netherlands	843	42.2	Indonesia[a]	145	3.8
Denmark	32	2.0			
Sweden	3,706	39.4	Union of South Africa	628	4.7
Norway	636	23.6	Australia[a]	283	1.0
Western Germany	952	5.0	New Zealand[a]	45	1.2

Sources: **43**, 1953–54, pp. 388–98; **60**, 1951, pp. 18–21. Cf. Table 126. (Data in **8**, 1952, p. 42, for some European countries, deviate slightly from those in Table 131.)

a. 1950.
b. 1947.
c. 1948.
d. Target for 1950 (**49**, pp. 62–64). According to **99**, 1952–53, p. 427, the USSR had 2,404 miles of electrically operated line in 1950, and electrification of a further 1,025 miles was under way.
e. **43**, 1953–54, p. 394, gives 4,755 miles of electrically operated railroads (state-owned mileage: 1,082; privately owned: 3,673).

districts, suburban trains for commuters and some other specialized trains. In freight transport, they operate slow trains for heavy bulk cargo (carload shipments) and fast trains for perishables and the more valuable freight, the so-called l.c.l. (less than carload lot).

PASSENGER TRAFFIC

The volume of passenger traffic in a country depends on many factors: the size of the country, density of the population, extent of urbanization and industrialization, development of the railway network, availability of other means of transportation, and so on.

Because the number of passenger-miles is the real indicator of the travel load carried by railroads, the United Nations presents international statistics on this point only.

Types of Passenger Traffic

Of the two types of passenger traffic, commuter and intercity, the first is handled in greater volume in densely populated and highly urbanized countries. In the United Kingdom, for ex-

ample, journeys in noncommuting travel at full fare represent only a small part of the total passenger traffic. In 1938 and 1952 the distribution of British passenger journeys by type of fare paid was as follows (in millions): [146]

	1938	1952
Total number of journeys	1,237.2	989.0
Full fare tickets	77.8	165.8
Season tickets (on basis of 600 trips per year)	387.1	278.2
Workmen's tickets	244.2	206.9
Monthly return, weekend, excursion tickets, etc.	474.5	290.0
Service and government trips	53.6	48.1

Even in the United States, where commuting by car is much more common than by train, commuting passengers exceed noncommuters in number: 308.9 and 246.0 million, respectively, in 1949; 277.7 and 208.5 million, respectively, in 1950. The relationship of passenger-miles traveled is inverse: 5.5 billion for commuters and

146. **20**, 1953, p. 225.

TABLE 132

RAILROAD OPERATIONS: PASSENGER TRAFFIC IN SELECTED COUNTRIES, 1929–51

(*Millions of Passenger-Miles*)

Country	1929	1937	1949	1950	1951
United States	31,165	24,695	35,133	31,790	34,640
Canada	2,897	1,929	3,193	2,816	3,085
Mexico	1,012	1,068	1,732	1,880	2,082
Cuba	. . .	127	313	345	347
Colombia	162	301	551	491	. . .
Ecuador	. . .	21	84	79	82
Brazil	2,753	3,168	6,093	6,228	6,462
Peru	. . .	85	162	150	153
Bolivia	34 [a]	109	86	98	121
Chile	574	744	798	987	1,123
Uruguay	. . .	146	221 [b]	. . .	. . .
Argentina	2,708	2,609	8,499	8,220	8,690
Great Britain	. . .	21,321	21,138	20,177	20,793
France [c]	17,566	16,777	18,312	16,405	17,460
Belgium [c]	3,955	3,820	4,422	4,379	4,507
Luxembourg	153	156	142	131	144
Netherlands	. . .	2,080	4,025	3,870	3,909
Denmark	819	1,026	2,108	2,051	1,850
Sweden	1,426	1,927	4,179	4,124	4,044
Norway	312	406	1,053	976	982
Finland	687	714	1,360	1,240	1,299
Germany [d]	25,513	26,618	19,100	18,805	18,624
Poland	4,395	4,317 [e]	12,956	16,375	19,200
Czechoslovakia	5,703	5,503	11,557	. . .	. . .
Switzerland	2,134	2,048	4,015	3,994	3,616
Austria [c]	2,278	1,481	2,557	2,668	2,904
Hungary	1,932	1,644	3,262	3,977	5,313
Portugal	. . .	461	917	861	897
Spain [f]	2,367	2,128 [g]	4,530	4,407	4,526
Italy [c]	5,030	6,089	13,724	12,391	12,915
Yugoslavia	1,352	1,755	4,470	5,160	4,709
Romania	1,893	2,223	3,378 [h]	4,698	6,214
Bulgaria	331 [a]	426	1,568 [i]	. . .	. . .
Greece	411 [a]	482	438	617	589 [c]
USSR	19,900	56,500	59,100	60,900	. . .
China	2,697 [a]	1,296	8,202 [b]	. . .	. . .
Korea	841	1,534	1,678 [j]	715 [j]	930 [j]
Japan [c]	13,264	18,052	39,832	42,877	47,875
Taiwan	315	446	1,519	1,361	. . .
Turkey	. . .	546	1,352	1,545	1,570
Iraq	60	156	322	330	311
Pakistan	} 22,295	18,847 {	5,485	5,676	6,118
India			40,021	40,052	37,864
Burma	634 [a]	465	74	107	206
Thailand	193	175	842	892	1,133
Indochina	301	469	49	46	71
Philippines [k]	208 [a]	262	232	225	258
French Morocco	76	137	400	357	396
Algeria	414	447	503	514	526

(*Continued on facing page*)

TABLE 132—*continued*

Country	1929	1937	1949	1950	1951
Tunisia [1]	97	98	165	167	171
Egypt	908	855	1,368	1,538	1,726
French West Africa	96	194	261	278	318
French Equatorial Africa	...	4	16	18	25
Belgian Congo	...	...	91	96	111
Nigeria	...	224	316	357	397
Mozambique	...	19[m]	48	75	75
Madagascar	...	36[m]	51	51	54

Sources: **5**, 1948, pp. 268–72; 1952, pp. 284–89; 1954, pp. 290–91; **8**, 1951, pp. 58–59; cf. **60**, 1951, pp. 72–75. Data for the USSR, 1929 and 1937: **49**, p. 83; cf. **37**, p. 77; 1949 and 1950: **57**, p. 16. For satellite countries, data for 1950 and 1951 represent the estimate of the Economic Commission for Europe, based on official percentages of plan fulfillment. (**8**, 1951, p. 83.)

a. 1931.
b. 1948.
c. State railways.
d. 1949–51: Western Germany; excludes occupation traffic.
e. Excludes livestock.
f. Broad gauge only.

g. 1935.
h. 1946.
i. 1947.
j. South Korea.
k. Manila Railway Company only.
l. Excludes military traffic.
m. 1938.

29.6 billion for others in 1949; 5.0 and 26.8 billion, respectively, in 1950. The average length of commuters' journeys was 17.8 miles in 1949 and 18.0 miles in 1950; that of noncommuters, 120.4 and 128.4 miles, respectively.[147]

In the USSR, where the railroads are used predominantly for travel to and from work and for government-controlled trips, three out of four or more passengers are commuters. The relation was almost the reverse in 1913, as shown by the following figures (in millions): [148]

	Commuters	Others
1913	59.3	125.5
1937	869.3	273.4
1939	980.9	286.1
1940	1,003.1	340.1

147. **15**, 1950, p. 39. One passenger-mile is figured as the equivalent of one passenger moved one mile. Countries use different methods to calculate the passenger-miles traveled during a year. In the United States, the calculation is on the basis of tickets sold for each journey. In Germany, receipts from tickets for each class of passengers are divided by kilometric rate, with travel tax deducted; in Belgium, receipts from ordinary tickets are divided by the fare per kilometer, which is the same for all distances, while season tickets are counted as 48 journeys and multiplied by the distance for which they are purchased. Italy multiplies the number of passengers by the average distance for each category of tickets sold; Denmark multiplies the number of journeys for one of several distance gradations by average distance, counting monthly tickets between all stations at 125 kilometers per journey and weekly tickets at 25 kilometers per journey. (**60**, 1951, pp. 146–47.)

148. **37**, p. 77.

Differences among Countries

The railroads of the USSR, Japan and India carry the heaviest passenger traffic in the world. Japan had about 14,000 passenger cars in 1950 as compared to nearly 44,000 in the United States, but recorded 42.9 billion passenger-miles, as compared to 31.8 billion in the United States. Overcrowding of passenger trains is an equally serious problem in India, Pakistan, China, Korea, Thailand and some other countries in the Far East. The main cause is inadequacy of the railroad network and rolling stock, aggravated in the Far East by generally unsettled conditions.[149]

Passenger traffic on railroads of the United States is about two thirds greater than that in the United Kingdom and double that in France. The American railroads would have considerably heavier traffic except for the general use of automobiles and the growing competition of highway and air transport.

In underdeveloped countries, travel on railroads is pitifully small, and millions of people have never been on a train. In 1951 Indochina had half the traffic, in passenger-miles, of tiny Luxembourg; French Equatorial Africa, one sixth. China, with 450 million people, has less passenger traffic than Argentina or Czechoslovakia; Turkey, Egypt and Taiwan, less than little Austria. (See Table 132.)

Despite the growth of population, the annual number of passenger-miles has changed little in

149. **2**, 1949, p. 68.

many countries, except in years of depression or war. Railroads in the United States reported 31.2 billion passenger-miles in 1929 and 34.6 billion in 1951 (31.8 billion in 1950); in Canada, 2.9 and 3.1 billion, respectively. For Belgium, the corresponding figures, in billions, are 4.0 and 4.5; for France, 17.6 and 17.5; for Austria, 2.3 and 2.9. This surprising stability is due, to a great extent, to the increasing use of private cars, particularly in the United States.

In contrast, passenger travel increased substantially during this period in a number of other areas where motoring is less developed and the railroads monopolize the traffic: from 2.7 to 8.7 billion passenger-miles in Argentina; from 2.8 to 6.5 billion in Brazil; from 13.3 to 47.9 billion in Japan; from 19.9 to 60.9 billion (1950) in the USSR; and from 22.3 to 37.9 billion in India.[150] (See Table 132.) In the last two countries, and particularly in the USSR, tremendous transports of population are largely responsible for this increase.

The average passenger journey is obviously longer in larger or more sparsely populated countries such as the United States, Canada and Australia than in countries where the population is heavily concentrated within a small territory. In 1951, for example, the average passenger trip in the United States was more than twice as long as the average in France and nearly five times Germany's average. In 1952 averages for some of the principal countries ranged as follows (in miles): [151]

Canada (1948)	91.0
United States (1951)	71.4
Greece	64.2
USSR (1939)	60.0
Spain	42.6
Italy	36.6
Finland	34.4
France	32.7
Turkey	32.0
Sweden (1951)	31.4
Yugoslavia	28.7
Netherlands	25.6
Norway	24.4
Austria	22.5
United Kingdom	20.9

150. India in 1929 includes Pakistan.

151. **14**, 1952, p. 172; **8**, 1952, p. 11. For the USSR, **49**, p. 83. The average for the United States is calculated per railroad and would be considerably greater on a through-passenger basis. For Italy and Greece: state railways; for Switzerland: federal railways.

Belgium	20.3
Denmark	18.3
Switzerland	18.1
Portugal	17.1
Western Germany	14.4
Luxembourg	13.2

FREIGHT TRAFFIC

The freight load of the railroads increases in prosperous times and shrinks in depression. Wars necessitate heavy shipments of equipment and munitions and rely mostly on railroads for this purpose. In the United States, for example, freight carried by the railways fluctuated as follows (in billions of short-ton-miles): [152]

1918	408.8
1921	309.5
1929	450.2
1932	235.3
1939	335.4
1944	740.6
1950	591.6
1951	649.8

The World's Freight Traffic

The world's freight traffic changed little from 1929 to 1938 (787 and 773 billion short-ton-miles, respectively) but increased to 1,239 billion, or by 60 per cent, from 1938 to 1948. In 1953, it was 23–24 per cent greater than in 1948. In 1953 North and Middle America accounted for about 44 per cent of the total; the USSR, for 32 per cent; Europe, for about 13 per cent; and all the rest of the world, for about 11 per cent. (See Table 133.)

Differences among Countries

The United States surpasses all other coun-

152. **26**, p. 1; **14**, 1952, p. 171. One ton carried one mile is equivalent to one ton-mile. Ton-miles are calculated in different ways. Railroads in the United States report the mileage for each year, as accounted for by the actual performance. Italy multiplies the number of tons carried by the railroads by the corresponding average distance, as estimated by the railroad administration. Denmark multiplies, for most traffic, the number of tons carried by distances actually covered; for transport of animals, the weight of a horse, cow and ox is set at 400 kilograms, of other animals, at 50 kilograms. Germany uses certain basic months to calculate the total weight of transported goods in various tariff classes grouped by distance gradations (the distance up to 59 kilometers, gradations of 10 kilometers; 60 to 199 kilometers, of 25; 200 to 499, of 50 kilometers, etc.) and multiplied by average length of distance gradations. (**60**, 1951, pp. 147–48.)

TABLE 133

RAILROAD OPERATIONS: FREIGHT TRAFFIC, BY CONTINENT, 1929–53

(*Billions of Short-Ton-Miles*)

Continent	1929	1932	1938	1948	1949	1950	1951	1952	1953
World	787	528	773	1,239	1,184	1,301	1,473	1,495	1,532
North and Middle America	489	261	323	707	592	653	721	694	681
South America	12	10	13	17	17	18	20	20	20
Europe	161	110	149	155	161	163	188	192	192
USSR	68	100	220	277	325	370	415	451	490
Asia	42	36	50	54	59	65	95	102	112
Africa	10	7	13	21	22	24	26	27	28
Oceania	5	4	5	8	8	8	8	9	9

Source: **5**, 1952, p. 283; 1954, p. 289. Estimate of the Statistical Office of the United Nations. Margin of error: for world, prewar, 3 per cent, postwar, 6–8 per cent; for North and Middle America and Oceania, 1 per cent through the entire period; for prewar Europe, 4 per cent and postwar years, 4–7 per cent; for Africa, 10 and 3–4 per cent, respectively; for Asia, 9 and 6–8 per cent, respectively.

tries in ton-mileage of railway freight traffic. Its railroads accounted for approximately 450 billion of the world's 787 billion short-ton-miles in 1929 and 650 billion of the total 1,473 billion in 1951. Regional specialization, great distances and the composition of freight — predominantly coal, iron ore, other mine products and steel — as well as the volume of national production are the main reasons. Railway freight traffic in the USSR is also very heavy, partly for the same reasons but also because it represents some nine tenths of the total ton-mileage; water transport is impossible during four or five months of the year, and motor traffic is comparatively insignificant.[153] Distances, moreover, are considerably greater than even in the United States. The geographic shift of industry to the east and much crosshauling are also responsible for the growth of ton-mileage.[154]

Western Germany has a greater ton-mileage than either France or Great Britain. Italy, where the railroads largely carry finished goods over short distances, has little more than half the traffic of the Union of South Africa, where there is heavy movement of mine products of all kinds. Argentina's railroads have about twice the ton-mileage of Brazil or Yugoslavia, and Australia is in the group with Sweden.

Freight traffic in Asia — except for India, Japan and, at a great distance, China and Pakistan — is insignificant. In the Philippines, Indochina and some other areas, it shows little tendency to increase. In most African regions, in contrast, traffic, though very small, is growing each year. (See Table 134.)

The average rail haul per ton in 1950 exceeded 416 miles in the United States and 400 miles in Canada and was considerably less in European countries: about 75 miles in the United Kingdom; 175 in Italy; 160 in France; 130 in Sweden; 129 in Western Germany and Yugoslavia (1951); 112 in Norway (1951); 104 in Portugal (1951); 94 in the Netherlands and Austria (1951); 74 in Switzerland (1951); 56 in Belgium; and 21 in Luxembourg. Indian railways report an average haul per ton of nearly 300 miles; Turkish, 213 miles; Russian, 491 miles in 1945 and were expected to have 429 miles in 1950.[155]

Distances are generally great in the USSR and the centers of raw materials, industry and consumption are widely separated in many cases. The average railroad hauls are therefore particularly long for some essential commodities needed throughout the country: 766 miles for petroleum; 633 miles for timber; and 600 miles for iron and steel.[156] The first postwar Five-Year Plan aimed

153. **94**, p. 151; **37**, p. 72. Freight traffic by rail in the United States amounts to some six tenths of the total ton-mileage.

154. Cf. **30**, pp. 128–46.

155. **14**, 1952, p. 171; **8**, 1950, pp. 54–55 and 1951, pp. 58–59; **66**, 1950, p. 114; for the USSR, **49**, p. 81.

156. **86**, p. 341. Data for 1940.

TABLE 134

RAILROAD OPERATIONS: FREIGHT TRAFFIC IN SELECTED COUNTRIES, 1929–51

(*Millions of Short-Ton-Miles*)

Country	1929	1937	1949	1950	1951
United States	450,189	362,815	529,146	591,550	649,831
Canada	35,026	26,925	56,338	55,538	64,071
Mexico	2,764	3,686	5,960	6,432	6,523
Cuba	. . .	492	758	723	795
Colombia	83 [a]	189	432	386	403
Ecuador	. . .	44	76	77	82
Brazil [b]	2,177	3,701	5,129	5,264	5,699
Peru	. . .	197	277	276	318
Bolivia	74 [c]	112	186	171	212
Chile	1,184	1,155	1,492	1,440	1,622
Uruguay	203	247	297	. . .	. . .
Argentina	9,651	9,184	11,182	11,583	11,685
Great Britain	20,580	20,087	24,651	24,792	25,650
Ireland [d]	274	273	345	351	353
France [e]	28,631	21,781	28,112	26,667	31,096
Belgium [f]	5,744	4,267	3,880	3,741	4,540
Luxembourg [b]	310	364	323	296	401
Netherlands [b, f]	. . .	1,545	1,909	2,066	2,230
Denmark	480	423	835	887	912
Sweden	3,149	3,840	5,553	5,918	6,863
Norway [b]	440	527	964	937	945
Finland	1,258	1,808	2,083	2,373	3,216
Germany [g]	55,682	60,161	32,772	32,931	37,714
Poland	14,550	13,623	20,411	24,044	26,437
Czechoslovakia	8,480	5,814	8,904	10,137	11,643
Switzerland	1,615	1,482	1,273	1,527	1,742
Austria [e]	3,044	2,843	3,953	3,890	5,021
Hungary	2,291	2,115	2,245 [h]	3,904	4,589
Portugal	. . .	401	390	357	401
Spain	3,904	2,868 [i]	3,788	4,417	4,799
Italy [e]	7,991	7,151	6,867	6,767	7,671
Yugoslavia	2,888	2,677	6,604	6,811	5,962
Romania	2,425	3,380	2,642 [j]	5,068	6,232
Bulgaria	451 [b]	512	846 [k]	2,466	2,808
Greece	145 [e]	182	85	108	151
USSR [l]	68,000	220,000	325,000	370,000	415,000

(*Continued on facing page*)

at reducing, by 1950, the average length of haul to about 606 miles for petroleum and 590 miles for ferrous metals, while that for ores, grain, timber and mineral construction materials was scheduled to remain about the same.[157]

RAILROAD ECONOMICS

EMPLOYMENT

The number of persons employed by the world's railroads may be estimated at 7.5–8.0

157. **30**, p. 140.

million. As of the end of 1951 the United States reported 1.3 million on its railways (Class I); Great Britain, 600,000; Western Germany, about 491,400; France, 403,600; Japan, 442,200; India, nearly 920,000. The USSR employed more than a million in 1937–38, and in 1948, according to Russian sources, several millions.[158]

Occupational Groups

In many countries, the largest group of em-

158. **49**, p. 12; **75**, p. 33; **57**, p. 20, gives approximately 3 million employees on Russian railroads for 1949.

TABLE 134—*continued*

Country	1929	1937	1949	1950	1951
China	3,053[a]	1,581	3,082[h]	. . .	. . .
Taiwan	347	514	543	603	. . .
Korea	888	1,827	912[m]	708[m]	1,884[m]
Japan[c]	8,615	12,503	19,517	21,038	25,261
Turkey[b]	. . .	697	1,784	1,714	1,862
Iraq	113	207	451	443	497
Pakistan	}23,216	25,510{	2,636	3,044	3,407
India			28,521	30,249	31,891
Burma	788[e]	747	112	63	137
Thailand	. . .	235	279	329	367
Indochina	96[e]	129	87	90	132
Malaya	. . .	179[n]	223	271	273
Philippines	107[e]	103	112	104	95
French Morocco	238	236	809	834	992
Algeria	691	595	821	851	937
Tunisia	. . .	527	569	539	621
Egypt	. . .	1,017	1,080	1,026	938
Anglo-Egyptian Sudan	. . .	366	503	501	663
French West Africa	112[e]	210	273	309	385
French Equatorial Africa	. . .	21	56	66	73
Belgian Congo	. . .	. . .	974	1,065	1,203
Nigeria	. . .	475	797	741	743
Kenya[b]	. . .	960	1,175	1,348	1,438
Mozambique	. . .	96	210	577	614
Madagascar	. . .	39	52	60	70
Southern Rhodesia[b]	1,103	1,651	2,218	2,524	2,805
Union of South Africa[b]	4,900	7,045	12,148	12,779	13,783
Australia	4,318	4,444	6,958	6,948	7,030
New Zealand	573	629	1,144	1,150	1,197

Sources: **5**, 1948, pp. 268–72; 1952, pp. 284–89; 1954, pp. 290–91; **4**, April 1953, pp. 72–77; cf. **60**, 1951, pp. 76–79. For satellite countries: **8**, 1951, p. 83.

a. 1931.
b. Excludes livestock.
c. 1930.
d. Two main railroads; includes some lines in Northern Ireland.
e. State railways.
f. Carload lots.
g. 1949–51: Western Germany; includes service and occupation traffic.
h. 1948.

i. 1935.
j. 1946.
k. 1947.
l. Cf. estimate, based on official percentages of the first postwar plan fulfillment, for 1950: 410.9 million short-ton-miles; for 1951: 461.6 million. (**8**, 1951, pp. 83–84.)
m. South Korea.
n. 1939.

ployees is engaged in the maintenance of equipment and stores: machinists, mechanics, electricians, blacksmiths, boilermakers, car cleaners, oilers, engineers and so on. This group accounted for 28.9 per cent of all employees in the United States in 1951, as compared with 19.7 per cent for employees engaged in maintenance of way and structure — roadmasters, ironworkers, carpenters, linemen, signal- and groundmen, and others. Labor engaged in transportation may be divided into two groups: train and engine force (conductors, ticket collectors, baggage-men, engineers, brakemen, flagmen, etc.) and station, yard and communications force (station masters, station agents, baggage- and parcelroom and station attendants, stewards and dining-room supervisors, waiters, train attendants, etc.). One out of three railroad employees in the United States was engaged in transportation in 1951 but only one out of five in the train and engine force. Clerical employees comprise stenographers, typists, switchboard operators, patrolmen, firemen, claims agents, janitors and cleaners (16.5 per cent). Executives, general officers, assistants and staff attendants accounted for a little more than one per cent.[159]

Employees per Mile of Line

Countries differ greatly in the number of employees per mile of railway length, though some reservation is in order in making international comparisons. Italian statistics, for example, exclude from railway personnel all persons engaged in maintenance of way, repair and similar services.[160] The volume and intensity of traffic must also be considered in comparing the number of employees per mile of length worked. The railroads of the United States and Algeria report about the same average number of employees, 5–6 per mile of line, though the number of short-ton-miles handled by one employee in the United States was about eight times that by an Algerian employee.

In the United Kingdom, where heavy passenger and freight traffic are concentrated within a small territory, more than 30 persons serve one mile, as compared to about 5 in Canada, Greece and Tunisia.

The number of employees per "unit of traffic" (one passenger-mile or one ton-mile) also varies from country to country. The smallest numbers of employees per million units of traffic are in the United States (1.9) and Canada (2.9). The rate is 10.1 in the Netherlands; 12.3 in Japan; 8.3 in France; 10.4 in Western Germany; 12.9 in Great Britain; and 14.6 in Portugal.[161] (See Table 135.) If the structure of the railroads and their role in the national economy were uniform, these figures would be an effective measure of productivity of labor. Actually, however, they reflect the interplay of many other factors, the most important among them the density of the railroad network and the average distance of shipments. Heavy traffic over a dense network of railroads and frequent shipments over short distances require a greater amount of labor than the same volume of traffic would necessitate for shipments over long distances on thinly spread lines.

Introduction of many automatic devices, increase in labor productivity and decline in traffic

TABLE 135

RAILROAD ECONOMICS: EMPLOYMENT IN SELECTED COUNTRIES, JANUARY 1, 1952

Country	Total, in Thousands	Per Mile of Line	Per Million Train-Miles	Per Million Units of Traffic [a]
United States [b]	1,275.7	5.7	1,443	1.9
Canada	193.6	4.7	1,609	2.9
Great Britain	599.9	30.9	1,593	12.9
France	403.6	15.7	1,706	8.3
Saar	13.1	38.2	2,767	...
Luxembourg	5.3	15.9	...	9.7
Belgium	77.3	24.9	1,625	8.5
Netherlands	34.6	17.3	998	10.1
Denmark	28.0	17.5	1,255	6.4
Sweden	70.2	7.5	853	13.1
Norway	25.3	9.4	1,448	8.0
Finland	36.8	12.3	1,625	8.7
Western Germany	491.4	26.0	1,578	10.4
Poland [c]	348.1	24.2	...	9.5
Czechoslovakia [d]	195.0	24.1	...	9.7
Austria	76.9	20.8	2,124	...
Hungary [e]	80.1	14.8	...	7.0
Switzerland	37.5	11.7	805 [f]	21.7
Portugal	28.2	12.8	2,478	14.6
Spain	136.1	12.2	2,446	8.1
Italy	167.5	16.1	1,416	...
Romania [g]	153.8	20.8	...	...
Bulgaria [g]	35.4	17.7	...	10.4
Greece [h]	7.7	5.1	2,220	6.1
Japan	442.2	36.2	2,317	12.3
Turkey	30.0	4.0	...	...
Iran	22.3	14.0	...	13.2
India	919.7	26.7	...	10.3
Algeria	15.1	5.5	...	6.9
Tunisia	5.5	5.0	1,625	...
Union of South Africa	191.8	13.8	...	...

Sources: **60**, 1951, pp. 46–49; **66**, 1952, p. 140; **14**, 1952, pp. 171 and 175; Tables 126, 131 and 133.

a. Units of traffic are the sums of passenger-miles and ton-miles.
b. Class I railways.
c. 1947; passenger and freight traffic: 1949.
d. 1948; passenger and freight traffic: 1949.
e. 1948.
f. Federal railways.
g. 1946.
h. State railways.

159. **14**, 1952, p. 175. Class I railways, excluding switching and terminal companies.
160. **66**, 1950, p. 108.
161. Data of the International Union of Railways, calculated on the basis of traffic units, deviate somewhat from figures in Table 134.

have led to the reduction of personnel. Despite an increase in railway traffic from 1950 to 1951, Sweden reduced its personnel by 3.8 per cent; Luxembourg, by 3.6 per cent; the Netherlands, by 3.3 per cent; and Austria, by 3.0 per cent.[162] In the United States the railways employed more than 2 million persons in 1920; 1.5 million in 1930 and 1.3 million in 1951.[163] In France, personnel has been reduced by nearly 20 per cent, from 490,350 in 1946 to 428,800 in 1950 and 403,600 at the end of 1951.[164]

OWNERSHIP OF RAILROADS

More than half the world's railway mileage (about 54 per cent in 1949) is government owned. The United States is the only country where almost the entire network is owned and operated by private companies.[165] In the rest of the world three fourths of the mileage is in public hands.

The government owns and operates all railroads in the United Kingdom, France, Germany, Belgium, the Netherlands, Poland, Czechoslovakia, Austria, Hungary, Romania, Bulgaria, Yugoslavia, the USSR, China, Pakistan, Ceylon, Thailand, Malaya, Iran, Iraq, Indochina, Argentina, New Zealand and many other countries. The share of public ownership ranges between about 83 per cent and 98 per cent in Colombia, Finland, Norway, Italy, Turkey, Australia, Japan, India and the Union of South Africa; it is 75–76 per cent in Mexico and Spain; exceeds 72 per cent in Sweden; [166] and ranges between about 54 per cent and 68 per cent in Switzerland, Denmark, Canada, Chile and Brazil. There are only a few countries outside of the United States in which the government controls less than half the mileage — Peru, Portugal, Greece and some other areas with an insignificant mileage. (See Table 136 and Figure 68.)

Development of Public Ownership

Government ownership of the world's railroads has been increasing throughout this century: from 30 per cent in 1900 to 33 per cent in 1913, 45 per cent in 1937 and about 54 per cent

in 1949. The issue of public versus private ownership has been with the railroads for almost a century. Public ownership of railroads, as it exists in the world, is not dependent on the size of a country or a particular type of economic or political system. It has been introduced in large and small countries and in countries that are industrial or agricultural, advanced or underdeveloped, democratic or totalitarian, peaceful or militaristic.[167]

Government ownership in the world as a whole has developed gradually. During the first decade of railroad building, railroads were considered merely improved highways which could be used by anybody with suitable equipment and the prescribed weight of load on payment of tolls.[168] This policy could not be followed for long since, when different vehicles ran on the rails, the slowest set the pace for all behind it. To accelerate traffic, sidings were built at frequent intervals.[169]

Not until later, about the middle of the nineteenth century, did the realization come in England and the United States that railways are different from canals and highways and must be managed exclusively by their owners as a monopoly, private or public.[170] The only feasible competition was among different lines, not among different carriers on the same railroad. However, the growing importance of railroads in the economic life of nations gave them a special character. Even when left in the hands of private owners, they were often put under public supervision and made subject to government regulations.

In France, the state participated from early days in the construction of the national railway

162. **8**, 1951, p. 48.
163. **15**, 1950, p. 159; **14**, 1952, p. 175.
164. **66**, 1952, p. 149; **60**, 1951, pp. 46–47.
165. The Alaska Railway, 536 miles long, is owned and operated by the federal government. The state of Georgia owns the Western and Atlantic Railroad, operated by a private company. A few municipalities — Cincinnati, for example — also own railroads. **31**, p. 646.
166. According to **23**, p. 93, about 80 per cent of Sweden's total trackage belongs to the state and accounts for a still greater percentage of the traffic, private lines being small and not heavily used.

167. **16**, p. 286.
168. **39**, p. 71. The charter of the Ithaca and Owego Railroad, 1827, stated in Section 12: "All persons paying the toll aforesaid may, with suitable and proper carriages, use and travel upon the said railroad." (**88**, pp. 35–36.) The charter of the Boston and Providence line authorized the company to erect toll houses and gates and appoint toll collectors to exact payment. A New Jersey statute permitted a farmer of that state to transport his produce of not more than half a ton in his own carriage, weighing not more than a ton, over the railroad, without paying the toll on his way to market, but he was to be charged toll for the empty carriage on his way back. Some railroads did operate for a time as toll roads but soon found this system impractical, particularly when steam power was introduced. (**69**, p. 92.) In England also the railroads were open to traffic in private vehicles.
169. **62**, p. 4.
170. **81**, p. 8.

TABLE 136

RAILROAD ECONOMICS: OWNERSHIP IN SELECTED COUNTRIES, 1937 AND 1949

| Country | Length of Line, in Miles | | | | Percentage of Government Owned Mileage [a] | |
| | Total | Government Owned | Total | Government Owned | | |
	1937		1949		1937	1949
World	788,672	355,724	783,679	419,093	45.1	53.5
United States	245,752	—	224,511	536	0.0	0.2
Canada	42,270	23,266	42,336	23,496	55.0	55.5
Mexico [b]	14,569	8,499	14,981	11,388	58.3	76.0
Colombia	2,051	1,115	2,106	1,955	54.4	92.8
Chile	5,589	3,763	5,726	3,234	67.3	56.5
Peru	2,613	568	1,947	461	21.7	23.7
Brazil	19,676	15,000	21,251	14,496	76.2	68.2
Argentina	23,704	5,764	26,710	26,710	24.3	100.0
United Kingdom	20,865	—	19,863	19,863	0.0	100.0
France [c]	26,388	4,750	25,700	25,700	18.0	100.0
Belgium	3,209	3,013	3,120	3,120	93.9	100.0
Netherlands	2,114	1,263	2,078	2,078	59.7	100.0
Denmark	3,326	1,542	2,263	1,486	46.4	65.7
Sweden	10,504	4,676	10,518	7,649	44.5	72.7
Norway	2,484	2,272	2,687	2,636	91.5	98.1
Finland	3,533	3,418	2,882	2,724	96.7	94.5
Germany [d]	36,256	33,461	19,086	19,086	92.3	100.0
Poland	13,375	12,349	14,400	14,400	92.3	100.0
Czechoslovakia	8,383	8,208	8,100	8,100	97.9	100.0
Switzerland	3,677	1,822	3,345	1,812	49.6	54.2
Austria	4,450	3,602	3,800	3,800	80.9	100.0
Hungary	4,773	4,047	5,400	5,400	84.8	100.0
Portugal	2,143	933	2,102	931	43.5	44.3
Spain	10,117	177	10,563	7,958	1.7	75.3
Italy	11,383	10,527	10,060	8,330	92.5	82.8
Yugoslavia	6,926	6,398	7,200	7,200	92.4	100.0
Romania	7,363	6,955	7,400	7,400	94.5	100.0
Bulgaria	1,996	1,996	2,000	2,000	100.0	100.0
Greece	1,621	826	1,500	690	51.0	46.0

(*Continued on facing page*)

network. The act of 1842 provided that the state should build the roadbeds and structures, while the railway companies were responsible for laying the track, supplying the rolling stock and carrying out the operations. Land was to be provided by the government. After a specified period of years, extended under Napoleon III to 99 years, the entire system was to revert to the state. This plan underwent various modifications to meet changing conditions, but the state control it established remained substantially in force for almost a century.[171] On the eve of World War II the French state and private railroads were welded into one system (Société Nationale des Chemins de Fer Français) and nationalized.

In Germany, Russia and Japan, government ownership was largely motivated by military considerations. Belgium and Switzerland adopted it partly to prevent foreign control of their railroads. In some countries, the state took over the railroads when they approached bankruptcy; in others, it built railroads because private capital was not available. In Italy, public ownership was an outgrowth of the efforts to unify the country. In Great Britain, all railroads were nationalized in 1947 by the Labor government. In Sweden, the state controls all important lines, leaving

171. **81**, pp. 62ff.

TABLE 136—*continued*

Country	Length of Line, in Miles				Percentage of Government Owned Mileage [a]	
	Total	Government Owned	Total	Government Owned	1937	1949
	1937		1949			
USSR	52,785	52,785	76,600 [e]	76,600 [e]	100.0	100.0
China	6,367	6,350	12,960	12,960	99.7	100.0
Japan [f]	18,776	13,132	12,308	10,991	69.9	89.3
Turkey	3,952	3,654	4,882	4,629	92.5	94.8
India [g]	43,021	31,670	34,021	33,245	73.6	97.7
Thailand	2,018	1,778	1,926	1,926	88.1	100.0
Malaya	1,068	1,068	1,068	1,068	100.0	100.0
Ceylon	951	951	913	913	100.0	100.0
Algeria	3,014	2,264	2,786	2,786	75.1	100.0
Morocco	1,111	1,111	1,080	1,080	100.0	100.0
Tunisia	1,849	1,576	1,273	1,000	85.2	78.6
Union of South Africa	16,203	13,195	13,931	13,258	81.4	95.2
Australia	28,555	27,128	28,045	27,212	95.0	97.0
New Zealand	3,336	3,336	3,528	3,528	100.0	100.0

Sources: **16**, p. 286; **43**, 1953–54, pp. 386–87; **59**, 1950, Table 3.

a. Data in **66**, 1952, p. 139, on the percentage of state ownership in 1949 differ from the figures in Table 136 with respect to several countries: Argentina (25 per cent); Denmark (100); Spain (100); Finland (100); Italy (100); Norway (100); Sweden (100); Switzerland (100); Morocco (0), etc.

b. According to **99** (1950, B21–33), 8,813 miles of main lines are government owned. A part of the privately owned lines is controlled by U.S. and British interests.

c. By decree of August 31, 1937, all French railways were nationalized.

d. Postwar: Western Germany.

e. 1950: first postwar plan. Includes mileage in annexed territories: eastern Poland, the Baltic states and others. **86**, p. 335.

f. Postwar data from **99**, 1952–53, pp. 498–503. According to **48** (1946–48, p. 415), the total length of main lines in 1947 was 15,929 miles, of which 12,266 miles (77 per cent) were state owned.

g. 1937: includes Burma. Postwar data from **99**, 1952–53, p. 488.

some feeder lines to private enterprise. In Belgium, all standard-gauge lines are state-owned but operated by a centralized railway company, on lease for seventy-five years (beginning in 1926).[172]

Public Control in the United States

In the United States the issue of government ownership of railroads was agitated in the 1870's by the Grangers, who complained about the high rates imposed by the railroads under the policy of charging "what the traffic will bear." The Windom Committee of Congress recommended in 1874 that the government build additional railways to protect the public through competition with private companies. No action was taken, however. The Act to Regulate Commerce, in 1887, laid the beginnings of government control over railroad rates and rate policy.

Congress created a special agency to administer the act — the Interstate Commerce Commission.

Further legislation was enacted from time to time to strengthen enforcement provisions and extend the jurisdiction of the Commission. The Transportation Act of 1920 revised the entire system of regulations, some of which had proved inadequate, and empowered the Commission to control the issuance of new securities by railroad companies, prescribe minimum freight rates to prevent cut-throat competition, supervise the use of existing equipment, and control extension and abandonment of facilities. During the depression, when the finances of the railroads were shattered and some went into receivership, the issue of public ownership arose again, but the railroads remained in private hands under effective government regulation.

However, the railroads, though privately built and run, are generally considered a public institution. The Supreme Court stated in one case

172. **99**, 1952–53, p. 333.

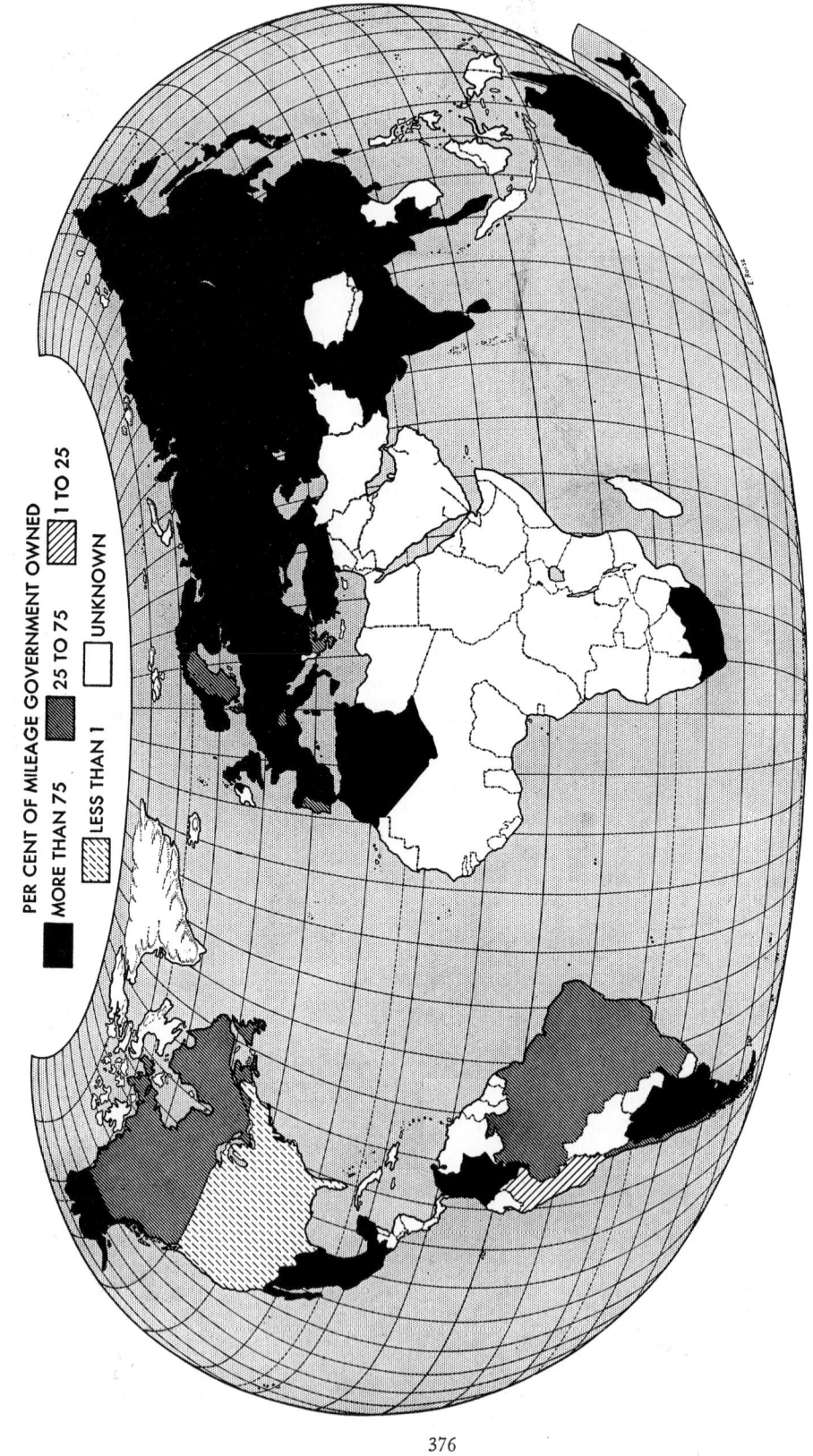

PER CENT OF MILEAGE GOVERNMENT OWNED

MORE THAN 75   25 TO 75   1 TO 25

LESS THAN 1   UNKNOWN

FIGURE 68. RAILROAD ECONOMICS: GEOGRAPHIC DISTRIBUTION BY TYPE OF OWNERSHIP IN THE WORLD, 1949

(Countries Classified by Percentage of Railroad Mileage Government Owned)

Source: Table 136

(Smyth *v.* Ames): "A railroad is a public highway, and none the less so because constructed and maintained through the agency of a corporation deriving its existence and power from the State. Such a corporation was created for public purposes. It performs a function of the State."[173] Railway companies in the United States have operated efficiently on the whole and, under government regulation, have improved service to the public considerably. The consensus among independent experts is that while there is no present need to nationalize railroads in the United States, no calamity would occur, despite dire predictions, if such a step should become necessary.[174]

Experience has shown that in many countries publicly owned railway systems have been efficiently operated and have yielded good returns while in others state railways are a burden to government finances and a source of public dissatisfaction. While the trend in the world at large is toward public ownership of railroads, the system of private railroads under public control has strong supporters.

FINANCES OF RAILROADS

Investment

Investment in railroads differs from country to country, depending not only on the mileage, and quality and size of equipment and installations, but also on methods of railroad capitalization, the topography of the country, the level of wages and prices for materials, the number of parallel tracks, and so on. Investment in United States railroads up to 1952 has been evaluated at more than $31 billion. After allowance for accrued depreciation, it is estimated by the railroad companies at $24 billion and by the Interstate Commerce Commission, at $21 billion.[175] The total outlay for German railroads amounts, according to the International Union of Railroads, to nearly $7.2 billion and for the British, to $4.1 billion. Canada has invested almost $3.6 billion. The four Scandinavian countries together have spent more than $1 billion, and Switzerland, about $840 million. These countries together represent about four tenths of the world's rail mileage but the investment per mile of railroad in the rest of the world has been considerably smaller, so that the world's total investment may be within

173. Quoted in **69**, p. 634.
174. **31**, pp. 659–60; **69**, pp. 634–47.
175. **14**, 1952, p. 168; **10**, p. 50.

TABLE 137

RAILROAD ECONOMICS: INVESTMENT [a] IN SELECTED COUNTRIES, JANUARY 1, 1952

Country	Total Investment, in Millions	Investment per Mile of Length, in Thousands
United States [b]	$31,077.8	$134.6
Canada	3,584.3	90.2 [c]
Great Britain	4,088.0	210.2
Luxembourg	11.9	23.6
Belgium	340.9	109.0
Netherlands	394.5	197.8
Denmark	92.6	56.4
Sweden	638.4	66.9
Norway	221.9	81.3
Finland	94.0	31.5
Germany	7,190.6	379.5
Switzerland	839.3	426.9 [d]
Portugal	42.3	19.0
India	1,700.7	49.9
Union of South Africa	765.5	57.2

Sources: **60**, 1951, pp. 106–09; for the United States: **14**, 1952, pp. 168–70.

a. All original and subsequent capital expenditures (acquisition of land, construction of lines and buildings, purchase of rolling stock and so on). **60**, 1951, p. 14.
b. Includes investment of lessor and proprietary companies ($3.4 million).
c. Canadian National Railways. Investment per mile of the Canadian Pacific Railway: $81,600.
d. Federal railroads. For Berne-Lötschberg railroad: $424,700.

$75–$80 billion, allowing for a broad margin of error.

The topography of Switzerland and that country's almost complete electrification of rail service have raised its investment per mile to triple the amount in the United States: $426,900 as against $134,600. Great Britain has the next highest outlay per mile — $210,200 — largely owing to the special circumstances in the early period of railroad building.[176] The smallest investment per mile among European countries is reported for Portugal, Luxembourg, Finland, and Denmark. Cheap labor has been an important factor in the fairly low outlay per mile in India and the Union of South Africa. (See Table 137.)

The reported investment in railroads in a country which has experienced a stormy inflation and subsequent substantial devaluation of

176. See pp. 343–44.

currency may appear too low or too high, depending on whether or not the railroad companies have recalculated capital values. For example, the total investment of French railroads by the end of 1951 is reported as some 170 billion francs or, at the current value of the franc, $483.7 million, which would indicate an outlay of about $18,800 per mile of line.[177] Actually, private outlays alone on French railroads have been estimated at more than $3 billion as of 1914,[178] an estimate in line with the reported data on construction cost per mile: $130,600 in 1894; $133,800 in 1900; $137,200 in 1907.[179]

Few industries can equal railroads in capital outlay in a country with a developed network — that is, expenditures for roadbeds, tracks, bridges, tunnels, rolling stock, stations, roundhouses and other structures. It has been estimated that an average manufacturing plant in the United States requires an investment of about 70 cents to produce one dollar of gross receipts per year, while the railroads' investment sometimes is as much as four or five dollars for each dollar of gross receipts.[180] This ratio varies from year to year, declining with increase in traffic and rising in bad years.

In the United States, for example, the railroads have reported the following varying amounts of investment and operating revenue (in millions of dollars):[181]

Year Ended [a]	Investment	Operating Revenue
1900	$10,263	$1,487
1910	14,558	2,812
1920	19,849	6,310
1930	26,051	5,356
1932	26,087	3,169
1940	25,646	4,355
1945	26,968	8,987
1950	30,174	9,473
1951	31,078	10,391

a. 1900 and 1910: year ending June 30; 1920–51: year ending December 31.

Thus, in 1900, the ratio of investment to gross revenue was nearly 7 to 1; in 1920, about 3 to 1;

in 1932, more than 8 to 1; in 1945 and 1951, about 3 to 1.[182]

Expenditures

Railroad expenses are of two types: constant and variable. The first are largely independent of the volume of traffic, while the latter tend to fluctuate with changes in the volume of business.

The constant character of a large part of railroad expenses was recognized soon after the railroads began to operate. The British railroad expert, Dionysius Lardner, called attention to it as early as 1850 in his survey of railway economy.[183] Some transportation experts estimate that from half to two thirds of railroad expenses are constant, while the rest does not increase in direct proportion to additional traffic.[184]

Interest on capital is the most important fixed charge. This must be paid whether business is large or small. Yet capital outlay is often much larger than is necessitated by the current volume of traffic. A railroad is ordinarily built and equipped to handle the traffic at the busiest season and at the peak of prosperity. Railroads also have been built in some countries, as the United States and Canada, in anticipation of growing demand. Moreover, there have been diversions of traffic to other means of transportation that could not be foreseen when the line was constructed.[185]

Many "operating expenses" are also constant to a large extent. Tracks and roadbeds must be maintained in proper condition at all times. Rails and bridges rust, and ties rot whether the traffic is heavy or light. Wear and tear is greater, of course, when use increases, but the bulk of the maintenance cost is relatively stable. Expenses for equipment are more dependent on the volume of traffic but do not vary in direct proportion to it. Locomotives become obsolete and freight cars

177. **60**, 1950, p. 110.
178. **62**, p. 73.
179. **81**, p. 77.
180. **31**, p. 163.
181. **15**, 1950, pp. 156–57; **14**, 1952, p. 170. Classes I, II and III, and lessor and proprietary companies are included.

182. The corresponding ratio for water carriers is about 1 to 1; for trucking carriers, 1 to 2. (**9**, p. 158.)
183. **67**, pp. 271ff.
184. **61**, p. 145; **83**, pp. 55–56; **69**, p. 137; **65**, p. 234; **42**, 1941, p. 315.
185. Cf. **31**, p. 165. Indeed, the capacity of the railroads to handle traffic is seldom utilized fully. In the United States, for example, in the peak business year 1929 track was used to about half its capacity; freight cars were utilized to not more than 70 per cent of capacity and passengers cars, to only 21 per cent. About one third of the potential power of locomotives was used, and about 70–75 per cent of the terminal facilities. **74**, pp. 351–56.

are subject to the action of the elements whether they are in use or idle. Wages, which constitute the main item in expenses for maintenance of way, structures and equipment and for transportation as such, also are not fully variable. In a protracted period of light traffic, the labor force is reduced, but there is a limit below which the railroads cannot go without endangering safety.

Two qualifications must be made, however: (1) when traffic is heavy, expenses tend to become more variable; (2) in the long run, expenditures are adjusted to a light volume of traffic through reorganization, closing of railroad yards, lease of idle buildings and so on.[186]

The variable, or "out-of-pocket," expenses increase and decline more or less proportionally with ups and downs in the volume of traffic.

Expenditures of the railways rose considerably in most countries between 1937 and 1951, partly because of rising prices, wages and taxes, and partly because of growing traffic. They more than doubled in the United States, Canada, Belgium, Sweden, Norway, Czechoslovakia, Finland, Switzerland, Greece, Turkey, Japan and other areas. In general, the rate of increase in expenditures has kept pace more or less with increase in revenues except in Great Britain, Finland, Austria, Italy and Australia.

Expenditures per mile of line worked vary greatly from country to country. In Portugal the cost in 1951 was below $10,000; in Norway, Turkey, India, the Union of South Africa and New Zealand (1950), below $20,000. In the United States, the Netherlands, Denmark, Italy and Japan the cost exceeded $30,000 per mile; in Great Britain and France, it approached $50,000. Even higher expenditures per mile worked were reported in 1951 by Switzerland ($63,900) and Belgium ($73,600). (See Table 138.)

Revenues

Comparison of the current financial returns of railroads shows a greater or smaller surplus of revenues over expenditures in 1951 in the United States (1950), Canada, Great Britain, Japan, India, the Union of South Africa, and many other countries. The railroads of Italy, Turkey and New Zealand reported a surplus before the war and a deficit in 1950. Some countries, among them Greece, Austria and Norway, almost closed the gap in prewar years but now are in the red.

186. **31**, pp. 167–68.

The Czechoslovakian railroads show a consistent excess of expenses over revenues. (See Table 138.)

The share of operating revenue in national income ranged in 1938 from 1.6–1.7 per cent in Denmark and Norway to 5.5 per cent in the United States and Australia and 6.7 per cent in Austria (1937). It decreased by 1950, probably because of competition from other forms of transportation, in almost all countries except Denmark, Sweden, Norway and the Netherlands, as is shown by the following percentages:[187]

	1938	1950
United States	5.5	4.0
Canada	8.3	5.6
United Kingdom	3.3	2.9
France	4.1	3.6
Belgium	4.0	3.2
Netherlands	2.0	2.0
Denmark	1.6	1.6
Sweden	2.9	2.9
Norway	1.7	2.1
Germany	5.5	4.7 [a]
Austria	6.7 [b]	5.0 [c]
Switzerland	4.2	3.8
Italy	2.9	2.1
Australia	5.5	2.8
New Zealand	4.7	3.4

a. Western Germany.
b. 1937.
c. 1948.

Few railroad experts were aware of the importance of the freight business when the railroads were introduced. The prevailing opinion was that passenger traffic would constitute the main source of revenue. Lardner and his associates, however, were foresighted enough to argue that income from freight traffic would constitute the backbone of total revenues.[188] Actually, the revenue from freight traffic exceeds that from passenger traffic in all countries except Denmark, the Netherlands, Greece and Japan. In countries which export or import bulky raw materials such as lumber, coal, ores and iron — among them Finland, Luxembourg, Canada, the Union of South Africa, Algeria and Tunisia — the propor-

187. **8**, 1951, p. 53.
188. **67**, pp. 271ff. To some extent, the general unawareness of the importance of freight can be explained by the fact that the early locomotives, of limited power and moving on too light tracks, could not carry heavy loads. **45**, p. 153.

TABLE 138

RAILROAD ECONOMICS: REVENUES AND EXPENDITURES IN SELECTED COUNTRIES, 1937 AND 1951

	1937		1951			
	Revenues [a] *Expenditures*		*Revenues* [a] *Expenditures*		*Revenues* [a] *Expenditures*	
Country	In Millions		In Millions		*Per Mile of Line Worked, in Thousands*	
United States [b]	$4,226.3	$3,165.2	$9,587.0	$7,135.1	$42.8	$31.9
Canada	334.6[c]	283.2	1,001.0	933.2	24.5[c]	22.8[c]
Mexico	35.8[d]	28.8[d]	60.2[e]	. . .	4.5[e]	5.5[e]
Great Britain	847.4	672.9	1,043.5	945.8	53.8	48.8
France	407.0	426.1[d]	1,283.8	1,265.6	50.4	49.7
Belgium	90.8	89.5	234.0	229.9	74.9	73.6
Netherlands	55.2	50.1	87.4	72.9	43.8	36.6
Denmark	27.3	27.4	54.4	56.9	33.1	34.6
Sweden	95.0	68.6	198.1	192.6	20.7	20.2
Norway	19.0	19.8	43.0	50.3	15.8	18.5
Finland	20.7	16.9	92.3	89.1	31.1	30.0
Germany [f]	1,775.1	1,608.4	1,121.7	1,127.3	59.4	59.5
Czechoslovakia	151.8[d]	159.5[d]	326.7[e]	343.4[e]	39.8	41.9
Austria	90.3	89.5	113.6	172.9	30.7	46.8
Switzerland	77.6	51.5	186.2	129.3	91.3	63.9
Portugal	11.2[d]	9.7[d]	21.7	21.1	9.7	9.5
Spain	88.6[g]	74.4[g]	. . .	. . .	. . .	. . .
Italy	228.5	185.3	273.2	337.5	26.9	33.3
Greece [h]	3.4[d]	3.3[d]	23.9	38.9	38.2	61.7
Japan	106.2[i]	73.8	482.4	432.7	39.3	35.2
Turkey [j]	18.0	13.1	67.7	73.6	19.5	15.6
India	386.5[d]	264.0[d]	555.7	450.1	16.0	13.0
Algeria	. . .	. . .	28.1	40.3	10.4	14.9
Egypt	. . .	. . .	38.4	36.0	. . .	. . .
Union of South Africa	157.3	101.5	256.7	166.0	19.2	12.5
Australia [j]	170.1	123.1	194.4	190.4	. . .	. . .
New Zealand [j]	31.1	27.5	54.7	57.7	15.6	16.5

Sources: **19**, 1938, pp. 104*–07*; **60**, 1951, pp. 92–103; for the United States: **15**, 1950, pp. 155 and 157; for Egypt: **43**, 1952–1953, p. 249.

a. Includes receipts arising from passenger and goods traffic, such as sale of tickets, warehouse and siding rent, charges for customs clearance, station concessions.
b. Postwar data for 1950. The last two columns: revenue and expenditure per mile of line owned by the railroads.
c. Canadian National Railways.

d. 1936.
e. 1948.
f. Postwar: Western Germany.
g. At official exchange rates.
h. State railways.
i. 1935–36.
j. Postwar data for 1950.

tion of total revenue derived from freight is particularly large. In 1951, for example, it amounted to 80.5 per cent in Iran; 79.8 per cent in Canada; and 84.5 per cent in Luxembourg. (See Table 139.)

In the United States also, where heavy materials are hauled over long distances, freight traffic is of preponderant importance in the total operating revenue. The percentage of total revenue derived from freight has increased considerably with the growing use of motor vehicles for

personal transportation and less weighty freight, and this trend is continuing: [189]

	Freight	Passenger
1909	67.8	22.8
1919	69.9	22.7
1929	76.9	13.6
1939	81.4	10.3

(*Continued on facing page*)

189. **15**, 1950, p. 158; **14**, 1952, p. 170. Data for 1950 refer to Class I railways.

TABLE 139

RAILROAD ECONOMICS: REVENUE FROM PASSENGER AND FREIGHT TRAFFIC, IN SELECTED COUNTRIES, 1951

(*Per Cent*)

Country	Pas- senger	Freight	Other Sources	Country	Pas- senger	Freight	Other Sources
United States [a]	8.7	83.1	8.2	Switzerland [e]	41.3	50.6	8.1
Canada [b]	14.6	79.8	5.6	Austria	21.7	61.9	16.4
Great Britain	37.6	61.1	1.3	Portugal	45.4	53.7	0.9
France	18.4	53.9	27.7	Spain	28.5	68.8	2.7
Luxembourg	10.0	84.5	5.5	Italy	44.8	46.3	8.9
Belgium	25.4	58.8	15.8	Greece [f]	54.0	43.7	2.3
Netherlands	56.7	40.4	2.9	Japan	50.5	47.2	2.3
Denmark	57.3	33.3	9.4	Iran	12.3	80.5	7.2
Sweden	35.8	60.3	3.9	India	37.6	52.8	9.6
Norway	43.9	51.4	4.7				
Finland	20.2	70.4	9.4	Algeria	25.6	72.0	2.4
Western Germany	27.4	64.8	7.8	Tunisia	23.3	75.6	1.1
Poland [c]	39.6	54.4	6.0	Union of South			
Czechoslovakia [d]	34.9	60.3	4.8	Africa	18.6	75.4	6.0

Sources: **60,** 1951, pp. 92–95; for the United States: **14,** 1952, p. 170.

a. Class I railways.
b. Canadian national railways; for the Canadian Pacific Railway, the corresponding figures are: 13.7; 81.9; 4.4.
c. 1947.

d. 1948.
e. Federal railways.
f. State railways.

1949	82.5	9.9
1950	82.8	8.6
1951	83.1	8.7

Railroad revenue per 100 passenger-miles or 100 ton-miles varies greatly. In the United States, the railroads derive nearly twice as much revenue from a passenger-mile as from a ton-mile; in Canada, more than twice. In contrast, each ton-mile yields about twice as much as a passenger-mile in Great Britain, more than double in Belgium, Portugal, Japan and India; and more than three times as much in Luxembourg. (See Table 140.)

Most of the total revenue from passenger traffic comes from the passengers using the so-called low-rate third class.[190] The recognition of this fact came gradually from practical experience, though it had been discussed by Lardner some

hundred years earlier.[191] The share of low-rate passengers in total traffic in all European countries varies from about 86 per cent to nearly 100 per cent, and the revenues from third-class traffic range from nearly 70 to 95 per cent. The explanation can be obtained by a glance at any passenger train in Europe, where the first-class cars ordinarily carry few passengers and are sometimes empty and the third-class cars are crowded to capacity.

The situation is strikingly different in countries with a sharp division between the European and native population. So as not to "mix" with the natives, Europeans use the higher-class cars. In the Union of South Africa, for example, nearly half the passengers ride in the first- and second-class cars. (See Table 141.)

In the United States, more than half of the 486.2 million passengers in 1950 were commuters who mostly use the coaches. Of the remaining 208.5 million, 185.8 million patronized coaches and 22.7 million, parlor and sleeping cars (89 and 11 per cent, respectively). Revenue from coach passengers represented nearly 59 per cent of the total; from the others, about 41 per cent. Revenue per passenger-mile was 2.47 and 3.25

190. In the United States, the railways provide coach and Pullman service, the latter at higher rates. The railroads in Europe and most other countries offer three distinct classes of service (four classes in some), and in many countries workers' trains are provided at especially low fares. In most western European countries, the difference between the second- and third-class service is not great, while the first class offers the maximum comfort of which the line is capable. Some railways have only two classes: second and third, or first and third.

191. **67,** pp. 271ff.

TABLE 140

RAILROAD ECONOMICS: REVENUE PER 100 PASSENGER-
MILES AND 100 TON-MILES, IN SELECTED
COUNTRIES, 1951

Country	Per 100 Passenger- Miles	Per 100 Ton- Miles
United States	$2.60	$1.35
Canada	2.75	1.22
Great Britain	1.44	2.74
France	1.33	2.28
Luxembourg	1.41	4.96
Belgium	1.31	3.14
Netherlands	1.23	. . .
Denmark	1.39	2.17
Sweden	1.77	2.02
Norway	1.96	3.15
Finland	1.41	2.30
Western Germany	1.34	2.34
Switzerland [a]	1.74	2.12
Austria	0.84	. . .
Portugal	1.22	2.93
Spain	0.71	1.60
Italy	0.90	. . .
Japan	0.40	0.91
Turkey	0.97	1.33
India	0.50	1.18
Union of South Africa	. . .	1.37

Sources: **60,** 1951, pp. 104–05; for the United States:
14, 1952, pp. 171–72.

a. Federal railways.

cents, respectively. The high total revenue from users of parlor and sleeping cars is due, in addition to the higher fare, to the fact that the average trip per passenger in coaches was 94 miles, and in more expensive accommodations, 411 miles.[192]

OUTLOOK

The history of railroads has entered a new phase since the motor vehicle and the airplane have appeared on the scene. These new products of technical progress have challenged the railroads' supremacy in economically advanced countries and have raised questions as to their merits in underdeveloped areas. At the end of the last century, none would have doubted that economic progress in Asia, Africa or the hinterland of South America required the building of railroads. Today it may be debated whether high-

192. **15,** 1950, pp. 39 and 53. Class I railways.

way transport and air travel cannot serve these areas more cheaply and effectively.

The great era of railroad construction in industrially developed countries came to a close before World War I. In other areas railroad building continued, but on a comparatively small scale. Between the two wars, the USSR built some new lines, mostly feeders or connecting links between existing railroads, and some new mileage is to be added in coming years.[193] The modest networks in Latin America, Asia and Africa have also been somewhat extended. It can be expected that sooner or later India and China will increase their railroad mileage, which is grossly insufficient for their vast territories. For them, as for the USSR, the railroads are a vital necessity since their small fleets of motor vehicles cannot cope with the transport of bulky and heavy raw materials, such as coal, iron ore, lumber and fertilizers. For such countries railroads are also the only feasible means of passenger mass transportation.

Essentially all new railroads in underdeveloped areas will be built or controlled by public agencies rather than by private enterprise.[194] Only government can now provide the necessary financing, whether from internal resources or loans. Private capital, particularly foreign capital, can hardly be lured into this field, as in the palmy days of the railroad boom during the nineteenth century. The fear of nationalization looms too heavily today, and the railroad is a venture from which quick profits cannot be expected. Foreign loans for railroad construction might be possible under the sponsorship of the International Bank, but they would then be conditioned by the Bank's decision on their economic need. In fact, railroads rank high in the development projects submitted to the Bank by various underdeveloped countries; India, Pakistan and Thailand have obtained Bank loans for railway rehabilitation.

Where the era of railroad construction is past history, the issues are entirely different. The tendency in such countries is toward coordination of all means of transportation — in some, through nationalization and in others, through government regulation and voluntary cooperation. In one form or another, the trend to coordi-

193. See p. 352.
194. This statement does not preclude the possibility of railroad construction by private companies in special cases. To get iron ore, private capital is building railroads in Labrador and Venezuela.

TABLE 141

RAILROAD ECONOMICS: DISTRIBUTION OF PASSENGERS AND OF REVENUE FROM PASSENGER TRAFFIC, BY CLASS, IN SELECTED COUNTRIES, 1951

(*Per Cent*)

Country	Passengers			Revenues		
	1st Class	2d Class	3d Class	1st Class	2d Class	3d Class
Mexico	7.0	93.0	—	34.3	65.7	—
Great Britain	2.4	0.1	97.5	…	…	…
France	0.4	5.7	93.9	6.2	21.0	72.8
Luxembourg	0.2	3.9	95.9	1.1	10.8	88.1
Belgium	0.1	5.7	94.2	1.3	12.6	86.1
Netherlands	a	7.6	92.4	0.3	14.1	85.6
Denmark	1.4	—	98.6	10.1	—	89.9
Sweden	a	1.3	98.7	0.7	11.1	88.2
Finland	a	3.8	96.2 b	—	14.8	85.2 b
Western Germany c	a	1.8	98.2	0.3	6.7	93.0
Czechoslovakia d	a	0.7	99.3	0.2	4.8	95.0
Switzerland e	0.1	5.3	94.6	1.3	16.2	82.5
Austria	a	0.4	99.6	…	…	…
Hungary f	a	1.9	98.1	—	9.2	90.8
Portugal	1.6	6.2	92.2	9.9	21.3	68.8
Spain	2.4	11.6	86.0	16.5	13.8	69.7
Italy	0.6	7.5	91.9	…	…	…
Bulgaria f	—	0.4	99.6	…	…	…
Greece g	2.0	4.4	93.6	6.0	10.8	83.2
Turkey	3.9	22.6	73.5	5.0	27.4	67.6
India	1.2	2.1	96.7	2.7	11.2	86.1
French Morocco	2.9	13.9	83.2 b	7.5	31.1	61.4 b
Algeria	0.8	8.4	90.8	5.0	23.8	71.2
Union of South Africa	24.2	21.6	54.2	22.1	33.0	44.9

Source: **60**, 1951, pp. 72–74 and 84–86.

a. Negligible.
b. Includes fourth class.
c. Excludes occupation traffic.
d. 1948.

e. Federal railways.
f. 1947.
g. State railways.

nate transportation is bound to be intensified as the competition within the transport system becomes stronger.

Although the railroads no longer dominate land transport, they remain the backbone of the transportation system in advanced countries with highly developed highway and air transport as well as in the world as a whole. They carry passengers and freight in all weathers; in transporting heavy and bulky goods in large quantities over long distances, their services have not been matched by any other means of transportation.

CHAPTER 9

LAND TRANSPORTATION: MOTOR VEHICLES
AND HIGHWAYS

ALTHOUGH RAILROADS were in existence in the early nineteenth century, their networks were so inadequate that attempts were made in various European countries to use steam power for road carriages.[1] In England, France, Germany and Belgium, a few steam-powered coaches were in operation on improved roads and turnpikes.[2] (See Figure 69,A.) The coaches enjoyed a certain popularity as a safer, cheaper and quicker means of transport than horse carriages. Their advocates believed they could be increased in size and made capable of competing with the railroads. (See Figure 69,B.) Friedrich List, the nineteenth-century German economist, disputed these claims, pointing out that travel in such coaches was perilous, slow and uncomfortable in comparison with rail transport and that they could carry only small loads. The success of steam coaches was short-lived. Their immense weight destroyed road surfaces; they were slow starting and needed much fuel. Turnpike trusts fought them by imposing prohibitive tolls, often twenty times as high as for horse coaches.[3] The railroad companies, in their turn, wanted no competition from other mechanized road vehicles and influenced legislation against steam coaches. An example of such legislation in England was the Red Flag Act, which required that a man carry a red flag by day and a red lantern by night before a horseless vehicle to warn people of danger, although the vehicular speed limit was four miles an hour.[4]

The spreading network of railroads drove steam coaches off the roads; mechanized land transport was thus relegated for more than half a century to railed tracks. The railroads virtually monopolized land transportation until the advent of another horseless vehicle, the automobile, early in the twentieth century.[5] The railroads took this new "toy" lightly at first but found out, after World War I, that it was a formidable rival. The impact was first felt in passenger traffic. In time, however, the competition of trucks became even more serious, since freight is more important to the railroads than passenger business.[6]

Motor vehicles soon became as characteristic of our century as railroads were of the nineteenth. They have brought effective transportation facilities to areas with insufficient or no railway service, have greatly increased the volume of transportation even in countries crisscrossed by railroads, and have generated new forms of passenger travel and new ways of handling and hauling cargo.

Motorization of transport changed the role of highways in the modern economy. From mere feeders to railroads, they became important arteries of freight and passenger traffic. Construction of highways suited to swift and heavy motor traffic has become an urgent problem in many countries. Indeed, "it was the Vehicle that made the Road," [7] and it has been the automobile that has created the need for new types of highways, capable of handling mass traffic.

The dispatch with which the motor vehicle conquered the highways is illustrated by conditions in the United Kingdom. In 1896, the red-flag law was annulled, and the first clattering motor vehicles were allowed to circulate on highways along with horse-driven buggies, pedestrians and cyclists. In the 1920's, cars began to rule the roads in the United States, the United Kingdom and other industrially developed countries, and by the 1930's they practically monopolized them.

Motor transportation has become one of the largest industries in the United States, and its

---

1. The first self-propelled steam vehicle was built in France by Cugnot in 1769. It made three miles per hour, but crashed through a wall during a test run, and the inventor was imprisoned. **67**, p. 32.

2. **53**, p. 216; **42**, p. 100. See illustrations of early steam coaches in **41**, Plates 113–122.

3. **67**, p. 32. For turnpikes, see Chapter 8, pp. 333–35.

4. **66**, p. 102; **67**, pp. 32 and 36. Speed of some later models exceeded ten miles per hour.

5. For the development of the automobile and the automobile industry, see **73**, pp. 1164–70.

6. See Chapter 8, pp. 379–81.

7. **41**, p. 27.

A. The Steam Coach in England, 1829

Sir Goldsworthy Gurney's steam carriage, London to Bath, 1829.

B. The Steam Coach of the Future

This picture of the highway steam coach appeared in the 1830's on the cover of a German magazine (*National Magazin für Haus- und Landwirtschaft . . .*). It shows how the enthusiasts of mechanical means of transportation visualized the steam-powered bus: a three-wheel contraption with the coachman in the customary place in front and an engine concealed somewhere within the ornate chassis.

FIGURE 69. THE STEAM COACH

TABLE 142

MOTOR VEHICLES IN THE WORLD, BY TYPE, 1938–53

Year, as of December 31	Number, in Thousands			Per Cent		
	Total	Passenger Cars	Trucks and Buses	Total	Passenger Cars	Trucks and Buses
1938	43,777	35,411	8,366	100.0	80.9	19.1
1939	45,422	36,581	8,841	100.0	80.5	19.5
1946	46,914	35,918	10,996	100.0	76.6	23.4
1947	53,068	39,543	13,525	100.0	74.5	25.5
1948	57,881	42,843	15,038	100.0	74.0	26.0
1949	63,584	47,582	16,002	100.0	74.8	25.2
1950	70,415	53,027	17,388	100.0	75.3	24.7
1951	74,019	56,001	18,018	100.0	75.6	24.4
1952	77,983	58,347	19,636	100.0	74.8	25.2
1953	83,057	62,501	20,556	100.0	75.2	24.8

Source: **37,** 1950, p. 30; 1951, p. 28; 1952, p. 26; 1953, p. 30 and 1954, p. 32.

importance in other countries is rising by leaps and bounds. Much progress has been made in the size and design of the body and engine of motor vehicles. The cars of today are as different from the first horseless vehicles as are Pullman cars from early railway passenger accommodations.

The problems of the role of motor vehicles in the modern economy are numerous, and only the most important are discussed in the following pages.[8]

MOTOR VEHICLES

NUMBER

Nearly 78 million motor vehicles rolled along the world highways in 1952 and over 83 million in 1953. The motor fleet has grown rapidly from 46.9 million vehicles in 1946 to 63.6 million in 1949 and 83.1 million (62.5 million passenger cars and 20.6 million trucks and buses) in 1953. This advance can no more be stopped than could King Canute stop the incoming tide.

Commercial vehicles are increasing in number more rapidly than passenger cars. At the end of 1952 and 1953 they constituted a fourth of all vehicles in the world as a whole as compared with one fifth in 1939. (See Table 142.)

8. The first section of this chapter discusses the size and composition of the motor fleet in the world and individual countries. The second deals with the volume and character of motor traffic; the third, with trends in highway development. The two concluding sections review financial questions relating to motor transport and the competition between motor vehicles and railroads.

Selected Countries

The United States leads, with 53.3 million vehicles: 43.8 million passenger cars and 9.5 million trucks and buses in 1952 (46.5 and 9.9 million, respectively, in 1953). Great Britain is next, then Canada, the USSR, France, Australia and Western Germany. In Asia, Japan and India rank first and second. In Africa, the Union of South Africa leads with a substantially greater number than either Japan or India. Australia has more motor vehicles than all Asia. (See Figure 70 and Table 143.)

In relation to national income the distribution of motor vehicles in the world appears more even, but very considerable contrasts remain. Motor vehicles are heavily concentrated in prosperous countries — the United States, Canada, the United Kingdom, northwestern Europe and Australia. (See Figure 71.)

In addition to the number of passenger cars and trucks reported in various countries (Table 143), the motor fleets in many areas include considerable numbers of motorcycles, which are in much greater use in other countries than in the United States. The United Kingdom reported more than 750,000 motorcycles on its highways in 1950 and had over a million in 1953.[9] In other European countries, the number of motorcycles and bicycles with auxiliary engine

9. **44,** 1951, p. 10 and **6,** 1953, p. 60. In 1951 the United States had some 420,000 private motorcycles and less than 10,000 publicly owned units. (**19,** 1951, p. 12.)

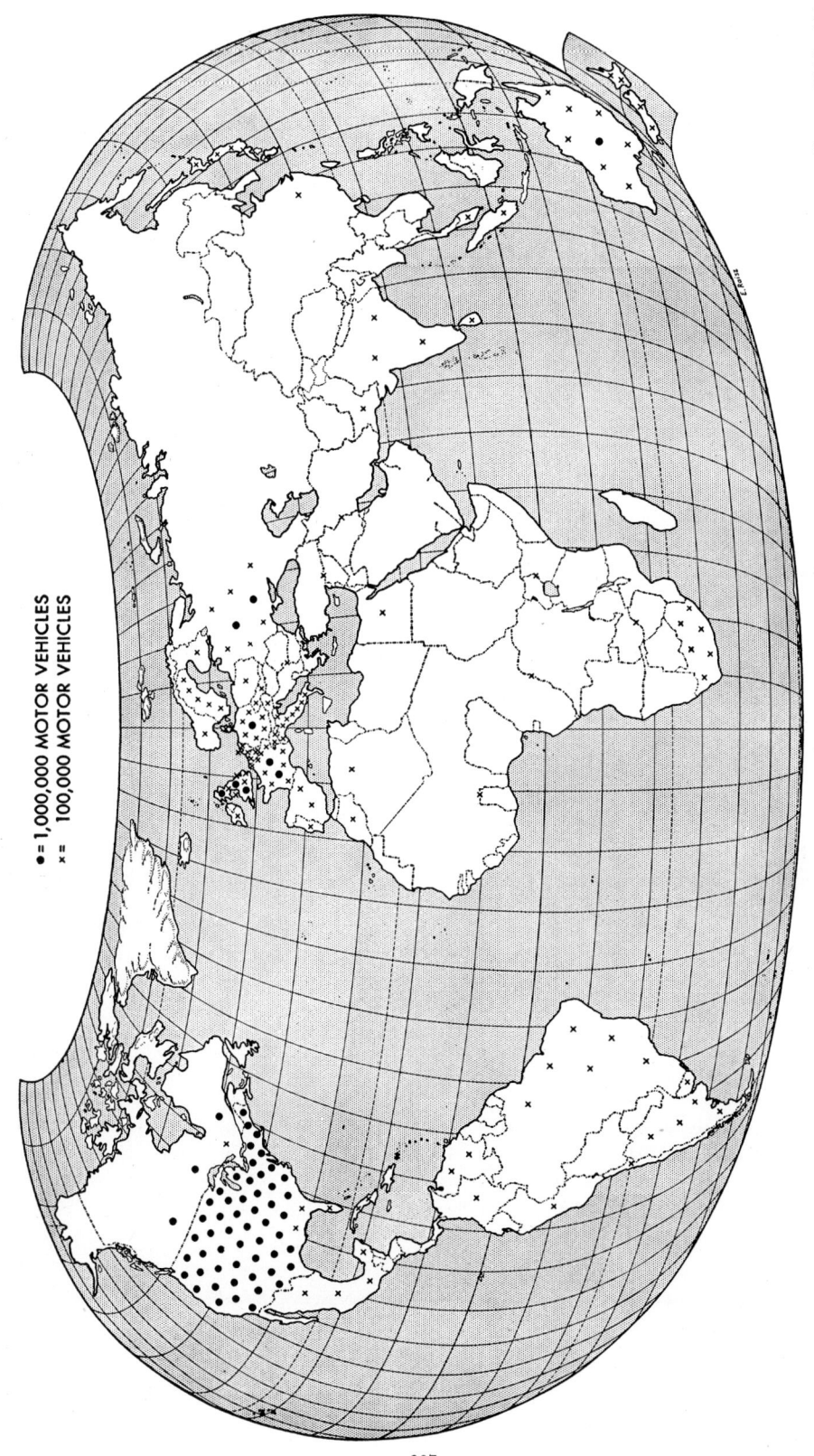

Source: Table 143

FIGURE 70. MOTOR VEHICLES: GEOGRAPHIC DISTRIBUTION IN THE WORLD, 1952

TABLE 143

MOTOR VEHICLES: REGISTRATIONS IN SELECTED COUNTRIES, 1928, 1937, 1952

(*Thousands*)

Country	1928 [a]			1937 [b]			1952		
	Total	Pas-senger Cars	Trucks and Buses	Total	Pas-senger Cars	Trucks and Buses	Total	Pas-senger Cars	Trucks and Buses
World	...	...	...	...	...	...	77,983 [c]	58,347	19,636
United States	24,512	21,308	3,203	29,706	25,391	4,315	53,294	43,811	9,484
Canada [d]	1,062	929	133	1,309	1,103	206	3,115	2,325	790
Mexico	67	49	18	120	78	42	369	215	154
Guatemala	3	2	1	4	3	2	15	8	7
El Salvador	...	...	...	3	2	1	11	6	5
Costa Rica	...	...	...	3	2	1	11	7	5
Panama [e]	6	5	2	11	9	2	23	16	7
Cuba	39	26	13	42	26	16	151	101	49
Dominican Republic	...	...	...	2	1	1	10	6	5
Puerto Rico	16	13	4	21	16	5	72	49	21
Venezuela	...	...	...	22	13	9	154	86	59
Colombia	...	...	...	22	13	9	84	41	43
Ecuador	...	...	...	2	1	1	16	5	11
Brazil	153	101	52	139	100	39	564	300	265
Peru	15	9	6	25	14	10	72	40	32
Bolivia	...	...	...	12	4	8	14	4	10
Chile	28	19	9	41	29	12	83	44	39
Uruguay	...	...	...	48	36	12	87	48	40
Argentina	334	273	61	387	297	90	367	222	145
Great Britain	1,288	934	354	2,359	1,833	526	3,610	2,504	1,105
Ireland	39	32	7	60	49	11	141	112	29
France	1,089	758	331	2,305	2,020	285	2,583	1,612	971
Luxembourg	8	6	2	12	8	4	518	358	160
Belgium	120	79	41	222	144	78	17	12	5
Netherlands	83	52	31	142	91	51	269	170	99
Denmark	89	63	26	142	101	41	209	131	78
Sweden	127	94	33	192	134	58	474	365	110
Norway	37	22	15	79	47	32	149	79	70
Finland	32	22	10	43	24	19	104	53	50
Germany [f]	484	343	141	1,489	1,108	381	1,556	1,010	547
Poland	22	17	5	27	20	7	76	29	47
Czechoslovakia	36	25	11	122	91	32	168	105	63
Switzerland	62	50	12	93	72	21	234	188	46
Austria	34	20	14	48	32	16	120	66	55
Hungary	24	20	4	30	26	4	16	6	11
Portugal	25	21	4	42	31	11	116	82	34
Spain	157	130	27	...	...	...	176	82	94
Italy	189	142	47	353	271	82	792	517	275
Yugoslavia	12	10	2	15	11	4	26	8	18
Romania	31	28	3	...	...	...	26	14	12
Bulgaria	...	...	...	...	...	...	15	5	10
Albania	...	...	...	...	...	...	2	1	1
Greece	17	13	4	18	9	9	34	10	23
USSR	19	...	...	760	167	593	2,600	250	2,350

(*Continued on facing page*)

TABLE 143—*continued*

Country	1928 [a]			1937 [b]			1952		
	Total	Passenger Cars	Trucks and Buses	Total	Passenger Cars	Trucks Buses and	Total	Passenger Cars	Trucks and Buses
China	...	...	...	65	36	29	53	3	50
Korea	...	...	...	9	5	4	15	4	11
Japan	74	51	23	113	35	78	530	88	442
Taiwan	...	...	...	...	...	...	20	5	15
Turkey	...	...	...	8	4	4	33	13	19
Cyprus	1	...	...	3	2	1	9	5	4
Lebanon	...	...	...	6	5	1	18	14	4
Israel [g]	...	...	...	9	6	4	31	14	17
Syria	...	...	...	4	3	1	14	7	7
Jordan	...	...	...	...	...	...	5	3	2
Saudi-Arabia	...	...	...	...	...	...	22	9	13
Iraq	...	...	...	7	5	2	19	12	7
Iran	...	...	...	...	...	...	43	23	20
Afghanistan	...	...	...	...	...	...	5	1	4
Pakistan	}125	106	19	124	88	36{	46	29	16
India							285	159	125
Burma	...	...	...	21	7	14	31	...	...
Thailand	...	...	...	10	5	5	30	17	13
Indochina	...	...	...	32	17	15	40	29	11
Ceylon	18	13	5	27	20	7	64	46	18
Malaya	...	...	...	27	20	7	65	45	20
Singapore	...	...	...	12	9	3	39	30	10
Indonesia	72	62	10	64	47	17	105	52	53
Philippines	30	20	10	49	30	18	106	51	55
French Morocco	18	13	5	59	45	14	99	64	35
Algeria	74	...	...	124	...	...	120	70	50
Tunisia	...	...	...	27	...	...	37	24	13
Egypt	25	20	4	31	27	4	88	68	20
Sudan	...	...	...	...	...	...	12	11	1
Ethiopia	...	...	...	...	...	...	9	5	4
French West Africa	...	...	...	17	6	10	46	19	28
Belgian Congo	...	...	...	9	4	5	37	15	22
Gold Coast [h]	...	...	...	...	...	...	33	10	24
Nigeria [h]	...	...	...	...	...	...	27	13	14
Kenya	...	...	...	12	9	3	40	19	21
Uganda	...	...	...	5	3	3	12	6	7
Tanganyika	...	...	...	...	...	...	17	9	8
Mozambique	...	...	...	6	4	2	16	12	4
Madagascar	...	...	...	...	...	...	14	6	8
Northern Rhodesia	...	...	...	...	...	...}	82	48	34
Southern Rhodesia	9	8	1	20	14	6{			
Union of South Africa	124	113	11	326	284	42	641	497	144
Australia	517	420	96	713	499	214	1,660	1,084	575
New Zealand	130	108	22	222	175	47	411	297	113
Hawaii	...	...	...	...	...	...	161	134	28

Sources: **4,** 1951, pp. 316–19; **51,** 1950, pp. 200–03; **37,** 1953, pp. 28–30; for the USSR: **40,** p. 495 and **37,** 1953, p. 29.

a. 1929 for Cuba, Guatemala, Austria, Algeria, Japan and Panama.

b. 1936 for Uruguay and Indonesia; 1938 for Bolivia, Indochina, Kenya and Uganda; 1939 for France and the Belgian Congo.

c. Excludes 65,000 vehicles not reported as to type.

d. Includes Newfoundland in 1952.

e. Figures for Canal Zone in 1928 and 1937.

f. 1952: Western Germany.

g. Prewar: Israel/Palestine.

h. Data in last columns for 1950.

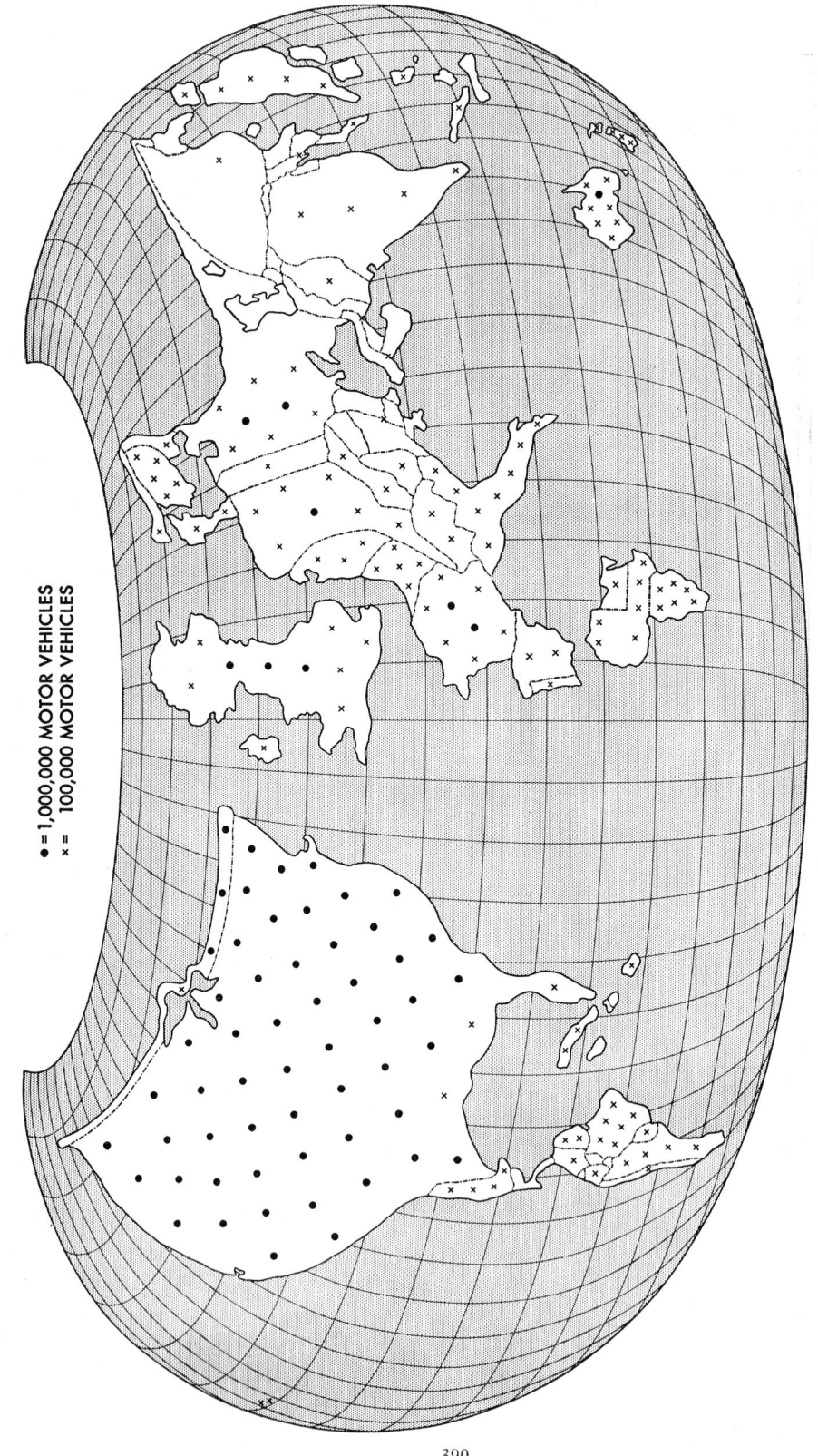

● = 1,000,000 MOTOR VEHICLES
× = 100,000 MOTOR VEHICLES

FIGURE 71. MOTOR VEHICLES: DISTRIBUTION IN THE WORLD IN 1952 IN RELATION TO NATIONAL INCOME, 1948

The dots and crosses showing the number of motor vehicles registered in 1952 are plotted on a distorted map of the world showing regions and countries on the scale of income in 1948. (See Figure 127, p. 397 in **73**.)

was as follows, in 1950 and 1953 (in thousands): [10]

	1950	1953
Belgium	140	204 [a]
Netherlands	151	401
Denmark	48	102
Sweden	213	291 [a]
Western Germany	914	1,665
Austria	137	202
Switzerland	76	172
Italy	652	1,740

a. 1952.

In recent years the increase in the total number of motor vehicles in many countries has been relatively greater than in the United States. Between 1937 and 1952, Canada, for example, more than doubled its motor fleet, which had remained nearly stationary during the 1928–37 decade. Brazil had fewer motor vehicles in 1937 than in 1928 — 139,000 and 153,000, respectively — but counted 564,000 in 1952. The number in Switzerland rose from 62,000 in 1928 to 93,000 in 1937 and 234,000 in 1952; for the Union of South Africa, the corresponding figures are 124,000, 326,000 and 641,000.

In many countries, trucks and buses have increased in number more rapidly than passenger cars, which remain an unattainable luxury in large areas of the world. Commercial vehicles, on the other hand, are often the only means of overland freight transport in underdeveloped countries. Turkey, for example, had 4,000 passenger cars and about an equal number of trucks and buses in 1937; in 1952, the numbers were 13,000 and 19,000, respectively. In the Philippines the number of passenger cars rose in this period from 30,000 to 51,000; of commercial vehicles, from 18,000 to 55,000. The same tendency appears in Mexico, Chile, Brazil, and also in Denmark, Finland, Austria, Italy, Egypt, the Union of South Africa, Australia and many other countries.

The United States

The first horseless vehicles in the United States appeared on the streets in the 1890's. Only four motor vehicles were registered by the end of 1895. Ten years later, there were 78,800; in 1915, nearly 2.5 million; and in 1925, almost 20 million. The number continued to increase,

TABLE 144

MOTOR VEHICLES: REGISTRATIONS IN THE UNITED STATES, 1897–1953

(*Thousands*)

Year, as of December 31	Total [a]	Passenger Cars	Trucks and Buses
1897	0.1	0.1	—
1898	0.8	0.8	—
1899	3.2	3.2	—
1900	8.0	8.0	—
1905	78.8	77.4	1.4
1910	468.5	458.4	10.1
1915	2,490.9	2,332.4	158.5
1920	9,239.2	8,131.5	1,107.6
1925	19,940.7	17,439.7	2,501.0
1930	26,532.0	22,972.7	3,559.3
1935	26,229.7	22,494.9	3,734.9
1940	32,035.4	27,372.4	4,663.0
1945	31,035.4	25,793.5	5,241.9
1946	34,373.0	28,213.3	6,159.6
1947	37,841.5	30,845.4	6,996.1
1948	41,085.5	33,350.9	7,734.6
1949	44,690.3	36,453.4	8,237.0
1950	49,195.2	40,333.6	8,861.7
1951	51,948.8	42,682.6	9,266.2
1952	53,294.5	43,810.5	9,484.0
1953	56,313.0	46,460.0	9,853.0

Sources: **14**, p. 223; **37**, 1953, p. 24 and 1954, p. 30.

a. Beginning with 1945, includes tax-exempt publicly owned vehicles, except military vehicles.

though less rapidly, then declined slightly during the depression but exceeded 34 million by Pearl Harbor Day. The wartime shortage of gasoline and rubber, coupled with interruption in the production of civilian motor vehicles, again held down the number but did not reduce it below 30 million. By the end of 1945, motor-vehicle registrations exceeded 31.0 million; five years later the number was 49.2 million and in 1953 the United States had more than 56 million motor vehicles.[11] (See Table 144.)

Although motor transportation has been growing rapidly elsewhere, the United States outdistances the rest of the world in the number of motor vehicles, with 75.1 per cent of the world's passenger fleet and 48.3 per cent of all commer-

---

10. **6**, 1953, p. 60. For Sweden: heavy motorcycles only.

11. This last figure does not include trailers, semi-trailers and motorcycles, which together exceed 3 million. Automotive equipment of the military forces is also excluded.

cial vehicles in 1952. Its share of the world's passenger cars rose between 1939 and 1953 from 71.5 to 74.3 per cent, but its share of trucks and buses fell from 50.6 to 47.9 per cent.

DENSITY

The density of the distribution of motor vehicles may be measured in relation to the size of the territory, the road mileage or the population. Because of the contrasts in the number of inhabitants per square mile and road mileage in relation to the area and population, the three measurements result in different rankings of countries.

Selected Countries

In 1950 Belgium and Brazil had about the same number of motor vehicles (429,500 and 443,100, respectively), but Belgium had 3,492 vehicles per 100 square miles as compared with Brazil's 13 — almost 270 times as many. In terms of population, Belgium, with 8.6 million inhabitants, counted 487 vehicles per 10,000 persons, while Brazil, with 52.1 million, had only 85 per 10,000. Because of its small territory, Belgium ranks first in density of vehicles per 100 square miles; Great Britain, Hawaii and the Netherlands are next, followed by the United States.

Density is very high in relation to road mileage in many areas which have relatively few vehicles in relation to area and population. Countries with an insignificant road mileage appear to have the greatest density. Thus Cuba, with 105,000 motor vehicles circulating over only 3,100 miles of roads, stands out with 33,871 vehicles per 1,000 miles of roads; Panama, reporting 24,000 vehicles and 1,400 miles of roads, has about the same density as Great Britain, with 3.3 million vehicles and more than 183,000 miles of highway. Egypt has more vehicles per 1,000 miles than Sweden, France and Switzerland — countries with a well-developed network of highways.

Motorization of transportation is best measured by the density of vehicles in relation to population. The United States tops the list, with 3,242 vehicles per 10,000 persons. The group of countries with more than 1,000 vehicles per 10,000 inhabitants also includes Hawaii, Canada, New Zealand and Australia. The number of motor vehicles per 10,000 persons ranges between 500 and 1,000 in Great Britain and France; between 100 and 500 in Sweden, Belgium, the Union of South Africa, Luxembourg, Switzerland, Ireland, Norway, Panama and many other coun-

tries. The USSR has 88 vehicles per 10,000 inhabitants; Brazil, 85; Czechoslovakia, 74. Most of the world has less than 20 vehicles per 10,000 persons: Japan, 19; Burma, 15; Indonesia and India, 8; Iran, Turkey and Ethiopia, 4; Pakistan, 3; the Gold Coast, 2 and China, 1. (See Table 145 and Figure 72.)

The United States

In 1910 the United States had one motor vehicle per 197.2 persons; in 1915, one per 40.4; in 1920, one per 11.5 and in 1925, one per 5.8 persons. By 1950, the increase in registrations lowered the ratio to one motor vehicle per 3.5 persons or an average of about one per family.

Density of motor vehicles varied widely from state to state when motor transportation was in its infancy. In 1910 there was one motor vehicle for 50–100 inhabitants in Rhode Island, California and the District of Columbia and one for more than 1,000 inhabitants in Florida, Mississippi, West Virginia, Alabama, Arkansas and Oklahoma. In relation to population, the District of Columbia and California had about fifty times as many motor vehicles as Oklahoma. The contrasts began to narrow rapidly, and five years later Arkansas was the only state with more than 200 inhabitants per motor vehicle. In 1920 all states except Alabama, Mississippi and Arkansas had less than 25 inhabitants per vehicle, and in 1930 every state in the Union had less than 10 persons per vehicle. (See Table 146.)

The controlling factors in the increase in registrations in a state have been the state's economic and industrial development and the distances which separate communities. Today distance is a stronger factor than income, and Oklahoma, in the last place in 1910, is now grouped with Connecticut, Indiana, Utah and Arizona, with fewer persons per vehicle than the average for the country as a whole. The continuing growth of the nation's tremendous motor fleet raises a question as to what the saturation point may be. Today, with the widespread ownership of two cars in a family, more than half the states average one motor vehicle for each 2–3 persons. From 1945 to 1950 the population of the United States increased 14.0 per cent and registrations, 58.4 per cent.[12]

Comparison between states of the United States and other countries shows that Turkey, Iran and Ethiopia have the same density of mo-

---

12. **19**, 1950, p. 15,

TABLE 145

MOTOR VEHICLES: DENSITY PER 100 SQUARE MILES, 1,000 MILES OF ROAD AND 10,000 INHABITANTS, IN
SELECTED COUNTRIES, 1950

Country	Per 100 Square Miles	Per 1,000 Miles of Road [a]	Per 10,000 Inhabitants	Country	Per 100 Square Miles	Per 1,000 Miles of Road [a]	Per 10,000 Inhabitants
United States	1,621	16,343	3,242	USSR	20	2,021	88
Canada	65	4,570	1,828	China	1	420	1
Mexico	37	6,491	134	Japan	110	272	19
Guatemala	31	3,714	46	Turkey	9	601	4
El Salvador	69	2,308	47	Lebanon	399	1,000	115
Costa Rica	40	8,000	100	Israel	240	2,000	185
Panama	83	17,143	300	Syria	21	3,750	47
Cuba	239	33,871	198	Iraq	11	2,794	37
Dominican Republic	42	4,000	38	Iran	3	1,350	4
Venezuela	37	11,391	267	Pakistan	9	562	3
Colombia	28	10,982	109	India	22	1,150	8
Ecuador	12	2,955	42	Burma	11	1,098	15
Brazil	13	2,746	85	Thailand	8	3,810	9
Peru	9	2,206	54	Indochina	11	1,304	11
Bolivia	3	1,348	30	Ceylon	192	2,743	64
Chile	25	2,408	124	Malaya	69	5,645	67
Uruguay	88	2,510	263	Indonesia	10	1,408	8
Argentina	40	1,664	251	Philippines	84	6,424	49
Great Britain	3,457	17,906	649	French Morocco	41	2,694	79
Ireland	437	2,379	393	Algeria	18	4,634	173
France	1,176	6,141	578	Tunisia	45	5,000	77
Luxembourg	1,400	5,185	467	Egypt	20	7,222	38
Belgium	3,492	14,549	487	Sudan	1	. . .	12
Netherlands	1,716	8,610	221	Ethiopia	15	1,395	4
Denmark	1,052	5,114	416	French West Africa	2	. . .	19
Sweden	198	3,255	493	Belgian Congo	3	438	24
Norway	87	4,203	352	Gold Coast	11	1,139	2
Finland	47	1,658	149	Nigeria	4	476	5
Western Germany	1,182	14,124	235	Kenya	3	353	11
Poland	57	. . .	28	Uganda	9	941	16
Czechoslovakia	186	2,104	74	Tanganyika	3	492	16
Switzerland	1,175	6,528	400	Mozambique	4	. . .	23
Austria	297	4,537	138	Madagascar	7	1,019	36
Hungary	61	. . .	24	Northern Rhodesia	3	991	47
Portugal	258	5,813	109	Southern Rhodesia	34	3,269	243
Spain	90	2,185	62	Union of South Africa	126	3,489	487
Italy	488	5,219	123	Australia	42	2,393	1,541
Yugoslavia	24	1,188	15	New Zealand	309	4,163	1,689
Romania	28	. . .	16	Hawaii	2,300	. . .	2,760
Bulgaria	35	. . .	21				
Greece	42	2,188	26				

Sources: Computed from **4**, 1951, pp. 316–19; **73**, pp. 48–49. Cf. **44**, 1951, p. 15.

a. Data on road mileage as of the beginning of 1948 (Table 148), except for the USSR and Burma, as of 1938.

tor vehicles as Oklahoma had in 1910: one vehicle for approximately 2,500 persons. Liberia, Thailand, India and Indonesia are in the group with one vehicle for 1,000–1,300 persons, as Alabama, Florida and Mississippi were in 1910.

Costa Rica, Brazil, Tunisia and French Morocco, with one vehicle for 100–130 inhabitants, compare with Virginia, West Virginia, the Carolinas, Georgia, Kentucky and Texas in 1915. Belgium, Luxembourg, Denmark, Ireland, Swit-

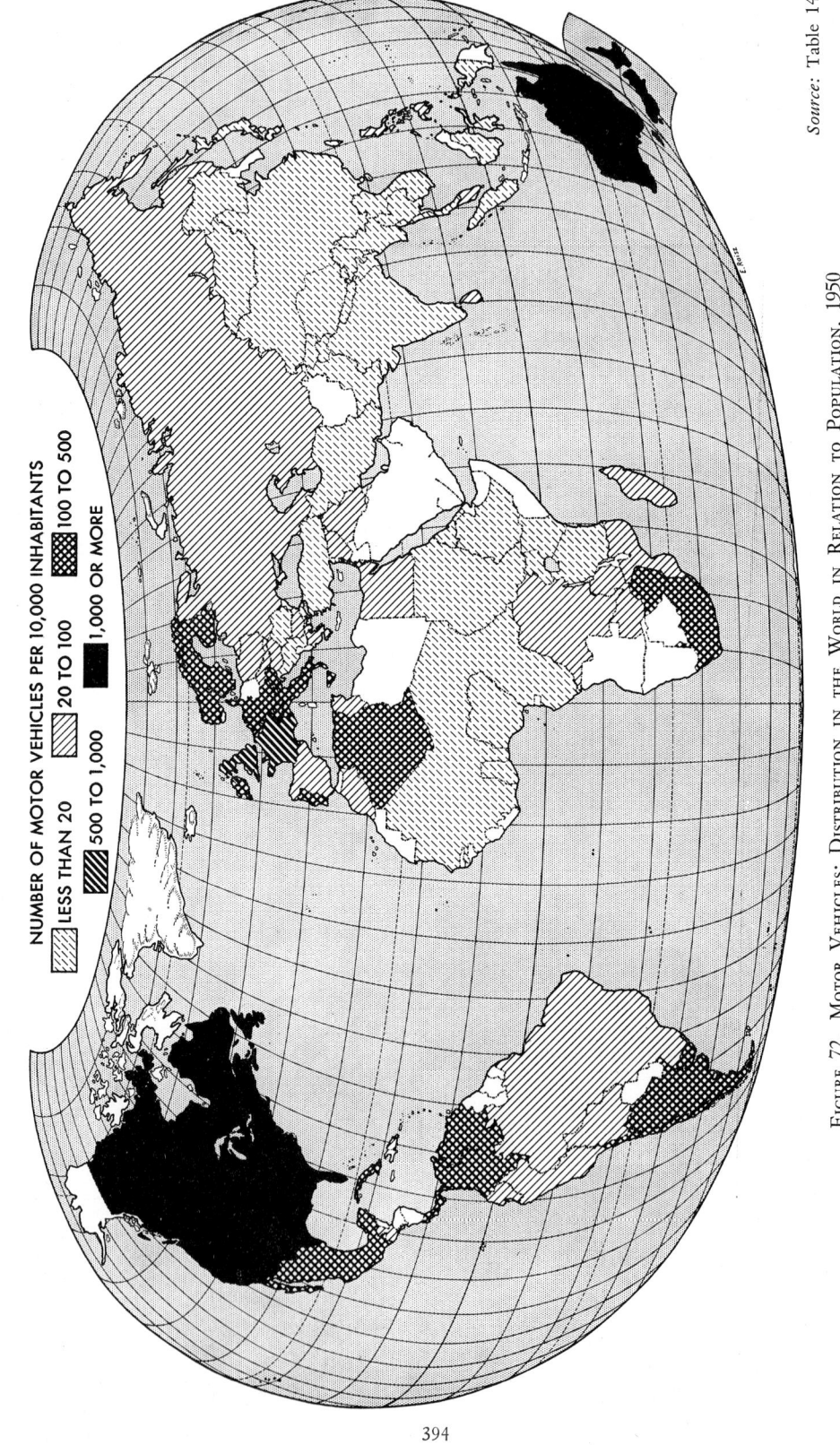

NUMBER OF MOTOR VEHICLES PER 10,000 INHABITANTS

LESS THAN 20   20 TO 100   100 TO 500

500 TO 1,000   1,000 OR MORE

FIGURE 72. MOTOR VEHICLES: DISTRIBUTION IN THE WORLD IN RELATION TO POPULATION, 1950

Source: Table 145

TABLE 146

MOTOR VEHICLES: DENSITY IN THE UNITED STATES, BY STATE, 1910–50

(Number of Persons per Motor Vehicle)

State	1910	1915	1920	1925	1930	1935	1940	1945	1950
United States	197.2	40.4	11.5	5.8	4.6	4.4	4.1	4.3	3.5
Maine	184.4	35.9	12.3	5.6	4.3	4.6	4.1	3.8	3.4
New Hampshire	122.9	32.9	12.8	5.6	4.2	4.1	3.6	3.5	3.2
Vermont	163.7	31.9	11.2	5.1	4.2	4.4	3.8	3.5	3.2
Massachusetts	107.7	36.1	14.1	6.5	5.0	5.5	4.8	4.9	3.7
Rhode Island	92.2	36.5	12.1	6.7	5.9	4.6	3.8	4.3	3.2
Connecticut	119.6	30.6	11.7	6.0	4.9	4.5	3.5	3.5	2.8
New York	145.8	38.0	15.2	6.9	5.5	5.7	4.9	5.4	4.0
New Jersey	154.9	34.8	14.0	6.3	4.8	4.6	3.8	4.1	3.1
Pennsylvania	206.3	52.2	15.3	7.1	5.5	5.6	4.6	4.7	3.5
Ohio	145.9	29.0	9.3	4.8	3.8	4.0	3.6	3.6	2.9
Indiana	268.4	29.6	8.8	4.3	3.7	3.9	3.4	3.5	2.8
Illinois	159.4	34.3	11.7	5.8	4.7	5.1	2.7	4.5	3.3
Michigan	137.0	28.4	9.0	4.4	3.6	3.9	3.4	3.8	2.6
Wisconsin	165.1	27.3	9.1	4.8	3.8	4.1	3.5	3.6	2.9
Minnesota	137.7	24.4	7.4	4.5	3.5	3.7	3.2	3.3	2.6
Iowa	214.1	16.3	5.5	3.7	3.2	3.6	3.2	3.3	2.5
Missouri	269.0	45.7	11.5	5.8	4.8	5.0	4.1	4.2	3.2
North Dakota	124.6	25.7	7.1	4.4	3.7	4.1	3.5	2.9	2.3
South Dakota	182.3	20.3	5.3	4.1	3.4	3.8	3.3	3.1	2.3
Nebraska	105.6	21.6	5.9	4.0	3.2	3.4	3.2	3.0	2.4
Kansas	161.3	23.3	6.0	4.0	3.2	3.4	3.1	2.9	2.3
Delaware	211.8	43.0	12.0	5.5	4.3	4.5	3.7	4.2	3.0
Maryland	232.9	45.1	14.2	6.6	5.1	5.0	4.1	4.6	3.5
District of Columbia	52.8	18.5	12.9	4.5	3.1	3.5	4.2	8.5	4.2
Virginia	688.0	107.4	20.3	8.6	6.5	6.5	5.4	5.6	3.7
West Virginia	1,399.1	104.4	18.2	7.3	6.5	7.2	6.3	6.1	4.2
North Carolina	689.8	117.7	18.4	8.5	7.0	7.2	6.1	5.8	3.9
South Carolina	676.9	109.0	18.0	10.2	6.0	7.5	5.7	5.7	3.7
Georgia	583.2	112.4	20.0	11.6	8.5	7.5	6.2	6.1	3.9
Florida	1,111.1	84.9	13.0	4.4	4.5	4.5	3.9	4.6	2.9
Kentucky	857.7	123.1	21.5	9.6	7.9	7.9	6.2	5.9	3.8
Tennessee	982.6	87.6	22.9	10.3	7.1	8.0	6.5	6.3	3.9
Alabama	1,208.0	201.6	31.6	13.0	9.5	11.1	8.4	7.8	4.5
Mississippi	1,185.3	188.8	26.3	10.8	8.5	11.1	8.5	7.9	4.6
Arkansas	1,376.2	212.2	29.7	9.9	8.4	9.1	7.6	6.5	4.1
Louisiana	456.8	154.2	24.8	9.5	7.6	8.3	6.5	6.1	3.8
Oklahoma	2,458.0	74.3	9.7	5.2	4.4	4.8	4.1	4.0	2.7
Texas	546.2	109.2	11.0	5.4	4.3	4.4	3.8	4.3	2.6
Montana	369.0	32.3	9.0	5.7	4.0	3.7	2.9	2.9	2.3
Idaho	700.5	55.8	8.5	5.3	3.8	4.1	3.2	3.3	2.2
Wyoming	408.8	42.1	8.2	4.5	3.7	3.4	2.9	3.0	2.0
Colorado	171.8	30.0	7.3	4.2	3.4	3.8	3.2	3.3	2.4
New Mexico	699.7	49.7	20.5	8.1	5.1	5.1	4.3	4.5	2.9
Arizona	245.6	33.9	9.8	5.8	3.9	4.2	3.6	4.4	2.8
Utah	278.9	46.9	10.6	6.6	4.5	5.0	4.0	4.0	2.8
Nevada	178.0	41.0	7.5	4.0	3.1	2.9	2.5	3.5	2.1
Washington	157.1	31.9	7.9	4.5	3.5	3.6	3.1	3.4	2.6
Oregon	127.5	31.6	6.8	4.1	3.8	3.4	2.8	2.9	2.2
California	54.5	18.4	6.1	3.3	2.8	2.9	2.5	3.1	2.3

Source: **19**, 1950, p. 17.

zerland, Norway and the Union of South Africa have one vehicle for 20–30 people, the 1920 rate in Virginia, Georgia, Kentucky, Tennessee, Mississippi, Arkansas, Louisiana and New Mexico. Canada, New Zealand and Australia, with one vehicle for 5.5, 5.9 and 6.5 persons, respectively, have rates similar to those in New York, Pennsylvania, Rhode Island and South Carolina in 1930.

MOTOR TRANSPORT

Uses of Motor Vehicles

The first and leading use of motor vehicles has been as a privately owned means of personal transportation. In the United States, more than nine out of ten private cars (92 per cent) serve for driving to and from work and for shopping; nearly three out of four are employed in making a living. More than three fourths (77 per cent) of persons living five to ten miles away from their place of employment, and more than five sixths (84 per cent) of those living more than ten miles away, depend on cars for home-to-work transportation.[13] According to the Bureau of Public Roads, some 63 million persons in the United States — about 80–90 per cent of all vacation travelers — took their vacation trips in 1950 in 31 million cars, averaging 1,000 miles in 9 days of travel.[14] The increasing numbers of passenger cars in other countries, especially in Western Europe, indicate a rising use of automobiles for personal travel, but figures are not available for a comparison with the United States.

Buses — local, suburban and intercity — are also used in passenger transportation. In the United States, more than 7 million children (28 per cent of the school enrollment) ride daily at public expense in more than 75,000 buses to more than 45,000 schools.[15] The use of buses in intercity travel is increasing: in 1939 they carried 225 million passengers and in 1950, 367 million, the average trip being some 53 miles.[16] Some 2,400 urban communities in the United States are entirely dependent on buses for local mass transportation.[17]

The use of cars and buses has greatly affected the layout of cities: while population once tended to cluster around streetcar lines, people now settle outside the city, along the highways leading to it. (See Figure 73.)

Truck haulage is of the greatest importance to farmers in the United States: nearly 90 per cent of their produce is trucked directly to initial markets (97 per cent in the northeastern region), and the rest is trucked by middlemen to railroads and docks for shipment to other points for grading, packing, processing and storing. Some 99 per cent of the tobacco output is trucked to market; 97 per cent of the milk; 96 per cent of poultry, eggs and cotton; 91 per cent of the grain.[18] Three fourths of all livestock received by stockyards in 1950 were hauled by truck.[19] The share of farm produce hauled to the largest cities in trucks is steadily growing. (See Figure 74.)

In Canada 95 per cent of the nation's milk supply is carried by highway transport, and fresh fruits and vegetables move mainly by truck.[20] In many other countries, likewise, manufacturers, wholesalers and retailers are using trucks increasingly. It has been estimated that, before World War II, industrialists, merchants, farmers and private persons, as a group, accounted for from 60 to 75 per cent of all highway freight transportation in the United States, the United Kingdom, Germany, Belgium and Switzerland.[21]

The United States

The Bureau of Public Roads estimates that one worker in 7 in the United States has work directly connected with highways and motor transportation.[22] In 1952, 5.6 million men drove trucks and buses,[23] more than 1.9 million traded in and serviced motor vehicles, and more than 280,000 worked for highway departments. Production of motor vehicles, parts and tires occupied some 900,000 persons, and 600,000 worked in associated industries and services (such as insurance, financing, battery manufacture); some 300,000 were engaged in producing

---

13. **37**, 1952, p. 62; 1953, p. 67.

14. **20**, p. 11.

15. **37**, 1950 p. 32; 1952, p. 30 and 1953, p. 37.

16. **60**, 1951, p. 4. Excludes passengers on local schedules. Corresponding figures for railroad passengers, exclusive of commuters, are 220 million and 209 million.

17. **37**, 1949, p. 30.

18. **13**, p. 23.

19. **38**, 1951, pp. 39 and 46; cf. **37**, 1952, pp. 66–67.

20. **45**, August 1951, p. 27.

21. **49**, p. 42.

22. **20**, p. 14.

23. Estimated by the Automobile Manufacturers Association, on the basis of 0.8 driver per nonfarm truck. Includes employees other than drivers of truck transportation companies.

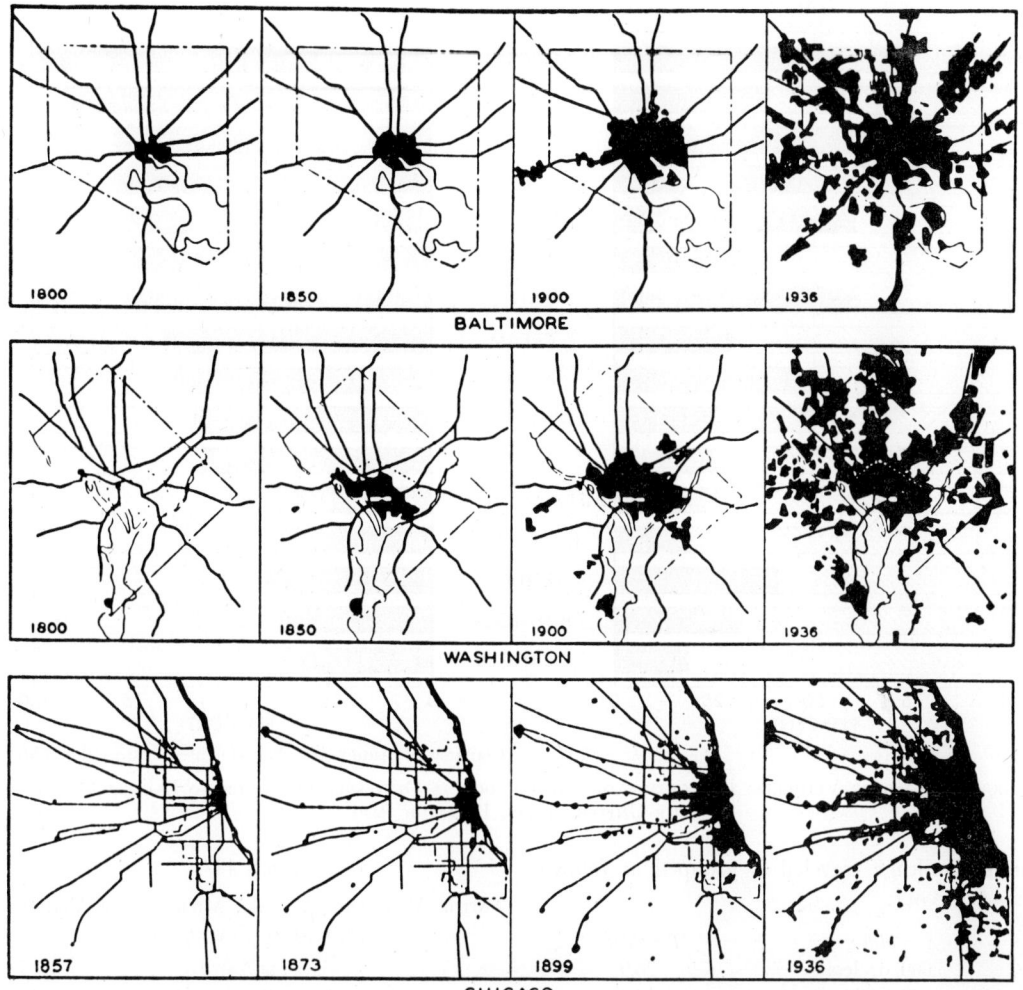

National Interregional Highway Committee (**9**)

FIGURE 73. MOTOR VEHICLES: IMPACT ON URBAN LAYOUT, IN BALTIMORE, WASHINGTON AND CHICAGO, 1800–1936

gasoline and oil. In all, nearly 9.6 million persons serviced highway transportation and worked in industries connected with it.[24]

In 1951 the motor fleet of the United States traveled more than 490 billion vehicle-miles, and in 1952 nearly 522 billion — a distance equal to more than 2,400 round trips from the earth to the sun. Rural traffic slightly exceeded urban in 1951, trucks accounting for the entire difference.[25] Of all motor traffic in the United States, 80 per cent is attributable to passenger cars, 19 per cent to trucks and one per cent to buses.

24. **37**, 1953, p. 62.
25. **37**, 1952, p. 34 and 1953, p. 65.

Between 1936 and 1952, the average mileage per vehicle increased about 10 per cent — except for a considerable decline in the war years, particularly in passenger traffic. The peak for passenger cars was reached in 1946, reflecting the return of wartime migrants to their homes and travel postponed during the war. (See Table 147.)

Canada

The use of cars in Canada, where 54 per cent of households own cars, is similar to that in the United States. In an average week, 70 per cent of the people use cars for making a living. The

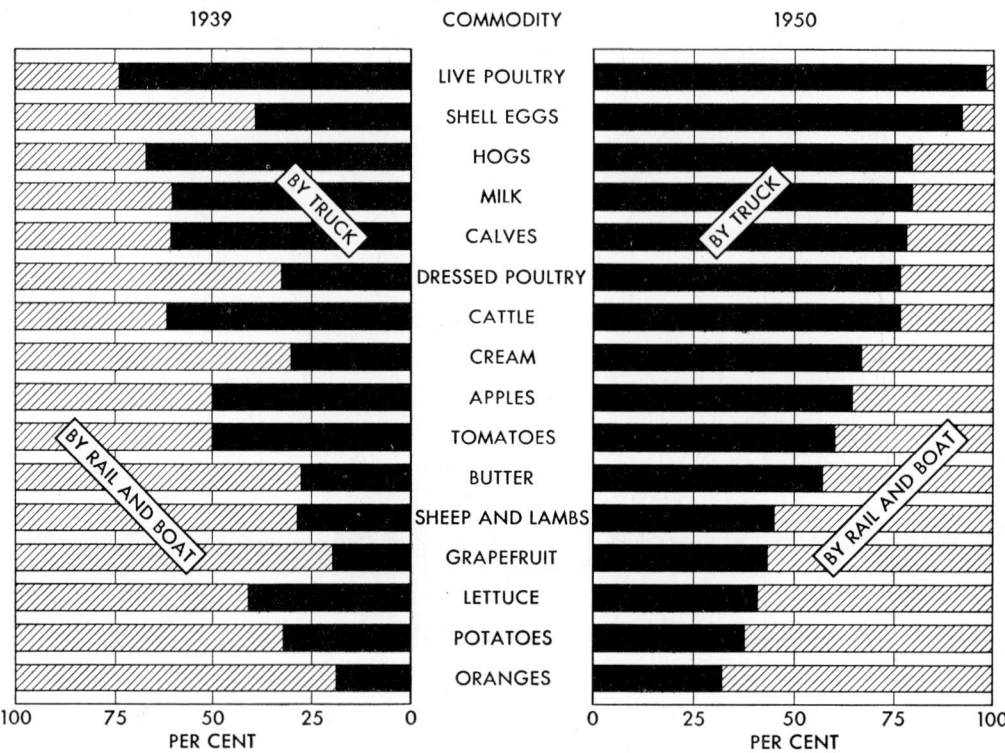

FIGURE 74. MOTOR VEHICLES: PROPORTION OF FARM PRODUCTS DELIVERED BY TRUCK TO LARGEST CITIES IN
THE UNITED STATES, 1939 AND 1950

annual mileage traveled is grouped as follows
(in per cent): [26]

Miles	Per Cent
3,000 or less	26.9
3,000–5,000	14.3
5,000–7,000	14.5
7,000–11,000	19.4
11,000–15,000	12.0
15,000 and over	12.9

The United Kingdom

The British Road Federation estimates that
1.8 million persons were employed in road transport in the United Kingdom in 1951. Of these,
1.1 million were drivers of trucks, buses and
taxis, and chauffeurs. Garage work and motor
sales accounted for 226,000; manufacture of vehicles and tires and the oil industry directly concerned with road transport, for 357,000; road
construction and maintenance, for 90,000.[27]

The Transport Act of 1947 authorized the
government to acquire all road-haulage enterprises engaged predominantly in ordinary long-

TABLE 147

MOTOR VEHICLES: AVERAGE MILEAGE PER VEHICLE
IN THE UNITED STATES, 1936–52

(*Miles*)

Year	Total	Passenger Cars	Trucks
1936	8,879	8,622	10,098
1938	9,134	8,871	10,383
1940	9,346	9,079	10,624
1942	8,123	7,803	9,602
1944	6,969	6,497	8,984
1946	9,958	9,942	9,615
1948	9,707	9,566	10,008
1950	9,373	9,041	10,700
1951	9,398	9,180	10,170
1952	9,844	9,577	10,878

Source: **37**, 1953, p. 65.

distance carriage for hire.[28] Permits to old and
new haulage firms were to be issued by the
Transport Commission. The purpose of the act
was to nationalize haulage and integrate it with

Courtesy of Automobile Manufacturers Association (**38**)

---

26. **37**, 1953, pp. 68–69.
27. **44**, 1951, p. 4.

28. Excludes carriage of meat, livestock, liquids in
bulk, felled timber in special vehicles and so on.

the railroads. There were a few very large concerns and about 20,000 small ones with one or two trucks each. By January 1951 about 2,900 haulage firms, including several major trucking concerns and many small firms, had been merged into a national network of some 40,000 vehicles and 75,000 employees.[29] By April 1951 the Transport Commission had also taken over nearly 24,000 buses, which accounted for practically all regular service in the country.[30]

HIGHWAYS

Without improved roads, motor transportation could never have grown to the present volume, since a poor road may defeat the best vehicle.

PROGRESS IN HIGHWAY ENGINEERING

From Coach Roads to Modern Highways

Roads were neglected during the unchallenged reign of the railways and reduced to the status of feeders. They lost national importance in all countries, became distinctly local and were little used for commercial and long-distance hauling, since only a limited number of commodities could support the high costs of horse-driven transport.[31] The jurisdictions responsible for roads had little money for permanent improvements, even for surfacing roads with gravel or stone. In the United States, highway construction was in eclipse for five or six decades after the appearance of the railroads, and most "highways" were unmanageable dirt roads until the end of the nineteenth century.[32] The federal government did not assist states and counties in building or maintaining roads.[33] A similar situation existed in Canada where the central government lost interest in roads, while favoring the railways.[34]

In the last decade of the nineteenth century it became clear that railroads were not the whole answer to the problem of overland transportation. Although the United States had some 2 million miles of rural dirt roads, the farmers, mud-bound in bad weather, began to agitate for all-year roads to haul their produce to the railroads. They clamored for roads extending two to five miles from the stations.[35] When the bicycle craze seized the country, city people also joined in the demand.[36] The League of American Wheelmen was organized to press for better roads. It may seem surprising that the railroads, now engaged in sharp competition with highway traffic, were in the forefront of the "good-roads" movement. They wanted mud-free feeder roads and ran "Good Roads" trains.[37] The introduction of free rural mail delivery strengthened the demand for road improvement. In England the cyclists were the first to call for better roads.[38]

This clamor for all-weather roads swelled tremendously with the advent of the motor vehicle. A hard surface that could take more punishment seemed to be the most vital need at that time. In the mid-1930's, at least all main roads in the United States and western Europe were hard surfaced. The length of rural surfaced roads in the United States increased from 153,530 miles in 1904 to 1.1 million miles in 1935 and 1.5 million in 1945.[39]

Along with hard surfacing, the United States and various European countries made many other improvements. These included widening of pavements, elimination of dangerous curves and hazardous crossings, the addition of traffic signs, and demarcation of highways. Though billions of dollars have been spent on road improvements, much still remains to be done. Many areas lack even such roads as would be held entirely unfit in countries with developed motor traffic. Others, such as Mexico and Guatemala, hold to the time-honored concept that a road should be available to anyone, whether on foot, on horseback or in a vehicle, be the vehicle horse-drawn, ox-drawn or an automobile. This catholicity impedes even the few paved highways these countries have built. In still others, such as Great Britain, Denmark and the Netherlands, cyclists commonly share the highways with motorists, with hazard to both. Many Canadian roads are rough and hard on both vehicle and driver.

Even in the United States and Great Britain, many highways are inadequate to handle the

---

29. **55,** pp. 95–98.
30. **30,** 1951 Series, No. 4, pp. 16–17.
31. **69,** p. 2; **57,** p. 666. For earlier conditions of roads, see Chapter 8, pp. 332–37.
32. **52,** p. 192.
33. **52,** p. 548.
34. **45,** August 1951, p. 30.

35. **21,** p. 4.
36. In the last decades of the nineteenth century millions of Americans used bicycles day and night. "By 1896 the lamps of some 4,000,000 bicycles flitted about on the highways at night like lightning bugs." (**53,** p. 86.)
37. **53,** pp. 227, 247.
38. **50,** Autumn 1950, p. 20.
39. **14,** p. 220.

volume, weight and speed of today's traffic. For a time it seemed a sound principle to adjust the quaint, winding roads of a more leisurely age to motor traffic; nobody did, and nobody could, anticipate the immense use of the motor vehicle. But motor traffic has grown beyond the wildest expectations and speed has almost doubled. The average speed on main rural highways in the United States in 1921–30 was 26 miles per hour, and 90 per cent of the drivers did not exceed 40 miles; in 1952–53, the average speed was 50 miles per hour; 90 per cent of the drivers did not exceed 62 miles.[40]

The change in the composition of the traffic imposes additional stresses on the highways as trucking increases more rapidly than passenger traffic. Moreover, the increase in traffic is greatest among the heaviest vehicles, the so-called truck-combinations. In the United States, for example, the ton-mileage of all trucks about tripled between 1936 and 1948, while that of truck-combinations alone more than quadrupled.[41]

More lanes are required when a large number of trucks use the highway than when all vehicles are passenger cars. In general, trucks have a greater effect on highway capacity than their physical dimensions would indicate. In flat country, it has been estimated, one truck is the traffic equivalent of two passenger cars on a multilane highway and of two and a half passenger cars on a two-lane road. In hilly stretches, one truck is equivalent to four passenger cars; in a mountainous terrain, the effect of one commercial vehicle on traffic may be as great as eight passenger cars.[42]

Ordinarily the volume of traffic grows in proximity to urban centers, mounting rapidly to loads far surpassing those on rural stretches. (See Figure 75.) The greatest congestion is at the approaches to large cities, where the efficiency of modern highways is compromised when long-distance traffic — speeding on intercity stretches — merges with local traffic. About 90 per cent of the traffic (passenger cars, buses and trucks) on main highways of the United States has its origin or destination, or both, in cities.[43]

To accommodate the new types, volume and speed of traffic, the expressway has been developed: a multilane arterial highway, with fully or partially controlled access to and from the surrounding territory, heavier pavement, a wider right of way, elimination of crossings through underpasses and overpasses, and sometimes segregation or restriction of types of vehicles.

Expressways

The main purpose of expressways is to assure safe and uninterrupted flow of traffic between points of greatest congestion by insulating it from the adjacent territory and segregating vehicles of widely different types. Though the expressway grants full franchise to motorists, it is not intended to be a race track.

The idea of separating fast, long-distance motoring from mixed and local traffic was tried out first in Italy and Germany — in Italy, mostly for national prestige and the attraction of tourists and in Germany, for military purposes. Italy's *autostrada,* opened in 1925, was the world's first expressway. Gradually such expressways linked Italy's chief cities and ports, from the north to Naples. Being the first of their kind, the *autostrade* have some features considered undesirable by today's standards of highway engineering, but credit for initiating the separation of fast, long-distance traffic and local traffic belongs to Italy.

Germany built a system of expressways, the *Autobahnen,* before World War II. Thoroughgoing standardization of alignment, junctions and road signs and visibility on curves and hills are considered their best features for combining speed with safety.

The United States has many superb highways, such as the Merritt, Wilbur Cross, Henry Hudson and Hutchinson River parkways in New York and Connecticut, the Outer Drive in Chicago, the Blue Ridge Parkway in North Carolina and Virginia, the Norris Freeway in Tennessee, the Natchez Trace Parkway in Alabama, Mississippi and Virginia, as well as many freeways in the West, expressways in California and many turnpikes in the East.[44]

France, which had the best roads in the world under Napoleon I and has since improved them considerably, recently built its first motorway, the *autoroute,* from Paris westward to Normandy and Brittany.[45] Many other countries are planning to redesign their highways according to the new concepts.

Expressways permit smoother and speedier

40. **33**, January 1953, p. 7.
41. **11**, p. 16.
42. **8**, p. 100; **12**, p. 40.
43. **9**, pp. 40–41; **22**, p. 3.

44. See p. 408.
45. **62**, pp. 54–55.

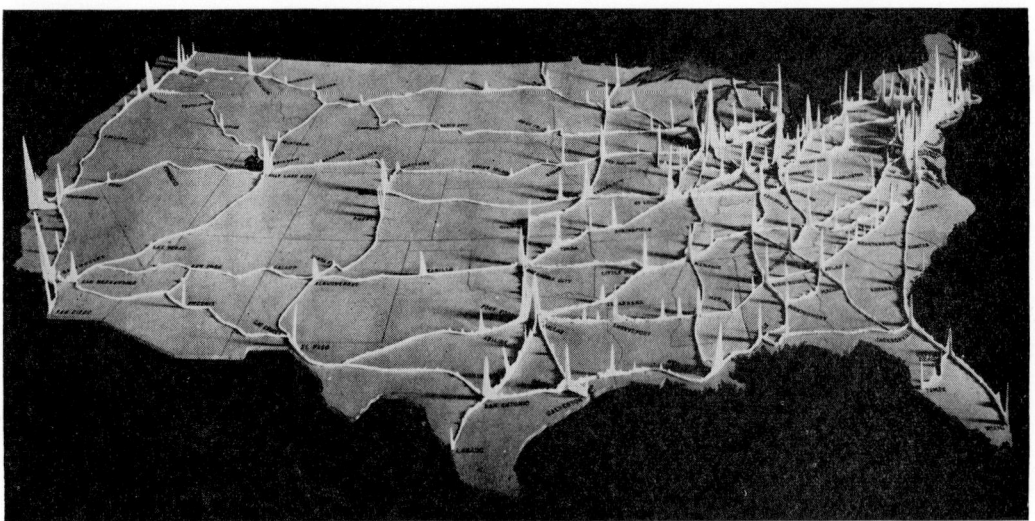

National Interregional Highway Committee

FIGURE 75. HIGHWAYS: PEAK TRAFFIC LOADS IN AND NEAR CITIES IN THE UNITED STATES

traffic on most heavily congested stretches and reduce the rate of accidents,[46] but they are expensive to build and for a long time will represent only a comparatively small mileage in any country. The expressways so far built and planned in the United States represent less than one per cent of the total highway mileage. Such roads, indeed, are not even needed for local purposes in rural areas. While some highways carry as many as 100,000 vehicles daily, the count on others is in dozens or scores per day. On the average, more than 80 per cent of road mileage in the United States is traveled by only twenty-two vehicles per day.[47] The need for expressways in other countries is much less pronounced. For the world as a whole, the greatest contribution of these marvels of modern highway engineering is not so much to relieve present congestion on highways — a problem in only a few countries on the heavily traveled segments of their arterial systems — as to exert influence on today's road construction so that difficulties may be avoided when traffic grows in the future.

EXTENT

Extension and improvement of roads has been stimulated by the increasing use of motor vehi-

cles, while better roads, in turn, encourage the growth of motor traffic. The world's network of highways has spread more rapidly than that of railroads.

Length

The length of the world's combined highways is estimated at more than ten million miles,[48] or more than ten times that of the world's railroads. Less than a third of the total is hard surfaced, however, and less than a fifth is "improved" — that is, graded and properly drained though without surfacing other than the natural soil. The remainder represents dirt roads passable only in good weather.

The United States has the largest highway system in the world, some 3 million miles, including about half the world's surfaced roads. The USSR had (1938) the next longest road mileage. Japan, Canada and Australia are next in line, followed, at some distance, by France and Argentina.

The ranking differs, however, when surfacing of roads is considered. The United Kingdom and Belgium are unique in that almost their entire highway mileage is hard surfaced. About three fourths of the mileage in France, about half in the United States and more than half in New Zealand are hard surfaced.[49] Unimproved

---

46. Except the Pennsylvania Turnpike in the United States, which shows about the same accident rate as the country's rural highways (10.0 and 10.3 fatalities per 100 million vehicle-miles, respectively). **48**, p. 44.

47. **39**, p. 21; **53**, pp. 207–08.

48. **53**, p. 337.

49. In the United States, 2 out of every 3 farms are on all-weather roads, and 20 per cent more are within two miles of such roads. (**20**, p. 11.)

dirt roads, on the other hand, comprise nearly seven tenths of the road mileage in the USSR and more than half in Canada, Australia and the Union of South Africa. Argentina, third in the Western Hemisphere in highway mileage, has about eight miles out of ten in dirt roads.[50] (See Table 148.)

Density

Factors controlling the density of highways in different areas and nations are similar to those which determine the density of railways: the level of economic development; density of population; size of the area; and availability of other means of transportation.

Highway mileage per 100 square miles of territory is greatest in such industrially developed and densely populated countries as Luxembourg (270 miles), Belgium (244), Denmark (211), Great Britain (195), the Netherlands (192), France (185) and Switzerland (180).[51] The United States has nearly 100 miles of highways per 100 square miles. Italy, Western Germany and Czechoslovakia have 83–88 miles; Norway and Finland, with comparatively large areas and sparse population, 22–28 miles. Density of highways ranges from one to 10 miles per 100 square miles in most Latin American countries, China, Thailand, Indonesia, Indochina, the greater part of Africa, the Near East and the USSR — in short, in the greater part of the world. (See Figure 76,A.)

Data on highway density in relation to population present a sharply contrasting picture. The mileage per 10,000 inhabitants is greatest in prosperous countries with a comparatively sparse population — Australia (695 miles), Canada (438), New Zealand (428), and the United States (208). Densely populated Western Germany is in the group with from 10–20 miles per 10,000 inhabitants along with Turkey, Mexico, El Salvador, Panama and Portugal. Belgium has less mileage in relation to population than the Belgian Congo or Madagascar; Italy is behind Ceylon and Venezuela, and the Netherlands, behind Paraguay and French Morocco. China, with 2.7 miles of highways per 10,000 inhabitants, and

50. International data are available only for 1948. The Economic Commission for Europe has drawn up a classification of highways based primarily on width and type of surface, but up to 1953 had received only two returns compiled on this principle. **6**, 1952, p. 44.

51. Ireland appears in this group in Table 149 partly because of a great mileage in dirt roads.

TABLE 148

HIGHWAYS: LENGTH, BY TYPE, IN SELECTED COUNTRIES, 1948

(*Thousands of Miles*)

Country	Total	Hard Surfaced	Im- proved [a]	Unim- proved [b]
United States	3,009.0	1,503.8 [e]	667.2	838.0
Canada	552.0	131.5	122.2	298.3
Mexico	43.6	10.8	1.8	31.0
Guatemala	3.5	—	1.9	1.6
El Salvador	3.9	0.2	1.1	2.6
Honduras	0.8	—	0.4	0.4
Nicaragua	0.6	0.1	0.3	0.2
Costa Rica	1.0	0.5	0.4	0.1
Panama	1.4	0.4	0.6	0.4
Cuba	3.1	1.9	0.4	0.8
Haiti	1.8	...	1.1	0.7
Dominican Republic	2.0	1.5	0.2	0.3
Venezuela	11.5	1.1	2.9	7.5
Colombia	11.2 [d]	8.6	—	2.6
Ecuador	4.4	0.6	1.1	2.7 [e]
Brazil	161.3	4.5	32.8	124.0
Peru	20.4	7.3	11.2	1.9
Bolivia	8.9	0.6	—	8.3
Paraguay	3.7	0.1	0.4	3.2
Chile	29.9	17.5	—	12.4
Uruguay	25.1	2.7	—	22.4
Argentina	259.0	39.8	7.6	211.6
Great Britain	183.4	183.4	f	f
Ireland	49.6	12.6	3.1	33.9
France	394.4 [g]	300.0	94.4	...
Luxembourg	2.7	1.3	0.8	0.6
Belgium	28.8	28.8	—	—
Netherlands	25.9	18.7	—	7.2
Denmark	35.0 [h]	5.1	29.9	.
Sweden	106.0	3.3	52.7	50.0
Norway	27.6 [h]	1.0	26.6	...
Finland	36.8 [h]	0.1	36.7	...
Western Germany	79.3	16.4	30.6	32.2
Czechoslovakia	44.2	...	...	...
Switzerland	28.8 [h]	3.8	25.0	...
Austria	21.6	2.3	1.8	17.5
Portugal	16.0	12.4	3.6	i
Spain	80.1	73.1	7.0	i
Italy	109.4	...	...	...
Yugoslavia	20.2	...	...	...
Greece	9.6	2.3	1.3	6.0
USSR [j]	841.3	54.3	205.5	581.5
China	126.3	...	...	...
South Korea	8.8	...	...	...
Japan	577.1	...	...	...
Turkey [k]	44.9	1.6	13.5	29.8

TABLE 148—*continued*

Country	Total	Hard Surfaced	Im-proved [a]	Unim-proved [b]
Cyprus	2.6	0.7	1.9	. . .
Lebanon	1.5	—	1.3	0.2
Israel	1.2	. . .	. . .	. . .
Syria	4.0	1.9	2.1	l
Iraq	6.8	1.8	5.0	l
Iran	16.3	1.2	8.5	6.6
Pakistan	90.0	12.6	77.4	l
India	239.1	85.8	153.3	l
Burma [j]	25.5	. . .	. . .	. . .
Thailand	4.2	0.3	3.3	0.6
Indochina	23.0	12.0	5.0	6.0
Ceylon	17.5 [l]	5.5	0.8	11.2
Malaya	6.2	4.1	1.4	0.7
Indonesia [j]	42.6	7.2	25.4	10.0
Philippines	15.1	12.7	2.4	l
French Morocco	24.5	5.7	18.8	l
Algeria	32.8	4.3	11.9	16.6
Tunisia	5.4	. . .	. . .	. . .
Egypt	10.8	1.4	7.6	1.8
Ethiopia	69.2	4.3	. . .	64.9
French Equatorial Africa	13.6	0.8	8.2	4.6
Belgian Congo	61.6	3.3	12.7	45.6
Gold Coast	7.9	2.6	2.8	2.5
Nigeria	25.2	0.8	5.8	18.6
Kenya	17.0	2.1	0.1	14.8
Uganda	8.5 [h]	2.5	6.0	. . .
Tanganyika	24.4	3.0	13.3	8.1
Nyasaland	4.0	—	1.9	2.1
Madagascar	15.7	0.1	1.9	13.7
Angola	21.8	5.4	16.4	l
Northern Rhodesia	10.1	0.4	8.3	1.4
Southern Rhodesia	15.6	2.5	8.1	5.0
Union of South Africa	171.7	40.1	24.5	107.1
Australia	528.2	100.8	108.4	319.0
New Zealand	77.1	45.4	8.7	23.0

Sources: **51**, pp. 1A–1B; **1**, 1949, p. 69; **2**, 1948, p. 173; **6**, 1950, pp. 64–66; for the USSR, **40**, pp. 495–96; for Turkey, **50**, Winter 1951, p. 61; for Pakistan, **5**, July-September 1951, p. 26.

a. Roads graded and with proper drainage, but with no other surfacing than the natural soil.
b. Roads on which no work has been done for grading or drainage.
c. Includes roads paved and with bituminous, gravel, stone and stabilized soil. According to **37**, 1953, p. 52, the United States had 1,666,000 miles of surfaced roads in 1951.
d. Excludes 30,500 mule and other tracks.
e. Includes 900 miles of mule tracks.
f. Negligible mileage.

Thailand, with 2.3 miles, have the lowest density among the eighty countries enumerated in Table 149. (See also Figure 76,B.)

RECENT DEVELOPMENTS AND PLANS

The world's network of highways is less stable than that of railroads, but is steadily expanding and improving in quality. While work on highways is highly advanced in some countries and only in the initial stages in others, highway construction has an important place almost everywhere in plans for the immediate or more remote future.

The United States

The Federal-Aid Highway Act of 1944 designated two new highway systems. The first, the National System of Interstate Highways, was limited by law to 40,000 miles of the most important highways, selected by the federal government and the states. It connects all the country's major cities and production centers, reaches 42 state capitals, serves 182 of the 199 cities with a population of more than 50,000, and includes the roads of greatest strategic significance.[52] This arterial system represents the backbone of the entire highway network and, though accounting for only a little more than one per cent of the total highway mileage (37,800 miles, as now designated), is expected to carry 20 per cent of the nation's traffic. (See Figure 77.)

The other new system consists of primary and secondary roads: farm-to-market roads, rural free-delivery mail routes, public school bus routes and other important highway traffic. As of June 1952, the Federal-Aid primary highway system comprised some 235,000 miles of rural roads and city streets, and the secondary highway system, some 438,000 miles.[53] It is estimated that the Federal-Aid system as a whole carries 83 per cent of the nation's traffic, while the remainder moves over 2.5 million miles of other roads.[54]

52. **21**, p. 14.
53. **19**, 1951, p. 105. For financial aspects of the program, see below, pp. 416–17.
54. **33**, January 1953, p. 29.

g. Excludes 187,000 miles of access roads not suitable for motor traffic.
h. Excludes unimproved roads.
i. Included in improved road mileage.
j. 1938.
k. 1951.
l. Excludes 8,200 miles of bridle paths.

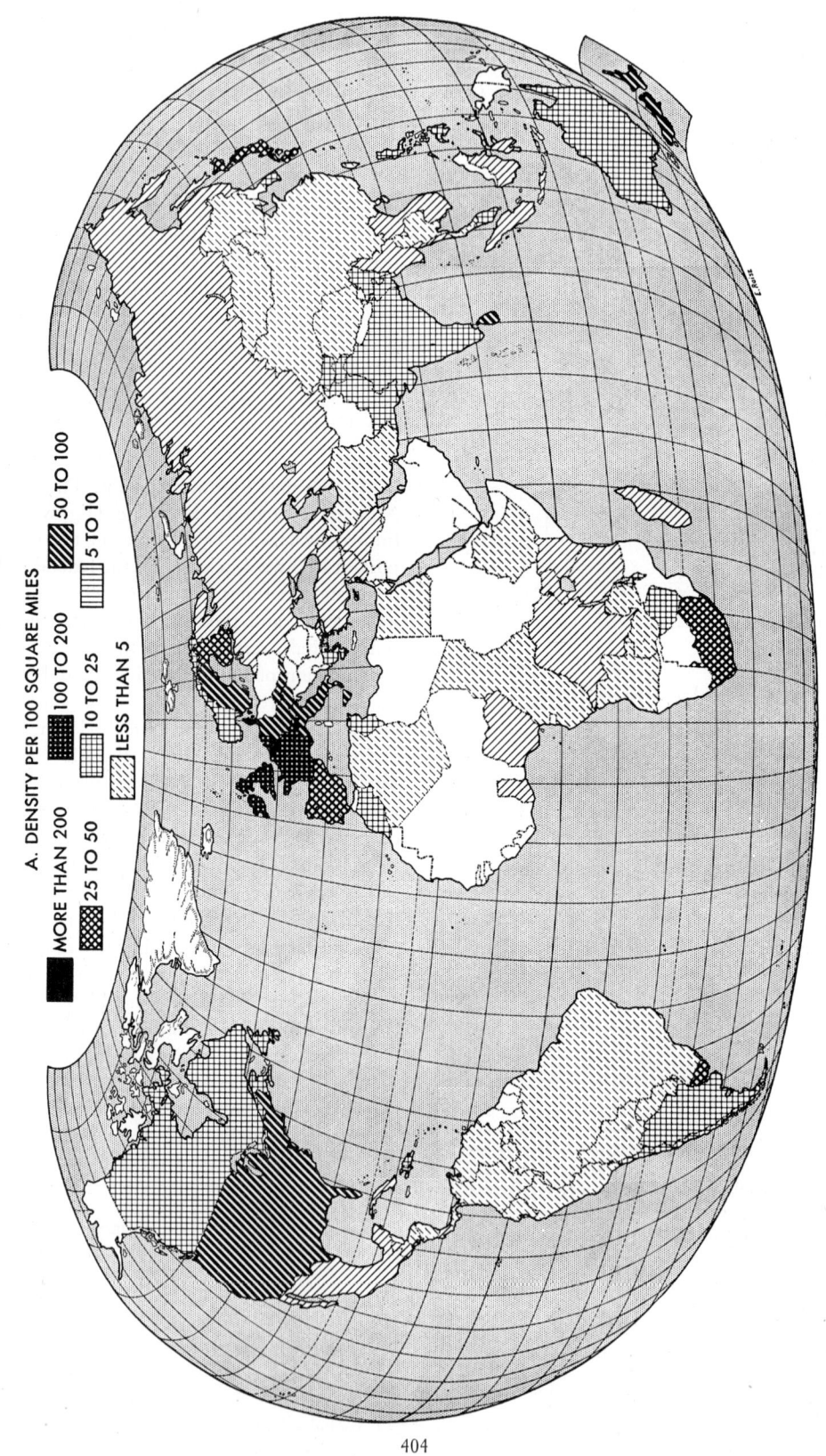

A. DENSITY PER 100 SQUARE MILES

MORE THAN 200

100 TO 200

50 TO 100

25 TO 50

10 TO 25

5 TO 10

LESS THAN 5

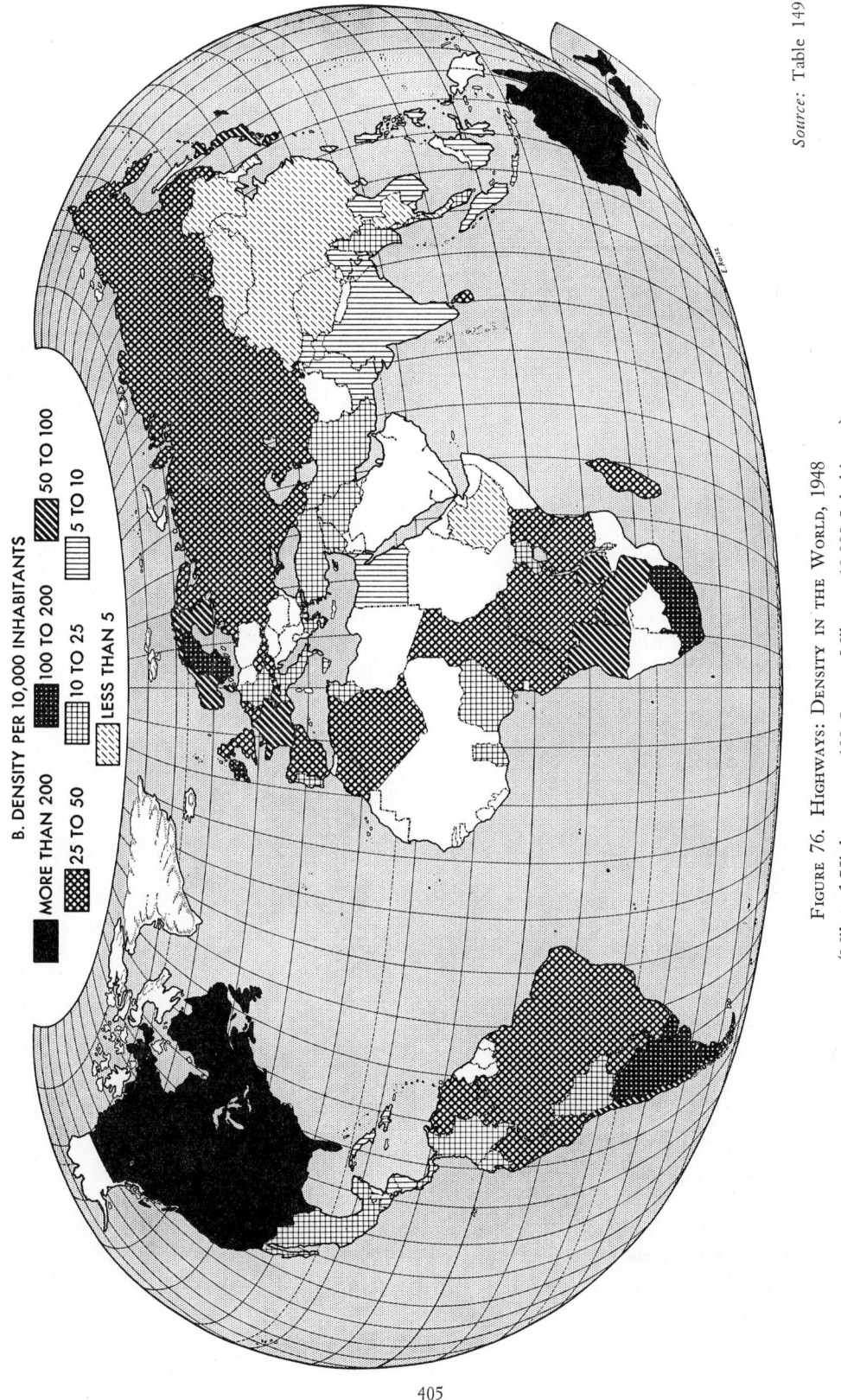

MORE THAN 200

100 TO 200

50 TO 100

25 TO 50

10 TO 25

5 TO 10

LESS THAN 5

FIGURE 76. HIGHWAYS: DENSITY IN THE WORLD, 1948

(Miles of Highway per 100 Square Miles or 10,000 Inhabitants)

Source: Table 149

TABLE 149

HIGHWAYS: DENSITY PER 100 SQUARE MILES AND PER 10,000 INHABITANTS, IN SELECTED COUNTRIES, 1948

(*Miles*)

Country [a]	Per 100 Square Miles	Per 10,000 Inhabitants	Country [a]	Per 100 Square Miles	Per 10,000 Inhabitants
Australia	17.8	695.0	Italy	83.5	24.0
Canada	15.3	438.1	Nyasaland	11.0	23.5
New Zealand	73.6	428.3	Bolivia	1.8	23.4
United States	99.6	207.8	Gold Coast	8.6	21.9
Ireland	186.5	165.3	Uganda	9.0	21.3
Argentina	24.0	160.9	Tunisia	12.0	20.8
Sweden	61.2	155.9	Portugal	46.4	19.3
Union of South Africa	36.3	151.9	Panama	4.9	19.2
Uruguay	34.8	109.1	El Salvador	29.8	19.1
France	185.2	96.7	Mexico	5.7	18.8
Southern Rhodesia	10.4	91.8	Western Germany	83.7	17.0
Luxembourg	270.0	90.0	Turkey	9.6	15.0
Finland	28.3	89.8	Iraq	5.9	14.2
Norway	22.2	89.0	Burma	9.7	14.1
Denmark	210.8	85.4	Ecuador	1.6	13.3
Japan	40.6	72.0	Greece	18.7	13.2
Switzerland	180.0	64.0	Costa Rica	5.1	12.8
Northern Rhodesia	3.5	63.1	Lebanon	37.5	12.5
Angola	4.5	54.5	Syria	5.6	11.4
Chile	10.3	54.4	Malaya	12.0	11.1
Cyprus	72.2	52.0	Nigeria	6.8	11.0
Kenya	7.6	45.9	Iran	2.6	10.9
Algeria	3.9	45.6	Colombia	2.5	10.7
Tanganyika	6.8	45.2	Israel	3.7	9.9
USSR	9.8	43.6	Guatemala	8.3	9.6
Belgian Congo	6.7	43.1	Dominican Republic	10.4	9.3
Great Britain	194.9	37.6	Indochina	8.0	8.6
Madagascar	6.8	36.5	Pakistan	15.8	8.1
Czechoslovakia	88.4	36.2	Philippines	13.1	7.7
Belgium	244.1	34.3	India	20.5	7.5
Brazil	4.9	33.6	Honduras	1.4	6.5
French Equatorial Africa	1.4	33.2	Cuba	7.0	6.1
Austria	66.9	31.3	Indonesia	5.8	5.8
French Morocco	15.1	30.6	Egypt	2.8	5.7
Paraguay	2.4	30.2	Nicaragua	1.1	5.3
Spain	40.7	29.1	Haiti	16.7	5.1
Peru	4.2	27.2	South Korea	24.4	4.4
Netherlands	191.9	27.0	Ethiopia	1.2	3.9
Venezuela	3.2	26.7	China	3.4	2.7
Ceylon	70.0	26.1	Thailand	2.1	2.3

Sources: **51**, pp. 8A–8B; Table 148.

   a. Countries arrayed by density in relation to population.

U.S. Department of Commerce: Bureau of Public Roads

Figure 77. Highways: National System of Interstate Highways in the United States

The National System of Interstate Highways is believed to be in vital need of reconstruction: of the total (37,800 miles), 26,000 miles must be completely reconstructed; 9,000 miles must be widened and resurfaced; only 2,800 miles are in satisfactory condition.[55] So far, federal aid has been used chiefly for various improvements, such as hard surfacing and widening of certain stretches, building and repairing bridges, and eliminating or relocating crossings.

One of the greatest impediments to establishing modern controlled-access highways is the acquisition of rights-of-way, which may entail staggering costs and time-consuming legal complications. When the highways were first laid out, provision was rarely made for future widening. With the growth of traffic and roadside ribbon development, real estate values have skyrocketed. Owners of adjacent land are often unwilling to sell their property, or they ask excessive prices. This difficulty besets road builders in practically all countries. Sometimes the cheapest and simplest solution is to lay out an entirely new highway across unused land, though it may parallel the existing highway.

Legal obstacles are also great.[56] Under common law, the owner has the right of access to a highway at any point at which his land adjoins it, i.e., the right of ingress to and egress from property adjacent to the highway, the right of visibility (for example, the right to display goods on property viewed from the highway) and the right to flow of light and air from the highway to the property. The needs of our mid-century's volume and speed of highway traffic have begun to make some dents in these sacred rights. The concept of controlled-access-highways is reflected in the legislation of many states of the United States. The first laws to this effect were enacted in 1937 in the states of New York and Rhode Island, and in May 1953 thirty-five states had legal authority to control, in one way or another, access to main highways.

The slow development of expressways, which depend on appropriation of public funds, has brought back the toll roads — common in the horse and buggy period — as the most direct, speedy and effective way to relieve congestion on trunkline highways.[57] Built to highest engineer-

ing standards, the "new look" turnpikes provide no technical features differing from modern freeways, but their toll-supported financing makes construction possible where other funds are unobtainable. The success of the Pennsylvania Turnpike, opened in 1940, encouraged toll-road projects in other states. On October 1, 1953, tolls were in effect on 762 miles of expressways, the three longest being the Pennsylvania Turnpike (327 miles), the New Jersey Turnpike (118 miles) and the Turner Turnpike (88 miles).[58] Under construction and scheduled for completion either in 1954 or 1955 are an additional 1,078 miles: the New York State Thruway (427 miles); the Ohio Turnpike (241 miles); the Garden State Parkway in New Jersey (165 miles); the West Virginia Turnpike (88 miles) and a number of shorter stretches. Fourteen states have authorized the building of toll roads totaling nearly 2,000 miles, but financing arrangements have not yet been completed.[59] Furthermore, toll roads recommended or authorized for consideration as to feasibility cover a projected 666 miles.

With few exceptions, all these roads are concentrated in the East. (See Figure 78.) Expressways in other states have also been built, but they are not toll roads. California, in particular, has many high-type facilities. Its mileage of divided highways exceeds by almost 25 per cent all toll-road mileage so far in operation in the United States, and a substantial percentage of it is in freeways.[60]

The United Kingdom

The Ribbon Development Act of 1935 represents an attempt to prevent disorderly ribbon development of a region, by controlling access to highway facilities. The act makes it unlawful to construct or lay out any means of access to or from main roads and to erect buildings on any land within 220 feet of the center of the road

---

55. **33,** January 1953, p. 28.

56. See **22** for a detailed discussion of the many-sided legal aspects of this problem.

57. For early turnpikes, see Chapter 8, pp. 333–37.

58. The 122-mile-long Florida Overseas Highway is not classed as a toll road, since tolls are collected only on bridges.

59. Among them are the Chicago–Twin Cities Turnpike in Wisconsin (287 miles); Dallas–Fort Worth–San Antonio (276 miles); the Indiana Turnpike (150 miles); and turnpikes, each 125 miles long, in Connecticut, North Carolina and Pennsylvania. Cf. **48**, pp. 10–12; **64**, pp. 4 and 190–92.

60. **48**, p. 63. Only a part of the freeway mileage, however, has complete separation of grades at interchanges, which is practically necessary on toll expressways.

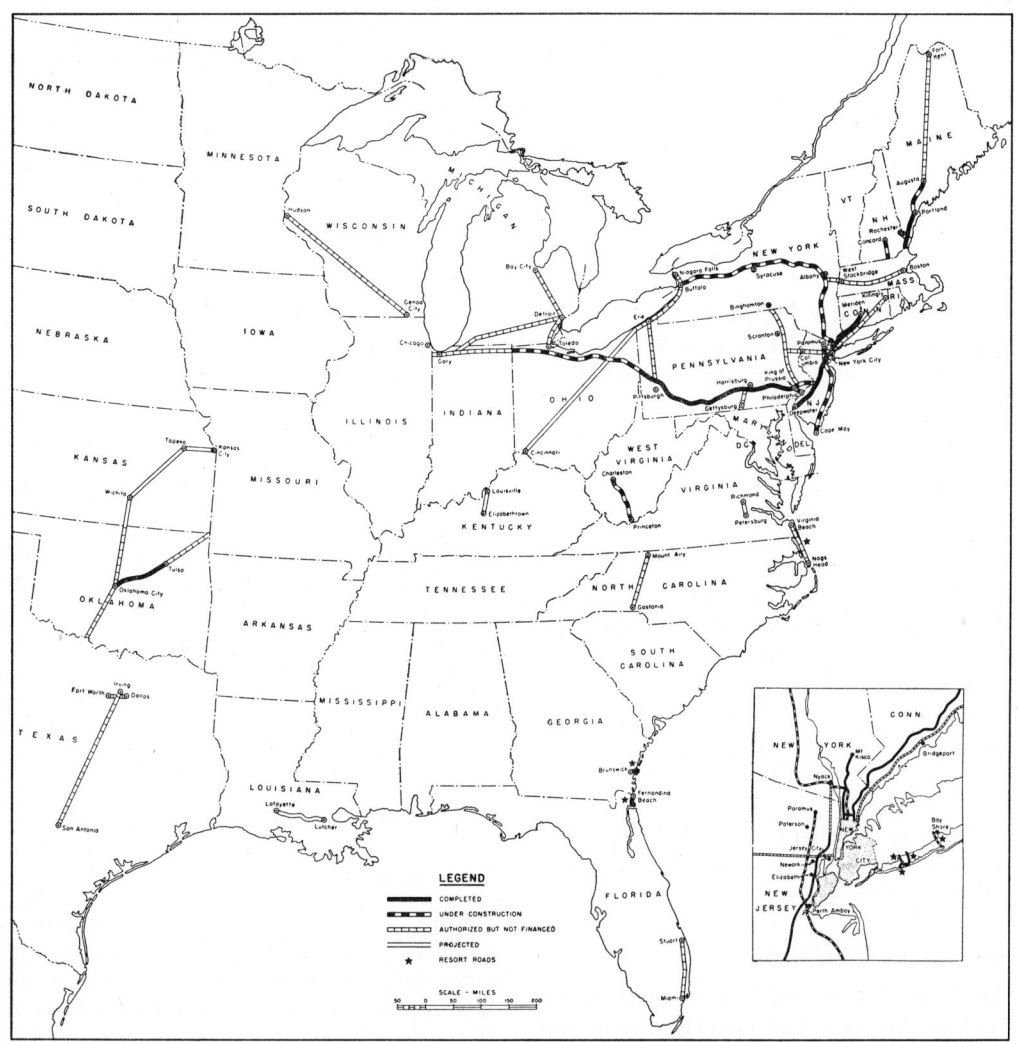

FIGURE 78. HIGHWAYS: TOLL ROADS IN THE UNITED STATES, EXISTING AND PROPOSED, 1953

In the western part of the United States (not shown on the map) there is only one toll road: from Denver to Boulder, Colorado. Another road from Tacoma to Everett, Washington, has been authorized but not financed.

without the consent of the highway authority. A right to compensation accrues only to owners whose interests or properties have been "injuriously affected" by the restrictions imposed. Developments which would clash with the natural beauty of the countryside, particularly in places of great scenic beauty and historic interest, have been consistently forbidden. How effective this act has been is uncertain because of the interplay of various other factors. Also, its principles may or may not be transferable to other countries with different legal, political and economic structures. Nevertheless, it is considered an important step forward in highway planning and thinking, as a device for the automatic protection of highways from disorderly real estate development along them. Some such devices are clearly necessary, and the British experiment may have a fruitful influence on highway planners and builders by directing their attention to the evils of ribbon development.[61]

In 1946 the British government announced a ten-year plan for highway modernization. The first five years were expected to effect repairs

<hr />

61. **21**, pp. 90–96 and 148–52.

of highways neglected during the war, rebuilding of destroyed bridges, resumption of projects interrupted by hostilities and various improvements at particular danger spots. The following five years were to be devoted to the construction of expressways, some of which were to be built from scratch, and of an orbital route around London. (See Figure 79.) The projected system of motorways greatly resembles the pattern of Roman roads laid out almost 2,000 years ago. (Cf. Figure 56,C, p. 331.) The second part of the program has not yet been implemented because of the economic difficulties besetting the United Kingdom.[62]

Italy and Belgium

A three-lane *autostrada* from Rome to Salerno and a two-lane highway around Rome are under construction. Road building is extensive throughout Italy, particularly in the south. It is being debated whether tolls would yield enough to defray the expenditures within a reasonable number of years. A counterproposal is to turn over to concession companies the revenues from gasoline and oil used on the expressway, on the basis of average consumption per mile and the present rate of taxation.[63]

Belgium is planning to build 600 miles of expressways, to be financed in one way or another by the immediate users.[64]

The Scandinavian Countries

Denmark plans to build three motorways patterned on American and German designs with fly-over crossings and twin carriageways. These highways will link all the main population centers with one another and with the ferries and bridges.

Sweden has built elevated highways, and fly-over crossings are in use on many roads. Many highways have lanes for cyclists.

Canada

A transcontinental highway, the dream of far-sighted Canadians since 1867, became a national project in December 1949 when the Parliament passed the Trans-Canada Highway Act.

The provinces must match each federal dollar of the $300 million appropriation; Quebec and Nova Scotia are the only provinces which have not yet signed an agreement to this effect.

Today traffic moves across Canada on roads of widely varying standards; the greatest part is gravel-surfaced, while some sections are paved. The present lack of a modern transcontinental highway is explained partly by the comparatively slow development of motor traffic in Canada before World War II and partly by the fact that motorists could dip below the United States border to travel over first-class highways and then re-enter Canada.[65]

The Trans-Canada Highway will be 22–24 feet wide, with ten-foot shoulders except where there are special difficulties. In heavily traveled stretches, it will have four lanes. It is agreed that the route will not be a superhighway, but it is believed that it will be a first-class road.[66] The most direct route from coast to coast will cover 4,975 miles. The plan is to traverse the southern, most populated provinces of Canada from east to west and to provide a link in British Columbia with the Alaska Highway, a 1,680-mile road hewn out of sheer wilderness during World War II by the United States government.[67] (See Figure 80.)

Latin America

Latin America's most important road project, the Pan-American Highway, will connect all Latin American capitals and will make it possible to drive the entire length of the Western Hemisphere, down the Alaska Highway and its Canadian connection, through the United States and all Latin America.

In the early 1800's Henry Clay proposed the building of a hemispheric highway.[68] The first steps were taken in 1923, at the Fifth Pan-American Conference in Santiago, Chile, and have been followed by several Pan-American Highway Congresses.

The international system consists of a chain of routes designated as links between meeting points at common frontiers. Of the total length (15,449 miles), 14,910 miles have been completed. About half (7,839 miles) is all-weather

---

62. **62**, p. 2.

63. **50**, Spring 1952, pp. 60–62. All prewar *autostrade* except the 30-mile motorway between Genoa and Serravalle were toll roads.

64. **50**, Spring 1951, pp. 66–67.

65. **5**, July–September 1952, p. 31.

66. **45**, August 1951, pp. 35–36 and 82.

67. Canada bought the Canadian section of the Alaska Highway at the end of the war.

68. **50**, Spring 1952, p. 12.

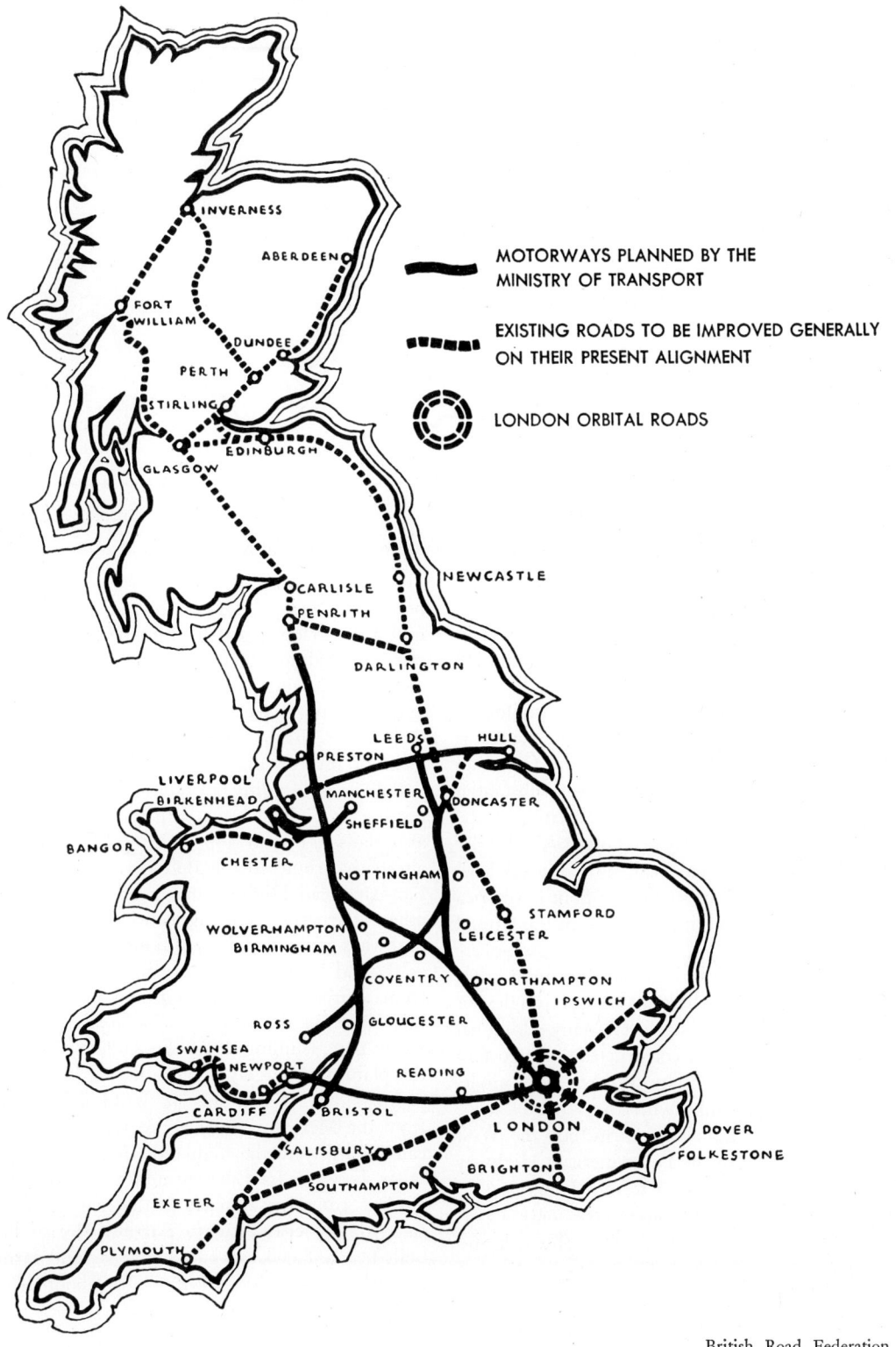

MOTORWAYS PLANNED BY THE
MINISTRY OF TRANSPORT

EXISTING ROADS TO BE IMPROVED GENERALLY
ON THEIR PRESENT ALIGNMENT

LONDON ORBITAL ROADS

British Road Federation

FIGURE 79. HIGHWAYS: MAJOR DEVELOPMENT SCHEMES IN THE UNITED KINGDOM

411

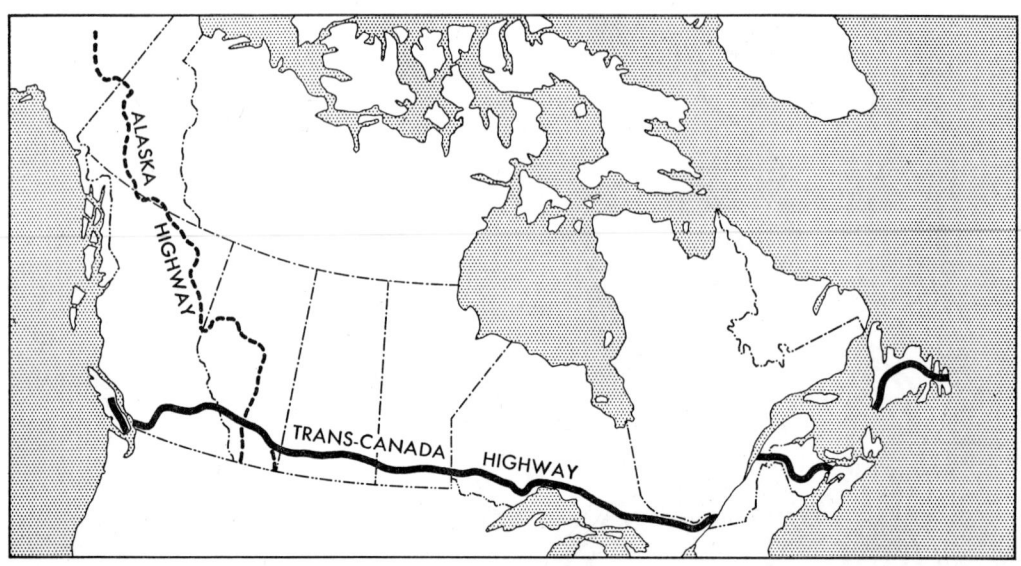

FIGURE 80. HIGHWAYS: PROPOSED TRANSCONTINENTAL ROUTE IN CANADA

road; more than one third (5,603 miles) is paved, and the rest (1,468 miles) is passable only in dry weather. Of the 539 miles not yet built, 410 miles are in Costa Rica and Panama, where the mountains in the first country and dense jungles in the second are the greatest obstacles; the rest is in western Colombia and Guatemala. (See Figure 81.) The United States has given substantial financial and technical aid in constructing the stretch between the Mexico-Guatemala border and Panama City, usually called the Inter-American Highway.[69] Construction in South America has been carried on without aid from the United States.

Building this great highway has been most difficult in places where it crosses jungles or rises 15,000 feet above sea level. Many additional connections have been constructed at important points at common frontiers. Mexico, for example, has built several links with the United States. Plans are under discussion to include the West Indies and Cuba in the Pan-American Highway system through ferries at terminal points.[70]

The Pan-American project solves only a part of Latin America's problem of highway trans-

portation. Most of Latin America needs more highways to open up the hinterland, which is sometimes almost completely isolated from the coastal areas and is occasionally provided both with railways and highways that run parallel to each other. Each country has some highway plans or projects under construction.

Bolivia is building a 350-mile highway connecting its high plateaus with the lowlands and also plans to extend some existing highways; an alternative route to the Bolivian section of the Pan-American Highway has been built and another alternative is being considered. Bolivian highways generally follow almost the same routes as the old Incan arteries crossing the highlands from southeast to northwest and are still the best roads in the country. The roads of more recent date, running down the Andes and across the plains, are largely makeshift.

Guatemala is planning to build a highway from the Mexican border across the Pan-American Highway to the highlands in the west; another, between La Libertad and Sebol, and still another from Los Amates to the main port on the Atlantic coast, Puerto Barrios. Mexico has built nearly 8,000 miles of highways and farm-to-market roads since 1948; Cuba, about 4,000 miles since March 1953.[71]

69. **50**, Spring 1952, p. 12. El Salvador completed its section of the Inter-American Highway without outside help, except for a stretch of about seventy-five miles.

70. **50**, Spring 1952, pp. 10–19; **5**, January–March 1952, pp. 19–26 and October–December 1954, p. 25.

71. **5**, January–March 1950, pp. 40–41 and October–December 1954, p. 27.

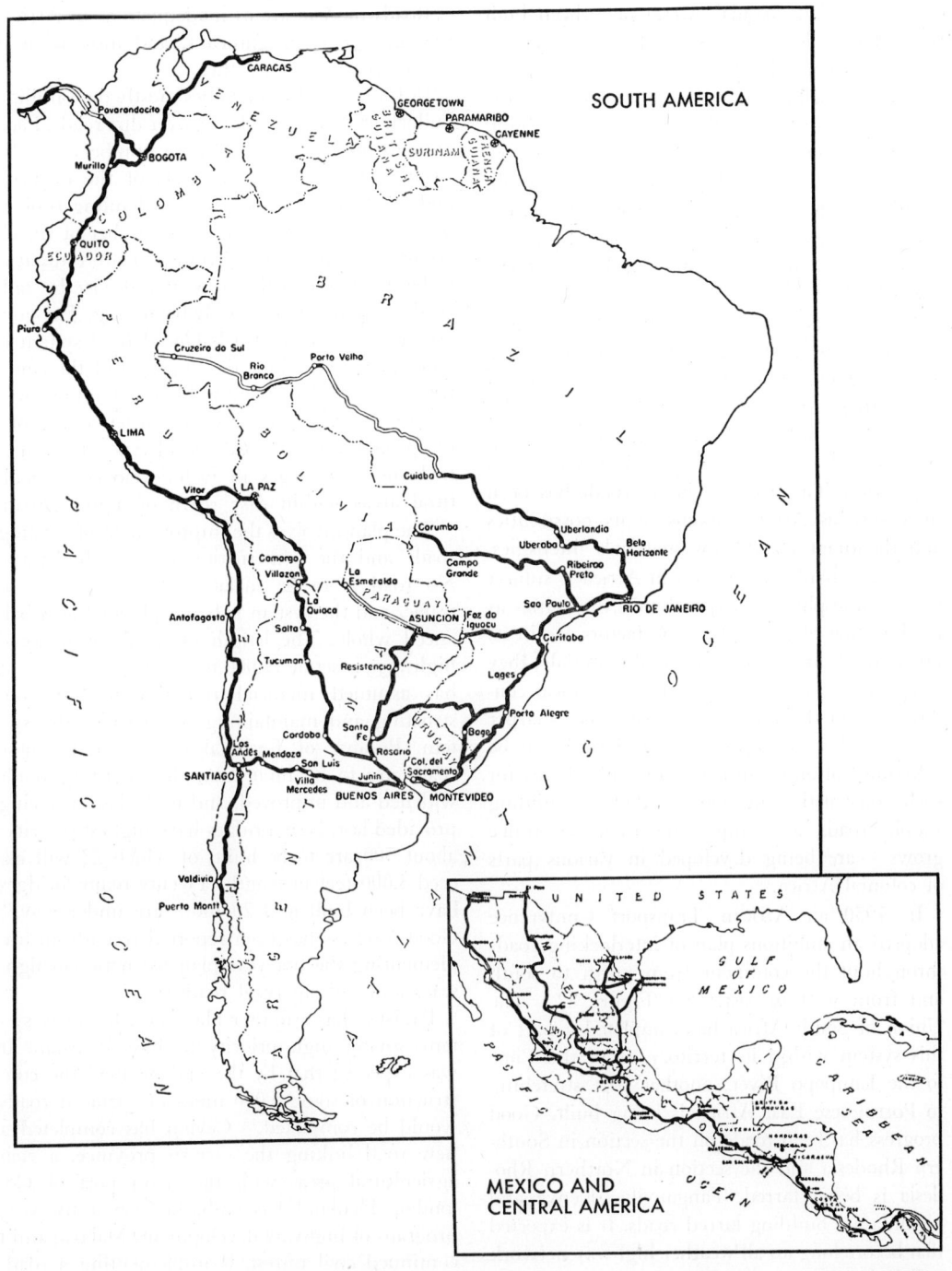

SOUTH AMERICA

MEXICO AND
CENTRAL AMERICA

United Nations

FIGURE 81. HIGHWAYS: PAN-AMERICAN SYSTEM IN LATIN AMERICA

Africa

Highways of colonial Africa have been built as feeders to local railroads, which connect the hinterland with the ports. The main exceptions are in the Belgian Congo and Uganda. In the first, a system of all-weather roads has been built, with ferry connections at the numerous rivers. Uganda has also developed a network of all-weather roads.[72] The Union of South Africa has the best highways on the continent and planned to complete a national system of hard-surfaced roads by 1954.

It is universally recognized that the lack of a comprehensive and properly integrated system of transportation, and specifically of a network of all-weather roads, is one of the main obstacles to the development of Africa's great natural resources and of higher living standards for its population. The need for better roads has been increasing as Africa wakens to its possibilities and the quest for its raw materials intensifies.

Though road construction in Africa is subject to the same physical and technical difficulties as the building of railroads, some factors are in its favor: roads may be built of local materials; they can be more easily adapted to geographical conditions than the railways and can take sharper curves and steeper gradients; and they can be experimental and improved gradually. Plans for such construction in stages — that is, building simple roads and improving them as traffic grows — are being developed in various parts of colonial Africa.[73]

In 1950 an African Transport Conference adopted an ambitious plan of interlocking roads throughout the continent from north to south and from west to east. (See Figure 82.) The Union of South Africa has completed a part of this system within its territory, from the Cape to the Limpopo River; another part stretching to Portuguese East Africa is being built. Good progress has been made on the section in Southern Rhodesia and the section in Northern Rhodesia is being tarred. Tanganyika, Kenya and Uganda are building tarred roads. It is expected that before long an all-weather highway network will link all parts of Africa, and, in particular, areas south of the Sahara.[74]

Asia

Roads in Asia are as inadequate as in Africa: the mileage is insignificant, and most of it is impassable in bad weather.

In India, rural traffic relies mostly on 8 million bullock carts moving slowly over dirt roads. Pack animals are still used in large numbers in relatively sparsely populated parts of the country, and elephants are important in hauling timber. The volume of goods and the number of travelers using such means of transport are estimated to be greater than the respective service by railroads.[75] Motor traffic is only beginning. The government realizes that a balanced road system is vital for the economic development of the country. The so-called Nagpur Plan, extending over twenty-five years, has for its target a network of 332,000 miles of roads of all types. Its aim is to bring all villages in well-developed agricultural areas within easy reach of a main road.

The plan involves the improvement of existing roads and the construction of new highways. No road is to be surfaced in anticipation of traffic, and the system is being planned as a balanced whole. The length of trunk or national highways is set at 16,000 miles. The government has assumed financial responsibility for constructing and maintaining this part of the system. Because of financial considerations, new roads are to be built first, then existing roads widened and improved, and high-class surfacing provided last. New bridges have highest priority; about 500 are to be built, of which 22 will exceed 3,000 feet in length. Twenty major bridges have been built and 20 more are under way.[76] Good progress has been reported recently in implementing the five-year plan for national highways and linking rural roads.[77]

Pakistan has a master plan for a highway system, giving high priority to East Pakistan. It was expected that by the end of 1953 the construction of some 5,000 miles of surfaced roads would be completed.[78] Ceylon has completed a new road linking the eastern province, a rich agricultural area, with the main port of Colombo. Thailand has embarked on a five-year program of highway development. Malaya, amid continued civil unrest, is implementing a road-building program financed by Marshall Plan

72. **50**, Winter 1951, pp. 45–46.

73. **50**, Winter 1951, pp. 45–50; **5**, July–September 1949, pp. 9–11.

74. **50**, Spring 1952, p. 28.

75. **61**, pp. 27–29.

76. **5**, October–December 1949, pp. 28–31 and October–December 1954, p. 29.

77. **1**, 1950, p. 264.

78. **5**, July–September 1951, p. 27.

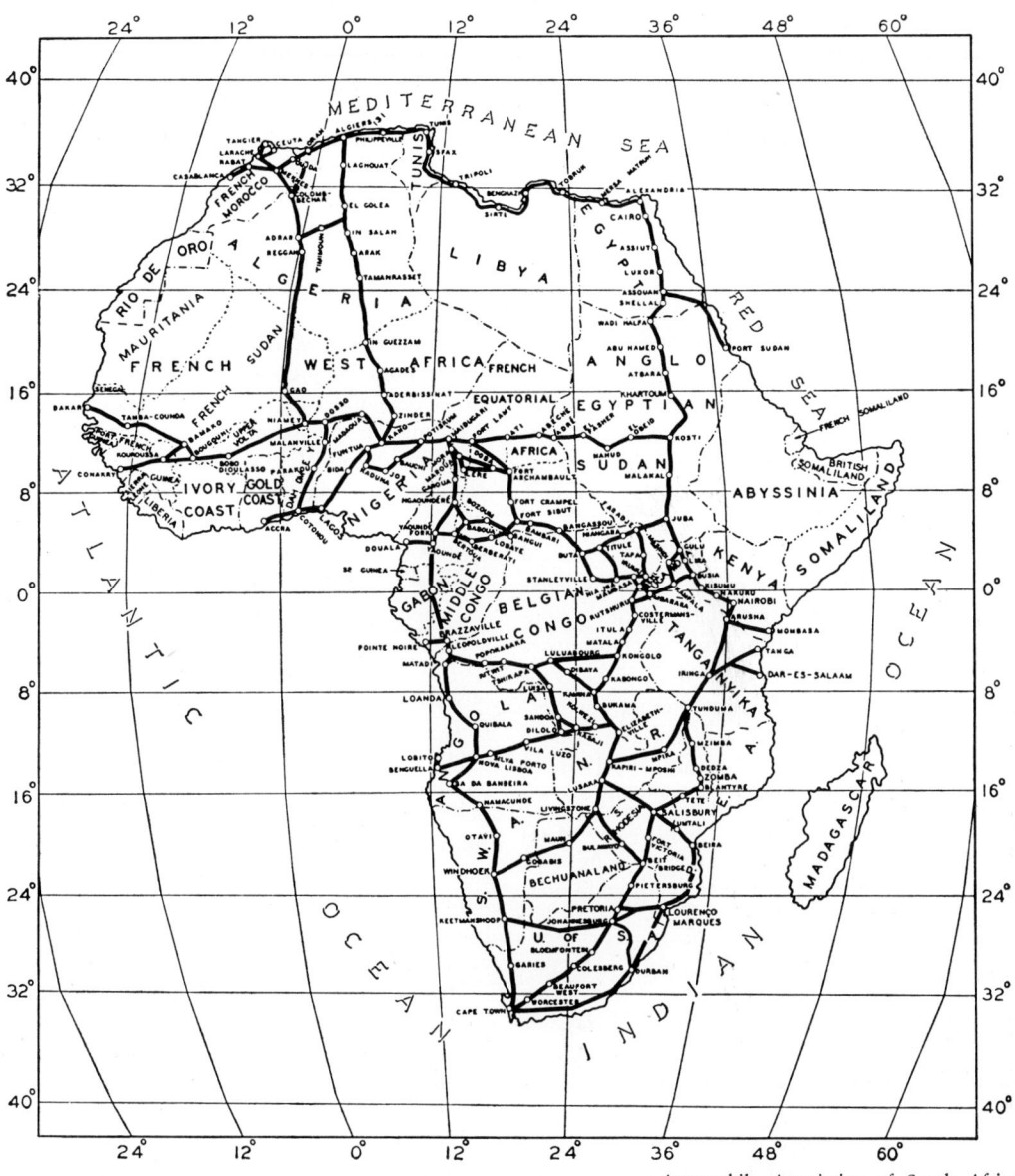

Automobile Association of South Africa

FIGURE 82. HIGHWAYS: PROPOSED TRANS-AFRICAN SYSTEM

This map shows the system of interlocking roads permitting safe travel at 40 miles per hour, as envisaged by the Central and Southern Africa Transport Conference, 1950. The Union of South Africa has completed 1,300 miles of asphalt road to the Limpopo, as part of its national road system, which was scheduled for completion in 1954.

funds via the United Kingdom. Indonesia has prepared a five-year plan for the construction of about a thousand miles of new highways, especially in Sumatra.[79] It is also planning to build four short modern highways from the capital, Djakarta, to four satellite towns, to draw off surplus population from the overcrowded capital. The first is under construction — a five-lane highway, with a 20-foot lane for streetcars, two 18-foot lanes on either side for fast traffic, two 12-foot center lanes for slow traffic (bullock carts, bicycles and so on) and two 6-foot footpaths.[80]

79. **1**, 1950, p. 264.

80. **50**, Autumn 1950, p. 34.

The Finances of Motor Transport

The world's motor fleet of 78 million units in 1952 represented an investment exceeding $100 billion. Its operation involves tremendous private expenditures and large public outlays for highway construction and maintenance.[81]

Expenditures for Highways

As long as roads were used chiefly for local transportation, local authorities met the costs of construction, repair and maintenance. As motor traffic developed, highways began to be used increasingly for long-distance traffic, and financing became the responsibility of national, state and regional authorities. To meet this new responsibility, special taxes — such as gasoline taxes and registration fees — on highway users have been introduced everywhere. In the United States, the gasoline tax represents, on the average, from 20 to 25 per cent of the price the consumer pays for the fuel. In most other countries it is considerably higher: more than 50 per cent in Belgium, Denmark, Norway, France, Switzerland, Iceland, Iran, Iraq and Pakistan; more than 60 per cent in Sweden and Israel; more than 70 per cent in Spain.[82]

In many countries, taxes on highway users do not provide enough to meet the costs of road construction and maintenance, and additional funds are appropriated from general taxation.

The United States

About $75 billion was spent on highways in the United States from 1920 through 1953, and nearly $54 billion was collected from 1925 through 1952 by taxation of highway users: taxes on motor fuel and lubricating oil, registration fees and federal motor-vehicle excise taxes.[83]

The federal government contributed in this entire period about $11 billion through the federal-aid program and work relief projects administered between 1935 and 1941.[84] In 1917, the first year of the federal-aid program, Congress provided $5 million for highways; in 1918,

$10 million. The appropriation was about $75 million a year during the next 12 years, rose to $125 million a year in 1931–36 and $200 million a year in 1938–39 and then fell to $142 a year during the next four years. The Federal-Aid Act of 1944 authorized the use of half a billion dollars a year for each of the first three postwar years for the improvement and construction of a designated system of highways.[85] Since funds were to be matched by the states, this represented a $3 billion program. Congress made the same amounts available through 1953 by subsequent annual appropriations. In 1952 it increased the federal-aid program by 10 per cent, from $500 million to $550 million, for 1954 and 1955, and an additional $25 million a year was specifically earmarked, for the first time, for improving the National System of Interstate Highways.

Total governmental expenditures — federal, state and local — amounted to $3.1 billion in 1949, $3.3 billion in 1950, $3.7 billion in 1951, $4.1 billion in 1952 and $4.5 billion in 1953, absorbing 1.2 to 1.3 per cent of the national income.[86] More than half is spent on construction, about a third on maintenance, and the rest on administration, highway police and other items. State taxes on highway users provided nearly $3.0 billion in 1952 and federal motor vehicle excise taxes yielded about $1.9 billion, but the latter go into the United States Treasury and bear no relation to the federal funds appropriated for highways.[87]

Diversion of highway-user taxes to nonhighway purposes has raised opposition in many states, and 27 states have constitutional amendments prohibiting this practice. The amendments are not fully effective in all cases, because of different accounting practices in various states, so that what is diversion in one state may not be so regarded in another. The percentage of highway-user taxes diverted to other purposes ranges from less than one in Minnesota, Mississippi, Montana, Vermont and Virginia to more than 42 per cent in New Jersey and 47 per cent in Rhode Island.[88] The Conference of State Highway Officials held in Kansas City in Decem-

---

81. The following pages outline problems of financing motor transport, including costs of building and maintaining the highways, costs of transportation in privately owned motor vehicles, and revenues and expenditures of commercial motor carriers.

82. **51**, Table 6.

83. **12**, p. 83; **37**, 1953, pp. 42 and 50.

84. **12**, p. 83; **28**, p. 253. During the depression

public funds were provided for highway improvements to create employment for people out of work.

85. See pp. 403 and 407–08.

86. **18**, Table HF–2; **17**, 1951, p. 148; **37**, 1953, p. 50. Data for 1953, forecast by Bureau of Public Roads.

87. **18**, Table HF–1; **20**, p. 8; **37**, 1953, p. 42.

88. **39**, pp. 75–76; **37**, 1953, p. 47.

ber 1952 voted that "all funds of the gasoline tax must be available for highway administration, construction, reconstruction and maintenance to fulfill the national demand for an extended highway program." [89]

Maintenance of highways is increasingly costly, since the roads deteriorate more rapidly as the volume and weight of traffic grow. The estimated lifetime of the average road surface is 12 years. This means that 44 per cent of the mileage of the high-type highways in use in 1950 will be worn out around 1960, along with 74 per cent of that of intermediate types and 94 per cent of low-type surfacing. Construction of needed highways would require from $42 billion to $47 billion at 1950 prices, according to the Bureau of Public Roads.[90]

Other Countries

The United Kingdom's expenditures on highway construction, maintenance and improvement exceeded $4 billion from 1920 to 1939 and amounted to about $1.2 billion from 1945 to 1950.[91] The amounts spent in the war years were not reported, but must have been very small. Highway expenditures absorbed less than one per cent of the national income in the first postwar years, as compared to about 1.5 per cent in 1938.[92] Taxation of motor vehicles and gasoline could approximately cover the annual expenditures on roads, but a substantial part of this revenue, sometimes two thirds of it, is used for general government purposes.[93]

Sweden spends less than one per cent of national income for highways, using about three fourths for maintenance and the rest for construction of roads and bridges.[94] France, the Netherlands and Denmark also spent a fraction of one per cent of national income in 1947; Australia, more than one per cent, and New Zealand, nearly 1.5 per cent.[95]

COSTS OF MOTOR TRANSPORTATION IN THE UNITED STATES

The United States spends about one eighth of its total national product on motor transporta-

tion each year.[96] Consumer expenditures for motor transportation many times exceed those for all other means of passenger travel combined.

Consumer Expenditures

Out of each dollar the consumer spent for personal transportation in 1953, 87.5 cents went for the purchase and operation of an automobile, in comparison with 8.1 cents for purchased local transportation (street cars, buses, taxis, commutation on railways and so on) and 4.4 cents for intercity transportation (railways except commutation, airlines, intercity buses, transfer by water, baggage and luggage).[97] Automobile transportation ranks fifth among total consumer expenditures in the United States, following food, clothing, housing and household operation.

The total outlay of the nation's car owners for purchase of cars, for repairs, gasoline and oil, insurance and related items is estimated at $5.7 billion for 1929, $5 billion for 1939, $16 billion for 1949 and nearly $23.5 billion for 1953. Throughout the depression and war years (except 1941) the largest item in car owners' expenditures was gasoline and oil; the next largest, buying a car. This relationship has been reversed in recent years, and the amount spent for purchase of cars now (1953) considerably exceeds the expenditure for gasoline: 46 per cent as against 28 per cent for gasoline. (See Table 150.)

The federal survey of consumer expenditures in 1935–36 showed that low-income and middle-income rural families spent a greater percentage of their income on cars than rural families in higher income brackets. Among urban families, in contrast, the higher income groups spent more, as illustrated by the following figures on the percentage of income spent for automobile transport: [98]

Income Group	Rural Families	Urban Families
Under $500	9.1	3.4
$1,000–$1,250	7.8	5.5
$2,000–$2,500	8.2	8.4
$4,000–$5,000	5.8	8.4
$5,000–$10,000	6.0	7.9

Cost per Mile

The cost of motor transportation per mile, particularly of passenger transportation, is vari-

89. **33**, January 1953, p. 37.
90. **20**, pp. 9-10.
91. **44**, 1951, p. 29.
92. Cf. **31**, 1953, pp. 216 and 265.
93. **43**, p. 163.
94. **32**, 1952, pp. 152 and 279.
95. **51**, 1950, Table 5; cf. **3**, *passim*.

96. **11**, p. 1.
97. **17**, 1954, pp. 206–07.
98. **27**, pp. 51 and 61.

TABLE 150

MOTOR TRANSPORTATION: EXPENDITURES ON OWNER-OPERATED MOTOR TRANSPORTATION IN THE UNITED STATES, 1929–53

(*Millions*)

Year	Total	Cars [a]	Tires and Tubes	Parts and Accessories	Repair and Other [b]	Gasoline and Oil	Tolls [c]	Automobile Insurance [d]
1929	$5,748	$2,588	$419	$221	$572	$1,814	$40	$94
1930	4,498	1,642	320	196	467	1,749	43	81
1931	3,617	1,144	264	162	386	1,540	45	76
1932	2,839	635	189	118	296	1,476	43	82
1933	2,940	779	154	117	306	1,466	42	76
1934	3,474	1,024	182	153	346	1,640	43	86
1935	4,102	1,508	175	181	354	1,743	42	99
1936	4,825	1,921	167	220	404	1,945	44	124
1937	5,147	1,988	176	238	421	2,143	44	137
1938	4,318	1,228	193	185	402	2,145	41	124
1939	4,967	1,679	237	220	462	2,181	46	142
1940	5,686	2,228	257	243	489	2,264	50	155
1941	6,777	2,708	318	316	577	2,628	57	173
1942	3,376	423	265		600	1,908	44	136
1943	2,844	463	334		660	1,198	34	155
1944	2,969	440	418		710	1,206	35	160
1945	3,691	484	603		770	1,616	43	175
1946	8,403	2,794	1,414		926	2,950	59	260
1947	11,619	4,934	1,626		1,087	3,528	63	381
1948	13,468	5,925	1,590		1,246	4,166	65	476
1949	15,995	7,878	1,511		1,369	4,635	67	535
1950	19,353	10,285	2,030		1,478	4,928	70	562
1951	18,690	8,900	1,967		1,670	5,405	78	670
1952	18,959	8,342	2,072		1,770	5,887	100	788
1953	23,461	10,696	2,416		2,727	6,619	129	874

Sources: **17**, 1951, pp. 194–95; **16**, July 1953, p. 22; for 1953: **17**, 1954, pp. 206–07.

a. New cars and net purchases of used cars.
b. Includes greasing, washing, parking, storage, rental.

c. Bridge, tunnel, ferry and road tolls.
d. Net payments.

able and rather difficult to determine precisely. It includes depreciation of the vehicle, its maintenance and repair, fuel, tires, insurance, gasoline taxes, registration fees, and often garage and parking expenses. The amount of such expenses on an annual or mileage basis depends on the price paid for the vehicle and the rate of depreciation for its particular type, its service life, the mileage traveled per year, types of road traveled, traffic conditions and many other factors.

In the first decade of this century, the cost of operating an automobile in the United States ranged from 10 to 18 cents per mile; in 1941, it was about 4 cents per mile for new cars covered by substantial insurance, including parking and garage fees. In the United States as a whole, one third of the car owners actually operated at less than 2 cents a mile; another third, at 2–3 cents a mile; one sixth, at 3–4 cents a mile, and only the last sixth, at more than 4 cents a mile.[99] Today the cost per mile is substantially higher because of the higher prices of cars and of gasoline and the higher charges for repair and maintenance.

Tires and oil, which were among the most important items of current expenditures in the early period of motoring, now account for only a small fraction of the total.

Despite the improvement in quality, the price of gasoline in 1950 (though 50 per cent higher than in 1939) was lower than in 1920: 26.8 and 29.8 cents per gallon, respectively.[100] Because of

99. **63**, pp. 12–16.
100. **34**, 1950, p. 367. Simple averages, including tax, at service stations in fifty representative cities.

heavier cars and the greater speed of motoring, the decline in price has not resulted, however, in reducing the cost per mile.[101]

Road surface is also a factor in the costs of motor vehicle operation. It has been estimated that in 1939 gasoline mileage was 2 miles per gallon less and oil mileage 50 per cent less on gravel-surfaced roads than on paved highways.[102] A similar comparison is considered valid for today between gravel surfaces and cement-concrete pavements. Tire wear on gravel roads is estimated to be double or more the wear on paved highways.[103] Thus, a recent study by the Pacific Northwest forest and range experiment station showed that the tire cost per mile for a 25–30 ton truck was 15.7 cents on earth-surfaced roads, 11.9 cents on gravel-surfaced roads and 4.7 cents on concrete highways.

THE FINANCES OF INTERCITY MOTOR CARRIERS

Some motor carriers transport property, others passengers, and few carry both. Buses are commercially operated, except for nonrevenue school buses, but much of the shipment of property in all countries is by means of private trucks.

Ownership

In 1940, 85 per cent of all trucks in the United States belonged to private persons and accounted for 76 per cent of all vehicle-miles on rural roads and 54 per cent of all ton-miles in the nation.[104] In 1948, about 6 million of the 7.2 million registered trucks were engaged in private hauling, including some 2 million trucks on farms.[105]

In the United Kingdom, France, Belgium, Norway, Western Germany, and Austria, from 80 to 91 per cent of all trucks operate on their own account. Trucks with less than a 2-ton load capacity are used almost exclusively for private purposes. (See Table 151.) In the United Kingdom, more than three fourths of all road freight is carried in trader-owned vehicles.[106]

In the United States, trucks operating "on own account" are ordinarily in the 1 to 3 ton group; trucks "for hire" have a considerably greater load capacity, some exceeding 20–25 tons.[107]

TABLE 151

MOTOR TRANSPORTATION: PERCENTAGE OF TRUCKS OPERATED ON OWN ACCOUNT, IN SELECTED COUNTRIES, 1952

Country	Among All Trucks	Among Trucks with Load Capacity of		
		Less than 2 Metric Tons	2 to 5 Metric Tons	5 Metric Tons and Over
United Kingdom	83	97	74	41
France [a]	87 [b]	96 [e]	87 [d]	71 [e]
Belgium [a]	91	97	74	64
Norway	82	96	63	49
Western Germany	81	94	66	56
Austria	80	95	71	59

Source: **6,** 1951, p. 41; 1952, p. 57.

  a. 1951.
  b. Excludes trucks with a capacity of less than one ton.
  c. Truck capacity: 0.5 to 0.9 tons.
  d. Truck capacity: 0.9 to 4.5 tons.
  e. Truck capacity: 4.5 tons and over.

Some states, among them Illinois and Rhode Island, permit the gross weight of trucks to reach 36–40 short tons.[108] The heavy load carried by for-hire trucks explains the fact that while they constitute about 15 per cent of all trucks in the United States, they transport about half the freight.

The for-hire truckers are divided into two groups — common and contract carriers. Common carriers work for the general public and ordinarily operate over regular routes on regular schedules, though some have irregular routes within a specified area. Contract carriers work under special arrangements with individual shippers, either on a long contract basis or on a job basis.

Commercial trucking is a small-scale business, as compared to railroads. A large number of operators have a few trucks each, though there are also common carriers with large truck fleets.[109] Among carriers subject to the jurisdiction of the Interstate Commerce Commission (ICC), about one fourth operated one truck in 1948 and less than 1 in 10 operated more than

101. **63,** p. 31.
102. **11,** p. 18.
103. **63,** p. 35; **11,** p. 18.
104. **57,** p. 676; **42,** p. 143.
105. **53,** p. 251.
106. **43,** p. 26.
107. There are only scattered statistics for the United

States on the weight and load capacity of trucks: in 1950, 6 states registered trucks by the manufacturer's rated capacity; 11 states, by the net weight of unladen vehicle; 26 states, by gross weight (combined weight of vehicle and load).
  108. **19,** 1950, p. 32.
  109. **57,** p. 680.

ten trucks.[110] Ownership is predominantly individual. Of the trucking enterprises regulated by the ICC in 1939, 70.3 per cent were run by individuals, 12.4 per cent by partners, and 17.3 per cent by corporations. The last, however, accounted for more than 49 per cent of all vehicle-miles, more than 52 per cent of the tonnage transported and more than 56 per cent of the total revenue.[111] Generally speaking, the corporations are predominantly family affairs, ownership being held by members of single families.

Concentration is much greater in the intercity bus business. In 1951, the 166 Class I reporting carriers of passengers in the United States operated 13,431 vehicles, or an average of 81 vehicles per company, as compared with an average of 17 trucks per reporting property carrier in Class I, or 122 total revenue vehicles (trucks, truck-tractors, semitrailers and full trailers).[112]

Major Financial Characteristics

The major financial characteristics of bus and truck transportation are similar. Both require a comparatively small capital outlay. Their total assets in the United States in 1941 have been estimated at some $1.2 billion, less than 5 per cent of the total investment in railroads, or about 25 per cent of that investment apart from outlays for roadbeds.[113] In trucking, an outlay of about 25–30 cents is required to obtain a dollar of annual gross receipts; in 1950 and 1951 Class I reporting property carriers in the United States received $3.18 per each dollar of investment.[114] A substantial proportion of the assets of both bus and truck companies is financed by current liabilities and working capital. The main outlay is for equipment, which can be disposed of if difficulties arise.

Unlike railroad costs, most of the expenses of motor carriers are variable — for fuel, supplies, wages and depreciation of equipment. Motor car-

riers do not need to maintain a "permanent way" or the numerous installations without which the railroad cannot operate. Terminal expenses and interest on investments, while less variable, are a comparatively small part of the total. Taxes are more or less in line with the amount of traffic. According to the ICC, at least nine tenths of all operating expenses, rents and taxes of motor freight carriers are variable.[115]

In 1951 revenue from the operation of commercial trucks (Class I carriers) in the United States amounted to $2,728 million; of buses to $393 million. Their expenditures were $2,603 and $345 million, respectively. About half the expenditures of commercial trucks and one third of those of buses were absorbed by transportation costs.[116]

The operating ratio — that is, the proportion of revenue absorbed by operating expenses, excluding taxes and fixed charges — is considerably higher than that of the railroads. Between 1939 and 1951, the operating ratio of Class I motor carriers of freight and that of Class I railroads fluctuated as follows (per cent): [117]

	Motor Carriers	Railroads
1939	95.1	73.1
1940	95.5	71.9
1941	94.8	68.5
1942	94.4	61.6
1943	96.6	62.5
1944	97.0	66.6
1945	. . .	79.2
1946	96.4	83.4
1947	95.3	78.3
1948	93.4	77.2
1949	94.7	80.3
1950	93.1	74.5
1951	95.4	77.4

Because of the relatively small investment of motor carriers in equipment and the small amounts for interest and other "fixed charges," it is considered that the operating ratio of motor carriers, though high, generally leaves enough margin for profit. How large the margin should be, is controversial. Some put the limit of the ratio at 90 per cent, others above 95 per cent,[118] while still others believe that the stability

---

110. **68**, p. 107. The average number of trucks operated by carriers in Germany was 1.4 in 1939; in the United Kingdom, 8. **65**, p. 295.

111. **28**, pp. 405–06.

112. **15**, 1954, pp. 587–88. Class I intercity carriers of property or passengers or both were subject to the jurisdiction of the ICC if their annual revenue was $100,000 or more. Since 1950 the requirement for inclusion in the Class I group has been raised to $200,000. Class I carriers are representative of the industry, in that they accounted in 1949 for 76 per cent of the revenue from trucking and 89 per cent of the passenger revenue. **25**, 1949, p. 3.

113. **10**, p. 146; cf. Chapter 8.

114. **25**, 1949, p. 4; **15**, 1954, p. 587.

115. **57**, p. 685. Common carriers have a larger proportion of constant costs than contract carriers. (*Ibid.*, p. 700.)

116. **15**, 1954, p. 587.

117. **57**, p. 683; **35**, p. 22; **15**, 1954, pp. 576 and 587.

118. **28**, p. 409; **57**, pp. 683–84.

of motor carriers is impaired when the ratio exceeds 95 per cent.[119]

Similar statistics for other countries are not available.

ROAD VERSUS RAIL

Both highway and rail transport offer their patrons specific advantages. Highway transport has made considerable inroads on the railroad business, though not all intercity motor traffic can be regarded as a direct diversion from railroad operations. Some transportation could not have been provided by the railroads in any event, either because it was created by the motor vehicle or because it is in areas not served by the railroads. Nevertheless, the railroads have lost a substantial portion of their potential freight and passenger traffic, and this loss is increasing.

ADVANTAGES OF ROAD TRANSPORT

In personal travel, the automobile provides many conveniences which no other form of transportation can match, as, for example, direct departure from home, without a rigid timetable and without need to pack as carefully and economically in terms of weight and space as otherwise would be necessary; freedom to stop at any desired place; considerably lower costs of travel, particularly for families; cheaper accommodations at overnight stops, and privacy.

The advantages of trucks, though of a different nature, are considerable. Truck hauling over a short distance is often more convenient than shipment by rail and requires less handling.[120] The truck picks up the product from the platform of the consignor and delivers it at the door of the consignee. Since the truck drivers usually load and unload, no extra expenditures for handling arise.[121]

Ordinarily, less damage is done in shipment by truck than by rail, particularly when goods are fragile or are difficult to load and unload, such as large pieces of machinery. Yet packaging is simpler and less costly; goods often can be sent unpacked or in cartons and light crates, while rail transport requires heavier and more elaborate packing.

Because they carry smaller loads than freight cars, the trucks also offer more frequent schedules. They can depart immediately and lose less time waiting for the assemblage of freight. The speedier service permits faster turnover of stock and reduces the amount of capital tied up in inventories which may, in certain circumstances, deteriorate or decrease in value if delayed.[122]

Trucks — the "road tramps" — can also perform many individual and specialized services, beyond the capacities of mass transportation facilities. Such services often involve small and light, but high-rated, freight which used to provide net income to railroads. A truck can accept an urgent shipment at any time and can change the route and schedule and adjust its services to the desires of the customer. A phone call brings a truck to the shipper's door, and in no time the loaded truck is on its way. A special train cannot be chartered, but a special truck can be hired. If the shipment is not ready, the truck can be held, but the train cannot. This difference is of special importance when goods are for export: a hauler may be able to delay his departure if the goods are not ready and still reach the port before the ship leaves, while similar delay in shipment by rail may mean that both the train and the ship are missed.[123]

Since World War II, the truck has become almost a part of the assembly line in manufacturing in the United States. It carries raw materials to processing plants, finished parts to subassembly shops, assembled units to the main production plant, and the completed products to wholesalers, thence to retailers and finally to the consumers.[124]

In addition to hauling operations as such, trucks connect shippers with rail, water and air terminals.

ADVANTAGES OF RAIL TRANSPORT

The railroads offer the most dependable overland mass transportation service, and in many areas where cars and buses are few, they are *the* means of transportation for the inhabitants. Even in the United States, the railroads have specific advantages over the other commercial carriers. Railroads handle commuter service around

---

119. **68**, p. 111. For the railroads so high an operating ratio is out of the question. According to the National Resources Planning Board, a ratio of about 75 per cent was considered favorable. (**28**, p. 409.)

120. A less-than-carload shipment of freight by rail may undergo as many as eight transfers, while the same shipment by truck may require only three. (**42**, p. 92.)

121. **68**, pp. 9-10.

122. **68**, p. 371.
123. **70**, pp. 116–17.
124. **20**, p. 12.

large cities on a scale not possible for buses. To the long-distance traveler, they offer accommodations and conveniences — such as eating and sleeping facilities, air conditioning and space to move about — that the buses cannot match. They are faster than the buses and much less affected by weather conditions. Their schedules are maintained except in extraordinary circumstances, and they are safer than any other means of transport on land or in the air.[125]

The chief advantage of railroads in freight traffic is their capacity to move great loads of heavy commodities, with which the trucking business cannot compete. The average load of all trucks and combinations in 1950 in the United States was 5.6 tons, and that of the heavier freighters alone, 10.6 tons.[126] In contrast, the average capacity of a freight car of Class I railways in 1950 was 52.6 short tons.[127] Thus, a locomotive hauling a train of 50 freight cars with a crew of five men can pull as much freight as some 250 truck-combinations driven by as many men.[128] To move by truck all the cargo hauled by the railroads would be out of the question.

Another important service that railroads provide and trucks do not is the storage of freight — on sidings, in special warehouses, in cars at freight stations.

Railroads ordinarily accept all kinds of commodities, at all times and in any quantity. They can move anything "movable" as trucking cannot. Moreover, they are expansible and can, if necessary, increase the volume of goods carried by adding more cars to a train and running more trains. This capacity was demonstrated most strikingly during World War II, when the railroads of the United States moved some 97 per cent of all military freight and about 70 per cent of all other intercity freight.[129] The Association of American Railroads points out that the increase in freight traffic from 1940 to 1944 was greater than the total growth in that traffic during the first 85 years of the railroad industry (1830–1915), and that the rise in passenger traffic was greater than in the first 110 years of the industry (1830–1940).[130]

125. Cf. **54,** pp. 98–100 and Chapter 7, p. 309.
126. **19,** 1950, p. 38.
127. **23,** 1950, p. 168.
128. Cf. **71,** p. 376.
129. **12,** p. 3.
130. **35,** p. 10.

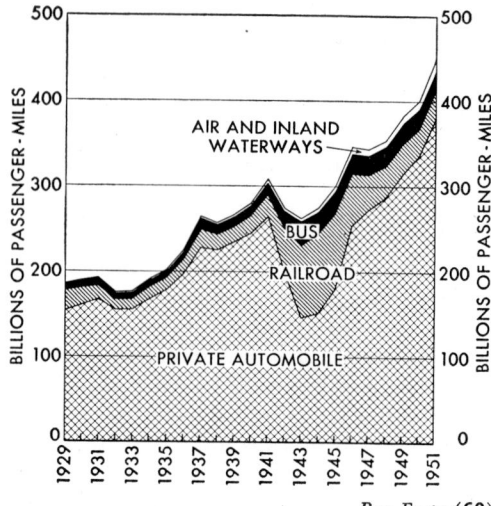

Bus Facts (**60**)

FIGURE 83. PASSENGER TRAFFIC: DISTRIBUTION, BY TYPE OF CARRIER, IN THE UNITED STATES, 1929–51

COMPETITION BETWEEN RAIL AND ROAD

Competition between the two mediums of land transportation — the motor vehicle and railroad — has become increasingly keen, even in Africa.[131] The proportion of traffic that road transport has captured from the railroads cannot be calculated exactly for any country. The available information on the volume of commercial intercity traffic, freight and passenger, indicates, however, that while highway traffic is growing, rail traffic is declining.

The United States

Nearly 85 per cent of all intercity travel in the United States was by private automobile in 1951, as compared to less than 8 per cent by train. Buses accounted for 4.8 per cent; airlines and waterways, for the remaining 2.7 per cent. More important is the fact that total intercity travel and travel by car, in terms of passenger-miles, more than doubled between 1929 and 1951 and travel by buses more than tripled, while railroad traffic increased about 30 per cent. (See Table 152 and Figure 83.) The only upswing in railroad traffic was during World War II when shortages of gasoline and rubber, interruption in car manufacture and priority of military transport increased passenger travel by train several times over. In addition, the railroads transported millions of members of the armed forces travel-

131. **5,** July–September 1949, p. 10.

TABLE 152

PASSENGER TRAFFIC: DISTRIBUTION, BY TYPE OF CARRIER, IN THE UNITED STATES, 1929–51

| | | | Public Carriers | | | | |
Year	Total	Private Automobiles	Total	Railroads	Buses	Airlines	Water-ways
			Billions of Passenger-Miles				
1929	186.6	154.3	32.3	24.2	6.8	—	1.3
1930	189.4	160.9	28.5	20.2	7.1	0.1	1.1
1931	192.3	168.6	23.7	15.9	6.7	0.1	1.0
1932	175.6	156.4	19.2	12.0	6.3	0.1	0.8
1933	176.2	156.5	19.7	12.0	6.4	0.2	1.1
1934	190.4	168.1	22.3	13.9	7.1	0.2	1.1
1935	201.8	178.3	23.5	14.4	7.6	0.3	1.2
1936	226.6	197.4	29.2	18.2	9.2	0.4	1.4
1937	264.3	228.4	35.9	21.5	12.7	0.4	1.3
1938	257.1	226.3	30.8	18.7	10.1	0.5	1.5
1939	267.7	234.7	33.0	19.6	11.2	0.7	1.7
1940	280.5	245.8	34.7	20.8	11.6	1.0	1.3
1941	307.6	264.3	45.3	26.5	13.6	1.4	1.8
1942	274.7	199.6	75.1	50.3	21.5	1.4	1.9
1943	262.6	147.1	115.5	84.6	27.4	1.6	1.9
1944	274.5	151.3	123.2	92.2	26.5	2.3	2.2
1945	300.3	179.8	120.5	88.1	26.9	3.4	2.1
1946	347.8	253.6	94.2	60.4	25.6	5.9	2.3
1947	345.6	273.0	72.6	40.8	23.9	6.1	1.8
1948	354.5	287.4	67.1	36.0	23.5	5.9	1.7
1949	383.3	316.7	66.6	36.0	22.4	6.8	1.4
1950	400.3	337.3	63.0	32.5	21.3	8.0	1.2
1951	448.1	379.3	68.8	35.3	21.5	10.7	1.3
			Per Cent				
1929	100.0	82.7	17.3	13.0	3.6	...	0.7
1930	100.0	85.0	15.0	10.7	3.7	...	0.6
1931	100.0	87.7	12.3	8.3	3.5	...	0.5
1932	100.0	89.1	10.9	6.8	3.6	...	0.5
1933	100.0	88.8	11.2	6.8	3.7	0.1	0.6
1934	100.0	88.3	11.7	7.3	3.7	0.1	0.6
1935	100.0	88.4	11.6	7.1	3.8	0.2	0.6
1936	100.0	87.1	12.9	8.0	4.1	0.2	0.6
1937	100.0	86.4	13.6	8.1	4.8	0.2	0.7
1938	100.0	88.0	12.0	7.3	3.9	0.2	0.6
1939	100.0	87.7	12.3	7.3	4.2	0.3	0.5
1940	100.0	87.6	12.4	7.4	4.1	0.4	0.5
1941	100.0	85.9	14.1	8.6	4.4	0.5	0.6
1942	100.0	72.7	27.3	18.3	7.8	0.5	0.7
1943	100.0	56.0	44.0	32.2	10.4	0.7	0.7
1944	100.0	55.1	44.9	33.6	9.7	0.8	0.8
1945	100.0	59.9	40.1	29.3	9.0	1.1	0.7
1946	100.0	72.9	27.1	17.4	7.3	1.7	0.7
1947	100.0	79.0	21.0	11.8	6.9	1.8	0.5
1948	100.0	81.1	18.9	10.1	6.6	1.7	0.5
1949	100.0	82.6	17.5	9.4	5.9	1.8	0.4
1950	100.0	84.3	15.7	8.1	5.3	2.0	0.3
1951	100.0	84.6	15.4	7.9	4.8	2.4	0.3

Sources: **60,** 1951, pp. 4 and 8; **23,** 1950, p. 18.

ing under orders and on furlough to and from their homes, camps and ports.

In freight traffic, motor carriers move a considerable tonnage, but much of it is hauled in urban and suburban areas, over short distances. In terms of ton-miles, the railroads, which haul most of the long-distance freight, account for the greater part of the nation's transport of goods: 78.3 per cent of the total in 1929; 63.3 per cent in 1939; 60.6 per cent in 1949; and 58.6 per cent in 1951. The share moved by highway transport in these years was 3.3, 8.1, 10.6 and 11.9 per cent, respectively.[132] (See Table 153.) Yet, as these figures show, the share of railroads in the growing volume of traffic is steadily declining. Between 1929 and 1951, the railroads' share of the freight business decreased by one fourth while the share of highway trucking nearly quadrupled.

Moreover, the composition of freight shipments is much more favorable for the truckers than for the railroads. The higher-rate freight, such as manufactured goods and perishables, generally goes by truck, while the railroads carry chiefly raw materials. Thus, about 60 per cent of the motor tonnage is in finished products and about 8 per cent in the products of mines, as compared with 28 and 56 per cent, respectively, for the railroads.[133]

The United Kingdom

Competition between rail and road for freight traffic in the United Kingdom is mostly for the transport of "general merchandise," that is, any goods but minerals and heavy merchandise, which are carried almost exclusively by the railroads. Traffic in general merchandise consists of small consignments, all less than a carload, conveyed over short hauls averaging about 100 miles or somewhat more.[134]

It is not known how much freight traffic has been diverted from the railroads. Some indication is given by an estimate based on the output and rail transportation of "general merchandise." This estimate assumes that total freight trans-

port is closely correlated with tonnage output of general merchandise. It takes 1907 as the base year, when road transport was not yet a serious competitor, and disregards water transport of freight, which is generally negligible in the United Kingdom. Without motor transportation, rail-borne traffic might have increased in later years in proportion to the increase in the output of general merchandise. The difference between the actual and hypothetical volume of rail traffic should therefore indicate the amount lost to road transport — about a third in 1930 and more than half in 1935. In fact, according to this estimate, the total share of road-borne traffic must have been considerably greater than these figures suggest, since a new, improved and cheaper means of transport generates additional production and traffic.[135] The proportion of traffic captured by road transport since 1935 has undoubtedly increased substantially, as it has in the United States.

Other Countries

Only scattered information is available on traffic competition in other countries. The indications are that in Western Germany, the Netherlands and Belgium the share of road transport in total traffic is increasing at the cost of both inland waterways and railroads.[136] In the Netherlands, in particular, where water transport is highly developed and distances are short, the position of the railroads has become exceptionally difficult with the capture of much of the transport business by a new rival.[137] In Norway, Denmark and Austria, too, the railroads are losing some business to competing road transport. No statistics are available, although in 1952 several European countries made sample surveys of freight traffic by road. According to the Economic Commission for Europe, such traffic by road has increased, but to a lesser extent than the increase in numbers of trucks would suggest. This is due to the fact that the increase in truck numbers has been chiefly in those operated on own account, and such trucks are used less intensively than commercial vehicles.[138]

In Egypt, also, highway transport competes seriously with the railroads in goods and passenger traffic.[139]

132. Water carriers and pipelines are also important freight carriers, but the competition between two surface carriers — highway and rail — is of greatest import. Airlines carry an insignificant tonnage of freight — 0.2 per cent of the total in 1950. For water carriers, see Chapter 10; for airlines, Chapter 11; for pipelines, see **73**, pp. 909–13.

133. **42**, p. 150. Cf. **26**, 1950, p. 40.

134. **70**, p. 19.

135. **70**, pp. 124–30.

136. **6**, 1951, pp. 7 and 16.

137. **72**, pp. 389–404.

138. **6**, 1952, pp. 20–24.

139. **46**, p. 84.

TABLE 153

FREIGHT TRAFFIC: DISTRIBUTION, BY TYPE OF CARRIER, IN THE UNITED STATES, 1929–51

| | Billions of Ton-Miles | | | | | Per Cent | | | |
Year	Total	Rail-roads [a]	Water Carriers [b]	Motor Carriers [c]	Pipe-lines [d]	Total	Rail-roads [a]	Water Carriers [b]	Motor Carriers [c]	Pipe-lines [d]
1929	575.3	450.2	106.0	18.9	...	100.0	78.3	18.4	3.3	...
1930	492.6	385.8	86.5	20.3	...	100.0	78.3	17.6	4.1	...
1931	389.5	311.1	58.3	20.2	...	100.0	79.9	15.0	5.2	...
1932	286.8	235.3	32.6	18.8	...	100.0	82.0	11.4	6.6	...
1933	324.6	250.7	55.3	18.7	...	100.0	77.2	17.0	5.8	...
1934	348.6	270.3	57.7	20.7	...	100.0	77.5	16.6	5.9	...
1935	376.4	283.6	68.1	24.6	...	100.0	75.3	18.1	6.5	...
1936	462.7	341.2	92.7	28.8	...	100.0	73.7	20.0	6.2	...
1937	563.0	362.8	110.1	32.3	57.8	100.0	64.4	19.6	5.7	10.3
1938	450.6	291.9	66.7	37.0	55.0	100.0	64.8	14.8	8.2	12.2
1939	530.2	335.4	96.2	43.0	55.5	100.0	63.3	18.2	8.1	10.5
1940	604.2	375.4	118.1	51.0	59.9	100.0	62.1	19.5	8.4	9.9
1941	743.7	477.6	140.5	57.1	68.6	100.0	64.2	18.9	7.7	9.2
1942	914.5	641.0	148.6	50.2	74.7	100.0	70.0	16.3	5.5	8.2
1943	1,016.2	730.1	141.7	48.2	96.3	100.0	71.8	13.9	4.7	9.5
1944	1,072.4	740.6	150.2	49.3	132.3	100.0	69.1	14.0	4.6	12.3
1945	1,006.3	684.1	142.7	56.2	123.0	100.0	68.0	14.2	5.6	12.3
1946	875.7	594.9	124.0	64.3	92.5	100.0	67.9	14.2	7.3	10.6
1947	986.6	657.9	146.7	77.9	104.2	100.0	66.7	14.9	7.9	10.6
1948	1,005.0	647.3	150.5	87.6	119.6	100.0	64.4	15.0	8.7	11.9
1949 [e]	882.9	534.7	139.4	93.7	114.9	100.0	60.6	15.8	10.6	13.0
1950 [e]	1,015.8	596.9	163.3	126.0	129.2	100.0	58.8	16.1	12.4	12.7
1951 [e]	1,119.0	655.4	178.0	133.2	152.1	100.0	58.6	15.9	11.9	13.6

Sources: **12**, p. 76; **23**, 1949, p. 22 and 1952, p. 18.

a. Classes I, II and III.
b. All inland and coastal rivers and the Great Lakes.
c. All trucks, including private and for hire.

d. Crude and refined oil. Includes gathering and non-reporting lines. Barrel-miles converted to ton-miles.
e. Includes small ton-mileage performed by airlines.

Effect on the Railroads

Diversion of traffic from rails to highways has forced the railroads to adjust and, first of all, to modernize many of their operations, unchanged during the long period of their monopoly in overland transport. Some authorities believe that the railroads have suffered their greatest losses not so much because of competition as because they neglected to modernize their service. In the attempt to recover traffic, the railroads in both the United States and the United Kingdom increased the speed of trains and service at the stations, introduced night traffic for goods, abandoned lines and stations with little business,[140] introduced pickup and delivery service by trucks for less-than-carload

lots of freight, and lowered rates on numerous commodities. A timetable for freight traffic (in use in Germany since 1929) was also introduced. In the United Kingdom, the railroads began to accept goods in bulk to be distributed among different consignees, thus giving such shippers the benefit of carload rates.

Railroads in France, Switzerland, Belgium and the Netherlands have taken similar measures. Before World War II most European railroads had introduced door-to-door delivery service in one form or another: in France, in all towns of 5,000 or more, representing 30 per cent of all communities and 70 per cent of the population; in the Netherlands, in principal cities and towns; in Great Britain, in all towns of any size. Even in Egypt, Nigeria and Rhodesia, the railroads provided various forms of collection and delivery service. In many countries they revised schedules and rates, accelerated acceptance and dispatch of

---

140. In the United States, 58 per cent of the rail mileage abandoned with authorization by the ICC had been affected by highway competition. (**57**, pp. 690–94.)

parcels and generally began to provide faster and more convenient service.[141]

On the other hand, the railroads "were not long in perceiving and utilizing for themselves the distinctive advantages of highway transport, both freight and passenger, in the fields where these advantages were most marked." [142] In the United States, they began to operate buses and trucks as early as 1925. In many instances they canceled some local trains that carried relatively few passengers and replaced them with buses with a considerably smaller seating capacity, at the same time making the schedule more frequent. They acquired large fleets of trucks, established the Railway Express Agency and entered into agreements with truck contractors to operate under railway supervision.

The stock of the Railway Express Agency is owned by 68 Class I railroads, and the company is the exclusive agent of some 300 rail carriers, including the 68 stockholding railroads. In 1950, its motor fleet of more than 64,000 units (some 48,061 trucks and 16,365 automobiles and trailers) operated on more than 15,000 route-miles. In addition, the Railway Express Agency used about 190,000 rail-miles, 13,000 steamboat-miles and nearly 100,000 airplane-miles.[143] It handles some 600,000 separate shipments daily, picks up and delivers less-than-carload shipments for the railways, and serves the railways in many other ways.[144]

In Canada, the United Kingdom, France and some other countries the railroads also use trucks for various services in freight transportation and own or rent buses to link various lines or to provide combination excursion trips, and the like.

Regulation of Highway Transport

Along with their adjustments to the new conditions, the railroads initiated a strong drive to subject road transport to government control. The main complaints of the railroads in the United States have been (1) the discriminative, sometimes cutthroat, rates at which individual truckers or small truck companies haul freight and (2) the free use of publicly built and maintained highways by their competitors, while the construction of roadbeds has necessitated large investments and maintenance imposes substantial expenditures every year.

Railroads in other countries have made similar complaints. In Germany, for example, the National Railway traced the losses in railroad business to the absence of established freight rates among motor carriers, their lesser liability for damage and their use of publicly built and maintained roads without fair payments in taxes.[145]

In the United States, the large trucking companies at first supported the railroads in their demand for regulation of road transport.[146] As a matter of fact, commercial trucking, free of restriction and regulation for about fifteen years, caused instability in transport conditions by discriminatory rates and services, especially in favor of large shippers. The rates were kept secret, and private arrangements were sometimes made with complete disregard of cost. In the "twilight zone," the so-called "gypsy" truckers operated as they pleased. Buses also competed with railroads, and among themselves, for customers. Passengers could shop around for bargain fares "to make a load." [147] Amidst this chaos, motor transport grew rapidly, with some contractors going bankrupt and others prospering. The situation was unhealthy, and not only the public and the railroads but also the stronger truck firms desired more stable conditions.

In 1935 Congress passed the Motor Carrier Act, which placed all commercial motor carriers under the jurisdiction of the ICC and established various regulations. Common carriers must set reasonable rates and charges; must make them public and observe them. Giving undue preference to any person or locality is unlawful. The ICC may prescribe the minimum, the maximum or the actual rate if it considers the rate of a common carrier unlawful. The contract carriers are not obliged to publish their rates but must file their schedules with the shippers, charge not less than the minimum rates and give thirty days' notice of a rate reduction. Private carriers are exempt from rate regulations, but must comply with the safety provisions of the act (such as speed limits, liability insurance and safety equipment).

The act permits consolidations and mergers of motor carriers when approved by the ICC as

141. **58,** pp. 339ff.
142. **36,** p. 46.
143. **26,** 1950, p. 210.
144. **54,** p. 122.

145. **47,** p. 619.
146. **54,** p. 423.
147. **28,** pp. 100–02.

consistent with the public interest. To obtain such approval for a combination of railroad with motor carriers, the ICC must be convinced that the transaction will promote the public interest and not restrain competition unduly. Like railroads, motor carriers must issue bills of lading and are liable to the shippers to the same extent. Motor carriers are also subject to various state regulations concerning the safety and protection of highways through the control of the weight and size of trucks and their speed.

Although the act was not designed to regulate motor transport for the benefit of other systems of transportation, it has given the railroads some support by imposing various regulations on the hitherto unrestricted activities of motor carriers.

In France, Germany and some other countries, where diversion of traffic from publicly owned railroads placed a burden on national finances, a solution was sought in a system of licensing for commercial trucks and the denial of licenses to new truck undertakings when this was considered contrary to the public interest — a concept broad enough to protect existing services against competition. In more recent years, national control over road transport has been considered more effective. This policy has been followed, to a lesser or greater extent, in a number of countries, industrialized as well as underdeveloped. The British Transport Act of 1947 put all types of commercial inland transport, including motor carriers, under public ownership and control. The provincial governments of Pakistan have been authorized to nationalize motor transport, particularly passenger transport.[148]

Taxation of Highway Users

In many countries the main controversy between rail carriers and road carriers is whether the latter pay their full share for the use of roads. The railroads maintain that their competitors obtain unfair advantages by their use of roads built and maintained by public funds.

It is true that continuous improvements of highways from public funds provide commercial motor carriers with facilities which they themselves could not have created. It is also true that heavy trucks, particularly truck-combinations, increase the costs of highway construction and maintenance. An adequate pavement for passenger cars and light trucks, with a capacity up to one and one half tons, costs much less than one designed for trucks with licensed capacities up to twenty tons. Damage caused by heavy trucks to the highways is also greater than from passenger cars. The railroads, which are hit mostly by competition from heavy freighters, want them taxed considerably more than they are today.

On the whole and on a national basis, the owners of motor vehicles in the United States are believed to pay highway costs for which they are responsible, although in some states they may pay too much and in others, not enough. If all highway-user taxes were applied only to road building and maintenance, they would actually meet most of the highway bill. Furthermore, in the United States, many thousands of miles of rural roads provide access to property and carry little traffic: the 2.5 million miles of rural roads in the United States — representing 83 per cent of total mileage — accounted for only 13 per cent of all traffic before the war; in 1952, 73 per cent of the road mileage carried only 9 per cent of total traffic.[149] Financial responsibility for such roads should therefore perhaps lie with property owners rather than with the users of motor vehicles.

The perennial problem of the division of highway costs among the various groups of vehicles does not lend itself easily to a neat mathematical solution. A large part of the highway system is designed to serve all vehicles jointly, and no specific cost can be readily attributed to any particular unit of traffic. The vehicles are of widely differing weights and dimensions which are constantly changing. They have different equipment, travel different mileages and speeds, and on different parts of the highway system; and this system itself comprises a diversity of pavement types, designs and costs.[150]

Even if it were possible to calculate exactly the use made of the highways by each type of vehicle, this information still would not solve all the difficulties, because of ignorance of the exact relationship between traffic volume and loads and the width, number, speed and driving characteristics of vehicles; the condition of soils and foundations; the influence of weather on pavements of various types and ages; factors affecting the costs of alignment, grading, paving depths and widths, and maintenance. To deter-

148. **1**, 1951, p. 34.

149. **28**, p. 263; **37**, 1953, pp. 21–22.
150. **28**, p. 261.

mine the relative effects on a particular pavement of different loadings with different types of vehicles, and to work out reasonable and uniform standards of maximum size and weight for motor vehicles, the National Research Council of the United States has carried out intensive tests on a highway section in Maryland (the so-called "Road Test One-Md.") [151] and is engaged in two other tests — in Idaho and Illinois. It is expected that these tests, when completed, may provide a scientific basis for regulating permissible loadings and calculating the appropriate taxation of motor vehicles of varying sizes and weights.

Whether higher charges on buses and heavy trucks would eliminate the difficulties experienced by the railroads from the competition of highway transport is another problem. Motor carriers of freight increasingly handle traffic able to pay about four times the average of rail revenue while their highway fees and taxes constitute only a small part of operating expenses. Increase of the latter would therefore have a relatively small effect.

Outlook

For the near future, highway transport has the brightest prospects of all means of transportation. In the United States and other advanced countries, motor traffic, both personal and commercial, has been growing each year. This trend is likely to continue with increasing population, rising standards of living, improvements in highways and possibly in motor vehicles themselves.

Highway traffic will grow even more rapidly in underdeveloped countries. In many of them, it is only at its beginning and is still beset by

various handicaps — poor roads, shortage of vehicles, tires, parts and gasoline, inadequate repair facilities and an insufficient number of mechanics. All these difficulties can and will be overcome. Experience has shown that people who have never seen a motor vehicle quickly learn to drive it efficiently. Highway transport offers so many tangible advantages to underdeveloped countries that, with the gradual removal of technical and financial obstacles, its increase can be taken for granted.

Motor vehicles of all kinds will be used in the world, and more and more highways will be built by stage construction in underdeveloped areas and of modern design in countries with heavy motor traffic.[152] In the latter, expressways will become increasingly important. Large international projects which seemed fantastic a decade or two ago, such as a highway under the English Channel, may someday become a reality. Pan-American and trans-African systems will be completed and effect closer contacts between Western civilization and remote corners of the earth.

In the race between the motor vehicle and other means of surface transportation, the odds will be on the side of the motor.

---

151. **59**, pp. 5–11 and 78ff.

152. While this book was in press, international data became available showing a considerable expansion in highway mileage in various countries since 1948. To give only a few examples: Australia had about 528,000 miles of highways in 1948 and 814,000 miles in 1951. Corresponding figures for Argentina are 259,000 and 417,-000; for Brazil, 161,000 and 275,000; for India, 239,000 and 433,000; for the Belgian Congo, 62,000 and 113,-000; for Greece, 10,000 and 23,000, and so on. (See **51**, 1953, pp. 12–14; cf. Table 148, p. 402 above.) Though this expansion may be due partly to statistical factors, the 1951 data nevertheless indicate a rapid growth in highway mileage.

CHAPTER 10

WATER TRANSPORTATION

SHIPPING IS ONE of the oldest forms of transportation and the most important in international trade. Ships carry more than three fourths of the total tonnage of goods exchanged among nations and continents.[1] No other means of transportation can replace them in the vital task of distributing raw materials and foodstuffs over long distances.

Passenger travel may be curtailed without serious national consequences; interference with the movement of overseas mails may now be mitigated by cable and radio communication and by air transport; stoppage of the trans-border movement of finished products would react unfavorably on both the exporting and the importing country; but stoppage of the world flow of basic commodities would have a paralyzing effect on the progress of nations. It [i.e., ocean] is the carrier of basic commodities in large quantities and at low rates which renders possible the concentration of materials, machines and men at strategic points where this combination may most efficiently produce an industrial product: it is the refrigerating ship which makes the food products of one area the daily diet of the world.[2]

Historically, it is shipping that populated the Western Hemisphere and Oceania, by carrying throngs of Europeans across the Atlantic and the Pacific. It has also fostered the industrial growth of Europe, providing it with raw materials from previously inaccessible regions, and has encouraged the growth of its population through additional, water-borne food supplies.

While practically all intercontinental trade is carried by ships, much intracontinental trade is also water-borne. Coastal and intercoastal traffic is of great importance to the United States, the United Kingdom, Norway, Japan and, in somewhat lesser degree, numerous other countries. Because of their forbidding topography and inadequate overland transport facilities, South America and Africa ship much of their east-west and north-south cargo along their coasts. Traffic in the Pacific archipelago moves either from island to island or along the coasts. Inland waterways account for a considerable share in the domestic and transit traffic of Germany, the Netherlands, Belgium, France and a score of other countries. In the United States, the Great Lakes with their canals have played an inestimable role in the movement of iron ore to the steel plants in the East and of coal to the West; grain moves from the northern Mississippi Valley and Canada via the Great Lakes to the eastern parts of both countries and to the seaboard for export. The economy of Germany, the Low Countries and Switzerland would be most adversely affected if the Rhine were closed to traffic. The importance of the Volga for the USSR, the Danube for eastern Europe, the Nile for Egypt, the Yangtze for China, can hardly be exaggerated.

The exchange of goods among continents, countries, and regions within countries would never have developed to the present level, except for waterways and progress in shipping — the means of cheap, though slow, transportation of bulky and heavy commodities.

FROM DUGOUT TO MODERN OCEAN VESSEL

Nature raises obstacles to overland transportation — mountains, swamps, deserts and impenetrable forests — but it provides waterways that man can use for communication and trade. In the beginning, much of humanity settled on river banks, around the lakes and along the sea coasts. Men moved about on rafts or in dugouts, hugging the coast, to engage in fishing and barter. Although much time passed before they learned to build boats that could brave the weather changes and whims of the sea, they avoided the labor of building and maintaining trails and roads by taking to the water.

Shipping, which has developed and grown in the keen competition of vessel against vessel, began when man discovered that what floated on water could be directed toward a goal.

Early Water Craft

The earliest craft must have been a single log of buoyant wood or several logs tied together

1. 71, p. x.
2. 79, p. 1.

to make a raft, though some primitive tribes also used reed rafts. Dugouts hollowed out by fire, dating from the Stone Age, have been found among the remains of Swiss lake dwellings. The next step was a canoe covered with bark or hide, first with a wicker framework, then built around planks; the outer covering was fastened to the wood with cord, later with pegs. A further advance came when rigid boards were fitted closely together.

Boats propelled by oars and sails were developed as early as three millenniums before our era. Used by the Phoenicians, the greatest seafarers of antiquity, and by the Egyptians, they gradually attained substantial carrying capacity. As commercial and military water-borne traffic developed, two distinct types of ships were built — the warship and the merchantman. The first was a long, narrow ship, fast and easily maneuvered, propelled chiefly by a crew of oarsmen though sails were used when possible. For the merchantman, carrying capacity was more important than speed, and a large crew would have been costly and would have taken too much precious space. A merchantman was therefore built as a broad, heavy sailing ship that moved with the wind and used oars only on rare occasions. These two basic types underwent many improvements and modifications but maintained their essential features for many centuries.[3]

The expansion of commerce throughout the length and breadth of the Mediterranean and other coastal regions led to the increase in the size of ships. Many could carry 250 tons, and occasionally much larger ships were built. For centuries, however, navigational instruments were unknown, and sailors followed only the seamarks, and the sun by day and the stars by night. In time, they developed charts which gave detailed descriptions of dangerous places, harbors, tides and prevailing winds. Lighthouses were erected at important harbors, such as Alexandria.

In all parts of the world people who lived close to water designed ships which resembled each other, because the same material and power were used — wood and human labor. The earliest known water craft in the British Isles was the coracle, a kind of canoe with a wicker framework covered with skins. Julius Caesar saw this contrivance for the first time in

Britain since more advanced types of ships were used in the Mediterranean in his day. He had some coracles made and described their construction.[4]

In the north, communication by sea was established between the Scandinavian countries in the Stone Age, again by means of rafts and hollowed tree trunks. By about 1000 B.C., the Norwegians were building ships of wood which could carry as many as fifty men. Much later came the long, swift viking ships of various sizes — some with 64 or more oars. In these ships, the intrepid Norwegians set out on voyages far from their shores and the usual trade routes. Some of their expeditions included an impressive number of ships. In A.D. 892 two viking fleets totaling 330 vessels attacked England.[5]

Galleys, Caravels and Indiamen

The medieval ship was a galley with heavy oars some 30–50 feet long, each oar requiring the strength of three or four men. As commerce expanded, it became increasingly necessary to protect heavily laden ships against pirates. The galley was too slow for safety and was gradually superseded by the sailing vessel, which, however, retained some of the galley's features. There was keen competition among French, English, Genoese, Spanish, Portuguese and others in designing ships better adapted to long voyages and better able to outride any weather. In the fifteenth century, ships of 1,000 tons were built, though most vessels averaged 400–500 tons. The sailing "caravel," introduced by the Spanish and Portuguese, was used in the great geographical discoveries of the fifteenth and sixteenth centuries. Before the adoption of steam power, other seafaring countries had built much larger ships, some 200 feet long.[6]

With the opening of the sea route to India by Vasco da Gama and the discovery of the New World, trade expanded rapidly. The powerful East India Company established regular service with the Far East, by means of a large fleet of "Indiamen." These ships had a gross weight of as much as 1,500 tons, carried large crews and were fully armed. For trade with other parts of the world, the Company built smaller ships, the "free traders," which had to be operated eco-

---

3. **52**, pp. 41–42.

4. **39**, p. 4. Coracles are still used along the Atlantic coast of Ireland. **49**, p. 1.

5. **54**, p. 109.

6. **39**, pp. 61-62.

nomically and to use every bit of cargo space to meet the keen competition of rival merchants.[7]

The sailing vessel that typifies advance in shipbuilding in the United States was the schooner, first built in 1713. It was faster, sailed closer to the wind and required a smaller crew than other sailing vessels of its time.[8]

Clipper Ships

In the first half of the nineteenth century, the shipyards of the United States developed the clipper, a sailing vessel of fine design and great speed — almost double the speed of English ships. With favoring trade winds, the clipper could make 12–15 miles an hour. Its ton registry was 3,000 or more.[9] Although the clipper, built of softwood, was less durable than the British ships made of oak or teak, it was a very efficient cargo carrier and, because of its speed, was used particularly for high-value goods. The tonnage of American shipping grew rapidly, and 90 per cent or more of foreign trade shipments were carried in national bottoms. The fame of the clippers was such that many were sold abroad.

The clipper was not only faster than foreign ships, but also initially cheaper, ton for ton, although the more solid, copper-bottomed and copper-fastened British ship was more economical in the long run. The hull of the softwood ship became waterlogged after a few voyages, and its sailing qualities deteriorated.[10] When the so-called California clippers appeared, with their tremendous spread of canvas, "there was nothing afloat that could live with them in strong winds . . . In beauty, power, and performance they were a revelation to the world." [11] With its greater length and spread of sail, the clipper had "a turn of speed which European shipowners had not only never achieved but never attempted." [12] The clipper, built for long voyages, was in great demand during the gold rush in California. Overland routes were slow and dangerous, and shipping companies were swamped with requests for space.[13]

After landing passengers at the Golden Gate,

the clippers proceeded to China to pick up a cargo for New York or London — tea, spices, silk, dried fruits. The clippers began to find their way into other trade, too. By the middle of the nineteenth century, they were a serious threat to British supremacy on the sea, but when the clipper was at the pinnacle of its glory, the days of sailing vessels were numbered.

The Advent of Steam and Iron

A new era opened in both shipbuilding and ocean transport when the steam engine replaced the sail as motive power, and when iron, and later steel, replaced wood in the ship's structure. There was a close interrelationship between these two developments, since the modern marine engine could not be used successfully in a wooden hull nor could sails propel a big iron ship.

The use of wood limited the length and size of ships: on ships more than 300 feet long, wood did not provide the stability necessary for an ocean voyage. Metal ships were stronger; the hull, thinner than that of a wooden ship, weighed less, and cargo capacity therefore could be greater without affecting buoyancy. Even more important was the fact that iron vessels could be much larger, the only limitations being the strength of the engine and the availability of cargo and port facilities. Steel, used for ocean-going vessels since 1879, proved to be an even better material.[14]

The earliest steamboat was built in France, in 1780. A small steam craft built in England in 1802 was found efficient for both freight and passenger service. A few steamboats of various types were also built in the United States about this time.[15] The first practical steamboat, Robert Fulton's "Clermont," began regular service over the 130 miles between New York and Albany in 1807.

Low-pressure steam engines were used first on small craft in passenger and mail service in European and American waters, but for some years the steamship remained less efficient than the sailing vessel for ocean voyages. The low-pressure engine consumed too much fuel, and the usual sea routes lacked conveniently located coaling stations. Not until 1837 was the first ship, the "Great Western," launched for transoceanic service at Bristol, England. The next

---

7. **66**, pp. 268–69.
8. **44**, p. 61.
9. **39**, p. 63; **44**, p. 50.
10. The British ship was splendidly finished and carried a double outfit of sails, rigging and other appurtenances. (**58**, p. 203.)
11. **52**, p. 235.
12. **85**, p. 7.
13. **51**, p. 241.

14. **57**, p. 542.
15. **40**, p. 54; **66**, p. 285.

year it made its initial trip to New York in thirteen and one half days.[16]

Sail and Wood versus Steam and Iron

Rivalry in shipbuilding — sail versus steam and wood versus iron — continued throughout the nineteenth century. The United Kingdom spearheaded the shift to the new source of power and the new material. Abundantly supplied with accessible coal, an advanced metallurgical industry and skilled labor, Britain led in developing ocean-going steamships of iron, later of steel, and established and fueled coaling stations along main routes. Geographic location made Britain's ports natural stopovers and entrepôts for world trade and its indented coast brought its harbors close to production centers. Its position as a great colonial power and the workshop of the world, its supply of coal for the return cargo, its capital resources, and the demand of its growing population for foodstuffs and raw materials from foreign lands were other decisive factors in securing Britannia's position as ruler of the waves.

The United States lagged far behind. Its shipbuilders had inexhaustible supplies of cheap softwood at hand, while the young iron industry was unable to produce plates at prices competitive with those of British shipyards and the high tariff made it impossible to import plates from the United Kingdom. The shipbuilding industry led in designing sailing vessels but was backward in the construction of iron hulls and steamships.[17] The country accordingly launched small wooden steamships and sailing vessels. Steamboats were used extensively on the excellent inland waters and in protected bays and sounds, but the proportion of the country's foreign trade carried by domestic merchant marine fell by more than half around 1870.[18]

---

16. A small American-built sailing vessel, the "Savannah," with an auxiliary steam engine, crossed the Atlantic in 1819 in twenty-seven days, operating partly by sail and partly by steam. (**51**, p. 240.)

17. **59**, p. 302.

18. Many other factors contributed to the decline of the United States merchant marine. The building of railroads promised greater profits and attracted capital (cf. Chap. 8, pp. 344–49); the opening of the West offered unlimited opportunities to venturous minds; the growing industries were profitable fields for investment and initiative. Also, the losses sustained in shipping during the Civil War and the sale of some shipping abroad further reduced the size of the merchant fleet, and the decreasing importance of some old trade routes made the shipping business less attractive.

Sailing vessels, however, held their own even on ocean routes for a time. Their great advantage was that steamers had to carry much coal for long voyages, since fueling stations were few and scattered. Freight rates were lower on the sailing ships, and some products, such as jute and rice, could not bear the high transportation charges of the steam vessels. Sail almost monopolized the shipment of grain from North America to Europe; in 1882, some 550 sailing vessels carried about a million and a quarter tons of wheat and barley. Through the 1880's, nearly all freight on the Australian run was carried in sailing vessels, together with a considerable proportion of the mail and passengers.[19]

Growth of Modern Merchant Fleets

Even with the advantages of free power, comparatively large cargo capacity and the need for only a small crew, the sailing vessel could not handle the growing volume of international trade and the large-scale emigration from Europe. Its dependence on weather and its comparative slowness and uncertainty of schedule were additional handicaps, and with the introduction of engines consuming less coal per unit of power, its defeat by the steamship became inevitable. In 1890 the world's registered tonnage in sail exceeded that in steam, but the opening of the twentieth century saw the doom of sail. In 1900, sailing vessels counted only 7.2 million gross registered tons out of the world's 29.6 million; in 1910, 4.6 million tons out of 41.9 million; in 1920, 3.4 million out of 57.3 million tons. In 1953, the tonnage of the world's sailing vessels represented only 0.6 million out of the total 94.0 million. (See Table 154 and cf. Figure 84.)

Technical Progress

The first steamers were propelled by paddle wheels and carried sails as auxiliary power and as a safeguard in case the propeller system broke down. Then the screw or propeller came into rather general use by shipbuilders in England and some other countries though the United States held back somewhat. Around 1880 twin screws were introduced on naval vessels, and later, three and four screws were used for the largest ocean liners.

The early steam engine had a pressure of only

---

19. **52**, pp. 242–45.

TABLE 154

MERCHANT VESSELS: SAILING SHIPS AND STEAMSHIPS
IN THE WORLD, 1850–1953

| Year | Number | | Gross Registered Tons, in Thousands[a] | |
	Sailing Ships	Steam-ships[b]	Sailing Ships	Steam-ships[c]
1850	...	...	9,092	279
1860	...	...	13,022	779
1870	...	...	13,500	2,050
1875	57,258	5,519	15,099	3,590
1880	48,584	6,392	13,872	4,401
1885	43,692	8,394	12,867	6,719
1890	33,879	9,638	10,540	8,286
1895	17,032	13,256	9,020	16,888
1900	11,942	15,898	7,245	22,369
1905	10,597	19,153	6,610	29,963
1910	8,050	22,008	4,624	37,291
1915	6,212	24,508	3,880	45,729
1920	5,082	26,513	3,409	53,905
1925	3,711	29,205	2,261	62,380
1930	2,717	29,996	1,584	68,024
1935	1,908	29,071	1,159	63,727
1939	1,423	29,763	930	68,509
1947	1,170	29,463	842	83,514
1950	880	30,852	720	84,583
1951	886	31,226	716	87,245
1952	857	31,461	688	90,180
1953	806	31,797	626	93,352

Sources: **88**, Vol. 5, pp. 60–65; **15**, 1936, p. 410; 1948, p. 561; 1954, p. 615; **68**, 1953, Appendix Volume, Section 6, p. 26.

a. The space within the hull of the ship and its enclosed superstructure is measured in either gross or net tons. *Gross tonnage* is the total cubic content of the ship in units of 100 cubic feet (2.83 cubic meters in the metric system), called tons. The registered *net tonnage* of a ship, measured by the same units, represents that part of the vessel which is available for cargo and passengers, after subtraction from gross tonnage of the space used for machinery, crew and the general operation of the ship. The table excludes vessels of less than 100 gross tons, wooden vessels on the Great Lakes and vessels on the Caspian Sea. For sailing ships: net registered tons, prior to 1920.

b. Since 1895: steamships and motorships.

c. 1875–90: net registered tons.

about 10–12 pounds to a square inch. It was replaced by a higher-pressure compound engine that gave the steamship greater speed and enabled it to compete with the sailing vessel in carrying cargo. In the last decades of the nineteenth century, efforts to make the marine engine more efficient and economical led to the introduction of the reciprocating engine of triple and quadruple expansion.

At about the same time, the turbine was invented almost simultaneously in Sweden and England. After many improvements, it came to have such compactness, lightness and freedom from vibration and, at the same time, such simplicity of construction, operation and repair, that it has become very popular for large, fast passenger liners. Some ships also use the turbine to advantage in combination with the reciprocating engine, or in combination with electric power (the turbo-electric drive).[20]

The diesel, an internal combustion engine, appeared in the twentieth century, and now rivals the turbine in popularity. The diesel needs no boilers, uses less fuel, and enables the ship to go further without refueling, but the initial cost is relatively high. While diesel engines continue to increase in number and are used on a share of the larger vessels of foreign flags and on all submarines, the turbine and the turbo-electric engine grew most rapidly in popularity between 1939 and 1952, particularly in the United States.[21]

Speed has risen from a few knots to more than thirty. The time for the Atlantic crossing has been shortened from more than twelve days to about four and a half, and passenger capacity has risen from about 100 to some 3,000.

Space does not permit even a brief description of all the changes in marine engineering in the last hundred years.[22] There has been a complete break with the past in the world's navigation and greater progress than in all preceding periods. The most experienced seafarer of ancient times would regard the modern ocean vessel as a leviathan propelled by devilish power.

The past, however, has not wholly disappeared from the world's waters. Buoyant logs and reed rafts still carry natives along the northwest coast of Australia and around the Pacific Islands as at the beginning of skill in navigation. The early British craft can still be seen on waters in some parts of Ireland and England, although the wicker framework of this canoe may be covered with tarred canvas, rather than hides.[23] As in other fields of human activity, various phases of the development through which mankind has passed are exemplified and recapitulated for posterity.

20. **44**, p. 65.
21. See Table 158, p. 458.
22. For such description, see **65**, pp. 366ff; **44**, pp. 48ff; **64**, pp. 261–66.
23. **39**, p. 4; **60**, p. 7.

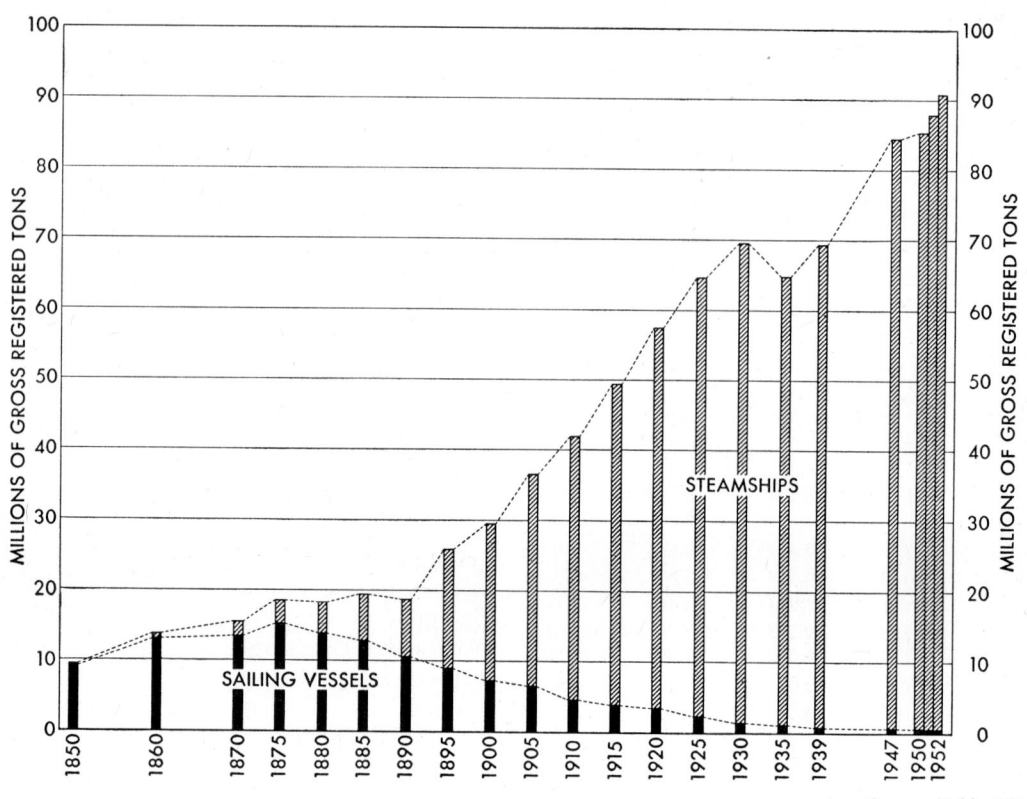

FIGURE 84. MERCHANT VESSELS: SAILING SHIPS AND STEAMSHIPS IN THE WORLD, 1850–1952

Source: Table 154

Marine Fuel

When steamships were introduced, coal was used to raise steam, and large vessels required considerable bunker space near the boilers. Much cargo space, and some of the best space, was sacrificed for fuel. Otherwise, the ship had to stop frequently at coaling stations, thus lengthening the voyage.

Fuel oil offered many advantages. In raising steam in marine boilers, one ton of oil, on the average, does the work of one and a half tons of coal. Moreover, it is cleaner and can be stored anywhere, thus freeing some of the best space for cargo. It can be pumped into the ship or, as was done at the beginning, even carried in ballast tanks. Transporting, storing and stowing oil require less labor; fewer firemen are needed, and therefore less food and wages and less space for crew accommodations. Also, while it required about 36 hours to coal a passenger liner for a transatlantic crossing, it takes only 12 hours to provide it with oil for both the crossing and the return trip, with resulting savings in the time spent in port and in wages.[24]

In view of these and other advantages, oil rapidly displaced coal and undermined the position of many coaling stations. In 1925, 28 per cent of the world's merchant shipping tonnage used oil as fuel for steam and internal-combustion engines; in 1952, 85 per cent.[25] Special ships — tankers — began to be built to transport oil and other liquids in bulk, the first in 1886. In 1900, the world had 109 tankers totaling 356,448 gross tons; in 1920, 540 tankers totaling 2.9 million gross tons; in 1939, 1,571 tankers of 11 million gross tons; in July 1952, 3,049 tankers of 20 million gross tons. In 1952, the United States owned 558 tankers of 4.4 million gross tons; Great Britain, 711 of 4.5 million gross tons and Norway, 361 of 3.1 million gross tons — together, more than half of the world's tankers and six tenths of the total tonnage.[26]

Oil-fueled ships are replacing many of the coal-burning ships sunk during World War II.[27] Many new tankers have come from the ship-

24. **46**, pp. 8–9.

25. **88**, Vol. 5, p. 72; **44**, pp. 66–67; **68**, 1953, Appendix Volume, Section 6, pp. 13–14.

26. **35**, 1950, p. 297; **19**, p. 58; **68**, 1953, Appendix Volume, Section 6, p. 14. Cf. **89**, pp. 912–13.

27. **78**, p. 365.

yards, some of them of 30,000 and even 45,000 tons deadweight.[28] The average speed of tankers rose from 9 to 11 knots between 1900 and 1939 and to about 14 knots in recent years.

OCEAN TRANSPORTATION

Shipping proceeds over natural and artificial waterways, inland waters and great ocean lanes. Some routes are of only local importance, others link the continents and serve worldwide traffic. Though the great ocean routes are of vital importance in foreign trade, inland waterways and coastwise navigation exceed them in volume of traffic. However, many rivers and canals serve as feeders to ocean traffic, and a substantial part of their cargo is for transoceanic shipments.

Currents and trade winds once determined the direction of sailing vessels across the oceans. As steam-powered ships came into use, such factors as the sphericity of the earth, the land masses between trading areas, location of fueling stations, cost of fuel and port and canal charges, storm areas and obstructions such as icebergs have come to influence the direction of ocean routes.[29]

OCEAN ROUTES

Ocean traffic follows seven major trunk routes and several auxiliary routes varying in importance. (See Figure 85.) Some of these routes have played a paramount role in world history ever since it became possible to ply them. Others, such as the Suez Canal route or the Panama Canal route, came into being when specific installations for shipping were created. The volume and character of traffic vary from route to route, depending on climatic, economic and political conditions. Shifts from one important source of a raw material to another may reduce traffic on one route and increase it on another. Politics may endanger a route and force traffic to shift elsewhere.

The movement of the most-traded commodities among continents and countries is described in Chapter 4; the main sea routes are briefly outlined below.

Steamship lines operate on a fixed route but may utilize from one to four major trunk routes in scheduling the sailings.[30] In contrast, tramp

vessels may follow any ocean route in their search for cargo.

The North Atlantic Route

This trunk line connects the chief commercial and industrial centers of the world. It carries the heaviest freight and passenger traffic in the world's fastest and largest vessels and engages more than one sixth of the world's shipping. A greater number of passenger liners ply this route than any other in the world, and freighters carry high-grade cargo and mail. To approximate a great circle as closely as possible, the North Atlantic route skirts the coast of North America northward to the Grand Bank off Newfoundland and then curves across the Atlantic.[31] Branches extend westward to the ports on the St. Lawrence River and southward to the Caribbean. The terminals are the ports of Europe, Mediterranean Africa and the eastern and Gulf coasts of North America. The ship lane is about fifty miles wide and like some other routes shifts with the season: equatorward during the winter and poleward during the summer.[32]

The Pacific Routes

Of the two Pacific routes, the more important and the more traveled is the northern trunk connecting North America and Asia, from San Diego to Prince Rupert and Alaska on the American side via the great circle of Yokohama, Shanghai and Manila, on the Asiatic side. Some transoceanic freight is shipped across the United States by rail to be transferred to ships taking this route.

The southern route runs from the western coast of North America via Hawaii and the Fiji Islands to Australia and New Zealand; or via Tahiti direct to Australia and New Zealand. Again, shipment over transcontinental railroads enables various parts of the United States to share in this trade with Oceania. This route has

---

28. **5**, July-September 1949, p. 23. Deadweight tonnage is the maximum weight of all cargo-fuel, passengers and goods that a vessel can carry when loaded to its deep-load line.

29. **58**, p. 256.

30. "Fixed route" should not be understood, however,

as an unchangeable and definite waterway. The expanse of the ocean is such that the outward and inward voyage may follow the same "fixed" route, but be many miles apart.

31. Because of the spherical shape of the earth, the shortest distance between any two points at approximately the same latitude is the arc of a great circle, rather than a line along the same parallel. Yokohama is directly west of San Francisco, but the shortest route between them curves from California to the Aleutian Islands, and then southward: 4,536 miles via the great circle; 4,709 miles by the direct route.

32. **67**, p. 26.

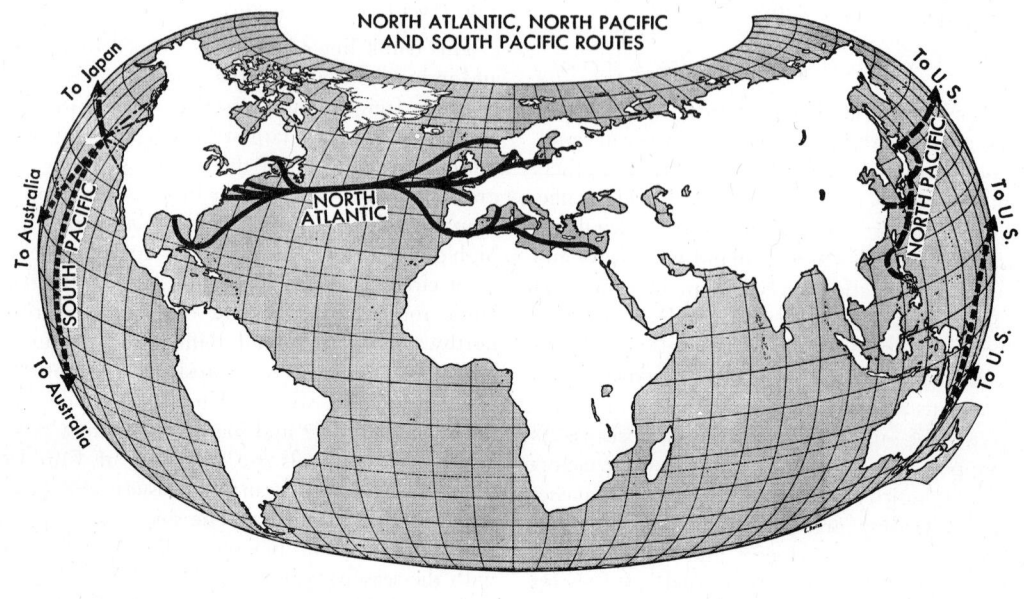

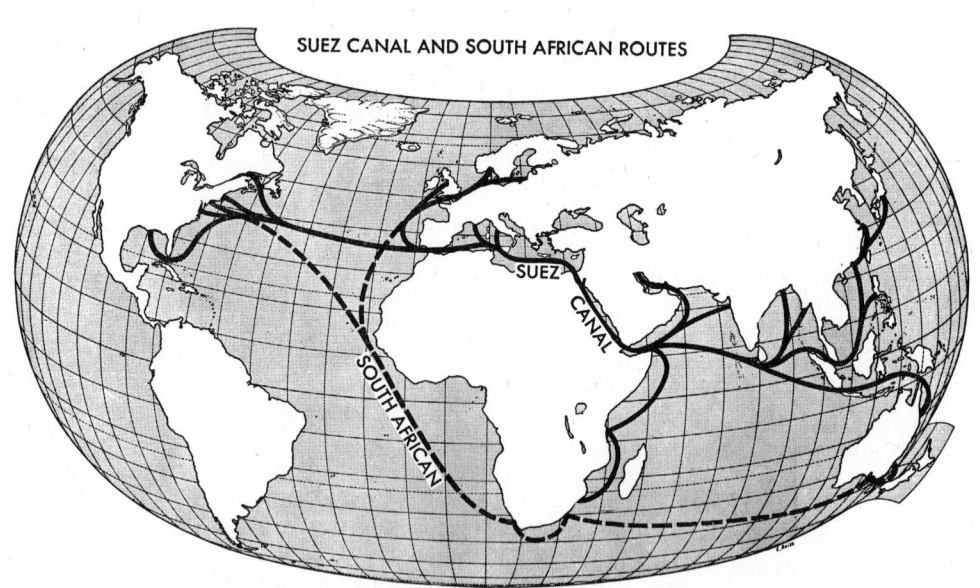

FIGURE 85. MAJOR OCEAN ROUTES OF THE WORLD

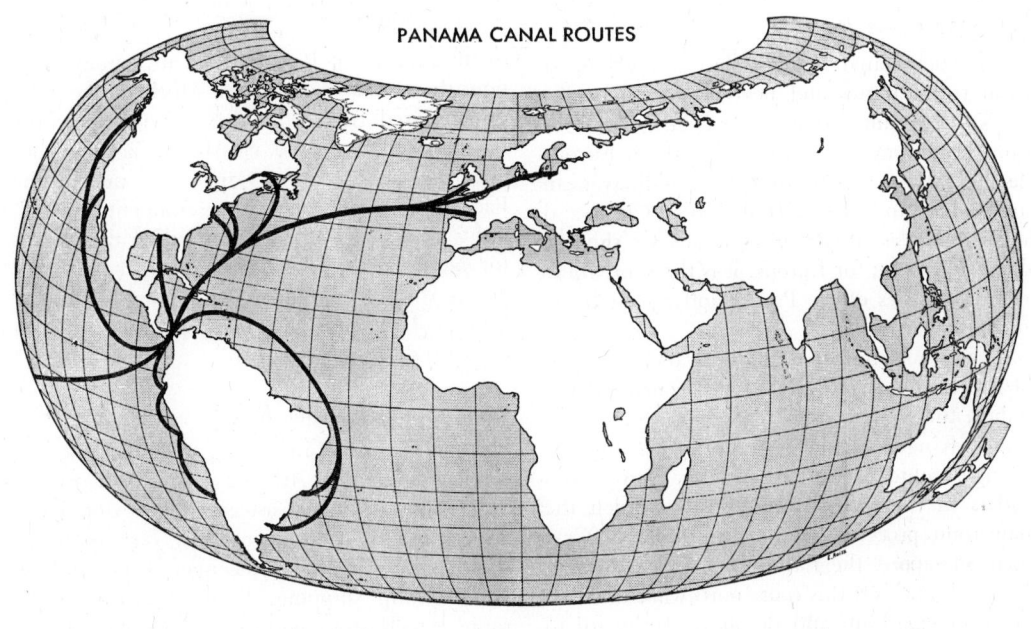

PANAMA CANAL ROUTES

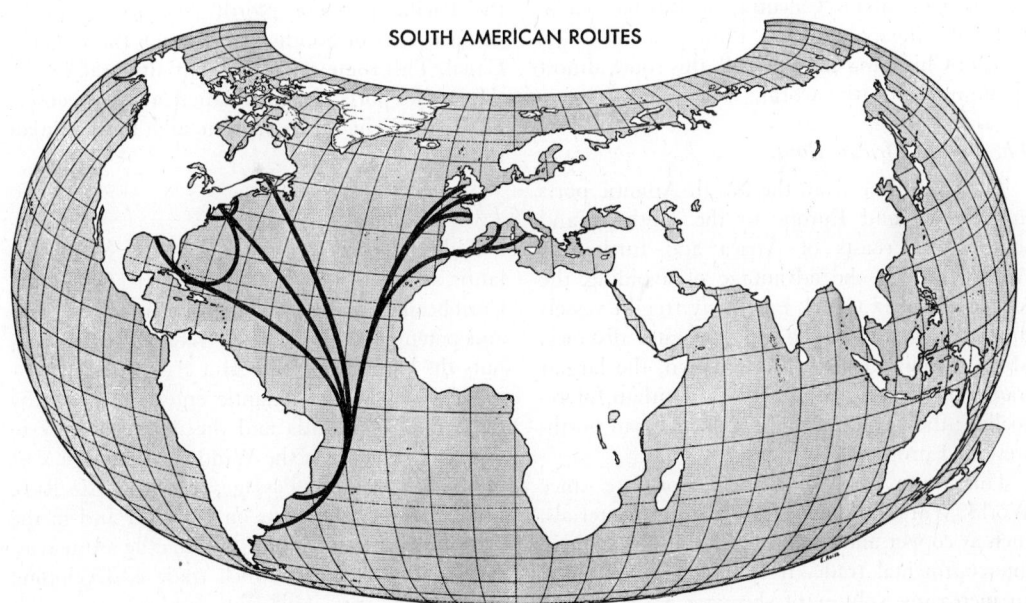

SOUTH AMERICAN ROUTES

FIGURE 85—*continued*

been increasing in importance since World War II.

The Suez Canal Route

The Suez Canal route is one of the longest ocean trunk routes and next in importance to the North Atlantic. It stretches from the eastern United States and western and southern Europe via the Suez Canal through the Mediterranean and Red Sea to India, the East Indies, China and Japan. Many essential raw materials are shipped along this route; for Europe, it is the short route to the countries of the Pacific and *the* highway for passenger traffic.

This trunk route has many branch lines or feeders east and west of the Suez Canal. At Gibraltar, the feeders from the United States, the United Kingdom and western Europe unite in a single route to Suez. Southern Europe has feeders in the Mediterranean. From Aden the main route proceeds eastward to Colombo (Ceylon), Singapore, the East Indies and Australia. Feeders branch off this route northward at Aden to the Persian Gulf and Bombay; southward to Zanzibar, Mauritius and Delagoa Bay; northward at Colombo to Calcutta and Burma; northward at Singapore to the Philippines and the ports of China and Japan. In all, this route almost circumnavigates the world.

The South African Route

The trunk line from the North Atlantic ports in America and Europe to the southern and southeastern coasts of Africa and further to Australasia has the advantage of avoiding the tolls at the Suez Canal. For many freight vessels this outweighs the handicap of greater distance. Much shipping calls at Cape Town, the largest trade center on this route, and at Durban for recoaling; the heaviest freight traffic is from northwestern Europe to Australasia.

This route has grown in importance since World War II. Many strategic raw materials, such as copper and uranium, are moved on it in intercontinental trade. It is likely to command an increasing volume of shipping as Africa expands production and develops inland transportation.

The Panama Canal Route

The opening of the Panama Canal in 1914 created a new ocean highway and stimulated the foreign trade of the United States and other countries of the Western Hemisphere. Steamships plying between North Atlantic ports and the west coast of South America used to go via the Straits of Magellan or transferred their cargo to the railroad at Panama and at Tehuantepec; now they cross the Isthmus. Much of the shipping cleared from United States ports for the Pacific once proceeded via the Suez Canal but now uses the Panama Canal. Far out in the Pacific, however, there is a competitive "twilight" zone about equally distant by either route: for New York, the line connecting equidistant points runs near Manila and Hong Kong; for Liverpool, near the large ports of Japan and east of Australia.

The South American Route

Traffic has been increasing on the trunk line connecting North Atlantic ports with Brazil, Argentina and other eastern countries of South America. This course is used by various steamship lines with heavy passenger traffic and by much tramp shipping. Feeders to this trunk route extend from ports in the Caribbean and the Gulf of Mexico. One branch line connects the Pacific ports of North America with the eastern ports of South America, via the Panama Canal. This route carries little, if any, traffic with the Pacific ports of South America: the steamers hauling freight for these ports take the Isthmian route.

The Caribbean Route

Although various branches of the North Atlantic route handle much of the traffic in the Caribbean and the Gulf of Mexico, the present and potential importance of trade with that area puts the Caribbean route in a class by itself.

Vessels from the Atlantic enter this route by the Straits of Florida and the main gateway to the Caribbean is via the Windward Passage, east of Cuba. The Mona Passage, east of Puerto Rico, is also used. Many ports on the Gulf and in the Caribbean serve this route and handle an increasing volume of traffic. Much trade is developing within the area itself and between the Gulf Coast and the ports to the south. There are so many separate routes in this region, sometimes called the "American Mediterranean," that what is generally called the Caribbean route represents virtually a system of routes.[33]

---

33. For more detailed descriptions of major trunk lines see **39**, pp. 98–103; **44**, pp. 181–200.

INTEROCEANIC CANALS

Canals are artificial channels built to accommodate and develop water-borne traffic. They may link two open seas, shortening the voyage between them, or may form part of a country's inland waterways.[34] The first are usually deep and comparatively short, the latter shallow and long. A third type comprises extensions of ocean routes to inland ports, with channels of sufficient depth to permit the passage of ocean-going ships. Such a canal makes an interior city virtually a seaport.

The Suez Canal

The Suez Canal, the oldest major oceanic canal, is a vital artery in the entire system of the world's water transportation. As H. J. Schonfield puts it, "The world without the Suez Canal is now almost unthinkable."[35] To Great Britain, more than any other country, it has been of great commercial and strategic importance from the beginning, as the "key to India" and Britain's other far-flung territories in the Far East.

The Suez Canal shortened the route to the Far East by several thousand miles. The distance from London to Bombay is 10,800 miles via the Cape of Good Hope and a little more than 6,300 miles via the Canal, saving some 24 days in those times. The Canal shortened the voyage between Trieste and Bombay by more than 7,000 miles.[36]

The advantages of a link between the Mediterranean and the Red Sea for trade with countries along the Persian Gulf were recognized as early as 2000 B.C. About that time, Pharaoh Sesostris connected one of the Nile's Delta channels, the Pelusiac Branch, with the Red Sea, via the Bitter Lakes. (See Figure 86.) This canal was open to small craft for some thousand years, then fell into disuse and was filled with silt. About 600 B.C. another Pharaoh, Necho, attempted to re-excavate the canal with the use of 120,000 slaves but was persuaded to abandon the enterprise in the midst of the work by the warning of an oracle that he was preparing the way for a barbarian invader. Less than a century later, Darius, a Persian ruler of Egypt, restored and enlarged the canal. The changing fortunes of Egypt, intermittently free or invaded, led at

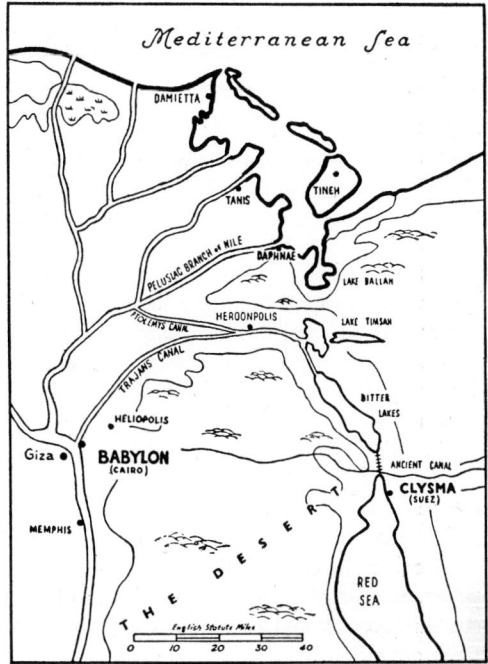

Courtesy of Constellation Books (**81**)

FIGURE 86. THE ISTHMUS OF SUEZ: LINK BETWEEN THE NILE AND THE RED SEA IN ANCIENT TIMES

times to the destruction of the canal or to its renovation.

The Roman emperor Trajan (A.D. 98) made it navigable by linking it with the main stream of the Nile. It was out of commission again from the third century until the Arab conquerors opened it in the seventh century. Finally, some 130–140 years later, it was closed by another ruler and remained in disuse for many centuries.[37]

From the seventeenth century on, many statesmen and merchants advocated a direct link between the Mediterranean and the Red Sea, but technicians believed this impossible because of a difference of over 30 feet in the level of the two. Not until 1853 did surveys establish that there was actually no such difference and that a direct channel through the Isthmus of Suez was entirely practical. The Suez Canal was built by a French company according to the plan of Ferdinand de Lesseps, whose vigor and perseverance triumphed over numerous difficulties and the strong opposition of Great Britain, which feared that a canal would compete with the Cape route, largely under British control.

---

34. For discussion of inland canals, see pp. 488–91.
35. **81**, p. 124.
36. **88**, Vol. V, p. 90.

37. **81**, pp. 4–5; cf. **43**, p. 1.

The Canal, opened in 1869, is about 101 miles long and is at sea level, without locks. After leaving Port Said it passes between banks created from dredged materials to the Bitter Lakes,[38] deep enough for free navigation, then resumes at the end of the lakes and continues to the Gulf of Suez. (See Figure 87.) The average speed of vessels passing through the Canal is 7.5 miles per hour.

Sailing vessels could not use the Canal since the Red Sea, about 1,200 miles long, is too calm for navigation by sail, but traffic increased rapidly with the development of steamship lines. Growth of through traffic has necessitated various improvements to enable ships of 20,000 or more tons to pass without difficulty.[39] The initial depth of 24 feet was increased gradually to 39 feet. In 1949 the Suez Canal Company and Egypt concluded an agreement for further deepening of the Canal, to be completed within five years. A by-pass, seven and a half miles long, is to be cut between Kantara and Balah, to speed up traffic in the opposite direction.

The Canal is held by the Suez Canal Company, an Egyptian joint stock company. The British government owns 353,000 out of 800,000 shares.[40] Toll charges are imposed on all ships, including warships. The rates were high; passenger dues were so high, in fact, that some liners used to disembark their passengers for transfer overland by rail and to re-embark them after the vessel had passed through the Canal. The steadily rising traffic after World War II enabled the Company to reduce the tolls in 1951 for both laden vessels and ships in ballast.

The Suez Canal has been an international waterway practically from its beginning. According to the Convention of 1888, signed by nine maritime countries, it must "always be free and open, in times of war as in times of peace, to

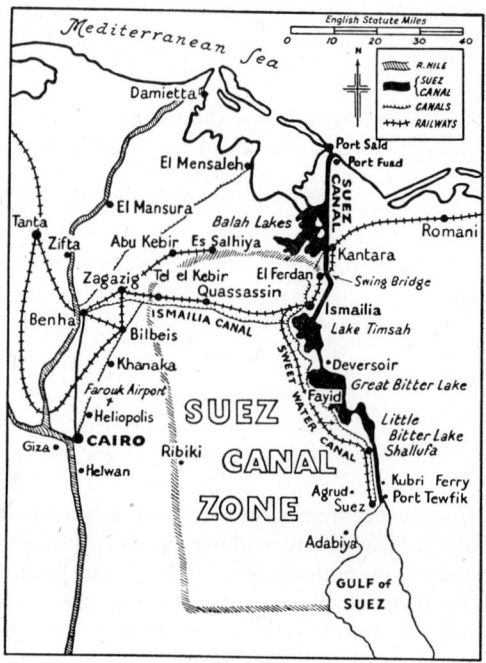

Courtesy of Constellation Books (81)

FIGURE 87. THE SUEZ CANAL

every vessel of commerce or of war without distinction of flag." During World War II, however, Italy and Germany defied the Convention (Article 4) forbidding any act of hostility against free navigation of the Canal, and bombed and mined it as much as they could. Great Britain, in turn, was prepared to block the Canal if worst came to worst, in disregard of the Convention.[41]

The concession under which the Canal was built expires in 1968. Since 1951 Egypt has been demanding the withdrawal of British troops from the Canal Zone and the restoration of its sovereignty over this area. The conflict was settled in 1954, when Great Britain agreed to withdraw its troops and technicians from the Suez within twenty months after the signing of a formal agreement. It reserved the right of re-entry in case any Arab state or Turkey is attacked during the next seven years.[42]

The Panama Canal

The Panama Canal, about 50 miles long, is the shortest route between points on the Atlantic

38. Both lakes (Great Bitter and Little Bitter) were dry for centuries. It took about half a year to fill them after the Suez Canal was built and the water began to flow in. **81**, pp. 127–28.

39. In 1947, for example, a giant floating dock of 50,000 tons was towed through the Canal in two sections; a U.S. aircraft carrier, 890 feet long, passed through in 1948 — the longest ship ever to make the transit. **81**, p. 126.

40. Initially blocks of shares were reserved for all Western countries but France and the Egyptian government acquired 384,802 shares out of 400,000, because of the lack of interest of other countries. The United Kingdom and the United States did not purchase a single share; Russia bought 174 shares, Germany 20, Denmark 7 and Sweden and Norway one. **81**, p. 35.

41. **81**, pp. 110–11.

42. This was not a conflict between Egypt and the Suez Canal Company, but between Egypt and Great Britain. Political issues such as the international status of the Sudan complicated the conflict.

and the Pacific. The distance from New York to San Francisco via the Straits of Magellan is 13,135 miles and via the Panama Canal, 5,262 miles; to Sydney, Australia, 13,743 miles and 9,811, respectively.

A French company headed by de Lesseps first attempted the construction of this canal but failed, partly on account of financial difficulties and partly because of the high mortality of workers from yellow fever and malaria. In 1902 the United States purchased the concession and the property of the French company and subsequently obtained the cession of the Canal Zone by the newly founded Republic of Panama. Work began in 1904 and continued for ten years, as on the Suez Canal. By that time, transmission of malaria by mosquitoes was known and one of the government's first tasks was to stamp out this disease.

The Canal itself was built according to a plan different from that tried by the French company — as a lock canal, rather than a sea-level canal. Vessels pass through three sets of large locks which lift them 87 feet above sea level and then return them to that level. All the locks are double, to permit two-way traffic. The largest man-made lake in the world, Gatun Lake, is a part of the route. (See Figure 88.) The Canal was opened in August 1914, on the eve of World War I. In October of the same year it was closed by a landslide but was soon reopened and formally declared completed in July 1915.[43] Traffic was rather light in its first years on account of the war, but expanded rapidly thereafter. In 1929, net tonnage almost equaled that passing through the Suez Canal. Traffic went down during World War II and returned afterward to the prewar level while that on the Suez Canal nearly tripled.[44]

International agreements regarding the Panama Canal are the same as for the Suez, the passage being open to all ships of all nations. The only legal difference is that the Suez regulations permitted passage of the warships of belligerents, even if Turkey (Egypt was then under Turkish suzerainty) was one of the belligerents. The Panama statute does not specify that warships of the enemies of Panama and the United States may use the Canal, and enemy ships would hardly find it "free and open." [45]

Other International Canals

The Kiel Canal, 61 miles long and 37 feet deep, connects the Baltic and the North Seas and serves as a link in the North Atlantic route, obviating the difficult journey around the Jutland peninsula. Completed in 1895, it has no locks, except those at each end for protection against violent tides. Although Germany built the canal for strategic purposes, it has become very important for that country's foreign trade, the port of Hamburg benefiting particularly.[46] The Treaty of Versailles opened the canal on equal terms to vessels of all nations at peace with Germany and established regulations similar to those for other international waterways.

About three fourths of the transit vessels before World War II carried the German flag. Many restrictions were imposed on merchant shipping as the role of naval bases became preponderant in German policy. After World War II, the restrictions were abolished, and commercial shipping of many countries is increasingly availing itself of the excellent facilities of this waterway. More than 52,000 vessels of all types and sizes, totaling almost 21 million net registered tons, passed through it in 1951. They carried westward 11.8 million metric tons of goods and eastward, 13.9 million, as compared with 8.0 and 8.6 million tons, respectively, in 1936.[47]

The Corinthian Canal in Greece cuts across the Isthmus of Corinth for four miles, connecting the Gulf of Corinth and the Gulf of Aegina. It shortens the distance between the Adriatic and the Black Seas by about 200 miles by eliminating the trip around the Peloponnesus. Use of this canal has not lived up to the expectations of its initiators, and it is not of great international importance.

PORTS

A port, the terminus of a water route, links water and land transport. The location of a port depends largely on the availability of a sheltered harbor deep enough for ocean vessels, but this factor alone is not decisive. Many natural harbors that offer secure refuge to ships have never been developed for lack of trade, difficulty of approach from the land side, or poverty of the hinterland. On the other hand, the absence of

---

43. **71**, p. 18.
44. See pp. 470–73.
45. **71**, pp. 16–18; **64**, p. 254.

46. **42**, p. 125.
47. **80**, June 25, 1952, pp. 8–9; **31**, August 1952, p. 373; **30**, 1952, p. 298.

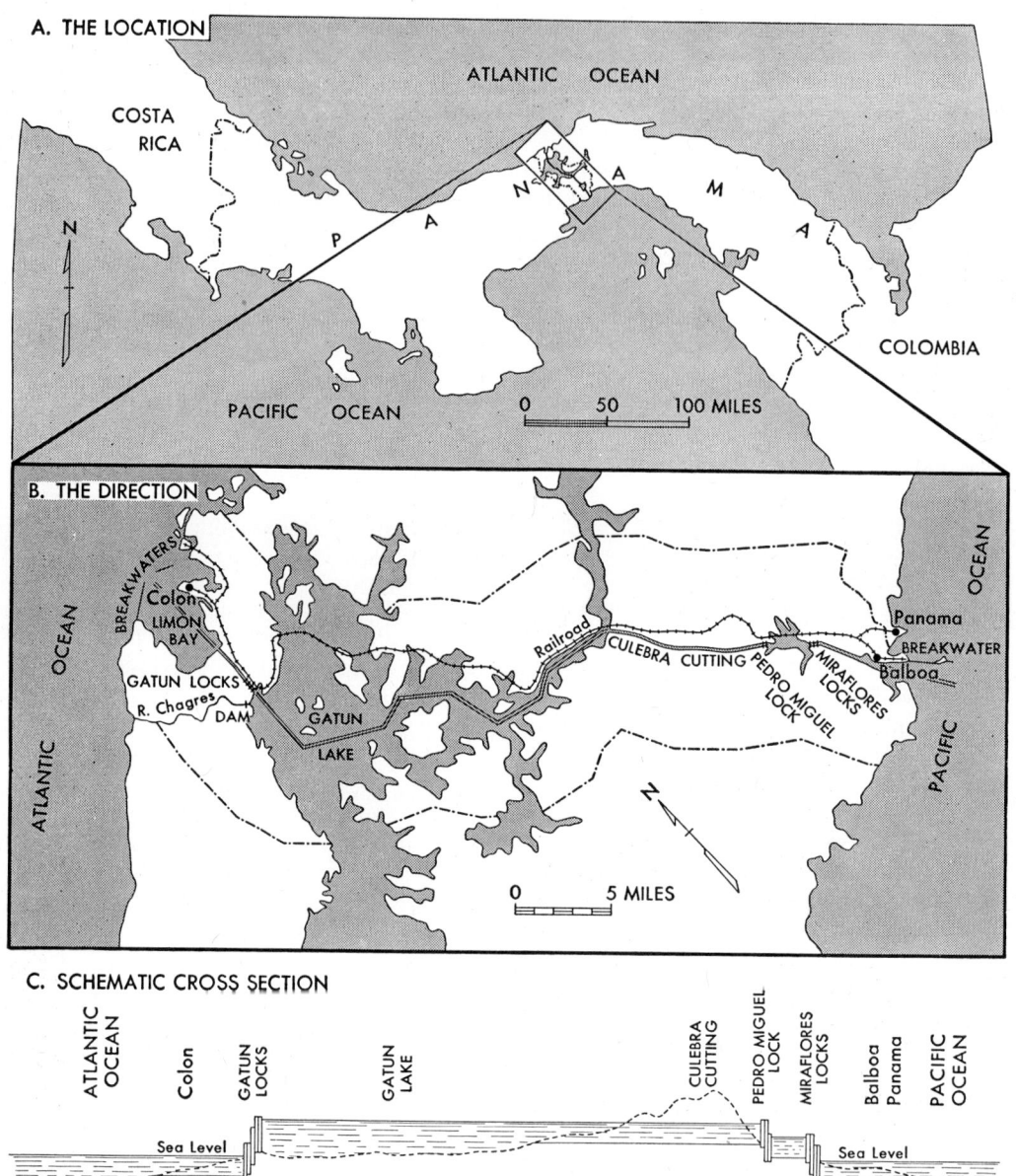

FIGURE 88. THE PANAMA CANAL

a good harbor does not preclude the establishment of a port at a point where trade demands it. In fact, many important world ports are man-made, among them Los Angeles, Boulogne and Dover.

A developed port provides not only quays and wharves to berth ships, but also repair facilities, open or wet docks depending on the tidal range, various accommodations for transferring, handling and storing cargo — warehouses and grain elevators, grain or other produce exchanges, refrigerating installations and the like. It also makes available various services, such as pilotage, towage, lighterage and stevedoring. It needs credit and insurance agencies and public provision for regulating traffic and customs. Serving the country from the water, the port is served from the land by rail and highway, and also from the air.

Ships go where cargo waits for them and

where their cargo is in demand. The port develops and prospers when the hinterland's industries are growing and both outflow and inflow of goods are expanding. The radius of the hinterland of a port extends further and further as transport facilities improve and freight rates make it possible to ship goods over greater distances.

The large ports tend to extend their territory by adding various installations as the need arises, and in time become clusters of wharves, sidings and other accommodations which may cover many square miles.

A major world port may have many hinterlands, a different one for each important commodity involved in its operations. The port of Vancouver, Canada, for example, draws timber from the nearby area, wheat from the western prairies, and manufactures from eastern Canada and even eastern United States. In contrast, the hinterland of a "primitive" port is the entire local area which has no easy or cheap access to another port on the coast. As soon as transportation facilities to neighboring areas are improved, differentiation among commodities moved to the port begins to take place, and the port's hinterland grows. A region may be hinterland to several ports. Thus West Virginia is in the hinterland of Norfolk for the shipment of coal and is in the hinterland of all large ports on the Atlantic coast for various other commodities.[48]

Number and Size of Ports

The world has thousands of commercial ports. The United States counts hundreds; the British Board of Trade enumerates 252 ports in its annual reports and another British source lists 282; French navigation returns name more than 100 ports; Sweden reports 270 in official surveys.[49]

Most of the ports are small and some are inconsequential for world trade; at many only a few ships may call during a year, despite comparatively good sheltering facilities, while ships at some busy ports may have to wait in the open sea until berth accommodations become available.

There is no standard method of determining the size and importance of port facilities, though various criteria may be used in appraising the ranking of ports: the controlling depth of approaches; draught of ships which can be accommodated; capacity for handling cargo; or the number of ships which enter and clear a port and their net tonnage. The last of these seems the most revealing. The depths of approaches to Southampton, for example, permit it to accommodate larger ships than Antwerp, but Antwerp is a much greater port. Though it is advantageous for a port to be able to receive the largest vessels, the bulk of the world's water-borne commerce is carried on in ships of more moderate size.[50] The capacity of ports for handling cargo depends on too many factors to be used as a single index of a port's efficiency. In contrast, the number and net tonnage of ships entered and cleared may be applied equally to all commercial ports and covers all classes of traffic and cargo — the passenger liner, cargo vessel, tanker, ferry steamer and so on.

This criterion, too, has its limitations, however. Some countries report gross tonnage instead of net, others count the arrival and departure of a foreign vessel at and from every port instead of the entrance and clearance of a ship during a single voyage at only its port of destination, as is done in countries with well-developed statistical services. The difference may be considerable: the shipping tonnage "arrived" at British ports in 1938 was one third greater than the net tonnage "entered."[51] In some statistical reports coastal shipping is merged with foreign trade.

It is even more difficult to define the ranking of ports in terms of their trade importance. Ship tonnage is not necessarily an index of the volume of goods imported or exported, since a ship may not be fully loaded. Cargo tonnage is not uniformly reported, many kinds of goods being counted by the piece rather than weight. The value of cargo presents even more problems because of fluctuations in prices and exchange rates from year to year or in shorter periods, which obscure comparisons from country to country and from one period to another.[52]

Using the criterion of net tonnage of ships entering a port, F. W. Morgan has compiled a list of 171 seaports which, in 1938, reported not less than one million net tons entered. These he considered to be the world's major ports. Of these, 77 ports reported a net tonnage of more

48. Cf. **73,** pp. 111–31.

49. **73,** pp. 13–14; **53,** p. 25.

50. The growth of tanker trade in vessels of increasing dimensions may influence the accommodations of ports and the direction of tanker trade.

51. **73,** p. 18.

52. Cf. **87,** pp. 116–19.

than 5 million (38 with 5–10 million net tons, and 39 with 10 or more million). Fifty of these largest ports are located on the Atlantic (including the Mexican Gulf), the Mediterranean and the North Sea, and 27 are scattered about the Pacific and Indian Oceans. The distribution among the continents is as follows: North America, 11; South America, 6; Europe, 31; Asia, 19; Africa, 8, and Australia, 2. (See Figure 89.[53]) For 1952, Morgan would add twelve more ports which had reached the mark of one million net tonnage entered.[54]

Development of Port Installations

Few European ports had quays in the eighteenth century. Ships had to drop anchor in the stream and transfer their cargo to lighters for delivery to the shore.[55] The entrance to Amsterdam was dangerous; that to London required intricate manipulations; the tide at Liverpool rose and fell some 30 feet. Large vessels had to drop anchor 60 miles off Hamburg. Conditions in some ports were more favorable, but nearly all had to deepen their channels as ships increased in size. There are only 48 important ports which can be entered by ships that draw 40 feet or more, and 5 of these can be entered only at high tide.[56] Where the water level changes greatly with the tides, wet, or tidal, docks have been built — a kind of artificial basin which a ship enters at high tide, to be kept afloat behind closed gates.

In time, piers and open quays were built, and later partially or wholly covered wharves. Equip-

ment was developed to handle general cargo and special commodities. Machinery supplanted hand labor in loading and unloading vessels — movable cranes, platform conveyors, automatic lifts, chutes and endless-chain arrangements. Grain is handled at many ports by stationary or floating elevators.

Warehouses were built, and transportation facilities to them were established, including railroad sidings, trailer systems, electric tractors and trailers. Lighter connections to the warehouses have been developed much more widely in Europe than in the United States.[57] Rotterdam's lightering traffic is very heavy, because, in addition to the usual volume in a large port, there is much transit traffic to and from the Rhine and other inland waterways. At Antwerp, Amsterdam and Hamburg, lightering is also important. At Rouen (France) coal is discharged partly on the quays but also into lighters which move up the Seine to Paris, some proceeding farther into the center of France.[58] Ports at which cargo is transferred mostly or entirely by lighters are very numerous. They are common on the west coast of South America, in West Africa, Greece, the Levant and other areas; many of these coasts are without harbors, since nature did not provide natural shelter and the hinterlands cannot afford to build artificial breakwaters.

The United States has introduced belt-line installations to coordinate rail and water transportation. Even in the port of New York, which has an extensive lighterage system, belt-line railroads are needed to serve the wharves and various other terminal facilities (such as warehouses and grain elevators); without them the several parts of the harbor would become separate ports.[59]

Types of Seaports

Ports may be classified by their physical characteristics; the nature of their traffic; the main distributive media in the hinterland; and on the basis of customs restrictions.

From the first point of view, ports are divided into natural bay ports, river ports, canal ports, combination river-and-bay ports and roadsteads.

Natural bay ports are located on waterways which provide ample room for ocean vessels to move and anchor, or on inlets within a large

---

53. In addition to ports listed by F. W. Morgan, Figure 89 shows 10 major ports of the USSR: Leningrad and Riga on the Baltic Sea, Arkhangelsk and Murmansk on the Arctic Ocean, Vladivostok on the Sea of Japan, Baku and Astrakhan on the Caspian Sea, and Odessa, Sebastopol and Batum on the Black Sea. The size of operations of these ports is not known. They are all marked on the map as having handled ships with a net tonnage of 5 to 10 million tons in 1938, although most of them may have operated on a considerably smaller scale.

54. **73,** p. 20. Probably more than 183 ports would fit Morgan's criterion in 1952: for example, Portland, Oregon, which he does not name, reported about 300,000 net tons of shipping entered in 1938 but 1.3 million in 1951.

55. Lighters are shallow craft with a capacity of some 500 tons and are more flexible and economical than various land carriers. In many cases, lighters ply between ship and warehouses on inland waterways inaccessible to seagoing ships. **5,** July-September 1953, p. 15.

56. **44,** p. 121.

57. **44,** p. 159.

58. **73,** p. 69.

59. **44,** pp. 166–68.

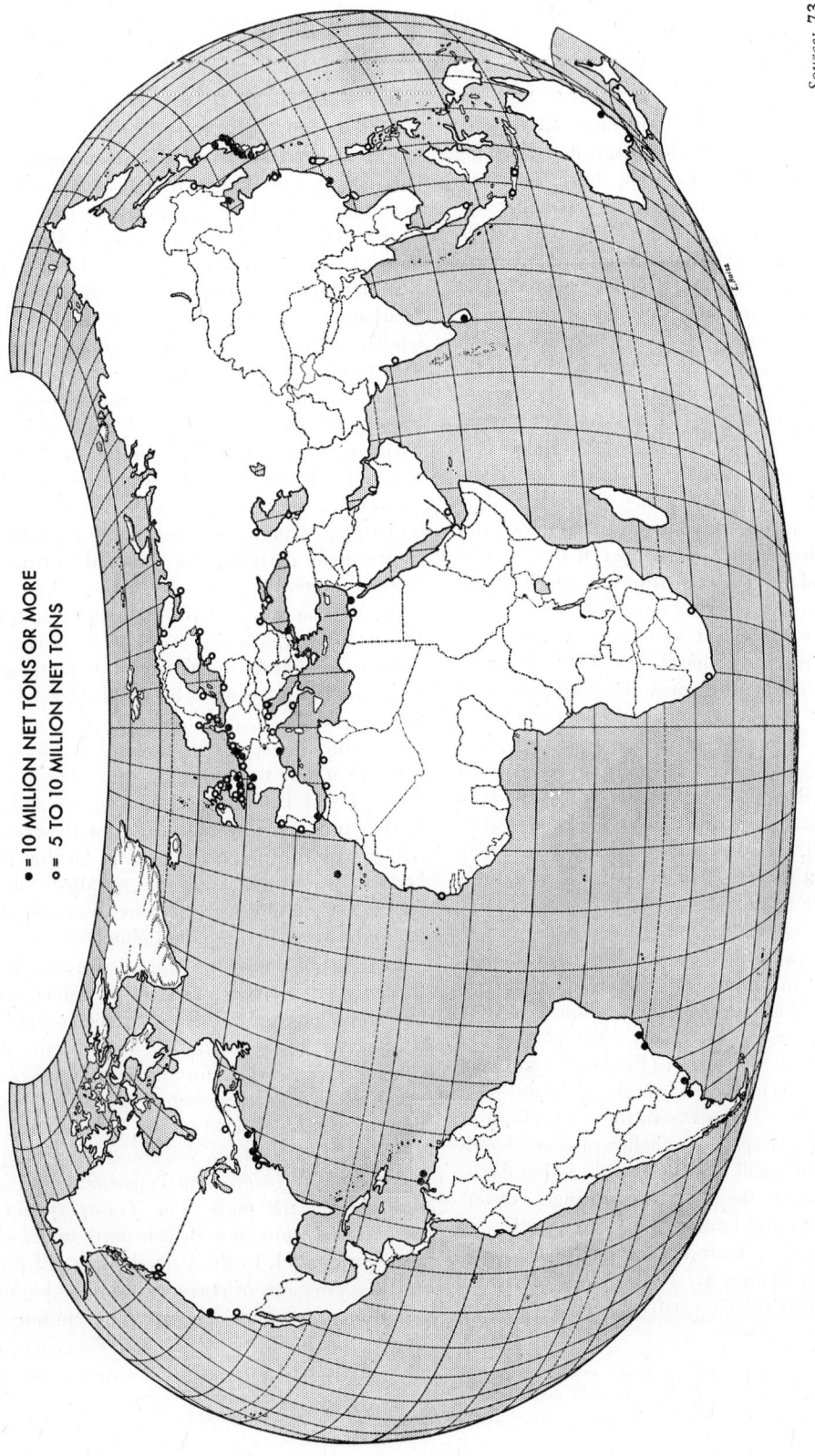

● = 10 MILLION NET TONS OR MORE
○ = 5 TO 10 MILLION NET TONS

FIGURE 89. MAJOR PORTS OF THE WORLD, 1938

This map shows all ports listed by F. W. Morgan as having more than 5 million net tons entered in 1938. To these are added the main ports of the USSR. They are classified as having 5–10 million net tons entered, but the exact volume of their operations is unknown.

Source: 73

bay or gulf — as for example, at Boston, San Francisco, Liverpool, Sydney, Rio de Janeiro, Istanbul and Yokohama. Bay ports lack one advantage of river ports — cheap river transportation to and from the hinterland. River ports include many of the world's greatest shipping centers, among them London, Rotterdam, Antwerp, Hamburg, Bremen, Rouen, Shanghai and, in the United States, Philadelphia and New Orleans, among others. New York is a combination bay and river port. Colón (Panama), Port Said and Suez are canal ports.

Some river ports — such as London, Bordeaux, Antwerp, Hamburg and Bremen, which developed a substantial business centuries ago — are located at a considerable distance from the sea: London, 67 miles; Antwerp, 50 miles; Bordeaux, 60 miles; Bremen, 54 miles; and Hamburg, 69 miles. When piracy flourished, ships proceeded as far as possible up riverways for safety. Moreover, it was cheaper at that time to shorten inland transportation of cargo; roads were inadequate, bridges were few and overland transport was difficult and risky. Later, when turnpikes were introduced, heavy tolls were imposed, which again favored the port located up the river.[60] To accommodate the increasing size of vessels, such ports have had to deepen their channels by continued dredging and sometimes must still depend on tidal changes.[61] The tidal rise is important for many world ports: Liverpool, Hull, London and Glasgow are among typical British ports that depend almost entirely on the tide to provide sufficient depth for large ships. The same situation is largely true of Lisbon and Oporto in Portugal; Bordeaux, Nantes and Rouen in France; Bremen and Hamburg in Germany; Tientsin in China; Philadelphia in the United States; and many other ports.[62]

Amsterdam, Manchester (England) and Houston (United States) are examples of inland ports that use artificial canals from the coast. Houston, for example, deepened a shallow channel barely navigable by small craft to provide a "big ditch" from the bay to the city, thus creating a convenient gateway and harbor.

Los Angeles, Dover, Boulogne, Cherbourg, Trieste and Madras are roadstead ports, created on coasts that offer no natural shelter for ships.

Strong breakwaters must be erected at such ports for safe anchorage, and the enclosed basins usually require dredging. There are also many roadsteads along the west coast of South America and both coasts of Africa.

The character of the predominant trade in a port determines its classification as a grain, raw materials, general or combination port. Montreal and Liverpool are grain ports, Valparaiso (Chile) is a raw materials port, and New York is an outstanding example of a combination type. Southampton is the only port in the world intended exclusively for passenger traffic en masse.

In terms of prevailing transportation facilities, a port may be classified as a railroad port or a barge port. Liverpool is a rail port, and so is Bremen, where 80 per cent of the cargo traffic is handled by railroads. In Rotterdam some 90 per cent of the total volume of cargo is carried on barges; Shanghai is also a barge port. In the future, some ports may be classified as truck or airplane ports.[63]

Ports either levy customs or permit free trade. Vessels enter, discharge, load and leave without customs formalities in the free-trade ports, separated from customs areas by established political boundaries. Bremen, Hamburg, Copenhagen, Stockholm, Singapore, Hong Kong and Panama City are among the free-trade ports. The United States, Great Britain, France, Belgium and the Netherlands have no free ports. In these countries re-export of imported goods is facilitated by bonded warehouses and the so-called "drawbacks," i.e., refunds of customs duties to shippers who re-export imported goods.[64]

In terms of ownership and administrative authority, ports may be classified as public, semi-public, public-trust or private. Public and public-trust ports prevail in Europe. In Italy, the state is mainly responsible for the ports; in France, chambers of commerce handle the actual operation of state-controlled ports. In Canada, the Union of South Africa and some states of Australia, various government departments exercise control over the ports. The Transport Act of 1947 placed numerous British ports under government control. In the United States, all forms and combinations of port ownership and administration are found. The two outstanding examples of public ports are San Francisco and New Orleans; Los Angeles is a municipal port,

---

60. **85**, p. 206.
61. Even so, the largest passenger vessels plying the Atlantic cannot enter the port of London and therefore dock at Southampton. (**74**, p. 24.)
62. **73**, p. 45.

---

63. **42**, p. 136; **44**, p. 111.
64. **73**, p. 75.

and New York is administered by the states of New York and New Jersey, with considerable influence by New York City. Many ports are private.

MERCHANT FLEETS

The registered tonnage of the world's merchant fleet increased steadily between 1850 and 1953 except for a few depression years in the early 1930's. Even then, the decrease in the worst year was only 5.5 per cent (68.7 million gross registered tons in the high year 1931 and 64.9 million at the low in 1935). The world's shipping tonnage has increased in the last hundred years as follows (in millions of gross registered tons): [65]

1850	9.4
1860	13.8
1870	15.6
1880	18.3
1890	18.8
1900	29.6
1910	41.9
1920	57.3
1930	69.6
1939	69.4
1950	85.3
1951	88.0
1952	90.9
1953	94.0

World War II recorded the loss of more than 4,000 seagoing ships together exceeding 20 million gross registered tons — close to one third of the world's shipping resources in 1939. Some of the surviving ships became obsolete; others were converted to wartime uses — passenger ships to troop transports, and specialized ships to tramp vessels, or vice versa. To overcome the war losses and provide facilities for moving men and supplies, the shipyards of the United States delivered about 40 million gross tons of shipping, primarily mass-produced freighters and tankers of relatively simple design.[66]

Since the end of the war, the world's merchant fleet has undergone significant changes in composition, quality and registry. Vessels built since the war are larger and faster, and incorporate many modern improvements in engineering. There are more freighters and tankers than in 1939, but fewer passenger ships. Fourteen countries have acquired merchant fleets for the first time — among them, Switzerland, Liberia, Ireland, Costa Rica and Ecuador. Some countries, such as Indonesia and Israel, which did not exist as independent entities before World War II now register merchant ships under their own flags. Liberia's fleet, owned primarily by United States companies or their affiliates, is larger than Brazil's. Individually, most of the countries with recently registered merchant ships are not important factors in international shipping, but in the aggregate they account for more than 1.2 million gross tons.[67]

DEVELOPMENT IN SELECTED COUNTRIES

The countries on the two sides of the North Atlantic control some four fifths of the world's merchant tonnage.

From the beginning of ocean traffic until 1944, the United Kingdom had the largest merchant fleet in the world. After the turn of the nineteenth century, however, its share in the world's tonnage decreased steadily. In 1900, it represented 45 per cent; in 1910, 42 per cent; in 1920 and 1930, 32 and 29 per cent, respectively; and in 1939, about 26 per cent. In 1950, the United Kingdom accounted for less than 22 per cent of the world's merchant tonnage and in 1952, for 20.6 per cent.

British marine tonnage has recorded some ups and downs during the past forty years, the highest figure being 20.3 million gross tons in 1930. Increases have been comparatively small, and the tonnage in 1952 was only a little greater than in 1920 (18.7 and 18.3 million tons, respectively).

Today the United States leads in merchant tonnage, with 27.9 million gross registered tons in 1950 and 27.6 million in 1952 — 30 per cent of the world's total.

Norway ranks third in the world and second to the United Kingdom in Europe. (See Table 155 and Figure 90.) Despite its great losses in 1940–45, it has more shipping tonnage than before the war. France, Italy and the Netherlands are next in line among European nations. The German merchant fleet, shrunk to insignificant proportions after the country's defeat, is being gradually rehabilitated; a comeback to its prewar size may be expected in the not too distant future.

The Japanese merchant fleet, almost entirely

---

65. Table 154, where, however, ships of less than 100 gross registered tons are excluded. For shipbuilding, see **89**, Chapter 30.

66. **19**, p. 2.

67. **19**, pp. 1–3 and Table 1.

TABLE 155

MERCHANT FLEETS OF SELECTED COUNTRIES, 1900–52 [a]

(*Thousands of Gross Registered Tons* [b])

Country	1900	1910	1920	1930	1939	1950	1951	1952
World	29,614	41,915	57,314	69,608	69,439	85,303	87,961	90,868
United States [c]	2,750	5,018	15,997	14,046	11,874	27,898	27,702	27,601
Canada [d]	. . .	. . .	976	1,235	1,223	2,039	1,765	1,804
Mexico	. . .	33	. . .	46	30	151	174	166
Honduras	. . .	. . .	. . .	98	84	523	508	468
Panama	. . .	. . .	. . .	75	718	3,370	3,618	3,749
Brazil	. . .	252	498	544	485	701	691	797
Peru	. . .	32	89	45	34	92	97	101
Chile	. . .	151	104	185	172	171	170	189
Argentina	88	163	150	298	291	923	994	1,047
United Kingdom [e]	13,242	17,517	18,331	20,322	17,891	18,318	18,657	18,733
France	1,350	1,882	3,245	3,471	2,934	3,211	3,371	3,641
Belgium	163	300	415	546	408	482	493	491
Netherlands	530	1,015	1,793	3,079	2,970	3,111	3,237	3,267
Denmark	519	737	803	1,072	1,175	1,269	1,344	1,391
Sweden	638	919	1,073	1,594	1,577	2,050	2,116	2,334
Norway	1,641	2,015	2,220	3,663	4,834	5,457	5,816	5,907
Finland	—	—	167	243	590	515	555	591
Germany	2,650	4,333	672	4,199	4,483	461	1,038	1,398
Poland	—	—	. . .	52	122	199	237	279
Portugal	. . .	110	276	239	257	547	502	538
Spain	695	766	997	1,207	902	1,193	1,220	1,219
Italy	983	1,321	2,242	3,262	3,425	2,583	2,918	3,290
Yugoslavia	—	—	. . .	320	410	217	240	252
Romania	. . .	32	75	69	112	. . .	. . .	. . .
Greece	178	528	530	1,391	1,781	1,349	1,277	1,274
Russia (USSR)	. . .	887	535	1,154	1,306	2,131	2,228	2,267
China	. . .	90	143	315	258	821	633	614
Japan [f]	488	1,147	2,996	4,317	5,630	1,871	2,182	2,787
Turkey	. . .	. . .	. . .	177	224	388	424	444
India [g]	. . .	176	. . .	182	238	421	455	480
Egypt	. . .	. . .	. . .	38	108	102	93	94
Union of South Africa	. . .	. . .	. . .	. . .	. . .	178	161	142
Australia	. . .	. . .	}649	685{	498	541	557	565
New Zealand	. . .	. . .			176	201	232	232

Sources: **4**, 1951, pp. 320–21; **68**, Appendix Volume, 1951, Section 7, Table 1 and 1953, Section 6, Table 1. Cf. **88**, Vol. 5, pp. 66–67.

a. Merchant vessels on June 30 of given year, excluding vessels of less than 100 gross tons and sailing ships of less than 100 net tons; ships trading on the Caspian Sea; wooden or composite ships on the Great Lakes; sailing ships of Greece, Japan, southern Russia and Turkey.

b. 1900 and 1910: totals comprise gross tons for steam- and motorships, and net tons for sailing vessels.

c. Includes vessels on the Great Lakes.

d. Excludes wooden or composite ships with auxiliary power under 300 tons, and, in 1900–20, sailing vessels.

e. Beginning in 1939, the figures include vessels on bare-boat charter from other countries, and those requisitioned by the United Kingdom.

f. Excludes wooden or composite ships and sailing vessels (about one million gross tons in 1938). (**76**, p. 106.)

g. 1930–39: includes Burma and Ceylon.

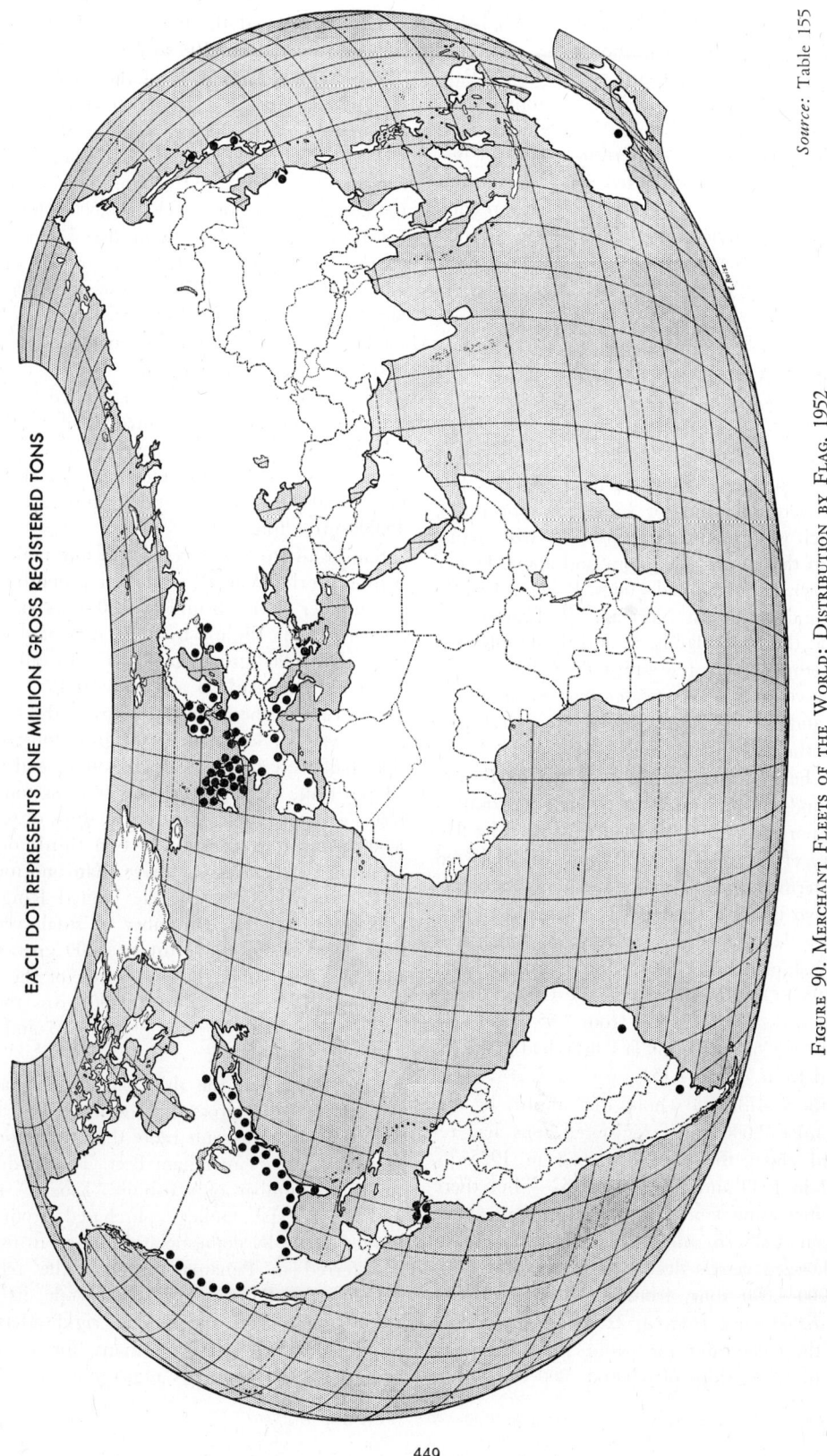

EACH DOT REPRESENTS ONE MILLION GROSS REGISTERED TONS

FIGURE 90. MERCHANT FLEETS OF THE WORLD: DISTRIBUTION BY FLAG, 1952

Source: Table 155

destroyed during World War II, is also being rebuilt and counted 2.8 million gross registered tons in 1952. The merchant fleet carrying Panama's flag more than quintupled in tonnage between 1939 and 1952. Much of the present fleet, however, is owned by American capital in one form or another: some United States shipowners register in Panama to avoid taxes and regulations under American registry. Canada, Sweden and the USSR have considerably increased their shipping tonnage.

Number and Size of Merchant Vessels

In 1952 the world had 31,461 steam- and motorships (of more than 100 gross tons). More than half of these — 19,133 — were of less than 2,000 gross tons. Only 2,569, or 8.2 per cent, had a gross tonnage of 8,000 or more. In this last group were 230 ships of 15,000 tons or more, of which more than one third (79) were registered in the United Kingdom and about 11 per cent (26), in the United States. Panama had 25 of these large ships; Norway, 29; France, 14; Italy, 9; the Netherlands, 7; and the USSR, 4.[68] The comparatively few ships of 8,000 tons or more account for the greater part of all ocean cargo and almost all long-distance sea-borne passenger traffic.

The heavy losses during World War II notwithstanding, the world's merchant fleet counted 1,698 more ships in 1952 than in 1939. The flag registry of the ships in 1952, however, reflected the aftermath of the war: Germany had less than two thirds its prewar number and only 7 of more than 8,000 tons, and Japan, which had had 10 ships exceeding 15,000 tons in 1939, had 2 in 1952. On the other hand, the United States had increased its total fleet from 2,853 vessels in 1939 to 4,876, and Canada's fleet had been increased from 792 to 1,151.

In the world as a whole, the number of vessels under 2,000 gross registered tons has remained about the same — 18,668 in 1925–26, 19,142 in 1939 and 19,133 in 1952 — but there is an increasing tendency to build larger ships. Between 1925–26 and 1952, the numbers of middle-sized vessels decreased as follows: ships of 2,000–4,000 tons, from 4,468 to 2,985; of 4,000–6,000 tons, from 3,522 to 1,896. In contrast, the 6,000–8,000-ton group increased from 1,724 to 4,878; ships of 8,000–15,000 tons, from

721 to 2,339; and the largest vessels, of 15,000 tons and over, from 102 to 230.

The aggregate tonnage of the world's steamers and motorships under 4,000 gross registered tons represented 37.8 per cent of the total in 1925–26, 30.8 per cent in 1939 and only 20.4 per cent in 1952. The largest group, in terms of total tonnage, was that of vessels of 6,000–8,000 tons, constituting 38.6 per cent of the world's merchant tonnage in 1952 (18.9 per cent in 1925–26 and 19.1 per cent in 1939). Vessels of 8,000 tons and over accounted for 14.8 per cent of the total tonnage in 1925–26; for 23.8 per cent in 1939 and for 30.5 per cent in 1952.

The merchant marine of the United States in the 1920's consisted predominantly of small vessels, with more than 55 per cent under 4,000 gross registered tons. It included 142 ships of 8,000–15,000 gross tons and 9 ships exceeding 15,000 gross tons.

Some shift to larger vessels became noticeable before World War II: although proportionally the number of vessels under 4,000 gross tons had decreased only slightly by 1939, that of ships of more than 8,000 gross tons had risen from about 4 per cent to nearly 8 per cent. In 1952, about 31 per cent of the merchant ships of the United States were of less than 4,000 gross tons; more than half were 6,000–8,000 gross tons, and some 14 per cent, of more than 8,000 gross tons. In terms of total tonnage, merchant ships of 6,000–8,000 gross tons constituted two thirds of the total, and larger vessels, more than one fourth.

The merchant fleet of the United Kingdom still includes a large number of small vessels, with 3,637 out of 5,912 under 2,000 gross tons. On the other hand, the proportion of the total tonnage in ships exceeding 8,000 gross tons is greater than in the United States: 43.7 and 25.8 per cent, respectively.

More than half the ships carrying Panama's flag are of 6,000 gross tons or more, and their total tonnage represents more than three fourths of that country's merchant fleet. This is due to the large number of war-built "Liberty" ships and "T-2"-type tankers purchased from the United States by domestic and foreign firms and transferred to Panama registry. The relative simplicity of Panama's maritime code, its relatively lower taxes and its less rigid safety requirements have attracted many foreign shipowners to that country's registry.[69]

---

68. **68,** 1953, Appendix Volume, Section 6, Table 3.

69. **19,** p. 27.

Greece has fewer ships and less tonnage under its own flag than before World War II, but Greek-owned ships under foreign flags far exceed, in tonnage, those under Greek registry. Because of various difficulties in obtaining ships from other nations, Greek shipowners have established companies abroad and dispersed their tonnage under various flags — British, Canadian, Panamanian, United States and so on.[70]

A substantial part of the merchant tonnage of Canada, Denmark, Sweden, Spain, Japan and the USSR — engaged more in coasting and cross-channel trade than in transoceanic shipping — is in comparatively small vessels. Two fifths of Western Germany's total tonnage is in ships of less than 2,000 tons. (See Table 156, A and B.)

Types of Merchant Vessels

Vessels, like railroad cars, are distinguished by the service for which they are built and used, although the demarcation is less pronounced. The U.S. Maritime Administration classifies ships as follows:[71]

Combination passenger and cargo vessels
Combination passenger and cargo-refrigerated vessels
Freighters
Freighters-refrigerated
Bulk carriers
Tankers

The classification on this basis for June 30, 1952 covers 13,788 ships of not less than 1,000 gross registered tons and a total gross tonnage of some 80 million.[72] Nearly 74 per cent of these vessels were used in freight service of all types exclusively; about 17 per cent represented tankers, and the rest carried both passengers and freight. In terms of tonnage, the distribution is somewhat different. Cargo carriers accounted for about 63 per cent of the total gross registered tonnage; tankers, for about 24 per cent; and the

combination passenger and cargo vessels, for some 12–13 per cent.

The percentage distribution, by type, of the world's merchant ships of not less than 1,000 gross tons changed between September 1, 1939 and June 30, 1952, as follows:[73]

	September 1, 1939	June 30, 1952
	Number	
Total	100.0	100.0
Combination (passenger-cargo)	14.4	9.5
Freighter	72.6	73.6
Tanker	13.0	16.9
	Tonnage	
Total	100.0	100.0
Combination (passenger-cargo)	21.3	12.5
Freighter	59.4	63.3
Tanker	19.3	24.2

Thus, the general tendency has been toward increase in freighter and tanker tonnage, in many cases at the expense of combination passenger-cargo shipping.

The distribution of a country's merchant vessels by type depends on the role of shipping in the national economy and defense. The United Kingdom, for example, needs a substantial passenger tonnage to maintain the ties with the Commonwealth and for reasons of balance of payments. On the other hand, Norway concentrates on freighters and tankers, while cargo-passenger ships represent only about 2 per cent of the total tonnage.

The United States, with its preference for larger vessels, had about 25 per cent of the world's ships (of not less than 1,000 gross tons) and 32 per cent of the tonnage. Within its merchant marine, the various freight carriers constituted nearly four fifths of the vessels and three fourths of the tonnage. Tankers accounted for some further 13 per cent of the vessels and more than 16 per cent of the tonnage. Relatively few ships were engaged in passenger service.[74]

In contrast, freighters accounted for some 68 per cent of the British ships and over 56 per cent

---

70. **19**, p. 17.

71. Another classification in use distinguishes four types of ocean carriers: (1) express liners carrying passengers, mail and high-class freight and making both rapid crossings and rapid turn-arounds in ports; (2) combination freight and passenger ships, concerned primarily with cargo, and varying greatly in type; (3) tramps, or slower ships, designed primarily for capacity and economy of operation and handling bulky raw materials; (4) industrial carriers owned by large enterprises, such as oil companies and plantation firms. **58**, pp. 257–59; cf. **90**.

72. Lloyd's Register covers 31,461 vessels of more than 100 gross registered tons, with an aggregate tonnage of more than 90 million for 1952.

73. For 1939: adapted from **19**, Appendix Tables, pp. 48–59; for 1952: data released by the Maritime Administration.

74. For the distribution of the United States merchant fleet by ownership, see pp. 461–62.

TABLE 156. MERCHANT VESSELS: DISTRIBUTION OF STEAM- AND

A. Number in Each Size Class

Country	Total Number	Size, in Gross Registered Tons					
		Under 2,000	2,000– 4,000	4,000– 6,000	6,000– 8,000	8,000– 15,000	15,000 and Over
1925–26							
World	29,205	18,668	4,468	3,522	1,724	721	102
United States	3,829	1,110	1,025	898	645	142	9
Canada	660	480	101	50	19	7	3
United Kingdom	8,161	5,182	917	1,174	513	309	66
France	1,527	936	275	183	66	63	4
Netherlands	1,046	624	175	100	98	43	6
Denmark	652	499	100	34	11	8	—
Sweden	1,203	1,050	91	50	7	3	2
Norway	1,745	1,340	216	138	44	7	—
Germany	1,947	1,524	183	122	68	45	5
Spain	789	550	184	44	5	6	—
Italy	1,035	498	196	215	91	31	4
Greece	448	247	139	58	3	1	—
Japan	2,087	1,378	354	234	90	31	—
1939							
World	29,763	19,142	3,669	3,594	1,906	1,269	183
United States	2,853	974	425	661	567	209	17
Canada	792	635	82	32	28	13	2
United Kingdom	6,722	4,247	484	991	488	428	84
France	1,231	770	207	126	42	76	10
Netherlands	1,523	1,091	153	91	96	80	12
Denmark	705	530	96	43	17	19	—
Sweden	1,231	1,035	99	62	15	15	5
Norway	1,987	1,272	203	238	140	131	3
Germany	2,459	1,836	230	175	126	70	22
Spain	777	595	124	40	13	5	—
Italy	1,227	691	159	240	79	41	17
Greece	607	239	134	211	22	—	1
Japan	2,337	1,373	382	314	167	91	10
1952							
World	31,461	19,133	2,985	1,896	4,878	2,339	230
United States	4,876	1,277	222	143	2,533	675	26
Canada	1,151	915	108	38	66	23	1
Panama	606	114	89	79	177	122	25
United Kingdom	5,912	3,637	362	376	800	658	79
France	1,251	736	171	98	124	108	14
Netherlands	1,617	1,183	116	65	124	122	7
Denmark	695	475	105	51	20	44	—
Sweden	1,266	917	164	89	40	54	2
Norway	2,181	1,406	174	195	143	234	29
Germany	1,522	1,321	111	56	27	7	—
Spain	1,089	865	142	43	26	13	—
Italy	1,101	671	67	81	192	81	9
Greece	372	179	33	51	101	7	1
USSR	1,019	625	220	86	71	13	4
Japan	1,587	1,163	168	75	135	44	2

MOTORSHIPS, BY SIZE, FOR SELECTED COUNTRIES, 1925–26, 1939 AND 1952

B. Tonnage in Each Size Class

Country	Total, in Millions of Gross Registered Tons	Percentage in Each Size Class					
		Under 2,000	2,000– 4,000	4,000– 6,000	6,000– 8,000	8,000– 15,000	15,000 and Over
1925–26							
World	62.4	17.1	20.7	28.5	18.9	11.4	3.4
United States	14.2	5.0	20.4	32.9	30.6	9.6	1.5
Canada	1.1	28.0	25.0	24.0	12.3	6.2	4.5
United Kingdom	19.3	13.6	14.4	30.3	18.4	16.2	7.1
France	3.3	14.4	22.8	27.3	13.9	18.9	2.7
Netherlands	2.6	14.0	20.0	19.7	26.2	15.7	4.4
Denmark	1.0	43.5	26.2	15.6	7.2	7.4	—
Sweden	1.3	50.9	20.1	20.0	3.9	2.6	2.6
Norway	2.6	36.2	24.1	25.7	11.4	2.6	—
Germany	3.0	28.0	17.5	20.3	15.6	15.0	3.7
Spain	1.1	21.4	49.7	20.5	4.5	3.9	—
Italy	2.9	9.5	20.4	37.2	20.7	9.4	2.8
Greece	0.9	17.6	48.9	30.5	2.1	0.9	—
Japan	3.9	19.9	25.7	30.8	15.7	7.9	—
1939							
World	68.5	15.3	15.5	26.4	19.1	17.9	5.9
United States	11.4	4.8	10.9	29.9	34.0	17.4	3.0
Canada	1.2	39.9	18.0	12.9	16.0	10.4	2.8
United Kingdom	17.9	11.6	8.0	27.9	18.9	23.3	10.2
France	2.9	12.8	20.6	21.2	9.8	25.9	9.7
Netherlands	3.0	14.2	14.4	15.5	22.4	25.2	8.3
Denmark	1.2	36.6	20.6	18.0	9.8	15.0	—
Sweden	1.6	41.1	17.6	20.1	6.3	8.8	6.2
Norway	4.8	16.9	12.1	24.4	19.8	25.6	1.1
Germany	4.5	19.3	14.6	19.6	19.7	15.4	11.4
Spain	0.9	21.9	40.6	21.8	9.5	6.1	—
Italy	3.4	11.3	13.5	35.8	15.2	11.6	12.5
Greece	1.8	9.2	24.1	57.5	8.2	—	1.0
Japan	5.6	13.3	19.6	28.3	20.3	15.4	3.1
1952							
World	90.2	10.7	9.7	10.6	38.6	25.4	5.1
United States	27.2	2.0	2.8	2.6	66.9	23.8	2.0
Canada	1.7	28.7	16.9	10.9	27.7	14.8	1.1
Panama	3.7	3.2	7.3	10.8	33.4	33.6	11.5
United Kingdom	18.6	9.9	5.7	10.4	30.4	34.2	9.5
France	3.6	9.5	13.8	13.1	24.0	30.7	8.8
Netherlands	3.3	13.5	9.8	10.2	27.2	34.9	4.4
Denmark	1.4	20.5	20.8	18.2	9.8	30.7	—
Sweden	2.3	24.2	20.0	19.0	12.0	23.2	1.5
Norway	5.9	10.8	8.3	17.0	16.8	39.1	8.0
Germany	1.4	40.2	22.5	19.6	12.9	4.8	—
Spain	1.2	23.1	34.1	17.7	14.6	10.4	—
Italy	3.3	10.0	5.8	12.5	41.3	24.2	6.3
Greece	1.3	8.0	7.9	19.9	57.1	5.8	1.3
USSR	2.3	21.8	27.5	19.5	22.0	5.8	3.4
Japan	2.8	20.3	16.0	13.2	33.0	16.3	1.3

Source: **68**, 1925–26, Vol. 2, pp. 1158–61; 1939–40, Vol. 2, Appendix Table 5 and 1953, Appendix Volume, Section 6, Table 3.

TABLE 157

MERCHANT VESSELS:[a] DISTRIBUTION, BY TYPE, FOR SELECTED COUNTRIES, 1952

Country	Number					Thousands of Gross Registered Tons				
	Total	Combina-tion[b]	Freight-ers[c]	Bulk Carriers	Tankers[d]	Total	Combina-tion[b]	Freight-ers[c]	Bulk Carriers	Tankers[d]
World	13,788	1,315	9,568	574	2,331	80,222	10,051	48,970	1,802	19,399
United States[e]	3,441	261	2,667	51	462	25,627	2,358	18,689	326	4,254
Canada	136	40	74	2	20	684	141	395	10	138
Mexico	30	—	9	1	20	152	—	23	6	123
Honduras	79	3	64	—	12	425	12	267	—	146
Costa Rica	17	2	14	—	1	88	4	77	—	7
Panama	550	26	300	31	193	3,730	193	1,575	115	1,847
Cuba	11	1	9	1	—	26	3	22	1	—
Venezuela	51	3	10	2	36	149	4	27	7	111
Colombia	12	—	11	—	1	33	—	32	—	1
Brazil	182	30	123	4	25	684	120	444	5	115
Peru	22	4	15	1	2	85	22	55	3	5
Chile	41	7	20	14	—	161	31	81	49	—
Uruguay	8	2	4	—	2	48	10	18	—	20
Argentina	141	24	70	4	43	903	172	394	6	331
United Kingdom	2,502	258	1,511	202	531	16,646	2,922	8,946	445	4,333
Ireland	12	—	9	3	—	36	—	24	12	—
France	559	78	337	47	97	3,276	756	1,537	142	841
Belgium	75	14	52	1	8	428	114	244	1	69
Netherlands	496	99	285	2	110	2,865	728	1,515	4	618
Denmark	312	28	241	11	32	1,260	90	844	27	299
Sweden	594	32	459	43	60	2,157	203	1,235	186	533
Norway	961	32	591	16	322	5,533	125	2,287	55	3,066
Finland	193	4	167	13	9	527	8	429	34	56
Germany	319	9	275	18	17	1,002	44	793	55	110
Poland	59	1	49	7	2	241	14	198	14	15
Switzerland	21	—	19	—	2	96	—	82	—	14

(Continued on facing page.)

of that country's tonnage. About one fifth of the vessels and one fourth of the tonnage was represented by tankers.

In Norway's merchant fleet, freight carriers comprised more than 63 per cent of the vessels and about 42 per cent of the total tonnage. Tankers, constituting three vessels out of ten, accounted for another 55 per cent of the tonnage.

The USSR, ranking tenth in tonnage (of ships of 1,000 tons or more), used about 67 per cent of it for cargo service, less than 10 per cent for tankers and the rest for combination passenger and cargo service. (See Table 157.)

Liners and Tramps

Liners — whether a passenger liner carrying cargo, a cargo-passenger liner or a cargo liner with few or no passengers — sail on an adver-tised schedule of ports, arrivals and departures. Their schedule is often fixed as much as a year ahead, and regularity may last over a period of years and entail monthly, fortnightly or weekly service. They operate between the same ports continuously, leave a port even when not fully loaded and stop at all designated ports whether or not they have a consignment to unload or pick up. Generally, liners are larger and speedier than "tramps."

The first "line" in the world was introduced by a United States company (the Black Ball Line) in 1816.[75] Line development was slow at first, and by 1870 several lines, mostly English,

75. On the first of each month, rain or shine, its ships left New York for Liverpool. This innovation in shipping has been characterized by a British expert as "nothing less than a stroke of imaginative genius." **85,** p. 7.

TABLE 157—*continued*

Country	Number					Thousands of Gross Registered Tons				
	Total	Combina-tion [b]	Freight-ers [c]	Bulk Carriers	Tankers [d]	Total	Combina-tion [b]	Freight-ers [c]	Bulk Carriers	Tankers [d]
Portugal	93	19	66	—	8	419	140	216	—	63
Spain	268	39	191	12	26	982	201	600	35	146
Italy	517	64	338	18	97	3,048	571	1,675	73	729
Yugoslavia	53	5	45	1	2	225	25	182	4	14
Romania	7	1	6	—	—	30	7	23	—	—
Greece	211	8	180	8	15	1,177	45	998	26	108
USSR	477	70	359	16	32	1,457	350	947	30	130
China	143	11	104	5	23	415	33	322	10	50
Japan	497	17	423	6	51	2,379	80	1,866	23	410
Turkey	109	29	75	1	4	387	120	243	1	23
Israel	23	3	20	—	—	105	13	92	—	—
Pakistan	24	2	19	1	2	126	17	95	5	9
India	85	15	68	1	1	419	68	343	5	3
Indonesia	8	1	5	—	2	34	6	24	—	4
Philippines	23	4	16	3	—	93	11	73	9	—
Egypt	20	12	8	—	—	80	50	30	—	—
Liberia	99	—	47	—	52	942	—	308	—	634
Union of South Africa	12	—	12	—	—	70	—	70	—	—
Australia	119	15	85	19	—	420	89	272	59	—
New Zealand	50	7	36	6	1	182	39	125	15	3

Source: **18**, 1952, pp. 66–67.

a. Seagoing steam and motor merchant vessels of 1,000 gross tons and more. Excludes vessels on the Great Lakes and inland waterways, special types (e.g., channel vessels, icebreakers, cable ships) and merchant vessels owned by any military force.

b. Combination passenger-cargo and passenger-cargo refrigerated ships.

c. Freighters and freighters-refrigerated.

d. Includes whaling tankers.

e. Includes 91 government-owned vessels transferred under lend-lease and other agreements to other flags: 83 of 518,000 gross tons to the USSR and 8 of 27,000 gross tons to the Philippines. Includes ships converted to transports, hospital, store and distilling ships (2.9 million gross tons).

connected Europe with only the most important transoceanic regions. Line shipping gathered momentum as European emigration increased, and as the demand grew for raw materials by European countries in process of rapid industrialization, and the capacity of countries across the oceans to purchase finished goods developed. By 1913, line shipping had spun a tight network around the world.

The cargo of liners comprises "general merchandise," any cargo not shipped in bulk — a variety of finished and semifinished goods and many raw materials, packed in bags, bales, boxes, cases and so on, such as cotton, wool, jute, hides and skins. Motor cars, crated or uncrated, are also general cargo, as are commodities requiring special handling, such as meat, butter and tropical fruit. Steel is an important cargo for liners because it is exported from a few sources to

nearly every port in the world and is valuable for stowage, making a good bottom cargo and comprising a large range of small pieces of all shapes and weights.[76]

Tramp ships differ in many respects from liners. They are not restricted by schedules and routes, as are the latter. Each tramp owner decides for himself what loads or routes his ship will take on each voyage and he may change the destination of a ship while it is on the high seas. A tramp ship can be chartered on time terms, or for one or more voyages, and the charterer is not limited, as he is when using space on a liner,

76. **73**, p. 98. Steel cargo is so valuable to liner trade that it increased the importance of many ports exporting steel. Antwerp, the largest steel-exporting port in the world, owes its leading position as a liner port partly to the fact that it draws on the steel works of Belgium, Luxembourg, France, the Saar and the German Ruhr.

by the needs of other shippers, by rigid delivery points, or by sailing orders from the line owners.

Tramps carry bulky freight of low value, such as coal, ores, fertilizers, grain, lumber. Generally speaking, they move products of primary industries, while liners carry those of secondary industries. Tramps are smaller and simpler in structure than liners; built for maximum carrying capacity and not for speed, they serve industries in which time is not a critical factor.

Despite the seemingly clear distinction between a liner and a tramp, there is actually no precise distinction between them.[77] Not infrequently a liner is sent tramping, or a line may develop from the routes formerly plied by tramp vessels.[78]

Assembled cargo ordinarily waits for liners in the ports, whereas tramps go as near as possible to the source of their cargo, be it a single mine or timber wharf or a port like Daiquirí in Cuba (iron ore) or Cardiff in Wales (coal). The same distinction applies to the discharge of cargo, though to a lesser degree.

As a group, tramps account for a considerable part of the cargo moved in international trade, but their share declined after World War I: 46 per cent of the tonnage in 1914; 33 per cent in 1933. The world's tramp tonnage declined between these years from 22.7 million gross tons to 21.3 million, and among the ten leading merchant fleets of the world, tramp tonnage gained in importance only in Italy and Greece.[79]

Tramp shipping was practically nonexistent under the United States flag prior to World War II. Tramps carried a third of the dry-cargo tonnage of U.S. foreign trade but except for a negligible quantity, it was moved in foreign-flag vessels.[80] The situation was reversed in the first postwar years. The wartime destruction of foreign merchant fleets, the strong demand for U.S.

bulk commodities, such as grain, fertilizers and coal financed by United States loans and gifts, and the legal requirement that at least half the shipments must be carried in U.S. bottoms, opened new opportunities to domestic merchant shipping as a whole, and to tramp shipping in particular. Of the 94 million long tons moved in all United States sea-borne foreign trade from July 1, 1947 to June 30, 1948, domestic tramps carried 27 million long tons and foreign tramps, 23 million. By 1951, however, competition of foreign-flag tramps, with their lower-cost services, began to force United States tramp ships from the seas: of the 66 million long tons of tramp cargoes in United States overseas trade, domestic tramps accounted for less than 26 million, or 39 per cent, as compared with 54 per cent in the former period.[81]

A substantial part of Japanese shipping was engaged in tramp service before World War II. At that time, the simultaneous reduction of tramp tonnage by British, Norwegian and other important merchant fleets made Japan second instead of tenth among the tramp-owning nations.[82]

Tramps are very important in British shipping: an uninterrupted flow of foodstuffs and raw materials — the lifeline of the British Isles — depends on a large volume of flexible shipping tonnage that can be moved at any season to and from different sources of supplies. They play a predominant role in coastwise trade, with coal as their main cargo. In 1948, tramps of over 100 gross registered tons in British coastwise shipping carried about 29.5 million long tons, as compared to 2.3 million tons handled by liners. In tramp coastal transport of that year, coal accounted for 24.7 million tons.[83]

The tramp ship, a "Jack-of-all-trades," began to lose ground before World War II, because of the growing competition from liners, the drastic decline in the British coal trade, the increased tonnage of tanker ships, the trend toward specialization in ship construction and the development of the industrial carrier.[84] Liners have also

77. The draftsman of the British Shipping Act of 1935 "gave up in despair the task of providing a statutory distinction." The 1935 Act consequently defined tramp ships by exclusion (Section 6, 1): "The vessels to which this Act applies are ships which are neither fishing vessels nor constructed or adapted for the carriage of liquid cargoes in bulk, nor so constructed or adapted that the space insulated for the carriage of special cargoes is in excess either of 50,000 cubic feet or of 10 per cent of the total space available for cargo."

78. **44**, pp. 71–72.

79. **71**, p. 68; **9**, p. 73. Later estimates for world tramp shipping are not available but it is believed that prior to World War II liners were steadily gaining business at the expense of the tramps.

80. **23**, pp. 1–2.

81. **20**, p. 2.

82. **76**, pp. 110–11; **9**, p. 73.

83. **53**, p. 16. In terms of tonnage, coal has been the major commodity in British shipping for some 200 years. Adam Smith wrote in 1776: "The coal trade from Newcastle to London . . . employs more shipping than all the carrying trade of England, though the ports are at no great distance." (**82**, p. 166.) Between the two world wars coal and coke accounted for four fifths of the total weight of the British export trade. (**23**, p. 18.)

84. **9**, p. 73.

made heavy inroads in grain transport, using grain — a clean cargo — to fill unoccupied space. Difficulties experienced by world tramp shipping became so great that Great Britain, the predominant tramp-owning nation, had to provide government subsidies in 1935 and 1936.[85] Nevertheless, the tramp ship remains an important adjunct to the cargo shipping of the world. It is cheap, flexible and specially important in carrying seasonal freight, since it can move from one part of the world to another as freight swells and declines.[86]

Tankers

Tank ships carry chiefly petroleum and petroleum products, but some are fitted to move other liquids and semiliquids in bulk, such as wine, latex and molasses.[87] The tank ship carries no return cargo and ordinarily travels in ballast, water being used for filling the tanks. Occasionally it takes on drinking water, as many tankers did on the return voyage from Plymouth, England, to Abadan, Iran.[88] Sweden has recently built special tank ships, with outer holds for petroleum and the central portion equipped for carrying iron ore.[89]

The size and efficiency of tank ships have been greatly increased in recent decades. Oil tankers are provided with many safety devices to prevent and control fires and explosions of their inflammable cargo, and with powerful pumps for discharging it. Even the largest tankers can be emptied in less than twelve hours.[90]

The trend is toward building larger tank ships. Before World War II, a 15,000-ton tanker was not very common, but today some tankers have 20,000 and more tons,[91] and a 45,000-gross-ton tanker has been launched. However, more than a fourth of the world's tanker fleet in 1952 (860 out of 3,049) were less than 2,000 gross tons. Tankers of 6,000 to 10,000 tons represented about a third of the ships and a little over a third of the total gross tonnage in the world;

those of 10,000 to 15,000 tons, about a fourth of the ships and more than four tenths of the tonnage: [92]

	Tank Ships	Gross Tonnage, in Millions
All tankers	3,049	20.0
Gross tons of:		
Under 1,000	652	0.3
1,000–2,000	208	0.3
2,000–6,000	341	1.3
6,000–10,000	930	7.5
10,000–15,000	810	8.7
15,000–20,000	103	1.8
Over 20,000	5	0.1

Type and Source of Power

In 1952, about 46 per cent of the world's merchant fleet, in terms of tonnage, was equipped with the reciprocating steam engine in combination with the turbine; less than half of the remainder was powered by the turbine in combination with the electric drive, and the rest, by the internal combustion engine.

The internal combustion engine is used more widely on European merchant vessels than in United States shipping. The gross tonnage of British motorships was 4.6 million in 1939 and 7.1 million in 1952; of Norwegian, 3 million and 4.5 million, respectively. In contrast, the United States had 0.7 million gross tons in motorships in 1939 and 1.2 million in 1952. In the latter year, it owned less than 5 per cent of the world's tonnage in motorships, about 36–37 per cent of that equipped with reciprocating engines and 48 per cent of tonnage fitted with turbines. (See Table 158.) Sweden and Denmark have more than twice, and Norway has nearly four times, as much merchant tonnage in motorships as in steamships.

Just as wood gave way to steel and sail to steam, coal is giving way to oil: in 1925, less than one third of the world's steamers, in terms of tonnage, were fitted to burn oil; in 1952, about eight out of ten. The United States led from the beginning: nearly 65 per cent of its steamship tonnage used oil in 1925, and more than 90 per cent in 1952. In other countries, the shift accelerated after World War II. One fourth of the steamship tonnage in the United Kingdom was fitted to burn oil, rather than coal, in

---

85. See pp. 465–66.
86. **44**, p. 73.
87. The first steamer provided with tanks to carry petroleum was built in Russia in 1879 to ply the Caspian Sea, from the Baku area to the Volga Basin. The first vessel constructed as a tank ship was built in England in 1886. **78**, pp. 33 and 146. For oil tankers, see **89**, pp. 912–13.
88. **73**, p. 87.
89. See **89**, p. 1162.
90. **78**, p. 33.
91. Cf. **73**, p. 92.

92. **68**, 1953, Appendix Volume, Section 6. Tank ships of not less than 100 gross tons. Includes vessels on the Great Lakes.

Table 158

Merchant Vessels: Distribution, by Type of Tractive Power, for Selected Countries, 1939 and 1952

(Thousands of Gross Registered Tons)

Country	1939				1952			
	Steamers		Motor-ships	Auxil-iaries [a]	Steamers		Motor-ships	Auxil-iaries [a]
	Recipro-cating Engine	Turbine			Recipro-cating Engine	Turbine		
World	41,847 [b]	9,728 [c]	16,601 [d]	334 [e]	41,634 [b]	22,391 [c]	25,903 [d]	253 [e]
United States:								
Sea	4,983	3,211	708	7	13,149	10,584	1,138	3
Great Lakes	2,348	65	39	...	2,072	234	65	—
Canada	965	113	138	8	1,208	225	239	20
Panama	...	...	...	...	1,824	1,344	572	1
Brazil	422	...	61	2	380	169	239	6
Argentina	...	...	...	...	300	318	415	1
United Kingdom	10,140	3,154	4,586	12	7,206	4,316	7,098	3
France	1,937	561	427	9	1,302	837	1,494	5
Netherlands	1,198	421	1,333	17	710	827	1,718	9
Denmark	529	32	595	20	347	44	975	24
Sweden	808	32	699	38	617	23	1,650	42
Norway	1,798	25	3,000	11	1,180	175	4,542	10
Germany	2,633	673	1,115	62	623	16	732	27
Spain	675	47	168	12	736	87	377	15
Italy	2,221	488	669	47	1,767	488	1,005	29
Greece	1,723	38	12	7	1,109	119	41	5
USSR	933	27	343	3	1,596	178	480	6
Japan	3,414	678	1,518	20	852	1,118	814	3
Australia	360	19	112	3	386	39	131	4
New Zealand	122	20	31	3	117	17	97	2

Source: **68,** 1939–1940, Vol. 2, Appendix Table 3 and 1953, Appendix Volume, Section 6, Table 4.

  a. Sailing vessels equipped with motor engines.
  b. Includes steamers of 2.9 million gross tons with re-ciprocating-turbine engine in 1939 and 1.9 million in 1952.
  c. Includes steamers of 0.5 million gross tons with turbo-electric drive in 1939 and 5.1 million in 1952.
  d. Includes motorships of 0.2 million tons fitted with diesel-electric drive.
  e. Includes 16,000 gross tons in sailing vessels equipped with steam engines in 1939 and 6,000 tons in 1952.

1925; four tenths consumed oil in 1939, and eight tenths in 1952. The change in French steamships was even more spectacular — about 12 per cent of the steamship tonnage used oil in 1925, 48 per cent in 1939, and 84 per cent in 1952. One tenth of the steamship tonnage of the USSR burned oil in 1939, and over four tenths in 1952. (See Table 159.)

The shift to oil spelled the doom of coaling stations along the ocean routes. For example, bunker coal loaded at the ports of the United Kingdom by vessels in foreign trade decreased from 13.5 million long tons in 1933 to 9.6 million in 1939 and 3.7 million in 1951.[93]

The Age Distribution of Merchant Vessels

Ships, except tankers, have a nominal longevity of 40–50 years but their economic life is considerably shorter because of technical progress. The stronger the competition, the speedier their obsolescence. Passenger liners, in particular, can face competition only if they offer the most modern accommodations and the greatest comfort and speed. Obsolescence therefore may hit them after only ten years of service. The lifetime of a tanker is estimated at not more than 10–15 years because of the effects of corrosion. In the tramp business, ships twenty years old and even older can be used.[94]

93. **45,** 1951–52, p. 156.

94. **58,** p. 263; **32,** p. 145.

TABLE 159

MERCHANT VESSELS: OIL-BURNING STEAMERS, BY COUNTRY, 1925, 1939 AND 1952

Country	Number			Millions of Gross Registered Tons			Percentage of Total Steamship Gross Tonnage		
	1925	1939	1952	1925	1939	1952	1925	1939	1952
World	3,490	4,202	8,801	17.8	20.6	50.3	30.0	39.9	78.6
United States	1,855	1,421	3,180	9.0	7.5	23.5	64.3	70.7	90.2
Canada	61	117	209	0.2	0.3	0.8	18.2	27.8	55.8
Panama	. . .	44	387	. . .	0.1	2.8	. . .	. . .	88.4
United Kingdom	730	839	1,710	4.7	5.3	9.2	25.4	39.9	79.8
France	87	213	351	0.4	1.2	1.8	12.1	48.0	84.1
Netherlands	178	169	242	0.8	0.8	1.4	33.3	49.4	91.1
Norway	99	230	420	0.5	0.7	1.1	21.8	38.4	81.2
Italy	72	229	299	0.4	1.2	1.8	14.8	44.3	79.8
Greece	. . .	. . .	164	. . .	. . .	1.0	. . .	. . .	81.4
USSR	. . .	31	142	. . .	0.1	0.8	. . .	10.4	45.1
Japan	85	153	134	0.5	0.7	0.8	13.2	17.1	40.6
Other [a]	323	756	1,563	1.3	2.7	5.3	. . .	24.3	55.2

Sources: **88**, Vol. 5, p. 72; **68**, 1925–1926, Vol. 2, p. 1165; 1939–1940, Vol. 2, Appendix Table 4 and 1953, Appendix Volume, Section 6, Table 5.

a. Includes countries enumerated above in years for which data are not available.

The bulk of the world's merchant fleet consists of tonnage built during and since the last war (see Table 160): [95]

Age, in Years	Millions of Gross Tons	Per Cent
Total	90.2	100.0
Under 5	14.8	16.4
5–10	38.1	42.3
10–15	11.0	12.2
15–20	3.7	4.1
20 and over	22.5	25.0

As after World War I, the youthfulness of the world's merchant fleet is due to the vast shipbuilding in the United States during the war and the energetic postwar efforts of other important maritime nations to reconstruct their decimated fleets.

The United States accounts for nearly half the world's tonnage of war-built vessels (18.9 million gross tons out of 38.1 million), but it has less than 4 per cent of the world's total tonnage of ships under five years of age. While the mass-produced freighters of World War II performed satisfactorily the functions for which they were intended, they are not as flexible as the more recently designed ships, credited with a more suitable relationship between space and weight capacity, greater speed and cargo-han-

dling facilities which permit a faster turn-around.[96]

According to the U.S. Maritime Administration, the overwhelming predominance of one age group within the United States merchant marine raises the specter of "block obsolescence." This threat is the greater because postwar construction has been negligible in the United States, which, with a very large shipping tonnage, has no immediate need for additional vessels. At the beginning of 1952, the United States had on order or under construction only 335,000 gross tons out of the world's total 13 million tons, as compared with 4.1 million tons for the United Kingdom and 2.2 million for Norway.[97] It should be pointed out, however, that a considerable proportion of the world's most modern tanker tonnage — new, on order and under construction — is owned or controlled by United States companies, either directly or through their subsidiaries.[98]

Several maritime nations, including Norway and France, which lost a substantial part of their merchant tonnage during the war and were forced to rehabilitate their fleets, now have a more balanced tonnage in terms of age groups.

96. **19**, p. 36. For world shipbuilding, see **89**, Chapter 30.

97. **19**, p. 31.

98. **19**, p. 36.

95. Figures in Table 160 are for July 1, 1952.

TABLE 160

MERCHANT VESSELS: DISTRIBUTION OF STEAM- AND MOTORSHIPS, BY AGE, FOR SELECTED COUNTRIES, 1952

(*Thousands of Gross Registered Tons*)

Country	Total	Age, in Years				
		Under 5	5–10	10–15	15–20	20 and Over
World	90,180	14,782	38,117	11,013	3,734	22,534
United States	27,245	548	18,893	4,581	237	2,986
Canada	1,692	199	617	53	21	802
Panama	3,740	582	1,537	241	54	1,326
Argentina	1,034	361	303	19	19	332
United Kingdom	18,624	3,892	6,389	2,900	1,493	3,950
France	3,638	1,140	1,130	283	201	884
Netherlands	3,264	591	1,062	624	234	753
Denmark	1,391	461	301	97	84	448
Sweden	2,332	552	724	213	98	745
Norway	5,906	2,457	1,192	635	480	1,142
Germany	1,398	499	63	79	92	665
Spain	1,216	151	131	23	33	878
Italy	3,289	337	1,276	315	49	1,312
Greece	1,274	7	770	87	17	393
USSR	2,261	75	313	143	175	1,555
Japan	2,787	1,063	1,020	132	125	447

Source: **68**, 1953, Appendix Volume, Section 6, Table 3.

On the other hand, about 70 per cent or more of the merchant fleets of Spain and the USSR consist of ships built before, or in, the early 1930's.

The difference in age distribution between the foreign merchant fleet as a whole and the privately owned and commercially operated merchant fleet of the United States is especially evident when the two are considered separately by type of vessel. In terms of tonnage, 40 per cent of the foreign ocean-going ships (of 1,000 gross tons and more) are of prewar construction, and 34 per cent were launched in wartime; much of this wartime tonnage has been purchased from the United States. The remaining 26 per cent has been built in recent years. The corresponding figures for the United States are 8, 83 and 9 per cent, respectively.

Two thirds of the foreign tonnage of combination passenger-cargo ships, three fifths of that of bulk carriers and one third of that of freighters and tankers are of prewar construction. About a fourth of the tonnage of combination vessels, freighters and bulk carriers and one third of that of tankers are in modern postwar ships, often custom-made for specialized trades. In contrast, the privately owned fleet of the United States consists, in terms of tonnage, predominantly of wartime vessels: freighters, 90

TABLE 161

MERCHANT VESSELS: COMPOSITION OF THE FOREIGN FLEET AND THE PRIVATELY OWNED UNITED STATES FLEET, BY AGE AND TYPE, 1951

(*Per Cent*)

Type of Ship	Foreign			United States		
	Pre-war	War-built	Post-war	Pre-war	War-built	Post-war
Total	40	34	26	8	83	9
Combination (passenger-cargo)	66	9	25	37	22	41
Freighter	35	42	23	2	90	8
Bulk carrier	60	14	26	14	67	19
Tanker	33	31	36	11	77	12

Source: **19**, pp. 35 and 37.

per cent; tankers, 77 per cent; bulk carriers, 67 per cent. Only the combination passenger-cargo vessels show a somewhat more balanced age distribution: 37 per cent of the tonnage of prewar construction, 22 per cent representing wartime launchings and 41 per cent postwar construction. (See Table 161.) The total tonnage of this latter type, however, is only about a half million gross tons.[99]

99. **19**, p. 8.

TABLE 162

MERCHANT FLEETS OF THE UNITED STATES AND GREAT BRITAIN, 1900–52

(*Millions of Gross Registered Tons* [a])

Year	United States	Great Britain	Year	United States	Great Britain [b]
1900	2.8	13.2	1928	14.5	19.9
1901	3.1	13.7	1929	14.3	20.2
1902	3.3	14.4	1930	14.0	20.4
1903	3.6	14.9	1931	13.6	20.3
1904	3.8	15.4	1932	13.5	19.7
1905	4.0	15.8	1933	13.3	18.7
1906	4.2	16.4	1934	13.0	17.7
1907	4.4	17.0	1935	12.8	17.4
1908	4.8	17.3	1936	12.5	17.3
1909	4.9	17.4	1937	12.3	17.5
1910	5.0	17.5	1938	12.0	17.8
1911	5.1	17.9	1939	11.9	17.9
1912	5.2	18.2	1940	11.4	17.9
1913	5.4	18.7	1941	11.0	16.6
1914	5.3	19.3	1942	11.1	15.4
1915	5.8	19.5	1943	14.1	15.6
1916	6.1	19.1	1944	23.2	17.1
1919	13.0	16.6	1945	30.2	17.7
1920	16.0	18.3	1946	35.9	17.7
1921	17.0	19.6	1947	32.9	17.8
1922	17.0	19.3	1948	29.6	18.1
1923	16.9	19.3	1949	28.2	18.2
1924	15.9	19.1	1950	27.9	18.3
1925	15.3	19.4	1951	27.7	18.7
1926	14.8	19.4	1952	27.6	18.7
1927	14.6	19.3			

Sources: **68**, 1953, Appendix Volume, Section 6, Table 10; for the period of World War II, United States: **15**, 1953, p. 585 and United Kingdom: **34**, 1938–1948, p. 213.

a. Ships of not less than 100 gross tons.
b. From 1939 to 1950, the figures include vessels on bare-boat charter from other countries, and those requisitioned by the United Kingdom.

Two Types of Development

In contrast to the course in Great Britain, the development of the merchant fleet of the United States has been spectacularly uneven, with growth in war years and rapid decline thereafter. The merchant marine reached its first peak in 1860 with 5.4 million gross registered tons, fell to 4.1 million in 1880, recorded 5.3 million on the eve of World War I, nearly tripled by 1920 (16.0 million tons) and, after a brief further expansion, fell back. In 1939 merchant shipping counted 11.9 million tons; in 1942, because of losses from submarines, 11.1 million. Wartime construction raised the figure to 23.2 million tons in 1944, and an all-time high of 35.9 million on January 1, 1946. (See Table 162 and Figure 91.) The share of the United States in the world's merchant tonnage fluctuated between 9.3 per cent in 1900 and 27.9 per cent in 1920; 17.1 per cent in 1939; 44.1 per cent in 1947; and 30.2 per cent in 1952.

The British merchant fleet has also recorded fluctuations since the end of the nineteenth century but within a much narrower range. Tonnage in 1951 was some 42 per cent greater than in 1900, and even in the record years 1929–31, was only about 54 per cent greater than in 1900. On the other hand, at no time did the figure fall below 15 million gross registered tons after 1903.

THE UNITED STATES MERCHANT MARINE

Ownership

The merchant marine of the United States consisted on June 30, 1952 of 1,271 privately owned vessels totaling 10.3 million gross tons and 2,079 government-owned ships totaling 14.8 million gross tons.[100]

100. Vessels of 1,000 gross tons and over. Excludes

The private fleet comprises the best types of freighters, tankers and combination passenger-freight vessels. Freighters constitute the largest part, and more than four fifths of freighter tonnage is from 8 to 11 years old. Tankers, the second largest group, also date from wartime and are of modern design. The weakest segment of the private fleet consists of the 47 combination passenger-freighter vessels, of which almost half are twenty or more years old. More than 90 per cent of the private merchant marine is in active service.

The government-owned merchant fleet is maintained primarily in reserve for defense purposes. Of the 2,079 ships only 289 vessels (2.2 million tons) were active on June 30, 1952, mostly servicing U.S. agencies; 34 ships (0.2 million tons) were temporarily inactive, and 1,756 (12.4 million tons) represented the reserve fleet. Thus, the reserve tonnage exceeds the privately operated tonnage.

Freighters constitute the bulk of the government-owned shipping (12.9 out of 14.8 million gross tons), mostly of the "Liberty" and "Victory" types. Some of these have been converted to troop transports and naval auxiliaries. Most of the combination passenger-cargo ships (202 out of 213) are also troop transport or hospital ships.

Ships held in reserve may be chartered to private operators for the government's account or for private operation. Before the outbreak of the war in Korea, 75 government-owned ships were in private operation — 41 in foreign trade and 34 in domestic commerce. By December 1951, 693 ships of all types were chartered to private operators or loaned to various government agencies.[101]

U.S. Flag Ships in the Country's Foreign Trade

The share of domestic shipping in United States imports and exports was greatest (90 per cent) in the first decades of the nineteenth century. It declined to some 34 per cent by 1870 and to 10 per cent during World War I. With the rapid increase in the merchant fleet by the end of that war, domestic bottoms carried some 40 per cent of United States foreign trade in 1920. In the 1930's, the ratio declined steadily from about 38 per cent in 1930 to a low of 22 per cent in 1939. The insignificant participation of na-

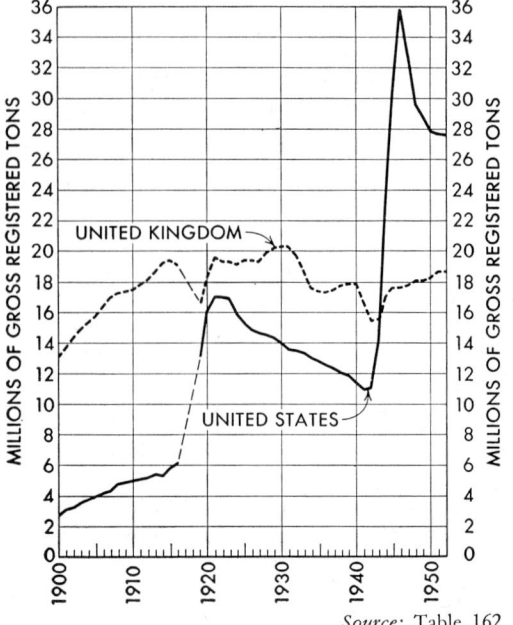

Source: Table 162

FIGURE 91. MERCHANT FLEETS OF THE UNITED STATES AND THE UNITED KINGDOM, 1900–52

tional flag ships in the foreign trade of the United States is to be attributed to many factors:

1. Most of the ships were old and slow and not sufficiently flexible in type to be moved from one trading area to another.

2. Operating costs were much higher than those of foreign flag ships.

3. Freight rates were often unremunerative to United States flag operators, who therefore laid up their ships.[102]

During World War II the situation was reversed, and the national flag ships carried a greater percentage of the total cargo in foreign trade: 63.6 per cent in 1943; 68.4 per cent in 1945. After the war, the ratio began to decline, though many factors favored operations of the United States merchant fleet:

1. Huge expansion of national shipping tonnage and depletion of the European fleet.

2. High freight rates.

3. Large foreign-aid exports, consisting to a considerable extent of bulk commodities (grain, coal and so on), coupled with the provision that at least 50 per cent of the aid shipments must be carried in United States flag ships.[103] On the other hand, after the war, the United States transferred much tonnage to the registry of countries which had suffered great wartime

vessels on inland waterways including the Great Lakes, ships owned by the Army and Navy, and special types, such as cable ships and tugs.

101. **19,** pp. 3–9.

102. **20,** p. 1.
103. **20,** p. 2.

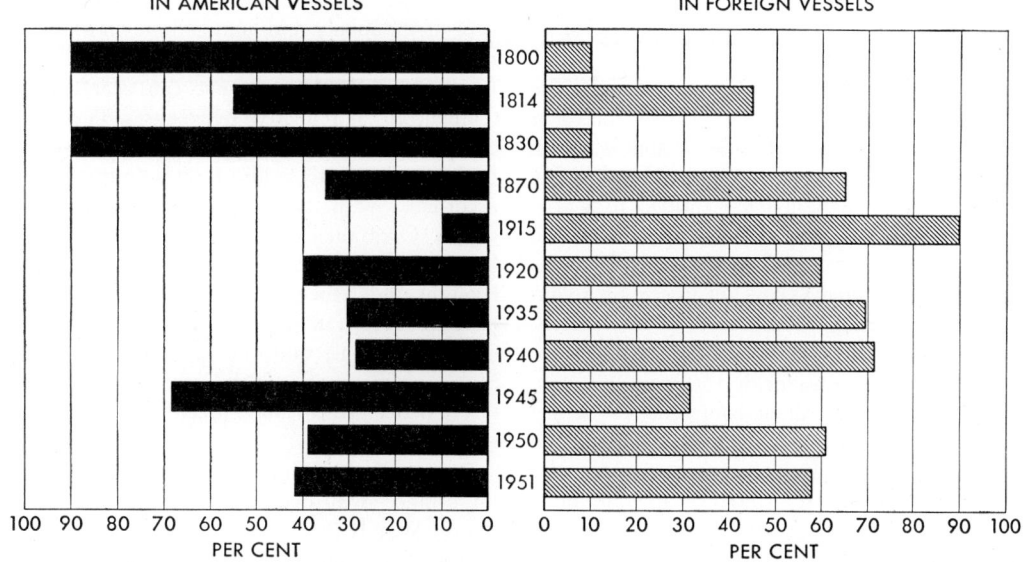

Source: **51**

FIGURE 92. MERCHANT VESSELS: SHARE OF THE UNITED STATES AND FOREIGN VESSELS IN THE FOREIGN TRADE OF THE UNITED STATES, 1800–1951

losses: "Liberty" and "Victory" ships, tankers and cargo ships were sold to Allied countries on terms favorable to them.[104]

In 1947, 51.6 per cent of United States cargo in foreign trade was carried by national ships; in 1949, 48.1 per cent; in 1951, 42.0 per cent.[105] (Cf. Figure 92.)

SHIPPING CONFERENCES

In water transport, as in rail, additional cargo and passenger traffic bring the carrier proportionately increasing returns. Competition is therefore very keen, particularly because it is relatively easy for tramp ships to enter the business. Competition is greatest when business is slack and the demand for space is low, as it was, for example, in the depression years, when nearly 13 million gross tons of the world's shipping lay idle and much of the tonnage in operation was underutilized.[106] When a liner has unused space, she competes for bulk cargo ordinarily carried by tramps. On the other hand, when demand for space is heavy, liners may charter additional ships to take up their top weight, though this is not always acceptable to shippers.[107]

Many instances of cutthroat competition can

be cited, some of which have resulted in an 80 per cent cut in freight rates.[108] To lessen competition and to raise rates or prevent rate declines, shipping lines have established so-called "conferences."

A conference ranges from informal meetings of shipowners and "gentlemen's agreements" to formal associations in a particular trade. It is not a financial merger, and the grouping is by trade rather than ownership. Lines of the same shipping combine may belong to different conferences, and a single conference may cover various combines operating in different countries. At times, conferences are practically universal. Territorially, a conference may cover lines serving ports in an area with more or less competitive traffic.

Many methods are used to control competition: fixing rates, apportioning traffic by limiting the number of sailings or the volume of cargo by lines, allotting ports of sailings, forming a united front against nonconference lines, and so on.[109] In its fight against an outside competitor, a conference may schedule a "fighting ship" to sail on the same day and offer undercutting rates. Financial losses are then distributed among members of the conference, lessening the burden to be borne otherwise by a single owner.[110] Some

104. **5**, July-September 1949, p. 19.
105. Excludes U.S. Army and Navy cargo and shipments on the Great Lakes. (**20**, Table 1.)
106. **72**, pp. 36–37.
107. **72**, pp. 224–25.

108. **32**, p. 181.
109. **13**, pp. 33–34.
110. **72**, p. 54.

conferences offer contract rates for stated periods in return for exclusive patronage to "tie" a shipper to their lines.[111]

The conference agrees that rates will be the same for each class of freight carried between the ports which its members serve jointly. Shippers who use the conference lines exclusively during a specified period are entitled to a "deferred rebate," usually 5–10 per cent of the charges. Deferred rebate by a single line is illegal in the United States, but its use by a conference has been approved.[112] It is used extensively in the rest of the world and many shipping companies consider it the most effective method at the disposal of conferences.[113] Since entrusting a single consignment to a line outside the conference results in forfeiting rebates, the conference gains a strong hold on its customers. Conference lines have also refused to accept cargo from shippers who do not use the rebate system.

The first successful shipping conference was established in 1875 in trade between the United Kingdom and Calcutta. The system spread rapidly; members of the first conferences, exclusively British lines, were soon joined by other nationals.[114] Activities of the conferences met with complaints of shippers about monopoly practices. In Great Britain, a Royal Commission on Shipping Rings (as conferences are also called) was created as early as 1906 to investigate the conditions in this trade; in the United States, the Committee on Merchant Marine of the House of Representatives engaged in 1912 in a study of the same problems. In their reports, presented in 1909 and 1914, respectively, both bodies came to the conclusion that conferences were necessary for the stabilization of rates, regulation of service and improvements in shipping facilities, though the disadvantages and abuses inherent in monopoly power were real. The British report stated that the entire history of steamship agreements showed "that in ocean commerce there is no middle ground between war and peace when several lines engage in the same trade. Most of the numerous agreements and conference arrangements . . . were the outcome of rate wars and represent a truce between the contending lines."[115]

In point of fact, conferences represent a mixture of monopoly and competition on all ocean routes. They keep their rates in great secrecy and fix them at the level "traffic can bear," rather than encourage reduction in expenses. The highly competitive nature of maritime traffic has forced them, however, to readjust rates frequently, in accordance with the supply of and demand for space. Occasionally they declare some rates "open" and competitive until these can be brought under their control. On the whole, they have reduced rate fluctuations and offer, with some exceptions, uniform rates to all shippers. Since conferences cover the principal lines, they offer better ships and greater regularity of sailings.[116]

Practically every liner route or "trade" of any importance was operated at the outbreak of World War II by a conference of the interested shipping companies. According to the Imperial Shipping Committee, at least sixty out of several hundred conferences were of major importance.[117] The International Shipping Conference, comprising some thirty shipowners' organizations in the most important maritime countries, was established in 1921, with headquarters in London. In January 1950, United States foreign trade was covered by 108 conferences, of which 100 concerned freight traffic, 4 dealt with passenger traffic and the other 4 — 2 in New York and 2 in London — handled local activities of conferences. Separate freight conferences may handle the outbound and inbound movement of goods between two areas because of differences in the commodities shipped and in shippers, though some are concerned with both segments of trade. Thus, of 100 freight conferences in U.S. foreign trade, 42 covered the outbound movement, 45 the inbound, 11 both directions of trade and 2 coordinated administrative activities.[118]

Line conferences have been hard on tramps, engaged in any event in wild competition among themselves, since all the world's shipping is a "free-for-all." The rates of tramps are subject to greater fluctuations because tramp owners are more prone to carry cargo for even less than full cost than to lay up a ship, yet have no access to

111. **13**, p. 163.
112. **44**, p. 312.
113. **72**, p. 55.
114. **13**, p. 5; **72**, p. 47.
115. **13**, pp. 33–34 and 48; **72**, p. 4.

116. **72**, p. 57; **32**, p. 166; **67**, pp. 340–41.
117. **70**, p. 95. The Imperial Committee consists of the important maritime countries of the British Commonwealth. Conferences in which shipping lines of the United States participate require the approval of the U.S. Maritime Administration.
118. **72**, pp. 137ff.

higher-paying freight to offset losses. Repeated attempts have been made by tramps to regulate rates and traffic among themselves. In some cases they have reached agreements of certain significance. For example, the British tramp owners complied with the request of the Tramp Act of 1935 to organize to avoid waste and the dissipation of subsidies,[119] enlisted foreign tramps in their organization and established minimum rates.[120] On the whole, however, tramp agreements have never exercised widespread influence. The extreme flexibility of tramp shipping, the small investment required to engage in it and the great number of operators militate against effective cooperation.[121]

GOVERNMENTAL SUPPORT OF THE MERCHANT MARINE

In almost all countries with a merchant marine of any importance, shipping has enjoyed government support in one form or another. Coastal trade is usually reserved for the national flag; the government may subsidize construction of special types of ships, exempt shipbuilding materials from import duties, grant loans to shipowners at low interest rates, pay higher rates for mail transport on national ships than on foreign-owned ships, and so on.[122]

The United States

The United States government supports the merchant marine in various ways. All internal and coastal shipping and shipping between the United States and its possessions must be carried in ships built, owned, operated and manned by nationals. The Merchant Marine Act of 1936 is aimed at fostering the development of a national merchant marine, capable of carrying domestic water-borne commerce and a substantial part of the foreign commerce and serving as a naval and military auxiliary. It provides that the United States merchant marine must be "composed of the best-equipped, safest and most suitable types of vessels, constructed in the United States." To support the merchant marine, the government may pay the difference between the cost of building a ship in American shipyards to Navy-approved specifications (except for coastal shipping) and of building the same ship

abroad, the so-called construction-differential subsidy. Public funds also provide all the features incorporated in a ship for purposes of national defense. The government also may refund the difference between operating costs under the United States flag and costs of operation under the flags of foreign competitors, the so-called operating-differential subsidy.[123]

Both types of subsidies are confined, however, to vessels engaged only in foreign trade and operating on trade routes considered by the Maritime Commission essential to the development of United States foreign commerce, in accordance with conditions stipulated by the Commission. Of the total number of ships before World War II, some two thirds were engaged in domestic commerce and consequently were not eligible for subsidies. World War II, with its unparalleled surge in government shipbuilding, made the United States the greatest maritime power of the world. The Merchant Ship Sales Act of 1946 was passed to reduce the fleet, expanded beyond need for commercial purposes, and to enable private ship companies to restore their fleets by purchasing vessels at roughly half the prewar cost of constructing equivalent dry-cargo vessels. A 25 per cent down payment was required with the remainder to be paid over a period up to 20 years.[124]

Great Britain

In contrast to the United States, Great Britain had never provided any shipping subsidies or other privileges to its merchant fleet until shortly before World War II. While the British government gave some financial aid for the building of a few transatlantic luxury liners such as the "Queen Mary," "navigation and construction bounty practices such as have been in force in France, Spain or Japan have been unnecessary and have had no place in British shipping development." [125] During 1935 and 1936, the gov-

---

119. See p. 466.
120. **13**, p. 65.
121. **52**, p. 272; **32**, pp. 166–67.
122. **58**, p. 286.

123. If the earnings of a subsidized ship over a 10-year period average more than 10 per cent on capital necessarily employed in the business, the operator must return to the government half of the excess up to the full amount of the subsidy accrual. The twelve subsidized lines for which the 10–year-of-first-recapture period expired on or before December 31, 1950 were obligated to refund $49.1 million of the government subsidy accrual of $70.1 million; $28.0 million was paid. **18**, 1952, p. 63.
124. Cf. **50**, pp. 497–500; **19**, p. 4. A substantial part of surplus tonnage was sold to Allied and neutral nations to rehabilitate their fleets.
125. **79**, pp. 194–95.

ernment accorded some subsidies to tramp vessels, then in a particularly difficult situation, but in 1937, when freight rates went up and business improved, these were discontinued. In 1939 the government announced plans to support tramp shipping and the construction of additional shipping tonnage, but the outbreak of the war interrupted the program. The decisive factor in the growth and efficiency of the British merchant marine has been the acute economic necessity for assured sea services in supplying essentials for the nation's life and production, rather than any aid from public sources. British shipowners have generally opposed extensive government assistance. Preference is given to national bottoms for carrying the mail but payments only slightly exceed the actual cost. Foreign flags are not excluded from coastal or intra-empire trade.

Other Countries

France has aided its shipping more extensively and over a longer period than most other countries. It has reserved coastal and colonial trade for French ships, subsidized construction and navigation, paid liberal mail rates and so on. Italy, without coal and without ore from which steel for ships can be made, has subsidized its shipbuilding industry in many direct and indirect ways.

In Japan, the merchant fleet came into being through the initiative of the government, and with its active financial and other support. The major conditions that compelled Japan to become a maritime and shipowning nation are similar to those in Great Britain: a dense population, living on islands; the necessity to import the essentials of life and raw materials and to export in order to pay for imports. Japan's historical development and level of industrial and commercial development have been entirely different, however. Thus, while private capital in Great Britain was strong enough to develop a large merchant fleet, the Japanese government assumed this responsibility and purchased the first vessels in 1875. Government aid underwent many changes afterwards but continued until World War II.[126]

Since World War II, shipping has been supported substantially by the governments of all maritime nations. Aid in construction has been granted by Australia and Italy and aid in operation by Brazil, Canada, France and the United States; loans, grants and government-guaranteed bonds have been provided in Belgium, Sweden, Norway and the Netherlands; tax privileges, more liberal than to other industries, have been accorded by various maritime countries. Various countries use many other forms of assistance to the national flag: the level of consular fees, request for payment of customs and port dues and charges in national currency, control of foreign trade and direction of its routing and so on.[127]

Sea-Borne Traffic

The Atlantic Ocean remains the area of the heaviest sea-borne traffic. It has been estimated that in 1908, 73 per cent of the world's commercial traffic was on that ocean, while the Pacific accounted for 20 per cent, the Indian Ocean for 6 per cent, and the rest for 1 per cent.[128] Shipping has increased on the Pacific Ocean but the Atlantic still holds the lead, though its share in the world's sea-borne transportation must have decreased somewhat. Passenger traffic on the Atlantic continues to be very heavy, with several score passenger liners shuttling on any day between the ports of Europe and the New World.

THE SHARES OF THE CONTINENTS AND COUNTRIES

The world's ocean fleet carried 430 million metric tons of goods in 1928, 470 million in 1938 and 660 million in 1952. The bulk of this traffic is intercontinental, but traffic in Asia and Africa is largely intercoastal.

Europe remains the leader in the world's sea-borne traffic, unloading a considerably greater tonnage than it loads. This difference is due not only to the fact that Europe has a passive trade balance [129] but also reflects the fact that that continent loads mainly high-priced manufactured goods of comparatively light weight and receives bulky, heavy raw materials and foodstuffs.

North and Middle America, as a unit, are next in importance. They used to export a greater tonnage than they imported, but today loadings and unloadings are more or less balanced. This is due to the larger quantities of heavy raw materials imported by North America, such as iron ore, manganese, bauxite, uranium, petroleum.

126. **79**, pp. 317ff; **32**, pp. 223–27.

127. **72**, pp. 38–39.
128. **88**, Vol. 5, p. 80.
129. See pp. 98–101 and p. 242.

TABLE 163

SEA-BORNE TRAFFIC: CARGO LOADED AND UNLOADED, BY CONTINENT, 1928–52

Continent	1928		1933		1938		1948		1951		1952	
	Loaded	Un-loaded	Loaded	Un-loaded	Loaded	Un-loaded	Loaded	Un-loaded	Loaded	Un-loaded	Loaded	Un-loaded
Millions of Metric Tons [a]												
World [b]	430.0		360.0		470.0		490.0		640.0		660.0	
North and Middle America	102.2	78.5	67.8	54.0	107.6	80.9	159.8	150.5	194.8	196.6	186.8	204.4
South America	45.9	23.5	40.4	13.6	52.3	19.5	98.3	28.7	113.2	31.0	116.3	30.1
Europe	196.0	238.0	166.0	212.0	185.0	266.0	108.0	226.0	165.0	294.0	170.0	303.0
Asia	56.1	64.7	56.3	57.1	83.8	67.8	84.4	49.7	121.7	72.2	144.1	76.0
Africa	26.4	21.0	20.2	17.3	28.2	23.4	31.1	26.6	37.7	32.7	36.0	32.8
Oceania	5.3	7.5	7.5	5.2	7.7	9.1	6.9	9.4	7.9	16.2	7.3	18.5
Per Cent												
World	100.0		100.0		100.0		100.0		100.0		100.0	
North and Middle America	23.7	18.2	18.9	15.1	23.2	17.3	32.7	30.6	30.4	30.6	28.3	30.7
South America	10.6	5.4	11.3	3.8	11.3	4.2	20.1	5.8	17.7	4.8	17.6	4.5
Europe	45.4	55.1	46.3	59.1	39.8	56.9	22.1	46.0	25.8	45.7	25.7	45.6
Asia	13.0	15.0	15.7	15.9	18.0	14.5	17.3	10.1	19.0	11.2	21.8	11.4
Africa	6.1	4.9	5.6	4.8	6.1	5.0	6.4	5.4	5.9	5.1	5.5	4.9
Oceania	1.2	1.7	2.1	1.5	1.7	1.9	1.4	1.9	1.2	2.5	1.1	2.8

Sources: **4,** 1952, p. 297; **2,** January 1954, p. xvii.

a. One metric ton = 1.1023 short tons.
b. Total tonnage loaded is approximately the same as the total tonnage unloaded in any year. Excludes the USSR. World totals: rounded figures.

Asia exports a considerably greater tonnage than before the war but its unloadings in 1951 and 1952 were only slightly above those in pre-war years. Oceania's loadings are about half the tonnage of unloadings.

Proportionately, the share of North and Middle America increased, in comparison with the prewar volume, in both loadings and unloadings; that of Europe fell substantially, particularly in loadings, and that of Africa fluctuated only slightly. Oceania's unloadings have increased substantially in recent years. (See Table 163).[130]

Ranking of Countries

The extent of the sea-borne traffic of a country is measured by two sets of statistics — the net registered tonnage of ships entering its ports and clearing from them for a foreign port (Table 164) and the tonnage of goods loaded and unloaded in its ports (Table 165).[131]

Until World War II, the United Kingdom ranked first in the cargo capacity (net registered tonnage) of the ships that visited its ports, and the United States followed closely. Today, international traffic in the ports of the United States is considerably greater. France, ranking after the United Kingdom, has not yet regained the volume of its prewar shipping. The cargo capacity of ships moving to and from Italian ports has fluctuated rather insignificantly. The volume of cargo entering and clearing from ports of the Philippines and Australia is greater than before World War II. (See Table 164.)

An excess of freight tonnage unloaded in the

130. The absolute data for this table were prepared by the Statistical Office of the United Nations, partly on the basis of official reports of individual countries, partly by estimates. The Office calls attention to a margin of possible error up to 10–15 per cent for Asia as a result of such estimates, and smaller margins for other continents and for the world as a whole. (**4,** 1952, p. 322.)

131. When a vessel in foreign trade enters or leaves several ports of a country in succession during a single voyage, as a rule only the first entrance or last clearance is counted. The net registered tonnage of ships entered or cleared may have little bearing on the volume of goods loaded or unloaded in a country.

TABLE 164

SEA-BORNE TRAFFIC: VESSELS ENTERED AND CLEARED IN PORTS OF SELECTED COUNTRIES, 1928–52

(*Millions of Net Registered Tons* [a])

Country	1928		1933		1938		1948		1950		1951		1952	
	En-tered	Cleared	En-tered	Cleared	En-tered	Cleared	En-tered	Cleared	En-tered	Cleared	En-tered	Cleared	En-tered	Cleared
United States [b]	57.3	63.5	44.9	49.8	47.9	59.1	53.9	68.5	66.8	60.2	70.3	81.1	...	...
Canada [c]	...	47.3 [d]	...	38.5	45.6	45.8	39.4	44.3	28.7	24.8	30.2	27.5	31.9	33.1
Mexico	1.5	3.8	1.3	3.3	1.0	2.7	1.2	2.1	1.8	3.1	1.6	2.7	1.8	2.5
Cuba [e]	7.9	7.8	5.6	5.7	4.1	3.9	...	5.2	...	6.2	...	6.4	...	...
Jamaica [e, f]	3.1	...	3.7	...	4.3	...	1.5	...	1.9	...	...	...	...	...
Curaçao [g]	...	...	17.1	...	26.3	...	44.3	...	...	...	...	...	...	...
Trinidad and Tobago	3.3	...	4.4	...	5.5	4.9	10.6	10.6	10.8	10.7	13.1	13.2	16.2	15.2
Venezuela	3.3	9.7	3.8	11.1	4.5	17.1	7.4	31.7	...	...	...	...	...	...
Colombia [f]	6.9	...	5.7	...	6.6	6.6	6.0	6.0	7.5	7.5	6.9	6.8	7.8	7.6
Brazil [h]	...	25.9	...	26.2	24.0	24.0	21.0	21.0	23.1	22.9	23.4	23.2	25.4	25.5
Peru [i, f]	...	18.5	...	14.0	16.5	16.5	8.3	8.3	10.4	...	10.6	9.6	12.1	12.2
Chile [f]	...	3.2	...	1.6	2.7	2.7	3.0	2.9	3.1	3.0	3.1	3.0	3.0	3.0
Uruguay [e, f]	16.0	...	10.4	...	11.5	...	...	...	...	...	...	...	...	...
Argentina [f]	...	...	9.5	...	9.2	...	9.7	...	9.5	...	9.2	...	8.9	...
United Kingdom	60.3	64.4	60.4	55.7	68.4	58.9	50.6	35.8	58.1	45.3	63.6	43.6	64.2	47.0
Ireland	6.7	5.0	6.8	4.9	8.2	5.3	5.5	3.7	7.5	4.8	7.5	4.7	7.3	4.7
France	52.4	46.4	53.7	44.9	51.9	42.6	30.3	20.5	34.3	27.5	42.0	31.8	46.0	34.8
Belgium	25.8	23.9	23.1	21.0	26.7	25.6	21.6	16.8	20.8	22.3	22.0	22.0	21.4	21.9
Netherlands	27.1 [d]	20.9 [d]	20.8	17.3	27.6	23.2	15.3	12.4	23.8	19.6	28.0	19.3	30.7	21.5
Denmark	8.0	4.2	8.3	4.2	9.4	5.2	6.5	3.6	9.6	4.8	9.4	5.2	9.7	5.7
Sweden	11.9	13.2	13.1	12.7	18.3	17.9	15.8	13.5	20.0	18.4	21.9	19.5	22.5	19.8
Norway	3.9	4.8	4.3	4.3	5.4	5.0	4.5	3.3	4.9	3.8	5.4	3.9	5.3	4.4
Finland	2.5	4.3	2.3	4.2	3.7	5.1	2.9	2.9	4.7	3.0	3.6	5.0	4.0	4.6
Germany [j]	31.8	23.9	24.5	21.5	31.9	24.5	10.8	6.5	16.4	15.0	17.8	12.6	21.8	14.9
Poland [k]	5.0	...	6.2	...	11.3	11.3	7.6	7.6	7.2	...	...	...	...	...
Portugal [f]	...	...	...	...	...	...	4.6	...	5.9	...	6.4	...	6.7	...
Spain [l]	16.4	24.1	15.1	23.2	...	...	7.0	9.7	7.3	...	9.0	...	...	...
Italy [f]	20.5	13.1	20.0	14.5	21.1	14.4	15.3	9.1	20.0	13.6	24.1	23.8	26.2	25.5
Greece [f]	...	...	...	...	6.3	6.0	4.0	3.8	5.3	5.3	4.5	...	...	...
Yugoslavia [f]	...	...	...	...	5.4	...	1.3	...	1.9	...	1.9	...	2.2	...
China [f]	23.9	...	20.6	...	14.8	...	...	...	...	...	...	...	...	...
Korea [f]	...	...	14.9	...	13.1	...	0.3 [m]	...	...	...	...	...	...	...
Japan [f]	54.8 [n]	...	59.3 [n]	...	59.2 [n]	58.7	5.1	5.1	10.1	10.0	14.4	14.9	17.8	18.2
Turkey [f, o]	11.5	...	8.3	...	7.1	...	5.7	...	4.3	...	...	...	...	...
Pakistan	} 8.1	8.3	7.2	7.6	9.1	9.5 {	2.9	2.1	3.8	3.1	4.5	3.4	4.9	4.1
India							7.8	6.8	8.0	7.3	9.3	7.8	9.3	8.9
Ceylon	9.7	9.0	9.8	10.1	11.0	10.7	5.7	5.6	8.0	7.0	7.9	7.0	8.5	7.6
Malaya	14.5 [p]	14.2 [p]	14.0	13.8	16.2	15.7	11.4	10.7	14.7	13.6	17.7	16.6	20.2	19.3
Philippines [q]	3.7	3.6	4.9	4.8	4.5	5.2	5.3	6.2	5.4	5.3	6.1	8.0	6.4	10.6
Algeria [e]	7.8	8.3	8.2	7.8	7.2	7.9	3.9	4.7	5.9	7.6	...	...	...	...
Tunisia [e, f]	4.4	...	4.6	...	4.8	4.8	3.0	3.0	3.9	3.9	4.0	4.0	4.3	4.3
French West Africa	9.7 [p]	...	9.3	...	11.7	...	6.8	...	11.1	...	11.6	...	...	...
Gold Coast [f]	2.7	...	1.9	...	2.4	2.4	2.8	2.8	3.2	3.2	3.3	3.3	3.3	3.2
Nigeria [f]	...	1.9	...	1.5	2.0	2.0	2.0	2.1	2.5	2.5	2.4	2.5	2.6	2.6
Kenya	1.8	...	3.9	...	4.8	...	3.4	...	3.6	...	...	...	...	...
Union of South Africa	4.6	5.0	4.5	4.6	8.7	8.8	...	...	8.4	8.0	8.1	7.7	8.1	7.4
Australia	5.0	4.8	4.3	5.2	5.9	6.1	4.8	4.7	8.0	6.2	8.2	6.2	8.6	7.2
New Zealand	2.0	1.7	2.0	2.0	2.5	2.1	1.9	1.4	2.5	1.7	2.3	1.6	2.7	1.8

Sources: **4**, 1948, pp. 277–80; 1953, pp. 304–07; **2**, September 1953, pp. xix-xxii.

a. Net registered tonnage of seagoing foreign and domestic merchant vessels (steam, motor and sailing). Refers to only one entrance or clearance for each foreign voyage. Excludes where possible vessels "in ballast," i.e., entering without unloading, or clearing without loading.

b. Includes Alaska, Hawaii, Puerto Rico, Virgin Islands and international trade of the Great Lakes.

c. Includes international traffic of the Great Lakes and St. Lawrence River; for 1929–48, includes vessels in ballast. Inclusion of vessels in ballast in 1950 raises the figures to 42.8 million tons for entered vessels and 47.3 million for cleared vessels (**2**, September 1952, p. xxii); 1929 and 1933: includes international ferry traffic (about 3.5 per cent).

d. 1929.

e. All entrances and/or clearances counted.

f. Includes vessels in ballast.

g. Includes Aruba and, possibly, coastwise traffic; also includes vessels in ballast.

h. Ports of Rio de Janeiro and Santos. Includes coastwise trade and vessels in ballast.

i. Includes coastwise trade.

j. Postwar: Western Germany; 1948–50 includes vessels in ballast.

k. 1928–39: Gdynia and Danzig only. Includes vessels in ballast.

l. Includes Balearic Islands.

m. South Korea.

n. Includes Korea.

o. Foreign vessels only.

p. 1931.

q. Prior to 1951: port of Manila only. Column for 1938 contains data for 1937.

TABLE 165

SEA-BORNE TRAFFIC: CARGO LOADED AND UNLOADED IN PORTS OF SELECTED COUNTRIES, 1930–52

(Millions of Metric Tons [a])

Country	1930 [b] Loaded	1930 [b] Un-loaded	1939 Loaded	1939 Un-loaded	1949 Loaded	1949 Un-loaded	1950 Loaded	1950 Un-loaded	1951 Loaded	1951 Un-loaded	1952 Loaded	1952 Un-loaded
United States [e]	50.5	48.3	56.0	38.2	65.2	70.2	56.9	87.7	109.9	98.8	98.3	105.3
Canada	9.6 [d]	7.0 [d]	15.7	9.5	20.3	25.7	19.2	33.4	24.7	34.7	29.5	35.2
Mexico	3.7 [e]	0.6 [e]	3.4	0.6	3.0	0.7	5.1	1.1	3.9	1.2	3.3	1.2
Cuba	...	...	...	...	6.7	3.4	7.3	4.1	7.4	4.4	...	...
Trinidad and Tobago	...	...	...	...	5.3	4.8	5.6	4.6	5.9	4.8	6.9	6.5
Venezuela [e]	20.6	0.5	29.7	0.7	65.5	2.3	74.1	1.7	85.3	1.9	92.1	1.8
Colombia	...	...	3.2	0.5	3.3	0.7	4.7	1.0	5.1	1.0	4.4	1.0
Brazil [e, f]	2.3	4.7	4.2	4.8	3.7	7.2	3.8	9.0	4.9	11.0	4.1	11.4
Peru [e]	2.0	0.4	2.1	0.5	1.8	0.6	1.8	0.6	1.8	0.8	1.9	0.8
Chile [g]	...	...	4.1	1.2	5.1	2.0	5.1	1.7	5.3	2.3	4.3	2.2
Argentina [e]	11.0	12.4	12.9	9.8	5.9	11.9	7.4	10.5	5.7	11.8	3.0	10.9
France [h]	...	...	12.6	35.9	15.2	36.1	19.2	31.5	22.6	40.9	22.3	42.5
Belgium	...	...	10.4	12.4	9.1	13.0	11.6	11.9	14.6	17.1	12.4	17.6
Netherlands [i]	...	...	15.4	27.3	10.3	18.7	15.0	23.9	13.8	34.2	14.2	37.0
Denmark	2.0	11.2	1.9	11.0	1.7	10.2	2.2	12.4	2.4	12.0	2.7	11.8
Sweden [j]	11.1	9.2	14.4	14.1	12.3	13.4	13.9	16.4	15.2	19.9	14.5	19.3
Finland	5.5	2.5	5.9	3.0	4.7	3.2	6.0	4.0	7.5	5.5	5.9	5.5
Germany [k]	...	...	12.4	24.0	5.3	15.6	9.9	13.5	10.3	20.5	10.6	24.4
Poland [j]	...	...	13.2	3.1	14.0	2.9	12.5	3.2	...	...	...	...
Portugal [l]	...	...	...	...	0.3	1.4	0.4	1.4	0.8	1.4	0.7	1.5
Spain [m]	...	...	...	...	4.0	4.6	4.1	5.0	6.0	4.5	6.3	5.4
Italy	3.6	22.4	3.8	20.4	3.5	21.0	4.1	22.0	5.3	27.5	5.6	28.1
Yugoslavia	1.8	0.5	1.4	0.5	2.0	1.0	2.0	0.9	1.8	1.3	1.7	1.6
Greece	...	...	0.6	2.2	0.2	2.9	0.2	3.1	0.5	3.5	...	...
Japan [n]	7.6	22.0	17.8	34.4	2.4	11.4	3.6	11.7	3.7	21.1	5.0	23.7
Burma	...	...	4.9	1.3	0.9	0.5	1.0	0.6	...	...	...	...
Indochina	2.9	0.5	3.9 [o]	0.6 [o]	0.4	0.7	0.4	0.7	0.8	1.1	0.7	1.5
Ceylon [p]	0.7	...	0.6	1.3	0.7	1.9	0.7	1.9	0.7	2.1	0.8	2.1
Indonesia	10.3	2.9	12.1	2.1	7.6	3.0	8.4	2.8	9.0	2.5	9.9	4.4
Philippines [q]	1.5 [e]	1.6 [e]	3.1 [o]	2.3 [o]	0.5	2.6	0.3	1.7	3.1	2.6	4.4	2.6
French Morocco [r]	2.1	0.9	2.9	1.0	5.6	2.0	6.0	2.1	6.8	2.8	6.3	3.2
Algeria	6.4	4.5	6.9	3.1	6.2	2.9	6.8	3.2	6.6	3.8	6.9	3.6
Tunisia [r]	4.1	1.0	3.1	0.8	3.5	0.9	3.3	1.0	3.7	1.0	3.5	1.0
Egypt [r]	2.4	5.6	3.7	6.2	2.7	5.1	2.8	5.5	3.1	6.2	2.0	4.9
French West Africa [r]	1.1	1.0	1.8 [o]	1.6 [o]	1.5	1.7	1.8	2.2	1.9	2.7	2.1	2.5
Gold Coast	...	...	0.7	0.4	1.4	0.9	1.4	0.9	1.5	1.1	1.4	1.1
Nigeria	0.8	0.5	1.0	0.4	1.5	1.0	1.5	1.1	1.7	1.3	1.6	1.3
Kenya	...	...	0.6	0.6	1.0	1.5	1.0	1.5	1.1	1.7	1.6	2.5
Mozambique [r]	...	...	0.8	0.8	2.5	2.0	3.4	2.2	2.7	2.2	...	...
Union of South Africa	...	...	3.0	4.4	3.1	6.4	4.2	7.0	3.3	6.5	2.8	6.2

(Continued on following page)

TABLE 165—*continued*

Country	1930 [b]		1939		1949		1950		1951		1952	
	Loaded	Un-loaded	Loaded	Un-loaded	Loaded	Un-loaded	Loaded	Un-loaded	Loaded	Un-loaded	Loaded	Un-loaded
Australia	4.5	6.0	6.0	5.8	6.4	7.7	6.1	10.2	6.4	11.9	5.4	13.1
New Zealand	0.8	2.1	1.0	2.9	1.2	3.4	1.3	3.7	1.2	4.0	1.4	5.0

Sources: **4,** 1949–1950, pp. 305–10; 1952, pp. 298–303; **2,** November 1953, pp. 78–82 and January 1954, pp. 80–82.

a. One metric ton = 1.1023 short tons.
b. The first year for which the United Nations has published the data.
c. Includes international traffic on the Great Lakes. Beginning 1950, excludes "special category" commodities. In 1930 and 1939 excludes goods in transit and imports and exports controlled by the U.S. Department of Defense; also excludes Alaska, Hawaii and Puerto Rico.
d. 1931. Excludes traffic on the Great Lakes.
e. Includes goods imported and exported other than by sea, the amount of which is believed small. For Argentina: 1930 and 1939 only.
f. Excludes goods to and from bonded warehouses.
g. Excludes goods re-exported and in transit to other countries.
h. Includes bunkers and ships' stores.

i. Includes ships, dredges and floating drydocks when delivered as goods, without being loaded on ships.
j. Excludes live animals.
k. Western Germany, except 1930; for 1939 and 1949: 12 largest ports in Western Germany. Figures comparable.
l. Goods carried by Portuguese vessels (27 per cent of loadings and 48 per cent of unloadings in 1950).
m. Includes the Balearic Islands.
n. Goods carried by steel vessels. Excludes military cargo.
o. 1938.
p. Port of Colombo only.
q. 1949 and 1950: port of Manila only. For 1951: 9 ports.
r. Includes coastwise traffic in prewar years; includes sea-borne traffic with the Sudan in postwar years.

ports of a country over the tonnage loaded may indicate that more heavy goods, possibly of lesser value, are imported than exported. Most European countries report considerably greater unloadings than loadings. The few European countries that export raw materials, such as Finland (lumber) and Yugoslavia (various ores), are exceptions. The extreme case in point is Venezuela, which exported 92.1 million metric tons via sea-borne traffic in 1952 and unloaded only 1.8 million.

The United States, with an active trade balance, ordinarily loads a greater tonnage on seagoing vessels (including international shipping on the Great Lakes) than it unloads. The surplus of loaded tonnage would be even greater were it not that its imports consist mostly of raw materials and its exports, of manufactured products. In recent years a substantial part of the loaded cargo has consisted of mineral fuels.

The sea-borne traffic of Japan, though recovering, is substantially below the prewar volume; that of Germany almost reached the prewar level in 1952. (See Table 165.)

Traffic on the Suez Canal

Except for interruptions and setbacks caused by two world wars, use of the Suez Canal has grown steadily, in terms of the net tonnage of transit vessels, from 3 to 6 million tons in the 1880's to about 20 million before World War I;

33 million in 1929; and more than 80 million in 1951.[132] More than twice as many vessels passed through the Canal in 1951 as in 1925 (11,694 and 5,337, respectively) while the net tonnage trebled, rising from 26.8 million net registered tons to 80.4 million, because of the increase in the average size of ships. (See Table 166.)

The British flag predominated among transit vessels from the opening of the Canal until recent years. It flew over 80 per cent of all shipping, in terms of net tonnage, in the 1880's; 60 or more per cent before World War I; some 57 per cent in 1929; and 50 per cent in 1939, but today the proportion is less than 35 per cent.[133]

An increasing number of tankers and ships in ballast pass through the Canal. Such ships represented only 18 per cent of the total in 1931 and about 24–25 per cent in 1938 but nearly 60 per cent in 1951. The loading capacity of all ships passing through in 1931 was 30 million net registered tons, of which tankers accounted for 2.2 million and ships in ballast, for 3.2 mil-

132. Suez Canal measurements, which are higher than those generally applied, tend to calculate the space capacity for cargo more closely. Tolls are paid on the basis of net tonnage, and the Suez Canal measurement has no uniform rules for its calculation. A. Berglund cites an example of two ships of 6,784 and 4,172 net tons, respectively, according to United States certificates. In terms of Suez Canal measurement, they paid for 9,118 and 11,661 net tons, respectively. (**39,** p. 44.)
133. **84,** various issues; **45,** various years.

TABLE 166

SEA-BORNE TRAFFIC: SHIPPING THROUGH THE SUEZ CANAL, 1871–1952

Year	Number of Vessels [a]	Tonnage, in Millions of Net Registered Tons [b]	Cargo, in Millions of Metric Tons	Year	Number of Vessels [a]	Tonnage, in Millions of Net Registered Tons [b]	Cargo, in Millions of Metric Tons
1871	765	0.6	...	1935	5,992	32.8	26.3
1880	2,026	3.1	...	1936	5,877	32.4	25.6
1890	3,389	6.9	...	1937	6,635	36.5	32.8
1900	3,441	9.7	...	1938	6,171	34.4	28.8
1910	4,533	16.3	...	1939	5,277	29.6	24.7
1913	5,085	19.8	...	1940	2,589	13.5	...
1920	4,009	16.8	...	1945	4,206	25.1	...
1925	5,337	26.8	...	1946	5,057	32.7	21.9
1929	6,274	33.2	34.5	1947	5,972	36.6	30.6
1930	5,761	31.4	28.5	1948	8,686	55.1	49.4
1931	5,366	30.0	25.3	1949	10,420	68.9	61.1
1932	5,032	28.3	23.6	1950	11,751	81.8	72.6
1933	5,423	30.7	26.9	1951	11,694	80.4	76.8
1934	5,663	31.8	28.5	1952	...	...	83.4

Sources: **84,** various issues; **45,** various years; **4,** 1951, p. 324.

a. Includes vessels in ballast.   b. Suez Canal measurement.

lion. For 1938 the corresponding figures were 34.4, 3.1 and 5.2 million net tons; for 1951, 80.4, 24.4 and 23.6 million net tons.[134]

Ships going northward through the Suez Canal carry a substantially greater tonnage of cargo than those moving southward. This difference reflects the passive trade balance of Europe with Asia and the character of commodities exchanged between the two continents: fabricated articles for raw materials. In recent years, shipments of oil from the Middle East have been increasing. The transit traffic in both directions in the last two decades has been as follows (in millions of metric tons): [135]

Year	Southward	Northward
1931	7.4	18.0
1933	7.2	19.7
1935	8.9	17.4
1937	10.2	22.6
1939	7.5	17.2
1947	7.8	22.8
1948	9.7	39.7
1949	13.0	48.0
1950	12.1	60.5
1951	17.4	59.3
1952	22.0	61.5

134. **45,** 1951/1952, p. 144. Total includes warships and government transports.

135. **4,** 1951, p. 325; **2,** November 1953, p. 82.

Traffic on the Panama Canal

In 1915, the first year of operation, traffic through the Panama Canal comprised more than a thousand vessels, with 4.9 million long tons of cargo. A record, never matched until 1952, was reached in 1929, with 6,289 vessels and 30.6 million tons of cargo. During World War II, traffic fell drastically, and in the worst year, 1944, only 1,562 vessels, carrying some 7 million long tons of cargo crossed the Isthmus. However, traffic is picking up — in 1952, 6,524 vessels with 33.6 million long tons of cargo.

The net tonnage of transit ships using the Canal reached a high point in 1930, with 27.7 million net registered tons.[136] It slumped in the depression years, fluctuated before World War II, shrank drastically in wartime under the menace of enemy submarine activity and in 1952 was the highest on record. (See Table 167.)

136. Panama Canal measurements differ from those generally accepted and also from Suez Canal measurements. The difference between United States and Panama Canal calculations of net tonnage can be seen from the following data for commercial through traffic (in thousands of net tons):

	U.S. Calculation	Panama Canal Calculation
1940	18,643	24,144
1952	24,243	30,674

(**15,** 1954, p. 604.)

TABLE 167

SEA-BORNE TRAFFIC: SHIPPING THROUGH THE PANAMA CANAL, 1915–52 [a]

	Ships				Ships		
Year	Number [b]	Tonnage, in Millions of Net Registered Tons	Cargo, in Millions of Long Tons [c]	Year	Number [b]	Tonnage, in Millions of Net Registered Tons	Cargo, in Millions of Long Tons [c]
1915	1,058	3.5	4.9	1934	5,234	26.4	24.7
1916 [d]	724	2.2	3.1	1935	5,180	25.7	25.3
1917	1,738	5.4	7.1	1936	5,382	25.9	26.5
1918	1,989	6.1	7.5	1937	5,387	25.4	28.1
1919	1,948	5.7	6.9	1938	5,524	26.0	27.4
1920	2,393	7.9	9.4	1939	5,903	27.2	27.9
1921	2,791	10.6	11.6	1940	5,370	24.1	27.3
1922	2,665	10.6	10.9	1941	4,727	20.6	25.0
1923	3,908	17.2	19.6	1942	2,688	11.0	13.6
1924	5,158	24.2	27.0	1943	1,822	8.2	10.6
1925	4,592	21.1	24.0	1944	1,562	6.1	7.0
1926	5,087	22.9	26.0	1945	1,939	8.4	8.6
1927	5,293	24.2	27.7	1946	3,747	17.5	15.0
1928	6,253	27.2	29.6	1947	4,260	20.2	21.7
1929	6,289	27.6	30.6	1948	4,678	22.9	24.1
1930	6,027	27.7	30.0	1949	4,793	23.5	25.3
1931	5,370	25.7	25.1	1950	5,448	28.0	28.9
1932	4,362	21.8	19.8	1951	5,593	27.2	30.1
1933	4,162	21.1	18.2	1952	6,524	30.7	33.6

Source: **25**, p. 55.

a. Includes only vessels of 300 or more net tons (Panama Canal measurement) for vessels rated on net tonnage, and 500 or more tons displacement for vessels rated on displacement tonnage. Net tonnage data before 1939 are estimates based on revised measurements, as established on March 1, 1938. (Panama Canal measurement.)

b. Excludes vessels operated or owned by the United States government until July 1, 1951; vessels of the Panama Republic and Colombia and vessels making the transit for ship repairs at the Canal repair shops.

c. One long ton = 2,240 pounds.

d. Canal closed to traffic during some seven months, because of the slides.

Considerably more cargo is shipped from the Pacific Ocean to the Atlantic in normal times than is transported in the opposite direction. This is shown by the following figures for 1941–52 (in millions of long tons).[137]

Year	Pacific-Atlantic	Atlantic-Pacific
1941	15.5	9.5
1942	8.9	4.7
1943	5.7	4.9
1944	3.6	3.4
1945	4.4	4.2
1946	8.8	6.1
1947	13.4	8.3
1948	15.4	8.7
1949	15.4	9.9
1950	19.4	9.5
1951	18.9	11.1
1952	18.5	15.1

137. **22**, various years; **25**, pp. 66–69.

Except in four early years and in 1945, when British vessels topped the list of transit vessels using the Canal, ships of the United States have been more numerous than those of any other flag. They carry 40 to 50 per cent of the total cargo — in 1949, 12.4 million long tons out of 25.3 million; in 1952, 13.7 out of 33.6 million tons. The United Kingdom is second, followed by Norway and Panama.

More than 80 per cent of the net tonnage passing through the Panama Canal is carried in vessels using eight main trade routes. Until recently the intracoastal trade route of the United States ranked first in tonnage among these routes, but after 1951 its importance declined and in 1952 two other United States routes, from the east coast to Asia and to the west coast of South America, were first and second in transit net tonnage. Among the trade routes from Europe using the Panama Canal, that to the

TABLE 168

SEA-BORNE TRAFFIC: MAIN STREAMS OF TRADE
THROUGH THE PANAMA CANAL, 1950–52

(*Millions of Net Registered Tons* [a])

Trading Region	1950	1951	1952
Total	28.0	27.2	30.7
United States			
Intracoastal trade	6.4	4.5	3.2
East coast			
To Asia	3.7	4.3	5.0
To west coast, South America	4.1	4.1	4.8
To west coast, Central America	1.5	1.4	1.7
To Canada and Oceania	0.8	0.8	1.4
Europe			
To west coast, United States and Canada	2.7	3.6	4.0
To west coast, South America	1.7	1.8	2.0
To Oceania	1.9	1.8	2.9
Other	5.2	4.9	5.7

Sources: **22**, 1951, p. 8; **25**, p. 7.

a. Panama Canal measurement.

west coast of the United States and Canada ranks first in importance. (See Table 168.)

The average cargo of a vessel using the Canal in recent years was 6,400 long tons (1949: 6,437; 1950: 6,419; 1951: 6,387; 1952: 6,243). Petroleum and its products have represented the largest shipments from the Atlantic to the Pacific, followed by coal and coke, and iron and steel. Ore, lumber, wheat, nitrates and canned food have constituted the main shipments from the Pacific to the Atlantic.[138]

Traffic in Ports

Water-borne trade in ports consists of exports, imports, transit trade and domestic commerce — coastal, internal and local. In many ports, such as New York, New Orleans and San Francisco, domestic trade accounts for a considerably greater share of the total cargo tonnage than foreign trade. Elsewhere, either foreign or domestic trade may represent almost the entire business. In Seattle, San Diego and Corpus Christi, domestic commerce accounted for more than 90 per cent of the total cargo tonnage in 1949; Cruz Grande, Chile, in contrast, operates exclusively for shipments abroad. Transit traffic also may be of great importance to a port, as it is to Rotterdam and, to a lesser degree, Antwerp.

The world's busiest ports include New York, London, Antwerp, Rotterdam, Marseilles, Liverpool, Rio de Janeiro, Genoa, Naples, Malmö, Gothenburg, Hong Kong, Singapore and Calcutta. The great German ports of Hamburg and Bremen have lost much of their importance since World War II, but are staging a rapid comeback.

Ports of the United States and Canada have expanded in recent years, accommodating more ships and handling substantially more cargo than before World War II. London and Liverpool have not fully recovered and the net registered tonnage of ships entered and cleared is below the 1938 level. In contrast, Antwerp has a flourishing business, with more cargo tonnage than before the war. (See Table 169; cf. Figure 93.)

COASTWISE TRAFFIC

Coastwise traffic is of a great importance to countries with extended coast lines and numerous harbors. The merchant marine of the United States carries more cargo in coastal trade than in foreign trade. The coastwise and intercoastal traffic of the country moves through 259 ports, of which 150 are on the Atlantic Ocean, 30 on the Gulf of Mexico, and 79 on the Pacific. It is concentrated, however, at 26 ports, which handled 88 per cent of the receipts and 70 per cent of the shipments in 1939. In 1951 New York handled 55.4 million short tons (receipts and shipments) in coastwise traffic, as compared to 35.0 million in foreign trade (imports and exports). The corresponding figures for San Francisco were 23.3 and 4.6 million tons; for Houston, 22.2 and 7.2 million tons; and for Los Angeles, 13.4 and 4.3 million tons.[139] Figure 94 shows the principal ports of the United States served by coastwise and intercoastal carriers.

Coastwise traffic in the USSR, accounting for the greatest part of its total sea-borne traffic, is carried on mostly on the land-locked Caspian Sea. About half of all water-borne cargo consists of shipments of petroleum from Baku to Astrakhan.[140]

Traffic between domestic seaports plays a considerable role in the economic life of the United Kingdom and Japan. In Australia and New

138. **22**, 1951, p. 17; **25**, p. 9.

139. **27**, 1952, Part 2, pp. xxvi–xxx.
140. **38**, p. 87.

TABLE 169

PORTS: SHIPS IN FOREIGN TRADE ENTERED AND CLEARED, AND IMPORTS AND EXPORTS, IN SELECTED MAJOR PORTS, 1936–51

Country, Port and Year	Ships Entered		Ships Cleared		Cargo Unloaded	Cargo Loaded
	Number	Millions of Net Registered Tons	Number	Millions of Net Registered Tons	Millions of Metric Tons [a]	
United States						
New York						
1938	3,584	20.4	3,844	20.9	10.9	6.0
1950	4,458	22.5	5,313	22.5	23.1	6.4
1951	4,642	24.3	5,321	24.3	25.2	9.8
Philadelphia						
1938	670	2.0	536	1.5	3.5	1.1
1950	1,667	9.1	1,229	7.1	12.1	1.0
1951	1,577	7.8	1,151	7.9	12.5	5.1
Baltimore						
1938	600	1.7	553	1.4	4.4	1.2
1950	...	...	...	...	10.9	2.6
1951	1,684	6.9	1,284	5.5	14.5	8.0
Boston						
1938	1,041	3.4	795	2.8	1.6	0.3
1951	993	3.7	627	2.6	5.1	0.4
Houston						
1938	541	2.2	546	2.3	5.6	0.5
1950	...	...	...	...	1.9	3.7
1951	591	2.2	660	2.6	1.8	5.4
New Orleans						
1938	1,350	3.6	1,240	3.3	...	...
1950	1,666	4.5	1,919	5.4	3.3	4.4
1951	1,712	4.5	1,921	5.4	4.3	6.0
San Francisco						
1938	398	1.7	577	2.3	0.9	3.5
1950	545	2.2	795	3.2	0.9	1.6
1951	842	3.6	819	3.5	1.6	3.0
Los Angeles						
1938	1,542	5.4	1,310	5.2	0.5	5.5
1950	1,572	4.0	1,031	3.8	0.8	1.4
1951	1,653	4.8	1,216	4.9	1.0	3.3
Seattle						
1938	1,848	3.3	1,743	3.3	0.2	0.4
1951	965	2.0	811	1.9	0.3	0.9
Portland, Oregon						
1938	104	0.3	80	0.3	0.1	0.6
1951	336	1.3	256	1.0	0.1	1.8
Canada						
Montreal						
1938	1,096	4.3	1,016	4.0	3.5	3.1
1951	1,188	4.2	1,189	4.2	6.2	7.3
Vancouver						
1938	2,876	6.4	2,808	6.3	1.7	1.8
1951	1,231	5.3	1,240	5.4	5.4	4.7
Quebec						
1938	387	1.9	377	1.7	0.2	0.3
1951	585	2.9	585	2.9	1.8	0.8

(*Continued on facing page*)

TABLE 169—*continued*

Country, Port and Year	Ships Entered		Ships Cleared		Cargo Unloaded	Cargo Loaded
	Number	Millions of Net Registered Tons	Number	Millions of Net Registered Tons	Millions of Metric Tons [a]	
Halifax						
1938	1,307	3.2	1,501	3.2	1.1	0.4
1951	1,475	5.0	1,464	5.0	2.0	1.4
Brazil						
Rio de Janeiro						
1938	4,411	12.4	4,415	12.4	...	...
1949	5,228	11.9	5,197	11.8	8.2	3.4
Santos						
1938	3,639	11.6	3,638	11.6	...	...
1949	5,228	10.6	4,514	10.6	8.7	10.2
United Kingdom						
London						
1938	...	22.5	...	20.4	...	...
1951	...	18.7	...	18.0	...	...
Liverpool						
1938	...	14.6	...	13.5	...	...
1951	...	12.5	...	12.1	...	...
Manchester [b]						
1938	...	3.5	...	2.9	...	...
1951	...	3.7	...	3.3	...	...
Southampton						
1938	...	11.5	...	11.6	...	...
1951	...	11.3	...	11.2	...	...
Dover						
1938	...	3.8	...	3.8	...	...
1951	...	4.1	...	4.1	...	...
Glasgow						
1938	...	4.9	...	4.9	...	...
1951	...	4.2	...	4.4	...	...
Hull						
1938	...	5.4	...	4.8	...	...
1950	...	4.6	...	4.4	...	...
1951	...	4.4	...	4.2	...	...
France						
Marseilles						
1938	7,837	16.0	7,895	16.1	6.7	2.7
1951	6,901	15.3	6,899	15.3	9.6	5.3
Bordeaux						
1938	2,667	3.6	2,687	3.7	3.0	1.1
1949	1,646	2.8	1,621	2.7	1.8	1.1
Rouen						
1938	3,818	3.9	3,844	3.9	6.5	1.2
1951	4,482	5.1	4,481	5.1	6.2	2.6
Le Havre						
1938	4,183	10.5	4,193	10.4	5.2	1.5
1951	4,176	15.2	4,184	15.2	9.3	3.7
Dunkirk						
1938	...	4.9	...	4.7	4.2	
1951	3,768	5.8	...	4.2	2.8	2.8

(*Continued on following page*)

TABLE 169—*continued*

Country, Port and Year	Ships Entered		Ships Cleared		Cargo Unloaded	Cargo Loaded
	Number	Millions of Net Regis- tered Tons	Number	Millions of Net Regis- tered Tons	Millions of Metric Tons [a]	
Belgium						
Antwerp						
1938	11,762	24.1	12,592	24.4	11.9	11.7
1951	11,425	26.5	...	...	15.1	14.0
Netherlands						
Rotterdam						
1938	15,360	24.7	...	...	42.4	
1951	13,709	23.2	...	32.7 [c]	38.0	
Amsterdam						
1938	...	5.0 [c]	...	5.0 [c]	...	
1951	4,354	4.9	...	6.7 [c]	6.3	
Denmark						
Copenhagen						
1936–38	9,865	5.2 [c]	7,683	3.3 [c]	4.4	0.8
1951	19,042	8.3	...	...	5.5	1.4
Sweden						
Stockholm						
1937	2,414	1.2	2,414	1.2	2.4	0.4
1950	4,128	4.6	[d]	[d]	4.4	0.3
Gothenburg						
1937	...	5.0	...	...	...	...
1950	8,347	11.1	[d]	[d]	3.5	1.5
Malmö						
1937	...	3.7	...	...	...	...
1950	12,590	5.9	[d]	[d]	1.6	0.5
Germany						
Hamburg						
1938	12,057	17.9	12,578	17.4	18.0	7.2
1951	8,852	11.4	9,364	11.4	9.9	4.4
Bremen						
1938	3,681	4.8	4,133	5.3	2.2	4.0
1951	3,906	5.5	4,459	5.7	3.9	3.4
Emden						
1938	968	1.9	773	1.6	3.7 [c]	4.2 [c]
1951	1,086	1.8	1,029	1.6	3.4	2.0
Italy						
Genoa						
1937	...	7.7	[d]	[d]	...	...
1951	5,337	11.2	5,342	11.3	6.5	1.2
Naples						
1937	...	5.9	[d]	[d]	...	...
1951	8,179	9.4	8,181	10.5	2.5	1.9
Venice						
1937	...	3.7	[d]	[d]	...	...
1951	2,858	3.0	2,829	3.0	3.8	0.3
Japan						
Yokohama						
1937	...	12.3	...	...	...	...
1950	1,590	6.4	...	...	...	...
Kobe						
1937	...	16.3	...	...	...	...
1950	1,353	5.1	...	...	...	...

(*Continued on facing page*)

TABLE 169—*continued*

| Country, Port and Year | Ships Entered | | Ships Cleared | | Cargo Unloaded | Cargo Loaded |
	Number	Millions of Net Registered Tons	Number	Millions of Net Registered Tons	Millions of Metric Tons [a]	
Taiwan						
Keelung (Kirun)						
1950	...	...	6,152	4.0	...	...
Pakistan						
Karachi						
1949	728	2.5	519	0.6	1.9	0.9
India						
Bombay						
1938–39	3,282 [f]	6.4 [f]	d	d		5.1
1949–50	...	7.3	d	d		8.8
Calcutta						
1939–40	...	...	...	...		9.7
1950–51	2,284	8.1	d	d		7.5
Indochina						
Saigon						
1936	...	3.6 [d]	...	...	...	...
1950	749	2.0	732	1.9	0.9	0.5
Philippines						
Manila						
1936	...	4.5	d	d	...	...
1950	1,282	5.4	...	...	0.3	1.7
Hong Kong						
1939	12,134	14.6	11,747	14.6	...	...
1950	6,792	11.7	6,864	11.7	3.9	2.3
Singapore						
1940	3,386	8.4	...	...	2.0	1.8
1950	2,905	8.3	...	...	3.9	2.4
Australia [g]						
Sydney						
1938–39	7,384	11.7	...	...	2.0	1.3
1949–50	3,927	8.1	...	...	3.2 [h]	2.1 [h]
Melbourne						
1938–39	3,384	8.5	...	...	1.8	0.8
1949–50	2,328	8.3	...	...	4.2	1.7
New Zealand						
Auckland						
1938	...	1.9	...	1.4	1.1	0.3
1950	...	1.2	...	1.0	1.4 [i]	0.3 [i]
Wellington						
1938	...	0.7	...	0.9	0.8	0.2
1950	...	0.8	...	1.0	0.9 [i]	0.2 [i]

Sources: For the United States: **17,** 1938, pp. 934–38; **16,** 1951 and 1952; **27,** Part 2, 1939, pp. 6–14; 1951, *passim* and 1952, *passim.* For the United Kingdom: **33,** February 9, 1952, p. 277. For Canada: **28,** 1939, pp. 692–93; **29,** 1951, *passim.* For India: **5,** October-December 1951, *passim* and statistical yearbooks. For other countries: statistical yearbooks and consular reports.

a. One metric ton = 1.1023 short tons.
b. Includes Runcorn.
c. Gross registered tons.
d. Included under "Ships entered."
e. 1936.

f. Steamships and their gross registered tonnage. Sailing vessels: 51,889, with 0.9 million gross registered tons.
g. Data on ships and tonnage entered include oversea, interstate and coastwise trade.
h. 1947–48.
i. 1949.

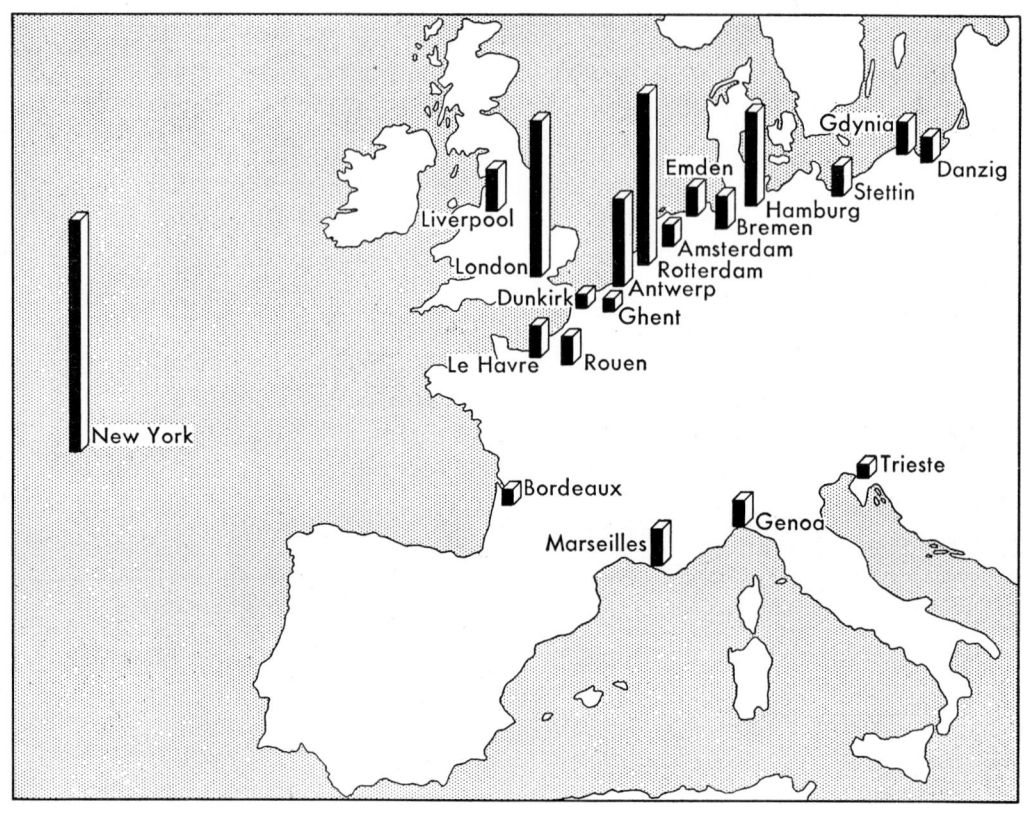

United Nations

FIGURE 93. COMPARATIVE TONNAGE HANDLED BY THE PRINCIPAL EUROPEAN PORTS AND NEW YORK, 1938

Zealand, likewise, the tonnage of cargo moved along the nations' coasts matches the foreign loadings and unloadings. (See Table 170.)

While the seas are open to ships of all nations, many countries reserve coastwise traffic for their own ships, as do the United States, France, Portugal, Spain, Japan and some others. Great Britain, the Scandinavian countries, Italy and Germany have opened their ports for coastal traffic either to ships of all nations or certain countries; Canada accepts only the British flag in its coastal traffic.

Coastwise traffic consists mostly of bulky and heavy commodities, such as lumber, coal, steel and clay, usually moved in barges especially adapted to them. A substantial proportion of the cargo is carried by industrial firms in their own vessels.

INLAND WATERWAYS

Since early days, rivers and lakes have been important avenues for internal commerce. Some rivers, such as the Rhine and the Danube, have been arteries of international traffic for centuries. In time, canals were built to connect natural inland water routes.

Transport by water is generally cheaper than by rail, chiefly because of two factors. Little tractive power is required to move heavy loads slowly over water so that one ordinary power unit can move more freight in a single row of barges than can be handled in several freight trains.[141] Moreover, waterways are provided by nature or at public expense and are improved and maintained from public funds.[142] In the United States, for example, the government spent more than $4 billion on rivers and harbors between 1791 and 1949.[143] On the other hand, water transportation is slow and subject to weather uncertainties. Much freight therefore has been diverted to the railroads, which offer many auxiliary services in addition to the advantages of speed and established schedules.

141. **40,** p. 150.
142. Cf. **69,** pp. 745–51.
143. **11,** p. 72.

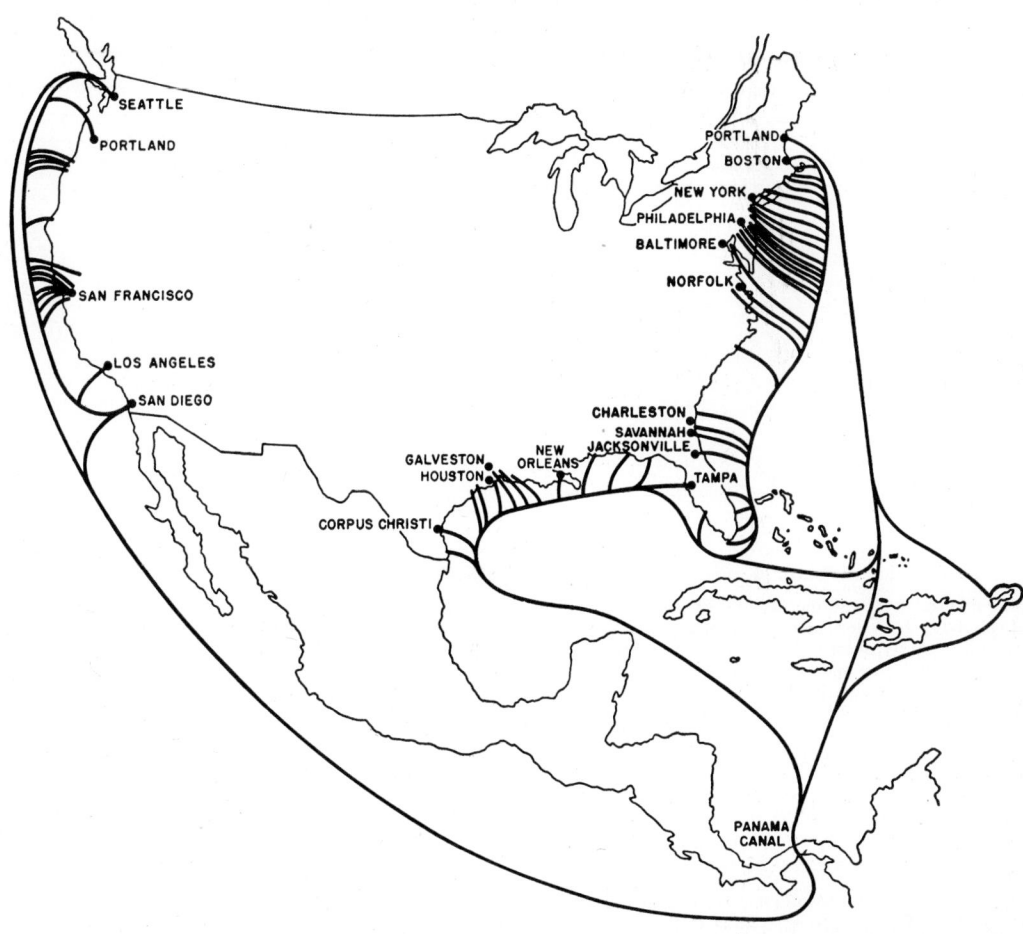

National Resources Planning Board

FIGURE 94. COASTWISE TRAFFIC: MAJOR PORTS OF THE UNITED STATES SERVED BY COASTWISE AND INTERCOASTAL CARRIERS

Nevertheless, inland waterways are still used largely for shipment of bulk commodities, and some nonnavigable rivers are used to float timber. Moreover, waterways sometimes offer facilities for storage. Thus, Belgian coal barges sent to Paris in the spring sometimes remain a long time in the Parisian basin until the coal is stored or distributed.[144]

Inland waterways are used to a great extent in the USSR and would account for an even larger share in total transport volume were it not for various physical difficulties. Most of the Russian waters follow a meridianal direction, south to north, in contrast to the predominant trade direction, which is east-west. Navigation is interrupted in the winter, when the rivers are frozen, and in summer on account of low water.[145]

Self-propelled barges and tankers are used increasingly on waterways of western Europe but dumb barges (without self-propulsion) are still important in many countries. The average carrying capacity of the self-propelled barge is less than 350 tons; of the dumb barge, slightly over 400 tons. Many obsolete craft are still in use. France, for example, has renewed only 13 per cent of its inland fleet within the last decade, and 28 per cent is more than 40 years old. Western Germany has intensified the construction of self-propelled barges and the conversion of dumb barges into self-propelled vessels, but 32 per cent of the former and 12 per cent of the

144. **39**, p. 6.

145. **41**, p. 13.

TABLE 170

SEA-BORNE TRAFFIC: GOODS UNLOADED IN COASTWISE SHIPPING OF SELECTED COUNTRIES, 1938–52

(*Millions of Metric Tons*)

Country [a]	1938	1948	1949	1950	1951	1952
United States	125.6	157.9	146.4	165.6	179.4	. . .
Canada	. . .	. . .	. . .	. . .	. . .	28.4
Mexico	1.1	1.4	1.7	1.7	1.6	2.0
Brazil	2.6	3.9	4.0	4.2	4.8	4.7
Chile	1.8	2.2	2.0	2.4	2.3	2.5
Denmark	2.6	3.8	3.4	3.1	3.6	3.1
Western Germany [b]	4.7	3.2	2.6	2.5	2.4	2.5
Italy [c]	10.5	4.2	5.5	5.8	6.4	7.0
Yugoslavia	0.2	1.3	1.5	1.4	1.2	1.1
Japan	95.6	46.1	47.4	44.7	64.3	52.2
Australia [d]	8.4	8.4	7.8	7.5	8.1	9.2
New Zealand	2.1	2.2	2.1	2.1	1.7	2.1

Sources: **2**, January 1954, p. 87; for the United States: **27**, Part II, various years.

a. Figures represent the weight of all goods which, after having been loaded on a seagoing vessel at some port of a country, were unloaded at another. Data exclude goods in vessels moving exclusively on rivers, lakes, canals or harbors without entering the sea; also goods transloaded from a vessel moving in coastwise traffic to another vessel moving in such traffic; data include goods unloaded to be reshipped for export.

b. Includes loadings destined for canal and river ports.
c. Includes traffic between Italy and Trieste.
d. Interstate traffic only.

latter are at least 50 years old.[146] In the United States, diesel-motored towboats, with a capacity of 2,000–3,000 tons, are commonly used. The country has some 8,000 vessels of this type. Such craft may carry as much as two or three freight trains.[147] The capacity of freighters on the Great Lakes exceeds 10,000 tons, and some of the new vessels can handle 18,000 tons of iron ore. In 1938, about one third of all inland freight traffic in Belgium, France, Germany and the Netherlands was carried by water; in the Netherlands, more than four fifths of the combined rail and inland water traffic moved over rivers and canals.[148] The tonnage handled in inland ports is considerable — sometimes larger than in big seaports. Thus, tonnage handled in the biggest European inland port, Duisburg-Ruhrort, amounted to some 20 million tons — about double that of Hamburg, Germany.

In areas where a subsistence economy predominates and transportation facilities are limited, natural waterways have preserved much of their historic role. Without them, many districts would be practically inaccessible. In contrast to advanced countries, where waterways are mostly used for freight transport, rivers in underdeveloped regions serve for passenger transportation as well. In prepartitioned India, for example, some 25 million passengers traveled on small canal boats in prewar years, and other millions used river boats.[149] In East Bengal (Pakistan), inland waterways are the major means of transporting both passengers and goods. In 1948, they moved some 20 million tons.[150] Small craft are used, since dredging and regularization of waterways are less common than in more advanced countries, and large mechanical equipment is lacking. They are often made of unseasoned wood, their carrying capacity is small, speed slow and life short. The total capacity of this type of craft — junks, country boats and the like — in India and Pakistan is conservatively estimated by the United Nations' Committee of Experts on Inland Transport at about 5 million tons. A large number of boatmen usually own only one craft, often manned by family members. The Committee estimates that several million people are engaged in the operation of such craft in the Far East. Some modern vessels also operate on inland waters in

146. **6**, 1951, pp. 41–42 and 78–79; 1952, pp. 58–62.
147. **50**, pp. 94–95.
148. **8**, 1949, pp. 99–100.

149. **75**, p. 100.
150. **21**, 1950, p. 242.

this area, but the ancient country boats account for a very large proportion of the traffic.[151]

The public authorities in underdeveloped regions often assume little or no responsibility for keeping the inland waterways in navigable condition. The United Nations' Mission of Technical Assistance to Bolivia reports, for example, that about all the government knows of Bolivia's navigable rivers — which, with a total length of 12,000 miles, are about as long as the Mississippi River system in the United States — is "that there are river ports on the tributaries of the Amazon which are used by private vessels." It is also known "that the level of water in the rivers varies considerably, that the beds and banks are shifting, that at each period of high water erosion takes place on a large scale, that trees are carried away, and that when the waters subside, these settle, hindering and even endangering navigation. The river users generally avoid these obstacles or remove them as far as their means permit and their needs require." [152]

Improvement and maintenance of navigable waterways is often linked with irrigation and drainage developments, and this often raises the problem of reconciling the normally opposed interests of navigation and other uses for water. Where inland waterways cross frontiers, as is the case in many regions, international problems arise which often lead to tension and even conflicts.[153]

THE UNITED STATES

The Mississippi System

The system of the Mississippi River with its tributaries (and their tributaries) exceeds 12,000 miles, thus comprising some 40 per cent of the total mileage (28,500 miles) of improved inland and intracoastal waterways of the United States. (See Figure 95.) A little over 4,000 miles have a ruling depth of 9 feet or more. This waterway was of great importance to the early settlers, until the railroad network blanketed the country. Around 1840, the internal commerce of the United States moved largely north and south via the Mississippi and its tributary, the Ohio River. New Orleans was then the fourth port in the world.[154]

Since the Mississippi River is the central trunk of the inland river system in the United States, the government has done much to improve conditions that originally were hazardous and difficult. Numerous bars and islands divided the waterway; rocks and snags blocked the main channel. Gradually, sand bars were removed by dredging, most snags were eliminated, reservoirs were built to hold water for release during the low-water season, depth was increased from the Ohio River to St. Louis, and secured by 26 locks and dams between the Missouri River and Minneapolis. Work continues to increase the controlling depth of some tributaries of the Mississippi. The largest project is to deepen the Missouri River bed from 9 to 12 feet up to Sioux City, and to about 9 feet up to Fort Benton. Other projects are to make some tributaries of the Ohio River navigable for larger vessels and connect the Tennessee River with the Intracoastal Waterway.

Most shipments on the Mississippi River and its tributaries are bulky commodities with low freight rates — coal, coke, lumber, iron and steel southbound; sugar and petroleum northbound. Most of the freight is hauled in steel barges, towed in groups by motor-driven tugs. In 1951, 72.5 million short tons of freight (without duplication) was moved on the Mississippi River, between Minneapolis and the Passes; the Ohio River (Pittsburgh to mouth) carried nearly 56.5 million short tons and the Monongahela, the Ohio's tributary, 32 million.[155] Coal is carried on the Monongahela directly from the mines to the steel mills of Pittsburgh without transshipment.

The Great Lakes

The Great Lakes, the most important system of inland waterways in the United States, occupy a strategic position between the iron ore and grain regions to the northwest and steel and coal areas to the southeast.[156] They carry freight traffic in products best suited for water transport and also excursion vessels, some accommodating as many as 1,200 passengers.[157] No other inland waterway of importance requires so little maintenance. All the Great Lakes, except Lake Michigan, are international waters.[158]

---

151. **8**, 1951, p. 98; **7**, pp. 36–37.
152. **3**, p. 79.
153. **5**, July-September 1953, p. 18. Cf. **75**, pp. 208 and 247 for the conflict of irrigation and navigation interests in India.
154. **40**, p. 55.

155. **27**, 1952, Part II, pp. xxxiv-xxxv.
156. See **89**, Chapters 10 and 29.
157. **44**, pp. 209–10.
158. **40**, p. 63; **24**, p. 360.

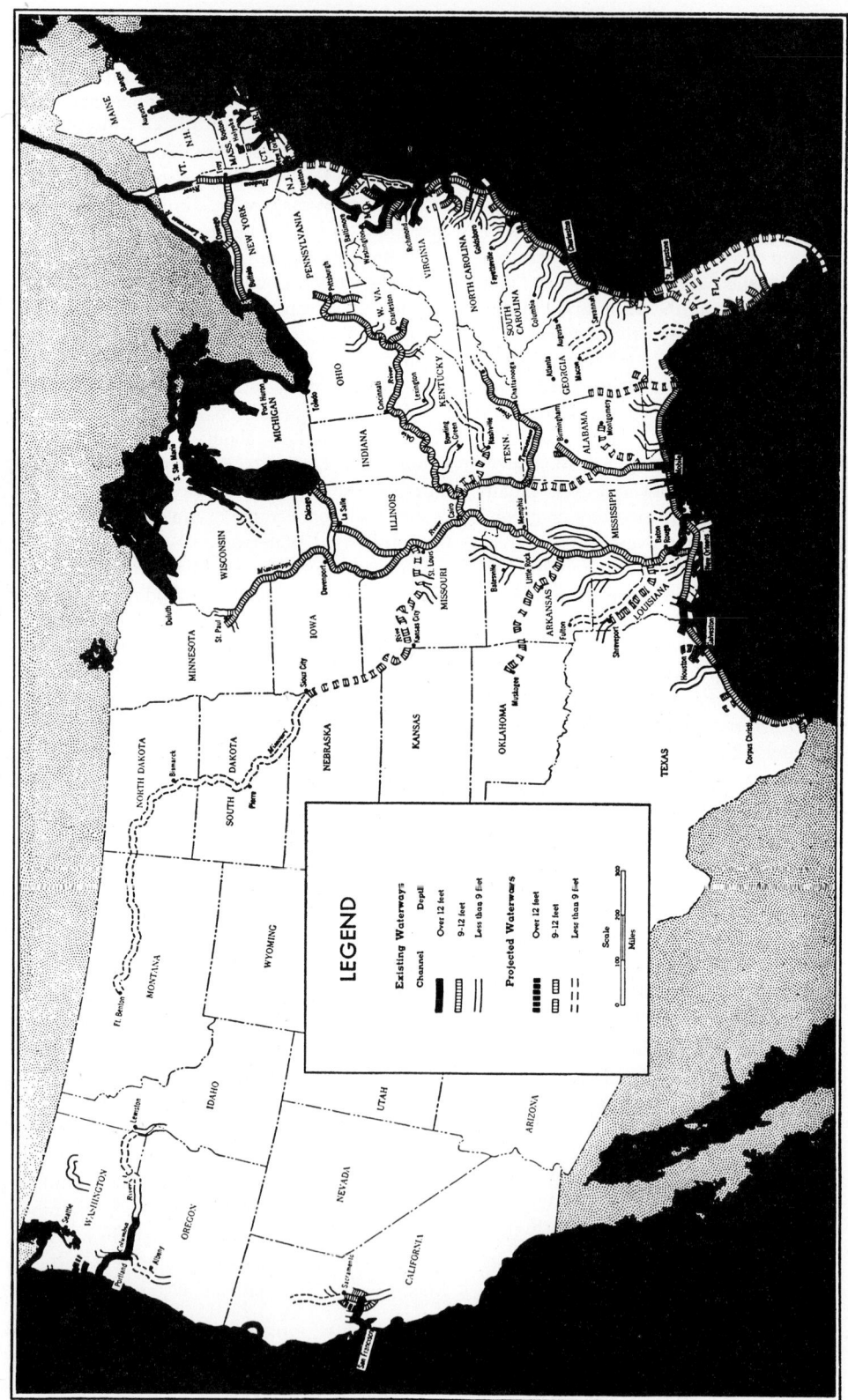

FIGURE 95. INLAND WATERWAYS OF THE UNITED STATES: PRESENT AND PROJECTED WATERWAYS

LEGEND

Existing Waterways
Channel   Depth
               Over 12 feet
               9-12 feet
               Less than 9 feet

Projected Waterways
               Over 12 feet
               9-12 feet
               Less than 9 feet

Scale
0   100   200   300
        Miles

482

The Great Lakes are virtually "tailor-made" for shipping, being of adequate depth and connected by natural or artificial links. Lake Superior was separated from Lake Huron by rapids at Sault Sainte Marie, and the Niagara Falls blocked navigation between Erie and Ontario. In 1855 Michigan completed the first "Soo" Canal at Sault Sainte Marie for through navigation to Lake Superior, and Canada added a canal on its side in 1895; the United States now operates four locks and Canada one. In 1829 Canada built the Welland Canal, circumventing Niagara Falls, and subsequently it was deepened to accommodate lake vessels of all sizes.[159] The navigable waterway of the Great Lakes is about 1,500 miles long from east to west; the area exceeds 95,000 square miles; the shore line, 8,300 miles, of which 3,774 miles are in the United States.[160]

A southern branch of the Great Lakes route, the Lakes-to-the-Gulf waterway, connects Lake Michigan with the Mississippi River via a system of canals and canalized rivers. This federal waterway, opened in 1933, is 326 miles long and has a controlling depth of 9 feet.

Vessels on the Great Lakes are comparable to ocean ships in size and frequently are specially designed for the goods to be transported. Many of the freighters have a cargo capacity exceeding 11,000 tons, and some are much larger. Industrial carriers, transporting coal, iron ore, grain and other products, account for most of the traffic. It is important for economical transportation that many vessels transport return loads, taking iron ore eastward, for example, and coal, westward.

The navigation season is about eight months, from April to December. Lake vessels are frequently used for storage during the winter. Shipping is closely coordinated with rail service, and terminals permit loading, unloading and interchange of cargoes with the utmost dispatch.[161] A 10,000-ton vessel carrying iron ore is unloaded in 3 to 4 hours.

The Great Lakes carry more than two thirds of all the inland transport in the United States.[162] The busiest ports are as follows: on Lake Erie: Detroit (Michigan), Buffalo (New York), Cleveland, Ashtabula, Conneaut, Toledo (Ohio); on

Lake Michigan: Chicago (Illinois), East Chicago, Gary (Indiana); on Lake Superior: Two Harbors (Minnesota), Duluth-Superior (Minnesota-Wisconsin); on Lake Huron: Rogers City (Michigan). Of the total cargo receipts of 185.4 million short tons and shipments of 204.2 short tons carried on the Great Lakes in 1951, these main ports accounted for the following percentages: [163]

	Receipts	Shipments
Duluth-Superior	4.3	31.9
Buffalo	10.0	1.0
Detroit	11.7	0.5
Chicago [a]	8.8	2.4
Cleveland	6.6	0.1
Conneaut	6.7	1.0
Toledo	2.3	12.7
Ashtabula	5.9	1.3
Gary	5.0	0.1
Two Harbors (Agate Bay)	0.1	10.7
East Chicago (Indiana Harbor)	5.7	2.6
Rogers City (Calcite)	0.1	7.6
All other ports	32.8	28.1

a. Includes Chicago Harbor and River, Calumet Harbor and River, Lake Calumet, Calumet-Sag Channel, and Chicago Sanitary and Ship Canal to Sag Junction.

Freight traffic through the Sault Sainte Marie Canals (Saint Marys Falls) is very heavy, most of it moving eastward. In 1937, the canals carried 72.1 million short tons eastward, and 15.5 million westward; in 1950, 89.2 and 16.9 million, respectively. Iron ore is the main commodity moving eastward: 80.0 million tons in 1950, about 90 per cent of all freight in this direction.

The importance of the Sault Sainte Marie Canals and the Great Lakes in general for the economy of the United States can hardly be exaggerated. The iron ore carried over these waterways to the eastern mills has been the foundation of the nation's iron and steel industry. (See Figure 96.) In 1951 it accounted for more than 85 per cent of the eastbound freight. Coal is the principal westbound commodity: in 1951, 10.7 million tons or 70 per cent of the westbound tonnage. United States vessels carry 85 per cent of all freight passing through the canals. The number of passengers traversing the canals increased from 32,937 in 1935 to 113,009 in 1949 but dropped to 49,855 in 1952.[164]

The New York State Barge Canal, formerly known as the Erie Canal, connects the Great

159. **10**, p. 1489; **48**, pp. 41–42.
160. **24**, p. 360.
161. **36**, pp. 54 and 322–23.
162. **10**, p. 199.

163. **15**, 1953, p. 574.
164. **15**, 1954, p. 605.

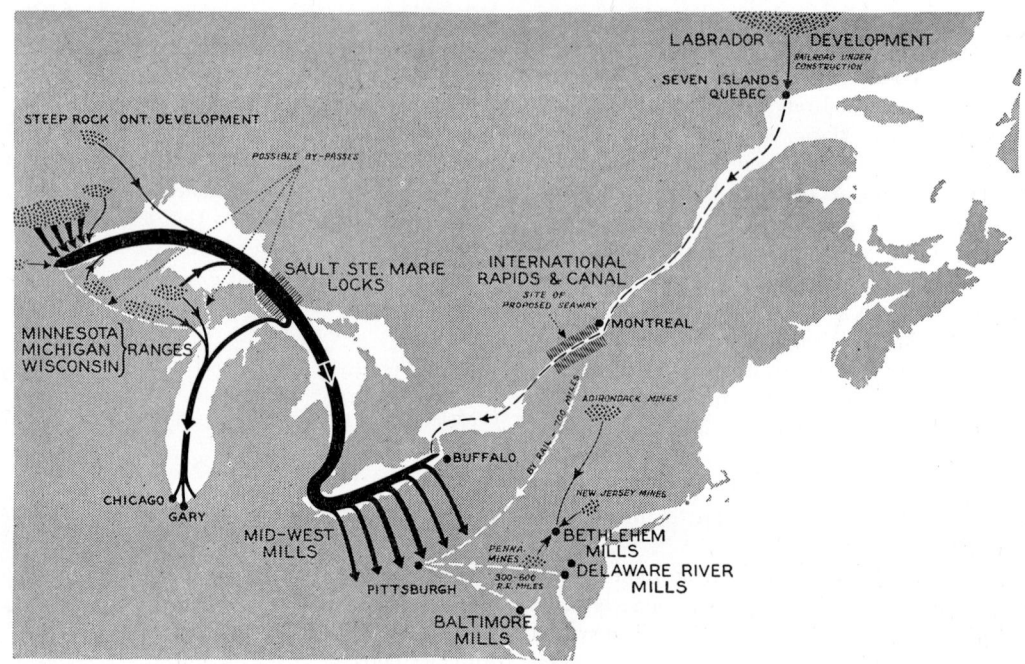

The President's Water Resources Policy Commission (**26**)

FIGURE 96. INLAND WATERWAYS OF THE UNITED STATES: THE GREAT LAKES AND SAULT SAINTE MARIE CANALS

The heavy line on the map indicates the intensity of transport of iron ore from Lake Superior to eastern mills.

Lakes and the Hudson River. It is about 525 miles long and has been enlarged to ship-canal dimensions, with a 12-foot controlling depth. Traffic is rather light and has shown no tendency to increase. The average tonnage on the Barge Canal has been as follows (in millions of short tons): [165]

1886–90	3.6
1906–10	2.2
1931–35	3.5
1936–40	3.8
1946–50	2.7
1951	3.7
1952	3.1
1953	3.2

The Intracoastal Waterway

The United States has embarked on a special project to combine rivers, lakes, lagoons, bays, swampy bayous, straits and existing artificial channels into one system of intracoastal waterways extending some 3,500 miles from Boston to the Rio Grande, on the Mexican border. Large stretches of the system are in operation.

The natural links in this chain are Long Island Sound, Chesapeake Bay, the Delaware River below Philadelphia and North Carolina's sounds. Artificial sections are the Cape Cod Canal, the Delaware and Raritan Canal, the Chesapeake and Delaware Canal, and a chain of channels and canals joining Chesapeake Bay and the sounds of North Carolina. A part of the route to the North Atlantic ports is exposed to the open ocean.[166]

A main difficulty in carrying out the project is the uneven and generally shallow depth of water at various points. The Cape Cod Canal, thanks to repeated dredging, is 30 feet deep at low water in the land cut and from 19 to 32 feet deep in the various sections of the mooring basin.[167]

Except for the Delaware and Raritan Canal which has not been used since 1932 by commercial vessels, boats drawing 11 feet can be and are used along the Atlantic waterway, the 770-mile course from Boston to Beaufort.[168]

Another link in operation is the Gulf Intra-

---

165. **15**, 1954, p. 606.

166. **40**, p. 65; **44**, p. 218.
167. The Cape Cod Canal, which was considered as a military measure by George Washington, was opened in 1914. It shortens the route between Boston and New York by sixty-six miles.
168. **47**, pp. 132–35; **27**, 1952, Part II, p. 415.

coastal Waterway, more than 1,100 miles long, from Apalachee Bay, Florida, to Corpus Christi, Texas and the Mexican border. The controlling depth is from 8 to 12 feet, and navigation is open all year. Traffic is growing: in 1940, 11.6 million tons were carried on the Gulf waterway; in 1944, 24.1 million; in 1949, 28.3 million; in 1951, 35.5 million.[169]

INLAND WATERS OF OTHER COUNTRIES

Europe's abundant supply of natural inland waterways has been an important factor in its economic development. The Rhine and the Danube are the main arteries, but the Elbe, the Oder, the Weser, the Vistula (Wisła) and other rivers, with their tributaries, have had a share in the settlement of population on this continent and in its water-borne trade. (See Figure 97.)

The Rhine

The Rhine system with its interconnecting canals and streams is about 850 miles long; the navigable length, from Basel to the North Sea, is about 550 miles. Though relatively short, the Rhine has been one of the most important European waterways since early times.

The Rhine flows through the densely populated and industrially most advanced part of Europe. Beginning in Switzerland, it serves as a natural outlet for Germany, the Netherlands and Belgium and empties into the sea opposite the British Isles. A system of canals connects it with France and the basin of the Danube.

Important tributaries and canals join the Rhine and add greatly to its traffic, among them the Main, Neckar and Moselle rivers, and the Rhine-Marne and Rhine-Rhone canals, each of which is a transportation artery for some manufacturing or commercial area of France and Germany. The Duisburg-Ruhrort Canal serves the Ruhr.

Traffic is heavy, especially on the lower Rhine, and largely international. It is estimated that coal, iron ore, fertilizers, sand and gravel, and cereals represented some 80 per cent of all cargo before the war. In 1937, 6.0 million metric tons of cargo crossed the Dutch-German frontier at Lobith, but in recent years this traffic has amounted to less than 4 million tons.[170]

Five countries have a vital stake in this river. Since the beginning of the nineteenth century,

from the time of the Congress of Vienna in 1815, they have generally followed a policy of keeping the Rhine free of obstructionist rules, restrictions and tolls. Navigation is open to vessels of all nations and their cargoes and crews [171] and is subject to the jurisdiction of the Central Commission for the Navigation of the Rhine, representing all riparian states. The Commission — the oldest international organization in the world — has worked successfully except for interruptions during wars and on the whole represents an example of international collaboration in transport.[172]

The Rhine system suffered great damage during World War II. The Germans bombed or demolished forty-six of the forty-nine fixed bridges between Basel and Rotterdam, and the wreckage obstructed navigation. In addition, about 3,000 vessels of various sizes were sunk in the channel, at the banks or in the ports.

Reconstruction proceeded rapidly after the end of the war. Navigation was resumed on September 1, 1945, but bottlenecks were frequent, and vessels moved precariously, circumventing dangerous spots. It has been a difficult task to clear the river of wreckage, build permanent bridges to replace emergency bridges with too low or too narrow openings for larger ships, and refloat or remove wrecked vessels. By the summer of 1948, all temporary bridges had been removed; eleven fixed bridges, with navigable passages equal to those in prewar bridges, and thirteen semipermanent bridges had been built. The channel has been completely cleared, and much dredging has been done; maintenance of the river has been resumed.[173]

The Rhine fleet of the five nations had an aggregate tonnage of 7.4 million tons in 1939 and 5.8 million in 1948, distributed as follows (in millions of gross tons): [174]

	1939	*1948*
Netherlands	3.8	2.9
Germany	2.2	1.5[a]
Belgium	0.9	0.8
France	0.4	0.4
Switzerland	0.1	0.2

a. British–U.S. Zones.

171. The Mannheim Convention of 1868 secured this privilege to its signatories only: France, the Netherlands and the German states of Baden, Bavaria, Prussia and Hesse. The Versailles Treaty extended it to all nations.
172. **5**, October-December 1949, pp. 19–20. Cf. Chapter 17.
173. **5**, October-December 1949, pp. 20–22.
174. **5**, April-June 1949, p. 10.

169. **27**, 1950, Part II, p. 1639, and 1952, Part II, p. 1788.
170. **2**, January 1954, p. 85.

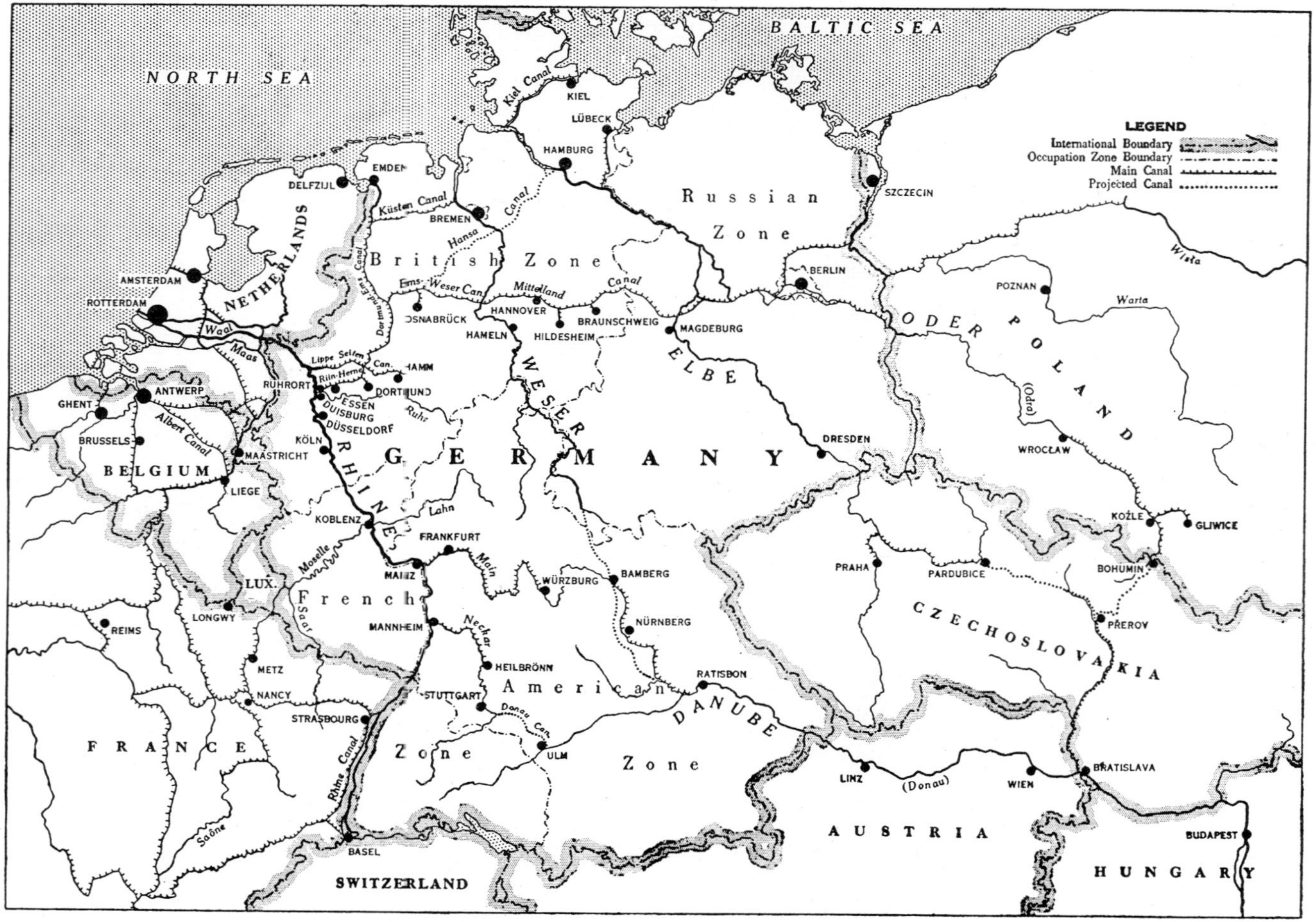

FIGURE 97. INLAND WATERWAYS: WESTERN AND CENTRAL EUROPE

United Nations

A novel development in the Rhine cargo fleet has been the great increase in diesel-powered, self-propelled barges, which give faster and more dependable service than towed barges. In 1935 they accounted for 19 per cent of the freight barged to Basel; in 1948, for 61 per cent.[175]

The Danube

The second river of international importance in Europe, the Danube, touches seven countries — Austria, Hungary, Romania, Bulgaria, Yugoslavia, the USSR and Czechoslovakia — in its flow from the Black Forest of Germany to the Black Sea. It is connected by a canal with the Main, a tributary of the Rhine. For purposes of navigation, it is usually divided into the maritime Danube, from the Black Sea to Romania's port Brăila, and the fluvial Danube, from that port to Regensburg (Ratisbon), Germany.

Seagoing vessels transfer their cargo to barges or the railroads at Brăila and Galatz, another Romanian port. Before World War II, the largest fleet on the Danube belonged to Yugoslavia and the chief commercial interests among non-riparian states were Greek.

Freezing interrupts navigation on the Danube for several winter months, and low water restricts it in summer. The most difficult stretches are the dangerous reefs and rapids at the Iron Gates in Romania, on Yugoslavia's boundary, where vessels need special assistance in proceeding upstream.

Although the Danube is the only major European navigable river which flows from west to east, its traffic has never developed to an extent commensurate with its geographic position. The Danube has more than three times the navigable length of the Rhine but only a fraction of the Rhine's traffic. In its middle and lower course, the Danube crosses comparatively poor agricultural countries, away from the main streams of commerce, and it ends in an almost enclosed sea little touched by international trade. Moreover, the bordering countries, often at loggerheads with one another, have resorted to various means to impede their neighbors' use of the river and at the same time have lacked financial means to make the improvements needed for navigation.

The Versailles Treaty established freedom of navigation on the Danube for all flags and prohibited fiscal and customs discrimination and higher duties than on other frontiers.[176] Two international commissions for the Danube (maritime and fluvial) were established and functioned until 1938, when Germany, and later the German-occupied riparian countries, withdrew from them. Postwar efforts to establish international control over the Danube have collapsed because of the opposition of the USSR and its satellites.

The new Danubian Convention adopted in Belgrade in 1948 established a single Danube Commission for the entire river except the Iron Gates sector and the Delta. Only Danubian states are represented.[177] Today the USSR's interests predominate in shipping on the Danube. That country has acquired, through majority control of Hungarian and Romanian shipping, a large part of the tonnage on the river and has blockaded all non-Soviet shipping at Ems.[178] In 1952, the USSR lifted its restrictions on the Austrian section of the Danube, and traffic there has increased considerably.

The Volga

The Volga River, with its tributaries, the Kama and Oka, is the chief inland water artery of the USSR. Almost half of all inland water traffic is carried by this system, which serves central Russia, with a population of some 50 million.[179] The Volga is 2,325 miles long, and the total navigable length of its system approaches 11,000 miles, while an additional 15,500 miles can be used for rafts.[180] The river abounds in shallows and sandbanks and, although dredging has increased the depth, very large craft cannot be employed. The aim is to secure a prevailing depth of 8.5 feet throughout its length.

The main cargoes on the Volga are petroleum, northbound, and lumber, southbound. Petroleum reaches Moscow, Leningrad and the Urals (via the Kama) without leaving the water, while a great part of the lumber is transferred to the railroad at Stalingrad. Grain moves from Stalingrad partly to Astrakhan on the Caspian Sea but mostly northward to the deficit areas of the USSR. Salt is also shipped from the Lower

---

175. **5**, July-September 1951, p. 59.

176. **70**, pp. 51ff.

177. In the prewar international commissions, Great Britain, France and Italy held membership, along with the riparian states.

178. **8**, 1949, pp. 104–05.

179. **38**, pp. 83–84. The Volga itself is navigable for 95 per cent of its length. **91**, p. 17.

180. **37**, p. 478.

Volga to the central districts. Coal, cement, cotton, fish and some other commodities are shipped in smaller quantities.

The Amazon

The total navigable length of the Amazon River system is not known, but some 15,000 miles are open to river steamers. Average-sized cargo vessels may ascend it to Iquitos, Peru, 2,300 miles from the Atlantic. The depth during the rainy season may reach 120 feet; the total basin drained is estimated at 2.7 million square miles, including parts of Brazil, Venezuela, Colombia, Peru and Bolivia.[181]

The internal port of Brazil, Manaus, is about a thousand miles from the Amazon's mouth, but the river is so wide and deep that ocean ships can bring cargo to it.[182] Because of lack of cooperation in customs and other matters, international traffic is little developed. Primitive canoes, rafts and small steamers are the prevailing craft.

The Paraná

South America's most important river system is the Paraná with its tributaries. It is much more active than the Amazon, which has no important port at its mouth. The Paraná has two first-class ports near the mouth of its wide estuary — Buenos Aires and Montevideo — and several important ports upstream. It provides an outlet for the great hinterland of Argentina, part of southern Brazil and western Uruguay and is Paraguay's chief means of communication with the outside world. Serving the periphery of Argentina's wheat zone, it has decisively influenced the economic life of that region. Rosario, on the Paraná about 400 miles from the coast, is the second largest port in Argentina. It is capable of handling large ocean-going vessels and is one of the chief grain markets of the country. Efficient modern vessels ply this system and compete with trucks and train.[183]

The Yangtze

China's most important riverway, the Yangtze, extends some 3,000 miles, distributing products throughout an area with almost half the total population of the country.[184] The depth

is sufficient to permit vessels of 5,000–6,000 tons to reach the port of Hankow, about 630 miles from the sea. Most traffic, however, is carried by small wooden craft powered by wind or oarsmen. These native boats and junks penetrate from the Yangtze into its tributaries and adjoining canals and thus afford communication to a considerable area.

The Nile and the Congo

The Nile, stretching over some 4,000 miles, is the longest river in Africa and one of the longest in the world.[185] Its basin, estimated at 1.1 million square miles, is drained by the Nile proper and fed by the great lakes of East Central Africa, the Nile's equatorial tributaries and the Abyssinian affluents; it contains Lake Victoria, the largest fresh water lake in the Eastern Hemisphere. The river is navigable without interruption for some 2,900 miles from the sea, until the rapids and cataracts are reached. Beyond this point, only some stretches are navigable.

The Congo, together with its great tributaries, the Ubangi and Kasai, is of great importance for a large area, particularly the Belgian Congo. Traffic is handicapped, as on the Nile, by many obstructions along the river's course. An additional handicap is that the Congo forms a great arc in its flow which lengthens navigation between many points.[186]

INLAND CANALS

It is not difficult to build a canal through level territory, and such canals have existed since antiquity. The Romans built two in England, one of which is still navigable. Since wind cannot be used for power on a canal, barges originally were hauled by fifteen or twenty men who towed them from the banks. This practice is still in use in China and some other regions, but in England and France, horses came into use when towpaths could be laid out. Later and until near the end of the nineteenth century, chain towage was used in Europe.[187]

The Invention of Locks

In the course of the many centuries between 486 B.C. and A.D. 1320 the Chinese built the

---

181. **1**, 1948, pp. 176–77.
182. **55**, pp. 174 and 181.
183. **1**, 1948, pp. 176–77; **44**, p. 216. Cf. **56**, pp. 123–24.
184. **44**, p. 216.

185. The Missouri-Mississippi is 3,988 miles long.
186. **5**, July-September 1949, pp. 6–7.
187. **63**, pp. 391ff.

Grand Canal — about 1,000 miles long — from Hangchow to Peking for both commerce and irrigation, but there is no indication that it passed through areas with different levels of ground; inland navigation through hilly country did not become possible until locks were invented.[188] A lock chamber with a double pair of gates is said to have been used for the first time in Italy in 1481. Before the end of that century, Leonardo da Vinci had connected the two chief canals of Milan by six locks.[189] A canal with locks was completed in Sweden in 1606, and France built two such canals during the seventeenth century; one of them, Canal du Midi (148 miles long and 119 locks), joined the Bay of Biscay and the Mediterranean.

The success of England's first modern canal with different levels, opened in 1761, led to an era of canal building which covered that country with a system of artificial waterways. By 1830, some 3,000 miles of canals were constructed in England and Wales alone.[190] Throughout this period, the Netherlands, Belgium, Germany and France were also engaged in intensive canal building.

Canal Building in the United States

In the United States, the canal period began later. The first canal of great commercial importance was the Erie (now called the New York State Barge Canal), which was opened in 1825 with 83 locks. It was such a financial success that tolls from the growing traffic defrayed the costs of construction within 10 years. It reduced the freight charges from Buffalo to New York from $100 to $5 per ton, and the time of delivery from 20 days to 6 days.[191] The impetus given by the Erie Canal was so great that by 1850 the United States had built 3,700 miles of canals and later had 4,600 miles. Pennsylvania built 400 miles, with one canal-railroad from Philadelphia to Pittsburgh, across the Alleghenies.[192] Maryland began the never-completed

Chesapeake and Ohio Canal. Indiana and Ohio built a system of canals to join the Ohio River and the Great Lakes; other states also were active in this field.

While the financial returns were generally unsatisfactory, canals facilitated the development of traffic between East and West. Along the eastern coast, a series of canals gave small and medium vessels an inside passage between northern and southern ports. The canals largely supplanted the turnpikes in the transport of bulky and heavy cargo. But the superior efficiency of the railroad, which became apparent by the middle of the nineteenth century, coupled with other factors, lessened interest in canals and with it the availability of capital for further canal building. Before the outbreak of the Civil War, large-scale construction of canals had practically ceased.[193]

The most important, in terms of tonnage carried, are the Sault Sainte Marie Canals between Lake Superior and Lake Huron. Freight passing through these canals in 1952 was about three times that carried through the Panama Canal the same year — 106.3 and 37.6 million short tons, respectively.[194]

Europe's Present and Projected Canals

In Europe, however, the canal era has not yet ended. Many important projects were under consideration before World War II. Belgium planned to connect the Scheldt with the Rhine; Germany, the Rhine with the Elbe, Oder, Vistula and Danube. Poland envisaged linking the Vistula with the Oder, Dniester and Pruth, thus establishing a through connection for 1,000-ton barges between the Vistula, the Danube and the Black Sea. The USSR planned to connect the bordering seas — the White, Baltic, Caspian, Azov and Black — by canals permitting passage of 10,000-ton vessels.[195] (See Figure 98.) Some of these projects have been completed since the war; others are now under way or may be revived in the near future.

Among Europe's important existing canals is the Manchester Ship Canal. As a link between

---

188. **66**, p. 20.
189. **63**, p. 409; cf. **42**, p. 141.
190. **39**, p. 111; **66**, pp. 19–23.
191. **67**, p. 9; **40**, pp. 56–57. Some short canals had been built before the Erie Canal, such as Dismal Swamp Canal (1794) and Middlesex Canal (1804). (**51**, pp. 277–78.)
192. Canal boats were built in two sections; each half was put on a specially designed railroad car. The passengers boarded the half-boat units in Philadelphia; the boat would be assembled in Columbia and move to Hollidaysburg, separated again, and placed on cars pulled by

cable up the mountain, and reassembled at Johnstown for the final stretch to Pittsburgh. **50**, pp. 32 and 696.
193. **39**, pp. 111–12. Of the 4,633 miles of canals built before 1909, 2,444 miles have been abandoned. (**51**, p. 511.)
194. **15**, 1954, p. 605. See p. 472.
195. **70**, pp. 74–75.

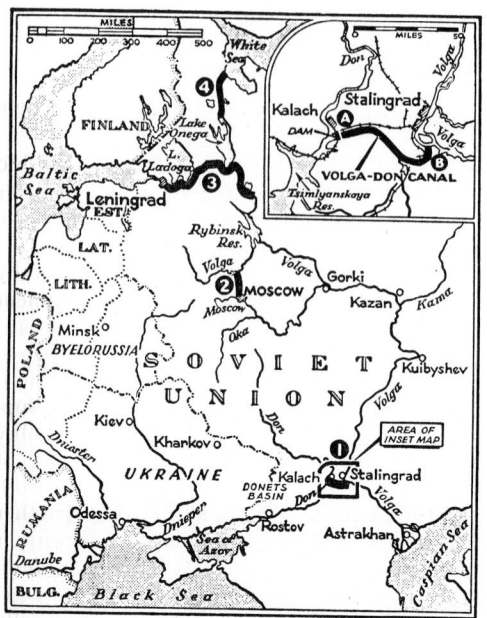

FIGURE 98. INLAND WATERWAYS: CANALS IN THE
USSR

The Volga-Don Canal (1) connects Kalach (A on in-
set) with Stalingrad (B). It is part of a system making
possible navigation from the Baltic to the Caspian by
means of the Moscow-Volga (2), Mariinsk (3) and
Baltic–White Sea (4) canals.

Liverpool and Manchester, it has made Manchester a great seaport. Seagoing vessels are
raised by four locks some 60 feet to dock level.
The minimum depth of the channel is 28 feet,
and the length 35.5 miles. Traffic is very heavy
and represents virtually all flags of the world.
Ships up to 10,000 tons deadweight can pass
through this canal.

The North Sea Canal, between IJmuiden on
the North Sea and Amsterdam, has been an
important factor in the economic life of the
Netherlands. It is less than 17 miles long, 164
feet wide at its bottom, and 41 feet deep.
Throughout its length it is connected with tributary canals to form a most efficient waterway
system. The canal is crossed twice by railroad
swing bridges, and the largest ocean locks in
the world are at IJmuiden, the Nordersluis being
1,320 feet long.

The Amsterdam-Rhine Canal was opened in
May 1952. It is 45 miles long and follows the
widened bed of the old Merwede Canal up to
Utrecht, makes a big bend around Utrecht and
continues to Tiel on the Waal, a tributary of

the Rhine. This canal is expected to ease the
traffic on the Merwede Canal, where no less than
105,000 vessels with 25 million tons of cargo had
to find their way in 1951.[196] It also affords a
more direct route between Amsterdam and the
Rhine even for the largest craft able to navigate
that river.

The New Waterway, a deep-water link between Rotterdam and the North Sea, is the shortest way from Rotterdam to the open sea and
was built to replace the more tortuous natural
channels.

The Göta Canal is a 360-mile river and lake
route connecting Stockholm with Gothenburg.
Only 56 miles are canalized, the rest being a
channel connecting two large lakes, Vänern and
Vättern, and one small lake. Part of the length
the boats move coastwise, then by a fjord and a
lake. The Göta Canal has 58 locks and does not
handle ocean or seagoing vessels.

The Mittelland Canal was completed by Germany in 1938. It links the rivers Ems, Weser
and Elbe and provides a convenient waterway
from the North Sea across the central part of
the country.

The USSR built the White Sea–Baltic Sea
Canal in the early 1930's to carry timber and
other cargo from the north to Leningrad and
on to the Volga. In 1937 it completed the
Moscow-Volga Canal, 128 miles long, with 11
locks and 11 dams, to enable ships to sail to
Moscow. Shortly before World War II, the
Dnieper-Bug-Vistula Canal was opened; it connects the Baltic and the Black Seas. In 1952 the
USSR completed the Volga-Don Canal, work
on which started at the beginning of the second
Five-Year Plan but was interrupted by the outbreak of war; work was resumed in 1948. This
canal, about 62 miles long, runs from the great
bend of the Volga south of Stalingrad and then
climbs 9 locks to the top of the watershed, 288
feet above sea level. On the other side it drops to
about 144 feet through 4 locks to the Don. (See
Figure 98.) While ocean ships now can pass
from the Baltic to the Black Sea only when the
Volga is at flood, it is expected that by 1956 the
connection will be open at all times.[197] This
system of canals has made Moscow a port accessible from five seas — the Baltic, White, Caspian, Black and Azov.

The Soviet government generally recruits

196. **83,** June 1952, p. 98.
197. **80,** February 1952, p. 182.

members of the kolkhozy (collective farms) for the work on canals. Thus, 160,000 of them have worked on the construction of the Great Fergana Canal in Central Asia, and tens of thousands on the Nevinnomusskiĭ Canal in North Caucasus.[198]

THE EXTENT OF INLAND WATERWAYS

What constitutes a navigable inland waterway is a matter of definition and depends on a country's means of transportation and its prevailing types of vessels. A waterway considered suitable for a raft or a small sailing vessel in China or Egypt would not be counted an "inland waterway" in the United States or the United Kingdom. Thus, the data reported by various countries should be regarded as approximations, not strictly comparable from country to country.

Length

In the length of its inland waterways, some 220,000 miles, the USSR ranks first in the world. The navigable length exceeds 62,000 miles, of which about 56,500 miles were utilized in 1938 — about the mileage of the railroad network.[199] Next comes the United States, with a total navigable length of 28,590 miles and Brazil, with 21,900 miles. The mileage in the United States ranges from shallow-draft channels kept open for limited navigation by occasional clearing to canalized waterways provided in developing major rivers. Some 80 per cent of all inland water-borne commerce is carried on fifteen major waterways.[200] Greece, Spain and Mexico have negligible inland waterways; Australia and Turkey have none.

While inland waterways comprise only the navigable rivers in some countries, in others artificially built waterways constitute a substantial proportion of the system. The Netherlands has 3,603 miles in canals, as compared with 695 miles in natural waterways. For the United Kingdom, the corresponding figures are 1,626 and 762 miles; for Ireland, 304 and 150 miles. Finland's inland waterway system consists of lakes interconnected by canals. (See Table 171.)

Small and seldom used canals are being abandoned in the United Kingdom and Western Germany. In the latter, for example, the Ludwig

Canal, built more than a hundred years ago, was recently closed as being totally unsuitable for modern traffic.[201]

Density

The Netherlands has the densest network of navigable inland waterways in relation to territory: 33.1 miles per 100 square miles. In relation to population, density is greatest in Bolivia: 30 miles per 10,000 inhabitants. The difference between the two countries is that the Netherlands has done an enormous amount of work and has used the highest engineering skill to crisscross the country with canals while nature has provided Bolivia with many streams. Another difference is that the inland waterways are the center of intensive shipping and commerce in the first country but are little used in the latter.[202]

The United States averages less than one mile of inland waters per 100 square miles and 1.8 miles per 10,000 inhabitants. The relationship is the opposite in the British Isles, with its small area and dense population: 2.5 miles per 100 square miles and 0.5 miles per 10,000 inhabitants. The corresponding figures for Belgium are 8.0 and 1.1; for Finland, 2.1 and 6.6; for the USSR, 0.7 and 3.2. (See Table 172.)

The proportion of waterways open to craft of over 350–400 tons varies from country to country. It is 22.7 per cent in France; 34.9 per cent in Italy; 38.1 per cent in the Netherlands; and 83.0 per cent in Western Germany. None of the inland waterways in the United Kingdom is open to barges exceeding 400 tons in carrying capacity.[203]

TRAFFIC ON INLAND WATERS

Traffic on inland waterways in many countries — carried on primitive boats, canoes and rafts — escapes statistics. Data for some other areas are incomplete or mixed with those for coastal ports or represent information on only some major river ports. Even European statistics are fragmentary and do not give a full picture of inland shipping.

In the United States, freight traffic on inland waterways increased slowly from about 114 million short tons in 1925 to 150 million tons in

198. **91,** pp. 11–12.
199. **38,** p. 62; **37,** p. 475.
200. **27,** 1951, Part I, Vol. 3, p. 129.

201. **6,** 1952, p. 45.
202. See p. 481.
203. **6,** 1952, p. 91.

TABLE 171

INLAND WATERWAYS: NAVIGABLE LENGTH IN SELECTED COUNTRIES, 1948–50

(*Miles*)

Country	Total	Rivers	Canals	Country	Total	Rivers	Canals
United States	28,590	...	...	Austria	229	218	11
Canada	2,700	2,200	500	Portugal	510	...	...
Venezuela	12,000	12,000	—	Italy [b]	1,536	877	659
Colombia	900	900	—	Yugoslavia	1,264	1,146	119
Brazil	21,900	21,900	—				
Bolivia	12,000	12,000	—	USSR	62,200	...	...
Chile	1,300	1,300	—	Iraq	300	300	—
Uruguay	800	800	—	Syria	400	400	—
Argentina	4,200	4,200	—	Pakistan	2,700	2,200	500
United Kingdom	2,388	762	1,626	Ceylon	200	—	200
Ireland	454	150	304	Egypt [c]	3,000	—	3,000
France	8,220	4,930	3,290	French Equatorial			
Belgium	964	460	504	Africa	1,800	...	...
Netherlands	4,298	695	3,603	Belgian Congo	7,700	7,700	—
Denmark	120 [a]	—	120	Gold Coast	200	200	—
Sweden [b]	754	559	195	Nigeria	4,000	4,000	—
Norway	190	—	190	Kenya, Uganda,			
Finland	2,700	—	40	Tanganyika [d]	6,000	...	...
Western Germany	2,654	1,918	736	Nyasaland [d]	400	...	...
Czechoslovakia	400	400	—	New Zealand	500	...	...
Switzerland	13	13	...				

Sources: **61**, Table 3; for Europe, 1951–52 (except Denmark, Norway, Finland, Czechoslovakia and Portugal); **6**, 1952, p. 91.

a. Ferry routes.
b. Includes waterway routes across lakes.
c. According to another source (**62**, pp. 100–01),

Egypt has less than 2,000 miles of navigable inland waterways.
d. Rivers and lakes.

1935. During World War II, it more than doubled, reaching nearly 344 million tons in 1941, then fell to 173 million in 1951. In terms of ton-miles, however, the relationship between the wartime and postwar periods was the reverse, indicating a longer average haul in later years: [204]

	Millions of Short Tons	Billions of Ton-Miles
1925	114.2	8.4
1930	132.6	9.1
1935	150.1	13.4
1940	259.2	22.4
1941	343.9	26.8
1942	334.0	26.4
1943	257.4	26.3
1944	268.4	31.4
1945	264.7	29.7
1949	243.3	40.0
1950	150.3	51.7
1951	173.1	62.2

204. **14**, p. 214; **27**, 1952, Part II, p. x; **10**, p. 198. Excludes the Great Lakes and Sault Sainte Marie Canals and Detroit River traffic, which are included in Great Lakes traffic. For Great Lakes traffic, see pp. 481, 483–84.

International statistics on inland-water traffic are scattered, particularly for underdeveloped areas. For example, data for Brazil (0.7 million metric tons of goods loaded and 0.5 million of goods unloaded in 1951) refer to goods originated and destined for coastal ports and major ports on the Amazon River; for Mozambique, for a few ports only.[205]

More complete data are available for several European countries. The greatest use of inland waterways is in Western Germany, the Netherlands, France and Belgium. A substantial proportion of tonnage loaded and unloaded on inland watercraft either originates in another country, or leaves for another country. (See Table 173.) In addition, transit traffic is of importance, exceeding, in the case of the Netherlands, 18 million tons in 1953.[206]

In the USSR, inland waterways are used not only for transport of goods but also for carrying

205. **4**, 1952, p. 308.
206. **6**, 1953, pp. 90–91.

TABLE 172

INLAND WATERWAYS: LENGTH PER 100 SQUARE MILES OF TERRITORY AND PER 10,000 INHABITANTS IN SELECTED COUNTRIES, 1948–50

(Miles)

Country	Per 100 Square Miles	Per 10,000 Inhabitants	Country	Per 100 Square Miles	Per 10,000 Inhabitants
United States	0.9	1.8	Austria	0.7	0.3
Canada	0.1	2.0	Portugal	1.4	0.6
Venezuela	3.4	24.5	Italy	1.3	0.4
Colombia	0.2	0.8	Yugoslavia	1.3	0.8
Brazil	0.7	4.2			
Bolivia	2.9	30.0	USSR	0.7	3.2
Chile	0.5	2.2	Iraq	0.2	0.6
Uruguay	1.1	3.3	Syria	0.6	1.3
Argentina	0.4	2.4	Pakistan	0.7	0.4
United Kingdom	2.5	0.5	Ceylon	0.8	0.3
Ireland	1.7	1.5	Egypt	0.8	1.5
France	4.0	2.0	French Equatorial Africa	0.2	4.1
Belgium	8.0	1.1	Belgian Congo	0.8	6.8
Netherlands	33.1	4.3	Gold Coast	0.3	0.5
Denmark	0.7	0.3	Nigeria	1.2	1.7
Sweden	0.4	1.1	Kenya, Uganda,		
Norway	0.1	0.6	Tanganyika	0.9	3.3
Finland	2.1	6.6	Nyasaland	0.8	1.7
Western Germany	2.8	0.6			
Czechoslovakia	0.8	0.3	New Zealand	0.5	2.6

Sources: Table 171; **89,** Table 19.

TABLE 173

INLAND WATERWAYS: CARGO LOADED AND UNLOADED, IN SELECTED COUNTRIES, 1938 AND 1952

(Millions of Metric Tons)

Country	1938		1952 Loaded		1952 Unloaded	
	Loaded	Unloaded	Total	Leaving the Country	Total	Entering the Country
Great Britain	13.2	13.2	12.6	—	12.6	—
Ireland	0.2	...	0.2	—	0.2	—
France	35.9	39.7	41.2	4.7	41.3	4.7
Belgium	20.3	20.0	26.4	9.2	31.6	12.3
Netherlands	52.5	50.6	62.8	24.5	51.8	13.5
Sweden	...	...	2.1	1.1	2.5	1.4
Western Germany	74.5[a]	66.3[a]	66.7	18.0	71.2	19.8
Austria [b]	...	...	0.5	0.4	1.7	1.6
Switzerland	0.2[c]	...	0.3	0.3	3.9	3.9
Italy	0.2[d]	...	1.1	0.3	1.4	0.2
Yugoslavia	1.9	2.7	2.6	0.3	2.8	0.1

Sources: **4,** 1953, pp. 319–20; **6,** 1952, pp. 80–81; **2,** January 1954, p. 85.

a. 1936.
b. Excludes traffic carried solely on the eastern stretch of the Danube.
c. Traffic on 13 lakes.
d. Lake service of "Società Concessionarie."

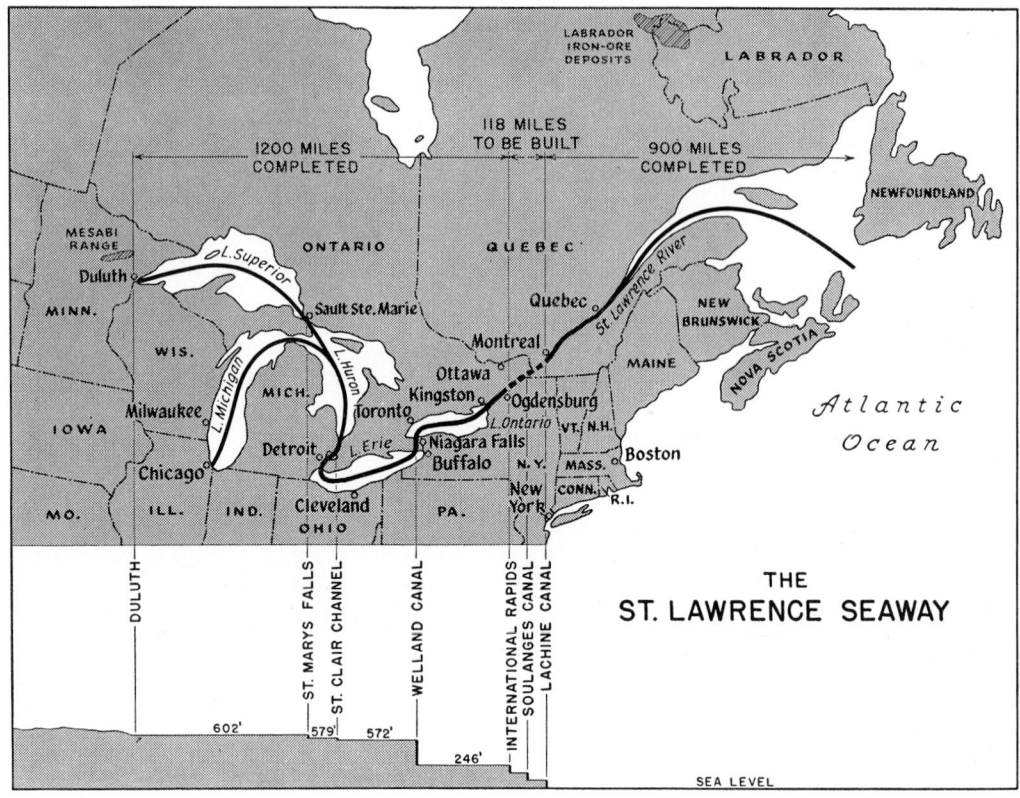

Source: *The Reporter*

FIGURE 99. INLAND WATERWAYS: THE ST. LAWRENCE SEAWAY

passengers. Some 75 million persons avail themselves annually of river vessels for traveling
within the country.[207] Great efforts are being
made to increase the tonnage of goods moved on
inland waters, so as to relieve the overburdened
railroads. The first Postwar Plan provided for
an increase in cargo tonnage by 38 per cent.

OUTLOOK

Freight transportation across the seven seas
has not been challenged and no effective rival is
in sight. It is likely to grow as international
trade expands. On the other hand, ocean passenger traffic has been affected by air transport,
and this competition is bound to become more
serious as time goes on.

Inland waterways — rivers, lakes and canals —
have lost some of their importance in countries well provided with other means of transport, but they still account for a substantial
part of all freight traffic, as do the Great Lakes
and the Mississippi River system in the United

States; the Rhine in Western Germany, the
Netherlands and Belgium; the Danube in eastern Europe; and many other inland systems.

Many projects to improve inland navigation,
shelved during World War II, have been revived. Some, such as the Amsterdam-Rhine
Canal and the Volga-Don Canal, have been completed, and others are under way or delayed
only because of problems of financing. In the
United States, some 189 projects for the deepening of water channels, river canalization, harbor
improvements and so on were under construction in 1951 and 369 projects, authorized by
Congress, had not yet been started.[208] (Cf. Figure 95.) Work on the Columbia River is pro-
gressing. Construction of the St. Lawrence Seaway — a project under discussion in the United
States and Canada for several decades and involving a vast investment — is expected to start
in the near future. The project was delayed by
the opposition of vested interests in the United
States. Finally, Canada announced its readiness

207. **41**, p. 13.   208. **27**, 1951, Part I, Vol. 3, p. 132.

to build the Seaway alone. In May 1954 the Congress decided on United States participation in the project.[209] The new Seaway is expected to handle from 65 to 84 million tons of cargo a year, according to an estimate by the U.S. Department of Commerce. When this Seaway is built, Chicago and Duluth will become seaports. (See Figure 99.) The completion of these and other projects will stimulate waterborne traffic in Europe and North Amercia.

In underdeveloped areas, bulky agricultural and mine products represent the main freight and are often transported over long distances to a port or into the interior. Development of cheap transportation is essential for the economic growth of these regions, and much attention is being given to the improvement of waterways, the traditional and often the only available medium of transport. When financial resources are meager, such projects are more feasible than the building of railroads.

Moreover, a new principle, that of multiple-purpose projects, so successful in the Tennessee Valley, has kindled the imagination of governments and experts of many countries. Various programs have been initiated which are designed to provide a combination of services: more efficient navigation; flood control; irrigation; and hydroelectric power. India has two such multiple-purpose projects under way: the Damodar Valley and the Mahanadi Valley, scheduled for completion in 1955–56. Mexico is developing the Papalcapan Valley on this basis. The Volga Canal project in the USSR also has as a goal the irrigation of the Volga steppes, development of hydroelectric power and raising the level of the Caspian Sea.[210] Other projects of this type will undoubtedly be launched. Thus in the world as a whole transport on both the oceans and inland waters is likely to expand in the years to come.

---

209. A part of this project — a joint power development by Ontario and the State of New York — was started in August 1954. The cost is estimated at $600 million, and the capacity of the plant at 1.9 million kilowatts.

210. **89**, pp. 342, 482–86.

CHAPTER 11

AIR TRANSPORTATION

AVIATION OPENED a new era in transportation. Waterways and roads had always been familiar to man. Whether he used a dugout or a modern ship, walked on a trail or motored along a modern parkway, he remained within the framework of traditional transportation. But use of the atmosphere for transport meant a break with tradition and fulfilled a dream nurtured through many centuries: "The air is an uninterrupted navigable ocean that comes to the threshold of every man's door. For centuries mankind has stood on the shore of this uncharted sea and yearned to enter it." [1] It took much inventiveness and experimentation, some productive and some premature, before man conquered this uncharted sea. Before his eyes was proof that flying was possible but hopes of imitating the birds remained a dream until in our century he created powerful birds of steel.

THE DEVELOPMENT OF AVIATION

From the Wings of Icarus to the Free Balloon

The Greek legend of Daedalus and Icarus gives the first description of an attempt to imitate the flight of birds. The experimenters fastened feathered wings to their bodies with wax and tried to fly from Crete to Sicily, but the sun melted the wax, and Icarus perished in the sea. Aulus Gellius (A.D. 130–180) mentions a wooden dove built for flying around 360 B.C.

For many centuries man's thoughts explored both branches of flying — aerostation (operation of lighter-than-air craft) and aviation (operation of heavier-than-air craft). Friar Roger Bacon predicted in the thirteenth century that "an instrument may be made to fly withall if one sits in the midst of the instrument, and doe turne an engine, by which the wings, being artificially composed, may beat the air after the manner of a flying bird." [2] Leonardo da Vinci patiently observed the movement of birds and published a study, "Flight of Birds," in 1505. He believed that a man provided with wings could lift and maintain himself in the air by manipulating the wings as birds do. [3] In the seventeenth century, Francesco de Lana, an Italian Jesuit, proposed an "air vessel" of about the type described by Bacon, with four hollow copper globes from which the air was to be withdrawn. The mechanics of construction seemed to him within man's abilities, but he feared that Providence would never permit men to fly: flyers might drop "fireworks, bullets and bombs" against helpless people on the ground! Early in the eighteenth century King John V of Portugal accorded a patent to another priest for building an airship. King John anticipated great advantages from this invention: communication between the metropolis and overseas colonies could be speeded up; Portugal's power would be enhanced by new discoveries, while its troops, in case of siege, could be supplied from the air with food and other necessities. [4]

Eighteenth-century inventors concentrated their attention on lighter-than-air craft. In 1783 the Montgolfier brothers achieved the first successful ascent in a captive balloon, fastened to the ground by ropes. A pot with burning straw and timber shavings was slung under an opening of the balloon and warmed the air within, causing the balloon to rise to a height of 6,000 feet. When this air cooled, the balloon lost its buoyancy and fell to the ground. Louis XVI ordered a repeat performance before his court in Versailles. This time the balloon also carried a basket with three passengers — a sheep, a duck and a rooster. It rose 1,500 feet and covered two miles in eight minutes.

In view of the great interest aroused by this ascent, the French Academy of Sciences offered a prize for a model inflated with "inflammable air" (hydrogen). Two Frenchmen, de Rozier

3. Mechanical models have been made from da Vinci's drawings, particularly of a helicopterlike structure intended to rise by means of a rotating screw. (2, October–December 1951, p. 2.)

4. Neither machine was actually built. Both priests were duly tried by the Inquisition for witchcraft; the first was acquitted, the second condemned.

1. 23, p. 329.
2. Quoted in 37, p. 8.

and d'Arlandes, made the first ascent in a modern free balloon, which floated five and a half miles over Paris. In 1784 the United States had its first ascent of a free balloon, in Baltimore, with a thirteen-year-old boy as the sole passenger. The next year saw the first flight of a balloon over the English Channel; it carried a few letters, including one for Benjamin Franklin. In 1793 George Washington watched J. P. Blanchard rise 5,800 feet in a hydrogen-filled balloon at Philadelphia. The balloon crossed the Delaware River and made for New Jersey, covering 15 miles in 46 minutes.

The information on pressure, temperature, wind velocity and air currents obtained in these and other experimental flights was of great value for the development of aerostation. In 1859 John Wise flew 809 air miles in 20 hours in a balloon in a flight from St. Louis, Missouri, to Henderson, New York. After France's defeat at Sedan during the Franco-Prussian war, Léon Gambetta, the French premier, used a balloon to fly from besieged Paris to organize resistance against the German troops. Mail was forwarded from Paris in pilotless free balloons, the first carrying some 500 pounds of letters. Several balloons drifted many miles over the Prussian lines before coming down, and others were lost.[5] John Wise's record in the flight from St. Louis to New York state was not broken until 1900, when a balloon flew from Paris to Russia, 1,193 air miles.

The Dirigible

The logical successor to the free balloon was the rigid or semirigid airship with an engine to control its movements, and no longer dependent on the wind's whims. Two French officers, C. Renard and A. C. Krebs, built a dirigible aircraft which had a 9-horsepower engine, a framework of bamboo and a bag of silk. In their five-mile flight they exceeded a speed of 14 miles an hour. Ferdinand von Zeppelin, a Prussian army officer, completed the building of his first ship in Germany in 1900 and made several flights in it.[6] Gradually improving the model, he built several airships and in a flight in 1907 broke all previous records, with a speed of 22

miles per hour and 12 hours in the air, despite adverse weather.

The success of Zeppelin's airships led to the formation of the German Airship Transportation Company (Delag), which made some 800 flights during the next four years, without a single accident.[7] About the same time, a young Brazilian inventor in Paris, A. Santos-Dumont, built several airships of his own design, all gasoline-powered, and attracted much attention by his daring stunts.

Between the turn of the century and World War I, Germany, France and the United States built a number of airships — nonrigid, semirigid and rigid. During the war, Germany built 88 Zeppelins as well as ships of various other models, more than all other countries combined. All these had been destroyed or seized by the Allies by the end of the war.

Some airships built during the following decades in Great Britain, Germany, the United States, France, Italy and the USSR made spectacularly successful flights but, in the end, for one reason or another they burned or crashed into the sea, with heavy loss of life.

Heavier-than-Air Craft

While many inventors and technicians centered their efforts on improving the airship, attempts to fly like birds were continued. Jean-Marie le Bris, a French sailor, built a glider to imitate the flight of the albatross, which he had observed during sea voyages. Towed by a horse and a cart, the glider ascended 300 feet, carrying Le Bris and another passenger, and landed safely after a flight of 200 yards. Otto Lilienthal, a German inventor, studied bird flight for years and described it in his book *Der Vogelflug als Grundlage der Fliegekunst*. He abandoned the idea of flapping wings, preferring the rigid wings of the hawk as a model for his glider.[8] Using a springboard to launch himself into the air, he made more than 2,000 successful flights but was killed in 1896 when his glider was upset in a storm. In the United States J. J. Montgomery performed many dashing flights in a glider launched from cables stretched between two mountain tops. Octave Chanute, who did much glider flying around Lake Michigan, contributed

---

5. **64**, p. 212.

6. Von Zeppelin had served as a volunteer in the Union army during the Civil War in the United States and operated a captive balloon to control artillery fire and observe the positions of opposing troops. (**47**, p. 259.)

7. **46**, p. 346.

8. Earlier experiments had shown that man's muscular ability was inferior to that of birds and could not propel him through the air. (**40**, p. 109.)

to the development of aerodynamics by his studies of air currents and wind velocities.

Despite progress in construction during the latter part of the nineteenth century and the first decade of the twentieth, airships and gliders still offered no prospect of commercial use. There was no engine with sufficient power to launch the craft into the air and maintain it there. Efforts to build such an engine continued in various countries and many persons helped to pave the way for modern aviation. The last to try before the flight of the Wrights was Samuel P. Langley, who constructed several heavier-than-air craft but failed in attempts to fly them from the Potomac River in Washington, D.C.

In December 1903, Wilbur and Orville Wright made the first flight in a power-driven airplane at Kill Devil Hill, Kitty Hawk, in North Carolina. The plane was in the air only 8 minutes, but it laid the foundation for air transportation in this short time, although the significance of the event was not generally realized: a telegram about the accomplishment did not get space in the newspapers. In 1908–09, in rapid succession, came the flights of Henri Farman in Paris with the first airplane passenger; of Louis Blériot across the English Channel; of Glenn Curtiss from Albany to New York; and the international speed race at Rheims, where France, England and Germany offered prizes for improved engines. The first transcontinental flight, from New York to Pasadena, California, was recorded in 1911 and the same year saw the establishment of the first airplane factory, in France.[9]

From World War I to World War II

World War I gave great impetus to aviation. Planes were used extensively in map-making, reconnaissance and some bombing operations. Pilots were trained, governments supported research in aeronautics, new aircraft models were designed. Engines were developed with greater power and speed but smaller consumption of fuel; twin-, triple- and multimotored planes were put in use. Altitude records soared — from less than 2,000 to more than 26,000 feet. More technical progress was achieved in the four wartime

years than would have been made in a decade of peace.[10]

Europe took the lead in establishing regular air service.[11] In most European countries the military and trade value of aeronautics induced the governments to subsidize commercial air transportation and technological research in this field. Many airlines were established, some wholly government owned. In the United States, however, business shied at the high costs of air transport, and the government was not ready to lend support to scheduled airlines though it eventually provided funds for the Post Office to introduce an experimental air mail service. At first, mail was carried by air only between Washington, D.C., and New York, but by September 1920, a transcontinental route for daylight flights had been established between New York and San Francisco.[12] The need for 24-hour service led the government to establish beacon lights along the route at about 10-mile intervals and to build emergency landing fields about every 30 miles. By the middle of 1924, round-the-clock air mail service was in operation and became the foundation of commercial aviation in the United States.[13] Accidents, frequent in the early stage because of prescribed flights in disregard of fog, wind and storm, were sharply reduced with the change in this policy, and in 1926 only one pilot fatality was recorded.

Although the air mail service was functioning very well, the United States had no regular passenger air service as late as 1926.[14] In contrast, the combined airlines of Great Britain, France, Germany, Italy and the Netherlands carried more than 100,000 passengers a year at that time and recorded some 9 million passenger-miles. Meanwhile spectacular flights by various avia-

---

10. **35**, p. 110.

11. As early as 1911, France had 353 certificated pilots, England 57, Germany 46, Italy 32 and Belgium 27, as compared to 26 in the United States. **54**, p. 21.

12. An early attempt to introduce air mail service was made in 1911 by E. L. Ovington, an aviator, over a short distance on Long Island. The Post Office authorized the service, but did not share in it financially. Some 37,000 pieces of mail were transported without accident, but the Post Office failed at that time to obtain appropriations for the establishment of an experimental air mail service. (**64**, pp. 212–13.)

13. **65**, p. 10.

14. If passengers were taken at all, they had to wedge themselves in among the mail sacks in small open-cockpit airplanes. In 1926, fewer than 6,000 passengers flew on scheduled airlines in the entire country. (**23**, p. 334.)

---

9. For a more detailed description of man's gradual conquest of the air, see **64**, pp. 1–28; **36**, pp. 10ff.; **37**, pp. 20ff. Cf. **70**, Vol. 5, pp. 98–101.

tors held the public's attention. In 1922 E. J. Faucett, an American, flew over the 22,000-foot Andes Mountains from Lima to a point sixty miles from Iquitos, Peru, covering a distance of 650 miles.[15] Nonstop transcontinental and transoceanic flights were made, as well as flights around the world and on polar expeditions. The spectacular flight of Charles A. Lindbergh from New York to Paris on May 20–21, 1927, was followed some two weeks later by an even longer nonstop transatlantic flight from New York to Germany, by D. Chamberlin and C. Levine. Altitude records were extended to 42,000 feet in 1929 and more than 72,000 feet in 1935. Endurance flights, in which the plane was refueled in the air, set one record after another — over 17 days in 1929 and 27 days the next year.[16] Lighter-than-air ships also attracted attention through their transcontinental crossings and round-the-world trips.

Despite the many crashes and fatalities resulting partly from stunt and "gypsy" flying and partly from inferior planes, public interest in aviation continued. Commercial airlines extended their routes, and passengers grew in number. The swiftly expanding airlines placed great emphasis upon the colonial routes. The United Kingdom's Imperial Airways extended its services toward the dominions and colonies along the "all-red route"; Air France linked metropolitan France with the colonies; the Netherlands concentrated on the East Indies service. Germany's Deutsche Lufthansa, without colonies to stimulate its development, devoted much attention to South America, where some German-controlled airlines were established. Pan American Airways, of the United States, with its partially owned affiliate, Panagra (Pan American-Grace Airways), extended its services down both coasts of South America and helped to establish local airlines in the interior.[17]

In the United States, a boom in aviation investments brought 44 scheduled airlines into existence by 1929 — many more lines than the immediate potential demand warranted. The collapse of the wave of speculation in 1929 forced the industry to readjust, while the government undertook encouragement of passenger traffic. Contracts for carrying air mail were made contingent on the degree of comfort and safety the airline provided for passengers. Largely as a result of this action, accommodations for travelers improved greatly, and passenger traffic began to increase. On the eve of World War II the scheduled airlines of the United States carried some 2 million passengers annually.[18]

By early 1939 the airways laced across almost every region of the world, with one notable exception — the North Atlantic. The first preparatory flights across this ocean had been carried out simultaneously from both sides of the Atlantic in 1937, when a Pan American Clipper and an Imperial Airways flying boat passed one another in mid-ocean. In the summer of 1939, Pan American began scheduled weekly flights on the southern route via the Azores and soon thereafter the United Kingdom air mail services began to operate across the Atlantic. In all, half a million miles of air routes encircled the globe in 1939, and the world's aircraft covered a distance of 300 million miles a year.[19] For the first time it became possible to fly around the world on scheduled airlines.

During World War II

World War II had an even stronger impact on aviation than World War I. Aircraft became a major factor in warfare, and a quarter of a century of peacetime development was telescoped into a few years.[20] New types of aircraft were developed and new fields opened for aviation. Radar and other electronic devices were introduced; jet-propelled planes were invented; a new raw material, magnesium, was used in aircraft; high-octane fuel was developed; weather services were greatly improved. Larger planes were built, the largest capable of carrying 400 fully equipped combat troops or 335 litter patients and attendants. Planes achieved higher speeds, with relatively less fuel consumption. Aircraft production reached an all-time high; pilots were

---

15. The trip from Lima to Iquitos was ordinarily made by boat from Lima to London and back to the east coast of South America, then some 2,300 miles up the Amazon River — a journey of three months. Today this trip is made in three hours. (**69**, p. 487.)

16. The first attempt to refuel in the air took place in the United States in 1923. The underlying principle is that a plane can carry a much heavier load during flight than at take-off. It therefore can take a maximum pay load but insufficient fuel and get the rest of its fuel in the air or can extend its trip by increasing its fuel supply in the air. Refueling in the air is now routine. (**25**, p. 42.)

17. **9**, p. 8.

18. **23**, p. 335.

19. **9**, p. 8; **53**, p. 60.

20. **9**, p. 11.

counted in hundreds of thousands, and cargoes of all types and great weight were transported on regular schedules.[21]

Military air transport service spanned the world. At the peak of operations, the United States Air Transport Command had a plane crossing the Atlantic every 6 minutes, and the Pacific, every 51 minutes. Its routes covered 200,000 miles along which 2,800 aircraft flew more than 600 million passenger-miles per month.[22] More than a million tons of military cargo were carried annually, and hundreds of millions of letters.[23] The Royal Air Force Air Transport Command of the United Kingdom ferried 27,000 aircraft from North America to the various combat areas during the war. In one month alone, its aircraft flew nearly 5 million miles, carrying 21,000 passengers and 23,000 tons of freight.[24] Landing fields were established throughout the world.

The global character of wartime aviation gave a fillip to international air traffic and wartime exigencies broke down many political barriers. Numerous technical and political problems had to be solved, however, before peacetime air services could be extended on an international scale.[25]

After World War II

Aviation emerged from the war as a major partner in the world's transportation system. Even the natural fear aroused by occasional airplane accidents now causes only a slight temporary slackening in air traffic. Air travel has become common even in remote parts of the world, in areas with few railroads and little highway traffic. Airfields have appeared in Ethiopia and the Belgian Congo, Iran and Burma. In tortuous valleys of Honduras and Guatemala, produce is brought to airfields by foot or on donkeys.

Progress in world aviation has manifested itself in better aircraft design and better navigational practices and aids. The existing aircraft models have undergone many modifications through increase in body length, seat capacity, power, weight and speed. The reciprocating (piston) engine in use has reached a very high degree of technical refinement. It weighs less than one pound per horsepower, is of proven durability, can fly up to 1,500–2,000 hours without overhauling and permits long-distance flights with a substantial pay load. Yet, just when the piston engine seems to have achieved its maximum development, a new type of engine — the turbine — appears to have a better chance of gaining ultimate supremacy in civil aircraft.[26] The turbine weighs no more than the piston engine and can develop several times as much power and much higher operational speed. It is smoother in operation, less complex to build, requires less overhauling, burns a cheaper fuel and has many other advantages.

Tremendous amounts of engineering research and testing have gone into the development of the turbine for civil aircraft. Europe, and particularly Great Britain, is ahead of the United States in this field, and so is Canada.[27] Great Britain produced the first turbo-propelled civil airplane and the British European Airways was the first airline to put such aircraft into regular scheduled passenger operation (in 1952). The new types of turbine aircraft are now in quantity production in Great Britain, and several international airlines, including some of the United States lines, are awaiting the delivery of ordered planes.[28]

According to the Civil Aeronautics Administration, the United States airlines may be operating domestic turbo-powered aircraft within three to five years — probably first on domestic, then on international routes; and similarly, first in flying cargo and afterward, passengers.[29]

In May 1952 Great Britain started civil jet transport and by the end of the year had jet aircraft in regular service: three round trips weekly between London and Johannesburg, two weekly trips to Singapore, and one to Ceylon.

21. For a description of the aircraft industry in various countries, see **71,** Chapter 30.

22. **9,** p. 11.

23. **64,** p. 346.

24. **9,** p. 11.

25. See pp. 556ff.

26. Two types of turbine have been developed: the turboprop engine harnessed to the propeller, and the turbojet engine. The first has a comparatively low rate of fuel consumption and can take off and land on shorter runways than the turbojet. The latter requires more fuel and operates best at altitudes as high as 40,000–50,000 feet and at very high speed.

27. **17,** p. 4.

28. **17,** pp. 36 and 75. The aircraft industry of the United States is now at work to produce turbine-powered civil aircraft and may possibly produce models superior to those in operation and in the design stage in other countries. However, foreign countries are considered to have a great advantage over the United States in accumulated operational knowledge. **17,** p. 7.

29. **29,** February 22, 1954, p. 14.

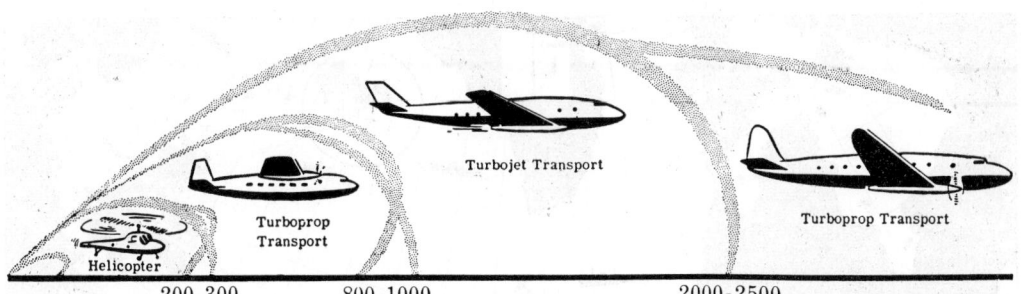

FIGURE 100. DEVELOPMENT OF AVIATION: COMING TYPES OF TRANSPORT AIRCRAFT—THE EUROPEAN VIEW

Operations were expanding throughout 1953, but early in 1954 three jet aircraft were involved in tragic accidents and jet transport was suspended. The investigation has revealed that the cause of trouble was metal fatigue.

The cruising speed of turbo-powered aircraft is 500 miles per hour; the altitude is about 35,000 feet. European manufacturers and operators believe that in the future three types of aircraft will be chiefly used, depending on the distance of stage flights: turboprops for flights averaging between 200–300 and 800–1,000 miles; turbojets for flights of 1,000 to 2,000–2,500 miles; for flights exceeding that length the turboprop may take over, since it is more economical in operation and consumes less fuel;[30] for stage lengths (flight distance) up to 200–300 miles helicopters may be the answer. (See Figure 100.) In other words, the helicopter may operate on local routes; the turboprop, on longer distances within a continent; and the turbojet, on transcontinental and transoceanic flights. On the longest transoceanic flights, the turboprop may compete with the turbojet.

There is general agreement, particularly among European manufacturers and operators, that turbine-powered aircraft will not only have a lower cost per ton-mile than the piston-engine aircraft, but also a longer depreciation period, of not less than ten years. The next new type of aircraft is expected to strive for supersonic speeds of some 900 miles per hour, but such aircraft would probably not be available for civil use for at least ten years.[31]

Many wartime improvements have been incorporated into civil aviation. A network of aids to air navigation now extends practically from pole to pole, even in areas where no human settlements exist. Observation posts on the high seas assure prompt and continuous weather information. In the North Atlantic, for example, 25 ships maintain weather patrol duty, taking upper-air observations every 12 hours by radiosonde balloon (a balloon carrying an automatic radio transmitter) and tracing it with radar equipment. (See Figure 101.) These and other aids to air navigation have become so extensive and reliable that the United States announced, in October 1953, the withdrawal of its weather patrol ships after the expiration of its agreement on June 30, 1954. However, it later agreed to continue the floating station service in the North Atlantic and signed the Paris agreement of February 25, 1954 to that effect. This agreement, calling for 9 ocean stations instead of 10 previously maintained, will run for two years, with 4 stations operated by North American states and 5 by European.

Civil aviation has made great strides in the postwar years, and this progress is reflected in the growing volume of traffic, increased frequency of service, faster schedules and the extension of routes all over the world.

CIVIL AVIATION

Civil aviation includes scheduled air operations and so-called "general aviation flying," or "utility flying."

Scheduled airlines operate on fixed routes, between specific terminals, according to regular timetables and published fares.

General aviation flying, as defined by the Civil Aeronautics Administration, includes a hetero-

---

30. Some U.S. experts estimate that direct operational costs of turboprops on domestic routes at about 500 miles per hour may be 15–20 per cent less than on turbojets, and on international routes, 20–25 per cent less. **30,** January 18, 1954, p. 16.

31. **17,** p. 11.

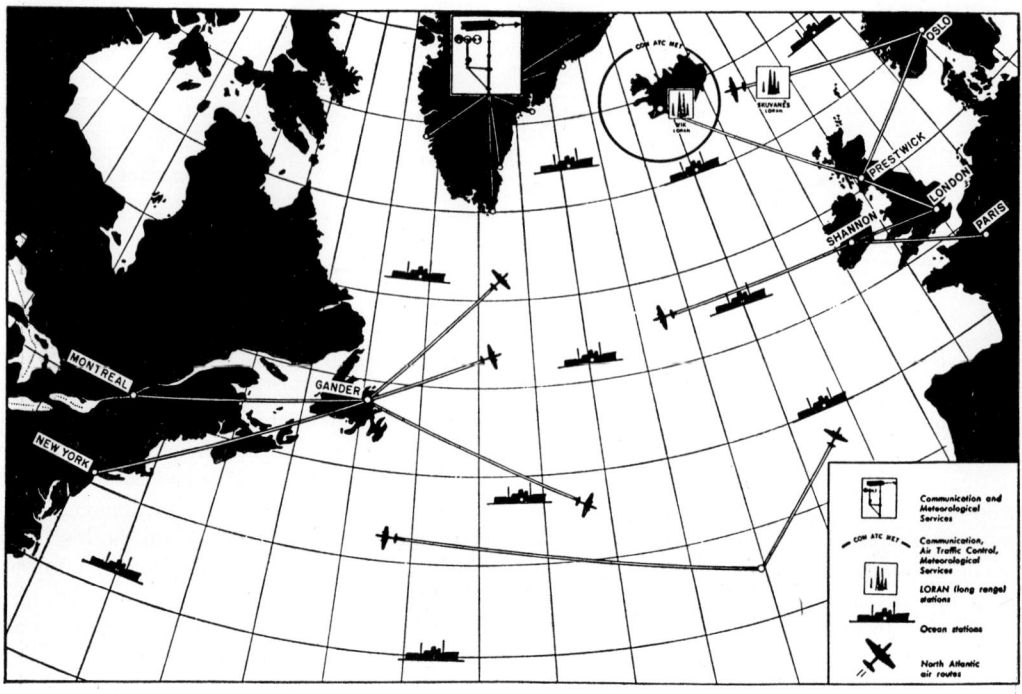

International Civil Aviation Organization

FIGURE 101. DEVELOPMENT OF AVIATION: SERVICES IN THE NORTH ATLANTIC, 1953

geneous group of operators, commercial and private. Among these are the nonscheduled operators who provide service to various points from "fixed bases" or offer charter service or work on a contract basis. Various types of industrial firms use their own airplanes for business purposes; farmers and pay contractors take to the air to seed, spray and dust crops. Aerial photography, surveying, advertising, sightseeing, flight training and pleasure flying are also included in general aviation flying.

Both types of civil aviation — scheduled and nonscheduled — depend on established airways and ground organization — airports, meteorological and communication services, navigational aids and all the paraphernalia that these require.

AIRWAYS

An airway is a lane through the airspace along which aircraft are guided from airport to airport. It is adequately equipped with intermediate landing fields at suitable intervals, various aids to navigation and an efficient communication system. The federal airways of the United States comprise the space extending horizontally for five miles on each side; vertically, they are limited only by maximum flying heights[32] and are divided into a number of traffic levels, spaced by 1,000-foot separations.

Development of commercial aviation has made it imperative to provide regular routes with various instrumentalities to enable pilots to maintain their course. The airway is usually equipped with radio stations transmitting information on weather and traffic conditions; radio range stations sending beams to direct the pilots along their course; instrument landing systems to guide them in overcast weather; radar, high-frequency

32. The legal question of the right to fly over private land was settled in the United States by a Supreme Court decision in 1946. The old maxim that "who owns the soil owns it to the sky, from the center of the earth to the Lord's abode" had often been used to support a landowner's right of airway over his property. If this contention had been upheld, the need to acquire rights of way would have created a tremendous, perhaps insuperable, obstacle to the development of air transportation. The Supreme Court declared that airspace is a public highway, the ancient doctrine having "no place in the modern world." It specified, however, that the landowner has "exclusive control of the immediate reaches of the enveloping atmosphere," since "otherwise buildings could not be erected, trees could not be planted, and even fences could not be run." (**51**, pp. 787–88; **63**, pp. 541–42.)

radio omnirange and other aids to navigation. Airways crisscrossing a country where aviation is developed are now as definite for pilots as highways for automobile drivers.

Although established airways are free and open to all, planes do not fly in boundless atmosphere at the mere whim of the pilot. The right to use existing airways is subject to strict rules and regulations, like the use of highways. Pilots and planes must be certified and must observe safety prescriptions.[33] They are guided not only at the take-off and landing but also during the entire flight. The pilot reports his position along the airway, and the control station knows his speed, altitude and exact location at all times. Planes must maintain a considerable distance from one another; because of their speed and the large turning radius — about a mile for the large passenger planes — safety requires substantial spacing.

Emergency landing fields are usually interspersed along the airways between airports, but the need for such fields is decreasing with the increase in the number of airports and in flying speeds and higher altitudes and the decline in mechanical failures. The number of intermediate fields in the United States declined from 404 in 1931 to 57 in 1951.[34]

No other country has built as complete and elaborate systems of airways for its lines as the United States. The domestic system was established at federal expense, but international carriers of the United States have developed their airways on a commercial basis. Before World War II, few airways were lighted, and both domestic and international operations were confined to daylight flights.[35] With the approach of the war, the federal government aided international carriers in establishing airways throughout the world. During the war, the armed forces of the United States extended the network of international airways and installed radio beams, weather stations and other facilities over the Atlantic and Pacific.[36] These facilities became available to the civil airlines of the United States at the end of the war.

In recent years the government has undertaken an extensive program of modernization of federal airways, and in 1952 nearly 46,000 miles of new "Victor" airways were opened. These new airways, superimposed upon or closely following the existing low-frequency airways,[37] are equipped with very-high-frequency omnidirectional transmitters.[38]

AIRPORTS

Airports are to aircraft what ports are to ships — links with the earth. Adapted for landings and take-offs, they have unobstructed approaches, runways and taxiways, facilities for sheltering, loading and unloading, servicing and repairing aircraft and for receiving and disembarking passengers, but they have almost none of the commercial and administrative installations without which a port is ineffective. Just as different port facilities are required for sailing ships, freighters and transatlantic liners, so do the requirements differ for pleasure planes of 2–3 passengers, slow local transport planes with some 15–20 passengers and large four-engine aircraft carrying 80–90 passengers and operating at a cruising speed of 300 or more miles.

In the pioneer days of aviation (1920–26), there were no airports — only "meets" of aviators. The small size of the planes and their slowness in taking off and landing made the use of level open ground possible. Between 1927 and 1933 a concrete apron was provided on many airfields; after 1933 runways became available; during 1941–47 complete runway systems of limited strength with taxi strips and aprons were built; 1948–51 saw the perfecting of runways.[39] However, ordinary grass fields are still used in many underdeveloped areas, as in Honduras, where "fields" for scheduled aircraft are literally pastures, provided with sheds to protect passengers from rain. This is possible because small light planes are still used in such regions.

Heavy aircraft need a paved landing surface, which is usually made of thick concrete, laid on a well-drained foundation and reinforced with steel rods or wire mesh. The artificial surface is laid in long strips to form runways. Hard surfaces are generally used in the United States and in many other countries.[40]

---

33. **65**, p. 63.

34. **18**, 1953, p. 4.

35. In the early days of aviation, bonfires were built to guide planes at night. Today heavy aircraft can fly an unlighted route with the help of navigational aids.

36. **65**, pp. 82–83.

37. Airways which provide navigation guidance and communication by low-frequency radio; such signals may be interrupted by stormy weather.

38. **18**, 1953, p. 18.

39. **44**, 1951, No. 4, p. 190.

40. **61**, p. 267; **66**, p. 306.

An airplane approaching an airport seems to assume larger and larger proportions, and as the number of aircraft increases the less space there is for each plane, particularly in bad weather. Congestion in some of the busiest airports is steadily increasing. During the summer of 1940 some airports in the United States averaged one landing or take-off per minute, and at Oakland, California, the rate was two planes per minute throughout the 24-hour period.[41]

The National Airport at Washington, D.C., averaged 88 landings and take-offs per hour during 1945. In 1950, thirteen airports in the United States averaged more than 500 departures and arrivals a day, and some seven or eight of the world's largest cities outside the United States, 200 landings and take-offs. Moreover, there are emergency periods during which an airport and the air over it become desperately overcrowded. Despite the many cubic miles above and around an airport, a few dozen planes circling, landing, and taking off may cause dangerous congestion. "Merely to visualize what would happen if the ship, tug, ferry and barge traffic of New York Harbor suddenly began to move at 150 miles per hour illustrates some of the fundamental differences between surface and air traffic." [42]

Planning

An airport should be close to the community it serves and easily accessible by land transport. Since a modern airport requires a great deal of surface space (the Newark airport, for example, occupies approximately seventy acres), the selection of its site is a difficult problem. Often natural surface defects have to be corrected by engineering efforts. New York's international airport (Idlewild) was built on a swamp, and scores of millions of cubic yards of sand were dredged from Jamaica Bay to raise its surface above the high-tide mark. At Gibraltar, a runway was lengthened by an extension over the sea. To build the new Zurich international airport, the level of the river was lowered some 15 feet to facilitate drainage.[43]

The coming of jet aircraft transport will place new demands on the airports. For reasons of economy such planes should remain on the ground for as short periods as possible, and their engines should be kept running. They must be kept from contact with one another to avoid damage to equipment, and at a safe distance from people to prevent injury from heat and the velocity of the exhaust blast.

Although the life of aircraft is relatively short because of rapid changes in design, the life of an airport, like a railroad station, must be long. In fact, the airport must outlive many generations of aircraft and be able to accommodate planes which today are but a dream of some imaginative designer.[44]

While some airports built a decade or so ago with greater spaciousness than aircraft then required were believed to be adequate for some fifty years, it is now estimated that most airports will need to be extended and adjusted to new requirements at intervals of fifteen years or possibly less.[45] Yet many countries, including the United States, have built airports haphazardly, without provision for expansion, as was shown by a study made before World War II of more than seventy airports in twenty countries of the Western Hemisphere and Europe.[46] At that time many of the world's largest airports were in the process of expansion; those incapable of enlargement were abandoned or duplicated. Croydon (London) had reached the saturation point, and a substantial part of its traffic was shifted to two other ports. Tempelhof (Berlin) had expanded its area. La Guardia Airport (New York), opened in 1939, had more traffic by 1941 than it could handle.[47]

Military requirements during World War II sometimes resulted in hasty construction of airports, to fit immediate emergencies. Many of them were located in out-of-the-way places not suited for civil use and were of such size and design that much of the initial investment was lost.[48] Even in countries with a well-developed air transport network, airports are frequently located at such a distance from the urban center that the greatest advantage of air transport, its speed, is almost nullified. Ground travel to and from the airport takes an hour in Chicago, Los Angeles, Seattle and Cleveland. Between Oslo and Stockholm, the flying time is actually shorter than surface-travel time between the airports and the city centers.

41. **23**, p. 336.
42. **67**, p. 41.
43. **61**, p. 299; **17**, p. 29.

44. **22**, p. 48.
45. **54**, pp. 108–09.
46. **66**, p. 3.
47. **61**, p. 282; **58**, p. 16.
48. **39**, p. 33; **18**, 1953, p. 3.

The USSR has many landing fields and airports, but until recently less than fifty were properly equipped. Even in many larger cities, some airports have had no hard-surfaced runways, hangars or adequate passenger terminals. Some of them cannot operate in winter for lack of proper facilities for snow removal.[49]

Runways

The length of the runway limits the size of the aircraft which can use the airport. Many experts believe that no single feature of the airport layout is more important for speed and safety of service than the strength and length of runways. In the early days of aviation, turf-surfaced runways were satisfactory; today hard surfaces are generally used in the United States and in many European countries.[50] Of the 6,042 airports listed in the United States in 1952, 5,966 were classified as follows by length of paved runways (in feet): [51]

Length	Number of Airports
1,800–2,500	3,685
2,500–3,500	976
3,500–4,500	571
4,500–5,500	437
5,500–6,500	181
6,500–7,500	116

In addition, all of these airports had about equal lengths of unpaved runway strips. The nation's longest runway (10,022 feet) is at Logan International Airport in Boston.

In the United Kingdom, some airports have runways 9,000 or more feet long — for example, the Manston airport at Ramsgate and the London airport. In Switzerland, the international airport opened in Zurich in 1952 has a runway length of 8,500 feet, with provision for extension to 11,500 feet.[52] In Egypt, the international airport in Cairo, covering some 2,000 acres, has two runways nearly 10,000 feet long, and one exceeding 8,500 feet.[53]

While it was exceptional in 1948–49 to plan a runway of more than 8,000 feet, runways of 10,000 feet were much discussed in 1951, and many experts believe that long-range operations of jet-propelled aircraft may call for a length of 12,000–15,000 feet.[54] The first airport built specifically for jet operation was opened in Uganda in November 1951.

It is also important to have a "flightway" beyond the runway — an unobstructed area near the airport's approaches, where incoming and outgoing aircraft can fly at low altitudes.[55]

Ownership

Airports are owned and operated by central governments, municipalities, or private enterprises. Some are owned by governments and leased to municipalities, and others are owned by municipalities and leased to private operators. According to the International Civil Aviation Organization (ICAO), nearly all large airports on the world's main air routes are publicly owned and operated.[56] The government of the United Kingdom owns and operates all airports; the United States government owns only one large airport, at Washington, D.C.

The total number of airports in the United States increased from 1,036 in 1927 to 2,280 in 1939, 4,026 in 1945 and 6,042 in 1952. In that last year, some 29 per cent were under nonpublic ownership or control and 39 per cent were publicly owned or controlled. In addition, the Civil Aeronautics Administration controlled a small number of intermediate airports, established for emergency stops and technical purposes; the rest consisted of private and military airports. With the increase in number of commercial and municipal airports, intermediate airports are passing out of existence. (See Table 174.)

HIGHWAYS OF THE AIR

The world's network of air routes multiplies every year, reaching into the remotest corners and bringing within its compass almost every town of commercial importance. Broadly, the international route system has been superimposed upon the old routes of land transportation.[57]

In the World

The unduplicated length of air routes (count-

49. **69**, p. 504.
50. **66**, p. 306.
51. **27**, 1953, p. 12. Includes 363 military airports.
52. **17**, p. 29.
53. **38**, pp. 82–83.

54. **10**, p. 18. When jet-assist take-off (JATO), now used in military aviation, becomes commercially feasible and is widely used, the length of runways will lose some of its importance.
55. **58**, p. 14.
56. **5**, p. 15.
57. **61**, p. 194.

TABLE 174

AIRPORTS: NUMBER BY TYPE OF OWNERSHIP OR CONTROL, IN THE UNITED STATES, 1927–52

Year Ending December 31	Total	Commercial	Municipal	Intermediate [a]	All Others [b]
1927	1,036	263	240	134	399 [c]
1929	1,550	495	453	285	317 [c]
1931	2,093	829	780	404	80
1933	2,188	938	827	265	158
1935	2,368	822	1,041	291	214
1937	2,299	727	1,053	283	236
1939	2,280	801	963	266	250
1941	2,484	930	1,086	283	185
1943	2,769	801	914	240	814
1945	4,026	1,509	1,220	216	1,081
1947	5,759	2,849	1,818	178	914
1949	6,484	2,585	2,200	139	1,560
1950	6,403	2,329	2,272	76	1,726
1951	6,237	2,042	2,316	57	1,818
1952 [d]	6,042	1,731	2,336	1,975	

Source: **18**, 1953, pp. 4–5.

a. Airports for emergency landings.
b. Includes military airports.
c. Includes auxiliary marked fields, later classified by ownership as municipal or commercial.
d. Since July 1952, the type definitions of airports have been revised, and five types established: (1) municipal airports (public use, public ownership and/or control, and aircraft services generally available); (2) commercial (public use, nonpublic ownership and/or control, and aircraft services generally available); (3) limited (intended for private use, but public not prohibited, public or nonpublic ownership and/or control, and aircraft services limited or not available); (4) military (some civil use, military ownership and/or control); (5) private (authorized use only, public or nonpublic ownership and/or control).

ing the route mileage only once even though more than one airline operates between two points) in the world, exclusive of the USSR, grew from 3,200 miles in 1919 to 385,600 miles in 1938, 867,100 in 1947–48 and 1.1 million in 1949. Between 1938 and 1949, air routes in North America, Europe and Oceania more than doubled in length; those in South America more than tripled; in Middle America, more than quadrupled; and in Asia, increased fivefold. (See Table 175.)

Information on routes in the USSR is contradictory, perhaps because some estimates disregard duplications. Russian sources claim that the route system of the USSR in 1945 was some 78,000 miles and considerably exceeded that of the United States.[58] The Fourth Five-Year Plan envisaged extending the route length to 109,000 miles in 1950.[59] In contrast, the Civil Aeronautics Board estimated the unduplicated length in 1950 at 46,933 miles.[60]

58. **55**, p. 44; cf. **57**, p. 354.
59. **34**, p. 89.
60. **21**, p. 8.

TABLE 175

AIR ROUTES: UNDUPLICATED LENGTH OF SCHEDULED AIRLINES, BY CONTINENT, 1938–49

(*Thousands of Miles*)

Continent	1938	1947–48	1949
World [a]	385.6	867.1	1,061.0
North America [b]	82.6	182.2	224.2
Middle America	10.2	43.9	49.3
South America	41.8	126.8	127.4
Europe	186.1	316.9	414.5
USSR	(65.9)	(90.0)	(49.0)
Asia	21.0	96.5	106.0
Africa	14.7	39.6	59.5
Oceania	29.2	61.2	80.2

Sources: For 1938 and 1947–48: **69**, p. 24; for 1949 (October 1): **68**, p. 10.

a. Excludes the USSR.
b. Excludes local Alaskan airlines and United States cargo carriers, certificated and noncertificated; includes Hawaii and Puerto Rico.

In Selected Countries

The United States has a longer system of air routes than any other country. Its unduplicated length of 184,000 miles in 1950 exceeded the combined mileage of the next two countries: the United Kingdom, with 82,014 miles and Australia, with 80,811. France and the Netherlands also have extensive networks. Brazil leads in South America and ranks sixth in the world. India and the Philippines lead in Asia; the Union of South Africa and Egypt, in Africa.

Almost all countries greatly extended the mileage of their air routes between 1938 and 1950. Mileage in the United Kingdom more than tripled and in many other countries was multiplied by five, six and even more. (See Table 176.)

In the United States, air routes developed gradually at first. The first major route was transcontinental, facilitating the flow of air mail among the large urban centers on both coasts. Since the single-engine aircraft of early aviation days required frequent refueling, many stops had to be made along the route. As passenger traffic grew, other air routes were developed to connect all large cities, until today practically all but the smallest cities have daily air service through an airport not more than thirty miles away.[61] The network of air routes in the United States resembles the railway network: the densely populated East has air connections in all directions, while the West has fewer. (See Figure 102; cf. Figure 61, p. 346.)

Domestic air routes of the United States are divided into trunk routes, which connect major cities, and local service routes confined to points relatively near one another. International routes connect the United States with foreign countries, but routes to Canada are considered domestic in statistics of the Civil Aeronautics Board. Routes within a territory of the United States — for example, Hawaii — or between two territories, such as Puerto Rico and the Virgin Islands, are called territorial, while a route between the United States and any one of its territories is considered an overseas route.

International air routes of United States carriers are mapped in Figure 103.

MAJOR WORLD ROUTES

As in shipping, major trunk routes of air navigation have evolved under the impact of many factors — potential traffic along the way and at terminals, the availability of adequate navigational aids and other facilities, length of unavoidable nonstop flights and of the route itself, weather conditions and so on. Airlines naturally try to establish routes in such a way as to minimize the distance between terminal points — that is, in general, to use the great-circle course. In flying, however, this rule cannot be followed to the same extent as on ocean lanes, especially when such a course requires long nonstop flights.

Of all forms of transportation, the airplane is the most sensitive to gross weight, which consists of the fuel load, the weight of the plane itself, crew, equipment, and the revenue load. The longer the flight, the greater the fuel load and the smaller the revenue load.[62] The present economical range of nonstop flying is slightly over 2,000 miles. For example, the air route between San Francisco and Manila is 8,000 miles via Hawaii, while the great-circle distance between the two cities is 6,965 miles. To take the latter course, however, would require a nonstop flight over the open sea for almost the entire distance, and no transport plane yet exists that would make this practicable on a commercial basis.[63] Even if such an aircraft existed, the amount of fuel needed for mere transportation would leave little or no capacity for cargo or passengers. The crew would merely be flying a gasoline tank across the ocean.[64]

One of the most important factors in determining an air route is the potential maximum traffic. On the whole, aviation has to cling to the focal points of existing streams of transportation, although it does strike out into new and unexploited areas and creates new traffic; in most northern parts of Canada, for example, the airplanes operate in areas where the only alternative is the use of dog sleds.[65]

The world's main routes have the newest and largest aircraft, the most frequent and speedy flights, the best accommodations for passengers. The focal centers of international routes are two North Atlantic areas — the northeastern part of the United States and Canada and the northwestern part of Europe. Between these two world centers lies the busiest thoroughfare of world aviation, the North Atlantic route. From

---

61. **54**, pp. 84–91; **65**, p. 33.

62. **60**, p. 29.
63. **60**, p. 24.
64. **62**, pp. 14–15.
65. **64**, p. 522.

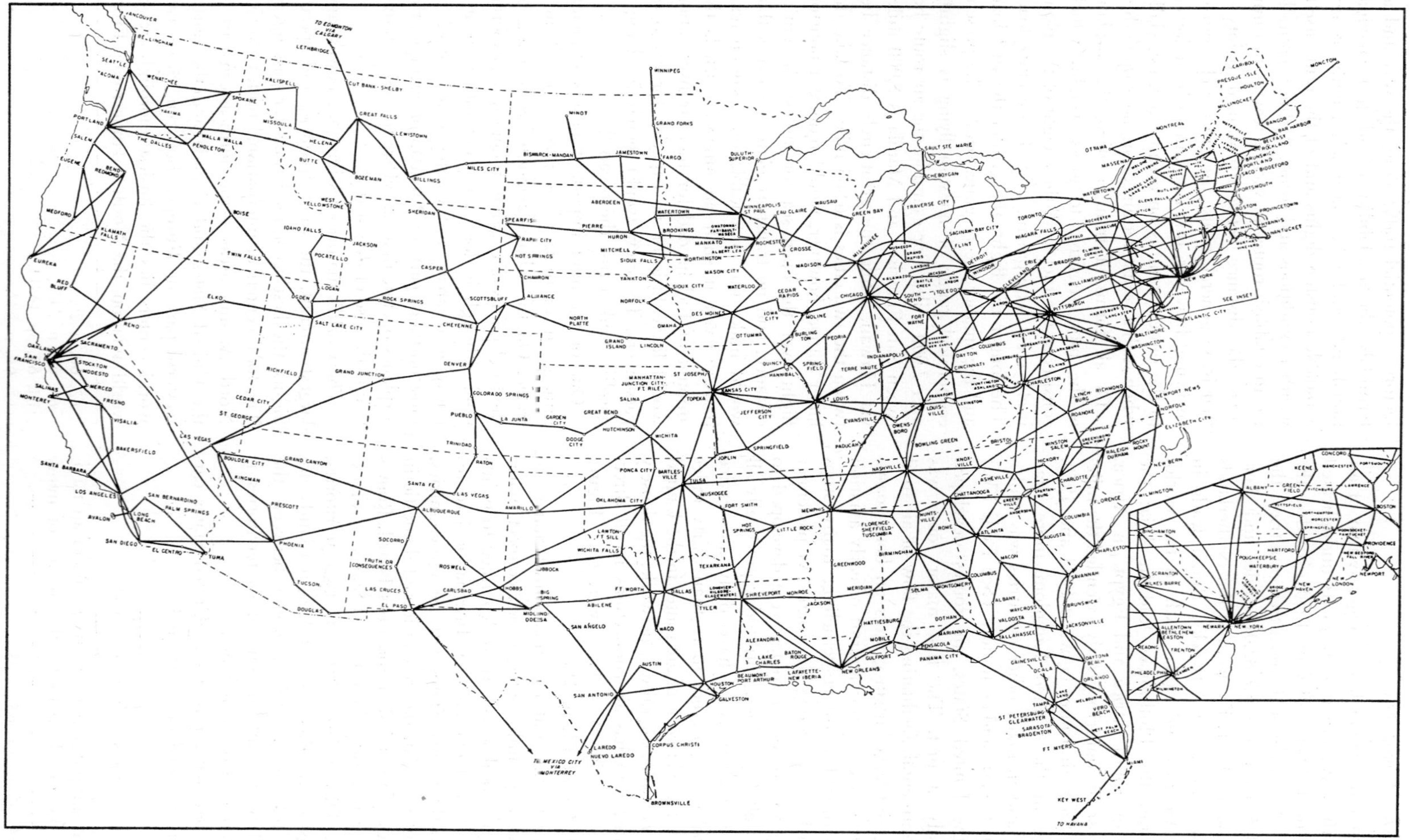

FIGURE 102. AIR ROUTES OF THE UNITED STATES: PERMANENTLY CERTIFICATED DOMESTIC ROUTES, 1953

Civil Aeronautics Board

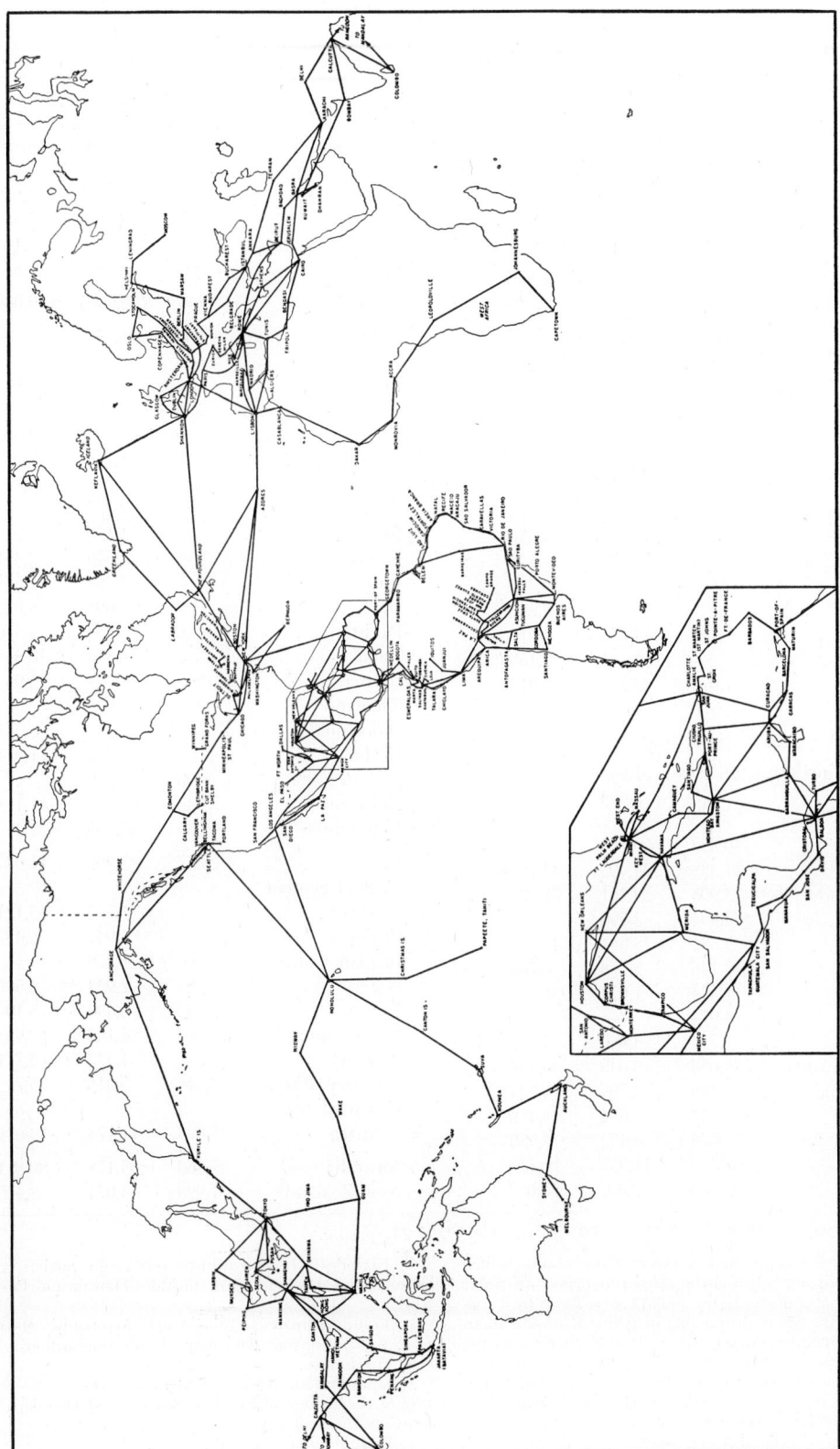

FIGURE 103. AIR ROUTES OF THE UNITED STATES: INTERNATIONAL AIRLINES, 1953

Civil Aeronautics Board

TABLE 176

AIR ROUTES: UNDUPLICATED LENGTH OF SCHEDULED AIRLINES, IN SELECTED COUNTRIES, 1938–50

(*Miles* [a])

Country	1938	1947–48	1950	Country	1938	1947–48	1950
United States [b]	70,718	158,098	184,000	Yugoslavia	3,483	2,845	2,049
Canada	11,917	24,084	45,481	Romania	6,309	2,760	1,589
Mexico	9,404	21,038	22,783	Bulgaria	. . .	. . .	1,168
Guatemala	—	286	1,830	Greece	547	846	6,883
El Salvador	—	. . .	2,326	USSR	(65,900)	(90,000)	(49,000) [c]
Honduras	—	. . .	2,576	China	4,956	26,058	. .
Nicaragua	—	. . .	849	Japan	8,694	—	—
Costa Rica	—	. . .	1,882	Hong Kong	—	. . .	5,022
Panama	—	476	542	Turkey	236	3,960	. . .
Cuba	796	2,709	8,003	Cyprus	. . .	. . .	2,993
Haiti	—	391	474	Lebanon	—	5,151	. . .
Dominican Republic	—	334	351	Israel	132	. . .	3,833
Venezuela	2,170	12,235	25,770	Syria	—	2,207	. . .
Colombia	5,314	16,245	24,656	Jordan	. . .	1,139	. . .
Ecuador	161	912	821	Saudi Arabia	—	1,545	2,391
Brazil	23,608	53,767	64,299	Iraq	—	2,363	1,578
Peru	3,935	. . .	5,886	Iran	—	8,695	6,010
Bolivia	3,129	4,396	4,010	Pakistan	}4,822{	654	4,510
Paraguay	—	1,161	2,169	India		14,354	30,546
Chile	1,075	3,199	4,912	Burma	545	—	2,953
Uruguay	860	1,143	1,433	Thailand	420	3,985	6,962
Argentina	1,577	23,182	27,302	Indochina	. . .	. . .	6,281
				Ceylon	—	434	11,971
United Kingdom	24,395	81,667	82,014	Malaya	390	719	. . .
Ireland	418	2,604	2,329	Indonesia	7,943	. . .	11,118
Iceland	. . .	. . .	6,834	Philippines	1,086	15,305	22,487
France	40,833	66,108	76,284 [d]	Egypt	2,047	2,906	11,047
Belgium	11,388	24,495	32,167	Anglo-Egyptian			
Netherlands	23,998	39,261	71,395	Sudan	—	1,572	3,121
Denmark	2,854	3,796	. . .	Ethiopia	—	3,947	6,437
Sweden	5,381	28,681	40,018 [e]	Belgian Congo	—	3,873	. . .
Norway	2,146	5,778	8,766 [f]	Nigeria	—	2,924	6,506
Finland	1,584	1,078	1,736	Kenya	2,932	4,499	5,196
Germany	24,974	—	—	Mozambique	—	2,143	2,695
Poland	3,744	3,960	4,442	Angola	—	1,572	2,711
Czechoslovakia	5,654	9,649	6,542	Southern Rhodesia	1,814	5,016	5,712
Switzerland	2,448	8,399	15,424	Union of South			
Hungary	1,740	694	1,478	Africa	7,893	11,173	13,046
Portugal	479	8,452	9,950				
Spain	—	11,858	16,217	Australia	27,160	55,178	80,811
Italy	23,583	9,497	21,082	New Zealand	1,990	3,071	8,408

Sources: Data for 1938 and 1947–48: **69**, *passim;* for 1950: **21**, *passim.*

a. Mileage for all carriers except those of the United States represents great-circle airport-to-airport distances and does not conform to the actual course flown by a particular airline where operational or political considerations require circuitous routings. For United States carriers, figures represent a weighted average when a change in route pattern occurs during the month. Although unduplicated route miles of the United States carriers and foreign carriers are computed on a slightly different basis, figures are, in general, comparable.

b. Excludes Alaskan airlines and cargo carriers, certificated and noncertificated; includes Hawaii and Puerto Rico.

c. 1950: estimate of the Civil Aeronautics Board. (**21**, p. 8.) Previous data may include duplications.

d. Air France.

e. Scandinavian Airlines System (SAS) — an association of the airlines of Sweden, Norway and Denmark for joint operation of scheduled services.

f. Excludes share in SAS.

the two centers air routes radiate toward other major centers on the Pacific coast of North America and the Atlantic coast of South America, in Africa, the Far East and Oceania. (See Figure 104.) Routes of the USSR form a separate system, connecting the country with a few areas outside its borders.

The existence of thousands of airports throughout the world makes it possible to shift air routes from time to time. On the whole, however, major world routes remain comparatively stable. Figure 105 shows the world's system of major intercontinental, transcontinental and regional routes in 1950, selected on the basis of permanency over a period of time, frequency of schedules throughout the year and volume of traffic.

Over the North Atlantic

The route between North America and Europe is the most important and also the most difficult, because of the length of the nonstop flight and the frequently adverse weather. The starting point is Gander (Newfoundland), about 1,000 miles northeast of New York.[66] Aircraft headed for London take the great-circle route via Newfoundland and then proceed either directly to Ireland (Shannon) and London, or via Iceland (Reykjavik) to Ireland; planes headed for southern Europe fly via Newfoundland with a stop at the Azores, and proceed to Lisbon, the European terminal for the southern route across the North Atlantic and for most of the South Atlantic routes.

The disadvantage of the Newfoundland route is the need to fly nonstop for more than 2,000 miles, nearly the limit of the economical range of modern aircraft. The Icelandic route, while providing a stop at Reykjavik, is some 200 miles longer, and weather conditions are uncertain during the winter. The southern route, via the Azores, has far better weather conditions but is some 900 miles longer. Despite the long nonstop flight, most traffic therefore goes via Newfoundland and Ireland.[67] (See Figure 106.)

When the United States and Great Britain finally established the North Atlantic air services in 1939 after years of research, experiment and preparation, the two countries at first intended to reserve the Newfoundland route for their own airlines, but this monopoly was short lived. At least nine countries — the United States, Great Britain (or, rather, the British Commonwealth), France, Germany, Italy, the Netherlands, Poland, Norway and Sweden — established or planned transatlantic service within a short time,[68] and transatlantic traffic grew by leaps and bounds.[69]

Another transatlantic route between the Western Hemisphere and Europe is via Bermuda and the Azores (Santa Maria) to Lisbon. It is longer than the northern route and entails at least as long a nonstop flight as any other course.

To South America

Air routes to South America from the United States and Europe can be described as South Atlantic routes. The approach to South America from the United States is via the Caribbean, making the entire southern part of the United States a gateway to all routes in this direction. Within South America, the airlines often must follow the old circuitous pattern of ground communications, hugging the coast, though additional hinterland points are opened to air transport each year.

The usual route from Europe to South America is either via New York or Bermuda to the points of destination, with intermediate stops in the Caribbean. Another route, which may possibly develop heavier traffic, is across the South Atlantic, via Dakar to Paramaribo (Surinam) and Brazil, a course that inherited many airway facilities from wartime operations. (See Figure 106.)

Australia is considering establishing a route to Chile, via Tahiti and Easter Island, presumably with flying boats, since Easter Island has no landing strip and it would be too expensive to build one. The distance from Australia to Santiago, Chile, via this route would be cut from some 13,700 miles by the most direct airline routing now available to about 8,900 miles.[70]

To Africa

Between North America and Africa planes may fly via Europe or via South America, but

---

66. During the war, the airport at Goose Bay, Labrador, was used jointly by the Allies. It is said to be one of the best natural air bases in North America, with much more favorable weather conditions than in Newfoundland. (**60**, p. 34.)

67. **65**, p. 52.

68. The Germans pioneered the transatlantic service even earlier, with the airship Graf Zeppelin on the South Atlantic route in 1933, and added heavier-than-air craft in 1934, with refueling in mid-ocean.

69. **54**, p. 59; **53**, pp. 60–62.

70. **10**, p. 11.

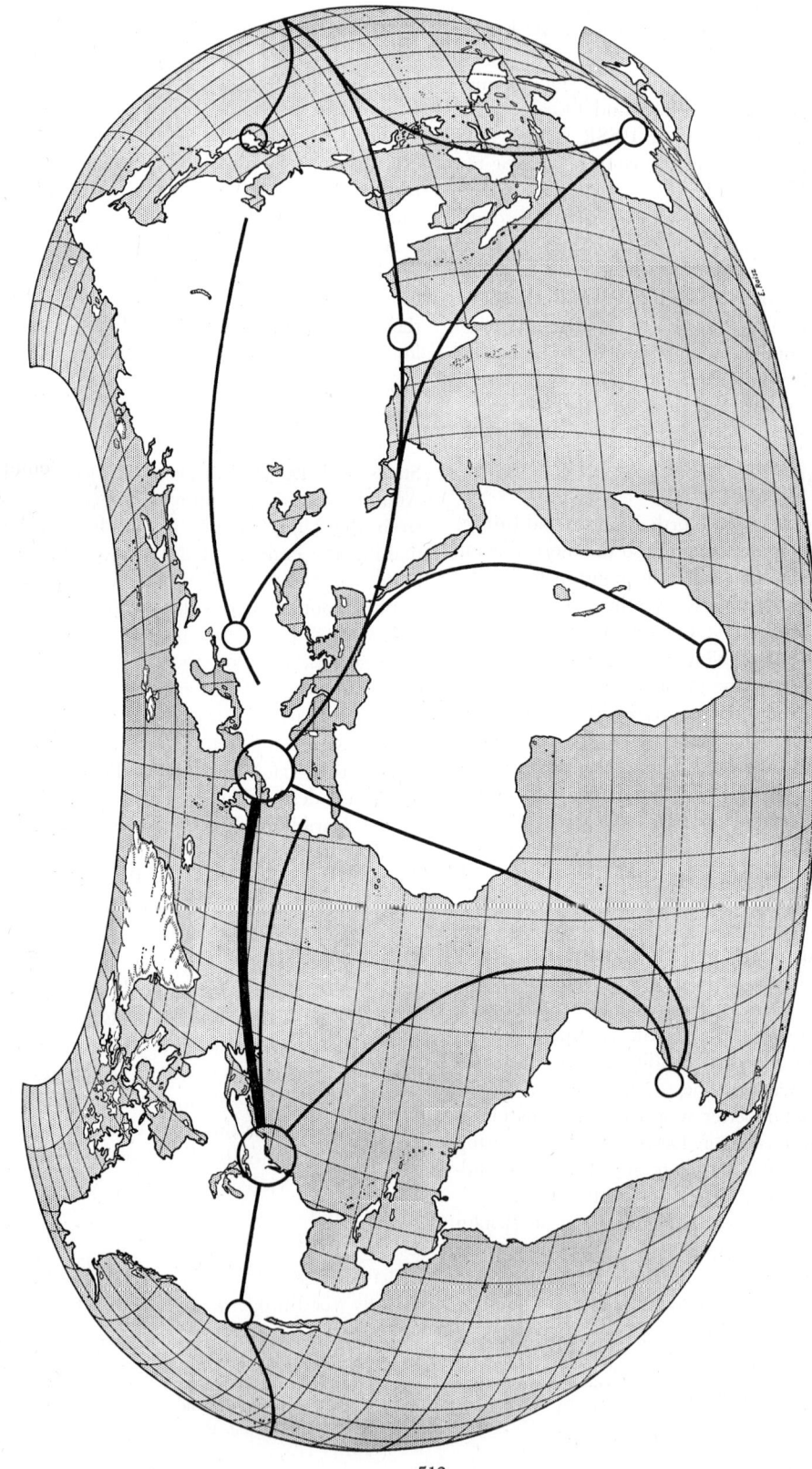

FIGURE 104. AIR ROUTES: GENERAL PATTERN IN THE WORLD, 1950

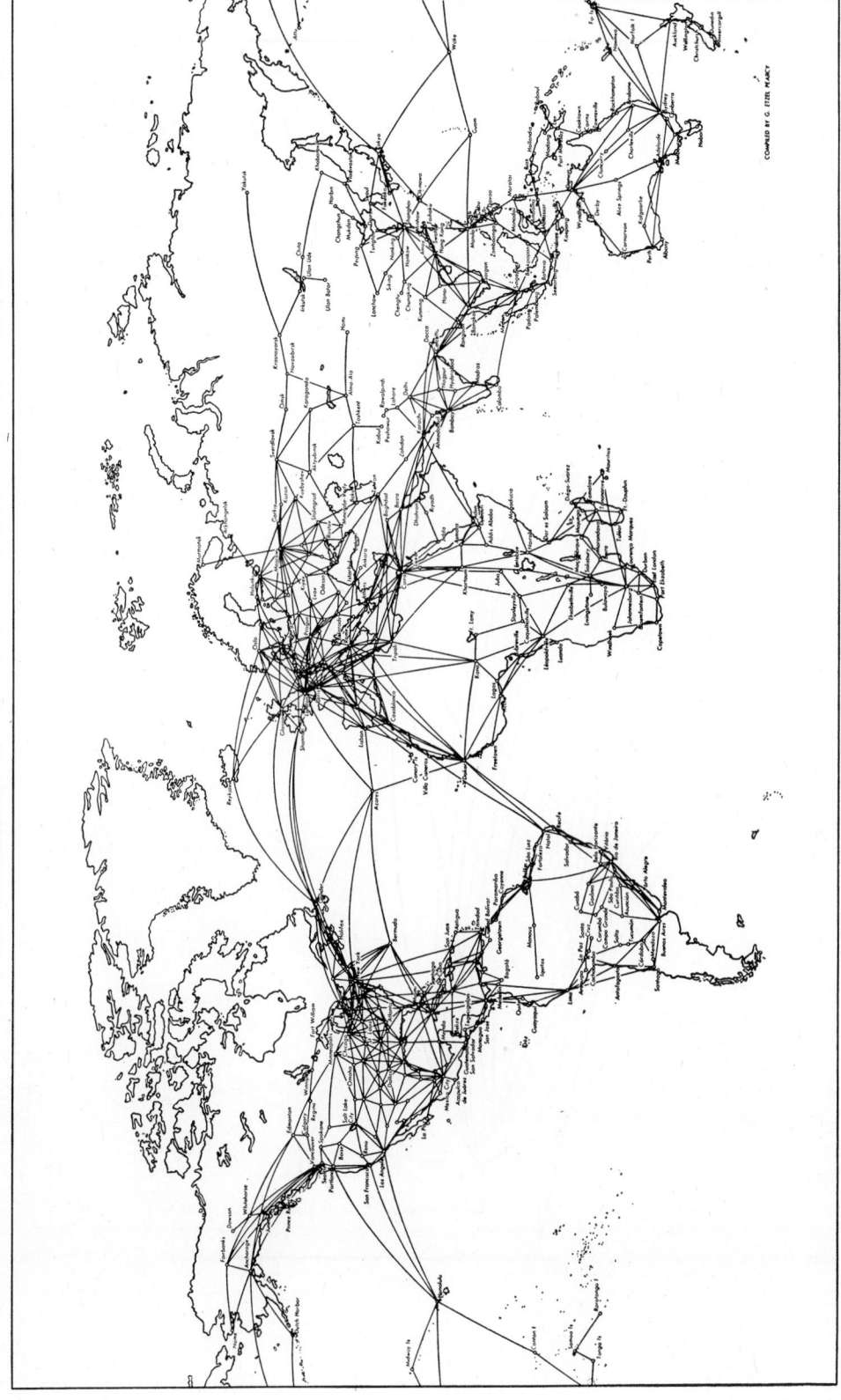

Source: Encyclopaedia Britannica World Atlas, 1951.

FIGURE 105. AIR ROUTES: MAJOR INTERCONTINENTAL, TRANSCONTINENTAL AND REGIONAL ROUTES, 1950

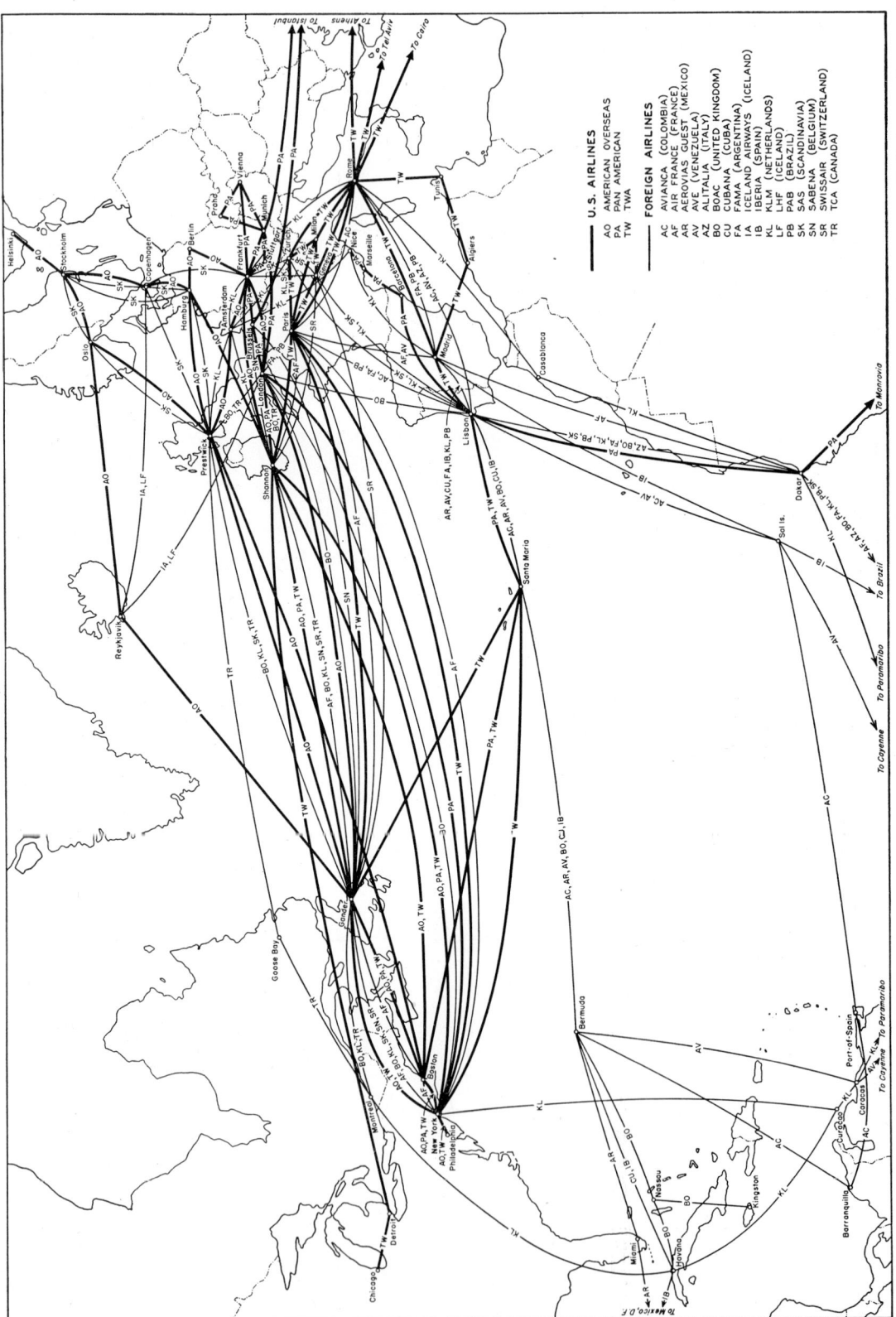

FIGURE 106. AIR ROUTES: SCHEDULED AIRLINES OPERATING IN THE NORTH ATLANTIC, 1950

U.S. AIRLINES

AO   AMERICAN OVERSEAS
PA   PAN AMERICAN
TW   TWA

FOREIGN AIRLINES

AC   AVIANCA (COLOMBIA)
AF   AIR FRANCE (FRANCE)
AR   AEROVIAS GUEST (MEXICO)
AV   AVE (VENEZUELA)
AZ   ALITALIA (ITALY)
BO   BOAC (UNITED KINGDOM)
CU   CUBANA (CUBA)
FA   FAMA (ARGENTINA)
IA   ICELAND AIRWAYS (ICELAND)
IB   IBERIA (SPAIN)
KL   KLM (NETHERLANDS)
LF   LHF (ICELAND)
PB   PAB (BRAZIL)
SK   SAS (SCANDINAVIA)
SN   SABENA (BELGIUM)
SR   SWISSAIR (SWITZERLAND)
TR   TCA (CANADA)

the route by way of Newfoundland or Labrador has the advantage of stops in advanced and densely populated countries with excellent facilities for air navigation. The distance is about the same — for example, from Dallas, Texas, to South Africa is roughly 10,200 miles via the European route and 10,600 miles via South America.[71]

Many routes link Africa and Europe. The main lines have been designed chiefly to connect metropolitan and colonial territories. Great Britain, France, Belgium and Italy were particularly active in establishing such connections. One route links northwestern Europe, via Madrid and Rome, with North Africa (Algiers and Tunis). Another runs from London, Paris and Rome, via Cairo, to southern and western Africa. Several routes follow the Atlantic coast of Africa, via Madrid and Lisbon, to Dakar, where they merge with the route connecting Africa with South America. Egypt, a focal point of three continents, has become a most important airline junction; all principal international airlines operate through one of Cairo's airports, which is reserved for international traffic.[72]

To Asia

Asia can be reached by air either from the east, over the Pacific route, or from the west, by way of the Mediterranean, Red Sea and Indian Ocean. The first route is the natural link between the United States and Canada and the Far East; the second connects Europe with the Middle and Far East and, in combination with the North Atlantic route, links the United States with the Middle East.

The route from North America to Asia begins with a 2,400-mile nonstop flight from San Francisco to Honolulu, Hawaii. Hawaii's position as an intermediate landing for various routes to the Orient gives the islands an importance in Pacific air transport which, in the opinion of some experts, can hardly be equaled by any other single spot on earth.[73] This route is also favored by good weather conditions. However, it is longer than a route via Alaska. New York, for example, is 1,500 miles nearer Shanghai via Alaska than via Honolulu, and Chicago is only 600 miles farther from Hong Kong via Alaska than is San Francisco. Alaska is a natural gate-

way between North America and Asia, and one airline operates this route from the United States to Japan.

The Hawaiian route proceeds with stops at Midway or Wake Island to Japan, or via Okinawa to Hong Kong, and via Guam to Manila. Branches extend in various directions — to Seoul in Korea, to Singapore and westward to Bangkok and Calcutta. (See Figure 107.) Singapore's position on the air routes to the Far East ranks in importance with its position as a sea port. Its civil airport, Kallang, handles all international and local traffic.[74]

The routes from northwestern Europe (and the Atlantic coast of North America) proceed via Cairo or Istanbul to the Middle East (Beirut, Basra, Dhahran) and further eastward to Karachi (Pakistan) and Bombay (India). (See Figure 108.) Local air services supplement American and European carriers.

To Oceania

San Francisco, Los Angeles and Vancouver are the terminals in the Western Hemisphere for the Pacific routes to Australia and New Zealand. The course is to Honolulu, then southward via Canton Island and Fiji to Sydney or Auckland.

From Europe (the United Kingdom) the route is via Cairo, Singapore, Jakarta (Indonesia) to Darwin, the nearest terminal in Australia, continuing to Sydney and on to New Zealand.

In 1953, a new route was opened from Johannesburg, the Union of South Africa, to Perth, Australia, via the Indian Ocean. This route has two stops — at Cocos Island and Mauritius — and the longest (2,670 miles) nonstop flight between these islands of any scheduled operation.

"Over the Top"

A new route, "over the top of the world" from the west coast of North America to Europe, was opened in November 1952 by the Scandinavian Airlines System (SAS). Stops are made at Edmonton, Canada, and Thule, Greenland. The route passes within 150 miles of the North Pole and is 13 hours shorter in flying time than the usual transatlantic route. This route may be extended for flying from Europe to the Orient via Thule and Alaska, with a 16-hour saving in

---

71. **65**, pp. 53–56; **60**, p. 32.
72. **38**, pp. 82–83.
73. **53**, p. 66.

74. **52**, p. 59.

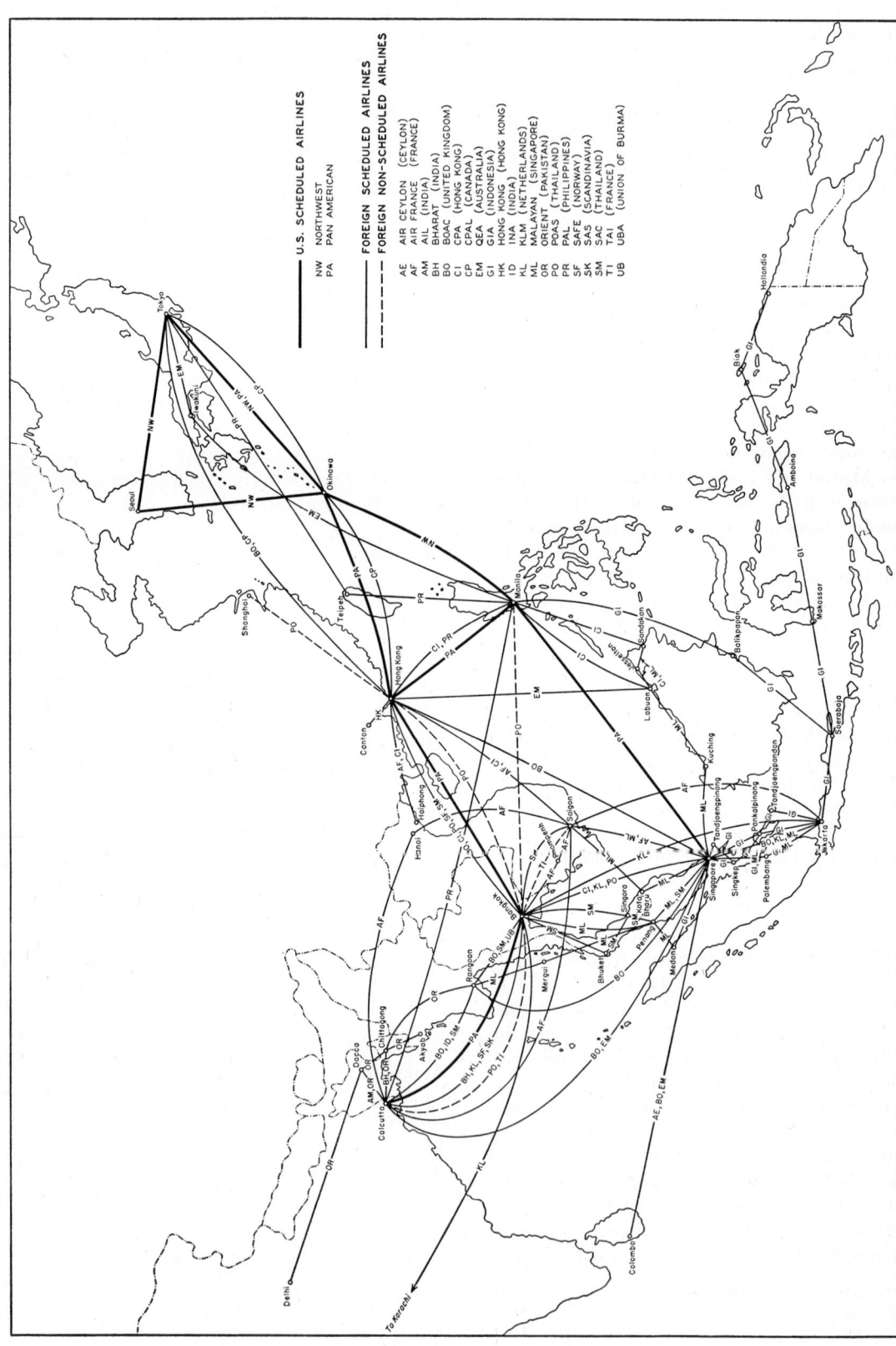

FIGURE 107. AIR ROUTES: SCHEDULED AIRLINES OPERATING IN THE FAR EAST, 1950

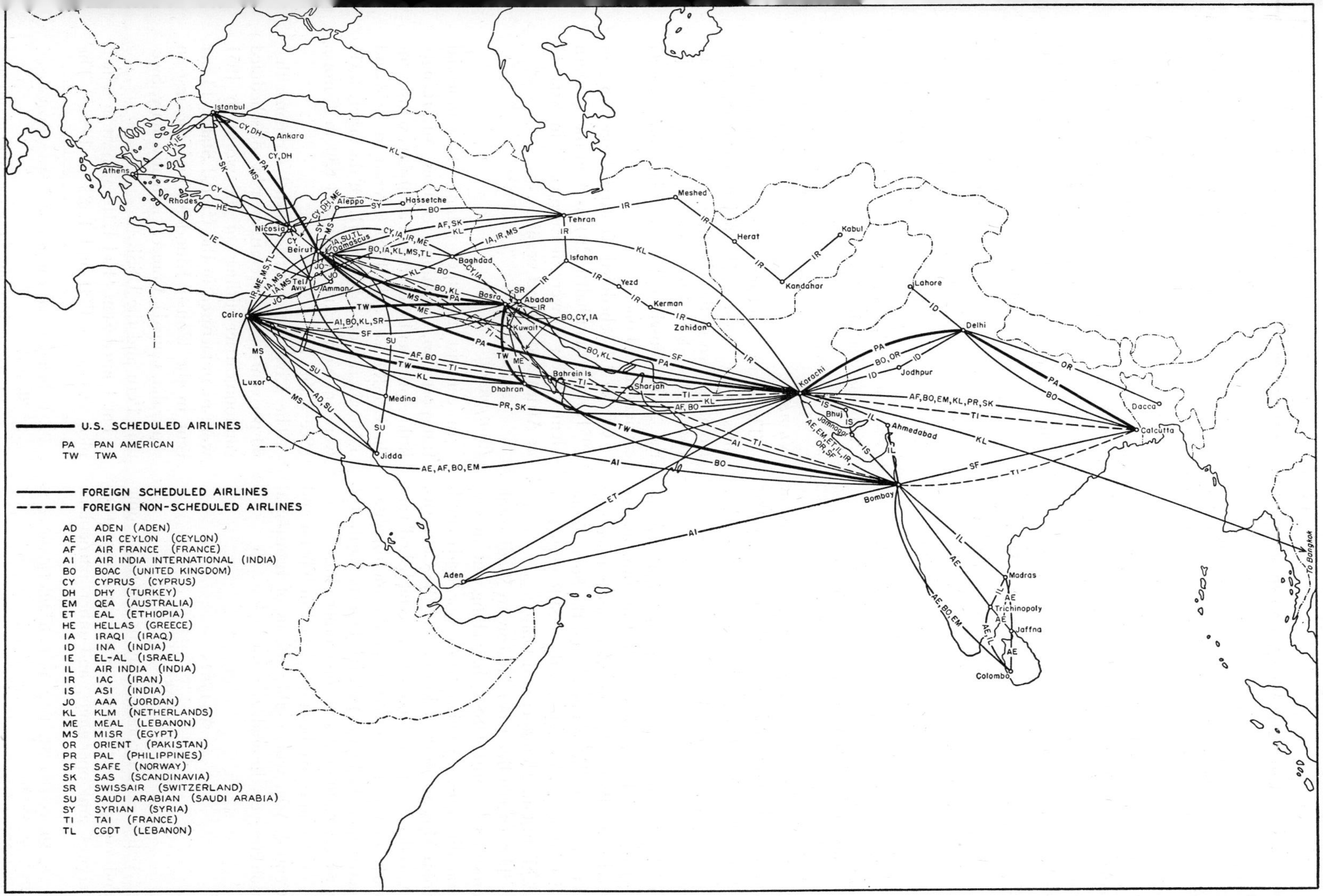

Figure 108. Air Routes: Scheduled Airlines Operating in the Middle East, 1950

Civil Aeronautics Board

TABLE 177

SCHEDULED AIRLINES: NUMBER OF LINES AND AIRCRAFT, BY CONTINENT, 1938–51

Continent	Airlines			Aircraft		
	1938	1947–48	1951	1938	1947–48	1951
World [a]	...	245	220	1,988	3,528	3,830
North America	...	67	62	457[b]	1,081	1,346[c]
Middle America	...	32	27	}270{	230	265
South America	...	34	37		425	472
Europe	...	50	30	877	936	880
USSR	...	(2)	...	(400)	(850)	...
Asia	...	30	32	153	472	434
Africa	...	13	12	81	160	188
Oceania	...	19	20	150	224	245

Sources: For 1938: **31**, p. 154; for 1947–48: **69**, p. 25 and *passim;* for 1951, **20**, *passim.*

a. Excludes the USSR.
b. **69** (p. 42) reports 724.

c. Includes 80 aircraft in U.S. territories.

time to Tokyo as compared with the present route via London and Thailand, and a 23.5-hour saving on the return trip.[75]

Soviet Routes

The USSR has signed no international air agreements. Its Aeroflot — the government-controlled air fleet — operates domestic service and services to satellite countries and the Soviet Zone in Germany, and connects the USSR with Iran, Afghanistan, Mongolia and China.

The arterial line from Moscow to Vladivostok crosses the entire USSR, branching out in several directions. Another trunk line leads south from Moscow to the Ukraine and the Caucasus. A feeder line from Moscow was established very early to transport matrices of the metropolitan newspapers to Leningrad, the Donets Basin, the Crimea, Stalingrad and some other cities.[76]

Air routes have been developed in Siberia and Central Asia, where other means of transportation are very limited.

AIRLINES

GENERAL CHARACTERISTICS

Airlines differ considerably in length of route and equipment, type of ownership, extent of services and operations, and other particulars.

Number

There are comparatively few scheduled airlines in the world — 245 in January 1948, apart from the two in the USSR, and 220 in 1951. In 1948, scheduled airlines were outnumbered by the 2,451 nonscheduled, irregular and contract carriers ten to one.

Of the 220 scheduled air carriers operating in 1951, more than half (126) were in the Western Hemisphere; 30 were in Europe, 32 in Asia, 12 in Africa and 20 in Oceania.

Equipment

In contrast to other means of commercial transportation, aviation requires surprisingly little equipment. Scheduled airlines (exclusive of the USSR) had only 1,988 aircraft in 1938 and 3,830 aircraft on July 1, 1951. Of the latter, 1,346 were in North America [77] and 880 in Europe. (See Table 177.)

The Civil Aeronautics Board estimates that 80 per cent of the aircraft used by all scheduled common-carrier airlines of the world in 1951 were manufactured in the United States, 13 per cent in the United Kingdom, and the rest in Australia, Canada, France, Germany, Italy, Sweden, Peru and the USSR.[78]

The United States had 1,218 aircraft in scheduled service in 1951 and 1,383 in 1953.[79] The

75. **59**, October 31, 1952, p. 613; **30**, December 8, 1952, pp. 35–36.
76. **33**, p. 501.

77. Including 80 aircraft in United States territories.
78. **20**, p. 1.
79. Does not include aircraft in operation by irregular

TABLE 178

SCHEDULED AIRLINES: NUMBER OF AIRCRAFT, IN SELECTED COUNTRIES, 1938–51

Country	1938	1947–48	Around 1951	Country	1938	1947–48	Around 1951
United States [a]	345	971	1,218	Italy	134	56	48
Canada	112	110	128	Yugoslavia	...	—	16
Mexico	83	111	155	Romania	...	23	22
Guatemala	...	3	9	Greece	...	6	22
El Salvador	...	11	10	USSR	400	850	...
Honduras	...	9	13				
Nicaragua	..	12	9	China	30	91	...
Costa Rica	...	14	13	Japan	55	—	—
Panama	...	14	2	Hong Kong	...	14	11
Cuba	...	22	22	Turkey	...	38	35
Haiti	...	5	4	Lebanon	...	15	13
Dominican Republic	...	3	7	Israel	...	9	16
Trinidad	...	5	12	Jordan	...	8	12
				Saudi Arabia	...	10	19
Venezuela	...	50	70	Iraq	...	6	4
Colombia	...	64	96	Iran	...	10	6
Ecuador	...	10	4	Pakistan	}27	156{	25
Brazil	41	150	186	India			117
Peru	...	32	20	Burma	...	—	16
Bolivia	...	7	7	Thailand	...	10	26
Chile	...	20	36	Ceylon	...	1	5
Uruguay	...	6	10	Indonesia	...	27	39
Argentina	10	73	37	Philippines	...	67	64
United Kingdom	173	335	240	Morocco	...	...	6
Ireland	...	22	15	Tunisia	...	...	4
Iceland	...	20	18	Egypt	...	18	17
France	159	145	135	Anglo-Egyptian			
Belgium	...	51	54	Sudan	...	4	4
Netherlands	...	61	69	Ethiopia	...	15	14
Denmark	...	22	[b]	Nigeria	...	...	12
Sweden	...	28	[b]	Kenya	...	...	20
Norway	...	23	5 [c]	Mozambique	...	7	26
Finland	...	9	10	Angola	...	16	21
Germany	146	—	—	Southern Rhodesia	...	21	30
Poland	...	30	35	Union of South			
Czechoslovakia	...	30	50	Africa	...	38	34
Switzerland	...	23	27	Australia	}150{	176	201
Portugal	...	19	12	New Zealand		43	44
Spain	...	25	29				

Sources: For 1938: **31**, p. 154; for 1947–48: **69**, *passim;* for 1951: **20**, pp. 26–29; **27**, 1952, p. 10 and 1953, p. 11.

a. Includes 80 aircraft in U.S. territories.
b. The Scandinavian Airlines System (SAS), a combination of the Swedish, Danish and Norwegian airlines, operating as one organization on international routes, had 65 aircraft in 1951.
c. Excludes Norway's aircraft in the SAS.

USSR had 850 planes in scheduled operations in 1948, the latest date for which figures are available. Next in line are the United Kingdom, with 240 planes in 1951; Australia with 201; Brazil with 186; Mexico with 155; France with carriers — 170 in 1951 and 177 in 1953. **19**, 1953, pp. 66–67.

135; and Canada with 128. Scheduled airlines of Southern Rhodesia operate more aircraft than those of Switzerland, and Kenya has more planes on scheduled routes than Finland. (See Table 178 and Figure 109.)

Two-engine planes predominate in the equipment of scheduled airlines, outnumbering four-

EACH DOT REPRESENTS 20 AIRCRAFT

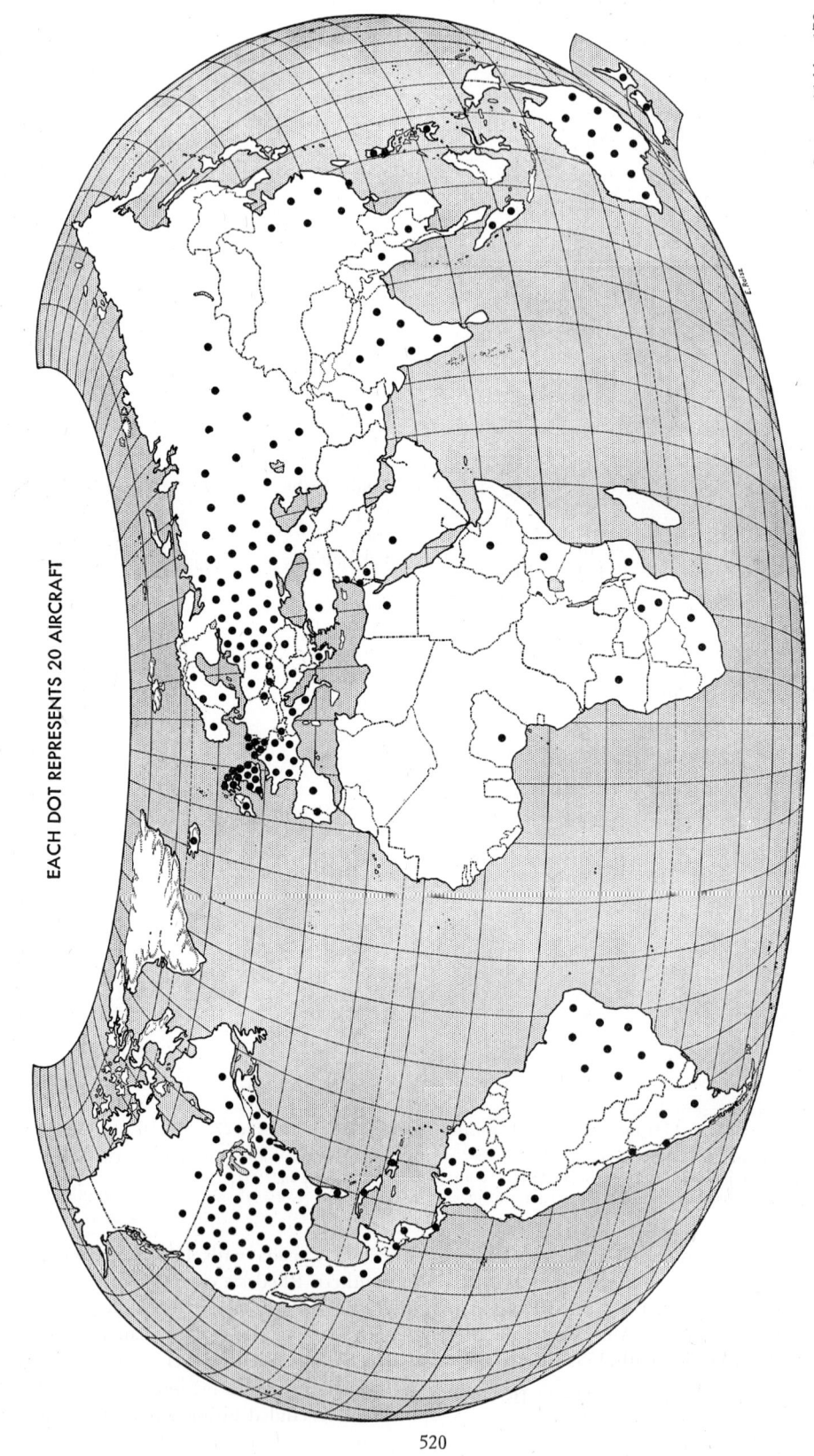

Source: Table 178

Figure 109. Scheduled Airlines: Geographic Distribution of Aircraft, Around 1951

engine planes by more than 2.5 to one. In July 1951, of the 3,830 planes operated by the world's scheduled airlines, 990 were four-engine; 99, three-engine; 2,561, two-engine; 180, one-engine.[80]

As in other fields of transportation, a mere numerical comparison of equipment owned by different airlines is not very meaningful. The struggle for supremacy in equipment is greater in aviation than in any other transport branch, because the rivalry among both domestic and international airlines is very keen. All important air carriers are busily engaged in retiring older types of equipment, bringing new types into service and placing orders for still newer designs. Traffic demands and the prospects of lower unit operating costs per seat-mile, despite the higher costs per aircraft-mile, are major influences on competing air carriers to modernize their equipment.[81]

Ownership

About one fourth of the world's aviation mileage is flown by government-operated lines and less than one tenth by airlines of mixed ownership — partly government and partly private. Seven of the thirty-five largest airlines in the world in 1950, each scheduling 100,000 miles or more per week, were government owned: British European Airways (BEA) and British Overseas Airways (BOAC), Air France, Trans-Canada Air Lines (TCA), South African Airways (SAA), Trans-Australia Airlines (TAA) and the Aeroflot of the USSR. Seven others were of mixed ownership: Swissair, the Scandinavian (SAS), Belgian Sabena, Philippine Air Lines (PAL), KLM of the Netherlands, Garuda of Indonesia and Avianca of Colombia.[82] The government operates air transport in all Soviet satellite countries and China. All air transport in India (nine airlines and their subsidiaries) was nationalized in the summer of 1953.

Airlines in the United States operate as private corporations under a competitive system but are subject to government regulation. A line must be approved by the Civil Aeronautics Board and may not abandon its assigned route without the Board's approval. Rates, tariffs, efficiency of operation, safety rules and various other aspects of an airline's activities are within the jurisdiction of the Board, and its records must be open to the Board.[83]

The total investment of the United States air carriers amounted to $742.3 million as of June 30, 1953 and was distributed among the various segments of the industry, as follows (in millions): [84]

Domestic trunk carriers [a]	$550.9
Local service carriers	17.5
International carriers [b]	160.2
Large irregular carriers [a]	13.7

a. Includes international operations of joint service carriers.
b. Includes Pan American, Panagra, Uraba, Medellin and Central.

Thus, the investment of all air carriers is smaller than that of a single company in some industries.

Aircraft represents the largest and most steadily increasing proportion of the total investment: 43 per cent for domestic trunk carriers in 1947; 52 per cent in 1951; and 63 per cent in 1953. The corresponding figures for international carriers of the United States are 39, 51 and 53 per cent; for local service carriers: 45, 51 and 77 per cent.[85]

Concentration

Scheduled operations in most countries are concentrated in one or a few airlines. Rapid technical progress in the field of aviation necessitates investments which only large, financially strong corporations can afford. Moreover, military considerations have led most governments to support or foster concentration of air transport in the hands of a few large lines. This tendency has often led to the designation of one airline, government-owned or government-subsidized, as a "chosen instrument," with ensuing monopoly in international operations. Nationalized Air France is the chosen instrument of France; KLM, of the Netherlands; Sabena, of

80. **20**, p. 1.
81. **13**, p. 12.
82. **68**, pp. 8–9. The full name of Swissair is Schweizerische Luftverkehr Aktien-Gesellschaft; of SAS, Scandinavian Airlines System, an association formed by Sweden's Aktiebolaget Aerotransport, Denmark's Det Danske Luftfartselskab and Norway's Det Norske Luftfartselskap; of KLM, Koninklijke Luchtvaart Maatschappij; of Avianca, Aerovias Nacionales de Colombia; of Sabena, Société Anonyme Belge d'Exploitation de la Navigation Aérienne.

83. **65**, p. 202.
84. **19**, 1953, pp. 54–55.
85. **19**, 1953, pp. 54–55.

TABLE 179

MAJOR AIRLINES OF THE WORLD: OPERATIONS, 1952

(*Millions*)

Country and Airline	Revenue Miles Flown	Passengers Carried	Passenger-Miles	Cargo Ton-Miles [a]	Mail Ton-Miles
World	1,059.0	45.0	24,500	623.0	178.0
13 major airlines	620.3	24.7	16,728	301.7	127.8
United States					
American	88.9	5.2	2,927	56.9	17.6
Capital	25.8	2.0	638	6.5	1.9
Eastern	66.6	3.9	2,021	11.3	6.2
National	17.1	0.8	484	6.1	1.4
Northwest	22.3	0.9	722	13.3	5.0
Pan American	59.2	1.4	1,807	51.6	16.9
Trans World	69.2	2.6	2,324	29.7	17.0
United	74.2	3.5	2,403	37.6	21.7
Canada					
Trans-Canada	27.3	1.2	652	6.7	4.9
United Kingdom					
BEA	79.3 [b]	1.3	357	5.7	2.5
BOAC	31.4 [b]	0.3	858	24.2	16.2
France					
Air France	33.7	1.1	907	30.5	11.7
Netherlands					
KLM	25.3	0.5	628	21.6	4.8

Source: **6,** No. 40, *passim.*

a. Express and freight.   b. Only international services.

Belgium; BOAC and BEA are the chosen instruments of the United Kingdom. In some countries, several airlines have been consolidated to form one strong line which the government owns in full or in part.

Of all the world's scheduled airlines in 1952, 13 accounted for nearly 55 per cent of all passengers, more than 68 per cent of all passenger-miles and more than 53 per cent of all ton-miles (cargo and mail). One United States airline (American) carried more passengers than the five leading Canadian, British, French and Dutch airlines combined. (See Table 179.)

In the United States, 4 out of 38 scheduled domestic airlines accounted in 1951 for nearly three fourths of the total ton-mileage (passengers, mail, express and freight). The next four carried more than one sixth of the total.[86] The doctrine of chosen instrument has found its exponents in the United States also. Pan American World Airways tried to prevent the entrance of other domestic airlines into the international field, arguing that the practice of foreign governments required the United States to adopt a similar policy in order to compete effectively. Bills to that effect have been introduced several times in Congress, but have all been defeated.[87]

MAJOR SCHEDULED AIRLINES

Of the world's 46 largest airlines in 1950, 17 operated from the United States, 2 from Canada, 8 from Latin America, 9 from Europe, 1 (centralized) from the USSR, 4 from Asia, 1 from Africa and 4 from Oceania.

In 1950, Air France had the longest unduplicated route mileage, followed by the Dutch KLM, the British BOAC, and Pan American World Airways of the United States. The USSR's Aeroflot was next in line. Except for Pan American, which engages exclusively in international operations, these lines operate both international and domestic traffic.

86. **30,** April 28, 1952, p. 115; cf. **23,** p. 339.   87. **63,** p. 607.

The scheduled weekly mileage, however, is a better reflection of the extent of an airline's operations than the route mileage operated. One airline may operate a long route, yet have only one or a few flights weekly, while another may handle a considerably greater volume of traffic over a comparatively short route. Thus, Braniff Airways has about the same route mileage as United Air Lines but only one fourth of the latter's weekly mileage. The USSR's Aeroflot operates a route only about half again as long as the Belgian Sabena, but has ten times the latter's scheduled weekly mileage. (See Table 180.)

The United States

Among the airlines of the United States, the "Big Five" are American, Trans World, Eastern and United — all domestic — and Pan American, which has no authorized domestic route and operates on an international basis exclusively. In 1950 the four large domestic airlines accounted for 54 per cent of all authorized route mileage and 61 per cent of the weekly scheduled mileage of all domestic airlines. Pan American, a giant among the world's international airlines, operated a greater weekly mileage than any other exclusively international airline. In addition, it has many subsidiaries and affiliates, holding from 33 to 52 per cent of common stock of several Latin American airlines.[88] For example, Pan American has a 48 per cent interest in Panair of Brazil and 52 per cent in the Cubana of Cuba.[89]

Canada

The chief Canadian company, Trans-Canada Air Lines, is controlled by the government-owned Canadian National Railways. Organized in 1937, it grew rapidly and now operates nearly 21,000 route miles. Canadian Pacific Airlines, another major carrier, serves nearly 23,000 route miles, with stops at northern prairie towns, fur trading posts and mining communities. It links Vancouver with Hong Kong via the great-circle route and with Sydney via Honolulu and other intermediate points.

Latin America

Middle and South America are served by several foreign airlines but most Latin American countries have established air services of their own or have increased their interest in the common stock of airlines organized by foreign capital to a controlling level. Colombia's Aerovias Nacionales operates nearly 20,000 route miles between domestic points, the United States, the Canal Zone and Ecuador.

Panair do Brasil, affiliated with Pan American Airways, serves numerous points in Brazil, with extensions to Uruguay, Argentina and Peru, and also operates over a transatlantic route to many European capitals and to Istanbul, Turkey. Emprêsa de Transportes Aerovias, another important Brazilian carrier, provides an extensive network in the eastern part of the country and maintains regular air service to the United States (Miami and New Orleans). Brazil's third major airline, Cruzeiro, has a somewhat shorter route but handles a greater weekly mileage. Aeroposta, Argentina's main airline, operates within the country and connects it with Chile, Paraguay and Uruguay. Mexico has a number of airlines, the largest of which is Compania Mexicana de Aviacion, with more than 5,000 miles of route between Mexico, Cuba and the United States (New Orleans).[90]

Europe

The United Kingdom has two major airlines: British Overseas Airways, formed by the merger of several companies, and British European Airways. Both are government owned and have a greater or smaller financial interest in various airlines within the British Commonwealth. Together, these two airlines operate more than 82,000 route miles and link all major points of the far-flung Commonwealth and all capitals in the Western Hemisphere.

The chief French airline, Air France, was created in 1933 through the consolidation of four carriers. It was nationalized in 1945 and is the only French company authorized to operate between the points it services. During the German occupation, Air France served only Free France, the eastern Mediterranean and Africa under mili-

---

88. **68**, p. 127.
89. **44**, 1953, No. 10, p. 573.

90. This line was organized in 1924 to deliver payroll gold throughout oil fields around Tampico, when thefts by bandits on isolated trails and roads had begun to increase. The airline had contracts with several oil producers guaranteeing it a certain monthly income. Later it was acquired by Pan American Airways but PAA's interest has been reduced to 42 per cent of the total through recapitalization and sale of stock to private Mexican citizens. (**68**, p. 203.)

TABLE 180
AIRLINES: UNDUPLICATED ROUTE LENGTH AND SCHEDULED WEEKLY MILEAGE, 1950

Country and Airline [a]	Undupli- cated Route Length, in Miles	Scheduled Weekly Mileage	Country and Airline [a]	Undupli- cated Route Length, in Miles	Scheduled Weekly Mileage
United States			United Kingdom		
Pan American	57,456	920,460	BOAC	69,024	521,018
Northwest	16,634	510,844	BEA	12,990 [e]	339,574
Trans World	16,237	1,038,059	Ireland		
United	9,489	1,020,221	Aer Lingus TTA	2,329	52,714
Braniff	9,203	254,874	France		
American	8,074	1,150,155	Air France	76,284	529,470
Eastern	7,108	1,030,601	Belgium		
American Overseas	6,146	97,918	Sabena	32,167	163,854
Panagra	6,098	109,921			
Chicago and Southern	4,874	191,123	Netherlands		
Capital	4,205	394,460	KLM	71,395	376,274
Delta	3,014	288,405	Scandinavia		
Mid-Continent	2,809	169,355	SAS [f]	40,018	289,938
National	2,745	259,617	Switzerland		
Western	2,709	143,339	Swissair [g]	15,424	93,090
Continental	2,414	112,742	Spain		
Colonial	2,010	62,752	Iberia [h]	16,217	80,984
Canada			USSR		
Canadian Pacific	22,848 [b]	101,567	Aeroflot	46,933	1,689,688
Trans-Canada	20,900	381,159	India		
Mexico			Air-India International	10,211	32,699
Compania Mexicana de Aviacion	5,115	148,902	Air-India	3,787	87,514
Cuba			Indonesia		
Compania Cubana de Aviacion	6,561	68,957	Garuda	11,118	116,303
Venezuela			Philippines		
Linea Aeropostal	6,896	84,195	PAL	22,487	136,030
Colombia			South Africa		
Aerovias Nacionales	19,256	112,559	South African Airways	13,046	133,998
Brazil			Australia		
Panair	20,543	166,192	Qantas Empire	27,816	111,859
Emprêsa de Trans- portes Aerovias	11,757	99,301	Trans-Australia	11,030	239,723
Cruzeiro [c]	10,622	132,139	Australian National	8,579	283,137
Argentina			New Zealand		
Aeroposta [d]	10,579	123,634	National	7,068	82,403

Source: **21**, *passim.*

a. Airlines in each country arrayed by unduplicated route length.
b. Includes service of subsidiary (Quebec Airways Ltd.).
c. Servicos Aereos Cruzeiro do Sul.
d. Aerolíneas Argentinas Aeroposta.

e. Excludes associated charter companies (4,384 route miles).
f. Association of Swedish, Danish and Norwegian airlines for joint international operations.
g. Schweizerische Luftverkehr A.G.
h. Compania Mercantil Anónima de Líneas Aëreas.

tary control, but after the country's liberation former commercial services were resumed and new ones inaugurated. Today Air France extends across all seas and touches all continents and has the longest unduplicated route mileage of any airline in the world (155,340 miles in 1953). Competition is keen in air transport of cargo over the North Atlantic but much less so in the Mediterranean area and the Middle East, where Air France retains much of the traffic, particularly to and from Madagascar, French Somaliland, Dakar and other colonial territories.[91]

The Dutch KLM is the world's oldest scheduled airline. Formed in October 1919 as a small company, it has developed into one of the major airlines of the world. During World War II, only its West Indies' division was in operation, but immediately after the war KLM resumed flights on its old routes and engaged in a major program of expansion to extend service to all continents except Oceania. In 1953, its unduplicated route mileage was nearly 130,000 miles. All its aircraft are of United States manufacture.

Belgium's principal airline, Sabena, operates European routes, a transatlantic service to the United States and five routes to the Belgian Congo, with an extension to the Union of South Africa.

Denmark, Norway and Sweden have, in addition to their domestic airlines, an international airline, the Scandinavian Airlines System (SAS), established in 1946 with a route length of some 40,000 miles. Each of the first two countries furnished two sevenths of the capital for SAS, and Sweden supplied the remaining three sevenths. (See Table 180.)

The USSR

Civil aviation in the USSR is under the direction of Aeroflot, which controls about 80 per cent of the country's air operations. Domestic service accounts for about 96 per cent of the total.[92] Glavmorput, a special organization for exploration in the north, operates in the Arctic. In 1948, a large helicopter accommodating some 20 passengers appeared in the skies over the USSR, but it is believed that such aircraft are not in quantity production.[93] In 1954 Aeroflot

concluded an interline agreement with the Scandinavian SAS for six weekly flights: Leningrad-Helsinki and Stockholm-Helsinki; both lines are entitled to sell tickets for either flight.[94]

Asia

India's largest airline is Air-India, owned and operated by nationals. It serves many domestic points as well as Pakistan, Ceylon and Thailand. After World War II the Indian government and Air-India organized Air-India International to operate the route from Bombay to London, via Cairo and Geneva. In 1950, Air-India International began operations on the route to East Africa, via Aden.

The Garuda Indonesian Airways was formed in 1950, with equal participation of the Indonesian government and the Dutch KLM. Its home base, Kemajoran airfield, is the largest in South Asia and can handle complete maintenance and overhauling of aircraft. The personnel is mostly foreign — Dutch, British and Australian — but Indonesians are being trained to replace nonnationals gradually.

In China, the Sino-Soviet Aviation Corporation (Hamiata) was formed in 1950, with alternating management of both governments. The USSR supplied the aircraft and equipment for three routes: Peking-Chita, Peking-Irkutsk and Peking-Alma-Ata.[95]

Africa

South African Airways operates over more than 13,000 route miles and is controlled by the government-owned railroads. It serves major internal points, with connections to Northern and Southern Rhodesia and, in cooperation with the British European Airways, to London.

The Misrair, Egypt's airline, is privately owned, in contrast to other government-operated African airlines, such as the Central African Airways (50 per cent of the capital provided by Southern Rhodesia, 35 per cent by Northern Rhodesia and 15 per cent by Nyasaland), the Central East African Airways and the West African Airways. The unduplicated route mileage of these four airlines is, respectively, 11,698, 12,320, 19,729 and 9,347.[96]

---

91. **28**, November 1952, pp. 7–10; **44**, 1953, No. 10, p. 571.
92. **21**, p. 1.
93. **45**, 1951–1953, p. 179.

94. **30**, February 1954, p. 74.
95. **59**, August 22, 1952, pp. 258–60. Some airports were built and others planned in China proper; airports were also established in Tibet.
96. **44**, 1953, No. 10, pp. 573–74.

Oceania

The two largest airlines of Australia are Australian National Airways, in operation since 1936–37, and Trans-Australia Airlines, organized by the government in 1946. The latter serves 53 centers throughout Australia, covering the largest internal network within the British Commonwealth.[97] National Airways of New Zealand operates all internal routes and some in the southwestern Pacific, accounting for more than 90 per cent of miles flown in New Zealand's domestic services.

GENERAL AVIATION FLYING

"General aviation" flying is a term used by the Civil Aeronautics Administration to include aviation other than the scheduled airlines — a heterogeneous group of air companies and individual owners, commercial and private.

Nonscheduled Aircraft

In 1938, business firms, private individuals and small charter and contract carriers owned 20,166 aircraft, more than 90 per cent of the world's registered 22,154 units. The proportion was even higher in 1947–48.[98] Most of these aircraft are in North America, where, in 1947–48, there were more than ninety times as many (95,613) as were used in scheduled operations (1,081).

In all continents except Europe, general aviation aircraft increased in number between 1938 and 1947–48: in North America, from 11,331 units to 95,613; in Latin America, from 508 to 3,543; in Asia, from 332 to 794. The number in Europe fell from 7,407 to 4,407. (See Table 181.)

In 1938, the United States had more than half the general aviation aircraft in the world — 10,855 out of 20,166; in 1947–48 the United States had nearly nine tenths — 93,850 out of 105,914; Canada, Brazil, the United Kingdom and France came next. While Canada and Brazil greatly increased general aviation flying during World War II, the number of craft thus engaged in the United Kingdom had declined somewhat by 1948 and in France, by more than half. The war also reduced Italy's general aviation air fleet to a small fraction of the peacetime size, and Germany's dropped completely out of the picture. (See Table 182.)

97. **68**, p. 257.
98. **69**, p. 25; **53** (p. 40) gives for 1938: 20,110 private aircraft and 1,798 units for regular airlines.

TABLE 181

GENERAL AVIATION FLYING: NUMBER OF AIRCRAFT, BY CONTINENT, 1938 AND 1947–48

Continent	1938	1947–48
World [a]	20,166	105,914
North America	11,331	95,613
Middle America	}508{	1,205
South America		2,338
Europe	7,407	4,407
USSR	(175)	(1,150)
Asia	332	794
Africa	284	874
Oceania	304	683

Sources: For 1938: **31**, p. 154; for 1947–48: **69**, p. 25.
a. Excludes the USSR.

Types of General Aviation Flying

As long as the GI flight training program was in full swing, instructional flying constituted the bulk of general aviation flying in the United States. Now many other types have been started or have grown in importance.

Among commercial carriers, the nonscheduled or irregular operators are the most important, particularly in the United States. Some of them antedate the introduction of regular air service by a number of years. Although they cannot publish or advertise a fixed time for departure and arrival, they find customers who are attracted by lower fares and are willing to accept simplified service. These carriers often enter into arrangements with ticket agencies to solicit business. In 1951, 54 large irregular carriers operated in the United States and transported nearly 600,000 passengers.[99]

Charter carriers operating from a "fixed base" take passengers and freight to desired destinations. Air taxis are available at almost every large airport to transport films and newspapers, to provide connections with ocean liners, homes and offices, and so on. In 1953, 1,375 air taxi operators, authorized by the Civil Aeronautics Board, were crisscrossing the country in short hops to large airports. Air taxi service, though still young, is already a substantial business. At many airports, there is a "fly-it-yourself" service for rental of planes.

Corporations are making increasing use of

99. **30**, April 28, 1952, p. 109.

TABLE 182

GENERAL AVIATION FLYING: NUMBER OF AIRCRAFT, IN SELECTED COUNTRIES, 1938 AND 1947–48

Country	1938	1947–48	Country	1938	1947–48
United States	10,855[a]	93,850	Ireland	. . .	6
Canada	476[b]	1,763	France [f]	2,829	1,155
			Belgium	. . .	200
Mexico	113	922	Netherlands	. . .	114
Guatemala	. . .	17	Denmark	. . .	75
El Salvador	. . .	9	Sweden	. . .	323
Honduras	. . .	6	Norway	. . .	93
Nicaragua	—	8	Finland	. . .	13
Costa Rica	. . .	22	Germany	1,420	—
Panama	—	53	Czechoslovakia	. . .	460
Cuba	. . .	122	Switzerland	. . .	388
Dominican Republic	—	17	Portugal [g]	. . .	56
Venezuela	. . .	50[c]	Spain	—	5
Colombia	. . .	39	Italy	558	34
Ecuador	—	10			
Brazil	52	1,550	Japan	64	—
Peru	—	28	India	}136{	. . .
Bolivia	. . .	8	Pakistan		. . .
Paraguay	—	5	Egypt	. . .	16
Chile	. . .	220	Belgian Congo	—	49
Uruguay	. . .	59	Union of South Africa	. . .	462
Argentina	230	369[d]			
			Australia	}304{	506
United Kingdom [e]	1,502	1,475	New Zealand		177

Sources: For 1938: **31**, p. 154; for 1947–48: **69**, *passim.*

a. Excludes Alaska; includes 137 aircraft in territorial nonscheduled operations.
b. Includes Newfoundland.
c. Data probably incomplete.
d. Number of aircraft reported, though exports to Argentina from the United States alone amounted to some 600 civil aircraft in 1947.
e. **24** (1938–1948, p. 220) gives 1,536 and 2,073 aircraft, respectively.
f. Includes French North Africa.
g. Includes the Azores.

company-owned aircraft.[100] In the United States, corporations owned about 9,500 planes in 1952, of which some 1,700 were multi-engined. This multi-engine fleet was larger than that of all the scheduled airlines of the United States. Planes are employed by oil and power companies in the inspection of their lines, prospecting and the like. Cattle men patrol boundaries; thousands of farmers own aircraft, and still other thousands engage the planes of commercial contractors to seed and fertilize, dust and spray fields, fight weeds and insects, check crops and livestock, get parts for farm equipment, and so on. About 12,000 aircraft were used by farmers and ranch-

ers in 1951; in that year commercial air dusting spread some 138,000 tons of chemicals over nearly 18 million acres, and air spraying treated more than 11 million acres.[101] Firms engaged in this business in the United States follow the seasons and the crops from border to border.

Personal, or pleasure, flying has been for years a major division of general aviation flying in the United States. Owning a plane as they would a yacht for occasional pleasure trips, 50,000 private fliers together logged almost 3 million hours of operation in each of the postwar years though, on the average, each used his aircraft less than 60 hours during a year.[102] However, pleasure flying experienced a decline after 1949. The following figures show the percentage distribution

100. **56**, November 1952, p. 3. For example, during 1950 one manufacturer of agricultural machinery in the United States made business visits in his own plane to more than 150 communities without regular airline service. (**10**, p. 14.)

101. **15**, pp. 7–10.
102. **18**, 1950, pp. 35–36.

of total mileage flown in different types of general aviation flying in the United States: [103]

	1939	1947	1949	1951
Instructional	37.3	56.5	33.5	19.1
Commercial [a]	19.3	10.0	14.7	21.1
Business	14.3	15.3	27.4	38.2
Pleasure	29.1	17.4	23.9	20.1
Unclassified	—	0.8	0.5	1.5

a. Includes noncertificated, contract, charter and other carriers; also includes firms engaged in aerial spraying, dusting and weed-killing.

General aviation flying for business and other purposes is well developed in many other countries. In Canada, which pioneered in air surveying, lumber companies use planes and flying boats to take stock of their timber resources and to control forest fires. Fire stations are alerted by radio; men and equipment are sent by air to the site of fire. Reportedly, large timber tracts have been saved from complete destruction by the use of air patrols.

In Australia, air ambulance service is firmly established. Hospitals send specially built aircraft with complete surgical equipment to settlements scattered through the vast expanses of the continent. Flying physicians and nurses regularly visit settlements which can now obtain emergency medical aid within two hours, in comparison with the two or three days required by surface transportation. As in the United States, farmers make considerable use of planes to fight weeds and other pests and to search for grazing grounds to which they can move livestock in time of drought.

Owners of remote rubber estates and tin mines in Malaya use planes to drop foodstuffs and pay to workers.[104]

According to the Civil Aeronautics Administration, the industrial classification of owners of 82,236 aircraft in continental United States in 1951 was as follows: [105]

	Number of Aircraft	Per Cent
Aviation, total	26,539	32
Manufacturing	1,215	1
Fixed-base operators [a]	24,719	30
Large and small irregular carriers	605	1
Farming and ranching	9,516	12
Automobiles and accessories	4,980	6
Construction and real estate	4,190	5
Transportation, communication, public utilities	1,956	2
Petroleum	1,723	2
Manufacturing and mining (exclusive of aircraft, automobiles and petroleum)	6,145	7
Trade	5,374	7
Services: business and repair (exclusive of aircraft and automobiles)	3,241	4
Professional and related services	4,735	6
Flying clubs	1,535	2
Government: federal, state, local	2,622	3
Other (inclusive of owners reporting more than one industry)	9,680	12

a. Scheduled airlines and aircraft operated by the CAA excluded.

Air Clubs and Private Pilots

Air clubs have mushroomed in many countries. In 1948 Canada had 61 clubs with 217 aircraft; the United Kingdom, 59 clubs with 283 planes; Sweden, 57 with 42 planes and 90 gliders; Chile, 50 with 210 planes; and Argentina, 59 with 304 planes. There were 433 clubs in France, 120 in Denmark, 6 in Spain, 10 in India, and so on.[106] The air clubs in the United Kingdom had more aircraft in 1948 than all that country's regular airlines.[107]

Certificated commercial and private pilots in the United States in 1952 exceeded half a million (566,020), and during that year, more than 30,000 student pilots obtained licenses for flying from the Civil Aeronautics Administration.[108]

AIR TRANSPORT OPERATIONS

In conquering the air, man has conquered space, at least in relation to our planet. Today a flight around the world takes only a few days. "The world is now actually smaller, measured in travel time, than were the Thirteen Original States that united to inaugurate George Washington as President," writes van Zandt.[109] Practically any spot on the globe can be reached by air transport, which surmounts such barriers to other means of transportation as mountains, deserts and ice fields. In 1929 the flight from New York to Los Angeles took 48 hours and required ten stops, with passengers traveling by

103. **18**, 1953, p. 37.
104. **52**, p. 61.
105. **15**, p. 40.
106. **69**, *passim.*
107. **24**, 1938–1948, p. 220.
108. **18**, 1953, p. 27. Excludes airline pilots; includes glider pilots.
109. **60**, p. 329.

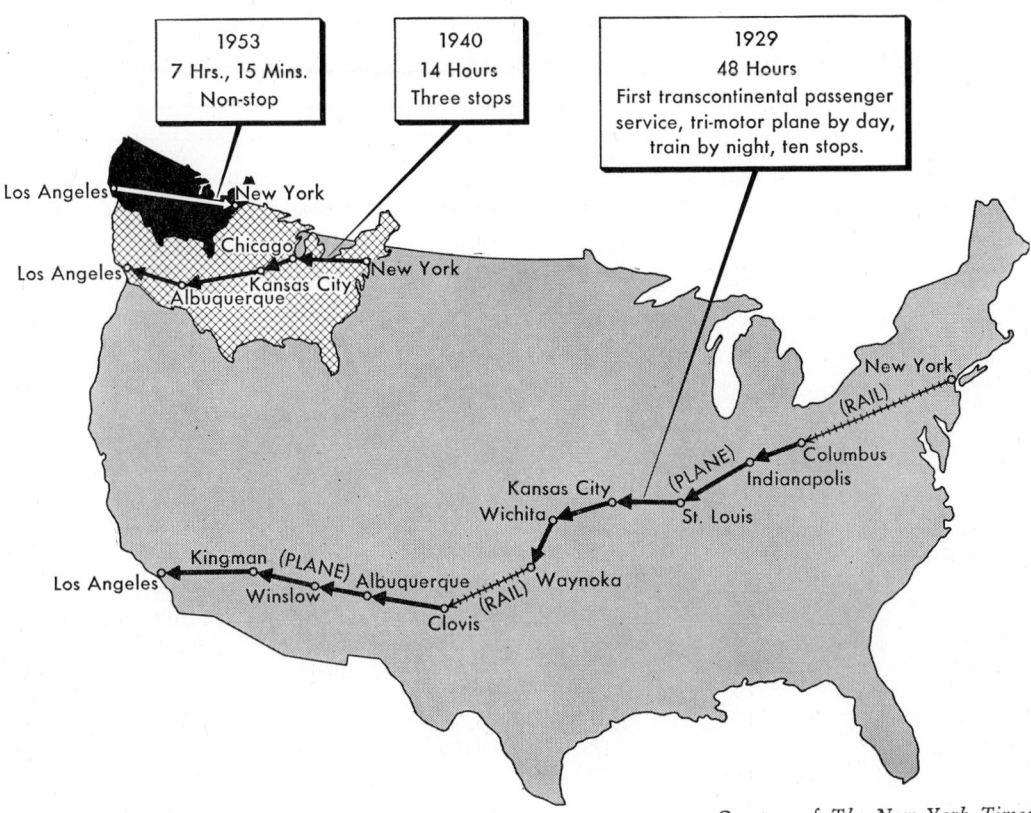

Courtesy of *The New York Times*

FIGURE 110. AIR TRANSPORT: TIME NEEDED TO CROSS THE UNITED STATES BY AIR, 1929, 1940 AND 1953

air during day hours and by train during the night; in 1940, the same trip took 14 hours and necessitated three stops; in 1953, the nonstop flight took only 7 hours and 15 minutes. (See Figure 110.)

Mileage Flown in the World

In 1929, the world's scheduled airlines flew 57 million aircraft miles; ten years later, 186 million miles in a year; after another decade, 836 million. In 1951 the total was 976 million; in 1952, 1.1 billion and in 1953, 1.2 billion miles, equivalent to some 40,000 flights around the world, following the equator or the great-circle route. The most rapid development came after World War II, as the following figures show (in millions of miles flown): [110]

1929	57
1931	86
1933	97
1935	127
1937	167
1939	186
1941	213
1943	203
1945	385
1947	718
1949	836
1950	890
1951	976
1952	1,059
1953	1,170

Mileage in Selected Countries

Scheduled airlines of the United States flew about 25 million miles in 1929 and more than 577 million in 1952 — nearly half the world's total in the first year and more than half in the second. Over this same period, Canadian lines increased their mileage from 6.3 million to 35.6 million, and the British, from 1.2 to 57.6 million. Australian airlines marked up about the same gain as the British: 1.1 million miles in 1931; 49.9 million in 1952. France, the Netherlands, Brazil, the Union of South Africa, India and many other countries also expanded aviation, some beginning practically from scratch. Den-

110. **6**, No. 40, p. iii; **10**, p. 3. Excludes the USSR for all years, Germany from 1941, Japan from 1945 and China from 1949.

TABLE 183

Air Transport: Miles Flown by Scheduled Airlines of Selected Countries, 1929-52

(*Thousands*)

Country	1929	1939	1949	1950	1951	1952
World	57,000	186,000	836,000	890,000	976,000	1,059,000
United States	25,142	90,841 [a]	459,022	471,617	518,121	577,263
Canada	6,284	9,620 [a]	26,413	29,281	32,711	35,624
Mexico	1,896	4,917	22,099 [b]	26,060	30,301	32,218
Cuba	. . .	734	. . .	4,598	5,046	5,348
Venezuela	. . .	3,299 [e]	11,247	12,427	15,534	16,156
Colombia [a]	789 [d]	3,144	14,837	19,024	19,804	19,014
Brazil [a]	400	2,994	35,605	40,389	51,958	53,581
Peru	267	2,052	4,053 [e]	1,988	2,874	2,704
Bolivia	119	478	1,359	1,542	1,832	1,649
Chile [d]	319	417	2,136	2,620	3,041	3,350
Argentina	. . .	355	7,717	9,025	9,168	8,421
United Kingdom	1,189	11,464	44,257	48,299	52,455	57,634
Ireland	. . .	385 [e]	2,550	2,952	3,288	3,724
France [f]	5,863	7,382	25,374	29,861	30,013	33,686
Belgium [g]	534	1,495	7,459	8,507	9,391	11,840
Netherlands [h]	1,234	5,878	18,796	20,917	22,366	25,320
Denmark [i]	96 [a]	772 [a]	3,721	4,469	4,664	4,890
Sweden [j]	176	1,709	5,745	6,764	7,322	7,798
Norway [k]	. . .	428	4,079	4,840	5,550	6,042
Finland	146	378	1,120	1,291	1,668	2,134
Germany	6,474	9,922	—	—	—	—
Poland	826	1,242 [a]	1,492	. . .	1,522 [l]	1,645 [l]
Czechoslovakia	536	1,640 [e]	3,652	3,098	1,475 [l]	1,009 [l]
Switzerland	372	894	5,194	5,561	6,485	6,425
Portugal	29	29	829	958	1,184	2,406 [l]
Spain	406	1,108	3,516	4,977	5,215	7,469
Italy	1,870	9,351	4,235	7,287	6,595	6,547
Yugoslavia [a]	119	331 [e]	491	1,191	1,349	1,260

(*Continued on facing page*)

mark reported 96,000 miles flown by its airlines in 1929 and 4.9 million in 1952. New Zealand's total air traffic, scheduled and nonscheduled, accounted for 190,000 miles in 1934, while scheduled airlines alone flew 6.8 million miles in 1952. (See Table 183.)

Load Capacity

The difference between the gross weight an aircraft can carry and its own weight represents its potential load in passengers or freight. Crew, gasoline and equipment aboard the aircraft limit the pay load, and airlines are constantly seeking to reduce the operating weight of an aircraft.

Airplanes are larger than in the early years. They are powered by several engines instead of a single motor, and their engines are more powerful. In recent years, the pay load has been limited more by space than weight-carrying capacity since changes in aircraft design have resulted in greater speed but relatively smaller hulls. The flying boats that crossed the Atlantic or Pacific between 1939 and 1946 often operated with unfilled space so as not to overstep maximum weight capacity. Today, the allowable gross weight of large planes is seldom attained, because of space limitations.[111] Efforts are being made to use space more economically by narrowing the aisles and seats, relocating baggage space, rearranging or eliminating coat rooms and so on.

Passengers ordinarily account for from 60 to 85 per cent or more of the total load carried by

111. **65,** p. 347.

TABLE 183—*continued*

Country	1929	1939	1949	1950	1951	1952
USSR	5,782[1]	70,918[e]	90,000[e]	...	...	...
China	58	1,304	14,396[b,d]	...	...	...
Japan	543	4,558	—	—	—	—
Turkey	...	114[e]	1,259[e]	1,659	1,933	...
Israel	...	...	...	...	1,591	2,189[a]
Iraq	...	...	744	602	593	636
Iran	...	...	1,663	926	744	718
Pakistan	}71[a]	1,686[a]{	...	2,997	2,124[1]	2,328
India			15,095	18,892	19,493	19,558
Thailand	29	98	1,220	1,277	1,381	1,583
Ceylon	...	...	1,189	608	1,444	1,404
Indonesia	...	1,245[e]	5,675	5,823	5,704	5,956
Philippines	...	940	7,419	7,099	7,159	7,553
Egypt	...	1,011[e]	1,813[e]	2,456	2,849[1]	2,486
Southern Rhodesia	...	850[e]	1,747	1,863	2,784	3,410
Union of South Africa	150[m]	1,751	7,614	7,305	6,482	6,339
Australia	1,102[m]	8,682	42,141	46,707	51,531	49,927
New Zealand	...	1,612	6,291	6,206	7,209	6,836

Sources: **6**, Nos. 29, 36, 40, *passim;* **1**, 1953, pp. 321–27; **59**, July 11, 1952, pp. 73–76; for the USSR: **69**, p. 501.

a. Includes nonscheduled traffic.
b. 1948.
c. 1938.
d. Incomplete.
e. 1947.
f. 1949–52: Air France.
g. Data for Sabena, which, in 1949, accounted for 88 per cent of total scheduled mileage; includes Sabena operations in the Belgian Congo.
h. 1949–52: KLM, all divisions.

i. Includes, from 1949, the Danish share (2/7) in the European and Overseas Division of SAS; in 1950–51, also includes the share (2/5) in the Asiatic Division.
j. Includes, from 1949, the Swedish share (3/7) in the European and Overseas Division of SAS; in 1950–51, also includes the share (3/5) in the Asiatic Division.
k. Includes, from 1949, the Norwegian share (2/7) in the European and Overseas Division of SAS.
l. Estimate of the ICAO.
m. 1931.

airlines; in 1949–51, they represented the following percentages: [112]

Airline	1949	1950	1951
American	82.8	81.5	81.5
National	83.8	87.2	86.1
Northwest	54.2	55.4	57.3
Pan American	68.7	68.0	69.4
United	85.4	87.1	88.2
Colonial	94.0	94.5	95.5
Trans-Canada	85.8	85.5	85.1
Cruzeiro	92.2	87.6	89.4
BEA	75.3	75.9	77.3
BOAC	62.4	63.8	66.0
Air France	70.1	69.0	68.8
KLM	72.1	71.8	71.1
Swissair	86.2	78.0	79.6
National (New Zealand)	90.5	86.8	83.3

The rest of the load consists of cargo and mail, which are of growing importance for some air-

lines. Thus, cargo and mail represented 13.5 per cent of total load in 1950 and 14.5 per cent in 1951 for one Australian line (British Commonwealth Pacific) and 54.3 and 51.0 per cent, respectively, for the other (Qantas Empire).

Number of Passenger Seats

The average number of seats per aircraft differs greatly from country to country, from airline to airline in the same country and from year to year for the same airline. It also differs in domestic and international transport. In 1951, for example, the average number of passenger seats on one New Zealand airline was 14.4 and on another, 37.0; in Brazil, the average ranged from line to line between 21.5 and 41.1. In the United States, the average number of seats on Eastern Air Lines in 1950 was 38.2 in domestic travel, and 52.2 in international. Changes from year to year are mostly upward. The following figures on the average number of passenger seats

112. **6**, No. 36, pp. 10–29.

available per aircraft reflect a general shift to larger aircraft and more economical use of space: [113]

Airline	1947	1951
American	37.5	50.9
Eastern	51.4	59.0
United	40.3	52.0
Pan American	33.9	44.8
Trans-Canada	20.8	36.3
BEA	17.4	21.4
BOAC	17.8	40.1
Sabena	29.0	35.4
KLM	31.5	38.8
SAS	29.5	40.3
Swissair	20.8	29.8
South African	25.7	41.3
Qantas Empire	14.6	29.7 [a]

a. 1950.

Utilization of Capacity

The seating capacity of aircraft is seldom utilized fully. The proportion of occupied seats ranges from 40 to 70 per cent or more. Utilization is generally greater in domestic than in international traffic. In 1950, for example, it was 60.2 per cent on American Airlines in international traffic and 69.6 per cent in domestic traffic. For Braniff, corresponding figures were 38.0 and 55.1 per cent; for Eastern Air Lines, 44.4 and 61.7.[114] The average number of passengers per aircraft in the world as a whole was 5.3 in 1937; 17.3 in 1949; 21.9 in 1951; and 24.5 in 1953.[115]

Complete utilization of capacity is as unrealistic a goal in airline operations as in other forms of transportation, but each airline tries to attain the highest possible ratio between capacity and revenue load. The International Civil Aviation Organization (ICAO) estimates utilization of capacity by most international airlines at 58 per cent for 1950 and 62 per cent for 1951,[116] holding that a load factor of 65 per cent on a year-round basis is as high as can be expected. Airlines of the United States that maintained such a load factor before World War II were reported to have broken even or profited from their operations.[117] In 1952 some of them had a load factor considerably lower (Eastern, 48.2 per cent; Braniff, 50.7 per cent; Colonial, 52.9 per cent);

but American had as high a load factor as 66.8 per cent and Trans World, 67.8 per cent.[118]

The ICAO recently investigated utilization of aircraft flying time, asking 40 airlines of 21 countries to report the number of hours flown by each plane during a year and the average number of hours flown per day "wheels off to wheels on." Answers, though scattered, showed a great variation in the extent of utilization not only among different airlines but among different planes used by the same airline for different types of operations. The volume of potential traffic, schedules and the number of available aircraft are among the main factors determining the degree of utilization. Belgian Sabena, for example, reported for 1949 an average flying time of 5 hours 21 minutes during the day for its largest aircraft (DC-6 Douglas with 51 passenger seats and take-off weight of 42.3 tons) and 2 hours 55 minutes for another (DC-3C Douglas with 21 seats and 12.7 tons take-off weight). In the United States in that year, National Airlines used DC-6 Douglas planes 7 hours 58 minutes daily, on the average, while DC-4 Douglas planes of Northwest Airlines averaged a daily flying time of 9 hours 34 minutes and their B-337 Boeings, 5 hours 16 minutes.[119]

Employment in Aviation

In comparison with other means of transportation, civil aviation employs relatively few persons. The scheduled airlines of the United States, which account for more than half the aircraft mileage flown in the world, employed only 82,786 persons in 1950 and 104,493 in 1952.[120] Complete data for other countries are not available, but the ICAO publishes figures on personnel of some airlines in individual countries. These data, though incomplete, reveal that comparatively few employees are needed in air transport. Air France, one of the largest airlines in the world and serving 151 destinations and all continents, employed some 15,000 persons in 1952.

Maintenance workers constitute the largest single group among airline employees — in Bel-

113. **6,** No. 36, pp. 11–27.
114. **6,** No. 25, pp. 17, 25, 27.
115. **30,** January 18, 1954, p. 67.
116. **10,** p. 6.
117. **65,** p. 352.

118. **8,** No. 43, Table 1.
119. **6,** No. 19, pp. 10, 88 and 90.
120. **32,** pp. 130–31. In 1950 U.S. railroads employed 1.4 million persons; local railways and bus lines, 156,000; highway passenger transportation, not elsewhere classified, 225,000; highway freight transportation and warehousing, 740,000; water transportation, 129,000. (**14,** p. 189.)

TABLE 184

EMPLOYMENT: AIRLINE PERSONNEL IN SELECTED COUNTRIES, 1949-53

Country, Airline and Year	Number of Aircraft	Personnel			
		Total	Flight	Maintenance	Other [a]
United States, all airlines, 1952	1,226	104,493	16,751	29,106	58,636
Canada, TCA and CPAL,[b] 1952	50	7,813	1,002	2,783	4,028
Brazil, Cruzeiro, Real, Panair, Varig, 1951	134	9,995	1,031	3,179	5,785
United Kingdom, BEA, 1952	106	8,223	1,074	2,508	4,641
BOAC, 1951	72	16,633	1,769	7,077	7,787
Ireland, Aer Lingus, 1953	17	1,501	148	403	950
France, Air France, 1952	133	15,012	1,400	6,142	7,470
Belgium, Sabena, 1951	. . .	4,426	324	2,199	1,903
Netherlands, KLM, 1952	72	13,000	1,313	3,826	7,861
Scandinavia, SAS, 1952	51	7,004	897	2,293	3,814
Denmark, Danske Luftfartselskab, 1949	14	1,545	116	756	673
Norway, Norske Luftfartselskap, 1949 [c]	17	1,364	175	586	603
Finland, Aero O/Y, 1952	8	618	63	273	282
Switzerland, Swissair, 1952	23	2,084	318	692	1,074
Portugal, Transportes Aereos, 1949	9	368	58	154	156
Iran, Iranian Airways, 1949	7	267	29	82	156
India, Air-India,[d] 1952	88	7,305	489	3,546	3,270
Thailand, Siamese Airways,[e] 1949	9	404	62	98	244
Ceylon, Air Ceylon, 1952	2	213	15	64	134
Union of South Africa, South African Airways, 1953	28	695	87	408	200
New Zealand, Tasman Empire Airways, 1953	5	699	96	410	193

Sources: **8,** Nos. 19, 42, *passim;* for the United States (domestic and international airlines): **32,** pp. 122–23 and 130–31.

a. Operations, traffic and sales, general, administrative and so on.
b. Trans-Canada and Canadian Pacific Airlines.
c. Includes Braathens South American & Far East Airtransport A/S (SAFE).

d. Includes India Airways, Air Services of India, Bharat Airways, Himalayan Aviation and Indian National Airways.
e. Includes Pacific Overseas Airlines.

gium and Denmark about half the total; in the Union of South Africa and New Zealand, about three fifths. (See Table 184.)

In the United States, productivity of airline personnel, measured in ton-miles of revenue traffic, more than doubled between 1946 and 1952. In 1946, 68,164 employees of 16 domestic trunk lines handled some 656 million ton-miles — more than 9,600 ton-miles per employee; in 1952, 72,059 employees of the same airlines piled up in excess of 1.4 billion ton-miles — 19,623 ton-miles per employee.[121]

PASSENGER TRAFFIC

Speed and frequency in schedule are the chief

121. **30,** April 28, 1953, p. 117. Ton-miles are calculated for total load: passengers, baggage, airmail, express and cargo. Weight of ten passengers with baggage = one short ton.

advantages that airlines offer in passenger traffic. No other means of transportation can match them in this combination of services. Because airports are generally remote from the center of the city, the time saving in air travel is relatively greater for long trips. Air transport offers particularly frequent service between busy centers of population. Thus scheduled airlines linking New York and Chicago provide 63 nonstop flights a day in each direction; between New York and Washington, D. C., there are 70 round trips a day.[122] The increase in passenger traffic is evidence that for many passengers these two features outweigh the advantages of lower cost and comparatively greater safety and reliability of railroad travel.

Speed in air travel results from the plane's cruising speed of up to 300 miles or somewhat

122. **27,** 1952, p. 4; **13,** p. 51.

more per hour on long-distance flights and also from the fact that the air distance between two points is always shorter — some 15–20 per cent, on the average, and often more — than the distance by rail or highway. Thus, the rail distance from New York to San Francisco is 3,169 miles; the airline distance, 2,588 miles. Corresponding figures for Chicago-Seattle are 2,161 and 1,809 miles; New York-New Orleans, 1,358 and 1,175. For nonstop flying, the distance differential is still greater. While express and local trains must often use the same tracks, nonstop air service can ordinarily take a straighter and shorter route than service with intermediate stops. For example, the air distance New York-Miami via intermediate stations is 1,225 miles and the nonstop distance, 1,095 miles; Los Angeles-Portland, Oregon, 989 and 838 miles, respectively.[123]

Promotional activities of airlines have also contributed to the growth of passenger travel in many countries. Free of traditional policies and routine procedures, this new industry was able to use a fresh approach to the problem of attracting patronage. Employing modern advertising methods and managed by people with a pioneering drive, it began to provide passengers with many extra conveniences to make the trip pleasanter, furnishing meals, stationery, maps, picture postcards, newspapers, magazines, blankets and first-aid medicines, and help in the care of children.[124]

Of much greater significance was the reduction in fares, which made air transport in the United States competitive with travel by train in Pullman cars. The price per passenger-mile in domestic air transport, 12 cents in 1926 and 8.3 cents in 1930, dropped to 5.2 cents in 1938 — a level maintained, with some fluctuations, through 1947. Air fare had been raised to 5.8 cents per mile by the end of 1948 and the rate at the close of 1953 was 5.5 cents.[125] The reduction in fares since 1926 was only partly due to increased efficiency of operation and competition among the air carriers: mail contracts, which permit the airlines to distribute the costs of operation over mail service and passenger transport, have also played their role.[126]

Number of Passengers

The world's air passenger traffic increased tenfold between 1938 and 1947 and has continued to grow rapidly. Some 3.4 million persons used scheduled air services in 1938; 24.3 million in 1947; 39 million in 1951; 45 million in 1952; and 52 million in 1953. Moreover, passenger air traffic in the world as a whole was growing, in terms of number of passengers, at an accelerated rate until 1952: by 12 per cent between 1948 and 1949, 18 per cent between 1949 and 1950, and 25 per cent between 1950 and 1951.[127] (See Table 185.) Between 1952 and 1953, the increase was only 15 per cent. Of the world's 52 million air passengers in 1953, the airlines of the United States carried 32 million or more than 61 per cent.[128]

Between 1938 and 1947, air passengers more than doubled in number in Europe and more than quintupled in the USSR. The increase was more than eightfold in Middle America and about tenfold in North and South America. Asia, Africa and Oceania also recorded great increases. The world's air passengers in these years were distributed among the continents, as follows (in thousands): [129]

	1938	1947
World	3,446	24,343
North America	1,402	14,848
Middle America	102	888
South America	184	1,826
Europe [a]	1,147	2,981
USSR	287	1,500
Asia [b]	113	947
Africa [c]	44	165
Oceania	167	1,188

a. Includes Mediterranean countries of Asia and Africa.
b. Excludes Mediterranean Asia.
c. Excludes Mediterranean Africa.

In most countries, the increase in air travel has been greatest since World War II. Between 1938 and 1952, the number of air passengers in the United Kingdom rose from 219,000 to 1.7 million; in France, from 91,000 to more than a million; in Australia, from 106,000 to 1.8 million; in India (and Pakistan), from 2,000 to

123. **54**, p. 39.
124. **63**, pp. 549–50.
125. **19**, 1953, p. 1. The fares of U.S. international airlines dropped between 1949 and 1953 from 7.9 to less than 7 cents per mile.
126. **13**, p. 15; **64**, pp. 278–79.

127. **10**, p. 3.
128. **30**, January 18, 1954, p. 67; **28**, February 1954, p. 28. For the United States: estimate of the Civil Aeronautics Administration.
129. **69**, p. 25. Later data by continent are not available.

TABLE 185

PASSENGER TRAFFIC: NUMBER OF TRAVELERS CARRIED BY SCHEDULED AIRLINES, IN SELECTED
COUNTRIES, 1938–52

(*Thousands*)

Country	1938	1948	1949	1950	1951	1952
World	3,446	23,600	26,500	31,200	39,000	45,000
United States	1,306	14,540	16,600	19,025	24,634	27,382
Canada	95[a]	...	898	1,128	1,326	1,393
United Kingdom	219	713	...	1,211	1,357	1,691
Ireland	4	176	189	218	264	289
France	91	563	641	765	1,020[b]	1,056
Belgium [c]	34	136	150	174	232	255
Netherlands [c]	114	415	382	416	461	496
Denmark [d]	18	119	118	147	152	169
Sweden [d]	42	156	168	189	224	262
Norway [d]	6	109	102	108	135	161
Finland	11	19	56	76	94	116
Germany	323	—	—	—	—	—
Czechoslovakia	40	116	117	...	...	...
Switzerland [c]	39	108	153	192	282	292
USSR	287	1,500[e]	...	...	...	...
Turkey	1	75[e]	...	85	122	...
Pakistan	}2	280[e]{	...	77	88	...
India			...	100	341	...
Indonesia	21	...	...	209	291	284
Philippines	16	306	252	243	291[f]	...
Union of South Africa	34	...	...	...	171	...
Australia	106	1,465	1,471	1,635	1,617	1,795[g]
New Zealand [h]	61	205	231	273	340	343

Sources: **69**, *passim;* **59**, July 1952, pp. 73–76; **30**, April 28, 1952, p. 82; **6**, various issues.

a. Includes nonrevenue traffic.
b. Air France and two other lines.
c. Main national airline: Sabena for Belgium; KLM for the Netherlands; Swissair for Switzerland.
d. Includes share in SAS, the Swedish-Danish-Norwegian airline.

e. 1947.
f. According to ICAO. Figure given in **59** (July 1952, p. 76): 525,796 passengers.
g. Domestic services.
h. National (NZNAC) and Tasman Empire (TEA).

341,000 for India and 88,000 for Pakistan (1951). In the United States, the number of air travelers grew from 5,772 in 1926 to 1.3 million in 1938; 14.5 million in 1948; 24.6 million in 1951; and 27.4 million in 1952. Canadian airlines carried 95,000 passengers in 1938 and 1.4 million in 1952. (See Table 185.)

About one third of all passengers between Paris and London and seven out of ten between the United States (and Canada) and South America travel by air.[130]

Passenger Mileage

Because each airline reports separately, and

passengers may change from one carrier to another during a journey, the total number reported includes some duplications. Revenue-passenger mileage flown is therefore a more precise criterion of changes in passenger traffic.

The world's airlines flew 132 million passenger-miles in 1929; 1.3 billion in 1939; 17.0 billion in 1950; 21.3 billion in 1951; and 24.5 billion in 1952. The last figure is the equivalent of about a million passenger flights around the world. Between 1929 and 1939, passenger traffic multiplied nearly ten times; between 1939 and 1949, more than eleven times; in 1952 it was more than one and one half times greater, in terms of passenger-miles, than in 1949. (See Table 186.)

130. **10**, p. 2.

TABLE 186

PASSENGER TRAFFIC: PASSENGER-MILES [a] FLOWN BY SCHEDULED AIRLINES, IN SELECTED COUNTRIES, 1929–52

(*Millions*)

Country	1929	1939	1948	1949	1950	1951	1952
World	132.0	1,275.0	13,173.0	14,478.0	16,963.0	21,308.0	24,500.0
United States	103.8	754.7	7,870.0	8,813.6	10,218.3	13,160.7	15,783.4
Canada	6.1	20.8	370.2	460.2	532.6	646.2	758.2
Mexico	5.4 [b]	21.4	342.9	349.0	389.1	541.5	608.8
Cuba	...	1.9	39.8	...	57.7	73.3	82.1
Colombia [e]	0.8	2.5	132.0	163.4	187.4	200.2	225.6
Brazil [e]	...	19.6	420.4	462.8	528.9	763.1	794.7
Bolivia	0.6	2.5	6.5	10.8	12.1	20.1	18.1
Chile	...	1.3	37.6	28.8	33.6	40.9	48.0
Argentina	...	1.7 [d]	55.1 [e]	122.9	157.5	181.0	145.2
United Kingdom	7.1	56.4	554.5	614.7	794.0	1,065.0	1,229.4
Ireland	—	0.5	40.2	42.5	49.8	60.2	65.6
France [f]	7.7	46.1	506.6	612.2	694.7	784.7	907.3
Belgium [g]	1.0	8.0	107.7	120.4	146.0	172.3	213.8
Netherlands [h]	4.4	37.7	449.4	377.9	479.8	544.5	628.3
Denmark [i]	0.3 [e]	4.7 [e]	41.1	73.3	92.1	104.4	117.3
Sweden [j]	0.7	11.3	81.0	112.4	138.2	160.6	182.4
Norway [k]	...	1.6	61.2	83.7	100.9	124.1	137.6
Finland	0.3	2.6	13.3	13.9	16.7	22.7	28.8
Germany	12.9	71.7 [l]	—	—	—	—	—
Poland	2.4	5.9 [d]	14.3	13.5	18.9	17.4	22.1
Czechoslovakia	1.3 [b]	13.5 [d]	34.3	25.5	...	16.2	11.1
Switzerland	0.8	6.8	49.8	74.8	91.5	122.5	138.6
Spain	1.8 [m]	13.1	63.1	71.9	112.8	137.2	151.9
Italy	3.4	63.3	—	—	—	115.0	128.0

(*Continued on facing page*)

The United States accounts for 60 or more per cent of the passenger mileage of the world's scheduled airlines: 60.2 per cent in 1950; 64.4 per cent in 1952. Next, at a great distance, is the United Kingdom, followed by Australia, France, Brazil, Canada, the Netherlands and Mexico. The passenger mileage of these seven countries together amounted to about a fourth (23.9 per cent) of the world's total in 1952.

The growth of passenger mileage is almost world-wide, Iraq and Iran being among the few exceptions. Many countries have had as high a rate of increase as the United States or even higher. Between 1939 and 1952, passenger mileage in the United States and Switzerland increased about twenty times; in the United Kingdom almost twenty-two times; in Canada more than thirty-six times; in Brazil more than forty times. (See Table 186.)

Length of Trip per Passenger

The average length of a passenger trip in the world as a whole (domestic and international traffic combined) increased from 360 miles in 1937 to 550 miles in 1953. There are, however, great variations from country to country and between domestic and international traffic. In a vast country where cities are frequently far apart, as in the United States, the average domestic trip is likely to be considerably longer than in a densely populated country like the United Kingdom: [131]

	United States	United Kingdom
1938	415	77
1940	375	125
1942	452	143
1944	538	138
1946	487	131
1948	454	150
1950	461	167
1951	466	167
1952	501	173

131. **18**, 1953, pp. 58 and 66. Cf. **27**, 1952, p. 12 and 1953, p. 4; for the United Kingdom: **24**, 1953, p. 234.

TABLE 186—*continued*

Country	1929	1939	1948	1949	1950	1951	1952
China	0.1	13.3	143.6[e]	...	...	...	...
Japan	0.7	29.6	—	—	—	—	42.9
Israel	—	—	...	...	...	46.9	61.0
Iraq	...	...	5.9	5.9	5.0	5.7	6.8
Iran	...	...	7.0	10.1	8.8	7.2	8.6
Pakistan	...		...	...	...	40.1	43.3
India	—	1.3[e]	176.3	190.6	233.4	257.2	242.0
Thailand	—	...	6.9	11.7	12.1	15.0	16.8
Ceylon	...	...	2.7	7.1	6.2	20.6	18.4
Indonesia	...	4.3	63.3	77.9	92.1	99.1	99.0
Philippines	—	1.4	108.7	101.8	116.5	130.2	132.5
Egypt [n]	—	...	...	12.4	29.3	33.9	32.1
Southern Rhodesia	—	...	18.6	20.0	24.5	35.7	45.1
Union of South Africa	—	8.8	105.1	104.6	124.9	136.6	136.2
Australia	3.5[e]	44.0	652.0	699.6	788.3	931.2	920.7
New Zealand	...	6.7[o]	78.4	78.4	97.6	135.5	132.6

Sources: **1**, 1948, pp. 283–87 and 1953, pp. 321–27; **6**, No. 40, *passim*.

a. Figures cover scheduled traffic, for which remuneration is received, of nationally registered airlines on domestic and international routes; United Kingdom portion of the joint United Kingdom-Australia service of Qantas Empire Airways included in the figures for both countries.

b. 1932.

c. Includes nonscheduled and nonrevenue traffic; for Brazil: a small percentage of such traffic.

d. 1938.

e. 1947.

f. Beginning 1948, operations of Air France only; includes traffic of service personnel.

g. Operations of Sabena only; includes its operations in Belgian Congo.

h. Operations of KLM.

i. Beginning 1948, includes Danish share of SAS.

j. From 1948, includes Swedish share of SAS.

k. From 1948, includes Norwegian share of SAS.

l. Includes Austria.

m. 1931.

n. Misrair only.

o. Domestic traffic only.

In international travel, however, the average number of miles in a passenger trip has been considerably greater for the United Kingdom than for the United States until 1950:

	United States	United Kingdom
1938	487	584
1940	614	1,593
1942	880	2,066
1944	909	1,814
1946	1,057	1,715
1948	1,376	1,494
1950	1,316	1,063
1951	1,273	1,101
1952	1,277	1,080

Passenger Travel in the United States

Every important center of population in the United States has an airport and is served by one or several airlines.

In recent years the air age has even reached, on the wings of local air service, communities with no more than 3,000 inhabitants. Local air service carried 25,118 passengers in 1946, its first full year of operation; in 1952, 1.7 million. Stops are made about every 60 miles, and routes operated by eighteen lines stretch from the Atlantic to the Pacific, and from Canada to the Gulf.[132] Practically all but the smallest cities are now within a 30-mile distance of daily air service.[133] This development of local air transport is obviously shortening the average length of air trips per passenger.

In domestic travel, airlines topped Pullman passenger-miles in 1951 for the first time. While in 1933 airlines operated less than 3 per cent of the passenger mileage served by Pullman cars, and in 1941, 14 per cent, they became serious competitors in postwar years: their passenger mileage amounted to 45.2 per cent of that of Pullmans in 1947; 64.0 per cent in 1949; 106.8 per cent in 1951; 134.2 per cent in 1952.[134]

132. **27**, 1953, p. 14.

133. **54**, p. 33.

134. **18**, 1953, p. 59. Cf. **30**, April 28, 1952, p. 103; 1953, p. 104. Excludes railroad commutation travel.

Air traffic is heavily concentrated at a few points. Of the 430 stations in the United States in 1949, 15 handled some 52 per cent of the passengers carried and 61 per cent of the passenger-miles flown. The greatest concentration of airline users is in the Northeast. New York, Newark and Chicago together account for about one fifth of all air passengers. Large urban centers on the Pacific coast and Washington, D.C., as the nation's capital, also record heavy passenger traffic. (See Figure 111.)

Passenger travel is particularly common between large commercial and industrial centers: Chicago and New York, Chicago and Detroit, New York and Detroit, New York and Pittsburgh, San Francisco and Los Angeles. Popular resort centers also attract airline users during certain seasons, for example, in travel between New York and Miami.[135] (See Figure 112.)

In view of the large number of United States air carriers servicing international traffic, it is difficult to present their flight frequencies all over the world in the same way as shown in Figure 112. This can be done more readily for foreign countries which have one or two international carriers. The main traffic of the British European Airways is between London, on the one hand, and Paris, Brussels, Dusseldorf, Amsterdam, Nice and Rome, on the other; and between Berlin and Hamburg, Dusseldorf and Hanover. The main traffic flow of the British Overseas Airways is between London and the Near East, via Rome, and Africa via Tripoli. Its transatlantic operations are less frequent. (See Figure 113, A and B.) The main traffic direction of Air France is between Paris and London. The traffic flow of Scandinavian Airlines is widely dispersed throughout Europe, with the main center in Copenhagen. (See Figures 114 and 115.)

Beginning in 1943, more travelers leaving the United States have gone by air than by sea: [136]

Year	By Sea	By Air
1939	981,129	60,646
1941	383,496	97,679
1943	86,208	156,648
1945	153,409	208,198
1947	645,905	816,085
1949	892,281	972,148

135. For detailed discussions, see **41**, pp. 174ff. and **54**, pp. 362–68.
136. **54**, pp. 78–79.

In 1951 over 300,000 more persons arrived at, or departed from, United States airports on international trips than were carried by steamship lines.[137]

AIR MAIL TRANSPORT

In the early years, the chief, or only, task of airlines in many countries was to carry the mails. The very modest beginnings of this service, hampered by small aircraft, inadequacy of ground facilities and very high postal rates, go back to World War I.

Development

The first regular air mail service in the world was introduced early in 1918, when the Royal Air Force began to carry military mail between London and Paris.[138] In the United States, air mail service between Washington and New York also dates from 1918 but was inefficient at the start.[139] In time, service improved considerably, and in 1920 daylight flights spanned the continent. Night flying, at first too hazardous, was established in the United States in 1924, after the government had placed beacon lights and emergency landings along the route. European airlines, however, did not undertake night mail service until close to the beginning of World War II.[140]

International air mail service was first developed in Europe. British airlines have maintained mail service to Cairo, Baghdad, India and Thailand since 1927.[141] By about that time, air mail service had been extended throughout the United States, where several hundred cities were served directly and thousands of others were served by a combination of air and surface carriers.

137. **56**, February 1953, p. 1.
138. **58**, p. 111.
139. This service was launched on May 15, 1918, in the presence of President Wilson, Cabinet members and diplomatic dignitaries. Four sacks of mail for New York were loaded aboard the plane but the engine refused to start for a very simple reason: its fuel tanks were empty. A nearby plane then was drained to provide fuel. The mail plane finally got under way but missed the route to New York and landed on a Maryland farm, 25 miles from Washington. The plane from New York to Washington made a better showing, reaching Washington in 3 hours and 20 minutes. In the first month, only one third of the scheduled trips between these two cities were completed; flying time averaged 4 hours. (**54**, p. 8.)
140. **65**, p. 10.
141. **58**, p. 111.

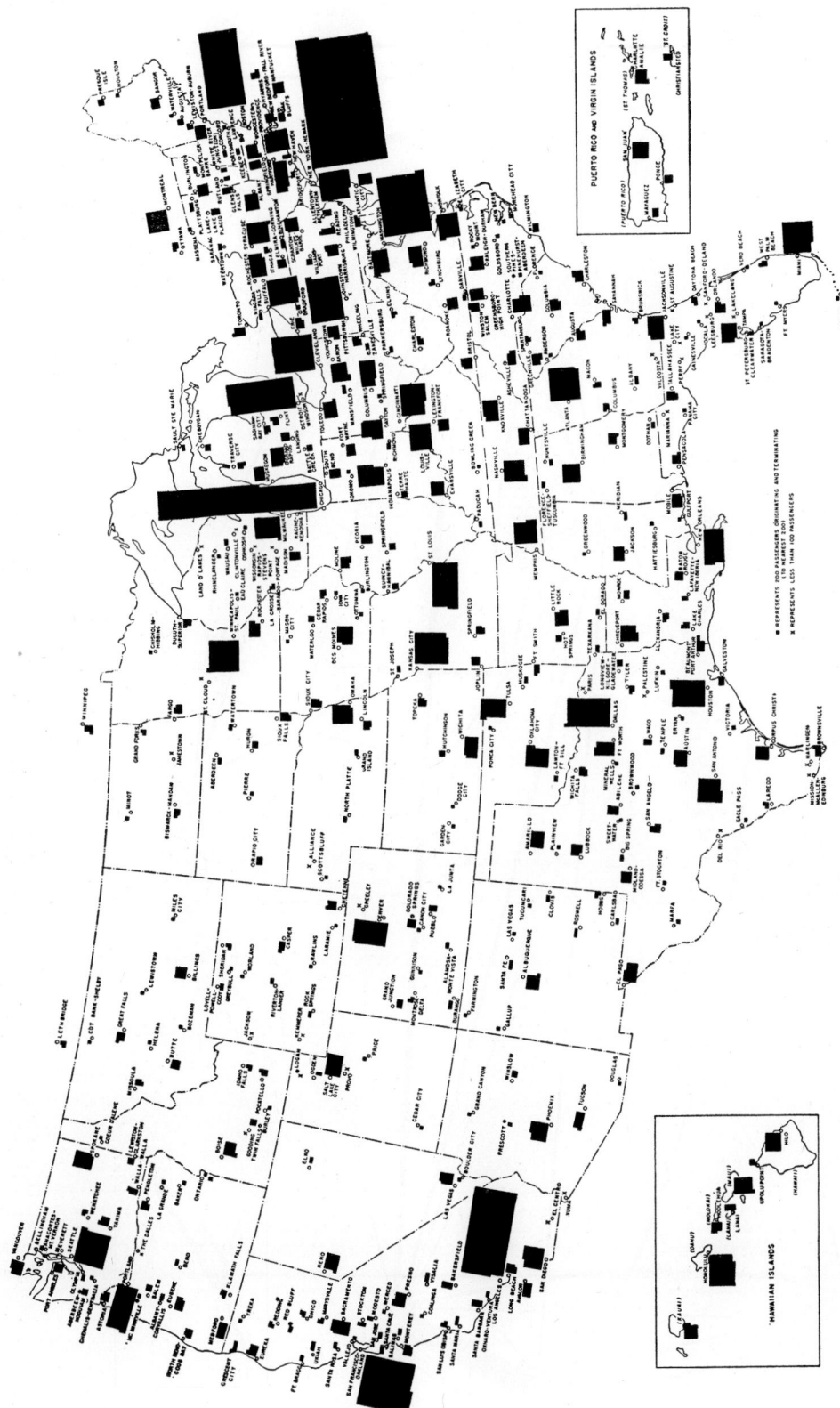

FIGURE 111. PASSENGER TRAFFIC: RELATIVE DISTRIBUTION OF PASSENGERS ARRIVING AT AND DEPARTING FROM AIRLINE STATIONS IN THE UNITED STATES, 1948

Civil Aeronautics Board

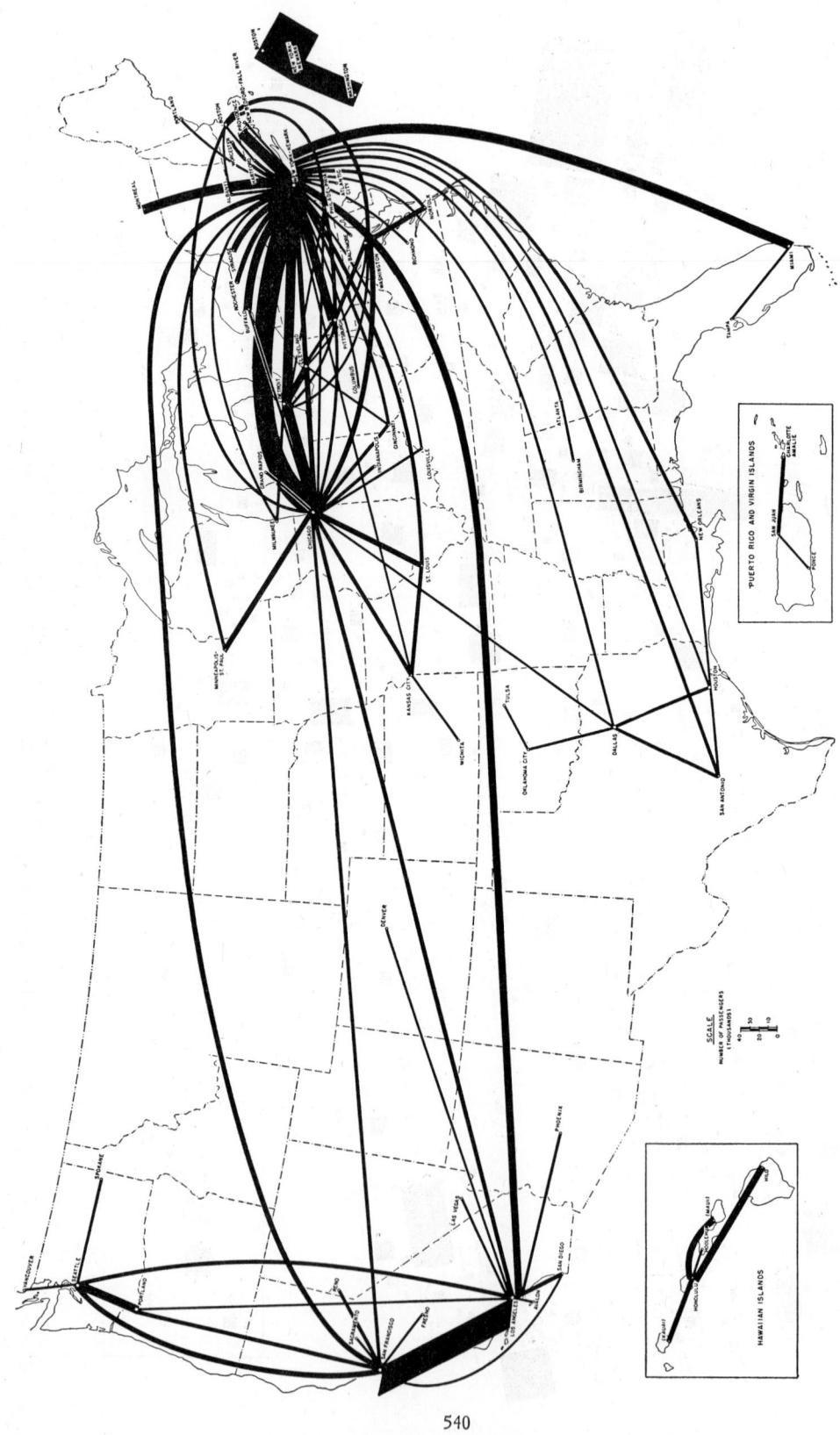

Civil Aeronautics Board

FIGURE 112. PASSENGER TRAFFIC: TRAVEL BETWEEN 100 TOP-RANKING PAIRS OF AIRLINE STATIONS IN THE UNITED STATES, 1948 (Domestic and Territorial Traffic)

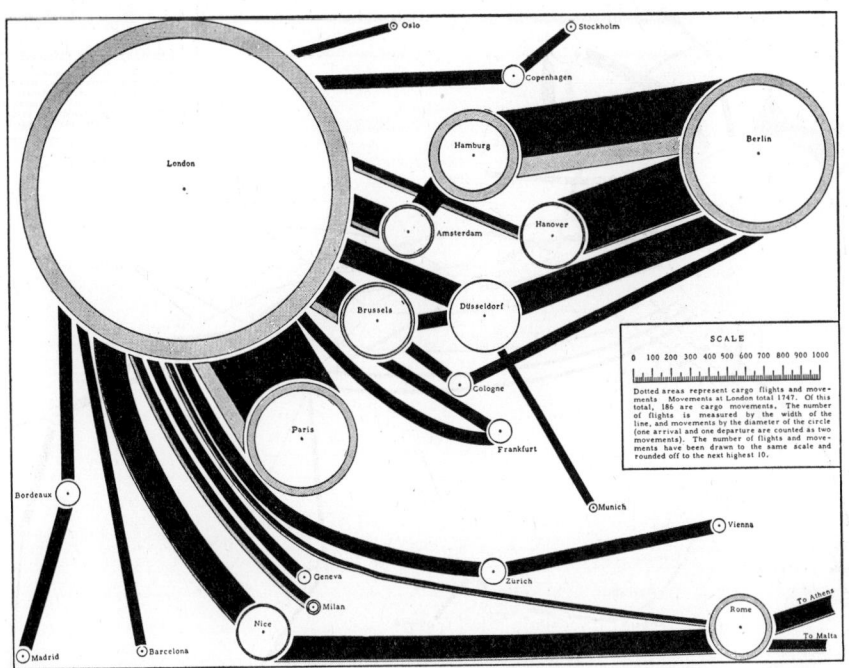

A. British European Airways

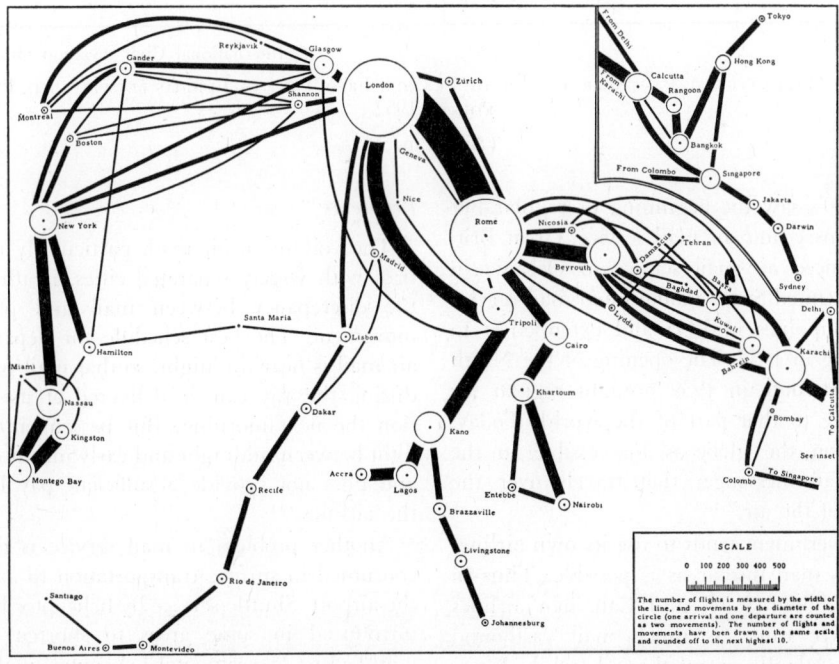

International Civil Aviation Organization

B. British Overseas Airways Corporation

FIGURE 113. INTERNATIONAL PASSENGER TRAFFIC OF THE UNITED KINGDOM: FREQUENCY OF FLIGHTS BETWEEN THE PRINCIPAL POINTS, 1952

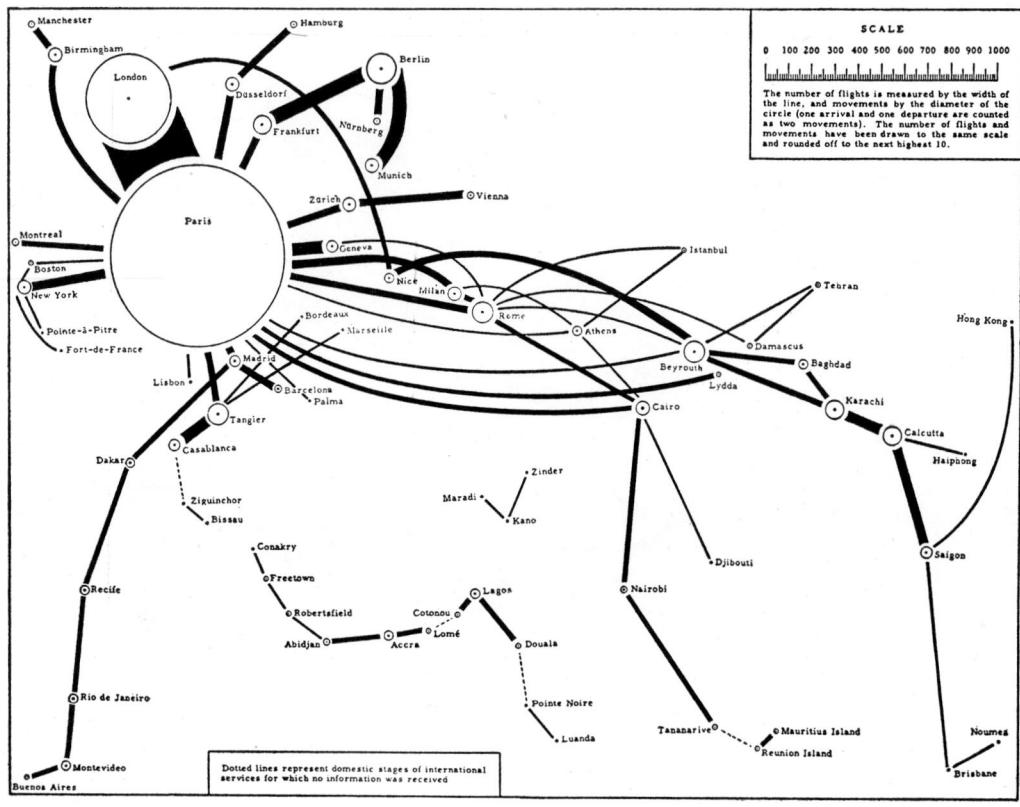

International Civil Aviation Organization

FIGURE 114. INTERNATIONAL PASSENGER TRAFFIC OF FRANCE: FREQUENCY OF FLIGHTS BETWEEN THE PRINCIPAL
POINTS, 1952

(Air France)

The 1930's saw the beginning of regular but limited transoceanic air mail service. Great Britain introduced air mail service to Oceania in 1933; the United States inaugurated mail service to the Philippines in 1935 and extended it to Hong Kong in 1937. The opening of the North Atlantic air route in 1939 brought regular air mail service to that part of the world. Today, "no spot on the globe is inaccessible to the winged mail messenger that travels over the highways of the air." [142]

Each government tends to use its own airlines to carry its mail insofar as is possible. Thus in 1951 the United States and Canadian airlines carried three times as much mail eastbound across the Atlantic as westbound, while European airlines carried three times as much mail westbound as eastbound. [143]

Problems

The volume of air mail, particularly in countries with widely separated cities, is affected by the discrepancy between mail and passenger movement. The best schedule for departure of air mail is near midnight, so that mail processed during the day can be delivered at its destination the next morning. But passenger traffic is light between midnight and early morning hours and does not provide a sufficient pay load for the airlines. [144]

Another problem in mail service is the time consumed in surface transportation to and from the airport. Shuttle service by helicopter has been introduced in some areas to shorten it. The world's first experimental helicopter mail service was established in 1947, between Los Angeles and some communities north of the city. The route has since been extended to serve some 50

142. **11**, p. 481.
143. **10**, p. 6.

144. **54**, pp. 348–49.

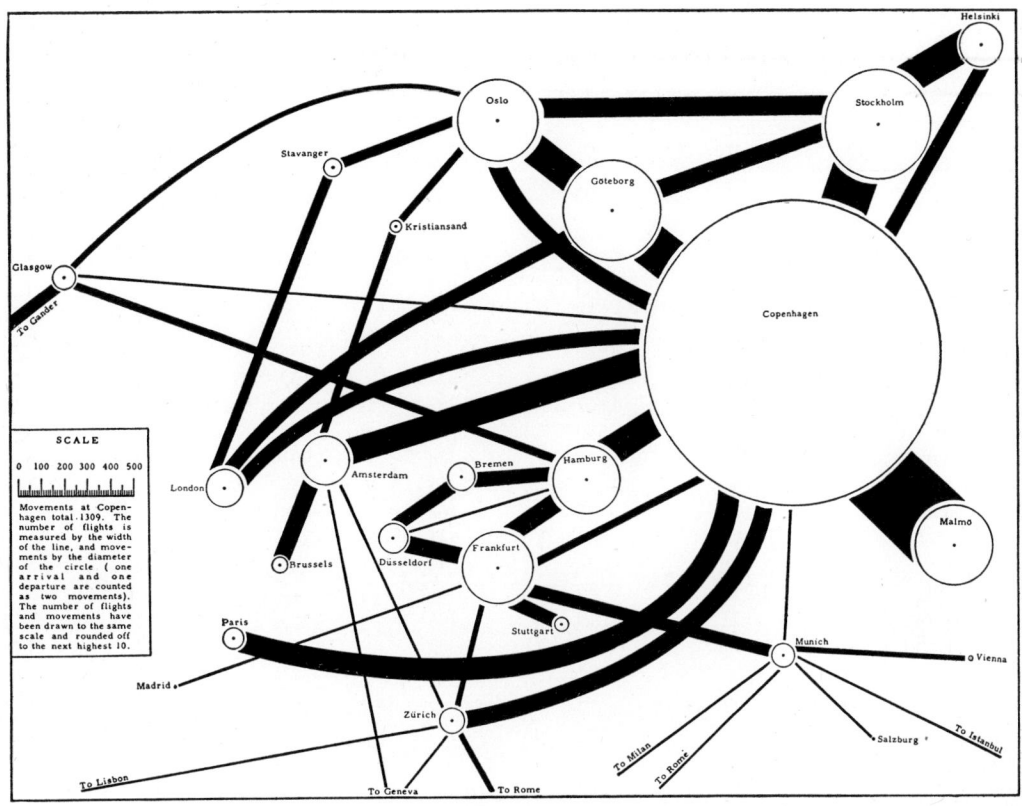

International Civil Aviation Organization

FIGURE 115. INTERNATIONAL PASSENGER TRAFFIC OF SCANDINAVIA: FREQUENCY OF FLIGHTS BETWEEN THE PRINCIPAL POINTS, 1952

(Scandinavian Airlines System)

cities and towns in the Los Angeles metropolitan area. Another helicopter service has operated since 1949 in the Chicago area. It consists of a shuttle — 18 times per day — between the Chicago airport and the roof of the main post office, and deliveries on three suburban routes covering forty-four suburbs, with a layover of only a minute and a half at each stop.[145] Helicopter service in and around New York City was inaugurated on October 15, 1952.

Similar services for mail pick-up and delivery are being introduced in other countries as well. In Belgium, for example, helicopters carry mail on a circuit of some 250 miles between 9 cities, with about four minutes on the ground at each stop.[146]

Air parcel-post services have been in operation in the United States since 1948 and are now available to more than 60 countries all over the world.[147]

Volume

In 1947 the world's scheduled airlines flew 88 million mail ton-miles; in 1949, 128 million; in 1951, 160 million; and in 1952, 178 million.[148] The United States accounts for more than half the total: 48.6 million ton-miles in 1947; 65.8 million in 1949; 90.8 million in 1951; and 97.0 million in 1952. The United Kingdom ranks next, with 18.5 million ton-miles in 1952, followed by France with 13.0 million and Australia with 7.7 million. The Netherlands and Canada have about equal volumes and India and the Union of South Africa also have substantial air mail traffic. (See Table 187.)

---

145. **54**, p. 426.
146. **10**, p. 11.

147. **11**, pp. 480–81.
148. **10**, p. 3. Data released by the ICAO. Excludes China since 1949, and the USSR.

TABLE 187

AIR MAIL TRANSPORT: OPERATIONS OF SCHEDULED AIRLINES, IN SELECTED COUNTRIES, 1937–52

(*Thousands of Short-Ton-Miles* [a])

Country [b]	1937	1947	1949	1950	1951	1952
World	...	88,000	128,000	143,000	160,000	178,000
United States	6,698	48,590	65,820	73,198	90,786	96,988
Canada	95	1,826	4,242	4,540	4,978	5,487
Brazil	149	614	845[c]	...	1,204	1,279
Chile	8	28	35	38	51	60
United Kingdom	4,317	9,229	11,823	13,565	17,292	18,531
Ireland	...	8	27	32	184	249
France	676	4,867	7,738	9,769	11,022	12,976
Belgium	92	590	871	1,113	1,561	2,153
Netherlands	965	5,643	6,134	4,901	4,282	5,293
Denmark	36	447[c]	473	655	810	1,058
Sweden	175	525	708	998	1,244	1,625
Norway	17	333	521	697	886	1,145
Finland	11[d]	23	45	53	57	88
Germany	1,252	—	—	—	...	...
Czechoslovakia	12	219	296	...	82	52
Switzerland	49	155	307	968	842	1,098
Spain	...	92	187	243	301	329
Italy	986	—	—	—	812	1,088
China	...	2,554	...	...	...	...
Japan	139	—	—	—	...	83
India	59	558	2,012	2,914	3,098	3,594
Thailand	5	11	36	31	39	190
Indonesia	31[d]	769[c]	1,085	920	1,038	1,203
Philippines	...	358	471	536	568	715
Southern Rhodesia	...	101	165	198	244	308
Union of South Africa	210	1,137	2,747	2,896	2,116	2,082
Australia	...	3,113	4,092	5,577	7,034	7,707
New Zealand	16	328	408	464	706	677

Sources: **6,** No. 40, *passim;* **1,** 1953, pp. 321–27.

a. One short-ton-mile = 1.46 metric ton-kilometers.
b. For France: Air France; for Belgium: Sabena, including its operations in Belgian Congo; for the Netherlands: KLM; for Denmark, Sweden and Norway: includes the respective national share in the operations of SAS; for Chile: Linea Aerea National.
c. 1948.
d. 1938.

CARGO TRANSPORT

Transportation of freight by air is still in a developmental stage. It holds third place in the operations of airlines, after passenger and mail service, except for air carriers that engage only in cargo transport.

Special Problems

Carrying freight by air creates various problems not encountered in surface transportation. Loading a plane is a slow and complex operation. Planes have limited floor and cubic space and the size of their doorways definitely limits the size of shipments. Weight must be distributed evenly so as not to disturb the center of gravity. Cargo, especially heavy shipments, must be packed securely, since shifts in load are dangerous at any time, whether at the take-off or landing or during flight.[149]

Efforts are made to place cargo according to the destination, so that the first to be unloaded

149. Several ways of securing cargo are used in the United States: a rope running through rings in the floor or reinforced walls; a large elastic net attached to the ceiling and floor of the cabin on either side, with cargo behind it; special equipment of bars, beams, ropes, hooks and tighteners. (**65,** p. 602.)

is nearest the door. Parachutes and ground pick-up and delivery, without landing of the plane, are used for small packages and mail in the United States and some countries abroad.[150] To increase the cargo capacity of an aircraft, a specially designed extra compartment, the so-called "Speed-Pack," is used, which can be attached to the bottom of the plane or detached from it in a few minutes.

Since the power plant of a plane cannot be detached during loading and unloading, like the engine of a train or the truck to which trailers are attached, cargo planes can fly only a few hours during a day.[151] Loss of time in loading, pick-up and delivery outweighs the advantages of air cargo transport except on long hauls. In fact, air cargo hauls in the United States are, on the average, three times longer than rail shipments of less-than-carload lots and more than five times as long as highway cargo consignments.[152]

The distance of airports from urban centers is another handicap. Much of the time gained in transport by air is lost in pick-up and delivery of merchandise carried to and from the air terminal by trucks. Helicopters may speed up this service as do those now operating in the New York area. They move freight from the Newark airport to Idlewild in 18 minutes, in contrast to the four hours required in truck service.[153]

Development

Air cargo transport was first developed abroad, particularly in Latin America and in Canada, countries where surface transportation facilities were less effective than in the United States and Europe. The Central American airline TACA was publicized before World War II as the largest cargo carrier in the world. In fact, its twenty small aircraft transported some 10,000 tons of freight in 1939 over jungles and snow-capped mountains, serving some 205 "airports," literally grassgrown fields, throughout the banana belt. They carried every kind of freight, including livestock, and occasionally hauled shipments weighing more than two and a half tons. Moving cargo by air has become so common in all Central American countries that planes there carry produce — such as salt or corn — which,

on account of its bulk and low value, would never be considered for air shipment in the United States or Europe.

Another example of what air cargo service may mean to a country is Colombia, with three great valleys separated by mountains and with surface transportation difficult and sometimes impossible. The country took to the air, and its national airline annually lifts some 2 million items of all kinds.[154]

Canada shipped valuable ores from the north by air long before freight was flown in the United States. Aircraft are used in New Guinea to transport gold ore from the mine at Bulolo, only 35 miles from the coastal town of Salamaua but separated from it by 12,000-foot mountains. Before air service was inaugurated, human carriers needed seven days to walk to Bulolo and six days to return, and their food took up about two fifths of their 50-pound loads.[155]

The Railway Express Company and its predecessor, the American Railway Express Company, pioneered in transporting cargo by air in the United States. Shipments consisted essentially of small parcels, ranging in weight from 1 to 21 pounds and averaging 6 pounds in 1939. In 1940, nearly a million parcels, weighing in all less than 3,000 tons, were shipped by air.[156]

World War II vastly increased air cargo transport, playing about the same role in its growth as World War I did for air passenger transport. Hundreds of thousands of tons of war materials were hurdled over the world's loftiest mountains by the Air Transport Command of the United States to support the Chinese war effort. Entire armies with all their equipment were carried by air. Within the United States, heavy machinery was delivered by air to speed up operations of war plants. In all, the Air Transport Command and the Naval Air Transport Services of the United States operated some 1.8 billion ton-miles around the globe in 1945.[157]

While the objective in wartime freight transport was speed, regardless of cost, the wartime services proved beyond doubt that cargo *could* be shipped by air over long distances, and provided valuable experience in handling and carrying air cargo. Moreover, manufacturers and other prospective air-cargo shippers, operating under the demanding time schedules of the war,

150. **65,** p. 60. The plane picks up packages with a hook device and drops them in special containers. (**16,** p. 23.)
151. **54,** p. 402.
152. **54,** p. 399.
153. **56,** February 1953, p. 2.

154. **44,** 1953, No. 12, pp. 648ff.
155. **42,** p. 29.
156. **23,** p. 348.
157. **54,** p. 391. Equipment, men and mail.

began to realize the advantages of moving their products by air.[158]

After the war, a number of all-cargo air carriers were organized in the United States, some by veterans of the armed transport services who acquired surplus aircraft at low cost. While most of the mushrooming companies soon went out of business, for lack of experience and sufficient capital or inability to obtain certification by the government, some survived and grew. Scheduled airlines also inaugurated cargo service after the war but were mostly absorbed in their spectacularly growing passenger traffic.[159] They did not begin to compete effectively with all-cargo carriers until a few years later. Since 1948, the ton-mileage of the regular trunk lines has considerably exceeded that of all-cargo carriers. Considered as a whole, air freight transport has grown by leaps and bounds in the United States since its start late in 1944.

Volume

The world's airlines reported 187 million ton-miles in cargo transport in 1947, 286 million in 1948, 390 million in 1949, 518 million in 1950, 602 million in 1951 and 623 million in 1952. Thus the volume of cargo more than tripled between 1947 and 1952.[160]

The greatest market for air freight has been in the United States, which accounts for more than half the world's ton-mileage, with 284 million ton-miles in 1950 and more than 348 million in 1952.[161] It is believed that air freight may become one of the major factors in the future growth of air transport in the United States.

Brazil and Colombia rank second and third, intermittently, though at a great distance from the United States in the volume of their air-cargo traffic, which, in each country, is several times that in Canada and greater than in any European country with a well-developed air network. Australia comes next, followed by France and the United Kingdom; in each, air freight traffic has grown remarkably since World War II. India ranks first in Asia, and the Philippines and Indonesia are next in line. (See Table 188.)

Composition

At first, air freight (air express in the United States) generally consisted mostly of articles of high value, small size and low weight: drugs, films, important documents, jewelry, precious metals, samples, style goods, emergency articles and perishables such as cut flowers — all goods which can stand the high costs of air transport. A machine part urgently needed and not locally available is often shipped by air. In general, speeding up production in plants is considered a more important factor than the distribution of finished goods.

After World War II, air cargo began to attract an increasing volume of shipments. Larger aircraft appeared on the scene, capable of handling tonnage cargo. Business discovered advantages of shipment by air. Speed of delivery permits lower inventories and faster turnover, lessening the risk of style and market changes, releasing otherwise tied-up capital and cutting warehouse expenses. Lighter packaging may often suffice in air transport, and shipments are less frequently damaged. For perishables there is less waste from spoilage, which otherwise may be as high as 20 to 30 per cent;[162] such shipments can stand high transport rates. As Wolfe puts it: "The orchid in the Mexican jungle has beauty but no commercial value until fast transportation brings it into the flower shops of the large cities where it brings a fabulous price."[163]

Almost any kind of freight may now be shipped by air around the world. England ships livestock for breeding: bulls to South America, sheep to Australia and New Zealand, hogs to Austria. Even equatorial Africa obtains calves and lambs by air. Jungle animals are shipped by air to the world's zoos. Millions of chicks travel in planes to tropical areas to replenish poultry stocks. Textiles reach Africa by air, and penicillin is flown to India and Pakistan.[164] Australia flies disjointed ox meat from the almost uninhabited interior to refrigerator ships at the ports and finds it economical to fly raw leather for making shoes to Singapore and to have the finished product flown back.[165] Loads

158. **13,** p. 33.

159. The inauguration of regular freight service brought about competition between air express handled by the Railway Express Agency and air freight carried at lower rates. A considerable proportion of air express traffic was diverted to air freight carriers.

160. Data released by the ICAO. Excludes the USSR and, in 1949–52, China. Mail not included.

161. Comparison of these figures with 3.3 million in 1939 highlights the striking increase over prewar years.

162. **30,** October 1952, pp. 10 and 32–33.

163. **65,** pp. 609–10.

164. **50,** January 1950, *passim*.

165. **44,** 1953, No. 12, p. 648; **59,** December 18, 1953, p. 808.

TABLE 188

AIR CARGO TRANSPORT: OPERATIONS OF SCHEDULED AIRLINES OF SELECTED COUNTRIES, 1929–52

(*Thousands of Short-Ton-Miles* [a])

Country	1929	1939	1949	1950	1951	1952
World	...	...	390,000	518,000	602,000	623,000
United States	...	3,311	200,863	284,212	308,994	348,569
Canada	...	966[b]	4,843	6,218	7,191	8,969
Colombia [c]	...	...	35,057	38,921	46,789	41,302
Brazil	...	523	21,284[d]	...	43,861	42,501
Chile	...	9	469	476	596	802
United Kingdom	245	945	20,255	24,533	31,111	30,378
Ireland	—	4[e]	440	547	759	679
France [f]	608	564	19,100	22,339	25,568	33,689
Belgium [g]	79	173	2,714	4,681	6,573	8,470
Netherlands [h]	...	778	9,242	16,667	19,337	23,806
Denmark [i]	28	124	1,317	2,350	2,952	2,889
Sweden [j]	27	381	2,049	3,641	4,519	4,423
Norway [j]	...	30	1,791	3,334	4,945	4,605
Finland [k]	...	57	264	318	413	516
Germany	518	1,535	—	—	—	—
Czechoslovakia	...	351[e]	1,243	...	372	281
Switzerland	20	65	933	1,733	2,424	2,640
Spain	6	...	251	...	794	811
Italy	64	512	785	...	2,397	2,411
Japan	1	203	—	—	—	101
Iraq	—	—	122	82	111	148
Iran	—	—	276	190	135	129
India	—	19	5,001	12,437	15,015	14,321
Thailand	...	1	201	295	425	509
Ceylon	—	—	51	75	1,558	1,210
Indonesia	—	—	3,156	3,469	3,853	3,686
Philippines	—	...	3,580	4,698	5,953	5,936
Southern Rhodesia	—	...	346	379	419	506
Union of South Africa	—	232[e]	980	1,792	1,421	1,366
Australia	...	966[l]	22,391	29,038	33,924	37,020
New Zealand	—	14	1,412	1,963	4,642	2,752

Sources: **1**, 1953, pp. 321–27; **6**, No. 29, pp. 3–9 and **41**, *passim.*

a. One short-ton-mile = 1.46 metric ton-kilometers. Cargo includes all goods carried for remuneration and as excess baggage. Excludes mail.

b. Nonscheduled flights and flights of Trans-Canada Air Lines.

c. Includes mail.

d. 1948.

e. 1938.

f. Excludes excess baggage. From 1949, Air France only.

g. Sabena only, with about 88 per cent of weekly scheduled mileage; includes its operations in Belgian Congo.

h. KLM.

i. Includes nonscheduled traffic in 1929 and 1939 and, since 1949, the Danish share of SAS operations.

j. From 1949, includes the country's share in SAS operations.

k. Aero O/Y, the country's major airline.

l. 1942.

of hats are flown to Paris from neighboring countries for stamping and labeling, and then reflown to the points of origin.[166]

In areas without adequate land transport, air cargo has supplied many newly opened mines with equipment and labor and delivered their products to industrial centers for processing.[167] For example, the recently developed iron mines in Labrador and Quebec were provided with equipment and personnel solely by air.

166. **17**, p. 59.

167. **40**, p. 122.

Because shocks can be avoided, aircraft transport delicate precision instruments and fragile articles, such as electronic devices, photographic cameras, telescopes, watches, glassware. Such commodities represent a sizable portion of the air freight.[168]

Newspapers are using air transport increasingly to extend the area of their circulation; weekly magazines in the United States are flown, if need be, to reach newsstands from coast to coast the day they are published.

Although a single plane can carry a comparatively small load, it is capable of producing a substantial ton-mileage over a period of time, because of its frequency of schedule and speed. It is believed that, averaging a five-ton load, it could reach 3.5 million ton-miles a year — the equivalent of 20 freight railroad cars of fifty-ton capacity at normal load and speed.[169]

In the United States, most air freight traffic originates in the Middle Atlantic and East North Central states, which ship their manufactured products to predominantly agricultural states. West- and southbound tonnage is about twice the east- and northbound. While air passenger traffic is concentrated over the weekend and during the day, air cargo transport is most active during the middle of the week and at night.[170]

The Economics of Air Transportation

Most of the world's airlines operate either with a close balance between revenues and expenses or with a deficit if government aid were excluded.[171] The ICAO concludes after a survey of financial results of operating airlines in many countries in 1951:

"If any special financial aid from governments were eliminated from consideration, a large proportion of the international airlines would probably still have an operating loss, though a much smaller one in most cases than they would have had three or four years ago."[172] This paradox of air transportation — phenomenal technical progress and consistently disappointing commercial results — is largely explained by the uneconomic principle of spending power to overcome the force of gravity, and the high rate of depreciation and obsolescence of aircraft.

Complete statistics on the revenues and expenses of airlines are available for the United States, where the law requires each carrier to file a full report of income and expenditures with the Civil Aeronautics Board. Information for other countries was scanty and fragmentary[173] until recently, but today comparable data are available for most of the principal national airlines.

REVENUES

Airlines classify their receipts as operating income and incidental revenue. Operating income is derived from three sources: transportation of passengers, of mail and of cargo. Incidental revenue comes from airline restaurants, limousine service, rental of equipment, various commissions and, in some cases, direct public grants.

Composition of Operating Receipts

In the developmental stage, revenue from mail was the financial backbone of many airlines in most countries. For the domestic airlines of the United States, for example, it represented 37 per cent of all revenue in 1938, and for its international air carriers, nearly 57 per cent. With the growth of passenger traffic, the share of air mail began to decline and in 1952 amounted to 7.2 and 16.4 per cent, respectively. For local airlines, revenue from mail still exceeds that from any other source.

Revenue from passengers is steadily increasing. Its share in the total receipts of the domestic airlines of the United States rose from about 58 per cent in 1938 to 87.2 per cent in 1946, when passenger travel postponed during war years was particularly heavy. It declined somewhat in the following years but is now again on the upgrade, with 85.1 per cent in 1952. For international airlines, the share of passenger revenue rose from 29.3 per cent in 1938 to the all-time high of 67.5 per cent in 1952.

Revenue from freight and various other sources is also increasing in importance. (See Table 189.)

Passengers provide the greatest part of revenue to all airlines except all-cargo carriers and some small carriers in the United States that live by mail contracts. Thus in 1952 almost all large airlines in the United States derived about 80

---

168. **49**, p. 134.
169. **40**, p. 122.
170. **54**, pp. 407–12.
171. **10**, p. 9; **65**, p. 265.
172. **10**, p. 9.

173. According to the ICAO, eighteen countries had never filed any of the reporting forms as of the end of 1951. (**10**, p. 45.)

TABLE 189

OPERATING REVENUES: SCHEDULED DOMESTIC, LOCAL AND INTERNATIONAL AIRLINES OF THE UNITED STATES, 1938–52

Airline and Year	Millions of Dollars					Percentage				
	Total	Passenger	Mail	Cargo	Other [a]	Total	Passenger	Mail	Cargo	Other [a]
Domestic Trunk										
1938	$ 42.9	$ 24.9	$15.9	$ 1.6	$ 0.6	100.0	57.9	37.0	3.7	1.4
1940	76.9	53.3	20.1	2.6	0.8	100.0	69.4	26.1	3.4	1.1
1942	108.2	74.8	23.5	7.0	3.0	100.0	69.2	21.7	6.4	2.7
1944	160.9	116.4	33.3	8.3	2.9	100.0	72.4	20.7	5.2	1.8
1946	316.2	275.6	21.0	13.6	6.0	100.0	87.2	6.6	4.3	1.9
1948	434.3	343.3	59.3	24.4	7.3	100.0	79.0	13.7	5.6	1.7
1950	557.8	444.5	63.8	35.1	14.4	100.0	79.7	11.4	6.3	2.6
1951	702.4	591.2	57.4	36.9	16.8	100.0	84.2	8.2	5.2	2.4
1952	817.8	695.5	59.0	42.8	20.5	100.0	85.1	7.2	5.2	2.5
Local Service										
1946	1.9	0.3	1.6	[b]	[b]	100.0	16.3	80.7	0.7	2.3
1948	16.3	4.7	11.3	0.1	0.2	100.0	28.6	69.3	0.9	1.2
1950	28.5	10.3	17.2	0.4	0.5	100.0	36.2	60.4	1.6	2.0
1951	37.6	16.3	19.7	0.7	1.0	100.0	43.2	52.5	1.8	2.6
1952	40.9	18.7	20.6	0.8	0.8	100.0	45.7	50.4	1.9	2.0
International										
1938	15.2	4.4	8.6	0.8	1.3	100.0	29.3	56.8	5.1	8.8
1940	26.9	8.8	13.4	1.2	3.5	100.0	32.8	49.9	4.4	12.9
1942	40.9	21.0	9.0	4.3	6.5	100.0	51.3	22.1	10.6	16.0
1944	38.9	24.3	2.9	5.4	6.3	100.0	62.5	7.4	13.9	16.2
1946	146.8	91.4	25.1	11.4	18.9	100.0	62.3	17.1	7.8	12.8
1948	249.2	151.3	57.3	20.8	19.8	100.0	60.7	23.0	8.3	8.0
1950	260.1	160.7	55.7	21.7	22.1	100.0	61.8	21.4	8.3	8.5
1951	287.9	184.7	53.2	25.2	24.8	100.0	64.1	18.5	8.8	8.6
1952	315.1	212.6	51.5	26.9	24.1	100.0	67.5	16.4	8.5	7.6

Sources: **18**, 1953, pp. 60 and 73; **27**, 1953, p. 15.

a. Excess baggage, nonscheduled transport service, incidental revenue, foreign mail and other, except in 1938 and 1940, when revenue from excess baggage and express is counted with cargo.

b. Negligible.

per cent, and some more than 85 per cent, of their revenue from passenger service. The corresponding figures for Air France, KLM and Swissair were between 67 and 72 per cent in that year; for Trans-Canada, 76.4 per cent and for BEA, 78 per cent.

The proportion of revenue derived from mail services varies from country to country and from airline to airline. In 1952 it represented more than 10 per cent of the total revenue of Swissair; for the Dutch KLM, 10 per cent; for British Overseas Airways and South African Airways, 23–28 per cent; and for Pan American Airways, 21.6 per cent. (See Table 190.)

Passengers

Demand for air transport is elastic, increasing with lower fares and shrinking when fares go up. Persons who travel by air for business purposes, mostly on expense accounts, and passengers using air services in an emergency are less responsive to travel costs than pleasure travelers. Of 6.5 million persons who used air services in the United States in 1945, it has been estimated that less than one million were different individuals, all others being "repeaters." Airlines began to tap a much larger potential market for their services in 1949 when they introduced promotional devices, such as round-trip discount fares, coach service, excursion and educational fares, and a family plan permitting the head of the family paying full fare to have with him other members of his family at half fare on off-peak days (Monday, Tuesday and Wednesday).

TABLE 190

OPERATING REVENUES: MAJOR WORLD AIRLINES, 1952

Country and Airline	Total (In Millions of Dollars)	Percentage Distribution				Country and Airline	Total (In Millions of Dollars)	Percentage Distribution			
		Passengers	Mail	Freight and Excess Baggage	Other [a]			Passengers	Mail	Freight and Excess Baggage	Other [a]
United States [b]						United Kingdom					
American	$187.3	85.9	4.2	8.4	1.5	BEA	$ 36.7	78.0	8.6	8.9	4.5
Braniff	31.9	84.0	9.7	5.3	1.0	BOAC	101.4	63.0	23.3	10.0	3.7
Colonial	7.3	82.4	13.4	2.3	1.9	France					
Chicago and						Air France	94.4	67.0	14.3	11.0	7.7
Southern	18.9	80.1	12.9	6.3	0.7	Netherlands					
Eastern	118.6	92.5	2.2	4.1	1.2	KLM	68.1	68.6	10.0	15.2	6.2
National	28.9	88.2	2.5	7.0	2.3	Scandinavia					
Northwest	55.7	75.1	13.4	9.2	2.3	SAS	45.3	71.9	11.8	10.1	6.2
Pan American	191.6	64.5	21.6	10.7	3.2	Finland					
Panagra	17.3	70.8	17.7	8.7	2.8	Aero O/Y	2.8	83.3	2.8	3.3	10.6
Trans World	160.5	84.3	7.3	7.0	1.4	Switzerland					
United	153.9	84.6	6.5	6.9	2.0	Swissair	15.8	71.1	10.3	9.2	9.4
Canada						Pakistan					
Trans-Canada	56.7	76.4	14.0	6.7	2.9	Orient Airways	4.5	57.7	3.9	14.7	23.7
Canadian Pacific	14.7	52.3	11.4	6.8	29.5	India					
						Airways India	3.0	54.7	2.8	34.4	8.1
Brazil						Philippines					
Panair	24.5	62.0	15.3	9.4	13.3	PAL	16.9	63.3	15.3	15.9	5.5
Real	9.9	77.7	5.2	10.1	7.0	Union of South Africa					
						South African					
Argentina						Airways	7.3	62.1	28.0	5.7	4.2
Aerolineas						New Zealand					
Argentinas	12.2	77.6	13.2	8.4	0.8	Tasman Empire	4.2	79.9	13.5	5.0	1.6

Source: **7,** No. 43, Table 2.

a. Includes charter and special flights.

b. Domestic and international operations.

Lower fares brought new customers who had never flown before and would not have traveled by air at regular rates.[174]

In the United States coach service has expanded each year. In 1951 scheduled domestic airlines operated 64 daily coach flights between 34 cities; in 1953, they provided 154 daily air coach flights serving 53 cities with a population totaling nearly 50 million.[175] The number of coach passengers on ten major airlines increased from 363,482 in 1949 to 1.5 million in 1951 and 2.4 million in 1952; the number of passenger-miles, from less than 100 million to 1.3 and 2.3 billion, respectively.[176] The load factor in coach service (the ratio between occupied and available seats) was much greater than in service of all trunk airlines.[177]

174. **54,** pp. 378–79. Increase in rail rates has been an additional stimulus by reducing the cost differential between air and surface travel.

175. **27,** 1952, p. 4; **19,** 1953, p. 1.

176. **30,** April 27, 1953, p. 41; **13,** p. 17.

177. Actually, the beginnings of low-fare coach service date from the first postwar year, when nonscheduled irregular operators, the so-called "non-skeds" (mostly veterans), entered the field. As the Senate Select Com-

Two thirds of the air coach passengers are traveling for pleasure, while three fifths of the first-class passengers travel on business. Women constitute the majority of coach passengers; men, of the first class. According to 58,000 answers received by the Institute of Transportation and Traffic Engineering of the University of California, the percentage distribution of passengers by the purpose of travel is as follows: [178]

	Total	*Men*	*Women*
First Class			
Total	100	63	37
Business	59	49	10
Pleasure	41	14	27
Coach			
Total	100	45	55
Business	35	26	9
Pleasure	65	19	46

The success of coach and tourist service in the United States led France and India to introduce it on some routes; many European countries and the Middle East have since followed suit.[179] After several years of discussion, all airlines operating on the North Atlantic routes agreed to introduce tourist service in May 1952 at a reduction of more than 30 per cent for a one-way ticket, with an additional 10 per cent reduction for a round trip.[180] The results were beyond expectations. The heaviest bookings in the airline history of the United States were recorded in the first summer season of coach travel abroad: the revenue passenger traffic across the Atlantic (between the United States and Canada to and from Europe) in 1952 showed a 31 per cent increase over 1951, as against less than 6 per cent in 1951 over 1950.[181]

Since April 1953 first-class services have been maintained by European airlines on only a few routes where the density of traffic permits catering to the demands and pocketbooks of varying groups of passengers. On the majority of European routes, tourist operations predominate and are expected to become the only type of pas-

senger air transport.[182] This is also the conclusion of the Senate Select Committee in its report *Future of Irregular Airlines:* "The aircoach service is destined to become the standard type of air travel." [183]

Thus, passenger air transport is shifting from a luxury status to a mass-consumption service.

Mail

Probably in no form of transport, particularly international transport, has mail service played so vital a part as in the development of aviation. In most countries mail contracts have been both a source of airline revenues and an instrument of government policy. Even with the present level of commercial air traffic, revenue from air mail remains a substantial source of income for most of the world's airlines.

The airlines of the United States would not have been able to operate passenger service in their early days without the mail and it is still "the indispensable keystone in the airway arch." [184] This is particularly true of local service carriers; some of them derived as much as 80 and even 90 per cent of their revenue from mail contracts in 1952,[185] and all of them, as a group, received more than half of their revenue from the mails.

Part of the mail payment in the United States covers the actual cost of service, while the remainder, often a much larger part, represents a subsidy. The Civil Aeronautics Act of 1938 provided that the Board should consider in determining compensation for mail service the "need" of an airline so as to enable it "together with all other revenue" to maintain its operations "to the extent and of the character and quality required for the commerce of the United States, the Postal Service, and the national defense." Thus, airlines with insufficient revenue from passenger and freight traffic receive a higher rate for mail service than those which show an operating profit. Rates change from year to year, depending on the fortunes of individual airlines, rising for an airline with a deficit, falling for one with profits. In general, mail payments represent a substantially smaller part of the total revenue of major airlines than in earlier days but even for these companies, mail contracts are very impor-

mittee on Small Business pointed out: "this was in part due to economic forces. The large certificated airlines had much greater equipment available and were able to meet the market demands for first-class service. Therefore, the irregular airlines were forced into developing a new field of air service." (**12**, p. 8.)

178. **26**, 1951, p. 223.
179. **30**, April 28, 1952, p. 68.
180. **10**, p. 10.
181. **27**, 1953, p. 3; **30**, April 27, 1953, p. 100.

182. **30**, April 27, 1953, pp. 57–59.
183. **12**, p. 16.
184. **35**, pp. 345–46.
185. **30**, April 27, 1953, pp. 50–51. Cf. Table 189.

tant as a source of revenue and a protection against potential losses.[186]

The Civil Aeronautics Board has calculated that in 1951 total mail payments to 33 scheduled domestic airlines operating within continental United States and to terminal points in Canada constituted 9.8 per cent of the aggregate revenue of $623.3 million: 4.3 per cent for mail service and 5.5 per cent as subsidy. The relative importance of mail subsidies to airlines, grouped by the amount of total revenues in 1951, is illustrated by the following figures: [187]

Number of Airlines	Total Airline Revenue, in Millions	Mail Payments as Percentage of Total Revenue	
		Service	Subsidy
33	$623.3	4.3	5.5
4	413.9	4.7	0.9
7	148.2	3.5	6.3
5	30.6	2.6	19.4
4	10.3	2.1	34.1
7	14.9	2.9	58.1
3	3.6	6.8	63.6
3	1.8	14.1	71.4

In many other countries air mail is an even more important source of revenue to airlines. Before World War II, the world's main airlines derived up to 50 per cent of their revenues from carrying mail, and may still obtain 15–20 per cent even though their income from passenger and freight traffic has increased considerably.[188] Trans-Canada Air Lines derived nearly 30 per cent of its total revenues in 1946 from mail service, and British Overseas Airways, nearly 30 per cent in 1946–1947.[189]

The problem of additional payment for air mail has been solved differently in various countries. In the United States, the extra charge for a first-class letter has amounted, since 1948, to double the regular cost. A number of European countries forwarded air mail at ordinary rates even before World War II. Sweden pioneered in this practice, which spread throughout Europe, so that by the summer of 1939 practically every European nation forwarded all first-class mail by air without extra postage when air service promised quicker delivery.[190] In 1937 the United Kingdom introduced the "all up" sys-

tem of carrying first-class mail without surcharge throughout the British Commonwealth. Only Canada remained outside the "all up" system because no transatlantic service was then in operation.[191]

Cargo

Cargo (freight, express and excess baggage) accounted for slightly less than one fifth of the world's airline traffic in 1951 (in terms of ton-miles) and nearly one sixth of the total revenue.[192] For many airlines, particularly in underdeveloped areas, and for carriers predominantly engaged in freight transport, cargo represents a much greater source of revenue, but it is still a minor partner in the business of the large combination airlines. (See Table 190.)

EXPENSES

Operating expenses of airlines are classified as (1) direct transportation costs (cost of flying, maintenance and depreciation of aircraft) and (2) ground and indirect expenses.

In the United States transportation cost has represented less than half the total on domestic lines, but in 1952 it rose to 50.0 per cent, of which the largest part, 28.9 per cent, was used for flying the aircraft, and the remaining 21.1 per cent, for aircraft maintenance and depreciation. The share of direct transportation cost in total expenses has fluctuated from year to year: 50.1 per cent in 1940, 48.8 in 1950 and 50.0 in 1952. On international airlines, this share amounted to 34 per cent in 1944, 49.5 per cent in 1950 and 48.3 per cent in 1952.

Ground and indirect expenses of United States airlines were particularly high in 1943–44, when they absorbed nearly two thirds of total costs, but have since declined. In 1950 and 1951, they were slightly more than half the total on domestic lines; in 1952, half the total. (See Table 191.)

The ratio between direct flying cost and ground and indirect expenses varies from country to country, from airline to airline and from year to year. Of the two major British airlines, one (BEA) spent 53.5 per cent of the total on direct transportation in 1952, and the other (BOAC), 64.1 per cent. Ground and indirect costs constituted in that year from less than 20

186. **54**, pp. 267–78; **51**, pp. 808–11 and 822–25.
187. **11**, pp. 63–64.
188. **3**, pp. 32–33.
189. **3**, p. 36.
190. **23**, p. 346; **58**, pp. 112–13.

191. **61**, p. 236. In 1953, Canada introduced air mail service for all first-class mail, without surcharge.
192. **10**, p. 5.

TABLE 191

OPERATING EXPENSES: SCHEDULED DOMESTIC AND INTERNATIONAL AIRLINES OF THE UNITED STATES, 1940–52

| Type of Airline and Year | Millions of Dollars | | | | Percentage Distribution | | | |
| | Total | Direct Transportation Costs | | Ground and Indirect Expenses | Total | Direct Transportation Costs | | Ground and Indirect Expenses |
		Flight	Other			Flight	Other	
				Domestic				
1940	$ 70.9[a]	$ 22.1	$ 13.1	$ 35.0	100.0[a]	31.5	18.6	49.9
1942	84.4	21.9	14.5	48.0	100.0	25.9	17.2	56.9
1944	124.5	28.2	16.9	79.4	100.0	22.7	13.6	63.7
1946	322.2	70.4	58.8	193.0	100.0	21.8	18.2	59.9
1948	431.6	109.6	90.4	231.6	100.0	25.4	20.9	53.7
1950	494.6	141.8	99.2	253.6	100.0	28.7	20.1	51.3
1951	595.4	173.0	114.9	307.4	100.0	29.1	19.3	51.6
1952	723.4	208.7	152.8	361.9	100.0	28.9	21.1	50.0
				International				
1944	39.2	8.5	4.9	25.9	100.0	21.6	12.4	66.0
1946	139.8	32.0	20.1	87.8	100.0	22.9	14.3	62.8
1948	235.3	67.2	43.8	124.3	100.0	28.6	18.6	52.8
1950	248.3	71.0	51.8	125.5	100.0	28.6	20.9	50.5
1951	269.9	75.1	54.1	140.6	100.0	27.8	20.1	52.1
1952	304.4	87.4	59.5	157.5	100.0	28.7	19.6	51.7

Source: **18**, 1953, pp. 61 and 74.

a. Includes Colonial Airline, for which distribution by type is not available.

per cent to 28 per cent on some airlines of India, Pakistan and New Zealand, but almost 52 per cent for the main Philippine airline (PAL). (See Table 192.)

According to the ICAO, average operating costs per mile for intra-European services are about the same as for transoceanic operations and for long flights across Europe and Asia. Domestic services in the United States and Australia, however, indicate much lower costs than have been attained in international operations anywhere. Though cost figures for Australian airlines are not as complete as those for the United States, the ICAO believes that average costs in Australia are probably lower.[193]

Direct Transportation Costs

The major direct costs are the salaries of flight crews and the cost of fuel and lubricants. In 1952, these constituted nearly 58 per cent of direct costs and about 29 per cent of the total expenses of domestic airlines of the United States.[194]

Maintenance of flying equipment is the next substantial expense. In contrast to highway vehicles, aircraft are checked and overhauled in relation not to mileage performed but to the number of hours in use. Some overhauling is done every time the plane is grounded, so that maintenance is practically continuous, and regular inspections are made every 130 hours. Engines used to be overhauled after every 1,000 hours of operations or less; with their improvement, the ceiling on overhaul time was raised to 1,500 hours; in 1952, to 1,700 hours for some aircraft. It was believed in 1953 that the piston engine will, before capitulating to the turbine, set a standard of a 2,000-hour overhaul span.[195] Longer overhaul periods generally lower overhaul cost per flight-hour.

In contrast to the practice in other branches of transportation, depreciation of flying equipment is considered a direct cost, although aircraft depreciate less on account of use than on account of obsolescence in design.

---

193. **10**, p. 7.
194. **18**, 1953, p. 61.

195. **30**, April 27, 1953, p. 124; **54**, pp. 320–22; **65**, p. 273.

TABLE 192

OPERATING EXPENSES: MAJOR WORLD AIRLINES, 1952

| Country and Airline | Total (In Millions of Dollars) | Percentage Distribution | | | | Country and Airline | Total (In Millions of Dollars) | Percentage Distribution | | | |
| | | Flight Operations | Flight Equipment | | | | | Flight Operations | Flight Equipment | | |
			Maintenance	Depreciation	Other [a]				Maintenance	Depreciation	Other [a]
United States [b]						United Kingdom					
American	$161.0	25.9	24.6	8.8	40.7	BEA	$ 39.8	31.3	19.1	3.1	46.5
Braniff	32.0	28.3	21.8	5.4	44.5	BOAC	98.3	31.3	25.7	7.1	35.9
Colonial	7.4	26.1	19.9	3.5	50.5	France					
Chicago and						Air France	100.1	31.5	22.0	6.6	39.9
Southern	16.3	30.1	15.6	8.7	45.6	Netherlands					
Eastern	102.6	32.3	18.4	11.5	37.8	KLM	65.4	32.4	16.0	10.5	41.1
National	25.6	28.8	20.0	4.5	46.7	Scandinavia					
Northwest	54.1	26.6	26.4	9.0	38.0	SAS	44.9	26.9	19.1	5.8	48.2
Pan						Finland					
American	185.1	28.8	18.2	8.4	44.6	Aero O/Y	2.7	26.6	20.6	2.6	50.2
Panagra	15.7	27.1	16.8	6.3	49.8	Switzerland					
Trans World	145.8	28.6	19.1	10.8	41.5	Swissair	15.8	23.7	18.7	8.3	49.3
United	129.6	29.1	17.1	8.8	45.0	Pakistan					
						Orient					
Canada						Airways	4.2	43.8	26.7	6.3	23.2
Trans-Canada	54.3	21.7	24.6	7.3	46.4	India					
Canadian						Airways India	3.0	62.0	15.5	2.8	19.7
Pacific	13.8	30.5	17.6	7.5	44.4	Philippines					
						PAL	16.4	33.4	8.0	6.8	51.8
Brazil						Union of South Africa					
Panair	25.5	26.4	10.6	7.6	55.4	South African					
Real	8.2	36.3	22.4	4.5	36.8	Airways	6.4	31.5	27.1	10.9	30.5
Argentina						New Zealand					
Aerolineas						Tasman Empire	4.5	34.7	25.5	11.9	27.9
Argentinas	18.4	29.7	14.7	3.1	52.5						

Source: **7,** No. 43, Table 2.

a. Ground and indirect costs.   b. Domestic and international operations.

Ground and Indirect Expenses

Ground and indirect expenses include salaries of all ground personnel, rent for airports, offices and buildings, maintenance and depreciation of ground equipment and so on. Maintenance cost includes repair of station communication equipment, hangars, shop and ramp equipment, motorized vehicles, and buildings. In comparison with maintenance, depreciation of ground equipment is a minor item, since such equipment does not require as large investments as aircraft and loses value less rapidly.

The ICAO has found that the world's airlines are, on the whole, exercising increasingly close control of overhead expenses (ground and indirect) and are trying to reduce costs. These vary greatly from country to country, as well as from airline to airline within a country.

According to the ICAO, ground and indirect expenses per short-ton-mile performed ranged,

TABLE 193

REVENUES AND EXPENSES: OPERATIONAL REVENUES AND EXPENSES OF SELECTED AIRLINES PER SHORT-TON-MILE PERFORMED, 1952

(*In U. S. Cents*)

Country and Airline	Revenues	Expenses Total	Flight	Flight Equipment [a]	Other [b]	Country and Airline	Revenues	Expenses Total	Flight	Flight Equipment [a]	Other [b]
United States [c]						France					
American	24.6	21.1	5.5	7.1	8.6	Air France	32.1	34.0	10.7	9.7	13.6
Braniff	30.8	30.9	8.8	8.4	13.8						
Chicago and						Netherlands					
Southern	32.1	27.8	8.4	6.8	12.7	KLM	30.6	29.4	9.5	7.8	12.1
Colonial	32.3	32.9	8.6	7.7	16.7						
Eastern	24.7	21.4	6.9	6.4	8.1	Scandinavia					
National	23.8	21.2	6.1	5.2	9.9	SAS	37.2	36.9	9.9	9.2	17.8
Northwest	29.2	28.4	7.5	10.1	10.9	Finland					
Pan American	35.1	33.8	9.7	9.0	15.1	Aero O/Y	41.5	40.5	10.8	9.5	20.3
Panagra	45.3	41.2	11.2	9.5	20.5						
Trans World	27.5	24.9	7.1	7.5	10.3	Switzerland					
United	24.8	20.9	6.1	5.3	9.5	Swissair	40.5	40.1	9.5	10.8	19.7
Canada						Pakistan					
Trans-Canada	34.2	32.8	7.1	10.5	15.3	Orient					
Canadian						Airways	33.4	31.1	13.6	10.3	7.2
Pacific	24.8	37.9	11.6	9.5	16.8	Philippines					
Brazil						PAL	36.7	35.5	11.8	5.3	18.4
Panair	45.9	47.7	12.6	8.7	26.4	Union of South Africa					
Argentina						South African					
Aerolineas						Airways	38.1	33.4	10.5	12.7	10.1
Argentinas	30.3	45.5	13.5	8.2	23.9	New Zealand					
United Kingdom						Tasman Empire					
BEA	39.6	42.9	13.4	9.5	20.0	Airways	30.6	33.6	11.6	12.6	9.3
BOAC	33.7	32.7	10.2	10.7	11.8						

Source: **7**, No. 43, Table 1.

a. Maintenance, overhaul and depreciation.

b. Ground and indirect costs.

c. Domestic and international operations.

in 1952, for United States airlines, from 8.1 cents for Eastern to 16.7 cents for Colonial and 20.5 cents for Panagra. Among the airlines of other countries, these expenses amounted to 11.8 cents for United Kingdom's BOAC and 20.0 cents for BEA; to 13.6 cents for Air France and 12.1 cents for KLM. (See Table 193.)

AIRPORT ECONOMICS

The construction costs of airports vary greatly in different parts of the world, depending on the nature of the terrain, runway dimensions, taxi tracts and aprons, landing aids provided, size and type of terminal buildings, and on the general level of wages and prices. An outlay ranging from $10 million to $150 million is required in building a modern airport.[196] In the United States, the total investment in civil airports increased from $42 million in 1926 to $326 million in 1939, $1,027 million in 1945 and $4 billion in 1952.[197]

Airport revenue comes partly from air traffic and, to a larger extent, from facilities and services not essential to air traffic as such: concessions for restaurants, shops, taxi service, sightseeing fees, rental of office space and newspaper and magazine stands. The revenues from landing charges are directly related to the volume of

196. **44**, 1951, No. 4, p. 190.
197. **32**, p. 189. For 1952, acquisition cost.

traffic in terms of the number and size of the aircraft, and to the level of landing charges, which vary greatly from airport to airport. The revenues from concessions are related to the number of embarking and disembarking passengers, but also depend on the proximity of the airport to large centers of population, its location in the route pattern and its attractiveness to airlines as a site for maintenance or administrative work.[198]

For many if not most airports, the largest items in annual costs are depreciation and interest charges. When fully accounted for, they generally amount to about half the total annual cost of maintaining an airport, and often to much more. For example, the ICAO estimated these charges for Le Bourget (Paris) airport at $1,046 million in 1951, as against the operating and maintenance costs of $808 million. For the same year the respective figures for some other international airports were as follows (in thousands of dollars): [199]

	Depreciation and Interest	Maintenance and Operating Costs
Montreal	$ 479	$ 596
Washington, D.C.	1,326	1,093
Miami	1,896	997
New York (La Guardia)	3,145	1,787
New York (Idlewild)	6,383	1,142
San Francisco	2,210	494
London (International)	2,113	2,198
London (Northolt)	384	1,698
Prestwick	385	1,178
Netherlands (Shipol)	1,026	524
Copenhagen	376	165
Stockholm	358	172
Oslo	190	78
Helsinki	171	141
Lisbon	290	111

The average airport cost per landing calculated on 750,000 scheduled international landings at 450 international airports was $97 in 1951, of which the airlines paid $24; other airport revenue provided $27; the deficit of $46 was borne by the airports.[200]

Until recently 99 out of 100 airports of the world were financial failures, if an accounting is made on a commercial basis.[201] But the ICAO believes that costs at most international airports

are not increasing as fast as revenue from traffic, since landing charges and concession revenues generally increase with the size of the aircraft. Thus, the financial position of many airports has begun to improve, except for those airports which need runway extensions and new terminal buildings. This trend will continue, according to the ICAO.[202]

INTERNATIONAL AGREEMENTS ON CIVIL AVIATION

In no other field of transportation is international cooperation as essential as in commercial aviation: the chief advantage of aviation is speed in overcoming great distances and many countries are too small for merely national operations. The establishment of international services requires a complex organization of aeronautics, radio and meteorology.

The greatest difficulties encountered in establishing such an organization have been political rather than technical. Because civil aviation is or can be linked with military aviation, it has been government controlled in nearly every country and used as an instrument of government in one way or another.

The Paris and Havana Air Conventions

The first general air convention was concluded in 1919 at the Paris Peace Conference. This convention recognized the complete and exclusive sovereignty of each nation over the air above its territory (metropolitan and colonial). Each contracting state undertook to permit innocent passage of the aircraft of the other parties above its territory in time of peace. It was entitled to prohibit, for military reasons or in the interest of public safety, the aircraft of the other contracting states from flying over certain parts of its territory.

By the summer of 1939, this convention had been ratified by 39 states, of which two (Austria and Czechoslovakia) had meanwhile been absorbed by Germany, and four (Bolivia, Chile, Panama and Iran) had subsequently withdrawn. The United States, Germany, the USSR, China, Brazil, Mexico, Cuba, Hungary and Turkey did not ratify the convention. The United States was developing its domestic service and had no particular interest in international agreements. Not until 1928, when the United States planned to extend its air routes to Latin Amer-

---

198. **4**, pp. 12–13.
199. **4**, p. 33.
200. **4**, p. 29.
201. **61**, pp. 286 and 291.

202. **4**, pp. 13 and 27.

ica, did arrangements with neighboring countries become necessary. A Pan-American Conference in Havana in 1928 adopted a convention similar in the main to the Paris convention.

Germany refused in 1923 to subscribe to the Paris convention except on equal footing and in 1929 initiated negotiations to this effect. After long deliberations, almost all obstacles to German accession were removed, the last being the question of languages for the publications of the International Commission for Air Navigation, set up by the Paris Conference. World War II broke out, however, before negotiations were concluded.

The USSR has kept aloof from international agreements and services, refusing to permit flying over its territory.

The principle of national sovereignty above a country's territory made air crossing of political boundaries subject to international agreement. The right to operate international air service was obtained through a unilateral concession or a bilateral agreement granting reciprocal privileges to contracting parties. Before World War II, concessions to foreign airlines became the subject of hard bargaining between governments, rather than between a government and a foreign airline.[203]

The complications of such bargaining may be seen from a few examples. In 1935 a British airline tried to establish service to Portugal via France and Spain. The Spanish government refused permission, even when asked to allow a nonstop flight over its territory. When it finally granted permission, in 1940, it was too late, since the increased range of aircraft made it possible to by-pass Spain. When British airlines tried to establish air mail service to India, Italy refused the use of its airports. Rerouting across Central Europe required new negotiations. Since Turkey had closed its air to foreign planes, the British tried to acquire flying rights over Greece, which then had a strong bargaining position. Britain, in turn, tried to bar foreign competition from the air over the Empire, for a time blocking a French route to Indochina and putting up a "No Admittance" sign at Hong Kong, thus depriving Pan American Airways of this trans-Pacific terminal. The United States refused landing rights in Hawaii to all foreign airlines, assuring its monopoly in trans-Pacific flying. Australia, thus prevented from establishing air services to

Canada, denied entry to Pan American Airways.[204]

The International Civil Aviation Conference

Global development of aviation during World War II revealed the inadequacy of most prewar regulations. The United States called an air conference in Chicago in 1944, which was attended by fifty-five Allied and neutral states. The conference reaffirmed the principle of air sovereignty over each state's territory and assured the right of each state to reserve domestic traffic to its own airlines. No scheduled international air service may operate over or into the territory of a contracting state without its consent. Each signatory state undertook to collaborate in securing the highest degree of uniformity in regulations and standards relating to aircraft, airways, and auxiliary services. An International Civil Aviation Organization was to come into existence when half the participating states had ratified the convention.[205] By April 1, 1951, 58 states had become affiliated with the ICAO, but one of these, China, withdrew on May 31, 1951. The USSR remains outside the organization.[206]

Commercial rights in international aviation were dealt with in two separate statements: the so-called Two Freedoms (or Air Transit Agreement) and the Five Freedoms (or International Air Transport Agreement) Agreements. The two freedoms of the air are the privilege of flying across the territory of any contracting state without landing; and of landing for nontraffic purposes (refueling or repair). (See Figure 116.)

The five freedoms grant, in addition, the privilege of discharging passengers, cargo and mail in any contracting state; taking on passengers, cargo and mail for the country under whose flag the aircraft flies; and carrying passengers, cargo and mail to and from the territory of any other contracting state. However, traffic from one point to another in a single country (domestic traffic) is prohibited; also, a plane must start in its own metropolitan territory and proceed to its most distant terminal with reasonable directness.

By May 1952, forty-one countries, including the United States, had subscribed to the Two Freedoms Agreement, while only twelve states had signed the Five Freedoms Agreement. The

---

203. **53**, p. 42.

204. **65**, pp. 121–22.
205. The ICAO began its work in April 1947.
206. **9**, p. 50.

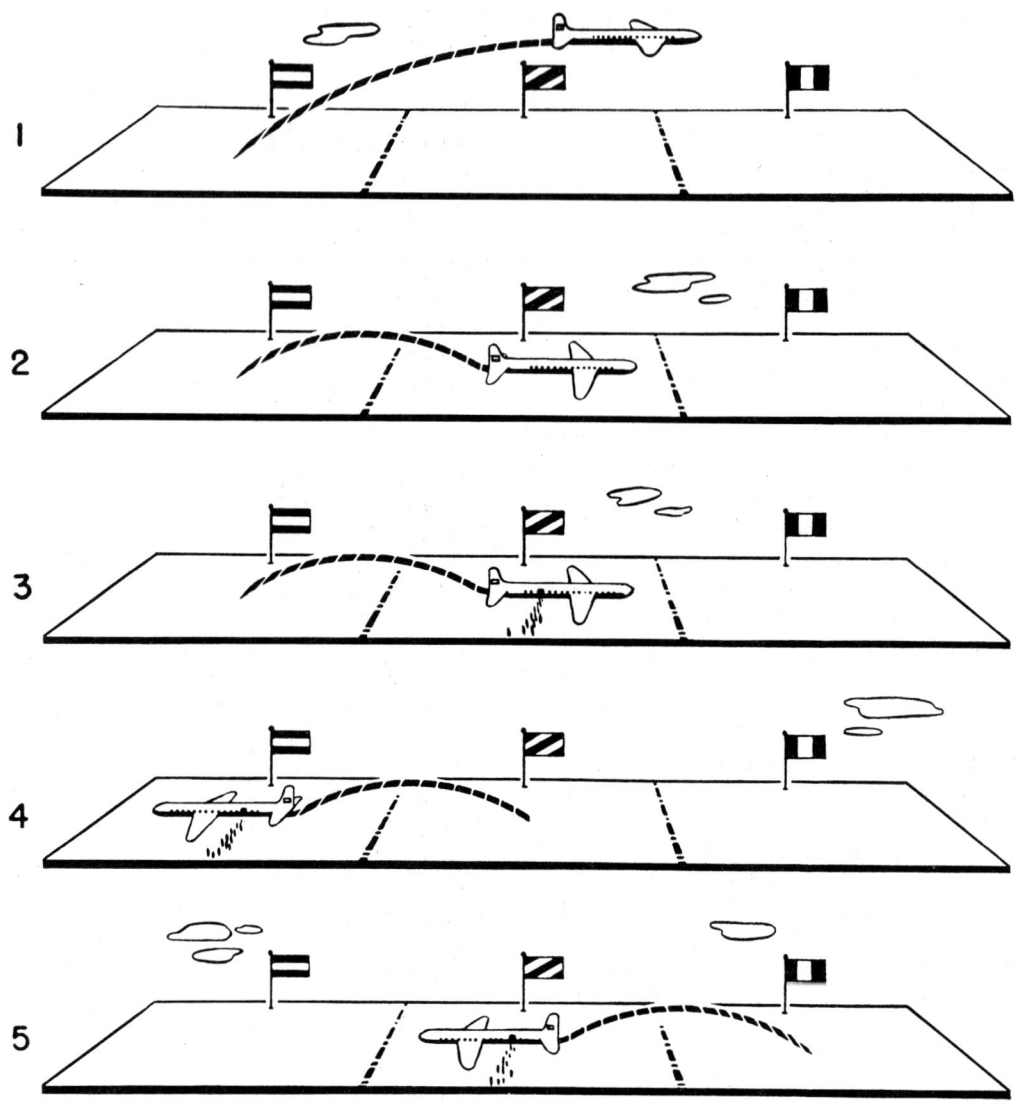

Courtesy of McGraw-Hill Book Company (**65**)

This figure illustrates the "Five Freedoms" embodied in the International Air Transport Agreement: 1. Flying across the territory of any contracting state without landing. 2. Landing rights for refueling and repair. 3. Discharging passengers, mail and cargo in any contracting state. 4. Taking on passengers, mail and cargo destined for the country under whose flag the aircraft flies. 5. Carrying passengers, mail and cargo to and from the territory of any contracting state.

FIGURE 116. INTERNATIONAL AGREEMENTS ON AVIATION: THE FIVE FREEDOMS OF THE AIR

United States signed the latter agreement but withdrew in 1947, as did also China, Nicaragua and the Dominican Republic.[207]

Since only a few states have been willing to accept the Five Freedoms Agreement, bilateral arrangement for international operations became necessary in most cases. A standard form for such agreements was adopted by the Chicago Conference and has been influential in all bilateral negotiations.[208] As of June 30, 1950, the United States had bilateral air agreements with 43 countries in which its carriers were permitted to serve 130 points.[209]

---

207. **10**, pp. 91–93; **65**, pp. 229–34.

208. For more detailed description of international regulations of air transport, see **53**, *passim;* **64**, pp. 608–31; **65**, pp. 225–43; and various publications of the ICAO.

209. **19**, 1950, p. 20.

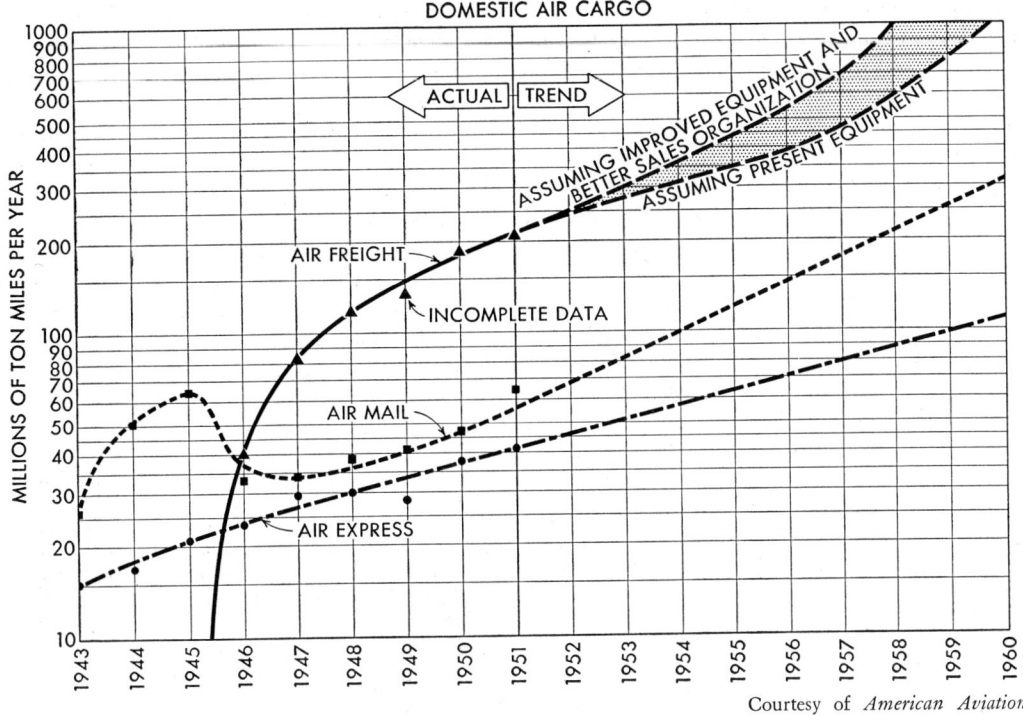

Courtesy of *American Aviation*

FIGURE 117. AIR CARGO OF THE UNITED STATES: TRENDS AND PROJECTIONS, 1943-60

OUTLOOK

Several decades ago a Canadian scholar, Charles Camsell, spent three and a half years exploring the northern part of his country on foot and in canoes. He met Eskimos who had never seen a white man, had no iron and barbed their lances with walrus bones. Some thirty-five years later, covering the same territory by airplane in ten days as Canada's Deputy Minister of Natural Resources, he found Eskimos using boats with outboard motors, repeating rifles, cameras and sewing machines, all of which had been delivered by plane.[210]

As the potentialities of the "age of flight" are fully realized, no place on the globe will be as completely isolated as northern Canada was until recently. The demand for transport in scattered and sparsely populated areas is not enough to attract capital to railroad or highway ventures, but the airplane is responding to an increasing demand in underdeveloped parts of the world and will do so more and more.

New air routes will be created and existing ones developed. New aircraft will be designed

to assure even speedier travel and new uses for airplanes will be devised.

The growth of the youthful air-service industry has been spectacular, and it has not known periods of drawn-out depression, such as older means of transportation have experienced. To some extent, this fact accounts for its dynamism and its easier acceptance of innovations in equipment. Further expansion is certain to come, provided the industry combines speed of transport with prices accessible to increasing numbers of consumers and continues to improve the safety and dependability of service.

Passenger service will continue to be the mainstay of air operations. The industry will probably try to cut time lost in ground transportation to and from airports by means of helicopter and air-taxi services and mid-city terminals. Though the helicopter has less speed, use of it will increase, since it can assure a quicker city-to-city schedule on distances up to 250 miles, which would include such routes as Paris-London and Washington-New York.[211] Large helicopters carrying from 20 to 30 passengers at cruising speeds exceeding 120 miles per hour were expected, in

210. **16**, pp. 6-7.

211. **10**, p. 12.

1952, to be in use within a few years.[212] In 1953 the Belgian Sabena initiated the world's first international helicopter passenger service between Liège and Antwerp and Lille in France, Rotterdam in the Netherlands, and Cologne and Bonn in Germany. The British BEA established helicopter flights between London and Birmingham.[213] For long-distance travel, commercial jet aircraft will become as common as stratocruisers are today.

Cargo service by air will also expand, though it will remain small in relation to total freight transport in countries well provided with other forms of transportation. Even there, however, air cargo potential may become considerable, and this service may generate additional traffic. *American Aviation* estimates, for example, that air freight in the United States may reach the level of a billion ton-miles a year by 1960 with present aircraft, but with new equipment and a stream-

lined sales organization will touch this mark by 1958.[214] (See Figure 117.)

Air transport will stimulate international trade in many commodities as remote markets come closer to hand. Some far inland cities are already more accessible to intercontinental traffic than many harbors.[215]

As the age of flight spreads its wings over our globe, the distance from industrial centers to markets will shrink. The decentralization of urban agglomerations started by the motor vehicle will be intensified. Private flying will expand, and the range of recreation will be extended within a country and beyond its borders to remote corners of the earth.

---

212. **56,** November 1952, p. 4.
213. **48,** October 1953, p. 11 and January 1954, p. 15.

214. Only domestic scheduled airlines and cargo carriers are considered in this projection. It does not allow for small irregular carriers, "air tramps," that operate for hire and account for a substantial aggregate volume of cargo traffic: about 33 million ton-miles in 1950 and nearly 80 million in 1951. (**30,** April 28, 1952, pp. 109–12.)
215. **43,** p. 290.

PART III. GOVERNMENTS

CHAPTER 12

NATIONS AND GOVERNMENTS

THE MODERN WORLD is organized politically as a system of units of two types: independent states and non-self-governing territories.[1]

INDEPENDENT STATES

Whether an area is an independent state (or part of such a state) or a non-self-governing territory is not always clear. The United Nations, for example, lists Alaska among "non-self-governing territories" and doubtless will continue to do so until it achieves statehood. On the other hand, satellites of the USSR, although completely controlled by the Kremlin, are classified among the independent states.[2]

The Number of States

The Statistical Office of the UN lists eighty-seven independent states.[3] The number, however, includes such political bodies as Vatican City (890 inhabitants in 1948), Andorra (5,000 inhabitants), Monaco (22,000), Liechtenstein (14,000), San Marino (13,000), Trucial Oman (80,000) and Qatar (20,000).[4] Without these, there would be eighty — 22 in the Western Hemisphere, 25 in Europe, 25 in Asia, 5 in Africa, 2 in Oceania, and the USSR. (See Table 194.) The UN list does not include Tibet and Taiwan and shows Germany and Korea as single nations.[5] When Western and Eastern Germany,

North and South Korea, Tibet and Taiwan are counted separately, the world has eighty-four independent states and seven small areas which possess certain characteristics of independent states.[6]

This number is surprisingly small when compared with the multitude of independent states — or statelike bodies — in the past. In Aristotle's time, there were some 160 city-republics and kingdoms on the Peloponnesian peninsula alone; in the Middle Ages, Europe, the present territory of Russia and the Middle East were divided among scores of independent princedoms. On the other hand, the number of states is much larger now than in the middle of the eighteenth century, when there were not more than two or three dozen independent states in the world and not a single one in the Western Hemisphere, which consisted solely of colonies and plantations of England, France, Spain and Portugal.

Processes of unification and disintegration have succeeded each other in the political history of different areas. Large empires absorbed dozens of formerly independent princedoms. The partition of Africa among colonial powers in the 1880's put an end to the existence of some 2,000 independent tribal "kingdoms." On the other hand, the disintegration of old empires and the emancipation of colonies called into being new independent states in America and Asia; the same process may now be discerned in Africa.

From the fifteenth through the nineteenth centuries, the prevailing trend in Europe and areas under the domination of European powers was toward integration and reduction of the number of states.[7] The same process resulted in

---

1. The United Nations emphasizes this distinction in statistical tables on world population. The distinction was less prominent in similar tables of the League of Nations. (Cf. **1**, 1942–44, pp. 12–23 for the League of Nations and **2**, 1949–50, pp. 17–27 and **6**, 1949–50, pp. 71–83 for the United Nations.)

2. The classification of the United Nations, followed in this chapter, does not use the term "independent states" but makes a clear distinction between "non-self-governing" and "dependent" areas on the one hand and other territories, on the other.

3. Adding Libya to 86 states listed in **2**, 1951, pp. 91–103 and **6**, 1951, pp. 21–33.

4. **4**. Cf. **2** and **6**.

5. For Germany this classification is justified by the fact that neither Berlin nor Eastern Germany can be regarded as an independent state. Eastern Germany can be classified either as an area under the Russian military occupation, like some islands in the Pacific occupied by

U.S. troops, or as a part of Germany temporarily separated from the rest by force of arms. The latter classification would also take care of the ambiguous international status of Berlin.

6. Vatican City, Monaco, Liechtenstein, San Marino, Andorra, Trucial Oman and Qatar. The data in Table 194 refer to midyear 1952 and do not take into account the political units that have emerged from the settlement of the war in Indochina.

7. **27**.

563

TABLE 194

POLITICAL ORGANIZATION OF THE WORLD: AREA AND POPULATION OF INDEPENDENT STATES, MIDYEAR 1952

State	Area, in Thousands of Square Miles	Population, in Millions	State	Area, in Thousands of Square Miles	Population, in Millions
North America			Europe (*continued*)		
United States			Spain [e]	130.3	28.3
(continental)	3,022.4	157.0	Italy	78.0	46.9
Canada	2,578.0	14.4	Yugoslavia	66.5	16.7
			Romania	61.5	16.5
Middle America			Bulgaria	28.7	7.5
Mexico	510.0	26.9	Albania	7.4	1.3
Guatemala	28.2	3.0	Greece [f]	34.3	7.8
El Salvador	8.8	2.0			
Honduras	39.7	1.6	USSR	5,768.0	210.0
Nicaragua	38.3	1.1	Asia		
Costa Rica	13.2	0.8	China [g]	2,521.7	463.5
Panama	19.2	0.8	Mongolia	419.8	1.0
Cuba	29.7	5.7	Korea [h]	57.2	29.3
Haiti	7.2	3.2	Japan	95.5	85.5
Dominican Republic	12.8	2.2	Turkey [i]	198.7	22.0
			Lebanon	2.4	1.3
South America			Israel	3.4	1.4
Venezuela	236.2	5.3	Syria	49.4	3.4
Colombia	295.0	11.8	Jordan	2.3	0.5
Ecuador	71.0	3.2	Saudi Arabia	500.0	6.0
Brazil	2,205.6	54.5	Yemen	50.5	4.6
Peru	323.5	8.9	Kuwait	5.4	0.2
Bolivia	276.9	3.1	Bahrein	0.2	0.1
Paraguay	105.4	1.3	Iraq	112.7	5.2
Chile	192.1	5.9	Iran	422.0	19.5
Uruguay	48.4	2.4	Afghanistan	250.0	12.0
Argentina	723.6	18.1	Pakistan	246.0	76.6
			India [j]	803.0	367.6
Europe			Nepal	36.3	7.1
United Kingdom	63.2	50.4	Bhutan	13.0	0.3
Ireland	18.2	2.9	Burma	175.5	18.9
Iceland	26.7	0.1	Thailand	133.0	19.2
France [a]	142.7	42.6	Ceylon	17.0	7.9
Luxembourg	0.7	0.3	Indonesia	386.3	78.2
Belgium	7.9	11.7	Philippines	77.4	20.6
Netherlands	8.7	10.4			
Denmark [b]	11.1	4.3	Africa		
Sweden	116.3	7.1	Egypt	260.0	21.4
Norway	84.0	3.3	Ethiopia	275.0	15.3
Finland	87.3	4.1	Libya	679.5	1.1
Germany [c]	91.5	70.4	Liberia	28.9	1.7
Poland	80.7	25.5	Union of South Africa	316.9	12.9
Czechoslovakia	33.1	12.7			
Switzerland	10.7	4.8	Oceania		
Austria	21.7	6.9	Australia	1,995.3	8.6 [k]
Hungary	24.9	9.5	New Zealand	69.4	2.0
Portugal [d]	23.8	8.5			

Sources: For area, **6**, 1949–50, pp. 71–83; for population, **5**, December 1952. Some figures estimated by the authors on the basis of data for preceding years.

a. Includes the Saar.
b. Includes the Faeroes.
c. All four zones and Berlin.
d. Includes the Azores and Madeira.
e. Includes the Balearic and Canary Islands.
f. Includes the Dodecanese.

g. Includes Tibet and Taiwan.
h. North and South Korea together.
i. Includes European part.
j. Includes Kashmir-Jammu.
k. Excludes aboriginals.

the unification of eastern Europe and northern Asia under the czars of Russia. The movement was reversed after World War I by the disintegration of the Austro-Hungarian and Ottoman empires, cession of limitrophes from Russia and the beginning of colonial emancipation. In the past three decades, the trend has been toward an increase in the number of independent states, mainly as a result of the liberation of colonies and the termination of mandates. This movement has been partly offset by the subjugation of adjacent states by Nazi Germany (nullified as a result of World War II) and the occupation of limitrophe areas by the USSR. All in all, the movement toward disintegration of empires based on conquest is still in progress.

Area and Population

The politically organized area of the world — excluding the Antarctic, certain uninhabited regions of the Arctic and a few small islands — is estimated by the Statistical Office of the UN at 35 million square miles. Independent states (including the British dominions) occupy approximately 80 per cent of this area, or 28 million square miles. Their population totaled, in the middle of 1952, approximately 2,258 million, or about 92 per cent of the world's total.[8] The distribution of this total area and population among continents is shown in Table 195.

Distribution by Size

Classification of states in terms of area or population is, of course, arbitrary, but the grouping in Table 196 does permit certain generalizations.

Roughly half the total population and 40 per cent of the area of all independent states are represented by the four states with the largest population — China, India, the USSR and the United States. At the other extreme, 23 states with less than 3 million inhabitants each had in all 29.4 million inhabitants in the middle of 1952, and 24 states in the group with 3–10 million inhabitants had a population of 141.9 million. Thirty-eight independent states had less than 7.0 million inhabitants each, and forty-two had more than 7.0 million. Nepal and Sweden, each with 7.1 million inhabitants, were in the median position. The states clustered around the

8. Cf. Chapter 14.

TABLE 195

POLITICAL ORGANIZATION OF THE WORLD: NUMBER, AREA AND POPULATION OF INDEPENDENT STATES IN EACH CONTINENT, MIDYEAR 1952

Continent	*Number*	*Area, in Thousands of Square Miles*	*Population, in Millions*
Total	80	28,016	2,258.0
North America	2	5,600	171.4
Middle America	10	707	47.3
South America	10	4,477	114.5
Europe	25	1,260	400.5
USSR	1	5,768	210.0
Asia	25	6,579	1,251.3
Africa	5	1,560	52.4
Oceania	2	2,065	10.6

Source: Table 194.

median point and their populations (in millions) were as follows:

Saudi Arabia	6.0
Austria	6.9
Nepal	7.1
Sweden	7.1
Bulgaria	7.5
Greece	7.8

The average (arithmetic mean) population of an independent state was 28.2 million.[9] Fourteen states were above this average and 66 below. The countries closest to the average had the following populations (in millions):

Poland	25.5
Spain	28.3
Korea	29.3

Size and Economic Development

The two states with the largest populations in the world — China and India — belong to the region in which a subsistence economy prevails. By modern standards, both countries have low per capita income, low levels of consumption, high mortality rates, and low expectation of life at birth — all features characteristic of underdeveloped areas.[10] With one third of mankind, these two countries have only 7–8 per cent of the

9. Excluding the seven minor areas with certain features of independent states; including Tibet and Taiwan in China; and counting Germany and Korea as one each.

10. See **35**, Chapter 13.

TABLE 196

SIZE OF INDEPENDENT STATES CLASSIFIED BY AREA AND POPULATION, 1952

(Area in Thousands of Square Miles; Population in Millions)

Area	Population				
	Very Large (*More than 100 Million*)	*Large* (*40–100 Million*)	*Medium* (*10–40 Million*)	*Small* (*3–10 Million*)	*Very Small* (*Less than 3 Million*)
More than 500,000 square miles	USSR United States China India	Brazil	Canada Argentina Mexico	Australia	Libya
Population Area	1,197.5 12,115.1	54.5 2,205.6	59.4 3,811.6	8.6 1,995.3	1.1 679.5
200,000 to 500,000 square miles		Pakistan Indonesia	Egypt Iran Ethiopia Afghanistan Union of South Africa Colombia	Peru Saudi Arabia Venezuela Bolivia	Mongolia
Population Area	— —	154.8 632.3	92.9 1,818.9	23.3 1,336.6	1.0 419.8
100,000 to 200,000 square miles		France	Spain Turkey Burma Thailand	Sweden Chile Iraq	Paraguay
Population Area	— —	42.6 142.7	88.4 637.5	18.2 421.1	1.3 105.4
50,000 to 100,000 square miles		Japan Germany United Kingdom Italy	Korea Poland Philippines Yugoslavia Romania	Yemen Finland Norway Ecuador	New Zealand
Population Area	— —	253.2 328.2	108.6 343.3	15.2 292.8	2.0 69.4
20,000 to 50,000 square miles			Czechoslovakia	Hungary Portugal Greece Bulgaria Austria Nepal Cuba Syria	Guatemala Uruguay Honduras Nicaragua Iceland Liberia
Population Area	— —	— —	12.7 33.1	56.4 248.8	9.9 210.2
Less than 20,000 square miles			Netherlands Belgium	Ceylon Switzerland Denmark Haiti	Ireland Dominican Republic El Salvador Albania Lebanon Israel Costa Rica Panama Jordan Luxembourg Bhutan Kuwait Bahrein
Population Area	— —	— —	22.1 16.6	20.2 46.0	14.1 107.0

Source: Based on Table 194.

world's income and an even smaller fraction of its industrial capacity.

Except possibly for these countries, there is no visible correlation between the size of a nation's population and its economic development. Both rich and poor countries are found among large, medium and small states. A large proportion of the comparatively prosperous, highly developed nations are in the group with 3–10 million inhabitants — Australia, Sweden, Switzerland, Denmark, Finland and Norway. The Netherlands, with a population just over 10 million, belongs in the same group.

Another cluster of modern, progressive states is in the group with 40–70 million inhabitants: Germany, the United Kingdom, France, Italy.

When independent countries and other areas for which data are available are arrayed by size of population — from China and India to Luxembourg and Iceland — the lack of correlation between the size of a state and the level of economic development becomes obvious. (See Table 197; cf. Figure 118.) This circumstance is worth noting since, other conditions being equal, a large state undeniably has a better chance for economic growth because of greater variety of natural resources, the possibility of regional specialization, a vast domestic market, and political power which ensures access to remote sources of raw materials and markets. The fact that despite these advantages prosperity does not parallel size, suggests that the advantages of bigness may be offset by other factors. A big state is more inclined than a small one to isolate itself from the rest of the world. Moreover, the conflict of interests among big states has often helped their smaller neighbors to preserve their independence and develop their resources.[11]

The question of the size of states has attracted the attention of political thinkers since the origin of political science. Plato and Aristotle noticed the striking contrast between the tiny city-republics in Greece and the huge empires and metropolitan cities in the Orient. They believed, however, that only very small states could be organized as free democratic republics. Both Plato and Aristotle visualized the "ideal

state" as a small closely knit community of some 5,000 households.[12]

Rome gave the Western world the idea of a large centralized nation — a pattern of political organization which the Greeks associated with the barbarian empires of the Orient.

After the disintegration of the Roman Empire, Western Europe became an agglomeration of petty princedoms and city republics, often without firmly established borders. The history of the Middle Ages is a record of bloody struggles among local feudal lords and of the gradual crystallization of their lands into larger political units. At that time the idea of small states became associated with pugnacity and continuous aimless clashes, while centralization and integration of political power began to mean peace and security. The emperors and the Roman Catholic Church became the proponents of the idea of the large centralized state.

Many political thinkers in the eighteenth and nineteenth centuries likewise were firmly convinced of the advantages of large states and this idea has left traces in modern political thinking.

Many students believe that modern industry and new means of transportation have outmoded small states of 3–5 million inhabitants, which are neither self-sufficient nor able to defend themselves. On the other hand, it can be argued that these criteria of the desirable size of a state do not apply to present conditions. No nation in the world today is completely self-sufficient; in fact, self-sufficiency is no longer regarded as the goal of a state. Moreover, experience has shown that no state is large enough and strong enough to rely on its own military and economic resources as a safeguard against attack by another state or a coalition of states. Alliances seem to be a better protection against aggression than the bigness of an individual state.[13]

---

11. Of course, a country with a population of a few million, such as Tibet, may likewise isolate itself from the surrounding world, and there are many examples of small states that have exhausted their resources in futile military ventures against their neighbors, such as the tiny republics and kingdoms of ancient Greece.

12. In the *Laws* Plato described the ideal state as a community consisting of 5,040 citizen families. (**24,** Vol. 4, p. 435.) In the *Republic* he expressed the opinion that a state does not need more than 1,000 well-trained warriors to defend it, suggesting that this is the ideal number of free citizen families in a state that is neither large nor small, but self-sufficient. (*Ibid.,* Vol. 2, p. 138.) For Aristotle a state with more than 5,000 citizens was a monstrosity: it "will require a territory as large as Babylon, or some other huge site, if so many persons are to be supported in idleness, together with their women and attendants, who will be a multitude many times as great." (**9,** pp. 93–94.)

13. Plato realized the importance of alliances for the security of a small state. Because of superior training, the

TABLE 197

SIZE AND PER CAPITA INCOME OF SELECTED STATES, ARRAYED BY POPULATION, 1949–52

(*Per Capita Income in U.S. Dollars*)

State	Population 1952, in Millions	Per Capita Income Around 1949–52		State	Population 1952, in Millions	Per Capita Income Around 1949–52	
China	463.5	$ 35	(1949)	Sweden	7.1	$1,000	(1951)
India	367.0	54	(1948)	Austria	6.9	374	(1952)
USSR	[210.0]	[200]	(1949)	Malaya	6.6	78	(1950)
United States	157.0	1,850	(1952)	Saudi Arabia	6.0	80	(1949)
Japan	85.5	160	(1951)	Chile	5.9	48	(1950)
Indonesia	78.2	35	(1949)	Kenya	5.8	41	(1950)
Pakistan	76.6	56	(1949)	Cuba	5.7	360	(1952)
Brazil	54.5	114	(1951)	Venezuela	5.3	423	(1951)
United Kingdom	50.4	752	(1952)	Iraq	5.2	85	(1949)
Western Germany	48.5	491	(1952)	Switzerland	4.8	976	(1951)
Italy	46.9	265	(1952)	Yemen	4.6	40	(1949)
France	42.6	685	(1952)	Denmark	4.3	698	(1951)
Spain	28.3	155	(1951)	Finland	4.1	646	(1951)
Mexico	26.9	170	(1950)	Syria	3.4	100	(1949)
Poland	25.5	[200]	(1949)	Norway	3.3	704	(1952)
Turkey	22.0	160	(1951)	Haiti	3.2	40	(1949)
Egypt	21.4	100	(1949)	Ecuador	3.2	40	(1949)
Philippines	20.6	125	(1951)	Bolivia	3.1	95	(1950)
Iran	19.5	85	(1949)	Guatemala	3.0	174	(1951)
South Korea	19.4	35	(1949)	Ireland	2.9	356	(1951)
Thailand	19.2	55	(1950)	Uruguay	2.4	331	(1949)
Burma	18.9	35	(1951)	Puerto Rico	2.2	400	(1951)
Argentina	18.1	282	(1951)	Southern Rhodesia	2.2	103	(1951)
Yugoslavia	16.7	271	(1951)	Dominican Republic	2.2	190	(1952)
Ethiopia	15.3	38	(1949)	El Salvador	2.0	92	(1949)
Canada	14.4	1,300	(1952)	New Zealand	2.0	861	(1951)
Union of South Africa	12.9	243	(1951)	Northern Rhodesia	2.0	50	(1950)
Czechoslovakia	12.7	345	(1951)	Liberia	1.7	38	(1949)
Afghanistan	12.0	50	(1949)	Honduras	1.6	83	(1949)
Colombia	11.8	196	(1950)	Jamaica	1.5	166	(1950)
Belgium	11.7	701	(1952)	Israel	1.4	389	(1949)
Netherlands	10.4	444	(1952)	Lebanon	1.3	125	(1949)
Hungary	9.5	269	(1949)	Paraguay	1.3	84	(1949)
Peru	8.9	110	(1951)	Nicaragua	1.1	90	(1949)
Australia	8.6	834	(1951)	Costa Rica	0.8	125	(1949)
Portugal	8.5	183	(1951)	Panama	0.8	183	(1949)
Ceylon	7.9	120	(1951)	Luxembourg	0.3	553	(1949)
Greece	7.8	252	(1949)	Iceland	0.1	476	(1949)

Sources: For population, **2**, 1952, pp. 89–102, and December 1953. Data for per capita income in 1949 are taken from **4**; data for more recent years are computed by the authors on the basis of **7** (for national income) and **3** (for population and exchange rates). Data in brackets are rough estimates.

Footnote 13 continued from page 567

warriors of his ideal state can withstand two or three times their own number, but in the face of an imminent aggression, this state sends an ambassador to the neighboring city telling it "what is the truth: Silver and gold we neither have nor are permitted to have, but you may; do you therefore come and help us in war, and take the spoils." And Plato asks, "Who, on hearing these words, would choose to fight against lean wiry dogs, rather than with the dogs on their side, against fat and tender sheep?" (**24**, Vol. 2, p. 137.)

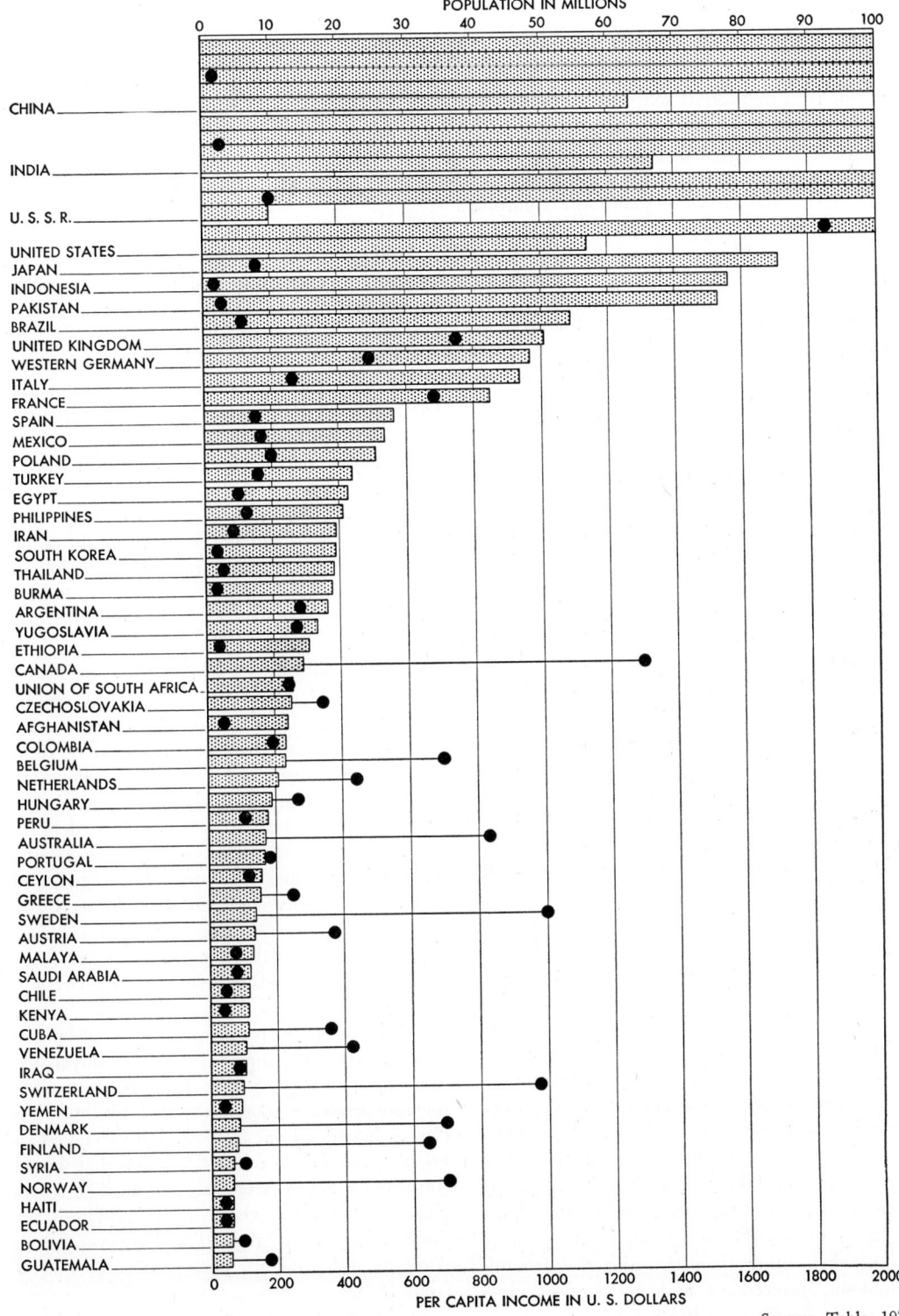

FIGURE 118. SIZE AND PER CAPITA INCOME OF SELECTED STATES ARRAYED BY POPULATION, 1949–52

States are arrayed by the number of inhabitants in midyear 1952. The population of each state is represented by the length of the bar or bars. Per capita income is shown by the position of the dot.

The Life Cycle of Independent States

Today's independent states are not much older than the trees in a forest: some are a hundred or a hundred and fifty years old and others are just taking root in the spaces cleared by the fall of old giants. A few thousand-year-old patriarchs tower above the crowd — some still vigorous, others approaching decay.

THE AGE OF STATES

The exact age of a state cannot always be established. Some existed for thousands of years as independent political units on approximately the same sites and under their present or similar names, then disappeared temporarily from the political scene, destroyed by invaders or absorbed by conquerors, only to return to political existence centuries later, often as bearers of a civilization imposed upon them by their foreign masters. The continuity of the political existence of ancient nations such as Egypt, Persia and India has been interrupted by foreign domination time and again; Spain was ruled by the Moors for five hundred years and needed another two hundred and fifty years to regain, step by step, its unity and independence; nearly all the Balkan Peninsula and Middle East were parts of the Ottoman Empire from the fifteenth to the nineteenth century. It is difficult to identify the Hungary within the borders fixed by the Treaty of Trianon after World War I as a direct successor to the kingdom of the same name established in A.D. 1001.

For an understanding of the present political organization of the world, traces of the earliest settlements on the territory of a nation are less significant than the time when, and the circumstances under which, it became an independent political unit. The United States, for example, came into existence as a state when the former British colonies along the Atlantic coast gained their independence and established a common government; the existence of Italy as a modern state dates from the year in which, after centuries of discord, it was united under the House of Savoy (1861); Germany entered the political scene when more than two dozen Germanic kingdoms, princedoms and independent cities merged in the German Reich (1871).

Even with this reservation, the date at which a nation achieved unity and independence is not always clear; some had been actually independent in internal affairs before they became independent units on the international scene; others, after having declared themselves independent, faced a long struggle, sometimes against their former masters, but more often among internal factions.[14]

The Western Hemisphere

All the states in the Western Hemisphere were built from parts of European colonial empires — British and French in the north, Spanish and Portuguese in the south.[15]

Whether the existence of the United States as an independent nation is dated from the Declaration of Independence (1776) or from the recognition of its independence by Great Britain (1783), it is the oldest existing nation in the Americas. Cuba is the youngest. (See Table 198).

In 1804 the island of Haiti, formerly dominated by France, obtained independence, but its two parts — Haiti and the Dominican Republic — did not become separate states until forty years later.

Internal political troubles in Spain and Portugal and the invasion of the Iberian Peninsula by Napoleon (1808) made untenable the vast overseas possessions of these countries. After 1810, the former Spanish and Portuguese colonies in the Western Hemisphere were in political and social turmoil. Mexico became independent in 1821, after a decade of bloody struggle. Guatemala, El Salvador, Honduras, Nicaragua and Costa Rica gained independence from Spain, almost by default, and formed the Central American Union. Two decades later, in 1838, the Union was dissolved, and the five small republics were established.

The birth of independence in Venezuela, Colombia, Ecuador, Panama, Peru and Bolivia was more dramatic. Starting in 1800, their struggle for independence soon developed into ruthless clashes between local factions. Bolivar failed in his desperate efforts to build a union that would constitute a South American nation. The struggle ended in 1830, when the six provinces became independent republics. However, Peru dates its independence from 1824 and Bolivia from 1825.

By that time other South American colonies — Brazil, Chile, Argentina, Paraguay and Uru-

---

14. Cf. **10, 12,** and **18.**
15. See **10.**

TABLE 198

AGE OF STATES, BY CONTINENT

Date of Establishment as Independent Nation	America	Europe	Asia	Africa and Oceania
Before A.D. 900		Denmark, France, Sweden	China, Japan, Iran, Afghanistan, Nepal, Bhutan, Thailand	Ethiopia
Before Peace of Westphalia, 900–1648		England, Spain-Portugal, Russia		
Before Congress of Vienna, 1648–1814	United States, 1776; Haiti-Dominican Republic, 1804	Switzerland, 1648		
Before World War I, 1815–1913	Argentina, 1815; Paraguay, 1815; Chile, 1818; Mexico, 1821; Brazil, 1822; Peru, 1824; Uruguay, 1825; Bolivia, 1825; Colombia, 1830; Venezuela, 1830; Ecuador, 1830; Panama, 1830; Guatemala, 1838; El Salvador, 1838; Honduras, 1838; Nicaragua, 1838; Costa Rica, 1838; Canada, 1867; Cuba, 1898	Netherlands, 1815; Luxembourg, 1815; Greece, 1829; Belgium, 1830; Romania, 1859; Italy, 1861; Germany, 1871; Norway, 1905; Bulgaria, 1908; Albania, 1913		Liberia, 1847; Australia, 1901; New Zealand, 1907; Union of South Africa, 1909
Before World War II, 1914–1939		Ireland, 1916; Finland, 1918; Poland, 1919; Czechoslovakia, 1919; Yugoslavia, 1919; Austria, 1919; Hungary, 1919	Kuwait, 1914; Turkey, 1921; Mongolian Republic, 1922; Jordan, 1923; Saudi Arabia, 1927; Bahrein, 1928; Iraq, 1932; Yemen, 1934	Egypt, 1922
During and after World War II, 1939–		Iceland, 1944	Syria, 1944; Lebanon, 1944; Korea, 1945; Philippines, 1946; India, 1947; Pakistan, 1947; Ceylon, 1947; Israel, 1948; Burma, 1948; Indonesia, 1949	Libya, 1951

Source: Computed by the authors. Grateful acknowledgment is made to Dr. James Robbins for his constructive suggestions.

guay — had constituted themselves into independent states, filling the political vacuum left by the withdrawal of Spain and Portugal. Brazil became a kingdom under the heir of the house of Portugal in 1822; the former Spanish colonies became republics in 1815–25, but in the following century repeatedly traded their republican institutions for dictatorial regimes.

In 1867, a new independent state appeared in North America: Canada — a British colony since 1763 — became a Dominion, the first state to join the British Commonwealth on the basis of a federal union.

After the Spanish-American War (1898), Cuba, the last remaining Spanish colony in the Caribbean, became independent.

All in all, of the present twenty-two independent states in the Americas, only the United States came into existence before 1800; nineteen states were established in the first half of the nineteenth century, most of them between 1810 and 1840.

Europe

Among the states of Europe (including the USSR), only seven have been independent continuously or with only brief interruptions for more than five centuries. Of these, Denmark, France and Sweden have existed within about their present boundaries for more than a thousand years and England, for nearly nine hundred.[16] Portugal has been an independent state since the twelfth century; Spain since the thirteenth, Russia since the fourteenth.[17] Switzerland was founded as a federation of three cantons in 1291, but did not become formally independent until 1648, after the Thirty Years War. The Peace of Westphalia, concluded in that year, was an attempt of the European powers to settle their disputes and consolidate the political boundaries of the continent by a multilateral agreement.

At that time, the map of modern Europe began to take shape. In addition to the states mentioned above, Poland was established in eastern Europe. But all central Europe, from France in the west to Poland and Russia in the east, remained a maze of fairly unstable kingdoms and princedoms and disputed possessions of the Spaniards, Swedes, Ottoman Turks and the House of Hapsburg.

The boundaries of Sweden and Norway remained fluid. Early in the eighteenth century, the border disputes between Sweden and Russia were settled, in favor of Russia. By the end of the century, the independence of Luxembourg, one of the smallest states in Europe, was recognized by its neighbors. Luxembourg and Switzerland are the only states in Europe born in the interval between the Thirty Years War and the Napoleonic wars.

Thus nine European states can look back on more than a century and a half of continuous independent existence. (See Table 198.) Poland, one of the most important states in Europe in the seventeenth century, is not among these; it disappeared from the map, the victim of repeated partitions among Russia, Prussia and Austria (1772, 1793 and 1795). Luxembourg is included in this group, though its independence and the integrity of its territory were not always respected by its neighbors.

At the beginning of the nineteenth century, the era of the Napoleonic wars, almost all historical boundaries were erased from the map of continental Europe. In 1815, at the Congress of Vienna, Europe's great powers made a new attempt to establish a durable order and a system of collective security. This Congress has been credited with drawing the main lines of the map of Europe as they were in the nineteenth century.[18] Actually, it left many questions unsettled. While the Austro-Hungarian monarchy gained new strength and the German Confederation, nucleus of the future German Empire, began to take shape, southeastern Europe was almost as chaotic as after the Peace of Westphalia.

Very soon the boundaries established in Vienna began to crumble: in 1829 Greece became independent of the Turks and in 1830 Belgium, of the Netherlands. In the second half of the nineteenth century, the most important changes in the political map of continental Europe were the unification of Italy (1861) and of Germany (1871).

Meanwhile, the dissolution of the Ottoman

---

16. We date the existence of France as a state from the Treaty of Verdun (A.D. 843) when Charlemagne's empire was broken up and the kingdom of western Franks was separated from the territory that later formed Germany and Italy. The beginning of England is dated from the invasion of the British Isles by William the Conqueror in 1066. The Danish kingdom is centuries older than England and France, its beginnings lost in mythological times. (Cf. **12**, *passim*.)

17. After Spain and Portugal regained independence from the Moors, and Russia broke the Tatar domination.

18. **29**, p. 780.

Empire went on. Romania, Bulgaria, Serbia and Montenegro (later absorbed by Yugoslavia) became formally independent, under the tutelage of Russia and Austria-Hungary.

Partial revision of political boundaries in Europe continued until World War I. In 1905, Norway severed its ties with Sweden. In 1913, Albania became independent.

World War I and the revolution in Russia brought radical changes: revision of the Franco-German border, with the return of Alsace-Lorraine to France; restoration of Poland; separation of the Saar and Danzig from Germany; partition of Austria-Hungary; separation of Ireland from Great Britain; [19] radical reshaping of the political map of the Balkans; redistribution of former German colonies; formation of three Baltic states (Lithuania, Latvia and Estonia); and the separation of Finland from Russia. In all, nine new states emerged in Europe.[20] Three of these (Lithuania, Latvia and Estonia) were annexed by the USSR after World War II, and two others (Poland and Czechoslovakia) fell under Soviet political and military domination, along with three Balkan states (Bulgaria, Romania and Albania). Only Ireland remained independent.

The youngest independent state in Europe is Iceland, which severed its ties with Denmark in 1944.

In summary, of twenty-five European states (apart from the USSR), seven (including Switzerland) existed as independent political units at the time of the Revolutionary War in North America; four (including Luxembourg) entered the political scene at the end of the eighteenth and in the first half of the nineteenth centuries; three (including Germany and Italy), in the second half of that century, and eleven, after the century ended. (See Table 198.)

Asia

Some states in Asia are very old, others very young; only a few are in the age group of 50–500 years.

China is supposed to have existed as a unified empire from the third century B.C. to 1912 (the end of the Manchu dynasty); [21] Japan, since 660 B.C.; Persia (now Iran) is probably as old as China and is known to have existed since the beginning of human history; Afghanistan, Thailand, Nepal and Bhutan are other ancient Asiatic kingdoms that have preserved their existence and national identity to our time. These seven states together represent about half the total population of Asia, more than 600 million of its 1,270 million inhabitants.[22]

Turkey, Korea, India and Pakistan are not in this list. India was the cradle of one of mankind's oldest civilizations but had ceased to exist as an independent and unified state long before it became a British colony. Pakistan, which emerged as an independent state from the partition of British India, had no political or administrative organization of its own before the partition. Korea had changed hands time and again before the recent attempt of the UN to make it an independent unified state. Turkey's present boundaries make it one of many fragments of the old Ottoman Empire rather than its continuation.

Apart from the seven ancient kingdoms mentioned above, all the independent states in Asia today have been founded recently — some on the site of the Ottoman Empire, after World War I; others in the course of liquidating the colonial system.[23]

Eight states in the Near East became independent between 1920 and 1948 — modern Turkey in 1921, Jordan in 1923, Iraq in 1932, Syria and Lebanon in 1944 and Israel in 1948. The independent kingdoms of Saudi Arabia and Yemen emerged from tribal conflicts on the Arabian peninsula around the 1930's. India, Pakistan and Ceylon became dominions of the British Commonwealth in 1947. The Philippines (once a Spanish colony and after 1898 under United States control) became independent in 1946; Burma (separated from India in 1937), in 1948; Indonesia (formerly the Netherlands Indies), in 1949.[24] The Mongolian People's Republic, a puppet state dominated by the USSR,

19. The independence of Ireland was proclaimed in 1916 but its final separation from the United Kingdom was effected by the Republic of Ireland Act, 1948, which came into operation on April 18, 1949. (**28**, 1951, p. 1151.)

20. Without counting short-lived states in the Transcaucasus and areas with special international status such as the Saar, Memel and Danzig.

21. **11**, p. 18.

22. Cf. Table 194.

23. Cf. **28**, *passim*.

24. The United States of Indonesia was established as a sovereign state, cooperating with the Netherlands on a voluntary and equal basis under the provisions of the statute of the Netherlands Union. This Union was dissolved in 1954.

was carved out of northern China in 1922, after the end of the civil war in Siberia.

Half of Asia's population lives in new political units, some few founded as long as thirty years ago, many still less than ten years old.

Africa and Oceania

Of the five independent states in Africa, Ethiopia (Abyssinia) is one of the oldest in the world. The continuity of Egypt's political existence was interrupted for more than a thousand years by the domination of the Arabs and, later, the Turks. Egypt was a part of the Ottoman Empire from 1517 to 1914, a British protectorate from 1914 to 1922, and has since been an independent state.

The Republic of Liberia — one of the oldest republics in the Eastern Hemisphere — was constituted in 1847 by an American philanthropic society as a national home for freed American Negro slaves and has continued to be an independent state.

The Union of South Africa has been a self-governing British Dominion since 1909.

Libya, the youngest independent state in the world, was a part of Turkey from the sixteenth century to 1911 and an Italian colony from 1911 to 1942. After ten years of Franco-British administration with growing autonomy in internal affairs, it became an independent kingdom in 1951.

The Commonwealth of Australia acquired its status as a Dominion in 1901, New Zealand in 1907.

Distribution by Age

In terms of the period since they became independent political units, 16 of the world's independent states are older than the United States; and sixty-three nations are younger. The eleven oldest states — with more than a thousand years of political life — are Denmark, Sweden and France in Europe; China, Japan, Iran, Afghanistan, Nepal, Bhutan and Thailand in Asia; and Ethiopia in Africa. Together they had about 675 million inhabitants in midyear 1952. Five other states older than the United States — the United Kingdom, Spain, Portugal, Russia and Switzerland — together had 303 million inhabitants. (See Table 198; cf. Figure 119.)

The United States is usually considered a young nation, but its reputation for youth has nothing to do with the country's actual political age. Indeed it is one of the oldest republics and one of the oldest "modern" states in the world. Sixty-three of the existing eighty states are younger than the United States; among these, twenty-one are in the Western Hemisphere and came into existence in their present form in the nineteenth century and thirty-four, many of them in Asia, were instituted after the turn of that century. The population of nations older than the United States totaled 353 million in the middle of 1952 while there were 749 million people in nations which came into existence as independent political units in the twentieth century. The latter include some states with very large populations (India, Pakistan, Indonesia), but most of them are comparatively small. Many of them were carved out of Austria-Hungary, the Ottoman Empire, or the disintegrating colonial empires of Western powers.

HOW STATES WERE BORN

In the remote past, new states emerged from tribal wars, the marriage of rulers, and the partition of inheritances. The founding of the United States marked the beginning of a new era. Of the sixty-four states now in existence that were formed after the revolt of the British colonies in America, forty once were colonies or possessions of other nations. These include:

Twenty-two states in the Americas: all of which are former British, French, Spanish or Portuguese colonies.

Twelve states in Asia, Africa and Oceania: seven of which are British Dominions — India, Pakistan, Burma, Ceylon, the Union of South Africa, Australia and New Zealand; the other five being Indonesia, the Philippines, Kuwait, Bahrein and Libya.

Six in Europe: Belgium and the Netherlands (formerly Spanish possessions); Poland, Finland, Ireland and Iceland.

Fifteen independent states were added as a result of the disintegration of the Holy Roman Empire (later the Austro-Hungarian monarchy) and the Ottoman Empire.[25] With Sweden and Norway, which took their present shape after the secession of Norway, fifty-seven states have been formed in the last hundred and seventy-five years as a result of the liberation of former colonies or the partition of larger political units.

During this period only seven states have been

---

25. This number includes the young state of Israel carved out of the remains of the old Ottoman Empire.

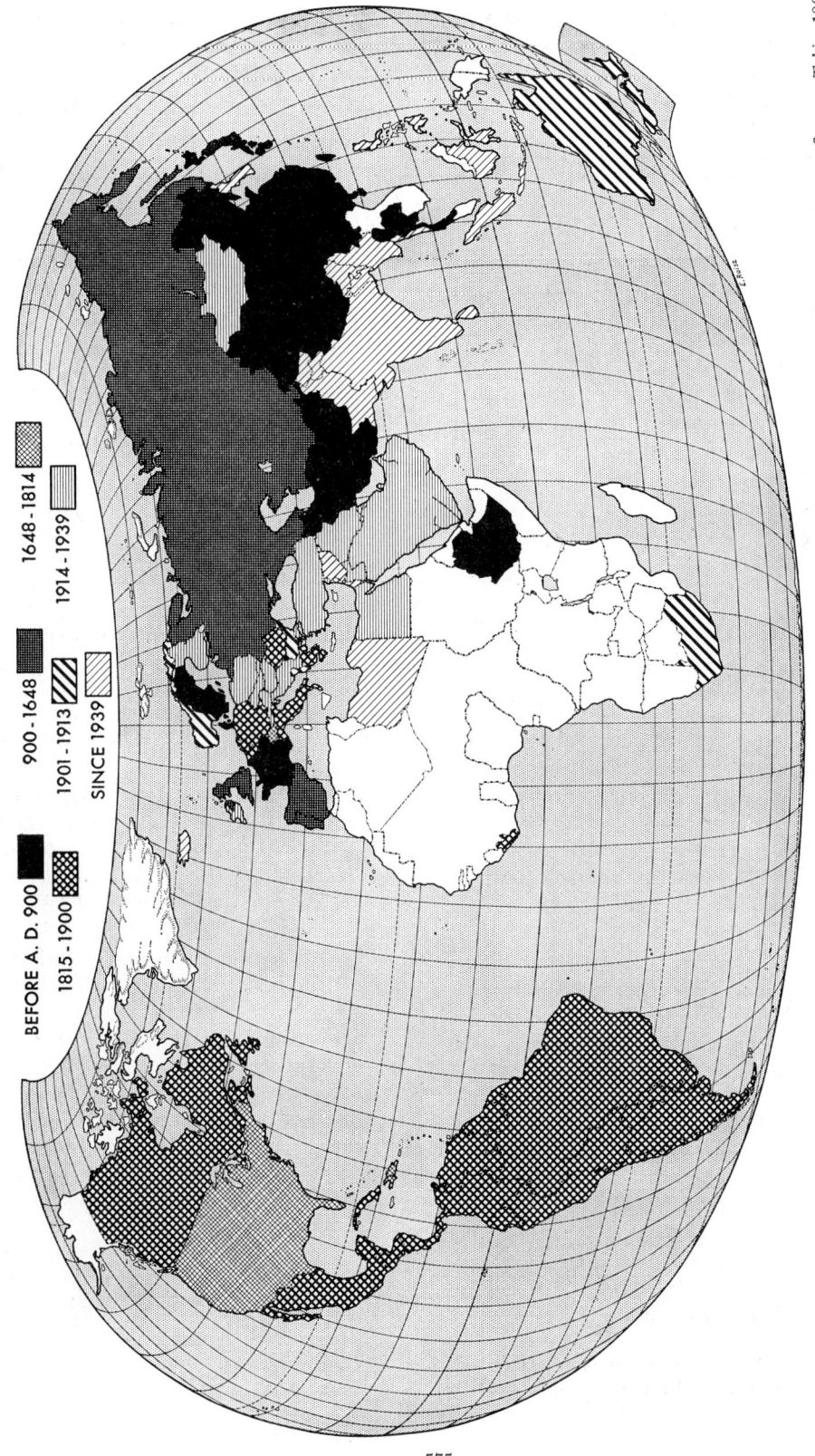

FIGURE 119. AGE OF STATES: GEOGRAPHIC DISTRIBUTION OF INDEPENDENT STATES CLASSIFIED BY DATE OF ESTABLISHMENT

Source: Table 198

575

created by other methods: Germany and Italy were formed by unification of nationally homogeneous territories, formerly split among descendents of feudal rulers; Saudi Arabia and Yemen emerged from old-style tribal wars; Luxembourg was established by an agreement among its neighbors; Liberia was founded by an American philanthropic society; and the USSR carved the Mongolian People's Republic out of China.

The unification of Germany (considered here as one nation) and Italy completed Europe's century-old process of liquidating medieval princedoms and forming national states. Except for them and the new kingdoms on the Arabian peninsula, all new states formed since the latter part of the eighteenth century have resulted from the splitting of larger units under the impact of centrifugal forces rather than from voluntary unification of smaller units into larger political agglomerations.

HOW STATES HAVE DIED

A state may cease to be an independent political unit by being split into several units or merged with another state. Either one may result from the free decision of the people or may be imposed upon them by external forces. In the past century, the death rate among states from any cause other than brute force has been negligible.[26] By force or a show of force, although often under the guise of an agreement, European powers extended their political control over hundreds of areas without explicit political organization in regions open to colonization in Africa and Asia. Nazi Germany used a similar technique in annexing Austria and Czechoslovakia, and the USSR, in annexing the Baltic states. Undisguised military force was used by both totalitarian countries in partitioning Poland early in World War II and by Italy in her seizure of Ethiopia. Earlier, military defeats of the Ottoman Empire and Austria-Hungary wiped both nations off the map and scattered their lands among a dozen new states.

In brief, states seldom fade away. They usually die a violent death.

Types of Governments

To appraise the prevailing trends in political organization in the world it is necessary to clas-

sify states by type of government. Never has this task been as difficult as in modern times.[27]

BASIC TYPES OF CONSTITUTIONS

Aristotle

The founder of political science, Aristotle, developed a classification of governments based on the distinction between ideal types and actually existing constitutions ("true" and "perverse" forms of government), declaring:

The government, which is the supreme authority in states, must be in the hands of one or of a few, or of the many. The true forms of government, therefore, are those in which the one, or the few, or the many, govern with a view to the common interest; but governments which rule with a view to the private interest, whether of the one or of the few, or of the many, are perversions.[28]

From this definition, Aristotle deduced the basic types of government: kingship or royalty, aristocracy, and constitutional government, which he defined as the government of all who possess arms. He confessed, however, that in all his experience he had not found a single true government but only perversions: tyranny, a perversion of royalty; oligarchy, a perversion of aristocracy; and democracy, a perversion of constitutional government.

"Tyranny," he explained, "is a kind of monarchy which has in view the interest of the monarch only; oligarchy has in view the interest of the wealthy; democracy, of the needy; none of them, the common good of all." [29]

It is noteworthy that the Aristotelian classification of "perverse" governments is much more realistic than his classification of ideal states. There never has been a government of the many or of all citizens.[30] Government is a specialized function in the society and can be exercised only by a comparatively small group of individuals. It may be questioned even whether "the many" or all citizens are able to exercise effective control over the government.[31] It is obvious, however, that the few actually in power, whether or not they are effectively controlled by the many, may have in view interests of different groups of population, and this distinction may be used as the basis of classifying states. The Aristotelian

---

26. **36.**

27. Cf. **13**, **15**, and **22**.
28. **9**, Book III, Chapter 7.
29. **9**, Book III, Chapter 7.
30. **17**, pp. 104–36.
31. **20**, p. 149.

distinction between the wealthy and the needy is insufficient, however: there may be different groups of the wealthy and the needy in a state, and describing a government in terms of the interests it has in view is a difficult task.

Despite this difficulty and changes in the concept of democracy, the Aristotelian distinction between a democratic regime, on the one hand, and tyrannies and oligarchies, on the other, remained the cornerstone of political thinking in Europe.

Machiavelli

In the Italy of the Renaissance — the bridge between the Middle Ages and modern times — Machiavelli was probably the shrewdest and most penetrating student of public affairs. He offered a simplified classification: "All states and dominions which hold or have held sway over mankind are either republics or monarchies," according to the first sentence of *The Prince*.[32] But like Aristotle, he saw about him more perversions of all kinds than true governments.

Montesquieu

Two millenniums after Aristotle, Montesquieu defined the basic types of government as follows:

There are three species of government: republican, monarchical, and despotic. . . . Republican government is that in which the body or only a part of the people, is possessed of the supreme power; monarchy, that in which a single person governs by fixed and established laws; a despotic government, that in which a single person directs everything by his own will and caprice.[33]

There were very few republics in the world at that time; Switzerland was probably the largest. The rest of the world was organized in kingdoms and princedoms of various sizes and types. Montesquieu's distinction between monarchies and despotisms went much further than Aristotle's concept of tyranny as a perversion of monarchy. While Aristotle's distinction depended on the "virtue" or "selfishness" of the ruler, Montesquieu stressed constitutional limitations on the ruler's power. Montesquieu's "monarchy" is a *constitutional* monarchy by definition; the ruler with unlimited power is a despot, whether or not he meets Aristotle's definition of a virtuous man. Montesquieu's influence on his generation and on the architects of the new independent states in the New World can hardly be overemphasized.

The current use of the term "constitutional" as the antithesis of "absolutist" or "despotic" goes back to Montesquieu. "Constitutionalism," remarks Robert G. Neumann, "is not identical with democracy . . . [but] in our days all democracies worthy of that name have constitutional government."[34] Among historical influences that have tended toward constitutionalism, Neumann mentions the spread of Christianity, with its doctrine of the limitation of temporal power and its insistence on individual responsibility.

The meaning of the words, however, changes as time goes on: not all modern constitutions protect the rights of minorities and individuals. Some have been designed to perpetuate a despotic regime, whether fascist or labeled a "people's republic." A constitution of this type establishes rules and procedures of government, including the election of a powerless sham parliament, but leaves no supreme power to the people. The classification of state forms offered by Montesquieu has no niche for such constitutions.

The Progress of Democracy, 1750–1900

The second half of the eighteenth century and the beginning of the nineteenth were marked by violent conflicts between republican and monarchistic forces on both sides of the Atlantic. In North America, republican forces fought a monarchy that was constitutional at home but failed to follow the same principles in its remote overseas possessions. In France, republican forces opposed a traditionally despotic monarchy that made an attempt to become constitutional when it was too late. The United States which emerged from the Revolutionary War became the model for all the states in the New World and gave a profound impetus to republican ideas in Europe and especially in France.[35]

The revolutionary struggle in France ended, however, in defeat. The French Republic degenerated into a new empire and the military collapse of the latter paved the way for the restoration of royal power. In the middle of the nineteenth century, after the futile upheavals in 1848 and the rebirth of the French Empire

---

32. **19.**
33. **21,** p. 8.

34. **22,** p. 591.
35. **8,** Vol. 1, p. 612.

under Napoleon III, Switzerland was the only republic in Europe. Not until 1870, after the disastrous war with Prussia, did France again become a republic, the second state in Europe to establish this form of government.

Between 1870 and the outbreak of World War I, republican ideas made no visible progress in the Old World. The progress of democracy in Europe found expression, rather, in the transformation of monarchies. Without sacrifice of the traditional pageantry around the palace, old kingdoms and empires became democratic in constitution and in spirit. The trend was toward universal suffrage and assumption of sovereign power by representative institutions. In the everyday political life of constitutional monarchies, "the kings just faded out of the picture." [36]

By the end of the nineteenth century, there were twenty-four republics in the world: twenty-one in America and three in the Eastern Hemisphere — France, Switzerland and Liberia. [37] The population of the republics totaled 180 million, in round numbers, while constitutional monarchies of various types continued to prevail in Europe, in an area with some 215 million inhabitants, and in the British dominions. At that time the world's population of 1.6 billion was distributed as follows (in millions):

Republics	180
Constitutional monarchies	290
Absolute monarchies	730
Colonies	400

Long before the end of the century Woodrow Wilson had summarized the political trends in the world as a triumphal advance of democracy:

If Aristocracy seems about to disappear, Democracy seems about universally to prevail. . . . [The advance of democratic institutions] has destroyed almost all pure forms of Monarchy and Aristocracy by introducing into them imperative forces of popular thought and the concrete institutions of popular representation; and the promise to reduce politics to a single form by excluding all other governing forces and institutions but those of a wide suffrage and a democratic representation — by reducing all forms of government to Democracy. [38]

The progress Wilson described was restricted to peoples of European stock, however. The nations of Asia and Africa had no part in it, and colonialism and absolutism continued to rule over more than 70 per cent of mankind.

Between the turn of the century and the outbreak of World War I, two important changes took place in the world's political structure. In 1905, after the first Russian revolution, the czarist empire began its transformation from a half-Asiatic despotism to a constitutional monarchy. [39] In 1912 a republic was established in China. The revolution in 1910 that transformed the kingdom of Portugal into a republic almost overnight was also symptomatic of the new times.

Impact of World War I

Then, after the brief curtain raiser of the Balkan wars, came the deadly clash between the Central European powers and the alliance of France, Great Britain and Russia, supported by the United States and the British dominions. If there was an undertone of conflicting political ideologies in World War I, it had no influence on the alignment of belligerents. The war, however, was followed by a series of revolutions. Four empires — the Russian, German, Austro-Hungarian and Ottoman — were destroyed: two of them divided up; two others plunged into revolutionary chaos.

Soon after the war ended, republican government was established in nearly all the areas formerly occupied by the four empires. The representative character of the Russian government was questionable even at that time. Some observers recognized that the Soviet government intended to rule "with military force . . . in accordance with the identical principle of the government of the czar." [40] Others professed to see in the emergencies of the civil war an excuse for its dictatorial practices. Some believed that that new form of government was an original development of the principles of democracy. [41] The

---

36. **15**, p. 31.

37. The South African Republic (Transvaal) had ceased to exist as an independent state shortly before the end of 1900.

38. **33**, p. 581.

39. The transformation was incomplete: the government appointed by the czar was not responsible to the Duma.

40. **8**, Vol. 2, p. 302.

41. Sidney and Beatrice Webb described the "novel representative system" of the Soviets as follows: "In contrast with every other community, the USSR has evolved a complex and multiform representative system of complete originality, based upon the principle of universal participation in public affairs, *under the guidance of a highly organized leadership of a unique kind*. . . . Man is represented in three separate capacities, as a citizen, as

question of the character of the Soviet regime is, however, irrelevant to its classification by type of constitution: the USSR emerged from the civil war without an hereditary monarch, and was explicitly described in its constitution, and even in its new name, as a union of *republics*. Few observers realized at that time that the new state was not a "perverse" republic but the prototype of a new antidemocratic form of government. Including the USSR (counted as one political unit), thirty-eight republics [42] existed in the world in the early 1920's. The world then had sixty independent states in all, which were distributed by type of constitution as follows: [43]

	Total	Absolute Monarchy	Constitutional Monarchy [a]	Republic
World	60	3	19	38
America	22	—	1	21
Europe	27	—	13	14
Asia	6	2	2	2
Africa	3	1	1	1
Oceania	2	—	2	—

a. Includes, besides European constitutional monarchies, Turkey and Japan; and four British dominions (Canada, Australia, New Zealand and the Union of South Africa).

Comparison of the political map of the world in 1913 and immediately after the end of World War I seemed to evidence tremendous progress in the direction envisaged by Woodrow Wilson: the dragon's teeth sown by the war had not yet yielded their harvest.

Recent Trends

The Soviet government in Russia proved to be the first of these fruits. It was followed by other governments of the same type, some radical, others reactionary, all extremist in their opposition to the liberal and democratic ideas of the nineteenth century. Born of revolution, military defeat or internal discord, all these governments claimed dictatorial power in the name of the absolute supremacy of the state over the in-

dividual. Planned as dictatorships of an organized, disciplined and indoctrinated minority over the rest of the people, the new-type governments degenerated into the absolute and unlimited power of the head of state. As time went on, the form of the new state became more complicated. Clusters of formally independent states developed and were controlled from a single center with all power invested in the deified leader of the central nucleus.

The new type of state appears to be a strange combination of all three "perversions" described by Aristotle: a democracy (in the Aristotelian sense) in theory, an oligarchy in everyday practice, a tyranny in spirit. Regimes of this type developed in Russia, Hungary (under Admiral Horthy), Italy, Germany, Spain and Portugal.[44]

Since the collapse of fascist Italy and Nazi Germany, communism, led by the USSR, has remained the main carrier of the idea of totalitarian absolutism. The same idea, however, has survived in variant forms in Spain and Portugal, and the same philosophy of government may be observed in some countries which have not broken completely with traditional democratic forms. Appraisal of the new type of government and analysis of its historical roots are beyond the scope of this study. Our main concern is rather to measure its expansion in the world in comparison with governments of other types.

Totalitarian States

The development of totalitarian regimes — some of them reactionary (Spain), others allegedly radical (the USSR before the Stalin-Hitler pact) — has wiped out the old distinction between monarchies and republics. Experience has shown that fascism can develop in a monarchy (Italy) as well as in a republic (Germany), or in a state which pretends to be neither republic

---

a producer and as a consumer. In each case the franchise is the widest in the world, though with peculiar and steadily dwindling disqualifications, whilst the extent to which the entire population actually participates in elections is without parallel." (**30**, Vol. 2, p. 1128. Italics added.)

42. Not counting three Transcaucasian republics reconquered by the Soviets.

43. **34**, Vol. VII, p. 98.

44. Such also was the regime Hitler tried to establish in France. (See **23**, pp. 15ff.)

Neumann points out that a similar regime, although in a milder form, existed in Austria under Dollfuss and Schuschnigg in 1934–38. (**22**, p. 582.)

Portugal is usually considered as an example of fascism in a mild form. The state has a fascist constitution (corporative republic). In the elections for the national assembly in 1934, 1938, 1942 and 1945, only lists of the official National Union party were presented, but the law permits the presentation of more than one list. In presidential elections in 1951, the opposition parties campaigned for their own candidate against one supported by the National Union and the government.

nor monarchy (Spain).[45] The Soviet regime in the USSR, in its fully developed form, with an absolutist government completely insulated against the criticism and rebuke of the people in general elections, no longer can be classified as a republic but lacks certain features of an hereditary monarchy.[46]

The crystallization of the new state took a decade or more. The end product was the synthesis of an omnipotent police state with a rigid thought-control system, demanding absolute acceptance of the doctrine enunciated by the deified head of government. Perhaps the regime which existed in Moscow until the death of Stalin can be described as a totalitarian atheistic theocracy. This definition, however, does not apply to the satellite countries, which have no deified national leaders, but are ruled by proconsuls who are sent by a foreign country and who are assisted by individuals hand-picked among the native inhabitants. Classification of Soviet satellites as independent states is not very accurate; describing them as Russian colonies or occupation zones would be more exact in many respects. On the other hand, not all "people's republics" are colonies of Moscow; it would be inappropriate, for example, to apply this term to China.

The classification of people's republics and fascist regimes by type of government is extremely difficult. The dissimilarity between them and democratic governments is not in the type of constitution, since the most despotic state of this sort may have the most liberal constitution on its books. A more promising basis for a classification that differentiates dictatorial governments, absolute monarchies and modern constitutional monarchies and republics is the actual relationship between the government and people, with the distinction between regimes that provide for popular control over the government and those based on governmental control over the people. Sometimes the difference is in the degree of control, and it is not always easy to decide who controls whom in a country. There

may be doubts, for example, concerning the proper classification of Argentina or Portugal. In most cases, however, the relationship between the government and the people is the fundamental criterion in defining the type of state.

GOVERNMENT AND PEOPLE

Aristotle's definition of government — in terms of the number of individuals who hold power — envisaged tiny city-states: communities of people "who live in the same place and intermarry" and attend "common sacrifices and amusements which draw men together." [47] In a modern state, the type of government is determined by the procedure through which the citizens form and express their will, and the extent to which their will controls the composition and policy of government.[48] Under republican and constitutional monarchistic regimes, the people are consulted periodically to determine the will of the majority. In people's republics, soviet republics and fascist dictatorships, elections and popular votes are used only as the means of propaganda ("political education") and under conditions which ensure the results desired by the rulers.[49] The latter are as free from popular control as the absolute monarchies or despotisms of ancient times. In any broad classification, the distinction between the USSR and the Muscovy of the sixteenth century is of minor significance in comparison with the contrast between a people's republic and a democratic regime. The essential difference is whether elections determine the policy of the government or not. When the rulers can predetermine the outcome of the popular vote, the procedure ceases to be an "election." The antidemocratic character of dictatorial regimes manifests itself in elections in which there is only one party or one list of candidates.[50]

This system is usually combined with governmental control over press and radio and may degenerate into grotesque sham elections like those in Hitler's Germany and in the USSR. But it may operate in milder forms as, for example,

---

45. There can be no doubt as to the close similarity of such regimes as the fascist state of Mussolini and the Nazi state of Hitler. The former, however, glorified monarchy as "the sacred symbol, glorious, traditional, millenary, of the Nation," while the latter proclaimed itself a people's republic. (Cf. **13**, p. 560.)

46. It is a matter of opinion whether Russia was still a republic in 1918 after the dissolution of the Constituent Assembly freely elected by the people. A country in the grip of a bitter civil war, however, cannot be classified exactly by type of constitution and government.

47. **9**, Book III, Chapter 10.

48. For purposes of a broad classification, the distinction between federal states (as the United States and Switzerland) and central states (as France) is not relevant. (Cf. **32** and **22**.)

49. The voting "under the guidance of a highly organized leadership of a unique kind" so highly praised by Sydney and Beatrice Webb. (See **30**, Vol. 2, p. 1128.)

50. Cf. **22**, pp. 580ff.

in Portugal.[51] The essential characteristic is an unopposed election.

As Herman Finer has pointed out:

The characteristic mark of selection of candidates in democracies is the openness and freedom of opportunity to all individuals to become candidates, and for any free grouping of citizens to propose them. The mark of candidacy in dictatorships is the reverse: The dictators or the ruling group and the dictator's party exercise the monopoly of nomination and conduct of the election campaign. To use the word "election" is, indeed, a misnomer, because the word implies a choice, whereas the dictatorial practice is the artful and forcible denial of choice — indeed, its deliberate seduction.[52]

This touchstone — more or less free elections or sham voting without choice of candidates — provides a classification of governments without arbitrary discrimination between good and bad parliamentary systems or good and bad dictatorial regimes.

Within the basic two groups of states — *parliamentary*[53] and *absolutist* — different types may be distinguished. A parliamentary regime, for example, may have an elected president or an hereditary monarch as its titular head. It may be democratic, as in the United States and Switzerland, or represent a "perversion" of parliamentarianism, as in Argentina and the Dominican Republic. An absolutist state may have a sham parliament fully controlled by the ruling party or no parliament at all. This classification makes the distinction between fascist governments and so-called people's republics immaterial, a distinction which is concerned with the background and intention of the ruling party rather than the philosophy and technique of government.

To the four basic types of states — two forms of parliamentary regime and two forms of absolutist regime — a fifth can be added: countries temporarily divided by opposing factions.

THE SCOPE OF PARLIAMENTARY AND ABSOLUTIST REGIMES

Area and Population

Of the eighty independent states in the middle of 1952, sixty can be described as parliamentary and eighteen as absolutist, while two (Germany and Korea) are divided by opposing forces.[54] (See Table 199; cf. Figures 120 and 121.)

Not all of the sixty parliamentary states meet the standards of democracy recognized in modern free nations. Where democratic procedures are not deeply rooted, their weakness appears most commonly in presidential elections.

For example, of the ten republics in South America at the beginning of 1953, only three (Brazil, Uruguay and Chile) had presidents elected in accordance with the constitution, by popular majority. In two (Paraguay and Peru), the president had been elected in one-man elections after his predecessor was deposed by the army. In two others (Bolivia and Venezuela), the army had nominated the president. In two republics, the latest elections took place under conditions which hardly left people a free choice: in Colombia, the liberal opposition refused to vote under the state of siege proclaimed by the incumbent president; in Ecuador, the election took place under the fear of a military coup. (Similarly, in Panama, the election, held amid political turmoil, raised to the presidency the police chief who was actually running the country.)[55]

---

51. A marginal case is an election in which the opposition is allowed to offer its candidates but is deprived of the free use of propaganda mediums: its newspapers are banned, leaflets confiscated, candidates arrested, and meetings dispersed. Such "perversions" of democracy occur often in Latin America (the Dominican Republic, El Salvador, Honduras, Colombia, Peru, Paraguay, Argentina; cf. Chapter 13, p. 630). Despite some similarity between these regimes and totalitarian states they can hardly be classified in the same group with the forced "unanimous" votes in Nazi Germany or the USSR and its satellites.

52. **13**, p. 255.

53. The term "parliamentary" as used here means simply that a country has a parliament, that is, an elected assembly with legislative power. In this sense the United States, the United Kingdom and France are parliamentary countries despite the differences in the role assigned by their constitutions to the parliaments. On the contrary, the system of the USSR is not parliamentary because its congress of soviets is neither really elected nor invested with legislative or any other real power. The term parliamentary is sometimes used in a narrower sense as characteristic of a particular type of governmental organization. The system is described as parliamentary when the government is directly responsible to the parliament and as "presidential" when it is appointed by the president and is not subject to a vote of confidence by the legislature. In this sense, the system of government is "parliamentary" in France but "presidential" in the United States. (Cf. **22**, pp. 610ff.)

54. Germany and Korea are counted as one political unit each. Tibet and Formosa are not counted separately. Also excluded are Monaco, Liechtenstein, Andorra, San Marino, Vatican City, Trucial Oman and Qatar. (See Table 194. Cf. **6**, 1949–50, pp. 71–83.)

55. Cf. **14**.

Argentina is described by many observers as a fascist dictatorship in disguise. This description may not be precise, but the varnish of parliamentary institutions is thin and it is hard to decide whether that country should be classified as a very weak ("perverse") parliamentary republic or a not fully developed fascist regime.[56]

In constitutional monarchies in Asia, the weakness of the parliamentary system appears in the selection of the prime minister and the extraordinary power given to the government. The regime of Mossadegh in Iran, for example, was close to a dictatorship behind a parliamentary façade. Such a situation, however, is regarded as a temporary deviation from legality and cannot be compared to the ruthless reign of force characteristic of fascist regimes and people's republics.

Among the 60 governments classified here as parliamentary, 38 are republics (21 in the Western Hemisphere, 7 in Europe, 8 in Asia and 2 in Africa) and 22 are constitutional monarchies (1 in America, 8 in Europe, 8 in Asia, 3 in Africa and 2 in Oceania).[57]

The spread of communist and fascist dictatorships is the most important trend of the last decade. Before World War II, there were five countries of this type: the USSR, Germany, Italy, Spain and Portugal. The war destroyed dictatorship in Germany and Italy, but it survived in Spain and Portugal and gained new strength in the USSR. Following the principle proclaimed in the Peace of Augsburg, *cuius regio, eius religio* (the people follow the religion of the ruler), the Kremlin established people's republics in all the areas under its control — Poland, Czechoslovakia, Hungary, Romania, Bulgaria, Yugoslavia, Albania and Mongolia. Yugoslavia has maintained an authoritarian form of government since its break with Moscow.

---

56. See **18, 26, 31.**

57. Some constitutional monarchies — for example, Afghanistan and Thailand — possess only rudimentary parliamentary institutions. Others — such as the United Kingdom, Belgium, the Netherlands, Denmark, Sweden and Norway — have achieved the highest level of democratic government while preserving the traditional form of hereditary monarchy.

The list of absolutist states includes six kingdoms and sheikdoms, all in Asia, and twelve dictatorships. Among the latter, two are of fascist-corporative type (Portugal and Spain); one is an independent people's republic (Yugoslavia) and the other nine form a bloc dominated by the USSR. Seven of them (Poland, Czechoslovakia, Hungary, Romania, Bulgaria, Albania and Mongolia) are actually controlled by the Kremlin.

The Soviets gained their greatest victory in 1949 in China, when the faction supported by Moscow defeated the national government of Chiang Kai-shek, supported by the United States. Sovietization of China brought to a dozen the countries of this type in the world. The USSR also holds Eastern Germany and North Korea in its grip.

Since political conditions in Germany and Korea are unsettled, those countries are classified in Table 199 as divided.

The world population of 2,460 million, in round numbers, in the middle of 1952 was distributed by type of government as follows (in millions): [58]

Parliamentary governments	
Republic	963
Constitutional monarchy	376
Absolutist governments	
Absolute monarchy	18
Dictatorship	801
Divided countries	100
Non-self-governing territories	201 [a]

a. This figure relates to mid-1950, and the number may have been 2 or 3 per cent higher by mid-1952. No adjustment has been made in view of the absence of official estimates and the considerable margin of error in population statistics for colonial areas. (See Chapter 14.)

When the population of Germany and Korea is divided between the West and the East, some 1.4 billion persons are living in parliamentary countries and almost as many — some 1.1 billion — are ruled by absolute monarchs, dictators or foreign masters.

Economic Power

When governments are classified in broad groups, as in Table 199, each group includes countries of very different economic structure. Among the republics are the United States, France, Switzerland and Austria and also Lebanon, Syria and Liberia. Among the constitutional monarchies, the United Kingdom, Belgium, the Netherlands, Denmark, Sweden and Norway meet Afghanistan, Thailand and Libya. People's republics have been established in Czechoslovakia and in Mongolia. The only homogeneous group is that of the absolute monarchies, which is limited to underdeveloped areas of Asia.

---

58. Computed from Table 199.

TABLE 199

GOVERNMENTS: POPULATION OF STATES CLASSIFIED BY POLITICAL REGIME

State	Population in Midyear 1952, in Millions	State	Population in Midyear 1952, in Millions
I. *Parliamentary government*		**B. Constitutional monarchy** (*cont.*)	
		Netherlands	10.4
A. Republic		Denmark	4.3
United States	157.0	Sweden	7.1
Mexico	26.9	Norway	3.3
Guatemala	3.0	Greece	7.8
El Salvador	2.0	Japan	85.5
Honduras	1.6	Jordan	0.5
Nicaragua	1.1	Iraq	5.2
Costa Rica	0.8	Iran	19.5
Panama	0.8	Afghanistan	12.0
Cuba	5.7	Pakistan	76.6
Haiti	3.2	Thailand	19.2
Dominican Republic	2.2	Ceylon	7.9
Venezuela	5.3	Ethiopia	15.3
Colombia	11.8	Libya	1.1
Ecuador	3.2	Union of South Africa	12.9
Brazil	54.5	Australia	8.6
Peru	8.9	New Zealand	2.0
Bolivia	3.1		
Paraguay	1.3	**II. *Absolutist government***	
Chile	5.9	**A. Absolute monarchy**	
Uruguay	2.4	Saudi Arabia	6.0
Argentina	18.1	Yemen	4.6
Ireland	2.9	Kuwait	0.2
Iceland	0.1	Bahrein	0.1
France	42.6	Nepal	7.1
Finland	4.1	Bhutan	0.3
Switzerland	4.8	**B. Dictatorship**	
Austria	6.9	Poland	25.5
Italy	46.9	Czechoslovakia	12.7
Turkey	22.0	Hungary	9.5
Lebanon	1.3	Portugal	8.5
Israel	1.4	Spain	28.3
Syria	3.4	Yugoslavia	16.7
India	367.0	Romania	16.5
Burma	18.9	Bulgaria	7.5
Indonesia	78.2	Albania	1.3
Philippines	20.6	USSR	210.0
Liberia	1.7	China	463.5
Egypt	21.4	Mongolia	1.0
B. Constitutional monarchy		**III. *Divided***	
Canada	14.4	Germany	70.4
United Kingdom	50.4	Korea	29.3
Luxembourg	0.3		
Belgium	11.7		

Sources: For population see Table 194. For description of government in each country see **25** and **28**.

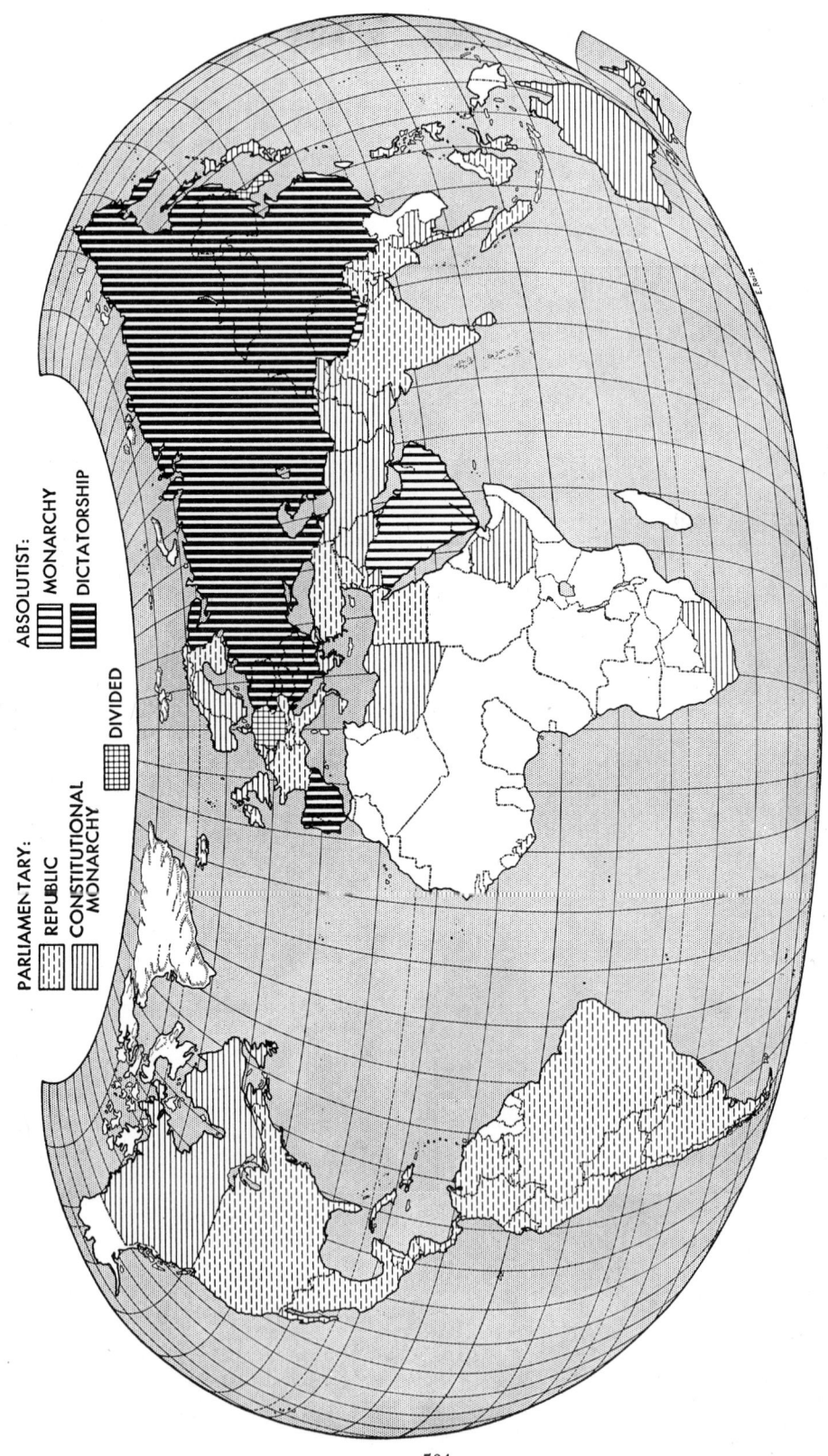

ABSOLUTIST:

PARLIAMENTARY:

REPUBLIC

CONSTITUTIONAL
MONARCHY

MONARCHY

DICTATORSHIP

DIVIDED

584

FIGURE 120. GOVERNMENTS: GEOGRAPHIC DISTRIBUTION OF INDEPENDENT STATES CLASSIFIED BY POLITICAL REGIME, 1952

Source: Table 199

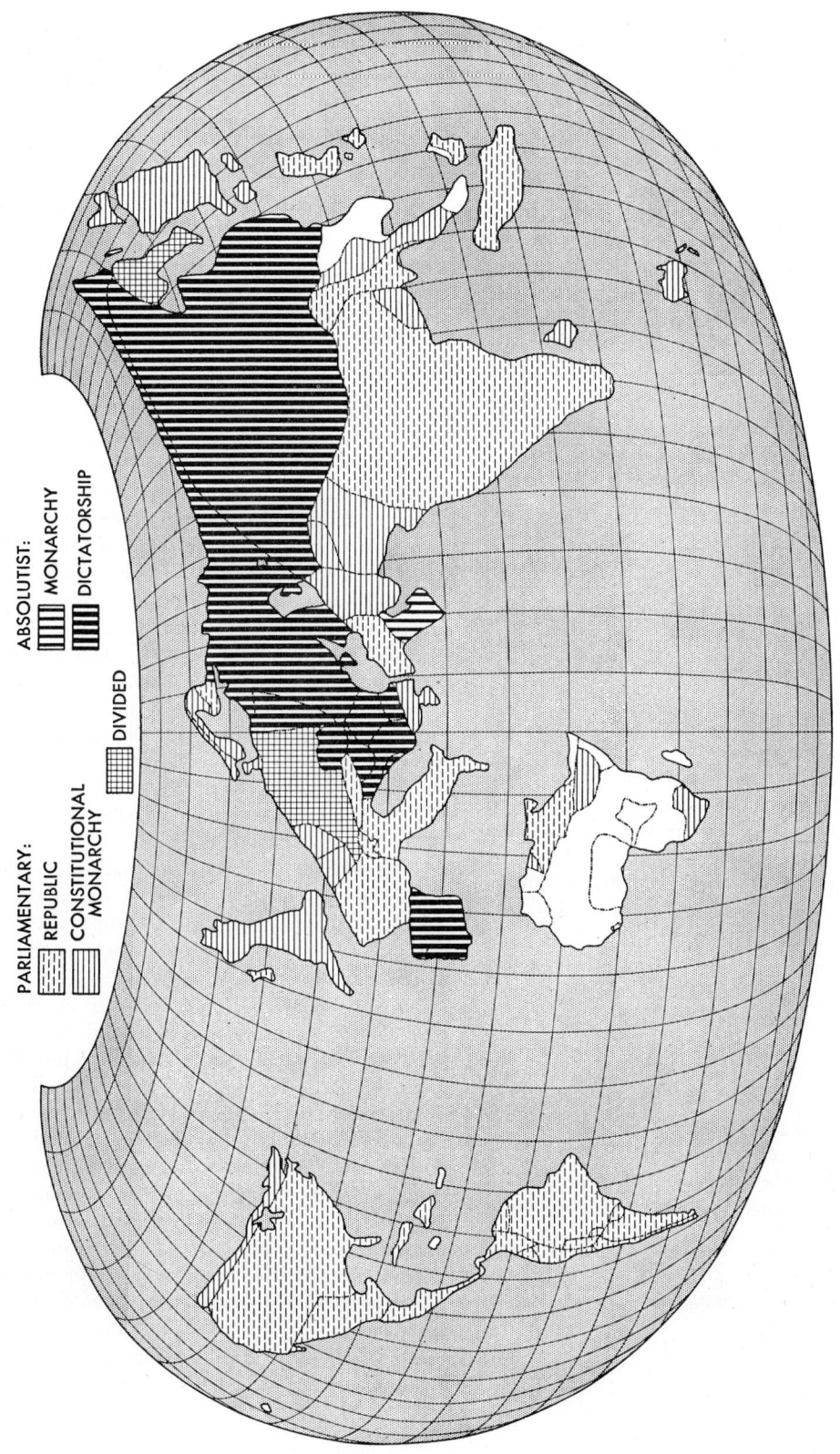

PARLIAMENTARY:
REPUBLIC
CONSTITUTIONAL
MONARCHY

ABSOLUTIST:
MONARCHY
DICTATORSHIP

DIVIDED

Source: Table 199

FIGURE 121. GOVERNMENTS: GEOGRAPHIC DISTRIBUTION OF INDEPENDENT STATES CLASSIFIED BY POLITICAL REGIME IN RELATION TO POPULATION, 1952

Continents and countries are shown on a scale proportionate to population.

Closer analysis reveals that almost all modern, economically developed countries are republics or constitutional monarchies. Among them, adherence to republican or monarchical forms is largely historical accident, as exemplified by the United States and France vs. the United Kingdom and Canada. Economically developed countries form the hard core of the parliamentary system. From this nucleus, parliamentary government spread to less developed areas, by way of imitation or as a result of the direct influence of the more advanced nations. The example of the United States largely determined the constitutions in Middle and South America; the United Kingdom brought constitutional monarchy to all its dominions except India. Introduction of parliamentary government marked the beginning of Europeanization in Turkey; rudimentary forms of parliamentarism marked the penetration of modern ideas into Afghanistan and Thailand.

Dictatorial regimes developed in Europe in areas as widely different as Portugal, Spain, Italy, Germany, Russia. Crushed by external force in Germany and Italy, dictatorship took root in other areas, spreading from Russia to countries which had fallen under its influence or domination.

The world's economic power is very unevenly distributed among nations with different types of government. (See Figure 122.)

In 1949 national income in the world totaled approximately $530 billion.[59] Of this total, some $13 billion represented non-self-governing areas and dependencies, and $517 billion, the approximate total income of all independent states. The share of the 38 republics (listed in Table 199) in this total was close to $307 billion; that of 22 constitutional monarchies, $93 billion. The absolute monarchies shared among themselves not more than $1 billion. The USSR claimed $59.5 billion, but its income hardly exceeded $40 billion when the real value of the Soviet ruble is substituted for the official rate of exchange. The rest was distributed as follows (in billions of dollars):

Satellite countries (Poland, Czechoslovakia,
  Hungary, Romania, Bulgaria and Albania) $21.0
China 18.5
Yugoslavia 2.3
Spain and Portugal 10.2
Western Germany 15.3
Eastern Germany 7.7
Korea 1.0

The resources of the USSR and its satellites and China, Eastern Germany and North Korea probably totaled close to $90 billion. At a rough approximation, this group of countries represented one third of the world's population and controlled one sixth of the world's income at that time.[60]

SUMMARY

Three developments characterize recent trends in types of government: (1) disintegration of old empires, liberation of colonies, formation of new states; (2) the growing participation of the people in government, and progress in democracy; and (3) development of dictatorial governments of the communist or fascist type.

The last development has often been held to represent a crisis in democracy due to the inability of democracies to defend themselves and to cope with the urgent problems of our time. There is no evidence, however, that dictatorial regimes have solved these problems. Even their superiority in military affairs has not been proved. Indeed, World War II started with three absolutist states — Germany, Italy and the USSR — representing one bloc, and the democracies of Western Europe, the other. It ended with complete disintegration of the absolutist bloc, a rift between Germany and Italy, open war between Germany and the USSR, originally allies, failure of Germany's planned war economy and collapse of its military machine, while the USSR was saved from defeat only by the aid of the United States and the superiority of the military force of the democracies over Hitler's war machine.

On the other hand, there is ample evidence of the internal stability of dictatorial regimes. Whatever the circumstances that have brought groups or parties to dictatorial power, they have shown an ability to remain at the helm indefinitely by continuing to use the same formula of government: concentration of all power in the hands of a small, well-organized and armed minority; political conditioning of the people by unceasing propaganda, control of public information and physical annihilation of opposition; preservation of the façade of popular elections with a single list of candidates.

Despotic regimes are older than parliamentary governments and have occurred at all stages of

59. Five billion dollars less than in 1948.
60. Estimated mainly on the basis of 4 and 7.

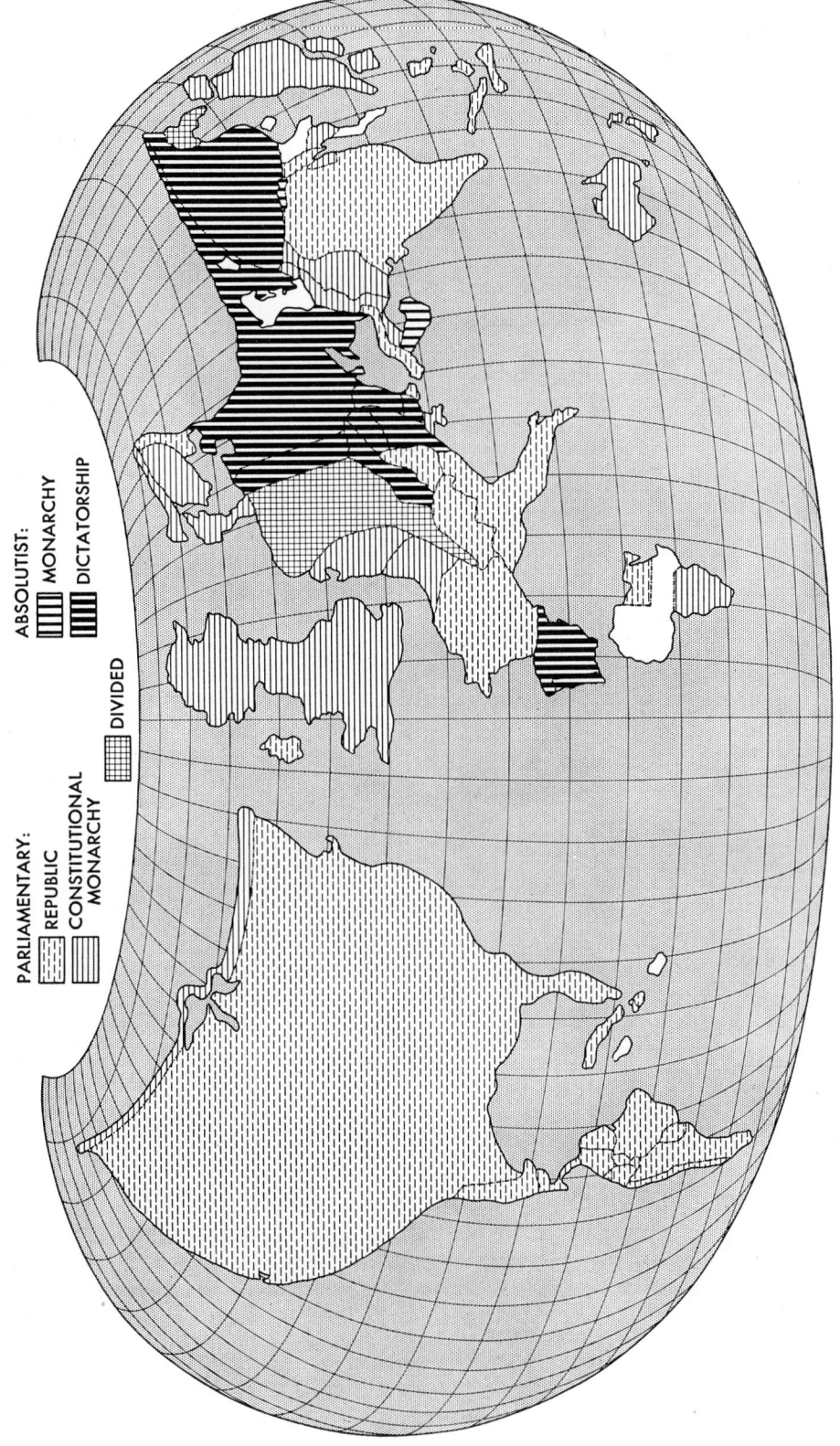

PARLIAMENTARY:

REPUBLIC

CONSTITUTIONAL
MONARCHY

ABSOLUTIST:

MONARCHY

DICTATORSHIP

DIVIDED

Source: Table 199

Figure 122. Governments: Geographic Distribution of Independent States Classified by Political Regime in Relation to National Income, Around 1950

civilization, usually emerging from wars, revolutions and internal anarchy.[61] The new feature in the political organization of the world is the ability of dictatorships to hold sway over a people indefinitely unless they are destroyed by external forces. The history of Central and South America in the nineteenth century and the beginning of the twentieth records many dictatorial regimes but most yielded to democratic forces sooner or later. On the contrary, no modern dictatorship has had to withdraw from power in face of mounting popular opposition.

Taking into account the scope of revolutions, wars and shifts in political boundaries, the number of dictatorships that have appeared on the scene in the last thirty-five years is not surpris-

61. Cf. **16.**

ingly large. The new feature has been the technique used by modern dictators for maintaining a grip on their peoples — a combination of ruthless terror with the appearance of democracy. Except for this, the spread of dictatorship from Russia to other countries has followed the old pattern of military conquest. No satellite country has accepted the new form of government voluntarily, through the free vote of the people; all have been sovietized by Russian tanks.

Though the annihilation of democratic freedom in the area overrun by the Russian army has been a heavy blow to world democracy, there may be some comfort in the fact that in camouflaging themselves as people's democracies, modern dictatorial governments recognize that they cannot exterminate the longing for freedom and self-government in their subjects.

CHAPTER 13

ELECTIONS AND PARLIAMENTS

SUFFRAGE

THE BEST SINGLE measure of the progress of democracy is the extent to which the people participate, directly or indirectly, in choosing their government and controlling its policy.

THE PROGRESS OF UNIVERSAL SUFFRAGE

It took many centuries to evolve political systems under which all citizens have a right to vote, regardless of their property holdings. The principle of universal suffrage was not firmly established in the world until two or three decades ago.[1]

The Ancient World and the Middle Ages

The republics of the ancient world and the Middle Ages were democracies of a small minority of the population: landowners and slave-holders in Greece,[2] merchants and handicraft masters in medieval Europe. The city-republics in various parts of Europe in the eighteenth and nineteenth centuries were ruled by small groups of substantial citizens and were plutocratic oligarchies rather than democracies in the modern sense.

The First Democratic Constitution

The question of voting limitations was avoided by the U.S. Continental Congress in the Articles of Confederation, which it adopted in 1777. Some members of the Congress were in favor of universal suffrage, others feared to antagonize their constituent states, all of which had some property qualifications.[3] Moreover, their immediate goal was to bring individual states into a union rather than to improve their electoral and other laws.[4] The Congress therefore established rules governing representation of individual states in the federal Congress and presidential elections but left each state to define its own qualifications for citizenship and the vote. Whoever was entitled to vote in the election of the larger legislative chamber in a state was automatically admitted to the federal polls.

This principle was retained in the Constitution of the United States, drawn up in 1787 and ratified by the required number (nine) of states by 1788. Article I provided that the members of the House of Representatives should be "chosen every second year by the people of the several States, and the electors in each State shall have the qualifications requisite for electors of the most numerous branch of the State Legislature." Each state was to have two Senators, "chosen by the Legislature thereof."

The property qualifications in the states were not very severe: 50 acres of vacant land (Delaware, Maryland, Virginia, North Carolina and South Carolina); property yielding an annual income of 36 to 40 shillings (Massachusetts, Connecticut, Rhode Island and New York); property worth £50 (New Hampshire and New Jersey). The most liberal were the requirements of Georgia (property of £10 value) and Pennsylvania (payment of any public taxes). In some cases the law provided alternative qualifications so that a citizen who failed to qualify under one requirement might meet another condition.[5]

Ideologically the U.S. Constitution followed the great French and British philosophers of the eighteenth century. That their ideas were accepted for guidance by a new nation overseas made a deep impression on the Old World and especially on France, which had paid only lip service to its radical thinkers.[6]

---

1. See **39, 40, 46, 47, 48, 53, 64.**

2. Aristotle expressed the ideas of his time when he insisted that husbandmen, craftsmen, laborers, and "any other class which is not a producer of virtue have no share in the state," and that the "ruling class should be the owners of property." (**41**, p. 296.) These qualifications excluded practically the whole economically productive population from citizenship. (Cf. **39.**)

3. **74**, Vol. I, pp. 497ff.

4. **74**, Vol. I, p. 392.

5. **68**, p. 13.

6. The American experiment, wrote Condorcet in *Influence of the American Revolution on Europe* (1786), was a realization of the great principles of liberty, equality and human rights "written in the books of philosophers and hearts of men of virtue." (**49**, Vol. 8, p. 11.) Two

The French Revolution

The first constitution of the New Regime in France, established by the Constituent Assembly in 1791, transformed France into a constitutional monarchy, with strict property qualifications in national and local elections. These qualifications were abolished after the suspension of the King, and the first republican National Convention (1792) was elected on the basis of universal suffrage for men. The government of 1793 was egalitarian but not democratic in the modern sense of this term and actually paved the way to military dictatorship.[7]

The French Revolution and the Napoleonic wars which followed left a deep rift in political thinking in Europe. Universal suffrage became a slogan of radical parties and of the rising labor movement, while moderate groups and political scientists more often favored some limited form of suffrage.[8]

---

years later he developed his views on current affairs in France in the form of *Letters of a Citizen of the United States to a Frenchman.* (**49**, Vol. 9, pp. 97–123.) Another French scholar of that time, De La Croix, gave a brilliant and penetrating analysis of the U.S. Constitution in the *Review of the Constitutions of the Principal States of Europe and the United States of America.* After an extensive survey of constitutions then existing in Europe, the author "ascends to the height of [his] subject." He writes, "I am going to speak of a constitution created by a principle of independence and a desire of equality . . . which has been constituted in all its parts by the energy of virtue, and produced in an age of knowledge." (**51**, p. 365.) This appraisal of the U.S. Constitution contrasts strikingly with the author's criticism of the republics of Venice, Genoa, Ragusa and others which excite "the attention of politicians, though in seeking there for liberty, they often find nothing but oppression." (*Ibid.,* p. 426.)

7. See Condorcet's appeal *Aux Citoyens Français, sur la Nouvelle Constitution* (**49**, Vol. 12, pp. 653–75 and "Extrait du Moniteur," *ibid.,* pp. 677–85). Condorcet paid with his life for criticism of that constitution.

8. "We think that [universal suffrage] is inadmissible," wrote a German scholar, Sebald Brendel, in 1817. "Most people are not even superficially aware of the necessary qualifications of a representative, often they are not familiar with common civic duties, their interest in public affairs is negligible, and they are easily influenced by the rich." He preferred therefore a "moderately limited" suffrage. All those who live from daily wages or occasional daily earnings should be excluded from the electorate; all those who have some property and are not on public relief rolls should be admitted to election. Furthermore, Brendel pleaded for fairly low property qualifications and decried as a fraud elections controlled or influenced by the government. (**46**, Vol. 2, pp. 288–89.)

The United States

In the United States, the problem of broadening the basis of suffrage remained essentially within the jurisdiction of the individual states. Before the end of the eighteenth century, property qualifications were abolished in South Carolina (1778), New Hampshire (1784), Georgia (1789) and Delaware (1792). They were followed by Maryland (1810), Connecticut (1818), Massachusetts and New York (both in 1821). The last vestiges of property qualification disappeared in the 1850's (Virginia, 1850, and North Carolina, 1856).[9]

After the Civil War the problem of universal suffrage emerged in a new form — extension of suffrage to the liberated Negroes, a problem still waiting a satisfactory solution in the South.[10]

Great Britain

Only 435,000 men, 2.5 per cent of the total population of Great Britain, were on the rolls of electors before the electoral reform of 1832. The reform eliminated some inequities in the distribution of constituencies and increased the number of potential voters by about 350,000. The second reform, in 1867, lowered property qualifications and doubled the size of the electorate, increasing it from 4 per cent to 8 per cent of the population. The Franchise Act of 1884 raised the number of electors to approximately 4 million, roughly 11 per cent of the total population or one third of all adult men.

The fourth electoral reform, the Representation of the People Act, 1918, entirely changed and simplified the procedure of registering voters,[11] and gave the franchise to all men aged 21 years or over — residence or occupation of business premises for six months in the constituency being the only requirement. At the same time, electoral rights were bestowed on women aged 30 years and over. This act increased the electorate from 6 million to 16 million. Ten years later, the People Equal Franchise Act made voting requirements the same for men and women, adding 6 million women to the Parliamentary Register. Thus nearly a century elapsed between the first electoral reform and the introduction of truly universal suffrage in the United Kingdom.[12] (See Table 200.)

---

9. **68**, p. 110.
10. See pp. 599ff.
11. **55**, p. 3.
12. **50**, pp. 160–61 and 276; **73**, pp. 169–70.

TABLE 200

ELECTORS: THE UNITED KINGDOM, 1886–1950

Year	Number, in Thousands		Ratio (Per Cent) of Electors to Population	Year	Number, in Thousands		Ratio (Per Cent) of Electors to Population
	Population	Electors			Population	Electors	
1886	36,860	4,132	11.2	1923	45,300	17,027	37.6
1892	38,700	4,518	11.7	1924	45,400	17,517	38.6
1895	40,100	4,682	11.7	1929	45,900	23,494	51.2
1900	41,800	4,993	11.9	1931	46,046	24,506	53.2
1906	43,340	5,495	12.7	1935	46,869	25,719	54.9
1910	45,000	5,864	13.0	1945	49,182	33,240	67.6
1922	45,200	16,051	35.5	1950	50,616	34,410	68.0

Sources: **50**, pp. 276–89; **23**, No. 84, 1935–1946, p. 71. Data for 1886–1910 (prior to the Representation of the People Act) rest on official estimates which imply a considerable margin of error.

Other Countries

A similar succession of electoral reforms brought the ratio of electors to population in Italy from 1.9 per cent in 1861 to 23.2 per cent in 1913, 62.2 per cent in 1948 and 64.5 in 1952.[13] (See Table 201.)

In Germany, Bismarck introduced universal suffrage for men in 1871, as a means of uniting the German Reich and increasing the authority of the central government in comparison with provincial (*Länder*) governments.

At the same time, France established universal suffrage, likewise for men only.

In the Netherlands, only 12–13 per cent of the men aged 25 years and over were on the electors' rolls in 1870–80; the percentage doubled by 1890 and almost doubled again by the turn of the century, but universal suffrage for both men and women was not established until 1920. (See Table 202.)

The general trend to broaden the electorate gained momentum in Europe after World War I. In the past two or three decades the principle of universal suffrage has been in effect in all democratic countries, but with some loopholes in its application. Few countries now have direct property qualifications for voting, but in many areas literacy tests, residence requirements, and registration formalities established to protect the ballot actually exclude certain groups of the population from the electorate or prevent them from exercising their rights as voters.

ENFRANCHISEMENT OF WOMEN

Woman suffrage did not attract the attention of the Founding Fathers of the United States, and the Constitution left the question open. At the time of the French Revolution, Condorcet pleaded with great eloquence for enfranchisement of women[14] but failed to convince his contemporaries. Not until the middle of the nineteenth century did women themselves enter an active claim to political equality with men.

In 1867 a petition demanding suffrage for women was presented to the British House of Commons and in the same year the question was brought before state constitutional conventions in New York and Michigan and the state legislature in Kansas. In the latter part of the century, the campaign for woman suffrage gained momentum, in both the United States and Europe.

The United States

Women obtained the right to vote in school elections in several states before the turn of the century. Woman suffrage was brought up repeatedly in state referendums and opposition to it decreased as the public became more familiar with the issue. When the United States entered World War I, the campaign was in full swing.[15] Fifteen states had already given women full voting rights, and the issue was pending before fourteen others. The activity of women's organizations during the war greatly increased their prestige in the nation. In 1919 Congress submitted to the state legislatures a proposed constitutional amendment that read in part: "The

---

13. **26**, 1944–1948, p. 149.

14. See his essay "Sur l'Admission des Femmes au Droit de Cité." (**49**, Vol. 10, pp. 121–30.)

15. See **70**.

TABLE 201

ELECTORS AND VOTERS: ITALY, 1861–1953

Year	Electors[a]		Votes Cast in General Elections	
	Number, in Thousands	Ratio (Per Cent) to Population	Number, in Thousands	Ratio (Per Cent) to Electors
1861	419	1.9	240	57.2
1865	504	2.0	272	53.9
1867	498	1.9	258	51.8
1870	530	2.0	241	45.5
1874	572	2.1	319	55.7
1876	605	2.2	358	59.2
1880	622	2.2	370	59.4
1882	2,018	6.9	1,224	60.7
1886	2,420	8.1	1,416	58.5
1890	2,753	9.0	1,477	53.7
1892	2,934	9.4	1,639	55.9
1895	2,120	6.7	1,251	59.0
1897	2,121	6.6	1,241	58.5
1900	2,249	6.9	1,310	58.3
1904	2,541	7.5	1,594	62.7
1909	2,930	8.3	1,904	65.0
1913	8,443	23.2	5,101	60.4
1919	10,239	27.3	5,794	56.6
1921	11,477	28.7	6,701	58.4
1924	11,939	29.0	7,614	63.8
1929	9,639	23.4	8,662	89.9
1934	10,426	24.3	10,060	96.5
1948	29,118	62.2	26,854	92.2
1953	30,273	64.5	28,406	93.9

Source: **26**, 1951, p. 138; 1954, p. 120.

a. For 1861–80, restricted franchise for men of 25 and over; for 1882–1909 more liberal, but still restricted, franchise for men of 21 and over; since 1913 universal franchise for adult men; in 1919 and 1921, proportional representation; in 1924, election by simple majority, all the country handled as a single district (fascist plebiscite); in 1929 and 1934, a similar procedure with compulsory voting; in 1948 and 1952, universal franchise for adult men and women, multiparty system, compulsory voting.

right of citizens of the United States to vote shall not be denied or abridged by the United States or by any State on account of sex." In 1920, after ratification by thirty-six states, this became the Nineteenth Amendment.

Great Britain

At almost the same time, woman suffrage triumphed in Great Britain. Here the movement had entered a militant phase in the 1890's, partly as a result of the enfranchisement of women in New Zealand (1893) and South Australia

TABLE 202

ELECTORS: THE NETHERLANDS, SECOND CHAMBER, 1870–1948

Year	Electors, in Thousands	Ratio (Per Cent) to Population Aged 25 and Over
	Men Only	
1870	104	12.1
1880	122	13.1
1890	296	28.6
1900	570	49.0
1910	855	63.2
	Men and Women	
1920	3,250	97.6
1930	3,884	98.1
1940	4,721	98.5
1946	4,761	97.8
1948	4,933	98.9

Source: **28**, 1940, p. 353, and 1950, p. 125.

(1894).[16] The press at first greeted the militant campaign of the suffragists with severe and contemptuous criticism, but though women lost their skirmishes with the British police, they won the support of public opinion. The decisive impetus to enfranchisement of women, however, was World War I, and especially the work of women in munitions industries.[17] In 1918 women aged 30 years and over were enfranchised by the Representation of the People Act.[18] A decade later the People Equal Franchise Act established equal suffrage for men and women. By an almost unanimous vote, the House of Commons overruled the last argument against equal suffrage for men and women — the fear that women would outnumber the stronger sex in the electorate and form a new women's party that would eventually destroy the British parliamentary system.

Scope of Woman Suffrage

Before World War II, woman suffrage, occasionally with minor restrictions, had been established in the United States, Great Britain, all the British dominions, Ireland, the Netherlands, Scandinavia, Finland, Germany, Austria, Czechoslovakia and Poland — areas with a total population of approximately 360 million. Women had

16. **71**, p. 286.
17. **71**, pp. 337ff.
18. Cf. p. 590.

TABLE 203

ELECTORS: WOMAN SUFFRAGE IN THE WORLD

(*As of November 30, 1952*)

A. COUNTRIES IN WHICH WOMEN HAVE THE SAME POLITICAL RIGHTS AS MEN			B. COUNTRIES WHERE WOMEN MAY VOTE IN ALL ELECTIONS WITH CERTAIN QUALIFICATIONS
Albania [a]	France	Netherlands	Guatemala. Constitution of 1945 made voting compulsory and secret for literate men; optional and secret for women with the required qualifications; optional and public for illiterate men.[b]
Argentina [a]	Germany	New Zealand	
Australia	Democratic	Norway	
Austria	Republic	Pakistan [a]	Lebanon. Women must have a certificate of primary education or its equivalent, not required for men. Rights granted in 1952.
Belgium [a]	(East)	Panama [a]	
Bolivia [a]	Federal Re-	Philippines	
Brazil	public	Poland	Portugal. Women are subject to higher educational requirements or, when fulfilling the tax qualifications prescribed for men, must be heads of families. Rights granted in 1945.
Bulgaria [a]	(West)	Romania	
Burma [a]	Greece [a]	Saar	
Canada	Hungary	Sweden	
Ceylon	Iceland	Thailand	Syria. Women must have an elementary school certificate, not required for men. Rights granted in 1949.
Chile [a]	India [a]	Turkey	
China [a]	Indonesia [a]	Union of South	
Costa Rica [a]	Ireland	Africa	
Cuba	Israel [a]	USSR	
Czechoslovakia	Italy [a]	United King-	C. COUNTRIES WHERE WOMEN HAVE NO VOTING RIGHTS IN GENERAL ELECTIONS
Denmark	Japan [a]	dom	
Dominican	Korea [a]	United States	
Republic	Liberia [a]	Uruguay	Colombia / Jordan / Peru
Ecuador [a]	Luxembourg	Venezuela [a]	Egypt / Libya / Saudi Arabia
El Salvador [a]	Mongolian Peo-	Yugoslavia [a]	Ethiopia / Mexico / Spain
Finland	ple's Republic		Haiti / Nicaragua / Switzerland
			Honduras / Paraguay / Yemen

Source: Adapted, with minor changes, from **2**, pp. 19, 20.

a. Countries in which women were enfranchised after June 26, 1945 (the date the UN Charter was signed).

b. The constitution was suspended after the revolution in June 1954. A new constitution is being drafted.

also full suffrage rights at the election to the Constituent Assembly in Russia in 1917, the only free election in that country after the revolution.

The principle of equal rights for men and women has been solemnly proclaimed by the United Nations — in the Preamble of the Charter and in the Universal Declaration of Human Rights.[19] A Commission on the Status of Women was established by the UN and its work has had some influence on legislation in member countries.[20]

In recent years women have gained the right to vote in areas with a total population of more than 600 million: Guatemala, El Salvador, Costa Rica, Chile, Argentina and Uruguay; France, Belgium and Italy; Japan, India, Pakistan, Ceylon, Thailand and Burma; the Union of South Africa. The question is under debate in several other countries.

In Asia, enfranchisement of women has become an indispensable element in democratic self-government.

Without counting the totalitarian countries, where women are entitled to, and often compelled to, participate in elections but, like men, actually have no political rights, they now have voting rights nearly or wholly equal to those of men in countries with a total population of approximately 1,000 million. Women have no vote in an area with a population of approximately 600 million, which includes non-self-governing territories, absolute monarchies, Spain, some parts of Latin America and some Asiatic countries. The scope of woman suffrage appears much broader when the USSR and other countries behind the Iron Curtain are included, as in the UN surveys. (See Table 203.)

VOTING AGE

The prevailing age requirement for voting in the Western Hemisphere is 21 years or over.

The United States Constitution leaves the mat-

19. **2**, p. 1.
20. **9**, April 13, 1953.

ter to the states, all but one of which specify a minimum age of 21 years; in Georgia, the minimum age is 18. Among the other American countries, 21 years is the age requirement in Canada and in Mexico, Guatemala, Honduras, Costa Rica, Panama, Haiti, Venezuela, Colombia, Ecuador, Peru, Bolivia and Chile. Four of these countries — Mexico, Guatemala, Costa Rica and Peru — permit married men to vote at the age of 18.

A minimum age of 18 is in effect in El Salvador, Brazil, Paraguay, Uruguay and Argentina and in the USSR, Yugoslavia, Indonesia and Turkey.[21] In Europe the pattern varies from country to country. Great Britain, France, Belgium, Denmark and Italy give the vote at age 21; Switzerland and Germany, at 20; Sweden and Norway, 23 years; Finland, 24 years; and the Netherlands, 25 years. Before Hungary fell under control of the USSR, that country required, for men, age 24 or over and at least 4 years of school attendance; for women, 30 years or over and not less than 6 years of school. In Japan the minimum voting age is 20 years.

It is generally believed that younger voters are more inclined to support extremist parties and older people, moderate groups.[22] This consideration probably has had some weight in determining the attitude of various political parties to the age requirement. The age of enrollment in the armed forces has been another important consideration. A strong argument can be made in favor of coordinating voting age and enrollment, especially in wartime. Lowering military age, therefore, raises the question of a similar change in voting age.[23]

---

21. See **66**, *passim*. The principle of differentiating voting age according to marital status, and sometimes according to education, was recognized in some of the early constitutions of Latin America in the period 1810–30. It is less popular in the Eastern Hemisphere, although different age limits for men and for women appeared in many European countries in the period of transition to universal suffrage for both sexes.

22. Cf. **75**, p. 112.

23. In U.S. elections in 1942 and 1944 members of the armed forces were handled as absentee voters in the constituency to which they had previously belonged. Qualified voters in the armed forces, scattered over the entire globe, were permitted to apply for state ballots and to cast their vote by mail. Except for the provision waiving the requirement of any poll tax for soldiers voting for federal offices, the federal legislation was strictly limited to facilitating absentee voting of persons in the armed forces abroad. The results were highly unsatisfactory in 1942, when only 137,000 persons applied for "war

THE ELECTORATE

Apart from property requirements, which are incompatible with the basic idea of universal suffrage, the relative size of the electorate depends on the following factors:

1. Whether or not women have the same rights as men.

2. The voting age and the composition of the population by age.

3. Voting requirements (literacy, residence and the like) and ability of people to meet these requirements.

4. The way in which voters' registers are established.

SEX AND AGE

In most countries in which women have the same electoral rights as men, they outnumber men in the electorate, as in the following examples (in thousands): [24]

	Men	Women
Great Britain, 1935	14,801	16,572
Bavaria, 1950	2,661	3,332
Belgium, 1949	2,705	2,930
Sweden, 1948	2,316	2,391
Norway, 1945	954	1,008
Finland, 1945	1,040	1,244
Austria, 1949	1,900	2,492
Australia, 1949	2,417	2,426
Japan, 1949	20,061	22,045

Men predominate in the electorate in countries that restrict voting by women and in areas where many voters fail to meet the literacy qualifications or do not care to register.[25]

Each one-year age class between ages 18 and 25 represents approximately 2 per cent of the population. Other conditions being equal, an electoral law which provides a voting age of 18 years and over implies that the percentage of po-

---

ballots" (58,000 in New Jersey and 79,000 in 42 other states). (**3**, p. 2.) Participation was better in 1944 when 4.5 million applications and 2.8 million votes were handled by the states. (**4**, p. 2.)

24. For Great Britain, **23**, No. 84, p. 71; for Bavaria, **22**, p. 82; for Belgium, **12**, 1950, p. 394; for Sweden, **33**, 1949, p. 320; for Norway, **30**, 1949, p. 352; for Australia, **10**, 1951, p. 82; for Austria, **11**, 1953, p. 70; for Japan, **27**, 1950, p. 394.

25. In the Union of South Africa the number of registered female voters is somewhat smaller than that of men (in 1948, 706,000 women and 746,000 men) because of the composition of the European (white) population. (**35**, 1948, pp. 98–101.)

tential voters will be about 6 points above that under a law with a minimum voting age of 21.

LITERACY

Many enlightened students supported literacy requirements for voting in the nineteenth century and they are still controversial issues. John Stuart Mill considered it wholly inadmissible in 1861 that any person should vote without being able to read, write and perform the common operations of arithmetic.[26] In modern countries, the question of literacy has been obviated by compulsory elementary education; it is irrelevant how the few remaining cases of illiteracy are handled under electoral laws. The question is very important, however, for countries with widespread illiteracy — not only in Asia and Middle and South America but even in some parts of Europe, where disfranchisement of those who cannot read and write amounts to disfranchising the poor.

Admittedly it is difficult to include illiterate voters in a system of secret ballots.[27] Orderly registration of eligible voters is difficult when a large proportion are illiterate, and voting by persons who can neither read the ballot nor sign their name creates the danger of irregularities and abuses. These difficulties, however, should be weighed against the advantages of enfranchising all citizens so far as possible and encouraging all to take part in political affairs. Moreover, a nation that has universal suffrage without literacy requirements is committed to provide compulsory education and to stamp out illiteracy.

The trend in modern constitutions has been away from literacy qualifications for suffrage. Such qualifications, however, have remained in electoral laws in Bolivia, Brazil, Ecuador, Peru and Chile as well as in some states of the United States. Guatemala's electoral law of 1945 (suspended in 1954 with the rest of the constitution) prohibited discrimination against illiterate voters.[28]

PROPERTY QUALIFICATIONS

Property qualifications for national suffrage are rare in modern constitutions and electoral laws.[29] The poll-tax requirement in force in some southern states of the United States and the occupational and income qualifications in electoral laws in Bolivia and Colombia are exceptions. More usual, both in the United States and in Europe, is the requirement of property qualification for voting on local affairs, especially on questions of local taxation, or the provision that nonresidents, otherwise ineligible to vote in a locality, may do so on matters involving taxes if they own property in the locality.

NATIONAL VARIATIONS

It is difficult to compare the numbers of registered voters in various countries because of differences in methods of establishing voters' lists. Registration may be compulsory or voluntary. Registers may be carried over (so-called permanent registration) or prepared for each election separately. The lists of the latter type usually show a lower ratio of voters to population than those based on permanent registration. The number of voters may also be affected by duplications resulting from the mobility of population and the rights of certain groups of electors to vote in more than one constituency.[30]

In most modern countries with a high level of literacy and a voting age of 21 and over, universal suffrage for men and women enfranchises

---

26. **63,** p. 160.
27. Indonesia, in view of its high percentage of illiteracy, conducts elections by means of party symbols on the ballot boxes rather than candidates' names.
28. The law contained special provision for voting by persons unable to read and write — in actuality, a large part of the Indian population in the highlands. For those who could read and write, it made registration obligatory and protected the secrecy of the ballot. For those who could not, registration was optional and illiterate voters were permitted to fill out the form in the presence of a witness of their choice. **(24, 25.)**

29. John Stuart Mill believed that the assembly which votes the taxes should be elected exclusively by those who pay something toward the taxes imposed. Voting on taxes by persons who do not have to pay them is, according to that writer, a violation of the fundamental principle of free government and amounts to "allowing them to put their hands into other people's pockets." **(63,** p. 162.)

An extreme case of suffrage based on property qualification is the three-class electoral system which existed in Prussia from 1849 to 1918. Voters in each district were divided among three classes, each of which paid approximately equal amounts of taxes, and each class elected one third of the representatives assigned to the district. Thus, 6 per cent of the voters elected one third of the Landtag. **(54,** p. 34.) The abolition of this system after World War I resulted in a drastic change in the composition of the Landtag and a shift of the majority from the Conservatives to the Social-Democrats. **(53,** Vol. 1, p. 409.)

30. A voter in Great Britain would vote in two constituencies — for example, in that of his residence and in that where his office or other rented premises were located.

TABLE 204

ELECTORS: SELECTED COUNTRIES, AROUND 1909 AND AROUND 1950

	Around 1909			Around 1950		
	Number, in Thousands		Ratio (Per Cent) of Electors to Population	Number, in Thousands		Ratio (Per Cent) of Electors to Population
Country	Population	Electors		Population	Electors	
United States	91,972	15,031[a]	16.3[b]	146,571	48,834[a]	33.3[b]
Canada	7,207	1,821	25.3	13,549	7,893	58.3
Guatemala	—	—	—	2,750	408[a]	14.8[b]
Colombia	—	—	—	10,545	2,614	24.8
Brazil	—	—	—	52,533	11,613	22.0
Uruguay	—	—	—	2,203	859	39.0
Chile	—	—	—	5,349	641.	12.0
United Kingdom	45,222	7,706	17.0	49,108	33,240	67.7
Ireland	—	—	—	2,998	1,800	60.0
France	39,602	11,463	28.9	39,100	24,218	61.9
Belgium	7,424	1,746	23.5	8,614	5,635	65.4
Netherlands	5,858	855	14.6	9,884	4,933[a]	49.9
Denmark	2,757	491	17.8	4,146	2,435	58.7
Sweden	5,222	1,066	20.4	6,883	4,708	68.4
Norway	2,394	810	33.9	3,088	1,962	63.5
Finland	3,115	1,430	45.9	3,989	1,736	43.5
Germany[c]	64,926	14,442	22.2	46,749	31,208	66.7
Bavaria	—	—	—	9,176	4,814	52.5
Switzerland	3,753	913	24.3	4,466	1,345	30.1
Austria	29,193	5,809	19.9	6,953	4,392	63.5
Italy	34,671	8,672	24.2	45,706	26,802	58.6
Bulgaria	4,055	988	24.4	—	—	—
Japan	52,523	1,504	2.9	82,636	42,105	51.0
Union of South Africa[d]	1,225	346	28.3	2,410	1,452	60.2
Australia	4,425	2,812	63.3	7,710	4,740	61.5
New Zealand	1,008	616	61.1	1,840	1,082	58.8

Sources: For 1909, **78**, Vol. 7, p. 103; for 1950, **1**, 1951, and official publications of the respective countries (**8, 15, 24, 31, 17, 13, 36, 16, 29**, and others).

a. Votes cast.   c. For 1950, Western Germany.
b. Ratio of votes cast to population.   d. Europeans only.

about 60–65 per cent of the population and universal suffrage for men, only some 30–32 per cent. Proportions substantially below these indicate that considerable numbers of potential electors are being disqualified on the basis of literacy and residence tests or are failing to register. (See Table 204; cf. Figure 123.)

The highest ratios of potential voters to population in recent years have been recorded in Sweden (68.4 per cent), Great Britain (67.7), Western Germany (66.7), Belgium (65.4), Norway (63.5), Austria (63.5), France (61.9) and Australia (61.5). The record of the United States in 1948 — which is based on the number of votes cast — was disappointing. If we assume that in the United States, as in other modern nations, some 20–25 per cent of the electorate normally fail to vote, the number of electors should be about one third larger than that of votes cast at elections — approximately 65 million in 1948. This hypothetical figure means that the electorate in that year represented some 44 per cent of the total population or less than 70 per cent of the population of voting age. The record was appreciably better in 1952.

REGIONAL VARIATIONS

Regional variations in the relative size of the

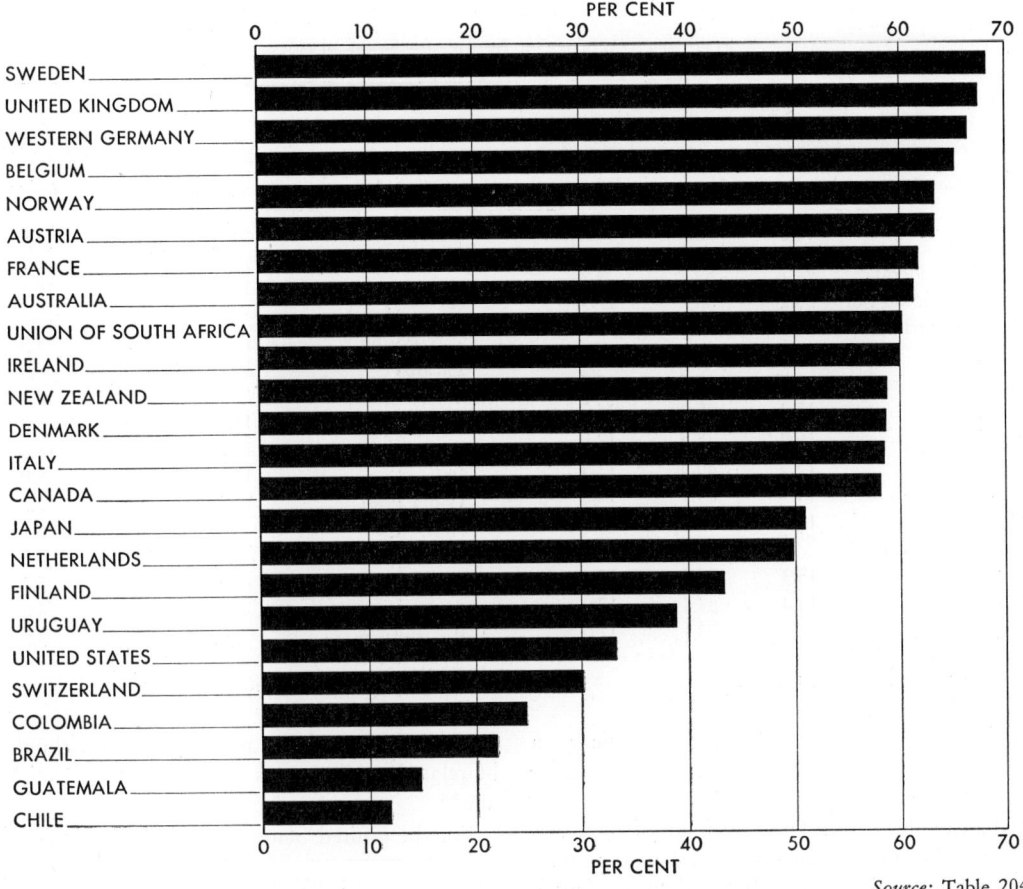

Source: Table 204

FIGURE 123. ELECTORS: RATIO OF ELECTORS TO POPULATION, IN SELECTED COUNTRIES, AROUND 1950

electorate are illustrated by the examples of Brazil, Peru and the United States.

Brazil

Brazil recorded the number of registered electors and voters at the general elections in 1945 by provincial units. (See Table 205.) With suffrage for men only, some 30 per cent of the population might have been eligible. This ratio, however, was drastically reduced by literacy requirements. Actually, only the most urbanized and industrialized and comparatively prosperous southeastern states — Distrito Federal, Rio Grande do Sul, Santa Catarina, São Paulo, Rio de Janeiro and Paraná — registered more than 16 per cent of the population as electors. In some sparsely populated and backward northwestern regions, less than 8 per cent of the population was registered, and in the extreme northwestern corner (Rio Branco), less than 5 per cent. Thus

illiteracy and other conditions characteristic of the underdeveloped areas disfranchised more than half, and in some cases more than two thirds, of the men of voting age.[31]

Moreover, in provinces with a comparatively high proportion of electors relatively more appeared at the polls than in backward areas: 80.1 to 89.2 per cent in the five states at the top of the list, 66.4 to 79.5 per cent in the five at the bottom.

Peru

Peru, which also has a literacy requirement, reported the number of electors as compared with total population and the number of men of 21 years and over, in each department in 1945. The ratio of electors to men of voting age

---

31. Racial discrimination is not among these conditions. Brazil has never had laws discriminating against Indians and Negroes. (**59**, p. 99.)

TABLE 205

ELECTORS AND VOTERS: BRAZIL, BY STATE, 1945

State[a]	*Ratio (Per Cent) of:*			State[a]	*Ratio (Per Cent) of:*		
	Electors to Population	Voters to Electors	Voters to Population		Electors to Population	Voters to Electors	Voters to Population
Total	16.2	78.7	12.8	Amapá	15.3	80.8	11.4
				Minas Gerais	16.3	67.8	11.1
Distrito Federal	27.7	89.2	24.7	Pará	15.3	68.6	10.5
Rio Grande do Sul	20.2	86.8	17.5	Fernando de			
Santa Catarina	19.6	83.8	16.9	Noronha	11.8	75.7	8.9
São Paulo	21.0	80.1	16.8	Paraíba	10.9	81.4	8.9
Rio de Janeiro	18.5	83.7	15.5	Guaporé	12.1	72.8	8.8
Paraná	17.3	85.0	14.7	Goiaz	11.1	76.9	8.8
Sergipe	16.0	78.5	12.6	Pernambuco	10.7	81.7	8.8
Iguaçú	15.4	80.3	12.4	Baía	10.1	86.9	8.0
Espírito Santo	14.5	84.9	12.3	Ponta Porá	10.2	75.3	7.7
Ceará	15.8	77.2	12.2	Acre	7.6	79.5	6.1
Rio Grande do				Alagoas	7.7	76.9	5.9
Norte	15.3	78.3	12.0	Maranhão	7.9	66.4	5.2
Piauí	14.4	83.4	12.0	Amazonas	6.7	68.3	4.6
Mato Grosso	16.1	73.1	11.7	Rio Branco	4.9	74.8	3.7

Source: **13**, pp. 520–21. Cf. **14**.

a. Arrayed by ratio of voters to total population.

averaged 51.6 per cent for the republic as a whole, ranging from 22.2 per cent in Apurímac to 79.9 per cent in Lima and 89.8 per cent in Callao (Table 206). Thus, suffrage of men was practically universal in some parts of the country, while in others probably less than one fourth of adult males could vote.

The United States

Conditions in the United States are less clear because of the absence of federal voter lists. We know only the approximate number of persons of voting age and the number of persons who register as voters and cast votes in presidential, congressional and gubernatorial elections in each state. Assuming that the ratio of votes to electors varies in the United States about as in other countries for which such data are available, the size of the electorate and its relation to the population of voting age can be roughly estimated.

For 1940, a census year, the number of votes cast in each state can be compared with the number of citizens (native and naturalized) of voting age.[32] For other years such a comparison is

more difficult and the number of votes should be related to all persons or all civilians of voting age.[33]

For the United States as a whole, the ratio of

dence requirements and those disfranchised on the ground of the poll-tax requirement, the literacy test, or by arbitrary action of local authorities. The ratio of votes cast to citizens of voting age is a product of two ratios: that of actual voters to potential voters and that of potential voters to all citizens of voting age.

33. The Bureau of the Census pointed out that "the population of voting age includes a great many persons who, although old enough to vote, may not do so because they have not satisfied registration, or payment of poll taxes. The alien population of the United States 21 years old and over, including foreign-born persons for whom citizenship was not reported, numbered 4,133,178 in 1940. However, by November 2, 1948 it is expected that there will be only in the neighborhood of 2,000,000 aliens of voting age in the United States. Among the citizens of voting age there are also many persons not qualified to vote because they are confined in penal institutions or are inmates of mental hospitals and kindred institutions. There are still others who may not vote because they reside elsewhere than in the State in which they have voting privileges. This group includes some members of the armed forces away from their place of voting residence, either in this country or abroad. In all these cases, eligibility to vote is determined by State laws which vary in many respects. Furthermore, there is an unascertainable number of persons in the District of Columbia who lack voting residence in any State." (**6**, No. 15, October 10, 1948, p. 1.)

32. See **42**, p. 178. Louis H. Bean uses the number of citizens aged 21 and over as equivalent to the number of persons entitled to vote. We think that correction should be introduced for persons who do not meet resi-

TABLE 206

ELECTORS: PERU, BY DEPARTMENT, 1945

| Department | Number, in Thousands | | | Ratio (Per Cent) of Electors to Men Aged 21 and Over |
	Total Population	Men Aged 21 and Over	Electors	
Total	6,837.6	1,508.8	779.2	51.6
Tumbes	28.0	5.9	4.3	72.9
Piura	449.9	93.9	35.7	38.0
Cajamarca	544.3	102.6	60.8	59.2
Lambayeque	212.6	49.2	27.6	56.1
La Libertad	421.9	92.1	60.1	65.3
Ancash	467.7	91.0	44.4	48.8
Huánuco	257.8	54.9	20.4	37.1
Pasco	99.8	22.4	10.7	47.8
Junín	372.6	79.9	55.9	70.0
Lima	912.1	236.8	189.1	79.9
Callao	90.9	25.5	22.9	89.8
Ica	155.2	37.2	31.0	83.3
Huancavelica	269.4	55.8	16.8	30.1
Ayacucho	305.2	79.1	21.2	26.8
Cuzco	536.1	130.7	33.3	25.5
Apurímac	284.4	62.0	13.8	22.2
Areguipa	289.9	65.2	46.6	71.5
Puno	603.8	133.0	29.9	22.5
Moquegua	37.6	8.3	5.7	68.7
Tacna	40.3	10.2	6.2	60.8
Loreto	186.0	38.4	17.7	46.1
Amazonas	71.8	14.3	10.8	75.5
San Martín	104.6	19.0	13.3	70.0
Madre de Dios	5.5	1.4	1.1	78.6

Source: **32,** 1946, pp. 601–03.

the number of votes cast to the estimated civilian population of voting age has varied in the past two decades as follows: [34]

	Population of Voting Age, in Millions	Votes Cast in Presidential Elections, in Millions	Votes Cast as Per Cent of Population of Voting Age
1932	75.6	39.8	52.6
1936	80.0	45.6	57.1
1940	84.0	49.8	59.3
1944	81.2	45.3[a]	55.8
1948	94.9	48.8	51.4
1952	98.4	61.6	62.6

a. Votes cast by civilians.

The range of annual fluctuations in the ratio of votes cast to population of voting age — from 51.4 to 62.6 per cent — was much narrower than the variations among the states. Indeed,

34. **5,** No. 63, August 31, 1952, p. 1.

the difference in 1940 between the deep South and West Virginia or Illinois, for example, was larger than that between the jungles of the upper Amazon river and the region around Rio de Janeiro in Brazil. (See Table 207.)

Assuming that the ratio of votes to electors varies from state to state in the United States as it varies from state to state in Brazil — 66 to 68 per cent in the most backward areas, 85 to 87 per cent in the most urbanized and industralized regions [35] — it is obvious that the contrasts in the ratios of votes to citizens aged 21 and over were due to some form of disfranchisement of a large proportion of such citizens. In fact, universal suffrage did not

35. Excluding the Distrito Federal. Brazil is taken as an example of a country with strong contrasts in the racial composition of the population and levels of economic development in different regions but without racial discrimination.

TABLE 207

ELECTIONS: UNITED STATES, POPULAR VOTE FOR PRESIDENT, BY STATE, 1940, 1948 AND 1952

(*Population of Voting Age and Votes in Thousands*)

State [a]	1940			1948			1952		
	Citizens [b] Aged 21 and Over	Votes Cast	Ratio (Per Cent) of Votes to Citizens Aged 21 and Over	Civilian Population of Voting Age [c]	Votes Cast	Ratio (Per Cent) of Votes to Civilian Population of Voting Age	Civilian Population of Voting Age [c]	Votes Cast	Ratio (Per Cent) of Votes to Civilian Population of Voting Age
Utah	298	248	83.1	370	276	74.5	414	330	79.7
West Virginia	1,046	868	83.0	1,103	749	67.9	1,128	873	77.4
Illinois	5,120	4,218	82.4	5,896	3,984	67.6	5,967	4,481	75.1
South Dakota	378	308	81.5	387	250	64.6	398	294	73.8
Indiana	2,199	1,783	81.1	2,557	1,656	64.7	2,626	1,955	74.4
Colorado	688	549	79.7	721	515	71.4	880	630	71.5
New Hampshire	296	235	79.6	365	231	63.2	351	273	77.8
Delaware	172	136	79.4	196	139	70.9	220	174	79.0
Massachusetts	2,575	2,027	78.7	3,228	2,155	66.8	3,220	2,383	74.0
North Dakota	358	281	78.4	332	221	66.5	350	270	71.4
Connecticut	1,012	782	77.2	1,376	884	64.2	1,445	1,097	75.9
Idaho	305	235	77.0	318	215	67.6	352	276	78.4
New Jersey	2,593	1,973	76.1	3,255	1,950	59.9	3,476	2,419	69.6
New York	8,328	6,302	75.7	10,035	6,275	62.5	10,478	7,216	68.9
Nevada	70	53	75.6	90	62	68.9	115	82	71.3
Iowa	1,609	1,215	75.5	1,718	1,038	60.9	1,688	1,269	75.2
Nebraska	817	616	75.4	846	489	57.8	882	610	69.2
Ohio	4,404	3,320	75.4	5,189	2,936	56.6	5,350	3,701	69.2
Rhode Island	429	320	75.2	503	326	64.8	533	414	77.7
Kansas	1,145	860	75.1	1,294	789	60.9	1,276	896	70.2
Wyoming	150	112	74.8	169	101	59.8	180	133	73.8
Missouri	2,464	1,834	74.4	2,623	1,579	60.2	2,656	1,892	71.2
California	4,456	3,269	73.4	6,714	4,022	59.9	7,333	5,142	70.1
Wisconsin	1,942	1,406	72.4	2,147	1,277	69.5	2,251	1,607	71.4

(*Continued on facing page*)

exist in the southern states.[36] In 1940, it was restricted by probably 20–25 per cent in North Carolina and Florida and more drastically, perhaps by 40–50 per cent, in Tennessee, Texas, Louisiana and Virginia, while Alabama, Arkansas, Georgia, Mississippi and South Carolina apparently denied the franchise to a great majority of the population of voting age, "poor whites" as well as Negroes. All in all, the literacy test, which usually was not offered to potential voters, the poll tax and other measures, including intimidation and violence, kept about 7.5 to 8 million persons or approximately 9 per cent of the civilian population of voting age from the polls.[37]

The situation changed remarkably after World War II. The civilian population of voting age increased by 10.9 million between November 1940 and November 1948 and by an additional 3.5 million between 1948 and 1952. At the same time, the number of aliens in this age group was steadily declining, so that the potential number of electors, under universal suffrage, may have increased by some 12 million between 1940 and 1948 and by 5 million between 1948 and 1952. The vote in 1948 was very light, but in 1952 the

36. Cf. André Siegfried (**69**, *passim*). The situation in the South in 1940 was not quite so gloomy as in the 1920's when Siegfried wrote his book but the main problem still exists as he saw it.

37. Cf. **60**, p. 506.

TABLE 207—*continued*

State [a]	1940			1948			1952		
	Citizens [b] *Aged 21 and Over*	*Votes Cast*	*Ratio (Per Cent) of Votes to Citizens Aged 21 and Over*	*Civilian Population of Voting Age* [c]	*Votes Cast*	*Ratio (Per Cent) of Votes to Civilian Population of Voting Age*	*Civilian Population of Voting Age* [c]	*Votes Cast*	*Ratio (Per Cent) of Votes to Civilian Population of Voting Age*
Minnesota	1,731	1,251	72.3	1,906	1,212	63.6	1,899	1,379	72.6
Montana	343	248	72.2	319	224	70.2	362	265	73.2
Washington	1,124	794	70.6	1,649	905	54.9	1,543	1,103	71.4
Pennsylvania	6,031	4,088	67.8	7,111	3,735	52.5	7,043	4,581	65.0
Oregon	717	481	67.1	1,109	524	47.2	1,035	695	67.1
Vermont	214	143	66.8	238	123	51.7	231	154	66.7
Michigan	3,132	2,086	66.6	3,981	2,110	53.0	4,264	2,799	65.6
New Mexico	275	183	66.5	295	186	63.0	376	239	63.5
Maine	494	321	65.0	568	265	46.6	545	352	64.6
Oklahoma	1,362	826	60.6	1,438	722	50.2	1,372	949	69.2
Kentucky	1,631	970	59.5	1,618	823	50.9	1,655	993	60.0
Maryland	1,154	660	57.2	1,363	597	43.8	1,570	902	57.4
Arizona	263	150	57.0	374	177	47.3	495	259	52.3
North Carolina	1,925	823	42.7	2,049	791	38.6	2,326	1,211	52.1
Florida	1,188	485	40.9	1,465	578	39.5	1,978	989	50.0
Tennessee	1,703	523	30.7	1,840	550	29.9	1,930	893	46.2
Texas	3,710	1,041	28.1	4,311	1,147	26.6	4,845	2,077	42.9
Louisiana	1,365	372	26.0	1,495	416	27.8	1,613	652	40.4
Virginia	1,568	346	22.1	1,772	419	23.6	1,979	620	31.3
Alabama	1,555	294	18.9	1,564	215	13.7	1,709	426	24.9
Arkansas	1,099	201	18.3	1,100	242	22.0	1,070	405	37.8
Georgia	1,769	313	17.7	1,917	419	21.8	2,114	651	30.8
Mississippi	1,195	176	14.7	1,155	192	16.6	1,176	286	24.3
South Carolina	990	100	10.1	1,029	142	13.8	1,112	341	30.7

Sources: For 1940, **42**, p. 178; for 1948, **8**, 1950, p. 318 and **6**, p. 6. For 1952, population of voting age as estimated by the Bureau of the Census (Current Population Reports, Population Estimates, Series P-25, No. 63); votes as reported by the United Press on the basis of official returns.

a. Arrayed by the ratio of votes to citizens aged 21 and over in 1940.
b. Native and naturalized.

c. Includes some 2 million aliens. In all states, except Georgia, voting age is 21 and over; in Georgia, 18 years and over.

representation of electors at the polls was about as heavy as in 1940 when the enfranchisement of former aliens is taken into account.

The ranking of individual states and geographic regions according to the ratio of votes cast to civilian population of voting age remained about the same throughout this period: densely populated industrial states (Illinois, West Virginia, Delaware, Massachusetts, Connecticut, New Jersey, New York) and "frontier" states were at or near the top of the list; the southern states, at the bottom. But the range of difference has been drastically reduced.

In the five states at the top of Table 207, votes were cast by an average 82.2 per cent of the civilian population of voting age in 1940, 67.9 per cent in 1948 and 76.1 per cent in 1952. The comparable averages for the five states at the bottom of the table were 15.9 per cent in 1940, 17.6 per cent in 1948 and 29.7 per cent in 1952.

In 1940, the rate was below 20 per cent in five states of the solid South and ranged between 22 and 40 per cent in four states. In 1952, no state had a rate below 24 per cent and only six states were below 40 per cent. (See Figure 124.)

The South still lagged behind the rest of the nation in the participation of the population in presidential and congressional elections, and the

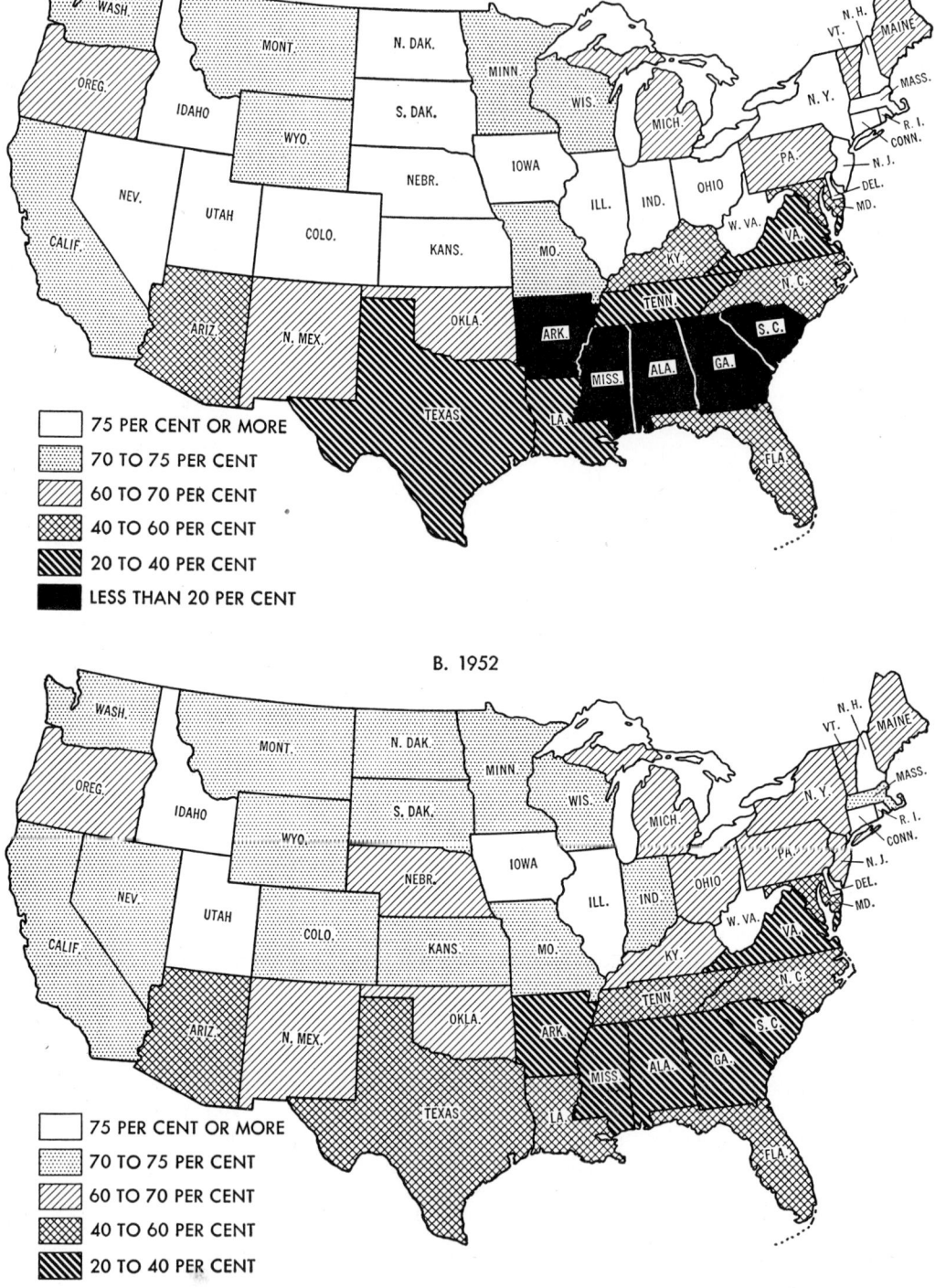

A. 1940

75 PER CENT OR MORE
70 TO 75 PER CENT
60 TO 70 PER CENT
40 TO 60 PER CENT
20 TO 40 PER CENT
LESS THAN 20 PER CENT

B. 1952

75 PER CENT OR MORE
70 TO 75 PER CENT
60 TO 70 PER CENT
40 TO 60 PER CENT
20 TO 40 PER CENT

Source: Table 207

FIGURE 124. ELECTIONS: THE UNITED STATES, POPULAR VOTE FOR PRESIDENT, BY STATE, 1940 AND 1952
(Votes Cast as Percentage of Civilian Population of Voting Age)

difference in voting in the South and the North was still too large to be explained by differences in education and interest in political affairs. Evidence of the disfranchisement of many Negroes and "poor whites" was clearly discernible on the political map of the United States for 1952 (see Figure 124,B), but equally striking was the contrast between this map and that for 1940. The trend has been decidedly toward truly universal suffrage.

ELECTIONS

Elections may be held by a single-member or multimember constituency, on the basis of proportional representation, or a plural vote, in one ballot or with provision for a second ballot if no list obtains an absolute majority.[38] Participation of voters may be compulsory or voluntary.

None of these characteristics, however, compares in significance with the fundamental distinction between a free vote designed to determine the people's wishes and mock elections which leave the voters no choice but to confirm the candidates picked by the government or the ruling party.

FREE AND MOCK ELECTIONS

Electoral abuses and irregularities are probably as old as balloting, but our generation is the first to witness the development of an electoral system that compels voters to vote according to the prescription of the government. The system was invented in the USSR, imitated in fascist Italy and Nazi Germany and recently introduced in all countries dominated by Moscow. The system is very simple: eligible voters are *ordered* to vote but *can* vote only for one list. The electoral campaign serves to make it clear to voters that a vote against the official list is an act of treason.

Under this system, it is irrelevant whether ballots are secret or open. In the booth, separated by a flimsy curtain from the supervising officer, the voter has no feeling of security. His identity

can be established by the order in which the ballots are arranged, or in some other way.

The statistical evidence that an election is a sham is the extent to which it endorses the government. An inexperienced totalitarian government, using only mild coercion, easily gets 90–95 per cent "yes" votes; a more ruthless ruler readily collects 99 per cent or more. Rates of 9,995 and more "yes" votes per 10,000 electors are not rare.

Germany under Hitler

The elections to the German Reichstag in April 1938 typify a forced vote under a dictatorial government.[39]

Electorate	45,091,735
Votes cast	44,906,256
Valid votes	44,836,557
For the *Führer's* lists	44,393,924
Against the *Führer's* lists	442,633

Less than one half of one per cent of the electorate failed to vote, and of those who voted, more than 99 per cent voted as ordered.

The Nazis, however, did not pretend that their candidates were acclaimed with the same enthusiasm in all electoral districts. In the plebiscite carried out simultaneously with the election, the government reported a victory of 96.95 per cent in Leipzig, 97.87 per cent in Weser-Ems, 98.11 per cent in Dresden-Bautzen, and even in the "best" districts, not more than 99.77 per cent.[40]

The Reichstag elected with such unanimity was called upon to represent Greater Germany, including Austria, which shortly before had been invaded by German troops. In view of the universally known resentment of the Austrians against the loss of independence of their country, it was important for the Nazis to obtain an eloquent demonstration of Austrian devotion to the *Führer*, who was himself a native of Austria. The elections did not fail to provide the expected endorsement. The ratio of votes cast to eligible voters was 99.71 per cent in Austria as compared with 99.59 per cent in Germany. The ratio of votes for the *Führer* to all valid votes was 99.74 per cent in Austria and only 99.01 per cent in Germany.

---

38. There are also various compromises between these alternatives. In the new electoral law of the German Federal Republic, some 60 per cent of the seats in the Bundestag are distributed on the basis of the one-member-constituency principle and 40 per cent on the basis of proportional representation applied to the whole country as a single constituency. The new French electoral law applies the principle of proportional representation to the constituencies in which no candidate has obtained an absolute majority.

39. **20**, 1938, p. 618.
40. **20**, 1938, p. 618.

The USSR under Stalin

The only free election Russia has ever held on the basis of universal suffrage was the election to the Constituent Assembly, in November 1917, soon after the Communist revolution. The Communists polled about 25 per cent of the votes and gained 156 seats out of 601 in the assembly.[41] Together with splinter groups which joined them, they could not muster more than 195 votes.

After dissolving the Constituent Assembly, the Communist government substituted for universal direct suffrage a system described as the "power of the soviets." In rural areas, the system worked as follows: The peasants in each village elected their soviet; the village soviets appointed deputies to a rural township congress of soviets; the latter sent representatives to a county congress of soviets, where they met representatives of urban-worker soviets; the county congresses nominated members of provincial congresses and these last appointed representatives to the Supreme Congress of Soviets, which elected the Executive Committee, the highest power in the country. Thus, elections were held in six stages, each time with open suffrage.

This system enabled the ruling party to obtain complete domination at the top of the pyramid despite weakness at the bottom. The operation of this system is illustrated by the following data on the percentage of Communists in the soviets at various stages of elections in the RSFSR in 1924–25 and 1925–26.[42]

	1924 25	1925 26
Village soviets	7.5	9.0
Rural township congresses of soviets	20.3	23.1
City soviets	53.1	44.1
County congresses of soviets	57.8	51.0
Provincial congresses of soviets	68.2	64.6
The RSFSR Congress of Soviets	90.2	78.1

After five siftings, only absolutely reliable delegates reached the top of the pyramid. Although some were registered as nonparty people, they never appeared in the Supreme Soviet as a faction independent of the Communist party. (See Figure 125.)

This system of the "power of the soviets" was used with minor modifications until 1937, when it was replaced by direct universal suffrage. Its results in 1931 are illustrated by the following figures, which also show the percentage of Communists among executive committees and presidiums of village and city soviets and congresses of soviets on different levels of the pyramid: [43]

	Members of Congresses of Soviets	Executive Committees	Presidiums [a]	Presidents
Elected by direct vote				
Village soviets	20	—	44	61
City soviets	56	—	71	73
Elected by indirect vote				
County congresses of soviets	51	70	90	99.7
Congresses of soviets in regions and autonomous republics	66–83	80–90	80	100
Congresses of soviets in constituent republics	74–90	77–85	100	100
Congress of soviets of the Union	75	81	100	—

a. Includes the president and several vice presidents of the respective bodies.

The new electoral law of July 9, 1937, amended in October 1945 and January 1950, is a model of simplicity.[44] The country is divided into electoral districts, each with approximately 300,000 inhabitants. Each district elects a deputy to the Supreme Soviet of the USSR.[45] All citizens 18 years and over are entitled to vote. Balloting is secret, with preprinted ballots.

The law permits the voter to choose from a list of several candidates. Actually, in all elections held since 1937, only one candidate, endorsed by the "Bloc of Communists and Non-Party People," has been presented in each electoral district.[46] Voting is compulsory.

The new system worked smoothly enough in 1937 but was further amended in 1945 and es-

41. **78**, Vol. 7, p. 27.

42. **37**, 1926, No. 8, p. 6. The RSFSR (Russian Soviet Federated Socialist Republic) — Russia proper — is the largest province in the USSR.

43. **56**, Vol. 1, p. 54.

44. **62**, pp. 267ff.

45. The Supreme Soviet of Nationalities is elected on a slightly different basis.

46. **76**, p. 35.

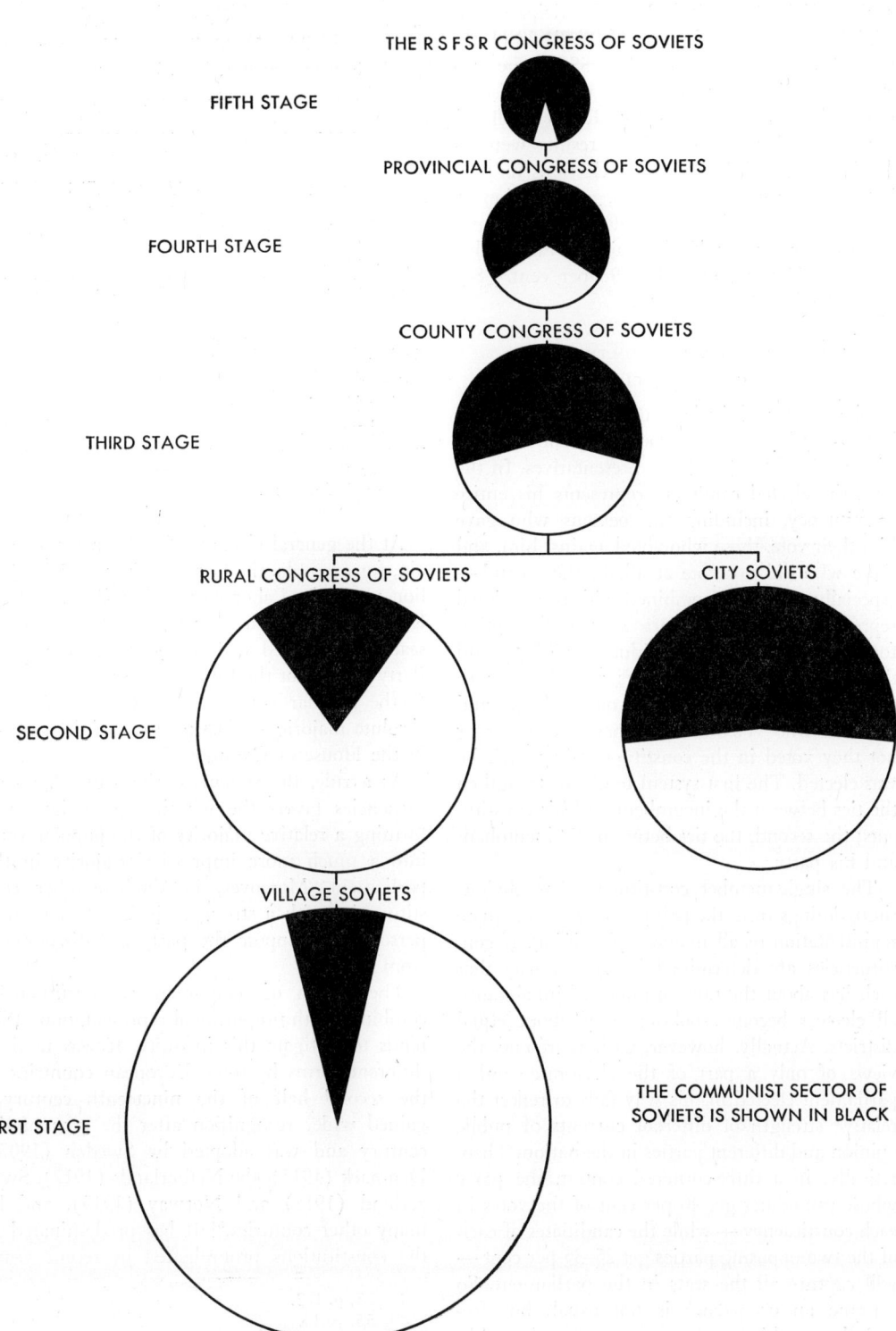

THE R S F S R CONGRESS OF SOVIETS

FIFTH STAGE

PROVINCIAL CONGRESS OF SOVIETS

FOURTH STAGE

COUNTY CONGRESS OF SOVIETS

THIRD STAGE

RURAL CONGRESS OF SOVIETS

CITY SOVIETS

SECOND STAGE

VILLAGE SOVIETS

THE COMMUNIST SECTOR OF
SOVIETS IS SHOWN IN BLACK

FIRST STAGE

FIGURE 125. ELECTIONS: THE USSR, FIVE-STAGE ELECTION TO THE RSFSR CONGRESS OF SOVIETS, 1924–25

pecially 1950. (See Table 208.) Participation of eligible voters in 1946 ranged from 91.78 (Lithuanian SSR) to 99.97 (Tadzhik SSR); the percentage of the total vote cast for the official candidate, from 94.59 (Estonian SSR) to 99.90 per cent (Georgian SSR).[47] These results were as good as those of the Reichstag elections in 1938 but not good enough. In 1950, participation in the election ranged between 99.82 per cent and 99.99 per cent; the bloc's majority ranged between 99.63 per cent and 99.98 per cent. (See Table 209.)

SINGLE-MEMBER AND MULTIMEMBER CONSTITUENCIES

The systems of single-member and multimember constituencies reflect two different concepts of the role of the people's representatives. In the first, the elected candidate represents his entire constituency, including the persons who gave him their vote, those who voted against him, and those who did not vote at all. In the second — especially when it is combined with proportional representation — people are supposedly voting for parties rather than individual candidates, and the candidate elected becomes a spokesman of the party which put his name on the ballot and of those who voted for this party, whether or not they voted in the constituency in which he was elected. The first system tends to strengthen the ties between the incumbent and his constituents; the second, the ties between the incumbent and his party.

The single-member constituency has obvious shortcomings from the point of view of adequate representation of all nuances of opinion. If constituencies are determined in such a way that each has about the same number of inhabitants, all electees become spokesmen of about equal districts. Actually, however, each represents the views of only a part of the electorate, and a parliament elected in this way fails to reflect the relative strength of different currents of public opinion and different parties in the nation. Theoretically, in a three-cornered contest, the party whose candidates get 40 per cent of the votes in each constituency — while the candidates of each of the two opposing parties get 25–35 per cent — will capture all the seats in the parliament. So extreme an occurrence is not usual, but frequently one third of the electorate remains without parliamentary representation.

47. **76,** p. 147.

TABLE 208

ELECTIONS: THE USSR, POPULAR VOTE FOR THE SUPREME SOVIET, 1937, 1946 AND 1950

Item	1937	1946	1950
	Thousands		
Eligible voters	94,138	101,718	111,116
Votes cast	91,113	101,451	111,090
Votes cast for the Bloc of Communists and Non-Party People	89,844	100,621	110,788
	Per Cent		
Ratio of votes to eligible voters	96.8	99.7	99.98
Ratio of Bloc's votes to total votes cast	98.6	99.2	99.73

Sources: For 1937 and 1946, **76,** p. 147; for 1950, **37,** March 25, 1950.

At the general election of 1922 in Great Britain, for example, the Conservatives won 5.4 million votes, the Labor party 4.2 million, and the Liberals 2.6 million. The Conservatives got 296 seats as compared with 138 seats for the Labor Party and 53 for the Liberals. Thus 44.3 per cent of the popular vote gave the Conservatives an absolute majority — 60.8 per cent of the seats — in the House of Commons.[48]

As a rule, the system of single-member constituencies favors the winning party by transforming a relative majority of the popular votes into a much more impressive majority in the parliament. Moreover, in single-member constituencies with a strong majority of one party, persons who oppose the party are discouraged from voting.[49]

The system of many-member constituencies combined with proportional representation (PR) tends to mitigate this inequity. It was used in different forms by some European countries in the second half of the nineteenth century,[50] gained wider recognition after the turn of the century and was adopted by Sweden (1907), Denmark (1915), the Netherlands (1917), Switzerland (1918) and Norway (1919), and by many other countries.[51] It has predominated in the constitutions promulgated in recent years.

48. **73,** p. 172.
49. **55,** p. 14.
50. In Denmark since 1855 (for election of the Upper House); in Switzerland since 1891 (in some cantonal elections); in Belgium since 1895 (in local elections).
51. **73,** p. 178.

TABLE 209

ELECTIONS: THE USSR, VOTES CAST FOR THE SUPREME SOVIET, MARCH 19, 1950

| Republic | Electors, in Thousands | Votes Cast, in Thousands | | Ratio (Per Cent) | |
		Total	For the Bloc	Votes to Electors	Votes for the Bloc to Total Votes
Total (USSR)	111,116	111,090	110,788	99.98	99.73
RSFSR	63,544	63,528	63,300	99.98	99.63
Ukrainian SSR	22,894	22,889	22,855	99.98	99.85
Byelorussian SSR	4,728	4,728	4,723	99.99	99.90
Uzbek SSR	3,498	3,498	3,494	99.99	99.90
Kazakh SSR	3,860	3,860	3,851	99.99	99.78
Georgian SSR	2,179	2,179	2,179	99.99	99.98
Azerbaijan SSR	1,677	1,677	1,676	99.99	99.90
Lithuanian SSR	1,599	1,598	1,594	99.88	99.76
Moldavian SSR	1,354	1,354	1,351	99.97	99.84
Latvian SSR	1,359	1,358	1,357	99.94	99.93
Kirghiz SSR	977	977	975	99.98	99.75
Tadzhik SSR	857	857	856	99.99	99.92
Armenian SSR	770	770	769	99.99	99.95
Turkmen SSR	725	725	724	99.98	99.91
Estonian SSR	800	798	795	99.82	99.63
Karelo-Finnish SSR	294	294	293	99.95	99.72

Source: **37,** March 25, 1950.

Despite its theoretical advantages, however, this system has not met all expectations. It has worked smoothly in comparatively small countries with strong democratic traditions and a high level of political education, such as the Scandinavian countries and the Netherlands, but has proved less successful in large nations in time of political crisis and internal strife. In Germany and France, in the interwar years, it produced a throng of splinter parties, parliaments without a clear majority, and shaky coalition governments which lacked effective support in the nation.

The controversy about the relative merits of either type of electoral system is nearly a century old [52] and is probably rooted in the dual purpose of the parliamentary elections: to reveal the thinking and feeling of the people and to lay the foundation for an efficient constitutional government. PR stresses the first objective; the system of single-member constituencies, the second. The single-member district is an old tradition in the United States, Great Britain and some British dominions. Plurality plans are in use throughout continental Europe and in Middle and South America. Some electoral laws combine the two systems. One-member constituencies may be used, for example, in the first election and PR applied in run-off elections in the constituencies where no candidate received an absolute majority.[53]

Neither system precludes the absolute predominance of a single party or coalition. A political group may command such universal respect in the nation that its candidates will be elected in most constituencies, large and small. On the other hand, both systems can be used by a dictatorial government for mock elections.

COMPULSORY AND VOLUNTARY VOTING

Compulsory voting in democratic countries leaves the citizen free to select any candidate or to cast a blank ballot. The compulsion is solely to appear at the polls or present a reasonable excuse for not appearing. The merits of this system are questionable. One can hardly anticipate a sensible vote from an individual who goes to the polls against his will. On the other hand, it can be argued that obligatory voting compels

52. Principles of proportional representation very similar to those used in the new electoral laws in France and Germany were developed by Thomas Hare in England in 1857. (See **58.**)

53. For discussion of comparative merits and shortcomings of both systems, see **57** and **59.**

politically indifferent citizens to think about public affairs and contributes to their political education.[54]

Countries with Compulsory Voting

Compulsory voting (or registering) exists in Belgium, Italy, Austria, Australia, Mexico, Costa Rica, Brazil, Paraguay, Peru, Uruguay and Argentina. In some of these, however, only registration of potential voters is compulsory and an elector is not obliged to go to the polls.

In democratic countries with compulsory voting a small percentage of the registered voters always fails to vote. In Australia, for example, ballots have been cast in general elections by the following percentages of the registered voters: [55]

1931	95.0	1943	96.3
1934	95.2	1946	94.0
1937	96.1	1949	95.9
1940	94.8	1951	96.0

In Belgium, absenteeism among registered electors averages 7 per cent and usually about 5 per cent of the ballots are blank or otherwise invalid.[56] In 1921–50 the percentages of absentees and blank and invalid ballots were as follows: [57]

	Absentees as Percentage of All Electors	Blank and Invalid Ballots as Percentage of All Votes
1921	8.9	4.8
1925	7.2	4.5
1929	6.0	5.0
1932	5.7	5.1
1936	5.3	5.9
1939	6.7	6.0
1946	9.7	3.9
1949	5.6	5.4
1950	7.4	5.3

Both rates also vary narrowly from province to province and from city to city; in 1949, the range

was from 3.9 per cent to 7.0 per cent for absentees and from 3.8 to 8.5 per cent for invalid votes.

In Italy, compulsory participation in elections has been tested under two regimes, under Mussolini and under the new democratic constitution. In 1934, 96.5 per cent of the registered electors went to the polls and 99.8 per cent of the ballots were cast for the candidates agreeable to the *Duce.* In 1946, at the general election for the constituent assembly, 89.1 per cent of the electors cast votes and 7.7 per cent of ballots were blank or null. The valid votes represented about 82 per cent of the eligible voters.

Regional variations in the proportion of invalid ballots are much wider in Italy than in Belgium, partly because of greater contrasts in local conditions, partly because of the briefer experience of the Italian people in democratic government. The following ratios were recorded for the four broad regions of Italy: [58]

	Absentees as Percentage of All Electors	Blank and Invalid Ballots as Percentage of All Votes
Northern Italy	9.2	5.6
Central Italy	11.1	6.9
Southern Italy	12.5	11.9
Islands	14.4	9.9

Valid ballots were cast by about 85 per cent of the eligible voters in the north and 76 per cent in the south. Although absenteeism was very high for a country where participation in elections is obligatory, universal suffrage in liberated Italy has fulfilled its purpose by revealing the state of mind of the Italian people.

From this point of view, the results of the Italian referendum on the type of government — monarchy or republic — held simultaneously with the general elections in 1946 are instructive. It showed a deep political rift in the nation: in northern and central Italy 64 per cent of the population voting for a republic and in southern Italy and the islands 66 per cent casting votes for a monarchy. Since the first area represents two thirds of Italy's population, the popular decision was in favor of the republic by 54.3 per cent to 45.7 per cent,[59] and the crisis was solved democratically.

---

54. The two systems — voluntary and compulsory — reflect two theories of suffrage: the individualistic and the collectivist. The former, based on the idea of natural rights of man, implies a voluntary vote. The second, imbued with the concept of the priority of the state over the individual, favors compulsory voting. (**54**, pp. 15–18; cf. **45**.)

55. **10**, 1951, pp. 82 and 1282; 1953, p. 71.

56. Under voluntary voting, some ballots may be voided for technical faults. The proportion of voided ballots, however, seldom exceeds 1–2 per cent. An appreciably higher proportion of blank ballots may indicate the protest of electors against conditions under which elections are being held or against candidates.

57. **12**, 1952, p. 501.

58. **26**, 1944–48, p. 151.

59. **26**, 1944–48, pp. 154–55.

Countries with Voluntary Voting

In countries with universal suffrage and voluntary voting, usually from 60 to 80 per cent of the electors appear at the polls in general elections. The ratio is higher in modern nations than in underdeveloped areas. The ratios vary widely from year to year and depend largely on the issues at stake, the personalities of candidates, the method of conducting the electoral campaigns and similar factors. The proportion is exceptionally high when political passions have been aroused. Heavy voting usually expresses growing opposition to the ruling party; absenteeism indicates that most people are satisfied with the government and desire no change.[60] The reverse may also be true: people may be induced to vote through fear that the government which they believe is defending their interests is threatened by the opposition. Usually, participation in local elections is smaller than in general elections, especially when the latter involve problems of national significance.

In the United Kingdom 58.9 per cent of the registered electors in contested constituencies voted in 1918; 79.5 per cent in 1929; 74.4 in 1936; 75.5 in 1945; 84.0 in 1950; 82.6 in 1951; and 76.8 in May 1955.[61] In France nearly 80 per cent of the registered voters participated in the general election in 1945, the first election after the liberation of France and the enfranchisement of women; only 2.5 per cent of the votes cast were voided.[62]

In Sweden, votes have been cast by the following percentages of the electorate: [63]

1911	57.0	1928	67.4
1914 (March–April)	69.9	1932	67.6
1914 (Sept.)	66.2	1936	74.5
1917	65.8	1940	70.3
1920	55.3	1944	71.9
1921	54.2	1948	82.7
1924	53.0		

In Norway, 76.4 per cent of the electors went to the polls in 1933; 84.0 per cent in 1936; 76.4 per cent in 1945; and 82.0 per cent in 1949.[64] Denmark has had a similar record: 79.7 per cent in 1946 and 81.9 per cent in 1950.[65]

In Germany, only 50.8 per cent of the registered electors appeared at the polls at the first Reichstag election in 1871; 60.9 per cent in 1874; 60.4 per cent in 1877; and 63.1 in 1878. At subsequent elections, the percentage increased as follows: [66]

1881	56.1	1893	72.2
1884	60.4	1898	67.8
1887	77.2	1903	75.8
1890	71.3	1907	84.4

Participation of eligible voters was higher in Germany before World War I than in other European countries and remained high at the election of the national assembly (*Nationalversammlung*) in 1919, but the percentage who voted declined in the 1920's, under the Weimar Republic: [67]

1919	82.7	1928	74.6
1920 (May)	78.4	1930	82.7
1924 (Dec.)	77.7		

Transformation of Germany into an authoritarian state began in 1933. One of the first steps was to make voting compulsory. All means of propaganda and psychological pressure short of direct terror were used to compel the German people to support the *Führer* unanimously. In the first Reichstag election under Hitler, in November 1933, 95.3 per cent of the eligible voters were brought to the polls and the *Führer's* candidates won 92.1 per cent of the valid votes.[68] Four years later, making full use of the electoral method developed by that time in the USSR, Hitler improved his record and obtained complete unanimity of the electorate.[69]

After its military defeat and political liberation, Western Germany returned to the system of universal suffrage for men and women with voluntary voting.[70] Participation in the election of the Bundestag in 1949 showed considerable interest in balloting. (See Table 210.)

Only fragmentary electoral statistics are available for South America. In Colombia, under a

60. **65,** p. 37.
61. **50,** p. 290; **23,** 1938–1948, p. 74.
62. **19,** 1940–1945, p. 296.
63. **33,** 1951, p. 328.
64. **30,** 1949, p. 352, and 1951, p. 334.
65. **18,** 1949, p. 218, and 1951, p. 237.

66. **78,** Vol. 7, p. 34.
67. **20,** 1931, p. 545.
68. **18,** 1934, p. 550.
69. Cf. p. 603.
70. The new electoral law is an intricate compromise between the proportional representation of the Weimar Republic and the system of single-member constituencies with election by simple majority, as in the United States and Great Britain.

TABLE 210

ELECTIONS: WESTERN GERMANY, VOTES CAST FOR THE BUNDESTAG, BY PROVINCE, AUGUST 14, 1949

| Province | Number, in Thousands | | Ratio (Per Cent) of Votes to Eligible Voters | Province | Number, in Thousands | | Ratio (Per Cent) of Votes to Eligible Voters |
	Electors	Votes Cast			Electors	Votes Cast	
Germany	31,179	24,491	78.5	Nordrhein-Westphalen	8,678	6,906	79.6
Baden	815	570	69.9	Rheinland-Pfalz	1,902	1,514	79.6
Bavaria	5,981	4,851	81.1	Schleswig-Holstein	1,730	1,431	82.7
Bremen	380	311	81.6				
Hamburg	1,131	926	81.9	Württemberg-Baden	2,519	1,825	72.4
Hesse	2,907	2,246	77.3	Württemberg-Hohenzollern	728	470	64.5
Niedersachsen	4,408	3,440	78.0				

Source: **21**, August 1949, p. 132.

system of universal suffrage for men, 55 per cent of the electors voted at general elections in 1947. At local elections, 40 per cent voted in 1941, 34 per cent in 1943 and 1945, 50 per cent in 1947.[71]

In Uruguay, 59.1 per cent of the electors voted in the election of national representatives in 1938 and 66.9 per cent in 1942.

In Japan, under the new constitution, votes were cast by the following percentages of the electors: in 1947, 74.9 per cent for men and 61.6 per cent for women; in 1949, 80.7 per cent for men and 67.9 per cent for women.[72]

Two conclusions can be drawn from the experience of free elections:

1. The rate of voluntary participation of electors at the polls tends to increase with the development of democratic institutions.

2. The rate often reaches 80 per cent and occasionally exceeds 85 per cent, which is not far from the proportion of valid votes among registered electors under compulsory voting.

VOTING BY MEN AND WOMEN

While universal suffrage tends to give women a slight majority in the electorate, usually relatively fewer women than men participate in elections. (See Tables 211 to 214.) A slight difference appears even in countries with compulsory voting for both sexes, such as Australia.[73] The

71. **17**, 1947, pp. 732–36.
72. **27**, 1950, p. 395.
73. In 1949, for example, votes were cast by 96.4 per cent of the eligible male voters and 95.4 per cent of the female. (**10**, 1951, p. 1282.)

TABLE 211

VOTING BY MEN AND WOMEN: SWEDEN, 1921–48

(*Percentage of Registered Electors Voting in Elections to the Second Chamber of Riksdag*)

| Year | Nation | | Cities | | Rural Communities | |
	Men	Women	Men	Women	Men	Women
1921	62.0	47.2	—	—	—	—
1924	60.0	46.7	—	—	—	—
1928	72.6	62.7	—	—	—	—
1932	73.1	62.5	74.0	65.6	72.7	60.6
1936	78.6	70.7	79.0	73.3	78.5	68.9
1940	72.6	68.1	73.9	72.3	71.9	65.0
1944	74.8	69.2	75.5	71.6	74.3	67.2
1948	84.9	80.7	85.7	82.8	84.2	78.7

Source: **33**, 1949, p. 320.

TABLE 212

VOTING BY MEN AND WOMEN: DENMARK, 1925 AND 1946

(*Percentage of Registered Electors Voting in Communal Elections*)

Sex	Nation	Capital	Provincial Cities	Rural Communities
		1925		
Men	—	82.4	89.5	81.4
Women	—	69.0	78.6	66.5
		1946		
Men	84.6	81.1	87.3	84.8
Women	86.5	74.9	80.1	76.6

Source: **18**, 1927, p. 147 and 1949, p. 219.

TABLE 213

VOTING BY MEN AND WOMEN: NORWAY, 1918–49

(*Percentage of Registered Electors Voting in Elections to the Storting, in Contested Constituencies*)

Year	Nation		Cities		Rural Districts	
	Men	Women	Men	Women	Men	Women
1918	70.7	51.3	77.0	68.5	68.3	43.4
1921	76.5	60.3	81.4	73.5	74.7	54.0
1924	76.5	64.1	82.6	78.3	74.2	57.3
1927	75.4	61.6	80.0	74.7	73.7	55.5
1930	81.5	74.0	82.9	80.7	80.9	70.9
1933	81.9	71.3	84.7	79.6	80.9	67.3
1936	87.8	80.7	89.3	86.3	87.2	78.0
1945	80.0	72.9	83.9	81.3	78.6	69.2
1949	85.3	78.9	88.0	85.4	84.1	75.4

Source: **30,** for the respective years.

TABLE 214

VOTING BY MEN AND WOMEN: AUSTRALIA, 1934–51

(*Percentage of Registered Electors Voting in Elections to the House of Representatives, in Contested Constituencies*)

Year	Men	Women
1934	95.5	94.8
1937	96.2	96.1
1940	94.2	95.4
1943	98.5	94.2
1946	95.1	92.9
1949	96.4	95.5
1951	96.5	95.5

Source: **10,** 1951, p. 82; 1953, p. 71.

trend in the number of women voting differs little, however, from that of men voters: [74] participation of women in the early years after their enfranchisement was no less than among men two or three decades earlier, and women rapidly caught up with the increasing rates for men.[75]

74. **78,** Vol. 7, p. 106.

75. Cf. **77,** p. 233 (for Australia and New Zealand at the beginning of the twentieth century).

On the basis of an analysis of electoral statistics for the period prior to 1934, Herbert Tingsten arrived at a different conclusion: "The women," he wrote, "nowhere make use of their vote to the same extent as the men; as a rule the difference in voting frequency between the sexes in recent years seems to have amounted to about ten per cent. A tendency toward equalization has been noticeable in several countries, but cannot be said to be general." (**75,** p. 229.) This conclusion was accepted by Nilson. (**65,** p. 38.) Although the difference between the voting frequencies of men and women in the period

VOTING IN CITIES AND RURAL AREAS

In almost all countries, voting is heavier in cities and densely populated areas than in sparsely populated rural communities. The difference is insignificant in countries with old democratic traditions and a high level of political education, such as Sweden, Norway, Denmark and Finland. (See Tables 211, 212 and 213; cf. Figure 126.) In politically youthful countries, however, and especially in areas with a heterogeneous population, it is considerable.

Moreover, in underdeveloped countries literacy tests frequently exclude a considerable part of the rural population from the electorate, and some who could pass this test are uninterested in voting. On the other hand, farmers in countries with a high level of political education and strong democratic traditions have learned how to use their ballots. In the United States, they are strongly represented, particularly in the Senate where the primarily rural states, relatively small in terms of population, have equal representation with the large and highly urbanized and industrialized states.

Only a few European countries record the votes in the urban and rural areas separately. More often the contrast in voting patterns of the cities and the country districts appears only in the difference in voting in primarily industrial and primarily agricultural regions.

Statistics of the 1950 election to the Landtag in Bavaria have been computed for urban and rural districts classified by the number of inhabitants in each community. They reveal several anomalies: participation at the polls (the ratio of votes cast to eligible voters) was higher in rural than in urban districts; in both types of district, it was highest in the smallest communities; the ratio of valid votes to all votes cast was higher in rural districts than in cities and was particularly high in the smallest rural communities. (See Table 215.)

Such occurrences, contrary to those observed in other countries, show that generalizations on the behavior of different population groups in elections do not establish sociological laws.

REGIONAL VARIATIONS

Regional differences in the participation of eligible voters often modify differences in the

studied by Tingsten allows more than one interpretation, his conclusion is defensible for that particular period, but has been invalidated by recent developments.

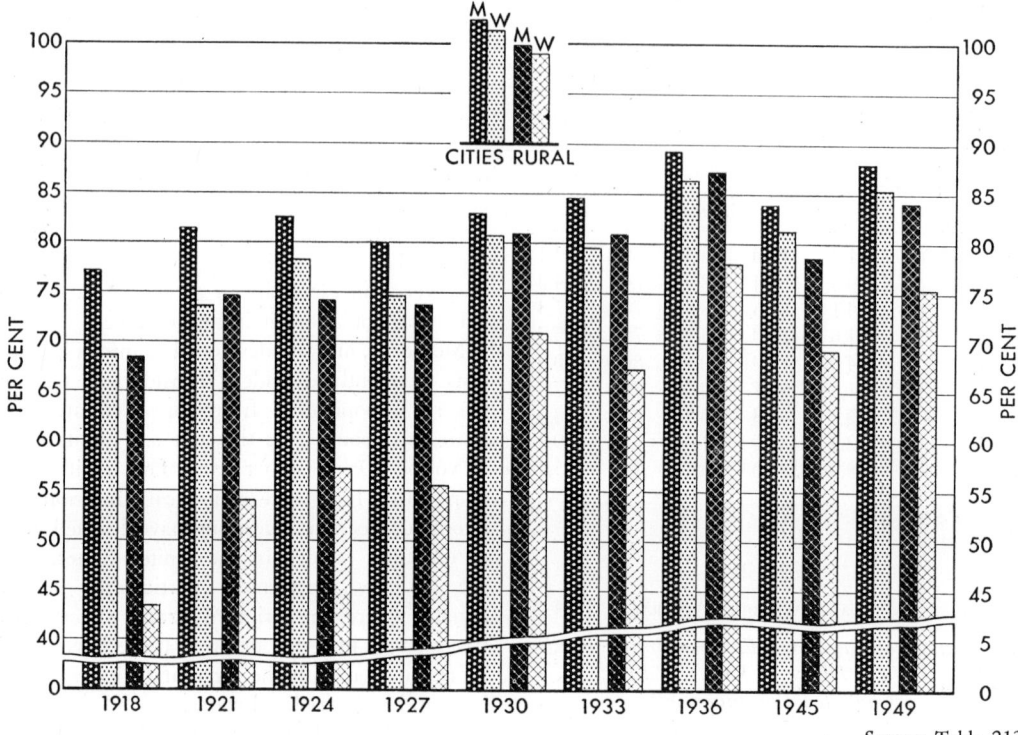

FIGURE 126. VOTING BY MEN AND WOMEN: NORWAY, 1918–49

TABLE 215

VOTING BY MEN AND WOMEN: BAVARIA, 1950

(*Percentage of Registered Electors Voting in Elections to Landtag*)

Size of Community (Number of Inhabitants)	Rural Districts		Cities	
	Men	Women	Men	Women
Less than 500	87.1	82.4	—	—
501–1,000	85.7	81.1	—	—
1,001–2,000	84.1	79.4	—	—
2,001–3,000	83.9	80.2	—	—
3,001–5,000	82.6	78.6	—	—
5,001–10,000	83.3	78.7	79.5	81.6
10,001–20,000	83.5	81.1	81.6	79.1
20,001–50,000	76.2	69.6	81.3	76.7
50,001–100,000	—	—	79.0	78.0
100,001 and more	—	—	74.6	70.3

Source: **22**, p. 80.

ratio of eligible voters to total population of voting age — for example, in the United States and Brazil. (See Tables 207 and 205.)

In France the ratio of voters to electors ranged in 1945 from 61 per cent in Corsica and around 69 per cent in the primarily agricultural departments of Charente-Maritime and Creuse to more than 85 per cent in Paris and its suburbs and the departments of Pas-de-Calais, Nord and Bouches-du-Rhône, all of which are densely populated and highly industrialized.[76] (See Table 216.) The general regional pattern is characterized by heavy voting in the northern and northwestern departments and comparatively light voting in the south. The percentage of voting electors is particularly low in Algeria. This pattern is very stable: it appeared clearly in elections in 1928[77] and Gosnell found a similar pattern in the composite picture of French elections in 1910, 1914, 1919 and 1924.[78] Similar differences occurred in Italy and Germany under the system of voluntary voting. Variations are less in Great Britain and the Scandinavian countries.

In general, participation in voting increases as one moves from rural to urban constituencies and is in turn correlated with density of population, level of education, circulation of newspapers, per capita income, level of public health

76. **19**, 1940–45, p. 296.
77. **61**, p. v.
78. **55**, p. 54.

TABLE 216

VOTING IN FRANCE, BY DEPARTMENT, 1945

Department	Number, in Thousands		Ratio (Per Cent) of Voters to Electors	Department	Number, in Thousands		Ratio (Per Cent) of Voters to Electors
	Electors	Voters			Electors	Voters	
Seine				Vaucluse	152	120	78.0
Paris	1,575	1,389	88.2	Charente	204	157	77.9
Banlieue (suburbs)	1,192	1,063	89.2	Lozère	63	49	77.7
Pas-de-Calais	648	574	88.6	Indre-et-Loire	219	170	77.6
Nord	1,156	1,006	87.0	Pyrénées-Orientales	139	108	77.4
Bouches-du-Rhône	501	428	85.4	Vienne	205	159	77.6
Oise	228	194	85.0	Moselle	315	249	77.4
Somme	273	232	85.0	Nièvre	164	127	77.4
Seine-et-Oise	850	722	84.9	Tarn	195	151	77.4
Gard	—	187	83.8	Finistère	483	374	77.4
Seine-et-Marne	248	207	83.5	Belfort	53	41	77.4
Aisne	267	219	82.0	Basses-Pyrénées	259	200	77.2
Ardennes	149	121	81.8	Maine-et-Loire	312	241	77.2
Alpes-Maritimes	238	194	81.5	Allier	240	191	76.7
Côte-d'Or	266	167	81.0	Corrèze	175	134	76.5
Vendée	253	205	81.0	Deux-Sèvres	204	156	76.4
Meuse	116	94	81.0	Haut-Rhin	285	218	76.4
Meurthe-et-Moselle	295	239	81.0	Drôme	169	129	76.3
Aube	140	113	80.7	Lot	109	83	76.1
Rhône	507	409	80.7	Tarn-et-Garonne	105	80	76.1
Mayenne	161	130	80.7	Var	217	165	76.0
Eure-et-Loir	155	125	80.6	Morbihan	318	241	75.7
Eure	185	149	80.5	Saône-et-Loire	330	249	75.5
Aveyron	205	162	80.4	Haute-Vienne	229	173	75.5
Cher	188	151	80.3	Basses-Alpes	57	43	75.4
Loir-et-Cher	157	126	80.3	Ain	191	144	75.3
Côtes-du-Nord	342	274	80.1	Manche	259	194	74.9
Loire	382	306	80.1	Isère	352	263	74.7
Calvados	222	176	80.0	Haute-Garonne	312	237	74.5
Doubs	172	139	80.0	Indre	171	127	74.2
Haute-Saône	135	108	80.0	Lot-et-Garonne	159	118	74.2
Loiret	218	174	79.8	Savoie	141	104	73.7
Haute-Marne	113	90	79.6	Cantal	122	90	73.7
Puy-de-Dôme	313	232	79.1	Gironde	521	384	73.7
Ardèche	173	137	79.1	Landes	173	127	73.4
Orne	167	132	79.0	Dordogne	259	190	73.3
Ille-et-Vilaine	358	283	79.0	Ariège	104	76	73.0
Sarthe	248	196	79.0	Hautes-Alpes	58	42	72.4
Yonne	172	136	79.0	Bas-Rhin	421	300	71.2
Hérault	269	212	78.8	Hautes-Pyrénées	128	91	71.0
Haute-Loire	155	122	78.7	Charente-Maritime	256	177	69.1
Haute-Savoie	160	126	78.7	Creuse	138	95	68.8
Loire-Inférieure	412	324	78.6	Gers	119	78	65.5
Jura	139	109	78.4	Corse	159	97	61.0
Aude	166	130	78.3	Algérie			
Marne	230	180	78.2	Oran	485	312	64.7
Seine-Inférieure	480	375	78.1	Alger	670	384	57.3
Vosges	224	175	78.1	Constantine	689	367	53.3

Source: **19**, 1940–1945, p. 296.

and other characteristics of the level of cultural and economic development of the area.

None of these conditions alone can be regarded as a factor controlling the political alertness and democratic maturity of a people. There is no evidence of a close correlation between interest in public affairs and income or wealth. In Germany and Austria, for example, factory workers have been traditionally among the most politically minded groups of the population. There are indications, however, that abstention is greater among eligible voters in the lower social strata than in the upper, as it appears to have been in Sweden's Riksdag election in 1948. (See Table 217.)

PLEBISCITES AND REFERENDUMS

The referendum is, to some extent, a return to the primitive form of democracy that operated in small communities of the ancient world — a direct decision by the people on legislative and administrative matters. It can be used on both a local and a national basis. The plebiscite is a direct decision by the people on some exceptionally important question, for example, on the form of government or national affiliation of an area.

THE PLEBISCITE

The plebiscite was first used during the French Revolution as a way of determining the destiny of an area. The inhabitants of territory occupied by revolutionary armies thus gained an opportunity to manifest their solidarity with their liberators. Napoleon I continued plebiscites in conquered countries.[79] The practice was revived in the middle of the nineteenth century by Napoleon III, who used it to confirm his *coup d'état* in 1851. He favored the plebiscite to determine the fate of Nice, Savoy and other territories on the border of France and Italy which were claimed by both France and Sardinia.

The peace conference at Versailles (1919) adopted the plebiscite as a universal method for determining the fate of disputed areas — in actuality, parts of the former territory of the defeated Central Powers. The treaty envisaged 17 plebiscites, but only 8 were held before the outbreak of World War II. Not all worked out in accordance with the victors' wishes. The plebiscite in Allenstein-Marienwerder returned these districts of East Prussia to Germany (1920). Ger-

79. **73**, p. 276.

TABLE 217

VOTING IN SWEDEN, BY SOCIAL CLASS, 1948

(*Percentage of Registered Electors Voting in Elections to the Second Chamber of Riksdag*)

Sex and Family Status	Employers, High Officials, Executive Officers	Craftsmen, Retail Dealers, Teachers, White Collar Employees	Workers
Men	93.3	87.7	82.2
Women			
Wives	94.8	89.4	86.5
Family members	79.2	66.1	58.3
Single	87.7	80.6	67.0

Source: **33**, 1949, p. 319.

many likewise received a majority of the votes in Upper Silesia (1921). Of the two zones of Schleswig, the northern voted for Denmark, while the southern decided to return to Germany (1920). Most significant was the plebiscite in the Saar in 1935: 98 per cent of the eligible voters appeared at the polls, and more than 90 per cent of the votes cast were for reunion with Germany.

Another free plebiscite was held in Iceland in 1944, when, by nearly unanimous vote, the people decided to dissolve their union with Denmark and establish a republic.[80]

In 1948 Newfoundland decided by plebiscite to join Canada. The choice was between self-government and membership in the Dominion of Canada. The proposal of confederation was accepted by 78,408 votes against 71,464.

These plebiscites contrast strikingly with votes that have been taken in various circumstances by totalitarian governments in Italy, Germany and the USSR. The results and statistical data of such mock plebiscites are meaningless. When one has studied the results of one totalitarian plebiscite, one need not look into the records of others. Hitler's plebiscite of April 1938 is typical.[81] (See Table 218.)

80. Iceland actually had been separated from Denmark since 1940, when the latter was occupied by Germany. (See **67**, 1952, pp. 105–06.)

81. The results of this plebiscite (*Volksabstimmung*) are characteristically published in the *Statistical Yearbook* for Germany without any reference to the issue on which the vote was taken (approval of annexation of Austria). This was the third plebiscite in Hitler's political career. The first was held in 1933 and gave approval to Germany's withdrawal from the League of Nations; the

TABLE 218

PLEBISCITE: NAZI GERMANY, VOTING BY DISTRICT, APRIL 10, 1938

District	Ratio (Per Cent) of:		District	Ratio (Per Cent) of:	
	Votes to Eligible Voters	Yes Votes to All Valid Voters		Votes to Eligible Voters	Yes Votes to All Valid Voters
Germany, total	99.59	99.01	Westphalia, South	99.37	99.11
			Hessen-Nassau	99.31	99.07
East Prussia	99.78	99.63	Cologne-Aachen	99.95	99.77
Berlin, West	99.12	99.17	Koblenz-Trier	99.98	99.54
Berlin, East	99.19	99.31	Düsseldorf, East	99.78	99.71
Potsdam	99.74	99.15			
Frankfurt an der Oder	99.72	99.52	Düsseldorf, West	99.80	99.63
Pommern	99.85	99.31	Oberbayern-Schwaben	99.89	99.37
Breslau	99.78	99.09	Niederbayern	99.82	98.23
Liegnitz	99.81	98.82	Franken	99.92	99.30
Oppeln	99.35	98.98	Rheinpfalz-Saar	99.98	99.91
Magdeburg	99.74	98.97	Dresden-Bautzen	99.14	98.11
Merseburg	99.79	99.00	Leipzig	98.75	96.95
Thüringen	99.96	99.19	Chemnitz-Zwickau	99.69	98.13
Schleswig-Holstein	99.31	98.52	Württemberg	99.96	99.39
Weser-Ems	99.35	97.87	Baden	99.73	98.33
East Hannover	99.35	98.55	Hessen-Darmstadt	99.26	98.80
South Hannover-			Hamburg	98.19	98.21
Braunschweig	99.27	99.48	Mecklenburg	99.78	99.04
Westphalia, North	99.82	98.50	Germans in Austria	98.75	99.40

Source: **20**, 1938, p. 618.

THE REFERENDUM

Referendums are widely used in local affairs in the United States, Canada, Australia, New Zealand, Ireland and many other countries. Switzerland uses them also as a customary method of effecting current federal legislation.[82]

Switzerland

Switzerland first used the referendum on a national scale in 1848 for popular decision on the proposed federal constitution. The constitution was approved by a great majority (70.2 per cent) of the voters, but only 55.3 per cent of the inscribed electors participated. Eighteen years later, in 1866, several proposals were put on referendum, and since that time direct consultation of the people on legislative matters has become usual. Most referendums have been held

second, in 1934, approved Hitler's decision to combine, in his own hands, the power of the Chancellor and that of the President of the Republic.

82. The new constitutions in France and Italy recognize the referendum as the normal device for changes in fundamental laws.

simultaneously with general elections, but occasionally a referendum is taken in interelection years.

Switzerland has four types of referendum: *obligatory* referendum on measures affecting the federal constitution; *facultative* referendum on legislative and administrative matters submitted by the federal government; *initiative* referendum on measures proposed by a group of citizens; and referendums on *countermeasures* submitted by the government in opposition to the measures advanced by popular initiative. In all cases, a proposal becomes law if it obtains a majority of popular votes in more than half of the cantons and in the country as a whole.

In more than a century, from 1848 to 1954, Switzerland has held 184 national referendums. (See Table 219.) Most of the measures put to vote before 1890 were rejected: of 33 proposals, only 9 were accepted by the majority of voters and cantons. The measures approved included the original constitution (1848), its revision (rejected in 1866, approved in 1872), a law on civil rights of immigrants, a law on factory work,

TABLE 219

REFERENDUMS: SWITZERLAND, NUMBER, BY TYPE AND OUTCOME, 1848–1954

Period	Total			Obligatory		Facultative		Initiative		Counter-proposal of Government	
	Total	Accepted	Re-jected	Accepted	Re-jected	Accepted	Re-jected	Accepted	Re-jected	Accepted	Re-jected
Total, 1848–1954 [a]	184	79	105	41	24	22	46	9	33	7	2
1848	1	1	—	1	—	—	—	—	—	—	—
1866	9	1	8	1	8	—	—	—	—	—	—
1872–79	11	4	7	1	1	3	6	—	—	—	—
1880–89	12	3	9	2	2	1	7	—	—	—	—
1890–99	22	11	11	7	3	3	6	1	2	—	—
1900–09	14	8	6	3	1	3	2	1	3	1	—
1910–19	11	8	3	6	1	1	—	1	2	—	—
1920–29	32	13	19	7	2	2	5	3	11	1	1
1930–39	23	10	13	6	—	1	7	—	6	3	—
1940–49	26	12	14	2	3	6	6	3	4	1	1
1950–54 [a]	23	8	15	5	3	2	7	—	5	1	—

Source: **34**, 1933, pp. 394–401; 1949, p. 486; 1950, pp. 470–71; 1953, pp. 510–11.

a. To June 20, 1954.

authorization of subventions for road building, restoration of the death penalty, prohibition and a patent law (rejected in 1882, approved in a new version in 1887).

Later the government learned to offer only measures which had a good chance of being approved. From 1890 to 1954, 49 proposals were put before the people as subject to obligatory referendum, and 9 as countermeasures to the action demanded by initiative referendum; 36 of the first group of proposals and 7 of the second were accepted by the majority of voters and cantons. During the same period, of 42 proposals voted according to the demand of electors' initiative, only 9 were accepted. Likewise, the majority of proposals subject to facultative referendum were rejected: 33 out of 51.

The rate of participation of eligible voters in referendums varies according to the significance of the issue: 41.6 per cent took part in a referendum in 1931 on the question whether Swiss citizens should accept decorations awarded by foreign governments; 84.4 per cent voted in 1935 on the program of full employment policy sponsored by the Swiss labor unions.[83]

The United States

In the United States, the referendum is a customary procedure in state and local legislation. Complete records are available on votes taken in states in 1938–46. Data on municipal voting are fragmentary.

In all, 1,026 state proposals were put to vote between 1938 and 1946. This procedure is most popular in Georgia (155 referendums in 8 years), Louisiana (122) and California (95). It has been used less frequently in New England and the Middle Atlantic States. (See Table 220; cf. Figure 127.) The geographic pattern is not clear, however. The referendum is widely used in some southern states but has not been very popular in Tennessee, Kentucky and Mississippi; it has been frequently used in some "frontier" states but not in all.

The proposals referred to the electorate cover a very broad range of questions. A majority of the constitutional proposals have been accepted, and the statutory proposals, rejected. (See Table 221.)

POLITICAL PARTIES

The role of political parties under a parliamentary system is to crystallize public opinion around definite legislative and administrative measures. Despite the corruption associated with partisan policy, democracy cannot, in the long run, operate without the competition of political parties for power. A parliament or congress

83. The proposal, known as *"Krisis Initiative,"* was rejected, 56.2 to 43.8 per cent of valid votes. (**34**, 1945, pp. 522–23.)

TABLE 220

REFERENDUMS: THE UNITED STATES, NUMBER SUBMITTED, BY STATE, 1938–46

State	Total, 1938–46 [a]	1938	1939	1940	1941	1942	1943	1944	1946
United States, total	1,026	201	61	189	83	124	39	153	176
Alabama	30	2	5	8	—	—	—	6	9
Arizona	22	3	—	10	—	1	—	2	6
Arkansas	39	11	—	11	—	6	—	7	4
California	95	25	5	17	—	18	—	13	17
Colorado	15	3	—	5	—	1	—	4	2
Connecticut	3	—	—	—	—	—	—	—	3
Delaware	—	—	—	—	—	—	—	—	—
Florida	34	4	—	6	—	9	—	9	6
Georgia	155	23	33	—	70	—	28	—	1
Idaho	23	1	—	5	—	5	—	5	7
Illinois	8	2	—	1	—	1	—	2	2
Indiana	3	—	—	3	—	—	—	—	—
Iowa	2	—	—	1	—	1	—	—	—
Kansas	3	—	—	1	—	—	—	1	1
Kentucky	4	—	—	—	2	—	2	—	—
Louisiana	122	28	—	32	—	10	—	21	31
Maine	8	1	1	2	1	—	—	1	2
Maryland	30	4	—	9	—	7	—	6	4
Massachusetts	12	3	—	—	—	1	—	5	3
Michigan	22	4	2	4	2	3	—	4	3
Minnesota	6	2	—	1	—	2	—	1	—
Mississippi	5	—	2	1	—	2	—	—	—
Missouri	25	9	—	7	—	5	1	2	1
Montana	15	4	—	3	—	4	—	3	1
Nebraska	13	6	—	2	—	1	—	2	2
Nevada	9	2	—	3	—	1	—	2	1
New Hampshire	8	4	—	—	—	3	—	—	1
New Jersey	5	—	2	—	—	—	1	1	1
New Mexico	13	1	1	2	—	6	—	1	2
New York	21	9	1	—	4	—	6	—	1
North Carolina	11	2	—	—	—	2	—	5	2
North Dakota	35	3	4	13	—	2	—	7	6
Ohio	8	1	4	—	—	1	—	2	—
Oklahoma	28	6	—	6	3	3	—	5	5
Oregon	46	12	—	9	—	7	—	9	9
Pennsylvania	1	—	—	—	—	—	1	—	—
Rhode Island	13	7	1	—	—	—	—	3	2
South Carolina	30	6	—	5	—	1	—	7	11
South Dakota	18	2	—	4	—	6	—	2	4
Tennessee	3	1	—	2	—	—	—	—	—
Texas	17	1	—	4	—	5	—	3	4
Utah	16	3	—	1	—	2	—	2	8
Vermont	1	—	—	—	—	1	—	—	—
Virginia	3	—	—	—	—	—	—	2	1
Washington	25	4	—	6	—	6	—	5	4
West Virginia	7	1	—	3	—	1	—	—	2
Wisconsin	5	—	—	—	1	—	—	1	3
Wyoming	9	1	—	2	—	—	—	2	4

Source: 5, p. 7.

a. Data for 1945 not compiled.

EACH DOT REPRESENTS 10 REFERENDUMS

Source: Table 220

Figure 127. Referendums: The United States, Number Submitted, by State, 1938–46

Table 221

Referendums: The United States, Number, by Type and Outcome, 1938–46

Item	Total, 1938–46 [a]	1938	1939	1940	1941	1942	1943	1944	1946
States submitting proposals	47	36	12	33	7	22	6	35	38
Proposals, total	1,026	201	61	189	83	124	39	153	176
Approved	664	115	47	91	80	61	36	109	125
Rejected	362	86	14	98	3	63	3	44	51
Constitutional proposals	849	154	50	151	82	98	38	130	146
Approved	590	97	43	76	80	51	35	99	109
Rejected	259	57	7	75	2	47	3	31	37
Statutory proposals	177	47	11	38	1	26	1	23	30
Approved	74	18	4	15	—	10	1	10	16
Rejected	103	29	7	23	1	16	—	13	14
Subject [b]									
Taxation	199	38	7	53	7	26	5	33	30
Bond issues	64	19	6	9	—	5	6	7	12
Regulations	125	37	6	27	—	15	2	21	17
Local government	278	42	21	30	64	26	15	33	48

Source: **5**, p. 7.

a. Data for 1945 not compiled.
b. Multiple-subject proposals have been classified under each appropriate title.

without party clashes is indeed a hollow form, a façade masking a dictatorial regime.[84]

The number and character of political parties determine the two basic types of parliamentary systems: those based on two strong parties that succeed each other at the helm of the state; and those in which seats in the parliament are distributed among many parties and the parliamentary majority is normally formed by a coalition of two or more groups.

A third type of parliamentary system is marked by the decisive dominance of one party. Such a situation often occurs in young countries early in the development of parliamentary institutions, preceding either a two-party or many-party system. It may also develop from either two-party or many-party rule as a result of the growth of one party.

A fourth type, clearly different from the predominance of a party in free competition, represents the monopoly of a ruling party that quells any opposition and inhibits the normal operation and growth of other parties. Such a situation is a "perversion" of the parliamentary system and marks the beginning of its transformation into a dictatorship.

TWO-PARTY SYSTEMS

The two-party system has found its fullest development in the United States and Great Britain and also prevails in Canada, Australia, New Zealand and some Latin American countries. It is conspicuous by its absence in continental Europe.

The United States

The two-party system in the United States is maintained by the single-member constituencies in congressional elections and the majority vote in presidential elections.[85] (See Table 222.) Although more than two tickets have been presented to the voters in most elections since 1828, the real contest has always been between the Democratic and Republican parties. Prohibitionists have had their own candidate in all presidential elections since 1872; the Socialist Labor party, in all elections from 1892 to 1936; the Socialist party, in all elections since 1900. Free-Soilers and Greenback-Labor (money reformers), Nationalists and Communists, Populists and others have added their candidates to the list, but for all these, the campaign has been only a means of disseminating ideas. Between 1828 [86] and 1952, the smooth operation of the two-party system was seriously disturbed only three times — in 1860, when two Democratic candidates ran for the presidency; in 1912, when the Republicans were split between Theodore Roosevelt and William H. Taft; and in 1924, when Robert La Follette (Progressive) received 4.8 million votes — much the largest popular vote ever obtained by a third-party candidate.[87]

The two-party system in presidential elections is supported by electoral laws as well as tradition: election of the whole state ticket by a simple plurality; preliminary registration of voters by party affiliation; and, in nearly all states, primary elections regulated by state law.

In congressional elections, likewise, a candidate has little chance of election without the support of one of the two principal parties. These parties, however, are not strictly centralized and neither is controlled by its national committee. Apart from the presidential election, they operate as loose federations of state and city organizations with broad autonomy in local affairs, among which is nomination of candidates for Congress.

This situation weakens the two-party principle in the everyday operation of Congress. Officially, almost all members of both chambers are either Democrats or Republicans (see Table 223), but some Democrats frequently vote with the Republicans and vice versa, so that the operating majority in Congress may consist of most

---

84. **64**, pp. 645–46.
85. The President of the United States is elected by a majority of the electoral votes, which does not necessarily represent the majority of the popular vote. Only twice, however, in the 120 years from 1828 to 1948 have the electoral majorities given the presidency to a candidate who received fewer popular votes than his opponents. In 1876, Rutherford B. Hayes (Republican) received 4,036,298 popular votes as compared with 4,300,590 votes cast for his opponent, Samuel J. Tilden. The electoral votes, however, gave Hayes a majority of 185 against 184, and he was elected. Twelve years later, in 1888, Benjamin Harrison was elected by 5,439,853 popular votes and 233 electoral votes, while his opponent,

Grover Cleveland, had 5,540,309 popular votes and only 168 electoral votes. In all other presidential elections the elected candidate has had a majority of the popular vote and a much larger majority of the electoral vote.
86. The first election with a clear-cut contest between Democrats (Andrew Jackson) and Republicans (John Quincy Adams).
87. For the regional pattern of distribution of popular votes in presidential elections, see **42** and **43**.

TABLE 222

PARTIES: THE UNITED STATES, POPULAR VOTE FOR PRESIDENT, BY PARTY, 1840–1952

(*Thousands*)

Year	Total	Democratic	Republican	Other	Year	Total	Democratic	Republican	Other
1840	2,411	1,129	1,275[a]	7	1900	13,965	6,358	7,220	387
1844	2,698	1,337	1,299[a]	62	1904	13,524	5,084	7,629	810[e]
1848	2,872	1,221	1,360[a]	291	1908	14,887	6,409	7,679	799[f]
1852	3,144	1,601	1,387[a]	156	1912	15,031	6,286	3,484	5,261[g]
1856	4,054	1,838	1,341	875[b]	1916	18,528	9,128	8,534	867
1860	4,480	1,375	1,866	1,239[c]	1920	26,813	9,141	16,147	1,525[h]
1864	4,019	1,805	2,214	—	1924	29,091	8,387	15,725	4,979[i]
1868	5,716	2,703	3,013	—	1928	36,812	15,016	21,391	404
1872	6,466	2,834	3,597	35	1932	39,751	22,822	15,762	1,168[j]
1876	8,431	4,301	4,036	94	1936	45,647	27,477	16,680	1,491[k]
1880	9,219	4,445	4,454	320	1940	49,820	26,827	22,304	689
1884	10,053	4,875	4,852	326	1944	47,976	24,777	22,006	1,193
1888	11,381	5,540	5,440	401	1948	48,834	24,106	21,969	2,759[l]
1892	12,044	5,554	5,191	1,298[d]	1952	61,552	27,315	33,824	413
1896	13,813	6,468	7,036	310					

Sources: For 1840–88, **7**, pp. 288–89; for 1892–1952, **8**, 1953, p. 321.

a. Whigs.
b. American party.
c. Includes 848,000 votes for the second Democratic ticket (Stephen A. Douglas).
d. Includes 1,041,000 votes for People's party.
e. Includes 402,000 votes for Socialist party (Eugene V. Debs).
f. Includes 421,000 votes for Debs.
g. Includes 4,120,000 votes for Progressive party (Theodore Roosevelt) and 901,000 votes for Debs.

h. Includes 920,000 votes for Debs.
i. Includes 4,823,000 votes for Progressive party (Robert La Follette).
j. Includes 882,000 votes for Socialist party (Norman Thomas).
k. Includes 882,000 votes for William Lemke cast under various party names.
l. Includes 1,169,000 votes for J. Strom Thurmond (States' Rights) and 1,156,000 votes for Henry A. Wallace (Progressive).

TABLE 223

PARLIAMENTS: THE UNITED STATES, COMPOSITION OF CONGRESS, 1951, 1953 AND 1955

Party	Number of Representatives	Party	Number of Senators
1951: After Elections of November 7, 1950			
Total	435	Total	96
Democratic	232	Democratic	50
Republican	200	Republican	46
Independent	1		
Vacant	2		
1953: After Elections of November 4, 1952			
Total	435	Total	96
Democratic	215	Democratic	48
Republican	219	Republican	47
Independent	1	Independent	1
1955: After Elections of November 2, 1954			
Total	435	Total	96
Democratic	232	Democratic	48
Republican	203	Republican	47
		Independent	1

Source: **67**, 1953–55.

of the representatives of one party supported by the minority of the other.

State and local elections, including the all-important contests for governorships, deviate even more from the two-party system. An individual campaigning independently may defeat opponents supported by the regular party organizations. Minorities of both parties may agree on a coalition candidate and bring about his victory over both regular party candidates.[88]

Great Britain

In Great Britain the voice of the majority in the House of Commons is supposed to express the will of the nation. A shift of the majority, and sometimes even an indication that the majority may be changing — as in the defeat of the majority candidate in a by-election — may lead to the fall of the government and new general elections. When the margin of the majority

88. Despite the flexibility of the U.S. electoral system, congressional and gubernatorial elections, even in mid-term years, clearly indicate shifts of public opinion between the two major parties. (See **43**.)

TABLE 224

PARLIAMENTS: GREAT BRITAIN, COMPOSITION OF THE HOUSE OF COMMONS AFTER GENERAL ELECTIONS, 1832–1955

(*Number of Representatives*)

Year	Total	Conservative	Liberal	Unionist	Nationalist	Labor	Other
1832	658	179	479	—	—	—	—
1835	658	275	383	—	—	—	—
1837	658	309	349	—	—	—	—
1841	657	368	289	—	—	—	—
1845	656	327	329	—	—	—	—
1852	654	331	323	—	—	—	—
1857	654	281	373	—	—	—	—
1859	654	307	347	—	—	—	—
1865	658	299	359	—	—	—	—
1868	658	279	379	—	—	—	—
1874	652	352	242	—	58	—	—
1880	652	238	349	—	65	—	—
1885	670	250	334	—	86	—	—
1886	670	316	191	78	85	—	—
1892	670	268	274	47	81	—	—
1895	670	341	177	70	82	—	—
1900	670	334	186	68	82	—	—
1906	670	134	376	23	83	54	—
1910 (Jan.)	670	242	275	31	82	40	—
1910 (Dec.)	670	240	270	34	84	42	—
1918	707	384[a]	165	—	80	72	6
1922	605	344[a]	114	—	3	142	2
1923	615	258[a]	159	—	—	191	7
1924	615	412	47	—	—	151	5
1929	615	260	59	—	—	288	8
1931	615	470	72	—	3	65	5
1935	615	387	54	—	3	166	5
1945	640	195	24	10	2	395	14[b]
1950	625	272	9	10	16	315	3[c]
1951[d]	625	294	6	9	8	294	14[e]
1955	630	344	6	—	—	277	3

Sources: **67**, 1950, p. 83; **50**, pp. 277–78. Cf. **48**, p. 55.

a. Unionists.
b. 10 Independents, 2 Nationalists, 2 Communists.
c. Vacant seats.

d. After election of October 25, for five-year term.
e. Includes 11 representatives supporting the governmental majority and 3 representatives of the opposition.

in the Commons is narrow, this system requires strict discipline of party members, and parliamentary votes are usually cast along party lines. The changes in the composition of the House of Commons from 1832 to 1955 offer the best example of the two-party system in operation. (See Table 224; cf. Figure 128.)

Until 1874, the system existed in pure culture — two and only two parties in elections and in the Commons. The Liberals were in power during most of the period but were unseated by the Conservatives in 1841 and 1852 and obtained only an insignificant majority in 1845.

The situation changed in the 1870's after the representatives of Ireland constituted a separate (Nationalist) faction. The factions in the Commons increased further to four when the Unionists appeared as a separate group. The contest for power, however, continued to be restricted to the Conservatives and Liberals. Between 1874 and 1900, general elections gave the victory to the Conservatives four times and to the Liberals three times.[89]

89. The Unionists, who played a significant role at that time, were a dissident Liberal group. Later they joined the Conservatives.

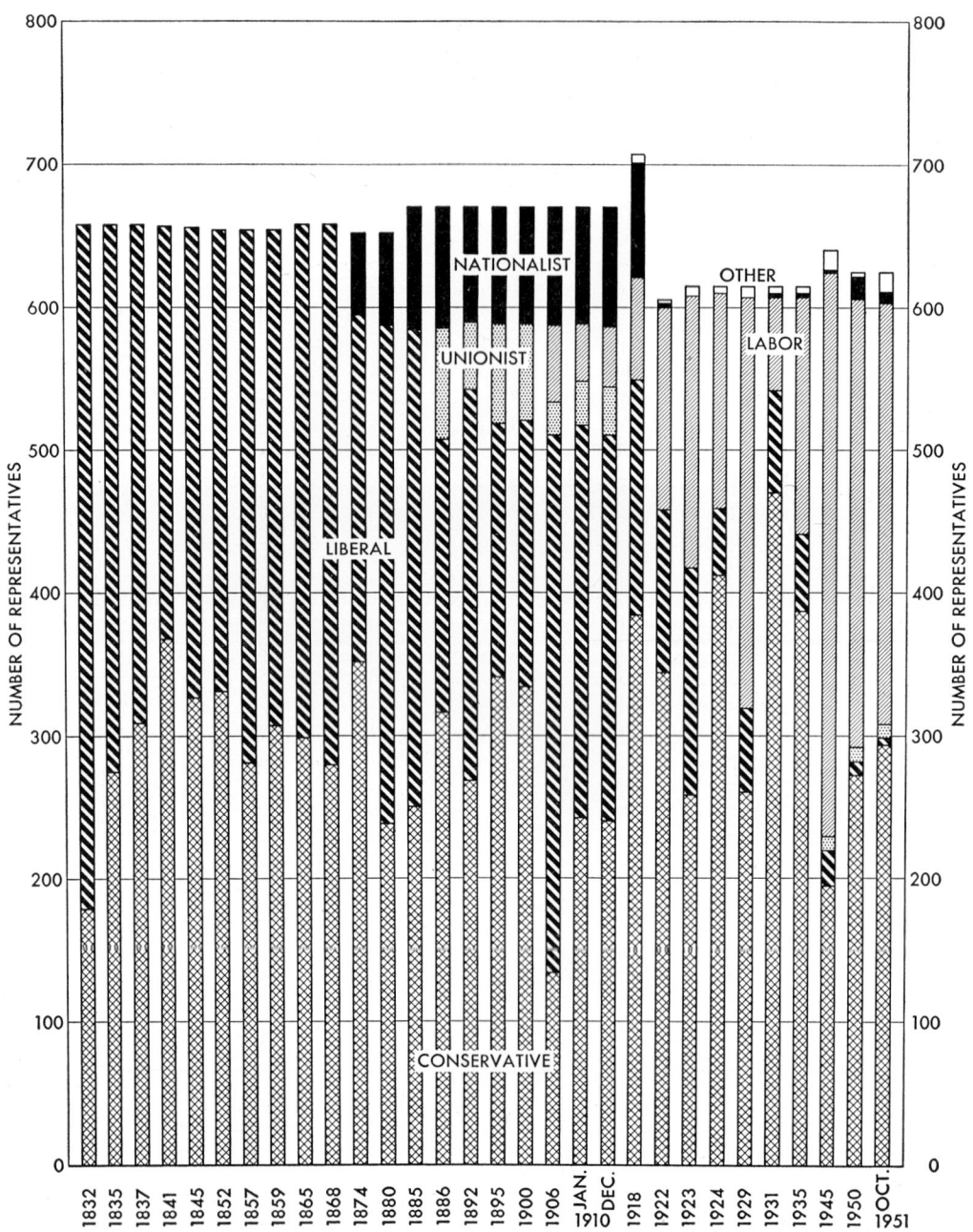

NATIONALIST

UNIONIST

OTHER

LABOR

LIBERAL

CONSERVATIVE

NUMBER OF REPRESENTATIVES

NUMBER OF REPRESENTATIVES

1832 1835 1837 1841 1845 1852 1857 1859 1865 1868 1874 1880 1885 1886 1892 1895 1900 1906 JAN. 1910 DEC. 1918 1922 1923 1924 1929 1931 1935 1945 1950 OCT. 1951

Source: Table 224

FIGURE 128. PARLIAMENTS: COMPOSITION OF THE BRITISH HOUSE OF COMMONS AFTER GENERAL ELECTIONS, 1832–1951

After the turn of the century a new power — the Labor party — appeared on the British political scene. Until World War I, however, it remained a mere splinter group. The Liberals were the strongest party, but did not have an absolute majority after the general elections in 1910. The two-party system had entered a critical period.

After the election in January 1910, the Liberals had a majority in the Commons only with the support of the Laborites and Irish Nationalists. The second election in the same year did not clarify the situation. Great Britain entered World

War I with a fairly unstable parliamentary situation but found an exceptionally able leader, David Lloyd George, who resolved the difficulty by forming a coalition government.

The first general election after the end of the war gave an absolute majority to the Conservatives, then campaigning under the name of Unionists. A Unionist-Liberal coalition was formed to cope with postwar difficulties. In 1922 the Unionists assumed power as the majority party. Under their old name, as Conservatives, they held the lead until 1945. During this period, a radical realignment of the British electorate was taking place: the Liberal party was fading away and its historical role passed to the Labor party. After 1931, Great Britain had a Conservative national government. In May 1940, in view of the war emergency, it became a coalition government under Winston Churchill, with strong Labor participation. The first postwar election in 1945 brought the Labor party to power. At the election in 1950 the Conservatives recovered a part of their losses, but the Labor party held the lead. The election in October 1951 gave the majority in the Commons to the Conservatives (together with Nationalists and Unionists), although they failed to obtain a majority of the popular vote. Following the election of 1951 the government and opposition forces in the House of Commons were distributed as follows: [90]

Total	625
Government coalition	322
Conservative	294
Unionist	9
Liberal Conservative [a]	19
Opposition	294
Labor	294
Other parties	9
Liberal	6
Irish	3

a. Includes five splinter groups.

Other Countries

The British dominions of Canada, the Union of South Africa, Australia and New Zealand have parliamentary systems of about the same type as Great Britain.

In *Canada* the principal parties are the Liberal and Conservative (which has recently changed its name to Progressive Conservative party). The Liberals have been in power since 1921.[91] (See Table 225.)

In *Australia,* the principal parties are the Liberal and Labor. Neither has an absolute majority, however, and the elections of April 1951 returned the Liberals to Parliament with 51 seats and the Laborites with 53 seats. (See Table 225.) The government is supported by a coalition of the Liberals and the Country party.

New Zealand's electoral votes and parliamentary seats are divided between the National and Labor parties. In the *Union of South Africa,* the two leading parties are the United and National. The latter represents extreme nationalism and, together with the Afrikaner party, has the parliamentary majority. (See Table 225.)

In some Latin American nations parliamentary practice seems to be developing toward the two-party system. *Nicaragua* and *Costa Rica,* for example, have only two parties: the National Liberal and Conservative parties in Nicaragua; the National Liberation and Democratic parties in Costa Rica. The situation in Uruguay is similar.

A situation similar to the two-party system exists likewise in the *Philippines* and *Austria.* In Austria the political contest is between the People's party (Catholic) and the Socialists, who have nearly equal strength in the lower chamber. (See Table 225.) The present government is supported by a coalition of the two parties.

However, the distinction between the two-party and multiparty systems becomes vague when several parties rally in two blocs which compete for power and succeed each other in the government. Such a situation existed, for example, in Chile before the elections in February 1953: the country had some fifteen parties, but they were grouped in two blocs — rightist and leftist — and the contest was between these blocs rather than between single parties.[92]

MULTIPARTY SYSTEMS

A multiparty system is often associated with proportional representation but is not necessarily a result of it. The relationship may be just the opposite: a country where many parties clamor for parliamentary seats may shape its electoral law accordingly, with many-member constituencies and PR.

---

90. See **67,** 1954, p. 86.

91. As in the United States, differences of opinion within each party are almost as wide as those that divide the two parties from each other.

92. Cf. **16,** 1945, pp. 3–31.

TABLE 225

PARLIAMENTS: SELECTED COUNTRIES, COMPOSITION OF THE LOWER CHAMBER UNDER THE TWO-PARTY SYSTEM, 1950–53

Country, Chamber and Party	Number of Representatives	Country, Chamber and Party	Number of Representatives
Canada, Lower Chamber elected in August 1953 and subsequent by-elections		*Nicaragua*, Parliament elected in 1950	
Total	265	Total	42
Liberal	170	National Liberal	28
Progressive Conservative	50	Conservative	14
Cooperative Commonwealth Federation	23	*Union of South Africa*, Lower Chamber elected in 1953	
Social Credit	15	Total	159
Other	6	National (inc. Afrikaner)	94
Vacant	1	United	52
Australia, Lower Chamber elected in 1951		South African Labor	5
		Representatives of the natives	3
Total	123	Independent	5
Liberal	51	*Costa Rica*, Parliament elected in 1953	
Country party	17		
Labor	53	Total	45
Nonvoting members	2	National Liberation	30
New Zealand, Parliament elected in 1951		Democratic and National Union	15
		Austria, Lower Chamber elected in 1953	
Total	80	Total	165
National	50	People's party	74
Labor	30	Socialist	73
		Communist	4
		Independent	14

Sources: **67**, 1954, and **72**, 1953, *passim.*

Multiparty systems are traditional in continental Europe. They are typified by the parliaments of prewar Germany, of France, Italy, Belgium, the Netherlands, the Scandinavian countries, Switzerland and Greece. Among the nations founded in recent years Indonesia and Israel seem to have adopted the multiparty system.

Germany

The parliamentary history of Germany presents strong arguments both for and against the multiparty system. From the time of Bismarck, the Reichstag always included a dozen parties, most of them ready to back the Kaiser's government. The Social-Democratic party and, on certain questions, the Centrum (Catholic) represented the opposition. Changes in the composition of the Reichstag reflected the growth of liberal forces in the nation: the reactionary wing counted 219 members in 1871 and only 102 in 1912; the Social-Democrats had 2 seats in 1871 and 110 in 1912.[93] The many-party system was successful throughout this period and became a political tradition.

Under the Weimar Republic, the Reichstag was split among fifteen to twenty factions, from the Nazis and the reactionary German National People's Party on the right to the Communists on the left. Of the 577 members, a total of more than 200 at both extremes were opposed to the republic and the democratic regime as such. The middle-way parties, from the conservative German People's Party to the moderate Socialists, had an absolute majority in the Reichstag but could not reach stable agreement among them-

93. **78**, Vol. 7, p. 34. Cf. **44**.

selves. The Conservatives looked to the right, the Social-Democrats to the left. Both feared, with good reason, the loss of support of their constituents. From 1919 to 1933, Germany experimented with some 20 coalition governments, all of the middle-way type, some stretching from the Centrum (Catholic) to the left, others to the right, a few including both left- and right-wing members but without the Nazis and Communists.[94]

The longevity of each coalition depended on the whim of any one of its partners. None proved stable enough to gain the respect and affection of the people. The continuous changes of the government created a cynicism bordering on contempt for democracy. Thus the way was paved for the surrender of the German Republic to Hitler. There is no evidence that the two-party system would have prevented the collapse of the Republic, but it seems clear that the Weimar constitution provided democracy with a very poor instrument for self-defense.

Although the new constitution of Western Germany tends to assure representation of all parties without weakening the working majority of moderate, middle-way groups it has not been very successful in this respect. The first Bundestag, elected in 1949, had 402 members; the second, elected in September 1953, had 487 members. They were distributed by party affiliation as follows: [95]

	1949	1953
Total	402	487
Christian Democratic Union	146	244
Social-Democrats	129	151
Free Democrats	57	48
German party	25	15
Bavarian party	12	a
Communists	14	b
Centrum (Catholic)	10	2
All-German bloc [c]	—	27
Other and vacant	9	—

a. Included in Christian Democratic Union.
b. The Communists participated in the elections of 1953, but failed to win any seats.
c. Organization of expellees and refugees from Eastern Germany.

In the Bundestag of 1953 the Christian Democratic Union had a majority of one vote, but the government was supported by a coalition of the Union, the Free Democrats, the German party and the All-German bloc.

94. **79**, p. 204.
95. **21**, August 1949; **67**, 1954, p. 79.

France

The French National Assembly, elected in 1946 on the basis of proportional representation, is another example of a parliament with too many parties. It had 16 official factions plus the Gaullist group, which cuts across the official factions, and 12 unaffiliated members. (See Table 226.) Of the 621 members of the Assembly, 167 were Communists, committed to opposition of any government. The Gaullists rejected any coalition with other groups. The required majority of at least 311 deputies could be provided only by a broad coalition.[96] The government's majority in the National Assembly has included Popular Republicans (MRP), Radical Socialists, Socialists (SFIO) and members of half a dozen splinter groups, though neither the Socialists nor all the moderate splinter groups have been continuously on the government side. In some coalitions, the majority's margin in the Assembly has been so narrow that withdrawal of a few "independent" or "unaffiliated" deputies could force the government to resign.

The elections to the new Chamber in 1951 were held on the basis of a new electoral law — a product of five years of dispute that introduced a modified majority system with multimember constituencies. The law provides that all seats of the constituency go to the party or coalition which obtains more than half the valid votes. The seats in constituencies in which no list has received an absolute majority are allocated to parties or coalitions of parties in proportion to the total number of votes cast for them in all such districts. Two departments — Seine and Seine-et-Oise — retained the system of proportional representation.[97]

96. Experience has shown that this parliamentary system fails to provide the necessary stability of government. France has had one parliamentary crisis after another, and despite the revision of the electoral law in 1951, changed governments eighteen times during 1947–52. Very often a government which succeeds a cabinet forced to resign because of lack of a chamber majority has been represented by the same parties and has been composed largely of the same men. The average life span of a French government has been 3 months, not counting the periods of "crisis" when France has been without a government.

97. The following examples show how this system works: In a department where 4 seats were at stake, 123,300 votes were cast, distributed as follows: Communists, 32,700 votes; Socialists, 28,600 votes; Gaullists (Reunion of the French People, or briefly, RPF), 21,600; Mouvement Republicain Populaire (MRP), 19,300; Conservatives, 12,400; Radicals, 7,400; splinter groups, 1,300

TABLE 226

PARLIAMENTS: FRANCE, COMPOSITION OF THE NATIONAL ASSEMBLY, 1946 AND 1951

Party	Number of Representatives [a]	Party	Number of Representatives [a]
Election of 1946, total	621	Election of 1951, total	627
Communists	167	Communists	98
Socialists (SFIO)	99	Socialists	105
Popular Republicans (MRP)	145	Popular Republicans	85
Radical Socialists	46	Overseas Independents	16
Republican Party of Liberty	29	Rally of Left Republicans	
Independent Republicans	24	Radical Socialist	76
Democratic and Social Action	16	Democratic and Socialist Union	24
Republican Peasant Action	19	Fourth Force	
Union of Democratic and Socialist Resistance	13	Republican Independent	54
Overseas Independents	12	Peasants	50
Democratic Union of Independents	9	Republican and Social Action	33
Union of Progressive Republicans	8	Gaullists (RPF)	72
African Democratic Rally	6	Other and vacant	14
Independent Popular Republicans	6		
Other and unaffiliated	22		

Source: **67**, 1950, p. 69 and 1954, p. 69.   a. Figures for each faction include affiliates.

The purpose of these provisions was to encourage electoral coalitions and strengthen representation of middle-way political groups. The new electoral law, however, did not improve the parliamentary situation in France. After the election in 1951, the Gaullists took part in the government for the first time since their appearance in the political arena. The Communists lost 69 seats, the Socialists and Radical Socialists made appreciable gains and the Popular Republicans lost to the Gaullists. (See Table 226.) The new Chamber was reminiscent of the German Reichstag under the Weimar Republic — strong groups on the right and the left and a weak and

votes. Next, the Socialists, MRP, Conservatives and Radicals pooled their votes, which gave them a total of 67,700 votes or an absolute majority. Of the 4 seats, 2 went to the Socialists while the Radicals and the MRP obtained 1 seat each.

In another department, likewise with 4 seats at stake, 136,900 votes were cast: 49,000 for the Communists, 34,400 for RPF, 16,800 for the Socialists, 12,600 for the Left Republicans, 11,300 for the Conservatives, 8,100 for MRP, 3,300 for the Resistance Movement and 1,400 for a minor party. The pooled votes for the Socialists, Left Republicans, Conservatives, MRP and Resistance gave them a total of 52,100. Through allocation of seats in proportion to votes, the coalition list obained 2 seats (1 for the Socialists, the other for the Left Republicans), while the Communists and the RPF won 1 seat each. (**73**, pp. 298–99.)

unstable center. Under this Chamber France suffered, in 1953, one of the longest and most disheartening crises in its parliamentary history and the situation remained unstable in 1954.

Italy

Like France, Italy is accustomed to the multiparty system and a fluid parliamentary majority. Its chief postwar political problem has been that of Communism. The first election (1948), held on the basis of the new republican constitution, gave an absolute majority to the Christian Democratic Party led by Alcide De Gasperi. The Communists emerged from the elections as the second strongest party in the Chamber of Deputies (see Table 227) and won control over most large cities, especially in the north. Although De Gasperi's party had an absolute majority in the Chamber, he tried to form a coalition government with the support of Socialists with anti-Communist leanings. The coalition of Christian Democrats, Socialists, Republicans and other splinter parties gave the government more than 380 votes out of 574 in the Chamber of Deputies, and its parliamentary position remained unshaken even after the withdrawal of the Socialists.

At local elections in 1951, a bloc of Christian

Democrats and moderate Socialists won from the Communists half the municipalities in which the latter had been entrenched since 1948.

A Chamber with an absolute majority of a single party was contrary to the political traditions of Italy, and the fluidity of party alignments in Italy made this majority uncertain in the long run. A new electoral law was enacted to ensure greater stability of the government. Its main feature is that it gives 64.5 per cent of the seats in parliament to the party or coalition which obtains more than half of the votes, thus converting a shaky popular majority into a solid majority in the Chamber. General elections held on the basis of the new law in June 1953 gave the coalition of Christian Democrats and other center parties, excluding right-wing Socialists, 49.8 per cent of the votes; 35.3 per cent went to Communists and left-wing Socialists; 12.7 per cent to the monarchists and neo-Fascists; and 1.7 per cent to right-wing Socialists. Thus, no group qualified for the majority bonus and none obtained an absolute majority in either the Chamber or the Senate. The left and right wings, together, had enough votes in Parliament to vote down any proposal of the center parties. To remain in power, the Christian Democrats were therefore compelled to seek the support of factions that had opposed them in the elections. If unable to obtain the support of the Socialists they must turn to the right, and thereby probably lose the support of moderate Socialists. (See Table 227.)

Switzerland

In Switzerland the Federal Assembly (composed of the National Council and the Council of State) elects the executive (the Federal Council of seven members). The various departments (foreign relations, tariff, etc.) are distributed among all the major parties. The Swiss arrangement typifies the smooth operation of the many-party system. It differs from the coalition cabinets in France and other European countries in that its purpose is not to obtain a working majority in the parliament but to make all major parties share responsibility for government. The system requires no preliminary agreement of government parties on a political program. In the event of disagreement within the Federal Council, the Council does not resign but refers the controversial issue to the National Council for decision.

The National Council had eight factions in 1951, three of almost equal numerical strength. All three and a fourth smaller faction are represented in the Federal Council. (See Table 227.)

Other Countries

Parliamentary contests in Belgium, the Netherlands, Denmark, Sweden, Norway, Finland and Austria are characterized by the competition between the moderate Socialist or Labor parties supported by the labor unions, on the one hand, and anti-Socialist parties on the other. The latter represent a wide range of political opinion and do not always act as a bloc; occasionally some join forces with the Socialists in a coalition government. The forces opposing the Socialists are often led by a party stressing its affiliation with the Church, but this is not a general rule. The parliamentary strength of the Communists in this group of countries is negligible.

This situation is somewhat similar to the two-party system but differs from it in that a coalition is always more or less fluid and under the rule of political blocs. No particular group is regarded as the presumptive heir of the party or coalition currently in power. (See Table 227.)

In *Belgium* the Social Christian party was in power until the last election (1954). Its policy in questions directly affecting labor was largely controlled by Christian labor unions, which avoided antagonizing the free unions aligned with the Socialists. The last election brought the Socialists to power, although the Social Christian party remained the strongest single party in the parliament.

In the *Netherlands* the government is supported by a broad coalition which includes all major parties — Catholic, Labor, Christian-Historical and Freedom. The cabinet represents all parties except the extreme left and extreme right.

The Socialists, as the strongest party, are at the helm in Denmark, Sweden and Norway. In *Denmark* they form a "minority" cabinet. In *Sweden* the Socialists have nearly an absolute majority in parliament; in *Norway* their absolute majority has not been challenged for a long time.

Finland has a coalition government with Agrarians in a leading position in the coalition. *Austria* has a coalition of the People's party and the Socialists.

The examples of these seven countries show how the multiparty system operates when all

Table 227

PARLIAMENTS: SELECTED COUNTRIES, COMPOSITION OF THE LOWER CHAMBER, UNDER THE MULTIPARTY SYSTEM, 1948–54

Country, Chamber and Party	Number of Representatives		Country, Chamber and Party	Number of Representatives

Italy, Chamber of Deputies elected in 1948 and 1953

	1948	1953
Total	574	590
Christian Democrat	306	269
Right-wing Socialists	13	19
Liberals	15	13
Other Center groups	10	10
Communists	132	143
Left-wing Socialists	71	75
Monarchists	13	32
Neo-Fascists	—	29
Other	14	—

Belgium, Lower Chamber elected in 1950 and 1954

	1950	1954
Total	212	212
Social Christian	108	95
Socialist	77	86
Liberal	20	25
Communist	7	4
Splinter groups	—	2

Netherlands, Lower Chamber elected in 1952

Total	100
Catholic People's party	30
Labor	30
Anti-Revolutionary	12
Christian-Historical	9
Freedom	9
Communist	6
Other	4

Denmark, Parliament elected in 1950 and 1953

	1950	1953
Total	151	179
Social-Democratic	59	74
Moderate Liberal	32	42
Conservative	27	30
Social Liberal	12	14
Communist	7	8
Other	14	11

Brazil, Chamber elected in 1954

Total	304
Social Democrat	108
National Democrat	76
Labor	61
Social Progressive	26
Republican	11
Other	22

Switzerland, National Council elected in 1951

Total	196
Radical Liberals	51
Social-Democratic	49
Catholic Conservative	48
Peasants, Artisans and Middle Class	23
Independent party	10
Liberal Democratic	5
Communist	5
Democratic	4
Nonparty	1

Sweden, Lower Chamber elected in 1952

Total	230
Social-Democratic	110
Liberal	58
Farmers (Agrarian)	26
Conservative	31
Communist	5

Norway, Parliament elected in 1949 and 1953

	1949	1953
Total	150	150
Labor	85	77
Conservative	23	27
Liberal	21	15
Agrarian	12	14
Christian People's party	9	14
Communist	—	3

Finland, Parliament elected in 1951

Total	200
Agrarian	51
Social-Democratic	53
Democratic Union	43
Conservative party	28
Swedish People	15
National	10

Japan, House of Representatives elected in 1953

Total	467
Liberal	185
Japan Democratic Party	120
Right-wing Socialist	61
Left-wing Socialist	72
Communist	1
Labor-Farmer	5
Independent	15
Vacant	8

Sources: **67**, 1954 and **72**, 1953, *passim.*

TABLE 228

PARLIAMENTS: GREECE, COMPOSITION OF THE PARLIAMENT, 1950 AND 1952

Party	Number of Representatives	Party	Number of Representatives
Election of 1950, total	250	Election of 1952, total	300
Populists (Tsaldaris)	62	Greek Rally (Papagos)	214
Liberal (Venizelos)	56	Liberals	36
National Progressive Union of the		Conservatives	24
Center	45	Progressives	14
Social Democrats	35	Democratic Party	5
Democratic Front (extreme Left)	18	Independent	7
PAP (extreme Right)	16		
Other	18		

Source: **67,** 1951, p. 96 and 1954, p. 95.

parties are well organized and experienced in parliamentary procedures.

Greece has passed through a period of political turmoil, with many parties, all poorly organized, inexperienced and held together largely by personal loyalty to the leader. With six parties in parliament, a brand new constitution, and unhealed wounds of civil war, Greece was bound to go from one parliamentary crisis to another. In 1951 a new electoral law was promulgated to foster concentration of political power in the hands of two or three parties. The law provides for two runs in the distribution of seats. First, seats are allocated to the candidates who obtained an absolute majority of votes in their respective constituencies. Next, all the seats not thus allocated are distributed proportionally among the parties (or coalitions) which obtained not less than 17 per cent of all votes. Thus, the law tends to encourage formation of electoral coalitions by moderate groups and parties and to eliminate splinter groups. The new law has radically changed the composition of the Greek parliament. (See Table 228.) Its long-range effect on the political life of Greece has yet to be tested.

The multiparty system, in various forms, also prevails in *Brazil* (see Table 227) and in *Panama;* in *Iceland, Ireland, Luxembourg;* in *Indonesia;* and in *Israel* (see Table 229).

In *Japan,* the ruling party seems to be able to adjust itself to modern needs and to assume leadership in economic and political reforms.

ONE-PARTY DOMINATION

A parliamentary system may record the continuing majority of a single party. Such a situation usually occurs early in a parliamentary regime and is followed by differentiation of political forces.

India, Egypt and Turkey are typical of youthful parliamentary regimes dominated by a single party. In *India,* Nehru's Congress Party won 362 seats out of 489 in the parliament in 1952. In *Turkey,* the Democratic party, opposed to the Republican People's party of Kemal Ataturk, founder of the Turkish Republic, gained an absolute majority and took over power in 1950, and gained an even larger majority in 1954. (See Table 230.)

In *Egypt,* the situation is more complicated. Elections of January 1950 to the Lower Chamber gave a majority of more than two thirds to the conservative Wafdist party supported by rich landowners and merchants. (See Table 230.) The Chamber was dissolved in March

TABLE 229

PARLIAMENTS: ISRAEL, COMPOSITION OF THE PARLIAMENT, 1951

Party	Number of Representatives
Total	120
Mapai (Israel Labor)	52
General Zionist	20
Mapam (United Workers)	7
Mizrahi Labor	8
Freedom	8
Communist	7
Progressive	4
Other	14

Source: **67,** 1955, p. 120.

TABLE 230

PARLIAMENTS: TURKEY AND EGYPT, COMPOSITION OF THE PARLIAMENT UNDER SINGLE-PARTY DOMINATION,
1950 AND 1954

Country and Party	Number of Representatives		Country and Party	Number of Representatives
Turkey, Assembly elected in 1950 and 1954	*1950*	*1954*	*Egypt*, Lower Chamber elected in 1950 [a]	
Total	487	541	Total	319
Democratic	386	504	WAFD	218
Republican People's party	52	31	SAAD	28
Nation's party	2	5	Liberal Constitutional	27
Turkish Peasant	6	—	Other	7
Independent	20	1	Independent	39
Vacancies	21	—		

Source: **67,** 1954, pp. 60, 188.

a. Dissolved, December 10, 1952, simultaneously with abolition of the monarchist constitution of 1923.

1952. The revolution of July 1952 which started the transformation of Egypt from a half-feudal kingdom into a republic was directed against the Wafdist party no less than against the king. In September 1952 all the old political parties were disbanded. On December 10, 1952 the government of General Naguib announced the abolition of the monarchist constitution of 1923 and the suspension of parliamentary life for three years. In February 1953 a new dictatorial three-year interim constitution was proclaimed. In June 1953 a republic was proclaimed and it was announced that the form of the republic would be decided by a plebiscite. In February 1954 the power passed to Lieutenant Colonel Nasser. This chain of events left Egypt a republic, temporarily without a constitution and parliament, ruled by a dictatorial military government.

One party, likewise, dominates the parliament in *Peru,* where the last general election gave 146 seats out of 156 to supporters of President Manuel A. Odría. However, no Odrísta party had campaigned in this election and no such party was organized in the Peruvian parliament. The unanimity of the electoral vote expressed rather support of the constitutional and parliamentary regime which the president had promised to restore and defend. The situation in Peru following the election of 1952 seems to suggest the possibility of consolidation of a constitutional regime under the domination of one party.

Similarly, one party dominates the political scene in *Mexico* and *Honduras*.[98]

98. Cf. Table 290 in Chapter 17.

ONE-PARTY DICTATORSHIPS

One-party parliaments are usually the products of one-candidate elections or a "purge." The following are typical mock parliaments that consist of candidates picked by the government:

The Supreme Soviet of the *USSR* (some 1,500 members, all candidates of the "bloc" of Communists and Non-Party People).

The national assembly of *Bulgaria* (293 members, all of the Fatherland Front).

The national assembly of *Czechoslovakia* (300 members, all of the National Front).

The national assembly of *Hungary* (415 members, all of the People's Front).

The parliament of *Romania* (423 members, all of the People's Democracy and other front organizations).

The assembly of *Yugoslavia* (620 members, all of the People's Front).

The parliament (*Sejm*) of *Poland* (425 members, all of the National Front).

The situation in the *Dominican Republic* and in *Paraguay* is very similar.

Less clear is the dictatorship of the ruling party in *Argentina*, where the Peronista party holds 146 seats out of 160 in the lower chamber and maintains its power by terrorizing opposition groups. For some reason, however, it has not converted the country into an openly fascist state or "people's republic." Likewise the situation in *Colombia* does not exactly fit the pattern of one-party dictatorship, although its parliament consists of 111 Conservatives, with 87 seats vacant, as a result of the decision of liberal and progressive elements to boycott elections which failed to give them the necessary freedom to campaign. Sooner or later the ruling party will either make concessions to the opposition and bring it back into parliament or abolish the constitution.

There are also marginal cases in which the balloting has had elements of mock parliamentarism and genuine democratic elections. In Asia and Africa, in some constitutional monarchies and republics without experience in democratic procedures, abuses are frequently reported. An official, for example, may give a voter a single ballot for the candidate picked by the local authorities, let the voter mark this ballot and then accept it as his vote.[99] The difference between such procedures and the mock elections in a "people's republic" is in the scope of abuse rather than in principle.

THE LONG-RANGE TREND AND OUTLOOK

A world survey of types of governments, voting, elections and parliaments reveals a great variety of patterns. None has proved perfect in all circumstances. Widely divergent methods have been successful under certain conditions and have failed in another setting.

There is as great a variety in the forms of tyranny as in those of democracy. The most dangerous is the dictatorial regime which poses as an advanced form of democracy and uses an imitation of parliamentary institutions as a means of cheating the people with an illusion of self-government.

Democracy, in the sense of a government of the people, by the people and for the people, has made vast gains since the end of the nine-

teenth century. This progress, measured by the scope of suffrage, has never been more spectacular than since World War I. The development of dictatorial regimes of various brands has not been able to block this progress. It is true that nations with a population of several hundred million have either surrendered their freedom to absolute rulers or have been conquered and enslaved. Some absolute rulers and their governments, however, have been expunged long before the end of the millennium for which they planned.

The temporary military success of dictatorial regimes has created a widespread feeling of "crisis in democracy." A survey of patterns of political life in the past three or four decades fails to substantiate this feeling. The democratic governments are not equally strong and equally successful everywhere. However, they have coped with peace and war more satisfactorily than the absolutist regimes — either the old-fashioned absolute empires or modern nazi, fascist and communist states. Freedom and self-government remain the most cherished possessions of peoples in democratic countries and the dream of peoples in enslaved nations. The ideological strength of democracy is evidenced by the fact that the dictatorial regimes feel compelled to pose as people's democracies, hiding behind the façade of parliamentary institutions and mock elections.[100] On the other hand, no democratic regime has ever attempted to gain support of the people by pretending that it is a dictatorship.

The world of today is half free and half slave, but the general trend in the past two centuries has been toward expansion of the scope of freedom.

---

99. Cf. **52,** p. 112.

100. Cf. Chapter 12.

CHAPTER 14

COLONIAL EMPIRES

SINCE THE END of the fifteenth century, colonization has been the major means of disseminating European ways of life and economic organization over the rest of the world. The system of colonial domination has not been static, however. Centralization and disintegration, colonization and decolonization have succeeded each other.[1]

The discovery of America was the greatest event in world history at the turn of the fifteenth century; the emancipation of the British, Spanish and Portuguese colonies in the Western Hemisphere, the greatest event at the turn of the eighteenth. The decolonization of the Americas did not restore these continents to their precolonial status. Free from foreign tutelage, the nations of the New World became bearers of the civilization brought to them in colonial days.

Similarly, the decolonization now in progress in Asia will not erase the impact of the colonial period. People in what were formerly colonies do not go back to the political and economic patterns of the precolonial era. They do not destroy the cities, railroads and highways the foreign masters have built but seek loans to develop them further. They do not close the factories, mines and power stations the invaders set up to exploit their resources but try to increase their industrial capacity, modernize their equipment and build up efficient economic systems according to Western patterns. Former colonies do not restore the power of their precolonial rulers but reshape their new state along Western lines with universal suffrage, a parliament, a responsible cabinet. Although people in what were once colonies strongly dislike their former masters, their nationalism is imitative. It is, indeed, as imitative as the nationalism of the United States at the time of the Revolutionary War or of the nations in Central and South America after their emancipation.

WHAT IS A COLONY?

The concepts of *colony, colonial power, colonial empire* and the like are rather vague and

often misleading. The source of confusion lies largely in the historical character of these concepts. The meanings of these terms changed in the course of centuries, and the word "colony" connotes different things in different parts of the world. The original meaning — "a company of people transplanted from their mother country to a new province or country, and remaining subject to the jurisdiction of the parent state" (*Webster*) — does not describe modern colonial systems.

In Search of a Definition

Some students have defined a colony as a group of people transplanted from their mother country to another, *less developed* country and stress the *superiority* of the settlers over the natives as a distinctive feature of colonial relations.[2] This definition, however, raises the question of measuring the conquerors' "superiority" to the natives.[3] A German student has defined colonies as "external territories under the administration of a nation which uses them for world economic and political purposes."[4] This definition does not fit the colonies that have been ruled by the selfish greed, ruthlessness and lawlessness of conquerors rather than by world considerations. If we reject the reference to world purposes, two characteristics remain: a colony is a territory administered by a foreign country but not assimilated as a part of the latter on the same basis as its other provinces; usually, a colony is not contiguous with the colonial power, but there are exceptions to this rule.[5] Ordinarily,

---

1. **49**, p. 22.

2. **46**, p. 14. Schäffle considered colonization as the influence exerted by a higher upon a lower grade of civilization, and classified colonies according to the distance between the relative degrees of development of the two societies, the mother country and the colony. He distinguished five degrees of civilization: the rural clan, the feudal society, the city-state, the territorial state and the national state. The first two are usually characteristic of colonial territories at the time of their occupation by the colonizing nation; the fifth is characteristic of modern colonial powers. (**53**, pp. 168ff.)

3. **62**, pp. 928–29.

4. **62**, p. 930.

5. Among the exceptions is South-West Africa, a trust territory of, and adjacent to, the Union of South Africa.

at least a small group of officials and business-men from the mother country settle in the col-ony. This group, however, may be numerically insignificant and can hardly be regarded as an essential feature of the concept of a colony. The essential is not the physical presence of the for-eigners but the control they exercise over the territory, even when such control is carried on from the deck of a gunboat off its coast.

The racial difference between the people in a colony and in the mother country may be a very important factor in their interrelations, but it is not decisive in determining the status of an area as a colony. What makes a colony is de-pendence on an external power.[6]

Dependence or Self-Government

A colonial power often introduces an admin-istration more or less similar to its own in the territories under its control. This was the policy of England in North America and of Spain and Portugal in their possessions in the Caribbean and South America. Another method of colonial administration, once used by the British in India, is indirect control through native rulers depend-ent on the colonial power for financial and military support. In both cases, the colonial sys-tem is compatible with some degree of self-government by the native population. Sometimes self-government in a colony is almost as com-prehensive as in the mother country, nearly wip-ing out the distinction between colonial and non-colonial areas.

Alaska is described in United States statistics as a "territory," outside the "continental United States." The term "territory" is reminiscent of the time when some areas of the country were not yet organized as member states of the Union.[7] It therefore connotes a definite stage in administrative development rather than colonial dependence. International statistics, however, have no equivalent term: in an international sur-vey "territory" means simply "land" or "area." Early publications of the League of Nations classified Alaska as a state, along with Canada and the United States;[8] later it was listed among "dependencies, colonies, etc." of the United States.[9] In publications of the United Nations, Alaska heads the list of United States "non-self-governing territories and dependencies," in the group of colonies, trust territories, protectorates and the like. Indeed, the United States includes Alaska in its annual reports to the UN on its non-self-governing territories.[10] Although this classification is defensible, the status of Alaska differs, of course, from that of most colonial territories.

Another example of the difficulty of classifying non-self-governing territories appears in the "overseas departments and territories" of France. One of these is Algeria, listed as a "non-self-governing territory" by the UN, although France does not include it in its annual reports to the UN. Algeria has broad self-government in local affairs, has elected a two-chamber as-sembly since 1948 and is also represented in both chambers of the French legislature. In 1946, France transformed its old colonies of Marti-nique, Guadeloupe, Réunion and French Guiana into "overseas departments" with a legal status like that of the departments in the homeland. France also has "overseas territories" and "trusts" (mandated territories) with varying degrees of self-government and different forms of repre-sentation in the national legislative assembly.[11] Are all these various territories French colonies or provinces?

The status of the overseas components of the French Union is characterized not by the con-trol the central government exercises over them or by their representation in the central legisla-tive assembly but by the status of the native population in comparison with settlers from the motherland. As long as the European settlers en-joy special privileges not extended to the natives in administration and local elections, the area is a colony, and its particular position in the ad-

---

6. "In international law," writes Emanuel Moresco, "the expressions *home country* and *colonies* designate organized collectivities inhabiting non-adjacent territories forming part of one and the same empire, but subject to different and unequal governmental systems, the home country exercising supreme authority throughout the whole empire." (**4**, p. 22.)

7. There were the Northwest Territory, beyond the Ohio River, in 1800; the Louisiana Territory, Illinois Territory, Michigan Territory, Indiana Territory, the Mississippi Territory and the Territory of Orleans in 1810; the Oregon and Minnesota Territories and vast unorganized territories in 1850. (**39**, pp. 46, 47, 51.) In official statistics, Alaska and Hawaii are described as "territories" while Guam, American Samoa, Puerto Rico, the Virgin Islands and the Panama Canal Zone appear

under the general heading of "territories and posses-sions." (**13**, 1950, p. 7.)

8. **1**, p. 11.

9. **3**, 1931–1932, p. 19.

10. **6**, 1946 and following years.

11. **56**, 1951, pp. 1000ff.

ministrative system of the Union does not change this hard fact of life.

There is also a subtle distinction between colonial possessions and protectorates.[12]

The status of British India between World War I and the Indian Independence Act of 1947 was most confusing. Pending negotiations on the future political status of the Indian subcontinent, the British classified it as a part of their Commonwealth and empire — but not as a dependency — even when India's association with the Commonwealth was uncertain.

In brief, the distinction between provinces of sovereign states and "non-self-governing territories and dependencies" is often a matter of opinion. This study follows the classification of the UN.

Types of Colonies

Apart from the great variety in their political and administrative status, colonial territories may be classified according to the purpose for which they are used by the mother country. The main types are trade colonies, settlement colonies and exploitation or plantation colonies.[13]

The Royal Institute of International Affairs offers a more detailed classification: [14]

1. Posts which have strategic value as bases controlling bottlenecks of traffic, such as refueling stations or centers of cable communication and wireless stations.

2. Colonies in which land is available for settlement. (The British dominions before they emerged from colonial status; parts of Mozambique and Angola; the highlands of Rhodesia, Nyasaland, Tanganyika and Kenya; the greater part of the coastal regions of French and Italian North Africa.)

3. Colonies offering opportunities for agricultural production directed by Europeans but carried out by native labor. (The West Indies, the Netherlands Indies, India and Ceylon before their emancipation; the Straits Settlements, the Guianas, parts of East Africa, the Congo and the Sudan.)

4. Colonies valuable especially for supplies of certain raw materials. (Malaya, for rubber; the Belgian Congo, Nigeria, Rhodesia and other territories, for mineral deposits.)

5. Countries in which native farming or semi-nomadic pastoral life predominates, where European estates and settlements are negligible, and the colonizing power is interested chiefly in trade.

For the purpose of the present study, a sharp distinction should be made between *point* colonization, which entails a firm hold over specific places and comparatively small areas around them, and *territorial* (or surface) colonization, which implies the mother country's control over large populated areas. Point colonization applies to types (1) and (5) in the Royal Institute's classification; territorial colonization, to the other three types. From this standpoint, colonies may be classified as follows:

A. Point colonization
   1. For trade
   2. For traffic and communication
   3. For military purposes
B. Territorial colonization
   4. For settlement
   5. For exploitation of natural resources
      a. Plantations
      b. Minerals

The same colony, of course, may present more than one advantage to the colonial power and the prime purpose may shift as a result of discoveries and changing economic conditions. Moreover, not all past drives for colonization can be classified under the headings above. The Spaniards overran South America in the sixteenth century in quest of gold, completely unprepared to extract it from the soil but well equipped to extort it from the natives. The Dutch and British who set sail for the East Indies in the sixteenth century were looking for spices, and their aim was to monopolize trade in these products rather than establish plantations. The purpose of point colonization on the West African coast in the seventeenth century was largely to provide slaves for plantations in the West Indies. One of the objectives of French colonization in North Africa has been to obtain additional manpower for the mother country in both war and peace.

THE SCOPE OF COLONIAL EMPIRES

The UN lists more than a hundred colonial territories and dependencies, some of them tiny, sparsely populated islands, others large expanses

---

12. **46**, pp. 109ff.
13. **38**, *passim;* **65**, pp. 934–35.
14. **49**, pp. 16–17.

with many millions of inhabitants. (See Table 231.) In all, non-self-governing territories covered an area of nearly 12.2 million square miles and had a population of more than 200 million in mid-1950.[15] These totals do not include land in Antarctica claimed by various powers; USSR possessions in Asia and its satellites in Eastern Europe; the Azores and Madeira islands (Portugal); the Canary Islands (Spain). They do include certain territories which are practically uninhabitable (for example, Greenland), all Indochina (though only part of it was under the control of French colonial authorities in mid-1950), and certain external possessions more like provinces of the mother countries than colonies (Alaska, the Channel Islands, the Isle of Man). Excluding Greenland and Alaska, the area of "non-self-governing territories and dependencies" totaled 10.8 million square miles and had 200.8 million inhabitants in mid-1950.

The list likewise includes territories whose political status has changed since 1950 or which are in the process of transformation:

	Area, in Thousands of Square Miles	Population, in Thousands
Total	1,880.6	37,587
Alaska and Hawaii (statehood under discussion in Congress)	592.8	633
Anglo-Egyptian Sudan (eventual unification with Egypt)	967.5	8,350
Eritrea (since 1952 part of Ethiopia)	47.9	1,104
Indochina	272.4	27,500

Excluding Greenland and these territories, colonial possessions covered an area of approximately 9.5 million square miles and had a population of approximately 163 million in 1950.

Distribution by Continent

Colonial territories are scattered over the world, but the most important are concentrated in two regions — in Africa and southeastern Asia. The distribution for the areas shown in Table 231 is as follows:

---

15. These figures and the detailed data in Table 231 require reservation since population statistics of colonial territories are not completely reliable. Data for the African colonies, in particular, have a considerable margin of error. (Cf. **37,** *passim.*)

	Area, in Thousands of Square Miles	Per Cent	Population, in Thousands (1950)	Per Cent
World	12,180.7	100.0	200,957	100.0
America [a]	1,631.0	13.4	6,662	3.3
Europe	0.7	0.0	793	0.4
Asia	692.1	5.7	43,254	21.5
Africa	9,630.6	79.1	147,428	73.4
Oceania	226.3	1.9	2,820	1.4

a. Including Greenland and Alaska.

Apart from Greenland and Alaska, most colonies in America are in the Caribbean, near the site of the oldest European settlements in the Western Hemisphere. The most important group of colonies in the Western Hemisphere is the British West Indies. (See Figure 129.) The British are planning to unite this group of colonies in a federation that will eventually become an independent dominion of the British Commonwealth.[16]

The non-self-governing territories in Europe include Gibraltar, Malta, the Channel Islands and the Isle of Man, all held by the British.

The population of Asiatic colonies totaled 43.3 million in the middle of 1950, as compared with 560 million in areas that had been colonial but have gained independence in recent years. Asia's most important colonies in 1950 were Indochina (27.5 million inhabitants) and the Federation of Malaya (5.2 million). Indochina is emerging now from a state of civil war and its future is uncertain, but hardly any part of it will maintain ties with the French Union.

Africa now comprises the bulk of the world's colonial possessions.

Australia, New Zealand and Tasmania are parts of the British Commonwealth of Nations; all other islands in Oceania are colonies — most of the largest and more important of them are under the control of Australia, Great Britain and New Zealand. (See Figure 130,A.)

Distribution by Colonial Power

After the emancipation of India, Pakistan, Burma, Ceylon and Indonesia, France became the largest colonial power in terms of both area and population (79.1 million) of the possessions. The United Kingdom was second (75.6 million). In 1950 these two countries together controlled

---

16. **60,** November 1949.

TABLE 231

NON-SELF-GOVERNING TERRITORIES: AREA AND POPULATION, MIDYEAR 1950

Colonial Power and Territory	Area, in Thousands of Square Miles	Population, in Thousands	Colonial Power and Territory	Area, in Thousands of Square Miles	Population, in Thousands
AMERICA	1,631.0	6,662	ASIA	692.1	47,254
United States,[a] total	590.4	2,432	*United States*		
Alaska	586.4	136	Bonin and Ryukyu Islands	1.7	917
Panama Canal Zone	0.5	53			
Puerto Rico	3.4	2,216	*United Kingdom,* total	249.6	11,878
Virgin Islands	0.1	27	Cyprus	3.8	484
			Aden protectorate and		
United Kingdom, total	109.0	3,232	colony	105.1	750
Bermudas	0.0	37	British Borneo	78.7	956
British Honduras	8.9	67	Federation of Malaya	50.6	5,227
British West Indies			Hong Kong	0.4	2,260
Bahama Islands	4.4	79	Singapore	0.3	1,018
Barbados	0.2	209	Maldive Islands	0.1	83
Jamaica (inc. dependencies)	4.7	1,403	Palestine [b]	10.6	1,100
Leeward Islands	0.4	112			
Windward Islands	0.8	276	*France,* total	272.6	27,830
Trinidad and Tobago	2.0	627	French India [c]	0.2	330
British Guiana	83.0	420	Indochina [d]	272.4	27,500
Falkland Islands	4.6	2			
			Netherlands		
France, total	36.3	593	New Guinea	159.4	1,018
Guadeloupe	0.7	289			
Martinique	0.4	273	*Portugal,* total	8.8	1,611
St. Pierre and Miquelon	0.1	5	Macao	0.0	500
French Guiana	35.1	26	Portuguese India	1.5	672
			Portuguese Timor	7.3	439
Denmark					
Greenland	839.8	23	AFRICA	9,630.6	147,428
Netherlands, total	55.5	382	*International administra-*		
Netherlands Antilles	0.4	163	*tion*		
Surinam	55.1	219	Tangier	0.2	111
EUROPE	0.7	793	*United Kingdom,*		
			total	1,270.1	58,433
International administra-			Gambia	4.1	273
tion			Sierra Leone	27.9	1,880
Trieste	0.3	298	Gold Coast	78.8	3,869
			Togoland [e]	13.0	397
United Kingdom, total	0.4	495	Cameroons [e]	34.1	1,000
Isle of Man and Channel			Nigeria	338.6	24,000
Islands	0.3	157	Uganda	34.0	5,125
Gibraltar	0.0	25	Kenya	225.0	5,555
Malta and Gozo	0.1	313			

(*Continued on facing page*)

TABLE 231—*continued*

Colonial Power and Territory	Area, in Thousands of Square Miles	Population, in Thousands	Colonial Power and Territory	Area, in Thousands of Square Miles	Population, in Thousands
Somaliland protectorate	68.0	500	*Portugal*, total	795.0	10,509
Tanganyika [e]	362.7	7,707	Portuguese Guinea	14.0	514
Zanzibar and Pemba	1.0	269	Angola	481.4	4,094
Nyasaland	47.9	2,330	Cape Verde Islands	1.5	143
Northern Rhodesia	290.3	1,866	Mozambique	297.7	5,698
Southern Rhodesia	150.3	2,095	St. Thomas Island	0.4	60
Bechuanaland	275.0	289	*Union of South Africa*		
Basutoland	11.7	574	South-West Africa [e]	317.7	379
Swaziland	6.7	197	*Military government*		
Mauritius	0.8	466	Eritrea (U. K.) [f]	47.9	1,104
St. Helena	0.0	5			
Seychelles	0.2	36	OCEANIA	226.3	2,820
Condominium			*United States*, total	7.5	630
Anglo-Egyptian Sudan	967.5	8,350	American Samoa	0.1	19
France, total	4,276.1	50,524	Guam	0.2	59
Morocco	161.6	8,410	Hawaii	6.4	497
Algeria	851.3	8,830	Pacific Islands [e]	0.8	55
Tunisia	60.2	3,470	*United Kingdom*, total	19.4	472
French West Africa	1,805.2	16,850	British Solomon Islands	11.7	100
Togoland [e]	20.5	990	Fiji Islands	7.0	289
Cameroons [e]	170.2	3,006	Gilbert and Ellice Islands	0.4	36
French Equatorial Africa	969.1	4,406	Tonga	0.3	47
French Somaliland	8.4	57	*France*, total	8.8	120
Madagascar and Comoro	228.6	4,250	French Oceania	1.7	60
Réunion	1.0	255	New Caledonia	7.1	60
Belgium, total	925.5	15,173	*Australia*, total	183.6	1,441
Belgian Congo	905.0	11,259	Papua and Norfolk Island	90.5	370
Ruanda-Urundi [e]	20.5	3,914	New Guinea	93.1	1,071
Italy			*New Zealand*, total	1.3	99
Somaliland [e]	198.1	1,246	Western Samoa [e]	1.1	79
Spain, total	132.5	1,599	Pacific Islands	0.2	20
Moroccan protectorate	17.7	1,180	*Condominium*, total	5.7	58
Possessions in North Africa	0.1	164	Nauru (U.K., Austr., N.Z.) [a]	0.0	3
Spanish West Africa	103.9	80	New Hebrides (U.K., Fr.) [a]	5.7	55
Spanish Guinea	10.8	175			

Sources: **5**, 1951, pp. 91–102; **9**, 1951, pp. 21–33.

a. Population as of April 1, 1950.
b. Former mandate territory (excludes Israel).
c. Pondichéry, Yanaon, Mahé and Chandernagor, settlements on the coasts of India.

d. Viet Nam, Cambodia and Laos. For population, rough estimate.
e. Trust territory.
f. Military government, since 1945; an autonomous part of Ethiopia since 1952.

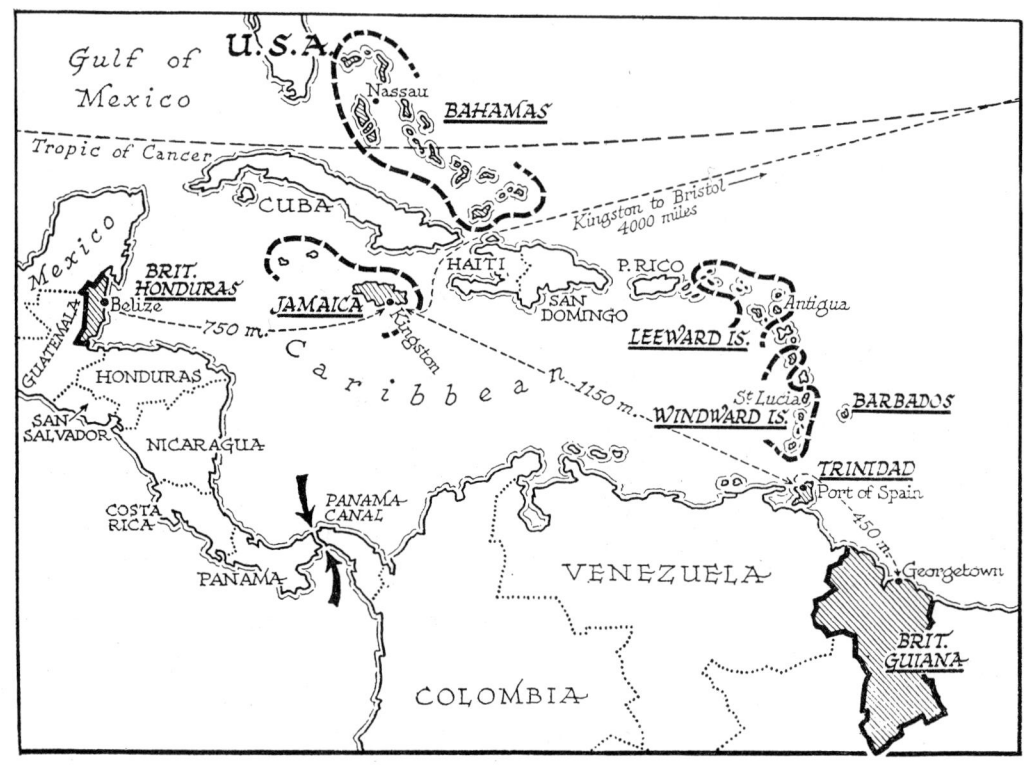

Map by J. F. Horrabin in *Venture*, November 1949

FIGURE 129. THE BRITISH WEST INDIES

The British West Indies include (from north to south, and west to east): the Bahama Islands, Jamaica, the Leeward and Windward Islands, Barbados, Trinidad and Tobago. The map also shows British Honduras in Mid- dle America and British Guiana in South America. British possessions in the Western Hemisphere also in- clude the Bermuda and Falkland islands.

some 77 per cent of the world's colonial popula- tion. (See Table 232.) The order of rank of these two countries would be reversed, however, if Eritrea and Indochina were excluded.[17] Other important colonial powers are Belgium (the Belgian Congo and Ruanda-Urundi with a total population of 15.2 million), and Portugal (Angola, Mozambique and some colonies in the Far East with a total population of 12.1 million). (See Figure 130,B.)

In mid-1950, the ratio of the population of non-self-governing territories to the population in the mother country represented the following percentages: [18]

France	188.7[a]	Spain	5.7
Belgium	175.6	New Zealand	5.2
United Kingdom	149.4	Union of South	
Portugal	140.6	Africa	3.1
Australia	17.6	Italy	2.7
Netherlands	13.8	United States	2.6

a. Includes entire population of Indochina.

France ranked first in the ratio of colonial population to population in the motherland. Bel- gium was second, and Great Britain and Portu- gal were in third and fourth places. After the loss of Indochina France shifted to fourth place, leaving Belgium at the head of the list. How- ever, even now France has more people in her colonial possessions than at home. The United States is at the bottom of the list, after the Union of South Africa and Italy.

The French colonial empire in Africa stretches from the Mediterranean to the Gulf of Guinea and the Congo River, covering most of north- ern, western and central Africa — a contiguous area of some 4 million square miles with a popu- lation of 50.5 million. It also includes the islands of Madagascar and Réunion and French Somali- land at the entrance to the Red Sea. France's

17. The Anglo-Egyptian Sudan is not included in these figures, nor is it included in the British colonial possessions in Figure 130,B and Table 232.

18. See Table 232.

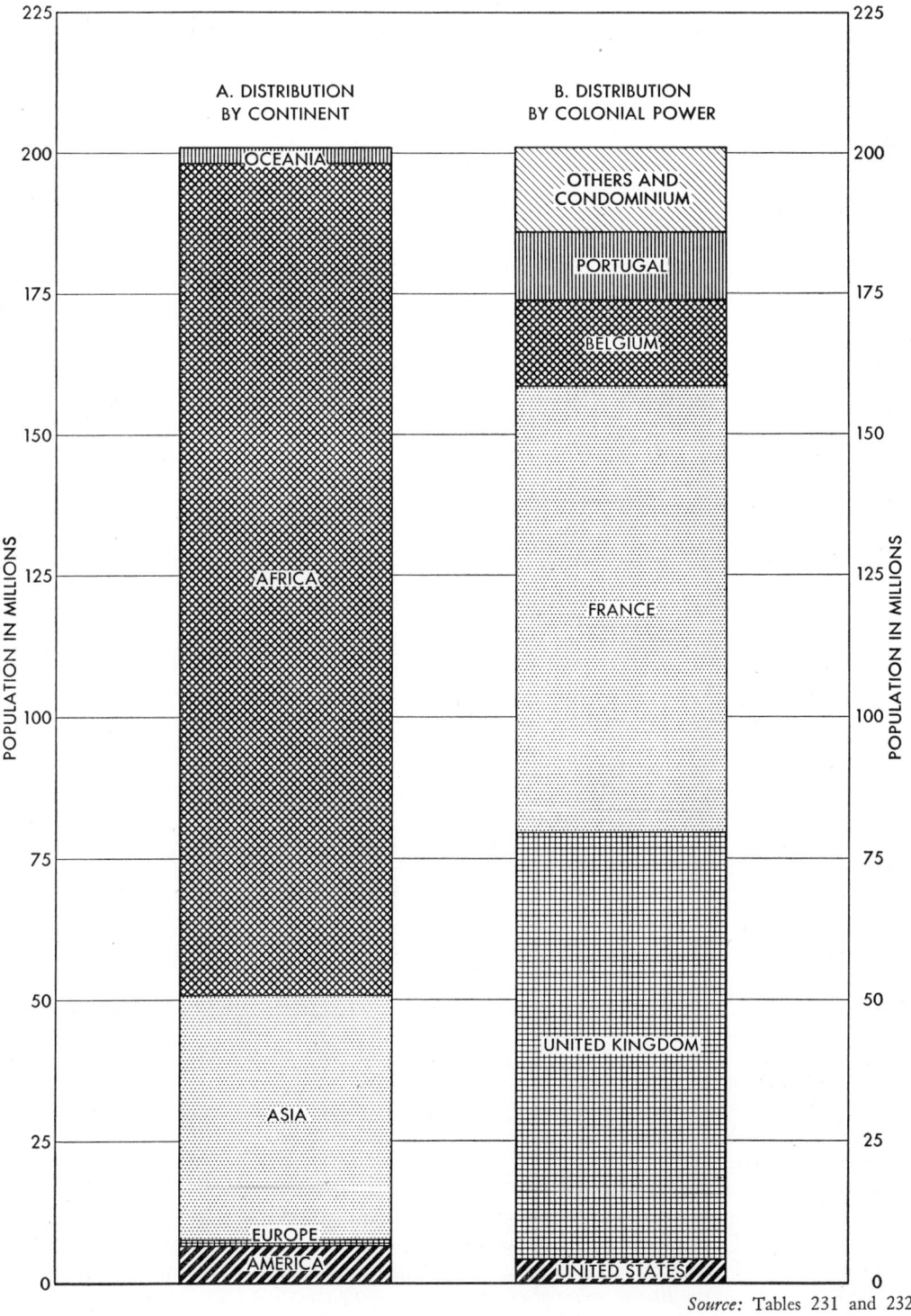

Source: Tables 231 and 232

FIGURE 130. POPULATION OF COLONIES: DISTRIBUTION BY CONTINENT AND COLONIAL POWER, 1950

TABLE 232

COLONIAL POWERS AND THEIR DEPENDENCIES: AREA AND POPULATION, MIDYEAR 1950

Colonial Power	Mother Country	Non-Self-Governing Territories					
		Total	In America	In Europe	In Asia	In Africa	In Oceania
Area, in Thousands of Square Miles							
Total	5,869.7	12,180.7	1,631.0	0.7	692.1	9,630.6	226.3
United States	3,022.4	599.6	590.4	—	1.7	—	7.5
United Kingdom	63.2	2,396.4	109.0	0.4	249.6	2,018.0 [a]	19.4
France	142.7	4,593.8	36.3	—	272.6	4,276.1	8.8
Belgium	7.9	925.5	—	—	—	925.5	—
Netherlands	8.7	214.9	55.5	—	159.4	—	—
Denmark	11.1	839.8	839.8	—	—	—	—
Portugal	23.8	803.8	—	—	8.8	795.0	—
Spain	130.3	132.5	—	—	—	132.5	—
Italy	78.0	198.1	—	—	—	198.1	—
Union of South Africa	316.9	317.7	—	—	—	317.7	—
Australia	1,995.3	183.6	—	—	—	—	183.6
New Zealand	69.4	1.3	—	—	—	—	1.3
Condominium	—	973.2	—	—	—	967.5 [b]	5.7
International administration	—	0.5	—	0.3 [c]	—	0.2 [d]	—
Population, in Thousands							
Total	372,834	200,957	6,662	793	43,254	147,428	2,820
United States	151,689	3,979	2,432	—	917	—	630
United Kingdom	50,618	75,614	3,232	495	11,878	59,537 [a]	472
France	41,900	79,067	593	—	27,830	50,524	120
Belgium	8,639	15,173	—	—	—	15,173	—
Netherlands	10,114	1,400	382	—	1,018	—	—
Denmark	4,271	23	23	—	—	—	—
Portugal	8,618	12,120	—	—	1,611	10,509	—
Spain	28,287	1,599	—	—	—	1,599	—
Italy	46,272	1,246	—	—	—	1,246	—
Union of South Africa	12,320	379	—	—	—	379	—
Australia	8,186	1,441	—	—	—	—	1,441
New Zealand	1,920	99	—	—	—	—	99
Condominium	—	8,408	—	—	—	8,350 [b]	58
International administration	—	409	—	298 [c]	—	111 [d]	—

Source: Computed from Table 231.

a. Includes Eritrea (military government), now an autonomous part of Ethiopia.
b. Anglo-Egyptian Sudan.
c. Trieste.
d. Tangier.

main colonial possession in Asia was, in mid-1950, Indochina, with an area of some 272,400 square miles and approximately 27.5 million inhabitants.[19] The French colonies in America and Oceania are of minor importance.

The largest part of the *British colonial empire* (roughly 85 per cent of the area and 80 per cent of the population) is now in Africa. Some British colonies are clustered along the western coast

19. Rough estimate.

of the continent from Gibraltar to the Gulf of Guinea, and others form an almost continuous belt throughout the length of eastern Africa, from the Sudan to the Union of South Africa. Among the British colonies in Asia, the Federation of Malaya is the most important.

The Royal Institute of International Affairs points out that "in current international controversies on the colonial question the British Colonial Empire is sometimes assumed to be identical with the area colored red on English maps." [20] Actually that color indicates the whole British *commonwealth and empire.* In recent years, liquidation of the empire has been paralleled by growth of the Commonwealth, a shift that has affected some 450 million inhabitants of India, Pakistan and Ceylon. The transformation of British colonies into dominions is still in progress. The British West Indies and Southern Rhodesia are probably the next in line.

The colonial empire of Belgium, the third in the world in both area and population, consists of the Belgian Congo and a small trust territory on its border, Ruanda-Urundi. It occupies a large area in central Africa, almost completely surrounded by British, French and Portuguese possessions. This territory, exceptionally rich in mineral deposits, is subject to international regulations which give it a special status; although under Belgian administration, it is open to all powers for trade and investment.

Portugal has colonies in Africa and Asia, among which Angola and Mozambique are the most important, but these possessions are small in comparison with the Portuguese colonial empire in the seventeenth and eighteenth centuries.

Four European powers in mid-1950 controlled a colonial area of 8.7 million square miles, with a total population of 182 million, distributed as follows:

	Area, in Thousands of Square Miles	Population, in Thousands (1950)
Total	8,719.5	181,974
French	4,593.8	79,067
British	2,396.4	75,614
Belgian	925.5	15,173
Portuguese	803.8	12,120

All other non-self-governing areas and colonies together had a population of some 19 million and an area of about 3.5 million square miles. These totals include the sparsely populated Anglo-Egyptian Sudan, Alaska and the almost uninhabitable Danish possessions in Greenland.

Among the minor colonial powers listed in Tables 231 and 232 are two nations that had sizable colonial possessions before World War II: the United States, which was in control of the Philippines until 1946, and the Netherlands,

which lost its centuries-old colonial empire in Indonesia in 1949.

THE INTERNATIONAL STATUS OF COLONIES

There are innumerable nuances in the administrative and political status of non-self-governing territories and dependencies.[21] Some provisions have been established by the colonial power alone, others rest on treaties between the powers and native rulers, confirmed to some extent by international agreements. The most important development in modern relationships between colonial powers and areas under their control has been the establishment of trusteeship.

Trust Territories

The system of trusteeship (or mandate) over colonial territories was established by the Covenant of the League of Nations incorporated in the Treaty of Versailles.[22] Article 22 of the Covenant reads as follows:

1. To those colonies and territories which as a consequence of the late war have ceased to be under the sovereignty of the States which formerly governed them and which are inhabited by peoples not yet able to stand by themselves under the strenuous conditions of the modern world, there should be applied the principle that the well-being and development of such peoples form a sacred trust of civilization and that securities for the performance of this trust should be embodied in this Covenant.

2. The best method of giving practical effect to this principle is that the tutelage of such peoples should be entrusted to advanced nations who, by reason of their resources, their experience or their geographical position can best undertake this responsibility, and who are willing to accept it, and that this tutelage should be exercised by them as Mandatories on behalf of the League.

3. The character of the mandate must differ ac-

---

20. **49**, p. 10.

21. See **29, 49, 48, 52**.

22. Concepts of "trusteeship" and "trust territories" have a long history. Edmund Burke, in a speech on the India bill in 1785, claimed that the British people should consider themselves trustees for the welfare of the people of India. In 1831, Chief Justice Marshall defined the position of the government of the United States as that of a trustee for the lands held by the Indians. In 1837 the British House of Commons explicitly adopted the term "trusteeship" in describing the attitude of Great Britain toward aboriginal tribes in colonies. (**31**, pp. 9–10.) What was new in the practice of the League of Nations was that it raised the trusteeship relationship between the ruling power and the colony to a principle of international law, at least for a dozen former possessions of Germany and the Ottoman Empire.

cording to the stage of the development of the people, the geographical situation of the territory, its economic conditions and other similar circumstances.

4. Certain communities formerly belonging to the Turkish Empire have reached a stage of development where their existence as independent nations can be provisionally recognized subject to the rendering of administrative advice and assistance by a Mandatory until such time as they are able to stand alone. The wishes of these communities must be a principal consideration in the selection of the Mandatory.

5. Other peoples, especially those of Central Africa, are at such a stage that the Mandatory must be responsible for the administration of the territory under conditions which will guarantee freedom of conscience and religion, subject only to the maintenance of public order and morals, the prohibition of abuses such as the slave trade, the arms traffic and the liquor traffic, and the prevention of the establishment of fortifications or military and naval bases and of military training of the natives for other than police purposes and the defense of territory, and will also secure equal opportunities for the trade and commerce of other Members of the League.

6. There are territories, such as South West Africa and certain of the South Pacific Islands, which, owing to the sparseness of their population, or their small size, or their remoteness from the centers of civilization, or their geographical contiguity to the territory of the Mandatory, and other circumstances, can be best administered under the laws of the Mandatory as integral portions of its territory, subject to the safeguards above mentioned in the interest of the indigenous populations.

Such are the general principles of trusteeship over non-self-governing territories as established by the League of Nations. To this declaration of principles more specific provisions were added:

7. In every case of mandate, the Mandatory shall render to the Council an annual report in reference to the territory committed to its charge.

8. The degree of authority, control or administration to be exercised by the Mandatory shall, if not previously agreed upon by the Members of the League, be explicitly defined in each case by the Council.

9. A permanent Commission shall be constituted to receive and examine the annual reports of the Mandatories and to advise the Council on all matters relating to the observance of the mandates.

This Magna Charta of colonial peoples applied originally to the former provinces of the Turkish Empire (Iraq, Palestine, Transjordania, Syria and Lebanon) and the former German colonies in Africa (Togoland, the Cameroons, German South-West Africa and East Africa) and in Oceania (the Caroline, Mariana and Marshall Islands, Samoa and so on.)

In accordance with paragraphs 3, 4 and 5 of Article 22 of the Covenant, the League of Nations established three types of mandates, which later became known as A, B and C mandates. The "A" mandates were applied to the former Turkish provinces as a temporary, transitional measure. France held the mandate over Syria and Lebanon; Great Britain, over Iraq, Palestine and Transjordania. All these mandates have expired and the respective territories have become independent.

The fundamental difference between the "B" and "C" mandates was that the former guaranteed equal opportunity for the trade and commerce of other nations (the "Open Door" policy), while the latter enabled the mandatory to run the trust territory more or less as a monopoly.[23] Both types of mandates contained safeguards for the civil rights of the natives. Actually, all major German colonies were ruled under "B" mandates: Togoland and the Cameroons, by the French and British; German East Africa, by the British (Tanganyika) and Belgians (Ruanda-Urundi); German South-West Africa, by the Union of South Africa. The "C" mandate was applied only to sparsely inhabited areas in Africa and islands in the Pacific.

The New International Status of Colonies

The general principles of Article 22 of the League Covenant have been restated and broadened in the Charter of the United Nations, in its "Declaration Regarding Non-Self-Governing Territories" (Chapter XI of the Charter), which reads in part as follows:

Article 73. Members of the United Nations which have or assume responsibilities for the administration of territories whose peoples have not yet attained a full measure of self-government recognize the principle that the interests of the inhabitants of these territories are paramount, and accept as a sacred trust the obligation to promote to the utmost, within the system of international peace and security established by the present Charter, the well-being of the inhabitants of these territories, and, to this end:

(a) To insure, with due respect for the culture of

23. **46**, pp. 91ff. The principle of the "C" mandates has been opposed by the United States.

the peoples concerned, their political, economic, social, and educational advancement, their just treatment, and their protection against abuses;

(b) To develop self-government, to take due account of the political aspirations of the peoples, and to assist them in the progressive development of their free political institutions, according to the particular circumstances of each territory and its peoples and their varying stages of advancement;

(c) To further international peace and security;

(d) To promote constructive measures of development, to encourage research, and to cooperate with one another and with appropriate international bodies with a view to the practical achievement of the social, economic, and scientific purposes set forth in this paragraph; and

(e) To transmit regularly to the Secretary General for information purposes, subject to such limitation as security and constitutional considerations may require, statistical and other information of a technical nature relating to economic, social, and educational conditions in the territories for which they are respectively responsible . . .

Article 74. Members of the United Nations agree that their policy in respect to the territories, to which this chapter applies, no less than in respect of their metropolitan areas, must be based on the general principle of good-neighborliness, due account being taken of the interests and well-being of the rest of the world, in social, economic and commercial matters.

At the same time, a new status was established for "trust territories," the term which officially replaced the old concept of "mandated territories":

Article 75. The United Nations shall establish under its authority an international trusteeship system for the administration and supervision of such territories as may be placed thereunder by subsequent individual agreements. These territories are hereafter referred to as trust territories.

Article 76. The basic objectives of the trusteeship system in accordance with the purposes of the United Nations laid down in Article 1 of the present Charter, shall be:

(a) To further international peace and security;

(b) To promote the political, economic, social and educational advancement of the inhabitants of the trust territories, and their progressive development toward self-government or independence as may be appropriate to the particular circumstances of each territory and its peoples and the freely expressed wishes of the peoples concerned, and as may be provided by the terms of each trusteeship agreement;

(c) To encourage respect for human rights and for fundamental freedoms for all without distinction as to race, sex, language or religion, and to en-

courage recognition of the interdependence of the peoples of the world; and

(d) To insure equal treatment in social, economic and commercial matters for all members of the United Nations and their nationals, and also equal treatment for the latter in the administration of justice, without prejudice to the attainment of the foregoing objectives, . . .

These and other provisions on trust territories (Articles 73–91 of the Charter) now apply mainly to the former German colonies, an area of about 900,000 square miles with a population of close to 19.5 million, distributed as follows: [24]

	Area, in Thousands of Square Miles	Population, in Thousands (1950)
Africa		
British Cameroons	34.1	1,000
French Cameroons	170.2	3,000
Italian Somaliland	198.1	1,206
Ruanda-Urundi (Belgium)	20.1	3,900
Tanganyika (Britain)	362.7	7,707
British Togoland	13.0	407
French Togoland	20.5	1,000
Oceania		
New Guinea (Australia)	93.1	1,071
Pacific Islands (United States)	0.8	55
Western Samoa (New Zealand)	1.1	79

The distinction between trust territories and other non-self-governing areas is less important today than the distinction between mandated colonies and other colonial possessions after World War I. At least in theory, *all* colonies have become subject to international control by virtue of Articles 73 and 74 of the UN Charter.

THE RISE AND FALL OF COLONIAL EMPIRES

What is happening today in the remaining colonial empires is the epilogue to an historical drama which had its prologue five centuries ago, in the era of great discoveries.[25]

Europe's Three Colonial Empires

The present phase of world colonial history can be described as the end of the liquidation of Europe's second colonial empire and the be-

---

24. See Table 231.
25. See **25, 26, 28, 32, 38, 42, 44, 52, 53, 54, 61, 62** and **63**. The principal sources are **58** (for the history of colonies before the end of the nineteenth century) and **49** (the modern problems of colonialism).

ginning of the liquidation of its third empire. Europe's first colonial empire rose in the sixteenth and seventeenth centuries in America, reached its zenith in the second half of the eighteenth century (Treaty of Paris, 1763) and was lost soon thereafter. The foundations of the second empire were laid in Asia and Oceania in the seventeenth century, and its rise began at the time when Europe was losing its American possessions. It reached its full expansion after the turn of the nineteenth century and is now in an advanced stage of liquidation. The third colonial empire was founded in Africa in the last quarter of the nineteenth century, reached its physical limits before the end of the century, and is now approaching its end.

The history of colonial relations casts light on current developments. It shows, indeed, that the emancipation of colonial peoples is an unavoidable phase in colonial relations; that the duration of colonial status in an area depends on the speed of economic and social progress; that the liquidation of colonial empires in the South Pacific is following the same pattern as the liquidation of colonial empires in the Western Hemisphere; that the emancipation of peoples of the second colonial empire differs from that of the first only in that it is being effected in a more orderly and peaceful way.

The Beginning of Modern Colonies

The colonial expansion of Europe began at the end of the fifteenth century, the age of the great mariners. Most of the great explorers were commissioned by their sponsors to find the route to the riches of the Orient — gold, precious stones, silk and, above all, spices. In 1486–87 Díaz reached the Cape of Good Hope in South Africa; in the years 1492–98 Columbus discovered the Caribbean islands and the mainland of South America; in 1497, Cabot entered the mouth of the St. Lawrence River and Da Gama found the sea lane to India; in 1498, Cabot explored the American North Atlantic coast and Pinzón, Ojeda and Vespucci visited the coast of Brazil. In 1520 Magellan reached East Asia by crossing the Atlantic and South Pacific and gave the seafaring nations of Western Europe new sea lanes to the other side of the world.

In the struggle for control over the new routes, forts and trading posts were built at strategic points along the coasts of remote lands. This was the beginning of point colonization in Asia and its archipelagoes. Discovery of the Caribbean islands and, later, the mainland of America gave adventurous sailors a new objective. The experience of Cortez and Pizarro showed that the shortest way to the treasure chests of primitive peoples was to take over the lands in which these riches were hidden. Thus began territorial colonization in the Western Hemisphere, laying the foundations of the first colonial empire.

COLONIES IN AMERICA

Spain had just regained freedom from the Moors when the New World fell into its lap. Strong and adventurous, it became the first European power to explore and exploit America. Very soon, however, Spain had to admit its neighbor, Portugal.

Spanish and Portuguese Conquests

The Portuguese had preceded the Spaniards in exploration along the western coast of Africa and, at the time of Columbus' voyages, had already established small settlements in the Azores, Madeira and Cape Verde Islands, along the Gulf of Guinea and, further to the south, at the mouth of the Congo. In 1454, the Pope bestowed upon them the right to all newly discovered lands south and west of Cape Bojador (just south of the Canary Islands) and in 1479 this right was recognized by Spain.[26] A new era in colonization began with Columbus' idea to search for new lands and a route to India by crossing the ocean westward, instead of following the African coast southward and eastward.[27]

---

26. **58**, p. 14. This allocation of newly discovered and still undiscovered lands by the Pope was based on the doctrine that all lands not in the possession of a Christian king belonged to the Holy Father in Rome.

27. Columbus shared the geographical knowledge of his time and, believing that the earth was round, also believed that the fabulous Orient, described by Marco Polo, could be reached by circling the globe in either direction. The question was the probable distance from the western coast of Europe (Portugal and Spain) to the eastern coast of India and China. Fifteenth-century European geographers calculated this distance by subtracting the estimated land distance from Europe to the Orient (in an eastward direction) from the estimated circumference of the earth. This essentially correct calculation led them to believe that India could not be reached by sea with the ships then available. Columbus' criticism of this conclusion was based on a curious mistake in his estimate of the size of the earth and upon his interpretation of two apocryphal verses of Esdras. Describing the earth's creation the Hebrew prophet declares that the Lord "commanded that the waters should

Taking possession of the lands discovered by Columbus, Spain desired to protect itself against future Portuguese claims.[28] The simplest solution seemed to be to divide the recently discovered and still undiscovered world between the two nations. This was accomplished by the famous Bull of Demarcation issued by Pope Alexander VI in 1493, which granted Spain "all the islands and mainlands, discovered and which thereafter may be discovered, toward the West and South . . . of a line from the Arctic Pole to the Antarctic Pole which line must be distant from the . . . Azores and Cape de Verde Islands a hundred Leagues toward the West and South." [29]

It is worth noticing that the demarcation between the Spanish and Portuguese possessions was related not to the newly discovered islands, whose exact geographic position was unknown at that time, but to the islands off the northwestern coast of Africa held by the Portuguese. The latter felt, however, that the line separating them from the future Spanish domains was too close to their own sphere of activity and proposed to the Spaniards that the line be transferred westward. The whole matter seemed of little practical significance to the Spanish government and in 1494, after brief negotiations, it was agreed that the line should be drawn not 100 but 370 leagues west of the Cape Verde Islands. (See Figure 131.)

When South America itself was discovered a few years later, its eastern bulge happened to lie east of the revised line and thus Brazil fell to the Portuguese. Later, the papal demarcation was forgotten. Portuguese administrators, seeking more territory in the hinterland, crossed the line without objection from the Spaniards and nearly half the South American mainland fell into their hands.

Haiti (Española) became the first Spanish stronghold in the New World. By 1513 there were seventeen Spanish settlements on this island, one of which, the city of Santo Domingo, had a population of 1,500. From here the Spaniards started exploration and conquest of the coast and islands of the Caribbean Sea and the Gulf of Mexico. They took possession of Puerto Rico (1508), Jamaica (1509), and Cuba (1511), founding on the last the important new settlements of Santiago (1514) and Havana (1515). The Spaniards now held the keys to the Americas. The daring drives of Cortez and Pizarro soon gave them Mexico (1521) and Peru (1531). A little later they also overran Bolivia (1535–36) and established themselves in Florida.

Officially, the Spanish-Portuguese colonial empire in the New World in the fourth quarter of the sixteenth century embraced all South and Central America, the Antilles and Florida. Actually, the conquerors had not penetrated very far from the coast and their domination over the hinterland was more or less nominal. Through plundering and plantations, they exploited the islands, the highlands along the Pacific coast of Central and South America and a comparatively narrow strip along the Atlantic coast, the Gulf of Mexico and Florida. Their hold over colonies in America depended largely on their sea power.

Meanwhile the Portuguese had taken possession of Brazil, which was reputed to be a poor country inhabited by nomadic cannibals. The colony seemed hardly worth exploitation. Contemporary Portuguese writers complained that for every grain of pepper Portugal had to pay a drop of blood.[30] By the middle of the sixteenth century, however, Portugal became more interested and began to set up its administration, founding forts and cities.

The Free-for-All Contest

The destruction of the Spanish Armada by the British (1588) was a heavy blow to Spain's colonial supremacy. Access to the New World, especially to the West Indies, was now open to all. In rapid succession, the Dutch, British and French appeared on the scene, and somewhat later, the Danes, Swedes, Belgians and even the Brandenburg-Germans.

Their interests originally centered on tropical plantations and the slave trade, but very soon they discovered other objectives for colonial

---

be gathered in the seventh part of the earth"; the remaining six sevenths were to be dry. Asserting his intention to navigate by the Bible, Columbus estimated the ocean route from Spain to the eastern coast of Asia as approximately 2,500 miles, or one seventh the earth's circumference. Actually, the distance was four to five times greater.

28. **40**, p. 242.

29. Quoted in **28**, p. 30. The language of this bull has puzzled geographers. The indicated line from pole to pole is a meridian cutting the globe into two hemispheres, along the Atlantic and Pacific Oceans. The reference to lands located south of that line is geographical nonsense. (**58**, p. 15.)

30. **22**, p. 72.

FIGURE 131. PARTITION OF THE NEW WORLD BETWEEN SPAIN AND PORTUGAL, BY THE PAPAL BULL OF 1493
In this map the demarcation line between Spanish and Portuguese claims is drawn to show its revision in 1494.

policy in North America: agricultural settlements, fisheries, the fur trade. The new orientation of colonial policy reflected the change in Europe's economic thinking. People became increasingly interested in foreign markets, and the acquisition of overseas possessions seemed to promise new outlets for domestic products. Under the influence of neo-mercantilism, monopoly of trade became the leading objective of colonial policy, replacing the early Spanish formula of colonization — to plunder gold, grab land and convert to Christianity the natives who survived the conquest.

Even the slave trade was appraised from the angle of its effect on the export of domestic products. A British writer, Sir Matthew Decker, praised the slave trade in the West Indies as a means of supporting British textile manufacturers by providing a new market for clothing. His argument, in brief, went as follows:

There must be a large importation of Negroes to raise . . . growths in our plantations and our clothing (industry) accordingly. . . . May not this be said to be transplanting of men for our benefit, by taking them from one climate, where (because of) heat they want no clothing, and carrying them to another (climate) where they cannot live without (clothing), nor be supplied by any but ourselves? [31]

The British increasingly stressed the use of the colonies as a source of agricultural produce and as a market for the products of the motherland and these objectives determined the location of new settlements. Preference was given to areas with a temperate climate which favored European types of agriculture, were easily approachable from the sea, and gave access to the hinterland. The new colonization shifted, accordingly, to a part of the New World which had neither spices nor precious metals — and therefore no Spaniards [32] — the Atlantic coast of North America.

After modest beginnings in the latter part of the sixteenth century (Newfoundland, 1583 and Virginia, 1584–87), the British took possession of selected spots on the Atlantic coast from the St. Lawrence River and Nova Scotia to Virginia, and established claims to lands stretching westward. At the beginning, the string of settlements was very thin, but by the middle of the seventeenth century the British had more settlers in North America than any other European power. In 1642, they had 24,000 settlers in New England alone, while the French had only 200 in all Canada.[33] The Dutch tried to establish control over the valley and mouth of the Hudson River (New Netherland); after a long struggle but with little bloodshed, the British took over the colony, complete with Fort Orange and New Amsterdam, which became Albany and New York. The colonial experiments of Sweden, Belgium and Denmark were short-lived because of lack of men and money, although seventeenth-century maps referred to the St. Lawrence River area as New Belgium or New Netherland. (See Figure 132.)

In 1686, the elector of Brandenburg, Frederick William, tried to gain a foothold in the West Indies by renting a tract of land on St. Thomas Island from the Danes and establishing a slave market. However, competition proved too strong at both ends of the business — in acquiring slaves on the African coast and selling them in the West Indies — and in 1731 the German installations were taken over by the Danes for debts.[34]

By 1670, the British faced only one dangerous competitor in the New World — France, their main opponent in Europe as well.

French-British Rivalry

French-British rivalry for colonial supremacy in North America lasted more than a century and played an important role in the American Revolution. The two powers clashed in the fishing grounds in Acadia and Newfoundland, in the fur trade in Hudson Bay, and at last, throughout Canada. The weakness of the French was their lack of men for settlement. In 1660 they had 3,418 settlers in Canada; by 1668 they had raised the number only to 5,870.[35] Meanwhile Great Britain was sending more and more people to its colonies, where population was also growing continuously as a result of immigration from other European countries. The contest ended in the complete victory of the British. By the Treaty of Paris (1763), France ceded Canada, with Cape Breton and Prince Edward Island; Spain gave up Florida.

The Treaty of Paris marked the high tide of Europe's colonial expansion in the Western Hemisphere. The continents, with their islands, were partitioned among Spain, Portugal and Great Britain. The British held all North America, from Newfoundland, Labrador and Hudson Bay to the Gulf of Mexico and from the Atlantic coast to the Mississippi River, roughly half the present area of Canada and one third that of the United States. Their possessions also included some islands in the West Indies. The Portuguese held Brazil. All the rest, except for a few spots in the Caribbean and on the northern coast of South America, was claimed by the Spaniards. Spain, however, did not actually control all this territory. Along with the organized colonies (New Spain), Spain claimed unexplored expanses — terra incognita — in South America and in North America west of the Mississippi. Including these territories, in three and a half centuries after its discovery, the New World had been parceled out among three European powers and only small pieces were left for other countries. (See Figure 133.)

The End of the First Colonial Empire

There is no need to recapitulate the events

---

31. Quoted in **35**, p. 19.
32. **27**, p. 14.
33. **58**, p. 67.
34. The Brandenburg colony in Africa was sold to a Dutch firm in 1718 for 7,200 ducats and 12 Negro boys,

who were later enrolled in the Prussian army as musicians. (**33**, p. 18.)
35. **58**, pp. 94–95.

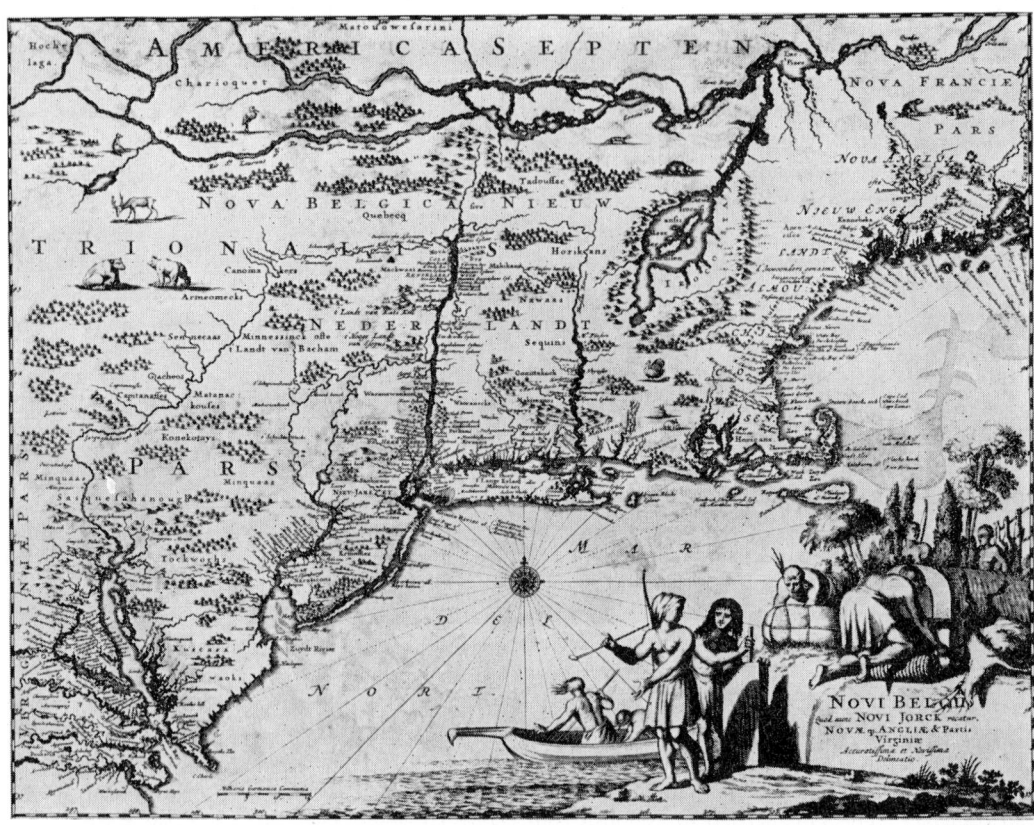

FIGURE 132. THE AREA BETWEEN THE ST. LAWRENCE RIVER AND THE ATLANTIC OCEAN, IN THE
MID-SEVENTEENTH CENTURY

This map appeared in Arnoldus Montanus' book *De
Nieuwe en Onbekende Weereld (The New and Unknown World)*, published in Amsterdam in 1671.

The upper portion of the map is inexact, but the
precision of the coastal area is evidence of the cartog-
rapher's familiarity with that area. The river running

east-west at the top is the St. Lawrence, and Chesapeake
Bay is shown at the lower left. The north central region
is called "New Belgium or New Netherland" (Nova
Belgica sive Nieuw Nederlandt). East of this vaguely
defined area can be seen a part of "New France" (Nova
Franciæ Pars) and "New England" (Nova Anglia).

which led to the emancipation of the British,
Spanish and Portuguese colonies in the New
World. The rebellious colonies in North America gained independence because they had
grown, economically and politically, beyond the
leading strings of their foreign masters. On the
other hand, Spain and Portugal lost South America because, weakened by war and political turmoil, they were unable to give their colonial
administrators and generals a sufficient supply
of men, arms and money.

The main difference between the North American and South American colonies at the time
of their emancipation was in the extent of their
political experience. In the north, the local self-
government introduced by the British had prepared men to organize a new state and lay
foundations for its further growth. In the south,
the Spanish and Portuguese colonies had been

ruled autocratically by local representatives of
the crown and this was the only form of government the colonists knew. Independence and
freedom appeared to them to lie in changes of
local rulers, and they had to undergo long years
of apprenticeship in democratic self-government
before they found the new forms of political
organization.

At the end of the Revolutionary War, some
farsighted people in England felt that the former
colonies were closer to them than to the continental European powers which had supported
them in their fight for independence. The borders of the United States were fixed at the four-
nation conference in Paris, in 1782. The American delegation, headed by Benjamin Franklin,
claimed the territory between the Atlantic coast
and the Mississippi River. But France and Spain
decided to block American designs on the hin-

terland and offered the new republic only a narrow strip of land extending from the coast to the Appalachian Mountains. The British shrewdly chose to support their erstwhile colonies. Thus Franklin, contrary to instructions from his government, entered into secret negotiations with the British and agreed with them upon more favorable terms of peace.[36]

The Paris treaty of 1783 left Spain with Florida and all North America west of the Mississippi River, from the Gulf of Mexico to the Arctic. Actually, the Spanish settlements did not reach further north than San Francisco, while the Russians had established outposts in Alaska for the fur trade and were moving quietly southward along the Pacific coast.[37]

The next steps in the decolonization of America were the emancipation of Haiti from French rule (1801); the purchase of Louisiana by the United States from Napoleon, who had obtained this area from the Spaniards but was unwilling to commit his forces to its defense against the British (1803); and the collapse of the Spanish and Portuguese colonial empires (1810–13). Cuba was the only significant colony retained by Spain.

The colonial system in the Western Hemisphere lingered in Canada until 1867, when that country became an independent dominion, and in Cuba until 1901; it still remains in the West Indies and a few other spots in the Caribbean and on the South American coast.

COLONIES IN ASIA

The main objective of Vasco da Gama's voyage to India was to find the shortest route to the land of spices and to establish direct trade with it, eliminating Arabian middlemen. Another great captain, Magellan, had a similar mission in his travels in the South Pacific.

Large-scale territorial colonization in Asia started later than in America, partly because the trade in spices could be secured by a few strategically located forts and trading posts, without substantial settlements; partly because Asia's kingdoms could not be overrun and conquered as easily as Mexico and Peru. The colonial powers had to wait for the hour when political turmoil, tribal wars and dynastic disputes gave them a chance to intervene. In India they waited nearly two centuries.

Portuguese and Spanish

After having landed in 1498 at Calicut, on the Malabar coast of India, Vasco da Gama returned to Europe with a friendly letter from the rajah of Malabar to the king of Portugal. "In my kingdom," wrote the rajah, "there is abundance of cinnamon, cloves, ginger, pepper, and precious stones. What I seek from thy country is gold, silver, coral and scarlet." When, however, following the rajah's invitation, the second Portuguese expedition arrived in India (1500–02), it was met by the natives with open hostility. This did not stop the Portuguese, and before sailing home they built two small forts, one in Calicut, the other in Cochin. The Pope promptly recognized the king of Portugal as the "lord of the navigation, conquest and trade of Ethiopia, Arabia, Persia and India" (1502) and the king appointed the first viceroy of India, of which the Portuguese had not yet seen more than a few coastal points. Very soon the Portuguese established themselves firmly on the Malabar coast, made Goa the capital of Portuguese India, captured Malacca and opened trade with Siam.

The Portuguese were exceptionally successful in this type of colonization and remained in control of the South Seas and the spice trade with India, Java and Sumatra to the end of the sixteenth century. Their colonial empire, however, hung on a long and very thin thread: Portugal was a small country and had neither ships nor men to defend its possessions against the increasing competition of the Dutch. Moreover, in 1580, Portugal was united with Spain and before long was absorbed by the latter politically.

The Spaniards found their way to the spice islands two decades after the Portuguese. After a clash between the two Iberian nations, the Treaty of Saragossa (1529) left the Spice Islands (the Celebes) in the hands of the Portuguese,[38] while the Spaniards remained in control of the Philippines, discovered by Magellan. They kept these islands until the Spanish-American War, which ended with the transfer of the Philippines to the United States (1898).[39] Except for domi-

---

36. **19**, pp. 287–88; **39**, p. 52; **58**, p. 144.
37. **58**, pp. 184–85.

38. This decision was based at least partly on the Papal Bull of 1493: the Celebes fall within the hemisphere awarded to Portugal.
39. By act of Congress, 1934, the United States withdrew from the Philippines and power was transferred to a republican government democratically elected by the local population. The Philippines were occupied by Japan during World War II and became independent in 1946.

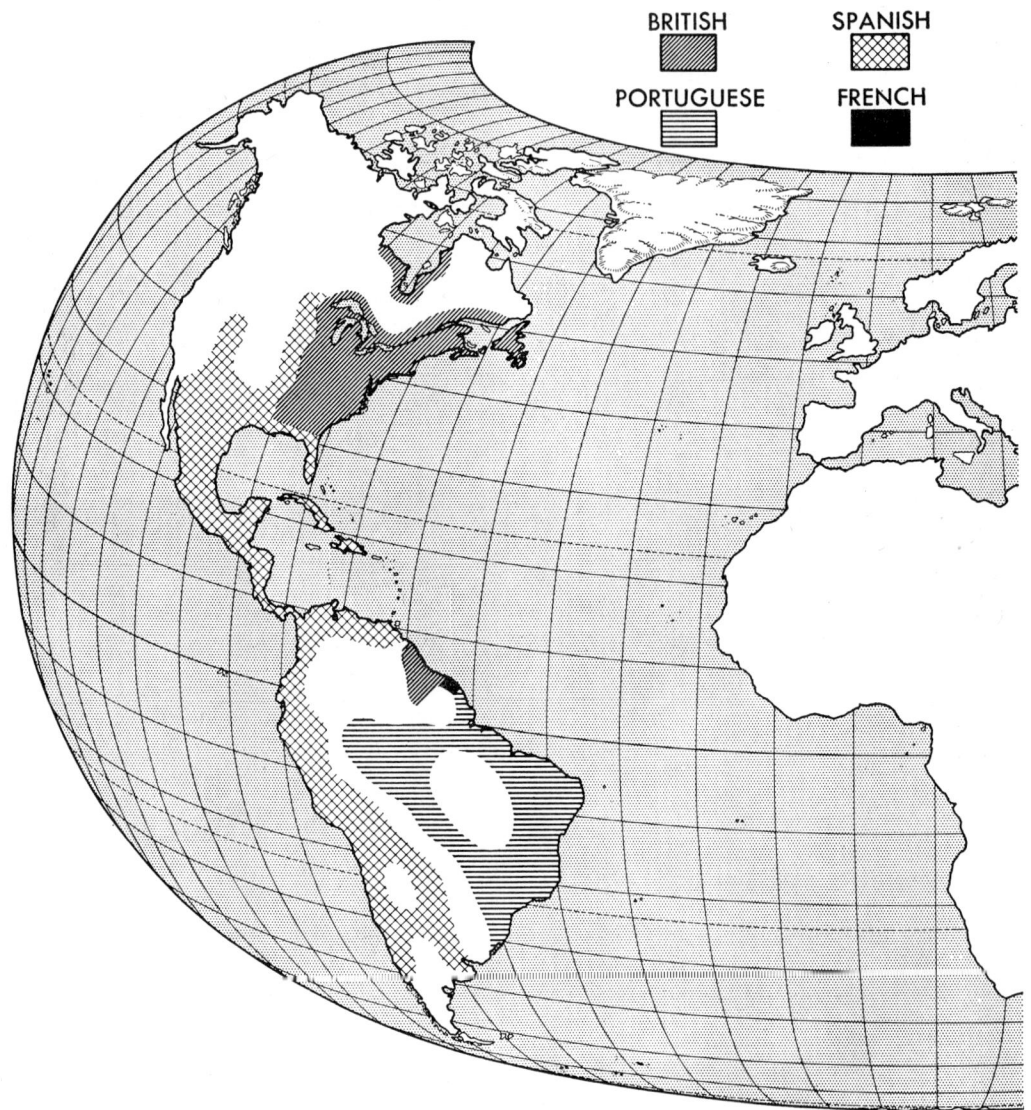

FIGURE 133. PARTITION OF THE AMERICAS AFTER THE TREATY OF PARIS, 1763

nation over the Philippines, Spain did not play an important role in the Far East.

The Dutch in the East Indies

At the beginning of the seventeenth century, supremacy in the South Seas shifted to the Dutch. Following the consolidation of their maritime and trade companies with interests in the Far East into the United East India Company of the Netherlands (1602), the Dutch established trading posts on the coasts of India, Ceylon, Sumatra and Java. They expelled the

Portuguese from the Celebes; in 1618 they laid the foundation of Batavia, which became the capital of their overseas possessions.

This was a colonial empire of a new type. The Dutch, like the Portuguese, were mainly interested in trade, but they were not satisfied with the role of middlemen between native producers and Europe. Long before the inauguration of the East India company, the Dutch had led in the European trade in spices as distributors of Indian products imported by the Portuguese. Now they moved into production. For this purpose, they concluded treaties with local rulers, playing off one against the other, and acquired huge tracts of land, not for settlement but for plantations.

In the second half of the eighteenth century, the Dutch lost their possessions on the mainland of India to the British, and their colonial empire was restricted to the islands of the East Indies.

Before the end of that century (1798) the United East India Company was dissolved. The position of the Dutch became extremely difficult after the British victory over the coalition of European powers allied with Napoleon. The remainder of the Dutch colonies in the South Seas became a crown colony of the Netherlands (1816). Gradually the borders of the colony were expanded. In the second half of the nineteenth century, they embraced the islands of Sumatra, Java, the Celebes, southern Borneo, the western part of New Guinea, and innumerable minor islands. Since 1901 the Dutch government has aimed at a gradual development of self-government in this area. First, municipal councils were instituted; after World War I a "people's council," a kind of national parliament with restricted power, was inaugurated.

Before the outbreak of World War II the Netherlands Indies was one of the world's most important colonies, with a population approaching 70 million. The whole area was occupied by Japan during the war. Since it was out of the question to restore colonial status after the liberation, the Dutch tried to transform their colonial possessions into an independent dominion by proclaiming the constitutional equality of Indonesia and the mother country (1942). This attempt failed, however. Before the new constitution could be worked out, a revolution broke out on the islands of Java, Madura and Sumatra, and a nationalist government seized power from the Japanese. After prolonged negotiations, the Netherlands recognized the complete independence and sovereignty of the United States of Indonesia (1949), which later was enlarged to include other areas and the name changed to the Republic of Indonesia.

Formally, Indonesia remained a member of the Netherlands-Indonesian Union under the Dutch crown, but this tie was very weak, and the Union was terminated in 1954. Apart from a comparatively small colony in New Guinea, claimed by Indonesia, nothing remains of the Dutch empire in the Far East.

The British in India

The first British settlement on the Indian coast, at Surat on the Gulf of Cambay, was founded in 1612, after a naval engagement with the Portuguese. Other clashes between the fleets of the two nations followed, and by 1622 the British had gained a decisive supremacy. The struggle between the British East India Company and its Dutch counterpart lasted until the middle of the seventeenth century and likewise ended in victory for the British, giving them a free hand on the subcontinent. By this time the British had acquired Bombay and founded Calcutta; had concluded treaties with local rulers and learned the art of local politics.

In the middle of the eighteenth century the British clashed with the French, who challenged their supremacy in India as in all other parts of the world. Initially, the French had the upper hand and they held temporarily the British settlement at Madras (1746), but the contest ended in the defeat of the French and the surrender of their stronghold, Pondichéry, on the Coromandel coast in 1761.

This ended the century and a half of preliminaries to the conquest of India, the period in which the British fought other European colonial powers — the Portuguese, Dutch and French. Actual conquest of India by the British East India Company began in the second half of the eighteenth century.[40]

Times had changed since the discovery of America. Clive and Hastings had little in common with Cortez and Pizarro, and the conquest of India differed from the conquest of South America. Force was used sparingly and few battles were fought, but unmanageable rulers were dethroned and the rulers raised to power gladly met the military expenses of the British by ceding them special rights and lands. In this way, at the time when Great Britain was losing its colonies in America, it was building a new and much larger colonial empire in Asia. In 1798, the British governor-general of India (appointed by the East India Company) inaugurated a policy aimed at unification of all India under the British, leaving the local princes only the appearance of independence within limits prescribed by Great Britain.

---

40. The India Act (1773) established parliamentary control over the Company and its activities. (See **17**, p. 387.)

The Napoleonic wars eliminated the last rivals of the British in the Far East, and by the middle of the nineteenth century the East India Company was actually the government of India. The great mutiny of local armed forces (the Sepoy Rebellion, 1857–58) showed that the situation was precarious and that far-reaching administrative reforms were urgently needed. In 1858, the Company was dissolved and all its rights were transferred to the crown. From that time until World War I, India remained a British colony with a complicated internal political organization and different degrees of self-government in its various provinces.

The French in the Far East

Nearly a century after the loss of India to the British (1761), the French fleet reappeared in the South Pacific in connection with military operations against China.

Under pretext of a police action in Annam, where a Spanish bishop had been killed by a mob, the French took possession of Saigon on the southeastern coast of Indochina and forced the Annamese government to cede part of the peninsula (1862). As the result of another colonial incident, the rest of Annam recognized the French protectorate (1874), and France became master of the eastern part of the Indochina peninsula. In the north, French possessions bordered on China and Burma. After protracted friction with the British, a demarcation between the interests of the two countries was established, and Siam (Thailand) was left an independent and neutral state between their possessions on the two coasts of the peninsula.

After World War II Indochina was in a state of civil war. In the later phase of the conflict the anti-French movement in the north was openly supported by China. The clash was settled in August 1954 by a partition of Indochina that gave complete independence from France to the northern provinces (Viet-Minh) and left unsettled the political state of the southern provinces.

The Partition of Southeastern Asia

Colonialism had reached the peak of expansion in the Far East by the end of the nineteenth century. Political boundaries in Asia seemed to be firmly established, and nothing indicated the possibility of their radical revision in the near future. The northern part of Asia, from the Caspian Sea and the Urals to the Pacific Ocean,

belonged to the Russian Empire. The western part, south of the Black Sea, was held by the Ottoman Empire. The southern part — India and Burma, Indochina and Malaya, Indonesia and the Philippines — was in the hands of Great Britain, France, the Netherlands, Portugal and the United States, which had succeeded Spain in the Philippines. In southeastern Asia, Japan had taken possession of Korea, Formosa and Kwantung.

In all, colonial powers in southeastern Asia controlled an area of some 3 million square miles, with a population of nearly 400 million.[41] (Cf. Figure 134.)

The Emancipation

The decolonization of Asia began during World War I when the British government promised India self-government (Declaration of August 20, 1917). This promise was implemented in 1919 by the solemn statement that the policy of Great Britain in India was to provide for "the increasing association of Indians in every branch of the administration and the gradual development of self-governing institutions with a view to the progressive realization of responsible government in British India as an integral part of the British Empire."[42]

The next important step in India's emancipation was its admission to the League of Nations as an original-state member. After that time India was no longer listed among British colonies and protectorates.[43] It remained in an ambiguous international status, neither a colony nor a completely independent nation, until the Indian Independence Act of 1947, when India and Pakistan became members of the British Commonwealth of Nations (the former as an independent republic). In 1947, Ceylon obtained independence, also as a dominion of the Commonwealth. Indonesia had gained its independence in 1949. These new countries were recognized as sovereign states by all the civilized world.[44]

---

41. These figures do not include Russian possessions in Siberia, Middle Asia and the Far East. Russian colonization in Asia was in many respects a migration within the boundaries of the nation, similar to the westward expansion of the United States after the middle of the nineteenth century. (See **64**, Chapter 3.)

42. **56**, 1948, p. 104.

43. **1**, p. 12.

44. The press and scientific publications of the USSR

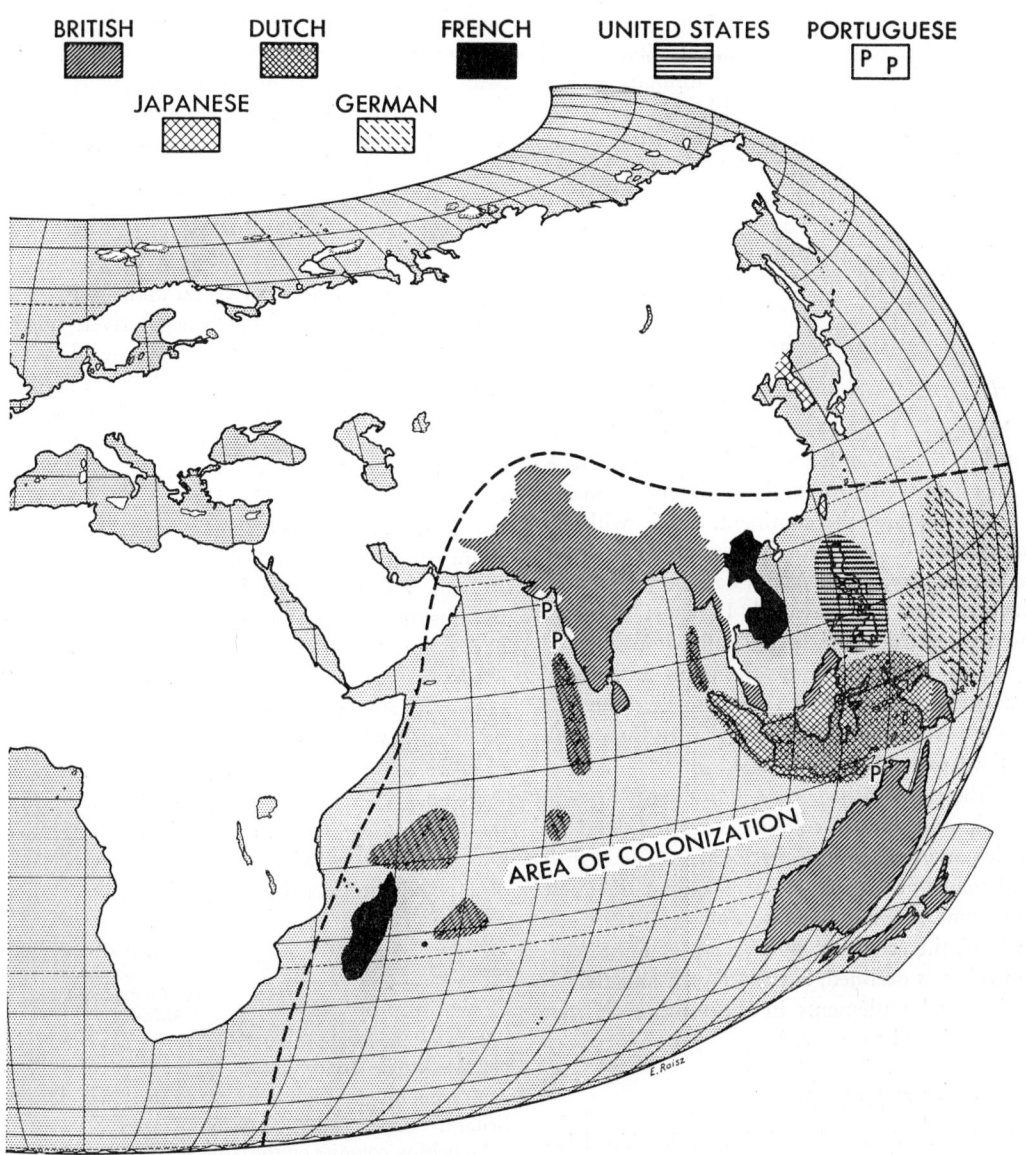

FIGURE 134. PARTITION OF FAR EASTERN REGIONS AMONG COLONIAL POWERS, 1900

The colonial system in this area of colonization reached its zenith at the end of the nineteenth century. India, Indochina, Korea, Australia, New Zealand, all the islands of Australasia and all the islands in the Indian Ocean were then in the hands of colonial powers.

Including the Philippines, Burma and the former Japanese colony of Korea, colonial domination in the Far East had come to an end in an area totaling nearly 1.7 million square miles, with a total population of more than 580 million in mid-1950:

continued to consider them as colonies of imperialist powers and described their "independence" (in quotation marks) as an attempt of the imperialists to preserve the colonial system. (**30**, pp. 6, 14 and *passim*.)

	Area, in Thousands of Square Miles	Population, in Millions (1950)
India	803.0	358.0
Pakistan	246.0	75.0
Burma	26.2	18.5
Ceylon	17.0	7.6
Indonesia	386.3	73.5
Korea	57.2	29.5
Formosa	31.1	7.8
Philippines	115.4	13.6

Colonial or semicolonial relations in Asia remained in a territory of 692,100 square miles with a total population of 43.3 million. Excluding Indochina this area would be reduced to approximately 420,000 square miles with a population of less than 16 million. Thus out of a population of about 630 million in present and former colonies in Asia, only 7 per cent remained under foreign rule in mid-1950 and less than 3 per cent at the end of 1954.

COLONIES IN AFRICA

Early Settlements

Modern colonization of Africa was inaugurated in the fifteenth century by the Portuguese, who established forts and trading posts on the western coast of the continent. Trade with the natives was disappointingly slow until the seventeenth century, when Africa became the leading slave market in the world. Purchase of slaves from tribal chieftains, occasionally supplemented by slave hunting, became the main business of the trading posts which mushroomed on the western African coast, from Dakar to the mouth of the Congo. Ivory was a sideline.

In the eighteenth century, Portuguese, French, British and Dutch colonies acquired land in Africa and pushed into the interior. The British settlements at Capetown were among the most important. After the abolition of the slave trade in 1807, the economic significance of most African colonies declined, but the Dutch and British agricultural settlements in the south took root and continued to grow.[45]

Progress of Colonization

In the 1830's a series of clashes developed between the French government and the ruler of the Arab state of Algeria. To protect their trade interests, the French seized some Algerian ports and the surrounding areas. In 1848, after having occupied the coastal part of Algeria, France proclaimed the annexation of the whole country, which was more than four times as large as France itself. Then, to secure the unknown

southern borders of the new colony against the attacks of Arab tribes, the French pushed southward. In the middle of the nineteenth century, some French statesmen dreamed of a colonial empire stretching from the Mediterranean to the Gulf of Guinea and embracing French settlements on both coasts, with a central trade post somewhere near Timbuktu.

The first step toward this goal was to establish a direct tie between Algeria and the French posts at the mouth of the Senegal river, north of Dakar.[46] Contemporary political conditions in North Africa favored France's designs. The disintegration of the Arab empire had created a political vacuum in North Africa. The French colony bordered on a no man's land. An indefinite part of this land had been claimed by the rulers of Algeria. Having annexed Algeria, France inherited these claims.

Thus, a century after losing its overseas possessions in America, France began to build a new empire — an empire separated only by the Mediterranean from its own national frontier. It moved slowly and cautiously, however, not quite sure whether the new empire would be of great value.

Around 1876, European powers claimed for their African colonies an area of about 1.25 million square miles with an estimated population of 11.4 million, distributed as follows: [47]

	Area, in Thousands of Square Miles	Population, in Millions (1876)
Portugal: the Azores, Madeira, Cape Verde Islands, Angola, Mozambique	696.0	5.9
Britain: Cape Colony, Natal, Mauritius, colonies on the Gulf of Guinea	273.0	2.3
France: Algeria, colonies on the Senegal River and others	270.0	2.9
Spain: Canary Islands	4.0	0.3

In addition, France and Great Britain together exercised political and economic control over Egypt, and the United States was the protector of Liberia, founded in 1816 as a haven for American freedmen.

With the single exception of the ancient kingdom of Abyssinia (Ethiopia), Africa was a maze

---

45. Cape Colony, founded by the Dutch in 1652, was ceded to Britain in 1814. The Orange region, colonized in 1810–20, was proclaimed a British possession in 1848 and became a free state in 1854. The Transvaal was colonized by the Boers in 1836–37, annexed by the British in 1877, recognized as independent in 1880. Natal was annexed by the British in 1843. (**32**.)

46. **58**, p. 203.
47. **58**, pp. 256–57. Cf. Tables 233 and 234.

of tribal states that had neither firmly established borders nor means of defending themselves,[48] when an American journalist, in search of a sensational scoop for his newspaper, blundered into the Upper Congo region.

Discovery of the Congo

Henry Morton Stanley, a roving correspondent of the New York *Herald,* was commissioned by the publisher, James Gordon Bennett, to go to Central Africa in search of the Scottish missionary and explorer, David Livingstone. In 1871–72, Stanley crossed the wilderness of Africa from Zanzibar on the western coast to the upper Congo, found Livingstone and returned to the coast with the latter's journals and a wealth of information on Africa's geography, anthropology and economic possibilities. He was the first white man to realize that large-scale economic exploitation of the African expanses was more promising than encroachment on the coast of the continent. He also realized the importance of African rivers and, in particular, the Congo, for colonization of this type.

In 1874–77 Stanley continued his exploration of the interior of Africa as the head of an Anglo-American expedition. This time he crossed the continent from the eastern coast westward and returned to the mouth of the Congo. On his return to Europe he approached the British government with a daring proposal of annexing the interior of Africa to the empire. The British, however, had enough trouble at that time with their other African colonies, especially Nigeria and Uganda, and showed little enthusiasm. Stanley's direct appeal to British businessmen likewise met with no response. In his address to the Manchester Chamber of Commerce he tried to kindle their imagination by the vision of exports to Africa: "There are 40 million people beyond the gateway of the Congo and the cotton spinners of Manchester are waiting to clothe them," he declared, pointing out that one Sunday dress for each inhabitant of the African jungles would mean 320 million yards of Manchester cloth.[49] The argument was not very convincing. The value of the new region from the viewpoint of colonial policy was not in its ability to purchase European fabrics but in its natural resources.

The Partition of Africa

What Stanley had discovered was a virgin region to colonize for plantations and exploitation. The first businessman to grasp this aspect of colonization in Africa was King Leopold II of Belgium, who had long dreamed of Belgian colonies in that continent.[50] Together with Stanley, he founded a private commercial company,[51] and in 1879 Stanley returned to Africa, no longer as an explorer but as an empire builder. He concluded treaties with more than 500 local chiefs, purchased or rented their lands, secured special privileges for his association, and actually brought native tribes in the Upper Congo area under its control.

Obviously, more than one party could play this game. A German explorer, Carl Peters, started a similar campaign in East Africa, moving from Zanzibar inland; a Frenchman, Pierre Brazza, enrolled local rulers on the right shore of the Congo; the Portuguese, supported by the British, started a drive inland from their coastal settlements in Angola and Mozambique. The French and Portuguese were so successful that they almost completely cut off the central Congo Basin from the sea.

Bismarck chose this moment to call an international conference on African affairs. The Conference, which met in Berlin in 1884–85, established definite rules for the acquisition of new lands by colonial powers and for their commercial and administrative policies in "the little-known or inadequately organized regions of the continent where slavery and slave trade still flourish."[52] According to the decisions of the Conference, reaffirmed thirty-five years later by the League of Nations, a vast area, described as the "Conventional Basin of the Congo" but actually stretching from the mouth of the Congo to the coast of the Indian Ocean, was put under international law. (See Figure 135.) Trade and waterways in this region were declared open to all nations; the colonial powers were committed to abolish slavery and to protect the natives, missionaries of all religions and travelers.[53]

---

48. **59**, p. 47.
49. **59**, p. 36.

50. **47**, pp. 73ff.
51. Originally, the organization had a modest name: "Committee for Studies of the Upper Congo." A year later it was secretly dissolved and replaced by the International Association for the Exploration and Civilization of the Congo, with far more ambitious designs. (**47**, p. 79.)
52. **49**, p. 50.
53. **58**, p. 270; **49**, p. 50.

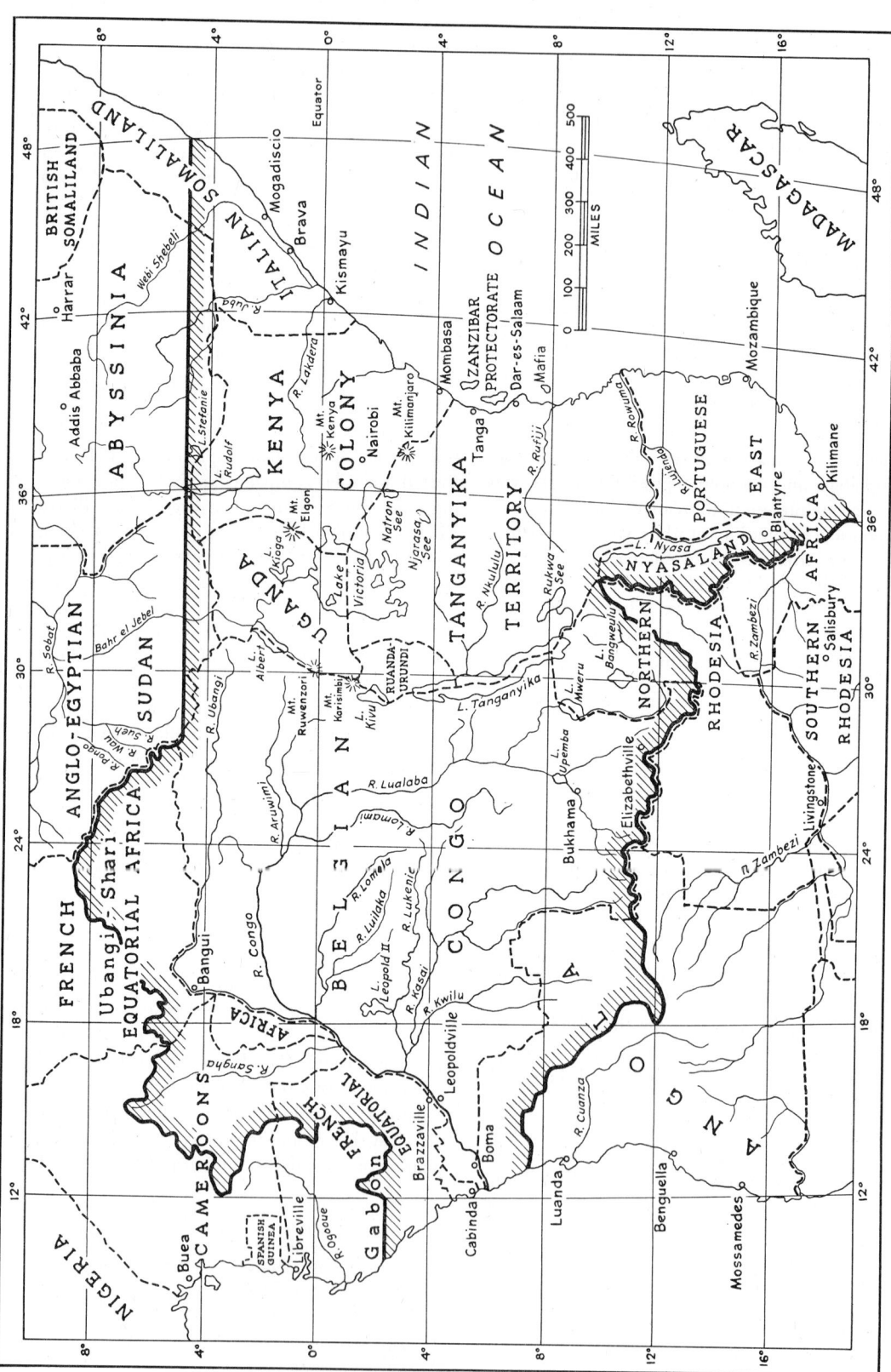

Figure 135. The Conventional Basin of the Congo

Courtesy of Oxford University Press (49)

In 1885, the Congo was proclaimed an independent neutral kingdom and Leopold II became its king. The new state had a strange form — a huge continental region with an area of 920,000 square miles and a long and narrow corridor giving it access to the sea, with some 20 miles of coast line. Actually, of course, the Congo has never been — and was never supposed to be — an independent state; it has been a Belgian colony since its inception. It was officially annexed to Belgium in 1908, shortly before the death of Leopold II.[54]

The Berlin Conference was the signal for a race of the European powers to partition Africa. The French easily took possession of Madagascar and the territories between the Mediterranean and the Gulf of Guinea: French West Africa comprising Senegal, French Guinea, the Ivory Coast, Dahomey, the French Sudan, Mauretania, Niger and Upper Volta, the region north of the lower Congo (the French Congo, now a part of French Equatorial Africa). The British expanded their possessions in western and southern Africa, always keeping an eye on their interests in other parts of the continent.

The clash between France and England on the Niger River was settled by an arrangement which gave the British Nigeria and left the French with a continuous tract of land stretching more than 2,500 miles from the Mediterranean to the lower Congo.

A more serious conflict developed between the two countries in East Africa, when French and British forces met face to face on the Upper Nile (the Fashoda Incident, 1898). Danger of a European war was imminent. The British were ready for a showdown, the French hesitated and finally withdrew to their possessions in the west. In March 1899, the two countries concluded a treaty delimiting their spheres of interest in North Africa, a treaty comparable to the Papal Bull of 1493.

The French-British disputes in Africa gave the Germans an opportunity to carve out sizable colonies for themselves: Togoland and the Cameroons on the Gulf of Guinea; German South-West Africa, between Britain's Cape Colony and Portugal's Angola; and German East Africa, facing the Indian Ocean north of Mozambique.

The Italians were less successful and had to satisfy themselves with comparatively poor strips of land in Libya, Eritrea and Somaliland.

While the European powers were partitioning Africa, gold was discovered in the Transvaal (1884). The influx of immigrants led to tension between the old and new colonists. The attempts of England to interfere in the dispute increased the tension, and in 1899 the South African war broke out. After initial reverses, the British regulars crushed the Boer volunteer army. The Transvaal and its ally, the Orange Free State, became British colonies in 1900.

Now the partition of Africa among the European powers was practically complete. Only two countries — Liberia and Abyssinia — remained independent.[55] The rest had been divided up as follows: [56]

	Area, in Thousands of Square Miles	Population, in Millions (1900)
Total	10,402	127.4
Britain: Gambia, Sierra Leone, Gold Coast, Nigeria, Egypt, Sudan, Kenya, Uganda, Zanzibar, British South Africa, etc.	3,553	53.1
France: Algeria, Morocco, Tunisia, French West Africa, French Equatorial Africa, Madagascar, etc.	3,939	31.5
Belgium: Congo	920	19.0
Germany: Togo, Cameroons, German South-West Africa, German East Africa	908	15.5
Portugal: Angola, Mozambique, Portuguese Guinea	800	6.9
Italy: Libya, Eritrea, Somaliland	197	0.7
Spain: Río de Oro, Canary Islands	85	0.7

The speed with which the colonial partition of Africa was effected explains the haphazard character of the present boundaries. Territories have been acquired at different times and for different reasons; many have changed hands more than once; frontiers have sometimes been drawn as a result of political bargaining and with entire dis-

---

54. Under the rule of Leopold II, the Congo was subject to ruthless and cruel exploitation. After its annexation the Belgian government declared its disapproval of the horrors of Leopold's regime and tried to remedy the damage that had been inflicted on Belgium's reputation as a colonial power. (**58**, pp. 187, 195–96.)

55. Abyssinia was occupied by the Italians from 1936 to 1941. Although marked as an Italian colony in a solid block with Eritrea and Somaliland in some maps published at that time, this temporary military occupation can hardly be regarded as an expansion of colonial rule in Africa beyond the 1900 limits.

56. **58**, p. 256. Data for 1900; partly rough estimates.

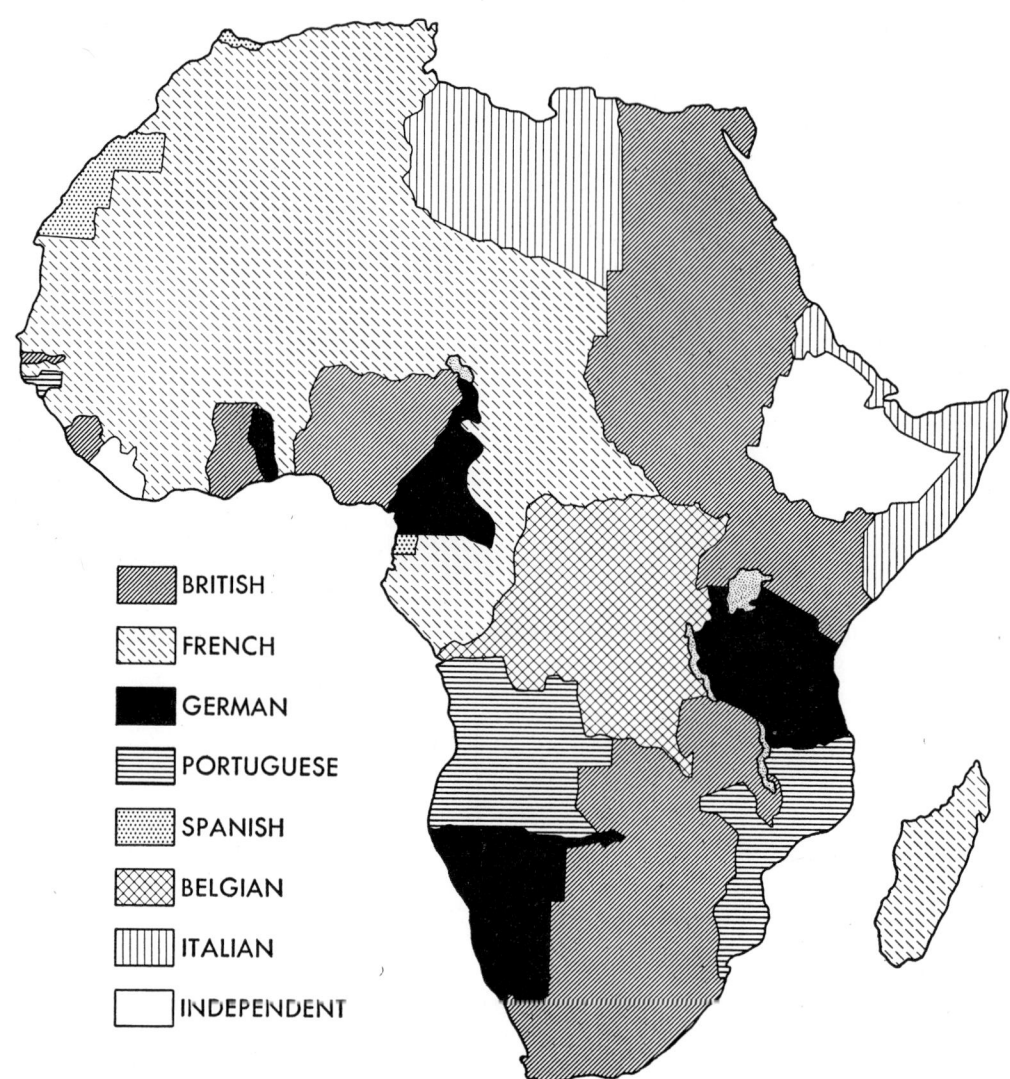

FIGURE 136. PARTITION OF AFRICA AMONG COLONIAL POWERS, 1900

regard of racial affinities or economic conditions. Boundaries in Africa are often straight lines cutting across tribes, rivers and natural communications; for political reasons, many enclaves have been left which present serious obstacles to the development of natural resources and an ordered economic life.[57]

After the beginning of the twentieth century only insignificant changes took place in the distribution of the African colonies. The most important was the transfer of the former German colonies to the trusteeship of Great Britain, France and the Union of South Africa.

Leonard Woolf gives a striking picture of the course of the partition of Africa, summarized in Table 233.[58] (Cf. Figure 136.)

The Beginning of Emancipation

In September 1909, the British Parliament passed the South Africa Act, bestowing full self-government on the former colonies of the Cape of Good Hope (Cape Colony), Natal, the Transvaal and the Orange River Colony, united under the name of the Union of South Africa. The act has not improved the state of the natives in that area, but it has put an end to the dependence of

57. **49**, p. 14.

58. **62**, pp. 52 and 67.

TABLE 233

COLONIAL POSSESSIONS: AREA AND POPULATION, IN AFRICA, 1815–1914

Region of Africa	Area, in Thousands of Square Miles				Population, in Millions			
	1815 [a]	1880 [a]	1890	1914	1815 [a]	1880 [a]	1890	1914
Total	500	1,000	5,998	11,574	3,000	10,000	74,661	122,876
North	...	...	1,546	3,636	...	...	18,700	28,700
West	...	...	2,500	5,147	...	...	33,000	64,400
East	...	...	1,461	1,584	...	...	19,086	21,586
South	120	250	491	1,207	...	2,000	3,875	8,190

Source: **62**, p. 67.   a. Approximate figures.

its white settlers on Great Britain. Termination of the British protectorate over Egypt (1922) was a further step in the direction of Africa's decolonization.

The growth of the nationalist movement in Egypt raised the question of the fate of the Anglo-Egyptian Sudan, an area of nearly a million square miles with a population of more than 8 million, officially described as an Anglo-Egyptian "condominium" but listed by British sources as a part of the British commonwealth and empire. In October 1951, the Egyptian government denounced the condominium treaty with Great Britain and a month later proclaimed the annexation of the Sudan. Ignoring this act, the British offered the Sudanese a new constitution, but this offer was rejected by the Egyptians and nationalists in the Sudan. In January 1953, an agreement was reached between the British government and the military ruler of Egypt, Mohammed Naguib. Both parties recognized the right of the Sudan to determine its political status by a plebiscite to be held in three years under the supervision of an international commission. There remained a dispute about the meaning of the agreement: the Egyptians interpreted the forthcoming plebiscite as a choice between complete independence or association with Egypt; the British insisted on the right of the Sudan to apply for the status of a British dominion. It is unlikely, however, that the Sudan would vote to join the Commonwealth and most observers believe that its merger with Egypt is merely a matter of time.

In December 1951, the former Italian colony Libya became independent. It consists of three provinces — Tripolitania, Cyrenaica and the Fezzan — in northern Africa, between Tunisia and Algeria to the west and Egypt to the east. This area was occupied by the Allies during World War II and later was under British and French administration. Recognition of the independence of this vast but sparsely populated and underdeveloped territory is another step in the general direction of decolonization of Africa. (See Figure 137.)

Southern Rhodesia is another African territory that has undergone a process of decolonization. In September 1923 this colony received a new constitution providing for a governor assisted by an executive council and an elected legislative assembly with restricted power, foreshadowing its transformation into Commonwealth status.[59] In 1951 the British government recommended a union of Southern and Northern Rhodesia and Nyasaland and admission into the Commonwealth as an independent entity, and in 1953 a bill authorizing such a merger was passed in the Commons. The Federation of Rhodesia and Nyasaland came into existence in 1954.[60]

A very different situation exists in Kenya, where part of the native population is in open revolt against the white masters.

The situation is similarly explosive in the French colonies in North Africa, especially in Algeria. This territory of some 850,000 square miles has a population of 8.8 million (1950), including a million Europeans. Until recently, administrative power over this area has been

59. Southern Rhodesia was affiliated with the British government through the Dominion Office; its representatives attended conferences of the British dominions, and its government negotiated and concluded trade agreements with the government of the United Kingdom. (**49**, pp. 18–19.)

60. The new federation's constitution leaves political power in the hands of the whites, and permits the natives only a limited voice in local self-government. Thus decolonization does not mean emancipation of the natives.

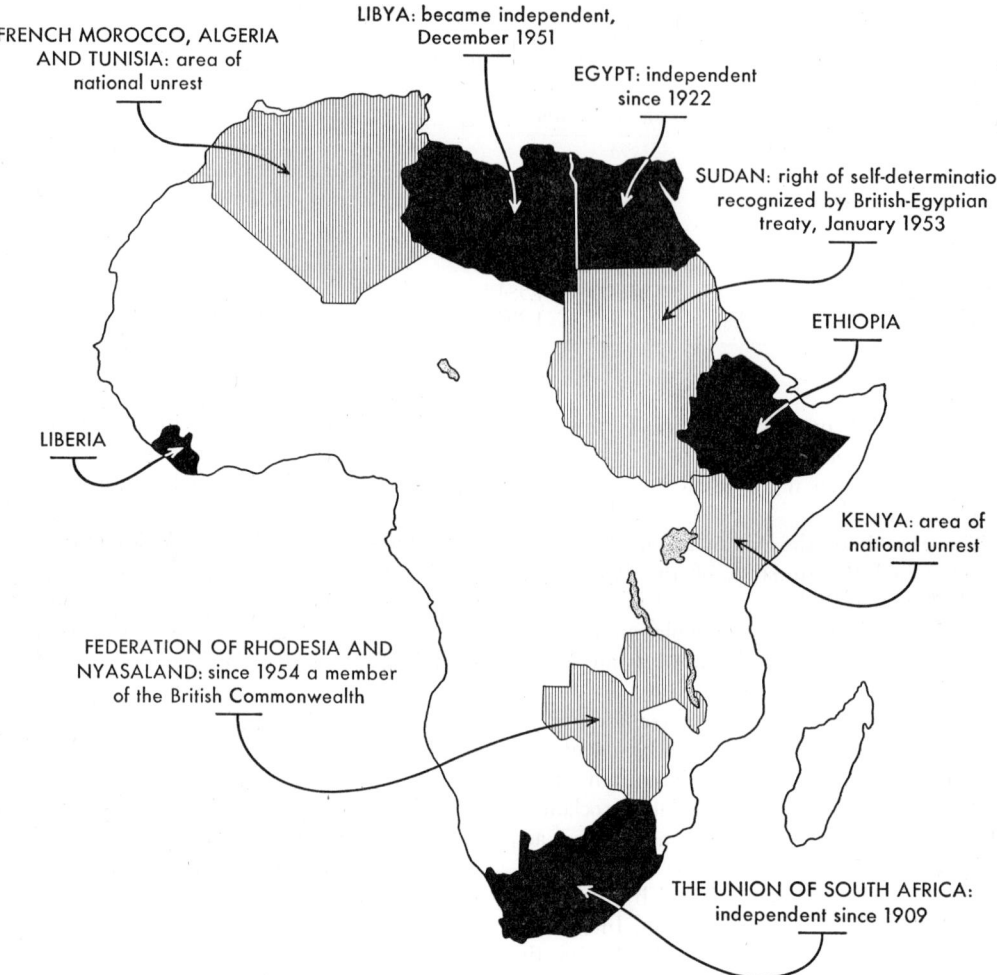

FRENCH MOROCCO, ALGERIA
AND TUNISIA: area of
national unrest

LIBYA: became independent,
December 1951

EGYPT: independent
since 1922

SUDAN: right of self-determination
recognized by British-Egyptian
treaty, January 1953

ETHIOPIA

LIBERIA

KENYA: area of
national unrest

FEDERATION OF RHODESIA AND
NYASALAND: since 1954 a member
of the British Commonwealth

THE UNION OF SOUTH AFRICA:
independent since 1909

FIGURE 137. THE PROGRESS OF DECOLONIZATION IN AFRICA, 1954

concentrated in the hands of the governor-general, and the native Moslems have had very little say even in local government. After World War II, racial and religious restrictions were abolished (decrees of 1946 and 1947). In 1948 the first Algerian assembly was elected. Formally, Algeria became a part of France as a government-general.

Actually the rights of self-government granted to the native Algerians lag far behind their aspirations. Many Moslems scorn the slow application of the principle of self-government and decline any arrangement short of complete independence. At the same time, nationalist movements are on the rise in the two French protectorates adjacent to Algeria: French Morocco to the west and Tunisia to the east. The three areas together, although widely different in eco-

nomic structure and level of development, form a continuous Arabic-Moslem area with a nationalist movement hostile to French domination. Political conditions in the northwestern corner of Africa, with an area of 1,073,000 square miles and a population of 20.7 million (1950), are suggestive of situations that preceded emancipation of many other colonial areas.

COLONIES IN OCEANIA

In 1788, after the voyages of Captain James Cook, the British founded a penal colony for deported criminals at Botany Bay, Australia. Another colony of the same type was established on Tasmania in 1803. A decade or two later, the first free settlers began to arrive in Australia. In 1821 the Australian colonies had 30,000 inhabitants, three fourths of them convicts; by the middle of the century the population approached 340,000, most of them free settlers. The discovery of gold in 1851 brought new throngs of immigrants. The settlements expanded rapidly along the coasts and gradually penetrated inland wherever conditions were favorable for agriculture and husbandry. The natives — tribes of hunters and fishermen with no permanent settlements or broad political organization — did not try to stop the white settlers, who took over the continent as though it were no man's land. Only in New Zealand did the British meet some resistance.

By the end of the nineteenth century, the whole continent was a flourishing British settlement, and on January 1, 1901, the six provinces were united as a dominion under the name of the Commonwealth of Australia.

New Zealand, originally settled as a resort by whalers and traders from Australia, became a British colony in 1840 by virtue of a treaty concluded by the settlers with the native Maori chiefs. It declined to join the other Australian colonies in the Commonwealth of Australia and became a separate dominion in 1907.

The Pacific islands that constitute a part of Oceania have changed hands more than once. Guam, discovered by Magellan in 1521, was conquered by the Spaniards in the seventeenth century and remained their possession until the Spanish-American War. In 1898 it was ceded to the United States. The Hawaiian Islands were discovered by Captain Cook in 1778 and remained independent until 1898. Then, after a period of internal unrest in which American settlers played an important role, the short-lived Hawaiian Republic decided to join the United States and was formally accepted as a colony. The question of its acceptance into the Union as a state is pending before Congress.

The Pacific Islands (the Caroline, Mariana and Marshall Islands) were occupied by the Spaniards step by step, sold to the Germans in 1899 (after the cession of Guam and the Philippines to the United States), and given to the Japanese under a mandate after World War I. They became a trust territory under United States administration in 1947.

Most of the more important inhabited islands of Oceania are in the hands of Australia and Great Britain.

According to the UN, the area and population

of non-self-governing territories of Oceania were distributed in 1950 as follows: [61]

	Area, in Thousands of Square Miles	Population, in Thousands (1950)
Total	226.3	2,810
British Commonwealth	204.3	2,000
Australia: eastern part of New Guinea, Papua and Norfolk Island	183.6	1,400
Britain: Solomon and Fiji Islands, Tonga and others	19.4	500
New Zealand: Western Samoa and some Pacific Islands	1.3	100
United States: Guam, Hawaii, Samoa and some Pacific Islands	7.5	630
France: French Oceania and New Caledonia	8.8	120
Condominium: New Hebrides and Nauru	5.7	60

CHANGES IN AREA AND POPULATION OF COLONIES

Two dates mark the high tide of colonial systems in the world. In the Western Hemisphere, the colonial system reached its maximum limits on the eve of the Revolutionary War; in the Eastern Hemisphere, at the end of the nineteenth century.

The Two Peaks

After the Treaty of Paris in 1763, all the mainland and islands of the Americas were in the hands of European colonial powers, mainly Spain, Portugal and England, with small morsels left for the French and Dutch and no single area organized as an independent state.

After the emancipation of most of these colonies in both North and South America, the colonial empires of the European powers were reduced to comparatively small possessions in Middle and South America, on the coasts of Africa, southern Asia and Australia and on islands in the Pacific and Indian Oceans. Great Britain, however, was already building a new colonial empire in India.

In 1876 the population of colonial territories all over the world was close to 300 million, most of it in the Indian subcontinent. The colonies in Africa, the Americas and Oceania together had less than 20 million inhabitants. The last quarter of the nineteenth century, especially the years

---

61. See Table 231.

1885–1900, was a period of colonial expansion,[62] which reached a new peak by the turn of the century. At that time, the colonial possessions of the European powers comprised all Africa, except Liberia and Abyssinia; southeastern Asia, except Siam; Australia and all the islands between Australia and Asia and in the Indian and Pacific Oceans. To European colonial possessions should be added the Japanese colonies in Asia, protectorates in the Near East and European colonies in the Caribbean.

At a rough approximation, the area of the colonial empires (including the Americas) of the eighteenth century now has a population of 300 million, while the lands which were under colonial domination at the end of the nineteenth century have more than 800 million.

There is very little overlapping of the two sets of colonial empires. In the eighteenth century, when the colonial empires in the Western Hemisphere were at their peak expansion, only point colonies and minute settlements of white men on the coasts of Africa and Asia marked the future nuclei of new colonial empires; when the latter were reaching their peak, only vestiges of colonies remained in the Western Hemisphere.

Today, nearly half the people in the world — about 1.1 billion — live in areas which once were colonial territories.

Recent Changes

More or less reliable information on the area and population of colonies goes back only to the second half of the nineteenth century. Alexander Supan, the German geographer, has compiled inclusive statistics for 1876, the beginning of the European powers' general assault on Africa.[63] More recent data collected by the League of Nations and the UN make it possible to survey changes in the scope of the colonial system from 1876 to 1950. (See Tables 234 and 235; cf. Figure 138.) From 1876 to 1900 more than 10.4 million square miles were added to the colonial empires: close to 9,150,000 square miles in Africa, 1,090,000 square miles in Asia, 200,000 in Oceania. France obtained the largest slice of Africa: 3,670,000 square miles; Great Britain acquired 3,280,000 square miles; Germany 908,000; and Belgium 905,000; minor tracts went to Italy, Spain and Portugal.

62. Cf. statistics on the growth of colonial empires in **36**, pp. 17–23.
63. **58**, pp. 256–57.

At the turn of the century, Great Britain was the leading colonial power in the world. Its colonies had an area nearly as large as that of all other powers together and a total population almost three times as large, as the following figures indicate:

	Area, in Thousands of Square Miles	Population, in Millions (1900)
World	18,563	499.1
Great Britain [a]	8,867	362.2
France	4,242	50.1
Germany	1,002	11.9
Belgium	905	19.0
Portugal	877	7.7
Denmark	840	0.1
Netherlands	795	37.9
United States [b]	706	8.8
Italy	197	0.7
Spain	132	0.7

a. Includes the Sudan and Australia, but does not include Canada.
b. Includes Alaska and the Philippines.

(See Tables 234 and 235.)

The bulk of the British colonial empire was in Asia; that of the French colonies, in Africa.

By 1925 the situation had changed. The area of the world's colonial empires had shrunk by one fourth and the colonial population, by more than half: from 499 million to 243 million people. If the growth of population in former colonial territory is taken into account, it appears that between 1900 and 1925 Europe lost a colonial domain of 4.7 million square miles with some 400 million inhabitants. Essentially, liquidation of colonies went hand in hand with the transformation of the British colonial empire into a commonwealth of nations voluntarily associated with the United Kingdom.

In the second quarter of the century, from 1925 to 1950, the transformation of the British Empire made further progress; the United States withdrew from the Philippines; the Netherlands recognized the independence of Indonesia; and Japan lost its colonies.

Liquidation of colonies is still in progress. A new dominion is likely to emerge from the British colonies in the Caribbean. This federation will unite a large part of the British West Indies — Jamaica, the Leeward and Windward Islands, Barbados, Trinidad and Tobago — with an area of some 8,000 square miles and a population of more than 2.6 million in 1950. Grenada

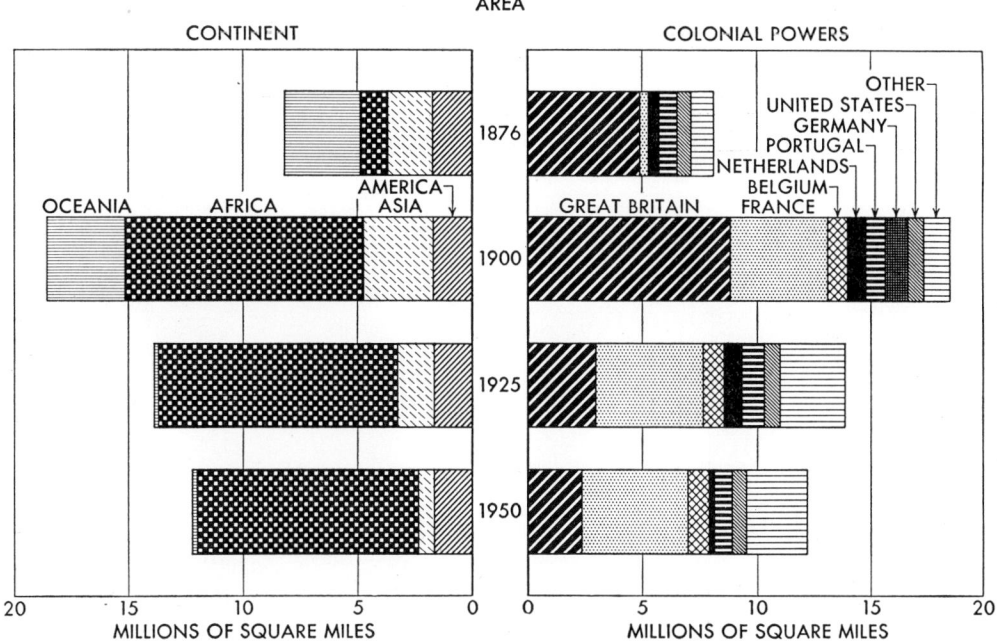

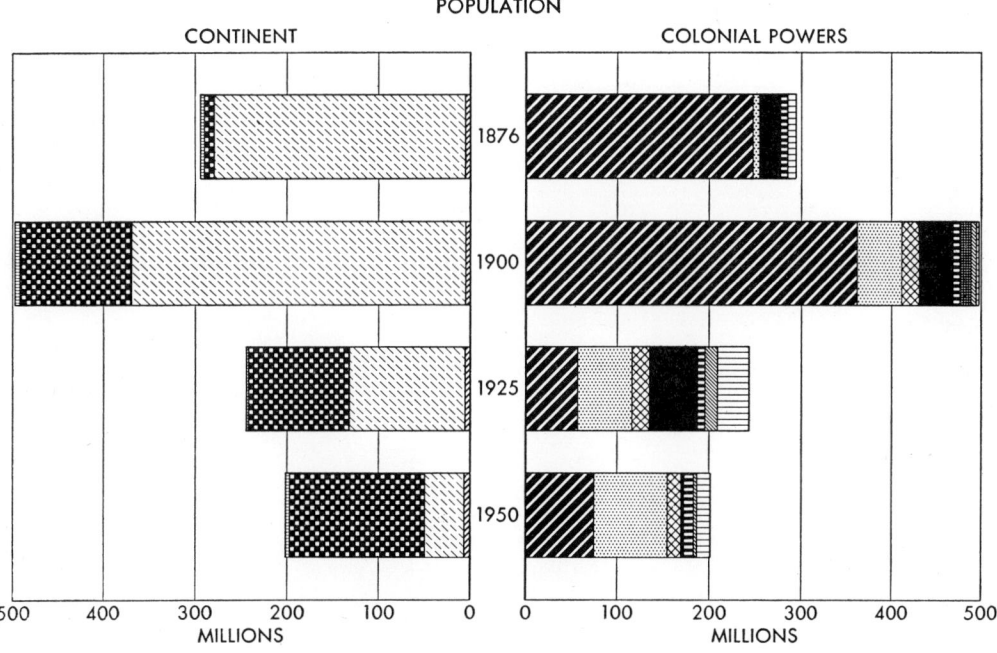

Source: Tables 234 and 235

FIGURE 138. COLONIAL POSSESSIONS: AREA AND POPULATION IN EACH CONTINENT, BY COLONIAL POWER, 1876–1950

Island in the Windward Islands has been designated as the site of the parliament of the new dominion and its capital. The Bahama Islands (located between the southern tip of Florida and the northern coast of Haiti), British Honduras and British Guiana remain, for various reasons, outside the proposed federation but may join it later, increasing the area of the federation to

GOVERNMENTS

TABLE 234

COLONIAL POSSESSIONS: AREA IN EACH CONTINENT, BY COLONIAL POWER, 1876–1950

(*Thousands of Square Miles*)

Colonial Power [a]	1876	1900	1925	1950
World	8,134	18,563	13,877	12,181
United States	590	706	706	600
Great Britain	4,921	8,867 [b]	2,979	2,396
France	376	4,242	4,671	4,594
Belgium	—	905	925	926
Netherlands	465	795	789	215
Germany	—	1,002	—	—
Denmark	840	840	840	840
Sweden	7	—	—	—
Portugal	773	877	934	804
Spain	162	132	132	133
Italy	—	197	816	198
Japan	—	—	114	—
Union of South Africa	—	—	—	318
Australia	—	—	—	184
New Zealand	—	—	—	1
Condominium	—	—	971 [e]	973 [e]
America	1,685	1,678	1,631	1,631
United States	590	590	590	590
Great Britain	109	109	109	109
France	36	36	36	36
Netherlands	56	56	56	56
Denmark	840	840	840	840
Sweden	7	—	—	—
Spain	47	47	—	—
Asia	1,960	3,047	1,595	692
United States	—	110	110	2
Great Britain	1,454	2,017	304	250
France	62	256	325	273
Netherlands	257	587	733	159
Germany	—	—	—	—
Portugal	77	77	9	9
Spain	110	—	—	—
Japan	—	—	114	—
Africa	1,243	10,390	10,425	9,631
Great Britain	273	3,553	2,360	2,018
France	270	3,942	4,302	4,276
Belgium	—	905	925	926
Germany	—	908	—	—
Portugal	696	800	925	795
Spain	4	85	132	133
Italy	—	197	814	198
Union of South Africa	—	—	—	318
Condominium	—	—	967 [e]	968 [e]
Oceania	3,246	3,448	226	226
United States	—	6	6	7 [d]
Great Britain	3,085	3,188	206	19
France	8	8	8	9
Netherlands	152	152	—	—
Germany	—	94	—	—
Spain	1	—	—	—
Japan	—	—	2	—
Australia	—	—	—	184
New Zealand	—	—	—	1
Condominium	—	—	4	6

Sources: For 1876 and 1900, data of Alexander Supan (**58,** pp. 256–57), rearranged, reclassified and corrected in accordance with more recent measurements; for 1925, **1,** pp. 10–16; for 1950, Table 232.

a. Colonial possessions in Europe (under British and international administration) are not included because of small size of respective areas.

b. Includes the Sudan and Australia, but not Canada.
c. The Sudan.
d. Includes Pacific Islands (military government).

TABLE 235

COLONIAL POSSESSIONS: POPULATION IN EACH CONTINENT, BY COLONIAL POWER, 1876–1950

(*Thousands*)

Colonial Power	1876	1900	1925	1950
World	293,887	499,117	243,471	200,957
United States	60	8,818	13,294	3,979
Great Britain	248,060	362,204 [a]	56,921	75,614
France	5,997	50,107	59,417	79,067
Belgium	—	19,000	18,000	15,173
Netherlands	24,520	37,874	53,429	1,400
Germany	—	11,914	—	—
Denmark	119	121	—	23
Sweden	1	—	—	—
Portugal	6,749	7,675	8,857	12,120
Spain	8,381	673	945	1,599
Italy	—	731	2,215	1,246
Japan	—	—	24,508	—
Union of South Africa	—	—	—	379
Australia	—	—	—	1,441
New Zealand	—	—	—	99
Condominium	—	—	5,885 [b]	8,408 [b]
International administration	—	—	—	409
America	4,021	3,838	4,799	6,662
United States	60	1,016	1,484	2,432 [a]
Great Britain	1,360	2,133	2,558	3,232
France	346	428	558	593
Netherlands	110	140	199	382
Denmark	119	121	—	23
Sweden	1	—	—	—
Spain	2,025	—	—	—
Europe	—	—	—	793
Great Britain	—	—	—	495
International administration	—	—	—	298
Asia	275,537	365,507	127,494	43,254
United States	—	7,635	11,465	917
Great Britain	241,835	301,495	14,915	11,878
France	2,683	18,073	22,178	27,830
Netherlands	24,170	37,494	53,230	1,018
Portugal	849	810	1,140	1,611
Spain	6,000	—	—	—
Italy	—	—	110	—
Japan	—	—	24,456	—
Africa	11,425	123,349	109,746	147,428
Great Britain	2,331	53,097	38,553	59,537
France	2,875	31,518	36,601	50,524
Belgium	—	19,000	18,000	15,173
Germany	—	11,465	—	—
Portugal	5,900	6,865	7,717	10,509
Spain	319	673	945	1,599
Italy	—	731	2,105	1,246
Union of South Africa	—	—	—	379
Condominium	—	—	5,825 [b]	8,350 [b]
International administration	—	—	—	111
Oceania	2,904	6,423	1,432	2,820
United States	—	167	345	630 [c]
Great Britain	2,534	5,479	895	472
France	93	88	80	120
Netherlands	240	240	—	—
Germany	—	449	—	—
Spain	37	—	—	—
Japan	—	—	52	—
Australia	—	—	—	1,441
New Zealand	—	—	—	99
Condominium	—	—	60	58

Sources: For 1876 and 1900, data of Alexander Supan (**58,** pp. 256–57), rearranged and reclassified; for 1925, **1,** pp. 10-16; for 1950, Table 232.

a. Includes the Sudan and Australia, but not Canada.   c. Includes Pacific Islands (military government).
b. The Sudan.

100,000 square miles and its population to 3.1 million (in 1950) in round numbers. (Cf. Table 231 and Figure 129.)

The trend toward dissolving colonial relations that has prevailed since the turn of the century contrasts with the recent conquests of the USSR in eastern Europe and Asia and the protectorate the USSR has established over its satellites. The contrast is as striking as that in political trends — toward iron dictatorship in the sphere dominated by Moscow, toward democracy in nearly all the rest of the world.

COLONIES IN THE WORLD ECONOMY

Colonies which have become independent in recent years include the Philippines, Indonesia, Ceylon, India, Pakistan and Burma, all areas in which economic development compares favorably with that in most other colonies. The areas still in colonial status are, with a few exceptions, among the least developed.[64] Some play an important role in the world economy because of their strategic location or natural resources, but the total share of colonies in the world's income and production is small in relation to their population and area.

Share in World Income

With a few exceptions, a subsistence economy prevails in colonial territories [65] and the available estimates of national income in these areas are not strictly comparable with the figures for modern industrial nations. However, even with allowance for understatement, the per capita income of the colonial population appears very low in comparison with the poorest independent countries in Europe and America. The average annual per capita income in the African and Asiatic colonies in 1948 was less than $50, probably not more than $40. The amount was higher in the Caribbean colonies, especially in Puerto Rico and Jamaica, but in the Pacific Islands it was lower.[66] Of the total world income of $549

billion in 1948, hardly more than $9 billion was attributable to the colonies.[67] Thus, non-self-governing territories, which represent about 8 per cent of the world's population, account for about 1.6 per cent of world income. Per capita income in colonial areas is about one fifth the average for the rest of the world.

Share in World Output

A committee of the League of Nations estimated before the outbreak of World War II that the share of colonies in the output of commercially important raw materials was not more than about 3 per cent of the world's total.[68] The rate may seem unexpectedly low, but becomes understandable when one realizes that the total world output of "commercially important raw materials" is dominated by such staple products as wheat, corn, meat, cotton, wool, wood and wood pulp, coal, petroleum and iron ore — all items which are not primarily colonial products. The economic value of overseas possessions to colonial powers is not in the colonies' share in the total value of world output but, rather, in their exports of particular crops and minerals.[69]

The Royal Institute of International Affairs has estimated the share of colonies in the world ouput of two score important products around 1935. (See Table 236.) This survey does not cover India, which was not regarded as a colony at that time, but does include the Netherlands Indies, Ceylon, the Philippines, Korea and Formosa. The list of commodities shown in Table 236 is not complete: it does not include pepper, kapok, cadmium, industrial diamonds and radium, of each of which the colonies supplied more than 80 per cent of world output before World War II.

The emancipation of the Asiatic colonies, espe-

---

64. This statement obviously does not apply to the territories which are listed for administrative and technical reasons as "non-self-governing territories and dependencies" but are not real colonies — for example, Alaska, the Isle of Man and the Channel Islands. Moreover, many colonial areas in Africa and Asia compare favorably with some independent states of the Middle East, such as Afghanistan, Yemen, Saudi Arabia and even Iran and Iraq. (Cf. **8**, pp. 12, 31–32 and *passim*.)

65. **64**, Chapter 13.

66. **64**, Chapter 12, Table 186.

67. This estimate is based on the assumption that the average per capita income for all colonial territories was $45.

68. **61**, p. 172.

69. Investments of foreign capital in colonial territories are often in export industries, the only enterprises that promise a large return. Colonial administration favors this type of colonial economy, and in the nineteenth century this policy was considered the development of the natural resources of colonies. In India, this one-sided economic policy was partly responsible for the famines which plagued the subcontinent in the latter part of the nineteenth century. (See **26**, *passim*.) Dutch administration in the Netherlands Indies avoided this mistake and tried to maintain some equilibrium between production of export crops and rice.

TABLE 236

PRODUCTION IN COLONIES: SHARE IN WORLD OUTPUT OF SELECTED COMMODITIES, AROUND 1935

(Per Cent)

Foodstuffs		Fibers		Other Agricultural Products		Minerals	
Cocoa	74.0	Hemp	6.2	Palm oil	98.8	Tin	56.9
Tea	48.0	Silk	3.1	Rubber	96.1	Phosphate	52.0
Cane sugar	35.9	Cotton	2.5	Copra	64.4	Graphite	46.0
Bananas	30.2	Wool	2.3	Groundnuts	28.5	Copper	21.3
Olive oil	12.9	Jute	0.3	Sesame	8.0	Tungsten	15.6
Soya	11.4			Cottonseed	2.6	Manganese	13.7
Citrus fruits	9.7			Linseed	0.1	Bauxite	13.1
Coffee	7.6					Chromite	12.3
Tobacco	4.8					Nickel	9.0
Wheat	1.9					Gold	6.4
Beef	1.5					Petroleum	3.7
Pork	1.0					Pyrite	3.4
Butter	0.7					Iron ore	3.4
						Zinc	1.5
						Silver	1.3
						Antimony	0.7
						Potash	0.7
						Asbestos	0.5
						Coal	0.3

Source: Based on **50**, tables following p. 22 and Appendix VI.

cially the Netherlands Indies,[70] drastically cut down the colonies' share in world output of such commodities as tin, rubber, graphite, copra, palm oil and tea. However, colonial empires still continue to play an important role in world output of such products as palm oil, cocoa, rubber, dates, bananas, groundnuts, figs, seasame seed, olive oil, coffee; bauxite, tin ore, phosphate rocks, manganese, copper, tungsten ore, chromite, asbestos and cadmium.[71] (See Tables 237 and 238.)

The colonial territories, however, are no longer the only source of so-called colonial products, and their share in production of spices, southern fruits and precious tropical wood is bound to decline with further decolonization.

In terms of the supply of raw materials demanded by industrial countries, the richest colonies today are probably Malaya, the French North African possessions (Algeria, Morocco, Tunisia), the Belgian Congo, the Gold Coast, Nigeria and the British West Indies.

70. The Netherlands Indies had almost a monopoly in production of quinine and pepper and accounted for 75 per cent of the world output of kapok and 20–40 per cent of that of palm oil, copra, rubber and tea. (**25**, p. 24; **49**, p. 290. Cf. **64**, Chapters 16, 17 and 19.)

71. Cf. **7**, pp. 24ff. and pp. 44ff. (data for Africa).

Share in World Trade

Apart from primitive plunder in the early phase of colonization, what the mother country obtains from its overseas possessions must appear in their exports.[72] Foreign trade therefore is one of the most significant measurements of a colony's economic value to the mother country. It is a tricky yardstick, however. Trade between a colony and adjacent areas, important as it may be for the colony itself, seldom brings direct gain to the mother country. On the other hand, in the event of three-cornered exchange, exports from the colony to a third country may be an important item in the mother country's balance of payments. Moreover, the economic significance to the mother country of a colony's foreign trade depends not only on the amount and direction of colonial trade but also on the national origin of the capital engaged in this trade. Under an open-door policy in a colony, the national status of trade capital may be even more important than that of the capital invested in

72. No country has ever succeeded in collecting from its colonies more taxes than the total it spends on their administration, development, policing and military protection.

TABLE 237

PRODUCTION IN COLONIES: SHARE IN WORLD OUTPUT OF SELECTED AGRICULTURAL PRODUCTS, 1948

Product	Percentage of World Output	Principal Producers and Percentage of World Output
Palm oil [a]	76	Nigeria, 43; Belgian Congo, 14; French West Africa, 6
Cocoa	65	Gold Coast, 30; Nigeria, 13; French Cameroons, 6; Ivory Coast, 6
Rubber	52	Malaya, 48
Dates	33	Algeria, 11; Tunisia, 5.5; Belgian Congo, 5.5; Morocco, 4.5
Bananas	25	Tanganyika, 12; Ruanda-Urundi, 6
Groundnuts	19	French West Africa, 7; Nigeria, 6
Figs	15	Algeria, 12; Morocco, 3
Sesame seed	14	Sudan, 8; Belgian Congo, 2
Olive oil	12	Tunisia, 6; Algeria, 3
Coffee	10	Angola, 2.5; French West Africa, 2.5
Sugar cane	7	Puerto Rico, 3
Cotton	6	Uganda, 1.1; Algeria, 0.7
Cottonseed	3	Uganda, 1
Tea	3	Nyasaland, 1.5; Kenya, 1
Tobacco	3	Southern Rhodesia, 1.1; Algeria, 0.7

Source: **11**, 1949, *passim.* Cf. **64**, Chapters 16 and 17.　　　　a. Prewar data. (**49**, p. 290.)

TABLE 238

PRODUCTION IN COLONIES: SHARE IN WORLD OUTPUT OF SELECTED MINERALS, 1948

Product	Percentage of World Output	Principal Producers and Percentage of World Output
Bauxite	51	Surinam, 26; Br. Guiana, 23
Tin ore	45	Malaya, 30; Belgian Congo, 9; Nigeria, 6
Phosphate rock	40	Morocco, 20; Tunisia, 12
Manganese	22	Gold Coast, 16; Morocco, 5
Copper	18	N. Rhodesia, 10; Belgian Congo, 7
Tungsten ore [a]	15	Malaya, 11
Chromite	15	S. Rhodesia, 11; New Caledonia, 3.5
Asbestos	11	S. Rhodesia, 6; Swaziland, 3
Cadmium	10	South West Africa, 9
Gold	7	Gold Coast, 2.2; S. Rhodesia, 2
Antimony	3	Algeria, 2; Morocco, 1
Zinc	1.5	N. Rhodesia, 1.5

Source: **14**, 1948, *passim.* Cf **64**, Chapter 22.　　　　a. Prewar data. (**49**, p. 290.)

local mines and plantations. Indeed, the colonial power may encourage a shift of production from plantations owned by its own citizens to native farmers provided that it controls exports.[73]

73. From the point of view of utilizing natural resources, production of export crops by native farmers serves the same purpose as plantations. From the political point of view, development of native farming and small plantations owned by native landholders is preferable to plantations operated by companies of the mother country. Since the turn of the century, the trend in many tropical

Overdevelopment of plantations and mines working for export, in comparison with production for the domestic market, is characteristic of the colonial economy. Colonial areas therefore have a conspicuously large share in world trade in comparison with their share in world produc-

colonies has been from large plantations to native farming. Large plantations no longer have a monopoly of any important crop except sisal and tea. Even in sugar production, the share of native farmers is increasing in some areas. (**45**, p. 184.)

tion and income. In 1951, for example, exports from sixty-six colonial territories, for which statistics are given in Table 239, exceeded $7.7 billion and imports of these territories totaled $8.4 billion. Total world exports in that year were estimated at $76.6 billion.[74] Thus, colonial areas with a total population of 160 million — less than 7 per cent of the world population — accounted for 10 per cent of the world's total exports and had a higher per capita export than the rest of the world: $48 for colonies, $30 for independent nations. This relationship in per capita export values contrasts with the disparity in national income. In colonial territories, the average value of exports in 1949–51 roughly approximated the national income in these areas.[75] For the rest of the world, exports averaged 10 per cent of national income in this period.

The overdevelopment of export industries is a serious problem for former colonial areas which have become independent. A colony that becomes master of its own destiny is likely to pay more attention to long-neglected domestic industries and native trades than to export industries that were built up and equipped by foreign companies.

A comparison of Ethiopia with Kenya, Uganda, Tanganyika, Nyasaland, and Northern and Southern Rhodesia illustrates this point. All these territories are located in tropical highlands; all are separated from foreign countries by mountains; all need foreign capital to develop natural resources. Ethiopia is probably the most developed of these areas. It differs also from its southern neighbors in being an independent nation while the others are colonies. In 1951, population, imports and exports of these areas compared as follows: [76]

	Population, in Thousands	Imports	Exports
		In Millions of U.S. Dollars	
Ethiopia	20,729	$104.2	$ 44.5
Kenya-Uganda	10,967	212.0	208.6
Tanganyika	7,827	78.4	110.7
Nyasaland	2,401	20.4	16.6
Northern Rhodesia	1,947	99.1	187.8
Southern Rhodesia	2,157	240.0	127.9

74. **10**, 1952, p. 361.

75. Disproportionate development of plantations and mining is characteristic of colonial economies. Mineral products, for example, account for more than 95 per cent of the exports from Northern Rhodesia; more than 50 per cent from the Belgian Congo; 40–50 per cent

Ethiopia had exports of $2.15 per capita, while Nyasaland had $6.91, Tanganyika $14.14, Southern Rhodesia $59.30 and Northern Rhodesia $96.46.[77]

It is difficult to predict what the economic policy of Kenya, Tanganyika and other African colonies would be in the event of the complete emancipation of their native populations from British tutelage. Probably none would fall into an economic isolationism such as that of Ethiopia, but it is unlikely that any would maintain export industries on the present level.

The Direction of Colonial Trade

Trade monopoly was one of the main motives for acquiring colonies in the sixteenth and seventeenth centuries. The principle that overseas possessions are the natural markets of the mother country prevailed until the middle of the nineteenth century. It has been abandoned in more recent times, and colonial powers have begun concluding agreements that ensure one another equal treatment in dealings with colonies. An international open-door agreement was concluded in 1885 for the conventional Congo Basin.[78] The same principle was applied to trust territories after World War II.

Thus colonial territories are no longer closed markets of the mother country. In principle, they are open to international competition in both import and export trade as well as in the development of plantations and mines and other forms of investment.[79] Indeed it is often impossible to ascertain the national origin of foreign capital invested in colonies.[80]

Despite this internationalization of colonial trade, the citizens of the mother country usually enjoy many special privileges. They hold the old concessions obtained in the early phase of colonization — lands and mines, often acquired at a

from Tunisia and Sierra Leone. (**7**, p. 43.) Since mines are operated by foreign companies, only a small part of the value of these products appears in the national income of the respective territories.

76. **9**, 1952, pp. 21–24 and 360–61.

77. Even more striking, Hong Kong, a typical trade colony with a population of nearly 2.3 million, had exports of $346 per capita in 1951 and the Federation of Malaya — a trade, plantation and mining colony with more than 5 million inhabitants — had exports of $372 per capita.

78. See Figure 135, p. 656, and the section on "The Partition of Africa," pp. 655–58.

79. **34**, p. 11.

80. **49**, pp. 279ff.

TABLE 239

FOREIGN TRADE OF COLONIES: VALUE OF IMPORTS AND EXPORTS, 1951

(*Millions of U.S. Dollars*)

Territory	Imports	Exports	Territory	Imports	Exports
United States			France		
Virgin Islands [a]	$ 10	$ 4	Guadeloupe	$ 26	$ 23
Guam [a]	14	1	Martinique	31	21
United Kingdom			Indochina	305	135
British Honduras	9	4	Morocco	456	252
Bermudas	30	3	Algeria	582	386
Bahama Islands	21	3	Tunisia	170	101
Barbados	30	21	Fr. West Africa	351	221
Jamaica	86	50	Togoland	13	15
Leeward Islands [a]	7	7	Cameroons	94	65
Windward Islands	13	8	Fr. Equatorial Africa	164	63
Trinidad & Tobago	129	125	Fr. Somaliland	15	6
British Guiana	49	34	Madagascar	131	77
Falkland Islands	9	10	Réunion	33	26
Malta & Gozo	55	6	French Oceania	11	10
Cyprus	54	43	Belgium		
Aden	141	74	Belgian Congo [c]	308	387
British Borneo	23	37	Netherlands		
Federation of Malaya	1,554	1,985	Neth. Lesser Antilles	767	703
Hong Kong	856	781	Surinam	24	21
Gambia	11	9	Denmark		
Sierra Leone	23	28	Greenland [a]	4	2
Gold Coast	177	232	Faeroes	10	11
Nigeria	237	365	Portugal		
Kenya & Uganda	212	209	Port. India [a]	16	2
Somaliland	5	3	Macao [b]	41	2
Tanganyika	78	111	Port. Guinea	6	6
Zanzibar & Pemba	14	17	Angola	76	111
Nyasaland	20	17	Cape Verde Islands	9	8
Northern Rhodesia	99	188	Mozambique	71	44
Southern Rhodesia	240	128	Spain		
Mauritius	43	50	Canary Islands	137	125
Eritrea [b] (military government)	12	8	Sp. Morocco [a]	36	33
Fiji Islands	24	15	Ceuta	30	16
Union of South Africa			Melilla	11	7
South West Africa	51	81	Italy		
Australia			Somaliland	5	3
Papua & Norfolk Island	10	4	Condominium		
New Guinea [a]	12	10	Sudan	121	184

Source: **9**, 1952, pp. 344–67.

a. 1950.
b. 1949.

c. Includes Ruanda-Urundi.

very low price. Their language is used in colonial administration and the courts. They have easier access to sources of economic information. In addition, the colonial system of taxes, tariffs, public roads and the like usually favors the interests of the mother country.

On the whole, the open-door policy has not weakened the economic ties between colonial territories and the mother country: British colonies are a part of the British economic bloc; the French "overseas departments and territories" belong economically to the French Union; the "outlying territories" of the United States are economically tied to that nation, as are the Belgian Congo and Portuguese colonies in Africa to their European motherlands.

In 1938 France controlled nearly two thirds of the imports and exports of its colonies. Belgium supplied more than two thirds the imports of its colonial possessions and absorbed more than half their exports — very high rates when one considers the international status of the Belgian Congo. Portugal's ties with its colonies were less close. Great Britain had a comparatively small share in the imports and exports of its colonies, slightly more than 25 per cent. The figures for 1938 for these countries are as follows (in millions of U.S. dollars):

		Share of Mother Country	
	Total		*Percentage*
Colonies	*Amount*	*Amount*	*of Total*
British			
Imports	$808	$225	27.8
Exports	778	204	26.2
French			
Imports	535	351	65.6
Exports	377	234	62.1
Belgian			
Imports	75	51	68.0
Exports	26	14	53.8
Portuguese			
Imports	28	10	35.7
Exports	50	7	14.0

Great Britain's comparatively small relative share in the foreign trade of its colonial territories is due to the fact that its colonial possessions include Malaya and Hong Kong, which trade intensively with all Asia. When these two colonies are segregated from other British overseas possessions, the figures for 1938 are as follows (in millions of U.S. dollars):

		Share of Mother Country	
	Total		*Percentage*
Colonies	*Amount*	*Amount*	*of Total*
Malaya and Hong Kong			
Imports	$400	$ 53	13.2
Exports	461	73	15.8
Other British colonies			
Imports	408	172	42.1
Exports	317	131	41.3

Moreover, the share of the British Commonwealth and Empire in the imports and exports of each British colony is considerably larger than that of Great Britain alone.

Despite the prevalence of the open-door policy in modern colonies, their foreign trade continues to be generally dominated by the mother country. (See Tables 240 and 241.)

THE MILITARY SIGNIFICANCE OF COLONIES

Strategic and military considerations have always been highly significant in shaping colonial policy. From the military standpoint, a colony is likely to be both an asset to, and a liability of, the mother country.

COLONIES AS MILITARY ASSETS

A colony is a military asset to the colonial power as a source of manpower and raw materials and occasionally as a strategic point.

Manpower

In World War I France and Great Britain made wide use of armed forces recruited in colonies. French-African troops fought in France on the German front. Indian troops were brought to France for a short time but were used mainly against the Turks in the Middle East. British-African troops participated in operations against the Germans and their colonial troops in East and West Africa.[81] During World War II, difficulties of transportation prevented the use of colonial troops in the European theater, but they played an important role in the resistance to Japanese aggression in the Far East.

The experience of the two wars suggests that colonial manpower cannot be inducted into the armed forces at the same or approximately the same rate as in the mother country. It is possible to mobilize colonial subjects on a smaller scale, but only a country controlling the sea can count on using them in the theater where they are needed.

Both French and British laws permit use of native levies in certain circumstances for service outside the colony. This course is forbidden in the trust territories except French Togo and the Cameroons.

It is possible that the psychological effect of the appearance of colonial troops on the battle front is greater than the material aid they bring

---

81. **47**, p. 29.

TABLE 240

FOREIGN TRADE OF COLONIES: VALUE OF IMPORTS OF SELECTED AREAS, BY PROVENANCE, 1938

(Millions of U.S. Dollars)

Colonial Power and Colony	World	Provenance of Imports						
		Continents				Countries		
		America	Europe	Africa	Asia and Oceania	Great Britain	France	United States
Great Britain								
Nyasaland, South-West Africa	$ 18	$ 1	$ 13	$ 4	—	$ 6	$ 1	$ 1
Northern and Southern Rhodesia	72	4	56	12	—	29	2	3
Sudan	27	1	21	5	$ 1	16	—	1
Br. East Africa	92	7	44	13	28	34	4	5
Br. West Africa	115	14	98	2	—	45	5	12
Br. West Indies	84	29	55	—	—	48	1	7
Malaya	347	128	107	2	110	48	16	116
Hong Kong	53	6	7	1	39	5	—	3
France								
Algeria, Tunisia	224	5	211	7	3	22	164	4
Fr. Morocco	58	1	48	2	2	3	25	1
Fr. Equatorial and West Africa	78	1	75	2	—	2	59	1
Other Fr. Africa	41	3	32	3	3	2	29	3
Guadeloupe, Martinique	20	—	20	—	—	—	20	—
Fr. Indochina	114	8	60	8	38	2	54	7
Belgium								
Congo [a]	75	2	72	1	—	—	—	2
Portugal								
Angola and Mozambique	28	1	23	3	1	—	1	1
Oceania	29	3	15	—	11	8	5	1

Source: **2**, pp. 112–71.　　　　　　　　　　　　　a. Includes Ruanda-Urundi.

to the mother country. The sight of the colonial soldiers and workers brought to France during World War I may have contributed to morale, reminding the French people that in addition to their own forty million, France could rely on a population half again as large in its overseas departments and territories. If this was the impression of the man in the street in hard-pressed France, it was not wholly warranted: a large part of the native troops came from Algeria, a region close to France and more assimilated than other colonies. Manpower from the more remote colonial possessions was not and could not be extensively utilized for military service.

Sources of Raw Materials

The significance of colonies as a source of raw materials during a war is illustrated by the flow of strategic materials from Africa to France during World War I.[82] Germany's experience in that war, however, was very different. The Reich was cut off from its colonies at the very beginning and later lost them. During World War II, the Allies were in a similar position: their colonies in Asia were overrun by the enemy and difficult logistic problems permitted only partial use of the resources of African colonies. On the other hand, when strategic materials were available within the area controlled by the sea and air power of the Allies, as in Middle and South America, it did not make much difference whether such materials were located in colonial territories or independent countries.

82. **51**, pp. 17–18.

TABLE 241

FOREIGN TRADE OF COLONIES: VALUE OF EXPORTS OF SELECTED AREAS, BY DESTINATION, 1938

(Millions of U.S. Dollars)

| | | Destination of Exports | | | | | | |
| | | Continents | | | | Countries | | |
Colonial Power and Colony	World	America	Europe	Africa	Asia and Oceania	Great Britain	France	United States
Great Britain								
Nyasaland, South-West Africa	$ 11	—	$ 3	$ 8	—	$ 2	—	—
Northern and Southern Rhodesia	58	$ 5	25	28	—	24	—	$ 3
Sudan	21	1	6	7	$ 7	6	—	1
Br. East Africa	69	4	31	13	21	21	$ 1	2
Br. West Africa	68	6	57	3	2	46	2	5
Br. West Indies	90	46	37	—	7	32	—	23
Malaya	297	13	68	2	214	54	1	10
Hong Kong	164	23	31	—	110	19	7	21
France								
Algeria, Tunisia	179	9	155	12	3	7	137	5
Fr. Morocco	49	4	36	1	8	2	20	2
Fr. Equatorial and West Africa	54	10	35	3	4	4	24	3
Other Fr. Africa	24	1	16	2	5	—	16	1
Guadeloupe, Martinique	12	3	9	—	—	—	10	2
Fr. Indochina	59	3	32	2	22	2	27	3
Belgium								
Congo [a]	26	2	19	3	2	2	—	2
Portugal								
Angola and Mozambique	55	11	26	7	11	9	—	7
Oceania	28	2	6	—	20	3	2	2

Source: **2,** pp. 112–71.　　　　　　　　　　a. Includes Ruanda-Urundi.

In the event of a new world war with extensive use of air power and atomic bombs, the role of colonies as suppliers of strategic materials is likely to be still more limited; the belligerents will appropriate strategic materials wherever they can find them.

Strategic Points

Strategic considerations played an important role in the selection of a site for a fort, trading post or settlement in early colonial times, when "the days of settled peace between maritime nations were few and far between." [83] It was important to be able to defend the colony. The site of a settlement was often chosen so as to pro-

vide a station for the fleet protecting the route between the colony, the mother country, and its other colonial possessions.

The strategic importance of certain points in colonies was proved during World War II, especially in the course of military operations in Africa. The Royal Institute of International Affairs lists the principal strategic points in the French colonial empire, as follows:

Bizerte
Dakar, the only great port in West Africa
Douala, a sea and river port in the Cameroons
Port Gentil, the best natural harbor in French Equatorial Africa
Djibouti
Diégo-Suarez, in northern Madagascar

83. **41,** p. 28.

Saigon, Camranh Bay and Haiphong, ports in the Far East

Fort-de-France and Papeete on the Atlantic-Panama-Pacific route

Nouméa, in New Caledonia

The list of strategic points in the British colonial empire is much longer. The security and very existence of the Commonwealth depend on freedom of the sea lanes that connect its parts with one another and Great Britain. Since the Commonwealth is dispersed over five continents, its communication lines cross all seven oceans. The principal lanes which Great Britain endeavors to secure are five: one to North America; two to the Far East (one, rounding the Cape of Good Hope; the other, through the Mediterranean and Suez Canal); and two to the Pacific (one, through the Panama Canal; the other, across the Indian Ocean).[84] Almost all colonies located along these lanes are of strategic significance as links between the members of the Commonwealth; most of the other colonies are integrated in the general defense system. Thus Tanganyika is considered the keystone in the defense of East Africa; Uganda and Kenya are links between Tanganyika and the strategic lane of the Mediterranean-Red Sea, and so on.

All external possessions of the United States are forward bastions of its defense system: Alaska (in combination with Canada) protects its northern border; Puerto Rico, the Virgin Islands and the Panama Canal Zone cover the Isthmus of Panama — the vital link between naval forces in the Atlantic and Pacific; Guam, Hawaii and the Pacific Islands are the first line of defense of the Pacific coast.

Although the strategic value of colonies is indisputable, it may be doubted whether their value, in the event of a new war, would depend on domination by the mother country of the respective areas. Indeed, during a major war, no colonial power can maintain control over a colonial territory against the resolute opposition of the native inhabitants. The strategic value of a colony is premised on its loyalty to the mother country, a loyalty that cannot be imposed during the war but must have been built up and earned in peacetime. If the local population is friendly toward the mother country, the relationship may be consolidated and sustained by an arrangement of equals — by some form of treaty between independent and sovereign parties; by a union (as between the members of the British Commonwealth); or by the political assimilation of the colony by the motherland (as in the relations between the United States and Hawaii).

Africa's Role

Since Africa now comprises most of the world's colonial empires, the strategic significance of colonies depends largely on the role of that continent in global strategy.

Africa played a minor role in World War I, but became the background for important events in the last war. Early in that war, after the collapse of the French defense, some farsighted French and British statesmen thought of removing the French government and troops to North Africa, believing that the French North African possessions could be converted into a new rallying point of the republic.[85]

D. H. Cole, in the most recent edition of his classic survey of imperial military geography, describes the military significance of Africa as follows:

Ports, railways and roads, the development of essential mineral resources, such as copper in Rhodesia, coal and tin in Nigeria, the vastly increased production of foodstuffs such as vegetable oils are obviously important in a strategic sense. Africa with its potential resources is becoming increasingly important as a supply base for the Western Powers; on its position, resources, communications, and manpower the defense of the Commonwealth and the Western Powers and the Mediterranean and Middle East areas may depend in no small degree in the future. It is, therefore, important that economic development is not hamstrung by political unrest, disruptive nationalist movements or communist infiltration.[86]

COLONIES AS A MILITARY LIABILITY

While contributing to the military potential, colonial possessions may also prove to be military liabilities of the colonial power, stretching its commitments and restricting its freedom of decision and action.

Overseas possessions have been lost by mother countries as easily as they were acquired. Possession of a colony implies a continuing commitment of the colonial power to protect it against aggression, and a nation unable to de-

---

84. **49**, pp. 29–30.

85. **23**, pp. 179, 201, 206ff.
86. **24**, pp. 19–20.

fend its overseas possessions is bound to lose them.

Napoleon's decision to sell Louisiana to the United States was based largely on his reluctance to carry out commitments that would have tied up military forces needed elsewhere.

Bismarck, for similar reasons, opposed any colonial entanglement of Germany. "I do not want colonies at all," he declared. "Their only use is to provide sinecures. That is all England at present gets out of her colonies, and Spain too. And as for us Germans, colonies would be exactly like the silks and sables of the Polish nobleman who has no shirt to wear under them." The vehemence of his language shows clearly that he was thinking of the military implications of colonial policy rather than of its impact on the national economy, a problem not so close to his heart.[87]

Colonial wars were a serious drain on the manpower and economic and financial resources of Spain and Portugal in the seventeenth and eighteenth centuries; of Great Britain in the eighteenth and nineteenth centuries; and of France in the latter part of the nineteenth and the first part of the twentieth. It is an open question whether the native divisions which appeared on the battlefields of Europe during World War I were worth the price in manpower and war material that the colonial powers had paid for their overseas empires.

Colonies have also been a military liability in another sense. Since the sixteenth century, colonial disputes have caused continual international conflicts. Great Britain and France have clashed in America, Africa and Asia. The attempt to prevent the emancipation of Cuba drove Spain into a disastrous war with the United States. Russia's attempt to "colonize" Korea (e.g., the forest concessions of Besobrasoff on the Yalu river) precipitated the Russo-Japanese war. The Anglo-French clash in the African desert (the Fashoda Incident) brought the two countries to the verge of war. The South African war, purely colonial, strained the relations of Great Britain and Germany to the utmost. Historians of World War I stress colonial quarrels as contributing largely to the causes of that war.[88]

On the chessboard of world politics, colonies often become a complicating factor, pressing the colonial power into a position which it would have liked to avoid.

The role of air forces in modern warfare has increased the military value of colonial territories but likewise the liability of the mother country. In fact, any colonial air base may fall into the hands of enemies unless it is protected against attack from the sea, land and air.

It can be argued that the military value of a colonial territory does not depend on its political status as a colony. The mother country may give such a territory self-government, recognize its independence, and use its bases and stations with the consent of its government on the basis of a treaty of friendship and mutual assistance. From the military point of view, such an arrangement would eliminate the necessity of policing the colony, but it would not free the mother country from a commitment to protect the territory in the event of war.

In 1942, for example, the British were faced with the difficult task of defending Singapore as a strategic point of their colonial empire in the Indian Ocean. Their task would not have been very different if Singapore had then been the port of a sovereign Malayan republic and the British navy had been using its facilities on a treaty basis.

Do Colonies Pay?

The question whether colonies are worth the price the mother country pays for them is very old, though not quite as old as modern colonization. It did not arise in the sixteenth century, when the discoverers of new worlds and the adventurous empire builders brought gold, spices and chained captives to their kings and sponsors: colonies then were easy to acquire and cheap to maintain.

As time went on, the maintenance of colonies became increasingly expensive and the profits expected from overseas possessions did not materialize. People began to wonder whether, after all, the acquisition of colonies had been good business.

THE CONTROVERSY

The grand debate about the value of colonies

---

87. **20**, Vol. 1, p. 522. Later, after the military supremacy of Germany was firmly established in continental Europe, Bismarck reversed his opinion on colonies and succeeded in acquiring sizable slices of Africa for Germany.

88. **49**, p. 26.

started in Great Britain in the middle of the eighteenth century and is still going on. Originally, it focused on the American colonies, which were — using the modern classification — typical settlement and trade colonies from the British viewpoint.

Adam Smith

The sharpest criticism of the colonial system was voiced by Adam Smith. To him, overseas colonies were a senseless waste of money. His *Inquiry into the Nature and Causes of the Wealth of Nations* ends with an eloquent peroration:

> The rulers of Great Britain have, for more than a century past, amused the people with the imagination that they possessed a great empire on the west side of the Atlantic. This empire, however, has hitherto existed in imagination only. It has hitherto been, not an empire, but the project of an empire; not a gold mine, but the project of a gold mine; a project which has cost, which continues to cost, and which, if pursued in the same way as it has been hitherto, is likely to cost immense expense, without being likely to bring any profit; for the effects of the monoply of the colony trade . . . are, to the great body of the people, mere loss instead of profit. It is surely now time that our rulers should either realize the golden dream . . . or that they should awake from it themselves, and endeavour to awaken the people. . . . If any of the provinces of the British empire cannot be made to contribute toward the support of the whole empire, it is surely time that Great Britain should free herself from the expense of defending these provinces in time of war, and . . . endeavour to accommodate her future views and designs to the real mediocrity of her circumstances.[89]

Adam Smith's argument was essentially financial, but it rested on his conviction of the economic uselessness of colonies as "a sort of splendid and showy equipage of the empire." His argument did not apply to exploitation colonies, such as those of Spain and Portugal in Middle and South America. It was directed against the conversion of overseas settlements into a closed market for British manufacturers, which was the central objective of British colonial policy,[90] and

his criticism amounted at that time to condemning the policy of colonial trade.

The liberal school in economic science remained true to Adam Smith's ideas on colonial policy. In 1793 Jeremy Bentham published a pamphlet under the title *Emancipate Your Colonies*. He pleaded:

> Give up your colonies, because you have no right to govern them, because they had rather not be governed by you, because it is against their interest to be governed by you, *because you get nothing by governing them,* because you cannot keep them, *because the expense of trying to keep them would be ruinous,* because your constitution would suffer by keeping them. . . .[91]

Nineteenth Century Liberalism

The loss of the American colonies left the British public disillusioned. When the foundations of Britain's second colonial empire were being laid in India, few people were interested in colonial expansion.

In the middle of the nineteenth century, however, the attitude of the liberal school in Great Britain toward colonial expansion began to change. Many of the British were opposed to the policy of the East India Company, but colonial expansion did not look like bad business to the average man. Criticism was directed against certain aspects of colonial policy rather than the colonial system as such. The colonial reform demanded by liberal statesmen from Richard Cobden to William Gladstone envisaged a gradual emancipation of colonies rather than immediate abandonment of overseas possessions.[92]

In the middle of the nineteenth century and even later, the colonial problem was primarily a British problem. Of the world's colonial population of close to 300 million, 250 million were in Britain's overseas possessions (including India), 25 million were in the Netherlands Indies, and more than 20 million were scattered among French, Spanish and Portuguese colonies. Germany had no colonies whatsoever, and the only "possession" of the United States was sparsely populated Alaska. (See Table 235.) The prevailing opinion among British statesmen and scholars was that colonies pay, but not very much.

---

89. **55**, p. 431.

90. In this respect the British government followed the mercantilist theory, which then prevailed in Great Britain and continental Europe. The charter of the Dutch East India Company contained a provision forbidding colonists to make any woolen, linen or cotton clothes or weave any other stuffs on pain of being banished from

the colony. (**61**, p. 163.) The British did not go to quite this length in their American colonies.

91. Quoted in **35**, p. 38. Italics added.

92. **35**, pp. 33ff.; **48**, pp. 63–64.

The New Imperialism

The situation changed in the 1880's, when spokesmen in favor of colonialism appeared on the scene — Joseph Chamberlain in Great Britain, Jules Ferry in France and Bismarck, who had become the promoter of colonial expansion for Germany. The origins of the new imperialism in Europe are not very clear.[93] It is fairly certain, however, that a change in the economic value of colonies, in terms of both current and anticipated gains for the mother country, was among the decisive factors. Colonialism became respectable and glamorous because colonies became, or promised to become, profitable.

That was when the center of colonial problems shifted to Africa. The new colonies seemed to promise profits, prestige and power, and it was so easy to acquire them! Africa, which for all practical purposes had been a coast line with a narrow strip of land along it, suddenly emerged as a continent with inexhaustible stores of wealth. As in the sixteenth century, after the discovery of the New World, a race for participating in the newly discovered riches developed. There was little doubt that the new colonies would pay! The question was, who would get there first?

It is noteworthy that the ideology of the new imperialism was essentially the same in Great Britain, France and Germany — the three countries that led in the partition of Africa. All three laid emphasis on the mission of the white race as the bearer of a higher civilization among benighted natives.

The Socialist Opposition

The socialists voiced the strongest opposition to colonialism at that time. Without denying that colonies would pay, they emphasized that all the gains derived from the exploitation of colonies would be appropriated by the rich, while the poor would foot the bill.

The best criticism of colonial expansion, from this point of view, was presented by J. A. Hobson.[94] Hobson tried to show that colonies bring profits to certain groups of capitalists but not to the nation as a whole. He pictured the colonial expansion sought by the captains of industry and finance as an attempt to offset the overproduction which resulted from underconsumption.

The colonial system appeared to him "clearly condemned as a business policy, in that at enormous expense it has procured a small, bad, unsafe increase of markets, and has jeopardized the entire wealth of the [British] nation in arousing the strong resentment of other nations." This system, he thought, was possible only because "the business interests of the nation as a whole are subordinated to those of certain sectional interests that usurp control of the national resources and use them for their private gain." [95]

Hobson's analysis of imperialism, however, left the controversy unsettled in Great Britain as well as in other countries. Aside from the distribution of the social product among different population groups, it was fairly obvious that such countries as Great Britain, France, the Netherlands and Belgium were obtaining sizable dividends from their colonial empires.

THE EXPERIENCE

Historical experience fails to give a yes-or-no answer to the question of the ultimate economic value of colonies.

Colonies did not stimulate economic progress in Spain and Portugal in the sixteenth and seventeenth centuries; in the period of full expansion of their colonial empires, both countries were losing ground politically and economically. Nor did the loss of the American colonies appreciably affect economic progress in Great Britain. The United States reached its high level of prosperity with negligible colonial possessions. The economic rise of Germany was not affected by the acquisition and loss of colonies.

On the other hand, most economists believe that colonial business — trade, investment, plantations and mining — has contributed to the national income of Great Britain, France, Belgium and the Netherlands. But the fundamental question remains: did the colonies bring these countries more gain than loss or were gains from certain colonies in certain years offset by losses in other colonies in other years?

Three Criteria

In appraising the value of colonies for mother countries, three criteria are frequently used. A colony is rated as an outlet for overpopulation, as a source of raw materials and as a market for exports and capital investment.

---

93. **35**, pp. 64ff.
94. See **36**.

95. **36**, p. 51.

The first test yields a negative result. It is doubtful whether emigration has ever relieved the pressure of overpopulation in a country. Colonies have absorbed only a very small part of emigration from colonial powers — hardly more than 3–4 per cent — and it is obvious that their role as a safety valve for overpopulation has been negligible.

The results of the raw-material and market tests appear positive but not wholly conclusive. Even under an open-door colonial policy, a colonial power has definite advantages in selling its products, buying raw materials and investing capital in colonies. More important is the flow of capital gains to the inhabitants of the colonial power. As a rule, a large part of these gains flows back to the mother country and is spent there, stimulating domestic industries.

This consideration, however, does not solve the problem. Even when we recognize the advantages and refrain from appraising them from the point of view of distribution among different social groups, there still remains the question of the price the colonial power pays for the advantages the colony offers its businessmen.

The Balance Sheet

The Royal Institute of International Affairs has developed a balance sheet in which the advantages a colony offers are set against its price: [96]

On the *credit* side:

1. Interest on the capital invested in the colony by the metropolitan country.

2. Benefits to consumers in the metropolitan country accruing from the low cost of production in the colony.

3. Benefits to producers in the metropolitan country accruing from the trade with the colony.

4. Payments of the colony to the metropolitan country for defense, administration, family remittances and the like.

On the *debit* side:

1. Losses of metropolitan investors on their investments in the colony.

2. Losses of traders and others doing business with the colony.

3. Subsidies, grants and subventions made by the metropolitan country or its citizens to the colony or its inhabitants.

4. The cost of acquiring the colony.

Furthermore, it can be argued that the contribution of a colony to the well-being of the metropolitan country is dubious if the capital invested in the colony yields a profit that could be obtained by investment in domestic business or in foreign countries. The colony's net return to the metropolitan country should be measured by the excess of profits and wages earned by metropolitan capital and labor in the colony over the profits and wages they could have earned elsewhere — at home, in foreign countries or foreign colonies.

When the economic return from colonies is measured in this way, it appears that only a few, such as the Netherlands Indies, the Belgian Congo, Malaya and perhaps India in certain periods, have brought substantial profits to the metropolitan countries. The net gains from most colonies have been uncertain and probably not very large in comparison with the role colonies have played in world politics.[97]

Colonial Policy

The dual character of colonization — settlement of emigrants from the mother country on foreign soil and domination over native population — raises two kinds of problems, one in settlement colonies, the other in exploitation colonies.

The controversy about the relationship between the mother country and the colonies established by its subjects was solved in the eighteenth century by the rebellion of the American colonies. In the nineteenth century, Great Britain was the only power with substantial numbers of "white" colonists, and its general policy was to establish a union with them, based on equality and recognition of common economic and political interests. More than a century elapsed before the present form of the British Commonwealth was evolved and Great Britain could offer its former exploitation colonies similar arrangements.

The core of the present colonial problem is in the relationship between colonial powers and their exploitation colonies.

---

96. **49**, pp. 43–44.

97. After assembling all the kinds of statistical data that can be used to determine the balance of gains and losses in colonial empires, the Royal Institute does not venture even a tentative answer to the question whether colonies pay. Stressing the open-door policy now prevailing in colonies, it suggests that the advantages accruing from the possession of colonies are becoming more and more problematic.

Colonies as Booty

The original attitude of European conquerors and colonizers to the new overseas possessions was well expressed by Sir George Peckham. In his eyes the spiritual salvation of the heathen was more than adequate payment for all the earthly belongings of which the white man robbed them. He wrote:

It shall fall out in proofe that the savages shall hereby have just cause to bless the houre when this enterprize was undertaken. First and chiefly, in respect of the most happy . . . tidings of the most glorious Gospel of our Savior Jesus Christ, whereby they may be brought from falsehood to trueth, from darkness to light. . . . And if in respect of all the commodities they can yield us (were they many more) that they should but receive this onely benefit of Christianity, they were more than fully recompenced.[98]

Such was the philosophy of colonial conquests of the sixteenth and seventeenth centuries. Not ecclesiastic but more cynical was the attitude of such empire builders as Clive in the eighteenth century and Leopold II in the nineteenth.

It would be erroneous to think that this philosophy left the natives without protection. Complaints of the natives — and occasionally of the Church — against abuses of Spanish colonial administration compelled the government to send investigating commissions to the New World. Columbus and his brother were sent back to Spain in chains under accusation of excessive cruelty toward the natives, an accusation their enemies did not substantiate. However, the protection occasionally accorded to the natives by colonial powers at that time was based on the white man's own moral code rather than on recognition of the rights of colonial peoples.

A French author describes this phase of colonial policy as follows:

When the Great Powers found themselves face to face with very different populations which we call native populations — some primitive, some deriving from a highly developed and ancient source — different policies were adopted. . . . First there is extermination, as in Tasmania, where we are shown the skull of the last native of the exterminated race. The second method of procedure has been crowding into reserves. . . . The third solution has been enslavement and the establishment of a human category destined to serve as labour for those in command.[99]

There have been various nuances in the application of these policies, but most students of colonial history agree that this approach to colonial problems was characteristic of the period of the slave trade and that some of its features reappeared in the nineteenth century after the partition of Africa. Criticism of this policy in the middle of the nineteenth century was based partly on humanitarian and political considerations, partly on doubt whether the policy was very successful. The opposition faded away after the great powers had learned that they could help themselves to generous portions of the Dark Continent.

The White Man's Burden

We do not know exactly when and where this term was invented, but it was made famous by the bard of British neo-imperialism, Rudyard Kipling:

Take up the White Man's burden —
    Send forth the best ye breed —
Go bind your sons to exile
    To serve your captives' need;
To wait in heavy harness,
    On fluttered folk and wild —
Your new-caught, sullen peoples,
    Half-devil and half-child.

Take up the White Man's burden —
    And reap his old reward:
The blame of those ye better,
    The hate of those ye guard —
The cry of hosts ye humour
    (Ah, slowly!) toward the light: —
"Why brought ye us from bondage,
    Our loved Egyptian night?"

The philosophy of the white man's burden ignores such trivial matters as trade, plantations and mines. Colonial peoples are the captives, the new-caught savages, half-devils and half-children. No question is raised about the right of the white man to catch them, but it is his burden to rule over his captives as their benevolent master. Joseph Chamberlain thus elaborated Kipling's thesis:

We have to carry civilization, British justice, British law, religion and Christianity, to millions and millions, to people who until our advent had lived in ignorance, in bitter conflict, and whose territories have fallen to us to develop. That is our duty. It is our great duty. It removes altogether from us the reproach of selfishness. . . .[100]

---

98. *A True Report of the Late Discoveries* (1583), quoted in **35**, p. 21.
99. **47**, p. 113.

---

100. Quoted in **57**, p. 79.

To some extent Chamberlain restated the philosophy of Sir George Peckham: the justification
for possession and exploitation of colonies lies in
the *civilization* the colonial administration brings
to the natives. But the emphasis was on the obligations of colonial powers toward the indigenous
population and neo-imperialism evolved toward
the concept of the "dual mandate" of colonial
powers: "as trustees to civilization for the adequate development of their resources, and as
trustees for the welfare of native races." [101] Too
often, however, the colonial powers put their
responsibility for the development of colonial
resources above their responsibilities for the well-
being of the natives. The neo-imperialism of the
latter part of the nineteenth century was characterized by reckless exploitation of colored labor
by white capital.[102] The allegedly sovereign
kingdom of the Congo — but actually the private
domain of the Belgian king — was the scene of
the worst abuses of this type of colonialism.[103]

Growth of Nationalism in Colonies

Under these conditions, the philosophy of the
white man's burden could not impress colonial
peoples as sincere and generous. Although Kipling invited the British to accept as a part of the
burden "the hate of those ye guard," the rising
hate of the natives against colonial powers threatened to make colonies untenable. Nationalist
movements in the colonies have risen not because of increasing colonial exploitation but in
part because of progress in education and self-
government. As time went on, a small group
of native intellectuals began to develop teachers,
officials, lawyers, journalists. Among them have
been men of the stature of Gandhi, thinkers and
statesmen second to none among the leaders of
the master race. These native intellectuals looked
with scorn and contempt on the conquerors who
treated their countrymen as half-devils and half-
children.

By the turn of the century, when the second
colonial empire reached the peak of expansion,
the system was nearing its end. The trend could
not be stopped or reversed. It was accelerated by
the advent of industrialization in colonial territories and especially by World War I.

The Turning Point

From the point of view of colonial peoples,
the war was a clash among the white masters.
The natives saw their proud rulers in a new
light — weak and frightened. They learned that
white armies could be destroyed. This was a
mortal blow to the prestige of the white man.
The grip of colonial powers over the native
populations was weakened and the nationalism
of colonial peoples gained new force. Insurrec-
tions in French North Africa had the same
origin as the spreading noncooperation movement in India.

The system of mandates introduced by the
League of Nations was another important step
toward liquidation of the colonial system. The
League of Nations had no jurisdiction over colonial possessions of individual powers, but was
charged with general supervision over mandated territories. A colonial power, however,
could not handle the population in its old colonies with less consideration than it showed toward the natives in mandated territories.

The activities of the International Labor Office
were a contributing factor in the evolution of
social relations in colonial territories in interwar
years. In many colonial areas, this was an era
of reforms aimed at improvement of living conditions, elimination of abuses in local administration and promotion of self-government.

The change of policy in the British colonies
found expression in the White Paper of 1923
and the report of the Parliamentary East Africa
Commission in 1925. The new French policy
was announced in the report of the Commission
on Closer Union of the Dependencies of Eastern
and Central Africa. At the same time comprehensive reforms were enacted in Portuguese colonies, in the Belgian Congo and in the Netherlands Indies.[104]

Recent Colonial Policies

The Royal Institute of International Affairs
classifies the aims of colonial policies of various
powers in different territories before the outbreak of World War II as follows:

(a) Maintaining the colony in perpetual economic
subordination to the metropolitan country, but providing at the same time for social and other services
for the well-being of the people.

101. **18**, pp. 151ff.
102. See **43**, Chapters 4 and 24.
103. **62**, Chapter 2.

104. **49**, pp. 114–15.

(b) The policy known as the "dual mandate" (with more emphasis on the interests of colonial peoples).

(c) The gradual ending of the colonial system by education of the people in self-government and by development of the resources of the territory, thus preparing them for eventual liberation from tutelage.

(d) The ending of the colonial system by incorporation of colonial territories within the boundaries of the metropolitan country, accompanied by the grant of rights and privileges for the native population equal to those enjoyed by other citizens of that country.[105]

No country, however, has openly recognized the policy described under (a) as its aim. In the 1930's the dual-mandate policy was the most conservative version of colonial policy openly proclaimed and defended by colonial powers. The policy of Great Britain, effected in a series of official acts, aimed at the gradual emancipation of colonies; the policy officially announced by the French envisaged the incorporation of colonial territories — originally described as "assimilation" and later labeled "association"; the colonial policy of the United States is shown in its withdrawal from the Philippines and the prospect of statehood for Hawaii. Practically, however, the policy of gradual emancipation and assimilation of colonies does not exclude a tendency toward continued white supremacy in some former colonial areas.

The Charter of the United Nations has brought more uniformity into colonial policies. Article 73 of the Charter states that colonial relationships are a strictly temporary status in the territories *whose peoples have not yet attained a full measure of self-government.* This language condemns both perpetual exploitation and a perpetual dual-mandate policy. The Charter recognizes colonies only as a temporary trust and obligates member nations to develop self-government in colonial territories, implying their eventual emancipation.[106] It fails to offer guidance, however, on what should be done after former colonies become masters of their destiny.

Recent developments suggest three possible courses of events:

1. The former colony, protectorate or trust territory may become completely independent of the power that has exercised control over it.

2. The former colony may join the former mother country in a union based on independence and equality.

3. The former colony may become an integral part of the former mother country, with the same rights and obligations as its other provinces and departments.

The first course is exemplified by the emancipation of the Philippines and Burma; the second, by India, Pakistan and Ceylon; the third is envisaged for Hawaii and is proclaimed officially by the French constitution of 1946.[107]

These are three ways of terminating colonial relations. The choice is very important for both colonial powers and colonial areas. The question is no longer whether the colonial system will be maintained but when and how it will be liquidated.

The Economic Development of Colonial Areas

The new trend in colonial policy has affected the economic development of colonial territories. Colonial powers have realized that the future of their colonial empires depends on their ability to persuade colonial peoples that a union with the mother country is in their interest. Hence the mushrooming plans for development. Such plans — some for two or three years, others for five years and even ten — are now in operation in almost all colonial territories. Some are very modest in scope, others more ambitious. Many have been revived and extended repeatedly. Most are being developed by local self-government councils working with representatives of the colonial administration and technical experts from the mother country. They are financed by

---

105. **49**, pp. 116–17.
106. See pp. 642–43.

107. Cf. **48**, *passim.* According to the constitution of 1946, the French Union consists of 90 departments of Metropolitan France; 7 overseas departments (3 in the Government General of Algeria, Martinique, Guadeloupe, Réunion and French Guiana); 9 overseas territories, including French West Africa and French Equatorial Africa with their administrative subdivisions; 2 territories under trusteeship (Cameroons and Togoland); 3 areas described as associated states (Viet-Nam, Cambodia and Laos); 2 protectorates (Morocco and Tunisia); and an Anglo-French condominium (New Hebrides). Administratively, the whole system is strictly centralized, and theoretically it offers each colonial area the possibility of becoming in due time a part of France proper, as an overseas department. This administrative system fails, however, to assure the natives in overseas territories equal rights with the white settlers. Even when an area rises to the status of an overseas department, with full representation in the national assembly, the natives may remain, in Kipling's words, in the position of "new-caught, sullen peoples, half-devil and half-child."

TABLE 242

DEVELOPMENT PLANS: TEN-YEAR INVESTMENT PLANS
FOR 21 BRITISH COLONIES, BY SOURCE OF
FINANCING, 1948–49

(Millions of Pounds)

Colony	Total	Source of Financing		
		Colonial Develop- ment and Welfare	Loans	Local Resources
Total	£199.4	£64.2	£63.9	£71.3
Nigeria	55.0	22.0	16.0	16.0
Sierra Leone	5.3	2.9	1.4	1.0
Gambia	2.0	1.3	0.3	0.4
Kenya	22.0	5.1	7.0	9.9
Tanganyika	18.0	7.1	6.9	4.0
Zanzibar	1.4	0.7	0.3	0.4
Uganda	13.9	2.5	2.0	9.4
Nyasaland	8.3	2.3	2.5	3.5
Northern Rhodesia	17.0	2.7	9.0	5.3
Jamaica	23.0	6.3	5.3	11.4
Barbados	3.4	0.8	1.0	1.6
St. Vincent	1.1	0.3	0.4	0.4
Cyprus	6.4	1.8	3.0	1.6
Mauritius	7.7	1.8	3.7	2.2
Seychelles	0.3	0.2	—	0.1
St. Helena	0.2	0.2	—	—
Aden	2.5	0.8	0.7	1.0
British Guiana	6.7	2.5	2.8	1.4
Grenada	1.7	0.4	0.5	0.8
North Borneo	3.5	1.2	1.3	1.0
Turks and Caicos Islands	0.1	0.1	—	—

Source: **16**, p. 129.

local funds, loans guaranteed by the mother country and, in part, by direct grants of the latter.

The ten-year development plans for twenty-one British colonies are typical of this new trend in colonial policy. (See Table 242.) The plans were developed in accordance with the Colonial Development and Welfare Act 1940, amended in 1945.[108] The idea was conceived in the early days of the war, when Great Britain could do little for its colonies except promise them care and aid in the future. It had become a reality by 1948–49. The main objective of the planned investment is to promote better health conditions (medical and health service, nutrition, water

108. See **15**.

supply and sanitation) and to raise the educational level of the population. Next in line are investments in agriculture including irrigation, drainage and soil conservation and veterinary service. Improvement of roads is also an important item. Only 2 per cent of the total outlay is earmarked for industrial development, electricity and power and 3 per cent, for ports, harbors and water transportation. (See Table 243.) On the whole, the plans emphasize strengthening the colonies' domestic economy rather than their export industries. In this sense, the long-range goal of the ten-year plans now in operation in British colonies is to facilitate decolonization.

OUTLOOK

The world is now in an advanced stage of liquidation of the remaining colonial empires. What will be the impact of the liberation of colonial areas on their inhabitants and on the colonial powers?

Emancipated colonial peoples inherit not only the ports, railroads, highways, mines, factories and electric power stations built by their foreign

TABLE 243

DEVELOPMENT PLANS: TEN-YEAR INVESTMENT PLANS
IN 21 BRITISH COLONIES, BY PURPOSE, 1948–49

(Millions of Pounds)

Purpose	Amount
Total [a]	£199.4
Social	
Education	26.3
Health service [b]	44.0
Housing	13.1
Welfare, etc.	1.9
Economic	
Agriculture [c]	31.7
Fisheries and forestry	4.7
Industry and electricity	4.4
Communications	
Roads	20.2
Ports, harbors, water transport	6.2
Aviation, railroads, etc.	7.7
Miscellaneous	10.1
Interest charges, reserve, etc.	18.4

Source: **16**, pp. 130–31.

a. Includes planning surveys and census.
b. Includes water supply, sanitation and nutrition.
c. Includes irrigation and drainage, land settlement and soil conservation.

masters but also a system of educational and health services that is pathetically inadequate according to modern standards but better than the conditions that prevailed in precolonial times.

When emancipated colonial peoples have a fair chance to develop economically and culturally as free nations, they will probably try to mold their economic life in forms other than those which have been forced upon them. They will not let their economy be merely supplementary to that of the mother country, geared to production for export. Even if they succeed in making this type of production more profitable for themselves, their main effort will probably be directed toward developing farming and industry for domestic consumption. Political decolonization is likely to be followed by decolonization of the economic system. The general trend will presumably be toward a more diversified and better integrated economy; practically, toward a larger extent of self-sufficiency.

This tendency may cause appreciable losses to industrial nations. They will have to pay more for products of the former colonial areas, and a larger part of the price will accrue to the native peoples. It is possible, however, that their losses will be offset in the long run by economic growth in the emancipated areas. In order to develop their natural resources, such areas will need the technical and financial help of industrial nations. The logical way in which they can obtain such aid without mortgaging their independence is by foreign loans to be repaid through future exports. As time goes on, exports from the former colonial areas may regain and surpass the level of colonial times, even if their ratio to national income declines.[109]

The liquidation of colonial empires will brighten the political outlook in the world. Colonies have always been a source of international friction. Since the end of the nineteenth century,

as a result of rising nationalism among the natives, colonial territories have been the setting for countless riots, clashes, punitive expeditions, minor colonial wars. These trends were developing long before the Communist revolution in Russia, but the government of the USSR has fully exploited colonial tensions and troubles in its struggle for world domination. Thus the only country in the world that maintains slave labor has become the spokesman for the emancipation of enslaved colonial peoples. In the long run, this appeared to be a clever maneuver. The colonies were bound to become independent, and by supporting their struggle against their present masters, Moscow would pave the way toward dominating them after their emancipation.

Moscow's plans have been frustrated by the decolonization of India, Pakistan, Burma, Indonesia, Ceylon and the Philippines. Politically and historically, the emancipation of the Asiatic colonies was a heavy blow to the idea of world revolution, but the Kremlin has not lost all hope. The former colonial areas have little experience in self-government and face difficult problems of organizing their domestic life. In this period of transition, internal turmoil and military conflict may give the Kremlin an opportunity to regain the strategic position it has been losing as a result of the orderly and peaceful liquidation of colonial empires in southeastern Asia. Similarly, the unsettled conditions in Africa give the Kremlin hope of new political and economic dislocations during the liquidation of the third and last colonial empire.

On the other hand, the former colonies which have gained independence in their struggle against the subjugation of one nation by another are becoming increasingly critical of the political system of the Soviet bloc, based on domination of the satellite countries by Moscow. The Bandung Conference of Asian and African nations in May 1955 branded this system as a new form of colonialism.

---

109. See Chapter 3.

CHAPTER 15

GOVERNMENT EXPENDITURES AND REVENUES

THE AMOUNTS OF governmental revenues and outlays, their relation to national income, the sources of public revenues and the purposes for which they are used reflect the scope of the government's activities and its place in a nation's economic life. They show what part of the people's purchasing power is being used for public needs and is directly controlled by the government, the amount of the goods and services which the government either uses directly for performing its functions or transfers to certain groups of the population in the form of subsidies, benefits, relief payments and the like. The term "government" includes not only the central administration but also all other public authorities — state or provincial governments, municipal councils and boards responsible for various aspects of administration in counties, districts, cities and other communities.

The structure of public finance of a nation depends largely on the distribution of administrative and fiscal responsibilities among the central and other governments.[1] In the United States in 1950, for example, the federal administration used for its own purposes 63 per cent of all public revenues, and state and local agencies, 37 per cent.[2] In some highly centralized countries such as France, the share of the central government in public outlays reaches 80–85 per cent,[3] while in Switzerland it fluctuates around 20 per cent.[4]

A comparison of the expenditures of central governments in various countries is therefore inconclusive unless expenditures of provincial and local governments are also taken into account. Unfortunately, few international statistics for local governments can be assembled.[5] In many instances, especially in the analysis of long-range trends in the development of public finance, one must rely essentially on the records of central governments.

GROWTH OF PUBLIC REVENUES AND EXPENDITURES

Two yardsticks, complementing each other, are commonly used for comparing the levels of public revenues or expenditures in various countries or at various times: per capita governmental revenues or expenses and the ratio of public revenues or expenses to national income.

"Wagner's Law"

In the last century the scope of public finances grew more rapidly than national income in almost all modern nations. A generalization of this tendency is sometimes called Wagner's law after the German economist, Adolph Wagner, who described it three quarters of a century ago as historical law. Wagner declared:

From the history of progressive civilized nations, on the basis of a comparison of their development in time as well as from comparison of nations and economic systems on different levels of development in different parts of the world, one can deduce a definite tendency or a so-called "law" of development of governmental activities among civilized

---

1. See pp. 702–04 and 717–19.
2. **25,** 1952, p. 356. Administrative and financial responsibilities of a government do not always match. The central government may be responsible for providing funds to provincial or local governments for functions within the area of their administrative responsibility. Because of this transfer of funds — or intergovernmental aid — distribution of revenues from own sources (financial responsibility) may differ from the distribution of revenues ultimately available for the functions of governments on different levels (administrative responsibility). The figures above refer to revenues available to different public bodies for their own purposes, after the transfer of federal aid to state and local authorities. (Cf. Table 252, p. 704.)
3. **27,** March 1951, pp. 43–45.
4. **37,** 1945, pp. 434, 448, 454; cf. **29,** 1949, p. 250,

for Denmark; **36,** 1950, p. 315, for Sweden; **35,** 1949, pp. 308–09, for Norway.
5. The Central Statistical Office in pre-Nazi Germany published an annual survey of the finances of central and local governments in thirty-six countries. (See **32,** 1934, pp. 226–31.) The French Central Statistical Office publishes a survey of revenues and expenditures of central governments in a score of countries. (See **31.**) Publications of the League of Nations and the UN contain data on the finances of central governments but little information on revenues and expenditures of local authorities. (See **1, 2, 16, 12, 13, 14** and **15**; cf. **5** and **17.**)

nations — expansion of the scope of the public or governmental functions.[6]

Changing Patterns

Like most historical generalizations, Wagner's "law" requires certain reservations.

First, it is extremely difficult to compare the volume of governmental activities and public finances in relation to all economic activities and total national income in periods remote from one another or in nations of different economic types.[7] There is no way to decide, for example, whether or not a modern democratic government, with all its agencies, absorbs a larger part of national income than was exacted from the people in the Middle Ages by what then represented the governmental system — the Church, the king and the nobles combined. It is difficult to determine whether the administration of modern Egypt has disposition over a larger share of Egypt's income — in products and services — than a Pharaoh controlled in the second millennium B.C., or whether the cost of government in Great Britain represented a heavier burden for the people in 1950 than in 1815, after the Napoleonic wars.[8]

Second, the financial requirements of a government vary widely from year to year, increasing in periods of international tension and war and declining in peace. In ancient times, the victorious country frequently obtained more in tribute after a major war than it could use for current expenditures, gifts to oracles and building temples. The surpluses were either hoarded or distributed among the soldiers and other citizens. On the other hand, heavy reverses during a long war, and especially defeat, resulted in various levies and taxes that absorbed a large part of the citizens' current income and eventually also their accumulated wealth.[9] The financial history of a state in the ancient world, from its mythological origin to its destruction — usually as the result of military defeat — begins with a Golden Age without taxes and ends with an era of unbearable levies. Indeed, the contrast between financial requirements in peace and war overshadows long-range trends in public finances.

The third reservation, which does not directly contradict Wagner's law, is that the limit to which taxes and levies can be raised without ruining the people depends on the economic and political structure of the nation, the way in which public funds are used and many other circumstances. When all these factors are taken into account, it appears that at all times public finances have expanded almost to the breaking point under the pressure of a national emergency and have contracted when the emergency was over. Complaints about taxes are as old as taxes themselves. As Harold M. Groves puts it,

> Every age is most alive to its own problems. The taxpayer, whatever age he lives in, is usually convinced that this generation is saddled with far heavier exactions than that of any other.[10]

Wagner's generalization is correct insofar as it suggests that public finances in several Western countries were growing in relation to national income in the second half of the nineteenth century. It is false in portraying such an event as a "law," that is, a continuous historical process. Public finances in most Western nations have reached their present status by leaps and bounds rather than gradual growth. Advances have been associated with major wars, while interwar periods have usually been marked by a standstill or a decline in the ratio of public expenditures to national income.

Even in this limited form, however, the "law" becomes questionable when the span of observation is lengthened. In the eighteenth century, public finances of the European nations engaged in the struggle for supremacy on the continent and overseas were greatly extended. The climax was reached under Louis XVI, on the eve of the revolution in France, and some twenty-five years later, at the end of the Napoleonic wars, in Great Britain. Subsequently public expenditures declined sharply in both countries and remained at about the same level for many decades. In the long run, the movement was cyclical rather than continuous.

In comparison with the recent growth in public finances, the increase from the middle of the nineteenth century to the eve of World War I was not very impressive. In terms of aggregate dollars, pounds and francs, public revenues and expenditures in 1913 were several times those of 1850 or 1860, but the increase was due largely to increases in population and per capita income. Rapid growth in the percentage of national income diverted to public use in many countries

---

6. **85**, Second Half Volume, pp. 883–84. Cf. **44**, p. 118; **79**, p. 514.

7. **62**, Volume 1, p. 78.

8. Cf. **47**, Vol. 2, pp. 249ff.

9. **60**, pp. 136ff.

10. **48**, p. 7.

is a relatively new development, dating from World War I.

Causes of Growth

Among the immediate causes of the expansion of governmental activities are increases in industrialization and urbanization; concentration of business; development of popular cultural interests that cannot be satisfied without the aid of public funds; wars and their economic, social and political implications; the growth of democracy and the rise to power of organized labor; the changing popular attitude toward the idea of governmental responsibility in economic affairs.[11] Not all these factors are equally important, however.

The growth of cities and industrialization and the increasing concentration of economic power in the hands of huge concerns have been continuous developments since the beginning, and especially the middle, of the nineteenth century. On the other hand, the striking feature of the growth in public finances has been its discontinuous character. Decade after decade elapsed without visible increase, then came an explosive expansion, followed by contraction or a long standstill until another upswing brought public expenditures to a new high level.

Two factors have been primarily responsible for this course of events: wars and changes in the distribution of political power in the nation. Although these factors have operated as unrelated impulses, they have had a cumulative effect on Western society.

THE DEVELOPMENT OF PUBLIC FINANCES

The pattern of fiscal expansion described above can be observed in many countries. The following pages examine it briefly in terms of developments in the United States, Great Britain, France and Sweden.

THE UNITED STATES

The rebellion of the American colonies against Great Britain was accelerated by disputes on fiscal matters — exemplified by the sugar tax and the Stamp Act (1765) — and by the attempt of the British government to impose duties on tea, glass, lead and a few other articles imported into British overseas possessions.[12] From a purely

11. **64**, pp. 513ff.
12. **40**, pp. 208ff.

fiscal point of view, these measures were not very important, but the colonists, reared in the ideas of the British constitution and self-government, vehemently resented Parliament's attempts to tax them without the consent of their legislatures.[13] The new taxes could not be enforced. The stamp tax brought the British Treasury about £4,000, while the expense of collecting it was close to £7,000.[14] Colonial opposition to import duties marked the beginning of the war for American independence.[15]

The United States began its existence with an empty federal treasury, a chaotic state of local finances and a Constitution which gave Congress the power "to lay and collect taxes, duties, imposts, and excises," [16] within strict limits: "No capitation or other direct tax shall be laid, unless in proportion to the census or [other] enumeration." [17] The purpose of this limitation was to protect property and commerce against the claims of frontiersmen, poor farmers and workers.[18] The clause, however, had regional implications in that it protected big landowners of the South against substantial taxation of their land. In fact, the Constitution gave property owners and prosperous regions assurance that they would not be called upon to support the national government in proportion to their property or income.[19]

Hamilton and Jefferson

The history of public finances in the United States opens with a clash between the opposite economic and political philosophies represented by Alexander Hamilton and Thomas Jefferson. Hamilton's goal was rapid industrialization of the Union on the British pattern. Jefferson dreamed of a primarily agricultural democracy and tried to protect the young Union from the evils of industrial capitalism. Practically, Hamilton's program demanded a strong central government, expansion of public finances, consolidation of public debts, protective tariffs and taxes on consumption high enough to cover growing governmental expenditures. Jefferson's program, on the contrary, called for a laissez-faire policy, a minimum of governmental inter-

13. **82**, p. 24.
14. **47**, p. 154.
15. **40**, p. 220.
16. Article I, Section 8, par. 1.
17. Article I, Section 9, par. 4.
18. **86**, p. 33.
19. **39**, pp. 169–71.

vention in economic affairs, limitation of public expenditures, withdrawal of public debts, fiscal (rather than protective) tariffs, repeal or reduction of taxes on consumption.[20]

Hamilton was Secretary of the Treasury when the first federal taxes were introduced — import duties and an excise on distilled liquors, later supplemented by excises on all alcoholic beverages, sugar, carriages and so on. The import duties proved highly productive; yields increased with the economic growth of the young nation and fairly well covered the growing financial requirements of the federal government, curtailing the demand for other taxes. Thus, the general fiscal pattern of the republic's finances was established and it did not change much under Hamilton's successors, although the Jeffersonian philosophy of government gained wide recognition in the nation by the beginning of the nineteenth century. Jefferson, spokesman of small farmers, wished to see the United States "happy rather than powerful" and believed "that government best which governs least." [21]

Frugality became the slogan of succeeding administrations and remained the guiding principle of financial policy until the outbreak of the Civil War. Except for periods of war and depression, the budget was kept in balance, the public debt was not permitted to rise, expenditures of the federal government were covered mainly by import duties.[22] Apart from temporary ups and downs related mainly to the vicissitudes in international affairs, federal revenues and expenditures kept pace with the growth of population but did not outdistance it. Per capita federal revenues were $1.45 in 1799 and $1.38 in 1849; per capita expenditures amounted to $1.88 in 1799 and $2.00 in 1849.[23] (See Table 244; cf. Figure 139.)

From the Civil War to World War I

During the Civil War the financial system was exposed to a strain it could not meet. The federal government financed war expenditures mainly by loans, at interest ranging from 5 to 7.3 per cent, and by issues of paper money.[24]

At the beginning of the conflict, Congress passed a revenue bill levying a $20 million direct tax on real property in both the northern and southern states; a 3 per cent income tax, effective January 1862, on all income over $800 earned in the calendar year 1861; and new or higher customs duties on sugar, coffee, tea and so on.[25] Actually, however, hardly any of the direct property tax was collected. It was apportioned among states according to population, but services rendered by the states in raising and equipping troops were credited against the levy. Less than $2 million in cash was collected in 1861–62 and still less in subsequent years, while credits for services rendered by the states were repaid to them in 1891.[26]

The income tax was repeatedly expanded and made more progressive by revenue acts in 1862, 1863 and 1869. The collections came in slowly at first. In 1862 only 11 per cent of federal expenditures, and 16 per cent in 1863, were covered by current revenues. In 1864, however, the ratio was more than 30 per cent and in 1865, nearly 26 per cent. These ratios, although insufficient according to modern views on war financing, appear fairly high when compared with the practices of financing war expenditures then prevailing throughout the world.

Per capita revenues of the federal government were very low in the early phase of the conflict but later they increased. (See Table 244.) Moreover, the dollar figures for that time reflect in part the general rise of prices. The real per capita rates expressed in 1860 dollars would be some 40 per cent less than those shown in Table 244.

On the other hand, it should be kept in mind that the per capita federal revenues and expenditures for 1861–63 shown in Table 244 are computed by prorating federal revenues and expenditures over the total estimated population of the United States, including the Confederacy; the amounts would be about 40 per cent higher if based only on the population of areas which remained under the control of the Union government.[27] The fact remains, however, that the Civil War, which was extremely expensive in relation to the current national income, was

---

20. **42**; **68**, pp. 30–31; **86**, pp. 35, 46, 47; **73**, pp. 187ff.

21. **82**, p. 65.

22. The public debt after a succession of rises and declines amounted to $64.7 million in 1860 as compared with $83.0 million in 1800.

23. **23**, pp. 295ff.

24. **73**, p. 323.

25. **82**, p. 141.

26. **82**, pp. 150 and 205.

27. Of the total population of 31.5 million enumerated by the Census of 1860, 22.7 million were in the northern states and 8.8 million (5.1 million white and 3.7 million Negro) in the area of the Confederacy.

TABLE 244

FEDERAL REVENUES AND EXPENDITURES IN THE UNITED STATES, 1789–91 TO 1955

| Year | Total, in Millions | | Per Capita [c] | | Expenditures as Percentage of National Income |
	Revenues [a]	Expenditures [b]	Revenues	Expenditures	
1789–91	$ 4.4	$ 4.3	$ 1.13	$ 1.10	...
1794	5.4	7.0	1.21	1.57	...
1799	7.5	9.7	1.45	1.88	1.4
1804	11.8	8.7	1.95	1.43	...
1809	7.8	10.3	1.11	1.46	1.1
1814	11.2	34.7	1.37	4.24	3.9
1819	24.6	21.5	2.62	2.29	2.5
1824	19.4	20.3	1.78	1.86	2.2
1829	24.8	15.2	1.97	1.21	1.6
1834	21.8	18.6	1.49	1.27	1.4
1839	31.5	26.9	1.88	1.61	1.6
1844	29.3	22.3	1.50	1.14	1.1
1849	31.2	45.1	1.38	2.00	1.9
1854	73.8	58.0	2.78	2.18	1.7
1859	53.5	69.1	2.00	2.58	1.6
1860	56.1	63.1	1.78	2.00	...
1861	41.5	66.5	1.28	2.06	...
1862	52.0	474.8	(1.57)	(14.30)	...
1863	112.7	714.7	(3.31)	(21.00)	...
1864	264.6	865.3	(7.59)	(24.82)	...
1865	333.7	1,297.6	(9.30)	(36.34)	...
1866	558.0	520.8	15.29	14.26	...
1867	490.6	357.5	13.12	9.57	...
1868	405.6	377.3	10.60	9.87	...
1869	370.9	322.9	9.50	8.27	4.7
1874	305.0	302.6	6.93	6.87	4.3
1879	273.8	266.9	5.50	5.42	3.7
1884	348.5	244.1	6.29	4.41	2.7
1889	387.1	299.3	6.26	4.84	2.8
1894	306.4	367.5	4.49	5.38	4.6
1899	516.0	605.1	6.90	8.09	3.9
1900	567.2	520.9	7.45	6.84	3.2
1901	587.7	524.6	7.57	6.78	3.1
1902	562.5	485.2	7.10	6.13	2.6
1903	561.9	517.0	6.97	6.41	2.6
1904	541.1	583.7	6.58	7.10	2.9
1905	544.3	567.3	6.50	6.77	2.6
1906	595.0	570.2	6.97	6.68	2.5
1907	665.9	579.1	7.65	6.66	2.4
1908	601.9	659.2	6.89	7.43	2.8
1909	604.3	693.7	6.68	7.66	2.6
1910	675.5	693.6	7.31	7.51	2.4
1911	701.8	691.2	7.47	7.36	2.5
1912	692.6	689.9	7.26	7.24	2.3
1913	724.1	724.5	7.45	7.45	2.3
1914	734.7	735.1	7.41	7.41	2.4

(Continued on facing page)

TABLE 244—*continued*

Year	Total, in Millions		Per Capita [c]		Expenditures as Percentage of National Income
	Revenues [a]	Expenditures [b]	Revenues	Expenditures	
1915	$ 697.9	$ 760.6	$ 6.94	$ 7.56	2.3
1916	782.5	734.1	7.67	7.20	1.9
1917	1,124.3	1,977.7	9.91	19.12	4.3
1918	3,664.6	12,696.7	35.05	121.44	22.3
1919	5,152.3	18,514.9	49.04	176.23	28.1
1920	6,694.6	6,403.3	62.86	60.12	8.4
1921	5,624.9	5,115.9	51.84	47.13	8.5
1922	4,109.1	3,372.6	37.35	30.66	5.5
1923	4,007.1	3,294.6	35.77	29.41	4.5
1924	4,012.0	3,048.7	35.16	26.71	4.2
1925	3,780.1	3,063.1	32.64	26.45	3.9
1926	3,962.8	3,097.6	33.75	26.38	3.7
1927	4,129.4	2,974.0	34.70	24.99	3.7
1928	4,042.3	3,103.3	33.54	25.75	3.7
1929	4,033.3	3,298.9	33.11	27.08	3.8
1930	4,177.9	3,440.3	33.94	27.95	4.6
1931	3,189.6	3,651.5	25.72	29.44	6.2
1932	1,923.9	4,659.2	15.41	37.32	11.2
1933	2,021.2	4,622.9	16.09	36.81	11.7
1934	3,064.3	6,693.9	24.24	52.90	13.8
1935	3,729.9	6,521.0	29.31	51.24	11.4
1936	4,068.9	8,493.5	31.77	66.33	13.1
1937	4,978.6	7,756.0	38.65	60.22	10.5
1938	5,761.6	6,938.2	44.37	53.76	10.3
1939	5,103.4	8,965.6	38.99	68.49	12.4
1940	5,264.7	9,182.7	39.90	69.58	11.3
1941	7,227.3	13,386.6	54.32	100.50	12.9
1942	12,696.3	34,186.5	94.92	253.87	24.9
1943	22,201.5	79,621.9	163.72	583.31	46.9
1944	43,891.7	95,315.1	330.95	690.29	51.8
1945	44,761.6	98,702.5	338.75	707.04	54.0
1946	40,026.9	60,703.1	286.12	433.90	33.7
1947	40,042.6	39,288.8	279.28	273.98	19.8
1948	42,210.8	33,791.3	289.02	231.96	15.1
1949	33,245.7	40,057.1	227.79	272.80	18.7
1950	37,044.7	40,166.8	244.93	266.53	17.3
1951	48,142.6	44,632.8	313.88	290.94	16.1
1952	62,128.6	66,145.2	396.10	421.31	22.7
1953	65,218.3	74,607.4	415.10	475.20	25.0
1954	64,356.0	68,131.0	400.04	423.52	21.2
1955	59,300.0	64,000.0	361.60	390.20	...

Sources: To 1931, **23**, pp. 295–301; for 1932–51, **25**, 1954, pp. 361–63. For ratio of federal expenditures to national income, before 1919, **58**, pp. 6–7 (partly interpolated by the authors); for 1919–28, **52**, p. 137; for 1929–51, **26**, p. 150. For 1952–55, releases of the Bureau of Internal Revenue.

a. Net receipts, excluding appropriations to federal Old-Age and Survivors Insurance Trust Fund beginning 1937, and refunds of receipts beginning 1931.

b. Total expenditures, excluding debt retirement and, beginning 1931, refunds of receipts and capital transfers.

c. Related to estimated population of continental United States. Per capita figures for the Civil War period are likewise related to total U.S. population rather than population of the area under Union control.

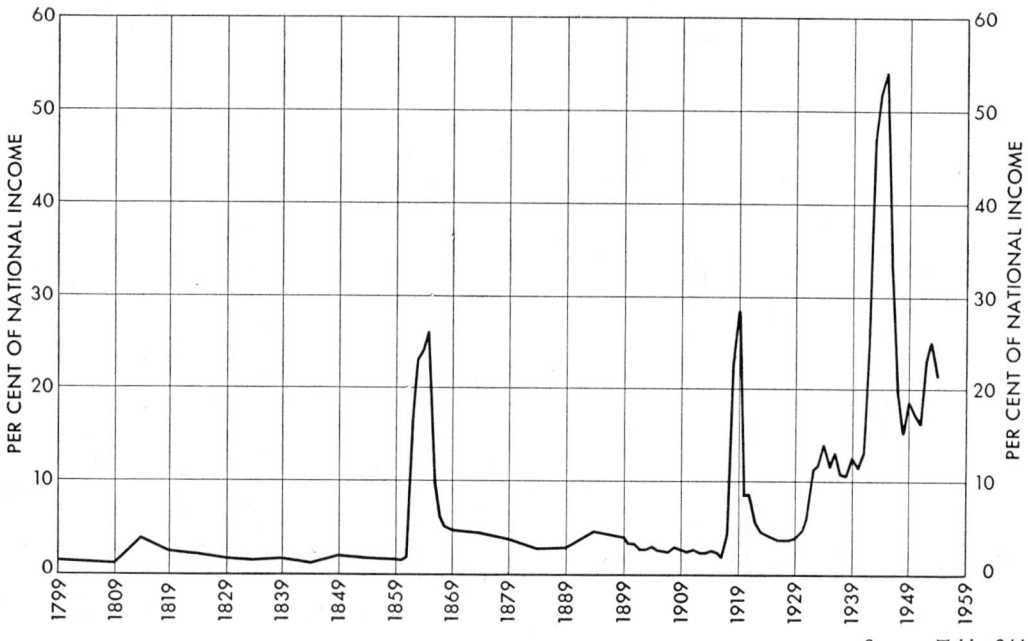

FIGURE 139. FEDERAL EXPENDITURES IN RELATION TO NATIONAL INCOME, IN THE UNITED STATES, 1799–1954
Data for 1860–68 as plotted on this chart are rough estimates.

financed largely by haphazard loans and left the nation saddled with a heavy national debt.

Depreciation of the dollar after the Civil War, combined with the financial commitments originated by the war, contributed to the increase in public expenditures and made a return of public finances to the prewar pattern impossible. In 1879 the federal government spent $266.9 million, $200 million more than in 1861. Of the increase, $101.3 million was attributable to interest on the public debt and $34 million to veterans pensions. The increase in other outlays was due partly to the rise of prices, partly to the growth of population.

From 1879 to the outbreak of World War I, per capita federal revenues and expenditures varied within a comparatively narrow range: for a large part of this period, between $6 and $8 per year.

Contrary to Wagner's law, the ratio of federal outlay to national income did not increase: in the decade 1905–14, it averaged 2.5 per cent, as in the decade 1805–14. (See Figure 139.) It is true that a comparison of selected years in the two decades indicates that the ratio was somewhat higher at the beginning of the twentieth century than a century earlier, but the difference becomes insignificant when payment of interest on national debt is excluded.

On the other hand, there are indications that state and local finances expanded more rapidly than the federal budget, but because of the lack of statistical data it is difficult to ascertain the trend by decade before and after the Civil War.

Studenski and Krooss describe the basic trends in public finances in the United States from 1799 to 1950, using a small sample of state and local government expenditures in the period 1799–1869. In their sample, New York State represents all state governments and Providence, all local governments. This method of comparison indicates a tremendous growth of per capita expenditures and their ratio to per capita income between 1799 and 1869: $3.64, or 2.8 per cent of per capita income in 1799, $24.54, or 14 per cent in 1869. It suggests, however, that the rise was halted and temporarily reversed after 1869. The comparable figures for 1913 were $25.92, or 8 per cent of per capita income.[28]

Thus, when the ratio of all government expenditures to national income on the eve of World War I is compared with the conditions which prevailed at the end of the eighteenth century or the beginning of the nineteenth, on the one hand, and after the end of the Civil War, on the other, it appears that the trend fol-

28. **82**, p. 7.

lowed Wagner's law before 1869 but not between 1869 and 1913. Through the whole period, from the beginning of the Union to the outbreak of World War I, the growth in the federal civil expenditures was the natural and normal result of the rapid growth of the territory, population and wealth of the nation, combined with a very slow and gradual expansion of functions of the federal government reflected in the creation of new departments and bureaus.[29] The increase, however, was so slow and uneven that it hardly supports Wagner's law in its general form.

World Wars I and II

After the entrance of the United States into World War I, federal expenditures skyrocketed from $735.1 million in 1914 to $12.7 billion in 1918 and $18.5 billion in 1919, never to return to the prewar level.

From 1922 to 1930, annual government expenditures fluctuated between $3 and $3.5 billion or, roughly, around 4 per cent of national income. Under the impact of depression outlays increased even before the inauguration of the New Deal, while federal revenues were declining. In 1932, government revenues totaled about $2.0 billion as compared with expenditures of $4.7 billion. Federal revenues represented 4.8 per cent of national income in that year, and federal expenditures, 11.2 per cent.

To some extent the growth of federal expenditures after World War I, as after the Civil War, was due to the increase in the national debt and veterans pensions. But these were not the decisive factors. From $724.5 million in 1913, federal expenditures rose to $4,659.2 million in 1932. Less than 30 per cent of the rise represented increase in appropriations for the War and Navy Departments, interest on the public debt and veterans pensions; most of it was for the civil departments.[30]

The expansion of public expenditures was due to a change in the political climate which began under Theodore Roosevelt and Woodrow Wilson and continued, with changes in pace, in subsequent administrations. On all governmental levels, both the executive and legislative branches were exposed to continuous pressure to expand their activities. William J. Shultz describes the legislative lobbying by social reformers as follows:

> Disinterested humanitarians and interested individuals or groups alike found it possible to bring pressure to bear upon legislatures and councils to vote for new governmental activities, generally meritorious, sometimes difficult to justify, and to provide funds for them. So more and better schools were built, improved methods of garbage disposal were provided, systems of mothers' pensions were voted, state hail insurance was developed, and funds were provided to combat the corn borer and the boll weevil.[31]

The pressure increased under the impact of World War I, which raised far-reaching hopes in the working population; subsided in the 1920's during the "Coolidge prosperity," and became particularly strong during the great depression. It was resisted by the Hoover administration, but received administration support after the inauguration of the New Deal. Expansion of governmental — especially federal — economic and social responsibilities became the cornerstone of the new policy, which called for free spending and growth of the public budget.

Before the great depression, expansion of federal activities was limited by the budget, which represented 3–4 per cent of national income in peacetime. Once public opinion had recognized additional responsibilities of government — such as social security, protection of farmers, development of natural resources and public works in times of mass unemployment — the ratio of governmental expenditures to national income was bound to increase.

Actually, this ratio became stabilized at about the level it reached at the depth of the depression in 1932 — 11.2 per cent. From that time until 1940 the ratio fluctuated between 10.3 and 13.8 per cent, averaging 11.8 per cent. Starting from this level it went up during World War II to an all-time peak of 54.0 per cent in 1945, and declined to 33.7 per cent in 1946, 19.8 per cent in 1947, and 15.1 per cent in 1948. The postwar trend was clearly back to the prewar pattern. Excluding appropriations for the Army and Navy Departments, veterans pensions and interest on the public debt, federal expenditures in 1948 amounted to 6.5 per cent of national income as compared with 6.55 per cent in 1938.[32]

---

29. **55**, pp. 44–45.
30. Cf. p. 708.

31. **75**, p. 27.
32. The comparison of government expenditures (or revenues) with national income (cf. Table 244) does not

This trend was reversed in 1949, mainly by the appropriations for foreign aid and support of farmers. A new upward spiral in federal spending started in 1951 under the impact of the new rearmament program. The expenditures of the federal government went down in 1953–54 and were further reduced in 1954–55. War again — the shooting war in Korea and the cold war in Europe — has played a decisive role in determining the trend in public finances in the United States.

THE UNITED KINGDOM

The growth of government expenditures in the United Kingdom can be followed with a reasonable degree of accuracy through more than 250 years.

The Eighteenth and Nineteenth Centuries

At the end of the seventeenth century the task of the Chancellor of the Exchequer was not overwhelmingly difficult: His Majesty's government spent £2 million in 1697, about 5s. per capita of population. During the eighteenth century, fiscal requirements of the government increased steadily under the impact of wars with the French and Spaniards. By 1797 they reached £58 million or about £3 5s. per capita. (See Table 245.) The British national income was estimated at £150 million in 1774, before the rebellion of the North American colonies, and probably had

not increased appreciably by 1797. Thus, government expenditures were close to 35–40 per cent of national income before the turn of the century.

During the long and expensive struggle with Napoleon, governmental outlays almost doubled. At the peak of the war, the Treasury was spending more than £100 million per year. In 1814 the outlay reached £112 million, or £5 10s. per capita. The size of the British national income in this period is unknown, but it hardly exceeded £220 million and it is fairly certain that governmental expenditures absorbed not less than 50 per cent of national income.[33]

After having secured a leading position in Europe, the United Kingdom concentrated its efforts on the development of its industries. In 1846, it became essentially a free-trade country, with only a few protective customs duties remaining in its tariff.[34] Governmental expenditures were kept low, and per capita expenditures even declined, despite the increase in national income. In 1865–66, the government spent £65 million, or £2 3s. per capita of population. In the following 30–35 years, per capita governmental expenditures fluctuated narrowly, in most years between £2 and £3, averaging £2 6s. (about $9).

In 1891–92, the Treasury spent £89 million while national income, according to A. L. Bowley, exceeded £1.6 billion. Thus, the ratio of expenditures of the central government to national income dropped to 5.5 per cent and was hardly higher than at the end of the seventeenth century, at the time of William Petty.[35]

The Twentieth Century

Governmental expenditures increased in the United Kingdom after the turn of the century under the impact of the South African war and the armament race. In 1913–14, the amount was £198 million or 8 per cent of national income (more than $830 million as compared with the U.S. federal budget of $725–$735 million). In

imply that national income is so distributed between the public and private sectors that part of it (for example, 54 per cent in 1945) goes to the federal government and the rest (46 per cent in that year) to private individuals and state and local governments. In fact, governmental expenditures and revenues include items which do not appear in national income. The most important of these are indirect taxes and costs of business maintenance and amortization which appear in the prices of goods purchased by the government. For some purposes it is preferable, therefore, to relate public expenditures not to national income but to gross national product, an aggregate which represents the value of all goods and services produced in the nation at market prices, including business taxes as well as maintenance cost of capital. In the past two decades, the gross national product (GNP) in the United States has usually been 10–20 per cent larger than national income, the ratio changing with business conditions and fiscal policy. In 1945, when national income amounted to $182.7 billion, GNP was estimated at $215.2 billion. Federal expenditures ($98.7 billion) represented 54.0 per cent of national income but only 45.9 per cent of GNP. The ratio of federal expenditures to GNP in 1929–50 was roughly 15 per cent lower than the ratio to national income given in Table 244.

33. This ratio may seem incredible at first sight, since the wars of that time were not "total wars" like those of the twentieth century. It should be kept in mind, however, that the British were waging war against Napoleon as a struggle for survival; that Great Britain then had 40 per cent fewer inhabitants than France; that the war had found the nation utterly unprepared and that naval warfare was very expensive even at that time. The ratio of governmental expenditures to national income given here should be reduced only if it could be proved that British national income at that time was considerably more than £220 million a year.

34. Cf. Chapter 6.

35. See **63**.

TABLE 245

CENTRAL GOVERNMENT EXPENDITURES: THE UNITED KINGDOM, 1697 TO 1954–55

(Pounds)

Year	Amount, in Millions	Per Capita		Year	Amount, in Millions	Per Capita	
	£	£	s.		£	£	s.
1697	2		5	1929–30	840	18	7
1747	11	1	1	1930–31	892	19	9
1797	58	3	5	1931–32	859	18	13
				1932–33	862	18	12
1809	72	4	5	1933–34	779	17	2
1814	112	5	10				
				1934–35	797	17	1
1865–66	65	2	3	1935–36	824	17	12
1874–75	74	2	5	1936–37	897	19	1
1881–82	85	2	9	1937–38	1,177	24	17
1891–92	89	2	6	1938–39	1,106	23	6
1901–02	182	4	8				
				1939–40	1,852	38	15
1904–05	141	3	6	1940–41	3,913	81	3
1913–14	198	4	6	1941–42	4,815	99	17
				1942–43	5,655	116	17
1914–15	560	12	3	1943–44	5,819	119	5
1915–16	1,559	33	14				
1916–17	2,198	47	3	1944–45	6,086	124	4
1917–18	2,696	57	14	1945–46	5,553	112	18
1918–19	2,579	55	1	1946–47	4,897	99	10
				1947–48	3,918	79	04
1919–20	1,666	35	7	1948–49	3,723	74	46
1920–21	1,195	25	5				
1921–22	1,079	22	12	1949–50	3,942	78	43
1922–23	813	18	3	1950–51	3,787	77	2
1923–24	789	17	1	1951–52	4,704	92	16
				1952–53	5,007	98	15
1924–25	796	17	2	1953–54	4,847	95	4
1925–26	827	18	4				
1926–27	842	18	11				
1927–28	839	18	8				
1928–29	805	17	12	1954–55	5,121	100	8

Sources: For 1697 to 1904–05, **62**, Vol. 1, p. 38; for 1904–05 to 1926–27, **87**, p. 6; for 1927–28 to 1937–38, **2**; for more recent years, **16**, 1951, pp. 514–15 and 1954, p. 487.

the latter phase of World War I expenditures rose to 50–55 per cent of national income and to 65–70 per cent in 1918–19. After the war, total expenditures declined from £2.6–£2.7 billion to £800 million, on the average, or from £55–£58 to £17–£19 per capita. (See Table 245.)

There was, however, no way back to the prewar pattern of public finances: in 1913–14, total central government expenditures had represented about 8 per cent of national income; in 1923, more than 8 per cent of national income was spent for interest on the public debt alone! This charge, together with war pensions, repayment of debts and the cost of collecting taxes, left the British with a postwar financial burden equivalent to more than 10 per cent — possibly 11 per

cent — of national income, making it practically impossible to cut total governmental expenditures to much less than 20 per cent of national income. The ratio of governmental expenditures to national income was fairly well stabilized at a little more than 20 per cent, as follows:

Period	*Percentage of National Income*
1922–23 to 1924–25	20.6
1925–26 to 1927–28	20.7
1928–29 to 1930–31	20.1
1931–32 to 1934–35	22.6
1935–36 to 1937–38	20.1

A parliamentary Treasury Committee found a great similarity between the patterns of public

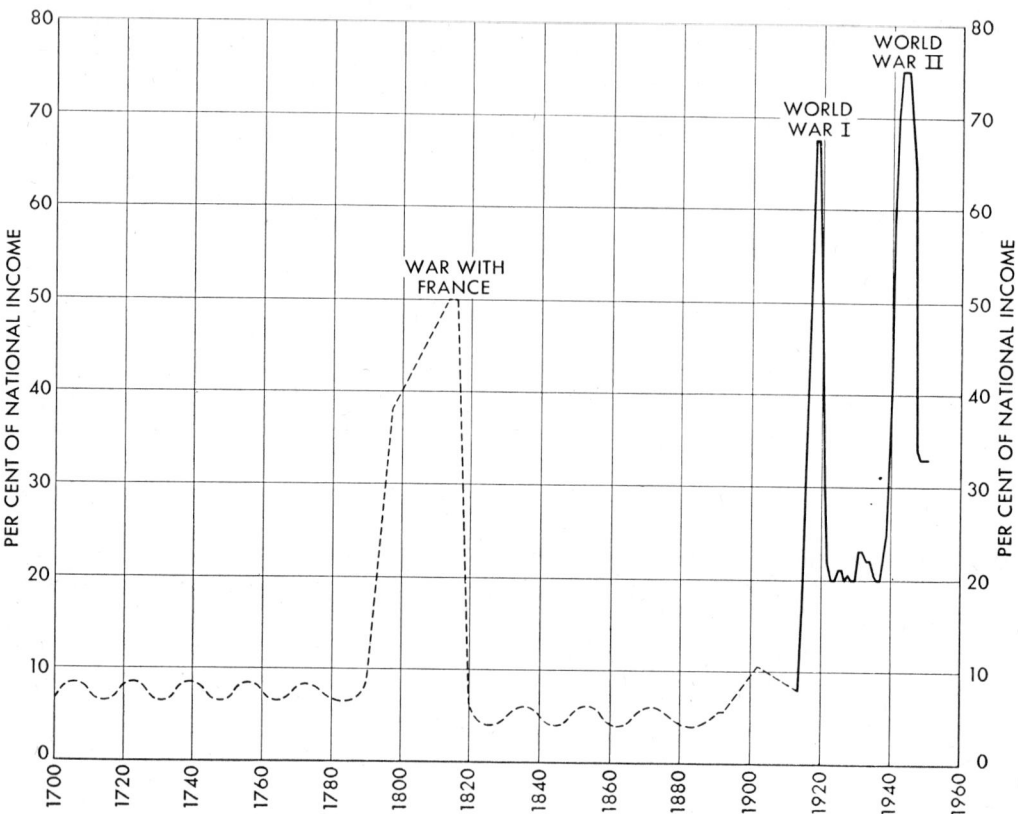

FIGURE 140. CENTRAL GOVERNMENT EXPENDITURES IN RELATION TO NATIONAL INCOME, IN THE UNITED KINGDOM, 1700–1951

The broken line on this chart shows the general trend in the ratio of central government expenditures to national income. Available data permit no precise estimate of this ratio for single years.

expenditures in 1923 and 1818.[36] It noted that the ratio of taxes to national income was higher in 1923 than in 1818 (19.5 per cent and 14.7 per cent, respectively) but the burden of taxes was lighter for the nation as a whole because the new system of taxes was more equitable and less oppressive to the poor. There was an important difference, however, between the trend in public finances in Great Britain after 1818 and after 1923. The Napoleonic wars were followed by a long period of peace, while World War I was succeeded by an even more terrible war.

From £1.1 billion in 1938–39, governmental expenditures jumped to £4.8 billion in 1941–42 and continued to rise as the struggle went on. In 1941–42 the ratio of government expenditures to national income averaged 66.8 per cent, about the same proportion as in the decisive phase of World War I. This time, however, the rise of public expenditures did not stop at that level.

From 1942–43 to 1944–45 the ratio ranged between 70 and 75 per cent. It dropped to 33.8 per cent in 1948–49 and has since declined slowly to 33.4 per cent in 1949–50 and 33.2 per cent in 1950–51. One third seems to correspond to the new peacetime conditions. (Cf. Figure 140.)

When the ratio of central government expenditures to national income after World War II, say in 1949, is compared with the average prewar ratio, say in 1930–39, it appears that the rise was from 22 to 33 per cent. This increase was much smaller than that due to World War I: from approximately 8 per cent in 1905–14 to more than 20 per cent in the 1920's. The immediate causes of the increase have also been different. After World War I, the largest increase was caused by the rise in appropriations for interest on national debt, defense and veterans pensions. After World War II, these items were overshadowed by outlays for public investments, price subsidies and current expenditures for social welfare and economic activities of the

36. **34**, p. 235; cf. **79**, p. 511.

government — fields reflecting the shift in public attitudes and political power.

On the whole, the ratio of public expenditures to national income in the United Kingdom has increased in the past 250 years in both peace and war. Of the three war peaks — the Napoleonic wars, 1917–18 and 1944–45 — the second was probably somewhat higher than the first, and the third decidedly higher than the second.[37]

The major increases in peacetime expenditures were made in two jumps, after the two world wars. Changes in this ratio before World War I may be represented by a waving horizontal line interrupted by a peak during the Napoleonic wars and a minor rise at the end of the nineteenth century. The jumps caused by the two world wars are perfectly clear. The trend in the interwar period is doubtful. The time elapsed since the end of World War II has been too short to permit generalization.

FRANCE

Some records of the finances of the French kings go back to the thirteenth century. When their expenditures are adjusted, roughly, to the purchasing power of money and prorated over the population,[38] it appears that centuries elapsed without substantial changes in the relative scope of public finances in peacetime, while each major war strained the fiscal resources of the nation and some wars left it economically exhausted for years to come. In the sixteenth and seventeenth centuries, the expenditures of French kings were three or four times larger than those authorized by the House of Commons to the British crown. In 1683, for example, the government of Louis XIV spent 229 million francs, roughly equivalent to £7.5 million, or 8s. per capita of population, as compared with the contemporary British national budget of £2 million, or 5s. per capita.

The French national budget increased further in the eighteenth century. For example, in 1789 — the first year of the French Revolution — the government of Louis XVI spent 475 million francs and the tax collectors extracted much more from the people.[39] Unbearable and badly

distributed taxes, combined with the high rents exacted by feudal landowners from the peasants, were among the main causes of the upheaval.

The fiscal system of the French revolutionary period rested on the printing of assignats secured by the value of land confiscated from the nobles. The catastrophic depreciation of this paper money contributed to the country's economic difficulties.

Under Napoleon, France emerged from the economic and political chaos as an empire with a claim to domination over Europe. As long as it could wage war on foreign soil and compel defeated enemies to foot the war bill, the budgetary outlays and revenues of the empire remained comparatively low. Both rose in the later phase of the Napoleonic wars, but only fragmentary statistics are available.

Until the middle of the nineteenth century, governmental expenditures in France increased very slowly, from 30 francs ($5.50) per capita in 1800 to 41 francs ($7.00) per capita in 1850. The rate was somewhat higher than in the United States (see Table 244), but the rise hardly kept pace with the increase in per capita income.

Under Napoleon III government expenditures increased, mainly those for the armed forces. After the disastrous war of 1870, the Third Republic started with a budget of 80–85 francs per capita per year. Public expenditures inched up until the outbreak of World War I but lagged behind the growth of national income: the ratio of public expenditures to national income was 15.0 per cent in 1878 and 11.8 per cent in 1913.[40] (See Table 246; cf. Figure 141.)

It is difficult to estimate national income in France during World War I, when the northern departments were overrun by the Germans and the franc was losing its purchasing power under the impact of creeping inflation. In 1920 governmental expenditures were estimated at 47.5 per cent of national income. The ratio declined to 38.1 per cent in 1921, 29.6 per cent in 1922 and 19.0 per cent in 1927. It increased again in the 1930's and averaged 26 per cent in 1934–38. Ap-

---

37. If the bare subsistence minimum of the people is excluded from national income, there is no evidence that the ratio of public expenditures to the excess of national income over this minimum was higher in World War II than in the late phase of the Napoleonic wars.

38. **62,** p. 56.

39. There is no reliable information concerning the total tax burden of the French people. Taine, the French historian, estimated that the combined levy of all types

of taxes and feudal dues took over 81 per cent of the meager income of the peasants. Some historians question this figure, pointing out that existence could not have been maintained on one fifth of a peasant's produce. (**48,** pp. 7–8.)

40. In view of the somewhat doubtful character of French statistics of national income, these rates are open to criticism, but the correction would hardly affect the conclusion.

TABLE 246

CENTRAL GOVERNMENT EXPENDITURES IN FRANCE, 1800–1954

Year	Total, in Millions	Per Capita	Expenditures as Percentage of National Income	Year	Total, in Millions	Per Capita	Expenditures as Percentage of National Income
1800	Fr. 835	Fr. 30	—	1923	Fr. 35,843	Fr. 900	—
1815	931	32	—	1924	39,825	996	—
1820	907	30	—	1925	33,137	824	—
1825	982	31	—	1926	37,338	924	27.9
1830	1,095	34	—	1927	39,541	973	19.0
1835	1,047	31	—	1928	42,445	1,040	20.2
1840	1,364	40	—	1929	45,366	1,106	20.0
1845	1,489	42	—	1930	50,358	1,222	20.6
1850	1,473	41	—	1931	50,640	1,226	20.8
1855	2,304	64	—	1932	41,422	1,000	18.1
1860	2,084	57	—	1933	54,945	1,323	26.7
1865	2,147	56	—	1934	49,883	1,196	25.1
1870	3,047	83	—	1935	49,868	1,196	27.1
1875	2,936	80 ⎫	15.0[a]	1936	46,450	1,111	26.4
1880	3,365	90 ⎭		1937	49,906	1,191	25.6
1885	3,467	85	—	1938	54,749	1,313	25.7
1890	3,288	96 ⎫	12.2[b]	1939	186,377	4,491	50.5
1895	3,434	85 ⎭		1940	189,834	4,596	—
1900	3,747	90	13.9	1941	265,000	6,447	—
1905	3,707	95	—	1942	291,848	7,118	—
1910	4,322	110	—	1943	410,000	10,000	—
1911	4,548	116	—	1944	346,000	8,480	—
1912	4,743	121	—	1945	313,000	7,690	12.0
1913	4,718	121	11.8	1946	587,000	14,460	17.1
1914	10,005	256	26.7	1947	821,000	20,020	27.1
1915	22,154	566	—	1948	1,675,000	40,560	30.9
1916	32,945	841	—	1949	2,251,000	54,380	34.4
1917	41,680	1,064	—	1950	2,460,000	59,100	34.6
1918	54,537	1,392	—	1951	2,949,000	69,100	32.1
1919	49,030	1,251	—	1952	3,720,000	87,500	36.1
1920	52,409	1,339	47.5	1953	3,850,000	89,700	36.8
1921	43,778	1,097	38.1	1954	3,387,000	78,200	…
1922	35,246	890	29.6				

Sources: For 1870–1927, **87**, p. 6 (cf. **31**, 1930, pp. 386–87); for 1928–51, **31**, various years; and **16**, 1954, p. 475.
   a. 1878.   b. Average for 1892 and 1893.

proximately 40 per cent of the increase in the ratio of public expenditures to national income — in comparison with the prewar ratio — was due to the appropriations for public debt service and the armed forces, the rest to the new responsibilities assumed by the government, mainly for price subsidies and social security. (See Table 247.)

During World War II financial conditions in France were chaotic. In 1939, government ex-

penditures amounted to 50.5 per cent of national income. No comparable data are available for the next five years, when France had no army and scarcely a national government. After the liberation of the country, public expenditures rose steadily, both in terms of francs adjusted to changes in prices and in relation to national income. (See Table 246, last column.) This increase reflected the gradual resumption of the prewar functions by the government.

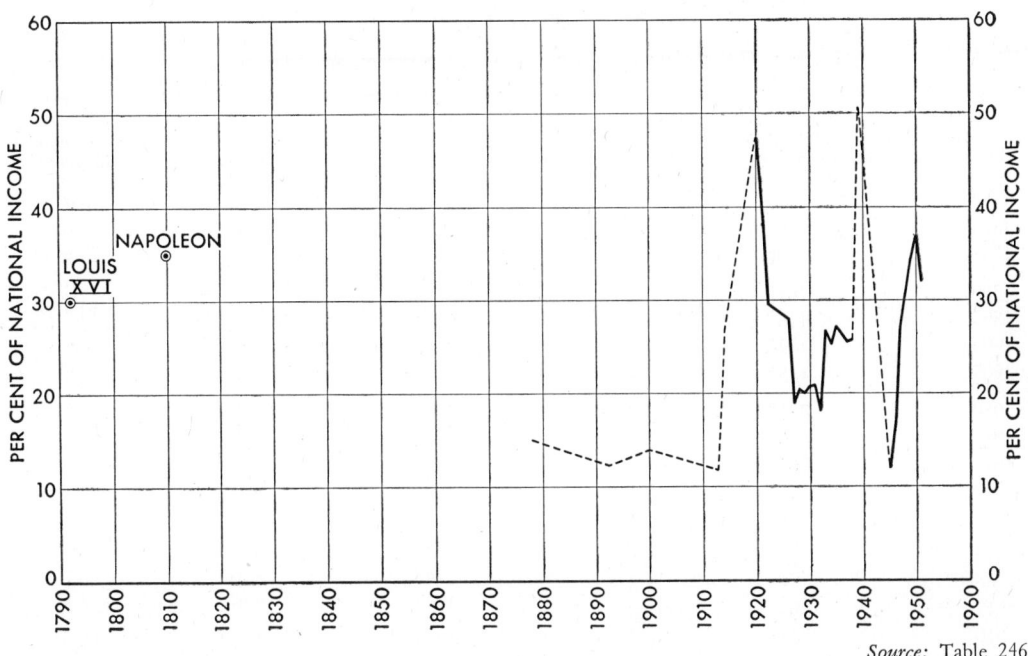

Source: Table 246

FIGURE 141. CENTRAL GOVERNMENT EXPENDITURES IN RELATION TO NATIONAL INCOME, IN FRANCE,
1792–1951

TABLE 247

CENTRAL GOVERNMENT EXPENDITURES, IN FRANCE,
CLASSIFIED BY PURPOSE IN RELATION TO
NATIONAL INCOME, 1910 AND 1938

(*Per Cent*)

Expenditure	1910	1938	Increase
Total	12.4	25.7	13.3
National debt	3.7	4.2	0.5
Defense	3.7	8.5	4.8
Price subsidies	—	3.7	3.7
Social security	—	4.0	4.0
Other current civil expenditures	4.2	4.2	—
Investments	0.8	1.1	0.3

Sources: For 1938: **18**, 1948, p. 40. For 1910: estimated by the authors following the same classification and method. Neither estimate is perfectly precise.

SWEDEN

Sweden exemplifies the trend in public finance in a modern industrial country that has escaped the ordeal of two world wars. Expenditures and revenues of the Swedish central government increased from 5.0 per cent of national income in 1864–66 to 8.8 per cent in 1895. Apart from a temporary rise during World War I and the period of postwar adjustments, this ratio did not rise appreciably between 1895 and 1929. (See Table 248.) It went up in the early 1930's under the impact of the depression, declined with the recovery and was higher again after World War II.

It is noteworthy that the pattern of public expenditures in prosperous years did not change appreciably from the 1890's (8.8 per cent of national income in 1895) to 1929 (9.1 per cent). The tremendous, truly revolutionary change to higher levels in the last decade has been due largely to the growth of the labor movement and its parliamentary strength.

OTHER COUNTRIES

All countries for which comparable data are available reveal similar changes in the ratio of government expenditures to national income. The upward trend was slow and uneven before World War I. In Germany, for example, government expenditures have represented the following percentages of national income: [41]

1890	5.5	1905	6.2
1895	5.0	1910	6.9
1900	7.1	1913	7.0

In Italy, government expenditures averaged 12.6 per cent of national income in 1901–05, 12.8

41. Computed from **31**, 1938, p. 478* and **10**, 1938–1948, p. 227.

Table 248

Central Government Expenditures, in Sweden, 1864–66 to 1955

Year	Amount, in Millions	Percentage of National Income [a]	Year	Amount, in Millions	Percentage of National Income [a]
1864–66	Kr. 33.6	5.0	1930	Kr. 811	9.8
1873–74	58.5	5.3	1931	819	11.0
1883	79.0	7.0	1932	991	14.5
1890	101[b]	7.2	1933	973	14.2
1895	116[b]	8.8	1934	1,106	14.2
1900	152[b]	7.6	1935	891	10.7
1905	185[b]	8.4	1936	957	10.5
1910	221[b]	7.4	1937	1,092	10.5
1911	236[b]	7.8	1938	1,295	10.7
1912	264	8.0	1939	1,363	. . .
1913	261	7.6	1940	2,514	. . .
1914	271	7.5	1941	3,414	. . .
1915	413	9.8	1942	3,604	. . .
1916	434	8.3	1943	4,037	22.3
1917	650	10.0	1944	4,072	22.2
1918	1,720	20.7	1945	4,103	20.8
1919	850	8.9	1946	3,329	15.3
1920	949	8.6	1947	3,155	13.5
1921	1,155	15.0	1948	3,971	16.2
1922	659	9.8	1949	4,643	16.1
1923	401	6.9	1950	5,762	21.3
1924	797	11.1	1951	6,303	19.1
1925	756	10.3	1952	7,614	21.0
1926	758	10.1	1953	9,145	24.7
1927	810	10.6	1954	10,146	. . .
1928	740	9.4	1955	10,141	. . .
1929	745	9.1			

Sources: **31**, 1938, p. 477; **10**, 1938–1948, pp. 227, 233; **18**, 1948, pp. 40–41 and 1949, p. 274; **16**, 1954, p. 485.

a. Government expenditures (for 1890–1911, revenues) are compared to national income for the respective years as shown in the series published by the United Nations (**10**). This series, however, is not uniform. Up to 1918, it refers to gross national product at market prices, excluding net income from abroad; for 1919–30, to national income at market prices, excluding government intermediate services and net income from abroad; for 1931–38, the same but including government intermediary services; since 1943, it has shown the gross national income at factor cost.

b. Revenues.

per cent in 1906–10 and 13.5 per cent in 1911–14, as compared with 13.8 per cent in 1871–75 and 14.0 per cent in 1876–80.[42] In the Netherlands, the proportion from 1900 to 1913 fluctuated very narrowly around 9 per cent. In Belgium, expenditures of the national government amounted to 12 per cent of national income in 1913–14, precisely as in 1940 and 1941.[43]

Before the outbreak of World War I the ratio of government expenditures to national income

varied from country to country and from year to year. In most countries for which more or less reliable data are available, the rates ranged between 6 and 12 per cent and were slowly increasing in the latter part of the nineteenth century.[44] World War I was the turning point. The financial strain in the countries directly involved was probably not much greater than in major wars of the past, but this war, unlike past wars, provided no booty to cover the military expenditures of the victorious nations. It left them saddled with heavy national debts and

42. Computed from same sources as Table 248.
43. Data on government expenditures from **79**, p. 505; national income data from **10**, 1938–1948, p. 227.

44. **74**; **56**.

veterans pensions. It also left a hopeless tangle of international debts.[45] The Germans succeeded in freeing themselves of their obligations by carrying inflation to the utmost limit at the price of ruining the middle classes. Other countries carried the burden left by the war through the 1920's, and this effort was the immediate cause of the rise in their governmental expenditures. The fiscal strain was alleviated temporarily by increasing national income, but the depression of the 1930's put an end to the illusion of a gradual return of public finances to prewar normalcy.

In the 1930's, a new factor appeared on the scene in the western world — a shift in political forces and increasing recognition of broader governmental responsibility in social welfare and economic affairs. Thus Wagner's law, whether it was true or half true when it was formulated, became incontestably true in the second quarter of the twentieth century.

INTERNATIONAL DIFFERENCES IN THE AMOUNT OF PUBLIC EXPENDITURES

The relative amount of governmental revenues and expenditures in various countries depends on many factors, including the scope of governmental activities, the distribution of responsibilities between the central and local governments, political and economic conditions in a particular year, and so on.

It is practically impossible to take account of each of these factors and to present the governmental expenditures of various countries, especially of countries that differ in political and economic structure, on a strictly comparable basis. The use of international financial statistics therefore requires substantial reservations.

Per Capita Expenditures

Governmental expenditures per capita of population ranged, around 1952–53, from less than $2 in Ethiopia and Liberia to $475 in the United States. (See Table 249.)

The data in Table 249 relate to total and per capita expenditures of the central government (national or colonial) in 70 countries around 1952–53,[46] including ordinary and extraordinary

budgets, additional appropriations and special accounts. In some budgets, the operating expenditures and investments of monopolies and business enterprises owned and operated by the government are likewise included; others incorporate only the net gains or losses of such enterprises. The data generally refer to the amount of appropriations by the parliament or the preliminary estimates submitted to the parliament by the government, rather than the records of the completed fiscal year. In converting governmental expenditures into U.S. dollars for the countries with controlled exchange, free-market exchange rates have been used when they could be ascertained.

A fairly clear pattern emerges from per capita governmental expenditures thus computed. The prosperous industrially developed nations top the list, with per capita expenditures of more than $200: the United States ($475), Canada ($303), the United Kingdom ($276), Luxembourg ($267), France ($256), Sweden ($247), New Zealand ($246), Australia ($216), Belgium ($205).

The group with per capita governmental expenditures of $100–$200 includes Finland ($195), Norway ($155), Hungary ($140), the Netherlands ($138), Venezuela ($133), Ireland ($122), Austria ($121), Western Germany ($107), Denmark ($103), Switzerland ($100). Among a number of comparatively prosperous primarily agricultural countries, the per capita figure ranges from $50 to $100. This group includes such countries as Argentina and Italy.

Surprisingly low public expenditures per capita appear for Portugal and Spain; surprisingly high, for Venezuela and some colonial areas, such as the Federation of Malaya ($38) and Southern Rhodesia ($41). Per capita expenditures in underdeveloped, predominantly agricultural regions vary in most cases between $20 and about $45: Panama ($45), Cuba ($42), Chile ($42), Greece ($41), the Dominican Republic ($38), Syria ($35), Ceylon ($33), Egypt ($28), El Salvador ($28), Turkey, ($24), Colombia ($22), Jamaica ($21).

In primarily agricultural regions where a subsistence economy prevails, the rate is usually below $20, often less than $10. The list of countries with per capita expenditures below $10 includes Honduras, Costa Rica, Haiti, India,

---

45. See Chapter 16.

46. The USSR and some of its satellites are excluded because their concepts of government and public finances differ fundamentally from those prevailing in countries with a free-enterprise economy. Data for Hungary are

---

listed on the theory that it was not completely sovietized when budgets for 1949 were prepared.

TABLE 249

CENTRAL GOVERNMENT EXPENDITURES, IN SELECTED COUNTRIES, AROUND 1952–53

(U.S. Dollars)

Country and Year	Total, in Millions	Per Capita	Country and Year	Total, in Millions	Per Capita
United States, 1953	$74,607	$475	Hungary, 1949	$1,297	$140
Canada, 1953	4,431	303	Portugal, 1951	164	19
Mexico, 1952	461	17	Spain, 1951	932	33
Guatemala, 1952	60	30	Italy, 1953	3,547	75
El Salvador, 1952	53	28	Greece, 1951	313	41
Honduras, 1952	14	9	Iceland, 1952	8	59
Nicaragua, 1951	13	12	Japan, 1952	817	10
Costa Rica, 1952	26	3	Hong Kong, 1951	21	10
Panama, 1951	37	45	Turkey, 1953	625	24
Cuba, 1950	223	42	Lebanon, 1952	26	20
Jamaica, 1950	29	21	Israel, 1953	138	86
Haiti, 1952	13	4	Syria, 1952	117	35
Dominican Republic, 1952	83	38	Iraq, 1952	81	16
Venezuela, 1952	690	133	Iran, 1952	305	16
Colombia, 1952	250	22	Pakistan, 1953	569	7
Ecuador, 1952	32	10	India, 1953	1,373	4
Brazil, 1952	696	13	Burma, 1953	230	13
Peru, 1952	156	18	Thailand, 1951	202	11
Bolivia, 1952	72	23	Malaya, 1951	200	38
Paraguay, 1950	39	20	Ceylon, 1952	265	33
Chile, 1952	255	42	Indonesia, 1951	736	10
Argentina, 1952	1,417	79	British Borneo, 1950	21	15
			Philippines, 1953	258	24
United Kingdom, 1953	14,020	276			
Ireland, 1953	367	122	Egypt, 1953	592	28
France, 1953	11,000	256	Anglo-Egyptian Sudan, 1949	33	4
Luxembourg, 1951	80	267	Ethiopia, 1950	25	1.6
Belgium, 1952	1,806	205	Liberia, 1950	3	1.9
Netherlands, 1953	1,383	138	Gold Coast, 1950	44	11
Denmark, 1951	444	103	Nigeria, 1950	76	3
Sweden, 1953	1,768	247	Tanganyika, 1950	35	4
Norway, 1952	509	155	Northern Rhodesia, 1951	40	20
Finland, 1951	788	195	Southern Rhodesia, 1951	89	41
Western Germany, 1952	7,355	107	Union of South Africa, 1953	815	63
Switzerland, 1952	480	100	Australia, 1951	1,855	216
Austria, 1952	848	121	New Zealand, 1952	485	246

Sources: **16**, 1952, pp. 21–32, 415–18, 442–77; **8**, 1953, *passim;* **18**, 1952, *passim.*

Pakistan, Ethiopia, Liberia, the Anglo-Egyptian Sudan, Nigeria and Tanganyika. China and many other underdeveloped countries not included in the table likewise belong in this group. It is noteworthy that more than half the population of the world pays less than $10 per capita per year for governmental services.

Relation to National Income

International comparison of the ratios of governmental expenditures to national income intro-duces a new variable into the analysis — differences in concepts and methods of estimating national income. On the other hand, such a comparison eliminates errors arising from the conversion of national currencies into dollars or any other international currency unit.

In 1935 the Swedish government published a survey of the comparative burden of taxation in Sweden, eight other European countries and the United States in 1925 and 1933 — before and after the great depression. The survey shows that ratios of tax collections to national income varied widely from country to country but increased from 1925 to 1933 in all these countries except Finland: [47]

Country	Tax Collections as Percentage of National Income	
	1925	1933
United States	11.0	23.4
United Kingdom	22.6	25.2
France	22.1	26.3
Netherlands	14.9	20.1
Denmark	19.6	20.1
Sweden	16.0	18.9
Norway	20.9	25.1
Finland	21.6	20.1
Germany	17.8	23.0
Italy	17.5	30.6

The relation of governmental expenditures to national income varies widely not only from country to country but also from year to year in the same country. Precise comparisons are available only for a limited number of countries. World-wide comparison can be ventured only with allowance for a rather wide margin of error and sometimes requires comparison of government expenditures with national income data which do not relate to the same span of time. (See Table 250.) Such a survey shows the lowest ratios (less than 10 per cent) in such underdeveloped areas as India, Brazil, Honduras and Bolivia. Moreover, national income in these areas is likely to be understated because of the difficulty inherent in appraising economic activities outside money and market operations,[48] and it is fairly probable that the actual ratios of public expenditures to national income in these countries are even lower than those shown in Table 250.

At the other extreme are countries where governmental expenditures amount to more than a third of national income, as in Luxembourg (45.5 per cent) and Northern Rhodesia (40 per cent). In some countries the ratio may be overstated because of understatement of the national income.

The high rate in some countries is due to their economic policy of development of economic activities and large investments covered by public funds.

Among countries similar in economic and so-

cial structure, it appears that government expenditures tend to increase in relation to national income as one moves — in terms of population — from bigger to smaller countries. The ratio is higher in Guatemala than in Mexico; higher in Paraguay, Colombia, Peru, Bolivia and Chile than in Brazil; higher in Luxembourg than in Belgium; higher in Pakistan than in India and still higher in Thailand, Burma and Ceylon.

When countries are arrayed by declining per capita governmental expenditures, as in Table 250, the ratio of public expenditures to national income declines from the top to the bottom of the list. It averages 30.2 per cent for the ten countries with the largest per capita governmental outlay; 22.2 per cent for the next ten countries; 18.3 per cent for the following ten countries; and 17.9 and 14.0 per cent, respectively, for the two groups of ten countries at the bottom of the list.

The same correlation is found when countries are arrayed by per capita income: the richer a country, the larger, in general, is the share of national income used for the services of the central government, though there are some exceptions to this rule.

Switzerland, for example, has the second highest per capita income in Europe but the expenditures of the federal government are unusually low in comparison with national income; in France, national expenditures are comparatively high. The explanation is obvious. Switzerland distributes many administrative and economic responsibilities among its cantons, while France has a highly centralized administration.

The three basic factors — the level of economic development (or per capita income), the size of population, and the degree of centralization in government — may be masked by other circumstances. For example, a dictatorial government is more expensive and more inclined to expand its activities than a democratic central government; a democratic government engaged in social and economic reforms tends to spend more than a more conservative administration. Most significant, however, is the state of international affairs. The experience of the United States in the past fifteen years illustrates the overwhelming importance of this factor. Under the impact of war in Europe, federal expenditures increased from $6.9 billion in 1938 to $13.4 billion in 1941; after the country entered the

47. **77**, pp. 135–36.
48. **89**, p. 382.

TABLE 250

CENTRAL GOVERNMENT EXPENDITURES IN RELATION TO POPULATION AND NATIONAL INCOME
IN SELECTED COUNTRIES, AROUND 1950–53

Country [a]	Amount Per Capita,[b] in Dollars		Government Expenditures as Percentage of National Income	Country [a]	Amount Per Capita,[b] in Dollars		Government Expenditures as Percentage of National Income
	Government Expenditures	National Income			Government Expenditures	National Income	
United States	$475	$1,900	25.0	Southern Rhodesia	$41	$133	30.8
Canada	303	1,336	22.7	Dominican Republic	38	195	19.5
United Kingdom	276	755	36.6	Spain	33	159	20.8
Luxembourg	267	587	45.5	Ceylon	33	123	26.8
France	256	724	35.8				
				Guatemala	30	181	16.6
Sweden	247	991	24.9	Egypt	28	(70)	(40.0)
New Zealand	246	884	27.8	Philippines	24	131	18.3
Australia	216	860	25.1	Turkey	24	178	13.4
Belgium	205	703	29.2	Bolivia	23	239	9.6
Finland	195	654	29.8				
				Colombia	22	251	8.8
Norway	155	710	21.8	Jamaica	21	170	12.4
Netherlands	138	462	29.9	Paraguay	20	(200)	(10.0)
Venezuela	133	430	30.9	Northern Rhodesia	20	50	40.0
Ireland	122	459	26.6	Portugal	19	185	10.3
Austria	121	371	32.6				
				Peru	18	118	15.3
Western Germany	107	447	23.9	Mexico	17	166	10.2
Denmark	103	696	14.8	Burma	13	(50)	26.0
Switzerland	100	972	10.3	Brazil	13	215	6.0
Israel	86	(500)	(17.2)	Nicaragua	12	140	8.6
Argentina	79	558	14.2				
				Thailand	11	55	20.0
Italy	75	266	28.2	Japan	10	160	6.2
Union of South Africa	63	248	25.4	Indonesia	10	(50)	(20.0)
Cuba	42	360	11.7	Honduras	9	120	7.5
Chile	42	375	11.2	Pakistan	7	(55)	(12.7)
Greece	41	504	8.1	India	4	55	7.2

Sources: Table 249; **16**, 1952; **9**; **10**; and **11**, various issues. Data in parentheses are rough estimates.

a. Arrayed by declining per capita government expenditures.

b. Per capita government expenditures around 1952–53 as shown in Table 249. Per capita national income in 1951–52 or the nearest year for which data are available.

war, its expenditures skyrocketed to $98.7 billion in 1945; after the end of the war, they dropped to $33.8 billion (1948). Increasing international tension and the threat of a new war brought them up again to $66.1 billion in 1952 and $74.6 billion in 1953.

THE STRUCTURE OF PUBLIC FINANCES

Public revenues and expenditures are usually distributed between the national government and a network of provincial and local governmental units. In the United States, 155,116 gov-

ernmental units were counted in 1942, and 116,743 units in 1952, distributed as follows: [49]

	1942	1952
Federal government	1	1
State governments	48	48
Counties	3,050	3,049
Townships and towns	18,919	17,202
Urban municipalities	3,332 ⎫	16,778
Rural municipalities	12,888 ⎭	
School districts	108,579	67,346
Special districts	8,299	12,319

49. **21**, p. 1; **25**, 1954, p. 412.

TABLE 251

FEDERAL, STATE AND LOCAL REVENUES IN THE UNITED STATES, 1890–1952

(Millions of Dollars)

Year [a]	Total	Federal	State	Local			
				County	City	School Districts	Other
1890	$ 968	$ 403	$ 107	$ 134		$ 324	
1902	1,584	562	176	198		648	
1913	2,393	724	345	373		951	
1932	10,327	2,006	2,317	1,264		4,740	
1942	24,159	13,623	6,100	1,650	$3,118	1,779	$492
1946	50,942	38,493	7,198	1,974	3,573	2,147	540
1947	52,071	37,936	8,481	2,253	4,071	2,496	600
1948	57,224	40,890	10,025	2,614	4,632	3,125	665
1949	56,512	38,602	10,986	3,035	5,019	3,662	767
1950	58,454	40,027	11,264	14,010			
1951	72,643	52,254	12,406	15,281			
1952	109,344	73,152	15,834	4,029	9,307	5,357	1,665

Sources: For 1890–1942: **23**, p. 314; for 1946–51: **25, 20** and **24,** for the respective years. Cf. **61.**

a. For 1890–1932 revenues from own resources. Since 1942 "total gross revenues," i.e., revenues from own resources, plus aid from other governments. Duplications arising from intergovernmental aid are excluded from totals. The data in columns for total revenues and federal revenues are not affected by the shift from "revenues from own resources" to "total gross revenues." In all other columns data for 1942–52 are not strictly comparable with those for 1890–1932.

Central and Local Finances

Each governmental unit has certain fiscal rights and responsibilities and their finances are often interwoven by a system of grants made by the national government to provincial or state governments and by the latter to local bodies. Often provincial and local governments are entitled to a definite share of the taxes collected by the central government.

As has been mentioned, the share of central government in total public revenues varies widely. In the United States it amounted to 41.6 per cent in 1890, 35.5 per cent in 1902, 30.3 per cent in 1913 and 19.4 per cent in 1932. The proportion increased under the New Deal administration and especially during World War II, reached 75.5 per cent in 1946, fell to 68.5 per cent in 1950, rose to 71.9 per cent in 1951 and was 66.9 per cent in 1952. (See Table 251.)

In recent years, the trend toward an increase in the budget of the national government in comparison with those of local authorities has prevailed in most countries. In the United Kingdom, for example, the central government controlled 85.9 per cent of the public revenues in 1949 as compared with 57.7 per cent in 1931; in

the Netherlands, the rates were 34.8 per cent in 1932 and 78.7 per cent in 1949; in Sweden, 48.6 per cent in 1930 and 66.7 per cent in 1948-49; in Norway, 53.2 per cent in 1931 and 68.6 per cent in 1949; in Switzerland, 29.9 per cent in 1931 and 52.4 per cent in 1949.

In countries where public finances were highly centralized before World War II, the shift has been toward increasing the financial responsibilities of provincial and local agencies. Thus, the share of the French central government in total public revenues declined from 70.4 per cent in 1929 to 65.0 per cent in 1949; of the Belgian, from 88.9 per cent in 1931 to 75.8 per cent in 1949. The trend was toward centralization in Canada (61.2 per cent in 1931 and 83 per cent in 1946–47) and away from it in Australia (84.7 per cent in 1931; 70.6 per cent in 1949–50).[50]

Intergovernmental Aid

The financial interdependence of different governmental units usually appears in the form of statutory contributions or grants-in-aid of the central government to the provinces. Often pro-

50. **31,** 1938, pp. 226*–30*; **18,** 1949, pp. 274–75.

TABLE 252

INTERGOVERNMENTAL AID IN THE UNITED STATES, 1950 AND 1951

(Millions of Dollars)

Item	Total		Federal		State		Local	
	1950	1951	1950	1951	1950	1951	1950	1951
Gross general revenues	$65,301	$79,940	$40,027	$52,254	$11,264	$12,406	$14,010	$15,281
Revenues from own sources	58,454	72,643	40,027	52,254	8,841	9,898	9,586	10,492
Aid from other governments (+)	6,847	7,297	—	—	2,423	2,508	4,424	4,789
Aid to other governments (−)	6,895	7,609	2,341	2,393	4,223	4,702	331	514
Revenues for own purposes	58,406	72,331	37,686	49,861	7,041	7,704	13,679	14,767

Source: **25,** 1953, p. 390.

vincial governments, in turn, contribute to the local agencies. In this way, part of the revenue of the national government is used for purposes for which local governments are responsible.

In the United States, the federal government had revenues totaling $40,027 million from its own sources in 1950; state governments collected $8,841 million from their own sources, and local governments, $9,586 million. But the federal government transferred $2,341 million to state and local governments and the states transferred $4,223 million to local authorities. (See Table 252.)

Similar intergovernmental transactions take place in all countries. Public expenditures are ordinarily more decentralized than public revenues.

Division of Responsibilities

The structure of public finance in a nation depends largely on its governmental structure. As Maxwell puts it, a distinction should be made between the fiscal problems of a federal and a unitary country. The lines of demarcation are never sharp, however, because no country is strictly unitary and none is completely federal.[51] The distribution of power and responsibilities among the central government and provincial (state) and local authorities is determined by conflicting forces and interests and changes as time goes on.

The principal and unique responsibility of the national administration is always national defense and the obligations arising from past wars — servicing of the national debt and veterans pensions. In the national budget, these items often outweigh all other current appropriations, but their share in total public expenditures, including those of local agencies, is less overwhelming. The main responsibilities of local governments usually are of economically productive types. They include internal security, fire protection, construction and maintenance of public highways and sanitation. Usually local governments are also in charge of social welfare programs and education. Social security and conservation of natural resources are often a joint responsibility of national and local governments.[52] Price subsidies are controlled primarily by central governments.

To some extent, the activities of central and local governments are mutually complementary. The absence of certain items in the budget of the central government is often due to the fact that the respective programs are administered by local authorities. The trend toward an increase of expenditures of the central government in comparison with those of provincial (state) and local authorities [53] after World War I has been due in part to the growth in military expenditures and outlays for interest on national debt and in part to the expansion in economic activities of central governments.

PUBLIC EXPENDITURES

Many students have tried to reduce the differ-

51. **59,** p. 31.

52. Social security operations are not always recorded in government budgets.
53. Cf. **50,** p. 45.

ence between public and private finances to the interrelationship between the expenditures and revenues in public and private budgets.

"While an individual's income determines the amount of his possible expenditure," writes Hugh Dalton, "a public authority's expenditure determines the amount of its necessary income. In other words, while an individual adjusts expenditure to income, a public authority adjusts income to expenditures."[54]

This difference is not fundamental, however. When the burden of taxation becomes excessive, the government is compelled to adjust its program to the available means. On the other hand, under the pressure of increasing expenditures, an individual and members of his family may try to increase the revenues of the household.

The basic difference between public and private expenditures lies in the fact that in a private budget the same individual carries the burden of expenditures and gets the satisfaction, while in public financing the decisions taken by the public authority impose sacrifices on a number of individuals but do not promise equivalent satisfactions to the same persons. In private finance, the relationship between sacrifice and satisfaction is direct and obvious, and budgeting follows the simple rule of equalizing the marginal utility of purchased goods or services.[55] In public finance, budgeting is brought about by a complex interplay of pressures and counterpressures of interested groups.

The results of the latter procedure — and therefore the distribution of the fiscal burden and the benefits of public expenditures — depend largely on the political weight of the respective groups of the population. Thus, the increase in recent decades in the political influence of organized labor and certain other population groups, such as farmers and the aged, has resulted in a shift in the distribution of both public expenditures and revenues and a change in the criteria used in appraising individual fiscal measures. This general statement refers to the final result of financial legislation and administration rather than the arguments used by framers of financial policy. Their arguments seldom reveal the political pressures to which they are exposed but stress rather the principles of justice and national interest.

Paul Studenski presents the ideal financial policy as consistent application of the principle of "maximum social advantage."[56] Social advantage is measured by the excess of the net social utility of public expenditures over and above the net social disutility of the taxes required. Maximum social advantage is obtained when public expenditures with the greatest net utility are made first and the others follow in order; when taxes with the least net disutility are imposed first and the others follow in order; and when the net utility of the marginal unit of expenditures equals the net disutility of the marginal unit of taxes.

This is, indeed, the principle which would logically control the extent and structure of public expenditures and taxes if they were not determined by the interplay of other forces. Studenski recognizes that modern governments fall far short of the ideal standard he describes but stresses that this ideal has value as a goal for public activity and as a yardstick for judging financial policy.

The growth of government expenditures since World War I has increased the significance of appraising national budgets from the point of view of social advantage. "As long as public expenditures formed only a small percentage of the social product, it was not so important how the government spent this money," wrote Gerhard Colm in 1936. "But with this proportion increasing, public spending becomes a decisive factor in economic policy. Public expenditures today can no longer be considered from a merely fiscal point of view; they must be considered also from the point of view of the whole economic system."[57]

TYPES OF EXPENDITURES

Public expenditures may be classified in many ways: according to the level of government (federal or national; state or provincial; local); according to the functions of government (defense, internal security, education and so on); according to the governmental agencies concerned (for example, the government department); or the character of the purchases made by the government (personal services, materials, munitions); in relation to time, such as expenses for payment for goods and services consumed in the past (service of the national debt), current expenses and expenses for goods which will be needed in

---

54. **46**, p. 17.
55. **89**, pp. 267ff.

56. **79**, p. 406.
57. **45**, p. 11.

the future (investments). A further distinction can be made between ordinary and extraordinary outlays, between different funds from which expenditures are financed, and between expenditures for self-supporting or productive enterprises and those met from general governmental revenues.[58]

These classifications are not mutually exclusive. In practice, the financial accounting of a nation is determined by administrative and legislative purposes, by budgetary procedures (formulating and adopting the budget) and budgetary management (program planning and execution and budgetary control).[59] Actually it is impossible to divorce budget classification and structure from budget procedure and management. This is one of the major sources of difficulty in international comparison of government expenditures and revenues; budgetary accounts rarely provide information necessary for such comparison, though it is feasible in many cases to rearrange budgetary accounts along the lines of an economically significant classification.

In analyzing economic and political trends in the past and in our time, the classification of public expenditures by the functions of government appears most enlightening, although many appropriations are designed for several purposes and fulfill several functions.

Studenski distinguishes six types of expenditures: (1) preparation for war and payment for its consequences; (2) internal protection of life and property; (3) general government (including miscellaneous undistributable items); (4) social and cultural services (education, health service, sanitation, recreation and social welfare); (5) economic services (coining money, customs service, conservation and development of natural resources, highways and waterways, scientific research and informational service, and the like); (6) government-owned enterprises (post offices, railroads, public utilities, municipal housing and so on).[60]

In international comparisons, only a very rough classification can be used. Indeed, the larger the number of countries covered by a survey and the wider the variety in their financial systems, the rougher necessarily is any classification which can be applied to all.

The attempts of the UN to establish comparable international statistics of the expenditures of central governments in various countries have not been very successful. Its *Statistical Yearbook,* 1951, pointed out that

. . . international comparisons of total government expenditures and receipts, and even more so of their components, are rendered extremely difficult by the following circumstances:
(a) The level of total expenditures and receipts depends mainly on the type of state organization and also on the scope of the government's economic activities. In centralized states the national government is partly or completely responsible for matters such as roads, education, health and police, which in federal states are the responsibility of regional authorities. Many governments own or operate railways, power plants, telegraph and telephone systems, etc., which in other states are private enterprises.
(b) Budgetary systems and accounting practices vary from country to country. In practically no case are all government expenditures and receipts included in a single budget account. Frequently distinctions are made between ordinary and extraordinary, current and capital, general and special budgets, revenue and loan accounts, war expenses accounts, public works budgets, etc. In some cases certain public undertakings, public health, education institutions, social insurance funds, etc., have their own budgets. Further, the national accounts may be shown on a gross or net basis, i.e., expenditures after deduction of certain receipts and refunds, and receipts after deduction of refunds and transfers; and in some cases they may include the gross working expenses and receipts of certain or all public undertakings, in others only the net receipts are included.[61]

The only items which can be singled out in budgetary accounts with reasonable precision are military expenditures and interest on the public debt.

MILITARY EXPENDITURES

In the history of public expenditures, wars appear like rugged peaks towering above the plain and throwing long shadows in two directions. Prewar years are marked by preparation for the approaching contest, and postwar years, by the payment of expenses originated by the war — veterans pensions, reparations, interest on war debts and the like.

It is not always possible to distinguish between war debts and other national debts. Most national debts have been accumulated during wars; others have resulted from the inability of a nation not at war to balance its budget under the burden of expenditures for military purposes,

---

58. **79**, pp. 432–34.
59. Cf. **3** and **7**.
60. Adapted, with minor changes, from **79**, p. 520.

61. **16**, 1951, p. 471. Cf. **7**.

veterans pensions and interest on its old loans for war and armaments. In all, more than 90 per cent — and probably not less than 95 per cent — of all public debt is due directly to military expenditures and the remainder is at least partly attributable to wars. It is therefore defensible in a broad historical survey to consider all appropriations for armaments, military installations, war pensions and the national debt under the same heading as expenditures for war, defense, national security and related purposes.[62]

Direct and indirect military expenditures in this broad sense constitute the bulk of the expenditures of national governments.

The United States

From the very beginning of the existence of the United States as an independent nation, national security has been the main responsibility of the national government, while attempts to expand its activities in other fields have been limited by the widely accepted Jeffersonian philosophy of government and the reluctance of the states to permit interference of federal administration in what they consider their affairs.

From 1789 to 1800, more than 85 per cent of all federal expenditures went for defense, including veterans pensions and interest on the national debt; 39 per cent, for defense proper, excluding debt service. Between 1826 and 1850, the rate fluctuated for most of the time between 65 and 75 per cent for defense including debt service and between 60 and 70 per cent for defense proper. Both rates fell in the 1850's, skyrocketed during the Civil War and then fell again. Most of the time from 1871 to 1915, the first rate ranged between 65 and 75 per cent and the second (defense proper) between 50 and 70 per cent.

The share of military appropriations in the federal budget in 1916–20 appears surprisingly low because many military expenditures, among others aid to the Allies, were recorded as civil appropriations. Together with these expenditures, the military budget in this five-year period

accounted for approximately 90 per cent of all federal expenditures. (See Table 253.)

After World War I, a new trend developed in the federal budget: the share of military appropriations began to decline. In 1931–40, for the first time in the history of the United States, less than one fourth of federal expenditures went for defense and veterans pensions.

World War II reversed this new trend. In 1941–45 more than 80 per cent of the tremendously expanded federal outlay was for the War and Navy Departments, veterans pensions and interest on the public debt. In 1946–50, appropriations under these titles averaged 59.9 per cent of total federal expenditures. In 1951–53 the rate averaged 74.6 per cent, without counting military and economic aid to foreign countries directly related to the war.[63] If this item also is considered a military expenditure in a broad sense, it appears that nearly $4 out of each $5 spent by the federal government in 1951–53 was appropriated either directly for national security or for commitments caused by the former wars.

The United Kingdom

In Great Britain as well, national defense, including interest payments on the debts accumulated in past wars, has been until recently the main burden of the national budget. A Treasury Committee on National Debt and Taxation estimated that in 1818 debt service absorbed 55 per cent of government expenditures and defense claimed 25 per cent, leaving only 20 per cent for all other needs.[64] The structure of public expenditures was different after World War I: in 1923, debt service accounted for 40 per cent and national defense, including war pensions, for somewhat less than 20 per cent, while more than 40 per cent went to other departments.[65] The share of military expenditures fell conspicuously in the 1930's and especially after World War II. As percentages of national income, expenditures of the British national government have changed as follows: [66]

	1939	1951
All expenditures	22.1	33.3
Defense	7.6	7.0
Interest on debt	4.3	4.4
Other purposes	10.2	21.9

---

62. Public debt may result from budgetary deficits during a depression. In the United States, for example, the national debt increased by $26 billion (from $17 billion to $43 billion) between June 1931 and June 1940. But these deficits in turn depended in part on military commitments of the government. In these nine years, the federal government spent more than $20 billion for the War and Navy Departments, veterans pensions, and for interest on public debts accumulated during World War I. Without these outlays, budgetary deficits would have totaled only $6 billion.

63. **25,** 1951, p. 309.
64. **81,** p. 571.
65. **34,** p. 235.
66. **16,** 1952, pp. 407 and 473.

TABLE 253

EXPENDITURES ON DEFENSE AND NATIONAL DEBT SERVICE IN THE UNITED STATES,
1789–95 TO 1946–50 ANNUAL AVERAGE, AND 1951, 1952 AND 1953

| | Millions of Dollars | | | | | | Percentage of Total Spent for: | |
| | | Expenditures on Defense | | | | Interest on National Debt | | Defense and Public Debt |
Period	Total Federal Expenditures	Total	War Department [a]	Navy	Veterans Pensions		Defense	
1789–1795	$ 5.6	$ 1.8	$ 1.6	$ 0.1	$ 0.1	$ 3.0	32.2	85.7
1796–1800	8.0	3.7	1.9	1.7	0.1	3.2	46.2	86.2
1801–1805	8.9	2.6	1.1	1.4	0.1	4.1	29.3	75.3
1806–1810	9.3	4.2	2.2	1.9	0.1	3.2	45.2	79.6
1811–1815	25.5	19.5	13.7	5.7	0.1	3.8	76.5	91.4
1816–1820	22.4	12.6	7.7	3.5	1.4	6.0	56.3	83.0
1821–1825	16.3	7.6	3.5	2.8	1.3	4.9	47.9	77.9
1826–1830	16.0	9.1	4.3	3.6	1.2	3.0	56.9	75.6
1831–1835	18.3	12.1	5.7	3.9	2.5	0.6	66.0	69.3
1836–1840	30.6	20.0	11.0	6.3	2.7	0.1	64.4	65.7
1841–1845	21.8	13.9	5.9	6.2	1.8	0.9	67.5	67.9
1846–1850	43.0	29.6	19.7	8.3	1.6	3.4	68.8	76.7
1851–1855	51.6	23.7	11.3	10.6	1.8	3.4	45.9	52.5
1856–1860	68.6	34.8	20.3	13.4	1.2	2.2	50.7	53.9
1861–1865	683.8	617.9	547.7	65.3	4.9	34.6	90.3	95.4
1866–1870	377.6	180.2	127.8	28.4	24.0	135.4	47.8	83.6
1871–1875	287.4	93.5	40.0	23.3	30.2	111.6	32.6	71.4
1876–1880	255.6	90.3	37.2	16.0	37.1	100.2	35.3	74.5
1881–1885	257.6	132.7	43.0	31.9	57.8	63.8	51.5	76.3
1886–1890	279.1	140.3	40.0	17.7	82.6	44.0	50.2	66.0
1891–1895	363.6	219.7	50.3	29.2	140.2	29.4	60.1	68.5
1896–1900	457.5	301.0	111.3	48.0	141.7	38.0	65.8	74.1
1901–1905	535.6	359.8	133.4	86.3	140.1	27.8	67.1	72.3
1906–1910	639.2	433.2	169.0	112.9	151.3	26.7	67.1	71.9
1911–1915	720.3	497.7	198.8	134.0	164.9	22.5	69.1	72.2
1916–1920	8,065.3	4,281.6	3,212.4	882.1	187.1	375.4	53.1	57.7
1921–1925	3,579.0	1,198.7	540.2	413.7	244.8	973.6	33.4	60.6
1926–1930	3,018.0	968.8	405.0	340.3	223.5	737.7	31.9	56.6
1931–1935	5,214.9	1,095.0	457.2	358.8	279.0	695.6	21.0	34.3
1936–1940	8,275.5	1,756.7	698.7	649.2	408.8	904.7	21.2	32.1
1941–1945	64,242.5	50,331.7	32,143.7	17,673.2	514.8	2,080.9	78.4	81.6
1946–1950	42,801.4	20,425.6	12,744.1	6,722.1	1,959.4	5,196.1	50.2	59.9
1951	44,058	26,154	15,182	5,583	5,389	5,615	59.4	72.1
1952	65,410	44,600	29,516	10,161	4,923	5,853	68.2	77.1
1953	73,982	48,757	32,548	11,875	4,334	6,504	65.9	74.7

Sources: For 1789–1945, **23**, pp. 299–301; for 1946–50, **25**, 1953, p. 340; for 1951–53, **25**, 1954, p. 364.

a. Since 1949 includes air forces.

Defense and debt expenditures together accounted for 53.8 per cent of all appropriations in 1939 and 34.2 per cent in 1951.

France

The Third Republic came into existence in 1870 loaded with internal and foreign debts, largely a result of the lost war and the reparations to be paid to Germany. Its main financial preoccupations were debt service and defense. These two items accounted for more than 70 per cent of its ordinary and extraordinary appropriations from 1870 to 1885. The ratio declined before World War I, as a result of a decrease in

TABLE 254

EXPENDITURES ON DEFENSE AND NATIONAL DEBT SERVICE IN FRANCE, AS PERCENTAGE OF TOTAL ORDINARY
EXPENDITURES, 1870–1954

| Year | Military Expenditures | | | Interest on National Debt | All Military Expenditures | All Military Expenditures and National Debt Service |
	Army and Navy	War Pensions	Reconstruction of War Damage			
1870	34.3	—	—	33.4	34.3	67.8
1875	24.2	—	—	46.9	24.2	71.1
1880	26.6	—	—	44.4	26.6	71.0
1885	28.4	—	—	41.2	28.4	69.6
1890	24.9	—,	—	40.9	24.9	65.8
1895	26.4	—	—	35.5	26.4	61.9
1900	27.9	—	—	33.5	27.9	61.4
1905	28.1	—	—	33.2	28.1	61.3
1910	29.6	—	—	29.5	29.6	59.1
1914	28.8	—	—	27.4	28.8	56.2
1922	12.0	0.6	29.9	35.9	42.5	78.4
1927	18.3	1.5	1.0	54.7	20.8	75.5
1938	29.8	8.2	—	14.4	38.0	52.4
1947	20.0	3.1	5.0	4.4	28.1	32.5
1948	18.8	3.1	7.0	3.2	28.9	32.1
1949	15.1	3.1	16.0	3.2	34.2	37.4
1950	25.6	2.7	14.2	3.9	42.5	46.4
1951	29.9	1.7	11.6	4.0	43.2	47.2
1952	37.3	1.8	10.4	3.5	49.6	53.1
1953	36.8	2.0	8.6	5.6	47.4	53.0
1954	43.0	...	9.2	5.3	52.2	55.5

Sources: For 1870–1914, 1922 and 1927: **87**, pp. 37–40; for 1938 and 1947–51: **16**, 1952, p. 465 and 1954, p. 475.

national debt in relation to national income. In 1914, the share of military expenditures in the ordinary budget of the Republic fell to 56.2 per cent, but the extraordinary war budget in that year was larger than the ordinary budget, and military expenditures totaled nearly 80 per cent of all government outlays.

After World War I, a new item appeared in the French national budget: expenditures for reconstruction of devastated areas, charged to the account of future German payments and temporarily covered by an increase in the national debt. In the late 1920's, the service of the national debt absorbed more than half of all governmental expenditures. These charges and appropriations for the army and navy and for war pensions together accounted for more than 75 per cent of all expenditures of the French government. (See Table 254.)

The 1930's were marked in France by the rise of the Socialist Party to power and a change in fiscal and economic policy. In 1938, according to the UN Economic Commission for Europe, defense and interest on the national debt represented less than half the expenditures of the French government (defense, 33.1 per cent; national debt, 16 per cent). Then came World War II, with military defeat, the German occupation, the abortive attempt to establish a fascist regime, the resistance movement, victory of the Allies and, finally, restoration of the republic.

The impact of these years on the social and political structure of the nation appears in changes in the structure of its public finance. The national debt was wiped out by inflation, and the share of military establishment in the national budget declined for a brief time and then went up again, largely because of the expensive war in Indochina. Together, military expenditures and debt service absorbed more than half of all government expenditures in 1952–54, about the same ratio as in 1938.

Other Countries

Despite the trend toward increase in civil expenditures, direct appropriations for the military establishment have remained the main item in national budgets of many countries. The ratio of

TABLE 255

CENTRAL GOVERNMENT EXPENDITURES: PERCENTAGE DISTRIBUTION BY PURPOSE IN SELECTED COUNTRIES, 1952

Country	Public Debt Service	Defense	Social Services			Subsidies	Other
			Education	Health	Other		
United States	8.3	71.6		8.7		—	11.4
Canada	12.1	40.3		20.1		0.7	26.8
Mexico	24.5	11.3	10.7	4.0		—	49.5
Guatemala	5.0	9.7	13.2	8.0		—	64.1
El Salvador	3.5	10.0	14.4	11.6		—	60.5
Honduras	5.5	16.6	12.1	7.3		—	58.5
Costa Rica	18.8	6.8	15.2	4.1	12.3	—	42.8
Panama [a]	13.4	—	22.4	11.6		—	52.6
Haiti	—	16.3	7.6	7.8	—	—	68.3
Venezuela	—	9.3	7.0	7.5		—	76.2
Colombia	18.0	16.6	6.9	6.2		—	51.3
Brazil	4.0	32.4	—	11.0	—	—	52.6
Peru	9.2	20.7	12.4	12.0		—	45.7
Chile	0.7	16.5	16.0	12.0		—	54.8
Argentina	9.7	22.4	10.7	3.8	13.1	—	40.3
United Kingdom	11.9	28.9	6.2	20.0		8.7	24.3
Ireland	3.6	5.0	7.5	—	9.0	13.0	61.9
France	—	34.3	—	—	—	—	65.7
Netherlands	9.0	26.9	8.0	0.6	—	2.7	52.8
Sweden [b]	5.2	20.0	9.0	3.4	24.0	6.0	32.4
Norway	5.0	27.6	4.9	2.0	8.5	—	52.0
Western Germany	2.1	23.7 [c]	—	—	—	2.5	71.7
Switzerland	13.7	37.6	2.2	0.5	19.0	—	27.0
Austria	0.8	2.3	6.7	0.1	28.2	6.6	55.3
Portugal [a]	6.0	24.0	9.0	—	—	—	61.0
Italy	5.7	23.3	10.0	11.1		—	49.9
USSR	—	23.9	12.6	4.8	8.8	—	49.9
Turkey	13.6	31.6	12.6	4.6	—	—	37.6
Lebanon	—	17.4	11.7	5.4	—	—	65.5
Israel	2.7	20.6	4.5	3.2	—	—	68.0
Syria	—	40.8	18.8	3.3	—	—	37.1
Jordan [b]	—	27.5	5.0	3.6	—	—	63.9
Iraq	—	26.6	15.4	8.9	—	—	4.9
Iran [b]	0.5	23.2	9.0	2.3	—	—	65.0
Pakistan	2.3	46.1	—	—	—	—	51.6
India	10.6	32.8	—	—	—	6.0	50.6
Burma	0.5	27.5	—	—	—	—	72.0
Thailand	2.7	19.7	5.3	3.8	—	—	68.5
Ceylon [a]	5.2	0.5	14.6	8.9	—	5.4	65.4
Malaya	1.4	23.0	9.6	6.2	—	—	59.8
Philippines	—	24.3	—	—	—	—	75.7
Egypt	2.6	21.2	12.4	3.9	2.6	7.8	49.5
Union of South Africa	4.9	8.9	4.3	2.4	—	8.0	71.5
Australia [a]	6.7	18.0	—	13.9		4.9	56.5
New Zealand	10.2	9.5	8.4	2.5	36.8	8.8	23.8

Sources: Computed from **16**, 1952, pp. 442–76. For the United States, **25**, 1954, p. 364. Total U.S. expenditures in this table include budget expenditures (as shown in Table 253) and trust account expenditures. Outlays for veterans are listed under defense (8.6 per cent of total expenditures).

a. 1951.   b. 1950.   c. Occupation costs.

military to total expenditures of the central government, however, does not necessarily indicate whether a militarist or a pacifist spirit prevails in a country.

This ratio is particularly high in the countries which believe that their national independence is endangered. It has been very high in the United States because of its commitments in Europe and the Pacific and its leading role in the organization of defense of free nations against aggression; it is very high in Pakistan because of tensions between that country and India; it is high in Syria as an aftermath of the war with Israel; it is high in Canada because of the threat to its northern border, which is open to air invasion; it is high in Switzerland because of its political organization, which makes military defense the main responsibility of the central government and leaves most civilian functions to the cantons. It was high in France in 1952–54 because of war in Indochina. On the other hand, the ratio is surprisingly low in the USSR, where all economic and financial resources of the nation are directed toward strengthening military power. (See Table 255.)

With these reservations, it is worthwhile to compare countries listed in Table 255 according to the ratio (per cent) of direct military outlays (excluding pensions and public debt service) to all expenditures of the national government in 1952:

United States	71.6	Argentina	22.4
Pakistan	46.1	Egypt	21.2
Syria	40.8	Peru	20.7
Canada	40.3	Israel	20.6
Switzerland	37.6	Sweden	20.0
France	34.3	Australia	18.0
India	32.8	Lebanon	17.4
Brazil	32.4	Colombia	16.6
Turkey	31.6	Honduras	16.6
United Kingdom	28.9	Chile	16.5
Norway	27.6	Haiti	16.3
Jordan	27.5	Mexico	11.3
Burma	27.5	El Salvador	10.0
Iraq	26.6	New Zealand	9.5
Philippines	24.3	Union of South	
Portugal	24.0	Africa	8.9
USSR	23.9	Costa Rica	6.8
Italy	23.3	Ireland	5.0
Iran	23.2	Austria	2.3
Malaya	23.0	Ceylon	0.5

The influence of political conditions seems to overshadow all other factors in determining the

TABLE 256

MILITARY EXPENDITURES IN RELATION TO GROSS NATIONAL PRODUCT, IN SELECTED COUNTRIES, 1938 AND 1949–50 TO 1952–53

(*Per Cent*)

Country	1938	1949–50	1950–51	1951–52	1952–53
United States	1.2	4.7	7.1	13.7	17.8
Canada	0.7	2.8	4.7	6.7	9.0
United Kingdom	6.5	5.7	6.7	8.4	9.9
France	7.3	6.5	7.8	9.8	10.1
Belgium–Luxembourg	2.5	2.6	2.9	5.6	7.7
Netherlands	2.3	4.2	4.2	6.6	7.0
Denmark	0.9	1.5	1.6	2.5	3.7
Norway	0.9	2.4	2.8	3.9	4.9
Germany [a]	15.8	5.1	4.9	6.7	8.3
Austria [b]	2.2	1.5	0.9	0.7	0.7
Portugal	2.7	2.0	2.1	2.3	2.6
Italy	6.0	3.5	4.2	4.8	5.7
Greece	5.5	7.1	9.8	8.8	7.5

Source: **41**, p. 134.

a. Except for 1938, occupation costs in Western Germany.

b. Except for 1938, occupation costs.

ranking of individual nations in the list above. It is worth noticing, however, that few small countries are found close to the top of the list.

Insofar as comparable data are available, it appears that the general trend in public finance after World War II was toward lessening the emphasis on war expenditures and increasing that on economic and social objectives. This trend, however, has been temporarily halted, or reversed, by the Korean war and the threat of a new worldwide conflict.

This observation is corroborated by statistics for twelve European countries computed by the Mutual Security Agency. In the MSA computation, military expenditures are expressed as a percentage of the gross national product of the respective countries. (See Table 256.)

ECONOMIC OBJECTIVES

The recent development in public finance in many countries — increasing emphasis on economic objectives — reflects a new philosophy that stresses a dual responsibility of government, for developing the natural resources of the nation and for maintaining full employment.

Development of natural resources often implies a drive toward relative self-sufficiency in
the event of war. The policy of full employment
requires measures to stabilize prices and prevent
excessive fluctuations in the volume of production. The principle of governmental spending as
a means of maintaining full employment gained
widespread attention in the 1930's. Lord Keynes
became the spokesman of the new economic
philosophy in Great Britain, and in continental
Europe it found expression in numerous plans
for implementing an expansionist economic
policy by means of public works.[67] The economic policy of the New Deal came closest to
the idea of using government spending as a
means of fighting the deflationary spiral and
mass unemployment.[68]

There was no opportunity to experiment along
these lines during and after World War II, when
the shortage of labor and the imminent danger
of inflation were the greatest concerns of governments, but the idea of using the national budget
as a device for maintaining equilibrium in the
economic system, preventing excessive fluctuations in money supply and ironing out the booms
and busts in business conditions gained wide
recognition. It was strongly supported by organized labor in the final phase of the war, when
many people anticipated a severe postwar depression and mass unemployment.

It also played a dominant role in the plans
for postwar economic policy developed by the
League of Nations and the International Labor
Organization and is now a guiding principle in
economic planning by experts of the UN. Its
influence on practical financial policy is less clear
than its impact on theoretical thinking.[69]

In recent years the economic objectives of the
federal budget of the United States have been
overshadowed by the requirements of foreign
aid and national defense.

In Great Britain the program of public investment gained importance in connection with
nationalization of transportation and certain
branches of industry. In France the new trend
found expression in Jean Monnet's plan for reconstruction and modernization of the French
economy.[70]

In Middle and South America, governmental
investment has become a part of planning for

industrial and economic expansion; in the former colonial and semicolonial areas in Asia, it
has become a part of the drive toward national
independence.

The contention that a national government
should engage in economic activities is not new.
In fact, the economic responsibility of governments in ancient times was as indisputable as
their responsibility for military security. The
ruins of temples, palaces and irrigation canals
are evidence of the wide scope of governmental
economic activities in the ancient world and in
the Middle Ages.[71]

The recent trend toward broadening governmental functions in economic fields, sometimes
described as economic planning, is too widespread to be explained as a temporary fashion
originated by new economic theories or inspired
by the example of economic planning in the
USSR.[72]

SOCIAL OBJECTIVES

Social objectives in governmental expenditures include social welfare and social security

67. **86,** pp. 6–8; **88,** *passim;* **19.** Cf. **28, 30, 45,
46;** and **83,** pp. 97ff. See also **53** and **54.**
68. See **28,** *passim.*
69. Cf. **67,** pp. 5–6.
70. **30,** and other publications of the same agency.

71. Athens' public works under Pericles are the classical example of "modern" economic thinking in the
ancient world. After the end of war with Persia, Pericles,
according to Plutarch, "informed the people that: . . .
they should convert the overplus of the wealth (of their
city) to such undertakings as would hereafter . . . give
them eternal honor, and, for the present, while in process,
freely supply all the inhabitants with plenty. With their
variety of workmanship and of occasions for service,
which summon all arts and trades and require all hands
to be employed about them, they do actually put the
whole city, in a manner, into state-pay. . . . For as those
who are of age and strength for war are provided for
and maintained in the armaments abroad by their pay
out of the public stock, so . . . he thought to bring in
among [the undisciplined mechanics who stayed at
home] these vast projects of buildings and designs of
work that . . . would give employment to numerous
arts. . . . (Thus) the part of the people that stayed at
home might . . . have a fair and just occasion of receiving the benefit and having their share of the public
money. . . . The materials were stone, brass, ivory, gold,
ebony, cypresswood; and the arts or trades that wrought
and fashioned them were smiths and carpenters, moul-
ders, founders and braziers, stonecutters, dyers, gold-
smiths, ivory-workers, painters, embroiderers, turners;
those again that conveyed them to the town for use,
merchants and mariners and shipmasters by sea, and by
land cartwrights, cattle breeders, waggoners, ropemakers,
flax-workers, shoemakers and leather dressers, road
makers, miners. And every trade . . . had its own
journeymen and laborers, belonging to it banded together as in array. . . . Thus, to say all in a word, the
occasions and services of these public works distributed
plenty through every age and condition." (**66,** p. 192.)
72. See **49,** p. 4.

programs, low-cost housing projects, public education and health services, price subsidies, and similar measures. A uniform classification of such projects in the national budgets of different countries is practically impossible. The data published by the UN are not inclusive and fail to show all the public expenditures for social objectives in nations with decentralized financial systems, as in the United States and Switzerland. In many cases, the national government's contributions to public education and health services are made through transfer of funds to the provincial and local governments. In some countries social insurance is administered by autonomous bodies outside the national budget.

In the United States, for example, the national budget for the fiscal year ended June 30, 1952, reported social security, welfare and health expenditures totaling $2,491 million. However, public expenditures for social services and social security in the country, including those of states and localities, totaled more than $20 billion. They comprised outlays on social insurance and related services and programs ($7,856 million); public aid ($2,584 million); health and medical services ($3,311 million); other welfare services ($1,064 million); public elementary and secondary schools ($5,838 million in 1950); and public institutions of higher education ($1,079 million in 1950).[73]

The share of public education is particularly high in the national budgets of some underdeveloped countries. Around 1952, it represented the following percentages of the total national budget: [74]

Panama	22.4	Sweden	9.0
Syria	18.8	Portugal	9.0
Chile	16.0	Iran	9.0
Iraq	15.4	New Zealand	8.4
Costa Rica	15.2	Netherlands	8.0
Ceylon	14.6	Haiti	7.6
El Salvador	14.4	Ireland	7.5
Guatemala	13.2	Venezuela	7.0
Turkey	12.6	Colombia	6.9
USSR	12.6	Austria	6.7
Peru	12.4	United Kingdom	6.2
Egypt	12.4	Thailand	5.3
Honduras	12.1	Jordan	5.0
Lebanon	11.7	Norway	4.9
Mexico	10.7	Israel	4.5
Argentina	10.7	Union of South	
Italy	10.0	Africa	4.3
Malaya	9.6	Switzerland	2.2

73. **25**, 1954, pp. 133–34 and 257.
74. Table 255.

It is noteworthy that the modern progressive countries in this list are at the bottom. The ranking changes when budgets of provincial and local governments are included. However, the total outlay on public education in the United States, including that of federal, state and local governments, does not exceed 9 per cent of total public expenditures. The fact remains that some underdeveloped countries spent a larger part of their public funds on their primitive schools than more prosperous nations pay for their elaborate systems of education. This relationship is characteristic of the order in which different types of expenditures appear in national budgets. The realization of the government's responsibility for elementary education often precedes the decision to build hospitals or launch expensive public works. Moreover, in countries on a higher level of economic development an increasing part of public expenditures is often absorbed by interest on the national debt and outlays for defense. The status of social security is not reflected satisfactorily in national budgets.

PUBLIC REVENUES

Whatever the responsibilities of the government in peace and war, it must have sufficient men and material resources at its disposal to meet them. One of the most important functions of government in all times and in all parts of the world has been to provide itself with the necessary means for performing its functions.

The broader the scope of governmental activities, the larger is the part of the national product which flows through the channels of public revenues and expenditures.

The transfer of a part of the resources of the nation to the government often results in a clash of interests between those who are called upon to pay taxes and those on whom public funds are being spent.[75]

75. Illustrative of disputes about taxes is the biblical story of the disintegration of the kingdom of Israel, under Rehoboam, the son of Solomon. The Book of Kings tells us that after the death of the builder of the Temple, the spokesmen of the people arrived at Shechem to ask the new king to repeal the taxes established by his father — in effect to ask him to cease fiscal exploitation of the land in order to increase the magnificence and glory of the capital. Before answering them, the king sought the advice of his officials and court. The "old men, that stood before Solomon," favored repeal of taxes. But "the young men that were grown up with him" insisted on an intransigent, high-tax policy. Rehoboam took their advice and rejected the plea of the people, thus provoking the division of the kingdom of Israel. Reho-

TYPES OF REVENUES

The revenues of a government can seldom be presented in the form of an internally consistent system.[76] The following remarks of William Withers on the fiscal structure in the United States apply more or less to nearly all nations at all times:

> The revenue systems of the various levels of government in the United States proliferated in unplanned and uncoordinated directions to meet the rising cost of government. . . . The taxes of one jurisdiction often overlap, conflict or compete with those of other jurisdictions. . . . Some government units are able to obtain surplus revenue while others are unable to meet expenses. In emergencies such as wars and depressions a unified national fiscal policy is difficult to establish and maintain. . . . The newer forms of taxation of income, business and consumption were adopted without regard for their duplicating effects. All governments exploited available sources of revenue as public expenditures rapidly increased.[77]

A classification of public revenues that is applicable to all countries at all times is impossible. Some items considered as revenue in one country are not regarded as such in another. Many taxes serve several purposes and can be classified only as "miscellaneous" revenues.[78]

Taxes and nontax revenues. In a very general way, most classifications make a distinction between taxes and nontax revenues.[79] *Taxes* are the part of income or property which individuals and corporations are compelled to give up to the public authorities.[80] *Nontax revenues* are the receipts that accrue to the government from the sale, operation or lease of lands, forests and mines; public enterprises and investments; tributes and reparations; coinage and depreciation of money; and fines and gifts. The most important nontax revenues usually are the profits of government monopolies conducted for revenue purposes, such as the monopoly on tobacco products in France or on the distribution of alcohol and liquor in czarist Russia. The economic effect of such revenues is similar to that of consumption taxes.[81] They differ, however, from consumption taxes not only in the method of collection but also in their underlying political philosophy. The same political forces that oppose indirect taxes often support expansion of governmental economic activities, including revenue monopolies. In many countries the share of nontax revenues in the national budget is increasing while the role of consumption taxes declines.

Less important are licenses and the service fees of public agencies, which are usually classified as nontax revenues. Some authors prefer to treat these as a separate type, intermediate between taxes and nontax revenues.

Among innumerable taxes, two major groups are usually distinguished: direct and indirect.[82] The distinction is not always clear, however. As a rule, *direct* taxes are levied on individuals, usually on the basis of a personal schedule, either per capita or in accordance with the income, occupation or property of the individual. The most important taxes of this group are the personal

---

boam kept Jerusalem and "an army of an hundred and fourscore thousand chosen men." The rest of the kingdom turned away from him saying: "What portion have we in David? . . . to your tents, O Israel." (I Kings 12.)

76. Germany under the Weimar Republic was one of the few exceptions: it had an almost perfectly streamlined fiscal system, which, however, proved fatal to the nation. In its preoccupation with preserving this system and maintaining a balanced budget, the government neglected other objectives of financial policy and did nothing to stop the deflationary spiral. More specifically, it took no measures against the rise of unemployment because it feared that outlays on public works would result in a budgetary deficit and endanger the stability of the currency. Thus its preoccupation with the budgetary equilibrium paved the way for Hitler's rise to power.

77. **86**, p. 353.

78. William J. Shultz distinguishes four types of classifications: historical, administrative, causal and functional. The first rests on the alleged historical sequence of development of certain types of governmental revenues: (a) gifts; (b) subsidies and tributes; (c) sovereign prerogatives of fines, coinage and the like; (d) forced contributions of personal services; (e) indirect taxation; (f) direct taxes. The administrative classification stresses the difference in the procedures used for providing the revenues. The causal classification distinguishes between gratuitous contributions (gifts), contractual (such as returns from the sale or lease of the public domain) and compulsory (taxes). The functional classification distinguishes (a) fees levied for public utility services; (b) fees, license charges and special assessments levied when a governmental activity confers a special benefit on the individual; (c) all other forms of governmental revenue. (**75**, pp. 185ff.)

79. Some authors consider this distinction less essential than the contrast between revenues based on the sovereign power of the government (taxes, franchises, licenses, fees, fines and so on) and commercial revenues (from land, property, business operations and similar sources). (Cf. **51**, p. 82.)

80. **62**, Vol. 1, p. 319.

81. **3**, p. 22.

82. This classification is close to Bastable's distinction between primary and secondary taxes, although Bastable considered death (or inheritance) duties a secondary tax. (**38**, p. 280.)

income tax and the general property tax. The land tax, however, is direct when it is paid by the owner out of his income and indirect when the landowner handles it as an item of production cost. Other direct taxes are death duties and capital levies. The distinction between direct taxes on income and capital is of considerable significance in countries in which the national budget is presented under two heads — current and capital expenditures and revenues [83] — but demands no elaboration within the scope of this study.

Indirect taxes are levied in association with definite transactions, such as purchase of goods or transfer of property independent of the individual circumstances of the taxpayer. Usually they affect prices of certain commodities or services, being chargeable to them as a cost item.[84] Two varieties of indirect taxes can be distinguished — consumption taxes and transfer taxes.

Consumption taxes are sometimes classified as taxes on necessaries (for example, salt or sugar excises) and taxes on luxuries.[85] This distinction is of little use in an international survey of taxation. A more formal classification is preferable: excise taxes, sales taxes, customs duties. Most business taxes, like excises, can be shifted to the price of the product and are therefore indirect taxes.

The place of corporation profit taxes in this classification is not clear. Formally, they are levied on the income of corporations and are often defended as a means of curtailing excessively high incomes. In international surveys of public finance, they are often classified with other levies on property and income.[86] They lack, however, the characteristic features of direct taxes and some experts describe them as a special form of indirect business tax.[87]

Very often a tax has contradictory features. The United States Supreme Court has been called upon to decide whether the income tax is direct or indirect.[88] Struggling with this problem, the Court tried to segregate the income tax

as it was voted by Congress into its components and determine when each component is a "direct" tax and when it becomes "indirect."

Frequent changes in tax laws make international comparison of them particularly difficult. Although some taxes have remained unchanged for many decades, most tax laws are voted only for one fiscal year and are revised or amended the next year. Some amendments are trivial, others affect important provisions of the tax law, such as rates and exemptions.

CRITERIA OF GOOD AND BAD TAXES

In 1782, Burke complained in the House of Commons: "We were already taxed if we rode or if we walked; if we kept at home or went abroad; if we were masters or if we were servants; if we drank wine or if we drank beer, and in short, we were taxed in every way possible." [89] According to our modern standards, these complaints were exaggerated. British taxes were badly distributed at that time, but the total fiscal burden of British taxpayers was not excessive.

Some economists of the laissez-faire school in the early part of the nineteenth century believed that any tax was an evil and the disagreements among them were only in degree: the higher a tax, the greater the evil. Other economists distinguished between good and bad taxes. In his famous treatise, Adam Smith expressed ideas which were widely accepted by his contemporaries when he offered four criteria for a good tax:

1. The subjects of every state ought to contribute toward the support of the government, as nearly as possible in proportion to their respective abilities; that is, in proportion to the revenue which they respectively enjoy. . . .

2. The tax which each individual is bound to pay ought to be certain and not arbitrary. . . .

3. Every tax ought to be levied at the time or in the manner in which it is most likely to be convenient for the contributor to pay it. . . .

4. Every tax must be so contrived as both to take out and to keep out of the pockets of the people as little as possible, over and above what it brings into the public treasury of the state.[90]

These four principles — equity, certainty, convenience and economy — are still in use, although interpretation of the terms has changed.[91]

---

83. **3**, p. 23.
84. **3**, p. 22.
85. **62**, Vol. 1, p. 344.
86. See **3**, p. 23.
87. See **80**.
88. The term "direct" tax was not used in this legal controversy in the sense in which it is used now. The task of the Court was rather to determine the nature of the income tax in relation to the concept of "direct" taxation as it was used in the U.S. Constitution. (See **72**, p. 10.)

89. Quoted in **47**, p. 174.
90. **76**, pp. 371–72. For an analysis of Smith's views see **57**.
91. **86**, pp. 18ff; **77**, Chapter 1.

Probably few modern students will accept Adam Smith's first maxim without reservations. Most will agree that a system of taxes which makes everyone give up the same proportion of his revenues would be unfair to the low-income groups of the population. They will argue that if an individual with an income close to the subsistence minimum is asked to give up 5 per cent of his income, a much higher rate should be imposed upon a rich man. The principle of progressive taxation, widely accepted in our day, was foreign to the thinking of the eighteenth century. Although Smith believed that taxation should be as nearly as possible proportionate to the taxpayer's "abilities," he did not go so far as to support a direct proportionate income tax. He considered it the most objectionable form of "capitation," a kind of poll tax with rates arbitrarily adjusted to the fortune of the taxpayer:

Capitation taxes, if it is attempted to proportion them to the fortune or revenue of each contributor, become altogether arbitrary. The state of a man's fortune varies from day to day, and without an inquisition more intolerable than any tax, and renewed at least once every year, can only be guessed at. His assessment, therefore, must in most cases depend upon the good or bad humor of his assessors, and must therefore be altogether arbitrary and uncertain.[92]

Smith held that the ideal system of taxation was a combination of land taxes, moderate taxes on profits, and excises and customs duties on selected articles.[93] He considered taxes on consumption a workable alternative to the impossible proportionate direct taxation of revenues:

The impossibility of taxing the people in proportion to their revenue, by any capitation, seems to have given occasion to the invention of taxes upon consummable commodities. The state not knowing how to tax directly and proportionally the revenue of its subjects, endeavours to tax it indirectly by taxing their expense, which, it is supposed, will in most cases be nearly in proportion to their revenues.[94]

Smith did not object to the progressiveness of certain taxes on consumption of luxuries. Such, in his eyes, was the tax on house rents, which "would in general fall heaviest upon the rich. . . . In this sort of inequality," he remarked, "there would not, perhaps, be anything very unreasonable. It is not very unreasonable that

the rich should contribute to the public expense, not only in proportion to their revenue, but something more than in that proportion."[95]

Whatever our interpretation of the equity of taxation, Adam Smith's four criteria may conflict with one another. Some types of taxes appear equitable and certain but inconvenient and uneconomical; others are economical, convenient and certain but contrary to our standard of equity. Pigou tried to reduce the various criteria to one single principle of taxation: the least aggregate sacrifice required of taxpayers.[96] This principle suggests a system of progressive taxes but provides no guidance in such questions as the optimum and most equitable degree of progressiveness, the economic implications of different fiscal measures, the ways of ensuring stability of the fiscal system and protecting it against excessive fluctuations resulting from changes in business conditions.

Moreover, whichever criteria are accepted for appraising particular taxes, in actuality the fiscal systems of nations develop and change as a result of compromises between different points of view and conflicting interests. Often a fiscal measure is used to fill gaps and to compensate for the weakness of another system. Thus, for example, direct taxes and levies have been used in emergencies because considerable funds could thus be raised quickly. Indirect taxes have been advocated as a supplement to direct taxation because the yield was less sensitive to changes in business conditions; moreover they are frequently less obvious to the taxpayer. The property tax has been used as a means of reaching income which evades general income taxation. It has been found that any new tax meets stronger objection than old taxes to which people have adjusted themselves. The common practice has therefore been to keep old taxes and add to them new taxes.

Moreover, modern fiscal policy goes beyond an appraisal of different taxes from the point of view of equity, certainty, convenience and economy, and compares their yield to the treasury with the sacrifices demanded from taxpayers. It also appraises each tax in terms of its effect on different sectors of the national economy, independent of the purpose for which its yield will be used. In other words, to the fiscal considerations stressed by the classical school, modern

92. **76**, p. 392.
93. **76**, pp. 372ff.
94. **76**, p. 393.

95. **76**, p. 379.
96. **64**, pp. 40–45, 60–61.

financial policy adds a broader economic criterion: to what extent does each tax fit into the economic program of the government? [97]

DISTRIBUTION OF FISCAL RESOURCES

Each country has its own way of distributing fiscal resources among federal and local governments. As a rule, the central government has customs duties at its disposal. Local governments usually, but not always, get the lion's share of property taxes, especially taxes on land. Income taxes are levied mainly by the central government in the United States, Canada, the United Kingdom, France and Italy, but are imposed primarily by local governments in Sweden, the Netherlands and Switzerland. Excises are divided almost evenly between central and local governments in the United States and Canada, but are used mainly by central governments in most European countries. Business and sales taxes are used by both central and local agencies. (See Table 257.)

TRENDS IN TAXATION

The historical development of taxation has been marked less by replacement of old practices by new than by a shift of emphasis from one type of taxation to another.

In ancient times, public finances rested mainly on public ownership of land. Control over land, forests and mines provided rulers of commonwealths with the means to carry out their functions. Occasionally this source was supplemented by monopolies, excises and customs duties.[98] In a national emergency special direct taxes and levies were used as a temporary measure.

The structure of public finances in the Middle Ages was largely determined by the idea that all land belonged to the sovereign and his subjects could hold it only under definite conditions. The land tax became a payment by the holder to the sovereign. The significance of other medieval taxes, direct and indirect, which were introduced as need arose to supplement the land tax, increased with the rise of cities and the development of large centralized kingdoms. Public

finances in Europe in the sixteenth and seventeenth centuries rested on a combination of the land tax with excises, monopolies and import duties. The campaign of the Physiocrats for a single land tax aroused little response. Adam Smith, although a friend and admirer of the Physiocrats, refused to follow them in this matter and stressed the advantage of a combination of diversified taxes, none of them burdensome enough to provoke the wrath of taxpayers but together able to provide enough funds for a thrifty government.

Taxes in the eighteenth century were regressive — exemplified by the system of taxation of the *ancien régime* in France, under which the nobility and clergy enjoyed liberal exemptions; consumption taxes, which fell heavily upon the poor, represented the backbone of the fiscal system.[99]

The shift toward direct taxes began in the nineteenth century but was very slow at the beginning. The income tax was considered an emergency measure rather than the foundation of sound and equitable finances in normal times.

This conception prevailed in public finances through the nineteenth century and even in the first quarter of the twentieth. Nitti wrote in the 1920's:

All fiscal systems of today are based on indirect taxes, consumption taxes. It is true that indirect taxes have resulted in many abuses . . . but they are the only really effective forms of taxation. Thus, indirect taxes remaining the foundation of the budget, they must be and are supplemented by direct taxes on property and especially on income. In many nations, the latter are used as supplementary taxes designed mainly to reach the income which otherwise would escape taxation.[100]

Nitti rejected the idea of a single tax as practicably impossible and fallacious even in principle:

Apart from the archaic conception of the Physiocrats, how could one visualize the single tax? A single tax on consumption is practically absurd. The only conceivable choice is between capital and income as the exclusive objective of taxation. However, the single tax on income and the single tax on capital are equally dubious and practically impossible.[101]

At that time many students of public finance were inclined to stress the advantages of taxes

---

97. **57,** pp. 342ff.

98. The Greek geographer Strabo described customs duties in Egypt: "The most valuable assignments come to Egypt from India and Ethiopia and are sent . . . to the rest of the world, so that Egypt gets double duties from them, on coming and on going out. And the duties are heavy in proportion to the value of the goods." (Quoted in **84,** p. 161.)

99. Cf. **71,** p. 485.

100. **62,** p. 338.

101. **62.**

TABLE 257

FISCAL RESOURCES: PERCENTAGE DISTRIBUTION BY LEVEL OF GOVERNMENT AND TYPE OF TAX, IN SELECTED COUNTRIES, BEFORE WORLD WAR II (According to Paul Studenski)

(*All Central and Local Tax Revenue* = 100)

Country, Year and Agency	All Taxes	Income	Property	Inheritance	Business	Sales	Excise	Customs	Other
United States, 1932–34									
Total	100.0	5.3	57.5	2.0	12.3	0.2	19.3	3.1	0.3
Federal	23.1	4.4	—	0.4	6.7	—	8.5	3.1	—
State and local	76.9	0.9	57.5	1.6	5.6	0.2	10.8	—	0.3
Canada, 1931–32									
Total	100.0	9.9	40.6	3.0	4.2	9.6	15.7	16.8	0.2
National	44.4	9.9	—	—	—	9.6	7.9	16.8	0.2
Provincial and local	55.6	—	40.6	3.0	4.2	—	7.8	—	—
United Kingdom, 1929–32									
Total	100.0	39.9	19.8	7.1	2.2	—	16.1	14.9	—
National	80.3	39.9	0.1	7.1	2.2	—	16.1	14.9	—
Local	19.7	—	19.7	—	—	—	—	—	—
France, 1929–33									
Total	100.0	20.1	11.7	—	14.1	13.0	21.9	9.5	9.7
National	72.9	20.1	—	—	11.9	13.0	18.4	9.5	—
Local	27.1	—	11.7	—	2.2	—	3.5	—	9.7
Belgium, 1931									
Total	100.0	34.2	0.3	3.0	26.6	2.8	12.2	15.5	5.4
National	82.6	19.5	0.2	3.0	26.6	2.8	11.2	15.5	3.8
Local	17.4	14.7	0.1	—	—	—	1.0	—	1.6
Netherlands, 1931									
Total	100.0	31.3	21.5	6.0	9.8	—	22.9	8.1	0.4
National	63.6	12.9	6.3	6.0	8.1	—	21.8	8.1	0.4
Local	36.4	18.4	15.2	—	1.7	—	1.1	—	—
Sweden, 1929–31									
Total	100.0	54.3	3.0	—	5.1	—	6.9	30.1	0.6
National	57.6	16.4	—	—	4.8	—	6.1	30.1	0.2
Local	42.4	37.9	3.0	—	0.3	—	0.8	—	0.4
Switzerland, 1932									
Total	100.0	49.5	1.5	2.1	7.7	—	5.9	32.7	0.6
National	41.5	3.0	—	—	5.8	—	—	32.7	—
Canton and local	58.5	46.5	1.5	2.1	1.9	—	5.9	—	0.6

Source: **81**, p. 29.

on consumption (customs duties and excises). They are "painless" when, paying them, the tax-payer is rewarded by special satisfaction, as in the case of tobacco and alcoholic beverages; they are easy to collect and yield substantial revenues; they can be easily enforced against evasion and fraud.

With a few significant exceptions, the prevailing opinion of experts before World War I was in favor of indirect taxes supplemented by mod-erate property and income taxes, with either a flat rate for all taxpayers or slightly progressive rates.

A decade or two later, all modern nations shifted toward the progressive income tax as the main foundation of national finance. Sir Josiah Stamp has described the new development as follows:

There is no country in which the whole system of taxation is one, logically worked out, from first principles. Everywhere the accidents of political and commercial considerations in past history are perpetuated and condition the present systems. But there is little doubt that these are gradually gravitating toward one or two common main types in which personal taxation of income is taking a predominant part, while various systems of indirect taxation and tariffs are taking a less important place relatively, even though their absolute yield is maintained.[102]

The decisive factor accounting for this development was the shift in political power. Under the system of indirect taxation, the largest part of the fiscal burden was shouldered by the poor and middle classes. The rise of organized labor made this system untenable. In their claim for direct taxation with graduated rates and higher charges upon the wealthy, the labor parties found broad support in the middle classes.

To political pressure was added a shift in economic thinking. The theory of diminishing utility (sometimes called the "marginal theory"), which became universally accepted by the end of the nineteenth century as the foundation of economic science, provided a theoretical basis for the principle of progressive taxation.[103] This theory does not require that every tax be progressive, but it shows convincingly that the tax system cannot pass the test of equity unless it results in progressive effective taxation.

The United States

The fiscal system introduced by Alexander Hamilton in the United States was in line with ideas which prevailed in England at that time — a combination of customs duties and excises. Of the two, the first proved to be nearly sufficient and customs duties remained the principal source of federal revenues until the Civil War; except during a short period of intensive sale of public land, customs met 80–90 per cent of fiscal needs of the government. During the Civil War, the federal government raised funds essentially by loans and issuance of paper money. When the destructive effect of these measures on the economic life of the nation became obvious, new taxes — among them a general income tax — were levied. The income tax was later repealed, while consumption taxes gained increasing significance in the 1870's and in the latter part of the century became the backbone of the federal budget.

After the outbreak of World War I, the system of indirect taxes proved completely inadequate. In 1916–20, customs provided 6.5 per cent of federal revenue, as compared with 40.7 per cent in 1911–15 and 49.4 per cent in 1906–10. Income and profit taxes became the foundation of the federal budget and maintained this leading position after the end of the war. (See Table 258; cf. Figure 142.) Their share in public revenues declined in the 1930's under the impact of the depression, but with the advent of World War II, income and profits taxes again became the fiscal pillars of the defense and rearmament program. These taxes financed more than two thirds of the war budgets of 1943–46.

In recent years, income and profit taxes have been recognized as the most reliable, and also the most flexible, element in the fiscal system.

The United Kingdom

As in other European countries, public finance in the United Kingdom depended until the end of the eighteenth century on a combination of land taxes, excises, import duties and direct levies. Indirect taxes and excises prevailed in peacetime, and direct taxes assessed on the property or means of individual taxpayers were regarded as an emergency measure.[104] Typical of such emergency taxes was the hearth-money tax introduced in 1662 — a levy of 2 shillings per year for every stove or hearth in every dwelling house except one-family cottages.[105] In 1689, this was the only direct tax in the kingdom. It yielded about £200,000, as compared with some £1,000,000 collected in import duties.[106]

During 1689–98, a per capita (poll) tax was levied repeatedly, each time in a different way, with an annual yield ranging from £6,000 in

102. **77**, p. 25.

103. The theory of diminishing utility rests on the observation that a consumer with a limited amount of money at his disposal uses each dollar for his most urgent need. Each additional dollar represents for him, therefore, a smaller utility than the preceding one. According to this general rule the value (utility) of the last dollar is larger for the poor taxpayer than for the rich. The corollary of this proposition is that a 10-percent tax represents a larger part of total utility of a small income than 10 per cent of a large income. In other words, taxation proportional to income is regressive in terms of the satisfactions taxed away from consumers on different levels of income. To be proportionate in terms of the sacrifice demanded of taxpayers, the income tax must be progressive.

104. **47**, pp. 3–5.
105. **47**, p. 29.
106. **47**, pp. 42–43.

TABLE 258

FEDERAL REVENUES BY SOURCE, IN THE UNITED STATES, 1789–1800 TO 1953

Period [a]	Total, in Millions of Dollars	Percentage Distribution				Period [a]	Total, in Millions of Dollars	Percentage Distribution			
		Cus- toms	Income and Profit Taxes	Other Taxes	Nontax Receipts			Cus- toms	Income and Profit Taxes	Other Taxes	Nontax Receipts
1789–1800	$ 5.7	87.8	—	6.6	5.6	1930	$ 4,177.9	14.0	57.7	15.0	13.3
1801–10	13.1	92.3	—	1.5	6.2	1931	3,189.6	11.9	58.3	17.9	11.9
1811–20	21.0	77.9	—	7.3	14.8	1932	2,005.7	16.3	52.7	25.1	5.9
1821–30	21.9	91.0	—	0.1	8.9	1933	2,079.7	12.0	35.9	41.3	10.8
1831–40	30.5	67.2	—	—	32.8	1934	3,115.6	10.1	26.3	58.5	5.1
1841–50	28.5	89.9	—	—	10.1	1935	3,800.5	9.0	28.9	57.3	4.8
1851–60	60.2	90.5	—	—	9.5	1936	4,116.0	9.4	34.7	50.7	5.2
1861–65	160.9	42.9	17.4	33.9	5.8	1937	5,293.6	9.2	40.9	46.0	3.9
1866–70	447.3	40.0	11.3	38.3	10.4	1938	6,241.7	5.8	42.3	48.8	3.1
1871–75	336.8	55.3	2.3	33.3	9.1	1939	5,667.8	5.6	38.6	52.4	3.4
1876–80	288.1	50.9	—	40.5	8.6	1940	5,893.4	5.9	36.1	53.9	4.1
1881–85	367.0	55.0	—	36.0	9.0	1941	7,995.6	4.9	43.4	48.7	3.0
1886–90	375.4	57.7	—	33.7	8.6	1942	13,676.7	2.8	58.2	36.8	2.2
1891–95	352.9	50.1	—	42.5	7.4	1943	23,402.3	1.4	68.7	25.9	4.0
1896–1900	434.9	42.5	—	47.5	10.0	1944	45,441.0	0.9	76.3	15.5	7.3
1901–05	559.5	46.5	—	45.7	7.8	1945	47,750.3	0.7	73.7	18.3	7.3
1906–10	628.5	49.4	3.3	40.9	6.4	1946	44,238.1	1.0	69.8	21.3	7.9
1911–15	710.2	40.7	7.0	43.2	9.1	1947	44,508.2	1.1	65.8	22.6	10.5
1916–20	3,483.7	6.5	56.0	25.6	11.9	1948	46,098.8	0.9	67.6	23.2	8.3
1921–25	4,306.7	10.7	49.1	24.4	15.8	1949	42,773.5	0.9	68.9	25.3	4.9
1926	3,962.8	14.6	50.0	21.6	13.8	1950	41,310.6	1.0	68.4	27.1	3.5
1927	4,129.4	14.7	53.9	15.6	15.8	1951	53,368.7	1.2	70.7	25.0	3.1
1928	4,042.3	14.1	53.8	15.4	16.7	1952	67,999.4	0.8	75.5	21.0	2.7
1929	4,033.2	14.9	57.8	15.0	12.3	1953	72,455.5	0.8	74.6	21.9	2.7

Sources: **23,** pp. 296–98; **25,** 1953, p. 337 and 1954, p. 361.

a. Year ended June 30. For 1789–1800 to 1921–25: annual average.

1693 to more than £600,000 the following year.

In the eighteenth century, the British government raised its revenues by means of customs duties, land and house taxes, taxes on various articles of consumption, stamp duties and the like. During the difficult struggle with France (1797), when all these sources seemed to have been exhausted, Pitt introduced a super tax based on the existing assessments and calculated in such a way as to levy 10 per cent on all income in excess of £200. This "triple assessment tax," the first income tax in England,[107] was revised in 1798 and 1799; repealed in 1802 after the Treaty of Amiens; restored in an improved form in 1803. It remained as an important but very unpopular source of public income until 1816, when it was abolished.

In 1842, the income tax was restored, essentially in the same form as in 1806. Since that time, it has remained a part of the British fiscal system in peace and war.[108]

The general structure of the British fiscal system changed little from the time of the Napoleonic wars to the 1880's. In 1815, 38 per cent of the ordinary revenues (excluding Ireland's contribution) was provided by direct taxes, 58 per cent by taxes on consumption and 4 per cent by stamp duties. In 1883, direct taxes accounted for 30 per cent of the revenues of the national government, taxes on consumption for 64 per cent,

107. **72,** pp. 66 and 113ff.

108. For details see pp. 723ff.

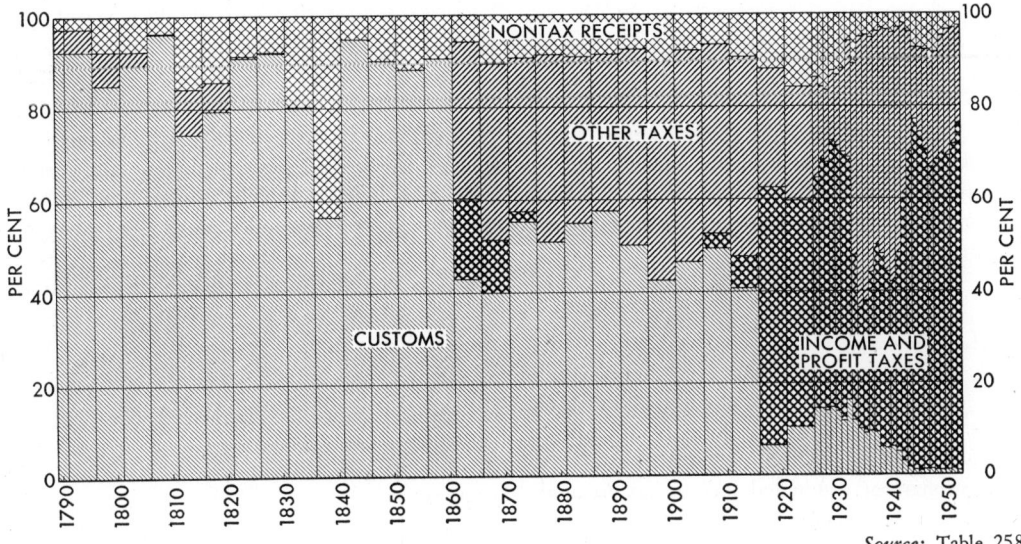

Source: Table 258

FIGURE 142. FEDERAL REVENUES: PERCENTAGE DISTRIBUTION BY SOURCE, IN THE UNITED STATES, 1789–1952

TABLE 259

CENTRAL GOVERNMENT REVENUES IN THE UNITED KINGDOM: PERCENTAGE DISTRIBUTION OF ORDINARY REVENUE, BY SOURCE, 1939–51

Source	1939	1943	1945	1947	1949	1951
Ordinary revenue	100.0	100.0	100.0	100.0	100.0	100.0
Inland revenue						
Income tax [a]	43.0	38.4	42.7	36.9	36.0	38.3
Death duties	8.4	3.3	3.4	4.4	4.2	4.5
Stamp duties	2.3	0.5	0.5	1.2	1.4	1.4
Profits tax	2.4	1.1	1.0	1.0	5.0	6.2
Excess profits tax	—	12.3	14.7	9.7	2.0	0.2
Other [b]	0.2	0.0	0.0	0.0	2.0	0.1
Customs and excises						
Customs	24.4	16.0	17.9	18.6	20.5	22.7
Excises	12.3	15.0	15.3	16.9	18.3	18.1
Other taxes and receipts [c]	7.0	13.4	4.5	11.3	10.6	8.5

Source: **33,** 1938–48, p. 222 and 1940–50, p. 252. Year ending March 31.

a. Includes surtax.
b. Includes special contributions in 1949 and 1951.

c. Includes motor vehicle duties; sales of surplus war stores (1947–51); Canadian government contribution (1943); and other nontax receipts.

stamp duties for 6 per cent.[109] During all this time, taxes on consumption, including customs duties, were mainly on beverages and tobacco.

The income tax provided 13.2 per cent of total revenues in 1883 and 18.2 per cent in 1900.[110] Direct taxes accounted for 54 per cent of governmental revenue in 1913–14, prevailed during

World War I, represented nearly 60 per cent of revenue in 1921–22 and slightly more than 50 per cent in 1927–28.[111] This rate increased during World War II but has declined in recent years. (See Table 259.)

Three phases may be distinguished in the modern history of British taxation:

1. From the end of the eighteenth to the end

109. **47,** pp. 396–97.
110. **62,** p. 359.

111. **87,** p. 33.

of the nineteenth century: predominance of customs duties and excises with a slow increase in direct taxation by the end of the period.

2. From the beginning of the twentieth century to the 1930's: a shift toward direct taxes, with increasing emphasis on the income tax.

3. From the 1930's to the present: consolidation of the fiscal system, essentially on the basis of direct taxes.

INCOME TAXES

When we speak of an income tax, we usually think of a tax with rates that are higher for high incomes than for low. This has not always been the practice. The road was long from indirect and poll taxes to the income tax and from the proportionate or graduated income tax to modern progressive income taxation.

Types of Income Taxes

There are many varieties of income taxes. Some are levied on particular types of income, others, on all income of the taxpayer. Some deal with income as such, regardless of its origin; others treat particular types of income differently (for example, "earned" and "unearned" income, "capital gains" and other income, and so on). The most significant classification of income taxes is by the rate structure and the method used to ascertain the taxpayer's income.

In terms of rate structure, three types of income tax can be distinguished: the scheduled or objective tax; the proportionate tax; and the progressive tax. Under the first, all citizens are divided into several classes according to their wealth, income or ability to pay, and members of each group are asked to pay a definite, stated sum. Income taxes of the second type charge all taxpayers in proportion to their income — so many cents for each dollar of income. Under a progressive income tax the rate of taxation increases with the amount of income. An income tax of the second type can be transformed into a progressive tax in several ways: by exempting part of an individual's income from taxation; by "abatement" of tax rates for low incomes; by levying a surtax on high incomes; by differentiating rates for different income classes or by a combination of several of these devices.

Three types of income taxes can likewise be distinguished in a classification of taxes by the method used to determine taxable income. Presumptive income taxes assess the taxpayer on the basis of some visible evidence of wealth or income, such as the type of dwelling, number of servants or value of furnishings.[112] A lump-sum income tax is assessed in accordance with all the income of the taxpayer, regardless of its origin. A scheduled tax asks the taxpayer to report on each of the several types of income and assesses each type separately. The distinction between the two latter types fades when the taxpayer is asked to report the individual items in his income so that the total sum can be ascertained.

Income Taxes in the Ancient World

Although the predominance of the income tax in public finance is characteristic of modern times, some rudimentary traces of it have been discovered in the ancient world and even in the Bible.[113]

Graduated taxes were used in ancient Greece and Rome as an emergency measure. A progressive income tax was enacted in Athens during the Peloponnesian war, on the insistence of Cleon, the illustrious leader of this city-republic immortalized by Aristophanes, his enemy.[114]

The people of Athens were familiar with such income tax problems as inequities in assessment, taxpayers' dishonesty and tax evasion. Plato has been credited with the observation: "When there is an income tax, the just man will pay more and the unjust less on the same amount of income." [115]

In the Middle Ages, income taxes and graduated levies appeared time and again on a national and local scale. In most cases flat rates were used so that, from the point of view of the modern classification, most of the income taxes of that time were regressive, though there were exceptions. A really progressive income tax, with rates that occasionally reached 50 per cent in the highest income brackets, existed in Florence in the fifteenth and sixteenth centuries, and was revived in 1710, with tax rates ranging from 10 to 20 per cent.[116]

---

112. In this sense, a general property tax can be described as a presumptive income tax in disguise.

113. ". . . and they shall not appear before the Lord empty [handed]: Every man shall give as he is able, according to the blessing of the Lord thy God which he hath given thee." Deut. 16:16–17.

114. **43**, p. 391.

115. This remark appears in Plato's *Republic* (**65**, Vol. 2, p. 26) in the outburst of Thrasymachus, who plays the role of a buffoon. It is clear from the context that Plato did not consider the complaints about tax evasion a serious objection to the income tax.

116. **62**, Vol. 1, p. 380.

Forced Loans in the French Revolution

The progressive taxes of the French Revolution were designed to serve several purposes: to stop inflation; to destroy the rich; and to give comfort to the poor, especially to the men in the revolutionary armies. "It is time to make the egoistic rich share in the burdens that so far have been carried by the poor alone" read the petition of the Commune of Paris, the spearhead of radical ideas. "We ask that a war tax be levied on this class of people." [117]

This proposal aroused enthusiasm in the National Convention and the principle of taxing the rich was adopted immediately. It took the Convention more time to convert this principle into law. Finally it took the form of a national forced loan of 1,000 million livres. Each member of the family was allowed an exemption of 1,000 livres (1,500 livres for married men and widows with children), and all income above the exemption was taxed at rates rising from 10 per cent on the first taxable 1,000 livres to 100 per cent (which was straight confiscation) on income over 9,000 livres.

The results of this measure were highly unsatisfactory. Although collection of the loan was spread over two years, only one fifth of the expected sum was collected. Two years later, under the Directory, a new forced loan was launched. This time the rates of assessment, although progressive, were very conservative; the highest assessments were fixed at 1,500 to 6,000 livres for persons with capital of more than 500,000 livres, with the provision that the taxpayers in this wealthy group were to pay "according to their faculties." This measure proved an even greater failure; instead of the anticipated 600 million livres, it yielded 8 million.

In 1798, the government ordered a new progressive forced loan of 100 million livres. The new loan was to supplement the real estate tax, with special assessments for taxpayers whose payments of that tax appeared too low in relation to their total income.[118] The yield of this loan was deplorably small. When Napoleon assumed power, the plan was abandoned and progressive taxation ended in France for a long time.[119]

The Income Tax in the United Kingdom

The modern progressive income tax was born in 1797 in Great Britain, and was fathered by William Pitt, the younger. His Triple Assessment Act was an ingenious attempt to establish progressive general taxation of income on the basis of the nonprogressive taxes then existing in England. Three groups of taxes were used as the basis of the new general surtax: assessments for carriages, horses and men servants; assessments for inhabited houses, windows, dogs, clocks and watches; and assessments for lodgings and shops. In computing the rates of the new tax at various presumed income levels, the assessments of old taxes were taken with appropriate weights to provide a fairly smooth progressiveness of taxation: no tax on income of less than £60; five sixths of one per cent on income of £60–£65; rates rising gradually from about 1 per cent to 10 per cent for income ranging between £65 and £200; 10 per cent on £200 and more.

The act did not live up to all anticipations, but the idea of progressive taxation with a ceiling of 10 per cent for high incomes took root. In 1799 Pitt introduced a new bill providing for progressive taxation of total income at the same rates as in the Triple Assessment Act. The law was fundamentally reshaped in 1803: a system of schedules was introduced for assessing different types of income and the ceiling was lowered to 5 per cent (1s. per pound) for income in excess of £150. Rates were increased in 1805 and again in 1806, and a ceiling of 10 per cent remained in force until 1816 when, soon after the final defeat of Napoleon at Waterloo, the tax was repealed.

In 1842 Sir Robert Peel reintroduced the income tax as part of a far-reaching financial reform. The new law followed essentially the pattern of the old income tax of 1806, with only one important difference: a flat rate of 6.33 per cent on all income over £150 replaced progressive rates.[120] In 1853, the principle of progressive taxation was partly restored in a simplified form: 5d. per pound on income of £100–150, 7d. per pound on income above £150. Practically, the progressiveness was applied to income from £100 to £2,000 and a flat rate (of slightly less than 3 per cent), to all income over £2,000.

With modifications in exemptions, abatements, deductions and general rates, this type of income

---

117. **71**, p. 32.

118. Provisions were somewhat similar to those used in the progressive income taxation established at that time in England.

119. **71**, pp. 36–37.

120. **71**, p. 42.

TABLE 260

TAXES IN THE UNITED KINGDOM: EFFECTIVE RATES, BY INCOME LEVEL, 1903–04 TO 1918–19
(According to Sir Herbert Samuel)

(*Rate of Taxation as Percentage of Income* [a])

Taxpayer's Annual Income	Income from Work			Income from Property		
	1903–04	*1913–14*	*1918–19*	*1903–04*	*1913–14*	*1918–19*
£ 50	9.1	8.1	—	9.1	8.7	—
100	6.2	6.0	13.8	6.2	6.0	13.8
150	5.0	4.9	11.0	5.0	4.9	11.0
200	5.6	4.8	10.3	7.8	7.0	12.4
500	6.6	5.8	13.1	8.8	9.9	18.1
1,000	7.4	6.6	19.4	10.3	12.2	26.5
2,000	6.6	5.8	25.6	9.8	12.0	33.6
5,000	5.6	6.8	37.2	9.6	12.4	43.5
10,000	5.1	8.1	42.6	9.5	15.1	50.3
20,000	4.9	8.3	47.6	10.0	16.0	58.1
50,000	4.8	8.4	50.6	10.2	18.1	63.9

Source: **69**, p. 179.

a. Assuming that all taxes on commodities are paid wholly by consumers.

tax remained in force until 1907. During this period, the United Kingdom had a proportional income tax, with a slight abatement of the general rate for the lowest incomes.[121] The general rate was changed repeatedly. It fluctuated between 6*d.* and 8*d.* per pound (2.5 per cent to 3.3 per cent) until the turn of the century and between 1*s.* and 1*s.* 2*d.* (5–6 per cent) after 1900.[122]

Although the nation then had some progressive taxes (for example, estate duties), its system of taxes was regressive on the whole. As a result of the predominance of excises and other taxes on consumption, the poor were asked to give the government a larger proportion of their income than the rich. The Finance Act of 1907 changed the situation by introducing a surtax of 2.5 per cent (6*d.* per pound) on all income over £5,000. During World War I, the progressiveness of the fiscal system was increased by heavy taxation of incomes in the upper brackets. Contrary to the experience after the Napoleonic wars, the principle of direct progressive taxation remained unchallenged after the end of the war. Indeed, it was strengthened in the first postwar budget (1918–19) under Lloyd George. The fiscal system was further tightened during World War II and its new features again remained in force after that war.

According to Sir Herbert Samuel, the transformation of the British system of taxation from regressive to progressive was effected during World War I.[123] (See Table 260.) The 1927 Treasury Committee on National Debt and Taxation (Colwyn Committee) revised Samuel's estimate, using another classification of income and other assumptions for the status of taxpayers, and carried the estimate through 1925–26. Its conclusions corroborate the statement that the British fiscal system was regressive before World War I, became progressive during the war and has retained this character.[124] (See Table 261.)

The United Kingdom's present income tax has a standard rate plus a surtax with progressive rates. The standard rate is very high: 9*s.* per pound, or 45 per cent, since 1946–47. The effective rate is reduced, however, by an abatement for income from work (one sixth of income, but not more than £250 in 1947–48); by personal allowances (£180 for a married couple and £60 for each child); and by reduction of the rate for the first £125 of income. Thus, a worker's family of five with an annual income of £600 pays an income tax on only £140 at the rate of 3*s.* per pound for the first £50, 6*s.* the next £75 and 9*s.* for £15. In all, the family is liable for a tax of £36 15*s.*, representing an

121. **71**, p. 44.
122. **71**, p. 219.

123. **69**, p. 179.
124. **34**, pp. 95–96.

TABLE 261

TAXES IN THE UNITED KINGDOM: EFFECTIVE RATES FOR A FAMILY OF FIVE, BY INCOME LEVEL, 1903–04 TO 1925–26 (According to Colwyn Committee)

(*Rate of Taxation as Percentage of Income* [a])

Taxpayer's Annual Income	Income Wholly from Work			Income Half from Work, Half from Property		
	1903–04	*1918–19*	*1925–26*	*1903–04*	*1918–19*	*1925–26*
£ 50	8.7	—	—	9.5	—	—
100	5.6	9.9	11.9	6.8	11.1	13.0
150	4.5	9.0	11.6	5.7	10.2	12.7
200	4.8	7.9	10.2	6.0	9.1	11.3
500	5.3	10.2	6.2	6.5	13.5	8.4
1,000	6.1	16.9	11.0	7.8	20.6	14.4
2,000	5.7	24.0	15.2	7.4	28.1	19.3
5,000	5.5	36.6	23.2	7.5	39.2	29.5
10,000	5.0	42.5	31.2	7.6	46.3	40.1
20,000	4.9	47.6	37.5	7.7	52.3	48.7
50,000	4.8	50.6	44.4	8.0	58.2	57.7

Source: **34,** pp. 95–96.

a. Assuming that all taxes on commodities are paid wholly by consumers and that the taxpayer is married and has three children under age 16.

effective rate of slightly more than 6 per cent on the entire income.

On the other hand, the surtax imposed on incomes in excess of £2,000 has progressive rates, which begin with 2s. per pound (10 per cent) for the first £500 in excess of £2,000 and rise to 48 per cent for amounts in excess of £20,000. The combination of both taxes results in highly progressive taxation, which constitutes the backbone of the British fiscal system. (See Table 262.)

The Income Tax in the United States

As in Great Britain, the development of income taxation in the United States is closely connected with wars. It came under discussion for the first time during the War of 1812, but the

TABLE 262

INCOME TAX IN THE UNITED KINGDOM: EFFECTIVE RATES FOR SINGLE PERSON, BY INCOME LEVEL, 1938–39 AND 1947–48

Actual Total Income [a]	1938–39				1947–48			
	Effective Rate per Pound [b]		Percentage of Income		Effective Rate per Pound [b]		Percentage of Income	
	s.	*d.*			*s.*	*d.*		
£ 100–120	—	—	0.0		—	—	0.0	
130	—	½	0.2		—	—	0.0	
150	—	2½	1.0		—	3½	1.5	
500	2	3	11.2		4	5½	22.3	
1,000	3	4	16.6		6	0	30.0	
2,000	4	1½	20.6		7	1½	35.6	
5,000	6	3	31.2		10	3½	51.5	
10,000	8	3	41.2		13	0	65.0	
50,000	11	10	59.2		18	0	90.0	
100,000	12	9	63.6		18	9	93.7	

Source: Adapted from **13** (United Kingdom), p. 35.

a. Income from work.   b. Tax and surtax.

TABLE 263. INCOME TAX IN THE UNITED STATES: EFFECTIVE RATES FOR

Revenue Act	Income Year	Income							
		$600	$1,000	$2,000	$5,000	$10,000	$25,000	$100,000	$500,000
		Single Person without Dependents							
1913	1913–15	—	—	—	.4	.7	1.1	2.5	5.0
1916	1916	—	—	—	.8	1.4	2.0	3.9	8.6
1917	1917	—	—	1.0	2.4	4.0	7.3	16.2	38.5
1918	1918	—	—	3.0	4.8	9.5	15.4	35.2	64.6
1918	1919–20	—	—	2.0	3.2	6.7	11.8	31.3	60.7
1921	1921	—	—	2.0	3.2	6.7	11.8	31.3	60.7
1921	1922	—	—	2.0	3.2	6.0	10.6	30.2	52.1
1921	1923	—	—	1.5	2.4	4.5	7.9	22.7	39.1
1924	1924	—	—	.8	1.2	2.3	6.5	22.7	39.9
1926	1925–27	—	—	.3	.8	1.5	4.9	16.1	23.2
1928	1928–31 [a]	—	—	.3	.8	1.5	4.4	15.8	23.2
1932	1932–33	—	—	2.0	3.2	6.0	10.6	30.2	52.7
1934	1934–35	—	—	1.6	2.8	5.6	11.2	31.4	53.0
1936	1936–39	—	—	1.6	2.8	5.6	11.2	33.4	61.0
1940	1940	—	.4	2.2	3.4	6.9	17.0	44.3	66.2
1941	1941	—	2.1	5.9	9.7	14.9	28.9	53.2	69.1
1942	1942	2.5	8.9	13.7	18.4	23.9	38.5	64.6	82.9
1942	1943 [b]	2.8	10.7	16.7	22.1	27.8	42.6	69.7	88.4
1944	1944–45	3.8	11.5	17.3	22.1	27.6	42.4	69.9	88.9
1945	1946–47	3.2	9.5	14.3	18.4	23.5	37.5	63.5	81.6
1948	1948–49	—	6.6	11.6	16.2	21.2	34.4	58.8	77.0 [e]
1950	1950	—	7.0	12.2	16.9	22.0	35.6	60.8	79.2
1951	1951	—	8.2	14.3	19.3	24.9	39.9	67.3	86.0
1951	1952–53	—	8.9	15.5	21.0	27.2	43.8	69.7	87.2
1954	1954–55	—	8.0	14.0	18.3	22.4	33.6	60.0	86.0

Source: **25,** 1954, pp. 373–75; Revenue Act, 1954.

war ended before plans for legislation were ready.

In 1861, Congress passed an act providing for a proportional tax on all income in excess of $800. The Treasury Department, however, did not try to enforce it. In 1862, another law provided for an income tax with progressive rates: 3 per cent on income of $600–$10,000; 5 per cent on $10,000 and over. Two years later new rates were established: 5 per cent on income of $600–$5,000; 7.5 per cent on $5,000–$10,000; 10 per cent on income over $10,000. In 1865, all income in excess of $5,000 was charged with a 10-per-cent tax.[125]

After the Civil War, when the need for large revenues diminished, tax rates were reduced and made uniform. Levels of exemption were gradually raised until the tax itself came to an end in 1872.[126]

125. **48,** pp. 154ff.
126. **75,** p. 102.

In 1892 President Cleveland proposed reintroduction of the income tax to offset the cuts in tariff rates. Two years later, after the panic of 1893, Congress passed an act providing for a proportional, 2-per-cent tax on all income over $4,000. Opponents of the tax attacked it on constitutional grounds, referring to the prohibition on the levying of capitation or other direct tax except in proportion to population (Article I, Section 9, paragraph 4). The controversy finally boiled down to the question of whether a proportional income tax is a direct tax. There was no doubt that the tax was "direct" in the sense in which the term was used at that time and is used now, but there was no evidence that the term meant the same thing to the authors of the Constitution and that it was their intention to bar fiscal measures like that passed by Congress in 1894. In fact, it could be proved that the controversial term was used loosely in the eighteenth century and had no universally accepted mean-

INDIVIDUALS, BY FAMILY STATUS AND INCOME LEVEL, 1913–55 (*Per Cent*)

Revenue Act	Income Year	Income							
		$600	$1,000	$2,000	$5,000	$10,000	$25,000	$100,000	$500,000
		Married Person with Two Dependents							
1913	1913–15	—	—	—	.2	.6	1.0	2.5	5.0
1916	1916	—	—	—	.4	1.2	1.9	3.9	8.6
1917	1917	—	—	—	1.3	3.4	7.1	16.2	38.5
1918	1918	—	—	—	3.1	7.8	14.7	35.0	64.6
1918	1919–20	—	—	—	2.1	5.6	11.4	31.2	60.6
1921	1921	—	—	—	1.4	5.3	11.3	31.1	60.6
1921	1922	—	—	—	1.4	4.6	10.0	30.1	52.1
1921	1923	—	—	—	1.0	3.4	7.5	25.6	39.1
1924	1924	—	—	—	.5	1.4	6.1	25.5	39.9
1926	1925–27	—	—	—	.2	.8	4.5	16.0	23.2
1928	1928–31 [a]	—	—	—	.2	.8	4.0	15.7	23.2
1932	1932–33	—	—	—	1.4	4.2	9.8	30.0	52.7
1934	1934–35	—	—	—	1.0	3.4	9.3	30.2	52.7
1936	1936–39	—	—	—	1.0	3.4	9.3	32.0	62.7
1940	1940	—	—	—	1.5	4.4	14.3	42.9	65.9
1941	1941	—	—	—	5.4	11.2	25.9	52.2	68.9
1942	1942	—	—	.7	11.8	19.1	35.3	63.5	82.7
1942	1943 [b]	.2	1.4	2.9	14.6	22.1	38.3	67.8	88.0
1944	1944–45	.5	1.5	2.3	15.1	22.5	38.8	68.6	88.6
1945	1946–47	—	—	—	11.8	18.6	34.1	62.3	81.3
1948	1948–49 [d]	—	—	—	8.6	13.6	21.9	45.6	71.7
1950	1950 [d]	—	—	—	9.0	14.2	22.7	47.2	73.9
1951	1951 [d]	—	—	—	10.6	16.2	25.6	52.6	80.7
1952	1952–53 [d]	—	—	—	11.5	17.7	28.0	56.0	82.2
1954	1954–55	—	—	—	10.4	15.9	25.1	51.9	79.8

a. Slightly lower rates in 1929.
b. Includes "victory tax."
c. Maximum rate.

d. Assuming that the reported income is split evenly between husband and wife.

ing. Further, it is fairly certain that the Constitution did not specifically intend to prohibit income taxation, since this subject was not under discussion when the Constitution was drafted.[127] The question of the constitutionality of the new income tax was answered by the Supreme Court in the negative, in a five to four decision.

In 1909, in view of the increasing pressure of public opinion for reform of the fiscal system, Congress proposed a constitutional amendment which would eliminate any doubt as to the constitutionality of federal income taxation. The Sixteenth Amendment, adopted by the statutory majority of states in 1913, was a straight repeal

of a part of Article I (Sec. 9, par. 4) of the Constitution. It reads:

The Congress shall have power to lay and collect taxes on incomes, from whatever sources derived, without apportionment among the several States, and without regard to any census or enumeration.

After the problem of constitutionality was settled, Congress passed an income tax law: a straight one per cent tax on income over $3,000 for single persons and over $4,000 for married persons, with a progressive rate of 1 to 6 per cent on income in excess of $20,000. This was a very mild income tax and yielded only some $60 million in the first year.

The real significance of the Sixteenth Amendment became apparent in 1917–18. Once more, the United States was at war and the government needed vast fiscal power. The income tax became the foundation of war financing.

127. When the Constitution was written, Seligman remarks, "almost every speaker used the term 'direct taxes' in a different way." (**72**, pp. 564–66.) Some used this term to describe taxes which are collected by the federal government directly, in contrast to those collected for the federal government by state and local authorities.

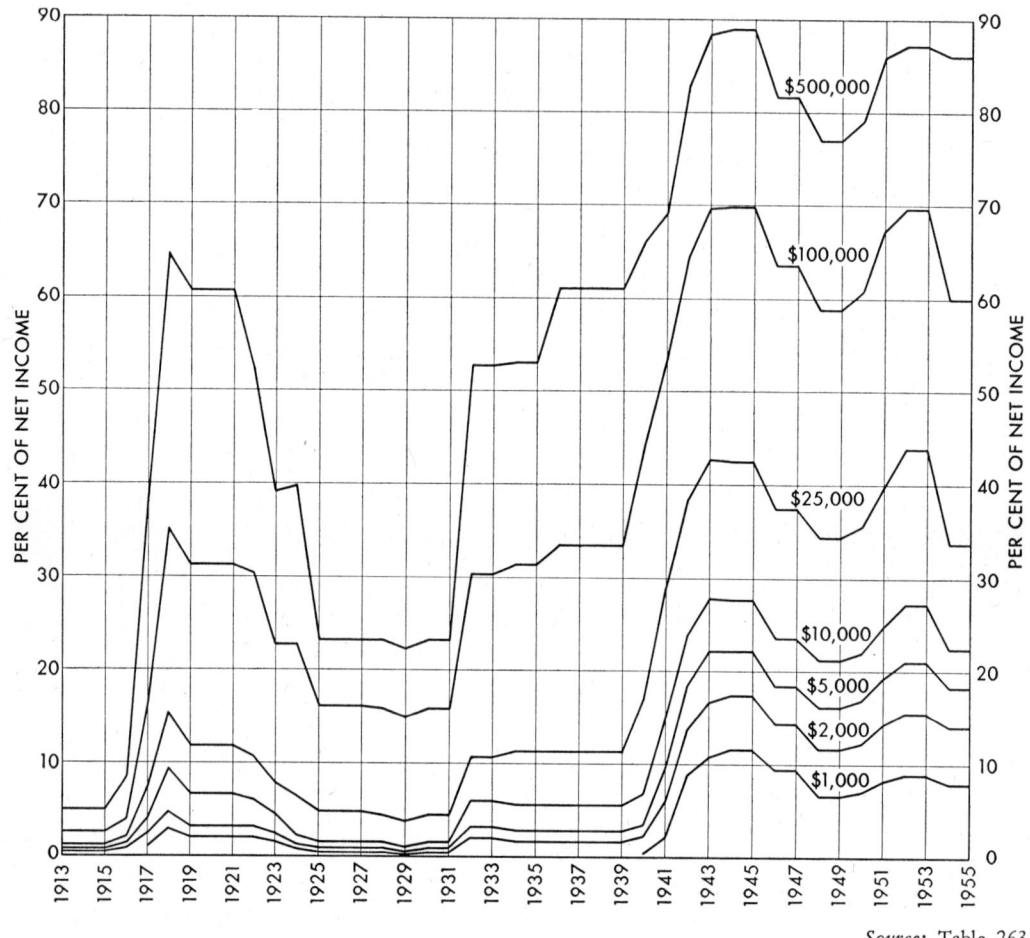

Source: Table 263

FIGURE 143. TAXES: EFFECTIVE RATES OF INDIVIDUAL INCOME TAX, IN THE UNITED STATES, 1913–55
(Effective Rates for Single Persons Without Dependents)

The income tax rates established in 1913 were about doubled by the Revenue Act of 1916 and further increased and made strongly progressive by the Revenue Acts of 1917 and 1918. The highest rate, on income of $500,000 and over, was raised to more than 60 per cent. The Revenue Act of 1921 established a plan for a gradual decrease in income tax rates, retaining their progressive character. Further and more drastic cuts were made by revenue acts in 1924, 1926 and 1928. Despite these cuts, the progressive income tax remained in force. In fact, it has been accepted as the basis of the fiscal system in peace as well as in war.

In 1932, in view of losses in other revenues, income tax rates were raised steeply, almost to the 1922 level. The revenue acts passed under the New Deal administration, before the out-

break of World War II, increased the progressiveness of the tax by cutting the rates on income under $10,000 and raising the rates in the high brackets. In 1936–39, persons with an annual income of $25,000 and over were taxed as heavily as in 1919–20, while the rates for lower incomes had been lowered.

The highly progressive income tax of 1936–39 became the starting point of defense financing after the outbreak of World War II. Since the highest tax rates already exceeded 60 per cent and not much could be gained by increasing them further, mobilization of the fiscal resources of the nation required an extension of the income tax to the low-income classes and a drastic increase in rates of the middle-income classes. Such was the goal of the Revenue Acts of 1940 and, in particular, 1941 and 1942. The last provided for a gradual increase of tax rates in 1942 and 1943.

The Individual Income Tax Act of 1944 introduced only minor adjustments into the tax structure, and apart from a slight increase in rates for the low-income groups, the Revenue Act of 1942 remained in force through 1945. After the war the effective tax rates were slightly reduced by the Revenue Acts of 1945 and 1948 but were raised again in 1950, 1951 and 1952. (See Table 263; cf. Figure 143.)

In the income tax established by the Revenue Act of 1951, the normal tax (3 per cent of taxable income) and the highly progressive surtax have been merged. The tax rates established by this act were increased in 1952 and cut in 1954. According to the Revenue Act of 1954 the lowest tax rate for the taxable net income of the head of the household (after deduction of exemptions and allowances) is 20.0 per cent and higher rates are assessed for each succeeding amount of net income:

Amount	Per Cent
Under $ 2,000	20.0
2,000–3,999	22.0
4,000–5,999	26.0
6,000–7,999	30.0
8,000–9,999	34.0
10,000–11,999	38.0
12,000–13,999	43.0
14,000–15,999	47.0
16,000–17,999	50.0
18,000–19,999	53.0
20,000–21,999	56.0
22,000–25,999	59.0
26,000–31,999	62.0
32,000–37,999	65.0
38,000–43,999	69.0
44,000–49,999	72.0
50,000–59,999	75.0
60,000–69,999	78.0
70,000–79,999	81.0
80,000–89,999	84.0
90,000–99,999	87.0
100,000–149,999	89.0
150,000–199,999	90.0
200,000–300,000	91.0
300,000 and over	92.0

The highest rate is 92 per cent, assessed on income exceeding $300,000, but the effective rate on total net income is limited to 87 per cent.

Income Taxes in Europe

The progressive income tax is now widely accepted in many countries as the foundation of the financial system. Tax rates differ widely from country to country but can be reduced to a comparable basis when taxpayers are classified by the relation of their income to net per capita income in the respective country. Thus a family of four with an income equal to four times the national per capita income can be described as having the *average* per capita income; a family of the same size with an income ten times the national per capita amount will be representative of people who have 2.5 times the *average* per capita income, and so on.

Using this method, the UN Economic Commission for Europe found that in European countries families of four with an income amounting to four times the national per capita income pay income taxes ranging from 9 to 18 per cent of the family income; families of four with an income twenty times the national per capita pay from 32 to 42 per cent in most countries; families which receive forty times the average income pay from 38 to 55 per cent in most countries. The charge on the very rich — families with an income 100 times the national per capita — amounts to 63 per cent in the Netherlands, 65 per cent in Western Germany, 70 per cent in Norway and 78 per cent in the United Kingdom. (See Table 264.)

These rates include national and local income taxes and are not strictly comparable with the data on the federal income tax in the United States presented in Table 263. To compare the system of income taxation in the United States with that of national and local governments in Europe, the federal tax rates should be increased, on the average, by 20–25 per cent, to allow for state, and sometimes also municipal, income taxes.

Per capita income in the United States in 1950 was $1,750. A family of four with an income three times this average received $5,250 and paid some $475 in federal income tax, an effective rate of over 9 per cent. The rate for a family with five times $1,750 was close to 14 per cent; that for a family with an income ten times $1,750 was 18 per cent; for an income twenty times $1,750, 27 per cent, and so on. Adjusted upward to include state and local income taxes the rates are in general lower than in the United Kingdom but higher than in France. At the given income levels families of four have

TABLE 264

INCOME TAX, IN SELECTED EUROPEAN COUNTRIES, FOR A FAMILY OF FOUR, BY INCOME LEVEL, 1949–50

(Rate of Taxation as Percentage of Family Income)

Country and Year	Family Income = Per Capita National Income Multiplied by:										
	3	4	5	10	15	20	25	30	40	50	100
United Kingdom, 1949	9	14	18	27	37	43	48	52	59	63	78
France, 1950	14	18	21	26	30	32	35	37	42	44	53
Netherlands, 1949	8	12	15	26	33	38	42	46	50	54	63
Denmark,[a] 1949	15	17	20	27	31	33	35	36	38	39	42
Sweden,[a] 1949	14	16	20	30	36	42	45	47	...	...	...
Norway,[a] 1949	12	15	18	31	37	42	45	48	55	58	70
Finland,[a] 1949	10	13	15	23	29	35	39	43	48	51	60
Western Germany, 1950	5	9	12	26	32	37	39	43	47	51	65
Austria, 1950	6	9	11	23	30	33	36	37	38	40	44

Source: **18**, 1950, p. 146.   a. The capital city.

been paying the following percentages of net income in income taxes: [128]

Family Income = Per Capita National Income Multiplied by:	Tax as Percentage of Family Income:		
	United States (1950)	United Kingdom (1949)	France (1950)
3	12	9	14
4	15	14	18
5	17	18	21
10	22	27	26
20	33	43	32
30	41	52	37
40	49	59	42
50	54	63	44
100	71	78	53

(See Figure 144.)

The progressiveness of taxation in a nation cannot be measured by the structure of its income tax rates alone but depends, rather, on the incidence of all direct and indirect taxes. Excises on articles of consumption, turnover and sales taxes and business taxes, including certain profit taxes, tend to be shifted to the prices paid by consumers. In most cases they are paid by the latter in rough proportion to their purchases of goods and services. Since consumers in the low-income classes spend practically all their income while upper-income families put aside a sizable part in savings, indirect taxes tend to be regressive on the whole. The laws must contain special provisions if the legislature intends to make the tax proportionate to consumers' incomes.

On the other hand, since property is usually concentrated in the hands of the rich, property taxes tend to be progressive even when the rates are not progressive.

A system of taxation is rarely as progressive as its income tax, but when 30–60 per cent of the total revenue is provided by income taxes with highly progressive rates, like those shown in Tables 259 to 264, the rich are asked to carry a large part of the fiscal burden. This pattern has become prevalent in most modern industrial countries in the past two or three decades.[129]

Income Taxes in Other Parts of the World

Less progress has been made toward an equitable distribution of fiscal burdens in industrially underdeveloped areas. Indirect taxes still prevail in Asia, except for Japan.[130] In South America, the recent trend has been toward replacement of customs duties by direct taxes on income and property.[131] (See Table 265.) Venezuela has in-

128. For the United States, data (interpolated) from Table 263, increased 25 per cent and rounded. For the United Kingdom and France, Table 264.

129. Since 1929 the role of import duties as a source of revenue has declined in most European countries (except Iceland, Portugal, Greece and Luxembourg). The share of consumption taxes in public revenues has not changed appreciably; the share of sales and turnover taxes has increased; that of income, capital and enterprise taxes has increased in eleven countries and decreased in seven. (**17**, 1950, No. 3, p. 60.) The main change has been in the structure of income taxes and the increase in the progressiveness of tax rates.

130. **6**, 1950, pp. 437–43a.

131. **5**, pp. 35–47.

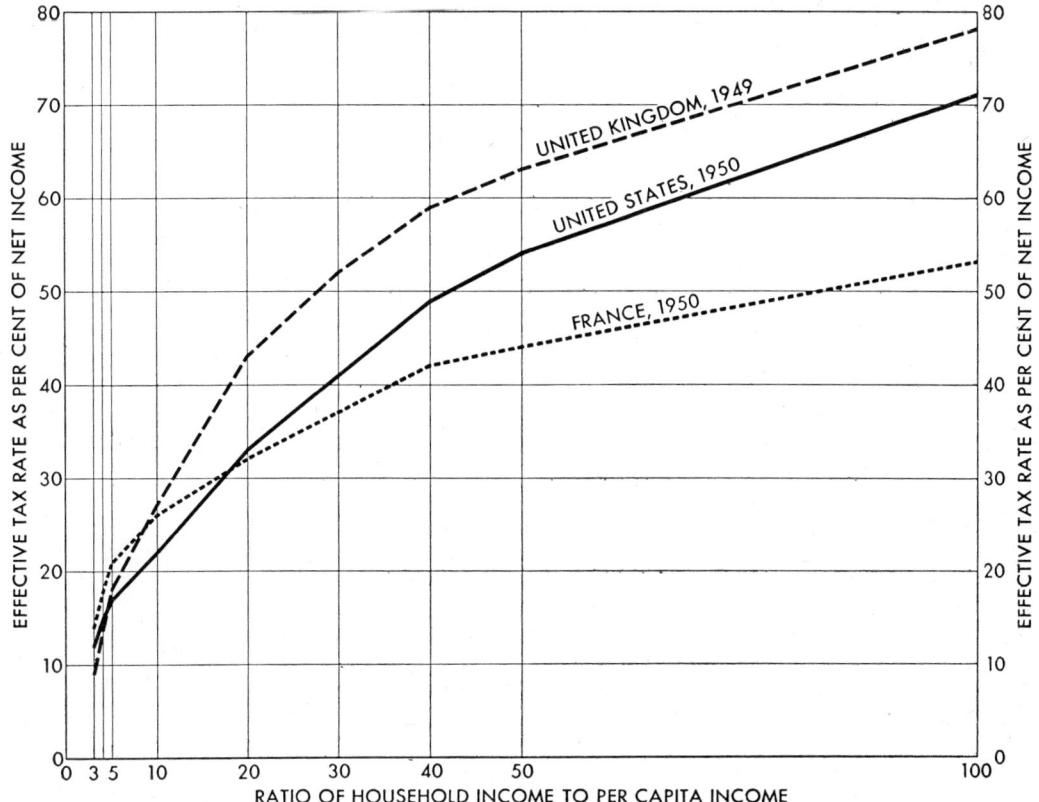

FIGURE 144. TAXES: EFFECTIVE RATES OF INCOME TAX FOR A FAMILY OF FOUR, IN THE UNITED STATES, THE UNITED KINGDOM AND FRANCE, AROUND 1950

TABLE 265

TAXATION SYSTEM: PERCENTAGE DISTRIBUTION OF TAX REVENUES, BY TYPE OF TAX, IN LATIN AMERICA, 1938 AND 1950

	1938			1950		
Country	*Taxes on Income and Property*	*Customs Duties*	*Other Indirect Taxes*	*Taxes on Income and Property*	*Customs Duties*	*Other Indirect Taxes*
Haiti	2.0	89.3	8.7	11.5	82.4	6.1
Colombia	23.6	49.5	26.9	48.3	18.1	33.6
Venezuela	27.1	42.6	30.3	58.4	19.9	21.7
Brazil	11.2	41.1	47.7	32.0	12.0	56.0
Peru	29.7	40.9	29.4	56.4	22.0	21.6
Chile	18.4	57.2	24.4	36.9	19.8	43.3
Argentina	20.3	34.6	45.1	40.8	7.7	51.5

Source: **5,** pp. 45–46.

TABLE 266

TAXATION SYSTEM: PERCENTAGE DISTRIBUTION OF GOVERNMENT REVENUES, BY SOURCE, IN SELECTED COUNTRIES, AROUND 1952–53

Country	Taxes on Income and Wealth	Customs Duties	Other Indirect Taxes	Other Receipts	Country	Taxes on Income and Wealth	Customs Duties	Other Indirect Taxes	Other Receipts
United States, 1953	84.1[a]	0.7	12.8	2.4	Switzerland, 1952	32.7	25.6	28.8	12.9
Canada, 1953	59.2	8.2	25.9	6.7	Austria, 1952	36.6	2.3	57.0	4.1
					Portugal, 1951	32.6	25.5	15.4	26.5
Mexico, 1950	22.4	28.8	33.6	15.2	Italy, 1953	17.8	73.5		8.7
Guatemala, 1952	9.0	36.3	35.4	19.3					
El Salvador, 1952	8.8	65.0[b]	17.5	8.8	USSR	10.1	...	55.8	34.1
Honduras, 1952	8.3	21.1	8.3	62.3					
Costa Rica, 1953	23.5	40.2	16.7	19.6	Turkey, 1953	21.4	11.0	60.2	7.4
Panama, 1951	18.5	29.3	19.7	32.5	Lebanon, 1952	15.6	24.4	47.9	12.1
Haiti, 1952	11.0	72.7	5.8	10.5	Israel, 1953	35.7	11.3	41.4	11.6
Venezuela, 1953	28.3	20.5	14.0	37.2	Syria, 1952	30.0	21.6	34.6	13.8
Colombia, 1952	38.8	32.5	18.4	10.3	Iraq, 1953	26.2	33.1	17.2	23.5
Brazil, 1952	31.9	7.0	52.7	8.4	Iran, 1950	14.9	21.6	34.3	29.2
Peru	21.7	50.6[b]	21.6	6.1	Pakistan	10.2	57.7[b]	13.7	18.4
Chile, 1952	40.2	17.2	30.0	12.6	India, 1953	20.6	32.7[b]	17.6	29.1
Argentina, 1952	32.5	5.6	24.9	37.0	Burma, 1953	5.7	26.7	9.9	57.7
					Ceylon, 1952	24.1	60.8	5.8	9.3
United Kingdom, 1953	53.7	33.5		12.8	Thailand, 1952	5.7	36.6[b]	31.2	26.5
Ireland, 1953	32.1	52.7		15.2	Malaya, 1952	15.3	64.3[b]	7.5	11.9
France, 1952	27.5	65.8		6.7	Philippines, 1953	17.8	3.4	64.0	14.8
Netherlands	32.0	8.0	40.5	19.5	Egypt, 1953	23.1	52.7		24.2
Sweden, 1950	57.2	29.8		13.0	Union of South Africa, 1953	54.3	13.3	16.9	15.3
Norway, 1951	32.9	7.2	53.1	6.8					
Western Germany, 1952	32.6	52.1		15.3	Australia, 1951	61.9	11.6	24.5	2.0
					New Zealand, 1952	59.1	17.9		23.0

Source: Computed from **16**, 1952, pp. 439–76.

a. Includes employment taxes.   b. Import and export duties.

troduced a modern income tax with progressive rates of surtax.[132]

SOURCES OF PUBLIC REVENUE IN SELECTED COUNTRIES

The Statistical Office of the UN distinguishes three economically meaningful types of taxes: direct taxes on income and wealth, customs duties, and other indirect taxes. All other governmental revenues are recorded under the title of "other receipts."

The taxes on income and wealth shown in Table 266 include taxes on corporations, land and buildings, although not all meet the usual definition of direct taxes. Customs duties include import and export duties, although the two types of taxes have little in common except the proce-

dure of collection. Other indirect taxes include excises, stamp duties and so on. Gains from monopolies and public enterprises are reported under "other receipts."

With reservation for the dissimilarity of taxes which appear under the same name in national budgets in different countries, these data permit a few generalizations.

The most significant is that taxes on income and wealth prevail in the modern progressive countries but usually play a subordinate role in underdeveloped areas. Such taxes represented the following percentages of the total revenue of national governments around 1952–53, ranging from about 84 per cent in the United States to less than 10 per cent in Thailand and Burma and several countries in Central America: [133]

132. **15** (Venezuela), pp. 63ff.   133. See Table 266.

United States	84.1	France	27.5
Australia	61.9	Iraq	26.2
Canada	59.2	Ceylon	24.1
New Zealand	59.1	Costa Rica	23.5
Sweden	57.2	Egypt	23.1
Union of South		Mexico	22.4
Africa	54.5	Peru	21.7
United Kingdom	53.7	Turkey	21.4
Chile	40.2	India	20.6
Colombia	38.8	Panama	18.5
Austria	36.6	Italy	17.8
Israel	35.7	Philippines	17.8
Norway	32.9	Malaya	15.3
Switzerland	32.7	Iran	14.9
Western Germany	32.6	Haiti	11.0
Portugal	32.6	Pakistan	10.2
Argentina	32.5	USSR	10.1
Ireland	32.1	Guatemala	9.0
Netherlands	32.0	El Salvador	8.8
Brazil	31.9	Honduras	8.3
Syria	30.0	Thailand	5.7
Venezuela	28.3	Burma	5.7

The exceptions are Chile and Colombia, where direct taxes yield a substantial part of governmental revenues, and Switzerland, where the federal budget rests mainly on customs duties and indirect taxes and income taxes are levied by the cantons. Customs duties play an important role in the national budget of such countries as Haiti (72.7 per cent), El Salvador (65.0), Malaya (64.3), Ceylon (60.8), Pakistan (57.7) and Peru (50.6). At the other extreme, the part of customs duties in the national budget is negligible in the United States, the United Kingdom, France, Norway and Austria.

In some underdeveloped areas, customs duties include duties on exported merchandise, usually raw materials produced in the area. Such duties are somewhat similar to the royalties the government obtains from exploitation of local natural resources by foreign capital.

A comparison of the system of taxation in the USSR with that in other countries is pointless in view of the difference between its economic structure and that of countries with a free-enterprise economy. In fact, a totalitarian country can finance its national budget without any taxes by manipulating prices and wages in such a way as to retain in its hands the difference necessary for maintaining the armed forces and police and carrying out other governmental services. The nearest thing to such an expedient is the general turnover tax, which forms the foundation of public financing in the USSR.

The expansion of the economic functions of governments began during World War I. The war economy demanded control over production, foreign trade, prices and exchange rates; rationing of scarce foodstuffs; allocation of scarce raw materials; subsidies to producers; and direct operation of mines and industrial plants. This was essentially an invasion by government of those fields of activities which had been dominated by private capital. After the war such economic functions of government were drastically reduced but they could not be discontinued completely. The same process occurred, on a much larger scale, during and after World War II.

In Europe this development was supported by changes in the distribution of political forces: the growing strength of organized labor and the rise to power of Socialists and Christian-Democrats. The two groups differed widely in their political philosophy but had two features in common: both groups spoke in the name of the common man and both demanded from government an expansion of economic activities for the benefit of workers and farmers.

CHAPTER 16

PUBLIC DEBTS

IN THE ANCIENT WORLD and the Middle Ages, kings and republics occasionally borrowed money in an emergency — usually in order to pay and feed their armies, build warships or pay tribute or ransom to the enemy. These were short-term and irregular operations, however. They often consisted of forced loans that differed little from confiscation or extortion. Sometimes usurious loans were raised by mortgages on crown jewels and public land. Some loans were repaid by grants of special privileges to the moneylenders; many were later repudiated. The procedure of long-term public debt, with sinking funds and regular budgetary appropriations for interest and amortization, is a modern invention.

The History of Public Debt

Governments began to borrow regularly from banks and professional moneylenders at the end of the seventeenth century. The Bank of England, from its foundation (1694), lent money to the government against anticipated tax revenues. By the middle of the eighteenth century, public borrowing, in various forms, had become a firmly established practice.

ADAM SMITH AND GEORGE WASHINGTON

Adam Smith, although recognizing that under certain conditions governments may be compelled to borrow, held this practice to be highly deplorable and denounced it in these words:

When war comes, there is no money in the treasury but what is necessary for carrying on the ordinary expense of the peace establishment. In war an establishment of three or four times that expense becomes necessary for the defense of the state. . . . The army must be augmented, the fleet must be fitted out, the garrisoned towns must be put into a posture of defense; that army, that fleet, those garrisoned towns, must be furnished with arms, munitions and provisions; an immediate and great expense must be incurred in that moment of immediate danger, which will not wait for the gradual and slow returns of the new taxes. In this exigency government can have no other resource but in borrowing.

When war comes the modern governments are both unwilling and unable to increase their revenue in proportion to the increase of their expense. They are unwilling, for fear of offending the people, who by so great and so sudden an increase of taxes, would soon be disgusted with the war; and they are unable, from not knowing what taxes would be sufficient to produce the revenue wanted. The facility of borrowing delivers them from the embarrassment which this fear and inability would otherwise occasion.[1]

Although he visualized the need for public borrowing in an emergency, Smith was deeply concerned about "the progress of the enormous debts which at present oppress, and will in the long run probably ruin, all the great nations of Europe."

George Washington expressed similar views in his *Farewell Address* (September 1796):

As a very important source of strength and security, cherish public credit. One method of preserving it is to use it as sparingly as possible; avoiding occasions of expense by cultivating peace, but remembering also that timely disbursements to prepare for danger frequently prevent much greater disbursements to repel it; avoiding likewise the accumulation of debt, not only by shunning occasions of expense, but by vigorous exertions in time of peace to discharge the debts which unavoidable wars may have occasioned; not ungenerously throwing upon posterity the burdens which we ourselves ought to bear.[2]

In their criticism of public borrowing, both Smith and Washington referred primarily to internal loans obtained from banks and private persons as a means of balancing the budget and, especially, of covering war expenditures. Through the whole nineteenth century and the first half of the twentieth, public debts were closely associated with wars. The history of national debt in the world reads like a history of armed clashes and their financial repercussions. Wars have not been the sole reason for piling up public debts, but they dwarf all the other factors. In no other country is the relation be-

---

1. **33**, pp. 412–13, 417.
2. Quoted in **20**, p. 12.

TABLE 267

NATIONAL DEBT OF THE UNITED STATES, 1791–1955

(*Millions of Dollars*)

Year [a]	Debt [b]	Year [a]	Debt [b]	Year [a]	Debt [b]	Year [a]	Debt [b]
1791	$ 75.5	1874	$2,160	1901	$ 1,222	1928	$ 17,604
1796	83.8	1875	2,156	1902	1,178	1929	16,931
1801	83.0	1876	2,131	1903	1,159	1930	16,185
1806	75.7	1877	2,108	1904	1,136	1931	16,801
1811	48.0	1878	2,159	1905	1,132	1932	19,487
1816	127.3	1879	2,291	1906	1,143	1933	22,539
1821	90.0	1880	2,099	1907	1,147	1934	27,053
1826	81.1	1881	2,019	1908	1,178	1935	28,701
1831	39.1	1882	1,857	1909	1,143	1936	33,779
1836	0.0	1883	1,722	1910	1,147	1937	36,465
1841	5.3	1884	1,625	1911	1,154	1938	37,165
1846	15.5	1885	1,579	1912	1,194	1939	40,440
1851	68.3	1886	1,556	1913	1,193	1940	42,968
1856	34.0	1887	1,466	1914	1,188	1941	48,961
1861	90.6	1888	1,385	1915	1,191	1942	72,422
1862	524	1889	1,250	1916	1,225	1943	136,696
1863	1,120	1890	1,122	1917	2,976	1944	201,003
1864	1,816	1891	1,006	1918	12,244	1945	258,682
1865	2,678	1892	968	1919	25,482	1946	269,422
1866	2,756	1893	961	1920	24,299	1947	258,286
1867	2,650	1894	1,017	1921	23,976	1948	252,292
1868	2,583	1895	1,097	1922	22,963	1949	252,770
1869	2,545	1896	1,223	1923	22,350	1950	257,357
1870	2,437	1897	1,227	1924	21,251	1951	255,222
1871	2,322	1898	1,233	1925	20,516	1952	259,105
1872	2,210	1899	1,437	1926	19,643	1953	266,071
1873	2,151	1900	1,263	1927	18,512	1954	271,260
						1955	276,649

Sources: **10**, pp. 304–06; **11**, 1954, p. 391; **12**, 1955.

a. Before 1841, as of January 1 of given year; subsequent years, as of June 30. For 1955, as of April 30.

b. Gross debt.

tween wars and national debt clearer than in the United States.

NATIONAL DEBT IN THE UNITED STATES

Five times the United States has incurred great national debts, and always to finance war: the Revolutionary War, the War of 1812, the Civil War, and the two world wars.[3] Apart from these crucial turning points, the national debt has gone up and down under the impact of changing political and economic conditions. (See Table 267.)

Before 1901

The original debt of the republic resulted mainly from funding federal and state loans and

obligations incurred during the Revolutionary War. It fluctuated around $80 million in the decade 1793–1802, increased to $86.4 million in 1804 and had been reduced to $45 million by the beginning of 1812. In the years 1812–15 it increased steadily and reached a new peak of $127.3 million at the beginning of 1816. As soon as peace was restored and in the succeeding years, the federal government, following the principles laid down in Washington's *Farewell Address,* began repaying its debts, domestic and foreign. By 1835, the national debt was only $38,000.

New deficits developed after the Florida war (1837–38), under the exceptionally unfortunate financial administration in the 1840's and as a result of the war with Mexico. The national debt reached a new peak ($68.3 million) in 1851, was

3. **20**, p. 12; cf. **30** and **36**, *passim.* See also **24**.

later reduced by more than half, and then sky-rocketed to nearly $2.8 billion during the Civil War. It took more than twenty years to pay half the debt accumulated during the struggle between the South and the North. Progress in repayment was interrupted in the 1890's and, under the impact of the war with Spain, the national debt had increased slightly by the end of the century.[4]

1901–54

After the turn of the century the national debt of the United States was stabilized at a little more than a billion dollars: $1,222 million in 1901; $1,225 million in 1916. The economy was growing rapidly at that time and it would not have been too difficult for the government to repay that amount. These obligations, however, presented no serious inconvenience to federal finance, and the policy of the administrations was to keep the budget in balance without spending current receipts to liquidate old debts.

World War I opened a new era in the history of the national debt. It jumped from $1,225 million in 1916 to $25,482 million in 1919, an increase which fundamentally changed its character and its role in national finances and the economic system.

As after the Civil War, the government began to reduce its debt immediately after the end of World War I, gradually redeeming maturing obligations. From 1919 to 1930, it repaid more than $9 billion — probably much less than should have been repaid to counteract the inflationary pressures which predominated in that time and became particularly dangerous by the end of the 1920's.

The great depression brought an upturn in the debt. As revenues shrank, a deficit developed in the federal budget and the outstanding debt began to rise. The rise was comparatively slow under the Hoover administration but gained momentum under the New Deal; from $19.5 billion in 1932, the national debt increased to $40.4 billion in 1939.

Several factors were responsible for this rise. Chief among them, of course, was the broaden-ing scope of the government's economic and social responsibilities. A shift in economic thinking was also of considerable significance. An unbalanced budget and an increase in national debt were officially recognized at that time as a sound policy in the fight against depression and mass unemployment. In the late 1930's, increasing outlays for defense and rearmament contributed to the growth of budgetary deficits and the debt. This factor, however, did not gain decisive significance until 1941.

That year was a new milestone in the history of the national debt: between mid-1941 and mid-1946, the federal debt increased from $49 billion to $269.4 billion. It had been reduced by some $14 billion by 1951, but increased again under the impact of the Korean war and the rearmament program to $271.3 billion on June 30, 1954 and $276.6 billion on April 30, 1955.

Relation to Population and National Income

These changes in the total dollar value of the national debt may convey a somewhat lopsided impression of the rate and implications of the increase. If the national debt had increased in the past 160 years, keeping pace with the growth of population and national income, its weight in the economic system would have remained unchanged and it would probably present the same problems that it presented in Washington's time. Changes in the dollar value, however, have not paralleled changes in either the size or income of the population. The amount of the debt per capita fluctuated widely before it jumped to the unprecedented level of recent years, as did also the ratio of national debt to national income.

National debt was about $20 per capita in the last decade of the eighteenth century, declined to $7 per capita at the beginning of 1812, rose to $15 in 1816 and sank practically to zero in 1835–36. It was as low as $1 per capita in the 1850's, before the outbreak of the Civil War, then reached $75 in 1865–66; it fluctuated between $11 and $12 per capita in 1914–16 and skyrocketed to $242 in 1919. In the 1920's during the postwar prosperity, the per capita national debt sank — to $132 by January 1930. It rose again during the great depression — to $309 in the middle of 1939 and $367 in 1941. From that unprecedented height it had increased fivefold by 1946 and has been reduced only slightly in recent years. (See Figure 145.)

---

4. Technically, the Spanish-American war lasted only four months and its direct cost was not large, but it was accompanied by an increase in the appropriations for the Army and Navy; the additional cost of military installations in 1898–1901 was close to $600 million. The national debt increased by half this amount. (**23**, pp. 465ff.)

A still better measurement of the real growth of the national debt is its relation to national income. It appears that the national debt of the United States amounted to more than 10 per cent of national income at the end of the eighteenth century, averaged less than one per cent from 1835 to 1860, rose to almost 50 per cent of current national income in 1865, and dropped again to 3–4 per cent of national income before World War I. The ratio of national debt to national income reached an all-time peak in 1945 (160 per cent); it has since declined, to 92 per cent in 1951 and 86 per cent in 1953, and amounted to 90 per cent in 1954. (See Figure 146.)

The recent decline in the ratio of national debt to national income has been due more to the rise in national income than to reduction in the dollar value of the debt. The ratio will decline further if the upward trend in national income continues, but it is highly unlikely that it will soon be lowered to the level considered normal before World War I.

Composition of the Public Debt

The increase in national debt in relation to national income has changed the role of federal indebtedness in the country's public debt system. At the beginning of this century, federal debt represented slightly more than one third of all public debt in the United States; state and local loans and credits accounted for two thirds. In 1944 the federal debt amounted to 92 per cent and in 1946 to 94.4 per cent of all public debt. The ratio declined somewhat in more recent years and dropped to slightly less than 90 per cent in 1952. (See Table 268). However, the portion of the gross national debt represented by federal obligations still exceeds the value of all other public and private debts in the nation and represents about half of all assets of banks and insurance companies. The manipulation and replacement of maturing securities can deeply influence the flow of money and purchasing power and, therefore, the nation's production, employment and welfare.[5]

Table 267 and Figures 145 and 146 provide a general outline of the variations in the size of the national debt in the United States. The following pages summarize the history of public debt in that and other countries for which comparable data are available.

---

5. **16**, p. 4; cf. **22**, *passim.*

TABLE 268

PUBLIC DEBT OF FEDERAL, STATE AND LOCAL GOVERNMENTS IN THE UNITED STATES, 1902–52

Year	Total	Federal	State	Local
Amount, in Billions of Dollars				
1902	$ 3.4	$ 1.2	$0.3	$ 1.9
1912	5.7	1.2	0.4	4.1
1922	33.2	23.0	1.2	9.1
1932	39.1	19.5	2.9	16.7
1940	63.2	43.0	3.5	16.7
1942	92.1	72.4	3.2	16.5
1944	218.5	201.0	2.8	14.7
1945	275.3	258.7	2.4	14.2
1946	285.5	269.4	2.4	13.6
1947	275.1	258.3	3.0	13.8
1948	271.0	252.3	3.7	15.0
1949	273.6	252.8	4.0	16.8
1950	281.5	257.4	5.4	18.8
1951	282.3	255.2	6.4	20.7
1952	289.2	259.1	6.9	23.2
Percentage Distribution				
1902	100.0	34.9	8.0	57.1
1912	100.0	21.0	7.4	71.6
1922	100.0	69.1	3.5	27.4
1932	100.0	49.9	7.4	42.7
1940	100.0	68.0	5.6	26.4
1942	100.0	78.6	3.5	17.9
1944	100.0	92.0	1.3	6.7
1945	100.0	94.0	.9	5.1
1946	100.0	94.4	.8	4.8
1947	100.0	93.9	1.1	5.0
1948	100.0	93.1	1.4	5.5
1949	100.0	92.4	1.5	6.2
1950	100.0	91.4	1.9	6.7
1951	100.0	90.4	2.3	7.3
1952	100.0	89.6	2.4	8.0

Sources: For 1902–46, **9**, 1949, p. 5; for 1947–53, **11**, 1954, p. 417.

NATIONAL DEBT IN VARIOUS COUNTRIES BEFORE WORLD WAR I

Public credit was tremendously strained at the end of the eighteenth century in the United States, Great Britain and France.

Heritage of Revolution: France and the U.S.

France's public debt reached astronomical dimensions during the French Revolution. It was

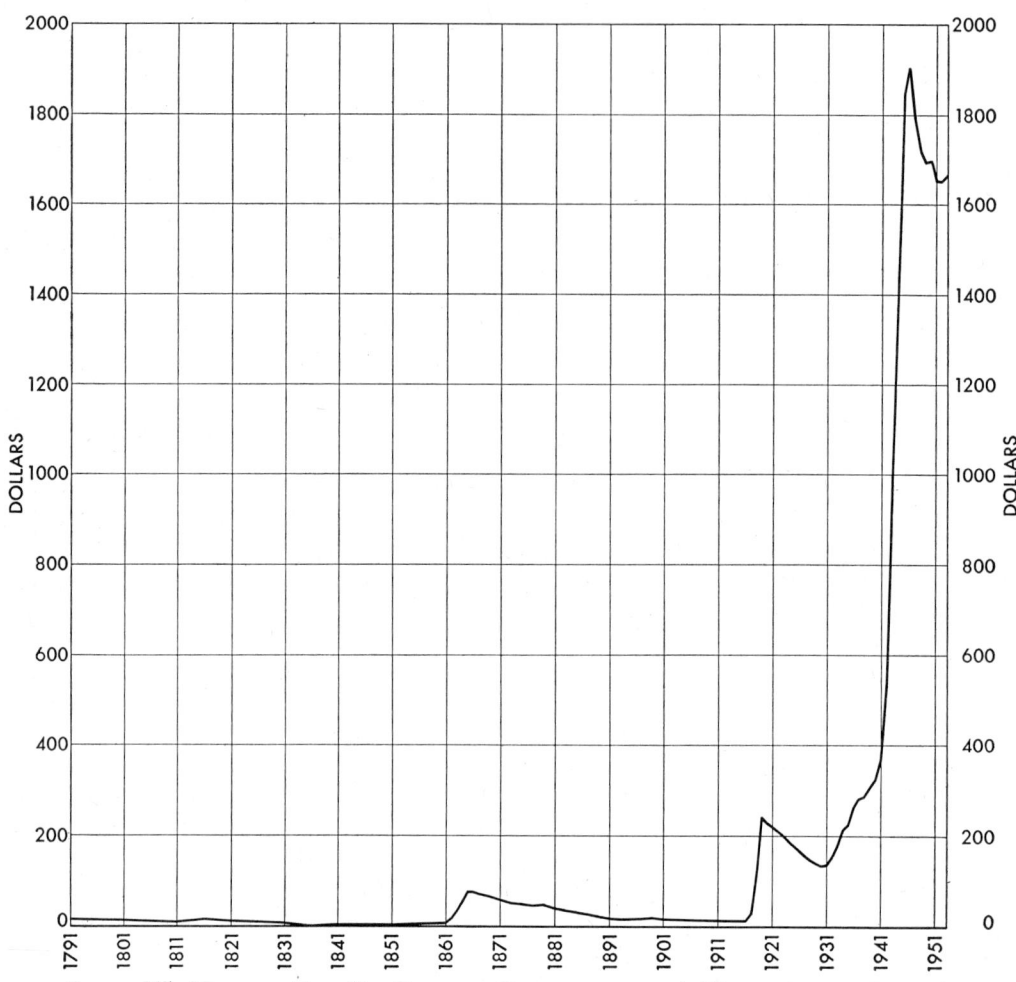

FIGURE 145   NATIONAL DEBT PER CAPITA OF POPULATION, IN THE UNITED STATES, 1791–1953

drastically cut, however, by devaluation of the currency and conversions.

The United States faced a similar problem in its early days — a maze of national and state debts, depreciated during the Revolutionary War to 10–15 per cent of their face value, and the practically valueless paper money issued by the Continental Congress. On the insistence of Alexander Hamilton, the first Congress decided to fund the entire national debt, domestic and foreign, principal and accrued interest, at face value. To this funded debt, which approximated $50 million, were added Revolutionary War obligations of the states totaling approximately $20 million. On the other hand, the paper money (bills of credit) issued by the Continental Congress was redeemed at a cent on the dollar.[6]

6. **18,** Part I, pp. 342–47.

The policy of funding depreciated loans at face value was highly controversial at that time. The opponents of this measure pointed out that most state and national obligations were no longer in the hands of those who had lent their money to the government during the war but had been purchased by speculators for a fraction of their original value. Refunding these obligations at face value amounted therefore to a bonus to speculators at the expense of the nation.

Whether or not this policy was sound, the obligations it imposed on the United States represented only a fraction of those the British had accumulated by that time as a result of their wars with France and their colonial policy.

National Debt around 1801

At the beginning of the nineteenth century,

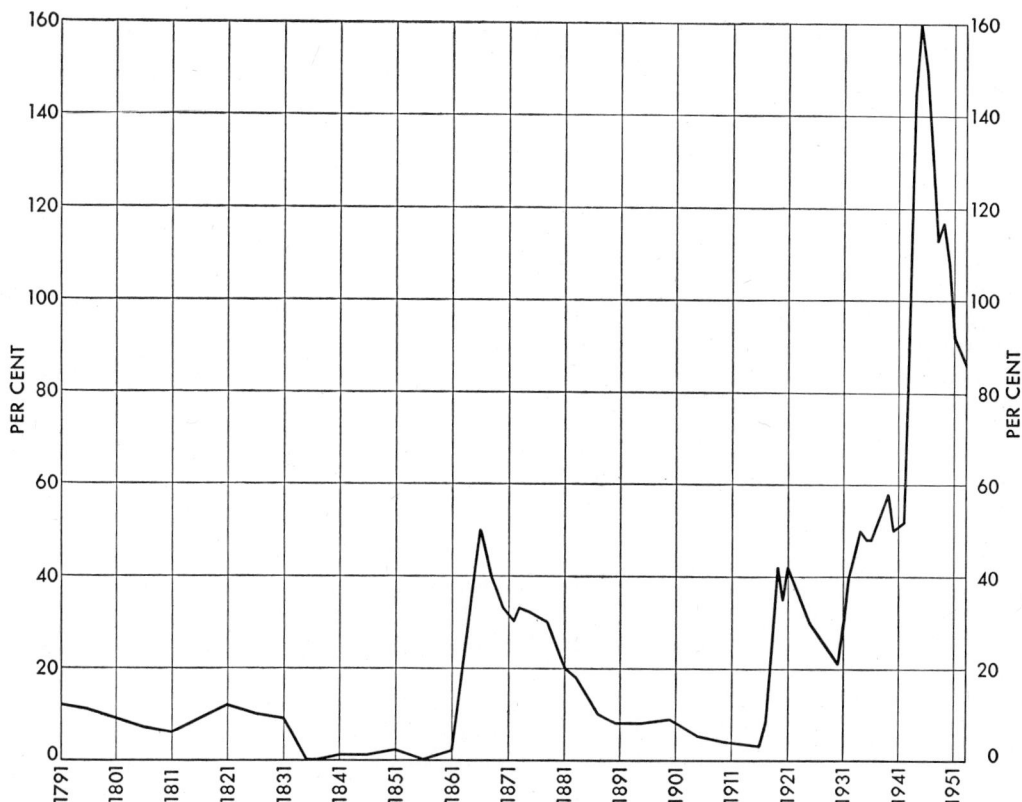

FIGURE 146. NATIONAL DEBT IN RELATION TO NATIONAL INCOME, IN THE UNITED STATES, 1791–1953

the sum of the public debts of the European countries and the United States approached $3,000 million. Great Britain accounted for about $2,400 million, or 80 per cent of this amount; Austria and France had debts of $140–$150 million each; the United States, with $83 million, ranked fourth, followed by Prussia ($40 million) and Russia ($26 million).[7]

Most public debt was in the form of domestic loans and credits. The United States had the largest foreign debt: some $12 million, including the obligations for financial assistance which Benjamin Franklin had obtained from Spain, Holland and France and the debt incurred for the Louisiana Purchase.[8]

From 1801 to World War I

From the beginning of the nineteenth century to the outbreak of World War I, wars continued to be the milestones in the course of public debt: the Napoleonic wars, in Great Britain and

France; the Crimean War in Russia; the Civil War in the United States; the Franco-Prussian War in France, and so on. In addition, the burden of armament accounted for budgetary deficits and the accumulation of debt in countries which were not directly engaged in war.

Another source of national debt — especially foreign debt — was the large-scale investment in public works, such as railroads, in the second half of the nineteenth century. The distinction between the economically constructive loans of that period and debts originated by wars and armament, however, is not always clear. Not infrequently a country sought a foreign loan for a productive project because its current revenues were pre-empted by defense appropriations. On the other hand, strategic considerations were often a decisive factor in building railroads, improving ports and digging canals.

The growth of public debt, however, was checked by the conservative financial policy most governments followed in the nineteenth century. The prevailing tendency was to repay at least part of the debt in good years. From 1801 to

7. **35**, p. 607; **37**, p. 135.
8. **35**, p. 651; **31**, p. 97.

TABLE 269

NATIONAL DEBT, DOMESTIC AND FOREIGN, IN SELECTED COUNTRIES, 1913–14

(*U.S. Dollars*)

Country	Total, in Millions			Per Capita	Country	Total, in Millions			Per Capita
	Total	Domestic	Foreign			Total	Domestic	Foreign	
United States	$1,188	$1,188	—	$12.3	Sweden	$ 186	$ 33	$ 153	$33.0
Canada	542	231	$311	73.1	Norway	96	6	90	39.0
Mexico	214	—	214	13.8	Finland	32	—	32	9.8
Guatemala	11	—	11	5.2	Germany	1,228	1,228	—	18.3
El Salvador	8	4	4	5.7	Switzerland	64	64	—	16.6
Honduras	29	2	27	50.0	Austria	2,556	2,556	—	87.5
Nicaragua	14	7	7	23.5	Hungary	1,254	665	598	58.6
Costa Rica	18	3	15	45.0	Portugal	636	436	200	10.6
Panama	4	2	2	11.1	Spain	1,821	1,626	195	89.4
Cuba	70	10	60	29.3	Italy	3,051	3,051	—	82.4
Haiti	31	9	22	12.4	Serbia	173	149	24	38.0
Dominican Republic	13	—	13	18.4	Romania	334	35	299	20.6
Venezuela	33	12	21	12.0	Bulgaria	192	24	168	39.7
Colombia	20	2	18	3.6	Greece	262	66	196	43.7
Ecuador	23	8	15	11.5	Russia (USSR)	4,571	3,097	1,474	31.5
Brazil	541	230	311	21.5	China	798	—	798	1.8
Peru	32	26	6	7.1	Japan	1,323	525	798	24.0
Bolivia	20	5	15	8.3	Turkey	567	—	567	29.1
Paraguay	11	5	5	12.2	Persia (Iran)	51	16	35	5.7
Chile	254	70	184	72.9	British India	1,819	593	1,226	5.7
Uruguay	130	10	120	10.0	Siam (Thailand)	27	—	27	3.2
Argentina	630	273	357	79.8	Egypt	438	—	438	35.2
United Kingdom	3,362	3,362	—	78.4	Union of South Africa	601	70	531	96.9
France	7,592	7,592	—	182.1					
Belgium	960	903	57	124.6	Australia	1,650	487	1,163	338.8
Netherlands	533	533	—	85.7	New Zealand	475	65	410	414.1
Denmark	97	24	73	32.3					

Sources: For the amount and distribution of national debt, **5,** *passim* and, for countries not listed in **5, 37,** p. 139. For population, **1,** pp. 10–15.

World War I, national debt in most countries increased at a lower rate than national income.

In the world as a whole, national debt totaled approximately $11–$12 billion in 1870 and probably somewhat more than $40 billion in 1913.

Great Britain's national debt was close to $2.4 billion in 1800, $3.8 billion in 1870 and $3.0 billion in 1913. It was considerably larger than the annual national income at the beginning of the nineteenth century; roughly equal to it in 1870; and hardly more than 30 per cent of it in 1913.[9] On the other hand, France's national debt increased from approximately $150 million in 1801 to more than $2.5 billion in 1870 and $7.6 billion in 1914. The last amount was about equal to the French annual national income.

9. **37,** pp. 135–37; **4,** 1938–1948, p. 228.

National Debt, 1913–14

The distribution and structure of public debts in 1913–14 deserve closer analysis.

Size. Before World War I, France had the largest national debt ($7.6 billion); Russia ranked second ($4.6 billion), followed by Austria-Hungary ($3.8 billion), the United Kingdom ($3.4 billion) and Italy ($3.1 billion). The national debt of these five nations totaled $22.5 billion. Other nations with obligations of more than a billion dollars were British India ($1,819 million), Spain ($1,821 million), Australia ($1,650 million), Japan ($1,323 million), Germany ($1,228 million) and, in the eleventh place, the United States ($1,188 million). (See Table 269.)

Per Capita. On a per capita basis, national

debt was particularly high in prosperous young nations — New Zealand ($414) and Australia ($339), followed by France ($182), Belgium ($125) and the Union of South Africa ($97). It was particularly low in such poor countries as India, Persia (Iran) and El Salvador (less than $6 in each), Guatemala ($5), Siam ($3) and China (less than $2). Except for the extremes, however, the correlation between per capita national debt and the level of economic development was rather weak.

National debt in 1913–14 ranged between $70 and $90 per capita in Canada, Chile, Argentina, the United Kingdom, the Netherlands, Austria, Italy and Spain. An equally heterogeneous group of countries had national debts of $10 to $20 per capita: Portugal, Mexico, Haiti, the Dominican Republic, Venezuela, Ecuador, Paraguay, Uruguay, on the one hand, and the United States, Germany and Switzerland, on the other. (See Figure 147.)

It appears that the poverty of some underdeveloped countries led them into debts beyond their ability to pay, while similar poverty in some others kept them from obtaining sizable credits either at home or abroad. Some of the most prosperous countries did not consider an increase in the national debt a serious inconvenience, while others avoided debts, especially foreign loans.

Public opinion and the attitude of the government toward budgetary deficits and public debt differed from country to country. Bastable exaggerated when he declared (1892): "We may say that any state that pretends to be civilized regards the creation of a debt as one of the essential marks of its having reached that position." [10]

The United States, like Switzerland and Germany, for example, followed a conservative financial policy and frowned on budgetary deficits in peacetime.

Domestic and Foreign Debt. In the world as a whole, three fourths of the total amount of national debt before World War I represented domestic (internal) loans and one fourth, foreign loans.[11] Almost all national debts consisted of loans by private individuals, corporations and banks to governments. Direct borrowing by one government from another was rather unusual at that time. Foreign loans were launched, as a rule, when a country needed foreign currency to purchase industrial equipment, railroad stock, ships or arms. Sometimes, however, industrially developed and prosperous nations found it advantageous to finance certain operations by floating public loans on foreign capital markets and some governments (for example, czarist Russia) borrowed money abroad in order to cope with internal financial and political difficulties.

China, Turkey and Egypt in the Eastern Hemisphere, and Mexico, Guatemala and the Dominican Republic in the Western, had sizable foreign debts before World War I although they could not or did not try to launch public loans among their own population.

The countries listed in Table 269 may be grouped as follows, according to the proportion that foreign loans represented in their total national debt:

Countries	*Foreign Loans as Percentage of National Debt*
United States, United Kingdom, France, Netherlands, Germany, Switzerland, Austria, Italy	0
Peru, Belgium, Spain, Serbia	0.1—19.9
Portugal, Russia	20.0—39.9
Canada, Nicaragua, El Salvador, Panama, Brazil, Paraguay, Argentina, Hungary	40.0—59.9
Haiti, Venezuela, Ecuador, Bolivia, Chile, Denmark, Greece, Japan, British India, Persia, Australia	60.0—79.9
Honduras, Costa Rica, Cuba, Colombia, Uruguay, Sweden, Norway, Romania, Bulgaria, Union of South Africa, New Zealand	80.0—99.9
Mexico, Guatemala, Dominican Republic, Finland, China, Turkey, Siam, Egypt	100

Neither a high national debt per capita of population nor the predominance of foreign

---

10. **17**, p. 626.

11. The distinction between internal and foreign debts, which is important in the classification of public debt, is not always based on the same criteria. In some countries, the distinction is made according to the currency in which the debt is expressed: in others, according to the place where the debt was contracted or the residence of the creditors. In the latter case, foreign bonds repurchased by residents of the home country are considered domestic debt, as in Sweden. (**5**, p. 8.)

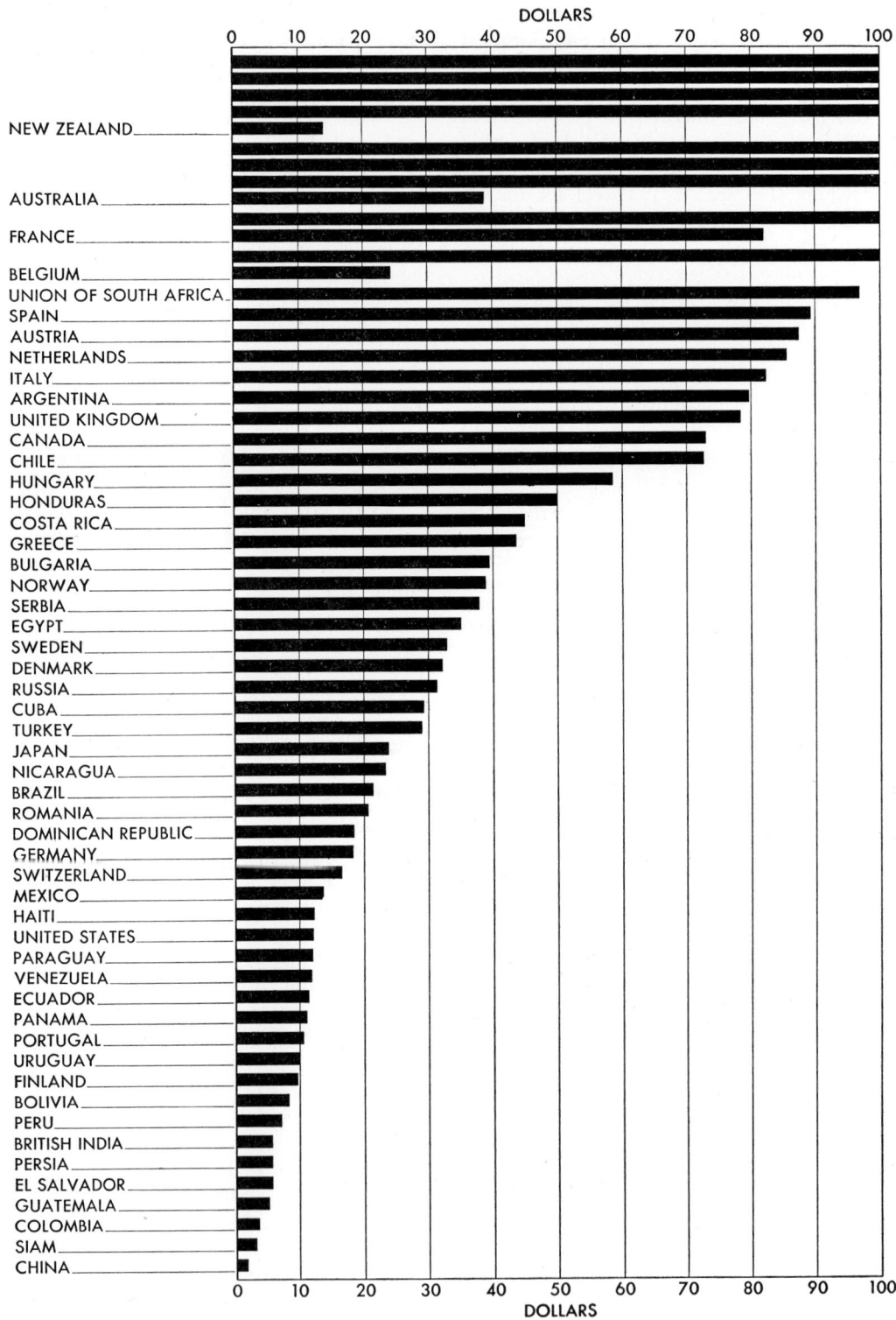

DOLLARS

NEW ZEALAND
AUSTRALIA
FRANCE
BELGIUM
UNION OF SOUTH AFRICA
SPAIN
AUSTRIA
NETHERLANDS
ITALY
ARGENTINA
UNITED KINGDOM
CANADA
CHILE
HUNGARY
HONDURAS
COSTA RICA
GREECE
BULGARIA
NORWAY
SERBIA
EGYPT
SWEDEN
DENMARK
RUSSIA
CUBA
TURKEY
JAPAN
NICARAGUA
BRAZIL
ROMANIA
DOMINICAN REPUBLIC
GERMANY
SWITZERLAND
MEXICO
HAITI
UNITED STATES
PARAGUAY
VENEZUELA
ECUADOR
PANAMA
PORTUGAL
URUGUAY
FINLAND
BOLIVIA
PERU
BRITISH INDIA
PERSIA
EL SALVADOR
GUATEMALA
COLOMBIA
SIAM
CHINA

DOLLARS

Source: Table 269

FIGURE 147. NATIONAL DEBT PER CAPITA OF POPULATION, IN SELECTED COUNTRIES, 1913–14

loans in the national debt was necessarily associated with a strain on national credit or the economic dependence of the debtor nation on the creditor.

THE IMPACT OF WORLD WAR I ON NATIONAL DEBT

The Cost of War

Apart from the destruction of human life, economic resources and property and the disorganization of production, the direct cost of World War I to the belligerent countries amounted to about $260 billion, distributed as follows (in billions of dollars): [12]

Allied Nations

Total	$176
United States	46
Great Britain	50
France	37
Russia	21
Italy	17
Belgium	3
Other	2

Central Powers

Total	$84
Germany	47
Austria-Hungary	28
Turkey and Bulgaria	9

In peacetime, the annual governmental expenditures of the belligerents had totaled $6 billion. If there had been no war, the governments would probably have spent about $40 billion in 1914–20. The war forced them to make additional outlays totaling about $260 billion, six and a half times the sum of all national debt which had been accumulated in the world from the end of the eighteenth century to the outbreak of World War I.

It is true that in the wartime bill expenditures are expressed in part in depreciated currencies. Converted, year by year, into gold, the cost of the war would be close to $200 billion, which is still five times the normal governmental expenditures of the belligerent countries in that length of time and five times the amount of all national debt in the world when World War I began.

---

12. Calculated as the difference between total governmental expenditures in 1915–20 and expenditures for the same period at the rate in 1913–14. For explanation of the method of calculation see **37**, pp. 144ff.

War Financing

Less than 20 per cent of the war expenditure was covered by increase in tax revenues. The rest was met by credit operations — Defense and Victory loans, borrowing from banks and, in some cases, issuance of paper money. The total amount of debt incurred by the belligerent countries cannot be estimated with reasonable precision. Roughly, it may be set at about 80 per cent of the direct financial cost of war, or $160 billion in gold. Adding this amount to the prewar national debt would give a total of about $200 billion for the world in 1919–20. Part of the war debt, however, together with some old debt, was wiped out by revolution, depreciation of currencies, and inflation. When the war was approaching its end, Germany had a national debt of 144 billion marks and Austria-Hungary, of nearly 100 billion marks — some $35 billion and $24 billion, respectively, at official rates of exchange.[13] Only a small fraction of these obligations remained in force after Germany had returned to peacetime normalcy. The Soviet Union repudiated all debts of the czarist government. A comparison of the actual status of national debt in 1919 with the hypothetical total of $200 billion suggests that obligations representing about $75 billion were wiped out, in one or another way, in the liquidation of war accounts.

National Debt, 1919

Immediately after the end of the war (after the dismemberment of Austria-Hungary and the repudiation of all internal and foreign debts by the Soviet government, but before the full development of inflation in Germany and France), national debt in the world totaled approximately $127 billion, more than three times the prewar total. The largest increases between 1914 and 1919 were those of the United Kingdom, the United States, France and Germany, the national debts of which had changed as follows (in billions of dollars):

	1914	*1919*	*Increase*
Total	$13.4	$98.4	$85.0
United Kingdom	3.4	35.6	32.2
United States	1.2	25.5	24.3
France	7.6	22.2	14.6
Germany	1.2	15.1	13.9

(See Table 270.)

---

13. **29**, pp. 53ff.

TABLE 270
NATIONAL DEBT IN SELECTED COUNTRIES, 1914–52

(*Millions of U.S. Dollars*)

Country	1914	1919	1924	1929	1934	1939	1944	1949	1952
United States	$1,188	$25,482	$21,251	$16,931	$27,734	$45,890	$202,627	$252,798	$259,151
Canada	542	2,622	2,735	2,620	3,141	3,708	10,370	16,950	17,544
Mexico	214	373	793	537	371	273	247	289	. . .
Guatemala	11	11	15	16	22	12	6	15	19 [a]
El Salvador	8	13	22	21	18	15	17	11	13 [b]
Honduras	29	29	32	15	14	9	7	13	5 [a]
Nicaragua	14	10	8	23	10	2	2	. . .	. . .
Costa Rica	18	. . .	16	20	20	24	40	53	65 [a]
Panama	4	7	10	18	19	21	19	27	33 [b]
Cuba	70	. . .	. . .	92	194	229	180	. . .	. . .
Haiti	31	29	24	18	12	10	16	36	31 [a]
Dominican Republic	13	12	15	19	19	18	18	27	21 [a]
Venezuela	33	29	29	12	7	1	7	5	5 [a]
Colombia	20	. . .	36	86	110	104	177	184	227 [a]
Ecuador	23	27	20	11	7	5	7	35	39 [b]
Brazil	541	595	1,000	1,050	620	800	850	840	696 [a]
Peru	32	38	56	126	159	144	225	126	103 [b]
Bolivia	20	. . .	34	69	114	116	135	180	192 [b]
Paraguay	11	. . .	. . .	8	1	10	72	. . .	. . .
Chile	254	323	231	325	423	219	308	252	151 [b]
Uruguay	130	180	183	207	251	150	322	. . .	. . .
Argentina	630	874	910	1,244	1,341	1,560	1,850	1,829	1,820 [e]
United Kingdom	3,362	35,624	33,513	36,290	40,150	39,052	78,972	102,088	73,150 [a]
Ireland	—	. . .	60	115	248	292	298	407	501 [a]
France	7,592	22,203	23,360	18,793	21,372 [e]	10,755	[16,800]	11,170	12,298 [a]
Belgium	960	1,992	1,998	1,459	2,271	1,975	3,843	5,751	5,085 [b]
Netherlands	533	1,070	1,326	1,100	2,272	2,243	6,478 [d]	5,742	6,379 [a]
Denmark	97	184	178	368	303	260	261	952	. . .
Sweden	186	336	434	491	610	635	2,608	3,271	2,400 [a]
Norway	96	255	209	421	387	373	1,202	1,266	692 [a]
Finland	32	118	57	76	74	102	136	. . .	. . .
Germany	1,228	15,080	528	2,126	5,702	12,388	11,000 [e]	. . .	5,259
Poland	—	332	343	466	881	1,003	. . .	. . .	. . .
Czechoslovakia	—	. . .	917	969	1,595	1,617	2,172 [f]	. . .	. . .
Switzerland	64	364	457	442	737	695	2,050	2,225	2,211 [a]
Austria	2,556	. . .	300 [g]	262	678	. . .	272 [d]	1,063	495
Hungary	1,254	. . .	147	253	457	565	. . .	. . .	. . .
Portugal	636	. . .	276	431	458	348	466	410	366 [b]
Spain	1,821	2,056	2,284	2,806	2,934	2,400	3,524	. . .	. . .
Italy	3,051	7,555	4,000	4,650	8,960	7,669	29,986	3,776	4,562 [a]
Romania	334	. . .	135	. . .	573	824 [h]	. . .	. . .	. . .
Bulgaria	192	114	37	161	264	274	1,007	. . .	. . .
Greece	262	. . .	151	491	402	447	. . .	. . .	. . .
Japan	1,323	1,661	2,167	2,865	2,672	4,896	. . .	1,458	. . .
Turkey	567	. . .	. . .	. . .	367	488	1,129	727	836 [a]
India	1,819	2,374	2,904	3,907	4,696	4,233	4,733	7,258	5,656 [i]
Thailand	27	33	39	57	47	31	. . .	. . .	. . .
Egypt	438	455	520	504	527	452	389	645	591 [i]
Union of South Africa	601	792	905	1,162	1,371	1,268	1,898	2,668	442 [a]
Australia	1,650	3,155	4,013	5,465	4,888	4,796	7,635	9,106	7,312
New Zealand	475	838	963	1,321	1,211	1,125	1,699	2,478	1,863 [a]

Sources: Adapted from **5**, *passim;* **6**, 1952, pp. 474–520; for conversion into U.S. dollars see **3**, December 1952. For 1919–29, see also **2**.

a. 1951.   b. 1950.   c. Does not include foreign debts.   d. 1945.
e. At lowest official exchange rate.   f. 1946.   g. 1925.   h. 1936–37.   i. 1953.

The increase of national debt between 1914 and 1919 consisted in part of international obligations of a completely new type, the inter-Ally debts.

Origin

During the war it became usual for the Allies to help each other financially. The United States credited $4.3 billion to Great Britain, $3.4 billion to France, $1.6 billion to Italy, $409 million to Belgium, and $600 million to other Allies.[14] Great Britain advanced $2.7 billion to Russia, $2 billion to France, an equal amount to Italy, and $1.6 billion to other belligerent countries. France, in turn, gave $1.3 billion to Russia and $600 million to Belgium. Such international transactions during and immediately after World War I totaled about $20 billion, and the resulting debts were strictly intergovernmental commitments.

These debts, however, were closely related to the internal debts of the creditor countries. Some originated directly in wartime purchases by the debtor government in the creditor country. The purchases were covered by the government of the country in which they were made and were defrayed in the same way as other military expenditures, largely through funds raised by internal loans. In general, for every million dollars one government owed to another, there was another million the latter owed to its citizens and banks. As long as the loan was not repaid, the creditor government was to collect interest from the debtor government and, in turn, pay interest to holders of its own bonds. Defaulting by the debtor could not free the creditor government from its domestic obligation.

The postwar international debts partly offset one another but they could not easily be cleared. Great Britain could not repay its debt to the United States by transferring to that country its claims against France; France could not compensate Great Britain by a transferal of claims against Russia.

Amount

By the end of 1924 the inter-Ally debts originated during and immediately after World War I, with accrued interest and after adjust-

---

14. These figures include the value of war materials left in Europe and food deliveries, 1919–20. (**13**, 1926, p. 579.)

ments agreed upon between debtor and creditor nations, amounted to $20.7 billion, without counting the Russian war debts. Clearing claims and obligations would have reduced the amount to approximately $15 billion, leaving the United States and Great Britain as the only creditors and the countries of continental Europe as the debtors. (See Table 271.)

Conflicting Views

However, neither France nor Britain was convinced that the balance in favor of the United States was justified by the conditions under which the war debts were contracted. A prominent British financial expert, Sir Josiah Stamp, offered several alternative plans for computing the mutual financial obligations of the Allies.

One of these plans proposed pooling all obligations contracted during the war as a common responsibility of all the Allies and redistributing them among the Allies in proportion to their ability to pay. Then the claims of each country would be compared with its share in the common responsibility. If its claims exceeded its responsibility, it would be credited with the difference; if its responsibility exceeded its claims, the difference would be charged against it. Stamp started with the following distribution of war foreign debts of the principal belligerents (in millions of dollars):

Total	$18,142
France	7,023
Great Britain	5,155
Italy	4,748
Belgium	1,216

He suggested distributing the responsibility for this debt among the four countries and the United States as follows (in millions of dollars):

France	$2,306
Great Britain	4,957
Italy	975
Belgium	244
United States	9,660

These figures would have left Great Britain with a net debt of $198 million and France with $4,717 million, while Italy and Belgium would have been entitled to repayments. The United States claims on Europe would have been reduced from $11.8 billion to $2.1 billion.

TABLE 271

INTER-ALLY DEBTS, BY CREDITOR AND DEBTOR NATION, 1924–25

(*Millions of U.S. Dollars*)

Debtor Nation	Total	Creditor Nation			
		United States [a]	Great Britain [b]	France [c]	Italy [d]
Europe, total	$20,714	$11,785	$7,190	$1,662	$78
Great Britain	4,575	4,575	—	—	—
France	7,185	4,135	3,050	—	—
Belgium	1,106	472	44	591	—
Finland	9	9	—	—	—
Baltic countries	35	30	2	3	—
Poland	402	179	24	185	15
Czechoslovakia	261	115	6	105	35
Austria	149	30	55	64	—
Hungary	3	2	1	—	—
Portugal	106	—	104	2	—
Italy	4,997	2,096	2,833	68	—
Yugoslavia	557	64	158	335	—
Romania	436	45	144	218	29
Greece	236	17	116	104	—
British dominions and colonies	631	—	631	—	—
Other areas	37	15	22	—	—

Source: Adapted from **14,** 1925, No. 16, p. 548.

a. November 5, 1924.　　　　　　　　　c. June 30, 1924.
b. March 31, 1925.　　　　　　　　　　d. December 31, 1924.

Another of Stamp's formulas tried to provide for an equitable redistribution among the Allies of not only war debts but also the total cost of the war, taking into account each country's ability to pay and the length of its participation in the war. This formula would have required the payment of $868 million by France; $1,319 million by Italy; and $1,240 by Belgium; Great Britain would have had a claim against it for $1,948 million and the United States, for $1,479.[15]

Attempts at Settlement

The attitude of the United States toward such proposals was determined by the rising tide of isolationism in the country. In the public mind, the debts of the former Allies to the U.S. Treasury were as undisputable as any other international obligation. There could be no question of waiving these claims, although concessions could be made in terms of repayment. Originally the United States asked the Allies for full repayment of all loans and credits with interest at the same rate it paid on its domestic debts. As long as the interest was paid, it would agree to stretch the repayment of principal over a fairly long period. This arrangement would have meant that the United States charged its European Allies with some 40 per cent of its internal debt service and obtained from them about $450 million per year.

It soon became obvious, however, that the European nations could not meet these conditions. In 1922 Congress appointed a special commission to negotiate a final settlement with the debtor countries. The general idea was that the interest on outstanding debts should be not less than $4\frac{1}{4}$ per cent and that all debts should be repaid in 25 years. Actually, much more liberal conditions were granted: repayment of the debts was stretched over sixty-two years; the interest rate was set at 3 per cent for the first ten years and $3\frac{1}{2}$ per cent thereafter, with special concessions to France, Belgium, Italy, Czechoslovakia and Yugoslavia; annual payments were arranged in such a way that most debtor coun-

15. **34,** pp. 94–97.

TABLE 272

WAR DEBTS OF EUROPEAN COUNTRIES TO THE UNITED STATES: THE SETTLEMENT OF 1925

(*Millions of U.S. Dollars*)

Country	Original Debt	Debt with Accrued Interest, as of June 15, 1925	Settlement		Interest and Repayment Plan
			First Payment	Total of 62 Further Annual Installments	
United Kingdom	$4,075	$4,520	$4.1	$4,600	3% for 10 years; then, 3½%
France	3,341	4,221	—	4,025	No interest for 5 years; then, rate rising from ⅛ to 3½%
Italy	1,648	2,042	0.2	2,042	$5 million annually for 5 years; then, rate rising from ⅛ to 2%
Czechoslovakia	83	—	—	115	No interest
Yugoslavia	51	63	—	63	No interest for 12 years; then, rate rising from ⅛ to 3½%
Romania	36	—	—	46 ⎫	3% for 10 years; then, 3½%
Hungary	1.7	1.9	—	1.9 ⎬	
Poland	160	179	—	179 ⎭	
Belgium	175	246	—	246	No interest
Finland	8	9	—	9 ⎫	3% for 10 years; later, 3½%
Lithuania	5	6	—	6 ⎬	
Latvia	5	6	—	6 ⎪	
Estonia	14	14	—	14 ⎭	

Sources: Based on information given in **13,** for the fiscal year ended June 30, 1926 (pp. 55–79, 255, 579–80 and *passim*); and summary given in **28,** July 1926, p. 164.

tries would not be pressed very heavily for the first ten or fifteen years.[16]

From the point of view of the United States, this seemed to be a workable compromise. It about halved that country's current claims but reaffirmed the principle of the sanctity of international debts and promised a continuous contribution by Europe to the national debt service in the United States. (See Table 272.)

Practically, the reduction in the annual payments to the United States amounted to a reduction in the debts. The "present value" of the latter, estimated on the basis of capitalization of forthcoming annual installments, was cut to one half — a little more than half when future payments were capitalized at an annual rate of 4¼ per cent and somewhat less than half if capitalized at 5 per cent. (See Table 273.)

This settlement did not solve the problem, however. The debtors could pay only in kind,

16. **13,** 1926; **37,** p. 187.

by increasing their exports to the United States. But the country had embarked on an extreme protectionist policy after World War I, surrounding itself by prohibitive tariffs and demanding payments in gold or dollars. Great Britain was the only European country able to effect such payments on a large scale. Moreover, the peoples of Europe were reluctant to make serious sacrifices to repay their rich overseas ally when they were unable to collect reparations payments from Germany.

War debts remained a major source of friction among the former Allies for more than a decade, contributing to isolationism in the United States, kindling anti-American feeling in Europe, undermining international credit and disorganizing international trade.

GERMAN REPARATIONS

The Treaty of Versailles made Germany responsible for all damage inflicted on the popu-

TABLE 273

WAR DEBTS OF EUROPEAN COUNTRIES TO THE
UNITED STATES: VALUE BEFORE AND AFTER
THE SETTLEMENT OF 1925

(*Millions of U.S. Dollars*)

Debtor Country	Outstanding Debt before Settlement	"Present Value" of Established Annual Installments	
		Discounted at 4¼%	Discounted at 5%
Total	$12,036.4	$6,862.3	$5,873.6
United Kingdom	4,715.3	3,788.5	3,296.9
France	4,230.8	1,996.5	1,681.4
Belgium	483.4	225.0	191.8
Finland	9.2	7.4	6.5
Czechoslovakia	123.9	92.0	78.0
Hungary	2.0	1.6	1.4
Romania	46.9	35.2	29.5
Italy	2,150.2	528.2	426.3
Yugoslavia	66.2	20.0	15.9
Lithuania	6.2	5.0	4.3
Latvia	5.9	4.8	4.1
Estonia	14.1	11.4	9.9
Other	182.3	146.7	127.6

Source: **14**, 1927, No. 1.

lations of the Allied countries and permitted the Allied governments to decide the amount to be paid and the terms of payment. The treaty did not ask Germany to reimburse the Allies for their war expenditures or their war debts but left it to the Allied governments to use the German reparations to reconstruct devastated regions, replace sunken ships and amortize their debts. Meanwhile Germany was compelled to make certain reparations in kind — cattle, railroad rolling stock, coal, lumber and so on.

Controversy

Immediately after the Versailles Treaty was signed, the Allied governments began to discuss the amount of reparations and ways to make Germany pay.

The first German delegation to the Paris Peace Conference offered a plan involving the payment of 20 billion gold marks in the first seven years and 80 billion in the following eighty years, stretching the whole operation through the year 2006.[17] This proposal was rejected without discussion.

17. **25**, p. 25.

In June 1920, the Allies set their reparation claims on Germany at 269 billion gold marks ($64 billion) payable in thirty-five annual installments (the Boulogne plan). In January 1921, the Allies announced a new plan: 247 billion gold marks ($59 billion) payable in forty-two years (the Paris plan). In March 1921, Germany offered to recognize a net reparations debt of 36 billion gold marks, and in April, to accept a debt of 50 billion gold marks ($12 billion). The Allies rejected these offers and countered with a plan to convert the German reparations debt fixed at a present net value of 132 billion gold marks ($31 billion) into funded marketable securities. The Germans scornfully rejected this plan.

The problem remained unsettled. France demanded that the Allies apply military pressure to compel Germany to pay. The United Kingdom, however, was opposed to military action at that point in the dispute. In January 1923, on the pretext of German default in delivering lumber, telegraph posts and coal as stipulated by the Versailles Treaty, the French and Belgian governments sent their troops to occupy the Ruhr. The Germans answered with passive resistance and a general strike in the occupied area.

Resistance in the Ruhr was lavishly financed by the Berlin government with paper money, which came back by the carload to unoccupied Germany. Since the German government took no measures to check this operation, Germany was flooded with paper money designed originally for the Ruhr; runaway inflation developed within a few months.

The depreciated German currency became an object of speculation all over Europe, and Germans were able to pay off their old commercial debts with worthless paper marks. The chaotic economic conditions in the country and the firm stand of the French compelled the resistance government (Cuno) to resign, and a new cabinet (Stresemann) asked the Allies to resume reparations negotiations. In April 1924 an international committee of experts appointed by the Reparations Commission and headed by the United States delegate, Charles G. Dawes, developed a plan which was adopted by the governments concerned in August.

The Dawes Plan

The Dawes Plan asked Germany to pay 1,000

million gold marks (about $240 million) in the first year; 1,220 and 1,200 million in the second and third years; 1,750 million in the fourth year; and 2,500 million marks (about $600 million) yearly beginning with the fifth year, in 1930–31. These annual payments were to be increased in the future in proportion to Germany's increasing ability to pay as measured by a special "prosperity index" computed on the basis of Germany's population growth, imports and exports, the revenues and expenditures of the national and provincial governments, railroad traffic, and per capita consumption of such items as sugar, tobacco, alcoholic beverages, and coal.

After thirty-three annual payments of 2,500 million marks with a prosperity bonus, payments were to be gradually reduced to 1,540 million marks, likewise with a supplement determined by the prosperity index. In all, Germany was to pay 123.3 billion marks in fifty-nine years apart from the prosperity index, but moderate growth of the country's ability to pay — at an annual rate of 1 per cent — would bring the total to 169.5 billion marks. However, the current value of the new German commitments — that is, the value of future payments discounted at a rate of 5½ per cent — was only 41.4 billion marks without the prosperity index, or 48.9 billion marks assuming a continuous increase of payments by 1 per cent per year.

The Allies also agreed to lend Germany 800 million gold marks to finance the first year's payment. With this assistance the Germans met their obligations for the first two years of the plan. Then difficulties developed. The Germans objected to having their obligations increased as a result of their economic advances and wanted no part in a prosperity which would enrich their enemies. To this psychological impasse was added the problem of transferring German payments to the creditor nations. The latter had no desire to see German merchandise invade their own and neutral markets. The German government, on the other hand, had no interest in making the Dawes Plan work. Its goal was, rather, to prove to the Allies that Germany was unable to pay. After four tentative years, the Plan collapsed.

The Young Plan

A new commission of experts was appointed in 1928, and in the summer of 1929 a new plan — known as the Young Plan — was presented to the respective governments. It provided for further reduction of the German debt, dissolution of the Reparations Commission, elimination of political and military pressure on Germany and the creation of a new organization to handle the transfer problem, namely, the Bank for International Payments. The most significant new feature in this Plan was the attempt to tie German reparations to international war debts.

The Young Plan asked Germany to make payments for fifty-nine years, beginning with 810 million gold marks in 1929–30 and rising to 2,438 million by 1965–66, with additional payments of 1.6–1.7 billion marks yearly in the subsequent nineteen years and smaller payments in the next three years. For the first thirty-seven years, German payments would be used partly to meet the claims of the European Entente nations and partly to repay their debts to the United States. In the last seventeen years, they would serve to repay the remainder of the European debts to the United States. The annual payments established in the Dawes Plan were reduced in accordance with the concessions the United States had made to its European debtors.

The Young Plan envisaged German payments totaling 116 billion gold marks in fifty-nine annual installments — 26.2 billion marks ($6.2 billion) for damages caused to European Entente countries; 84.5 billion marks ($20.1 billion) to liquidate inter-Ally debts, and 5 billion marks ($1.2 billion) to repay the Dawes loan and satisfy certain claims of the United States and Belgium.

The End of Reparations

The new plan became effective in May 1930. A year later it was suspended, for a year, by President Hoover's moratorium. It has never been reinstated and enforced. The moratorium proved to be the end of both German reparations and inter-Allied debts.[18]

Technically the war debts of the Allies have not been canceled; they are still carried as "debts in default" in the official balance sheet of the liabilities and assets of the United States.

Ultimately the German reparations debt was settled in the following manner: According to the German experts, German payments before the occupation of the Ruhr were close to 56 billion gold marks, but the Reparations Commission credited Germany with payments and de-

18. See **37**, pp. 189–223. Cf. **19, 25, 26, 32**.

TABLE 274

FOREIGN PUBLIC DEBT, BY DEBTOR AND CREDITOR NATION, END OF 1924

(*Millions of U.S. Dollars*)

Debtor Nation	Total	Creditor Nation				
		United States	Europe			Other Nations
			Great Britain	Other Entente Nations	Rest of Europe	
World	$45,411	$14,554	$19,685	$4,700	$6,078	$393
Europe ("Entente")	20,140	11,961	6,571	1,167	332	109
Great Britain	5,456	4,761	—	350	292	52
France	7,824	4,443	3,310	—	22	50
Belgium-Luxembourg	1,554	660	133	736	18	7
Italy	5,000	2,097	2,835	68	—	—
Portugal	306	—	293	13	—	—
Russia (USSR)	7,933	251	3,682	1,264	2,609	127
Neutral Europe	990	470	20	—	500	—
Netherlands	100	100	—	—	—	—
Denmark	198	124	—	—	74	—
Sweden	214	55	—	—	159	—
Norway	207	96	20	—	91	—
Switzerland	95	95	—	—	—	—
Spain	176	—	—	—	176	—
Other European countries	3,943	823	1,009	1,410	692	8
Finland	224	37	12	21	154	—
Germany	243	110	58	41	33	—
Poland	562	238	24	288	12	—
Danzig	8	—	8	—	—	—
Baltic states	42	31	8	3	—	—
Czechoslovakia	302	164	33	105	—	—
Austria	351	52	123	140	36	—
Hungary	167	10	50	94	14	—
Yugoslavia	676	79	159	287	151	—
Romania	578	75	177	300	25	—
Bulgaria	285	—	—	18	267	—
Greece	506	27	357	114	—	8

(Continued on facing page)

liveries in kind totaling only 7.9 billion gold marks (1.9 billion marks in cash, 3.5 billion in kind and 2.6 billion in the value of seized property).[19] Part of this went to cover the cost of occupation, and part could not be distributed among the creditors, so that the net yield of reparations transferred to the respective governments before the Ruhr operation was 2,344 million marks ($558 million). All later German payments are estimated at approximately 7 billion marks. In the same period, however, much larger amounts were transferred to Germany in the form of loans, credits and sales against worthless paper money.

THE INTERWAR YEARS

Inter-Ally debts and German reparations represented the core of the problem of public debt in the interwar years. Apart from revisions of such obligations, national debts fluctuated within a comparatively narrow range. The prevailing trend was downward in the decade 1919–29 and upward in 1929–39.

19. **37**, p. 208.

TABLE 274—*continued*

Debtor Nation	Total	Creditor Nation				
		United States	Europe			Other Nations
			Great Britain	Other Entente Nations	Rest of Europe	
Middle America	$ 550	$ 55	$ 161	$ 12	$322	—
South America	1,987	242	1,524	189	29	$ 2
Brazil	633	69	500	64	—	—
Chile	161	31	119	—	11	—
Uruguay	145	15	69	59	—	2
Argentina	966	115	782	61	7	—
Other	82	12	54	5	11	—
Asia	2,337	175	839	264	321	137
China	781	25	261	178	202	115
Japan	755	150	518	86	—	—
Turkey	719	—	—	—	719	—
Persia (Iran)	20	—	20	—	—	—
Siam (Thailand)	62	—	40	—	—	22
Africa	453	—	2	—	451	—
Egypt	451	—	—	—	451	—
Liberia	2	—	2	—	—	—
British dominions and colonies	6,041	226	5,806	—	—	10
Canada	520	211	309	—	—	—
British India	1,660	—	1,660	—	—	—
Union of South Africa	641	—	641	—	—	—
Australia	2,119	—	2,119	—	—	—
New Zealand	569	—	559	—	—	10
Other	533	15	518	—	—	—
Non-British colonies	1,038	351	71	394	222	—

Source: Adapted from **14**, 1925, No. 16, p. 549; cf. **37**, pp. 164–65. Minor discrepancies in additions are due to rounding.

The total for the countries listed in Table 270 changed as follows (in billions of dollars):

1919	$125.2
1924	109.6
1929	110.9
1934	133.7
1939	147.1

These changes in the total were due in part to the accumulation of budgetary deficits or repayment of maturing debts in individual countries. Other factors were the disappearance of the German internal debt (some $15 billion) engulfed in the runaway inflation (1923); monetary reform in France (1929); and variations in exchange rates, especially the effects of the devaluation of the pound (1931) and the dollar (1933). Monetary and political factors prevailed in the interwar years and dwarfed even such economic factors as the postwar recovery in the 1920's and the depression in the following decade.

Foreign national debts changed little in this period. Actually, they were frozen at the level of 1924–25, when the obligations of European countries toward the United States were settled. Foreign public debt then totaled $45.4 billion, including the fictitious item of $7.9 billion for the Russian debt repudiated by the Soviet government, or $37.5 billion when this item is excluded. (See Table 274.)

This total represented more than one third of all public debt, internal and foreign, in 1924

($109.6 billion). It does not include the reparations debt of Germany, which never was an economic reality. The total does include, at face value, the debts of the Allies to the United States, which actually were halved by negotiated settlements and later, under the Young Plan, became as unreal as German reparations.

A few years later, approximately two thirds of the foreign public debt, as it stood on the books at the end of 1924, proved to be "bad" debts. A large part of the inter-Ally war debts proved as unrecoverable for the creditors as were the German reparations debts for the victors.

This experience helped the United States government to shape its financial policy during World War II. Indeed, not only the lend-lease program but the management of the reparations problem since World War II and the foreign-aid policy have been greatly influenced by the fate of war debts after World War I.

THE IMPACT OF WORLD WAR II ON NATIONAL DEBT

The total cost of World War II, including losses in human life and other resources and the destruction suffered by belligerent nations, is unknown, and no attempt will be made here to estimate it. In terms of military expenditures, the financial cost can be roughly estimated as the difference between the governmental expenditure during and immediately after the war and in the last prewar year.

Expenditures for War

In the United States the federal government spent $382 billion in the six years 1941–46, while its expenditures in 1940 amounted to $9.2 billion. Assuming that under normal peacetime conditions federal expenditures would have totaled $55 billion in six years, war expenditures of the United States are set at $327 billion. This estimate is on the conservative side, first, because some military expenditures were included in the 1940 federal budget, and, second, because war expenditures did not end with 1946. In fact, in the four years 1947–50, the United States spent some $10 billion for veterans pensions and rehabilitation programs, $17 billion in interest on war loans and credits, and $12 billion (net) in foreign aid. Thus, to cope with war and its repercussions, the United States had spent approximately $366 billion by 1950.

Similarly, war expenditures of the United Kingdom from 1940 to 1950 can be roughly

estimated at $150 billion and those of the USSR and Japan, at $100 billion and $40 billion, respectively. Approximately $25 billion was spent by Canada, $15 billion by Australia, $5 billion by India. To these sums should be added the expenditures of Germany and Italy, of countries overrun and occupied by Germany and of the neutral countries which kept their armed forces in readiness as a measure of precaution.

Less than half the estimated total war expenditure of $1,000 billion was covered by taxes; the rest was financed by all kinds of loans, credits and other operations, including issuance of paper money. In the United States, $151 billion of the estimated $366 billion of military and postwar expenditures was provided by the increase in federal revenues, while $215 billion was covered by loans. In the United Kingdom, the share of loans in war and postwar national budgets was close to 40 per cent, and in most other countries it was larger. In all, we are probably on the conservative side in assuming that loans and other credit operations provided governments of belligerent nations with some $500 to $550 billion at current prices. Not all this amount appears, however, in the increase in national debt.

Increase in National Debt

The total dollar value of the national debt of the countries listed in Table 270 almost trebled between 1939 and 1949, rising from $147.1 billion to $436.8 billion. The increase — about $290 billion — was very unevenly distributed among belligerent and neutral countries

National debt increased in countries which succeeded in avoiding a runaway inflation and preserved the stability of their currency in relation to the gold standard, such as the United States and Canada, or devalued it in an orderly way, as did the United Kingdom, Belgium, the Netherlands, Sweden, Norway and Denmark. The debt figures for these countries, converted into U.S. dollars at the current exchange rate, are as follows (in millions of dollars):

	1939	1949	Percentage Change
United States	$45,890	$252,798	+451
Canada	3,708	16,950	+357
United Kingdom	39,052	102,088	+161
Belgium	1,975	5,751	+191
Netherlands	2,243	5,742	+156
Denmark	260	952	+266
Sweden	635	3,271	+415
Norway	373	1,266	+239

Debts increased less rapidly in the belligerent countries which waged war less intensively, as follows (in millions of dollars):

	1939	1949	Percentage Change
Australia	$4,796	$9,106	+ 90
New Zealand	1,125	2,478	+120
Union of South Africa	1,268	2,668	+110
India	4,233	7,258	+ 71

On the other side, Axis countries emerged from the war and postwar economic and financial chaos with less national debt than they had before the war (in millions of dollars):

	1939	1949	Percentage Change
Italy	$7,669	$3,776	–51
Japan	4,896	1,458	–70

At the same time some non-European countries that engaged in extensive projects of industrialization and development of natural resources, such as Argentina, Brazil, Peru, Bolivia and Turkey, increased their national debt in terms of national currency, but their value in terms of U.S. dollars did not increase in the same proportion because of depreciation of the national currencies. The debt of these countries changed as follows (in millions of dollars):

	1939	1949	Percentage Change
Brazil	$800	$840	+ 5
Peru	144	126	–12
Bolivia	116	180	+55
Argentina	1,560	1,829	+17
Turkey	488	727	+49

Of the world's total net increase of some $290 billion, the United States accounted for $207 billion, the United Kingdom for more than $63 billion, and all other countries for only $20 billion.

When the diminished purchasing power of the U.S. dollar is taken into account, and the 1950 dollar is set at 60 cents, at 1939 prices, it appears that the total national debt of the surveyed countries increased between 1939 and 1949 from $147 billion to approximately $262 billion (at 1939 prices). Almost all the rise ($115 billion) was due to the increase of the national debt of the United States ($108 billion at 1939 prices), while increases in the rest of the world (mainly in the United Kingdom) were almost completely offset by decreases.

Thus the increase in national debt after World War II was not as widespread as after World War I, but was heavily concentrated in a single nation, the United States. Other nations sustained heavier losses in human life, property and the standard of living of the population but, in terms of national debt, the United States has chiefly footed the bill.

To a large extent, this result reflects the role of the arsenal of democracy which the nation assumed in the world conflict. To a large extent the final distribution of the increase in national debt was due to its lend-lease and foreign aid programs, which prevented the development of inter-Ally debts during and after World War II.

Lend-Lease and Foreign Aid

The Lend-Lease Act was signed by President Roosevelt on March 10, 1941, nine months before Pearl Harbor. The program expired with the end of the war but was followed by a series of other emergency-aid and rehabilitation programs: UNRRA, post-UNRRA, interim aid, the ECA European program, the civilian supply action, Philippine rehabilitation, Korean and Far Eastern aid, the Mutual Security Program, and so on. (See Table 275.)

By the end of 1952 the United States had dispersed more than $90 billion in foreign aid — $48.7 billion under the lend-lease program, and $41.6 billion in grants and credits under other programs.[20] In 1953 an additional $6.4 billion was allocated; in 1954, $4.7 billion.

Part of the lend-lease disbursements has been offset by reverse lend-lease operations and return of lend-lease ships (over $8 billion). Part of some grants has been offset by credit agreements ($1,256 million), cash settlements and counterpart funds credited to foreign countries. Part of the principal has been reimbursed. With these corrections, net outlays of the United States for military assistance and economic and technical aid to foreign countries totaled $78.6 billion by the end of 1952 and $90 billion by the end of 1954. Of this total more than $40 billion represents net disbursements under the lend-lease program, the rest postwar grants and credits.

It can be misleading, however, to pool lend-lease operations, grants and credits to foreign

20. For lend-lease operations through 1951, see Chapter 5, Table 84; for other programs through June 1953, see Table 87.

TABLE 275

FOREIGN AID BY THE UNITED STATES GOVERNMENT, JULY 1, 1940 THROUGH DECEMBER 1952

(Millions of Dollars)

Program	Total	War Period	Postwar Period
Gross foreign aid	$90,258	$49,224	$41,034
Grants utilized	78,375	48,128	30,247
Less: credit agreement offsets	1,256	—	1,256
Credits	13,140	1,096	12,044
Returns:			
Grants	9,103	7,873	1,230
Credits	2,571	380	2,191
Net foreign aid	78,583	40,971	37,612
Grants			
Lend-lease	48,660	46,728	1,932
Civilian supplies	6,153	813	5,340
UNRRA, post-UNRRA and interim aid	3,526	83	3,443
Mutual Security Program			
Economic and technical assistance	12,711	—	12,711
Military aid	4,687	—	4,687
Philippine rehabilitation	634	—	634
Korean and Far Eastern aid	310	—	310
Chinese stabilization and military aid	623	380	243
Greek-Turkish aid	659	—	659
Other	721	124	597
Credits utilized	13,140	1,096	12,044
Special British loan	3,750	—	3,750
Export-Import Bank	3,744	329	3,415
Credit-agreement offsets to grants	1,256	—	1,256
Surplus property	1,487	—	1,487
Mutual Security Program [a]	1,608	—	1,608
Lend-lease	420	349	71
Other	875	417	458

Sources: **8,** p. 81; **12,** March 1953, p. 15.   a. Includes loans to Spain and India.

countries under a common title of "foreign aid." Lend-lease deliveries consisted largely of defense articles — tanks, airplanes, guns, munitions, trucks and other tools of war. (See Table 84, page 218.) Whether these tools were used by the troops of the United States or those of its Allies, they served the same purpose.[21] Nearly every lend-lease operation had a twofold military meaning: the United States supplied weapons to the Allies and the latter supplied the men to operate the engines of war turned out in the United States.

There was nothing new in this arrangement.

During World War I the United States had acted as an arsenal of democracy although the term had not been coined at that time. In both wars it began this operation long before it became a belligerent. The only difference was in the financial side of the arrangement: in World War I, delivery for cash payment, loans and credits; in World War II, transfer of foodstuffs, strategic materials, military equipment and munitions to friendly nations, and later to the Allies, without financial commitment on their part. If all lend-lease deliveries had been effected in the same way as military deliveries during World War I, they would have resulted in foreign debts to the United States totaling approximately $40 billion at the end of the war, or some $55 billion,

21. This reasoning applies also to other lend-lease deliveries. During a total war, raw materials and foodstuffs are tools of war, precisely as are airplanes and munitions.

including moderate accrued interest, by 1955. The purpose of the lend-lease program was to prevent this impact of the war on international finance.

This purpose has been achieved. The net value of lend-lease deliveries has been covered by the United States as a part of its own military expenditures and does not appear in postwar international debts.

This is likewise true of part of the United States foreign aid after the end of the war. Of the total of some $40 billion, approximately $10 billion has been formalized as regular long-term debt of the respective countries to the United States. The remaining $30 billion represents grants and gifts motivated by humanitarian and political considerations. The UNRRA program represents gifts based chiefly on humanitarian and moral motives; Chinese stabilization and military aid, Greek-Turkish aid and the mutual defense assistance program typify foreign aid inspired by farsighted national policy. Both considerations determined the Mutual Security Program and aid to the East. All these outlays have contributed to the growth of the internal debt of the United States but have not increased the indebtedness of the receiving countries. Thus, the growth of foreign debts of the free European nations has been prevented to some extent by the growth of internal debts of the United States.

The Present Status of National Debt

AMOUNT

National debts of the countries listed in Table 270 totaled approximately $400–$410 billion in 1951–52. A more precise estimate is impossible because not more than a score of countries report their current debt status. For many countries, the most recent data available are for 1950, while some have published no reports since 1946 or 1948.[22] The estimated total therefore includes numerous items which have been adjusted to changes in exchange rates but are not up to date in terms of new debts incurred by the government or the settlement of old debts.

The downward change in the dollar value of national debt between 1949 and 1951–52 was due mainly to the devaluation of the pound in the autumn of 1949. This resulted in reduction by a third of the dollar value of all debts written in pounds or other currencies within the sterling

area (in Table 270, the United Kingdom, Australia, New Zealand, Sweden, Norway and India). This adjustment was partly offset by the increased indebtedness of the United States and Italy.

It is noteworthy that the domestic national debt of the United States in the middle of 1952 ($259 billion) exceeded the sum of the domestic and foreign debts of all other countries of the world, which then totaled $152 billion (for all countries listed in Table 276, not including the USSR and its satellites).

DOMESTIC AND FOREIGN DEBTS

Information on the amount of the domestic and foreign debts of individual countries is incomplete. The UN has published detailed statistics for 1946 [23] and more general data for two-score countries around 1952. The latter are summarized in Table 276. These data, however, are not strictly comparable. As the *Statistical Yearbook* of the UN points out, some countries record all liabilities of the state in the national debt, while others include only definite types of liabilities, such as loans and bank credits; some countries consider money in circulation issued by the government as a part of its debt, others do not. Different methods are used in computing the value of outstanding debt and in converting foreign debt into the national currency.

Table 276 excludes all debts of World War I. The national currencies have been converted into U.S. dollars at the current exchange rate. This may have resulted in some overstatement in foreign debts in countries with controlled currencies.

The survey reveals a decline in the share of foreign obligations in national debt. Excluding the United States, the debts of the other thirty-eight countries listed in Table 276 totaled about $152 billion around 1952. Of this total, domestic debt amounted to more than $134 billion, and foreign obligations to $18 billion. When the United States is included, the total for national debt rises to more than $410 billion, of which less than 5 per cent was in foreign loans.

Foreign commitments represented more than 50 per cent of the national debt of Ecuador (82 per cent), El Salvador (77 per cent), Bolivia (76 per cent), Italy (74 per cent) and Burma (70 per cent). The ratio ranged between 20 and 50

22. **6**, 1952, pp. 459–76; **7**, 1953, *passim*.

23. **5**; **6**, 1952, pp. 459–76. Cf. **3, 4** and **7**.

TABLE 276

NATIONAL DEBT: DOMESTIC AND FOREIGN, IN SELECTED COUNTRIES, AROUND 1950–53

Country and Year	Amount, in Millions of U.S. Dollars			Per Capita, in Dollars	National Debt as Percentage of National Income
	Total	Domestic	Foreign		
United States, 1952	$259,151	$259,151	—	$1,650	91
Canada, 1952	17,544	17,134	$410	1,226	98
Mexico, 1949	289	260	29	12	10
Guatemala, 1951	19	19	—	6	[6]
El Salvador, 1950	13	3	10	7	[7]
Honduras, 1951	5	4	1	3	[3]
Costa Rica, 1951	65	35	30	79	[79]
Haiti, 1951	31	31	—	10	[10]
Dominican Republic, 1951	21	21	—	10	[10]
Panama, 1950	33	20	13	40	. . .
Venezuela, 1951	5	5	—	1	[1]
Colombia, 1951	227	146	81	20	[10]
Ecuador, 1950	39	7	32	12	[12]
Brazil, 1951	696	515	181	13	[13]
Peru, 1950	103	75	28	12	18
Bolivia, 1950	192	46	146	64	. . .
Chile, 1950	151	110	41	32	7
Argentina, 1949	1,829	1,811	16	109	36
United Kingdom, 1951	73,150	67,442	5,708	1,446	229
Ireland, 1951	501	390	111	165	49
France, 1951	12,298	8,706	3,592	291	47
Belgium, 1950	5,085	4,777	308	588	85
Netherlands, 1951	6,379	5,479	900	621	143
Sweden, 1951	2,400	1,739	661	340	30
Norway, 1951	692	531	161	210	32
Western Germany, 1952	5,269	5,239	30	84	45
Austria, 1952	495	485	10	70	35
Switzerland, 1951	2,211	2,211	—	465	50
Portugal, 1950	366	344	22	43	30
Italy, 1951	4,562	1,190	3,372	98	26
Turkey, 1951	836	559	277	40	27
India, 1953	5,656	5,412	244	16	30
Burma, 1953	255	76	179	13	[26]
Ceylon, 1950	136	108	28	18	12
Philippines, 1951	283	215	68	14	11
Egypt, 1953	591	591	—	28	. . .
Union of South Africa, 1951	442	442	—	35	24
Australia, 1952	7,312	6,412	900	867	99
New Zealand, 1951	1,868	1,650	218	959	107

Sources: Chiefly **6**, 1952, pp. 21–52, 406–07, 439–76. Figures in brackets represent rough estimates based on the hypothetical estimate of per capita income in the respective Latin American republics at $100 and in Burma at $50.

per cent for Costa Rica (46), Panama (39), Colombia (36), Turkey (33), France (29), Sweden (28), Ireland (22), Peru (27), Chile (27), Brazil (26), the Philippines (24) and Ceylon (21). For the other twenty-one countries, it was below 20 per cent; for most of them, below 10 per cent.

Moreover, about half the total foreign public debt represents intergovernmental commitments held by the government of the United States.

The agreement for annual installments to be paid as interest and amortization has substantially reduced the present value of thcsc commitments computed on the basis of capitalization of future payments.

Foreign Indebtedness to the United States

According to governmental accounts, the indebtedness of foreign countries to the United States totaled $11,780 million on December 31, 1954, distributed by debtor country as follows (in millions of dollars): [24]

United Kingdom	$4,643
France	1,859
Germany	1,193
Brazil	458
India	361
Netherlands	309
Italy	290
USSR	222
China	155
Belgium-Luxembourg	154
Indonesia	136
Mexico	133
Ireland	128
Israel	123
Finland	103
Norway	102
Turkey	94
Union of South Africa	92
Argentina	91
Japan	85
Philippines	78
Greece	77
Chile	77
Poland	68
Spain	65
United Nations	60
European Coal and Steel Community	59
Yugoslavia	54
Portugal	50
Denmark	49
Other countries	412

(Cf. Figure 49, page 232.)

Some of these debts are hardly recoverable, and for some no schedule of repayment has been established. Formal arrangements were made for reimbursement of $9.6 billion, with interest,

24. **12**, April 1955, p. 12. The figures include only loans and credits of the U.S. government to foreign governments. Accounts of foreign governments showing their debts to the United States may include commercial loans issued in the name of those governments on the U.S. market. For the state of U.S. loans to foreign countries as of June 30, 1951, see p. 232.

in annual payments extending partly to 1984 and partly to the end of the century.

Beginning with 1951, payments under the Anglo-American Financial Agreement and under the French war-account settlement have similar types of repayment schedules. The annual payment under each agreement remains constant — $138.5 million for the British through the year 2000 and $30.6 million for the French through the year 1980 — with an increasing portion each year applicable to amortization of principal and a decreasing portion to interest. In this respect the terms differ from those on credits extended by the United States to other countries. On all other credits for which debt-service projections have been made, the payments of principal, though in many cases not constant, are a fixed amount each year and interest payments are to be made on the basis of a stated rate on the unpaid balance. In a few instances interest is not stipulated or implied.

The established plans foresee a fairly constant decline after 1952 in total debt service on present formalized obligations. From total payments of $509 million in 1952, scheduled payments are halved by 1980. From 1984 through the year 2000, the sole remaining payments are those of $138.5 million annually by the United Kingdom.

Scheduled payments amount to almost $9.6 billion in amortization and more than $4.3 billion in interest, bringing to $13.9 billion the total scheduled payment by foreign countries on their indebtedness to the United States government in the next forty-nine years. Countries participating in the European Recovery Program are scheduled to pay 88 per cent of the total: the United Kingdom, 54 per cent; France, 20 per cent; other ERP countries, about 14 per cent. Of the remainder, the other European countries are scheduled for 5 per cent; American republics, for 4 per cent, and countries in the Far East, for 2 per cent.[25] (See Figure 50, page 233.)

NATIONAL DEBT PER CAPITA

The United States, the United Kingdom, Canada, New Zealand and Australia have by far the largest national debt per capita of population:

United States	$1,650
United Kingdom	1,446
Canada	1,226
New Zealand	959
Australia	867

25. **12**, January 1952, pp. 19–20.

Next in line are the comparatively prosperous countries of continental Europe:

Netherlands	$621
Belgium	588
Switzerland	465
Sweden	340
France	291
Norway	210

These countries are followed by Ireland ($165), Argentina ($109), Italy ($98), Western Germany ($84), Costa Rica ($79) and Austria ($70).

National debt is also comparatively high per capita in Bolivia ($64), Portugal ($43), Panama ($40) and Turkey ($40). It is low, even with allowance for low per capita income, in Mexico, Guatemala, El Salvador, Honduras, Haiti, the Dominican Republic, Venezuela, Ecuador, Brazil, Peru and the Philippines.[26]

RELATION TO NATIONAL INCOME

Since neither national debt statistics nor national income estimates for different countries are strictly comparable, data on the ratio of national debt to national income (Table 276) should be regarded as rough approximations. The range of variation is so wide from country to country, however, that discrepancies due to the method of computation do not affect the general conclusions.

In the six following countries the national debt exceeds the current annual national income or is close to it, and represented the following percentages of the national income around 1950–52:

United Kingdom	229
Netherlands	143
New Zealand	107
Australia	99
Canada	98
United States	91

Belgium is just below this group with 85 per cent, followed by Costa Rica (79 per cent).

At a substantial distance follow countries in which national debt represents from one third to

one half the annual national income: Switzerland (50 per cent), Ireland (49), France (47), Western Germany (45), Argentina (36) and Austria (35).

Next come Norway (32 per cent), Sweden (30), Portugal (30), India (30), Turkey (27), Italy (26), Burma (26), the Union of South Africa (24), Peru (18), Brazil (13), Ecuador (12), Ceylon (12) and the Philippines (11).

Two conclusions are inescapable. (1) There is a fairly clear correlation between the level of economic development and the relative indebtedness of nations. With a few exceptions, it appears to be the privilege of prosperous modern nations to carry a national debt amounting to more than half the annual national income. (2) In relation to national income, national debt in the United States is lower than in the Netherlands, New Zealand, Australia and Canada, and less than half that in the United Kingdom.

DEBT SERVICE

The relative fiscal burden of national debt appears in the share of debt service in the national budget.

It is noteworthy that in the early years of the United States interest on public debt was the principal item of federal expenditures. It averaged 53.5 per cent of the federal budget in 1789–95; 40.0 per cent in 1796–1800; 46.0 per cent in 1801–06. It declined gradually after 1806 and dropped to 0.3–0.4 per cent of all federal expenditures in 1836–40. After some ups and downs it reached a level of 3.2 per cent before 1856–60. The Civil War brought it back close to the post-Revolutionary War figure: 35.8 per cent, on the average, in 1866–70; 38.8 per cent in 1871–75; 39.2 per cent in 1876–80. In this period, debt service represented a very serious financial burden for the nation.

The ratio of public debt interest to total expenditures declined gradually in the following period until it dropped to 3.1 per cent in 1911–15 — a ratio close to that before the outbreak of the Civil War. It skyrocketed after World War I, averaged 27.2 per cent in 1921–25 and dropped to 10.9 in 1936–40. The subsequent variations are most characteristic. As a result of the tremendous growth of federal expenses during World War II, the share of debt service in the national budget declined in significance. In 1941–45 the federal government spent more than $2 billion annually on public debt interest, but

---

26. Because of changes in exchange rates and variations in years to which these computations refer, per capita rates discussed here have a considerable margin of error. The ranking of individual countries changes slightly from year to year. The figures above refer to the years shown in Table 276.

this amount — although 700 times that at the time of Alexander Hamilton — represented only 3.2 per cent of total government expenditures. After World War II interest on the public debt exceeded $5 billion yearly, more than the total annual expenditures of the government in 1931–35. However, the share of this item in the federal budget did not increase: it averaged 13.3 per cent in 1931–35 and 12.1 per cent in 1946–50, was 12.6 per cent in the fiscal year 1950–51, declined to 8.9 and 8.8 per cent in 1951–52 and 1952–53. (See Table 253, page 708.)

The share of national debt service in the total expenditures of central governments in other countries varies widely. In 1952 it ranged from 0.5 per cent in Burma and Iran and 0.7 per cent in Chile to 18.0 per cent in Colombia, 18.8 per cent in Costa Rica and 24.5 per cent in Mexico. In the following countries the share was between 8 and 14 per cent: the United States (8.9), the Netherlands (9.0), Peru (9.2), Argentina (9.7), New Zealand (10.2), India (10.6), the United Kingdom (11.9), Canada (12.1), Panama (13.4), Turkey (13.6), Switzerland (13.7). (See Table 255, page 710.)

The Impact of National Debt

A large national debt can greatly influence public finance, the monetary system and the whole economic life of a nation. This influence, however, depends less on the size of the debt than on changes in the amount, business conditions, the tax system, treasury policy and many other factors.

A large national debt can affect the economic welfare of the nation directly through the obligations it imposes on national finance or indirectly, by creating a psychological climate unfavorable for business. Such an effect is not automatic, however. It is not predetermined by the size of the debt in relation to national income and can be prevented or minimized by a sound financial and monetary policy of the government and by proper management of the debt. A poorly managed national debt amounting to 30–40 per cent of annual national income may represent a greater danger to the economic system than a debt three or four times as large but well distributed among different sectors of the national economy, skillfully funded and properly managed. On the other hand, a mistake in management of the national debt, comparatively harmless when the debt amounts to 10 per cent of

national income, may have disastrous results when the debt equals or exceeds annual national income. A huge national debt increases the economic responsibilities of the government but does not necessarily ruin the nation.

THE DANGER OF NATIONAL DEBT

The Committee on Public Debt Policy headed by W. Randolph Burgess described the imaginary and real dangers of national debt as follows:

Many people in thinking of the debt are worrying about some vast but vague cataclysm. They think the towering debt of 250 billion dollars is likely, somehow, to topple over and crush them. To be more specific, they worry about some form of national bankruptcy under which the national debt might be repudiated — in the sense of the government being unwilling or unable to meet its obligations as they fall due. . . . Or they refer to the fact that some 50 billions of debt matures within a year, and they wonder whether the Treasury will always be able to sell new securities to pay this debt on maturity.

These fears of some great catastrophe in connection with the debt are based on the feeling that we as individuals have about our own debts. We know from experience that a debt can be not only a millstone about the neck, but also at times a source of disaster like the loss of a home when the mortgage cannot be met.

Actually, the real threat of the debt is more subtle than the danger of sudden catastrophe. For national debt is different from the debt of an individual or family in at least two respects. First, governments have the power to tax in order to raise funds to support their debts. . . . Second, governments control the money supply and make the laws and regulations to govern what citizens who are creditors of the government can do with the securities they own.

In short, national debt is just as serious as private debt, perhaps more so, but its impact on the people is different.[27]

Charles C. Abbott likewise stresses the difference between the real and imaginary threat of a large national debt:

Contrary to much popular belief, the debt does not bring with it a threat of some cataclysm, or even the presumption that national bankruptcy is inevitable. The dangers lie in other directions.[28]

27. **22**, p. 6.
28. **16**, p. 9.

The Committee on Public Debt Policy pointed out four dangers:

1. Dilution of the dollar, that is, depreciation of the currency and rise of prices as the result of an excessive money supply.

2. Risk of boom and bust, that is, economic instability resulting from debt management which interferes with sound governmental monetary and fiscal policy.

3. Smothering of an enterprise economy through the drain of taxes and government controls necessitated by the difficult task of debt management.

4. Loss of human freedom as a result of the increasing concentration of economic power in the hands of governments.[29]

A large national debt necessarily means a broadening scope of governmental interference in the economic life of the nation and implies a danger that the government will not use its augmented power with necessary skill and wisdom. The danger is not imminent when national monetary policy and national debt management are in strong and able hands.

The National Association of Manufacturers, in its campaign against deficit financing and accumulation of heavy national indebtedness, pointed out in 1948:

The necessary flow of risk capital, or venture capital, into private business will diminish, if taxes become too high as a result of having to make payments for interest and for reducing the principal of a large public debt. . . . It will diminish because people are becoming less inclined to take a chance due to high taxes and poor opportunities for making business profits. This will in turn discourage the establishment of new businesses and hinder the growth of existing firms. If this happens, the level of production will be below what it would otherwise be. The same would hold true for job opportunities. The volume of consumption goods would also be less than it would otherwise be and the standard of living would be lower.[30]

In general, the argument of the inflationary danger of an *increase* in national debt (through accumulation of budgetary deficits) and the deflationary danger of a sudden drastic *reduction* of the debt is stronger than the contention that a large national debt in itself represents an imminent threat to the national economy.

The potential dangers of a large debt — more exactly, of mistakes in its management — cannot

be belittled by the consideration that in the case of a domestic debt the nation owes and pays to itself. The high taxes required for transfer payments can represent a serious burden on the nation's finances and economy. The burden remains real even when such taxes are collected from the same groups of the population that hold the national debt obligations in the way pictured in the following deliberately simplified example given by the National Association of Manufacturers:

Suppose that the Federal Government obligations are distributed among all taxpayers in proportion to the amount of tax that each one pays to the Federal Government. If we could realize such a perfect distribution of the internal federal debt, the amount of interest received by each holder of government securities would, of course, be equal to or at least proportional to the share of his tax payments which are used to pay the interest charges on the federal debt.[31]

The NAM considered such an equilibrium between the tax payments and the receipts of security holders contrary to the principle that in the U.S. economic system everyone is entitled to some income on his savings or capital funds. In this case, indeed, buyers of government securities would have lent their money to the government free of charge.

It is highly probable, however, that even if governmental securities are distributed among different *groups* of taxpayers in the same proportion as taxes, government bonds will not be distributed evenly among *individuals* in each group: some members of each group will have bought national securities, others will not. All will be called to pay taxes required for debt service, but the yield will be distributed among the holders of governmental securities and the latter will be paid for their money at the expense of other taxpayers.

Here again the economic impact of a large national debt appears to depend on the patterns of distribution of government securities and taxes rather than the size of the debt. In other words, the core of the problem is in the management of the national debt — the policies of issuing, converting, renewing and repaying national loans.

Moreover, in its more recent publications the NAM does not assail the present national indebtedness as excessive and threatening the well-being of the nation. In its statement adopted in

---

29. **22,** pp. 7–11; cf. **16,** pp. 9–10.
30. **27,** pp. 11–12.

31. **27,** p. 12.

February 1955 it insists only that the limit of the national debt be kept at $275 billion, with the following safeguard clause:

To avoid resort in future to temporary debt limit increases — which always involve the threat of permanency — and as a means of providing flexibility in Treasury operations, it is recommended that tax anticipation certificates issued and maturing within a given fiscal year be excluded from the statutory debt limit.

THE DISTRIBUTION OF NATIONAL DEBT

The management of the national debt is concerned also with its distribution among different types of obligations and different groups of holders of securities.

Type of Obligations

In most countries with a large national debt, the debt is made up of obligations issued at different times and on different terms. Bonds and loans differ not only in interest rate but in retirement schedule and marketability and sometimes in special provisions, such as tax exemption and limited convertibility into cash. The heterogeneity of the obligations included in a national debt depends partly on differences in the market conditions under which the respective securities were offered to the public or banks and partly on consideration of the needs and preferences of prospective buyers. Some securities could be sold at a very low interest rate; others were issued when only comparatively high interest and promise of other advantages could induce banks, corporations and private individuals to subscribe. As a rule, the government has to pay higher interest for long-term nonmarketable loans than for short-term credits.

Special inducements must be offered to reach particular groups of investors. This policy has been described by a spokesman of the U.S. Treasury as follows:

. . . we have arranged the debt so that each investor class holds securities which are appropriate to it. Over 60 per cent of the securities held by the commercial banks are due or callable in less than five years. On the other hand, insurance companies hold about 10 per cent of their portfolios in the form of securities due or callable within five years, and 90 per cent in longer categories. Individuals largely hold Series E, F, and G savings bonds, which they may either cash when the need arises or continue to hold at an ascending rate of interest. About half of the holdings of individuals is in the form of Series

E bonds, a security designed exclusively for the average small investor.

Corporations other than banks and insurance companies hold close to one third of their Government securities in the form of savings notes — a highly flexible instrument which may be turned in on taxes, redeemed for cash or held for investment at increasing rates of interest. The bulk of the remainder of corporation holdings is in the form of short-term securities, largely certificates of indebtedness.

This "tailoring" of securities to the needs of the investor is a healthy thing for the economy.[32]

The composition of the national debt changes continuously. Some loans mature and must be repaid; some securities are cashed by the holders. Often at least part of the matured or redeemed obligations can be replaced by new securities of the same type, but the turnover permits, and sometimes requires, reshaping the composition of the debt.

When the national debt consists largely of floating short-term obligations, the amount of securities redeemed and sold during a year may be larger than the whole debt. On the other hand, some governmental securities are held as long-term investments by the purchasers, and seldom change hands.

The federal debt of the United States in 1947 consisted of sixty types of interest-bearing loans, bonds, notes, certificates and special issues and several types of obligations bearing no interest.[33] Almost equally long is the list of France's outstanding debts.[34] The national debt of the United Kingdom on March 31, 1951 amounted to £26.0 billion and consisted of the following types of debt (in billions of pounds):

Funded, internal	£ 3.9
Unfunded, internal	19.9
Foreign	2.2

The funded internal debt included nine kinds of obligations; the unfunded debt included Treasury bills, Treasury deposits by banks and "ways and means advances," tax reserve certificates and twenty-nine different loans.[35]

Interest rates on government obligations also vary widely: between a fraction of 1 per cent and 3¼ per cent in the United States; between 2½

32. Quoted in **16**, p. 39.
33. **5**, pp. 150–52.
34. **5**, pp. 62–67.
35. **15**, 1938–1950, p. 256.

and 4 per cent in the United Kingdom; between 3 and 5½ per cent in France and Belgium; between 4 and 5 per cent in Australia.[36]

When government securities are traded in the open market, the price varies in accordance with the yield and other terms, such as maturity date, conditions of redemption and special advantages. The price also tends to vary with changes in business conditions. When money becomes scarce, the price of low-interest bonds declines; when money is cheap and the prevailing interest rate sinks, the price rises. On the other hand, when governmental low-interest securities are high, the government can obtain new loans and credits on favorable terms, while depreciation of low-interest bonds compels it to offer higher interest on new issues.

Ownership

Government securities are usually distributed among private individuals, business enterprises, banks, insurance companies, and governmental agencies which have assets of their own. The economic impact of an increase or decrease in the national debt depends largely on its distribution among major owner classes. A change in the distribution of government securities among different economic sectors may have the same economic effect as a change in the amount of the national debt.

When private individuals subscribe to a government loan, they transfer part of their purchasing power to the treasury. When the government uses the proceeds of such a loan to purchase goods and services, the operation results in a shift in consumption and production but does not increase the total demand for goods and services and consequently does not generate inflationary pressure. On the contrary, when a bank subscribes to a government loan, it does not necessarily transfer to the government purchasing power which it otherwise would have put at the disposal of its private clients. As long as reserves of the bank are not exhausted, the purchase of government securities does not compete with its other operations. Therefore, large-scale borrowing from banks may become as inflationary as arbitrary creation of new money by the government. To be economically sound, sale

of government securities to banks should be accompanied by restriction of bank credits to private persons and corporations.

Similarly, an inflationary situation may develop when the total amount of the national debt remains unchanged but an increasing part passes from private investors to commercial banks. Such a redistribution may be due to the sale of bonds by private holders to banks or redemption of bonds by private holders and purchase of securities of a different type by banks. In both cases the change in ownership of the national debt creates additional purchasing power in the hands of consumers without reducing the money supply at the disposal of the banks.

These problems appear in one form or another in all countries with a large national debt. Little attention was paid to them before World War I, when national debt was small in relation to national income, but such questions have become important to heavily indebted nations since World War II.

NATIONAL DEBT POLICY

The specific problems of public debt policy vary from country to country and change with business conditions. The task of the treasury is to reconcile the needs of public credit with requirements for economic stability and economic growth. There is general agreement that a large part of the national debt should be kept in long-term obligations held by private individuals and such savings institutions as life insurance companies and trust corporations. It is recognized that securities of this type cannot be sold in large quantity unless they provide a substantial interest rate, and that although they do not represent the cheapest form of public credit, it is sound policy to hold a large part of the national debt in loans of this type. By this operation, the government sacrifices the narrow fiscal viewpoint to broader considerations of general economic welfare. There is less agreement among experts on specific points within the framework of this general debt policy.

The highly technical character of the related problems, however, makes public discussion of them difficult and not very fruitful. In the United States, discussion was prompted in the 1930's by the clash of opinion on the New Deal deficit spending and after World War II, by the conflict between the Treasury and the Federal Reserve Board.

---

36. Interest rates are considerably higher in some underdeveloped countries: as much as 6–8 per cent on some domestic and foreign loans of such countries as Brazil, Bolivia, Chile and Greece.

The National Association of Manufacturers recommended (1948) the following conservative public debt policy: [37]

1. A balanced budget.

2. Retirement of the federal debt should begin promptly after the achievement of a balanced budget.

3. Transfer of a much larger portion of the outstanding public debt to permanent or long-term investors.

4. Renouncement of the low-interest-rate policy by the Treasury.

5. Reduction of the portion of the national debt held by banks.

In its more recent statement (1955) the NAM stresses the general principles of management of the marketable and nonmarketable securities:

The marketable debt should not be channeled into the hands of predetermined groups of owners by restrictions on amounts, negotiability, and other terms. It should be allowed to find its own distribution, in a free market, among various classes of owners according to their investment needs and preferences . . .

The policy of creating non-marketable demand debt should be applied hereafter as follows:

a. Continue to offer savings bonds in amounts and denominations as required to refund maturing savings bonds;

b. to the extent practicable, future sales of savings bonds in excess of the amount required under paragraph a. should be limited to individuals and personal trust estates. Institutional owners should be encouraged to shift to non-demand debt.

The program developed by the Committee on Public Debt Policy (1948) presented the same principles in a more cautious and flexible form:

1. Careful watch over the budget, but not necessarily a balanced budget in peacetime at any price and under all conditions.

2. A planned policy of debt reduction, related to the state of business activity of the country. Heavy retirement of debt in prosperity and "reduced retirement in times of adversity."

3. Redistribution of the debt, with a shift of securities from banks to actual investors.

4. A flexible policy on interest rates.

5. Alleviation of the relative burden of the national debt by "preserving and increasing the dynamic energy of our economic life." [38]

The core of the conflict between the Treasury and the Federal Reserve Board was the policy of supporting the price of low-interest government securities. As Abbott puts it:

The Treasury, charged with managing a tremendous debt, confronted with a serious refunding problem and living always under the shadow of having to raise new money when and as deficits return, found a low and stable interest policy ideally suited to its needs. Such a policy kept the interest burden at a minimum and greatly aided the refunding of government securities as they fell due or moved within the call period. [39]

Practically, this policy required the Federal Reserve System to support a stable price for low-rate government bonds. The Reserve banks were instructed to purchase such bonds at face value, not permitting their price to fall. When business was active, this policy encouraged bond holders to sell them to banks and use the cash for more attractive investments. It also tended to weaken the individual's incentive to save. [40] Thus, the policy of low interest and stable prices for government obligations led to expansion of purchasing power in the nation, enhanced inflationary pressures and interfered with the responsibility of the Federal Reserve System for controlling the money supply. Indeed, this policy was in obvious conflict with the traditional methods of monetary policy — to manipulate discount rates and adjust the prices of securities to current business conditions. [41]

The story of the conflict between the two agencies and its settlement, by a compromise, is outside the scope of this study. What is of interest from the broad international viewpoint is the conflict between the two approaches to the problem of debt management — the purely fiscal approach of the Treasury and the monetary and economic approach of the Reserve Board. Whatever the administrative organization of debt management, the conflict between the two viewpoints is likely to arise sooner or later in any country with a large national debt. The conflict between the two U.S. agencies thus has general significance.

A detailed analysis of this conflict leads Abbott to the conclusion that the Treasury continued its cheap-money policy "irrespective of war, peace or cold war, irrespective of whether

---

37. **27**, p. 19.
38. **22**, pp. 24–25.

39. **16**, p. 87.
40. See **21**, pp. 17–18.
41. **16**, p. 88.

the federal government had a surplus or a deficit, irrespective of the changes that took place in business conditions" and was unwilling "to consider what the consequences were to other segments of the economy." [42]

The program of debt management recommended by the Twentieth Century Fund's Committee on the Federal Debt on the basis of Abbott's study considers debt management a part of monetary policy. The Committee recommended:

1. That the Employment Act of 1946 be amended to include a directive that attention be given to maintenance of the value of money.

2. That better coordination be established between the many federal lending agencies.

3. The adoption of a regular program of extinguishing part of the federal debt.

4. That the proportion of debt taking the form of short-term maturities be reduced.

5. That maturities should be distributed over time.

6. That federal debt management should use the market place more and . . . special-purpose issues less. The proper principle for federal borrowing is to use marketable issues, bearing whatever rates of interest and terms of payment are necessary to elicit funds from individuals and from each particular type of savings institution.

7. Transferring as much as possible of the debt from commercial banks and other less permanent holders into the hands of true savers and savings institutions.

8. That we should not retire that portion of the debt which backs our hand-to-hand currency. With the growth of population and productivity, the percentage of the debt devoted to this purpose and held accordingly in banking hands may be expected to increase.

9. We do not recommend such a heroic debt reduction as to threaten us with deflation of the price level.

10. That we must recognize the potentiality of the national debt as a tool to maintain high employment.

11. That monetary policy be installed as a regular weapon in the arsenal of economic stabilization. [43]

Elaborating the last point, the Committee remarks: "The Federal Reserve System should be free to deal with the money market on the basis of its effects on employment and prices, and not on the basis of the needs of the Treasury for securing low-cost funds."

This last remark answers the question raised by the controversy between the two agencies in 1949–51 and, at the same time, a more general question which is not limited to the United States — the question of the meaning of debt management in countries with a large national debt. The Fund's Committee strongly recommended that the debt policy be integrated with monetary policy and planned as part of the measures taken for economic stabilization.

Comparison of the three debt-management programs summarized on the preceding pages shows that, despite differences in political philosophy, they agree on two important points: (1) the necessity of transferring a larger part of the national debt from banks to real savers and investors; and (2) the necessity of subordinating the interest-rate policy to broader economic considerations. Agreeing on the need for a program for retirement of the national debt, they differed on the character of such a program: the NAM advised "prompt retirement"; the Committee on Public Debt Policy and the Fund's Committee recommended plans related to business conditions.

SUMMARY

As time passes, it becomes increasingly clear that the absolute amount of a national debt and its size in relation to national income are less important than the way in which the debt is managed. The danger of inflationary or deflationary pressure arises not from the size of the government's liabilities but from the precipitate cashing of securities by holders, excessive expansion of bank credits supported by securities held by the banks or, inversely, from precipitate contraction of government debt through taxation that exceeds current budgetary requirements. The problem of the national debt becomes more and more a problem of a farsighted monetary and economic policy. Within the framework of such a policy, a large national debt may become a stabilizing factor, increasing not only the scope of a government's responsibilities but also its ability to influence the national economy without recourse to direct controls and regulations.

During the postwar readjustment, this aspect of the growth of national debt in industrialized and economically developed countries has been obscured by such pressing tasks as the restoration and expansion of productive facilities, re-

42. **16**, p. 190.
43. **16**, pp. 220–22.

sumption of foreign exchange, balancing of payments and stabilization of currencies. All these tasks have tended to broaden the scope of government responsibilities and have been reflected in the growth of public finance in relation to national income. The growth of national debt has acted in the same direction, not only because of its direct impact on government expenses, but still more because of the economic implications of debt management.

CHAPTER 17

INTERNATIONAL COOPERATION

FROM ANTIQUITY TO THE NAPOLEONIC WARS

ONE OF THE OLDEST FORMS of international cooperation is military alliance for defense or conquest. Alliances for siege and defense of cities — as in ancient Troy — are older than recorded history. Even in the time of Homer, such alliances were not limited to purely military operations but involved agreements on the disposal of spoils or tribute and mutual aid in providing arms, troopships and so on.[1]

Arbitration of disputes between nations is another form of international cooperation which also antedates recorded history. Settlement of territorial differences through mediation or arbitration can be traced back to ancient myths.[2]

Intertribal trade is still another form of international cooperation in primitive society. Indeed, the prerequisite of such trade — even in a rudimentary form and on a modest scale — is some kind of agreement on the place, time and other conditions of exchange. Such agreements sometimes rested on customs respected by both parties and sometimes were formalized by treaties. The barter agreement between King Solomon and Hiram of Tyrus implied their cooperation not only in trade but also in the transport of goods and in public works.

Most military alliances and commercial arrangements in ancient times were bilateral. Alliances which included more than two members were usually established through a system of bilateral pacts. The oldest form of multilateral association is a confederation for common worship, centered around a shrine or oracle, such as the amphictyonic leagues in ancient Greece.[3] From occasional contacts among isolated communities during war, arbitration of disputes, trade and worship, there emerged the concept of a permanent supranational organization ensuring peace and justice to all its members. Originally, this was a religious, moral and sentimental ideal. Its proponents dreamed of the unity of mankind as a moral objective and preached humanitarianism in international as well as personal affairs.[4]

The medieval idea of international union as a means of ensuring peace was advocated by both clerical and lay writers. At the beginning of the fourteenth century, Pierre Dubois, adviser to King Philip IV of France, proposed a federation of Christian nations with the dual purpose of liberating the Holy Land and of maintaining peace in Europe. A fifteenth-century proposal for a federation of the Christian princes of France, Germany, Hungary, Poland, Italy and Spain was discussed by the respective governments. The objectives were the preservation of European peace and the defense of Christianity against Turkish attacks. Planned as an organization independent of the Catholic Church, the project was opposed by Rome. Erasmus in the sixteenth century was among the most eloquent proponents of a European federation designed to protect the peace.[5] Throughout the Middle Ages the popes made numerous attempts to arbitrate and mediate disputes between princes, and to establish rules (or laws) of war based on the authority of the Church.[6]

In 1603 Henry IV of France submitted Sully's "Great Design" to the European kings. The plan envisaged a European federation of fifteen states (the universal republic) with a joint military force, including navy and land troops, and sovereign power vested in a senate.[7]

In 1623 a French monk, Emeric Crucé, published an essay on the means of establishing a general peace and freedom of commerce throughout the world.[8] His plan was not limited to a federation of Christian princes but was universal in scope. His assembly of ambassadors would be composed of representatives of all the rulers of the world, temporal and spiritual, and would include envoys from the European princes and the pope, from the emperor of China, the grand

---

4. Such, for example, were Isaiah the prophet; the Greek philosophers; Marcus Aurelius the Roman; and Tertullian and other Church Fathers. See **146**.
5. **155**, pp. 1–4, 14–17 and 18–20.
6. **177**, pp. 83ff.
7. **156**, p. 37; **146**, p. 28.
8. See **151**.

---

1. **173**, pp. 7–8.
2. **167**, p. 153; cf. **177**, p. 80.
3. **155**, p. xi.

duke of Moscovy, the Tatar Khan, and from the sovereigns of Morocco, Persia, India and other lands. Meetings were to be held in a neutral city — preferably Venice. Crucé's interest in international economic cooperation and in standards of domestic policy foreshadows concepts that were later to be incorporated in the Covenant of the League of Nations and in the Charter of the United Nations.

Among the more remarkable eighteenth-century schemes are the proposals of the French philosophers, the Abbé de Saint-Pierre, Jean Jacques Rousseau and the Comte de Saint-Simon; the British philosopher, Jeremy Bentham; and the German, Immanuel Kant.[9] Widely different in approach and details, these plans had two features in common: (1) their ultimate aim was to prevent war as a means of settling disputes between nations; and (2) they proposed to ensure peace through international cooperation by means of a supranational tribunal or government, its authority based on agreement between independent nations.

Although these plans appeared unrealistic to their contemporaries, they left traces in the thinking of men, and some of their ideas were eventually to materialize in the League of Nations Covenant and the United Nations Charter.

While philosophers were dreaming of the unification of mankind, economic expansion brought nations closer to one another and multiplied the contacts among them. Foreign trade by land and by sea steadily increased from the sixteenth, and especially the seventeenth, century. There was urgent need to regulate international relations; to codify customs and usages; and to develop procedures for settling disputes between nations. The principles of international law in peace and in war, which Grotius [10] defined in the early seventeenth century, gained universal recognition and became the foundation of international arbitration. As F. P. Walters puts it, "in so far as individual genius or power contributed to make the League possible, it may be said that, looking back from the days of Woodrow Wilson, no

figure stands out so high as that of Grotius." [11] The direct ancestors of the League Covenant are the dreams of humanists and pacifists, on the one hand, and international law, on the other.

FROM THE NAPOLEONIC WARS TO WORLD WAR II

ALLIANCES

The end of the Napoleonic wars saw two attempts to guarantee peace through broad international alliances.

The first was the Quadruple Alliance between Great Britain, Austria, Prussia and Russia, concluded in 1814 (the Treaty of Chaumont) and reaffirmed in 1815 (Paris) and 1818 (Aix-la-Chapelle). Its immediate aim was to stabilize the political order the allies had established in Europe after their victory over Napoleon. The foundations of the Quadruple Alliance were laid at the Congress of Vienna, attended by a score of European countries but actually dominated by the four great powers. Bilateral agreements among the attending countries were summarized in the Final Act, which was signed at the only plenary session ever held by the Congress. Along with the preservation of political boundaries, the Final Act proposed to maintain order in Europe by supporting legitimate monarchs against revolutionary forces.

Another attempt at international alliance, made about the same time by Alexander I of Russia, is known as the Holy Alliance. The political goal of this plan — so far as it can be discerned through the mystical phraseology — was to transform and expand the Quadruple Alliance into a pledge by all European monarchs to follow the principles of justice, Christian charity, peace, fraternity and "the sublime truths which the Holy Religion of our Savior teaches." These principles were to guide the signatories in their relations with one another and with their subjects. The monarchs assembled in Vienna did not share the Czar's religious exaltation, nor did their foreign ministers. The proposal was looked upon as sheer nonsense. However, out of respect to the Czar, two of his allies, the emperor of Austria and the king of Prussia, signed the agreement; [12] later, other princes of Europe joined them. Only the king of Great Britain, the pope and the sultan withheld their signatures — the first for constitutional reasons, the other two for religious considerations. There is no indication that the

---

9. Charles de Saint-Pierre, *Memoires pour rendre La Paix Perpetuelle en Europe* (1712); Jean Jacques Rousseau, *Extrait du Projet de Paix Perpetuelle* (1761); Jeremy Bentham, "A Plan for an Universal and Perpetual Peace" in his *Principles of International Law* (1793); Immanuel Kant, *Perpetual Peace* (1795); Saint-Simon, *De la Reorganisation de la Société Européenne* (1814). See also **155, 160**; cf. **148, 159, 169, 178**.
10. See **153**.

11. See **174**.
12. For the full text see **166**, pp. 575–77.

solemn declaration of the monarchs affected international conditions in Europe, but more than three decades later Nicholas I of Russia was to cite this document as justification for sending troops to Hungary and crushing the liberal revolution in that country.

The Quadruple Alliance which emerged from the Vienna Congress dominated European politics until 1848 and formed with France the "concert" of European powers.[13] The period 1848–71 was characterized by a series of armed clashes in Europe: the wars between Austria and Hungary and between Austria and Sardinia (1848–49); the Crimean War (1853–56); the war of Italian liberation (France and Sardinia against Austria, 1859); the rape of Denmark by Prussia and Austria (1864); the Austro-Prussian War (1866); and the Franco-Prussian War (1870–71).

The Congress of Berlin (1878) stabilized political conditions in Europe. A compromise between the ambitions of Russia, Great Britain and Austria in southeastern Europe was achieved. In historical significance the Congress was comparable to that of Vienna in 1815. For more than three decades the peace of Europe was to be maintained by a system of alliances and secret agreements which tended to counterbalance one another. In 1879 Germany and Austria-Hungary entered into a political and military alliance. Italy joined them in 1882, thus forming the Triple Alliance of the central powers. Although its declared purpose was the preservation of peace and resistance to possible aggression by Russia and France, both the latter countries felt threatened. After long diplomatic maneuvering (1891–94), an alliance of the two countries was formed and in 1895 the Dual Alliance was publicly recognized by both. After that time, Europe was formally divided into two coalitions, and this division was one of the major factors in the race of armaments which led to World War I. Between 1918 and 1939 numerous nonagression, friendship and guarantee pacts were signed, but durable alliances such as those of the nineteenth century did not develop. After World War II the world returned to a system of alliances, such as that of the United States and its Allies; the USSR and its satellites; and the Arab League.

ARBITRATION

Arbitration of disputes between governments

13. See **162**.

by a neutral party or the Church was not uncommon in Europe in the Middle Ages and the seventeenth and eighteenth centuries. Often such arbitration followed a protracted war, but occasionally a dispute was settled before it developed into a *casus belli*. Many old treaties combined a promise of peace with more or less vague promises of peaceful settlement of future claims.

A direct reference to arbitration — at least for a definite type of claim — appears in Jay's Treaty concluded between the United States and Great Britain in 1794. This treaty seemed to fulfill the hopes of Benjamin Franklin for "the discovery of a plan that would induce and oblige nations to settle their disputes without first cutting one another's throats." [14] In the eyes of the American people, however, the arbitration clause was completely overshadowed by the concessions made to the British. The treaty raised a storm of indignation in the United States and was vehemently denounced by Jefferson. Washington and Hamilton had to use all their influence to obtain its ratification by the Senate.[15]

After the Napoleonic wars, arbitration of international disputes became a common practice in Europe. Between 1815 and 1900, 177 disputes between European states were submitted to arbitration.[16] In most cases, the arbitrator's decision was duly carried out by both parties; in no case was a question submitted to arbitration later made a case for war.[17] There were numerous attempts to make peaceful settlement of disputes obligatory and to establish legal procedures for international arbitration. Resolutions to this end were adopted by the legislatures of the United States, Great Britain, Italy and many other countries. In 1890 eleven American republics, including the United States, signed a Pan-American treaty of arbitration; and in 1897 a similar treaty was concluded between the United States and Great Britain. All these treaties remained unratified, however.[18] The movement gained momentum after the turn of the century: 140 bipartite arbitration treaties were concluded in the decade 1901–10.[19]

The Hague Conferences of 1899 and 1907 — often called the First and Second Peace Conferences — were significant milestones in the his-

14. **146**, p. 48.
15. **147**, pp. 369–70.
16. **146**, p. 11.
17. **174**, p. 9.
18. **146**, p. 11.
19. **163**, p. 15.

tory of international arbitration. Initiated by Nicholas II of Russia and attended by representatives of twenty-six nations, the first was planned as a disarmament conference. Germany, however, blocked discussion of military questions. As a compromise, the Conference concentrated on adopting conventions for the pacific settlement of international disputes and establishing more humane laws of war — such as prohibiting aerial bombardment, the use of poisonous gases and bullets designed to expand or explode in the human body. The second Hague Conference, attended by forty-four nations (including seventeen republics of Central and South America), again waived the question of disarmament but agreed on a series of important conventions, all of which were ratified by the respective governments. These conventions sought to protect civilians in the event of war, on land and at sea, and established procedures for the settlement of international differences. They did not "outlaw" war but committed the signatories "to use their best efforts to insure the pacific settlement of international differences." Three types of disputes were distinguished, and the means for settling them indicated: [20]

Type of Disagreement	*Means of Settlement*
1. Serious disagreement or dispute	1. The good offices or mediation of one or more friendly powers
2. Disputes arising from a difference of opinion on points of fact, and involving neither honor nor vital interests	2. An international commission of inquiry
3. Questions of a legal nature, particularly in connection with international conventions	3. Arbitration

The Permanent Court of Arbitration (Hague Tribunal) was established in 1899 by a convention of the first Hague Conference. Until the outbreak of World War I the Hague system of arbitration operated smoothly. The organization of the court proved less successful. Despite its name, this was not a permanently and continuously operating body, but had to be organized *ad hoc* each time the need arose. After World War I, the Permanent Court of International

Justice (World Court), based on an international agreement concluded in Geneva in 1920, was set up under the auspices of the League of Nations. From 1922 to 1937 inclusive, the court heard some sixty cases; it handed down twenty-eight judgments and gave twenty-seven advisory opinions.[21]

During World War II only a few minor disputes were brought before the court. In 1945 it was dissolved and its functions taken over by the International Court of Justice, an autonomous "specialized agency" of the United Nations. The new court operates on the basis of a constitution similar to that of its predecessor.[22]

INTERNATIONAL ORGANIZATIONS

International cooperation is not limited to the conferences of top governmental representatives of nations. Common interest has called into being international conferences of physicians, geologists, architects, teachers, statisticians, criminologists, churchmen, labor leaders, chambers of commerce, experts in transportation and communication and so forth. Such conferences have been followed by the formation of permanent bureaus, institutes and committees. Some conferences have been private, others have brought together representatives of governments. Some have been regional, others global.

International organizations have a long history but it was not until the second half of the nineteenth century that they began to extend widely into different fields of science, technology and politics.[23]

---

20. For the full text of the convention for the pacific settlement of international disputes signed at The Hague in 1907, see **166**, pp. 544–59.

21. **157**, p. 7.

22. For a comparison of the statutes of the two courts, see **149**, pp. 265–83.

23. One of the earliest international organizations to gain notice was the International Workingmen's Association (the First International) founded in 1864 in London. Under the leadership of Karl Marx, it became the rallying point of revolutionary and socialist forces all over Western Europe. It was at the peak of its glory in 1871, in the days of the Paris Commune, and disintegrated in 1872–74 as a result of the internal struggle between the socialists (Marx) and anarchists (Bakunin).

In 1889 the Socialist International (the Second International) was organized. It gained considerable influence in the early part of the twentieth century but collapsed during World War I under the strain of international differences and internal discord within national parties.

In the interwar years, a federation of Communist parties directed by the Kremlin was organized under the name of the Communist International (also known as the Third International). Attempts were made to restore the Socialist International on a platform combining democratic principles and socialist ideals with internationalism,

The Brussels Union

The Union of International Associations (Brussels) listed 503 international organizations in 1912.[24] The *Handbook* (1938) of the League of Nations listed 806 associations, bureaus and committees, without counting the League's own organizations, commercial organizations and associations which, though international in object, existed on a purely national basis.[25] This list includes international associations of national unions and their federations but not United States labor unions which call themselves "international" but are so only in the sense that they admit members regardless of their origin and nationality and may have locals in Canada and Mexico.

For the year 1951–52, the Brussels Union lists 951 international associations, institutes, bureaus and commissions of the following types:

UN and associated intergovernmental bodies	22
Other intergovernmental bodies	99
National organizations related to the UN	9
Nongovernmental organizations	821

Of the last group, 48 were purely inter-American, 74 purely inter-European. The central offices of these various organizations were distributed geographically as follows:

Europe, total	762	North America	127
		Latin America	32
Western Europe		Africa	9
France	224	Middle East	2
Switzerland	158	India, Pakistan,	
United Kingdom	143	Ceylon	10
Belgium	100	Other Asian countries	3
Other	123	Oceania	2
Eastern Europe	14	Unknown	4

The objectives of the organizations range from sport and recreation to religion and moral betterment, from the sciences and arts to politics, from bibliography to the furtherance of professional interests. The Union groups them in 20 broad classes:

Bibliography	27
Philosophy, religion and moral improvement	77
Social and political sciences	36
International relations and peace	92
Law and administration	31
Relief and social insurance	34
Employers, labor and professions	78
Politics	10
Economics and finance	14
Commerce and industry	40
Agriculture	28
Transport and communication	29
Engineering techniques	35
Pure and natural sciences	55
Medicine	76
Education and youth	46
Arts, literature	34
Sport, touring, recreation	49
Women's organizations	20
Miscellaneous and nonclassified	140

A listing by decades in which these organizations were founded shows a rapid increase in the number of international associations in the 1920's and again in 1941–51: [26]

Before 1851	6
1851–1900	71
1901–10	58
1911–20	81
1921–30	192
1931–40	101
1941–51	395
Date unknown	47

United States Participation

The United States government is officially represented in more than sixty international organizations, including such agencies of the UN as the International Labor Organization (ILO), the Food and Agriculture Organization (FAO), the Economic, Social and Cultural Organization (UNESCO), the International Bank for Reconstruction and Development, the International Monetary Fund, the International Court of Justice, the International Refugee Organization (IRO), and the World Health Organization (WHO). Its affiliations also include nine commissions and boards that handle various problems related to the aftermath of World War II. (See Table 277.) The oldest international organizations of which the United States was a participating member in 1949 are as follows: [27]

	Year Founded
The Central Commission for Navigation of the Rhine	1815
Universal Postal Union	1865

(*Continued on facing page*)

but the associations were unstable and lacked the prestige of the Second International. They collapsed during World War II. The World Federation of Socialist Parties organized after World War II is a loose organization trying to activate and coordinate democratic forces in the political labor movement.

24. **165**, p. 43.
25. **9**, pp. 6 and 435–69.

26. **172**, p. 1223.
27. **118**, pp. v–vi and *passim*.

	Year Founded
International Bureau of Weights and Measures	1870
International Meteorological Organization	1872
International Union for the Protection of Industrial Property	1873
Interparliamentary Union for the Promotion of International Arbitration	1878
International Penal and Penitentiary Commission	1880
Permanent International Association of Navigation Congresses	1889
Central International Office for the Control of the Liquor Traffic in Africa	1890
International Union for the Publication of Customs Tariffs	1890
Central Bureau of the International Map of the World on the Millionth Scale	1891

These are likewise among the oldest international organizations listed by the Brussels Union.

THE LEAGUE OF NATIONS

The League of Nations was the first attempt in world history to end war and achieve disarmament by establishing a community of nations that was worldwide, at least in principle. The experiment aroused exaggerated hopes at the start and ended in bitter disappointment. Betrayed from within in the tragic hour when the world was facing its hitherto most destructive war, the Geneva organization had ceased to exist long before it was formally dissolved. Its experience, however, proved invaluable in the creation of the United Nations, designed to carry on the League's unfinished work.

ORIGIN OF THE LEAGUE

At the time of the short-lived successes of the League, in the 1920's, some people thought that its establishment had been one of the objectives of World War I,[28] but there is no evidence to support this view. The League of Nations was not among the controversial issues on which the European powers clashed in 1914. But if it was not an objective of the war, it was decidedly one of its most significant results.

The Covenant of the League was born of the disasters of World War I, just as Saint-Simon's plans for unifying Europe were inspired by the Napoleonic wars. Pacifism increased as war went on, partly under the influence of the revolution in Russia. Public opinion demanded a positive policy for preventing future armed conflicts.

Catchwords like "disarmament" and "arbitration" of international disputes gained universal support, and they could be readily combined with a plan for permanent mutual Allied aid to maintain international security. Thus emerged the idea of a new grand alliance.

In the United States a movement in favor of such an organization had developed before the country entered the war and the Russian revolution had added strength to the campaign. The movement was headed by William Howard Taft and Woodrow Wilson. In both the United States and Great Britain, the governments felt that "people needed to be convinced that victory would be followed by a sweeping reform of the conditions which had allowed such disasters to fall upon them unawares. Thus alone could their longing for peace help to keep them fighting and working to the bitter end."[29]

For President Wilson, however, the League of Nations was more than an effective slogan to keep tired men fighting. He was convinced that a new supranational organization would change the course of world history. Probably no European government fully shared his enthusiasm, but the idea stirred the imagination of the ordinary man and was not too controversial from the viewpoint of the immediate national interests of Europe's great powers. This fact gave the President his first victory in Paris: almost without discussion, the peace conference adopted his resolution "that a League of Nations be created." Wilson likewise encountered little opposition to his proposal that the Covenant of the League be made a part of the peace treaties — an idea that in retrospect does not appear to have been very good.

THE COVENANT

The Covenant reflects the conditions under which it was conceived. It combines the lofty principles of Woodrow Wilson with provisions which permit member-nations to evade responsibilities without openly renouncing their obligations. It is questionable whether all signatories to the Covenant took its general principles as seriously as they took the escape clauses. Indeed, the great powers have never observed the principles which Wilson held to be the core of the whole plan.

The Preamble of the Covenant describes the aims of the League:

---

28. **164**, p. 1.

29. **174**, p. 20.

TABLE 277

INTERNATIONAL ORGANIZATIONS IN WHICH THE UNITED STATES PARTICIPATES, 1949

Organization	Year Founded	Organization	Year Founded
General		International Authority for the Ruhr	1948
United Nations	1945	Tripartite Boards of the Western Zones	
Organization of American States	1948	of Germany	1947
Inter-American Defense Board [a]	1942	Tripartite Commission for the Restitution	
Agriculture and fisheries		of Monetary Gold	1946
Food and Agriculture Organization of		**Political and legal**	
the United Nations	1945	Committee of Control of the Interna-	
Inter-American Institute of Agricultural		tional Zone of Tangier	1923
Sciences	1944	Interparliamentary Union for the Pro-	
International Seed-Testing Association	1924	motion of International Arbitration	1878
International Whaling Commission	1949	Permanent Court of Arbitration	1907
Commodity		**Regional**	
Combined Tin Committee	1945	Caribbean Commission	1942
International Cotton Advisory Committee	1939	South Pacific Commission	1944
International Sugar Council	1937		
International Tin Study Group	1947	**Social and health**	
International Wheat Council	1942	American International Institute for the	
International Wool Study Group	1946	Protection of Childhood	1924
Rubber Study Group	1947	Central International Office for the Con-	
		trol of the Liquor Traffic in Africa	1890
Economic and financial		Inter-American Commission of Women	1928
Interim Commission for the International		Inter-American Conference on Social Se-	
Trade Organization [b]	1946	curity	1940
International Bank for Reconstruction and		Inter-American Indian Institute	1933
Development	1946	International Bodies for Narcotic Control	1912
International Monetary Fund	1945	International Criminal Police Commission	1905
International Union for the Protection of		International Labor Organization	1919
Industrial Property	1873	International Penal and Penitentiary	
International Union for the Publication of		Commission	1880
Customs Tariffs	1890	International Refugee Organization	1946
Organization for European Economic		Pan American Sanitary Organization	1902
Cooperation	1948	United Nations International Children's	
Educational, scientific, and cultural		Emergency Fund	1946
Central Bureau of the International Map		World Health Organization	1946
of the World on the Millionth Scale	1891	**Transport and communications**	
Inter-American Statistical Institute	1948	Central Commission for Navigation of	
International Bureau of Weights and		the Rhine	1815
Measures	1870	Inter-American Radio Office	1937
International Council of Scientific Unions		International Civil Aviation Organiza-	
and Associated Unions	1919	tion	1944
International Hydrographic Bureau	1919	International Commission of the Cape	
International Meteorological Organization	1872	Spartel Light	1865
Pan American Institute of Geography		International Telecommunication Union	1925
and History	1928	International Union of Official Travel	
United Nations Educational, Scientific		Organizations	1935
and Cultural Organization	1945	Pan American Railway Congress Associa-	
Occupation and peacemaking		tion	1910
Allied Commission for Austria	1944	Permanent International Association of	
Allied Control Council for Germany	1945	Navigation Congresses	1889
Allied Council for Japan	1945	Postal Union of the Americas and Spain	1911
Council of Foreign Ministers	1945	Provisional Maritime Consultative Coun-	
Far Eastern Commission	1945	cil	1946
Inter-Allied Reparation Agency	1945	Universal Postal Union	1863

Source: **115**, pp. v–vi and *passim.*

a. Concerned solely with technical military problems.   b. Dissolved in 1950.

The High Contracting Parties,

In order to promote international co-operation and to achieve international peace and security

    by the acceptance of obligations not to resort to war, by the prescription of open, just and honourable relations between nations,

    by the firm establishment of the understandings of international law as the actual rule of conduct among Governments, and

    by the maintenance of justice and a scrupulous respect for all treaty obligations in the dealings of organised peoples with one another,

Agree to this Covenant of the League of Nations.

Obligations of Member Nations

The obligations of members of the League in the event of war or threat of war are outlined in Articles 10 and 11 of the Covenant:

Article 10

The Members of the League undertake to respect and preserve as against external aggression the territorial integrity and existing political independence of all Members of the League. In case of any such aggression or in case of any threat or danger of such aggression the Council shall advise upon the means by which this obligation shall be fulfilled.

Article 11

1. Any war or threat of war, whether immediately affecting any of the Members of the League or not, is hereby declared a matter of concern to the whole League, and the League shall take any action that may be deemed wise and effectual to safeguard the peace of nations. . . .

2. It is also declared to be the friendly right of each Member of the League to bring to the attention of the Assembly or of the Council any circumstance whatever affecting international relations which threatens to disturb international peace or the good understanding between nations upon which peace depends.

Articles 12–14 deal with arbitration of disputes which the members of the League consider "suitable for submission to arbitration." This part of the Covenant established the Permanent Court of International Justice and tightened the provisions of the Hague Convention of 1907 for the peaceful settlement of international disputes.

Settlement of Disputes and Sanctions

Of crucial significance from the viewpoint of international cooperation are Articles 15 and 16. The first provided for the handling of disputes between members which had not been submitted to arbitration. The latter established the principle of economic and military sanctions against members which resorted to war in disregard of the Covenant.

Because of the crucial importance of these articles in the League's later history, they are given in full.

Article 15

1. If there should arise between Members of the League any dispute likely to lead to a rupture, which is not submitted to arbitration in accordance with Article 13, the Members of the League agree that they will submit the matter to the Council. Any party to the dispute may effect such submission by giving notice of the existence of the dispute to the Secretary-General who will make all necessary arrangements for a full investigation and consideration thereof.

2. For this purpose, the parties to the dispute will communicate to the Secretary-General, as promptly as possible, statements of their case with all the relevant facts and papers, and the Council may forthwith direct the publication thereof.

3. The Council shall endeavour to effect a settlement of the dispute, and if such efforts are successful, a statement shall be made public giving such facts and explanations regarding the dispute and the terms of settlement thereof as the Council may deem appropriate.

4. If the dispute is not thus settled, the Council either unanimously or by a majority vote shall make and publish a report containing a statement of the facts of the dispute and the recommendations which are deemed just and proper in regard thereto.

5. Any Member of the League represented on the Council may make public a statement of the facts of the dispute and of its conclusions regarding the same.

6. If a report by the Council is unanimously agreed to by the members thereof other than the Representatives of one or more of the parties of the dispute, the Members of the League agree that they will not go to war with any party to the dispute which complies with the recommendations of the report.

7. If the Council fails to reach a report which is unanimously agreed to by the members thereof, other than the Representatives of one or more of the parties to the dispute, the Members of the League reserve to themselves the right to take such action as they shall consider necessary for the maintenance of right and justice.

8. If the dispute between the parties is claimed by one of them, and is found by the Council, to arise out of a matter which by international law is solely within the domestic jurisdiction of that party, the Council shall so report, and shall make no recommendation as to its settlement.

9. The Council may in any case under this Article refer the dispute to the Assembly. The dispute shall be so referred at the request of either party to the dispute, provided that such request be made within fourteen days after the submission of the dispute to the Council.

10. In any case referred to the Assembly, all the provisions of this Article and of Article 12 relating to the action and powers of the Council shall apply to the action and powers of the Assembly, provided that a report made by the Assembly, if concurred in by the Representatives of those Members of the League represented on the Council and of a majority of the other Members of the League, exclusive in each case of the Representatives of the parties to the dispute, shall have the same force as a report by the Council, concurred in by all the members thereof other than the Representatives of one or more of the parties to the dispute.

Article 16

1. Should any Member of the League resort to war in disregard of its covenants under Articles 12, 13 or 15, it shall *ipso facto* be deemed to have committed an act of war against all other Members of the League, which hereby undertake immediately to subject it to the severance of all trade or financial relations, the prohibition of all intercourse between their nationals and the nationals of the covenant-breaking State, and the prevention of all financial, commercial or personal intercourse between the nationals of the covenant-breaking State and the nationals of any other State, whether a Member of the League or not.

2. It shall be the duty of the Council in such case to recommend to the several Governments concerned what effective military, naval or air force the Members of the League shall severally contribute to the armed forces to be used to protect the covenants of the League.

3. The Members of the League agree, further, that they will mutually support one another in the financial and economic measures which are taken under this Article, in order to minimise the loss and inconvenience resulting from the above measures, and that they will mutually support one another in resisting any special measures aimed at one of their number by the covenant-breaking State, and that they will take the necessary steps to afford passage through their territory to the forces of any of the Members of the League which are cooperating to protect the covenants of the League.

4. Any Member of the League which has violated any covenant of the League may be declared to be no longer a Member of the League by a vote of the Council concurred in by the Representatives of all the other Members of the League represented thereon.

Article 17 extends the provisions of Article 16 to countries which are not members of the League.

During the discussion of the Covenant by the Big Four in Paris, the French suggested that a military force be placed at the disposal of the League as a means of preventing or repelling aggression.[30] This proposal was rejected, but the Covenant established a procedure which, if followed, would be more effective. In fact, a military force under direct command of the League under the conditions which existed in Europe at that time would scarcely have been larger than a guard of honor. Rather than relying on such a force Section 1 of Article 16 declares that aggression committed by any member of the League places all members in a state of war. Declaration of war against the aggressor and economic sanctions (including total embargo) are to follow automatically. Each aggressive war becomes a common war of the League against the aggressor, and the League assumes the responsibility for coordinating the military efforts of all member nations.

It will be noticed that Section 2 of Article 16 committed the Council to "recommend" to the member nations what effective military force they should contribute, thereby leaving the ultimate decision to the several states. This was hardly a weakness of the Covenant. The obligations of member nations were outlined in the Preamble and a nation which betrayed the spirit of the Covenant could violate any of its articles. Moreover, in the matter of economic sanctions, the language was perfectly clear, but it did not prevent the European powers from ignoring their obligations in the face of Italy's aggression against Ethiopia and Hitler's seizure of Austria and Czechoslovakia.

Peacetime Cooperation

In addition to the provisions for settling international disputes and preventing war, and determining the status of the former German colonies and territories taken from the Ottoman Empire, the Covenant outlined a program of international cooperation in peacetime. The respective article reads as follows:

Article 23

Subject to and in accordance with the provisions of international conventions existing or hereafter to be agreed upon, the Members of the League:

(*a*) will endeavour to secure and maintain fair

---

30. **174**, p. 61.

and humane conditions of labour for men, women, and children, both in their own countries and in all countries to which their commercial and industrial relations extend, and for that purpose will establish and maintain the necessary international organizations;

(*b*) undertake to secure just treatment of the native inhabitants of territories under their control;

(*c*) will entrust the League with the general supervision over the execution of agreements with regard to the traffic in women and children, and the traffic in opium and other dangerous drugs;

(*d*) will entrust the League with the general supervision of the trade in arms and ammunition with the countries in which the control of this traffic is necessary in the common interest;

(*e*) will make provision to secure and maintain freedom of communications and of transit and equitable treatment for the commerce of all Members of the League. In this connection, the special necessities of the regions devastated during the war of 1914–1918 shall be borne in mind;

(*f*) will endeavour to take steps in matters of international concern for the prevention and control of disease.

The genesis of this program can be traced to the influence of General Jan Christiaan Smuts of South Africa, the first statesman to look on the League not only as a possible instrument for preventing wars but, even more important, as an integral part of the ordinary peaceful life of civilization and as the foundation of a new international system and the starting point from which to make arrangements for peace. He wrote:

It is not sufficient for the League merely to be a sort of *deus ex machina,* called in in very grave emergencies when the spectre of war appears; if it is to last, it must be much more. It must become part and parcel of the common international life of States, it must be an ever visible, living, working organ of the polity of civilisation. It must function so strongly in the ordinary peaceful intercourse of States that it becomes irresistible in their disputes; its peace activity must be the foundation and guarantee of its war power.[31]

ORGANIZATION

At its zenith in the mid-1920's, the League had sixty-two members: thirty were signatories to the peace treaties; thirteen acceded to the Covenant

31. **171**, p. 8.

within two months of its coming into force; and nineteen were elected by the Assembly. Spain, Costa Rica and Brazil withdrew from the League in the latter part of the 1920's. Japan withdrew in 1933. Germany was admitted in 1926 and withdrew in 1933. The USSR was admitted in 1934 and expelled in 1939.

The principal organs of the League were the Assembly and the Council. In the Assembly, each member country might be represented by as many as three delegates, but each delegation had only one vote. The Council, the executive organ of the League, consisted of representatives of the "Principal Allied and Associated Powers" (the permanent members of the Council) and the representatives of four other members designated by the Assembly.

The Covenant required, as a general rule, unanimous decisions in both the Assembly and the Council. Section 1 of Article 5 declared:

Except where otherwise expressly provided in this Covenant or by the terms of the present Treaty, decisions at any meeting of the Assembly or of the Council shall require the agreement of all the Members of the League represented at the meeting.

Strict observance of this principle, which gave the veto right to each member of the Assembly and Council, would have paralyzed the whole organization. The principle of unanimity was, however, qualified by provisions allowing decisions on certain types of questions by a simple or qualified majority. For example, a simple majority was required for procedural questions (Article 5, Sec. 2); a two-thirds majority, for the admission of new members (Article 1, Sec. 2). The Council was authorized to release reports adopted by simple majority (Article 15, Sec. 4). No special rights were reserved to the principal powers, but each had the same veto power as other members of the Council.

Actually, the right of veto was seldom used in either the Council or the Assembly; the great powers controlled the League by behind-the-scene arrangements.

THE ABSTENTION OF THE UNITED STATES

As soon as the Treaty of Versailles — with the League Covenant incorporated in it — was signed by the Allies (June 28, 1919), strong opposition to both the treaty and the Covenant developed in the United States. The treaty was criticized for its territorial concessions to France, Italy and Japan. The Covenant was assailed for the commitments that League members were required to make. A bitter fight between the supporters and the opponents of Wilson's policy developed in Congress and in the press.

The President's authority over Congress had been weakened — in part, by his long absence from the country, and in part by the same factors that brought about the breakup of the wartime cabinets in Great Britain, France and Italy. His uncompromising defense of the Covenant contributed to the bitterness of the controversy, which finally centered in the question of Senate ratification of the Covenant as a part of the peace treaty.

After long discussion and much congressional maneuvering, the Foreign Relations Committee, headed by Senator Henry Cabot Lodge, submitted to the Senate a resolution recommending ratification of the treaty (i.e., United States participation in the League). To the resolution was added an amendment with fourteen reservations which were finally accepted by the Senate:

1. The United States shall be the sole judge as to whether all its international obligations and all its obligations under the said Covenant have been fulfilled, and notice of withdrawal by the United States may be given by a concurrent resolution of the Congress of the United States.

2. The United States assumes no obligation to preserve the territorial integrity or political independence of any other country or to interfere in controversies between nations — whether members of the League or not — under the provisions of Article 10; or to employ the military or naval forces of the United States under any article of the treaty for any purpose, . . .

3. No mandate shall be accepted by the United States under Article 22, Part I, or any other provision of the treaty . . . except by action of the Congress of the United States.

4. The United States reserves to itself exclusively the right to decide what questions are within its domestic jurisdiction . . .

5. The United States will not submit to arbitration or to inquiry by . . . the League of Nations . . . any questions which in the judgment of the United States depend upon or relate to its long-established policy, commonly known as the Monroe Doctrine; said doctrine is to be interpreted by the United States alone and is hereby declared to be wholly outside the jurisdiction of said League of Nations and entirely unaffected by any provision contained in the said treaty of peace with Germany.

6. The United States withholds its assent to Articles 156, 157, and 158, and reserves full liberty of action with respect to any controversy which may arise under said articles.

7. The Congress of the United States will provide by law for the appointment of the representatives of the United States in the Assembly and the Council [and associated agencies] . . .

8. The United States understands that the reparation commission will regulate or interfere with exports from the United States to Germany, or from Germany to the United States, only when . . . Congress approves such regulation or interference.

9. The United States shall not be obliged to contribute to any expenses of the League of Nations [or any of its agencies], unless and until an appropriation of funds . . . shall have been made by the Congress of the United States.

10. If the United States shall at any time adopt any plan for the limitation of armaments proposed by the Council of the League of Nations under the provisions of Article 8, it reserves the right to increase such armaments without the consent of the Council whenever the United States is threatened with invasion or engaged in war.

11. The United States reserves the right to permit, in its discretion, the nationals of a covenant-breaking State, as defined in Article 16 of the Covenant of the League of Nations, residing within the United States or in countries other than that violating said Article 16, to continue their commercial, financial, and personal relations with the nationals of the United States.

12. Nothing in Article 296, 297, . . . shall, as against citizens of the United States, be taken to mean any confirmation, ratification, or approval of any act otherwise illegal or in contravention of the rights of citizens of the United States.

13. The United States withholds its assent to Part XIII (Articles 387 to 427 inclusive) [the I.L.O.] unless Congress . . . shall hereafter make provision for representation in the organization established by said Part XIII, . . .

14. The United States assumes no obligations to be bound by any election, decision, report, or finding of the Council or Assembly in which any member of the League and its self-governing dominions, colonies, or parts of empire, in the aggregate have cast more than one vote, . . .

Reservations 3, 7 and 9, which stressed the rights of Congress, conformed to the United States Constitution and would not have jeopardized either the League or the position of the United States in that organization. Reservations 1, 4, 8 and 10 sounded more alarming than they really were: many countries which joined the League probably made similar mental reservations. Reservations 6 and 12 referred to comparatively minor issues. The question of the participation of the United States in the International Labor Organization (Reservation 13) could have been left open for a time. But the adherence of

the United States to the League was made pointless by Reservations 2 and 11. In addition, Reservation 14 amounted to a request that Canada,
Australia, New Zealand, India and the Union of
South Africa be excluded from the League.

In the vote in the Senate in November 1919,
55 votes were cast for ratification of the Covenant
with the fourteen reservations and 39 against.
Among the dissenting votes were twenty-three
supporters of the Covenant in its original form
without reservations. Since the vote in favor of
ratification fell short of two thirds, ratification
was defeated. The election campaign waged by
the Democratic party in 1920 was a fight for
acceptance of the League by the United States.
Its defeat confirmed the policy of isolationism
represented by Senator Lodge.

It is useless to speculate what the situation
would have been if the supporters of President
Wilson had voted to ratify the Covenant with
the fourteen reservations. Conditional United
States participation in the League would hardly
have been accepted by other member nations,
and if accepted, the country's position in the
League would have been untenable. One won-
ders, rather, what the course of world events
would have been if the United States had joined
the League *without* reservations. There is no
doubt that its participation would have strengthened the League. It is less certain whether it
could have prevented Japanese aggression in
China; Italian aggression in Africa; the rearmament of Germany; the dissensions among the
great powers of Europe; Hitler's seizure of Austria and Czechoslovakia; his pact with Stalin; and
other events which finally led to World War II.
It is possible, however, that at least some of these
developments could have been altered if the
League had not been undermined from the very
beginning by the refusal of the United States to
join.

ACHIEVEMENTS AND FAILURES OF THE LEAGUE

The activities of the League of Nations during
the two decades of its existence covered a broad
range of political and economic issues, of which
only the most important can be mentioned in the
following pages.[32]

Settlement of Disputes

The political activity of the League was limited by the tendency of the great powers to handle crucial matters through the old diplomatic
channels. The questions they brought to the
Council were mostly of local significance, but
the League very soon became a world tribunal
to which the smaller and weaker nations could
appeal against the wrongdoing of more powerful
nations.

In 1920 the British government submitted to
the Council the dispute between Sweden and
Finland over the Åland Islands. Sweden demanded that the question be solved by a plebiscite among the islanders; Finland, which was not
a member of the League at that time, insisted
that the islands were an integral part of its territory. The Council, after a thorough investigation
of the problem, supported the Finnish point of
view.

In the same year, the League tried to mediate
a boundary dispute between Poland and Lithuania. The dispute was aggravated by Poland's
seizure and annexation of Vilna, which Lithuania considered its capital. The dispute remained
unsettled until 1939, when the USSR overran
Lithuanian and Polish territory, including Vilna.

In 1921 the Council mediated in two minor
frontier disputes — one between Albania and
Yugoslavia, the other between Czechoslovakia
and Poland. It also took part in settling a
German-Polish dispute on the administration of
Upper Silesia.

In 1923 the Council intervened in a conflict
between Greece and Italy provoked by the mur-
der of an Italian official on Greek territory. The
Council's decision was invalidated by the dissenting vote of Italy, but was upheld by the Conference of Ambassadors and, on the urging of
the latter, accepted by both parties. About the
same time, the Council successfully arbitrated
the frontier differences between Hungary and
Czechoslovakia and took part in settling new differences between Czechoslovakia and Poland.

In 1924–25, the League settled a dispute between Turkey and Iraq (at that time under
a British mandate) concerning the district of
Mosul, important because of rich oil fields. In
1925 the Council's intervention averted hostilities between Greece and Bulgaria. In 1926 the
Council settled a dispute involving actions of
Lithuania in Memel; and in 1927–28 it mediated
between Hungary and Romania.

In 1929 the Council took part in mediation
between Bolivia and Paraguay in their dispute
over the Chaco region.[33] In later years it tried

---

32. For a complete survey of the activities of the
League, see **145** and **174**.

33. **164**, pp. 272–81.

to arbitrate the differences between Bolivia and Paraguay but could not bring the parties to a settlement of the dispute.

Ethiopia's complaint against the United Kingdom and Italy was one of the most noteworthy events in the early history of the League. In June 1926, the ministers of both powers in Addis Ababa informed the Ethiopian government that their governments had concluded an agreement on the promotion of their respective interests in Ethiopia. The British intended to construct a dam on Lake Tana to control the waters of the Blue Nile and to build a motor road on Ethiopian territory from the Sudanese frontier to the lake. To connect their colonies in Eritrea and Somaliland the Italians planned a 1,000-mile railway, which would cross Ethiopia from north to south, and they sought exclusive economic influence in the territory traversed by the railway.

The then-regent of Ethiopia, Ras Tafari (later Emperor Haile Selassie), asked the members of the League whether they considered the Anglo-Italian agreement compatible with the independence of Ethiopia. Before the League could discuss the matter, the British and Italian governments declared that it had never been their intention to bring pressure on Ethiopia but merely to renounce possible competition with each other. Ras Tafari answered with a formal note to the League in which he placed on record the assurances which his protest had gained for his country.

The Anglo-Italian agreement, which was totally inconsistent with the principles of the League, was an example of earlier diplomatic processes which continued with the new system established by the Covenant.[34] The result of the conflict between the two systems was highly reassuring to small nations: the African David had met two Goliaths and defeated them before the world forum of public opinion.

In February 1933 the Colombian government appealed to the Council, complaining of the seizure (September 1932) of its territory (Leticia, a village on the Amazon River) by Peruvian troops. The League's action prevented a war between the two countries and by May 1934 was able to report that "traditional bonds of friendship" between the two countries had been restored.[35]

In 1934–35, the League helped to lessen the friction between Yugoslavia and Hungary caused by the assassination of Yugoslavia's King Alexander by terrorists who operated from within Hungary. In the years 1934–37, it mediated between Iran and Iraq.

The most serious political problems the League faced were those of Japanese aggression in China and Italian aggression in Ethiopia.

The League seemed to have been successful in the initial phase of the Sino-Japanese conflict — the Mukden incident — in 1931. In response to the seizure of Mukden by Japanese troops, China requested the application of Articles 10 and 15 of the Covenant. The Council referred the dispute to the Assembly where forty-two member states adopted a resolution condemning the aggression. Soon thereafter, Japan notified the League of its intention to withdraw troops from Mukden.[36] This incident, however, did not stop Japanese penetration into China. Japan had converted the northern provinces of China into the "independent" state of Manchukuo under a puppet government and was ready to use it as a springboard for further conquests. It resumed aggression after the defeat of the League in the Italo-Ethiopian conflict, which is discussed subsequently.[37]

Disarmament

In addition to the mediation and arbitration of international disputes, the most important political task of the League was disarmament, which was considered in Article 8 of the Covenant:

1. The Members of the League recognise that the maintenance of peace requires the reduction of national armaments to the lowest point consistent with national safety and the enforcement by common action of international obligations.

2. The Council, taking account of the geographical situation and circumstances of each State, shall formulate plans for such reduction for the consideration and action of the several Governments.

3. Such plans shall be subject to reconsideration and revision at least every ten years.

4. After these plans shall have been adopted by the several Governments, the limits of armaments therein fixed shall not be exceeded without the concurrence of the Council.

5. The Members of the League agree that the manufacture by private enterprise of munitions and implements of war is open to grave objections. The Council shall advise how the evil effects attendant

34. **174**, p. 397.
35. **145**, p. 316.

36. **145**, p. 320.
37. See p. 781.

upon such manufacture can be prevented, due regard being had to the necessities of those Members of the League which are not able to manufacture the munitions and implements of war necessary for their safety.

6. The Members of the League undertake to interchange full and frank information as to the scale of their armaments, their military, naval and air programmes and the condition of such of their industries as are adaptable to warlike purposes.

After twelve years of negotiation, the League's permanent Commission for Disarmament met for the last time in September 1932. On February 2, 1932 the Conference for the Reduction and Limitation of Armaments met. The opening of the conference can be definitely ascertained, but as Hans Aufricht says, "League historians disagree on when or whether [it] was ever adjourned." Aufricht summarizes the work of the League in this field as follows:

The League studied the problem of the reduction and limitation of armaments from many angles. In particular, the ways and means of extending the League's system of war prevention were explored time and again. Numerous theories of and proposals for war prevention were advanced. Yet, unfortunately, no general agreement was reached, either on the theory or on the practice of war prevention.[38]

The failure of the disarmament proposals did not lead to a general armaments race — the consequences were more disastrous. It furnished the militarist elements in Germany — and, in part, also in Italy — with an excellent pretext for rearming at a time when military defense was rapidly disintegrating in the nations most reluctant to make sacrifices for national security. Instead of general disarmament based on international agreement, munitions were dumped by peace-loving nations and stockpiled by nations that expected to gain from a new war.

Economic and Financial Problems

The League of Nations was more successful in promoting the financial and economic rehabilitation of Austria, Hungary, Bulgaria, Greece, Estonia and Danzig. Threatened with economic collapse and political upheaval, they applied for financial aid and accepted the programs of monetary and fiscal reform outlined by the Council. These programs included the withdrawal of depreciated notes and their replacement by a stable and duly guaranteed currency; sound monetary

and credit policies; and fiscal measures to ensure balanced budgets. Having restored the credit of the respective governments, the Council floated loans for them through private banks in New York, London and other money markets: some $150 million for Austria; $60 million for Hungary; $85 million for Greece; $25 million for Bulgaria; $7.5 million for Estonia; $10 million for the municipality of Danzig, and $4.5 million for the Danzig Harbor Board.[39]

In line with the then prevailing conditions on the money market, the loans were made at rather high interest rates (6 to $7\frac{1}{2}$ per cent yearly). The purpose was not only to stabilize the currency but also to finance urgent economic measures; to resettle refugees; to restore transportation facilities and the like. The entire operation, extending over six years (1922–27), amounted to less than $350 million and was carried out on a strictly commercial basis, at no cost to the taxpayers in the countries where the loans were floated.

To promote broader international cooperation in economic reconstruction and combat inflation, the League called two world economic conferences, in Geneva in 1927 and in London in 1933. The first was unanimous in stressing the international character of the economic difficulties which individual governments were trying to meet by raising customs barriers, controlling exchange rates and similar measures. It called on all governments to reduce trade barriers and enter into multilateral agreements on matters of common concern.

The second conference met when Europe was recovering from the depression but when the United States had just begun its fight against unemployment. It revealed a deep cleavage of opinion on monetary policy between the United States and the European countries which had anchored their currency officially to the gold standard. In view of this disagreement, the conference was unable to make recommendations acceptable to both parties.

The League was active in the spheres of trade and international transport and communication, taxation, the press, statistics, intellectual cooperation and in suppression of the traffic in opium.[40] Numerous conferences were held and agreements reached on the desirability of unifying trade regulations and practices. Only a few

---

38. **145**, p. 292.

39. **164**, p. 75; see also **1, 2, 6, 8.**
40. See, for example, **12, 13, 14** and **16.**

such agreements were formalized as treaties, but the international exchange of views was of value to the technicians in various countries. The League deserves particular credit for having raised the question of nutrition as an issue of national and international policy.[41]

International cooperation in the interwar years was conspicuously successful in the fields of labor legislation and social welfare, which were handled by the International Labor Organization.[42]

THE DECLINE AND END OF THE LEAGUE

As a world tribunal the League's success was short-lived and in part illusory.

Throughout its existence it suffered from a structural imbalance. It never included the United States; Germany and Russia were short-lived members. The great nations of Asia — China, India and Japan — played minor parts in its activities; the interest of the Latin American republics was not impressive. In effect, the League depended on Great Britain, France and Italy, and its strength declined as friction increased among these three. Moreover, the Covenant was part of the Versailles treaty, and the League could be no stronger than the political system established by this treaty.

The first warning came soon after the end of the war, in April 1922, when Russia, declining the offers of the former Allies to resume economic relations with them, signed a treaty of good will with Germany at Rapallo. This was an early indication of the forthcoming alignment of forces hostile to the political system established at Versailles.

Unrest in Europe

Mussolini's rise to power (October 1922) and the occupation of the Ruhr by French and Belgian forces as a means of obtaining productive guarantees of reparations payments were heavy blows to the League. The vitality of the League was questioned. Canada introduced a resolution to give each member freedom to accept or reject appeals for military assistance against aggression. Essentially, this was a paraphrase of Senator Lodge's second reservation to the resolution to ratify the peace treaty. Had it not been for the dissenting vote of the Persian delegation, the Canadian resolution would have been accepted by the Assembly unanimously.

The settlement of the Ruhr conflict and the reparations dispute [43] somewhat cleared the political atmosphere, but the fact that both were settled through old-fashioned diplomatic channels, outside the League, did not strengthen its position.

Europe's chances for peace seemed to improve with the signing of the Locarno Pact by Great Britain, France, Belgium and Italy, on the one hand, and Germany on the other, in October 1925. Essentially this was a series of multilateral nonaggression and arbitration treaties based on the recognition of the inviolability of existing boundaries. But, characteristically, this pact also was concluded outside the League.

In 1926 Germany became a member of the League with a permanent seat on the Council. Simultaneously Spain and Brazil, offended by the Assembly's rejection of their claims for Council seats, withdrew from the League. Friction between the great powers became increasingly bitter. Despite the Locarno Pact, Germany made no secret of its desire to have the Versailles treaty revised. Disarmament negotiations were deadlocked. The famous Kellogg-Briand Pact (1928) outlawing war was negotiated and signed without regard to the Covenant.

The Great Depression

The already precarious situation in Europe in the late 1920's was aggravated by the downturn in business conditions in the autumn of 1929. Walters describes the consequences of the great depression for the League as follows:

Its direct and immediate consequence was to tear down the structure of economic co-operation which was gradually being built up. Its indirect consequence was to poison and embitter relations between Germany and France, Italy and France, and, in general, between the so-called dissatisfied powers on the one hand and satisfied on the other; to encourage the worst forms of nationalist and bellicose ambition in Germany, Japan and Italy; to weaken the cohesion and confuse the purposes of the peace-loving States. . . . No skill or power was available to hold back the darkening clouds of distress, poverty, and unemployment which were spreading over the greater part of the world. And the coming storm not only swept aside the gradual and partial action of the League in the economic sphere, but also began with almost equal swiftness to undermine the slow process of rebuilding the political stability of Europe.[44]

41. See **7, 11,** and **15.**
42. See pp. 783ff.

43. See Chapter 16.
44. **174,** pp. 428–30.

No other European country felt the depression as painfully as Germany. Unemployment reached staggering proportions. In the middle of 1932, less than 40 per cent of the workers were employed full time, as many were out of jobs, and the rest worked only part time.[45] The growing despair of the masses of the population fostered the extremist parties — the Nazi and the Communist — which joined forces in attacking the moderate elements and the Weimar Republic.

Hitler and Mussolini

Hitler became Chancellor of Germany in January 1933 as the result of a series of parliamentary crises created by the Nazis and Communists. Two months later, following the burning of the Reichstag building, he abolished the Weimar constitution and seized absolute power. In October of the same year, he announced Germany's withdrawal from the International Disarmament Commission and the League of Nations. In 1934 the USSR joined the League.

A new war was approaching. Germany and Italy put all their energy into rearmament, while the peace-loving countries seemed paralyzed by fear of the imminent disaster. Mussolini chose this time to resume the offensive in Africa, beginning in December 1934 (the Walwal incident). On March 17, 1935 the Ethiopian government demanded that the League investigate the situation. In September the Commission of Conciliation and Arbitration released its decision in which the "incident" was explained as the result of "an unfortunate chain of circumstances" for which neither the Ethiopian nor Italian government was held responsible.[46]

The Italian government took this decision as an invitation to further aggression. On October 3, the Italian army, supported by the air force, invaded Ethiopia. A week later the Council declared the existence of a state of war in Africa, and the Assembly approved economic sanctions against Italy. A coordination committee drafted a program of action — an embargo on arms and a few harmless financial and economic measures. When compared with the language of Article 16, it appears that the program was formulated so as to look like a sanction without weakening Mussolini's striking forces in Africa.

With superior weapons and indiscriminate use of mustard gas against the civilian population, the Italians crushed the Ethiopian army and entered Addis Ababa on May 5. Four days later Mussolini declared the annexation of Ethiopia and conferred upon the Italian king the title of Emperor of Ethiopia.

When the British and French governments made an attempt to appease the *Duce* by recognizing his conquests in Africa as a *fait accompli* (Hoare-Laval plan), Mussolini demanded expulsion of the Ethiopian delegation from the League. Ethiopia's representative appealed to the Council:

Ethiopia requests the Council vigorously to condemn the new act of violence of the Italian Government and its claim to suppress by force a State Member of the League of Nations. The Ethiopian delegation asks that all the provisions of Article 16 of the Covenant should at last be enforced, so that all States, weak or powerful, which are threatened by the ambition and covetousness of an unscrupulous Government, may be reassured. The moment is a tragic one for the League of Nations. On the resolution that the Council takes today depends the future and the very existence of the League of Nations.[47]

The Council took no action, but on July 15 the coordination committee proposed abrogation of the restrictive measures taken against Italy under Article 16. The League's submission did not satisfy Mussolini. His attitude toward the Geneva organization remained hostile and contemptuous, although Italy did not formally withdraw from the League until December 1937.

The League's enemies called it a moribund organization when Hitler sent (March 7, 1936) his army to occupy the demilitarized Rhine zone. On the same day, Hitler denounced the non-aggression agreements at Locarno. France demanded immediate action from the League but showed no willingness to use its military forces against Hitler's troops in the Rhineland. Britain was unwilling to interfere; Belgium claimed neutrality; Italy jubilantly supported Germany. Completely demoralized, the League failed even to take a stand on these developments. Germany and Japan concluded the Anti-Comintern Pact in 1936. This pact later included Italy as well as other nations. Soon after, the civil war in Spain reached a decisive phase. Although half a dozen members of the League were involved in the conflict, directly or indirectly, the great powers kept the League out of the Spanish turmoil.

---

45. **175**, p. 100.
46. **145**, p. 322.

47. **145**, p. 323.

The Collapse

In March 1938 Hitler invaded and annexed Austria. Great Britain and France did not move and kept the League from taking any action. A year later, after the agreement between the great powers at Munich, Hitler invaded Czechoslovakia. The League scarcely took note of this event, but the British and French governments suddenly realized how close the zero hour had come and they made desperate attempts to reverse their policies. They offered the Kremlin a plan for the revival of the League of Nations, restoration of the Covenant, and the application of vigorous sanctions in the event of new aggression. Stalin rejected this offer. He had made his decision: the USSR would side with Hitler in the approaching war.[48]

On August 23, 1939, the USSR and Germany signed a ten-year nonaggression pact, which was in reality a military alliance. On September 1, German armies entered Poland from the north, west and south. Two days later, Great Britain and France declared war on Germany, but before their troops could come to the rescue of the crumbling Polish army, the Russians had invaded Poland from the east.

The League had no role in the fast-moving drama. It was no longer a living political organization.

Only once did the League awake from its lethargy. In December 1939, Finland, attacked by the USSR, appealed to the League. The latter condemned the aggression and expelled the USSR — the only time such a measure was ever taken against a member of the Geneva organization.

Even when war was raging in the world, however, the technical services of the League remained active. Reduced to a skeleton staff in Geneva and its technical services removed to Princeton, Washington and Montreal, the League experts continued their work, trying to digest the experience they had accumulated[49] and to outline plans for international cooperation after the war.[50]

The League formally dissolved itself in a quiet meeting of the Assembly in Geneva on April 8, 1946. Its obituary was pronounced by the British

delegate: "The League is dead, long live the United Nations."[51]

LESSONS OF THE LEAGUE

The lessons of the League of Nations have been judiciously summarized by Arthur Sweetser:

> The League of Nations, by its success in some ways and its failure in others, . . . demonstrated conclusively that it is possible to build a system of organized international cooperation complete in all its parts; that such a system will function effectively as long as it is moderately supported and not too greatly strained; but that it will not be able to withstand the greater shocks unless the world's principal governments give it their full support. The governments and peoples of the world can have peace if they want it, but they cannot hope to get it by default or half-effort.[52]

Apart from such general considerations, it appears that the League was handicapped from the start by the fact that the Covenant assigned it functions which the great powers reserved for themselves. The disintegration of the alliances created by World War I left it in a political vacuum.

Despite the infamy of its last years, the League did vindicate the basic idea of the Covenant — the creation of an international organization which would intervene in disputes among states, settle the differences and, if necessary, call for sanctions against the aggressor. The experience of the League also proved the value of Smuts's idea of combining political activities with peacetime pursuits in economic, social and cultural fields within the framework of the same international organization.[53]

---

48. **174**, p. 800.
49. See **174**, **3**, **10** and **16**.
50. See **4**, **5**, **17** and **18**.

51. **174**, p. 815.
52. **152**, pp. 6–7.
53. There are of course other and different interpretations of the record of the League of Nations. Many hold that the League's failure to prevent World War II is evidence of the futility of international agreements and organizations of sovereign nations. According to this school of thought, lawlessness in international life, conquests and wars can be eliminated only by the merging of individual nations in a world-wide political organization under a world government. (See, for example, **168**, and **161**, *passim*.) In the opinion of the present writers the concepts of a world state and a world government have distinct merits as long-range philosophical generalizations but destroy their own purpose when they are used as arguments against international cooperation on a limited — and therefore more realistic — scale. (Cf. **156**, pp. 572–608.)

THE INTERNATIONAL LABOR ORGANIZATION

Proposals for an international organization to further the interests of labor had been made more than a century before such a body came into existence under the League of Nations.

In 1818 Robert Owen submitted a memorandum to the meeting of the Quadruple Alliance at Aix-la-Chapelle, requesting the nomination of an international commission of labor to protect workers against ignorance and exploitation.[54]

ORIGIN OF THE ILO

The idea of international cooperation in the field of labor legislation gained strength in the latter part of the nineteenth century as the international labor movement grew. Organized labor, represented by socialist parties and labor unions, was largely responsible for the revival of the idea in 1916–18, in the final years of World War I. The revolutions in Russia, Germany and Austria persuaded representatives assembled at the Paris Peace Conference that the new international order should recognize the aspirations of workers and give them a new role in the community of nations.[55]

The Conference appointed a commission for international labor legislation under the presidency of Samuel Gompers, and this commission developed a plan for a permanent international organization designed to promote uniform labor legislation throughout the world. The plan was accepted with only minor changes by the Conference and became the constitution of the ILO. For political expediency rather than for logical considerations, it was incorporated in the peace treaties [56] and became a part of them, like the Covenant of the League of Nations.

Later, certain provisions of the constitution of the ILO were revised and amended. In part because of the personality of Albert Thomas, its first director, the ILO achieved a large degree of independence from the League Secretariat. Indeed it established a policy of its own and has maintained continuity of purpose and methods from its first conference in Washington in 1919 to the present day. The ILO was an autonomous institution of the League of Nations until 1946, when it became one of the specialized agencies of the United Nations.[57] Its headquarters remains in Geneva.

PURPOSE

The Preamble of the constitution outlines the purposes of the ILO as follows:

Whereas the League of Nations has for its object the establishment of universal peace, and such a peace can be established only if it is based upon social justice;

And whereas conditions of labour exist involving such injustice, hardship and privation to large numbers of people as to produce unrest so great that the peace and harmony of the world are imperiled; and an improvement of those conditions is urgently required: as, for example, by the regulation of the hours of work, including establishment of a maximum working day and week, the regulation of the labour supply, the prevention of unemployment, the provision of an adequate living wage, the protection of the worker against sickness, disease and injury arising out of his employment, the protection of children, young persons and women, provision for old age and injury, protection of the interests of workers when employed in countries other than their own, recognition of the principle of freedom of association, the organisation of vocational and technical education and other measures;

Whereas also the failure of any nation to adopt humane conditions of labour is an obstacle in the way of other nations which desire to improve the conditions in their own countries;

The High Contracting Parties, moved by sentiments of justice and humanity, as well as by the desire to secure the permanent peace of the world, agree to the following.[58]

ORGANIZATION AND PROCEDURE

The principal organs of the ILO are the general conference of representatives of the members, which usually convenes once a year; a governing body of thirty-two members; and the permanent International Labor Office.

Each member nation is represented in the general conference by four delegates — two for the government, one for employers and one for employees. Although appointed by the respective governments, the representatives of employers and employees constitute separate groups within the conference, giving it the character of an international parliament. Differences among the national delegations are less important in this

---

54. **68**, pp. 4–5.
55. **68**, p. 9.
56. Part XIII of the Treaties of Versailles, Saint-Germain and Trianon; Part XII of the Treaty of Neuilly.

57. **53**, 1947–48, p. 818; cf. **65**.
58. **57**, p. 4.

body than those among the employers' and employees' representatives. Since each of these groups represents only a fourth of the votes, both must seek the support of the governmental delegates.

A majority of two thirds of the delegates present is required in voting on labor legislation. Theoretically, this gives the deciding vote to the governmental representative. In most cases, however, government delegates from countries with strong unions and highly developed labor laws will vote for similar legislation in other countries. Therefore the labor representatives can count on the support of at least some of the government delegates so long as their demands do not go beyond the standards accepted in modern progressive countries. Thus, the general conference of the ILO acts, to some extent, as an international arbitration panel.

The ILO deals with such subjects as protection of labor; social security; wages and hours of work; collective bargaining; the right of workers to organize. Its decisions are of two kinds: "recommendations," which are brought to the attention of national governments; and drafts of "conventions," which are submitted to them for ratification.

Recommendations and conventions are usually drafted by the Office staff of the ILO but the proposed convention can be amended and changed by the conference until the text is acceptable to a two-thirds majority. Occasionally, the draft of a convention appears in the agenda of several consecutive conferences before it is finally accepted or rejected.

The decisions of the conference are not binding on member nations. Their responsibilities in regard to conventions are defined in the constitution as follows:

(*b*) each of the Members undertakes that it will, within the period of one year at most from the closing of the session of the Conference, or if it is impossible owing to exceptional circumstances to do so within the period of one year, then at the earliest practicable moment and in no case later than eighteen months from the closing of the session of the Conference, bring the Convention before the authority or authorities within whose competence the matter lies, for the enactment of legislation or other action;

(*e*) if the Member does not obtain the consent of the authority or authorities within whose competence the matter lies, no further obligation shall rest

upon the Member except that it shall report to the Director-General . . . the position of its law and practice in regard to the matters dealt with in the Convention, . . .[59]

Similar procedures are to be followed by members in the case of recommendations.

The language of these provisions may convey the impression that the ILO is primarily a consultative body. Actually, it has been a potent factor in promoting international labor legislation and channeling the aspirations of workers toward definite practical goals. The strength of the ILO has been in the education of statesmen, labor leaders and businessmen. The conferences in Geneva have become international seminars not only on labor problems but also on the art of reconciling divergent opinions, settling controversies and arriving at practical decisions. Thousands of labor leaders and statesmen have attended this "school" in the past three and a half decades, and what they have learned is embodied in a long series of recommendations and conventions that have strongly influenced labor legislation in some three dozen countries.[60]

The ILO has also undertaken studies on social conditions in various countries; old-age insurance and other forms of social security; arbitration of labor disputes; the social implications of rationalization; unemployment; housing problems; the form of wages and minimum wage legislation; [61] and studies on occupational and vocational training. From the beginning it has worked to standardize international labor statistics and continues to do so as a specialized agency of the United Nations.[62]

CONVENTIONS

Between 1919 and December 1954 a total of 103 conventions were adopted by the ILO. Fifteen of these were revisions of previously adopted conventions, reducing the number of original conventions to 88. Occasionally several conventions have dealt with the same problem in different industries. Such, for example, are the conventions on old-age, invalidity and survivors insurance in industry and agriculture (numbers 35–40 in Table 278) or those on minimum age

---

59. **57**, p. 11.
60. See **69**.
61. For publications of the ILO on these subjects see, for example, **54** through **56**, **58** through **61**, **66**, **70** and **71**.
62. See **63** and **72**.

TABLE 278

THE INTERNATIONAL LABOR ORGANIZATION: CONVENTIONS ADOPTED AND RATIFIED, 1919–54

Convention Number	Title of Convention	Number of Countries Ratifying	Convention Number	Title of Convention	Number of Countries Ratifying
	First Session (Washington) 1919			*Eleventh Session (Geneva) 1928*	
1	Hours of Work (Industry)	29	26	Minimum Wage-Fixing Machinery	26
2	Unemployment	34			
3	Maternity Protection	19		*Twelfth Session (Geneva) 1929*	
4	Night Work (Women)	35	27	Marking of Weight (Packages Transported by Vessels)	40
5	Minimum Age (Industry)	33			
6	Night Work of Young Persons (Industry)	35	28	Protection against Accidents (Dockers)	4
	Second Session (Genoa) 1920			*Fourteenth Session (Geneva) 1930*	
7	Minimum Age (Sea)	35	29	Forced Labour	28
8	Unemployment Indemnity (Shipwreck)	30	30	Hours of Work (Commerce and Offices)	14
9	Placing of Seamen	28			
	Third Session (Geneva) 1921			*Fifteenth Session (Geneva) 1931*	
10	Minimum Age (Agriculture)	23	31	Hours of Work (Coal Mines)	1
11	Right of Association (Agriculture)	38			
12	Workmen's Compensation (Agriculture)	25		*Sixteenth Session (Geneva) 1932*	
13	White Lead (Painting)	29	32	Protection against Accidents (Dockers) (Revised)	16
14	Weekly Rest (Industry)	40			
15	Minimum Age (Trimmers and Stokers)	35	33	Minimum Age (Non-Industrial Employment)	8
16	Medical Examination of Young Persons (Sea)	36		*Seventeenth Session (Geneva) 1933*	
	Seventh Session (Geneva) 1925		34	Fee-Charging Employment Agencies	10
17	Workmen's Compensation (Accidents)	25	35	Old-Age Insurance (Industry, etc.)	8
			36	Old-Age Insurance (Agriculture)	7
18	Workmen's Compensation (Occupational Diseases)	33	37	Invalidity Insurance (Industry, etc.)	8
19	Equality of Treatment (Accident Compensation)	43	38	Invalidity Insurance (Agriculture)	7
20	Night Work (Bakeries)	13	39	Survivors' Insurance (Industry, etc.)	6
	Eighth Session (Geneva) 1926		40	Survivors' Insurance (Agriculture)	5
21	Inspection of Emigrants	25		*Eighteenth Session (Geneva) 1934*	
			41	Night Work (Women) (Revised)	22
	Ninth Session (Geneva) 1926		42	Workmen's Compensation (Occupational Diseases) (Revised)	26
22	Seamen's Articles of Agreement	30	43	Sheet-Glass Works	9
23	Repatriation of Seamen	19	44	Unemployment Provision	8
	Tenth Session (Geneva) 1927			*Nineteenth Session (Geneva) 1935*	
24	Sickness Insurance (Industry)	19	45	Underground Work (Women)	37
25	Sickness Insurance (Agriculture)	13	46	Hours of Work (Coal Mines) (Revised)	2

(*Continued on following page*)

TABLE 278—*continued*

Convention Number	Title of Convention	Number of Countries Ratifying	Convention Number	Title of Convention	Number of Countries Ratifying
47	Forty-Hour Week	1	72	Paid Vacations (Seafarers)	3
48	Maintenance of Migrants' Pension Rights	6	73	Medical Examination (Seafarers)	6
			74	Certification of Able Seamen	8
49	Reduction of Hours of Work (Glass-Bottle Works)	7	75	Accommodation of Crews	5
			76	Wages, Hours of Work and Manning (Sea)	1
	Twentieth Session (Geneva) 1936			*Twenty-Ninth Session (Montreal) 1946*	
50	Recruiting of Indigenous Workers	6	77	Medical Examination of Young Persons (Industry)	9
51	Reduction of Hours of Work (Public Works)	1	78	Medical Examination of Young Persons (Non-Industrial Occupations)	6
52	Holidays with Pay	16			
	Twenty-First Session (Geneva) 1936		79	Night Work of Young Persons (Non-Industrial Occupations)	7
53	Officers' Competency Certificates	13	80	Final Articles Revision	39
54	Holidays with Pay (Sea)	6			
55	Shipowners' Liability (Sick and Injured Seamen)	6		*Thirtieth Session (Geneva) 1947*	
56	Sickness Insurance (Sea)	4	81	Labour Inspection	19
57	Hours of Work and Manning (Sea)	5	82	Social Policy (Non-Metropolitan Territories)	1
	Twenty-Second Session (Geneva) 1936		83	Labour Standards (Non-Metropolitan Territories)	1
58	Minimum Age (Sea) (Revised)	15	84	Right of Association (Non-Metropolitan Territories)	2
	Twenty-Third Session (Geneva) 1937		85	Labour Inspectorates (Non-Metropolitan Territories)	1
59	Minimum Age (Industry) (Revised)	5	86	Contracts of Employment (Indigenous Workers)	2
60	Minimum Age (Non-Industrial Employment) (Revised)	4			
61	Reduction of Hours of Work (Textiles)	1		*Thirty-First Session (San Francisco) 1948*	
62	Safety Provisions (Building)	9	87	Freedom of Association and Protection of the Right to Organise	16
	Twenty-Fourth Session (Geneva) 1938		88	Employment Service	20
63	Statistics of Wages and Hours of Work	18	89	Night Work (Women) (Revised)	17
			90	Night Work of Young Persons (Industry) (Revised)	9
	Twenty-Fifth Session (Geneva) 1939			*Thirty-Second Session (Geneva) 1949*	
64	Contracts of Employment (Indigenous Workers)	3	91	Paid Vacations (Seafarers) (Revised)	6
65	Penal Sanctions (Indigenous Workers)	2	92	Accommodation of Crews (Revised)	8
66	Migration for Employment	0			
67	Hours of Work and Rest Periods (Road Transport)	0	93	Wages, Hours of Work and Manning (Sea) (Revised)	1
			94	Labour Clauses (Public Contracts)	12
	Twenty-Eighth Session (Seattle) 1946		95	Protection of Wages	10
68	Food and Catering (Ships' Crews)	9	96	Fee-Charging Employment Agencies (Revised)	10
69	Certification of Ships' Cooks	10			
70	Social Security (Seafarers)	1	97	Migration for Employment (Revised)	10
71	Seafarers' Pensions	3			

(*Continued on facing page*)

TABLE 278—*continued*

Convention Number	Title of Convention	Number of Countries Ratifying	Convention Number	Title of Convention	Number of Countries Ratifying
98	Right to Organise and Collective Bargaining	16		*Thirty-Fifth Session (Geneva) 1952*	
			101	Holidays with Pay (Agriculture)	6
	Thirty-Fourth Session (Geneva) 1951		102	Social Security (Minimum Standards)	0
99	Minimum Wage-Fixing Machinery (Agriculture)	2	103	Maternity Protection (Revised)	0
100	Equal Remuneration	3			

Source: **62.**

in various industries and occupations. The conventions may be grouped as follows: [63]

Issue	Number of Conventions
All issues	103
Hours of work	10
Night work	7
Minimum age	8
Weekly rest and holidays	5
Social security, unemployment benefits and workmen's compensation	20
Placement and employment services	4
Minimum wage	2
Right of association	3
Labor conditions of seamen	16
Labor conditions in nonmetropolitan areas (colonies)	8
Maternity protection	2
Medical examination of young workers	3
Dangerous occupations	3
Migrants	2
Miscellaneous	10

RATIFICATION OF CONVENTIONS

These 103 ILO conventions have been submitted for ratification to seventy-two countries, but only six have been ratified by half that number or more.[64] Characteristically, all six are either formal (80: Final articles revision), purely technical (27: Marking of weight), or are easy to comply with (14: Weekly rest; 16: Medical examination of young persons; 11: Right of association; 19: Equality of treatment).

Other conventions which have been ratified by thirty to thirty-five countries deal with unemployment; night work of women and young

63. **62**, March 31, 1953. For details see **67.**
64. Cf. **67**, 1952.

persons; underground work of women; and the work of seamen.

Table 278 shows that, chronologically, the number of ratifying countries has tended to decline sharply. In fact, there is often a lag of several years between the adoption of a convention and its ratification. Public opinion must become familiar with the new convention; organized labor needs time to muster support for ratification; parliamentary or administrative procedures in some countries may cause further delay. There are, however, other reasons for the larger number of ratifications of the early conventions as compared with those of more recent years. In its first fourteen or sixteen sessions — up to 1930–32 — the ILO fairly well covered those aspects of labor legislation on which international agreement could be reached readily. It has since become increasingly difficult to find new issues that are generally acceptable. On the other hand, however, many countries have tended to adjust their domestic labor legislation to the standards of the ILO conventions without formally ratifying them.

The ranking of the seventy-two nations to which ILO conventions have been submitted for ratification is shown in Table 279. It is supplemented by Figure 148, which indicates the conventions that have been ratified by each country.

The table reveals strange anomalies in the ranking of countries. The group of nations with the largest number of ratifications (63–48) includes, on the one hand, France, the United Kingdom and Belgium, which have been leaders in the ILO since the beginning, and, on the other hand, Italy and Bulgaria. Likewise, among the next twelve countries (with 39–34 ratifications)

TABLE 279

THE INTERNATIONAL LABOR ORGANIZATION: NUMBER OF CONVENTIONS RATIFIED, BY COUNTRY, 1919–52

Country	Ratifi-cations	Country	Ratifi-cations	Country	Ratifi-cations
France	63	Greece	23	Lithuania	7
Bulgaria	62	Denmark	22	Egypt	6
Italy	54	Estonia	22	United States	6
United Kingdom	51	Pakistan	21	Afghanistan	5
Belgium	48	Hungary	20	Dominican Republic	5
Netherlands	39	India	20	Israel	5
Cuba	38	Switzerland	20	Albania	4
New Zealand	37	Venezuela	19	Haiti	4
Finland	37	Canada	18	Indonesia	4
Mexico	36	Romania	17	Iceland	3
Chile	35	Western Germany	17	Ethiopia	1
Czechoslovakia	35	Latvia	17	Liberia	1
Norway	35	Australia	15	Syria	1
Argentina	34	Guatemala	15	Thailand	1
Ireland	34	Portugal	15	Bolivia	0
Poland	34	Brazil	14	Costa Rica	0
Spain	34	Burma	14	Ecuador	0
Sweden	33	Ceylon	14	Iran	0
Nicaragua	30	China	14	Lebanon	0
Uruguay	30	Japan	14	Libya	0
Luxembourg	28	Peru	11	Panama	0
Yugoslavia	26	Union of So. Africa	11	Philippines	0
Austria	26	Turkey	10	El Salvador	0
Colombia	25	Iraq	9	Viet-Nam	0

Source: Computed from **62**.

are the Netherlands, New Zealand, Finland, Czechoslovakia and Norway, on the one hand, and Cuba, Chile and Argentina, on the other.

The number of ratifications does not necessarily reflect the ranking of different nations in the development of labor legislation. Up to 1932–33, Bulgaria, Spain, Cuba, Nicaragua, Colombia, Chile, Argentina and Uruguay ratified almost all the conventions adopted by the ILO, as did the United Kingdom, France, Luxembourg, Belgium, Czechoslovakia and several other countries. Some countries — for example, the United Kingdom, Belgium and Czechoslovakia — found it easy to ratify conventions that did not go further than their labor laws. Others, such as Nicaragua, Colombia and Chile, hardly contemplated strict and immediate application of the proposed measures. Later it became usual in underdeveloped countries to adopt generous and expensive social security plans in principle, but to put them into effect only gradually and on a small scale. On the other hand, such countries as the United States, Australia, Canada and

Switzerland have ratified few conventions but have achieved the ILO goals through domestic legislation.[65]

Thus Figure 118 illustrates the visible influence of the ILO on various countries rather than the actual progress in their labor legislation.

TECHNICAL ASSISTANCE

The regular ILO program has included, since its inception, awards of fellowships for studying industrial relations, labor legislation, vocational training, social security, industrial welfare, labor statistics and related matters. These activities have been continued on a larger scale under the UN's technical assistance program.[66]

Missions have been sent to underdeveloped areas (Guatemala, El Salvador, Panama, Peru, Paraguay, Greece, Iran, Burma, Ceylon, Indo-

65. The United States has ratified six conventions: five dealing with labor conditions of seamen (Nos. 53, 54, 55, 57 and 58 in Table 278) and one of purely technical character (No. 80).

66. See pp. 806ff.

china, Liberia); training institutes and seminars have been held (among others, in India, Pakistan, Indonesia, Thailand, Libya); surveys of labor conditions have been organized and foundations laid for labor statistics; experts have been appointed to advise public authorities in underdeveloped areas on industrial hygiene, accident prevention, administration of employment services, organization of cooperatives and so forth.

In 1952, for example, Ceylon asked the ILO for advice on problems involving vocational training; economic and social surveys; organization of a cooperative fruit canning plant; cooperative marketing of vegetables; training within industry; and the management of cement, plywood and other industries.

Pakistan listed the following subjects: a training center for motor vehicle drivers and mechanics; industrial welfare; small-scale industries; training of mechanics for heavy earth-moving equipment; a survey of labor conditions in agriculture; labor force statistics; and a demonstration training center.[67]

The ILO has recruited experts for the underdeveloped areas in all parts of the world. In some projects it works jointly with other specialized agencies of the UN such as the Food and Agriculture Organization (FAO), the World Health Organization (WHO) and the United Nations Educational, Scientific and Cultural Organization (UNESCO).[68]

THE UNITED NATIONS

The term "United Nations" was first used, on the suggestion of President Franklin D. Roosevelt, in the title "Declaration of the United Nations," on January 1, 1942, and was adopted as the name of the new international organization as a tribute to the late President of the United States.[69]

ORIGIN OF THE UN

Plans for this organization were developed in August–October 1944 during conversations at Dumbarton Oaks between representatives of the United States, the United Kingdom, the USSR and China.[70] The General Assembly of the UN met for the first time in London, on January 10, 1946.

Although called upon to continue the work of the League of Nations, the UN does not consider itself the successor of the Geneva organization. It took over the assets and some technical functions of the League and has used its experience widely, but the tendency has been to accept the UN as a completely new organization.[71]

MEMBERSHIP AND BUDGET

The UN counted 60 members in 1953, among them the 51 original signatories of the Charter adopted at the San Francisco Conference. The original members are:

Western Hemisphere

United States	Dominican Republic
Canada	Venezuela
Mexico	Colombia
Guatemala	Ecuador
El Salvador	Brazil
Honduras	Peru
Nicaragua	Bolivia
Costa Rica	Paraguay
Panama	Chile
Cuba	Uruguay
Haiti	Argentina

Europe

United Kingdom	Norway
France	Poland
Luxembourg	Czechoslovakia
Belgium	Yugoslavia
Netherlands	Greece
Denmark	

The Soviet Union

USSR	Ukraine
Byelorussia	

Asia

China [a]	Iraq
Turkey	Iran
Lebanon	India
Syria	Philippines
Saudi Arabia	

Africa

Egypt	Liberia
Ethiopia	Union of South Africa

Oceania

Australia	New Zealand

a. Represented now by the Nationalist government of Formosa.

67. **20**, 1953, p. 66.
68. See pp. 808ff.
69. **53**, 1947–48, p. 3.
70. **53**, 1947–48, p. 5.

71. This may have been due in part to courtesy to the USSR, which was expelled from the League after its aggression against Finland.

FIGURE 148. THE INTERNATIONAL LABOR ORGANIZATION:

STATES	Number of ratifications	1st Session (1919)						2nd Session (1920)			3rd Session (1921)										7th Session (1925)				8th S. 1926	9th Session (1926)			10th Session (1927)	11th S. 1928	12th Session (1929)				14th Session (1930)		15th S. 1931	16th Session (1932)		17th Session (1933)							18th Session (1934)				19th Session (1935)				
		1	2	3	4	5	6	7	8	9	10	11	12	13	14	15	16	17	18	19	20	21	22	23	24	25	26	27	28	29	30	31	32	33	34	35	36	37	38	39	40	41	42	43	44	45	46	47	48	49
Afghanistan	5																																																	
Albania	4																																																	
Argentina	34																																																	
Australia	15																																																	
Austria	26																																																	
Belgium	48																																																	
Bolivia	0																																																	
Brazil	14																																																	
Bulgaria	62																																																	
Burma	14																																																	
Canada	18																																																	
Ceylon	14																																																	
Chile	35																																																	
China	14																																																	
Colombia	25																																																	
Costa Rica	0																																																	
Cuba	38																																																	
Czechoslovakia	35																																																	
Denmark	22																																																	
Dominican Republic	5																																																	
Ecuador	0																																																	
Egypt	6																																																	
Estonia	22																																																	
Ethiopia	1																																																	
Finland	37																																																	
France	63																																																	
Western Germany	17																																																	
Greece	23																																																	
Guatemala	15																																																	
Haiti	4																																																	
Hungary	20																																																	
Iceland	3																																																	
India	20																																																	
Indonesia	4																																																	
Iran	0																																																	
Iraq	9																																																	
Ireland	34																																																	
Israel	5																																																	
Italy	54																																																	
Japan	14																																																	
Latvia	17																																																	
Lebanon	0																																																	
Liberia	1																																																	
Libya	0																																																	
Lithuania	7																																																	
Luxembourg	28																																																	
Mexico	36																																																	
Netherlands	39																																																	
New Zealand	37																																																	
Nicaragua	30																																																	
Norway	35																																																	
Pakistan	11																																																	
Panama	0																																																	
Peru	11																																																	
Philippines	0																																																	
Poland	34																																																	
Portugal	15																																																	
Romania	17																																																	
El Salvador	0																																																	
Spain	34																																																	
Sweden	33																																																	
Switzerland	20																																																	
Syria	1																																																	
Thailand	1																																																	
Turkey	10																																																	
Union of South Africa	11																																																	
United Kingdom	51																																																	
United States	6																																																	
Uruguay	30																																																	
Venezuela	19																																																	
Viet-Nam	0																																																	
Yugoslavia	26																																																	
TOTAL OF RATIFICATIONS	1349	29	34	19	35	31	34	35	30	28	22	38	25	28	39	35	36	25	33	43	13	25	30	19	19	13	26	39	4	26	13		1	16	8	10	8	7	8	7	6	5	22	25	8	8	34	2	1	7	7
Convention No.		1	2	3	4	5	6	7	8	9	10	11	12	13	14	15	16	17	18	19	20	21	22	23	24	25	26	27	28	29	30	31	32	33	34	35	36	37	38	39	40	41	42	43	44	45	46	47	48	49

■ RATIFICATIONS REGISTERED INCLUDE CONVENTIONS WHICH STATES HAVE UNDERTAKEN TO IMPLEMENT IN VIRTUE OF A PREVIOUS RATIFICATION BY A STATE OF WHICH THEY FORMED A PART.

This chart lists all the ratifications communicated at any time since the establishment of the International Labor Organization without regard to the current legal position of the state having communicated the ratification, which, in certain cases, presents problems on which the ILO is not competent to express an opinion.

RATIFICATIONS OF CONVENTIONS, BY COUNTRY, 1919–52

20th Session (1936)			21st Session (1936)					22nd S. 1936	23rd Session (1937)				24th S. 1938	25th Session (1939)				28th Session (1946)									29th Session (1946)				30th Session (1947)						31st Session (1948)				32nd Session (1949)								34th Session (1951)		35th Session (1952)			STATES
50	51	52	53	54	55	56	57	58	59	60	61	62	63	64	65	66	67	68	69	70	71	72	73	74	75	76	77	78	79	80	81	82	83	84	85	86	87	88	89	90	91	92	93	94	95	96	97	98	99	100	101	102	103	
																																																						Afghanistan
																																																						Albania
■		■																												■																								Argentina
							■						■													■				■								■																Australia
																														■	■						■		■					■	■			■						Austria
■			■	■	■	■	■	■				■		■				■	■				■	■						■							■		■					■						■				Belgium
																																																					Bolivia
		■	■					■																						■																		■						Brazil
		■	■	■	■	■	■	■		■		■						■	■		■	■	■		■		■	■	■		■							■																Bulgaria
																																																					Burma
								■					■					■	■				■	■						■								■																Canada
													■																■																								Ceylon
																													■																								Chile
									■																				■																								China
																													■																								Colombia
																																																					Costa Rica
																																				■	■	■	■	■	■	■	■	■	■	■	■						Cuba
		■											■																■								■	■	■														Czechoslovakia
		■	■										■																■							■					■												Denmark
																													■																								Dominican Republic
																																																					Ecuador
			■										■																■																								Egypt
			■																																																		Estonia
																													■																								Ethiopia
		■	■									■	■									■			○					■	■						■					■	■		■		■		■						Finland
		■	■	■	■	■		■				■	■					■	■	■	■	■	■	■	○		■	■		■	■						■	■				■	■		■	■			■						France
																																																					Western Germany
		■																											■																								Greece
																											■	■	■	■	■					■	■	■	■	■				■	■	■	■	■						Guatemala
																														■																							Haiti
																																																					Hungary
																																				■					■							■						Iceland
																													■	■								■	■														India
																																																					Indonesia
																																																					Iran
								■																			■			■	■							■															Iraq
													■						■										■	■								■			■												Ireland
		■																																																			Israel
		■	■		■			■	■	■								■	■				■				■	■	■	■	■							■	■	■				■	■	■	■							Italy
■																																																				Japan
																																																				Latvia
																																																				Lebanon
																																																					Liberia
																																																					Libya
																																																					Lithuania
																													■																								Luxembourg
		■	■	■	■			■				■	■																■							■												■	■				Mexico
								■				■	■						■					■					■	■						■	■						■	■	■	■							Netherlands
■	■	■	■					■	■	■	■		■	■	■														■				■				■	■								■		■					New Zealand
																																																					Nicaragua
■			■					■	■				■						■		■				○					■	■						■	■			■	■			■	■								Norway
																													■							■		■	■						■		■						Pakistan
																																																					Panama
																																																					Peru
																																																					Philippines
												■															■	■	■	■																							Poland
																	■	■				■	■																	■	■												Portugal
																																																					Romania
																																																					El Salvador
																																																					Spain
							◩	■					■											○					■	■						■	■				■				■		■						Sweden
												■	■																■	■							■	■															Switzerland
																																						■															Syria
																													■																								Thailand
																													■	■							■								■		■						Turkey
													■																■									■															Union of South Africa
■						■							■	■	■				■					■						■	■	■	■	■	■	■	■	■						■	■		■	■						United Kingdom
			■	■	■		■	■																					■																								United States
																																																					Uruguay
																													■																								Venezuela
																																																					Viet-Nam
																													■																				■				Yugoslavia
6	1	12	13	5	6	4	5	13	4	3	1	8	17	3	2			6	10	1	3	3	6	6	5	1	6	5	4	39	16	1	1	2	1	2	14	16	13	6	6	8	1	9	8	9	6	11	2	3				TOTAL OF RATIFICATIONS
50	51	52	53	54	55	56	57	58	59	60	61	62	63	64	65	66	67	68	69	70	71	72	73	74	75	76	77	78	79	80	81	82	83	84	85	86	87	88	89	90	91	92	93	94	95	96	97	98	99	100	101	102	103	Convention No.

◩ CONDITIONAL RATIFICATIONS REGISTERED.
○ RATIFICATIONS DENOUNCED.

Source: 63

Three countries present special circumstances: (1) Burma remains bound by the fourteen conventions which India had ratified up to April 1, 1937, the date on which Burma ceased to be part of India. (2) Indonesia remains bound by the four conventions which had previously been ratified by the Netherlands. (3) The list above includes the fifteen conventions which India had ratified up to August 15, 1947, the date of the partition of India.

With its constituent republics of the Ukraine and Byelorussia the USSR was given three votes.

Nine countries were admitted to the UN in 1946–50: Sweden, Iceland, Afghanistan and Thailand in 1946; Yemen and Pakistan in 1947; Burma in 1948; Israel in 1949; and Indonesia in 1950. (See Figure 149.)

The admission of Ireland, Finland, Austria, Portugal, Italy, the Republic of Korea, Transjordan, Ceylon and Nepal has been vetoed repeatedly by the USSR in the Security Council. The admission of USSR satellites — Hungary, Romania, Bulgaria, Albania and the Mongolian People's Republic — has been barred by majority votes of the Western powers.

Membership in the specialized agencies of the UN is distinct from membership in the UN itself. Many nonmember countries adhere to the ILO, the FAO, the WHO and other agencies. On the other hand, the USSR (including the Ukraine and Byelorussia), Saudi Arabia, Yemen and several other countries, although members of the UN, participate in few of these agencies. (See Figure 150.)

The annual budget of the UN has fluctuated in successive fiscal years as follows (in millions of U.S. dollars):

1948	$39.4
1949	43.5
1950	44.5
1951	48.6
1952	50.3
1953	48.3
1954	48.1

These amounts do not include the operating expenses of the specialized agencies nor outlays for the UN's technical assistance program.

Contributions to the UN are distributed among member states according to assessment quotas, which change slightly from year to year. The assessment of each member for fiscal year 1953 represented the following percentages of the UN's budget.[72]

United States	35.12	Ukraine	1.63
USSR	12.28	Poland	1.58
United Kingdom	10.30	Argentina	1.45
France	5.75	Brazil	1.45
China	5.62	Belgium	1.37
India	3.45	Netherlands	1.25
Canada	3.30	Czechoslovakia	1.05
Australia	1.75	Union of So. Africa	0.83
Sweden	1.65	Pakistan	0.79

Denmark	0.78	Ethiopia	0.10
Mexico	0.70	Syria	0.08
Turkey	0.65	Afghanistan	0.08
Indonesia	0.60	Saudi Arabia	0.07
Norway	0.50	Bolivia	0.06
Egypt	0.50	Guatemala	0.06
New Zealand	0.48	El Salvador	0.05
Yugoslavia	0.44	Dominican	
Byelorussia	0.43	Republic	0.05
Philippines	0.39	Panama	0.05
Colombia	0.35	Luxembourg	0.05
Venezuela	0.35	Lebanon	0.05
Cuba	0.34	Honduras	0.04
Chile	0.33	Costa Rica	0.04
Iran	0.33	Nicaragua	0.04
Greece	0.19	Haiti	0.04
Peru	0.18	Ecuador	0.04
Uruguay	0.18	Paraguay	0.04
Thailand	0.18	Iceland	0.04
Israel	0.17	Yemen	0.04
Burma	0.13	Liberia	0.04
Iraq	0.12		

THE CHARTER

The Charter of the UN resembles the Covenant of the League of Nations in many respects, but differs in wording, details of organization, and in its approach to the problems of securing peace and resisting aggression.[73]

Purpose

The purpose of the organization is stated in the Preamble:

We the peoples of the United Nations determined

to save succeeding generations from the scourge of war, which twice in our lifetime has brought untold sorrow to mankind, and

to reaffirm faith in fundamental human rights, in the dignity and worth of the human person, in the equal rights of men and women and of nations large and small, and

to establish conditions under which justice and respect for the obligations arising from treaties and other sources of international law can be maintained, and

to promote social progress and better standards of life in larger freedom,

And for these ends

to practice tolerance and live together in peace with one another as good neighbors, and

to unite our strength to maintain international peace and security, and

to ensure, by the acceptance of principles and the institution of methods, that armed force shall not be used, save in the common interest, and

72. **53**, 1952, p. 123. Countries arrayed by size of assessment.

73. For a history of the Charter see **160**, pp. 42–57.

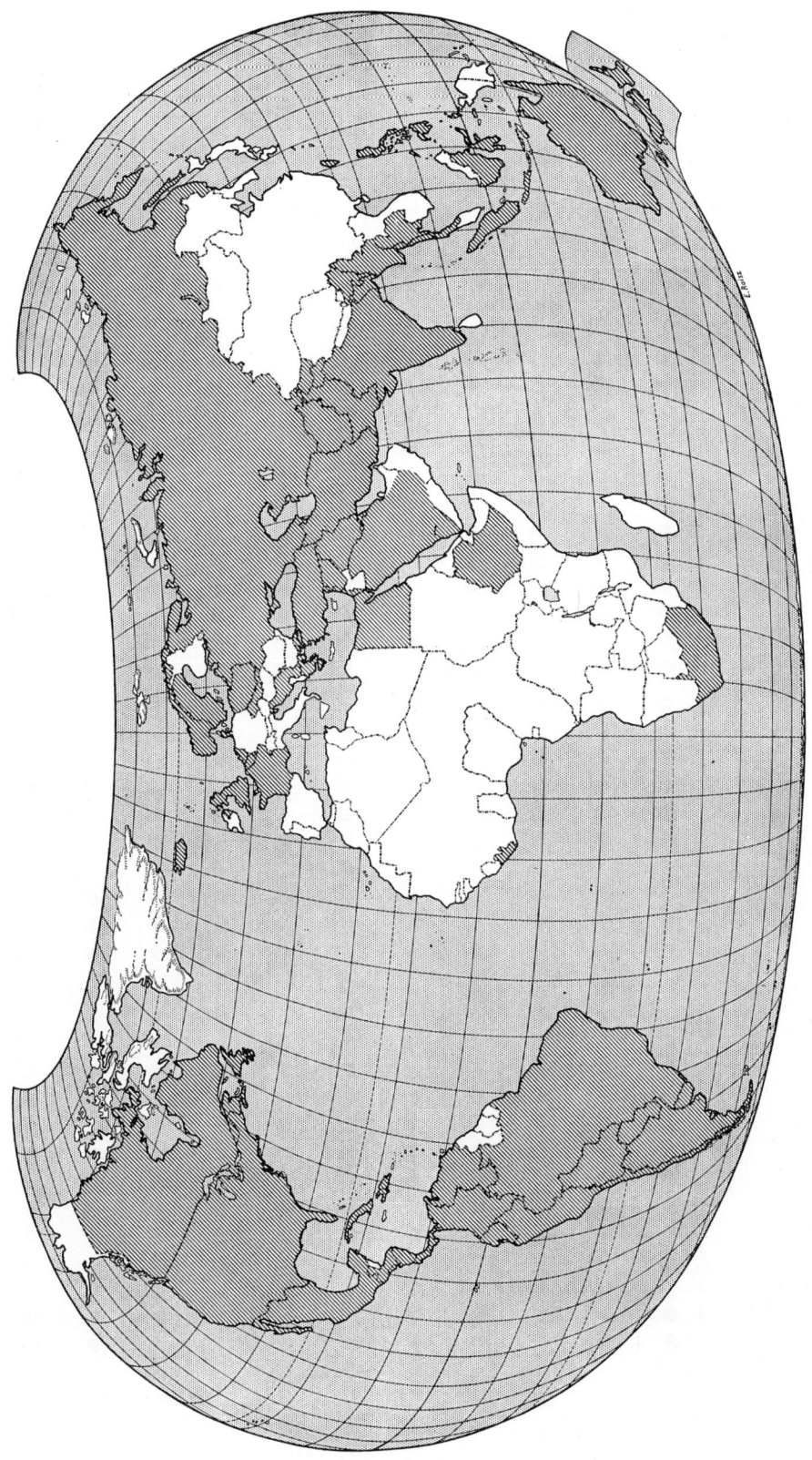

FIGURE 149. THE UNITED NATIONS: GEOGRAPHIC DISTRIBUTION OF MEMBERS, 1954

This map differs from official maps of the United Nations, which show members them struggling for independence — as being represented in the UN. (Cf. **53**, 1952, of the UN and their dependencies. It seems unrealistic to list colonies — some of map following page 150.)

FIGURE 150. MEMBERSHIP IN THE UNITED NATIONS

UN — UNITED NATIONS
ILO — INTERNATIONAL LABOR ORGANIZATION
FAO — FOOD AND AGRICULTURE ORGANIZATION
UNESCO — EDUCATIONAL, SCIENTIFIC AND CULTURAL ORGANIZATION
ICAO — INTERNATIONAL CIVIL AVIATION ORGANIZATION
BANK — INTERNATIONAL BANK FOR RECONSTRUCTION AND DEVELOPMENT
FUND — INTERNATIONAL MONETARY FUND
WHO — WORLD HEALTH ORGANIZATION
UPU — UNIVERSAL POSTAL UNION
ITU — INTERNATIONAL TELECOMMUNICATION UNION
WMO — WORLD METEOROLOGICAL ORGANIZATION

	UN	ILO	FAO	UNESCO	ICAO	BANK	FUND	WHO	UPU	ITU	WMO
TOTAL	60	66	71	69	61	55	55	81	93	90	82
UNITED STATES	●	●	●	●	●	●	●	●	●	●	●
CANADA	●	●	●	●	●	●	●	●	●	●	●
MEXICO	●	●	●	●	●	●	●	●	●	●	●
GUATEMALA	●	●	●	●	●	●	●	●	●	●	●
EL SALVADOR	●	●	●	●		●	●	●	●	●	
HONDURAS	●		●	●		●	●	●	●	●	
NICARAGUA	●		●	●	●	●	●	●	●	●	
COSTA RICA	●	●	●	●		●	●	●	●	●	
PANAMA	●	●	●	●		●	●	●	●	●	
CUBA	●	●	●	●	●	●	●	●	●	●	●
HAITI	●	●	●	●	●	●	●	●	●	●	●
DOMINICAN REPUBLIC	●	●	●	●	●	●	●	●	●	●	●
VENEZUELA	●	●	●	●	●	●	●	●	●	●	●
COLOMBIA	●	●	●	●	●	●	●		●	●	
ECUADOR	●	●	●	●		●	●	●	●	●	
BRAZIL	●	●	●	●	●	●	●	●	●	●	●
PERU	●	●	●	●	●	●	●	●	●	●	●
BOLIVIA	●	●	●	●	●	●	●	●	●	●	
PARAGUAY	●		●		●	●	●	●	●	●	●
CHILE	●	●	●	●	●	●	●	●	●	●	
URUGUAY	●	●	●	●	●	●	●	●	●	●	●
ARGENTINA	●	●	●	●	●			●	●	●	●
UNITED KINGDOM	●	●	●	●	●	●	●	●	●	●	●
IRELAND		●	●		●			●	●	●	●
ICELAND	●	●	●		●	●	●	●	●	●	●
FRANCE	●	●	●	●	●	●	●	●	●	●	●
LUXEMBOURG	●	●	●	●	●	●	●	●	●	●	●
BELGIUM	●	●	●	●	●	●	●	●	●	●	●
NETHERLANDS	●	●	●	●	●	●	●	●	●	●	●
DENMARK	●	●	●	●	●	●	●	●	●	●	●
SWEDEN	●	●	●	●	●	●	●	●	●	●	●
NORWAY	●	●	●	●	●	●	●	●	●	●	●
FINLAND		●	●		●	●	●	●	●	●	●
WESTERN GERMANY		●	●	●	●	●	●	●	●	●	
POLAND	●	●		●	●				●	●	●
CZECHOSLOVAKIA	●	●		●	●	●	●		●	●	●

	UN	ILO	FAO	UNESCO	ICAO	BANK	FUND	WHO	UPU	ITU	WMO
SWITZERLAND		●	●	●	●			●	●	●	●
AUSTRIA		●	●	●	●	●	●	●	●	●	
HUNGARY		●		●					●	●	●
PORTUGAL		●	●		●			●	●	●	●
SPAIN			●	●	●			●	●	●	●
ITALY		●	●	●	●	●	●	●	●	●	●
YUGOSLAVIA	●	●	●	●		●	●	●	●	●	●
ROMANIA									●	●	●
BULGARIA		●							●	●	●
ALBANIA		●							●	●	
GREECE	●	●	●	●	●	●	●	●	●	●	●
U. S. S. R.	●								●	●	●
UKRAINE	●								●	●	●
BYELORUSSIA	●								●	●	●
CHINA (TAIWAN)	●	●		●	●	●	●	●	●	●	●
SOUTH KOREA			●	●	●			●	●	●	●
JAPAN		●	●	●	●	●	●	●	●	●	●
TURKEY	●	●	●	●	●	●	●	●	●	●	●
LEBANON	●	●	●	●	●	●	●	●	●	●	●
ISRAEL	●	●	●	●	●			●	●	●	●
SYRIA	●	●	●	●	●	●	●	●	●	●	●
JORDAN			●	●	●	●	●	●	●	●	
SAUDI ARABIA	●		●	●				●	●	●	
YEMEN	●		●						●	●	
IRAN	●	●	●	●	●	●	●	●	●	●	
IRAQ	●	●	●	●	●	●	●	●	●	●	●
AFGHANISTAN	●	●	●	●	●			●	●	●	
PAKISTAN	●	●	●	●	●	●	●	●	●	●	●
INDIA	●	●	●	●	●	●	●	●	●	●	●
NEPAL			●	●				●			
BURMA	●	●	●	●	●	●	●	●	●	●	●
VIET NAM		●	●	●				●	●	●	
CAMBODIA			●	●				●	●		
LAOS			●	●				●	●	●	
THAILAND	●	●	●	●	●	●	●	●	●	●	●
CEYLON		●	●	●	●	●	●	●	●	●	●
INDONESIA	●	●	●	●				●	●	●	●
PHILIPPINES	●	●	●	●	●	●	●	●	●	●	●
EGYPT	●	●	●	●	●	●	●	●	●	●	●
ETHIOPIA	●	●	●		●	●	●	●	●	●	●
LIBYA		●	●	●	●			●	●	●	
LIBERIA	●	●	●	●	●			●	●	●	
UNION OF SOUTH AFRICA	●	●	●	●	●	●	●	●	●	●	●
AUSTRALIA	●	●	●	●	●	●	●	●	●	●	●
NEW ZEALAND	●	●	●	●	●			●	●	●	●

The totals for some of the specialized agencies include some members, such as the Vatican City, Monaco, San Marino and possessions of Great Britain, France and other colonial powers, not named in the chart.

In 1954 the USSR joined the International Labor Organization.

to employ international machinery for the promotion of the economic and social advancement of all peoples,

Have resolved to combine our efforts to accomplish these aims.[74]

Chapter I describes the purposes and principles of the UN:

Article 1

The Purposes of the United Nations are:

1. To maintain international peace and security, and to that end: to take effective collective measures for the prevention and removal of threats to the peace, and for the suppression of acts of aggression or other breaches of the peace, and to bring about by peaceful means, and in conformity with the principles of justice and international law, adjustment or settlement of international disputes or situations which might lead to a breach of the peace;

2. To develop friendly relations among nations based on respect for the principle of equal rights and self-determination of peoples, and to take other appropriate measures to strengthen universal peace;

3. To achieve international cooperation in solving international problems of an economic, social, cultural or humanitarian character, and in promoting and encouraging respect for human rights and for fundamental freedoms for all without distinction as to race, sex, language, or religion; and

4. To be a center for harmonizing the actions of nations in the attainment of these common ends.

Article 2

The Organization and its Members, in pursuit of the Purposes stated in Article 1, shall act in accordance with the following Principles.

1. The Organization is based on the principle of the sovereign equality of all its Members.

2. All Members, in order to ensure to all of them the rights and benefits resulting from membership, shall fulfil in good faith the obligations assumed by them in accordance with the present Charter.

3. All Members shall settle their international disputes by peaceful means in such manner that international peace and security, and justice, are not endangered.

4. All Members shall refrain in their international relations from the threat or use of force against the territorial integrity or political independence of any state, or in any other manner inconsistent with the Purposes of the United Nations.

5. All Members shall give the United Nations every assistance in any action it takes in accordance with the present Charter, and shall refrain from giving assistance to any state against which the United Nations is taking preventive or enforcement action.

---

74. See **21, 115** and **116.**

6. The Organization shall ensure that states which are not Members of the United Nations act in accordance with these Principles so far as may be necessary for the maintenance of international peace and security.

7. Nothing contained in the present Charter shall authorize the United Nations to intervene in matters which are essentially within the domestic jurisdiction of any State or shall require the Members to submit such matters to settlement under the present Charter; but this principle shall not prejudice the application of enforcement measures under Chapter VII.

Procedures

The core of the Charter is in Chapter VI, "Pacific Settlement of Disputes" (Articles 33–38), and Chapter VII, "Action with Respect to Threats to the Peace, Breaches of the Peace, and Acts of Aggression" (Articles 39–51). The procedure for settling disputes is similar to that in the Covenant of the League of Nations, but the provisions (Articles 41 and 42) dealing with aggressors go beyond those of the Covenant.

Article 41

The Security Council may decide what measures not involving the use of armed force are to be employed to give effect to its decisions, and it may call upon the Members of the United Nations to apply such measures. These may include complete or partial interruption of economic relations and of rail, sea, air, postal, telegraphic, radio, and other means of communication, and the severance of diplomatic relations.

Article 42

Should the Security Council consider that measures provided for in Article 41 would be inadequate or have proved to be inadequate, it may take such action by air, sea, or land forces as may be necessary to maintain or restore international peace and security. Such action may include demonstrations, blockade, and other operations by air, sea, or land forces of Members of the United Nations.

Article 43

1. All Members of the United Nations, in order to contribute to the maintenance of international peace and security, undertake to make available to the Security Council, on its call and in accordance with a special agreement or agreements, armed forces, assistance, and facilities, including rights of passage, necessary for the purpose of maintaining international peace and security.

2. Such agreement or agreements shall govern the numbers and types of forces, their degree of readi-

ness and general location, and the nature of the facilities and assistance to be provided.

Article 45

In order to enable the United Nations to take urgent military measures, Members shall hold immediately available national air-force contingents for combined international enforcement action. The strength and degree of readiness of these contingents and plans for their combined action shall be determined, within the limits laid down in the special agreement or agreements referred to in Article 43, by the Security Council with the assistance of the Military Staff Committee.

Article 46

Plans for the application of armed force shall be made by the Security Council with the assistance of the Military Staff Committee.

These are the most important parts of the Charter from the viewpoint of international political cooperation. In addition, it provides for international economic and social cooperation, the administration of non-self-governing and trust territories and the establishment of the International Court of Justice. The Charter has been amended by UN agreements with other international bodies — such as the ILO and the FAO — thus bringing together a throng of autonomous specialized agencies.

ORGANIZATION

The principal organs of the UN are the General Assembly, the Security Council, the Economic and Social Council, the Trusteeship Council and the Secretariat. They are supplemented by the International Court of Justice and by the specialized agencies. (See Figure 151.)

Theoretically, the highest authority is the General Assembly. In practice, the organization has two political centers — the General Assembly and the Security Council. The General Assembly has only indirect control over the Security Council, but the latter can exercise effective control over the Assembly — its composition, the scope of questions admitted to discussion, and, particularly important, action taken in fulfilling the principal obligation of the UN: securing peace and preventing war. In fact, all political questions such as admitting new members, settling disputes, safeguarding peace and resisting aggression are under the direct jurisdiction of the Security Council, a provision of decisive importance in view of the differences in the composi-

tion and in the voting procedures in the two bodies.

The General Assembly

The General Assembly is primarily a deliberative, overseeing and reviewing body. It consists of all the members of the UN, each one entitled to as many as five representatives but having only one vote, except for the USSR's three votes.

The General Assembly meets in regular annual sessions and in special sessions if required. It has numerous committees, some of them permanent and with important functions. (See Figure 151.)

The Assembly may discuss any question within the scope of the Charter with one limitation: it may not make recommendations on questions relating to peace that are being dealt with by the Security Council unless the latter so requests. This limitation gives the Council control over the Assembly. Decisions are made in the Assembly by a simple majority, but in political matters a two-thirds majority is required.[75]

The Security Council

The Security Council consists of five permanent members (the United States, Great Britain, the USSR, France and China) and six nonpermanent members elected by the General Assembly for two-year terms. Members of the Council each have one representative and one vote. Decisions are made by affirmative vote of seven members, but, except for procedural matters, the affirmative votes must include those of all five permanent members. Thus, any one of the latter may invalidate an otherwise unanimous decision. This veto power extends to recommendations of the General Assembly and, in certain cases, to the execution of its decisions.[76]

This right of veto of the great powers is somewhat reminiscent of Senator Lodge's "reservations" to the Covenant. It gives the great powers a guarantee that the UN will make no important decisions contrary to their interests. In the first eight years (1946–54) of existence no great power except the USSR had used its veto right in the Council; the USSR had used the veto against the Western world more than a hundred

---

75. For details, see **154.**
76. There is one exception to the veto right of the permanent members: they may not vote on the settlement of a dispute to which they are a party.

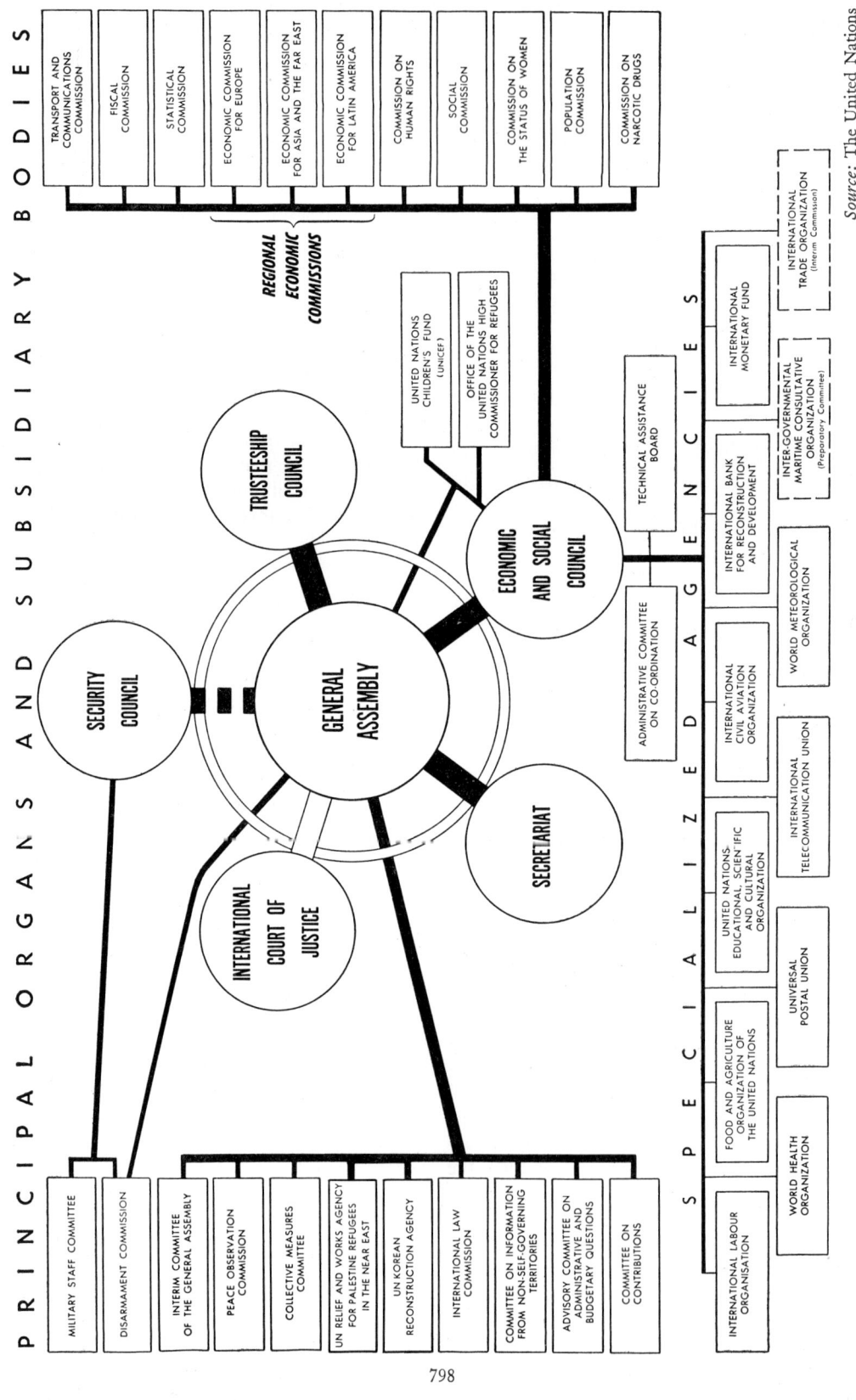

FIGURE 151. THE UNITED NATIONS: PRINCIPAL ORGANS AND SUBSIDIARY BODIES, AS OF DECEMBER 1953

Source: The United Nations

times.[77] The veto principle has thus tremendously strengthened the position of the USSR at the expense of the democratic nations.

The power vested in the Security Council is set forth in the Charter (Chapter V) as follows:

Article 24

1. In order to ensure prompt and effective action by the United Nations, its Members confer on the Security Council primary responsibility for the maintenance of international peace and security, and agree that in carrying out its duties under this responsibility the Security Council acts on their behalf.

2. In discharging these duties the Security Council shall act in accordance with the Purposes and Principles of the United Nations.

The Economic and Social Council

The primary responsibility of this organ is to promote international cooperation in matters of economic and social policy. The Council consists of eighteen members elected by the General Assembly for three-year terms. All decisions are taken by a simple majority of members present and voting.

The functions of the Economic and Social Council are described in Article 62 (Chapter X) of the Charter:

Article 62

1. The Economic and Social Council may make or initiate studies and reports with respect to international economic, social, cultural, educational, health, and related matters and may make recommendations with respect to any such matters to the General Assembly, to the Members of the United Nations, and to the specialized agencies concerned.

2. It may make recommendations for the purpose of promoting respect for, and observance of, human rights and fundamental freedoms for all.

3. It may prepare draft conventions for submission to the General Assembly, with respect to matters falling within its competence.

4. It may call, in accordance with the rules prescribed by the United Nations, international conferences on matters falling within its competence.

The Council coordinates the economic and social activities of the permanent commissions and the specialized agencies of the UN. (See Figure 151.) It has initiated regional economic commissions for Europe, Asia and the Far East and Latin America;[78] numerous technical committees for exploring fundamental problems of economic policy;[79] and it is primarily responsible for the statistical and economic publications of the UN.[80] The Council has also contributed to the resettlement of refugees and displaced persons and has initiated the expanded program of technical assistance of underdeveloped areas.[81]

POLITICAL ACTION BY THE UNITED NATIONS

Unlike the League of Nations, which was barred from any discussion of urgent political questions by the persistence of the great powers in using the old diplomatic channels, the UN has been from its beginning an international forum where world politics have been discussed, and the East-West controversy has been aired. The United States, the United Kingdom and France, despite differences on many important questions, have been determined to shape their foreign policy within the framework of the UN, even when this course has entailed serious limitations on their freedom of action. For the United States, the UN has become the alternative to political isolation; for the free countries of Europe, the common ground on which to meet their powerful American ally; for the less developed countries, the possibility to face the great powers under conditions that approach equality and occasionally to take advantage of their numerical strength in the General Assembly.

All this has made a striking difference between the political climate of the UN and the League. There has been some similarity, however, in the problems faced by the two organizations. Both emerged out of global war and both were dedicated to peace. Like the League, the UN was founded by a victorious coalition which began to disintegrate before peace was established. As with the League, the greatest threat to peace has come from the division within the great powers.

THE WEST AND THE EAST

Since the second half of 1946, discussions in the General Assembly and the Security Council have been dominated by the clash between the

---

77. The exact number of vetoes cannot be ascertained since many proposals have never been put to a vote in the Council because of the USSR representative's declared intention to veto.

78. See **24, 26, 27, 28** and **29**.
79. See, for example, **23, 25, 36, 40**.
80. See especially **22, 35** and **46**.
81. See pp. 806ff.

Western bloc, led by the United States and the United Kingdom, and the USSR, supported by its satellites, Czechoslovakia and Poland.[82] Apart from a few irrelevant questions, mainly on procedure, the two groups have clashed on all political and economic issues. Mutual accusations and counteraccusations have consumed the larger part of the proceedings of the Assembly, the Council, and the various commissions. The Secretary General's annual reports read like blow-by-blow accounts of the struggle between the East and the West.

The UN was destined to become the arena for this battle because world affairs have been dominated, since 1945, by the aggressive moves of the USSR, as they were dominated by the aggressive moves of Nazi Germany in the late 1930's. The political vacuum created westward and eastward of the USSR by the defeat of Germany and Japan, combined with the exhaustion and spontaneous disarmament of the European powers, brought world domination within reach of the Kremlin. The United States was the only power capable of halting the USSR, but it could do so only on the basis of broad international cooperation, and by promoting the rearmament and the economic reconstruction of the free world. Once more the United States had to become the arsenal of democracy. It was able to play this role not only because of its superior economic and financial power but also because of the lead it had gained, during World War II, in developing a new and destructive weapon.

DISARMAMENT

The history of the disarmament issue before the UN epitomizes the source of political tensions since World War II.

The UN has been as unsuccessful in achieving disarmament as the League of Nations, but for different reasons. The League failed because of disagreement between the Western great powers — the United Kingdom, France and Italy. In the UN, on the contrary, the leading Western powers have been ready to accept a universal disarmament plan, including outlawing of atomic weapons, but up to 1955 the USSR has wrecked all such proposals.

One of the first political steps of the UN was to establish the Atomic Energy Commission, consisting of twelve members, eleven of them

members of the Security Council. The Commission, appointed in January 1946, submitted its first report to the Security Council by the end of that year. The report was signed by ten members, the USSR and Poland abstaining. At the request of the Council, the Commission continued its work. The second report was completed in September 1947. Again it recommended the same plan, which again was signed by ten members, and again opposed by the USSR and its satellite.

The core of this lengthy report was summarized in its annex as follows:

An international agreement to outlaw the national production, possession and use of atomic weapons is an essential part of any effective international system of control. But an international treaty to this effect, if standing alone, would fail (a) to ensure the use of atomic energy only for peaceful purposes, and (b) to provide for effective safeguards by way of inspection and other means to protect complying States against the hazards of violation and evasions, . . . To be effective, such agreement must be embodied in a treaty providing for a comprehensive international system of control, and including guarantees and safeguards adequate to ensure the carrying out of the terms of the treaty. . . .

As an integral part of such a comprehensive system of control, the treaty would:

1. Prohibit the manufacture, possession and use of atomic weapons by all nations parties thereto and by all persons under their jurisdiction;

2. Provide for the disposal of any existing stocks of atomic weapons and for the proper use of nuclear fuel adaptable for use in weapons.[83]

The Commission stressed that whether the end product is destined for peaceful or destructive uses, the production processes are identical and inseparable up to an advanced stage of manufacture, since atomic energy once produced, even for peaceful purposes, readily lends itself to the manufacture of atomic weapons. The Commission recommended that the danger of diversion of materials and clandestine operations be met by internationalization of the production of atomic energy. An international control agency established by treaty would own, operate and manage all chemical and metallurgical plants for treating uranium and thorium ores and all facilities capable of producing nuclear fuel, including isotope-separation plants and primary and secondary reactors. It would also own all nuclear

---

82. The Soviet bloc in the UN includes the two satellites and the USSR with its three votes.

83. **53,** 1947–48, p. 465. The Commission's recommendations are essentially the same as those submitted by the U.S. government and known as the Baruch Plan.

fuel produced in the world. In brief, the Commission offered a plan of complete atomic disarmament on the basis of close international cooperation in the production of atomic energy.

From the outset of the Atomic Energy Commission's deliberations, the USSR opposed the recommendations embodied in the two Commission reports. In June 1946 the Russians offered their own program: prohibition of production, storage and use of atomic weapons; destruction of all stocks of such weapons whether in a finished or unfinished condition; and granting to each nation freedom to produce atomic energy — even adaptable for use in weapons — without any international control except such measures as would be established subsequently by separate conventions within the framework of the Security Council. The last qualification implied that all subsequent control measures would be subject to veto by any great power which found them undesirable. The Commission rejected the USSR plan by a majority vote of ten.

In June 1947 the USSR submitted to the Atomic Energy Commission a more elaborate plan which would establish a commission responsible to the Security Council with the right to periodic inspection of atomic plants in all countries engaged in such production. This plan was rejected by the Atomic Energy Commission, and in its third report to the Council (May 1948) it acknowledged that an "impasse" had been reached.[84] The impasse was caused by the unwillingness of the USSR to accept effective international control over its production of atomic energy and, eventually, atomic weapons, and by the unwillingness of the United States to destroy its stockpiles of atomic weapons without an effective guarantee against the production and use of such weapons by the USSR.

In November 1948 the General Assembly adopted a resolution (by a vote of 40 in favor, 6 nays, and 5 abstentions) approving the findings and general recommendations of the Commission and requesting it to continue its work.[85] Discussion in the Commission continued until January 1950, when the USSR demanded the exclusion of the representative of the Chinese Nationalist government. When this was rejected, the USSR withdrew from the Commission.[86] This brought to a halt the attempts to achieve

atomic disarmament on the basis of worldwide internationalization of the production of atomic energy.

Officially, the Kremlin objected to this plan on the principle of sovereignty, but its insistence on the prohibition of atomic weapons *without* safeguards against their future production made the Western powers suspicious. It would seem that the real purpose of the Russian proposals was to gain time for stockpiling atomic resources which could be transformed into weapons on short notice. If carried out, this plan would have given the Kremlin a monopoly of atomic armament and absolute military supremacy, at least for the limited period of time needed to destroy the military and industrial forces of the free nations.

There is, of course, no evidence that such were the intentions of the Kremlin, but the records of the UN show, beyond any possible doubt, that in June 1946 the USSR submitted a plan which could have had these results; that this plan has been the main objective of the USSR in the UN; that it has fought relentlessly for this plan, supporting it by "peace offensives"; and that until 1955 it made no concessions in either of the two main points of the plan: immediate and complete atomic disarmament of complying nations and unlimited potentialities of Russian atomic rearmament. Unable to impose this plan upon the UN, the USSR succeeded in defeating the plan of the Atomic Energy Commission: its program could not be carried out against the opposition of the USSR, which has made the free world believe that its goal is to obtain supremacy — and, if possible, monopoly — in atomic weapons.

The failure of a workable plan for atomic disarmament made any discussion of the limitation of conventional arms fruitless. In January 1952, the General Assembly dissolved the Atomic Energy Commission and the Commission for Conventional Armaments. The two commissions were replaced by a Disarmament Commission under the Security Council.[87] The new commission has been unable to break the deadlock caused by the insistence of the USSR that atomic warfare be outlawed and stockpiles of atomic weapons destroyed by the Western nations without prejudice to the production and stockpiling of such weapons behind the Iron Curtain. The Soviet bloc reworded its proposals but remained

84. **53**, 1947–48, p. 471.
85. **53**, 1948–49, p. 351.
86. **53**, 1950, p. 416.

87. **53**, 1951, p. 177.

opposed to international controls.[88] In May 1955 the Kremlin announced a change in its policy. It accepted the principles of gradual reduction in all types of arms, general limitation of armaments and international control over production of atomic energy. This has made possible the reopening of disarmament negotiations (in a preliminary phase when this book was printed).

SETTLEMENT OF DISPUTES

The most important — or, perhaps, most typical — political questions and disputes brought before the UN in the years 1947–53 were the Iranian question; guerrilla warfare in Greece; the Indonesian question; disputes between India and Pakistan; the racial problem in South Africa; the problem of Palestine; and the Korean war.

The Iranian Question

In January 1946 the Iranian government addressed a letter to the Secretary General of the UN protesting the presence of Russian armed forces in Iran and their interference in the domestic affairs of the country. Under the threat of an investigation, the troops were evacuated.

The Greek Question

In 1946 a commission was sent to investigate Greek complaints about the support given by Yugoslavia, Albania and Bulgaria to guerrilla activities in Greece. The commission's report (signed by eight members) recognized the validity of the Greek complaint. In October 1947, the General Assembly, opposed by the Soviet bloc, adopted a resolution declaring that Albania, Bulgaria and Yugoslavia had aided the guerrillas and called on them to refrain from such actions. In July 1949, the UN Commission on the Balkans found that not only Albania and Bulgaria had continued to support the guerrillas in Greece but that such support was also coming from "certain states not bordering upon Greece."

The Greek question assumed the proportions of a major international conflict. The USSR accused the United States of occupying Greece and preparing an invasion of other Balkan countries. In December 1949, the General Assembly adopted a resolution condemning the actions of Bulgaria, Albania and Romania and called for the economic support of Greece.

The technical, financial and economic assistance given to Greece by the United States in conformity with UN policy saved Greek independence and halted Communist aggression at the nation's borders.

The Indonesian Question

In August 1947, the Security Council adopted a resolution calling on the Netherlands and Indonesia to cease hostilities and submit their dispute to arbitration. The Council arranged a truce but was unable to bring the parties to agreement on political issues. In December 1948, the government of the Netherlands resumed military action against the Indonesian Republic and arrested its president and members of the government. The UN demanded that the Netherlands cease hostilities and release prisoners and offered its good offices as mediator of the conflict. The dispute was settled (1949) in accordance with the recommendations of the UN at a round-table conference at The Hague. The Netherlands has recognized, without reservations, the sovereignty of the United States of Indonesia.

Disputes between India and Pakistan

Partition of the Indian subcontinent left bitter feelings between the Hindus and Moslems. Religious and racial friction was aggravated by territorial disputes between the two nations.

In January 1948 India called the attention of the Security Council to the threat of war between India and Pakistan, as a result of disputes over Kashmir. The Council was able to prevent large-scale hostilities but could not persuade the two countries to negotiate their differences.[89]

The problem of Hyderabad arose from Indian military action against this predominantly Hindu principality, which was supported by Pakistan. The UN did little more than exhort both sides to moderate their actions. Ultimately the dispute was settled in accordance with the views of the Indian government.

The Racial Problem in South Africa

In 1946 India accused the Union of South Africa of discrimination against persons of Indian descent residing in the Union. Overruling the objections of the Union of South Africa, the General Assembly asked both governments to present their case to its next session.

---

88. **53**, 1952, pp. 312–23; 1953, pp. 258–69.

89. See **53**, 1952, pp. 232–41.

The Assembly referred the question to one of the permanent committees, where the discussion centered on the problem of competence. The committee rejected the resolution proposed by the South African representative, who asserted that the question was wholly domestic. The Indian resolution requesting an investigation was adopted. The Assembly limited itself to inviting both parties to a round-table conference (May 1949), which produced no tangible results. The measures against Indians were part of the nationalist policy of the Union and the UN found itself powerless against the country's campaign for "white supremacy."

The Problem of Palestine

During 1948 and 1949 the UN mediated between Israel, on the one side, and Egypt, Lebanon, Jordan and Syria, on the other. Its intervention was not wholly successful. An armistice was concluded and Israel's borders were defined. The armistice left uncertain the resettlement of Arab refugees and the disposition of their land and other property which had been taken over by Israel. The return of refugees to their villages and the restoration of their property are considered by the Arab states to be the fundamental conditions of peace. Since Israel rejected these claims no peace negotiations were held.

The Arab countries have remained, technically, in a state of war with Israel and have not recognized its independence. At the same time, Israel has maintained its claim to Jerusalem.

Unable to bring the two sides closer together, the UN has limited itself to assisting Arab refugees and to general supervision of the armistice between Israel and its neighbors.[90] Despite all efforts border skirmishes — such as the Kibya incident of November 1953 — have continued. The stand taken by the UN has satisfied neither party in the dispute. Israel has charged that the UN's commission was biased in favor of the Arab group of states, while the Arab countries have accused it of a pro-Israel bias.

THE KOREAN WAR

Since the end of World War II no event has been of greater significance than the Korean war. It has become a milestone in the history of the UN, demonstrating both the possibilities of international action in securing peace and the limitations of such actions.

World War II left Korea divided by an arbitrary line (latitude 38° N) cutting it in two without regard to cultural or economic conditions. The line had been drawn originally following the expulsion of the Japanese as a demarcation between the areas under the military control of the United States and the USSR. As long as the two powers acted in concert in Korea, the line was irrelevant. The split between the USSR and the Western powers transformed the 38th parallel into a frontier on which the East and the West came into armed conflict.

On November 14, 1947 the General Assembly appointed a temporary commission on Korea to facilitate the unification of the country under a national government based on free nationwide elections. The Russian military command did not permit the commission to proceed north of the 38th parallel, but on May 10, 1948 the people of South Korea had an opportunity to elect their representatives freely. In December of the same year, the UN replaced the temporary commission with a new commission which was to seek the unification of Korea and its economic integration under a freely elected government and to observe the actual withdrawal of the occupying forces. The USSR denied this commission entrance to North Korea, but the commission observed, and reported to the UN, the evacuation of United States forces from South Korea. Then on June 24, 1950, North Korean forces crossed the 38th parallel at several points and invaded South Korea.

At the request of the United States, the Security Council met to deal with the aggression in Korea. The USSR was absent; its representative had withdrawn on January 13, 1950, declining to participate in the Council's work while the representative of the Nationalist government of China remained.[91] On June 25 the Council called on North Korea to withdraw its troops to the 38th parallel; on June 27 a second resolution was adopted, which read as follows:

The Security Council,

Having determined that the armed attack on the Republic of Korea by forces from North Korea constitutes a breach of the peace,

Having called for an immediate cessation of hostilities, and

Having called upon the authorities of North Korea

---

90. **53**, 1952, pp. 241–62.

91. The USSR returned to the Council on August 1, 1950, when the presidency of the Council devolved upon its representative, according to the rule of monthly rotation.

to withdraw forthwith their armed forces to the 38th parallel, and

Having noted from the report of the United Nations Commission for Korea that the authorities in North Korea have neither ceased hostilities nor withdrawn their armed forces to the 38th parallel and that urgent military measures are required to restore international peace and security, and

Having noted the appeal from the Republic of Korea to the United Nations for immediate and effective steps to secure peace and security,

Recommends that the Members of the United Nations furnish such assistance to the Republic of Korea as may be necessary to repel the armed attack and to restore international peace and security in the area.[92]

This resolution inaugurated an unprecedented international armed operation in defense of peace.

The USSR declared the resolution illegal on the ground that it was taken in the absence of its representative and that the Chinese representative of the Nationalist government had no authority to speak for that country. In the free world, however, the decision of the UN caused a wave of enthusiasm: thirty-nine member states, one nonmember state and nine international organizations joined the United States in offering troops, ships, planes, medical personnel and supplies, foodstuffs and other materials in support of the UN action. Some were modest contributions: Liberia offered 10 tons of natural rubber; Nicaragua, 150 tons of rice and 5,000 quarts of alcohol; Iceland, 125 tons of cod-liver oil; Paraguay and Israel, medical supplies. But troops, ships and planes were sent to Korea by fifteen nations: the United Kingdom, France, Belgium, the Netherlands and Greece; the United States, Canada and Colombia; the Philippines, Thailand and Turkey; Ethiopia and the Union of South Africa; Australia and New Zealand. Volunteers came from a few of the smaller nations.[93]

On July 7, 1950, the Security Council asked the United States to designate the commander of the UN military forces in Korea and authorized the unified command to use the UN flag.

North Korea held all the initial advantages of preparedness and surprise. The South Korean army was crushed, and UN reinforcements were pushed southward until, by the middle of July, only the southeastern corner of the peninsula and the adjacent islands remained uninvaded. In September, after having built up the necessary

strength, the UN command opened a counteroffensive and in two weeks had reoccupied almost all the South Korean territory. In October a second amphibious maneuver was launched. In November overwhelming numbers of Chinese "volunteers" joined the armies of the North. Again the UN forces were pushed south of the 38th parallel. Early in 1951 the UN opened a new offensive, but was halted just north of the original demarcation line by truce negotiations begun on the initiative of the USSR. After a year of active and mobile warfare, with heavy losses on both sides, a stalemate in the negotiations developed which was to last for two years, largely caused by the dispute over repatriation of war prisoners.

During all this time, the fighting in Korea continued as a UN action against North Korean aggression, supported by Chinese "volunteers." Actually, however, the North Korean army had ceased to exist. The reconstituted South Korean army and the United States forces, supported by smaller units from other nations, were facing Russian-equipped Chinese troops. The original cause of the conflict was overshadowed by its larger political significance: a Kremlin-inspired offensive — carried out by its Chinese ally — against South Korea as the advance United States post in the Pacific and guarding other bases there — Japan, the Philippines and the Pacific Islands.

The UN attitude toward the Korean war was beginning to change. The enthusiasm of the summer of 1950 faded away. UN members were becoming increasingly apprehensive over the Far Eastern military actions under the UN flag. They wanted the war limited to operations that would not provoke direct interference by the USSR. Devotion to the Charter was increasingly tempered by considerations of real policy.

An armistice between the UN command and North Korea and China was concluded on July 27, 1953. It fell far short of South Korean hopes of unification under a freely elected government, but it did provide for a demarcation line running somewhat north of the 38th parallel. In general, the armistice accepted the UN principles in regard to the repatriation of war prisoners. The Communist demand for the forced repatriation of war prisoners held by the Allies was denied, but both sides were given opportunity to interview war prisoners who declined to return to the country of their origin. A cumbersome machinery for screening, interviewing and per-

---

92. **53**, 1950, pp. 222–24.
93. **53**, 1950, pp. 226–28.

suading prisoners was established and the exchange was handled in the following manner.

The UN held more than 110,000 prisoners. During the truce negotiations, in June 1953, the South Korean government freed 27,000. Of those remaining in custody, 23,000 rejected repatriation and were transferred to a Neutral Repatriation Commission. However, only 2,014 persons were subjected to Communist "explanations" and only 137 of these decided to be repatriated. Finally, 1,000 changed their minds and decided to return to their homes in Communist-dominated areas. In all, the United Nations Command has returned to Communist control 61,415 prisoners.

The Communists announced that they held 13,000 prisoners, all of whom, except 200 South Koreans, 20 Americans and one Briton, were repatriated.

Preliminary negotiations for the arrangement of a peace conference were begun in November 1953. The peace had not been concluded by the middle of 1955 when these pages went to press.

The number of casualties in the Korean war was very high in relation to the limited scope of military operations. The number of killed, wounded and missing on the side of South Korea and the United Nations was more than 450,000 (141,000 from the United States, 14,000 from the other allied countries and the rest South Koreans). The North Korean and Chinese casualties have been estimated at 1,500,000 to 2,000,000.

ECONOMIC ACTION OF THE UNITED NATIONS

The international cooperation begun by the League of Nations in economic and financial fields has been continued, on a broader scale, by economic and regional commissions and by the specialized agencies of the UN, with the Economic and Social Council and the Secretariat acting as planning and coordinating organs. (See Figure 151.)

The UN has ten specialized agencies and eleven economic and regional commissions. The specialized agencies include the International Labor Organization (ILO, Geneva); the Food and Agriculture Organization (FAO, Rome); the Educational, Scientific and Cultural Organization (UNESCO, Paris); the International Civil Aviation Organization (ICAO, Montreal); the International Bank for Reconstruction and Development (IBRD, Washington); the Interna-

tional Monetary Fund (IMF, Washington); the World Health Organization (WHO, Geneva); the Universal Postal Union (UPU, Berne); the International Telecommunication Union (ITU, Geneva); and the World Meteorological Organization (WMO, Lausanne).

Regional commissions have been established for Europe, Latin America, and Asia and the Far East. Other permanent commissions handle such subjects as population; human rights; social problems; the status of women; fiscal policy; transport and communication; narcotics; and statistics.

The following observations are not intended to give a complete picture of the activities of all these organizations. Only the work of five principal specialized agencies is discussed in any detail.

INTERNATIONAL COOPERATION

Close cooperation has been established between the UN and the International Meteorological Organization, one of the oldest international associations in the world.[94] International conferences have been called on problems of road and air transport. A convention on road traffic has been accepted by interested governments. A campaign to standardize road signs and signals has been launched.[95] International conferences have been held for the coordination of railway transport. The UN has taken the initiative in developing international conventions on air transport.[96]

The Economic and Social Council and the specialized agencies are also continuing the work of the League in developing integrated and uniform international statistics. They compile and disseminate international statistics of population and try to improve their comparability.[97] They have initiated the unification of foreign trade statistics and promoted development of national income statistics.[98] The extent of their work in the field of international statistics is revealed by the steadily expanding scope of subjects covered in current statistical publications of the UN.[99]

The UN publications on economic development in the world and its major areas are based on the cooperation of the statistical agencies of the respective countries and contribute to better

94. **52,** April–June 1950.
95. **52,** July–September 1951.
96. Cf. Chapter 11.
97. See **22, 35, 32, 34, 38** and **39.**
98. See **45, 19, 47.**
99. See **22, 35** and **46**; cf. **20.**

understanding among governments.[100] UN special reports on matters of economic policy, such as the development of natural resources, measures in support of full employment, taxation, trade, banking and money are other examples of international scientific cooperation.[101] The Scientific Conference on the Conservation and Utilization of Resources, which met in New York in 1949,[102] was a noteworthy event in international exchange of ideas on urgent economic problems.

TECHNICAL ASSISTANCE TO UNDERDEVELOPED AREAS

The UN has given particular attention to cooperation between industrially developed and underdeveloped areas.[103] The objective of such cooperation was trenchantly stated in the annual report of the Secretary-General:

The gap between the most and the least developed countries is one of the most significant and alarming aspects of our contemporary society; and, in spite of the growing interdependence of the world, it has tended to become progressively wider in recent decades, for the more advanced countries, by very reason of their progress, have an important advantage over the retarded ones. Their higher levels of output and better economic organization make it easier to accumulate capital for further development and to direct it into productive channels. The existence of highly developed and differentiated industry and agriculture automatically provides the best kind of training facilities for managers, technicians and skilled workers and each technological advance helps to stimulate further inventions, by creating new demands and suggesting new solutions to technical problems. The under-developed areas thus tend to fall farther and farther behind, and they are likely to continue to do so unless deliberate and effective measures are taken to bring to them the benefits of modern science and technology.

The report stressed the political implications of the problem:

It has become clear that the wide gap between unprecedented wealth in a few countries and grinding poverty in most of the others constitutes a basic source of economic and social instability in the world. The narrowing of this economic gap, by accelerating development in the less advanced areas, is thus an imperative and urgent task from the standpoint of the more and the less developed countries alike.

---

100. See **24** through **29, 41, 48** and **49.**
101. See **36, 40, 44.**
102. See **42.**
103. See **120, 50, 43, 30, 31, 33.** Cf. publications mentioned above.

The rate of economic development must be fast enough not only to keep up with population growth, but to exceed it by a substantial margin. For a little development may sometimes be a dangerous thing, if it provides only a temporary palliative for starvation and misery without bringing about a continuing, balanced rise in welfare and productivity. Such limited, partial development may serve in the long run, as it has in the past, only to increase social tensions and permit a more reckless waste of both human and natural resources.

A response to this challenge has come in the technical assistance provided by the industrially developed nations for the less developed areas.

The idea was not new even when it was announced by President Truman in his inaugural address in January 1949 as "a bold new program for making the benefits of our scientific advances and industrial progress available for the improvement and growth of underdeveloped areas." The President went on to say:

I believe that we should make available to peace-loving peoples the benefits of our store of technical knowledge in order to help them realize their aspirations for a better life. And, in cooperation with other nations, we should foster capital investment in areas needing development.

Our aim should be to help the free peoples of the world, through their own efforts, to produce more food, more clothing, more materials for housing, and more mechanical power to lighten their burdens.

We invite other countries to pool their technological resources in this undertaking. Their contributions will be warmly welcomed. This should be a cooperative enterprise in which all nations work together through the United Nations and its specialized agencies wherever practicable. It must be a world-wide effort for the achievement of peace, plenty, and freedom.

"The bold new program" — better known in the United States as "Point Four" — has called into existence the expanded technical assistance program of the UN. The report of the Secretary-General developed its leading principle as follows:

The under-developed countries may profitably draw upon the experience of countries with a longer history of development in fields of economic and social policy, financial measures and administrative methods as well as in the more limited sphere of production. But it will not be enough simply to apply in a new environment the techniques evolved from such experience. Under-developed countries differ widely in their climate, resources, population, and history — both among themselves and in relation to the more advanced countries — and for each the first step in development must be a realistic appraisal of its special conditions and needs. The basic aim of outside technical assistance to underdeveloped countries must be to help themselves, and to diminish their dependence on external aid.

This program is carried out by the UN Technical Assistance Administration in cooperation with the specialized agencies and the governments and peoples of underdeveloped countries. It is not intended to replace foreign investment and domestic capital formation as a means of developing local resources but is designed to create conditions favorable for investment. Sometimes technical and financial assistance go hand in hand, as in the operations of the International Bank for Reconstruction and Development.[104]

Close to seventy states have participated in this technical assistance, which is financed by a special fund subscribed by both member and nonmember nations of the UN. The largest part of the fund has been provided by the United States (60.5 per cent in 1950–51, 62 per cent in 1952, 60 per cent in 1953). Modest contributions have been made by even the smallest and poorest nations, such as Liberia, Libya and Yemen, but there has been a conspicuous absence of contributions from the Soviet-bloc countries. (See Table 280.)

The annual budget of the program amounts to approximately $20 million. In 1952 the funds were distributed as follows: FAO, 29 per cent; WHO, 22 per cent; UNESCO, 14 per cent; ILO, 11 per cent; ICAO, 1 per cent; the remaining 23 per cent was under direct control of the United Nations.[105]

Between July 1950 and October 1952, 1,600 experts were sent, either singly or in teams, to some 65 countries requesting technical assistance. During the same period about 2,700 fellowships and scholarships were awarded. In 1953, 495 experts, recruited from 50 countries, worked in 55 countries.[106]

The idea of international technical assistance has gained great popularity all over the world. The United States program of Technical Cooperation (Point Four) is similar to the expanded technical assistance program of the UN, but on a much larger scale. Four international regional

organizations have been established for the same purpose:

1. The Organization of American States (OAS) specializes in projects which promise to benefit several American nations rather than one individual country. The United States provides 70 per cent of the necessary funds and the rest is allocated among the other member states.

2. The Caribbean Commission, composed of the governments of France, the Netherlands, the United Kingdom and the United States, provides technical assistance, on a comparatively modest scale, in the Caribbean region.

3. The South Pacific Commission carries on a score of projects in the fields of health and economic and social development in that area.

4. The British Commonwealth Plan, supported by the United Kingdom, Canada, India, Pakistan, Ceylon, Australia and New Zealand, envisages outlays of up to £8 million ($19.2 million) within the Commonwealth over a three-year period.

Similar operations are performed under the program of Cooperative Economic Development in Southeast Asia (Colombo Plan).

The total contribution of the United States to international technical assistance plans and its own Point Four program ran to nearly $170 million in 1953.[107]

Largely under the impetus of the willingness of industrial countries to share their technical resources with underdeveloped areas, development plans are mushrooming in the Middle and Far East and in Africa. Some of the plans are geared to obtaining grants and loans that have a remote chance of repayment, but most of them represent serious efforts of local leaders to put an end to illiteracy, devastating diseases, premature death, hunger and poverty.[108]

SPECIALIZED AGENCIES OF THE UNITED NATIONS

The activities of the UN specialized agencies are outlined on the following pages from the viewpoint of their contributions to international cooperation. For details, see the *Yearbook of the United Nations* and reports of the agencies.[109]

---

104. See pp. 813ff.
105. **51,** p. 4.
106. **72,** 1952, p. 360; **53,** 1953, p. 316.

107. $12.8 million for the UN's expanded Technical Assistance program and $155.6 million for the TCA program (see pp. 808 and 848).
108. For a brief survey of development plans see **150,** pp. 51–82.
109. See **72, 73, 77, 83, 96, 105** and **106.**

TABLE 280

UN Expanded Technical Assistance Program: Pledges and Payments, 1950–51 to 1953

(*Thousands of Dollars*)

Country	1950–51		1952		1953
	Pledges	*Payments*	*Pledges*	*Payments*	*Pledges*
Total	$20,070	$19,822	$18,796	$17,310	$22,396
United States	12,008	12,008	11,400	10,750	12,767
Canada	773	773	750	750	800
Mexico	35	—	35	35	35
Guatemala	5	—	8	—	8
El Salvador	5	5	5	5	6
Honduras	8	8	8	8	10
Nicaragua	—	—	5	5	5
Costa Rica	5	5	5	5	5
Panama	—	—	3	—	3
Cuba	50	50	50	—	50
Haiti	6	6	12	12	12
Dominican Republic	—	—	6	6	10
Venezuela	44	4	20	—	25
Colombia	51	51	100	100	100
Ecuador	6	6	0	6	6
Brazil	459	459	459	—	459
Peru	—	—	—	—	10
Bolivia	13	—	13	—	25
Paraguay	—	—	5	—	5
Chile	90	90	174	174	209
Uruguay	99	—	50	—	75
Argentina	200	200	200	200	200
United Kingdom	2,128	2,128	1,260	1,260	1,400
Ireland	14	14	14	14	—
France	1,208	1,208	1,065	1,065	1,208
Luxembourg	3	3	3	3	3
Belgium	270	270	270	276	284
Netherlands	400	400	400	400	421
Denmark	96	96	109	109	434
Sweden	97	97	357	357	387
Norway	35	35	56	56	70
Finland	5	5	10	10	10
Germany	—	—	119	71	149
Poland	—	—	—	—	15
Switzerland	234	234	219	219	233

(*Continued on facing page*)

THE FOOD AND AGRICULTURE ORGANIZATION

Origin and Constitution

Plans for the Food and Agriculture Organization were laid at a United Nations conference at Hot Springs in May 1943, and its constitution was formally adopted in October 1945, at Quebec, when it took over and greatly enlarged the functions of the League's Mixed Committee on the Problem of Nutrition [110] and the Inter-national Institute of Agriculture in Rome (liquidated in January 1948). The purposes of the FAO are stated in the Preamble of its constitution as follows:

raising levels of nutrition and standards of living of the peoples . . . securing improvements in the efficiency of the production and distribution of all food and agricultural products,
bettering the condition of rural populations, and thus contributing toward an expanding world economy.

110. See **7** and **11**.

TABLE 280—*continued*

| Country | 1950–51 | | 1952 | | 1953 |
	Pledges	*Payments*	*Pledges*	*Payments*	*Pledges*
Austria	$ 19	$ 19	$ 19	$ 7	$ 19
Italy	93	88	93	—	93
Yugoslavia	50	50	50	50	63
Greece	20	20	20	20	20
Iceland	—	—	3	3	3
Monaco	3	3	3	3	1
USSR	—	—	—	—	1,000
China	10	10	10	10	10
Korea	5	5	5	—	3
Japan	—	—	80	80	80
Turkey	184	184	182	182	184
Lebanon	7	7	7	—	7
Israel	28	28	28	28	40
Syria	11	—	11	—	11
Saudi Arabia	—	—	15	15	15
Yemen	4	4	—	—	2
Iraq	5	5	5	—	11
Iran	40	—	40	40	40
Afghanistan	7	7	7	7	10
Pakistan	140	140	151	151	166
India	250	250	275	275	275
Burma	8	8	8	8	12
Thailand	20	20	34	34	40
Cambodia	—	—	5	5	5
Laos	—	—	5	—	5
Viet-Nam	—	—	8	8	8
Ceylon	15	15	15	15	15
Indonesia	122	122	44	44	64
Philippines	50	50	50	25	50
Libya	—	—	—	—	3
Egypt	82	82	82	82	86
Ethiopia	20	20	20	—	20
Liberia	8	8	12	12	12
Australia	200	200	200	200	400
New Zealand	124	124	124	126	126

Sources: 112, p. 109; for 1953, **53,** 1953, pp. 313–14. These figures represent contributions to the UN technical assistance special account, from which allocations to the participating agencies are made. They do not include contributions made by recipient governments to the cost of projects carried out in their own countries in local currency or goods and services. These local contributions are estimated to be approximately equal to the cost borne by the participating agencies financed from the special account.

The functions of the FAO are outlined in Article 1:

1. The Organization shall collect, analyse, interpret, and disseminate information relating to nutrition, food and agriculture.

2. The Organization shall promote and, where appropriate, shall recommend national and international action with respect to

(*a*) scientific, technological, social and economic research relating to nutrition, food and agriculture;

(*b*) the improvement of education and administration relating to nutrition, food and agriculture, and the spread of public knowledge of nutritional and agricultural science and practice;

(*c*) the conservation of natural resources and the adoption of improved methods of agricultural production;

(*d*) the improvement of the processing, marketing, and distribution of food and agricultural products;

(*e*) the adoption of policies for the provision of adequate agricultural credit, national and international;

(*f*) the adoption of international policies with respect to agricultural commodity arrangements.

3. It shall also be the function of the Organization

(*a*) to furnish such technical assistance as governments may request;

(*b*) to organize, in cooperation with the governments concerned, such missions as may be needed to assist them to fulfil the obligations arising from their acceptance of the recommendations of the United Nations Conference on Food and Agriculture; and

(*c*) generally to take all necessary and appropriate action to implement the purposes of the Organization as set forth in the Preamble.

Section 3 has become the cornerstone of the expanded technical assistance program of the United Nations.

Operations

The educational activities of the FAO include not only dissemination of agricultural knowledge but also the practical training of technical personnel in underdeveloped areas, coordination of governmental efforts directed toward raising agricultural output by improved methods of farming, and operation of special programs wherever and whenever the need arises.

The FAO called an international conference on cereals in 1947 and established a special international Rice Commission in 1949. Under a hybrid-maize program it shipped seed to some twenty countries. To stimulate production and utilization of fishery products, it organized Fisheries Councils for the Indo-Pacific and the Mediterranean areas. In 1947, it called a timber conference and established regional forest-products commissions for Europe, Latin America, Asia and the Pacific. It is estimated that European countries, following recommendations of the timber conference, have increased their timber output 19 per cent.

International conferences on locust control were held in Karachi (1949) and New Delhi (1950), and a Committee of Coordination of Locust Control was established in Central America and Mexico. A special agency has been established for control of the desert locust. An international conference was held in Lucknow to discuss ways of increasing livestock production in the tropics and subtropics. Mass immunization of cattle against rinderpest was started in Hong Kong, Thailand and Ethiopia in 1949–50. In 1951 the FAO submitted to twenty-four govern-

ments the draft of a plant protection convention which would provide for a worldwide reporting service on plant diseases and insect pests and for more effective plant quarantine measures. Twelve FAO–WHO centers have been set up throughout the world for research on brucellosis, an animal disease transmissible to human beings. A conference on land-use practices in underdeveloped countries in the tropics was held in Ceylon. An important meeting was held in London on the organization of agricultural work in Europe.

Arrangements were made for fishery training seminars in Indonesia, Thailand, and Latin America. Special studies have been made of fishery technology, and suggestions for improvements in the design of fishing boats were offered to Canada, Newfoundland, Ireland and several countries in the Far East. In 1951 direct technical assistance was given to Haiti and Thailand (on fish-culture methods); to Pakistan (on the construction of a fishery harbor); to Chile (on expansion of fish consumption); to Ecuador (on locating new fish resources); and to Libya (on development of sponge fisheries).

Forestry experts of the FAO have worked on problems of tree pests, the improvement of forest seed, and fire prevention. An interesting case of the West following the East was the FAO decision to endorse the proposal of India for a world festival of the trees, designed to arouse consciousness of the aesthetic, physical and economic value of trees.[111]

The FAO has achieved considerable success in coordinating agricultural statistics and in bringing together information on agricultural production from all parts of the world, except the area behind the Iron Curtain. In addition to a monthly bulletin, it publishes yearbooks covering the whole scope of its activities, two quarterly reviews of forestry and a bimonthly bulletin on fisheries.[112]

The Expanded Technical Assistance Program

At the end of 1951, FAO experts from thirty-eight countries were working under the UN's expanded program of technical assistance in thirty-five countries, principally on questions of land and water development, crop improvement, control of animal diseases, nutrition, agricultural

---

111. See **77**, 1952.
112. See, respectively, **76**; **80, 81, 82**; **78, 79: 74**.

economics, the conservation and management of forests, and the development of fisheries.[113]

Technical assistance projects of this type have the greatest appeal to peoples and governments in underdeveloped areas because they promise the quickest returns. The Secretary-General of the UN has said:

Agricultural production can undoubtedly be substantially increased. Many means of doing so are known and hundreds of examples could be given of how the requisite knowledge could be applied. In many cases, relatively simple improvements in methods of husbandry, the provision of more effective tools and small-scale implements would bring about important changes. The use of better seed and of fertilizers would have immediate results. It is conservatively estimated, for example, that yields in the rice-producing countries could be increased by 10 per cent if the best varieties were generally utilized, while the introduction of hybrid varieties of corn (maize) can add 20 or 30 per cent to the crops. Similarly, it is estimated that livestock production on a world scale could be increased by 25 per cent in ten years through selective breeding. The control of animal diseases, and better feeding could have similar results: rinderpest, the major livestock disease in Africa and Asia, which accounts for the loss of 2 million cattle annually, can now be eradicated by the use of vaccines; grass and other forms of forage are among the most important of crops and are frequently the most neglected. Technical assistance in these fields can readily be made available.

Apart from production as such, substantial increases could be made in the quantity and quality of agricultural and forestry products by the prevention of losses and the better utilization of available resources. Among many examples the following are cited. The present annual loss of stored grains and edible legumes throughout the world is estimated at 30 million tons a year or 10 per cent of the total world crop, a quantity sufficient to feed 150 million persons. These losses, caused by insects, rodents and fungi, can be vastly reduced by known methods of controlling infestation and by the provision of more and better storage, especially in tropical and subtropical areas.

The application of modern techniques to the processing and the handling of agricultural, fishery and forest products would result in a substantial increase, both in efficiency of production and in output. Shortages of essential foodstuffs could be overcome. The yields of marketable products could be increased. Waste products could be utilized and the nutritional value of foodstuffs improved. Thus, improvements in sea fishing and pond culture would greatly augment the supply of high-quality protein.

Fish liver oils, rich in vitamin A, now wasted, would make a badly needed improvement in diet in many areas. Improvement in the nutritive value of cereals, particularly rice, as consumed, could be brought about by improved milling practices. Examples of this nature could be multiplied many times.

"Progress of a fundamental nature"[114] was reported by the Director-General for the first time in the annual report of the FAO for 1951–52. This had been achieved through the work of the FAO experts and the native technicians whom they had trained in fifty-one countries. (See Figure 152.) The FAO could point to the worldwide coverage of its work: a foundation had been laid for the sugar industry in Ceylon and El Salvador; cotton had been introduced in Haiti, Venezuela and Ethiopia; fisheries had been improved in Brazil, Ecuador, Finland, Liberia, Somaliland; forestry improvement was under way in Guatemala, Chile, Iran, Burma and Indonesia.[115] The fight against plant and animal disease conducted by the FAO in a score of countries was showing results.

In March 1953 the FAO took inventory of its field workers and found that nearly 800 expert technicians had finished their work, were at work or had been requested under FAO's current technical assistance program. They came from 51 countries at last count, and they work in every region of the world.

In Afghanistan a Chinese silk man was at work, as well as a Swiss expert on small tools, and a Swedish expert in seeds. At work in Brazil were a Dutchman, an Australian, and a Frenchman. In Burma, under FAO auspices, were an Austrian and a Japanese. The mission chief in Ceylon was Canadian; working with him were a Dutchman, a Finn, a Jordanese, and a South African. There was a Dane in Chile, a Czech in Ecuador, an Italian in Honduras.

Working in Ethiopia were a Canadian, a Chilean, a Belgian, an Australian, a Peruvian, a Haitian, and a Swiss. In Haiti, an Israeli and a Chinese taught pond-fish culture. A Yugoslav statistician was helping Indonesians. In Iran were Frenchmen, Italians, Chinese, and Dutchmen. Rhodesians, Greeks, Canadians, Frenchmen, Australians, Englishmen, and Swiss were in Libya.[116]

---

113. **53**, 1951, pp. 872–77.

114. **77**, 1951–52, p. vii.
115. **73**, 1950–52, pp. 11–13.
116. See **75**.

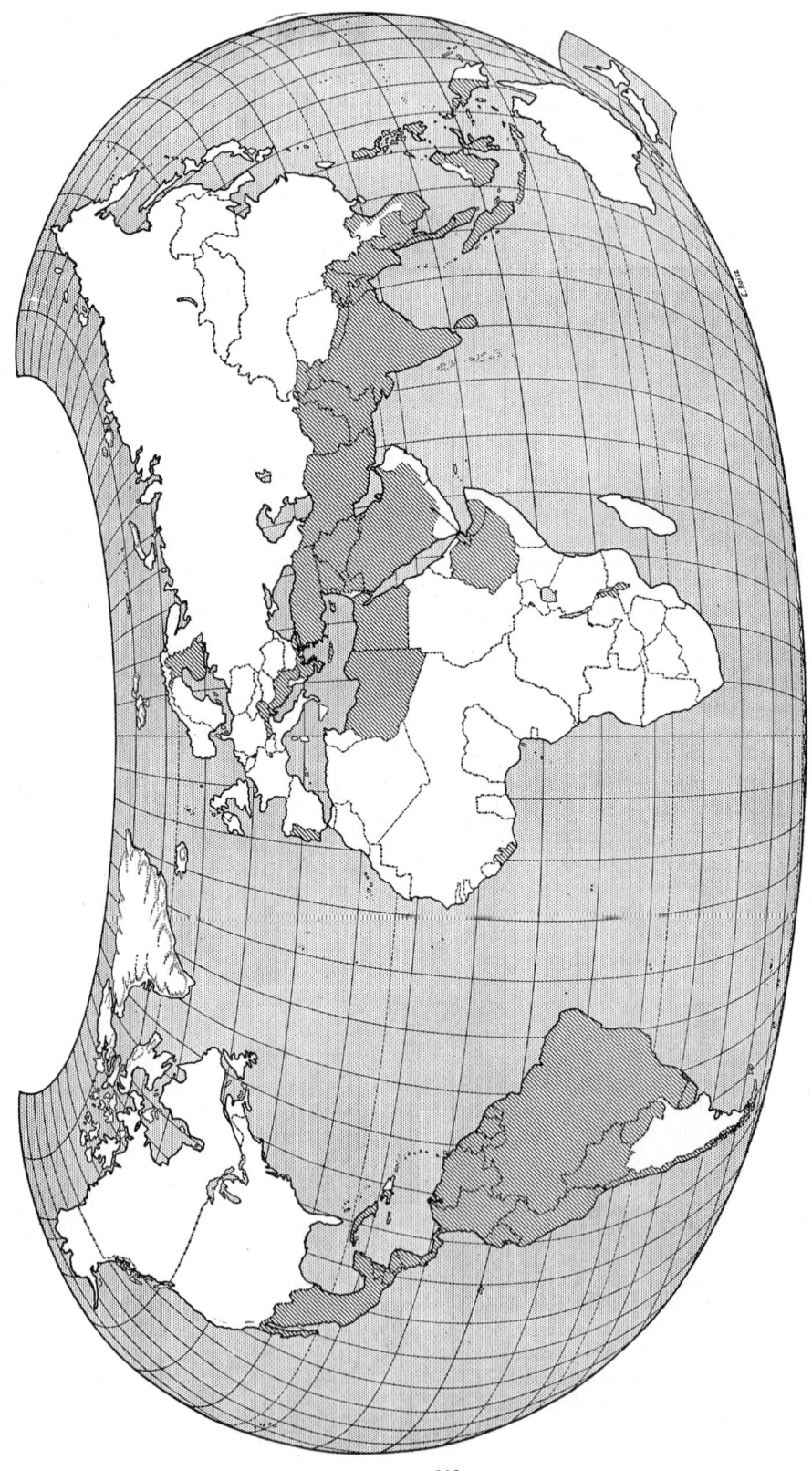

Source: 73

Figure 152. The Food and Agriculture Organization of the UN: Geographic Distribution of Activities under the Expanded Technical Assistance Program, 1952

THE INTERNATIONAL BANK FOR RECONSTRUCTION AND DEVELOPMENT

Origin and Constitution

An agreement to establish the International Bank was reached at the United Nations Monetary and Financial Conference at Bretton Woods, New Hampshire, in July 1944. The Bank was organized in December 1945, and it became a specialized agency of the United Nations in August 1947.

The Bank is an independent international organization associated with the UN through an exchange of representatives (without vote) in the respective governing bodies (Article II), and the two organizations consult one another on matters of mutual interest (Article IV). The UN makes no recommendations to the Bank with respect to specific loans but may advise it on the technical aspects of reconstruction and development plans.

The Bank falls short of any ambitious project for preventing wars through unification of the world's financial systems. Essentially it is a sober business organization. Its special purposes are outlined in Article I of the Articles of Agreement as follows:

(i) To assist in reconstruction and development of territories of members by facilitating the investment of capital for productive purposes, including the restoration of economies destroyed or disrupted by war, the reconversion of productive facilities to peacetime needs and the encouragement of the development of productive facilities and resources in less developed countries.

(ii) To promote private foreign investment by means of guarantees or participations in loans and other investments made by private investors; and when private capital is not available on reasonable terms, to supplement private investment by providing, on suitable conditions, finance for productive purposes out of its own capital, funds raised by it and its other resources.

(iii) To promote the long-range balanced growth of international trade and the maintenance of equilibrium in balances of payments by encouraging international investment for the development of the productive resources of members, . . .

(iv) To arrange the loans made or guaranteed by it in relation to international loans through other channels so that the more useful and urgent projects, large and small alike, will be dealt with first.

(v) To conduct its operations with due regard to the effect of international investment on business conditions in the territories of members. . . .

The subscribed capital stock of the Bank totaled more than $9 billion by June 30, 1954. According to the Articles of Agreement, each member of the organization pays 2 per cent of its subscription in gold or U.S. dollars and 18 per cent in national currency; 80 per cent is held by the respective country, subject to call by the Bank only to meet obligations that country has created by borrowing from the Bank, or to guarantee loans made by the Bank. Payments in national currency may be replaced by non-interest-bearing nonnegotiable demand notes. Including these notes, the capital stock at the disposal of the Bank amounted to approximately $1.8 billion: less than half of it in U.S. dollars, the rest in other currencies, in part convertible, in part nonconvertible. (See Table 281.)

Operations

The Bank operates by making loans to governments or private concerns under governmental guaranty; and by participating in loans, or guaranteeing, in whole or in part, loans made by private investors.

The fundamental concepts of the Bank's functions, which underlie its activities, were formulated in its second *Annual Report* (1946–47) as follows:

The first of these fundamental concepts is that the Bank cannot, and was never intended to, provide the external financing required for all meritorious projects of reconstruction and development. Rather, the Bank's function is to provide a catalyst by which production may be generally stimulated and private investment encouraged. The Bank believes that its funds must be used chiefly to finance programs or projects which will eliminate bottlenecks to production, or which will generate increases in production of related goods or in related areas, or which will otherwise serve effectively to stimulate the revival or development of industry and agriculture. The strategic use of comparatively modest sums can in this way have beneficial effects out of all proportion to the size of the investment.

In the second place, the Bank believes that it should encourage necessary action by its member governments to assure that the Bank's loans will actually prove productive. The promotion of sound financial programs, the removal of unnecessary trade barriers, and the regional integration of production plans, where appropriate, are some of the fields in which the Bank, as it acquires experience and builds up the confidence of the responsible officials of its members, may be able to exert a helpful influence.

Implicit in what has already been said is the third

TABLE 281

INTERNATIONAL BANK FOR RECONSTRUCTION AND DEVELOPMENT: SUBSCRIPTION TO CAPITAL STOCK, AS OF JUNE 30, 1954

(*Millions of U.S. Dollars*)

| Member [a] | Number of Shares | Subscriptions, Total | Amount Paid in | | | Amounts Due | Subject to Call to Meet Obligations of Bank |
			U.S. Dollars	Other Currencies	Demand Notes		
Total	91,485	$9,148.5	$750.98	$182.60	$892.70	$3.49	$7,318.80
United States	31,750	3,175.0	635.00	—	—	—	2,540.00
Canada	3,250	325.0	6.50	40.69	17.81	—	260.00
Mexico	650	65.0	1.30	11.70	—	—	52.00
Guatemala	20	2.0	0.04	0.36	—	—	1.60
El Salvador	10	1.0	0.02	0.18	—	—	0.80
Honduras	10	1.0	0.02	0.18	—	—	0.80
Nicaragua	8	0.8	0.02	0.14	—	—	0.64
Costa Rica	20	2.0	0.04	0.36	—	—	1.60
Panama	2	0.2	0.00	0.04	—	—	0.16
Cuba	350	35.0	0.70	0.06	6.24	—	28.00
Haiti	20	2.0	0.04	0.01	0.36	—	1.60
Dominican Republic	20	2.0	0.04	0.00	0.36	—	1.60
Venezuela	105	10.5	0.21	1.36	0.53	—	8.40
Colombia	350	35.0	0.70	6.30	—	—	28.00
Ecuador	32	3.2	0.06	0.58	—	—	2.56
Brazil	1,050	105.0	2.10	18.90	—	—	84.00
Peru	175	17.5	0.35	0.06	3.09	—	14.00
Bolivia	70	7.0	0.14	0.01	1.25	—	5.60
Paraguay	14	1.4	0.03	0.25	—	—	1.12
Chile	350	35.0	0.70	6.30	—	—	28.00
Uruguay	105	10.5	0.21	1.89	—	—	8.40
United Kingdom	13,000	1,300.0	26.00	9.09	224.91	—	1,040.00
France	5,250	525.0	10.50	22.93	71.57	—	420.00
Luxembourg	100	10.0	0.20	0.02	1.78	—	8.00
Belgium	2,250	225.0	4.50	4.84	35.66	—	180.00
Netherlands	2,750	275.0	5.50	2.13	47.37	—	220.00
Denmark	680	68.0	1.36	1.57	10.67	—	54.40

(*Continued on facing page*)

fundamental concept which has been developed, that the Bank must play an active rather than a passive role. The Executive Directors and the management are convinced that it is not enough simply to examine and pass judgment upon loan applications as they are presented. Rather the Bank must take advantage of its international cooperative character to initiate and develop plans to the end that the Bank's resources are used not only prudently from the standpoint of its investors but wisely from the standpoint of the world.[117]

These purposes add a new feature to the direct responsibility of the Bank as a money-lending institute and make it a consultative organ in the world's struggle with poverty. The constitution prohibits the Bank from lending money for relief purposes or political needs, including defense. All its loans must serve the reconstruction or economic development of the borrowing country and must have reasonable prospects of repayment. They must be used to finance definite projects recommended by a competent committee after careful study. The Bank lends money only when there is evidence that the borrower is unable to obtain the loan elsewhere under conditions that the Bank considers reasonable.[118]

117. **83**, 1946–47, p. 8.

118. **83**, 1946–47, p. 15.

TABLE 281—*continued*

Member [a]	Number of Shares	Subscrip- tions, Total	Amount Paid in			Amounts Due	Subject to Call to Meet Obligations of Bank
			U.S. Dollars	Other Currencies	Demand Notes		
Sweden	1,000	$100.0	$2.00	$18.00	—	—	$ 80.00
Norway	500	50.0	1.00	0.37	$ 8.69	—	40.00
Finland	380	38.0	0.76	6.84	—	—	30.40
Western Germany	3,300	330.0	6.60	1.28	58.12	—	264.00
Czechoslovakia	1,250	125.0	1.88	0.22	22.28	$0.62	100.00
Austria	500	50.0	1.00	0.30	8.70	—	40.00
Italy	1,800	180.0	3.60	3.69	28.71	—	144.00
Yugoslavia	400	40.0	0.80	7.20	—	—	32.00
Greece	250	25.0	0.50	4.50	—	—	20.00
Iceland	10	1.0	0.02	0.18	—	—	0.80
China	6,000	600.0	9.13	1.08	106.92	2.87	480.00
Japan	2,500	250.0	5.00	0.45	44.55	—	200.00
Turkey	430	43.0	0.86	0.11	7.63	—	34.40
Lebanon	45	4.5	0.09	0.81	—	—	3.60
Syria	65	6.5	0.13	0.04	1.13	—	5.20
Jordan	30	3.0	0.06	0.00	0.53	—	2.40
Iraq	60	6.0	0.12	0.02	1.06	—	4.80
Iran	336	33.6	0.67	0.06	5.99	—	26.88
Pakistan	1,000	100.0	2.00	0.18	17.82	—	80.00
India	4,000	400.0	8.00	0.72	71.28	—	320.00
Burma	150	15.0	0.30	0.03	2.67	—	12.00
Thailand	125	12.5	0.25	0.04	2.21	—	10.00
Ceylon	150	15.0	0.30	0.03	2.67	—	12.00
Indonesia	1,100	110.0	2.20	0.20	19.60	—	88.00
Philippines	150	15.0	0.30	1.20	1.50	—	12.00
Egypt	533	53.3	1.07	0.10	9.50	—	42.64
Ethiopia	30	3.0	0.06	0.54	—	—	2.40
Union of South Africa	1,000	100.0	2.00	4.10	13.90	—	80.00
Australia	2,000	200.0	4.00	0.36	35.64	—	160.00

Source: **83**, 1953–54, p. 52. Cf. **84**.

a. Czechoslovakia was suspended from membership on January 1, 1954. Israel became a member of the organization in 1954. The number of members remained unchanged as in this table (**58**).

In the case of long-run reconstruction or development projects, the Bank does not commit itself for the whole duration of the project but makes loans sufficient to cover the needs of a limited period and at the end of this period, in response to a new application, decides whether or not a new loan should be made. This policy gives the Bank control over the use of its funds. Most loans are made at yearly interest rates ranging from $3\frac{1}{4}$ to 4 per cent. For guarantees and loans made from borrowed funds, the Bank charges a commission ranging between one and $1\frac{1}{2}$ per cent a year.

In its first year of operation the Bank received applications for loans totaling approximately $2.5 billion; France asked for $500 million; the Netherlands for $535 million; Poland $600 million; Czechoslovakia $350 million; Denmark $50 million; Luxembourg $20 million; Mexico, Chile and Iran applied for loans for various development projects. Not all of these requests were granted.

During the first seven years of lending, the Bank made 104 loans to thirty-four countries totaling $1,914 million, of which $40 million was canceled or refunded, leaving loans totaling $1,874 million outstanding as of June 30, 1954. (See Table 282.)

TABLE 282

INTERNATIONAL BANK FOR RECONSTRUCTION AND DEVELOPMENT: LOANS OUTSTANDING, BY PURPOSE AND AREA, AS OF JUNE 30, 1954

(*Millions of U.S. Dollars*)

Purpose	Total	Western Hemisphere	Europe	Asia and Middle East	Africa	Australasia
				Area		
Total loans	$1,874	$457	$782	$232	$199	$204
Reconstruction loans						
Total: France, the Netherlands, Denmark, Luxembourg	497	—	497	—	—	—
Other loans						
Total	1,377	457	285	232	199	204
Electric power: machinery, equipment & construction materials	509	290	35	63	88	33
Transportation	397	103	63	86	71	74
Railroads: locomotives, rolling stock, rails & shop supplies	201	50	3	63	68	17
Shipping: vessels & marine equipment	37	—	37	—	—	—
Airlines: planes & parts	34	—	7	—	—	27
Roads: building machinery & equipment	87	50	—	5	2	30
Ports: docks, loading & dredging machinery; harbor craft	24	3	16	4	1	—
Pipelines	14	—	—	14	—	—
Communications: telephone & telegraph equipment; supplies	26	24	—	2	—	—
Agriculture and forestry, total	167	20	29	47	—	71
Mechanization: general farm machinery and equipment	76	16	2	—	—	58
Irrigation and flood control: construction equipment & materials	57	1	13	37	—	6
Land improvement: machinery equipment and construction materials	22	2	3	10	—	7
Grain storage: construction materials	5	1	4	—	—	—
Timber production: machinery and vehicles	7	—	7	—	—	—
Industry	168	20	90	32	—	26
Manufacturing machinery	145	20	74	32	—	19
Mining equipment	23	—	16	—	—	7
General development	110	—	68	2	40	—
Development banks	20	—	18	2	—	—
General development plans	90	—	50	—	40	—

Source: **83**, 1953–54, p. 12.

The loans made by the Bank by June 30, 1954 were distributed, by purpose, as follows (in millions of dollars):

Reconstruction	$497
Electric power	509
Transportation	397
Communications	26
Agriculture and forestry	167
Industry	168
General development	110

Nearly two thirds of the loans were granted for twenty-five years or more. The largest sums were awarded to the following countries (in millions of dollars): [119]

France	$257.5
Brazil	234.7
Netherlands	229.0
Australia	204.0
India	113.5
Union of South Africa	110.0
Mexico	99.8
Belgium	86.0
Colombia	69.4
Yugoslavia	60.7
Turkey	54.4
United Kingdom	52.0
Pakistan	44.5
Japan	40.2
Denmark	40.0
Chile	37.5
Finland	36.0
Uruguay	33.0
Thailand	25.4
Norway	25.0
Italy	20.0

Approximately half the loans were made to prosperous countries, particularly in the early period of the Bank's operations; the rest, to underdeveloped areas. (See Figure 153.)

Development Projects

In recent years, the Bank has made loans mainly for specific developmental projects; 276 individual projects have been completed or started with its help. The seventh *Annual Report* summarizes this work as follows:

The amounts lent do not measure the magnitude or the total costs of these projects. The Bank normally finances only the foreign-exchange costs of imported equipment and services needed to com-plete projects; usually the larger part of the cost of any project is met by the borrower. The total cost of projects completed or started with the help of Bank financing amounts to more than $3 billion.

The Bank's first four loans, amounting to $497 million, were made in 1947 to France, Denmark, Luxembourg and the Netherlands to assist postwar reconstruction during the period before the European Recovery Program was in operation. Since that time nearly all of the Bank's lending has been devoted to providing basic utilities in the less developed areas.

It is the loans made after the reconstruction loans of 1947 that are discussed in the following paragraphs.

Agriculture: The Bank has engaged in a wide variety of lending to increase agricultural production. Among other things, it has helped to finance farm mechanization (in Australia, Chile, Colombia, Nicaragua and Paraguay), land clearance (in India and Pakistan), irrigation (in Chile, India, Iraq, Thailand and Turkey), flood control (in Iraq and Turkey), grain storage (in Nicaragua and Turkey) and improvements on individual farms (in Iceland). . . . In addition, many of the Bank's loans for electric power and transportation have been made to countries that are predominantly agricultural, and have been designed in part to promote agricultural production and earnings.

Transportation: The less developed countries need basic transportation facilities, to quicken internal and international trade and to provide new incentives for production. . . . The Bank's lending for transportation . . . includes the financing of highway construction (in Colombia, Ethiopia and Nicaragua), railway rehabilitation (in Australia, Brazil, India, Pakistan, Thailand and the Union of South Africa), and port development (in Peru, South Africa, Thailand and Turkey).

Electric power: Bank-financed power projects, for the most part still under construction, are situated in Australia, Belgium, Finland, Iceland, India, South Africa, Southern Rhodesia, Turkey, Yugoslavia, and in six countries of Latin America: Brazil, Chile, Colombia, El Salvador, Mexico and Uruguay. The Bank's lending in the Western Hemisphere has been predominantly for electric power, and the contribution being made to the power capacity of Latin American countries is noteworthy.

Industry: The requirement of the Bank's charter that loans to private borrowers be government-guaranteed has, as a practical matter, limited the extent to which the Bank can make loans direct to industry. . . .

Program lending: Some of the Bank's lending in less developed areas has been in support of broad programs covering an entire country or region.[120]

---

119. These sums include direct loans to governments and loans to private concerns guaranteed by the respective governments.

120. **83**, 1951–1952, pp. 8 and 10.

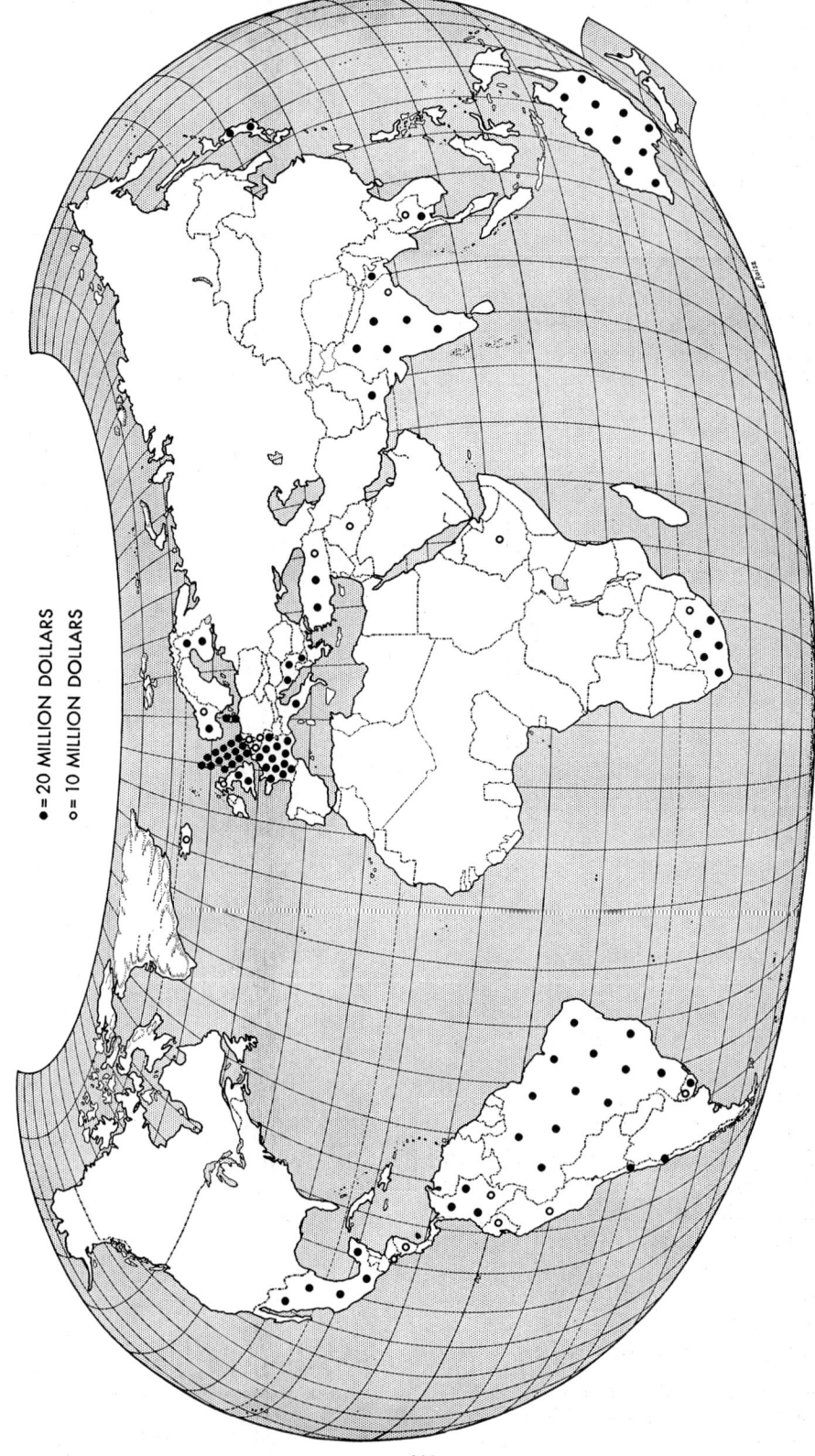

FIGURE 153. THE INTERNATIONAL BANK FOR RECONSTRUCTION AND DEVELOPMENT: GEOGRAPHIC DISTRIBUTION OF LOANS, AS OF JUNE 30, 1954

Typical Loans

The role of the Bank in international economic cooperation is illustrated by its loans to the Belgian Congo and to India.

The loan to the former consisted of two operations: one loan of $40 million directly to the Belgian Congo, fully guaranteed by Belgium; another, of $30 million to Belgium, designed to finance its outlays on development of the African colony. Both are parts of the ten-year development plan for the Congo, begun in 1950, which envisages expansion of production and a rise in the standard of living in the area.[121]

The Bank's financial contribution to the Congo development plan is a 25-year loan for an amount representing little more than 5 per cent of the total investment envisaged for the ten-year period.

The Bank's loans to India have consisted of five operations. The first loan of $34 million, made in August 1949, was to aid the Indian government in the rehabilitation and improvement of the railway system. The total dollar cost of the program, which involved the importation of 653 locomotives and 350 tank cars, was approximately $84 million, of which $34 million was supplied by the Bank.[122]

The second loan of $10 million, made in September 1949, was to help the Indian government to purchase agricultural machinery for use in jungle clearance and in eradicating kans grass.

The total capital cost of the program is close to $25 million. The Bank's loan financed the dollar costs of the program, amounting to $8,750,000, for the purchase in the United States of 345 heavy tractors. Other costs covered by the Indian government include the purchase in the United Kingdom of cultivating equipment; the cost of buildings, vehicles, fuels, lubricants and labor.

The plans include also the clearance of scrub jungle land covering 2.2 million acres, where heavy brush and undergrowth and other factors have made cultivation impossible. Experiments conducted on a small scale with old equipment obtained from United States Army surpluses have been sufficiently encouraging to warrant the undertaking of a pilot program of jungle clearance.

The Bank's loan will help finance a pilot program for the clearance of about 100,000 acres of scrub jungle land east of New Delhi. Cultivation will be carried on by the provincial government for the first two or three years and later the land will be sold in units of 10 to 20 acres to individual farmers.

The Bank's loan financed the purchase of 30 heavy tractors. As in the case of the kans grass eradication program, the major portion of the total cost of the program is to be met by India out of its own resources.[123]

The third and fourth loans, totaling $38 million, were granted for development work in the Damodar River Valley, the country's most important industrial area. The full program included construction of eight flood control storage dams with hydroelectric plants having a total installed capacity of 182,000 kilowatts; two additional hydroelectric plants; a thermal plant at Bokaro of 200,000 kilowatt ultimate capacity (the largest in India); about 600 miles of transmission lines; an 80-mile navigation canal, and an irrigation barrage to divert water into a network of 477 miles of main line and branch line canals and to provide irrigation for about 967,000 acres, including 185,000 acres now irrigated from existing canals only during the monsoon season.

The total cost of the program was estimated at $142 million, including dollar outlays for heavy equipment and electrical machinery. The Bank made the first loan for financing the Bokaro thermal station in April 1950. The total capital cost of this project was estimated at about $53 million, of which the Bank's loan covered $18 million — payments in the United States and Canada for power house equipment, construction equipment, conductors and accessories for the transmission lines. The remainder of the cost, about $34 million, was financed out of India's own resources.[124]

A supplementary loan of $19.5 million, made in January 1953, when the construction of the Bokaro plant was nearing completion, was to be used in the building of two multipurpose dams, each with a hydroelectric plant; an extensive irrigation system, including a diversion dam on the Damodar River; and for canals to carry barge traffic.[125]

The fifth loan, of $31.5 million, was made in December 1952 to the privately owned Indian Iron and Steel Company, with works in West

121. See **84,** September 13, 1951.
122. See **84,** August 18, 1949.

123. See **84,** September 29, 1949.
124. See **84,** April 18, 1950.
125. See **84,** January 26, 1953.

Bengal. The loan is for a term of fifteen years and is guaranteed by the government of India.

The loan will help the company carry out a five-year project for increasing its blast-furnace capacity from 640,000 tons to 1,400,000 tons and its finished steel capacity from 350,000 to 700,000 tons annually. When completed, the company's program will double the quantity of foundry iron now available from domestic sources in India, and will increase the country's present output of finished steel by about one third.[126]

The loans described above are not overwhelming in amount when compared with prewar international investments. All are of the portfolio type, all are made either directly to governments or guaranteed by them, and all are related to long-term development plans. The loans cover only part of the costs of the approved projects and finance outlays which require foreign currency, thereby removing a financial bottleneck that might have threatened the execution of the project.

Technical Assistance

The Bank's technical assistance program [127] is the outgrowth of its conviction that external financing will be of the most value in countries that already are making the best possible use of their own resources. The principal way in which it has helped member countries to achieve this objective has been through survey missions, comprising groups of experts specially organized to make intensive studies of national resources and to formulate recommendations which can serve as the basis of long-term development programs. Beginning with the general survey mission to Colombia in 1949, the Bank has sent such groups to many other countries.[128]

Usually, the missions have included advisers on public finance and economics, industry, power, transportation, and one or two agricultural specialists provided by the FAO. On occasion, experts in public health and education, nominated by WHO and UNESCO, have been added. Additional experts in such fields as mining and irrigation have been recruited as needed, on an international basis. At least one or two Bank staff members have served in every case.

The broad purpose of each group has been to work out long-range programs designed to raise the level of productivity and to improve the standard of living. There is evidence that the work done by the survey missions is achieving results in most of the countries to which they have gone.

In Colombia, for example, a nonpartisan development committee of leading private citizens was appointed by the government to outline a long-term program based on the mission's recommendations. Following this program, the government has effected budgetary and banking reforms; lifted restrictions on imports; relaxed exchange controls; and adopted a liberal and encouraging attitude toward foreign capital. Inflation has been checked.

In Guatemala, construction has begun on a highway between Guatemala City and the Atlantic coast — a project to which the survey mission gave top priority. A commission has been appointed to make recommendations for reorganizing the nationalized rural estates, an essential reform stressed in the recommendations presented to the government.

Recent development budgets of Turkey and Iraq indicate that governmental thinking has been substantially influenced by the recommendations of the Bank's missions.[129] Cuba has framed a comprehensive request for technical assistance and reorganized the National Economic Planning Commission.[130] Nicaragua has brought into effective operation a national economic council and a development corporation; it has adopted a five-year development program and a budget for the first year; and has undertaken major changes in fiscal, budgetary and tariff policies.[131]

Plans for Expanded Operations

Lending operations of the Bank — approximately $250 million per year, on the average — do not fill the gap left by the contraction of private foreign investments but have important advantages over private investment of equal amounts. The capital transferred to the borrowing country directly serves its long-term development plans rather than the interest of the investing firm, ensuring more balanced development of local resources and eliminating the danger inherent in a monoculture economy. The borrowing country does not have to fear imperial-

126. See **84**, December 19, 1952.
127. **83**, 1951–52, pp. 10–12.
128. See **85, 87** through **95**.

129. **91** and **95**.
130. **85**.
131. See **94**.

istic and colonial aspirations of the lending agency. On the lender's side, the loans are secure even if extreme nationalists come to power, and the lender has a reasonable amount of control over the use made of the borrowed funds.

In recent years, numerous suggestions have been made to expand the Bank's functions. The U.S. International Development Advisory Board recommended that an international finance corporation be created as an affiliate of the Bank.[132] The corporation would be empowered to make loans to private concerns without a guarantee by the government or the central bank of the country in which the project to be financed is located.

. . . the capital of the Corporation would be subscribed by member governments and not by the Bank. The purpose of the Corporation would be to promote economic development through the stimulation of private investment, "by bringing together investment opportunities, capital (both domestic and foreign) and experienced management, and by helping to finance private productive undertakings through equity investment and loans without government guarantee." The Corporation would not accept responsibility for managing an enterprise in which it invested, and would not hold a controlling equity interest in it. No special immunity or status would attach to any enterprise solely by reason of the Corporation's participation. The Corporation would attempt to revolve its funds as rapidly as possible by selling securities in its portfolio whenever possible at a fair price.[133]

A group of experts appointed by the Secretary-General of the UN advised an expansion of the International Bank, with the objective of lending $1 billion annually to underdeveloped countries. They recommended the establishment by the UN of an international development authority to assist the underdeveloped countries in preparing, coordinating and implementing their development programs: to make grants-in-aid for specific purposes; to verify the proper utilization of such grants; and to study and report on the progress of development programs.[134]

Another commission has recommended that the operations of the Bank and the proposed international finance corporation be supplemented by a special UN fund supplying underdeveloped areas with noncommercial capital in the form of grants-in-aid or long-term, low-interest loans. The funds should be raised by governments, in either convertible or inconvertible currency, with the provision that local currency could be used for the purchase of required commodities or for services available in the respective country. Decisions on applications would be made by an executive board of from eight to twelve members, with equal representation of the major contributors to the fund and of the other members. The group cautioned that the fund should have at least the equivalent of $250 million pledged for its initial operations by at least thirty contributing governments.[135]

In brief, the commission envisages an international Marshall Plan on a small scale. Whether it proves workable or not, it stresses an important point: the operations of the International Bank, even when expanded and supplemented by other agencies operating on a commercial basis, cannot solve all the financial difficulties of underdeveloped areas whose needs for foreign capital exceed their credit and ability to pay.

THE INTERNATIONAL MONETARY FUND

Plans for the International Monetary Fund were formulated at the United Nations Monetary and Financial Conference held at Bretton Woods in July 1944. The organization is closely related to the International Bank for Reconstruction and Development: the purpose of the Bank is to promote economic development; the Fund's task is to maintain the stability of the world economic system by assuring equilibrium in its monetary systems. The latter involves more than purely monetary measures. Article 1 of the Articles of Agreement describes the Fund's purposes as follows:

(i) To promote international monetary cooperation through a permanent institution which provides the machinery for consultation and collaboration on international monetary problems.

(ii) To facilitate the expansion and balanced growth of international trade, and to contribute thereby to the promotion and maintenance of high levels of employment and real income and to the development of the productive resources of all members as primary objectives of economic policy.

(iii) To promote exchange stability, to maintain orderly exchange arrangements among members, and to avoid competitive exchange depreciation.

(iv) To assist in the establishment of a multilateral system of payments in respect of current transactions between members and in the elimina-

132. See **119** and **124**.
133. **83**, 1951–1952, p. 13; cf. **86**.
134. See **33**, p. 95.

135. See **42**.

TABLE 283

INTERNATIONAL MONETARY FUND: SUBSCRIPTIONS, BY COUNTRY, AS OF APRIL 30, 1954

(Millions of U.S. Dollars)

Member	Quota	Paid in Gold or U.S. Dollars	Paid in Member Currency	Member	Quota	Paid in Gold or U.S. Dollars	Paid in Member Currency
Total	$8,848.5	$1,608.21	$6,351.49	Sweden	$100.0	$17.00	$ 83.00
				Norway	50.0	12.50	37.50
United States	2,750.0	687.78	2,062.22	Finland	38.0	0.76	37.24
Canada	300.0	75.00	225.00	Western Germany	330.0	33.01	296.99
Mexico	90.0	22.50	67.50	Czechoslovakia	125.0	2.37	122.63
Guatemala	5.0	1.25	3.75	Austria	50.0	5.00	45.00
El Salvador	2.5	0.63	1.87	Italy	180.0	0.02	—
Honduras	2.5	0.63	1.87	Yugoslavia	60.0	7.90	52.10
Nicaragua	2.0	0.50	1.50	Greece	40.0	—	—
Costa Rica	5.0	0.37	4.63	Iceland	1.0	0.25	0.75
Panama	0.5	0.13	0.37	China	550.0	0.06	—
Cuba	50.0	12.50	37.50	Japan	250.0	62.50	187.50
Venezuela	15.0	3.75	11.25	Turkey	43.0	10.75	32.25
Colombia	50.0	12.50	37.50	Lebanon	4.5	0.27	4.23
Ecuador	5.0	1.25	3.75	Syria	6.5	0.17	6.33
Brazil	150.0	37.50	112.50	Jordan	3.0	0.10	2.90
Peru	25.0	3.15	21.85	Iraq	8.0	—	8.00
Bolivia	10.0	2.50	7.50	Iran	35.0	8.77	26.23
Paraguay	3.5	0.88	2.62	Pakistan	100.0	3.50	96.50
Chile	50.0	8.82	41.18	India	400.0	27.53	372.47
Uruguay	15.0	—	—	Burma	15.0	0.50	14.50
Dominican Republic	5.0	1.25	3.75	Thailand	12.5	3.13	—
Haiti	2.0	0.50	1.50	Ceylon	15.0	0.75	14.25
				Indonesia	110.0	15.50	—
United Kingdom	1,300.0	236.27	1,063.73	Philippines	15.0	3.75	11.25
France	525.0	108.11	416.89	Egypt	60.0	9.50	50.50
Luxembourg	10.0	0.48	9.52	Ethiopia	6.0	0.06	5.94
Belgium	225.0	56.25	168.75	Union of South Africa	100.0	25.00	75.00
Netherlands	275.0	68.75	206.25				
Denmark	68.0	5.94	62.06	Australia	200.0	8.40	191.60

Source: **96**, 1954, pp. 166, 167.

tion of foreign exchange restrictions which hamper the growth of world trade.

(v) To give confidence to members by making the Fund's resources available to them under adequate safeguards, thus providing them with opportunity to correct maladjustments in their balance of payments without resorting to measures destructive of national or international prosperity.

(vi) In accordance with the above, to shorten the duration and lessen the degree of disequilibrium in the international balances of payments of members.[136]

Practically, the Fund's transactions are limited to

136. **97**, pp. 1–9.

supplying a member, on the initiative of such member, with the currency of another member in exchange for gold or for the currency of the member desiring to make the purchase. [Article V, Sec. 2.]

These functions put the Fund in a strategic position for coordinating monetary and financial policy among member countries.

The Fund's capital is supplied by the members according to quotas established either in the Agreement or subsequently. Power is vested in a Board of Governors. Each member appoints one governor and one alternate. Voting rights are the same as in the International Bank: each Governor has 250 votes, with an additional vote for each $100,000 of his country's quota.

As of April 30, 1954 the Fund had fifty-six members and their quotas totaled $8,848.5 million. Of this amount $7,959.7 million had actually been subscribed: $1,608.2 million had been paid in gold or U.S. dollars and the rest ($6,351.5 million) in member currencies. (See Table 283.) The share of the United States was $2,750 million, which gave it 27,750 votes out of a total of more than 100,000 votes represented in the Board.[137]

From the beginning of its operations in 1947, the Fund has sold to its members currency equivalent to $1,155 million, mainly U.S. dollars. The members, however, have repurchased $410 million worth of their currencies and transferred to the Fund gold or dollars, so that net transactions effected by the Fund by April 30, 1954 amounted to $745 million. The operations were distributed as follows, in the equivalent of millions of U.S. dollars: [138]

Currency Sold	
United States	$948
United Kingdom	192
Other	15
Currency Taken in Payment [a]	
United Kingdom	$300
Brazil	169
France	125
Japan	124
India	100
Netherlands	75
Australia	50
Mexico	45
Union of South Africa	35
Belgium	33
Other	92

a. Currency worth $6 million was sold against gold.

By advancing hard currency to countries with nonconvertible currency and by facilitating the flow of foreign trade, the Fund has prevented economic dislocations that might have cost the world many billions of dollars. Its transactions, however, have not prevented recurrence of the payments difficulties of individual countries which result from inflationary pressures and lack of free movement of capital and which are aggravated by trade and exchange restrictions.[139]

The Fund, with its limited means, cannot straighten out the monetary system of the world, but it can contribute to the solution of monetary and other economic problems by advising national governments. Its *Annual Report* for 1952 contains this statement:

The countries which, through their membership in the Fund, have subscribed to the objectives of expansion and balanced growth of international trade and currency convertibility have other economic objectives as well, such as a high level of employment, economic development or economic stability, high or minimum standards of living. In the short run for particular countries there may be difficulty in reconciling the claims of all these objectives. In such circumstances it is the function of the Fund to provide a forum for discussion. The judgment is embodied in the Fund Agreement that the balanced growth of international trade, with the highest degree of multilateralism, currency convertibility, and currency stability, will itself be of major assistance in helping countries to attain their other basic economic objectives. It is the duty of the Fund constantly to remind countries of the weakening effects on the world economic structure of the mere symptomatic treatment of exchange difficulties, and to urge them to give careful consideration to the question whether the policies they adopt set up incentives that lead, over a period of time, in the direction of international balance, or in the opposite direction.[140]

THE UN EDUCATIONAL, SCIENTIFIC AND CULTURAL ORGANIZATION (UNESCO)

The constitution for this organization was drawn up by the representatives of forty-four nations at a conference which met in London in November 1945 on the invitation of the British and French governments. The Preamble links the scientific and cultural cooperation of nations to the problem of peace:

. . . since wars begin in the minds of men, it is in the minds of men that the defences of peace must be constructed; . . .

The purpose of UNESCO as defined in Article 1 is

to contribute to peace and security by promoting collaboration among the nations through education, science and culture in order to further universal respect for justice, for the rule of law and for the human rights and fundamental freedoms which are affirmed for the peoples of the world, without distinction of race, sex, language or religion, by the Charter of the United Nations.

137. **96**, 1952, p. 93.
138. See **96**, 1954, pp. 138–39.
139. See **99**.

140. **96**, 1952, p. 34.

The tasks of the organization within this general framework include publications and conferences to promote the general principles of international solidarity; support of international scientific and cultural associations; translation of classics; surveys of press, radio and film facilities; and exchange of students and books.

The basic program of UNESCO, as adopted by its General Conference in 1950, emphasizes the following fields of action:

1. The elimination of illiteracy and the encouragement of fundamental education.

2. Obtaining for each person an education conforming to his aptitudes and to the needs of society, including technological training and higher education.

3. Promotion, through education, of respect for human rights throughout all nations.

4. Removing the obstacles to the free flow of persons, ideas and knowledge between the countries of the world.

5. Promoting the progress and utilization of science for mankind.

6. Study of the causes of tensions that may lead to war and their eradication through education.

7. Demonstration of world cultural interdependence.

8. The advancement of the cause of truth, freedom and peace through the press, radio and motion pictures.

9. Bringing about better understanding among the peoples of the world and convincing them of the necessity of cooperating loyally with one another through the instrumentality of the United Nations.

10. Rendering clearing-house and exchange services in all UNESCO fields of action, together with services in reconstruction and relief assistance.

Some parts of this program — for example, 6 and 7 — hardly require a worldwide international organization; some — for example, 3 and 5 — are almost as general as the proclamation of the Holy Alliance; still others, such as 2 and 4, greatly exceed the means at the disposal of the organization. However, the program includes at least two practical tasks: promoting the idea of the United Nations (9) and technical assistance in the field of education (10).

The achievements of UNESCO are modest in comparison with its announced goals, but appreciable when measured by less ambitious stand-

ards. It has held seminars on problems related to schools and libraries in various countries; it has sent educational missions to numerous countries; arranged national conferences on adult education, vagrant children and the like; awarded grants to international scientific and technological organizations; established an international university bureau and a score of scientific and cultural associations; launched numerous research projects; and organized traveling scientific exhibitions. In addition to popular pamphlets and leaflets, it publishes international directories and surveys of developments in political science in various countries.[141] It has tried to explore the origin of social and international tensions.[142] It has started a monumental project — a scientific and cultural history of mankind — which is being prepared on the basis of broad cooperation among scholars of many nations.

Its least controversial activity is its participation in the expanded technical assistance program of the UN. By December 1951 UNESCO had signed seventy agreements with thirty-four countries and had eighty-five experts working in twenty-seven countries. Their responsibilities range from advising governments on school system plans to organizing demonstration schools, libraries and documentary centers. From April 1951 through December 31, 1952, eighty-three projects requiring 272 experts were in operation in thirty-two countries.

During this period Libya was among the countries receiving generous assistance from UNESCO. This country had asked for experts and advisers to develop a center for business, handicrafts and mechanical skills; to establish a teacher-training center and a manual-work department at the teachers college; to study the education of adults and nomads; to explore problems of aridity; and to survey its long-term needs in the field of education.[143] To meet these requests, twenty-eight UNESCO experts worked in Libya in 1951–52.

Other countries asked for assistance in developing educational programs (Costa Rica, Ecuador, Indochina, Taiwan); for advice on such problems as educational broadcasting (Iran, Pakistan, Panama); the eradication of illiteracy (Indonesia); vocational and teacher training; establishment of libraries; and improvement and

---

141. See **102, 104; 100.**

142. See **101, 103.**

143. **20,** pp. 85–86.

reorganization of institutes of higher education.

In some projects UNESCO works with other specialized agencies, such as the ILO, the WHO and the FAO.

THE WORLD HEALTH ORGANIZATION (WHO)

The World Health Organization is the direct successor to the Health Organization of the League of Nations.

Under its constitution, the World Health Organization is empowered (a) to act as the directing and coordinating authority on international health work; (b) to place at the disposal of all countries advanced knowledge and techniques for the promotion of health and the prevention of illness; and (c) to adapt to local needs and conditions whatever assistance is needed for strengthening the public health services of individual countries.

Commenting on the trends in world health, the *Annual Report* of the WHO Director-General on the work of WHO for 1952 emphasized health in relation to economic and social development. In this connection, the report noted the development of preventive and social medicine, the increased use of practical techniques in training both professional and auxiliary personnel, the importance of environmental sanitation and certain experiments in the control of several communicable diseases.[144]

Since its inception, the work of WHO, like that of its predecessor, has been international in scope.[145] It has collected international health statistics, operated research laboratories, organized exploratory missions, established training centers and advised interested public authorities on all branches of health legislation, especially on protection against communicable diseases.

In recent years, WHO has paid increasing attention to underdeveloped areas, supplying them with advisory services, in part under the expanded technical assistance program. It has dealt with insect control; the fight against tuberculosis; control of venereal and other communicable diseases; nursing, maternal and child-health services; and public health administration. Fellowships have been supplied for all areas. (See Figure 154.) Its staff consisted in 1953 of 717 persons recruited from 53 different countries. Its own regular budget (apart from contribu-

tions from the UN technical assistance program) amounted to $9.8 million in 1953.

UNITED STATES FOREIGN AID

The total amount of United States foreign aid has been discussed elsewhere in this study.[146] From the outbreak of World War II through June 30, 1954 (including appropriation for fiscal year 1953–54) the United States spent $99.5 billion on military and economic aid to foreign countries: $49.2 billion during the war; $28.2 billion from August 1945 (the surrender of Japan) to the beginning of war in Korea; and $22.1 billion from June 25, 1950 through June 30, 1954. Excluding wartime aid to the Allies (mainly lend-lease operations), U.S. outlays on foreign aid came to more than $50 billion gross, while the net amount was about $46.8 billion — $35,841 million in net grants and $11,005 million in net credits.

Before the Korean war, the larger part of United States foreign aid consisted of civilian goods and capital equipment. After the middle of 1950, emphasis shifted toward military aid.

The largest single program of foreign economic aid has been that of the Economic Cooperation Administration (ECA), widely known as the Marshall Plan. It was replaced by the Mutual Security Agency set up by the Mutual Security Act of 1951 (amended 1952).

THE ECONOMIC COOPERATION ADMINISTRATION (MARSHALL PLAN)

The immediate purpose of the ECA was to help European countries in the difficult period of postwar reconstruction and readjustment and to check the danger of economic collapse and political upheaval. The program included shipments to Europe of foodstuffs, raw materials, machinery and other goods, fully paid for by the U.S. government. The so-called ECA countries obtained these goods free of charge, as grants. In this way Europe's "dollar shortage" or need for capital and consumer goods was met on a noncommerical basis, just as Europe's wartime needs for arms and ammunition had been met under the lend-lease plan.

Expenditures, 1948–51

The ECA was in operation from 1948 through 1951. During the first two years, all U.S. grants

144. See **105.**
145. See **106** and **107.**

146. See Chapter 5, pp. 223ff.

Figure 154. The World Health Organization: Geographic Distribution of Advisory Services in Non-European Countries, 1952

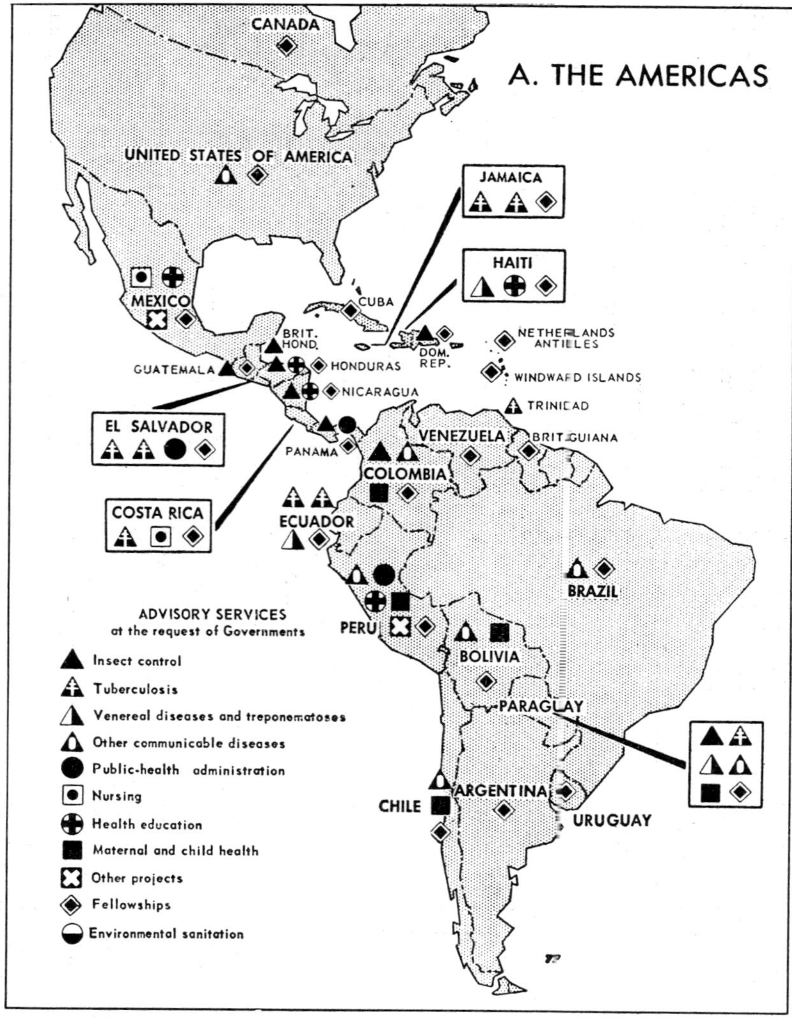

A. THE AMERICAS

B. AFRICA

ADVISORY SERVICES
at the request of Governments

◀ Insect control
△ Tuberculosis
▽ Venereal diseases and treponematoses
◁ Other communicable diseases
● Public-health administration
◉ Nursing
✚ Health education
■ Maternal and child health
✖ Other projects
◈ Fellowships
◐ Environmental sanitation

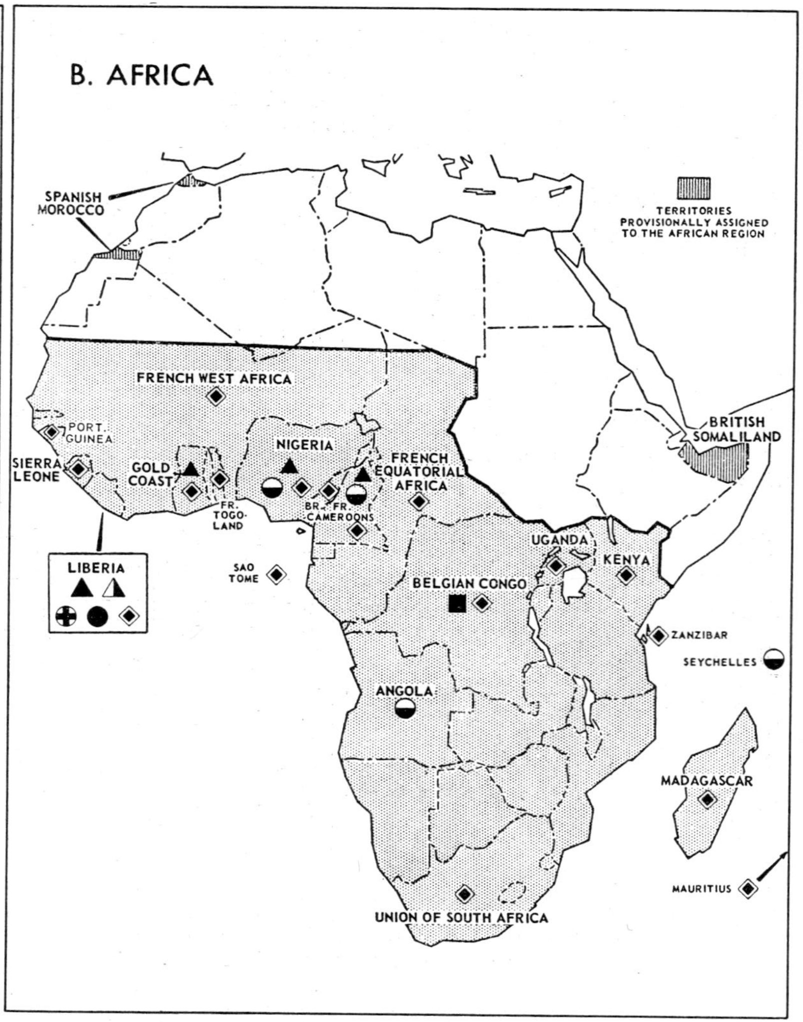

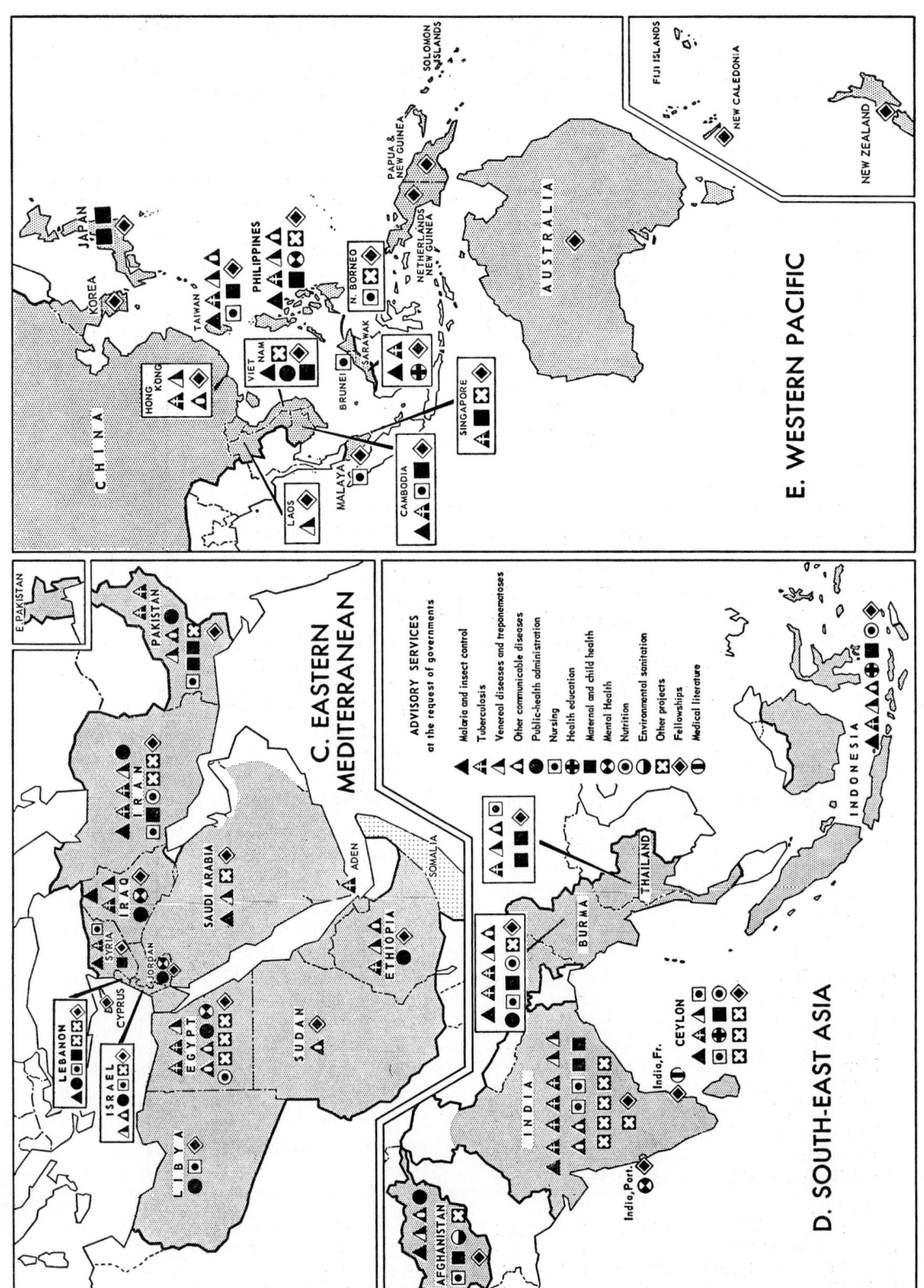

C. EASTERN MEDITERRANEAN

D. SOUTH-EAST ASIA

E. WESTERN PACIFIC

ADVISORY SERVICES
at the request of governments

▲ Malaria and insect control
▲ Tuberculosis
△ Venereal diseases and treponematoses
△ Other communicable diseases
● Public-health administration
◒ Nursing
⊕ Health education
■ Maternal and child health
◓ Mental Health
◐ Nutrition
○ Environmental sanitation
◈ Other projects
⊗ Fellowships
⊖ Medical literature

were used for civilian goods, including capital equipment; later grants were used partly for economic and technical assistance and partly for military aid. Through 1951, $12,763 million was disbursed under this program as follows (in millions of dollars): [147]

Period	Total	Economic Assistance	Military Aid
1948–51	$12,763	$10,717	$2,046
1948	1,493	1,493	—
1949	3,821	3,821	—
1950	3,309	2,841	468
1951	4,140	2,562	1,578

Including $585 million for economic and military assistance to Greece and Turkey, $512 million to the Philippines and $123 million to China, the United States spent about $14 billion for foreign aid in this period.

Use of Counterpart Funds

A distinctive feature of ECA — and later of the Mutual Security and similar programs — was that the operation was not limited to the delivery of agreed-on shipments, as under the purely humanitarian relief programs such as the distribution of civilian supplies, UNRRA, post-UNRRA and interim aid.[148] U.S. grants were used, rather, as the starting point of a far-reaching policy of reconstruction, stabilization and development:

In each country where defense-support assistance is provided on a grant basis by the Mutual Security Agency, there is created a special local currency account pursuant to the provision of bilateral agreements entered into by the United States and the participating countries. Each participating European country has agreed to deposit in its special account amounts of local currency equivalent to the dollar grant aid it receives. These deposits, which are called counterpart funds, are used in general by the depositing country to carry out Mutual Security objectives agreed jointly with the United States.

Mutual Security Agency notifies each country monthly of the amount of grant dollars expended for its benefit. The participating country then, with certain minor exceptions, deposits in its special account an amount of local currency commensurate to the dollar grant aid. Most of the local currency

required to fulfill the deposit obligation is secured from firms which import goods financed by Mutual Security Agency. The recipient country, however, is committed to deposit the full commensurate value of all grant aid received regardless of the amounts collected from importers who purchase dollar exchange.

There is reserved for United States use at least 5 percent of the counterpart funds deposited to match the dollar funds obligated prior to June 20, 1952, and 10 percent of the counterpart deposited to match dollar funds obligated on and after that date.

The United States portion of counterpart funds is used to defray certain costs payable in local currencies including administrative expenses of the aid program, certain expenses connected with technical assistance and informational activities, and the cost of acquiring strategic materials or developing their production.

The bulk of the counterpart funds is available for use by the depositing countries. Under the Economic Cooperation Act of 1948, counterpart funds were employed for the promotion of internal monetary and financial stability, for the stimulation of production, and for other purposes consistent with the aims of the Economic Recovery Program. The Mutual Security Act of 1951 extended the uses of counterpart to include "military production, construction, equipment, and matériel."

The Mutual Security Act of 1952 directed that, except as otherwise specifically authorized by law, counterpart funds were to be used only to carry out purposes for which new funds authorized by the Act would themselves be available — that is, primarily for military assistance and defense support.[149]

Counterpart funds have played an important role in the reconstruction of European countries and in the development of Far Eastern areas. From the inauguration of the ECA and MS programs, withdrawals of more than $10 billion of counterpart funds have been authorized by the U.S. government: $2.5 billion for debt retirement (an anti-inflationary measure); almost $1.8 billion for military purposes; over $1 billion for housing, relief and special welfare programs; $4.8 billion for promotion of agricultural and industrial production, development of transportation, communication and power, and other productive purposes. (See Table 284.)

THE MUTUAL SECURITY PROGRAM

The ECA was succeeded by the Mutual Security Agency and, later, the Foreign Operations Administration (FOA). (After June 30, 1955 all activities of the latter were to be transferred to

---

147. **131.**

148. Supplies worth $6,252 million were distributed in areas devastated by war ($2,831 million during the war and through 1947; and $3,421 million in 1948–51). Under UNRRA, post-UNRRA and interim aid, grants totaled $3,526 million ($2,900 million through 1947; $626 million in 1948).

149. **125,** p. iv.

TABLE 284

UNITED STATES FOREIGN AID: APPROVALS FOR WITH-
DRAWAL OF COUNTERPART FUNDS UNDER THE
ECA AND THE MSA PROGRAMS, CUMU-
LATIVE TO APRIL 30, 1954

(*Millions of Dollars*)

Purpose	Total	Europe	Far East
Total	$10,368	$10,047	$321
Monetary and financial stabilization (debt retirement)	2,511	2,511	—
Promotion of production			
Agriculture	1,031	949	82
Mining	503	502	1
Manufacturing	783	776	7
Transportation, communication and utilities	1,966	1,903	63
Other productive purposes	398	389	9
Productivity projects	91	91	—
Public welfare			
Public health	34	18	16
Housing and public building	886	886	—
Relief and other public welfare purposes	134	131	3
Military purposes	1,769	1,661	108
Other	261	230	31

Sources: **125**, p. 5; **126**, p. 4.

the International Cooperation Administration in the State Department.) United States outlays on foreign aid were substantially increased and distributed more widely throughout the world. In many countries MS programs appeared as a direct continuation of the Marshall Plan, although the change of agency reflected a change in the orientation of the program. The reports of the FOA in the *Survey of Current Business* often merge expenditures under these and related programs as "foreign grants and credits" of the government. Through June 30, 1954 such outlays totaled $46.8 billion including appropriations for fiscal year 1953–54. (See Table 285.) Of the $46.8 billion, nearly $12.2 billion was earmarked for military assistance in strategic areas, as follows (in millions of dollars):

Europe	$9,107
Asia and the Pacific	2,769
Western Hemisphere	181
Unspecified	124

The remaining $34.7 billion ($23.7 billion in grants and $11.0 billion in credits) went mainly to economic and technical assistance, although part of this amount was spent on development of strategic raw materials and munitions industries and mutual defense financing.

Early in 1951, when Chinese troops appeared on the Korean front, the character of U.S. foreign aid changed conspicuously. The immediate goals of the ECA had been reached: the acute dollar shortage was overcome; agricultural and industrial production, disorganized by the war, had, in most ECA countries, been resumed and expanded above the prewar level. The European economy could stand on its own feet, although it had not reached the stable equilibrium it had before World War I or in the late 1920's.

Under these conditions, the United States could have reduced or discontinued its grants to foreign countries, at least to the comparatively prosperous countries of Europe, without any immediate danger of acute economic dislocations. The free world, however, was facing a new danger — the threat of Communist military aggression. The challenge called for a joint military effort by the free nations. Rearmament and the organization of powerful standing armies had become, temporarily, the prime objectives.

However, many countries which were important links in the defense plans because of their strategic locations were unable to finance the new military program without endangering the standard of living of their people. It was thus obvious that an economic setback would make the rearmament program politically impossible in such areas. The United States again had to become an arsenal of democracy — to supply its Allies with arms and provide them with funds to buy raw materials for an expanded arms-production program at home.

The transition from economic to military aid was gradual. In 1947 the United States had supplied both types to Greece, Turkey and China. The Mutual Defense Assistance Act of 1949 had authorized military assistance grants. But the Mutual Security program as such, with decisive emphasis on military cooperation, did not begin until October 1951, when the Mutual Security Act of 1951 became law. (See Figure 155.)

Operations

The program included three operations and read as follows:

The Department of Defense administers the military assistance programs designed to bring about a

TABLE 285

UNITED STATES FOREIGN AID: FOREIGN NET GRANTS AND CREDITS, JULY 1, 1945 THROUGH JUNE 30, 1954

(Millions of Dollars)

	Total *Postwar* *Period*	*Before* *Korean* *Invasion*	After Korean Invasion				
				Fiscal Year			
			Total	*1951*	*1952*	*1953*	*1954*
Grand total	$46,847	$26,269	$20,578	$4,910	$4,610	$6,365	$5,193
Military grants	12,181	1,372	10,809	1,132	1,805	4,329	3,543
Western Europe [a]	9,107	567	8,539	914	1,364	3,496	2,765
Asia and Pacific	2,769	799	1,970	189	284	777	721
American republics	181	—	181	—	115	21	45
Unspecified	124	6	118	29	42	35	12
Other grants and credits	34,666	24,898	9,769	3,277	2,805	2,036	1,650
Grants	23,661	15,610	8,051	3,121	2,470	1,930	530
Credits	11,005	9,288	1,718	156	335	106	1,120
Western Europe [b]	25,089	18,746	6,344	2,429	1,961	1,244	709
Grants	18,072	11,440	6,632	2,436	1,912	1,368	916
Credits	7,017	7,305	−288	−7	49	−124	−207
Eastern Europe	1,095	1,107	−12	−2	−15	−4	9
Grants	1,010	1,011	−1	—	−13	—	13
Credits	85	96	−12	−2	−2	−4	−4
Near East and Africa	579	−5	584	88	167	136	193
Grants	345	−71	416	45	110	102	158
Credits	233	65	168	43	56	35	34
Other Asia and Pacific	6,090	3,976	2,114	611	623	423	457
Grants	5,439	3,666	1,773	582	416	404	371
Credits	652	310	342	29	207	20	86
American republics	906	343	563	94	28	196	246
Grants	209	127	82	15	17	21	30
Credits	697	217	481	79	11	175	216
International organizations and unspecified areas	907	731	176	57	41	41	36
Grants	841	692	149	42	28	36	42
Credits	66	38	27	15	13	6	6

Source: *Survey of Current Business,* October 1954, pp. 9–10.

a. Includes Turkey and Greece.   b. Includes dependent areas.

rapid increase in the combined effective military strength of the free nations; the Mutual Security Agency administers defense support (economic aid) programs in Europe and Southeast Asia to enable these nations to make a greater contribution to the mutual defense than would be possible otherwise; and the Technical Cooperation Administration (of the Department of State) administers the Point 4 Program, which brings to the so-called underdeveloped areas technical assistance and "know how" enabling these nations to make economic and social progress.[150]

Politically, the first two operations (military

150. **131**, p. 1.

assistance and defense support) were closely related; the Point Four program rested on other premises, and had other roots and a different orientation. The present phase of U.S. foreign aid can be examined under two broad headings — military aid (including defense financing) and measures to promote economic and social progress in the world. Practically, the distinction between the two is not always clear, however. Some programs served both purposes, and emphasis on one or the other objective may be a question of political expediency.

The scope of operations in the fiscal years 1950–53 as well as those planned for the fiscal

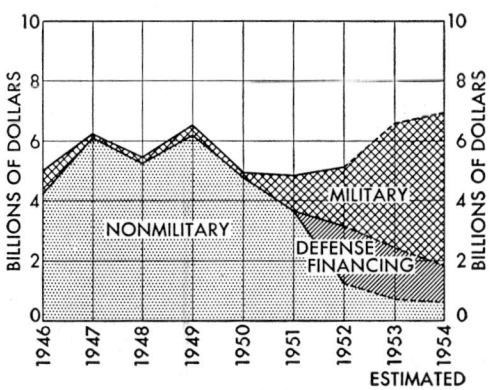

Source: **111**

FIGURE 155. UNITED STATES FOREIGN AID: MILITARY
AND NONMILITARY AID, 1946–54

Grants and credits are shown before deduction of
returned principal and reverse grants and are measured
in terms of goods delivered or shipped by the U.S. government, services rendered, or cash disbursed to or for
the account of a foreign government or other foreign
entity.

Fiscal year 1954 is an estimate for the Mutual Security
program only; the first nine months of fiscal 1953 are
based on actual data.

year 1954 is characterized, in a very general way,
by the following figures (in millions of dollars):

Fiscal Year	Total	Military	Economic, Technical and Other
1950	$5,288	$1,314	$3,974
1951	7,622	5,223	2,399
1952	7,284	5,744	1,540
1953	6,002	4,220	1,782
1954	5,319	3,782	1,537

(See Table 286.)

Military Aid

The MS program is international cooperation
to secure peace by military force. Contrary to the
Marshall Plan, it rests not on the ideal of world-
wide solidarity but on the recognition of the
wide rift in the modern world, divided into two
mutually hostile camps. Indeed, as early as in
December 1951, President Truman reported to
Congress on MS measures to rearm the free
world against the imminent onslaught from the
East.[151] (See Figure 156.) To the numerical
strength of the enemy, the President urged, the
free nations must oppose their superior techniques and economic organization. Together,
they could maintain superiority in resources.
(See Figure 157.) On the other hand, the
Soviet bloc would gain the balance of power if
it could overrun Western Europe, the Near East,
South and Southeast Asia and Japan, adding the
resources of all these areas to its own. (See Figure 158.)

"The Mutual Security program is directed
toward peace, not war," President Truman declared, but there remained the grim reality that
the new program sought peace primarily in rearmament and gave priority to military assistance. The comparatively modest economic aid
the Mutual Security program provided was also
subordinated to the strategy of defense against
Communism. "Basic data" given to Congress
during discussions of the program for the fiscal
year 1954 reflect the planning against the background of the political strength of Communists

151. See **127**.

TABLE 286

UNITED STATES FOREIGN AID: APPROPRIATIONS FOR MILITARY AND ECONOMIC AID, FISCAL YEARS 1950–54

(*Millions of Dollars*)

Purpose	1950	1951	1952	1953	1954
Total	$5,288	$7,622	$7,284	$6,002	$5,319
Military aid	1,314	5,223	5,744	4,220	3,782
Europe	1,000	4,504	4,774	3,128	2,180
Non-Europe	314	719	970	1,092	1,502
Other [a]	—	—	—	—	100
Economic and technical aid	3,954	2,399	1,540	1,754	1,413
Europe	3,823	2,250	1,122	1,282	500
Non-Europe	131	149	418	472	913
Other aid	20	—	—	28	125

Source: **111**, p. 4.

a. Appropriations which are not distributed by geographic areas.

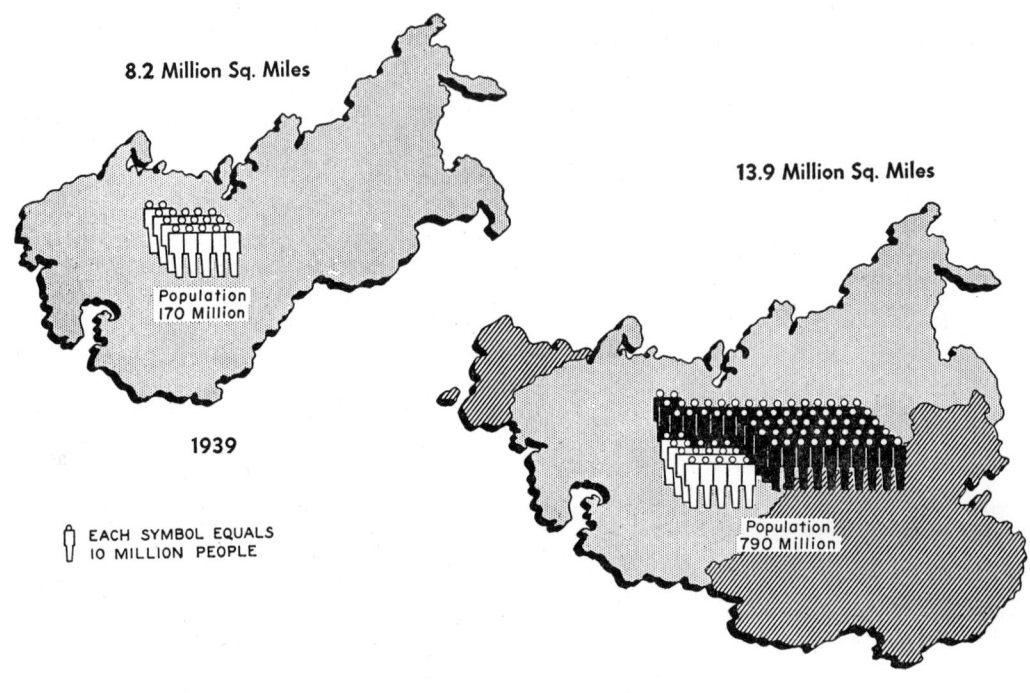

8.2 Million Sq. Miles

Population
170 Million

1939

EACH SYMBOL EQUALS
10 MILLION PEOPLE

13.9 Million Sq. Miles

Population
790 Million

1951

Source: **113,** December 31, 1951

FIGURE 156. THE GREATER SOVIET BLOC: A CHALLENGE TO THE FREE WORLD

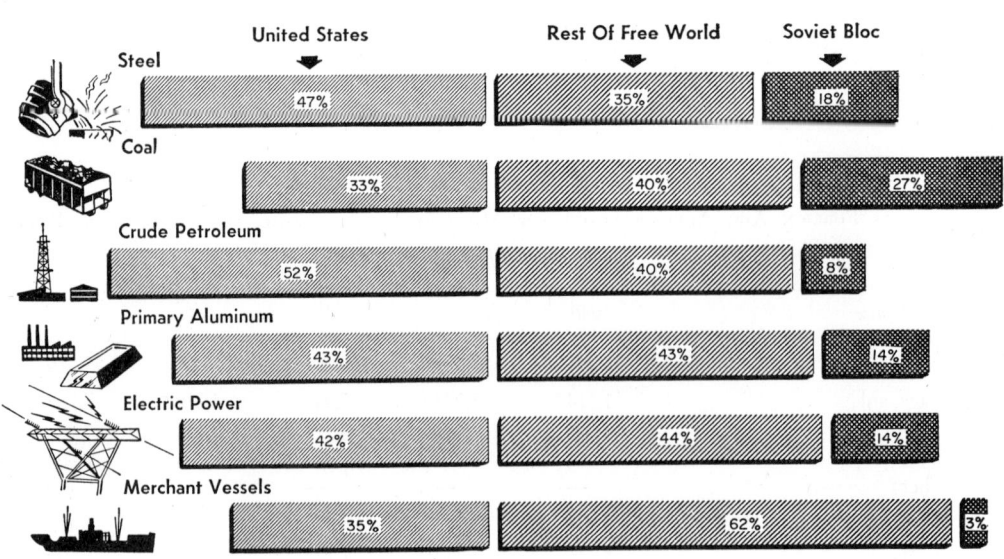

	United States	Rest Of Free World	Soviet Bloc
Steel	47%	35%	18%
Coal	33%	40%	27%
Crude Petroleum	52%	40%	8%
Primary Aluminum	43%	43%	14%
Electric Power	42%	44%	14%
Merchant Vessels	35%	62%	3%

Source: **113,** December 31, 1951

FIGURE 157. THE MUTUAL SECURITY PROGRAM: RESOURCES OF THE FREE NATIONS AND THE SOVIET BLOC

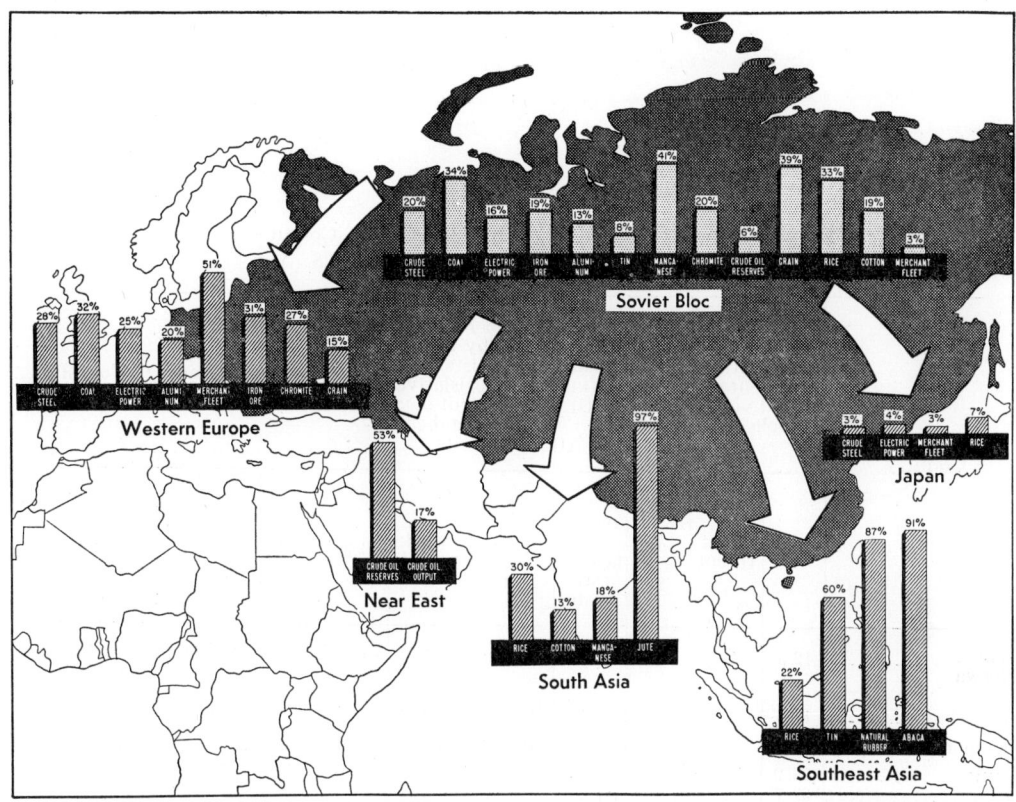

Source: **114**, 1953

FIGURE 158. STRATEGIC RESOURCES OF THE SOVIET BLOC AND SURROUNDING AREAS

All data are given as percentages of world totals (latest data available, 1951 or 1952).

The Soviet bloc would gain the balance of power if the resources of the surrounding areas should be added to its own.

in various parts of the world. (See Tables 287 to 290.)

The United States provides direct military aid to 50 countries: reimbursable aid to 24; reimbursable aid and grants to 21; and grants only to 5. Military Assistance Advisory Groups (MAAG's), which assure close military cooperation between these countries and the United States, are located in 23 countries. (See Figure 159.)

The program in Europe centers on the collective defense build-up of the North Atlantic Treaty Organization (NATO), which now includes the United States, Canada and 13 European nations: the United Kingdom, France, Germany, Luxembourg, Belgium, the Netherlands, Denmark, Norway, Portugal, Italy, Greece, Turkey and Iceland. Sweden is not a member. Germany's part in an integrated European defense system was determined by the Paris Agreements of October 1954. After a long delay caused by

the hesitation of France, the Agreements were ratified by the Parliaments and governments of all NATO states and Germany.

Military Expenditures in Europe

The armament program of the European Defense Community (EDC) was fluid and its targets were revised repeatedly. By the end of 1952 the NATO countries had some fifty divisions, over half of them in combat readiness and the remainder in rapidly mobilizable reserve units. They had some 4,000 combat aircraft, together with necessary airfields, supporting installations and communication systems; and naval forces consisting of 704 major combat vessels and 925 smaller combat ships. These figures do not include forces to be supplied by Greece, Turkey and Germany. According to the Paris Agreements of October 1954, Germany is authorized and committed to maintain a standing army of 12 divisions, with air forces and navy designed

Table 287

POLITICAL BACKGROUND OF THE MUTUAL SECURITY PROGRAM: COMMUNIST STRENGTH IN WESTERN EUROPEAN COUNTRIES RECEIVING U.S. AID

Country	Voting strength (percent of total vote polled)		Party membership (in thousands)		Number of seats held by Communists in main legislative body out of total number of seats		Circulation of leading Communist Party newspaper (in thousands)		
	1946	Most recent	1946	Most recent satisfactory estimate	1946	Most recent	1946	Most recent	Newspaper
Belgium	12.7	4.7	100	30	23/202	7/212	(¹)	35	Drapeau Rogue (French), Rhode Vaan (Flemish edition).
Netherlands	11.4	6.16	50	33	10/100	6/100	400	100	de Waarheid.
Denmark	²12.5	4.84	60	16	² 18/149	7/149	35	{ 19 / 29	Land og Folk, daily. / Land og Folk, Sunday
France	28.2	25.7	850	550	181/621	100/625	1,200	174	L'Humanité.
Italy	³39.7	⁴34.7	⁵2,300	1,700	219/556	178/555	330	340	L'Unita.
Norway	²11.9	5.8	35	9	² 11/150	0/185	40	11	Friheten.
Western Germany	7.9	5.7	300	126	6/104	15/402	------	48	Freies Volk.
United Kingdom	.4	.07	48	35	2/640	0/625	121	95–100	London Daily Worker.
Greece	⁶9.3	⁷11.4	175	50	³ 18/250	0/300	50	8	Avgi.
Austria	5.4	5.28	100	60	4/165	4/165	180	100	Volkstimme.
Iceland	20.0	19.5	1	1	10/52	9/52	7.5	6.5	Thjod Villjinn.
Turkey	Communist Party and all front organizations are illegal.						------		No organ published.
Yugoslavia	Under Tito's control the Communist Party dominates the political life of Yugoslavia.						664		Borba.

¹ Not available.
² 1945 elections.
³ Includes vote of parties allied with Communists.
⁴ The figures used here are for the Communist-led electoral alliance in those areas voting in the local elections, May-June 1951. The first column for Italy gives the results of the 1948 national elections, and the 2d column indicates the results of the 1951-52 local balloting in areas where elections were held.
⁵ Party claims January 1948.
⁶ The Communists boycotted the elections and this figure represents an estimate of the number of voters who abstained in obedience to the party's orders.
⁷ Pro-Communist United Democratic Left; Greek Communist Party has been banned since December 1947.

Source: **112,** 1954, p. 51.

TABLE 288

POLITICAL BACKGROUND OF THE MUTUAL SECURITY PROGRAM: COMMUNIST STRENGTH
IN THE NEAR EAST AND AFRICA

Country	Communist	Communist Party membership
Anglo-Egyptian Sudan	Illegal	Less than 100 (estimate).
Egypt	do	Less than 3,000 (estimate). No unified party organization or coordinated leadership.
Ethiopia	None	None.
Iran	Tudeh Party declared illegal Feb. 5, 1949.	Tudeh Party hard core estimated at not more than 15,000.
Iraq	Illegal	12,000 (estimate).
Israel	The Communist Part of Israel; 27,300 votes, 5 seats (4 held previously).	6,000 Jewish members; 4,000 Arab members (estimate April 1950); 25,000 Jewish members; 10,000 Arab members (Communist claim).
Jordan	Illegal	Estimated at about 2,000.
Lebanon	do	8,000 (estimate, January 1952).
Liberia	None	None.
Saudi-Arabia	No anti-Communist legislation, but Government would not tolerate Communists.	Do.
Syria	Illegal	10,000 (estimate, January 1952).
Turkey	Communist Party and all front organizations illegal.	No Communist Party members; the number of pro-Communists is extremely small.
Yemen	No anti-Communist legislation known, but Government presumably would not tolerate communism.	None.

Source: **112,** 1954, p. 51.

TABLE 289

POLITICAL BACKGROUND OF THE MUTUAL SECURITY PROGRAM: COMMUNIST STRENGTH IN ASIA

Country and date of last national parliamentary election	Communist or Communist-controlled party	Bloc supported by Communists	Non-Communist parties	Communist Party membership
Burma: 1951	Burma Communist Party (BCP). The major Communist organization. Maintains international Communist contacts. Not represented in the legislature. Communist Party (Burma), A small national Communist group which split from the BCP in 1946. Not represented in the legislature. Burma Workers and Peasants Party (BWPP). A pro-Communist group which broke with the Burma Socialist Party in December 1950. Holds 9 seats in the chamber of deputies.		The Anti-Fascist People's Freedom League (AFPFL): A nationalist coalition dominates the legislature. The AFPFL, including the Burma Socialist Party, its principal component controls 196 seats in the Chamber of Deputies. People's Peace Front: A leftist group. Has 3 seats in Chamber of Deputies; members usually follow BWPP. Mahabama: Now represents little more than personal following of Ba Maw. Has 1 seat; follows BWPP.	
Ceylon: May 1952, 2,331,306 votes polled; 95 elected seats and 6 appointed seats.	Communist Party of Ceylon. 134,527 votes (5.8 percent), 4 seats (4.2 percent). Lanka Sama Samaj Party (Trotskyite), 305,114 votes (13.0 percent), 9 seats (9.5 percent).		Complete data not available.	5,000 (estimate)
National Government of the Republic of China (Taiwan).	Communist Party and pro-Communist parties are illegal.		Kuomintang dominates the Government and activities of the 2 legal minor parties. The Young China Party and Democratic Socialist Party, each of which has had a few seats in the Legislative Yuan and 1 nonministerial portfolio in the Executive Yuan.	No estimate.
India: Election of October 1951–February 1952 House of the People.	Communist Party of India (CPI): 4,712,009 votes (4.5 percent), 23 seats (4.7 percent).			30,000 (claim, October 1951). Probably has increased since then.
Indochina (Vietnam)	Vietnam Workers Party: The Indochinese Communist Party, officially dissolved in November 1945, reemerged in the "Democratic Republic of Vietnam" as the "National Vietnam Workers' Party at a congress held in February 1951. In areas under Franco-Vietnamese control, Communist organizations and activities are prohibited.	The Workers Party is in full control of the "Democratic Republic of Vietnam," and the "National United Front (Lien Viet)" which involves the numerous subsidiary front organizations within the regime.	Major non-Communist political groupings in Vietnam are the Catholics, the Caodaists, and the Dai Viet and Vietnam Nationalist Parties. Some of these groupings, notably the Catholics, survive in the Communist zones, although they have been largely driven underground. For the most part these groupings support the anti-Communist policies of the Government of Vietnam under Bao Dai.	No estimate.
Indochina (Laos): National Assembly, Aug. 26, 1951, 39 seats.	The "Laotian Resistance Government", and the "Laotian National United Front", organized in August 1950 operate in close	The Laotian "resistance movement," headed by Prince Souphanouvong.	The Laos Union National Party, Progressive Party, and Democratic Party and a number of independents make up the	Negligible.

			representation of the Laos National Assembly.	
Indochina (Cambodia): National Assembly, Sept. 9, 1951, 78 seats.	conjunction with Communist-dominated groups in Vietnam. There is no overt Communist activity in areas under control of French Union forces and the Laotian National Army. The "Cambodian National United Front" and "Western Cambodia Mouta Seiha Party" operate in close conjunction with Communist-dominated groups in Vietnam. There is no overt Communist activity in areas under control of French Union forces and Royal Cambodian forces.	The Cambodian "resistance" movement.	The Khmer Renovation, Democratic, National Recovery, Liberal, People's, Democratic-Progressive, National Union and Victorious Northeastern Khmer Parties, as well as a number of independents are all opposed to communism.	Negligible.
Indonesia	Pending the holding of general elections, party representation in the unicameral Parliament continues to be determined by Government fiat. Indonesian Communist Party (Stalinist) has 15 votes (6.8 percent), plus 12 votes (5.5 percent) from satellite and allied groups, and 11 votes (5 percent) from nonparty members, giving a theoretical maximum of 38 votes (17.3 percent). Proletarian Party Murba (National Communist) has 4 votes (1.8 percent).	None in Parliament.	Non-Communist leftist parties: Indonesian Socialist Party, Labor Party, PSII (Moslem party), Indonesian Nationalist Party (PNI) a nonreligious national party currently disunited by virtue of the actions of its more extreme left wing. Nonreligious centrist and rightist parties: Party of Great Indonesia (Parindra), Great Indonesia Association (PIR), National People's Party (PRN), Indonesian People's League (SKI), Democratic People's Faction. Religious Parties: Moslem League (Masjumi), Nahdatul Ulama, Catholic Party, Protestant Party (Parkindo). To this may be added 11 votes (5 percent from nonparty members, giving a theoretical total of 178 non-Communist votes in Parliament (80.7 percent).	Indonesian Communist Party: 30,000 (claim 1951); 15,000 estimate. Proletarian Party: 70,000 (claim 1951).
Pakistan: None. One planned for late 1953.	Communist Party of Pakistan (CPP).		Jinnah Awami Muslim League, Azad Pakistan Party,[1] Socialist Party of Pakistan.	
Thailand: 1948. Communists take no part in overt party politics.	Thai Communist Party: Thai CP appendage of the Chinese Communist Party (Thailand) composed largely of intellectuals. Chinese Communist Party (Thailand): A potential threat to the Thai Government because of its influence among the 3 million Chinese in Thailand and its support from Communist China. Indochinese Communists in Thailand support the "Democratic Republic of Vietnam" military activities in Indochina.		Formal political parties are banned. The 1947 Coup Group and its adherents, forming the government's parliamentary majority, and opposition MP's of the former Democratic Party are the major non-Communist groups in the National Assembly.	5,000 maximum (estimate). Thai Communist Party: 50-100 (estimate). Chinese Communist Party (Thailand): 2,000. Indochinese Communists (no estimate).

[1] Certain significant element sympathetic with the Stalinist Party.

Source: **112**, 1954, pp. 52-53.

TABLE 290

POLITICAL BACKGROUND OF THE MUTUAL SECURITY PROGRAM: COMMUNIST STRENGTH IN LATIN AMERICA

Country and date of last national parliamentary election	Communist	Left-wing parties	Center and right-wing parties		Communist Party membership
			Ruling party or coalition	Opposition parties	
Argentina, November 1951	Communist Party (PCA), no seats.	Socialist Party, no seats.	Peronista Party, 165 seats (92 percent).	Radical, Progressive Democrat, 14 seats (8 percent).	Not over 40,000.
Bolivia, May 1951	Communist Party (PCB) (illegal); Revolutionary Workers Party (POR), Trotskyist.	Revolutionary Left Party (PIR).	Nationalist Revolutionary Movement (MNR). (This party includes both leftist and rightist elements.) (Military Junta which took power in May 1951 was ousted by MNR coup in April 1952.)	Socialist Falange (FSB), Social Democratic Party (PSD), Republican Socialist Union Party (PUSR), Liberal Party.	PCB under 2,000 (estimate).
Brazil, October 1950	Communist Party (PCB) (illegal, 1 deputy elected on non-Communist ticket).	Socialist Party (PSB) 36,638 votes (0.6 percent), 2 seats (0.6 percent).	Social Democratic Party (PSD), 2,068,405 votes (35 percent), 141 seats (38 percent); Brazilian Workers Party (PTB), 1,262,000 votes (20.7 percent), 63 seats (17 percent); Social Progressive (PSP), 558,792 votes (9.2 percent), 31 seats (8 percent).	National Democratic Union (UDN), 1,301,459 votes (21.3 percent), 90 seats (25 percent); Republican Party (PR), 216,207 votes (3.5 percent), 15 seats (4 percent).	55,000 (estimate).
Chile, March 1949	Communist Party (PCCh) (illegal), 2 seats (1 percent).	Socialist Party (PS), 9 seats (5 percent). (PSP faction and PSCh merged in October 1951 to form PS).	Agrarian Labor (major wing), Popular Socialist (PSP) (major wing), (Democratic Front, People's Democratic, Independent, 23 seats (12 percent).	Radical, Social Christian, Falange, Democratic (major wing), 77 seats (40.1 percent); Traditional Conservative, Liberal, Liberal Progressive, Democratic (minor wing), Agrarian (minor wing), 81 seats (42.2 percent).	35,000 (estimate).
Columbia, September 1951	Communist Party (PCC), 4,471 votes (0.5 percent), no seats.	Liberal Populist Party, 5,478 votes (0.6 percent), no seats.	Conservative Party, 845,000 votes (98.6 percent), 111 seats (56 percent), (87 seats vacant).	Liberal Party, party abstained in 1951 elections.	About 2,000.
Costa Rica, October 1949	Popular Vanguard (VP) (illegal). (Communist-front Progressive Independent Party (PPI) gained official registration in October 1952).	Social Democratic Party, 5,034 votes (7 percent), 3 seats (7 percent).	National Union Party, 54,375 votes (72 percent), 33 seats (73 percent).	Constitutional Party, etc., 16,422 votes (22 percent), 9 seats (20 percent); National Republican (Calderonista) Party.	About 1,000.
Cuba, June 1950	Popular Socialist Party (PSP).		Unitary Action Party (PAU) (Batista, head of the PAU, took power in coup of March 1952, postponed elections, and dissolved Congress).	Cuban Revolutionary Party (Auténtico), Party of the Cuban People (Orthodoxo), Democrata, Liberal Parties, etc.	25,000 (estimate).
Dominican Republic, May 1947.	Popular Socialist Party (PSPD) (illegal, based in Guatemala).	None.	Dominican Party, 840,340 votes (100 percent), all seats.	Dominican Revolutionary Party (in exile).	Not over several hundred.
Ecuador, June 1950.	Communist Party (PCE), 1 seat (0.9 percent).	Socialist Party (PSE), 4 seats (3.7 percent).	Velasquista Organization, 34 seats (31.2 percent).	Conservative Party, 30 seats (27.5 percent), Catholics, 15	Not over 5,000.

Country, election date	Communist Party	Other parties	Principal election results	Other parties' results	Estimated Communist strength
El Salvador, March 1952	Communist Party (PCS), (illegal).	Revolutionary Action Party (PAR), Democratic Party (PD). Parties abstained in 1952 elections.	Revolutionary Party of Democratic Unification (PRUD), 700,979 votes (99.9 percent), all seats.	seats (13.8 percent), Liberal Party, 22 seats (20.1 percent), Concentration of Popular Forces (CFP), 2 seats (1.8 percent).	Not over 1,000.
Guatemala, December 1950	Guatemalan Labor Party (PGT). Dropped name of Communist Party and registered as legal party in December 1952. Constitution prohibits "formation of * * * political organizations of international or foreign character." In 1950 elections 4 communists were elected on administration party slates.	Revolutionary Action Party (PAR), 19 seats (32.7 percent), Party of the Guatemalan Revolution (PRG), 19 seats (32.7 percent); National Renovation (RN), 4 seats (6.9 percent).	Left-wing coalition is ruling in Guatemala.	National Electoral Union, Patriotic Union, etc., 12 seats (20.7 percent).	Under 1,000.
Haiti, October 1950	Communist Party (illegal).	Popular Socialist Party (PSP) (illegal). Democratic Revolutionary Party (PDRH) (illegal).	Magloire group.	Workers and Peasants Party.	Not over several hundred.
Honduras, October 1948	No party (illegal).		Nationalist Party, 255,974 votes (99.9 percent) all seats.	Liberal Party, etc., 514 votes.	Do.
Mexico, July 1952	Communist Party (PCM) (lacks membership required for electoral registration).	Popular Party (PP), 2 seats (0.9 percent); Federation of People's Parties (FPPM), 1 seat (0.5 percent).	Revolutionary Institutional Party (PRI), 204 seats (90 percent); Nationalist Party (PNM), 2 seats (0.9 percent).	National Action Party (PAN). 5 seats (2.3 percent).	About 3,000.
Nicaragua, May 1950	Socialist Party of Nicaragua (PSN) (illegal).		National Liberal Party, 153,297 votes (75 percent), 40 seats (67 percent).	Conservative Party, 49,401 votes (25 percent), 20 seats (33 percent).	500 (estimate).
Panama, May 1952	People's Party (PDP) (lacks membership required for national electoral registration).	Patriotic Front Party (PFP), 1 seat (1.9 percent); Independent Revolutionary Party (PRI), 1 seat (1.9 percent).	Administration Coalition: Reform (PR), Liberal (PL), National Revolutionary (PNR), Popular Union (UP) Parties, 40 seats (75.5 percent); National Democratic Party (PND), 7 seats (13 percent).	National Liberal Party (PLN), 3 seats: Independent, 1 seat (1.9 percent).	Under 1,000.
Paraguay, July 1950	Communist Party (PCP) (illegal).		Colorado Party, 218,172 votes (100 percent) all seats.	Liberal, Febrerista Parties (not allowed to participate in elections).	Under 2,000.
Peru, July 1950	Communist Party (PCP) (illegal).	Aprista Party (illegal); Socialist Party, 4 seats (2 percent).	Pro-Odria Group, 194 seats (95.6 percent).	Anti-Odria Independents, 5 seats (2.4 percent).	Under 10,000.
Uruguay, November 1950	Communist Party (PCU), 19,026 votes (2.3 percent), 2 seats (1.5 percent).	Socialist Party, 17,041 votes (2.1 percent), 2 seats (1.5 percent).	Colorado Party, 433,164 votes (52.3 percent), 71 seats (54.3 percent).	Herrerista, Independent Nationalist, Civic Union, 358,349 votes (43.3 percent), 55 seats (42.7 percent).	15,000 estimate.
Venezuela, December 1947	Communist Party (PCV) (illegal), Revolutionary Proletarian Party (PRP-e) (Dissident).	Democratic Action (AD), (illegal); Democratic Republican Union (URD); Venezuelan Socialist Party (PSV).	Junta of Government (Venezuelan Congress dissolved following 1948 military coup).	Copei-----------	Under 20,000.

839

Source: 112, 1954, pp. 54–55.

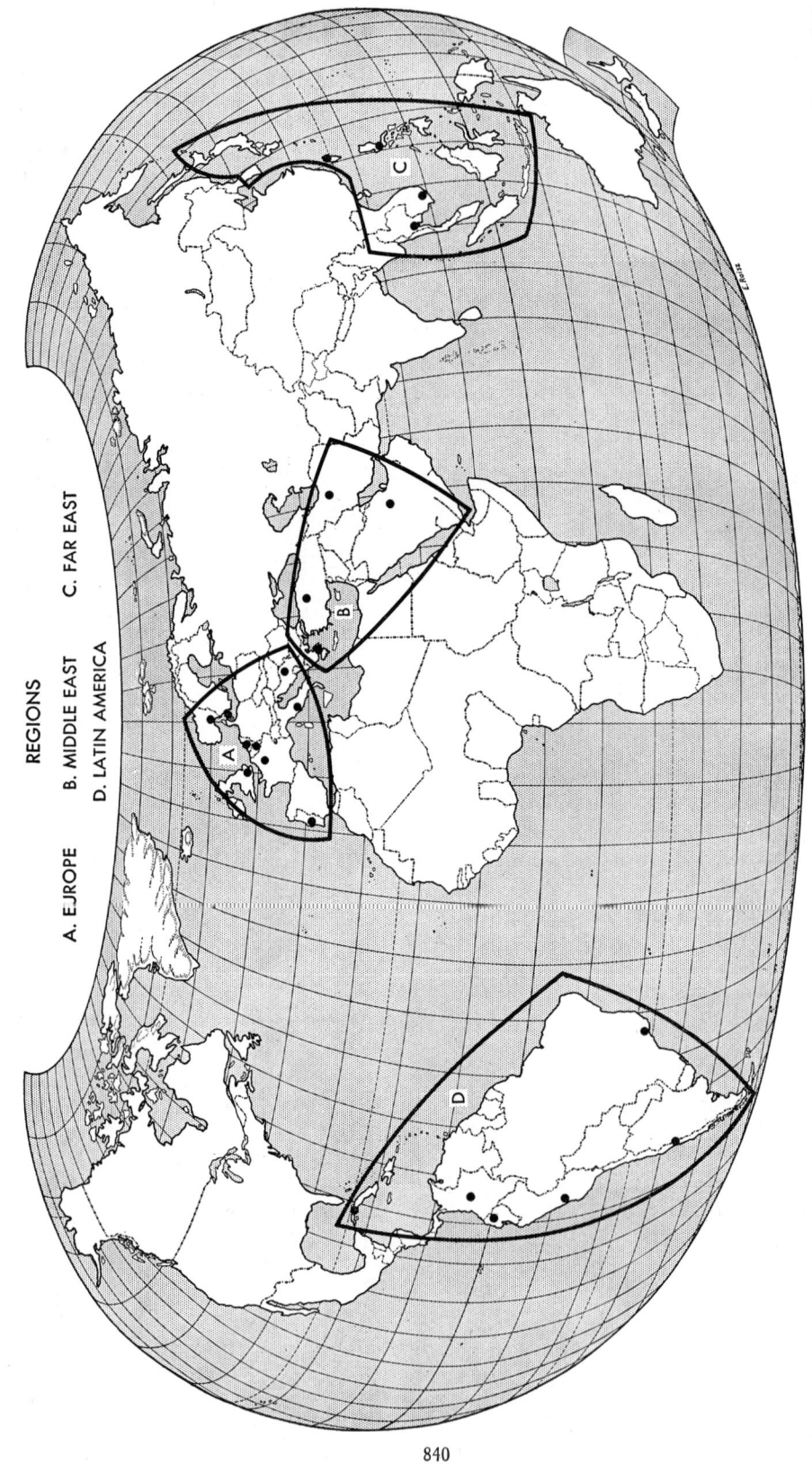

REGIONS

A. EUROPE   B. MIDDLE EAST   C. FAR EAST

D. LATIN AMERICA

FIGURE 159. THE MUTUAL DEFENSE ASSISTANCE PROGRAM: LOCATION OF MILITARY ASSISTANCE ADVISORY GROUPS (MAAG)

for defensive operations. The armed forces are limited to 500,000. The organization of the armed forces will hardly be completed before 1957.

Europe's defense expenditures increased from $6.4 billion in 1950 to $11.5 billion in 1952 and were estimated at $13.7 billion in 1953 and $14.9 billion in 1954. (See Figure 160,A.) Each of the NATO members is building up its armed forces separately in accordance with a common plan. The United States is to supply a large portion of the major matériel and to provide the European countries with raw materials for their own defense production. The financial contribution of the United States to the military defense of Europe amounted to $1 billion in the fiscal year 1950; $4.4 billion in 1951; $4.2 billion in 1952; and was estimated at $3.0 billion in 1953 and $2.2 billion in 1954. (See Figure 160, B.) These outlays were supplemented by nearly $10 billion spent on economic aid. Basically, however, almost all the military expenditures of the United States ($22 billion in 1951; $45.6 billion in 1952; more than $60 billion in 1953; and the $40 billion appropriated for 1954) can be regarded as the U.S. contribution to the military defense of the free world.

Productivity for Defense

The Mutual Security Agency in Europe carries on the productivity campaign inaugurated by the ECA as part of postwar reconstruction and economic growth. Little has changed in the campaign, but the emphasis has shifted toward resistance to the military and political aggression of the Kremlin. As the MSA phrases it:

By increasing productivity, the Europeans will be able to:

Produce more of materials required by their NATO defense forces in the protection of the Free World against the possibility of armed attack.

Increase the production of civilian goods at lower prices, share the resulting benefits more equitably, and thus strengthen faith in free institutions.[152]

Numerous labor and management teams from Western European countries have toured the United States to study its methods of production, its industrial relations and the administration of labor laws and related problems. On their return home, many productivity missions have published reports — some of them highly technical — with practical suggestions for domestic industry on ways of raising productivity to U.S. levels. It is impossible to measure the results of these study trips and to ascertain their share in the growth of industrial production in Europe since 1949, when the project began. But there is no doubt that European teams have had unique opportunities to become familiar with U.S. ways of life; to consider the problems of productivity; and to evaluate the social and political implications of these problems.

Control of Trade with the Soviet Bloc

To supplement its policy of collective rearmament the United States sought to induce the free nations to deny strategic goods to the Soviet bloc. The campaign was launched by the Mutual Defense Assistance Control Act of 1951 (known as the Battle Act), which declares that it is the policy of the United States to embargo shipments of arms, ammunition and certain other materials of primary strategic significance to nations that threaten the security of the United States. By a provision that no United States aid shall go to any country unless it adopts the same embargo — with certain exceptions — the act transforms a unilateral policy into a program of mutual security.[153]

While all NATO countries are committed not to sell arms to their potential enemies, the Battle Act goes further and, by establishing a partial embargo on raw materials, tries to stop the flow of strategic goods from the free world to the USSR and its satellites. The weak point of the act lies in the concept of "strategic goods." Broadly speaking, nearly all products in foreign trade are strategic goods during a war or in preparation for war. Since the foreign trade policy of Russia emphasizes the goods needed to increase the military strength of the nation, no measure short of complete embargo can deny the Soviet bloc strategic goods in the broad sense of the term. The Western European countries would oppose such measures, however, since trade with eastern Europe is much more significant for them than for the United States. Normally these countries import from Russia and its satellites many articles which are, for them, strategic goods in the broad sense, such as manganese and timber. The term strategic goods is therefore used more narrowly in the Mutual Defense Assistance Control Act.

---

152. **130**, p. ii.

153. See **110**; cf. **127** and **128**.

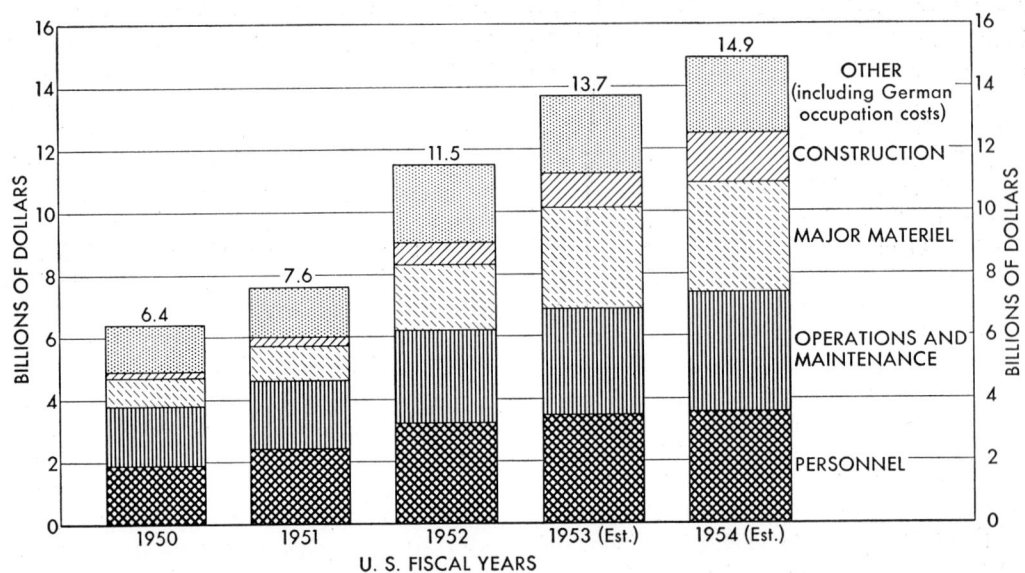

A. European Defense Expenditures: NATO and Germany

From 1950 to 1953 the entire German defense expenditure was for occupation costs. In fiscal year 1954 an additional German expenditure of $1,274 million for the EDC contribution is included in the categories shown on the chart.

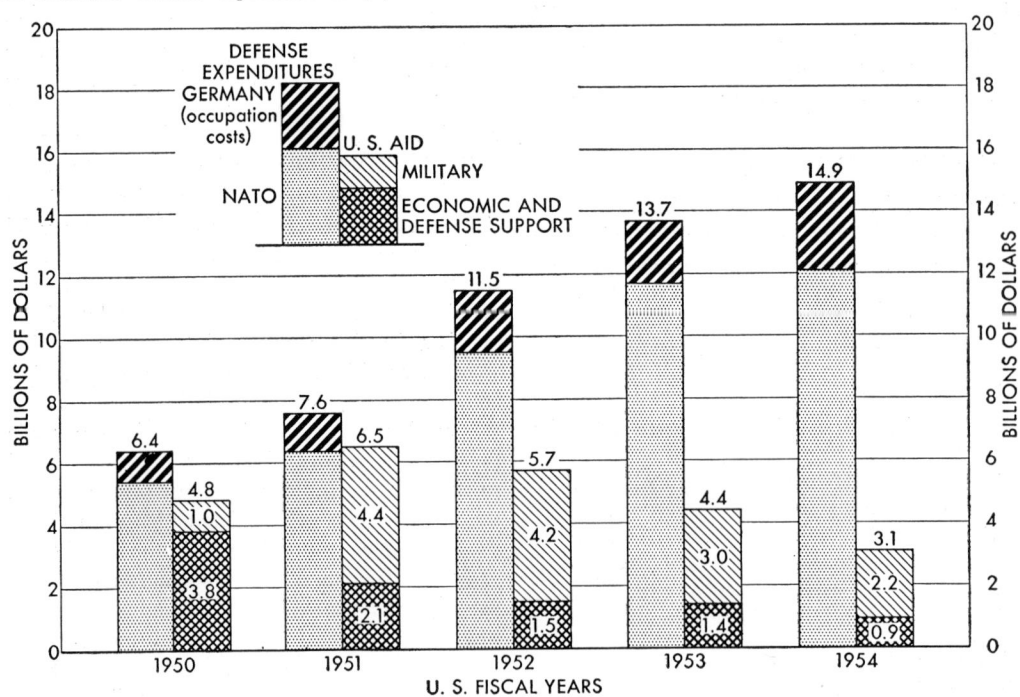

Source: 129

B. European Defense Expenditures and U.S. Economic and Military Aid to Europe

The actual U.S. appropriations have been adjusted to reflect interappropriation transfers.

The authorization request for 1954 excludes an estimated saving of $300 million carry-over from fiscal year 1953 funds.

FIGURE 160. THE MUTUAL DEFENSE ASSISTANCE PROGRAM: EXPENDITURES IN EUROPE, 1950–54

A partial embargo serves no useful purpose, however, when the Soviet countries can readily shift their orders to a country which does not adhere to the program — for example, Sweden, Switzerland and Argentina. Indeed, even a complete embargo by a group of nations would not be effective unless supported by a blockade. In the absence of such a blockade, the selective embargo is likely to create certain inconveniences but will hardly cripple the military industries of Russia and its satellites. The practical effects of the program were not very clear in mid-1955. The first Administration reports to Congress failed to provide evidence that the act had met expectations.

Development of Strategic Materials

A more significant aspect of the MS program is the development of production of strategic materials throughout the world, in part for stockpiling in the event of war. This should not be confused with U.S. financial and technical assistance to underdeveloped countries to develop their resources, which is determined by the needs and requests of the respective countries, whereas the strategic-materials-development projects are motivated by the grim threat of war. However, these projects also encourage the local economy. They are dispersed throughout the world from Greenland (lead) to Southern Rhodesia (asbestos, copper); from Jamaica (bauxite) to Norway (aluminum, columbite); from Greece (bauxite, lead, zinc, manganese) to New Caledonia (chrome). (See Figure 161.)

Appraisal of the Program

It is difficult to appraise the effect of the MS program on the world's chances for peace and the survival of freedom. The strategy of the West in its conflict with the East has been the subject of bitter criticism. Many controversial issues are involved; differences in the views of France and Germany, Great Britain and France, the United States and Great Britain have made decisions particularly difficult. It seems, however, that the program has achieved some practical results.

In his report to Congress for the second half of 1952, President Truman summarized the results as follows:

The first international military command in the peacetime history of the world has become a going concern.

The NATO nations, originally twelve and now fifteen in number, have agreed on a common strategic plan for the common defense.

These nations are building, together, balanced collective forces.

Armed forces of the original NATO nations have more than doubled and to those have been added the armed forces of Turkey and Greece.

Intensive joint training exercises and war games have been carried out on land, sea, and in the air by the armed forces of many nations.

The consultative machinery originally established under NATO has been transformed into a permanent working organization.

While the nations of Western Europe and the Atlantic world are not yet secure against Soviet invasion, they have created and will continue to strengthen a powerful military deterrent to any aggression.

At the same time there has been real progress toward the establishment of a Western European community of nations, including the Federal Republic of Germany. The Schuman Plan — one of the most imaginative acts of statesmanship in our times — has led to the establishment of a six-nation merger of coal and steel resources. Projects are pending for economic integration; and work has been started on a draft constitution for political federation. There have been disappointments and setbacks; we face a number of difficult problems right now. But, over-all, the movement toward greater unity in Europe is still continuing.

In short, what began as international cooperation for economic recovery in Western Europe is growing into collective defense, economic integration, and political unity. This is one of the most hopeful — and essential — developments in our time.

THE TECHNICAL COOPERATION ADMINISTRATION:
POINT FOUR PROGRAM

The program of the Technical Cooperation Administration (TCA) had its genesis in 1949 in the Point Four proposal. It is a modest venture in comparison with the Marshall Plan or the Mutual Assistance program. It has features, however, which justify it as a "bold new program" and ensure it a unique place in the history of international cooperation. After June 30, 1955 the program will be entrusted to the State Department. The scope for the year 1955–56 has not been fixed, but it is expected that the emphasis will be shifted to Asia.

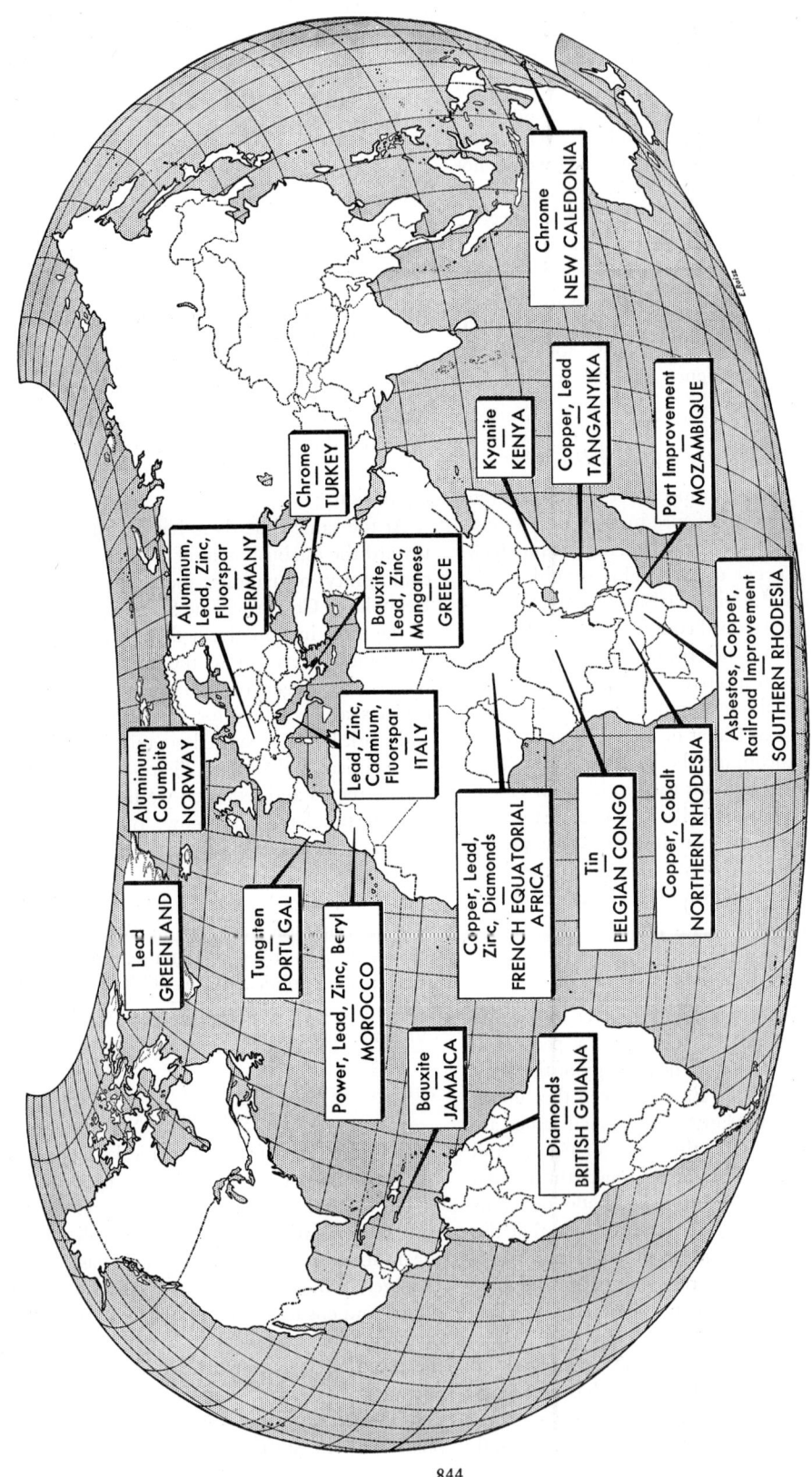

FIGURE 161. THE MUTUAL SECURITY PROGRAM: GEOGRAPHIC DISTRIBUTION OF PROJECTS TO DEVELOP STRATEGIC MATERIALS, AS OF JUNE 30, 1952

Origin and Organization

Point Four is the U.S. program of technical assistance to underdeveloped countries on a non-commercial basis. It was carried on by the Foreign Operations Administration, in areas which include Latin America, the independent countries of Africa, the Middle East and South Asia.

The name under which this program has become known was first used by President Truman in his inaugural address on January 20, 1949 — when it was defined as the fourth major point in U.S. foreign policy.[154] Authority for the program was provided by the Act for International Development of 1950.[155] Continuation of the program was authorized by the Mutual Security Acts of 1951 and 1952.[156] Under the new Administration the original name was dropped in official documents and it became known as the Technical Assistance (or Technical Cooperation) program.[157]

The program, however, considerably antedates the President's inaugural address of 1949. It may be regarded as an expansion of activities which the U.S. government had been carrying on in Latin America since 1942 through the Institute of Inter-American Affairs. In June 1950 the Institute became the Inter-American Regional Office of the TCA.[158]

The Act for International Development combined technical cooperation (or assistance) with encouragement of U.S. private investment abroad:

It is declared to be the policy of the United States to aid the efforts of the peoples of economically underdeveloped areas to develop their resources and improve their working and living conditions by encouraging the exchange of technical knowledge and skills and flow of investment capital to countries which provide conditions under which such technical assistance and capital can effectively and constructively contribute to raising standards of living, creating new sources of wealth, increasing productivity and expanding purchasing power.[159]

It may be questioned whether the combination of the two ideas in one legislative act was sound. To attract investment capital, a development project must promise profits high enough to offset risks. When a company plans foreign investments it thinks of "expanding purchasing power" in terms of its stockholders. Foreign investment may create new sources of wealth in an underdeveloped country, but that is rarely the purpose or criterion in determining investment policy. The Act for International Development, however, establishes procedures for selecting assistance projects based solely on the interests of the underdeveloped countries. Assistance is given either through multilateral technical cooperation programs carried on by the UN, its specialized agencies and the Organization of American States, or through bilateral agreements with individual countries. Assistance may be provided to a country only if the country meets the following conditions:

1. Pays a fair share of the cost of the program.
2. Provides all necessary information concerning such program and gives the program full publicity.
3. Seeks to the maximum extent possible full coordination and integration of technical cooperation programs being carried on in that country.
4. Endeavors to make effective use of the results of the program.
5. Cooperates with other countries participating in the program in the mutual exchange of technical knowledge and skills.[160]

All programs are initiated by the governments that request assistance, usually as a part of their own plans for development.

Technical Cooperation Agreements

Action under Point Four begins with the signing of a "general agreement" for technical cooperation between the United States and the recipient state. Between November 1950 and September 1953, such bilateral agreements were signed with thirty-nine countries.[161]

The agreements are not identical, but contain similar provisions. They state the objectives of the program and the intentions of the two governments; outline the nature of contributions to be made by both parties; confirm the intention of the recipient government to coordinate this program with other related plans; ensure information and public reports on the progress of the program; authorize detailed agreements for particular projects; provide for the duration of the program and the conditions of its termination.[162]

---

154. **117**, pp. 1–2.
155. **110**, pp. 99–100.
156. **110**, pp. 1–34.
157. See **122**.
158. See **135, 136** through **141, 158**.
159. **110**, p. 91.

160. See **110**.
161. See **133**.
162. **137**, pp. 14–15; cf. **134**.

In view of the considerable role these agreements play in developing the program, two typical agreements are examined below in some detail. Both were signed with India. The first is a general agreement, while the second establishes operating procedures.

The general agreement, signed on December 28, 1950, consists of five articles, which respectively establish the scope of assistance and cooperation; deal with information related to the cooperative projects; relate technical and administrative problems to special agreements; define the status of U.S. personnel employed on the projects; and define procedures of entry. The last three articles are essentially formal. The policy of the whole operation is outlined in Articles I and II, which read as follows:

Article I
Assistance and Cooperation

1. The Government of the United States of America and the Government of India undertake to cooperate with each other in the interchange of technical knowledge and skills and in related activities designed to contribute to the balanced and integrated development of the economic resources and productive capacities in India. Particular technical cooperation programs and projects will be carried out pursuant to the provisions of such separate written agreements or understandings as may later be reached by the duly designated representatives of India and the Technical Cooperation Administration of the United States of America, or by other persons, agencies, or organizations designated by the governments.

2. The Government of India through its duly designated representatives in cooperation with representatives of the Technical Cooperation Administration of the United States of America and representatives of appropriate international organizations will endeavor to coordinate and integrate all technical cooperation programs being carried on in India.

3. The Government of India will cooperate in the mutual exchange of technical knowledge and skills with other countries participating in technical cooperation programs associated with that carried on under this agreement.

4. The Government of India will endeavor to make effective use of the results of technical projects carried on in India in cooperation with the United States of America.

5. The two governments will, upon the request of either of them, consult with regard to any matter relating to the application of this Agreement to project agreements heretofore or hereafter concluded between them, or to operations or arrangements carried out pursuant to such agreements.

Article II
Information and Publicity

1. The Government of India will communicate to the Government of the United States of America in a form and at intervals to be mutually agreed upon:

(a) Information concerning projects, programs, measures and operations carried on under this Agreement, including a statement of the use of funds, materials, equipment and services provided thereunder;

(b) Information regarding technical assistance which has been or is being requested of other countries or of international organizations.

2. Not less frequently than once a year, the Governments of India and of the United States of America will in mutual consultation make public in their respective countries periodic reports on the technical cooperation programs carried on pursuant to this Agreement. Such reports shall include information as to the use of funds, materials, equipment and services.

3. The Governments of the United States of America and India will endeavor in mutual consultation to give full publicity to the objectives and progress of the technical cooperation program carried on under this Agreement.

The language of these articles is clear, and they contain nothing which might be construed or interpreted as interference by the United States in the domestic affairs of India or as a desire to exercise political or economic pressure on the Indian government.

The second agreement, signed on January 5, 1952, is more technical. Its core is in Articles II, III and IV. The first two establish the system of operating funds and the procedure of allocations and disbursements:

Article II

1. The two Governments agree that there shall be established an Indo-American Technical Cooperation Fund (hereinafter known as Fund A) in which the Government of the United States of America will deposit, up to the 30th June, 1952, the sum of 50 million dollars for agreed projects. This Fund shall be jointly administered by a duly appointed officer of the Government of India and by the [U.S.] Director and shall be utilized only for the execution of agreed projects of technical cooperation. Allocations will be made . . . whereby agreed amounts shall be transferred from Fund A to the Consolidated Funds of the Government of India or shall otherwise be authorized to be expended. Such transfers . . . shall be in the forms of grants-in-aid and loans in proportion to be agreed — to the Government of India in support of the Technical Coopera-

tion Program which, by this Agreement, the two Governments undertake to execute. . . .

2. The Government of India has an established Special Development Fund (hereinafter referred to as Fund B) which exceeds 25 crores of rupees. The Government of India agrees that, for each duly agreed project, it will, itself or in cooperation with the Government of the States in India, make available supplementary finance, in rupees, in agreed proportions, as required, by authorizing expenditures against Fund B or otherwise.

Article III

1. The two Governments agree that with respect to the funds to be made available by the Government of the United States of America to Fund A, any part thereof may, with the concurrence of the Government of India, be withheld in the United States of America for the procurement of agreed goods, materials and contractors' services from sources outside of India; funds so withheld shall be regarded as having been deposited in Fund A.

2. Sums disbursed in furtherance of projects may be disbursed either as grants-in-aid or as loans, or any combination thereof. If funds are disbursed as loans, there shall be a stipulation for repayment in rupees to the Government of India; funds accruing to the Government of India by virtue of such repayments of loans attributable to Fund A as well as sales proceeds of saleable goods imported under this Technical Cooperation Programme shall be deposited in Fund B and shall, during the period this Agreement remains in force, be utilized only for the prosecution of further projects of economic development agreed to between the two Governments.

3. The two Governments agree that the salaries and expenses of all technical experts employed for the programme by the Government of the United States of America, the travel outside India, tuition and other expenses of any nationals of India to whom training facilities outside India are made available by the Government of the United States of America, and the costs of technical assistance provided by the Government of the United States of America through contract with private agencies, shall be borne by the Government of the United States of America out of funds other than those agreed to be deposited in Fund A. The Government of India on its part shall arrange to provide such local facilities as may be required and agreed in each case.

Article IV states that the government of India alone is responsible for selecting and planning the development projects. The U.S. director is to serve only as a consultant:

Article IV

1. The Government of India agrees to constitute a Central Committee . . . The Committee shall lay down the broad policies and provide the general supervision under which agreed projects of Technical Cooperation shall be executed. The membership of the Committee shall consist of such persons (not to exceed 7) as may be appointed by the Government of India.

2. The Committee shall be responsible for developing, in consultation with the appropriate authorities in the various States in India, programmes of economic development and technical cooperation in which the assistance provided by the Government of the United States of America can be most advantageously utilized.

3. The Director shall make his services available as a consultant to the Committee and he shall be consulted with respect to all programme recommendations of the Committee and his concurrence shall be required with respect to any recommendations involving the allocation or expenditure of funds made available by the Government of the United States of America.

4. The Government of India shall ensure that all projects undertaken pursuant to this Agreement are properly coordinated with the economic development programmes and activities of the Government of India, including those carried on with the cooperation of other governments, of international organizations, and of private agencies.

These passages reveal the spirit in which the program is operated in India. Care has been taken to establish mutual confidence and to eliminate any suspicion of colonialism in the guise of assistance.

During the discussion of the extension of the Mutual Security Act before the House Committee on Foreign Affairs, the Assistant Secretary of State emphasized the importance of simple phrasing in the agreements:

We are in an area of the world here where personal confidence and contacts and friendships mean everything. . . . The agreements we are sometimes required to make are so long and so legal and so complicated that the good will we try to obtain by a small amount of assistance is offset by the fact that they just are suspicious of what all this legal language means. I cannot stress that too much.[163]

The attempt to crowd too much into the general agreements with Burma and Indonesia proved a serious obstacle to the technical assistance programs in those countries.

---

163. **109**, p. 1043.

Scope of Operations

Funds for carrying out the TCA program in five fiscal years have been appropriated by Congress as follows (in millions of dollars):

1951	$ 34.5
1952	159.5
1953	155.6
1954	328.3
1955	302.0

The appropriation for fiscal year 1954 included $106.3 million for technical assistance proper and $222 million for economic development projects ($147 million for the Near East and $75 million for India and Pakistan). For fiscal year 1955, $117 million was appropriated for TCA proper and $185 million for development assistance. The projects included construction of roads, dams, power stations; irrigation and drainage works; and development of local industries. Approximately 10 per cent of the outlays must be in the form of loans, the rest may be spent as straight grants.

Projects have been carried on in thirty-five countries. (See Figure 162.) In January 1953, 1,424 TCA experts were at work in these countries as follows: [164]

Latin America	598	Near East and	
Mexico	38	Africa	533
Guatemala	9	Libya	48
El Salvador	25	Egypt	38
Honduras	24	Ethiopia	16
Nicaragua	26	Liberia	60
Costa Rica	30	Lebanon	72
Panama	29	Israel	34
Cuba	8	Jordan	38
Haiti	22	Saudi Arabia	24
Dominican		Iraq	63
Republic	12	Iran	137
Venezuela	5	Regional	3
Colombia	18		
Ecuador	40	Asia	293
Brazil	88		
Peru	57	Afghanistan	11
Bolivia	40	Pakistan	45
Paraguay	43	India	113
Chile	28	Nepal	11
Uruguay	8	Burma	73
Regional	48	Indonesia	40

Furthermore, underdeveloped countries send technicians, students, labor and business leaders to the United States to observe and obtain advanced training not available in their own countries. *Project News* of the FOA describes this part of the program as follows:

There are scattered throughout the world today over 13,000 nationals from Europe, Asia, Africa, the Far East and the Caribbean who have visited the United States since 1949 under technical assistance sponsorship to observe and study the practices, principles and philosophies that have come to be known as the "American way."

Some come for a few weeks, some for several months, some for a year or more. Some have been high-placed government officials, scientists, engineers, industrialists, businessmen and skilled technicians. Others have been farmers, bench workers in factories and vocational students. But executive or worker, manufacturer or merchant, civil servant or cabinet minister, all have had a common aim and purpose in their visits: to find ways of thinking and doing that would make their skills more productive, their lives fuller and more satisfying, and their freedoms and those of the collective free world more secure.

More than 2,800 European project participants came to the United States in 1953. They were sent by Austria, Belgium, Luxembourg, Denmark, France, Germany, Greece, Iceland, Italy (including Trieste), the Netherlands, Norway, Portugal, Turkey, the United Kingdom, Yugoslavia, Sweden and Switzerland. The two latter countries have participated in the program at no expense to the U.S. Government. Almost 400 persons came from Free China, Indochina, the Philippines and Thailand during 1953. [165]

The many and various activities of TCA technicians may be grouped under four broad headings: (1) agriculture, including forestry and fisheries; (2) health and sanitation; (3) education; and (4) resource development, including general planning, industries and handicrafts, mining, transportation and communication, labor, public works, public administration and other services. (See Figure 162.)

Throughout the developing areas of Latin America, Asia and Africa, in which the Point 4 Program operates, the major problems of the more than a billion people grow out of widespread hunger, disease and illiteracy. Consequently, Point 4 concentrates its efforts on helping the people achieve their basic aims: improved agriculture, health and education. About 85 per cent of the TCA budget and personnel are directed to projects in these broad fields. However, as the program develops, increasing attention is being given to related fields of labor and industry, transportation, mineral and water development and the various phases of public administration.

164. See **136**.

165. **123**, December 1953, p. 3.

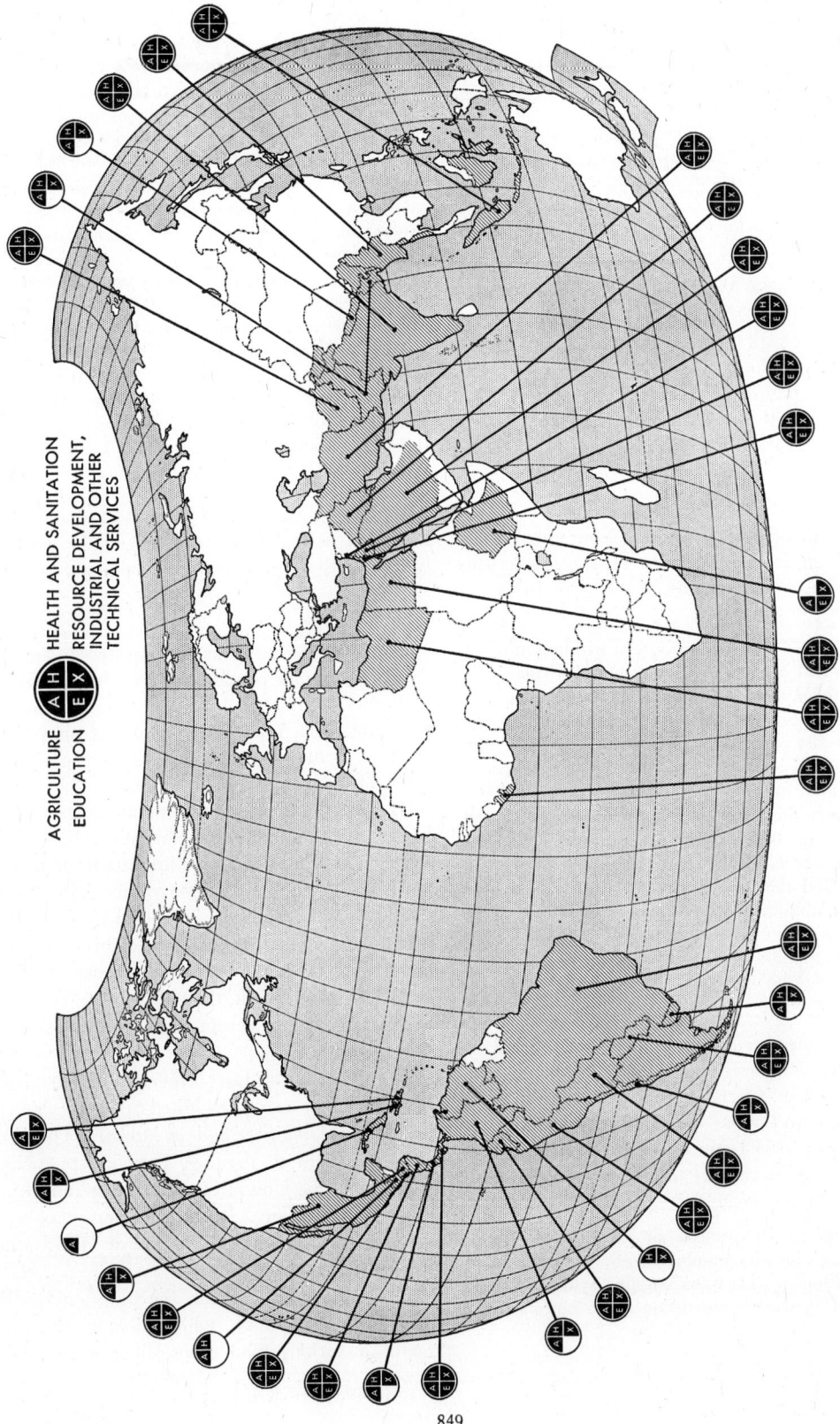

AGRICULTURE HEALTH AND SANITATION

EDUCATION RESOURCE DEVELOPMENT, INDUSTRIAL AND OTHER TECHNICAL SERVICES

Source: U.S. Department of State

FIGURE 162. POINT FOUR PROGRAM: GEOGRAPHIC DISTRIBUTION OF OPERATIONS, JANUARY 1953

Point 4 is essentially a program of education and training. It attempts, through education and training, to make available to great masses of people the knowledge and the techniques they need to produce more, earn more, and live better. Most of the education and training takes place through close working relationships between a few Americans and many local government officials, technicians and students, who in turn apply their new ideas and skills to the problems of the country and the training of others.[166]

The Technical Assistance program, like similar projects of the UN, is flexible. The United States supplies the experts, but the cooperating government — with the advice of these experts — determines the nature of the particular project. The character of the work varies from country to country and from region to region.

Latin America

In Latin America, the Point Four program is carried on by the Institute of Inter-American Affairs through *servicios*. (See Figure 163.)

The *servicio* is an agency set up by the Latin American government as a bureau within a ministry to carry out a given type of technical assistance in which the United States participates by supplying technicians and part of the program funds. Operations are cooperatively planned, directed and administered by United States and Latin American technicians.

At the beginning of 1953, 44 cooperatively financed programs of this type were in operation: 18 in the field of health, welfare and housing; 14 in agriculture and the development of natural resources; 10 in education; and 2 to provide assistance to industry and government services. About 600 United States technicians were participating in these programs, working with over 14,000 Latin American nationals.[167]

When the *servicio* programs were started in 1942, the U.S. government generally financed the whole project. Over the years, its contributions decreased and those of recipient countries increased. By 1954 Latin American countries were providing $3 to each $1 the United States appropriated for *servicios*.[168]

In 1952, active projects in the eighteen Latin American countries numbered 609. These included construction of 72 water supply systems and 8 sewerage systems; construction of 26 hospitals and

operation of 27; construction of 21 health centers and operation of 69; construction of 1 nursing school; operation of 26 mobile units, 69 local training courses, 24 health education projects, 12 malaria control projects, and assistance to industries to improve industrial hygiene in 5 countries. During that year, 119 United States technicians worked with 2,535 Latin American doctors, nurses, sanitary engineers, and other professional personnel; 1,183 subprofessional and administrative personnel, and 3,416 unskilled workmen.

In the Amazon River Valley, 56 health centers and their subposts minister to 2 million people scattered over an immense area. Efforts have been concentrated on reducing malaria and intestinal diseases that affected almost the entire population. As a result of the cooperative programs, these diseases have been virtually eliminated, not only from the great Amazon Valley but also from the Rio Doce Valley. When work first began in 1942, there were 40 United States technicians cooperating with 500 Brazilians. Today not a single United States technician is in the Amazon Valley. The work is being carried forward by 1,000 Brazilians, most of whom were trained as a part of the cooperative program.[169]

Another interesting example is the industrial hygiene program being carried on in the mines of Peru. The mines in the Andes mountains of Peru are from 14,000 to 16,000 feet above sea level, and only the Peruvians who are native to these altitudes can work in them.

These high-altitude mines contain copper, zinc, lead, vanadium, antimony, bismuth, and other strategic products that are important in world markets. In 1947, the Peruvian government passed a law making an industrial hygiene program mandatory, to start in the high mining areas, and made provision to finance it. The Peruvian government then asked the cooperative health staff to accept responsibility for this program.

The Institute of Inter-American Affairs borrowed the best available United States personnel, an industrial engineer and an industrial chemist, and sent them to Peru. A Peruvian physician was sent to the United States to study industrial hygiene and safety. Remarkable progress was made in controlling the incidence of silicosis, the main scourge of the area.

In the agricultural field, the program has as its objectives: research, which aims at improvement in various food crops, fiber plants, and

166. See **132**.
167. **139**, p. 2.
168. **138**, p. 8.

169. **139**, p. 3; cf. **121**, p. 11.

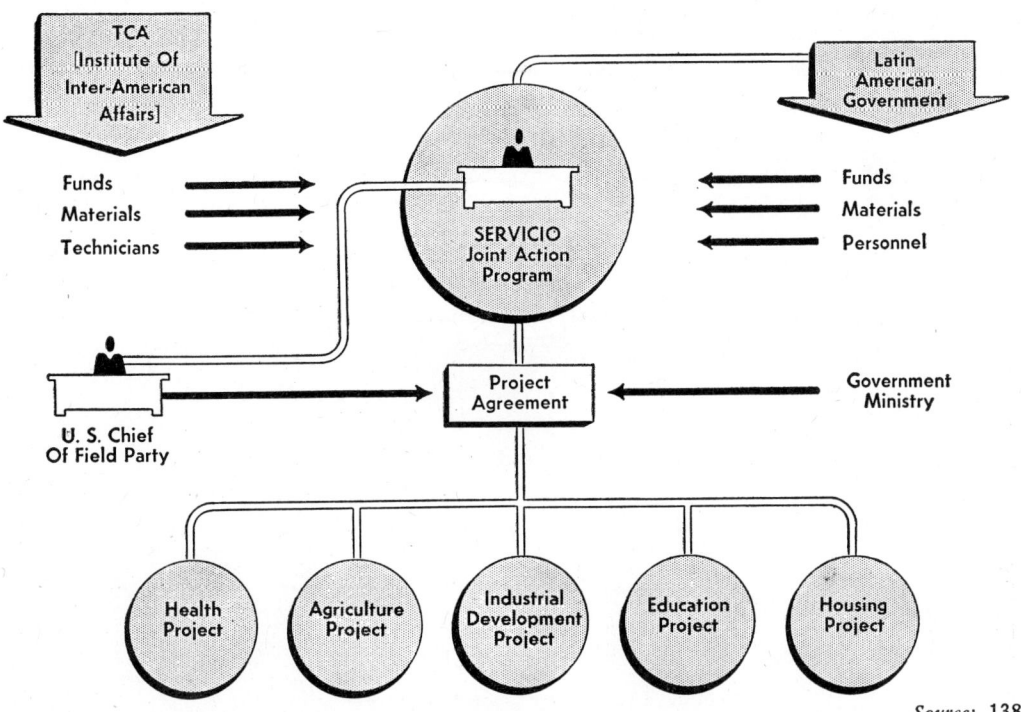

FIGURE 163. POINT FOUR PROGRAM: THE ORGANIZATION AND OPERATION OF THE SERVICIO IN LATIN AMERICA

Source: 138

livestock; education and vocational training in agriculture and home economics; rural development, which encompasses land clearing, forest utilization, colonization, irrigation and drainage, land classification, soil conservation, road building, storage and drying facilities, marketing, food processing, supervised credit, machinery pool operations, fertilizers, range and livestock management, seed and nursery production, and insect, disease and weed control.

In the natural resources fields, the activities point toward development of land and water resources, forestry, fisheries and minerals.

Plant insect and disease control programs have proved particularly effective in many Latin American countries. Technical assistance of this type frequently starts a chain reaction. In Peru, for example, when the agriculture program began in 1943, it was hard to convince farmers that they should spend money for chemicals, the use of which seemed to them wasted effort as well as money.

Most of the early requests for insecticides were calls of desperation when 25 to 50 per cent of a crop was already lost and a farmer feared he might lose his crop completely.

Since the program began in Peru in 1943, *servicio* technicians have carried on many insect control projects. They include control of the fruit fly on tomatoes; late blight on potatoes; cotton insects such as bucculatrix, thrips, boll worm, red stainer, boll weevil, and soil worms; soil worms and cut worms on corn; insects in stored grains; snails and ants.

During 1952 control of the cotton boll weevil increased yields one third by saving the portion of the crop normally lost to this pest.

In 1952 a nationwide rat control program began in Peru.

C. O. Rowe of the Institute of Inter-American Affairs summarized his survey of eleven years of technical assistance in Latin America as follows:

The cooperative technical assistance program is a quiet, long-range constructive effort of one neighbor helping others. By its very nature it creates closer bonds of human relations. The thousands of Latin Americans who come to the United States to study, and the hundreds of United States technicians who go south to offer their know-how to help their good neighbors, build better understanding and closer friendship between the Americas. This is freedom's fight where the battleground is in the hearts and

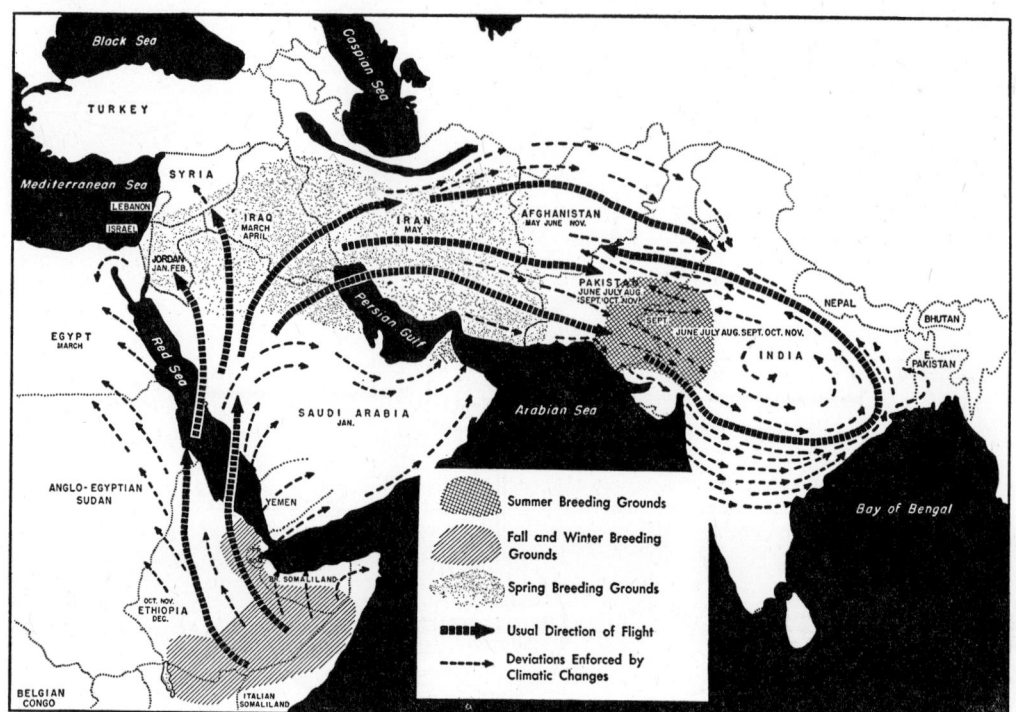

Source: **113**

FIGURE 164. POINT FOUR PROGRAM: LOCUST INVASIONS IN AFRICA, THE MIDDLE EAST AND SOUTH ASIA

minds of men. Freedom wins where confidence, hope and enlightenment prevail.[170]

The Near East and Africa

About half the funds for the Technical Cooperation program in the Near East and Africa are devoted to improving the food situation.

In Iran, which was one of the first underdeveloped countries to sign a general agreement with TCA, ten regional headquarters were established. Agricultural extension services have been given to 800 villages. A large well-drilling program was begun. Efforts were made to improve seed and to introduce better breeds of cattle. In Ethiopia, an institute of agriculture was established. In Liberia, the local agricultural industrial institute was expanded. In Libya, U.S. technical experts gave help in improving wool production and settling nomadic tribes. In Lebanon, plans for the utilization of water resources were completed.

International locust control is another project carried out by TCA in the Near East. Locust invasions are a constant threat to grain crops

170. See **139.**

in the area from eastern Ethiopia to western India, causing farmers damage ranging from $80 to $200 million a year. From their breeding grounds in the highlands of Ethiopia, swarms of locusts move toward Arabia, Egypt, Jordan and Syria, Iraq and Iran. Other swarms move from northern Arabia and Iran to Pakistan and India; still others circle the Indian Peninsula. (See Figure 164.)

The problem is international and requires international control. In 1951–52 U.S. entomologists, assisted by FAO technicians, and the British Desert Locust Control waged war against the locusts with planes and national ground-control organizations. The U.S. contribution to this campaign totaled about $1 million in 1951 and 1952, mainly for planes and personnel and insecticides. The eventual success of the undertaking will free the region from a plague which has devastated it since biblical times.

South Asia

TCA activities in South Asia range from the organization of health services to aid in developing hydroelectric power, but the main problem

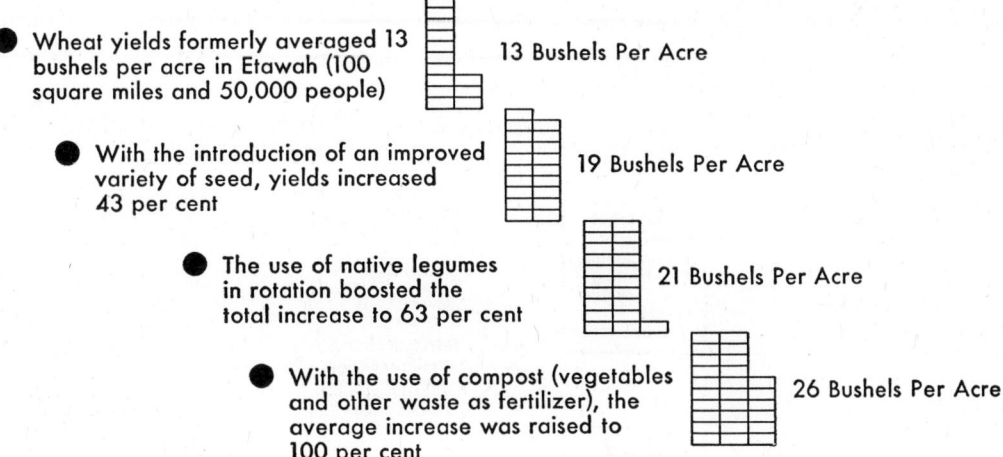

WHEAT YIELDS DOUBLED WITH SIMPLE IMPROVEMENTS IN METHODS

● Wheat yields formerly averaged 13 bushels per acre in Etawah (100 square miles and 50,000 people)   13 Bushels Per Acre

    ● With the introduction of an improved variety of seed, yields increased 43 per cent   19 Bushels Per Acre

        ● The use of native legumes in rotation boosted the total increase to 63 per cent   21 Bushels Per Acre

            ● With the use of compost (vegetables and other waste as fertilizer), the average increase was raised to 100 per cent   26 Bushels Per Acre

THE LESSONS OF ETAWAH ARE BEING APPLIED IN OTHER POINT 4 AREAS

Source: **113**

FIGURE 165. POINT FOUR PROGRAM: THE ETAWAH PROJECT IN INDIA

is food — to increase the yield of wheat and other crops.

Many of the most interesting projects are in India, where the three-year development project at Etawah yielded much valuable experience. The purpose was to test the extent to which Indian farmers, with the advice of U.S. agricultural experts, could improve their lot. An area with 102 villages and a population of 50,000 was selected for the experiment. Improved varieties of seed were provided. The farmers were taught to use native legumes in rotation and to use compost as fertilizer. The average yield doubled, and in some cases tripled or even quintupled. Hunger and poverty could be fought with simple methods. (See Figure 165.)

Relying on this experience, the Indian government started a larger project — the Community Development Program. Fifty-five areas, in various parts of the country, were selected. Each area represents roughly a circle with a ten-mile radius and includes, on the average, 300 villages with approximately 200,000 inhabitants. A team of Indian workers trained and led by U.S. technicians was installed in each area to help people to help themselves. Their program includes not only agricultural development but the organization of schools, improvement of health conditions, community services, introduction of small-scale home industries and home building. (See Figure 166.) They use no expensive machinery, no power tools, no tractors, only such tools as are within the reach of every Indian tiller of the soil, plus know-how and the achievements of modern science. In every village and every group of population they seek supporters for the ideas they have brought to ancient India from the New World.

The lay missionaries from the United States who carry on this program are bound by a code which embodies the principles of international cooperation. The manual tasks which they expect of the farmers they must themselves be able to perform. They are taught to ask no gratitude for their work, but seek only friendship.

Similar plans of community development were being considered for Pakistan and remote areas in the upper Amazon basin.

Development of the Program

In a report submitted to the President in June 1952, the International Development Advisory Board stressed the fundamental difference between technical assistance and other aspects of the MS program, in which the grim requirements of the struggle against Communist aggression predominate over all other considerations:

The Act for International Development contains no indication that the Point 4 program is to be related directly or indirectly to military activity

The Community Development Program In India

Its Aims • More Food
          • Better Living Conditions

55 projects under Point 4 sponsorship will have a direct effect on the farming and living conditions of 11 million people in 16,500 villages.

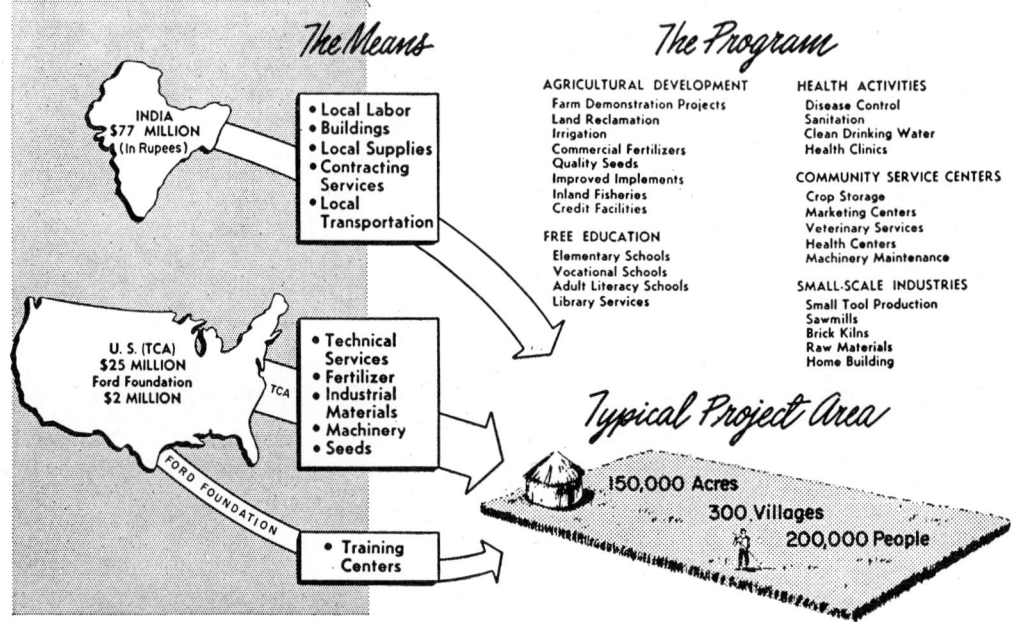

The Means

INDIA
$77 MILLION
(In Rupees)

• Local Labor
• Buildings
• Local Supplies
• Contracting
  Services
• Local
  Transportation

U. S. (TCA)
$25 MILLION
Ford Foundation
$2 MILLION

TCA

• Technical
  Services
• Fertilizer
• Industrial
  Materials
• Machinery
• Seeds

FORD FOUNDATION

• Training
  Centers

The Program

AGRICULTURAL DEVELOPMENT
  Farm Demonstration Projects
  Land Reclamation
  Irrigation
  Commercial Fertilizers
  Quality Seeds
  Improved Implements
  Inland Fisheries
  Credit Facilities

FREE EDUCATION
  Elementary Schools
  Vocational Schools
  Adult Literacy Schools
  Library Services

HEALTH ACTIVITIES
  Disease Control
  Sanitation
  Clean Drinking Water
  Health Clinics

COMMUNITY SERVICE CENTERS
  Crop Storage
  Marketing Centers
  Veterinary Services
  Health Centers
  Machinery Maintenance

SMALL-SCALE INDUSTRIES
  Small Tool Production
  Sawmills
  Brick Kilns
  Raw Materials
  Home Building

Typical Project Area

150,000 Acres
300 Villages
200,000 People

Source: 113

FIGURE 166. POINT FOUR PROGRAM: COMMUNITY DEVELOPMENT IN INDIA

abroad. Other agencies functioning under the Mutual Security Act are concerned with programs of direct military aid and economic assistance. The Board believes there is a fundamental distinction between the philosophy underlying Point 4 and the philosophy underlying programs of military assistance. It believes these philosophies and the programs deriving from them should be kept separate and apart. It believes that Point 4 operations are fully justifiable without reference to military or military-support objectives. The Board feels that the creation of sound economic defenses against political aggression is as necessary as the creation of military defenses against armed aggressions.[171]

The report of the Advisory Committee on Underdeveloped Areas in May 1953 emphasized that the main objective of the program is a stronger and increasingly prosperous free world. The foreign development programs must serve these objectives:

(a) by helping to build economic, political, social and psychological strength in the nations of the free world;

(b) by widening opportunities for individual self-realization and by increasing the ability of individuals to make the most of these opportunities; and

(c) by promoting increased production and consumption through more effective utilization and distribution of economic resources.

Programs designed to attain these objectives must take into account the area's technology, its capital investment, its financial stability, its labor situation, its psychological traits, its social structure, its economic and political institutions.

Economic and technical programs cannot be limited to the international transfer of capital and technology, but must lay stress also on changes in customs and institutions and in underlying values and attitudes, since such changes are often prerequisite to effective utilization of additional capital or improved technology.

Concern for the customs, institutions, underlying values and attitudes of other peoples must take into account (a) the sensitivity of other peoples about external interference, (b) the difficulty we often experience in making clear to the less developed areas the mutuality of our interests and theirs, and (c) the severe limits on our own understanding of

171. **117**, p. 4.

the values and attitudes, customs and institutions most conducive to economic development of the kind serving our mutually agreed objectives.

It is essential (a) to move slowly in deciding that particular changes must be brought about, (b) to limit proposals for change to those recognized and supported by competent and responsible persons in the participating country, and (c) not to emphasize American initiative in getting such changes considered and promoted.[172]

It is from this general point of view that the Advisory Committee approached the problem of the direction of economic development in areas applying for assistance. It recommended the following guidelines:

(a) the underdeveloped countries should be encouraged to weigh carefully the possible lines of economic development before rushing into industrialization; (b) the United States has a responsibility to warn these countries of the dangers to themselves of diverting resources too rapidly away from the production of primary materials needed by themselves as well as by the rest of the free world; (c) most of our assistance in development financing should be designed to encourage the production and some processing of primary materials and foods and the development of related transportation and power facilities with a very close examination of projects for direct industrial development to make certain that they are justified economically; (d) positive steps should be taken to iron out wide fluctuations in the prices of the major primary commodities; and (e) steps should be taken to assure the less developed countries that they will receive their fair share of manufactured goods, including capital goods, even in times of emergency and shortages.[173]

The Committee has also taken a position on two difficult and controversial issues: (1) should the main concern of the development programs be direct improvement of living conditions or development and support of those groups of the local population which can be "expected to provide leadership in business, government and the professions"? and (2) how should the danger of rapid population growth which results from improved health conditions be met? Answering the first question the Advisory Committee expressed its belief

that on both economic and political grounds substantial weight should be given in U.S. foreign development programs to measures and activities affect-

ing primarily the groups that provide the experts and leaders and make the investments. At the same time, there must be adequate provision in our programs for projects of the impact type that will help the recipient governments to increase the extent and improve the quality of their services to the people.

The Advisory Committee's answer to the second question was more cautious. It recognized that "industrialization, urbanization, better education, more economic security and higher incomes tend to be associated with gradually falling birth rates." On the other hand it recognized that at least in the early years of modernization declining death rates will not be matched by declining birth rates and concludes that "real steps in the direction of conscious promotion of population limitation seem to be required."

The report, however, offers no Malthusian program and merely directs the attention of the respective governments to the problem: "We do ourselves and our friends in the less developed countries a disservice if we pretend that the poverty in these countries reflects only the inadequacy of resources, or their ineffective utilization." [174]

The Committee concluded its recommendations with a plea for the continuance of U.S. technical and economic assistance to the less developed areas, aside from the military emergency which has determined the MS program:

One of the most important principles in the operation of the development program for the less developed areas, either bilaterally as a U.S. program or multilaterally under international auspices, should be a sense of permanence and continuity. . . . The broad program . . . should shake off the "emergency" tag that has been associated with the program up to the present. There should be some assurance to the free world that we are "in the world for good" and that our interest in the less developed areas is not a short-run emergency policy. Recognition of the inevitable and continuing role and responsibilities of the United States in today's interdependent world is a fundamental problem of American public policy.[175]

The whole problem was reappraised in 1953 by the International Development Advisory Board. The Board, headed by Eric Johnston, recommended vigorous support of the technical cooperation programs of both the United States and the UN as a part of the long-range foreign

---

172. **124**, pp. iv-v.
173. **124**, p. vi.

174. See **124**, p. 18.
175. **124**, p. 36.

policy of the United States: "because it is politi- cally, economically and morally the right thing to do." It considered expenditures for such programs as "ordinary and necessary business expenses" and not as "giveaways" and recom- mended planning and budgeting for such pro- grams on a long-range, rather than annual, basis.

The conclusions and recommendations of the Board stress the moral (or psychological) value of the technical cooperation programs:

In the underdeveloped countries, Technical Co- operation is not just a program of material help. Though its tools are mainly material, the long-term goal is to mobilize the energies of the small but rapidly growing educated minority in these coun- tries for the cause of freedom, peace and construc- tive achievement. It is this group that will largely decide the fate of the underdeveloped half of the world.

Technical Cooperation offers these men leadership in building rather than in destroying, a life's work of self-fulfillment rather than of frustration. It directs their idealism, their energies and patriotism towards freedom rather than enslavement, towards peace and friendship with the West rather than blind anti-Western hatred that can only deliver their countries to a totalitarian foreign oppressor, and towards justice and equality based on creating new health rather than misery.

In this role as a lodestar for the new educated middle classes of the underdeveloped areas may well lie the most important contribution Technical Co- operation can make to our victory in the ideological world conflict of our time.

And as the underdeveloped areas increase in strength, their physical capacity to defend themselves and their moral resistance to the totalitarian poisons will increase too. What this means to the American taxpayer, weighted down as he is under a heavy burden of military expenditures, can be seen when it is realized that the entire cost of the Program for a whole year is less than the cost of equipping and maintaining one single United States division.

Technical Cooperation is of all the parts of our foreign policy the one that goes furthest beyond mere "containment" of the threat that faces all of us in the Free World. By showing men how they can liberate themselves from the crushing burden of ignorance, disease and destitution, it makes them ready to assume the responsibilities of free men.[176]

EUROPEAN INTEGRATION

After World War II several attempts were made to promote the economic, political and

military unification of Western Europe. Impelled by external pressures rather than by a spon- taneous surge of international good will, these attempts were only partially successful. New organizations were created and vast projects for international cooperation were launched, but many difficult problems still remained unsettled. In mid-1954 there were five official organizations which united the Western European nations. (See Table 291.)

The Organization for European Economic Co- operation (OEEC)

The OEEC was founded in response to the historic speech of the U.S. Secretary of State, George Marshall, at Harvard on June 5, 1947. It was established as a permanent organization in April 1948, at about the same time that the Economic Cooperation Act was passed by the U.S. Congress.[177] In the course of international discussions on the OEEC, the foundations were laid for two other agencies of European coopera- tion, the European Customs Union Study Group and the European Payments Union.[178]

Under the terms of the Convention for Euro- pean Economic Co-operation of April 16, 1948, the contracting parties agreed "to work in close cooperation in their economic relations with one another." They defined their immediate task as the drawing up and execution of a joint recovery program permitting them to achieve as soon as possible a satisfactory level of economic activity without extraordinary outside assistance. To this end, the member countries undertook certain general obligations and set up an international body to implement these obligations.

The general obligations refer to undertakings given by the member countries individually, and to the efforts to be made toward cooperation and mutual help. In the former sphere, each country undertakes to increase its production, to stabilize its currency and its internal financial position and to make the fullest use of its available man- power. In the sphere of cooperation, the Euro- pean countries agree to draw up joint general programs as often as may be necessary, to de- velop their trade to the maximum extent, and, to this end, to achieve as soon as possible a multi- lateral system of payments. Lastly, they agree to strengthen their economic links, by all means which they consider appropriate for the achieve-

---

176. **121**, p. 3.

177. **108**, pp. 9–11.
178. See Chapters 5 and 6.

TABLE 291

OFFICIAL EUROPEAN ORGANIZATIONS

Organization for European Economic Cooperation (April 16, 1948 [a])	North Atlantic Treaty Organization (August 24, 1949 [a])	Council of Europe (May 5, 1949 [a])	European Payments Union (July 1, 1950 [a])	Coal and Steel Community (July 25, 1952 [a])
United Kingdom	United Kingdom	United Kingdom	United Kingdom	
Norway	Norway	Norway	Norway	
Denmark	Denmark	Denmark	Denmark	
Iceland	Iceland	Iceland	Iceland	
France	France	France	France	France
Germany	Germany [b]	Germany	Germany	Germany
Italy	Italy	Italy	Italy	Italy
Netherlands	Netherlands	Netherlands	Netherlands	Netherlands
Belgium	Belgium	Belgium	Belgium	Belgium
Luxembourg	Luxembourg	Luxembourg	Luxembourg	Luxembourg
Greece	Greece	Greece	Greece	
Turkey	Turkey	Turkey	Turkey	
Portugal	Portugal		Portugal	
Austria			Austria	
Switzerland			Switzerland	
Sweden		Sweden	Sweden	
Ireland		Ireland	Ireland	
United States [c]	United States			
Canada [c]	Canada			

Source: **109.**

a. Date of ratification.　　　　b. Since May 1955.　　　　c. Associated members.

ment of the aims laid down in the Convention. Furthermore, the contracting governments propose to cooperate with other countries in reducing present obstacles to the expansion of trade.

The OEEC has not been an integral part of the European Recovery Program. Founded as an organ of European cooperation, it has remained a permanent institution in the political structure of Western Europe. It is difficult to appraise its role in terms of the specific activities for which it has been responsible and which could not have been effectuated without it.

The OEEC is, essentially, a consultative body:

[It] provides a new constructive element in the life of Western Europe. The continual exchange of views and information facilitated by the Organisation, acting as a kind of permanent conference, accustoms Governments to comparing their points of view and promotes a "European way of thinking." This implies, in essence, that each Government, when faced with an important decision, considers the effect this might have on the economy of other

members of the group and usually consults them before determining its position.[179]

The Council of Europe

The Council of Europe supplements the OEEC to some extent as a forum of European nations. It differs from the OEEC and other international organizations in structure and it spearheads the drive toward the political and economic unification of Europe. It emerged from the fifty-year multilateral treaty "for collaboration in economic, social and cultural matters and for collective self-defense" signed by the foreign ministers of the United Kingdom, France, Luxembourg, Belgium and the Netherlands in Brussels on March 17, 1948. The Brussels treaty provided a Consultative Council for mutual consultation among the signatories. The Council was composed of the foreign ministers, which were to meet whenever the need arose — as they could have done with-

179. **108,** p. 21.

out a special treaty. In January 1949, however, the Consultative Council decided to strengthen the group. The Council of Europe was established, consisting of a Committee of Ministers and a Consultative Assembly. Additional nations joined, and by the end of 1953 the Council included the following:

United Kingdom	Netherlands	Western Germany
Ireland	Denmark	Italy
France	Sweden	Greece
Luxembourg	Norway	Turkey
Belgium	Saar	Iceland

Permanent headquarters are maintained in Strasbourg. Members of the Assembly are appointed by their respective parliaments.[180] The Council is a deliberative body with somewhat loosely defined powers and a strong tendency to consider itself as a European parliament. An annual meeting is statutory, but extraordinary sessions may be called at any time.[181]

The Council seeks to unify all forms of European cooperation, including the European Coal and Steel Community (Schuman Plan).[182]

It has also tried to improve the ties between European nations and their overseas colonies and possessions (the Strasbourg Plan) but has been unable to establish direct relations with the British colonies and members of the British Commonwealth.[183]

Apart from its contribution to intra-European cooperation in such matters as passports and tariffs, perhaps the most interesting aspect of the work of the Council is its hope of transforming the European Coal and Steel Community into a political community which would include the same six states — France, Luxembourg, Belgium, the Netherlands, Germany and Italy. The community would have a parliament consisting of a chamber of peoples elected by direct universal suffrage and a senate elected by national parliaments. It would form the center of integration for all European countries.[184]

---

180. In the Assembly the United Kingdom, France, Western Germany and Italy have 18 representatives each; Turkey, 10; Belgium, the Netherlands and Greece, 7; Sweden, 6; Norway and Denmark, 5; Ireland, 4; Luxembourg, the Saar and Iceland, 3.

181. See **142** and **143**.

182. See **142**, **143** and **144**, August 1952.

183. **144**, February 1953.

184. **144**, January 1953.

The North Atlantic Treaty Organization (NATO)

Although often considered a European affair (see Figure 160), NATO brings together the Western European nations, the United States and Canada and can be described as a regional association within the UN. Its purpose is joint action against aggression. Since this is likewise one of the principal purposes of the UN, NATO takes over the commitments of the UN with respect to the North Atlantic area.

The Preamble of the treaty reads as follows:

The Parties to this Treaty reaffirm their faith in the purposes and principles of the Charter of the United Nations and their desire to live in peace with all peoples and all governments.

They are determined to safeguard the freedom, common heritage and civilization of their peoples, founded on the principles of democracy, individual liberty and the rule of law.

They seek to promote stability and well-being in the North Atlantic area.

They are resolved to unite their efforts for collective defense and for the preservation of peace and security.

They therefore agree to this North Atlantic Treaty.[185]

The treaty reaffirms the commitments imposed upon all UN members by the Charter, but in three important clauses it goes further: the obligation of the NATO countries to develop their "individual and collective capacity to resist armed attack"; their obligation to consult on defense matters; and agreement that an armed attack against any member of NATO shall be considered an attack against all. The respective articles of the treaty read as follows:

Article 3

In order more effectively to achieve the objectives of this Treaty, the Parties, separately and jointly, by means of continuous and effective self-help and mutual aid, will maintain and develop their individual and collective capacity to resist armed attack.

Article 4

The Parties will consult together whenever, in the opinion of any of them, the territorial integrity, political independence or security of any of the Parties is threatened.

---

185. **110**, p. 114.

Article 5

The Parties agree that an armed attack against one or more of them in Europe or North America shall be considered an attack against them all; and consequently they agree that, if such an armed attack occurs, each of them, in exercise of the right of individual or collective self-defense recognized by Article 51 of the Charter of the United Nations, will assist the Party or Parties so attacked by taking forthwith, individually and in concert with the other Parties, such action as it deems necessary, including the use of armed force, to restore and maintain the security of the North Atlantic area.

Any such armed attack and all measures taken as a result thereof shall immediately be reported to the Security Council. Such measures shall be terminated when the Security Council has taken the measures necessary to restore and maintain international peace and security.[186]

The treaty was signed for a period of twenty years, with provision for revision after ten years.

On the basis of the treaty, joint plans for defense against the USSR were developed; the share of each member nation in the joint military effort was established; and a joint command in the event of war was provided. Plans were also made for building up the necessary land, sea and air forces. The role assigned to the United States was primarily that of providing an adequately strong air force and aiding the European countries with arms and military equipment. The main responsibilities of the European countries were to raise the land forces, train and maintain them, and to provide at least a part of the necessary equipment. The U.S. contribution to the program through the fiscal year 1953–54 was over $20 billion.

Even before Germany became a member of NATO, U.S. military experts considered it an important link in the defense of Western Europe. The delay in its participation in the joint defense organization was due to the fact that NATO is essentially a military alliance requiring its members to rearm and maintain considerable armed forces. Germany was forcibly disarmed by the Allies after World War II. To Germany's neighbors, the victims of Nazi aggression, the rearmament of their former enemy seemed like a revival of Prussian militarism. On the other hand, the Germans themselves were not eager to take part in the armed defense of Europe unless invited to do so on the basis of complete equality.

A solution of the problem appeared to have been found in a plan to merge the armed forces of those European countries directly threatened by Russian aggression into a common European army. German units could be absorbed into this army in the same way as troops of other nations, but there would be no German army under the command of a German general staff. The plan was to have included France, Western Germany, Italy, Belgium, the Netherlands and Luxembourg, the six nations in the Coal and Steel Community, and was known as the European Defense Community (EDC). It was signed by all six but was ratified — conditionally — only by the Benelux countries and was abandoned in August 1954 after its ratification was rejected by the French Parliament. In October 1954 the United States, the United Kingdom and France signed an agreement with Western Germany restoring its sovereignty, recognizing its right to keep an army and inviting it to join NATO as a member of the Western European Union. This treaty (Paris Agreements) has practically terminated occupation of Western Germany by the Allies. It became effective in May 1955.

The European Payments Union (EPU)

The EPU is an auxiliary of the OEEC. Its purposes are to stimulate intra-European trade and to protect the stability of European currencies. This dual purpose is effected by clearing operations and settlement of deficits in the bilateral trade balances between member nations. The methods are as follows:

At the end of each accounting period (usually one month) each member reports the bilateral end-of-month balances of its monetary area with other members and their monetary areas to the Agent (Bank for International Settlements), which establishes a net surplus or deficit for each member. These net deficits or surpluses are settled in the following ways: (a) Through the use of "existing resources" representing bilateral debts outstanding as of June 30, 1950, for which no specific amortization plan has been agreed bilaterally. Existing resources may be used at the request of the holding country to settle a net deficit. (b) Through the use of "initial credit or debit balances." For the first year of the EPU operations certain prospective debtors were allotted initial credit balances with the EPU to facilitate the settling of their deficits. On the other hand, certain prospective creditors were allotted

---

186. **110**, p. 115.

initial debit positions for which they received an equivalent amount of conditional ECA aid. (c) Through the use of "special resources." For the second year of operations certain prospective debtors were allotted special resources by the U.S. government to cover anticipated deficits with the Union. As these special resources are used, equal amounts in dollars are paid to the Union by ECA. (d) Through the use of credit and gold payments.

For the purpose of determining the maximum cumulative accounting surplus or deficit that can be settled in this way the member countries have been assigned quotas. The following table shows how the monthly accounting deficits and surpluses are settled by gold and credit:

Monthly Accounting Surplus or Deficit Is Settled:

When Cumulative Accounting Surplus or Deficit Equals:	For Cumulative Creditors		For Cumulative Debtors	
	By Credit to or from EPU (Per Cent)	By Gold Payments to or from EPU (Per Cent)	By Credit to or from EPU (Per Cent)	By Gold Payments to or from EPU (Per Cent)
First 20 per cent of quota	100	0	100	0
Second 20 per cent of quota	50	50	80	20
Third 20 per cent of quota	50	50	60	40
Fourth 20 per cent of quota	50	50	40	60
Fifth 20 per cent of quota	50	50	20	80

A deficit in excess of the assigned quota shall be settled in gold unless the OEEC decides otherwise. An obligation to pay gold by a member or by the Union may be discharged by payment in U.S. dollars.

The U.S. government undertook the obligation of making available an amount of not less than $350 million so that the Union might meet any excess in gold and dollar out-payments.[187]

The Coal and Steel Community

This organization is perhaps Europe's bravest attempt at international cooperation. Its purpose is to combine the steel-plant capacity of the leading steel-making nations of continental Europe;

to modernize their equipment; and to raise their productivity for the common benefit of all European consumers. It is, in a sense, an international public cartel to end all national and private cartels.[188]

By 1954 the Community was functioning and had not yet met the real difficulties which may be in store for it. In 1954 the United States government granted it a $100 million loan for the modernization of the European steel industry.

SUMMARY AND OUTLOOK

Despite continued tensions in various parts of the world, the gradual deterioration of alliances established during World War II and the less-than-satisfactory success of the UN to prevent aggression in Korea, progress in international cooperation in recent years, in comparison with the past, is undeniable. The League of Nations visualized by Woodrow Wilson was a gallant attempt to realize an old dream. It was frustrated by compromises in the Covenant, the absence of the United States and by a lack of sincerity, courage and vision among European statesmen when the organization was put to the test.

World War II, with its wanton destruction, was the price the world had to pay for its failure to stop violations of the peace and of treaties when they could have been stopped with comparative ease — in China, Ethiopia, the Rhineland, Prague, Vienna. As the war approached its end, blueprints were being readied for a new world organization. Situations similar to those which had brought the League of Nations to an ignominious end were anticipated and efforts made to assure the success of the UN.

In some fields, international cooperation has proved successful beyond expectation. The European Recovery Program is an inspiring page in world history. The specialized agencies of the UN, especially the FAO, the WHO and the International Bank for Reconstruction and Development, are examples of international cooperation of unprecedented scope and diversity. The Point Four Program of the United States will leave a deep imprint on the lives of the people in underdeveloped areas.

But despite these manifestations of international cooperation in recent years, they have all, without exception, one feature in common: the world is split into two camps and all interna-

---

187. See **98**.

188. **176**, pp. 1140–42.

tional cooperation takes place in one camp; the other camp makes frantic efforts to discredit and ruin every cooperative program. NATO and the action in Korea are merely episodes in the struggle between the East and the West.

There has been no international cooperation program in which Russia and its satellites have worked with the West. They have declined to support the FAO, the WHO, and the International Bank. When Soviet representatives have taken part in international organizations, such as the Assembly and the Security Council of the UN, the Economic Commission for Europe and UNESCO, their aim has been either propaganda or sabotage. They succeeded in wrecking the disarmament program of the West and especially its plan for atomic disarmament. They have undermined the vitality of the UN and have paralyzed the Security Council by their ruthless use of the veto.

This same split between the East and the West also explains the reorientation of U.S. foreign aid from economic assistance to arming the free nations in anticipation of a new war.

Since 1950–51, international cooperation has largely been developing in the form of rearmament for joint resistance to aggression. It has returned to the oldest form of international action — military alliance. What has changed basically is the character of future war. Most experts agree that another war will begin with a surprise attack with atomic weapons and launched under conditions which promise the aggressor the greatest advantage. Whether the experts are right or not, that is the threat the free world tries to meet through the MS program and NATO, subordinating all other forms of cooperation to the international strategy of defense.

Every major war is a break in the continuity of history. If it succeeds in solving some perennial problem, at the same time it creates new problems. An atomic war, should it come, will cause a more profound break in the continuity of economic and social progress than has any previous war.

There is no way of determining the outlook for international cooperation. Only an *if* forecast can be ventured.

If the danger of a sudden atomic attack and total war were eliminated; *if* the split between the East and the West were healed; and *if* the Iron Curtain were raised, the outlook for international cooperation would be bright — perhaps brighter than at any time in world history. As time goes on, the results of cultural cooperation and technical assistance will become more and more evident. The success of the pioneers of Western civilization, working on the virgin soil of less developed areas, will stimulate further efforts in that direction. Where hundreds toiled a few years ago and thousands are working now, tens and scores of thousands will toil in the years to come. When the people of both the less developed areas and of the modern industrial countries realize how much can be achieved by a handful of experts equipped with modern scientific methods and good will, there will be no difficulty in finding ways to finance their work. Technical and cultural cooperation through bilateral and multilateral projects will penetrate farther and farther into underdeveloped countries to conquer sickness and poverty; and to transform the school systems, communal organizations, agriculture and industry, transportation and trade systems, patterns of consumption.

This is not a forecast, however, but only an *if* projection based on the assumption that Western civilization will be freed from the fear of an Eastern onslaught.

A change in this basic assumption would result in other projections, some of them very gloomy, indeed.

SOURCE REFERENCES

PART I. TRADE

CHAPTER 1

TRADE IN THE WORLD ECONOMY

1. United Nations, *Demographic Yearbook*, New York.
2. ———, *Monthly Bulletin of Statistics*.
3. ———, *National Income Statistics, Supplement 1938–1950*, New York, 1951.
4. ———, *Statistical Yearbook*, New York.
5. International Labor Office, *Yearbook of Labour Statistics*, Geneva.
6. International Monetary Fund, *International Financial Statistics*.

UNITED STATES

7. Department of Commerce, *Survey of Current Business*.
8. ———, Bureau of the Census, Sixteenth Census of the United States (1940), *Population, Comparative Occupational Statistics for the United States, 1870–1940*, 1943.
9. ———, ———, Sixteenth Census of the United States (1940), *Population: The Labor Force* (Sample Statistics) *Industrial Characteristics*, 1943.
10. ———, ———, *Statistical Abstract of the United States*.
11. ———, ———, *Historical Statistics of the United States, 1789–1945*, 1949.
12. FRANCE. Statistique Générale, *Résultats Statistiques du Recensement Général de la Population en 1936*, Paris, 1938.

GERMANY

13. Länderrat des Amerikanischen Besatzungsgebiets, *Statistisches Handbuch von Deutschland, 1928–1944*, Munich, 1949.
14. Statistisches Reichsamt, *Statistisches Jahrbuch für das Deutsche Reich*, Berlin.

15. SWEDEN. Central Bureau of Statistics, *Statistisk Årsbok, 1950*, Stockholm.

16. Aristotle, *Politics* (Benjamin Jowett, trans.), Oxford University Press, New York, 1943.
17. Condliffe, John B., *The Commerce of Nations*, W. W. Norton, New York, 1950.
18. Gillespie, James E., *A History of Geographical Discovery, 1400–1800*, Henry Holt, New York, 1933.
19. Hamilton, Alexander, "Report on the Subject of Manufactures," in *State Papers and Speeches on the Tariff*, edited by F. W. Taussig, Harvard University, Cambridge, 1892.
20. Herrmann, Albert, *Die alten Seidenstrassen zwischen China und Syrien*. Beiträge zur alten Geographie Asiens (Quellen und Forschungen zur alten Geschichte und Geographie), Weidmann, Berlin, 1910.
21. Homer, *Works*, Modern Library, New York, 1935.
22. Hoyt, Elizabeth E., *Primitive Trade: Its Psychology and Economics*, K. Paul, Trench, Trubner and Company, London, 1926.
23. List, Friedrich, *Schriften, Reden, Briefe*, 10 vols., Reimar Hobbing, Berlin, 1927–35.
24. Mataja, Victor, "Handel," in *Handwörterbuch der Staatswissenschaften*, Gustav Fischer, Jena, 1909–11.
25. Newton, Arthur Percival, *The Great Age of Discovery*, University of London Press, London, 1932.
26. Pirenne, Henri, *Medieval Cities, Their Origins and the Revival of Trade* (trans. from the French by Frank D. Halsey), Princeton University Press, Princeton, 1925.
27. Pohl, Frederick J., *Amerigo Vespucci: Pilot Major*, Columbia University Press, New York, 1944.
28. Polo, Marco, *Travels*, Modern Library, New York, 1931.
29. Rostovtzeff, M. I., *Caravan Cities*, Oxford University Press, London, 1932.
30. Selfridge, H. Gordon, *The Romance of Commerce*, John Lane, London, 1918.
31. Smith, Adam, *An Inquiry into the Nature and Causes of the Wealth of Nations* (with notes, etc., by J. R. M'Culloch), new ed., A. & C. Black, Edinburgh, 1863.
32. Stewart, Paul W., and Dewhurst, J. Frederic, *Does Distribution Cost Too Much?*, Twentieth Century Fund, New York, 1939.
33. Teggart, Frederick J., *Rome and China; a Study of Correlations in Historical Events*, University of California Press, Berkeley, 1939.
34. Unwin, George, *Studies in Economic History* (Collected Papers), Macmillan Company, London, 1927.
35. Woytinsky, Wl. (W. S.), *Die Welt in Zahlen*, 7 volumes, Rudolf Mosse, Berlin, 1925–1928.
36. Woytinsky, W. S., *Labor in the United States: Basic Statistics for Social Security*, Committee on Social Security, Social Science Research Council, 1938.
37. ———, *The Labor Supply in the United States*, Committee on Social Security, Social Science Research Council, June 1937.
38. ———, and Woytinsky, E. S., *World Population and Production: Trends and Outlook*, Twentieth Century Fund, New York, 1953.

CHAPTER 2

THE VALUE AND VOLUME OF FOREIGN TRADE

1. League of Nations, *Balances of Payments, 1939–45*, Geneva, 1948.
2. ———, *Industrialization and Foreign Trade*, Geneva, 1945.
3. ———, *International Statistical Year Book*, 1926, 1928.
4. ———, *Memorandum on Balances of Payments and Foreign Trade Balances*, Geneva, 1928.
5. ———, *Review of World Trade*, Geneva.
6. ———, *Statistical Year Book*.
7. ———, *World Economic Survey*.
8. ———, *World Production and Prices*.
9. United Nations, *Demographic Yearbook*, New York.
10. ———, *Statistical Yearbook*, New York.
11. ———, *Monthly Bulletin of Statistics*.

12. ——, *National and Per Capita Incomes, Seventy Countries, 1949,* New York, 1950.

13. ——, *1950 Supplement to the Monthly Bulletin of Statistics, Definitions and Explanatory Notes,* New York, December 1950.

14. ——, *Statistics of National Income and Expenditures,* New York, 1952.

15. ——, *Yearbook of International Trade Statistics.*

16. International Monetary Fund, *International Financial Statistics.*

UNITED STATES

17. The President, *Thirty-third Report to Congress on Lend-Lease Operations,* 1952.

18. Department of Commerce, *Survey of Current Business.*

19. ——, Bureau of the Census, *Historical Statistics of the United States, 1789–1945,* 1949.

20. ——, ——, *Statistical Abstract of the United States.*

21. AUSTRIA. *Monatsberichte des Österreichischen Instituts für Konjunkturforschung,* Vienna.

22. FRANCE. Statistique Générale, *Annuaire Statistique,* Paris.

GERMANY

23. Institut für Konjunkturforschung, *Die Industriewirtschaft,* Vierteljahrshefte zur Konjunkturforschung, Sonderheft 31, R. Hobbing, Berlin, 1933.

24. Statistisches Reichsamt, *Das Deutsche Volkseinkommen vor und nach dem Kriege,* Berlin, 1932.

25. ——, *Statistisches Jahrbuch für das Deutsche Reich,* Berlin.

---

26. Bastable, Charles Francis, *The Theory of International Trade with Some of Its Applications to Economic Policy,* 4th ed., Macmillan Company, London, 1903.

27. Cairnes, John Elliott, *Some Leading Principles of Political Economy, Newly Expounded,* Harper & Brothers, New York, 1874.

28. Condliffe, John B., *The Commerce of Nations,* W. W. Norton, New York, 1950.

29. Dugé de Bernonville, Léo, "Les Revenus Privés," *Revue d'Économie Politique,* March–April 1937.

30. ——, "Les Revenus Privés et les Consommations," *Revue d'Économie Politique,* May–August 1939.

31. Ellsworth, Paul T., *International Economics,* Macmillan Company, New York, 1938.

32. Gerschenkron, Alexander, "Russia's Trade in the Postwar Years," *Annals of the American Academy of Political and Social Science,* May 1949.

33. Haberler, Gottfried, *The Theory of International Trade with Its Application to Commercial Policy* (trans. from the German by A. Stonier and F. Benham), W. Hodge and Company, London, 1936.

34. Hamilton, Alexander, "Report on the Subject of Manufactures," in *State Papers and Speeches on the Tariff,* edited by F. W. Taussig, Harvard University, Cambridge, 1892.

35. Harrod, Roy Forbes, *International Economics,* Nisbet & Company, London, 1933.

36. Jevons, W. Stanley, *The Theory of Political Economy,* 4th ed., Macmillan Company, London, 1911.

37. List, Friedrich, *Das Nationale System der Politischen Ökonomie,* Vol. VI of *Schriften, Reden, Briefe,* 10 vols., Reimar Hobbing, Berlin, 1927–35.

38. Marsh, Donald Bailey, *World Trade and Investment, the Economics of Interdependence,* Harcourt, Brace and Company, New York, 1951.

39. Martin, Robert F., *National Income in the United States, 1799–1938,* National Industrial Conference Board, New York, 1939.

40. Meerwarth, Rudolf, *Nationalökonomie und Statistik: Eine Einführung in die Empirische Nationalökonomie,* W. de Gruyter Company, Berlin, 1925.

41. Mill, John Stuart, *Principles of Political Economy, with Some of Their Applications to Social Philosophy,* Longmans, Green and Company, London, 1909.

42. Ricardo, David, *Principles of Political Economy and Taxation,* Everyman's Library, E. P. Dutton & Co., New York, 1933.

43. Schwartz, Harry, *Russia's Soviet Economy,* Prentice-Hall, New York, 1950.

44. Scobel, Albert, *Geographisches Handbuch zu Andrees Allgemeiner Handatlas,* Velhagen & Klasing, Bielefeld, 1899.

45. Smith, Adam, *An Inquiry into the Nature and Causes of the Wealth of Nations* (with notes, etc., by J. R. M'Culloch), new ed., A. & C. Black, Edinburgh, 1863.

46. Studenski, Paul, and Wyler, Julius, *International Survey of National Income,* National Bureau of Economic Research, New York. (Unpublished study.)

47. Taussig, F. W., *International Trade,* Macmillan, New York, 1927.

48. ——, *Protection of Young Industries as Applied in the United States: a Study in Economic History,* G. P. Putnam's Sons, New York, 1884.

49. Woytinsky, Wl. (W. S.), *Die Welt in Zahlen,* Vol. V: *Handel und Verkehr,* Rudolf Mosse, Berlin, 1927.

50. ——, *Internationale Hebung der Preise als Ausweg aus der Krise* (Frankfurter Gesellschaft für Konjunkturforschung), Hans Buske, Leipzig, 1931.

51. Woytinsky, W. S., *The Social Consequences of the Economic Depression,* International Labor Office, Geneva, 1936.

52. ——, *Earnings and Social Security in the United States,* Committee on Social Security, Social Science Research Council, 1943.

53. ——, and Woytinsky, E. S., *World Population and Production: Trends and Outlook,* Twentieth Century Fund, New York, 1953.

CHAPTER 3

DIRECTION OF WORLD TRADE

1. League of Nations, *Europe's Trade,* Geneva, 1942.

2. ——, *International Currency Experiment,* Geneva, 1944.

3. ——, *International Trade Statistics,* Geneva.

4. ———, *Memorandum on Balances of Payments and Foreign Trade Balances, 1913–1927*, Geneva, 1928.
5. ———, *Memorandum on Production and Trade*, Geneva.
6. ———, *The Network of World Trade*, Geneva, 1942.
7. ———, *World Production and Prices, 1925–37*, Geneva, 1935–38.
8. ———, Gold Delegation, *Selected Documents*, Geneva, 1930.
9. United Nations, *Balance of Payments Trends and Policies, 1950–1951*, New York, 1951.
10. ———, *Direction of International Trade*.
11. ———, *Economic Report: Salient Features of the World Economic Situation, 1945–1947*, New York, 1948.
12. ———, *Economic Survey of Asia and the Far East*.
13. ———, *Economic Survey of Europe*.
14. ———, *Economic Survey of Latin America*.
15. ———, *World Economic Report*.
16. ———, *Yearbook of International Trade Statistics*.
17. International Monetary Fund, *International Financial Statistics*.

UNITED STATES

18. Department of Commerce, *Foreign Commerce Yearbook*.
19. ———, *Foreign Trade of the United States, 1936–49*, 1951.
20. ———, *Survey of Current Business*.
21. ———, Bureau of the Census, *Foreign Commerce and Navigation of the United States, Annual Report*.
22. ———, ———, *Historical Statistics of the United States, 1789–1945*, 1949.
23. ———, ———, *Statistical Abstract of the United States*.
24. Economic Cooperation Administration, Special Mission to the United Kingdom, *The Sterling Area, An American Analysis*, 1951.

25. GREAT BRITAIN. *Economic Survey for 1947*, Cmd. 7046, H.M.S.O., London.

26. Condliffe, John B., *The Commerce of Nations*, W. W. Norton, New York, 1950.
27. Hilgerdt, Folke, "The Case for Multilateral Trade," *American Economic Review*, March 1943, Supplement (*Papers and Proceedings* of the Fifty-fifth Annual Meeting of the American Economic Association).
28. List, Friedrich, *Das Nationale System der Politischen Ökonomie*, Vol. 6 of *Schriften, Reden, Briefe*, 10 vols., Reimar Hobbing, Berlin, 1927–35.
29. Machlup, F., "Three Concepts of the Balance of Payments and the So-Called Dollar Shortage," *Economic Journal*, March 1950.
30. Marsh, Donald Bailey, *World Trade and Investment, the Economics of Interdependence*, Harcourt, Brace and Company, New York, 1951.
31. Sprague, O. M. W., "Price Stabilization," *American Economic Review*, March 1929 (reprinted in *Selected Documents* of the Gold Delegation, League of Nations, 1930).

32. Woytinsky, Wl. (W. S.), *Die Welt in Zahlen*, Vol. V: *Handel und Verkehr*, Rudolf Mosse, Berlin, 1927.
33. ———, *Tatsachen und Zahlen Europas*, Peneuropa Verlag, Vienna, 1930.
34. Woytinsky, W. S., and Woytinsky, E. S., *World Population and Production: Trends and Outlook*, Twentieth Century Fund, New York, 1953.

CHAPTER 4

THE COMPOSITION OF FOREIGN TRADE

1. League of Nations, *International Trade Statistics*, Geneva.
2. ———, *Minimum List of Commodities for International Trade Statistics*, rev. ed., 1938.
3. ———, *The Network of World Trade*, Geneva, 1942.
4. ———, *Review of World Trade*, Geneva.
5. United Nations, *Commodity Trade Statistics*.
6. ———, *Review of International Commodity Problems*.
7. ———, *Standard International Trade Classification*, 1951.
8. ———, *Statistical Yearbook*.
9. ———, *Yearbook of International Trade Statistics*.
10. ———, Economic Commission for Europe, *Economic Bulletin for Europe*.
11. ———, ———, *Economic Survey of Europe*.
12. ———, ———, *European Steel Trends in the Setting of the World Market*, 1st rev., Geneva, 1951.
13. ———, ———, *A General Survey of the European Engineering Industry*, Geneva, 1951.
14. ———, ———, *Quarterly Bulletin of Steel Statistics*.
15. Food and Agriculture Organization (FAO), *European Timber, Trends and Prospects*, Geneva, 1953.
16. ———, *Food and Agricultural Statistics, 1948–April 1952*.
17. ———, *Forestry and Forest Products*, Washington, 1946.
18. ———, *Grain Exports by Source and Destination, July 1951–June 1952*, October 1952.
19. ———, *Monthly Bulletin of Agricultural Economics and Statistics* (since May 1952).
20. ———, *Yearbook of Food and Agricultural Statistics*, Rome.
21. ———, *Yearbook of Forest Products Statistics*.
22. International Institute of Agriculture, *Agricultural Commodities and Raw Materials*, Rome, 1944.
23. ———, *Les Grands Produits Agricoles*, Rome, 1944.
24. ———, *Yearbook of Forest Products Statistics*.

UNITED STATES

25. Department of Agriculture, *Fats and Oils, World Production and Trade*.
26. Department of Commerce, *Foreign Commerce Yearbook*.
27. ———, *Foreign Trade of the United States, 1936–49*.
28. ———, Bureau of the Census, *Historical Statistics of the United States, 1789–1945*, 1949.
29. ———, ———, *Statistical Abstract of the United States*.
30. Department of the Interior, Bureau of Mines, *Minerals Yearbook*.

31. Department of State, *Energy Resources of the World*, 1949.
32. Tariff Commission, *Hides and Skins and Leather*, 1946.
33. President's Materials Policy Commission, *Resources for Freedom*, 5 volumes, 1952.

34. FRANCE. Statistique Générale, *Annuaire Statistique*, Paris.

35. GERMANY. Statistisches Reichsamt, *Statistisches Jahrbuch für das Deutsche Reich*.

36. American Petroleum Institute, *Petroleum Facts and Figures*, 9th ed., New York, 1951.
37. British Iron and Steel Federation, *Statistical Yearbook*, Part II: "Statistics of the Iron and Steel Industries of Overseas Countries," London.
38. Leith, G. K., Furness, J. W., and Lewis, Cleona, *World Minerals and World Peace*, Brookings Institution, Washington, 1943.
39. Pratt, Wallace, and Good, Dorothy (Editors), *World Geography of Petroleum* (American Geographical Society, Special Publication No. 31), Princeton University Press, Princeton, 1950.
40. Woytinsky, Wl. (W. S.), *Die Welt in Zahlen*, 7 volumes, Rudolf Mosse, Berlin, 1925–1928.
41. Woytinsky, W. S., *The Social Consequences of the Economic Depression*, International Labor Office, Geneva, 1936.
42. ———, and Woytinsky, E. S., *World Population and Production: Trends and Outlook*, Twentieth Century Fund, New York, 1953.

CHAPTER 5

BALANCES OF PAYMENTS AND INTERNATIONAL INVESTMENTS

1. League of Nations, *Balances of Payments.*
2. ———, *Course and Phases of the World Economic Depression*, 1931.
3. ———, *Memorandum on Balances of Payments and Foreign Trade Balances* (for 1910–1924 and 1911–1925).
4. ———, *Memorandum on International Trade and Balances of Payments* (for 1912–26, 1913–27, 1926–28 and 1927–29).
5. ———, *Statistical Year Book.*
6. United Nations, *Balances of Payments.*
7. ———, *The Economic Development of Latin America and Its Principal Problems*, 1950.
8. ———, *Economic Report: Salient Features of the World Economic Situation, 1945–1947*, New York, 1948.
9. ———, *International Capital Movements during the Inter-War Period*, 1949.
10. ———, *Statistical Yearbook*, New York.
11. ———, *A Study of Trade between Latin America and Europe*, 1953.
12. ———, *A Survey of the Economic Situation and Prospects of Europe*, Geneva, 1948.
13. ———, *World Economic Report.*
14. ———, Economic Commission for Europe, *Economic Survey of Europe.*

15. Food and Agriculture Organization (FAO), *Current Development of and Prospects for Agriculture in Latin America.*
16. International Monetary Fund, *Annual Report.*
17. ———, *Balance of Payments Manual.*
18. ———, *Balance of Payments Yearbook.*
19. ———, *International Financial Statistics.*

UNITED STATES
20. The President, *Thirty-third Report to Congress on Lend-Lease Operations*, 1952.
21. Department of Commerce, *Balance of International Payments of the United States, 1946–1948.*
22. ———, *Balance of Payments of the United States, 1949–51*, 1952.
23. ———, *Foreign Commerce Weekly.*
24. ———, *International Transactions of the United States during the War, 1940–45*, 1948.
25. ———, *Survey of Current Business.*
26. ———, *The United States in the World Economy*, 1949.
27. ———, *United States Direct Investments in Foreign Countries*, 1953.
28. ———, Bureau of the Census, *Historical Statistics of the United States, 1789–1945*, 1949.
29. ———, ———, *Statistical Abstract of the United States.*
30. *Report to the President on Foreign Economic Policy.*
31. Treasury Department, *Census of American Owned Assets in Foreign Countries*, 1947.

GREAT BRITAIN
32. Board of Trade, *Journal.*
33. Central Statistical Office, *Statistical Abstract of the United Kingdom.*
34. Chancellor of the Exchequer, *Statistical Material Presented during the Washington Negotiations*, Cmd. 6070, H.M.S.O.

35. Buchanan, Norman S., and Lutz, Friedrich A., *Rebuilding the World Economy: America's Role in Foreign Trade and Investment*, Twentieth Century Fund, New York, 1947.
36. Condliffe, John B., *The Commerce of Nations*, W. W. Norton, New York, 1950.
37. Feis, Herbert, *Europe, The World's Banker, 1870–1914: An Account of European Foreign Investment and the Connection of World Finance with Diplomacy before the War*, Yale University Press, New Haven, 1930.
38. Frankel, Sally, *Capital Investment in Africa, Its Course and Effects*, Oxford University Press, London, 1938.
39. Jenks, Leland H., *The Migration of British Capital to 1875*, Alfred A. Knopf, New York, 1927.
40. Lewis, Cleona, *Debtor and Creditor Countries: 1938, 1944*, Brookings Institution, Washington, 1945.
41. Madden, John T., Nadler, Marcus, and Sauvain, Harry C., *America's Experience as a Creditor Nation*, Prentice-Hall, New York, 1937.
42. *Manchester Guardian Commercial*, "Der Wiederaufbau in Europe," April 20, 1922.
43. Staley, Eugene, *War and the Private Investor*, Doubleday, Doran, New York, 1935.

44. Viner, Jacob, *Studies in the Theory of International Trade,* Harper and Brothers, New York, 1937.
45. Woytinsky, Wl. (W. S.), *Die Welt in Zahlen,* Vol. V: *Handel und Verkehr,* Rudolf Mosse, Berlin, 1927.
46. Woytinsky, W. S., *The Social Consequences of the Economic Depression,* International Labor Office, Geneva, 1936.

CHAPTER 6

TARIFFS, TRADE AGREEMENTS AND TRADE RESTRICTIONS

1. League of Nations, *Commercial Policy in the Interwar Period: International Proposals and National Policies,* Geneva, 1942.
2. ———, *Commercial Policy in the Postwar World,* Report of the Economic and Financial Committees, Geneva, 1945.
3. ———, *The Transition from War to Peace Economy,* Geneva, 1943.
4. ———, International Economic Conference (Geneva, May 1927), *Customs Classification,* Geneva, 1927.
5. ———, International Economic Conference (Geneva, May 1927), *Tariff Level Indices,* Geneva, 1927.
6. United Nations, *A Survey of the Economic Situation and Prospects of Europe,* Geneva, 1948.
7. ———, *General Agreement on Tariffs and Trade,* 4 volumes, New York, 1947.
8. ———, *Statistical Yearbook,* New York.
9. ———, *World Economic Report.*
10. ———, Economic Commission for Europe, *Economic Survey of Europe.*
11. ———, ———, *Economic Bulletin for Europe.*
12. Groupe d'Études pour l'Union Douanière Européénne, Comité Douanier, Comité Spécial Restreint de la Nomenclature, *Average Rates of Duty, 31 August 1949.*
13. ———, ———, *Draft Revised Tariff Nomenclature* (Main Headings), 2 volumes, Brussels, 1950.
14. ———, ———, *Moyenne de Tariffs Basée sur la Nomenclature de Bruxelles de 1949,* 5 volumes, Brussels, 1950.
15. The Contracting Parties to the GATT, *A New Proposal for the Reduction of Customs Tariffs,* Geneva, January 1954.
16. ———, *GATT in Action,* Geneva, February 1952.
17. ———, *International Trade, 1952,* Geneva, June 1953.
18. The International Customs Tariff Bureau, *Germany* (Federal Republic), February 1952.
19. ———, *Great Britain and Northern Ireland,* June 1952.

UNITED STATES

20. Department of Commerce, *Foreign Commerce Weekly.*
21. ———, Bureau of the Census, *Historical Statistics of the United States, 1789–1945,* 1949.
22. ———, ———, *Statistical Abstract of the United States.*
23. Department of State, *How a Trade Agreement Is Made* (Commercial Policy Series), October 1950.

24. ———, *Proposals for Expansion of World Trade and Employment* (Commercial Policy Series), 1945.
25. Commission on Foreign Economic Policy (Randall Commission), *Report to the President and the Congress,* January 1954.
26. Public Advisory Board for Mutual Security, *A Trade and Tariff Policy in the National Interest,* February 1953.
27. Tariff Commission, *Annual Report.*
28. ———, *Dictionary of Tariff Information,* 1924.
29. ———, *Effect of Trade Agreement Concessions on United States Tariff Levels Based on Imports in 1930,* October 1931.
30. ———, *Effect of Trade Agreement Concessions on United States Tariff Levels Based on Imports in 1952,* rev., September 1953.
31. ———, *Extent of Equal Tariff Treatment in Foreign Countries* (Report No. 119), 1937.
32. ———, *Operation of the Trade Agreements Program, June 1934 to April 1948,* 5 Parts, 1948–49.
33. ———, *Operation of Trade Agreements Program* (Annual Report).
34. ———, *Reciprocity and Commercial Treaties,* 1919.
35. ———, *Trade-Agreement Concessions of the United States,* rev., August 1949.
36. ———, *Summaries of Tariff Information,* Volumes 1–16, 1948.
37. ———, *Watches* (War Changes in Industry Series, No. 20), 1947.

38. FRANCE. Ministère de Finances, "Décret portant Fixation de Tarif des Douanes," *Journal Official,* January 18, 1938.

39. GERMANY. Bundesministerium der Finanzen, *Zolltarifgesetz vom 16 August 1951 und Gebruchszolltarif mit Anhang,* Bonn, October 1951.

40. RUSSIA. Ministerstvo Torgovli i Promyshlennosti, *Voprosy Vneshneĭ Torgovoĭ Politiki,* Petrograd, 1916.

41. Angier, Charles, and Marvaud, Angel, *La Politique Douanière de la France dans ses Rapports avec Celle des Autres Pays,* Felix Alcan, Paris, 1911.
42. Ashley, Percy W. L., *Modern Tariff History: Germany, United States, France,* 2d edition, J. Murray, London, 1910.
43. Barnes, Donald G., *A History of the English Corn Laws from 1660–1846,* F. S. Crofts & Company, New York, 1930.
44. Bidwell, Percy Wells, *Our Trade with Britain: Bases for a Reciprocal Tariff Agreement,* Council on Foreign Relations, New York, 1938.
45. ———, *The Invisible Tariff, a Study of the Control of Imports into the United States,* Council on Foreign Relations, New York, 1939.
46. ———, and Diebold, William, Jr., *The United States and the International Trade Organization* (International Conciliation, No. 449), Carnegie Endowment for International Peace, New York, 1949.

47. Buchanan, Norman S., and Lutz, Friedrich A., *Rebuilding the World Economy: America's Role in Foreign Trade and Investment,* Twentieth Century Fund, New York, 1947.

48. Chalmers, Henry, "Tariffs" in *Encyclopaedia Britannica,* Vol. 21.

49. ———, *World Trade Policies,* University of California Press, Berkeley, 1953.

50. Chamber of Commerce of the United States, *International Trade Policy Issues,* Washington, 1953.

51. Condliffe, John B., *The Commerce of Nations,* W. W. Norton & Company, New York, 1950.

52. ———, *The Reconstruction of World Trade* (International Studies Conference), W. W. Norton & Company, New York, 1940.

53. Cunningham, W., *The Rise and Decline of the Free Trade Movement,* 2d ed., Cambridge University Press, Cambridge, 1912.

54. De la Salle, J. Perthuis, *La Politique Française de Contingentement,* Université de Paris, 1935.

55. Delle-Donne, Ottavio, *European Tariff Policies since the World War,* Adelphi Company, New York, 1928.

56. Dewey, Davis Rich, *Financial History of the United States,* Longmans, Green & Company, New York, 1931.

57. Fisk, George M., and Peirce, Paul S., *International Commercial Policies with Special Reference to the United States,* Macmillan Company, New York, 1923.

58. Fouchet, Jacques, *La Politique Commerciale en France depuis 1930,* Les Presses Modernes, Paris, 1938.

59. Gordon, Margaret S., *Barriers to World Trade, a Study of Recent Commercial Policy,* Macmillan Company, New York, 1941.

60. Gras, Norman S. B., *The Early English Customs System,* Harvard University Press, Cambridge, 1918.

61. ———, "English Customs Revenue up to 1275," in *Annual Report* of the American Historical Association, 1917, Washington, 1920.

62. Gregory, T. E. G., *Tariffs: a Study in Method,* J. B. Lippincott Company, Philadelphia, 1921.

63. Grunzel, Josef, *Economic Protectionism* (Carnegie Endowment for International Peace, Division of Economics and History), Oxford University Press, New York, 1916.

64. ———, *System der Handelspolitik,* Julius Springer, Vienna, 1928.

65. Haight, Frank Arnold, *French Import Quotas, a New Instrument of Commercial Policy,* P. S. King and Son, London, 1935.

66. Hamilton, Alexander, "Report on the Subject of Manufactures," in *State Papers and Speeches on the Tariff,* edited by F. W. Taussig, Harvard University, Cambridge, 1892.

67. Harms, Bernard, *Die Zukunft der Deutschen Handelspolitik im Rahmen des Neuaufbaus der Deutschen Volkswirtschaft und Ihrer Weltwirtschaftlichen Beziehungen,* Gustav Fischer, Jena, 1925.

68. Higginson, John Hadley, *Tariffs at Work, an Outline of Practical Tariff Administration with Special Reference to the United States and Canada,* P. S. King, London, 1913.

69. Hill, William, *First Stages of the Tariff Policy of the United States,* American Economic Association, Evanston, Illinois, 1893.

70. Högel, Max, *Die Auswärtige Handelspolitik Frankreichs nach dem Kriege* (Münchener Volkswirtschaftliche Studien), Gustav Fischer, Jena, 1929.

71. Holland, Bernard, *The Fall of Protection, 1840–1850,* Longmans, Green & Company, New York, 1913.

72. Jones, Joseph M., *Tariff Retaliation, Repercussions of the Hawley-Smoot Bill,* University of Pennsylvania Press, Philadelphia, 1934.

73. Leser, A., "Merkantilsystem," *in Handwörterbuch der Staatswissenschaften,* Gustav Fischer, Jena, 1910.

74. Liepmann, Heinrich, *Tariff Levels and Economic Unity of Europe* (trans. from the German, by H. Stenning), Macmillan Company, New York, 1938.

75. List, Friedrich, *Das Natürliche System der Politischen Ökonomie,* Vol. IV in *Schriften, Reden, Briefe,* 10 volumes, R. Hobbing, Berlin, 1927–35.

76. Lynch, David, "Tariffs," in *Britannica Book of the Year,* 1953.

77. Marsh, Donald Bailey, *World Trade and Investment, the Economics of Interdependence,* Harcourt, Brace and Company, New York, 1951.

78. Oncken, A., "Handelsverträge," in *Handwörterbuch der Staatswissenschaften,* Vol. V, Gustav Fischer, Jena, 1910.

79. Piquet, Howard S., *Aid, Trade and the Tariff,* Thomas Y. Crowell Company, New York, 1953.

80. Polo, Marco, *Travels,* Modern Library, New York, 1931.

81. Rathenau, Walther, *Deutschlands Rohstoffversorgung,* S. Fisher, Berlin, 1917.

82. Rausch, Ernst, *Französische Handelspolitik vom Frankfurter Frieden bis zur Tarifreform von 1882,* Duncker & Humblot, Leipzig, 1900.

83. Salter, Sir Arthur, *Recovery, the Second Effort,* Century Company, New York; G. Bell and Son, London, 1932.

84. Sommerland, T., "Zollverein," in *Handwörterbuch der Staatswissenschaften,* Vol. VIII, Gustav Fischer, Jena, 1911.

85. Stanwood, Edward, *American Tariff Controversies in the Nineteenth Century,* 2 volumes, Houghton, Mifflin and Company, Boston, 1903.

86. Taussig, F. W., *The Tariff History of the United States,* 8th ed., G. P. Putnam's Sons, New York, 1931.

87. Whelpley, James Davenport, *The Trade of the World,* Century Company, New York, 1913.

88. Wilcox, Clair, *A Charter for World Trade,* Macmillan Company, New York, 1949.

89. Woytinsky, W. S., *The Social Consequences of the Economic Depression,* International Labor Office, Geneva, 1936.

90. Zimmermann, Alfred, *Geschichte der Preussich-Deutschen Handelspolitik, Aktenmässig Dargestellt,* A. Schwartz, Oldenburg, 1892.

PART II. TRANSPORTATION

CHAPTER 7

TRANSPORTATION IN THE WORLD ECONOMY

1. United Nations, *Statistical Yearbook*, New York.
2. ———, *Statistics of National Income and Expenditures*, New York.
3. ———, *Transport and Communications Review*.
4. ———, Economic Commission for Europe, *Annual Bulletin of Transport Statistics*, Geneva.
5. International Labor Office, *General Report*, Geneva.
6. ———, *Yearbook of Labour Statistics*, Geneva.

UNITED STATES

7. Department of Commerce, *Transportation Routes and Systems of the World, Development of Steam-Carrying Power on Land and Sea, 1808 to 1908*, 1909.
8. ———, Bureau of the Census, *Historical Statistics of the United States, 1789–1945*, 1949.
9. ———, ———, *Statistical Abstract of the United States*.
10. ———, Bureau of Foreign and Domestic Commerce, *Foreign Commerce Weekly*.
11. ———, ———, *Survey of Current Business*.
12. ———, ———, *National Income*, Supplement to *Survey of Current Business*.
13. ———, Civil Aeronautics Administration, *Statistical Handbook of Civil Aviation*.
14. Interstate Commerce Commission, *Annual Report*.

15. FRANCE. Institut National de la Statistique et des Études Économiques pour la Metropole et la France d'Outre-mer, *Annuaire Statistique*, Paris.

16. GERMANY. Statistisches Bundesamt, *Statistisches Jahrbuch der Bundesrepublik Deutschland*, Wiesbaden.

17. GREAT BRITAIN. Central Statistical Office, *Annual Abstract of Statistics*, London.

18. NORWAY. Statistisk Sentralbyrå, *Statistisk Årbok før Norge*, Oslo.

19. SWEDEN. Central Bureau of Statistics, *Statistisk Årsbok*, Stockholm.

---

20. Barger, Harold, *The Transportation Industries 1889–1946, a Study of Output, Employment and Productivity*, National Bureau of Economic Research, New York, 1951.
21. Blum, Otto, *Die Entwicklung des Verkehrs*, Vol. I, Julius Springer, Berlin, 1941.
22. Bonavia, Michael R., *The Economics of Transport*, Nisbet and Company, London, 1936.
23. Daggett, Stuart, *Principles of Inland Transportation*, Harper and Brothers, New York, 1941.
24. D'Avenel, Georges, *L'Évolution des Moyens de Transport*, Ernest Flammarion, Paris, 1919.
25. De Foville, Alfred, *La Transformation des Moyens de Transport et ses Conséquences Économiques et Sociales*, Guillaumin et Cie., Paris, 1880.
26. Fair, Marvin L. and Williams, Ernest W., Jr., *Economics of Transportation*, Harper and Brothers, New York, 1950.
27. Frickey, Edwin, *Production in the United States, 1860–1914* (Harvard Economic Studies, Vol. 82), Harvard University Press, Cambridge, 1947.
28. Healy, Kent T., *The Economics of Transportation in America; the Dynamic Forces in Development, Organization, Functioning and Regulation*, Ronald Press Company, New York, 1940.
29. Huber, F. C., "Verkehrsmittel und Verkehrswege," in *Handwörterbuch der Staatswissenschaften*, Vol. 8, 3d ed., Gustav Fischer, Jena, 1911.
30. *Journal of Railroads*.
31. Landon, Charles E., *Transportation: Principles, Practices, Problems*, William Sloane Associates, New York, 1951.
32. Locklin, D. P., *Economics of Transportation*, 3d ed., Richard D. Irwin, Chicago, 1947.
33. Miller, Sidney L., *Inland Transportation, Principles and Policies*, McGraw-Hill Book Company, New York, 1933.
34. National Safety Council, *Accident Facts*, Chicago.
35. Pirath, Carl, *Die Grundlagen der Verkehrswirtschaft*, 2d ed., J. Springer, Berlin, 1949.
36. Renner, George T. and Associates, *Global Geography*, Thomas Y. Crowell Company, New York, 1944.
37. Smith, Adam, *An Inquiry into the Nature and Causes of the Wealth of Nations* (with notes, etc., by J. R. M'Culloch), new ed., A. & C. Black, Edinburgh, 1863.
38. Transportation Association of America, *Sound Transportation for the National Welfare*, Chicago, 1953.
39. Westmeyer, Russell E., *Economics of Transportation*, Prentice-Hall, Inc., New York, 1952.
40. Wilson, G. L., *The Elements of Transportation Economics*, Simmons-Boardman Publishing Corporation, New York, 1950.
41. Woytinsky, W. S., and Woytinsky, E. S., *World Population and Production: Trends and Outlook*, Twentieth Century Fund, New York, 1953.

CHAPTER 8

LAND TRANSPORTATION: THE PREMECHANICAL ERA AND THE RAILROADS

1. League of Nations, *International Statistical Yearbook*, Geneva.
2. United Nations, *Economic Survey of Asia and the Far East*.
3. ———, *Economic Survey of Latin America*.
4. ———, *Monthly Bulletin of Statistics*.
5. ———, *Statistical Yearbook*, New York.
6. ———, *Statistics of National Income and Expenditures*, New York.
7. ———, *Transport and Communications Review*.

8. ———, Economic Commission for Europe, *Annual Bulletin of Transport Statistics,* Geneva.

UNITED STATES

9. Seventy-ninth Congress, First Session, Board of Investigation and Research, *Technological Trends in Transportation* (Senate Document No. 76), 1945.

10. Eighty-second Congress, Senate Committee on Interstate and Foreign Commerce, *Domestic Land and Water Transportation* (Report No. 1039), 1951.

11. Department of Commerce, *Foreign Commerce Yearbook.*

12. ———, Bureau of the Census, *Historical Statistics of the United States, 1789–1945,* 1949.

13. Department of Commerce and Labor, *Transportation Routes and Systems of the World, Development of Steam-Carrying Power on Land and Sea, 1808 to 1908,* 1909.

14. Interstate Commerce Commission, *Annual Report.*

15. ———, *Statistics of Railways in the United States.*

16. National Resources Planning Board, *Transportation and National Policy in the United States,* 1942.

17. Office of the Federal Coordinator of Transportation, *Public Aid to Transportation,* 2 volumes, 1938.

18. CANADA. Dominion Bureau of Statistics, *The Canada Year Book,* Ottawa.

19. GERMANY. Statistisches Reichsamt, *Statistisches Jahrbuch für das Deutsche Reich,* Berlin.

20. GREAT BRITAIN. Central Statistical Office, *Annual Abstract of Statistics, 1938–1948,* London.

21. SWEDEN. Central Bureau of Statistics, *Statistisk Årsbok,* Stockholm.

22. *American Railroad Journal.*

23. Anderson, Ingvar, and Associates, *Introduction to Sweden* (Swedish Institute, Publications), Bonniers, New York, 1949.

24. *Archiv für Eisenbahnwesen* (early editions, Carl Heymann's Verlag; later editions, J. Springer Verlag), Berlin.

25. Association of American Railroads, *Transportation in America,* Washington, 1947.

26. ———, Bureau of Railway Economics, *Railroad Transportation, a Statistical Record, 1911–1947,* Washington, 1948.

27. Balzak, S. S., Vasyutin, V. F., and Feigin, Y. G., *Economic Geography of the USSR* (translated from the Russian by the American Council of Learned Societies), Macmillan Company, New York, 1949.

28. Baranskiĭ, N. N., *Ekonomicheskaia Geografía SSSR,* 8th ed., Uchpegdiz, Moscow, 1950.

29. Bateman, John H., *Introduction to Highway Engineering,* 5th ed., John Wiley and Sons, New York; Chapman and Hall, London, 1948.

30. Bergson, Abram (Editor), *Soviet Economic Growth; Conditions and Perspectives,* Row, Peterson and Company, Evanston, Illinois, 1953.

31. Bigham, Truman C., and Roberts, Merrill J., *Transportation: Principles and Problems,* 2d ed., McGraw-Hill Book Company, New York, 1952.

32. Biruliả, A. K., *Obshchù Kurs Puteǔ Soobshcheniià,* Dopisdat, Moscow, 1950.

33. Blanqui, L. A., *Cours d'Économie Politique,* Paris, 1845.

34. Bruce, Arthur C., and Clarkeson, John, *Highway Design and Construction,* 3d ed., International Textbook Company, Scranton, Pennsylvania, 1950.

35. Cavaillès, Henri, *La Route Française,* Armand Collin, Paris, 1946.

36. Chatburn, George R., *Highways and Highway Transportation,* Thomas Y. Crowell Company, New York, 1923.

37. Chudov, A. S. (Editor), *Planirovanie na Zhelezno-Dorozhnom Transporte,* Part I, Gosudarstvennoe Transportnoe Zhelezno-Dorozhnoe Izdatelstvo, Moscow, 1948.

38. Clapham, J. H., *An Economic History of Modern Britain, the Early Railway Age, 1820–1850,* Macmillan Company, 1927.

39. Cleveland, F. A., and Powell, F. W., *Railroad Promotion and Capitalization in the United States,* Longmans, Green and Company, New York, 1909.

40. Clough, Shepard B., *France: History of National Economics, 1789–1939,* Charles Scribner's Sons, New York, 1939.

41. Cohn, Gustav, "Eisenbahnen," in *Handwörterbuch der Staatswissenschaften,* Vol. 3, 3d ed., Gustav Fischer Verlag, Jena, 1909.

42. Daggett, Stuart, *Principles of Inland Transportation,* rev. ed., Harper and Brothers, New York, 1941.

43. *Directory of Railway Officials & Year Book,* Tothill Press, London,

44. Dunbar, Seymour, *History of Travel in America,* Tudor Publishing Company, New York, 1937.

45. Fair, Marvin L., and Williams, Ernest W., Jr., *Economics of Transportation,* Harper and Brothers, New York, 1950.

46. Faulkner, Harold U., *American Economic History,* 5th ed., Harper and Brothers, New York, 1943.

47. Feis, Herbert, *Europe, the World's Banker, 1870–1914* (Council on Foreign Relations, Publications), Yale University Press, New Haven, 1930.

48. Foreign Press Association of Japan, *The Japan Year Book,* Japan Press Times, Tokyo.

49. Garbutt, P. E., *The Russian Railways,* Sampson Low, Marston and Company, London, 1949.

50. Glazebrook, G. P. de T., *A History of Transportation in Canada,* Yale University Press, New Haven, 1938.

51. Glover, John G., and Cornell, William B. (Editors), *The Development of American Industries,* 3d ed., Prentice-Hall, New York, 1951.

52. Hadley, Arthur T., *Railroad Transportation, Its History and Its Laws,* G. P. Putnam's Sons, New York, 1903.

53. Heaton, Herbert, *Economic History of Europe,* rev. ed., Harper and Brothers, New York, 1948.

54. Henry, Robert S., "Railroads in the United States," *Transport and Communication Review,* April–June 1949.

55. Holmstrom, J. (Editor), *Railways and Roads in Pioneer Development Overseas: a Study of Their Comparative Economics,* P. S. King and Son, London, 1934.

56. Hunnicut, Benjamin H., *Brazil Looks Forward,* Instituto Brasileiro de Geografia e Estatistica, Rio de Janeiro, 1945.

57. Hunter, Holland, "Soviet Railroads since 1940," in *Bulletin on Soviet Economic Development* (Report No. 4), University of Birmingham, September 1950.

58. International Road Federation, *Road International,* London.

59. ———, *World Road Statistics,* London, 1950.

60. International Union of Railways, *International Railway Statistics,* Paris.

61. Johnson, Emory R., and Associates, *Transportation: Economic Principles and Practices,* D. Appleton-Century Company, New York, 1940.

62. Kirkaldy, Adam W., and Evans, Alfred T. D., *The History and Economics of Transport,* 3d ed., Sir Isaac Pitman and Sons, London, 1924.

63. Kovalevskiĭ, V. J. (Editor), *Rossiĭâ v Kontsie XIX Veka,* Ministry of Finances, St. Petersburg, 1900.

64. Labatut, Jean, and Lane, W. J. (Editors), *Highways in Our National Life: a Symposium,* Princeton University Press, Princeton, 1950.

65. Landon, Charles E., *Transportation: Principles, Practices, Problems,* William Sloane Associates, New York, 1951.

66. *L'Année Ferroviaire,* Librairie Plon, Paris.

67. Lardner, Dionysius, *Railway Economy: a Treatise on the New Art of Transport Management, Prospect and Relations,* Taylor, Walton, and Maberly, London, 1850.

68. Lee, Charles E., "The Evolution of Railways," *The Railway Gazette,* 1937.

69. Locklin, D. Philip, *Economics of Transportation,* 3d ed., Richard D. Irwin, Chicago, 1947.

70. Macaulay, Thomas Babington, *The History of England from the Accession of James the Second,* 5 volumes, Harper and Brothers, New York, 1849.

71. Middleton, P. H., *Railways and Public Opinion, Eleven Decades,* Railway Business Association, Chicago, 1941.

72. Minkswell, Lord, *Railways and Their Future,* Ernest Benn, London, 1946.

73. Moakes, Lilian, *History of Travel and Communications,* John Growther, Sussex, England, 1945.

74. Nourse, Edwin G., and Associates, *America's Capacity to Produce,* Brookings Institution, Washington, 1934.

75. Obraztsov, V. N., *Die Eisenbahnen der Sowjetunion,* Verlag der Sowjetischen Militärverwaltung in Deutschland, Berlin, 1946.

76. ———, *Transport i ego Budushchee,* Academy of Sciences, Moscow-Leningrad, 1948.

77. Peyret, Henry, *Histoire des Chemins de Fer en France et dans le Monde.* Societé d'Éditions Françaises et Internationales, Paris, 1949.

78. Pratt, Edwin A., *A History of Inland Transport and Communication in England,* E. P. Dutton and Company, New York; Kegan Paul, Trench, Trubner and Company, London, 1912.

79. Prescott, William H., *History of the Conquest of Mexico* and *History of the Conquest of Peru,* Modern Library, New York, 1936.

80. *Railway Age.*

81. Raper, Charles Lee, *Railway Transportation, a History of Its Economics and of Its Relation to the State,* G. P. Putnam's Sons, New York, 1912.

82. Ringwalt, J. L., *Development of Transportation Systems in the United States* (published by the author), Philadelphia, 1888.

83. Ripley, William Z., *Railroads: Rates and Regulations,* Longmans, Green and Company, New York, 1912.

84. Rudchenko, P. T., *Ocherk Rasvitiĭâ i Sovremennogo Sostoĭaniĭâ Miestnych Puteĭ Soobscheniĭâ v Niekotorych Inostrannych Gosudarstvach i v Rossii,* St. Petersburg, 1904.

85. St. Clair, Labert, *Transportation since Time Began: Land, Air, Water,* rev. ed., Dodd, Mead & Company, New York, 1942.

86. Schwartz, Harry, *Russia's Soviet Economy,* Prentice-Hall, New York, 1950.

87. Stamp, L. Dudley, and Beaver, S. H., *The British Isles,* 3d ed., Longmans, Green and Company, New York, 1941.

88. Sterne, Simon, *Railways in the United States,* G. P. Putnam's Sons, New York, 1912.

89. Syme, Ronald, *The Story of British Roads,* British Road Federation, London, 1950.

90. Thomson, Lesslie R., *The Canadian Railway Problem,* Macmillan Company, Toronto, 1938.

91. Thornburg, Max W., Spry, Graham, and Soule, George, *Turkey: an Economic Appraisal,* Twentieth Century Fund, New York, 1949.

92. Wedgwood, Ralph L., and Wheeler, J. E., *International Rail Transport,* Oxford University Press, New York, 1946.

93. Westmeyer, Russell E., *Economics of Transportation,* Prentice-Hall, New York, 1952.

94. Whitworth, Charles E., "The Russian Railways," *Annals of the American Academy of Political and Social Science,* November 1943.

95. Wiedenfeld, K., "Eisenbahnstatistik," in *Handwörterbuch der Staatswissenschaften,* Vol. 3, Gustav Fischer, Jena, 1909.

96. Wilber, Donald N., *Iran: Past and Present,* 1st ed., Princeton University Press, Princeton, 1948.

97. Williams, Sydney Charles, *The Economics of Railway Transport,* Macmillan Company, London, 1909.

98. Wood, W. V., and Stamp, Josiah, *Railways,* Thornton Butterworth, London, 1928.

99. *World Railways, a Survey of the Operation and Equipment of Representative Rail Systems* (edited by Henry Sampson), Sampson Low, Marston and Company, London, 1952.

100. Woytinsky, Wl. (W. S.), *Die Welt in Zahlen,* 7 volumes, Rudolf Mosse, Berlin, 1925–1928.

101. Woytinsky, W. S., and Woytinsky, E. S., *World Population and Production: Trends and Outlook,* Twentieth Century Fund, New York, 1953.

102. Wythe, George, Wight, Royce A., and Midkiff, Harold M., *Brazil: an Expanding Economy,* Twentieth Century Fund, New York, 1949.

103. Zimmermann, Erich W., *World Resources and Industries,* rev. ed., Harper and Brothers, New York, 1951.

CHAPTER 9

LAND TRANSPORTATION: MOTOR VEHICLES AND HIGHWAYS

1. United Nations, *Economic Survey of Asia and the Far East,* New York.

2. ———, *Economic Survey of Latin America,* New York.

3. ———, *National Income Statistics, 1938–1948,* New York, 1950.

4. ———, *Statistical Yearbook,* New York.

5. ———, *Transport and Communications Review.*

6. ———, Economic Commission for Europe, *Annual Bulletin of Transportation Statistics,* Geneva.

7. International Labor Office, Inland Transport Committee, *General Report,* Geneva.

UNITED STATES

8. The President, *Highway Needs of the National Defense* (Message to the Eighty-first Congress, House Document No. 249), 1949.

9. Seventy-eighth Congress, National Interregional Highway Committee, *Interregional Highways* (House Document No. 379), 1944.

10. Seventy-ninth Congress, First Session, Board of Investigation and Research, *Technological Trends in Transportation* (Senate Document No. 76), 1945.

11. Eighty-first Congress, Joint Committee on the Economic Report, *Highways and the Nation's Economy,* 1950.

12. Eighty-second Congress, Senate Committee on Interstate and Foreign Commerce, *Domestic Land and Water Transportation* (Report No. 1039), 1951.

13. Department of Agriculture, *Statistical Findings of Survey of Transportation from Farms to Initial Markets,* 1949.

14. Department of Commerce, Bureau of the Census, *Historical Statistics of the United States, 1789–1945,* 1949.

15. ———, ———, *Statistical Abstract of the United States.*

16. ———, Bureau of Foreign and Domestic Commerce, *Survey of Current Business.*

17. ———, ———, *National Income,* Supplement to *Survey of Current Business.*

18. ———, Bureau of Public Roads, *Highway Finance, 1945–1950,* 1951.

19. ———, ———, *Highway Statistics.*

20. ———, ———, *Highways in the United States,* 1951.

21. Federal Works Agency, Public Road Administration, *Highway Practice in the United States of America,* 1949.

22. ———, ———, *Public Control of Highway Access and Roadside Development,* 1947.

23. Interstate Commerce Commission, *Annual Report.*

24. ———, *Preliminary Abstract of Railway Statistics,* 1951.

25. ———, *Statistics of Class I Motor Carriers.*

26. ———, *Statistics of Railways in the United States.*

27. National Resources Planning Board, *Family Expenditures in the United States,* 1941.

28. ———, *Transportation and National Policy in the United States,* 1942.

29. GERMANY. Statistisches Reichsamt, *Statistisches Jahrbuch für das Deutsche Reich,* Berlin.

GREAT BRITAIN

30. British Transport Commission, *Transport Statistics,* London.

31. Central Statistical Office, *Annual Abstract of Statistics,* London.

32. SWEDEN. Central Bureau of Statistics, *Statistik Årsbok för Sverige,* Stockholm.

33. American Association of State Highway Officials, *American Highways.*

34. American Petroleum Institute, *Petroleum Facts and Figures,* New York.

35. Association of American Railroads, *The Railroad Situation, 1950,* Washington, 1950.

36. ———, *Transportation in America,* Washington, 1947.

37. Automobile Manufacturers Association, *Automobile Facts and Figures,* Washington.

38. ———, *Motor Truck Facts,* Washington.

39. Automobile Safety Foundation, *Highway Facts,* Washington, 1952.

40. Balzak, S. S., Vasyutin, V. F., and Feigin, Y. G., *Economic Geography of the USSR* (translated from the Russian by the American Council of Learned Societies), Macmillan Company, New York, 1949.

41. Belloc, Hilaire, *The Highway and Its Vehicles* (Geoffrey Holme, editor), The Studio Ltd., London, 1926.

42. Bigham, Truman C., and Roberts, Merrill J., *Transportation: Principles and Problems,* 2d ed., McGraw-Hill Book Company, New York, 1952.

43. Bonavia, Michael R., *The Economics of Transport,* Nisbet and Company, London, 1936.

44. British Road Federation, *Basic Road Statistics— Great Britain,* London.

45. *Canadian Business.*

46. Cumberbatch, A. N., *Egypt* (Overseas Economic Surveys), Board of Trade, London, 1951.

47. Daggett, Stuart, *Principles of Inland Transportation,* rev. ed., Harper and Brothers, New York, 1941.

48. Davis, Harmer E., and Associates, *Toll Road Developments and Their Significance in the Provision of Expressways,* University of California, Institute of Transportation and Traffic Engineering, Richmond, 1953.

49. Delmer, Alexandre, *Les Transports de Marchandises: Étude Économique,* Editions Techniques et Scientifiques, Brussels, 1950.

50. International Road Federation, *Road International,* London.

51. ———, *World Road Statistics,* London, 1950.

Horn, Paul V., *International Trade: Principles and Practices,* 3d ed., Prentice-Hall, New York, 1951.

Interavia, Geneva.

Jane's All the World's Aircraft, Sampson Low, Marston and Company, London; McGraw-Hill Book Company, New York.

Johnson, Emory R., *Transport Facilities, Services and Policies,* D. Appleton-Century Company, New York, 1947.

——, and Associates, *Transportation: Economic Principles and Practices,* D. Appleton-Century Company, New York, 1940.

L'Air, Paris.

Landon, Charles E., *Transportation: Principles, Practices, Problems,* William Sloane Associates, New York, 1951.

L'Aviation Marchande, Paris.

Locklin, D. P., *Economics of Transportation,* 3d ed., Richard D. Irwin, Chicago, 1947.

Mackenzie, K. G., *Malaya* (Overseas Economic Surveys), Board of Trade, London, 1952.

Mance, Sir Harry Osborne, *International Air Transport* (American ed.), Oxford University Press, New York, 1944.

Nicholson, Joseph L., *Air Transportation Management; Its Practices and Policies,* John Wiley and Sons, New York, 1951; Chapman and Hall, London, 1952.

Ordin, A. G., *Vosdushnyi Flot Strany Sovetov,* All-Soviet Society for Political and Scientific Knowledge, Moscow, 1949.

Planes, Aircraft Industries Association of America, Washington.

Schwartz, Harry, *Russia's Soviet Economy,* Prentice-Hall, New York, 1950.

58. Stuart, F. S., and Biard, H. C., *Modern Air Transport,* John Long, London, 1947.

59. *The Aeroplane,* London.

60. Van Zandt, J. P., *The Geography of World Air Transport,* Brookings Institution, Washington, 1944.

61. Veale, S. E., *Airliners and Airways of Today,* Pilot Press, London, 1948.

62. Weiss, D. E., *Air Transport,* Art & Educational Publishers, London, 1946.

63. Westmeyer, Russell E., *Economics of Transportation,* Prentice-Hall, New York, 1952.

64. Wilson, G. L., and Bryan, L. A., *Air Transportation,* Prentice-Hall, New York, 1949.

65. Wolfe, Thomas, *Air Transportation—Traffic and Management,* McGraw-Hill Book Company, New York, 1950.

66. Wood, John W., *Airports; Some Elements of Design and Future Development,* Coward-McCann, New York, 1940.

67. ——, *Airports and Air Traffic; the Airport Needs of Your Community,* Coward-McCann, New York, 1949.

68. *World Airline Record, 1950–51,* Roy R. Roadcap and Associates, Chicago.

69. *World Aviation Annual, 1948,* Aviation Research Institute, Washington, D. C., and James Jackson Cabot Professorship of Air Transportation of Norwich University, Northfield, Vermont.

70. Woytinsky, Wl. (W. S.), *Die Welt in Zahlen,* 7 volumes, Rudolf Mosse, Berlin, 1925–1928.

71. ——, W. S., and Woytinsky, E. S., *World Population and Production: Trends and Outlook,* Twentieth Century Fund, New York, 1953.

52. Johnson, Emory R., and Associates, *Transportation: Economic Principles and Practices,* D. Appleton-Century Company, New York, 1940.

53. Labatut, Jean, and Lane, W. J. (Editors), *Highways in Our National Life: a Symposium,* Princeton University Press, Princeton, 1950.

54. Landon, Charles E., *Transportation: Principles, Practices, Problems,* William Sloane Associates, New York, 1951.

55. Lewis, Ben W., *British Planning and Nationalization,* Twentieth Century Fund, New York, 1952.

56. List, Friedrich, "Die Dampfwagen auf Chausseen und ihre mögliche Konkurrenz mit den Eisenbahnen betreffend," in Vol. III of *Schriften, Reden, Briefe* (10 Vols.), Reimar Hobbing, Berlin, 1931.

57. Locklin, D. P., *Economics of Transportation,* 3d ed., Richard D. Irwin, Chicago, 1947.

58. Long, W. Rodney, *Transport Control Abroad: Recent Outstanding Measures, Trends and Developments,* U. S. Department of Commerce, 1938.

59. National Academy of Sciences, Highway Research Board, *Road Test One-Md.* (Special Report No. 4), Washington, 1952.

60. National Association of Motor-Bus Operators, *Bus Facts,* Washington.

61. National Planning Committee, *Transport Services,* Vora and Company, Bombay, 1949.

62. Nockolds, Harold, *Roads: the New Way,* British Road Federation, London, 1950.

63. Owen, Wilfred, *Automotive Transportation: Trends and Problems,* Brookings Institution, Washington, 1949.

64. ——, and Dearing, Charles L., *Toll Roads and the Problem of Highway Modernization,* Brookings Institution, Washington, 1951.

65. Pirath, Carl, *Die Grundlagen der Verkehrswirtschaft,* 2d ed., Springer Verlag, Berlin, 1949.

66. Plummer, Alfred, *New British Industries in the Twentieth Century, a Survey of Development and Structure,* Sir Isaac Pitman & Sons, London, 1937.

67. Redmayne, Paul (Editor), *Transport by Land,* John Murray, London, 1948.

68. Taff, Charles A., *Commercial Motor Transportation,* Richard D. Irwin, Chicago, 1950.

69. Tucker, Harry, and Leager, Marc C., *Highway Economics,* International Textbook Company, Scranton, 1942.

70. Walker, Gilbert J., *Road and Rail, an Enquiry into the Economics of Competition and State Control,* 2d rev. ed., G. Allen and Unwin, London, 1947.

71. Westmeyer, Russell E., *Economics of Transportation,* Prentice-Hall, New York, 1952.

72. Wohl, Paul, and Albitreccia, A., *Road and Rail in Forty Countries,* Oxford University Press, London, 1935.

73. Woytinsky, W. S., and Woytinsky, E. S., *World Population and Production: Trends and Outlook,* Twentieth Century Fund, New York, 1953.

CHAPTER 10

WATER TRANSPORTATION

1. United Nations, *Economic Survey of Latin America,* New York.

2. ——, *Monthly Bulletin of Statistics.*

3. ——, *Report of the Mission of Technical Assistance to Bolivia,* New York, 1951.

4. ——, *Statistical Yearbook,* New York.

5. ——, *Transport and Communications Review.*

6. ——, Economic Commission for Europe, *Annual Bulletin of Transportation Statistics,* Geneva.

7. International Labor Office, Inland Transport Committee, *Coordination of Transport Labour Problems,* Geneva, 1951.

8. ——, ——, *General Report,* Geneva.

UNITED STATES

9. Eighty-first Congress, Second Session, Subcommittee on Maritime Affairs, *Encouragement of the Development and Expansion of Privately Owned Tramp Shipping Operations under the United States Flag* (Hearings), 1950.

10. ——, ——, Senate Committee on Interstate and Foreign Commerce, *Study of Domestic Land and Water Transportation,* 1950.

11. Eighty-second Congress, Senate Committee on Interstate and Foreign Commerce, *Domestic Land and Water Transportation* (Report No. 1039), 1951.

12. Department of Commerce and Labor, *Transportation Routes and Systems of the World, Development of Steam-Carrying Power on Land and Sea, 1808 to 1908,* 1909.

13. Department of Commerce, Bureau of the Census, *Control of Ocean Freight Rates in Foreign Trade* (Trade Promotion Series, No. 185), 1938.

14. ——, ——, *Historical Statistics of the United States, 1789–1945,* 1949.

15. ——, ——, *Statistical Abstract of the United States.*

16. ——, ——, *United States Foreign Trade, Summary Report, F975.*

17. ——, Bureau of Foreign and Domestic Commerce, *Foreign Commerce and Navigation of the United States, 1938,* 1940.

18. ——, Federal Maritime Board and Maritime Administration, *Annual Report.*

19. ——, Maritime Administration, *Merchant Fleets of the World, September 1, 1939–December 31, 1951,* 1952.

20. ——, ——, *Participation of United States Flag Ships in American Overseas Trade, 1921–51,* 1952.

21. ——, Office of International Trade, *Foreign Commerce Yearbook.*

22. Governor of the Panama Canal, *Annual Report.*

23. Maritime Commission, *A Study of Tramp Shipping under the American Flag,* 1949.

24. National Resources Planning Board, *Transportation and National Policy in the United States,* 1942.

25. Panama Canal Company and Canal Zone Government, *First Annual Reports, 1952, 1953.*

26. *A Water Policy for the American People,* Report of the President's Water Resources Policy Commission, 1950.

27. U.S. Army, Office of Board of Engineers for Rivers and Harbors, *Annual Report of the Chief of Engineers.*

CANADA

28. Dominion Bureau of Statistics, *The Canada Year Book,* Ottawa.

29. National Harbours Board, *Annual Report*, Ottawa, 1951.

GERMANY

30. Statistisches Bundesamt, *Statistisches Jahrbuch für die Bundesrepublik Deutschland*, Wiesbaden.
31. ———, *Wirtschaft und Statistik*, Wiesbaden.
32. Verkehrswissenschaftlicher Forschungsrat beim Reichsverkehrsministerium, *Der Wettbewerb in der Seeschiffahrt*, Gustav Fischer, Jena, 1940.

GREAT BRITAIN

33. Board of Trade, *Journal*.
34. Central Statistical Office, *Annual Abstract of Statistics*, London.

———

35. American Petroleum Institute, *Petroleum Facts and Figures*, New York.
36. Association of American Railroads, *Transportation in America*, Washington, 1947.
37. Balzak, S. S., Vasyutin, V. F., and Feigin, Y. G., *Economic Geography of the USSR* (translated from the Russian by the American Council of Learned Societies), Macmillan Company, New York, 1949.
38. Baranskiĭ, N. N., *Ekonomicheskaia Geografiia SSSR*, 8th ed., Uchpegdiz, Moscow, 1950.
39. Berglund, Abraham, *Ocean Transportation*, Longmans, Green and Company, New York, 1931.
40. Bigham, Truman C., and Roberts, Merrill J., *Transportation: Principles and Problems*, 2d ed., McGraw-Hill Book Company, New York, 1952.
41. Biruliâ, A. K., *Obshchiĭ Kurs Puteĭ Soobshcheniia*, Dopisdat, Moscow, 1950.
42. Blum, Otto, *Die Entwicklung des Verkehrs*, Vol. I, Julius Springer, Berlin, 1941.
43. Borgognon, Pierre, *Les Transports Internationaux par Voie de Terre*, R. Pichon and R. Durant-Anzias, Paris, 1951.
44. Bryan, Leslie A., *Principles of Water Transportation*, Ronald Press Company, New York, 1939.
45. Chamber of Shipping of the United Kingdom, *Annual Report*, H. F. and G. Witherby, London.
46. Chamberlain, E. T., *Liner Predominance in Transoceanic Shipping* (Trade Information Bulletin No. 448), U. S. Department of Commerce, 1952.
47. Clowes, Ernest S., *Shipways to the Sea: Our Inland and Coastal Waterways*, Williams and Wilkins Company, Baltimore, 1929.
48. Daggett, Stuart, *Principles of Inland Transportation*, rev. ed., Harper and Brothers, New York, 1941.
49. Deihl, D. George, *Water Transportation*, University Press, Des Moines, Iowa, 1940.
50. Fair, Marvin L., and Williams, Ernest W., Jr., *Economics of Transportation*, Harper and Brothers, New York, 1950.
51. Faulkner, Harold U., *American Economic History*, 5th ed., Harper and Brothers, New York, 1943.
52. Fayle, C. Ernest, *A Short History of the World's Shipping Industry*, Dial Press, New York, 1933.
53. Ford, P., and Bound, J. A., *Coastwise Shipping and the Small Ports*, B. Blackwell, Oxford, 1951.
54. Haaland, Christian, "The Norwegian Shipping Industry," in *Norway's Export Trade*, Blix Publishing Company, Oslo, 1939.

55. Hardy, A. C., *Seaways and Sea Trade*, D. Van Nostrand Company, New York, 1928.
56. ———, *World Shipping*, Penguin Books, New York, 1941.
57. Heaton, Herbert, *Economic History of Europe*, rev. ed., Harper and Brothers, New York, 1948.
58. Horn, Paul V., *International Trade: Principles and Practices*, 3d ed., Prentice-Hall Inc., New York, 1951.
59. Hutchins, John G. B., *The American Maritime Industries and Public Policy, 1789–1914: an Economic History* (Harvard Economic Studies, Vol. 71), Harvard University Press, Cambridge, 1941.
60. Insull, Thomas, *Transport by Sea* (designed and edited by Paul Redmayne), Transatlantic Arts, Florida; John Murray, London, 1950.
61. International Road Federation, *World Road Statistics, 1950*, London, 1951.
62. Issawi, Charles P., *Egypt, an Economic and Social Analysis* (Royal Institute of International Affairs), Oxford University Press, London, 1947.
63. Jeans, J. Stephen, *Waterways and Water Transport in Different Countries, with a Description of the Panama, Suez, Manchester, Nicaraguan and Other Canals*, E. and F. N. Spon, London, 1890.
64. Johnson, Emory R., *Transport Facilities, Services and Policies*, D. Appleton-Century Company, New York, 1947.
65. ———, and Associates, *Transportation: Economic Principles and Practices*, D. Appleton-Century Company, New York, 1940.
66. Kirkaldy, Adam W., and Evans, Alfred T. D., *The History and Economics of Transport*, 3d ed., Sir Isaac Pitman and Sons, London, 1924.
67. Landon, Charles E., *Transportation: Principles, Practices, Problems*, William Sloane Associates, New York, 1951.
68. *Lloyd's Register of Shipping*, London.
69. Locklin, D. P., *Economics of Transportation*, 3d ed., Richard D. Irwin, Chicago, 1947.
70. Mance, Osborne, and Wheeler, J. E., *International River and Canal Transport* (Royal Institute of International Affairs), Oxford University Press, London, 1945.
71. ———, and ———, *International Sea Transport* (Royal Institute of International Affairs), Oxford University Press, London, 1946.
72. Marx, Daniel, Jr., *International Shipping Cartels: a Study of Industrial Self-Regulation by Shipping Conferences*, Princeton University Press, Princeton, 1953.
73. Morgan, F. W., *Ports and Harbours* (Hutchinson's University Library), Longmans, Green and Company, New York; Hutchinson, London, 1952.
74. Mott, George Fox, *A Survey of United States Ports*, Arco Publishing Company, New York, 1951.
75. National Planning Committee, *Transport Services*, Vora and Company, Bombay, 1949.
76. *The Orient Yearbook, 1942*, Asia Statistics Co., Tokyo, 1942. (Republished by the Interdepartmental Committee for the Acquisition of Foreign Publications.)
77. Pirath, Carl *Die Grundlagen der Verkehrswirtschaft*, 2d ed., J. Springer Verlag, Berlin, 1949.
78. Pratt, Wallace E., and Good, Dorothy (Editors), *World Geography of Petroleum* (American Geo-

graphical Society, Special Publication No. 31), Princeton University Press, Princeton, 1950.
79. Saugstad, Jesse E., *Shipping and Shipbuilding Subsidies*, U.S. Department of Commerce, 1932.
80. *Scandinavian Shipping Gazette*, Copenhagen.
81. Schonfield, Hugh J., *The Suez Canal in World Affairs*, Constellation Books, London, 1952.
82. Smith, Adam, *An Inquiry into the Nature and Causes of the Wealth of Nations* (with notes, etc., by J. R. M'Culloch), new ed., A. & C. Black, Edinburgh, 1863.
83. *Strom und See*, Basel.
84. Suez Canal Company, *Monthly Bulletin*.
85. Thornton, R. H., *British Shipping*, Macmillan, New York, 1939.
86. Todd, John A. (Editor), *The Shipping World Afloat and Ashore*, Sir Isaac Pitman and Sons, London, 1929.
87. Van Cleef, Eugene, *Trade Centers and Trade Routes*, D. Appleton-Century Company, New York, 1937.
88. Woytinsky, Wl. (W. S.), *Die Welt in Zahlen*, 7 volumes, Rudolf Mosse, Berlin, 1925–1928.
89. Woytinsky, W. S., and Woytinsky, E. S., *World Population and Production: Trends and Outlook*, Twentieth Century Fund, New York, 1953.
90. Zimmermann, Erich W., *Ocean Shipping*, Prentice-Hall Inc., New York, 1921.
91. Zvonkov, V. V., *Velikie Stroiki Kommunisma i Transport*, Academy of Sciences, Moscow, 1952.

CHAPTER 11

AIR TRANSPORTATION

1. United Nations, *Statistical Yearbook*, New York.
2. ———, *Transport and Communications Review*.
3. International Civil Aviation Organization, *Air Mail Study*, Montreal, 1948.
4. ———, *Airport Charges in August 1953*.
5. ———, *Airport Economics* (Preliminary Study), 1948.
6. ———, *Digest of Statistics* (Scheduled Airline Operations).
7. ———, *Financial Data*.
8. ———, *Fleet Personnel*.
9. ———, *Memorandum on ICAO: The Story of the Civil Aviation Organization*, 1951.
10. ———, *Report of the Council to the Assembly on the Activities of the Organization in 1951*, May 1952.

UNITED STATES

11. Eighty-second Congress, House of Representatives, Committee on Interstate and Foreign Commerce, *Air Mail Subsidies*, 1952.
12. Eighty-third Congress, Senate, Select Committee on Small Business, *Future of Irregular Airlines*, July 1953.
13. ———, ———, ———, *The Role of Competition in Commercial Air Transportation*, November 1952.
14. Department of Commerce, Bureau of Foreign and Domestic Commerce, *National Income, 1951*, Supplement to *Survey of Current Business*, 1951.
15. ———, Civil Aeronautics Administration, *Aircraft Use in 1951*, December 1952.

16. ———, ———, *Civil Aviation Economy*, 1945.
17. ———, ———, *Foreign Development Progress,*
18. ———, ———, *Statistical tion.*
19. ———, Civil Aeronautics
20. ———, ———, *Equipment uled Common Carrier*
21. ———, *World Common Carrier Airl*
22. Civil Aeronautics Authority to the Congress, 1939
23. National Resources Plan and National Policy,

24. GREAT BRITAIN. Centr *Abstract of Statistics*

———

25. *Aircraft Annual, 194* including *Specifica* Ian Allan, London
26. Aircraft Industries *Aircraft Year Boo*
27. "Air Transport Fact tion (Annual Air
28. *Air Transportation.*
29. *Air Week.*
30. *American Aviation*
31. *Aviation Facts an* dolf Modley, A America), McG York, 1945.
32. *Aviation Facts an* Modley and T tries Associatio Washington.
33. Balzak, S. S., V *Economic Ge* from the Ru Learned Soci York, 1949.
34. Baranskiĭ, N. N 8th ed., Uch
35. Bigham, Trum *portation: P* Graw-Hill I
36. Black, Archib House), Mc 1940.
37. Brown, C. L. University
38. Cumberbatch Surveys),
39. Dearing, Ch *Transport* Washingt
40. Fair, Marvi *nomics* New Yo
41. Frederick, rev. ed.
42. Hocking, *Transp* Sydney

PART III. GOVERNMENTS

CHAPTER 12

NATIONS AND GOVERNMENTS

1. League of Nations, *Statistical Year Book*.
2. United Nations, *Demographic Yearbook*, New York.
3. ———, *Monthly Bulletin of Statistics*.
4. ———, *National and Per Capita Incomes, Seventy Countries, 1949*, New York, 1950.
5. ———, *Population and Vital Statistics Reports*.
6. ———, *Statistical Yearbook*, New York.
7. ———, *Statistics of National Income and Expenditures*, Series H, No. 4, New York, 1953.

8. Allen, Stephen Haley, *The Evolution of Governments and Laws, Exhibiting the Governmental Structure of Ancient and Modern States, Their Growth and Decay and the Leading Principles of Their Laws*, Princeton University Press, Princeton, 1916.
9. Aristotle, *Politics* (Benjamin Jowett, trans.), Oxford University Press, New York, 1943.
10. Bowman, Isaiah, *The New World: Problems in Political Geography*, 4th ed., World Book Company, New York, 1928.
11. Ch'ien, Tuan-sheng, *The Government and Politics of China*, Harvard University Press, Cambridge, 1950.
12. East, Gordon, *An Historical Geography of Europe*, Methuen and Company, London, 1935.
13. Finer, Herman, *Theory and Practice of Modern Government*, rev. ed., Henry Holt & Company, New York, 1949.
14. Fitzgibbon, Russell, "A Political Scientist's Point of View," in "Pathology of Democracy in Latin America: a Symposium" (ed. by W. W. Pierson), *American Political Science Review*, March 1950.
15. Friedrich, Carl J., *Constitutional Government and Democracy, Theory and Practice in Europe and America*, Little, Brown and Company, Boston, 1941.
16. Fromm, Erich, *Escape from Freedom*, Farrar & Rinehart, New York, 1941.
17. Loewenstein, Karl, *Political Reconstruction*, Macmillan Company, New York, 1946.
18. Macdonald, Austin F., *Government of the Argentine Republic*, Thomas Y. Crowell Company, New York, 1942.
19. Machiavelli, Niccolò, *The Prince* (trans. by Luigi Ricci; rev. by E. R. P. Vincent), Oxford University Press, New York, 1935.
20. MacIver, Robert M., *The Web of Government*, Macmillan Company, New York, 1947.
21. Montesquieu, C. L. de S., Baron de, *The Spirit of Laws*, translated from the French by Thomas Nugent, George Bell and Sons, London, 1902.
22. Neumann, Robert G., *European and Comparative Government*, McGraw-Hill Book Company, New York, 1951.
23. Ogg, Frederic A., *The Rise of Dictatorship in France*, 1941; supplement to *European Governments and Politics*, 2d ed., 1940, Macmillan Company, New York.
24. Plato, *The Works of* (trans., with analysis and introduction, by B. Jowett), Dial Press, New York.
25. *Political Handbook of the World* (annual), Council on Foreign Relations, New York.
26. Rennie, Ysabel F., *The Argentine Republic*, Macmillan Company, New York, 1945.
27. Schuman, F. L., *International Politics; the Western State System in Transition*, 3d ed., McGraw-Hill Book Company, New York, 1941.
28. *The Statesman's Year-Book: Statistical and Historical Annual of the States of the World*, Macmillan Company, New York.
29. Valkenburg, Samuel V., *Elements of Political Geography*, Sir Isaac Pitman and Sons, London, 1949.
30. Webb, Sidney, and Webb, Beatrice, *Soviet Communism: a New Civilization*, 2d ed., 2 vols., Charles Scribner's Sons, New York, 1938.
31. Weil, Felix José, *Argentine Riddle*, John Day, New York, 1944.
32. Wheare, Kenneth C., *Federal Government*, Oxford University Press, New York, 1946.
33. Wilson, Woodrow, *The State: Elements of Historical and Practical Politics*, D. C. Heath and Company, Boston, 1889.
34. Woytinsky, Wl. (W.S.), *Die Welt in Zahlen*, 7 volumes, Rudolf Mosse, Berlin, 1925–1928.
35. ———, W. S. and Woytinsky, E. S., *World Population and Production: Trends and Outlook*, Twentieth Century Fund, New York, 1953.
36. Wright, Quincy, *A Study of War*, 2 vols., University of Chicago Press, Chicago, 1942.

CHAPTER 13

ELECTIONS AND PARLIAMENTS

1. United Nations, *Demographic Yearbook*, New York.
2. ———, *The Road to Equality: Political Rights of Women*, 1953.

UNITED STATES

3. Department of Commerce, Bureau of the Census, Elections: 1942; *The Soldier Vote in 1942*.
4. ———, ———, Elections: 1944; *Army and Navy Voting in 1944*.
5. ———, ———, Elections: 1946; *State Proposals Voted upon in 1946*.
6. ———, ———, *Estimates of the Population of Voting Age, by States*, Current Population Reports, Population Estimates, Series P-25, 1948.
7. ———, ———, *Historical Statistics of the United States, 1789–1945*, 1949.
8. ———, ———, *Statistical Abstract of the United States*.
9. Department of State, *Bulletin*.

10. AUSTRALIA. Commonwealth Bureau of Census and Statistics, *Official Year Book of the Commonwealth of Australia*, Canberra.

11. Austria. Österreichisches Statistisches Zentralamt, *Statistisches Handbuch für die Republik Österreich*, Vienna.

12. Belgium. Institut National de Statistique, *Annuaire Statistique de la Belgique et du Congo Belge*, Brussels.

Brazil
13. *Anuario Estatistico de Brasil, 1941–45*, Rio de Janeiro, 1946.
14. *Sinopse Estatistica de Brasil*, Rio de Janeiro, 1947.

15. Canada. Dominion Bureau of Statistics, *The Canada Year Book*, Ottawa.

16. Chile. Direcion General de Estatistica, *Politica, Administracion, Justicia y Educacion*, Santiago de Chile.

17. Colombia. *Anuario General de Estadistica*, Bogota.

18. Denmark. *Statistisk Årbog*, Copenhagen.

19. France. Statistique Générale, *Annuaire Statistique*, Paris.

Germany
20. Statistisches Reichsamt, *Statistisches Jahrbuch für das Deutsche Reich*, Berlin.
21. Statistisches Amt des Vereinigten Wirtschaftsgebietes, *Wirtschaft und Statistik*, Stuttgart.
22. Bayerisches Statistisches Landesamt, Beiträge zur Statistik Bayerns, *Wahl zum Bayerischen Landtag am 26. November 1950*, Munich, 1951.

23. Great Britain. Central Statistical Office, *Annual Abstract of Statistics*, London.

Guatemala
24. *Informe del Ciudadano Presidente de la Republica, Doctors Juan Jose Arevalo al Congresso Nacional*, March 1951.
25. *Lei Electoral* (Decretos 255, 313, 324, 533, 552), 1950.

26. Italy. Instituto Centrale di Statistica, *Annuario Statistico Italiano*, Rome.

27. Japan. Statistics Bureau of the Prime Minister's Office, *Japan Statistical Yearbook*, Tokyo.

28. The Netherlands. Central Bureau voor de Statistiek, *Jaarcijfers voor Nederland*, The Hague.

29. New Zealand. *The New Zealand Official Year Book*, Wellington.

30. Norway. Norges Offisielle Statistisk, *Statistisk Årbok for Norge*, Oslo.

31. Panama. *Anuario de Estadistica*, Panama.

32. Peru. *Anuario Estadistico del Peru*, Lima.

33. Sweden. Central Bureau of Statistics, *Statistisk Årsbok*, Stockholm.

34. Switzerland. Eidgenoessisches Statistisches Amt, *Statistisches Jahrbuch der Schweiz*, Bern.

35. Union of South Africa. *Official Year Book of the Union of South Africa*, Pretoria.

36. Uruguay. *Anuario Estadistico*, Montevideo.

USSR
37. *Trud*, Moscow.
38. *Vlast' Sovetov*, Moscow.

---

39. Allen, Stephen Haley, *The Evolution of Governments and Laws, Exhibiting the Governmental Structure of Ancient and Modern States, Their Growth and Decay and the Leading Principles of Their Laws*, Princeton University Press, Princeton, 1916.

40. Andrew, Milton H., *Twelve Leading Constitutions, with Their Historical Backgrounds*, American University Series, Compton, California, 1931.

41. Aristotle, *Politics* (Benjamin Jowett, trans.), Oxford University Press, New York, 1943.

42. Bean, Louis H., *How to Predict Elections*, Alfred A. Knopf, New York, 1948.

43. ———, *The Mid-Term Battle*, Cantillon Books, Washington, 1950.

44. Bergsträsser, Ludwig, *Geschichte der Politischen Parteien in Deutschland*, 7th ed., Isar Verlag, Munich, 1952.

45. Braunias, Karl, *Das Parlamentarische Wahlrecht*, W. de Gruyter, Berlin, 1932.

46. Brendel, Sebald, *Die Geschichte, das Wesen und der Werth der National Repräsentation, Ein Handbuch für Wirkliche oder Künftige Volksvertreter*, 2 vols., C. F. Kunz, Bamberg, 1817.

47. Buck, Philip W., and Masland, John W., *The Governments of Foreign Powers*, rev. ed., Henry Holt and Company, New York, 1950.

48. Carter, Gwendolen M., Ranney, John C., and Herz, John H., *Major Foreign Powers, the Governments of Great Britain, France, the Soviet Union and Germany*, rev. ed., Harcourt, Brace and Company, New York, 1952.

49. Condorcet, M. J. A. N. C., marquis de, *Oeuvres* (publiées par A. Condorcet O'Connor et M. F. Arago), 12 vols., Firmin Didot Frères, Paris, 1847.

50. *Constitutional Year Book, 1939*, Harrison & Sons, London, 1938.

51. De la Croix, Jacques V., *A Review of the Constitutions of the Principal States of Europe and of the United States of America* (trans. from the French, with notes), G. G. T. and T. Robinson, London, 1792.

52. Douglas, William O., *Strange Lands and Friendly People*, Harper Brothers, New York, 1951.

53. Finer, H., *Theory and Practice of Modern Government*, Methuen & Company, London, 1932.

54. Gosnell, Harold F., *Democracy, the Threshold of Freedom*, Ronald Press Company, New York, 1948.

55. ———, *Why Europe Votes*, University of Chicago Press, Chicago, 1930.

56. Gsovski, Vladimir, *Soviet Civil Law, Private Rights and Their Background under the Soviet Regime,*

2 vols., University of Michigan Law School, Ann Arbor, 1949.

57. Hallett, George H., and Hoag, Clarence G., *Proportional Representation — the Key to Democracy,* The National Home Library Foundation, Washington, D.C., 1937.

58. Hare, Thomas, *The Election of Representatives, Parliamentary and Municipal. A Treatise,* 3d ed., Longmans, Green and Company, London, 1865.

59. Hermens, F. A., *Democracy or Anarchy? a Study of Proportional Representation,* Univ. of Notre Dame, Notre Dame, 1941.

60. Key, V. O., Jr., *Southern Politics in State and Nation,* Alfred A. Knopf, New York, 1949.

61. Lachapelle, Georges, *Élections Législatives, 22–29 Avril 1928,* F. Alcan, Paris, 1928.

62. Meisel, James H., and Kozera, Edward S., *Materials for the Study of the Soviet System. State and Party Constitutions, Laws, Decrees, Decisions and Official Statements of the Leaders, in Translation,* George Wahr Publishing Company, Ann Arbor, 1950.

63. Mill, John Stuart, *Considerations on Representative Government,* Parker, Son & Bourn, London, 1861.

64. Neumann, Robert G., *European and Comparative Government,* McGraw-Hill Book Company, New York, 1951.

65. Nilson, Sten 'S., *Histoire et Sciences Politiques,* J. Grieg, Bergen, 1950.

66. *Pan American Yearbook, 1945,* Pan American Associates, New York, 1945.

67. *Political Handbook of the World* (annual), Council on Foreign Relations, New York.

68. Porter, Kirk H., *A History of Suffrage in the United States,* University of Chicago Press, Chicago, 1918.

69. Siegfried, André, *America Comes of Age,* Harcourt, Brace and Company, New York, 1927.

70. Stanton, Elizabeth C. (Editor), *History of Woman Suffrage,* 3 vols., S. B. Anthony, Rochester, 1881–89.

71. Starchey, Ray, *"The Cause:" a short History of the Women's Movement in Great Britain,* G. Bell and Sons, London, 1928.

72. *The Statesman's Year-Book: Statistical and Historical Annual of the States of the World,* Macmillan Company, New York.

73. Strong, Charles F., *Modern Political Constitutions: an Introduction to the Comparative Study of Their History and Existing Form,* 3d ed., Sidgwick and Jackson, London, 1949.

74. Thorpe, Francis N., *The Constitutional History of the United States, 1765–1895,* 3 vols., Callaghan and Company, Chicago, 1901.

75. Tingsten, Herbert, *Political Behavior, Studies in Election Statistics,* P. S. King and Son, London, 1937.

76. Towster, Julian, *Political Power in the U.S.S.R., 1917–1947,* Oxford University Press, New York, 1948.

77. Webb, Augustus, D., *The New Dictionary of Statistics,* George Routledge and Sons, London, 1911.

78. Woytinsky, Wl. (W.S.), *Die Welt in Zahlen,* 7 volumes, Rudolf Mosse, Berlin, 1925–1928.

79. ———, *Zehn Jahre Neues Deutschland,* Rudolf Mosse, Berlin, 1929.

CHAPTER 14

COLONIAL EMPIRES

1. League of Nations, *International Statistical Yearbook, 1926,* Geneva, 1927.

2. ———, *The Network of World Trade,* Geneva, 1942.

3. ———, *Statistical Year Book.*

4. ———, International Institute of Intellectual Cooperation, *Colonial Questions and Peace* (a survey prepared under the direction of Emanuel Moresco), 1939.

5. United Nations, *Demographic Yearbook,* New York.

6. ———, *Non-Self-Governing Territories* (summaries and analyses of information transmitted to the Secretary General), New York.

7. ———, *Review of Economic Conditions in Africa* (Supplement to *World Economic Report, 1949–50*), New York, 1951.

8. ———, *Review of Economic Conditions in the Middle East,* New York, 1951.

9. ———, *Statistical Yearbook,* New York.

10. ———, *World Economic Report,* New York.

11. ———, Food and Agriculture Organization (FAO), *Yearbook of Agricultural Statistics, 1949* (Part 1. Production), Washington, 1950.

UNITED STATES

12. Department of Commerce, *Foreign Commerce Yearbook.*

13. ———, Bureau of the Census, *Statistical Abstract of the United States.*

14. Department of the Interior, Bureau of Mines, *Minerals Yearbook.*

GREAT BRITAIN

15. Secretary of State for Colonies, *Colonial Development and Welfare,* Cmd. 6713, H.M.S.O., 1945.

16. ———, *The Colonial Territories (1948–1949),* Cmd. 7715, H.M.S.O., 1949. (Excerpts used by permission of the Controller of Her Britannic Majesty's Stationery Office.)

17. Adams, James Truslow, *Building the British Empire,* Charles Scribner's Sons, New York, 1938.

18. Barnes, Leonard, *The Duty of Empire,* V. Gallancz, London, 1935.

19. Beard, Charles A., and Beard, Mary R., *The Rise of American Civilization,* Macmillan Company, New York, 1930.

20. Busch, Moritz, *Bismarck, Some Secret Pages of His History,* Macmillan Company, New York, 1898.

21. Carnegie Endowment for International Peace, *International Conciliation* (various issues), New York.

22. Chapman, Charles E., *Colonial Hispanic America: a History,* Macmillan Company, New York, 1933.

23. Churchill, Sir Winston, *The Second World War* (6 vols., 1948–53), Vol. II: *Their Finest Hour,* Houghton Mifflin Company, Boston, 1951.

24. Cole, D. H., *Imperial Military Geography*, 10th ed., S. Praed & Company, London, 1950.

25. Deschamps, Hubert J., *La Fin des Empires Coloniaux*, Presses Universitaires de France, Paris, 1950.

26. Dutt, Romesh C., *The Economic History of India under Early British Rule*, 4th ed., Kegan Paul, Trench, Trübner and Company, London, 1917.

27. Egerton, H. E., *Is the British Empire the Result of Wholesale Robbery?* (Oxford Pamphlets, 1914), Oxford University Press, London, 1914.

28. ———, *Origin and Growth of Greater Britain*, Clarendon Press, Oxford, 1920.

29. Girault, Arthur, *Principes de Colonisation et de Législation Coloniale*, 5 vols., Recueil Sirey, Paris, 1927–1936.

30. Guber, A. A., *Krisis Colonialnoĭ Systemy Posle Vtoroĭ Mirovoĭ Voĭny*, Pravda, Moscow, 1947.

31. Hailey, Malcolm Hailey, Baron, *The Future of Colonial Peoples*, Princeton University Press, Princeton, 1944.

32. Hart, Albert Bushnell, *A Reference History of the World, from the Earliest Times to the Present*, G. and G. Merriam Company, Springfield, 1921.

33. Hasser, Kurt, *Deutschlands Kolonien, Erwerbungs- und Entwicklungsgeschichte, Landes- und Volkskunde und Wirtschaftliche Bedeutung Unserer Schutzgebiete*, Seele and Company, Leipzig, 1910.

34. Henderson, H. D., *Colonies and Raw Materials* (Oxford Pamphlets on World Affairs, No. 7), Clarendon Press, Oxford, 1939.

35. Hinden, Rita, *Empire and After, a Study of British Imperial Attitudes*, Essential Books, London, 1949.

36. Hobson, J. A., *Imperialism, a Study*, James Pott and Company, New York, 1902; 3d ed., G. Allen & Unwin, London, 1938.

37. Kuczynski, Robert R., *Colonial Population*, Oxford University Press, London, 1937.

38. Leroy-Beaulieu, Paul, *De la Colonisation chez les Peuples Modernes*, 5th ed., 2 vols., Guillaumin and Company, Paris, 1902.

39. Lord, Clifford L., and Lord, Elizabeth H., *Historical Atlas of the United States*, Henry Holt and Company, New York, 1944.

40. Madariaga, Salvador de, *Christopher Columbus: Being the Life of the Very Magnificent Lord Don Cristobal Colon*, Macmillan Company, New York, 1940.

41. Mahan, Alfred T., *The Influence of Sea Power upon History, 1660–1783*, Little, Brown and Company, Boston, 1890.

42. Morris, Henry C., *History of Colonization, from the Earliest Times to the Present Day*, 2 vols., Macmillan Company, New York, 1908.

43. Olivier, S. H. O., Baron Olivier, *White Capital and Coloured Labour*, new ed., L. & V. Woolf, London, 1929.

44. Palmer, R. R., *A History of the Modern World*, Alfred A. Knopf, New York, 1950.

45. Pim, Sir Alan W., *Colonial Agricultural Production; the Contribution Made by Native Peasants and by Foreign Enterprise*, Oxford University Press, London, 1946.

46. Reinsch, Paul S., *Colonial Government, an Introduction to the Study of Colonial Institutions*, Macmillan Company, New York, 1902.

47. Renouvin, Pierre, *Les Politiques d'Expansion Imperialiste, Colonie et Empires*, Presses Universitaires de France, Paris, 1949.

48. Royal Institute of International Affairs, *Colonial Administration by European Powers* (a series of papers read at King's College, London, 1946), London, 1947.

49. ———, *The Colonial Problem*, Oxford University Press, London, 1937.

50. ———, *Raw Materials and Colonies* (Information Department, Paper No. 18), London, 1936.

51. Saraut, Albert, *La Mise-en-Valeurs des Colonies Françaises*, Rayot, Paris, 1923.

52. Sayre, Francis B., *Dependent Peoples and World Order* (Foundations for World Order), University of Denver, Denver, 1948.

53. Schäffle, Albert, *Deutsche Kern- und Zeitfragen*, E. Hofmann and Company, Berlin, 1894.

54. Shiels, Sir Drummond, *The Colonies, Today and Tomorrow* (British Commonwealth Affairs, No. 1), Longmans, Green and Company, London, 1947.

55. Smith, Adam, *An Inquiry into the Nature and Causes of the Wealth of Nations* (with notes, etc., by J. R. M'Culloch), new ed., A. & C. Black, Edinburgh, 1863.

56. *The Statesman's Year-Book: Statistical and Historical Annual of the States of the World*, Macmillan Company, New York.

57. Strauss, W. L., *Joseph Chamberlain and the Theory of Imperialism*, American Council on Public Affairs, Washington, 1942.

58. Supan, Alexander G., *Die Territoriale Entwicklung der Europäischen Kolonien*, J. Perthes, Gotha, 1906.

59. Townsend, Mary Evelyn, *European Colonial Expansion since 1871*, J. B. Lippincott Company, Philadelphia, 1941.

60. *Venture* (monthly publication of the Fabian Colonial Bureau, London).

61. Whybrow, S. J. B., and Edwards, H. E., *Europe Overseas, a Survey of Modern Empires*, J. M. Dent & Sons, London, 1939.

62. Woolf, L., *Empire and Commerce in Africa, a Study in Economic Imperialism*, Labour Research Department, Westminster, 1920.

63. Woytinsky, Wl. (W.S.), *Die Welt in Zahlen*, Vol. I: *Die Erde — Die Bevölkerung — Der Volksreichtum*, Rudolf Mosse, Berlin, 1925.

64. ———, and Woytinsky, E. S., *World Population and Production: Trends and Outlook*, Twentieth Century Fund, New York, 1953.

65. Zoepfl, G., "Kolonien und Kolonialpolitik," in *Handwörterbuch der Staatswissenschaften*, 3d ed., Vol. 5, Gustav Fischer, Jena, 1910.

CHAPTER 15

GOVERNMENT EXPENDITURES AND REVENUES

1. League of Nations, *International Statistical Yearbook*, Geneva.

2. ———, *Statistical Year Book*.

3. United Nations, *Budgetary Structure and Classification of Government Accounts*, 1951.

4. ———, *Demographic Yearbook*, New York.

5. ———, *Desorrollo de las Financus Publicas en America Latina*, May 1951.

6. ———, *Economic Survey of Asia and the Near East*.

7. ———, *Government Accounting and Budget Execution*.

8. ———, *Monthly Bulletin of Statistics*.

9. ———, *National and Per Capita Incomes, Seventy Countries, 1949*, New York, 1950.

10. ———, *National Income Statistics, 1938–1948*, New York, 1950.

11. ———, *Population and Vital Statistics Reports*.

12. ———, *Public Debt, 1914–1946*, New York, 1948.

13. ———, *Public Finance Data, 1937–1948*.

14. ———, *Public Finance Information Data*.

15. ———, *Public Finance Surveys*, New York, 1951.

16. ———, *Statistical Yearbook*, New York.

17. ———, Economic Commission for Europe, *Economic Bulletin for Europe*.

18. ———, ———, *Economic Survey of Europe*.

19. International Labor Office, *Public Investment and Full Employment*, Montreal, 1946.

UNITED STATES

20. Department of Commerce, Bureau of the Census, *Governmental Revenue*.

21. ———, ———, *Governmental Units in the United States*, 1942.

22. ———, ———, *Historical Review of State and Local Government Finances*, 1948.

23. ———, ———, *Historical Statistics of the United States, 1789–1945*, 1949.

24. ———, ———, *State Government Finances*.

25. ———, ———, *Statistical Abstract of the United States*.

26. ———, Bureau of Foreign and Domestic Commerce, *National Income*, Supplement to *Survey of Current Business*.

27. Economic Cooperation Administration, Special Mission to France, *France Data Book*.

28. National Resources Planning Board, *Development of Resources and Stabilization of Employment in the United States*, 1941.

29. DENMARK. *Statistisk Årbog*, Copenhagen.

FRANCE

30. Commissariat Général du Plan de Modernisation et d'Équipement, *Rapport Général sur le Premier Plan de Modernisation et d'Équipement*, 1946–1947.

31. Statistique Général, *Annuaire Statistique*, Paris.

32. GERMANY. Statistisches Reichsamt, *Statistisches Jahrbuch für das Deutsche Reich*, Berlin.

GREAT BRITAIN

33. Central Statistical Office, *Annual Abstract of Statistics*, London.

34. *Report of the Treasury Committee on National Debt and Taxation*, Cmd. 2800, H.M.S.O., 1927. (Excerpts used by permission of the Controller of Her Britannic Majesty's Stationery Office.)

35. NORWAY. Norges Offisielle Statistisk, *Statistisk Årbok for Norge*, Oslo.

36. SWEDEN. Central Bureau of Statistics, *Statistisk Årsbok*, Stockholm.

37. SWITZERLAND. Eidgenoessisches Statistisches Amt, *Statistisches Jahrbuch der Schweiz*, Bern.

---

38. Bastable, C. F., *Public Finance*, 3d ed., Macmillan Company, London, 1903.

39. Beard, Charles A., *An Economic Interpretation of the Constitution of the United States*, Macmillan Company, New York, 1935.

40. ———, and Beard, Mary R., *The Rise of American Civilization*, Macmillan Company, New York, 1930.

41. Berolzheimer, Joseph, "The Impact of U.S. Foreign Aid since the Marshall Plan on Western Europe's Gross National Product and Government Finances," in *Finanzarchiv*, Vol. 14, No. 1, J. C. B. Mohr, Tübingen, 1953.

42. Bolles, Albert S., *The Financial History of the United States from 1789 to 1860*, D. Appleton and Company, New York, 1883.

43. Breasted, James H., *The Conquest of Civilization*, Harper and Brothers, New York, 1926.

44. Buehler, Alfred G., *Public Finance*, 1st ed., McGraw-Hill Book Company, New York, 1936.

45. Colm, Gerhard, "Theory of Public Expenditures," *Annals of the American Academy of Political and Social Science*, January 1936.

46. Dalton, Hugh, *Principles of Public Finance*, 9th ed., George Routledge and Sons, London, 1936.

47. Dowell, Stephen, *A History of Taxation and Taxes in England*, Longmans, Green and Company, London, 1884.

48. Groves, Harold M., *Financing Government*, Henry Holt and Company, New York, 1939.

49. Harris, Seymour E., *Economic Planning, the Plans of Fourteen Countries, with Analyses of the Plans*, 1st ed., Alfred A. Knopf, New York, 1949.

50. Jensen, Jens P., *Government Finance*, Thomas Y. Crowell Company, New York, 1937.

51. Kendrick, Myron S., *Public Finance; Principles and Problems*, Houghton Mifflin Company, Boston, 1951.

52. Kuznets, Simon, *National Income and Its Composition*, 2 vols., National Bureau of Economic Research, New York, 1941.

53. Lerner, Abba P., *Economics of Employment*, McGraw-Hill Book Company New York, 1951.

54. ———, *The Economics of Control; Principles of Welfare Economics*, Macmillan Company, New York, 1944.

55. Lutz, Harley L., *Public Finance*, 3d ed., D. Appleton-Century Company, New York, 1936.

56. Mann, Fritz K., "Die Staatswirtschaft Unserer Zeit," in *Finanzwissenschaftliche Forschungen*, No. 1, Gustav Fischer, Jena, 1930.

57. ———, "Steuerpolitische Ideale," in *Finanzwissenschaftliche Forschungen*, No. 5, Gustav Fischer, Jena, 1937.

58. Martin, Robert F., *National Income in the United States, 1799–1938,* National Industrial Conference Board, New York, 1939.

59. Maxwell, James A., *The Fiscal Impact of Federalism in the United States,* Harvard University Press, Cambridge, 1946.

60. Meyer, Eduard, "Griechische Finanzen," in *Handwörterbuch der Staatswissenschaften,* Vol. 4, Gustav Fischer, Jena, 1909.

61. National Industrial Conference Board, *Cost of Government in the United States, 1928–29,* New York, 1931.

62. Nitti, Francesco S., *Principes de Science des Finances* (traduits de l'italien par Stefan Freund), Marcel Giard, Paris, 1928.

63. Petty, Sir William, *Political arithmetik, or A discourse concerning the . . . value of lands, people, buildings . . . As the same relates to every country in general, but more particularly to the territories of His Majesty of Great Britain, and his neighbours of Holland, Zealand and France,* published by R. Clavel, London, 1691.

64. Pigou, A. C., *A Study in Public Finance,* Macmillan Company, London, 1928.

65. Plato, *The Works of* (trans. with analysis and introduction, by B. Jowett), Dial Press, New York.

66. Plutarch, *The Lives of the Noble Grecians and Romans* (trans. by John Dryden), Modern Library, New York, 1932.

67. Poole, Kenyon E. (Editor), *Fiscal Policies and the American Economy,* Prentice-Hall, New York, 1951.

68. Ratner, Sidney, *American Taxation,* W. W. Norton and Company, New York, 1942.

69. Samuel, Sir Herbert, "The Taxation of Various Classes of the People," *Journal of the Royal Statistical Society,* March 1919.

70. Schatz, O., "Die Finanzen der Europäischen und Wichtigeren Aussereuropäischen Staaten," in *Finanzarchiv,* Vol. 37.

71. Seligman, Edwin R. A., "Progressive Taxation in Theory and Practice," *American Economic Association Quarterly,* December 1908.

72. ———, *The Income Tax, a Study of the History, Theory and Practice of Income Taxation at Home and Abroad,* Macmillan Company, New York, 1914.

73. Shannon, Fred A., *America's Economic Growth,* 3d ed., Macmillan Company, New York, 1951.

74. Shirras, G. Findlay, *Volkseinkommen und Besteuerung,* Gustav Fischer, Jena, 1926.

75. Shultz, William J., *American Public Finance and Taxation,* Prentice-Hall, New York, 1931.

76. Smith, Adam, *An Inquiry into the Nature and Causes of the Wealth of Nations* (with notes, etc., by J. R. M'Culloch), new ed., A. & C. Black, Edinburgh, 1863.

77. Stamp, Sir Josiah, *The Fundamental Principles of Taxation in the Light of Modern Developments,* new, rev. ed., Macmillan Company, London, 1936.

78. *The Statesman's Year-Book: Statistical and Historical Annual of the States of the World,* Macmillan Company, New York.

79. Studenski, Paul, *Chapters in Public Finance* (reprinted from Vol. 2 of *Economic Principles and*

Problems, by Walther E. Spahr and others), R. Long and R. R. Smith, New York, 1933.

80. ———, "Toward a Theory of Business Taxation," *Journal of Political Economy,* October 1940.

81. ———, "Modern Fiscal Systems, Their Characteristics and Trends of Development," *Annals of the American Academy of Political and Social Science,* January 1936.

82. ———, and Krooss, Herman E., *Financial History of the United States,* McGraw-Hill Book Company, New York, 1952.

83. Taylor, Philip E., *The Economics of Public Finance,* Macmillan Company, New York, 1948.

84. Toutain, Jules F., *The Economic Life of the Ancient World,* Alfred A. Knopf, New York, 1930.

85. Wagner, Adolf, *Grundlegung der Politischen Oekonomie* (Part I: Grundlagen der Volkswirtschaft), C. F. Winter'sche Verlagshandlung, Leipzig, 1892–93.

86. Withers, William, *Public Finance,* American Book Company, New York, 1948.

87. Woytinsky, Wl. (W.S.), *Die Welt in Zahlen,* Vol. VI: *Die Öffentlichen Finanzen,* Rudolf Mosse, Berlin, 1928.

88. ———, *Internationale Hebung der Preise als Ausweg aus der Krise* (Frankfurter Gesellschaft für Konjunkturforschung, Veröffentlichungen), Hans Buske, Leipzig, 1931.

89. ———, and Woytinsky, E. S., *World Population and Production: Trends and Outlook,* Twentieth Century Fund, New York, 1953.

CHAPTER 16

PUBLIC DEBTS

1. League of Nations, *International Statistical Yearbook,* Geneva.

2. ———, *Statistical Year Book.*

3. United Nations, *Monthly Bulletin of Statistics.*

4. ———, *National Income Statistics,* New York.

5. ———, *Public Debt, 1914–1946,* New York, 1948.

6. ———, *Statistical Yearbook,* New York.

7. International Monetary Fund, *International Financial Statistics.*

UNITED STATES

8. Department of Commerce, *Foreign Aid by the United States Government, 1940–1951* (Supplement to the *Survey of Current Business*).

9. ———, Bureau of the Census, *Governmental Debt.*

10. ———, ———, *Historical Statistics of the United States, 1789–1945,* 1949.

11. ———, ———, *Statistical Abstract of the United States.*

12. ———, Bureau of Foreign and Domestic Commerce, *Survey of Current Business.*

13. Department of the Treasury, *Annual Report of the Treasury.*

14. GERMANY. Statistisches Reichsamt, *Wirtschaft und Statistik,* Berlin, 1939.

15. GREAT BRITAIN. Central Statistical Office, *Annual Abstract of Statistics,* London.

16. Abbott, Charles C., *The Federal Debt: Structure and Impact,* Twentieth Century Fund, New York, 1953.
17. Bastable, C. F., *Public Finance,* 3d ed., Macmillan Company, London, 1903.
18. Beard, Charles A., *An Economic Interpretation of the Constitution of the United States,* Macmillan Company, New York, 1935.
19. Bergmann, Karl, *Der Weg der Reparationen,* Societäts Druckerei, Frankfurt am Main, 1926.
20. Committee on Public Debt Policy, *Our National Debt after Great Wars* (National Debt Series, No. 1), New York, 1946.
21. ———, *Our National Debt and Our Savings* (National Debt Series, No. 5), New York, 1948.
22. ———, *Our National Debt and the National Welfare* (National Debt Series, No. 7), New York, 1948.
23. Dewey, Davis Rich, *Financial History of the United States,* Longmans, Green & Company, New York, 1931.
24. Groves, Harold M., *Financing Government,* Henry Holt and Company, New York, 1939.
25. Kautsky, Benedikt, *Reparationen und Rüstungen,* Hess & Company, Vienna, 1931.
26. Keynes, John M., *The Economic Consequences of the Peace,* Harcourt, Brace and Company, New York, 1920.
27. National Association of Manufacturers, *You and Your Nation's Debt,* New York, 1946.
28. Rotterdamische Bankvereinigung, *Monatsberichte,* Rotterdam.
29. Schatz, O., "Die Finanzen der Europäischen und Wichtigeren Aussereuropäischen Staaten," in *Finanzarchiv,* Vol. 37.
30. Shannon, Fred A., *America's Economic Growth,* 3d ed., Macmillan Company, New York, 1951.
31. Shultz, W. J., and Caine, M. R., *Financial Development of the United States,* Prentice-Hall, New York, 1937.
32. Simon, H. F., *Reparation und Wiederaufbau,* C. Heymann, Berlin, 1925.
33. Smith, Adam, *An Inquiry into the Nature and Causes of the Wealth of Nations* (with notes, etc., by J. R. M'Culloch), new ed., A. & C. Black, Edinburgh, 1863.
34. Stamp, Sir Josiah, "Internationale Finanzprobleme," in *Weltpolitik und Weltwirtschaft,* No. 3, 1925.
35. Studenski, Paul, *Chapters in Public Finance* (reprinted from Vol. 2 of *Economic Principles and Problems,* by Walther E. Spahr and others), R. Long and R. R. Smith, New York, 1933.
36. ———, and Krooss, Herman E., *Financial History of the United States,* McGraw-Hill Book Company, New York, 1952.
37. Woytinsky, Wl. (W.S.), *Die Welt in Zahlen,* Vol. VI: *Die Offentlichen Finanzen,* Rudolf Mosse, Berlin, 1928.

Chapter 17

International Cooperation

League of Nations

1. *Banking and Currency Reform in Estonia,* 1927.
2. *Bulgarian Stabilisation Loan: Protocol and Annexes,* 1928.
3. *Commercial Policy in the Inter-War Period. International Proposals and National Policies,* 1942.
4. *Commercial Policy in the Post-War World,* 1945.
5. *Economic Stability in the Postwar World: the Conditions of Prosperity after the Transition from War to Peace,* 1945.
6. *Financial Reconstruction of Austria. General Survey and Principal Documents,* 1926.
7. *Food, Famine and Relief, 1940–46,* 1946.
8. *Greek Stabilisation and Refugee Loan. Protocol and Annexes,* 1927.
9. *Handbook of International Organisations* (final edition), 1938.
10. *International Currency Experience: Lessons of the Inter-War Period,* 1944.
11. *Final Report of the Mixed Committee of the League of Nations on the Relation of Nutrition to Health, Agriculture and Economic Policy,* 1937.
12. *Prevention of International Double Taxation and Fiscal Evasion: Two Decades of Progress under the League of Nations,* 1939.
13. *Report of the Committee for the Study of International Loan Contracts,* 1939.
14. *Report on Exchange Control,* 1938.
15. *Survey of National Nutrition Policies, 1937–38,* 1938.
16. *The Course and Control of Inflation: a Review of Monetary Experience in Europe after World War I,* 1946.
17. *The Transition from War to Peace Economy,* 1943.
18. *Trade Relations between Free Market and Controlled Economies,* 1943.

United Nations

19. *A System of National Accounts and Supporting Tables,* 1953.
20. *Catalogue of Economic and Social Projects of the UN and the Specialized Agencies.*
21. *Charter of the United Nations and Statute of the International Court of Justice.*
22. *Demographic Yearbook.*
23. *Domestic Financing of Economic Development,* 1950.
24. *Economic Bulletin for Europe.*
25. *Economic Development in Selected Countries: Plans, Programs and Agencies,* 1947.
26. *Economic Survey of Asia and the Far East.*
27. *Economic Survey of Europe.*
28. *Economic Survey of Europe since the War: a Reappraisal of Problems and Processes,* 1953.
29. *Economic Survey of Latin America.*
30. *Formulation and Economic Appraisal of Development Projects,* Vols. 1 and 2, 1951.
31. *Measures for the Economic Development of Underdeveloped Countries,* 1951.
32. *Methods of Estimating Total Population for Current Dates,* 1952.
33. *Methods of Financing Economic Development in Under-developed Countries,* 1949.
34. *Methods of Using Census Statistics for the Calculation of Life Tables and Other Demographic Measures,* 1950.
35. *Monthly Bulletin of Statistics.*
36. *National International Measures for Full Employment,* 1949.

37. *Population Bulletin.*
38. *Population Census Handbook,* 1953.
39. *Population Census Methods,* 1949.
40. *Problems of Unemployment and Inflation,* 1950 and 1951.
41. *Proceedings of the Regional Technical Conference on Flood Control in Asia and the Far East* (Flood Control Series No. 3), Bangkok, 1952.
42. *Proceedings of the United Nations Scientific Conference on the Conservation and Utilization of Resources, 1949,* Vol. 1–6, New York, 1950–51.
43. *Report on a Special United Nations Fund for Economic Development,* 1953.
44. *Review of International Commodity Problems,* 1952.
45. *Standard International Trade Classification,* 1951.
46. *Statistical Yearbook.*
47. *Statistics of National Income and Expenditures* (Statistical Papers, Series 4).
48. *Summary of Recent Economic Developments in Africa,* 1952.
49. *Summary of Recent Economic Developments in the Middle East,* 1952.
50. *Technical Assistance for Economic Development,* 1949.
51. *Technical Assistance under the International Agencies,* 1951.
52. *Transport and Communication Review.*
53. *Yearbook of the United Nations.*

INTERNATIONAL LABOR ORGANIZATION
54. *Action against Unemployment.*
55. *Arbitration of Labor Disputes.*
56. *Compulsory Old-Age and Life Insurance.*
57. *Constitution and Standing Orders of the ILO.*
58. *Economic and Social Reconstruction of the United States.*
59. *Housing Policy in Europe.*
60. *Industrial Labor in Japan.*
61. *Industrial Relations in Great Britain.*
62. *International Labour Conventions.*
63. *International Labour Review.*
64. *International Survey of Social Security.*
65. *Report of the Director-General,* 1952.
66. *Social Aspects of Rationalization,* 1952.
67. *Summary of Reports of Ratified Conventions,* 1954.
68. *Ten Years of the ILO.*
69. *The International Labor Code.*
70. *The Minimum Wage: an International Survey.*
71. *Three Sources of Unemployment.*
72. *Yearbook of Labor Statistics.*

FOOD AND AGRICULTURE ORGANIZATION
73. *Activities of FAO under Expanded Technical Assistance Program, 1950–52.*
74. *FAO Fisheries Bulletin.*
75. *FAO Memo.*
76. *Monthly Bulletin of Agricultural Economics and Statistics.*
77. *The Work of FAO.*
78. *Timber Statistics.*
79. *Unasylva.*
80. *Yearbook of Fisheries Statistics.*
81. *Yearbook of Food and Agricultural Statistics.* (Part I: Production; Part II: Trade.)
82. *Yearbook of Forest Products Statistics.*

INTERNATIONAL BANK FOR RECONSTRUCTION AND DEVELOPMENT
83. *Annual Report.*
84. Press Releases.
85. *Report on Cuba,* Johns Hopkins Press, Baltimore, 1951.
86. *Report on the Proposal for an International Finance Corporation,* 1953.
87. *Report on Surinam,* Johns Hopkins Press, Baltimore, 1952.
88. *The Basis of a Development Program for Colombia,* Johns Hopkins Press, Baltimore, 1950.
89. *The Economic Development of Ceylon,* Johns Hopkins Press, Baltimore, 1953.
90. *The Economic Development of Guatemala,* Johns Hopkins Press, Baltimore, 1951.
91. *The Economic Development of Iraq,* Johns Hopkins Press, Baltimore, 1952.
92. *The Economic Development of Jamaica,* Johns Hopkins Press, Baltimore, 1952.
93. *The Economic Development of Mexico,* Johns Hopkins Press, Baltimore, 1953.
94. *The Economic Development of Nicaragua,* Johns Hopkins Press, Baltimore, 1953.
95. *The Economic Development of Turkey,* Johns Hopkins Press, Baltimore, 1951.

INTERNATIONAL MONETARY FUND
96. *Annual Report of the Executive Directors,* Washington.
97. *Articles of Agreement of the International Monetary Fund,* 1952.
98. *International Financial Statistics.*
99. *The World Payments Situation.*

UNITED NATIONS EDUCATIONAL, SCIENTIFIC AND CULTURAL ORGANIZATION
100. *Contemporary Political Science, a Survey of Methods, Research and Teaching,* 1951.
101. *Cultural Patterns and Technical Change,* 1952.
102. *Directory of International Scientific Organizations,* 1952.
103. *Tensions That Cause Wars,* University of Illinois Press, Urbana, 1952.
104. *World Handbook of Educational Organizations and Statistics.*

WORLD HEALTH ORGANIZATION
105. *The Work of WHO,* Annual Report of the Director-General to the World Health Assembly and to the United Nations (Official Records, No. 45, Geneva, 1953, and N51, Geneva, 1954).
106. *Chronicle of the WHO.*
107. *Epidemiological and Vital Statistics Report.*

ORGANIZATION FOR EUROPEAN ECONOMIC COOPERATION
108. *OEEC, History and Structure,* Paris, 1953.

UNITED STATES CONGRESS
109. Eighty-second Congress, First Session. Mutual Security Act Extension: Hearings before the Committee on Foreign Affairs on H.R. 5710, 1953.
110. Eighty-second Congress, House of Representatives, Committee on Foreign Affairs. Mutual Security

Legislation and Related Documents with Explanatory Notes, November 1952.

111. *The Mutual Security Act of 1953,* Report of the Committee on Foreign Relations, June 1953.

112. *The Mutual Security Program for Fiscal Year 1954; Basic Data Supplied by the Executive Branch,* June 5, 1953.

113. *The Mutual Security Program . . . for a Strong and Free World.* Half-Year Report of the President to Congress.

114. *Report to Congress on the Mutual Security Program.*

U.S. DEPARTMENT OF STATE

115. *Charter of the United Nations.*

116. *Dumbarton Oaks Documents.*

117. *Guidelines for Point 4: Recommendations of the International Development Advisory Board,* 1952.

118. *International Organizations in Which the United States Participates,* 1949.

119. *Partners in Progress.*

120. *Technical Assistance under the International Agencies,* 1951.

U.S. FOREIGN OPERATIONS ADMINISTRATION

121. *Conclusions and Recommendations of the International Development Advisory Board,* December 1953.

122. *Monthly Operations Report.*

123. *Project News.*

U.S. MUTUAL SECURITY AGENCY

124. *Economic Strength for the Free World, Principles of a United States Foreign Development Program,* a report to the Director for Mutual Security by the Advisory Committee on Underdeveloped Areas, May 1953.

125. *European Program, Local Currency Counterpart Funds,* June 30, 1954.

126. *Far East Program, Local Currency Counterpart Funds,* June 30, 1954.

127. *Mutual Defense Assistance Control Act of 1951, First Report to Congress . . . a Program for the Denial of Strategic Goods to the Soviet Bloc,* 1952.

128. *Mutual Defense Assistance Control Act of 1951, Second Report to Congress . . . Problems of Economic Defense,* 1953.

129. *Mutual Defense Financing in Western Europe — a Part of the Mutual Security Program for 1953–54,* May 1953.

130. *Technical Assistance for Productivity,* 1953.

131. *Questions and Answers on the Mutual Security Program,* 1953.

U.S. TECHNICAL COOPERATION ADMINISTRATION

132. *Outline of Point 4 Organization, Policy and Operation,* 1952.

133. *Point 4 Chronological Summary,* 1952.

134. *Point 4, What It Is, How It Works,* 1953.

135. *Statement by Stanley Andrew* (TCA Administrator) before the Senate Foreign Relations Committee, May 1953.

136. *Status of Point 4 Field Activities,* 1953.

137. *What Is Point 4?* 1952.

INTER-AMERICAN AFFAIRS INSTITUTE

138. Iverson, Kenneth R., *The Servicio in Theory and Practice* (Building a Better Hemisphere Series, No. 1), 1951.

139. Rowe, C. O., *Eleven Years of Point 4 in Latin America,* 1953.

140. Stone, Wyman R., *Building Better Health in Latin America,* 1952.

141. White, John W., *Miracle on the Amazon* (Building a Better Hemisphere Series, No. 11), 1952.

COUNCIL OF EUROPE

142. Consultative Assembly, *Official Report of Debate.*

143. Consultative Assembly, *Texts Adopted by the Assembly.*

144. Consultative Assembly, *News.*

---

145. Aufricht, Hans, *Guide to League of Nations Publications; a Bibliographical Survey of the Work of the League, 1920–1947,* Columbia University Press, New York, 1951.

146. Beales, A. C. F., *The History of Peace,* The Dial Press, New York, 1931.

147. Beard, Charles A., and Beard, Mary R., *The Rise of American Civilization,* new edition, Macmillan Company, New York, 1935.

148. Bentham, Jeremy, *Plan for an Universal and Perpetual Peace,* Sweet and Maxwell, London, 1927.

149. Carlston, Kenneth S., *The Process of International Arbitration,* Columbia University Press, New York, 1946.

150. Cook, Morris L., and Associates, *Groundwork for Action* (Bold New Program Series, No. 3), Public Affairs Institute, Washington, 1950.

151. Crucé, Emeric, *The New Cyneas* (ed. with an introd. and tr. into English from the original French text of 1623 by Thomas W. Balch), Allen, Lane and Scott, Philadelphia, 1909.

152. Davis, Harriet E. (Ed.), *Pioneers in World Order; an American Appraisal of the League of Nations,* Columbia University Press, New York, 1944.

153. Grotius, Hugo, *The Law of War and Peace — De Jure Belli ac Pacis,* W. J. Black, New York, 1949.

154. Haviland, H. Field, Jr., *The Political Role of the General Assembly* (United Nations Studies, No. 7), Carnegie Endowment for International Peace, New York, 1951.

155. Hemleben, Sylvester J., *Plans for World Peace through Six Centuries,* University of Chicago Press, Chicago, 1943.

156. Hill, Norman L., *International Organization,* Harper and Brothers, New York, 1952.

157. Hudson, Manley O., *The World Court, 1921–1938,* World Peace Foundation, Boston, 1938.

158. Iverson, Kenneth R., "Ten Years of Point 4 in Action in Latin America," *Foreign Commerce Weekly,* February 4, 1953.

159. Kant, Immanuel, *Perpetual Peace, a Philosophical Essay,* The American Peace Society, Boston, 1897.

160. Leonard, L. Larry, *International Organization,* McGraw-Hill Book Company, New York, 1951.

161. Mangone, Gerard J., *The Idea and Practice of World Government,* Columbia University Press, New York, 1951.

162. Mowat, Robert B., *The Concert of Europe,* Macmillan Company, New York, 1930.

163. Myers, Denis P., *List of Arbitration Treaties,* World Peace Foundation, Boston, 1911.

164. ———, *Handbook of the League of Nations since 1920,* World Peace Foundation, Boston, 1930.

165. Office Central des Associations Internationales, *L'Union des Associations Inernationales,* Brussels, 1912.

166. Potter, Pitman B., *An Introduction to the Study of International Organization,* 3d ed., The Century Company, New York, 1928.

167. Ralston, Jackson H., *International Arbitration from Athens to Locarno,* Stanford University Press, Stanford, 1929.

168. Reves, Emery, *The Anatomy of Peace,* Harper and Brothers, New York, 1945.

169. Saint-Simon, C. H. de R., *De la Reorganisation de la Société Européenne* (Bibliotheque Romantique), Les Presses Françaises, Paris, 1925.

170. Shotwell, J. T., *War as an Instrument of National Policy and Its Renunciation in the Pact of Paris,* Harcourt, Brace and Company, New York, 1929.

171. Smuts, Jan C., *The League of Nations, a Practical Suggestion,* Hodder and Stoughton, London, 1918.

172. The Union of International Associations, *Yearbook of International Organizations, 1951–52,* Columbia University Press, New York, 1952.

173. Thucydides, *The Complete Writings; the Peloponnesian War,* The Modern Library, New York, 1934.

174. Walters, F. P., *A History of the League of Nations,* 2 vols., Oxford University Press, New York, 1952.

175. Woytinsky, Wl. (W. S.), "Der Deutsche Arbeitsmarkt in der Krise," in *Schmollers Jahrbuch,* Munich, 1933.

176. ———, W. S., and Woytinsky, E. S., *World Population and Production: Trends and Outlook,* Twentieth Century Fund, New York, 1953.

177. Wright, Robert F., *Medieval Internationalism; the Contribution of the Medieval Church to International Law and Peace,* Williams and Norgate, London, 1930.

178. Wynner, Edith, and Lloyd, Georgia, *Searchlight on Peace Plans,* rev. ed., E. P. Dutton and Company, New York, 1949.

INDEX

INDEX

BECAUSE THIS BOOK is principally concerned with the whole world rather than its separate nations, states and cities, as such, this is essentially a subject index rather than a geographical one. It gives the location of information on the main topics and subtopics covered by the study — trade, capital movement, foreign debts, tariffs; transportation by land, water and air; forms of government, public finances and debts; international cooperation, etc. References to particular regions, continents, countries and cities are included only when there is extended or special discussion of them.

The book contains a vast quantity of information about geographical areas — mainly in the form of comparative statistics under each subject division. The reader wanting information about India, for example, will find it by referring first to the heading "India" for special discussions of the country and then to the various subject headings under "World, *data for selected countries*." The same is true for continents and cities, information for which can be found by referring to the subject headings listed under "World, *data by continent*" and "Cities." The United States is an exception to this rule and is more fully indexed than any other country, under "United States," "United States, *data by state*," and by important subjects under these headings.

Personal entries include only the names of persons specifically mentioned or quoted in the text or footnotes. A separate Alphabetical List of Authors appears on pages 889–891 and a complete chapter-by-chapter listing of authors and source materials in the Source References section on pages 863–888.

An extensive Table of Contents will be found on pages ix-xxi and detailed lists of the statistical tables and figures (maps, graphs and charts) on pages xxiii–xxxvii in the front of the book.

The designation (t) following a page number in the index indicates a reference to a table; the designation (f) to a map, graph or chart. These designations are used only when a subject is covered in tabular or graphic form alone; they are not used with a group of pages that includes text as well as tables and graphs relating to the subject.